WITHDRAWN

# The New York Times
## Current History

# THE
# EUROPEAN
# WAR

### VOLUME XIII
OCTOBER—DECEMBER, 1917

With Alphabetical and Analytical Index
Illustrations, Maps and Diagrams

NEW YORK
THE NEW YORK TIMES COMPANY

# INDEX AND TABLE OF CONTENTS

## Volume XIII.

[This Index constitutes a Table of Contents and an Analytical Index of Authors, Subject Matter, and Titles.]

[Titles of articles appear in *italics*]

VAUGHAN, Crawford, 162.

VENICE, historical sketch, 383.
See also CAMPAIGN in Europe, Austro-Italian Border.

VENIZELOS, Eleutherios, statement on final trial of monarchy, 154; disclosure of war policy of King Constantine before Commission of Inquiry, 256.

VEDEROSKI, (Admiral) Dmitri N., 72.

VERSKOVSKY (Col), 72.

VIENNA, see CONGRESS of Vienna.

VIRGILI, (Lieut.) Alberto, 450.

VITAL Statistics, article showing effect of war on births and deaths in England and Germany, 247.

## W

WANG, (Hon.) C. T., on Chinese issue, 346; on Chinese crisis and American influence, 353.

WAR Council, see SUPREME War Council.

WAR Industries Board, see COUNCIL of National Defense.

War Record of the British Dependencies, 359.

WAR Revenue Bill, 243.

WAR Trade Board, organization, 233.

WAR museums, in France, 453.

WAR Trade Council, advisory to War Trade Board, 233.

WARNER, Arthur H., "Slang and Slogans of War in France," 250.

WASHINGTON, George, speech of Viscount Ishii at tomb at Mount Vernon, 51.

WEDGWOOD (Commander), VIII. (Dec. supplement).

WESTCOTT, Allan, "A Historic Peace Conference," 538.

WESTMINSTER Gazette, account of events preceding entry of Turkey into war, 334.

WHEAT, control by U. S. Govt., 236.

WHEELER, W. Reginald, "The Attempted Restoration of the Manchus in China," 346.

WHITE, (Rev.) George E., account of Armenian atrocities, 339.

Who Was Responsible for the War? 91.

WILLIAM II., Emperor of Germany, address on Aug. 24 to German battalions, expressing hatred toward England, 2; secret treaty with Czar of Russia destroyed through efforts of Count Witte, 7; congratulations on capture of Riga, 69; resolutions of loyalty by Hamburg and Bremen Chambers of Commerce, 87; correspondence with Emperor William in 1904-1907 aiming at treaty between Germany, Russia, and France, with object of isolating England, 331; negotiations for entry of Turkey into war, 334; letter to Dr. Michaelis on resignation, 451; telegrams from King and Queen of Greece, and reply, 457; extract from letter to Pres. Wilson on outbreak of war, 487; dispatches to Czar on outbreak of war, 488; statement on invasion of Belgium in letter to Pres. Wilson, 490; responsibility discussed by D. J. Hill in analysis of documents bearing on outbreak of war, 496; documents of correspondence with King George on outbreak of war, 508.

WILLIAM, Crown Prince of Germany, at Verdun, 116.

"WILLY - NICKY" correspondence, see WILLIAM II., Emperor of Germany.

WILSON, Havelock, 131.

WILSON, (Gen. Sir) Henry Hughes, 434.

WILSON, (Pres.) Woodrow, message to national army; letter to T. L. Chadbourne, Jr., 11; reply to speech of Viscount Ishii, 50; message to National Council Assembly at Moscow, 67; text of reply to Pope Benedict's peace proposal, 81; comment on reply by New-Yorker Staats-Zeitung and by foreign press, 83; resolution of Hamburg and Bremen Chambers of Commerce protesting against reply to the Pope, 87; comment by Lord Cecil on reply, 89; war aims supported by American labor, 90; editorial comment on ascendency over Congress, 192; statement on determination for price of wheat, letter to M. Eastman on censorship, 236; reply to address of G. Roussos, 258; comment by Dr. Michaelis on reply to Papal note, 288; attitude toward German peace agitation as expressed to League of National Unity, 293; telegram to King Albert on Belgian fete day and telegram to loyalty conference at St. Paul, 386; foreword to regulations for classification of registered men, 424; indorsement of Supreme War Council, 438; telegram to Pres. of Brazil on entry into war, 439; text of address before American Federation of Labor, 441; extract from letter from German Emperor on outbreak of war, 487, 490.

WINN, Robert Sumner, "Australasia's Record in the War," 526.

WITTE, (Count) Sergius Y., forces Czar to destroy treaty with Germany against England, 7, 333.

WOMEN, employment in Germany on railways; anxiety as to future of workers, 156; appeal by M. Provost to French for cheering letters, 254; rumor of use of hair in place of leather in Germany, 449.

WOOD, Bryan, 514.

WOOD, H., "The Dogs of War," 161.

WORFOLK, Ellen, 450.

World at War, 5.

Worldwide Embargo Against Germany, 239.

Written on Going Into Action, 295.

WU TING-FANG (Dr.), appointed acting Premier, 349; Minister of Foreign Affairs, 352; address at American University Club on America's duty to China, 353.

## Y

YANUSHKEVITCH (Gen.), testimony on Russian mobilization, 92, 505.

YOUNG Men's Christian Association, work at cantonments, 426.

YOUSSOUF Izeddin, Prince, 335.

YUGOSLAVIA, declaration of formation of State, 111; memoranda of A. Radovitch to King Nicholas suggesting union of Montenegro and Serbia as Slav State, suggestions of Gen. Matanovitch and of Mr. Ilitch, 163.
See also CROATIA.

## Z

ZENNECK, Jonathan, 22.

ZIMMERMANN, (Dr.) Alfred, telegrams to Bernstorff in connection with German plots, 280.

## Portraits

## Illustrations

## Maps

## Cartoons

# THE EUROPEAN WAR
## Period October, 1917—December, 1917

# INTRODUCTION

THE opening of a new phase of the Russian revolution, in which the radical wing of the Socialist movement gained the ascendency and began to work for peace, was the most important aspect of the world war during the months of September, October, and November, 1917. Another setback to the allied cause, but more local in its effects, was the retreat of the Italian armies and the invasion of Northern Italy by Austro-German forces. This success of the Teutonic arms, combined with the overthrow of the Kerensky Government in Russia and the establishment of a proletarian régime under the leadership of the Bolsheviki, disturbed allied policy and at the same time gave the German Government fresh encouragement in its hopes, if not of ultimate victory, at any rate of a negotiated peace which would result in substantial territorial and other advantages.

From the military standpoint the principal fact was the continuance of the determined fighting by the allied armies on the western front, but the successes gained were largely neutralized by the fact that the whole plan of campaign of 1917 had been weakened ever since the Russian armies had begun to demand peace and to refuse to fight. The Central Empires no longer felt any considerable pressure in the eastern theatre of the war, and were thus enabled to strengthen their forces in Flanders, France, and Italy. After a series of hard-won victories, which produced valuable tactical gains, the British ended the year's fighting with a surprise attack at Cambrai that began with a brilliant victory but was transformed into the one serious reverse they had sustained during the year. Nevertheless, Field Marshal Haig reported at the conclusion of the campaign that the additional strength which the Teutonic Empires had been able to obtain from events in Russia and Italy had already been largely discounted and that the ultimate destruction of the Teutonic field forces had been brought appreciably nearer.

The scene of the British offensive continued to be in Flanders, where it was carried on almost without intermission throughout nearly the whole period under review. After a short pause, operations were resumed with renewed energy, and until the conclusion of the offensive in November the Germans were steadily forced back.

The first of the new series of attacks, that of Sept. 20, was on an eight-mile front, between the Ypres-Comines Canal and the Ypres-Staden railway. It resulted in the capture of several important positions. Six days later came another smashing drive, this time on a six-mile front, through a maze of fortified farms and concrete redoubts. Zonnebeke was occupied and the Tower Hamlets spur was reached.

Terrific counterattacks by the Germans failed to dislodge the British, who, on Oct. 4, launched a still more formidable attack on an eight-mile front from south of Tower Hamlets to the Ypres-Staden railway, north of Langemarck. The British gained possession of the main ridge up to 1,000 yards of Broodseinde. At this time the British had taken 10,000 prisoners since the resumption of the offensive on Sept. 20.

Bad weather caused a lull in the fighting, and then, on Oct. 9 and 12, the British again attacked, in both cases throwing their main strength over Passchendaele Ridge. The second of these two drives extended over a front of ten miles. The French, who co-operated on the north, captured the villages of St. Jean Mangelaere and the northern hamlet of Veldhoek, with numerous intervening concrete redoubts, or " pillboxes," while the British drove beyond Poelcapelle.

The British and French were now within long-range gunshot of Roulers, and had gained the principal heights commanding the plain of Flanders. As a result of the five attacks between Sept. 20 and Oct. 12, the Allies had advanced to the Ypres-Roulers road on the northeast and the neighborhood of Passchendaele, a distance of over three miles, had gained nearly a mile to the southeast over the Ypres-Menin road, and so reconquered an area of about twenty-three square miles.

A new phase of the battle of Flanders opened on Oct. 16, developing along the Ypres-Roulers road to the northeast, embracing the village of Passchendaele, along the Ypres-Staden railway, north through the outskirts of the Forest of Houthulst, where the French were engaged, and still further north, until it included the Mercken Peninsula, just south of Dixmude. On Oct. 22 the British secured important positions on both sides of the Ypres-Staden railway, while the French occupied the southern defenses of Houthulst Forest; on Oct. 26 both the British and the French took additional German positions; and on Oct. 27 the British extended their positions west and south of Passchendaele, while the French advanced on both sides of the Bixschoote-Dixmude road, capturing various villages and fortified farms. On Oct. 28 French and Belgian troops advanced across the morasses two miles south of Dixmude and captured the Mercken Peninsula. On Oct. 30 the British attacked toward Passchendaele, but, owing to

heavy German reinforcements, had to wait a week until the artillery prepared the way for the successful advance which was made on Nov. 6. That day the British swept clear through Passchendaele, and on Nov. 10 the ridge which bears that name, the chief objective of the offensive in Flanders, passed entirely into their hands.

As evidence of the terrible character of the struggle for Passchendaele Ridge, it was announced that the British General Staff had obtained information showing that in two months the Germans had used up ninety-one divisions in vainly defending the ridge and in furitless counterattacks. During the same period the British casualties of all kinds numbered more than 180,000.

The Flanders offensive, now at an end, was followed by one of the most brilliant and dramatic attacks of the whole war, namely, the British drive at Cambrai which broke the Hindenburg line between St. Quentin and the River Scarpe. The operation was carried out by the 3d British Army under Sir Julian Byng. It was remarkable for two features: One, that there was no preliminary bombardment; the other, that the tanks, far more numerous than in any previous battle, opened the way for the infantry by smashing through all obstacles. The attack, which was totally unexpected by the Germans, was launched on Nov. 20 on a front of thirty-two miles and resulted in an advance of five miles, reaching the village of Cantaing, less than three miles southwest of Cambrai. Two days later the Germans began to counterattack and regain some of their lost territory. On Nov. 24 a fierce struggle commenced for Bourlon Wood, three and a half miles west of Cambrai. After two days' fighting it remained in the possession of the Germans, who now began to get the upper hand and to drive the British back by intense artillery fire. On Nov. 30 the Germans made two simultaneous attacks which were just as much of a surprise as that of the British ten days before. The southern part of the salient newly formed by the British was broken through and all positions commanding the German approaches to

Cambrai and several dominating Cambrai itself had to be surrendered.

## THE FRENCH

The two most notable successes gained by the French during 1917 were those at Malmaison in October and on the Chemin des Dames in November. Earlier in the year the French offensive had come to a standstill at the ridge between the Aisne and Ailette Valleys northeast of Soissons, a position of great defensive value to the Germans who occupied it. On Oct. 23 the French attacked on a six-mile front between the villages of Allemant and Filian, near Soissons, captured the old fort of Malmaison, which the enemy had transformed into a very strongly fortified position, and drove the Germans down the ridge in the direction of the Ailette River. The counteroffensive was feeble, and on Oct. 25 the Germans were forced back to the Aisne-Oise Canal, hotly pursued by the French, who took many prisoners and guns, and who on Oct. 26 and 27 again added to their gains. On Nov. 2 the Germans were once more forced back on a front of twelve and a half miles between Froidmont Farm and a point east of Craonne.

The value of this successful advance by the French was enormous, for it made the whole of the German position along the Chemin des Dames untenable. The Germans retreated, and the French occupied the northern slopes of the famous ridge and the terrain which lay between the ridge and the Ailette, between Braye-en-Laonnais and Cerny, as well as several villages. All hope of a German movement south of the Chemin des Dames was destroyed, and the enemy had to take up new defensive positions on the heights which form the last line in front of Laon.

## THE AMERICANS ON THE FIGHTING LINE

Before we conclude the story of the fighting in the western theatre of the war we have to note the first appearance of American troops on the firing line. On Oct. 27 it was officially announced that the Americans in France had begun to finish their intensive training in the trenches " of a quiet sector on the French front." A few days later, just as the Germans were completing their retreat across the Ailette, they announced the capture of some American patrols on the front of the Marne Canal, which connects the Rhine with the Marne via Toul and Nancy. From that day onward casualty lists told of Americans killed or wounded in action or by German shell-fire. The Americans were mainly engaged in trench raiding and minor forms of warfare for purposes of training, but to their fellow-countrymen at home these preliminary encounters drove home the lesson that they were now being called upon in earnest to offer their share of sacrifice in the struggle they had undertaken.

## THE ITALIAN DISASTER

Following the collapse of the Russian armies earlier in the year and preceding the virtual withdrawal of Russia from the war after Kerensky's downfall, the Allies suffered another setback through the retreat of the Italian armies and the invasion of Northern Italy by Austro-German forces. The Italian armies had been sorely in need of a continuous stream of supplies all the year, and had thus been prevented from following up several of their successful attacks. This was one of the initial and contributory causes of the disaster. Another was the growth of disaffection in the ranks, largely stimulated by pacifist propaganda.

After elaborate preparations had been made and German troops sent to join the Austrians, a concentrated attack was begun on Oct. 24 on the Italian front along the Isonzo. The Austro-Germans exerted their greatest pressure on a twenty-mile front between Plezzo and Tolmino. It was here that the Italian line was broken, the troops finding the enemy pressing forward on their flanks and toward their rear. The Italians had no choice except to retreat. On Oct. 26 the Italian high command ordered a retirement on the whole line between Monte Maggiore and Auzza. Teutonic forces were now moving down the Mattisone Valley toward the rear of the troops holding the Bainsizza Plateau. On Oct.

27 the enemy occupied Cividale, and the retreat spread out over a still longer line. On Oct. 28 the Austrians entered Gorizia, while the Italians began to abandon the Carso. On Oct. 29 Udine, a railroad centre and the former Italian general headquarters, was taken. On this, the fifth day of the retreat, the Italians were retiring right across the whole Venetian plain.

The first attempt by the Italians to hold back the invaders was made behind the Tagliamento. On Nov. 4 this river had been reached, and the positions on the Carnic Alps were being evacuated. But successful as were Cadorna's efforts to reorganize his forces, the Italians were forced three days later to resume their retirement. Another stand was made on the Livenza, but, despite the great improvement in the Italians' powers of resistance, the retreat went on. The real stand was made on the Piave, which was reached on Nov. 9. Here, for the first time, the invaders were held back. Attacking along the Piave, and through the mountains between the Piave and the Brenta, the Teutons were only moderately successful in their attempts to cross the river. One crossing was made near the sea, another at Zenson, a few miles south of the railroad from Motte to the important junction at Treviso, and at Folina Fagare, above Zenson. In the mountains the fighting was particularly fierce. The Italians held the heights about Asiago against tremendous assaults. But the Teutonic forces succeeded in pushing through between the Brenta and the Piave, past Feltre and Cismon. On Nov. 19 they captured Quero and the protecting height of Monte Cornella. Soon they reached the line on Monte Tomba and Monte Monfenera, which formed the last defensive position before the Venetian plain, now only eight miles away. On Nov. 21 the invaders captured the summits of Monte Fontana Secca and Monte Spinoncia, between the Piave and the Brenta, an important tactical gain. The attack was shifted two days later to the Asiago region, but failed to secure its objectives, while the Italians recaptured the slopes of Monte Tomba. From that date 'till the end of the month there was a lull in the fighting, during which large masses of troops were concentrated by the Teutonic Generals for another offensive.

## THE RUSSIAN FRONT

The German advance on Riga, which had begun in August, was pressed with increased vigor, and on Sept. 2 the Dvina was crossed near Uxkull. Despite Russian counterattacks the Germans pushed on northward to Riga, eighteen miles away. Another column at the same time moved against Riga on the Mitau-Riga road across the Tirul marshes. But the main attack was that which was made at Uxkull. The Russian line was broken, and General Lechitzky, the Russian commander, ordered the whole region to be evacuated. On the night of Sept. 2-3 the Germans entered Riga. The Russians retreated along the coast, falling back on a semicircular line from behind the River Melupe, on the Gulf of Riga, and beyond the River Aa in Livonia, through Segevold, Moritzberg, Kastran to Friedrichstadt on the Dvina. At this point the line joined positions which had not been affected by the German advance. On Sept. 8 and 9 fighting took place on the main Petrograd road in the direction of Pskoff. On Sept. 12 the Russians forced the Germans back south of the road. At this point the Germans ceased to advance in this region, and turned their attention further south, capturing Jacobstadt on Sept. 21.

The possession of Riga being of little value to the Germans unless they also controlled the waters of the Gulf of Riga, the next important operations were conducted for the purpose of occupying the two islands of Oesel and Dagö. On Oct. 13 German troops, protected by guns of warships, were landed on the shore of the Gulf of Tagalah, a northern inlet of Oesel Island, and near the village of Serro on the southern shore of Dagö Island. On Oct. 15 Arensburg, the chief city of Oesel, was taken by the Germans, while the Russian garrisons fled eastward to the mainland. On Oct. 21 the Germans, operating from Moon Island, landed on the mainland at Werder. The Russian Baltic fleet, in the meantime, after having been apparently trapped in

Moon Sound, made its escape. The Germans did not push their advance any further because troops were needed to assist the Austrians in Italy. As a result of the overthrow of the Kerensky Government it was possible to withdraw forty-seven Teutonic divisions, or about 650,000 men, from the eastern front and replace them with half as many men in the first stages of training from Germany and Austria-Hungary. The German lines were thus actually consolidated in the rear to the east of Riga and by a withdrawal toward the Skuli-Lemberg line in the south. The development of the expedition against the mainland east of the Gulf of Riga was postponed. The net result of these operations during August, September, and October, however, was to add to the list of German conquests part of the long-coveted Baltic provinces of Russia and thereby strike another blow at the territorial integrity of the new republic.

The long series of postponements in launching an offensive on the Macedonian front was described in an official report, dated Nov. 15, 1917, from Lieut. Gen. G. F. Milne, commander of the British Saloniki force, under the supreme direction of General Sarrail, the Commander in Chief of the allied forces in Macedonia. On four occasions in April and May, 1917, the British attacked the enemy, and each time General Sarrail halted operations. Finally, on May 24, General Milne received definite instructions from General Sarrail that offensive operations were to cease all along the front, and from that date there had been no essential change on the Doiran-Vardar sector, which was held by the British. One of the causes of the postponed offensive mentioned by General Milne was bad climatic conditions; but, as we have seen in the record of events leading up to the abdication of King Constantine, the main reasons had to do with the political situation in Greece.

In Palestine the advance of the British expedition was resumed in October. During the last week of the month the military railroad from Shellal, fourteen miles south of Gaza, was rapidly carried forward, and on Oct. 30 the bombardment of Gaza was begun. Under cover of heavy artillery fire the British made a final attack on Beersheba, which they captured the following day. On Nov. 6 Gaza fell, and three days later the whole Turkish Army was moving rapidly northward. The British advance on Jerusalem had now begun, and during the next couple of weeks was maintained at a steady rate. Jaffa, the port of Jerusalem, was occupied on Nov. 17, after which there was a pause before the movement on the Holy City itself was initiated.

In Mesopotamia also good progress was made. The Anglo-Indian Army, commanded by Sir Stanley Maude, on Sept. 29 captured Ramadie, on the Euphrates, 130 miles south of Mosul, and with it an entire Turkish army under Ahmed Bey. On Oct. 5 the Russian Army of the Caucasus took the village of Nereman, 50 miles north of Mosul. Then, on Nov. 6, the British occupied Tekrit, on the Tigris, 97 miles northwest of Bagdad, forcing the Turks to retire from 30 to 50 miles north in the direction of Mosul, the southern terminal of the Bagdad Railway, and the largest inland city still in Turkish possession.

## AIR FIGHTING

Both the allied and the German aviators engaged in numerous raids upon cities in addition to their ordinary duties as air fighters. Ostend, Zeebrugge, and other Belgian towns were frequently attacked by British airmen, and in retaliation for the German raids on English and French cities several aerial expeditions were carried out by the Allies into Germany. In one of these raids considerable damage was done in the German Rhenish industrial centres. Constantinople was attacked by British naval aviators, and Venice by Austrian airmen.

The attacks on London were frequent and caused considerable loss of life, particularly in the month of September. During the period under review more than 200 persons were killed in London and other parts of England, and very many more injured. Nearly all these attacks were made by airplanes, but on Oct. 19 the Germans sent a squadron of thirteen Zeppelins to raid the northeast coast of

England. On their return voyage the Zeppelins were attacked by French airmen. Four of the airships were destroyed and three captured, one, the L-49, being brought down intact at Bourbonne-les-Bains in France.

## NAVAL EVENTS

In the German campaign in the Baltic provinces of Russia naval forces cooperated with the military. When German troops were landed on Oesel and Dagö Islands on Oct. 13, the Russian shore batteries were silenced by German warships. Next day there was an engagement between German and Russian naval forces in Soeia Sound. Two German torpedo boats were sunk and two damaged. The Russians lost one torpedo boat. On Oct. 18 the Germans seized Moon Island and sunk the Russian battleship Slava. The whole of the Russian Baltic fleet was driven into the inner waters of Moon Sound behind a barrier of mines planted by German submarines, but, managing to escape from its awkward position, inflicted considerable loss on the German fleet in an engagement in and near the Gulf of Riga on Oct. 21. Six German torpedo boats were sunk, while two dreadnoughts, one cruiser, six torpedo boats, and one transport were put out of action. The other naval episodes worth mentioning were the sinking by a British naval force of a German auxiliary cruiser and ten patrol boats in the Cattegat on Nov. 3 and the sinking of one German light cruiser and the crippling of another off the coast of Heligoland on Nov. 17.

No new important factor entered into the submarine situation during the period under review. The German U-boats continued to sink very nearly the average number of allied and neutral ships which they had destroyed each week since the opening of their unrestricted warfare. Sir Eric Geddes, in his first speech in the House of Commons as First Lord of the Admiralty, on Nov. 1 declared that the German official figures were greatly exaggerated and that Germany was losing larger numbers of U-boats than ever before. Nevertheless, the loss in shipping was considerable, as was indicated in the official figures relating to British vessels. During the thirteen weeks ended Dec. 2, 150 ships over 1,600 tons and seventy-four under 1,600 tons were reported sunk by German submarines or mines. To these have to be added the lost ships of other allied countries and of the neutral nations carrying freight for the Allies.

## AMERICA IN THE WAR

The best indication of the progress of America's preparations for fighting was the announcement, already mentioned, that the training of the troops in France had reached the stage when men were being exposed to the enemy's fire in the trenches. At the beginning of September the combined strength of the regular army, National Guard, and other branches of the military forces was over 800,000 officers and men, to which an almost equally large number began to be added as the draft recruits for the national army assembled at the sixteen new camps specially prepared for their training. The calling up of the conscripts was only gradual, and at the end of the period under review a considerable number of the 687,000 men in the first draft had yet to be summoned to duty.

The figures so far given represented only the beginnings of America's contribution in men to the allied cause. When asking Congress on Sept. 19 for emergency appropriations the Secretary of War stated that the money would be required to equip and supply an army of 2,300,000 men. Secretary Baker had previously said that by Jan. 1, 1918, the United States Army would have a strength of 2,030,000. This force was to consist of the regular army recruited up to 450,000, the National Guard expanded to 470,000, the first draft army of 687,000, auxiliary troops, including aviators and engineers, to the number of 170,000, a hospital corps of 140,000, and Quartermaster and other supply troops. The progress made up to Nov. 7 was shown by the figures made public by Secretary Baker on that date. The army was then over 1,800,000 strong, distributed as follows: National (draft) army, 616,820; National Guard called into Federal service, 469,000; regular army, 370,000; special branches, 200,000; reserves, 80,000; officers, 80,000; total, 1,815,820.

Military necessity precluded public statements as to how many of these men were with Pershing in France, but Secretary Baker, in the first announcement regarding the increase in the size of the expeditionary force, issued on Nov. 23, said that troops were departing from the United States and arriving in France as rapidly as intended in the War Department's plans. A further announcement was made on Nov. 29 that National Guardsmen from every State in the Union had arrived in France and that some were already in training within sound of the guns on the battle front.

The growth of the United States Navy was no less satisfactory. At the end of November the personnel had increased since the beginning of the year from 4,500 officers and 68,000 men to 15,000 officers and 254,000 men; the number of stations of all kinds from 130 to 363; the number of civil employes from 35,000 to 60,000; the strength of the Naval Reserve from a few hundred to 49,246 men; the average monthly expenditure from $8,000,000 to $60,000,000; the number of ships in commission from a little more than 300 to more than 1,000; the Marine Corps from 344 officers and 9,921 men to 1,197 officers and 30,000 men; the national naval volunteers from zero to 16,-000 men.

The special session of Congress—the most memorable in the history of the United States—which ended on Oct. 6, made ample financial provision for the carrying out of the vast war measures enacted since April. Appropriations for the fiscal year ending June 30, 1918, totaled just under $17,000,000,000, but of this sum $7,000,000,000 represented loans to the Allies. The cost of the war to the United States, combined with the ordinary expenses of the Government, amounted for the year to $14,390,373,940. These expenditures were provided for by ordinary revenues, new taxation, and loans. A sum of $2,500,000,000 was expected from the new taxes on incomes and profits, while additional bond issues were authorized for over $3,500,000,000, leaving almost another $4,000,000,000 to be provided for by Congress in its next session.

The Second Liberty Loan, announced on Sept. 27, at 4 per cent., but subject to estate or inheritance tax and to graduated additional income taxation, was a greater success than the first loan. When applications closed on Oct. 27 the amount subscribed for was $4,617,532,300, or 54 per cent. more than was asked for by the Government. The bonds allotted to subscribers amounted to $3,808,766,150. The number of subscribers—9,400,000—had never been equaled in history.

While the growth of the army and navy proceeded with very little friction, the nation's great enterprise in building up a mercantile marine occasioned much controversy. The need of ships, it was recognized, was paramount. As the weeks and months went on it became clear that no effort could be too strenuous to produce vessels with the utmost rapidity to transport troops and supplies across the ocean and to provide the Allies with food and materials for their war industries. Bound up with the Government's plans for the building of new ships were other measures, such as the control of existing vessels and of the trade in which they were employed. Thus, a development of far-reaching import was the control assumed by the Shipping Board on Sept. 6 over the chartering of all American ships and over the acts of American shippers. For this purpose a Chartering Commission was established, and through it a system of co-operation between the American and allied shipping authorities came into existence. At the same time the Shipping Board, in conjunction with the Exports Administrative Board, subsequently reorganized as the War Trade Board, obtained virtually complete control over alien tonnage. The Trading with the Enemy act, passed Oct. 6, armed the Government with new powers over trade, and thereby over shipping. On the ground of war necessity the Shipping Board was authorized to commandeer neutral tonnage tied up in American ports, while all American vessels, according to an order which became effective on Oct. 15, were placed under

Government direction in so far as their deadweight capacity was not under 2,500 tons and they were available for ocean service. The approximate number of vessels affected was 500, aggregating 2,000,000 tons. The ships were turned back to their owners to be operated on Government account under a system similar to that created by the British Government.

A valuable addition to the shipping resources of the Allies was secured by the agreement, announced on Nov. 13, whereby the United States acquired over 400,-000 tons of ships belonging to the neutral nations of Northern Europe. These nations were induced to turn over their ships in exchange for foodstuffs which only America could supply.

A building program for a fleet of merchant vessels of from 10,000 to 12,000 tons, capable of sixteen knots or better, was outlined on Sept. 7. The Shipping Board announced on Sept. 26 that there were then under construction 1,036 cargo vessels, aggregating 5,924,700 tons, there being included in these figures 400 vessels, aggregating 2,800,000 tons, of foreign ownership, which had been requisitioned on the stocks. On Nov. 4 the largest single order so far placed by the Emergency Fleet Corporation was awarded to the American International Corporation, operating the great Government fabricating yard at Hog Island, on the Delaware River, in close association with the American Bridge Company. The contract was for seventy 8,000-ton vessels to be built within twelve months at a cost of $100,000,000. The American International Corporation had previously received a contract for fifty 7,500-ton vessels at a cost of $50,000,000.

For various reasons the Shipping Board and the Emergency Fleet Corporation had not been functioning altogether smoothly. There were personal disagreements as well as disputes in regard to policy and method. Reorganization was therefore once more necessary, and on Nov. 12 Charles A. Piez, a Chicago engineer, who had recently become Vice President of the Fleet Corporation, was placed in charge of all construction work, taking over many of the duties which

had been performed by Rear Admiral Capps, General Manager of the Corporation. The goal which was now being aimed at was the production of 6,000,000 tons of ships by the end of 1918.

The greatest difficulty which confronted the Shipping Board was the shortage of labor, both skilled and unskilled. More than 300,000 additional workers were reported on Oct. 26 as necessary for the construction of tonnage needed at once, and it was far from easy to secure this new labor force because of the withdrawal of 2,000,000 men for the army and navy and the demand by every kind of industry which had been stimulated by the war.

Government control of food was rapidly extended by the exercise of the powers conferred on the President and the Food Administrator. Through the United States Grain Corporation, which was capitalized at $50,000,000, the Food Administration made its first appearance in the wheat market on Sept. 5. Government agents at central zone offices throughout the country went into the market at the opening of the business day and took possession of the wheat in the elevators at the basic price of $2.20 a bushel. From that day onward every bushel of wheat on sale in the United States passed through the Grain Corporation on the way from the elevators and terminals to the mills. This was the first large application of Government control to foodstuffs.

To save the millions of bushels of grain used annually in the manufacture of whisky, the provision of the Food Control act which prohibited the making or importation of distilled liquors was made effective on Sept. 8. Of the 100,-000,000 bushels of grain which had previously gone to the distilleries each year, it was calculated that about 40,000,000 had been used to make whisky and other distilled liquors.

The people were made to realize the necessity of conserving food by the institution, late in September, of " meatless " Tuesdays and " wheatless " Wednesdays in public eating houses. The food situation now reflected war conditions, since the enormous quantities of food exported to the allied countries had created a shortage and sent up prices to about two and a half times those prevailing on the outbreak of the war in 1914. Only the fact that employment was at a higher mark than at almost any time in the history of the nation, and that wages had risen considerably, though not high enough to keep pace with the increased cost of living, limited the growth of popular discontent.

The extraordinary condition of so-called " war prosperity " was fairly well diffused among all classes, and if profiteering was rife, the people were not greatly disposed to raise objections or make them grounds for agitation. The organized labor movement, as represented by the American Federation of Labor, was committed to a policy of co-operation with the Government for the successful prosecution of the war, and so 2,500,000 workers, who could have constituted themselves a formidable opposition, remained satisfied.

Another branch of the labor movement, embracing for the most part unskilled and nomadic workers, and inspired by ideas of class warfare, was not so quiescent. These men either belonged to or sympathized with the organization known as the Industrial Workers of the World, more popularly known as the I. W. W., whose leader was William D. Haywood, and whose agitation against the war was carried on chiefly in the Western States. One great feature which made the United States Government regard the I. W. W. as a menace was the advocacy by some of its members of sabotage and the suspicion that acts of violence and destruction were in contemplation. Early in September, therefore, Haywood was arrested by the Federal authorities, and documents found at I. W. W. offices throughout the country were seized. Many more I. W. W. leaders and agitators were arrested and with Haywood indicted on charges of sedition and conspiracy. Meanwhile a special labor commission, appointed by President Wilson, was investigating conditions in the States where the I. W. W. doctrine was spreading, and discovered that, however reprehensible the views of the agitators, employers were also responsible by refusing to concede the reasonable demands of the workers and taking up a generally unsocial attitude. It was the President's policy to try to establish smoother relations between employer and employed, so that there should be no interruption to industrial activities which would militate against national efficiency for war purposes.

## RUSSIA'S AFFAIRS

Russia was now rapidly moving toward the culmination of one of the most extraordinary developments in modern history. The political revolution in March which had destroyed Czarism was but the prelude to a newer revolution, such as Marx and his followers had advocated for nearly seventy years, namely, the revolution which would destroy not merely political autocracy, but the power of the propertied classes as well. In other words, a war of the classes, bourgeoisie and proletariat, was begun by the Bolsheviki, the left wing of the Social Democratic Labor Party, led by Lenine and Trotzky. The Provisional Government, in which Kerensky was Prime Minister and Terestchenko directed foreign affairs, was branded by the Bolsheviki as a bourgeois Government, and the demand was made that all power be transferred to the Soviets, the councils of Workingmen's and Soldiers' Delegates. The Bolsheviki secured the support of the soldiers by their program of an immediate general peace, of the peasants by proposing to expropriate the landowners without delay, and of the workingmen by proclaiming that they should control industry. Here, then, were the beginnings of the first attempt since Marx had formulated his ideas to put them into practice.

The course of events favored the plans of the Bolsheviki. No sooner had Korniloff addressed the Moscow conference at the end of August than he hurried away to his headquarters to initiate an armed movement against what he believed to be the disloyal trend of affairs at Petrograd. On Sept. 9 he sent a message to Kerensky demanding the surrender of all power into his hands. The bearer of this message was Vladimir Lvoff, brother of Prince Lvoff, the first head of the Provisional Government. The full story of the differences between Kerensky and Korniloff and of Vladimir Lvoff's part as intermediary is not yet known, but in his appeal to the Cossacks Korniloff charged actual treason on the part of some members of the Provisional Government. Kerensky refused to accede to Korniloff's demands, and at once found the workmen's, peasants', and soldiers' organizations rallying to his support. Korniloff, after failing to receive adequate support from either the army or the civil population, and after advancing some distance toward Petrograd with comparatively a handful of men, admitted defeat, and on Sept. 14 submitted to the Provisional Government.

The belief that a counter-revolutionary attempt had been made frightened the people, and the propaganda of the Bolsheviki began steadily to exert an ever-greater influence. Although Kerensky took immediate steps to safeguard the results of the revolution by proclaiming a republic on Sept. 15 and summoning the Constituent Assembly to meet in December, his handling of the Bolshevist menace was weak, and the masses rapidly lost confidence in him. On Sept. 27 a Democratic Congress met in Moscow, and in addition to other important resolutions adopted one demanding that without its consent no coalition should be formed; and another that a pre-Parliament, to be called the Temporary Council of the Russian Republic, be set up to act as an advisory body until the Constituent Assembly should meet and decide the form of the future Government of Russia. Again Kerensky's influence with the moderate Socialists, his temporizing, and the pressure of the bourgeois interests had results which were to prove fatal to the Provisional Government. The representation of the Soviets in the Council of the Republic, as originally agreed upon, was reduced and that of the bourgeois interests increased; while the opposition of the Democratic Congress to the formation of a Coalition Cabinet was flouted, as was seen on Oct. 7 when Kerensky announced

the names of the members of the new Government. Eleven days later the Bolsheviki took the decisive step which led to Kerensky's downfall.

The Bolsheviki, with their demand that all power should be in the hands of the Soviets, had opposed the establishment of the Council of the Republic, but they were represented at its first meeting in Petrograd on Oct. 18. Trotzky, speaking on their behalf, once more stated the Bolshevist program, and then, with his followers, withdrew from the council in a body. The Constitutionalist-Democrats (Cadets) and moderate Socialists who were left behind realized what the withdrawal of the Bolsheviki would mean in creating new conditions of insecurity and disorder, and in vain tried to induce them to come back and take part in planning for Russia's future. But the Bolsheviki were determined to pursue their own course, since they now had reason to believe that the great majority of the peasants, workmen, and soldiers would support them. For three weeks the Council of the Republic continued to exist, endeavoring in its last days to frame measures to solve the land question and to initiate a movement to bring about peace. That Kerensky was well aware of the impending climax was shown in a statement he made to a press correspondent on Nov. 1 in which he declared that Russia was worn out and that the Allies should shoulder the whole burden of the war.

The issue on which the clash came between the Bolsheviki and the Provisional Government arose from the demand of the Revolutionary Military Committee of the Workmen's and Soldiers' Delegates to control all orders of the General Staff in the Petrograd district. This was refused, whereupon the committee appointed special commissioners to undertake the direction of the military forces and invited the troops to observe only orders signed by the committee. At the same time the committee moved machine-gun detachments to the Workmen's and Soldiers' headquarters and made other military preparations for the overthrow of the Provisional Government.

The blow fell on Nov. 7. The Petrograd garrison, acting under the direction of the Revolutionary Military Committee, and assisted by sailors from the cruiser Aurora, after comparatively little fighting, gained control of the city. Kerensky fled, no one knew where, while several of his colleagues in the Cabinet, including Terestchenko, were arrested and imprisoned. A proclamation addressed by the Military Revolutionary Committee to the army committees, to all councils of Workmen's and Soldiers' Delegates, and to the garrison and proletariat of Petrograd announced that the Kerensky Government had been deposed and that the supreme power had been confided to the Military Revolutionary Committee pending the creation of the Government by the Soviets. Further, an offer of an immediate democratic peace was to be made, the land was to be handed over to the peasants without delay, and the Constituent Assembly was to be summoned. Trotzky appeared at a meeting of the Petrograd Soviet and there introduced Lenine as " an old comrade whom we welcome back." Lenine received a vociferous reception and proceeded to outline his program. Two days later he was named by the All-Russian Congress of Workmen's and Soldiers' Delegates as Premier of the Government, with Trotzky as Foreign Minister. Abram Krylenko, who was appointed one of a committee of three to perform the functions of the former Ministers of War and Marine, became Commander in Chief of the armies.

The new authority was rapidly recognized by the working classes throughout Russia, except in Finland and the Ukraine, the two territories which had the most completely developed nationalist and separatist movements. In Moscow there was more fighting than in Petrograd before the Bolsheviki established themselves; near Tsarskoe Selo troops supporting Kerensky were defeated. On the whole, the new régime was ushered in with comparatively little bloodshed. The great majority of the people—the peasants, the workmen, and the soldiers who were recruited from the toiling masses—were behind the uprising and desired to give the Bolshe-

viki every opportunity to carry out their program of making Russia a Socialist republic. The bourgeoisie was either cowed into silence or gagged by the suppression of its organs of opinion. Its property rights were ignored. In many cases individuals belonging to the propertied classes were no longer safe from violence. Never since Marx and Engels had drawn up the communist manifesto had the dictatorship of the proletariat been made such an actual concrete reality as in these days of November, 1917. The peasants ruled throughout the country districts, and in the cities and towns the workmen either expelled from the workshops and factories, or reduced to impotence, the men who once owned and controlled industry.

Among the circumstances which it is asserted impeded the creation of the Cooperative Commonwealth, which is held up as the ultimate aim of socialism, were the state of war which still existed and which left Russia at the mercy of the Teutonic armies; the absence of a properly organized industrial system; the backwardness of agriculture, and the general lack of the equipment and methods which make a modern nation efficient in its economic and social activities. The new Government had to set about its task under conditions little short of chaotic, but its promulgation of orders of confiscation of property, repudiation of debts, and general disregard of the fundamentals of honest relationships between Government and people foreshadowed certain disaster.

The Bolsheviki promptly proceeded to take steps which they asserted might bring about a general peace. The day after the new Cabinet was appointed, (Nov. 10,) the Workmen's and Soldiers' Congress adopted a series of peace resolutions in which the formula of " No annexations, no indemnities, and the free self-determination of nationalities " was again set forth and defined. An immediate armistice was suggested so that " all the nations in the war or its victims " might participate in the negotiations.

General Dukhonine, the Commander in Chief of the Russian armies, was instructed on Nov. 20 to offer an armistice to "all nations, allied and hostile," but, ignoring the order, he was the following day dismissed from his position and replaced by Ensign Krylenko. Shortly afterward he was murdered by a Bolshevist mob. With the change of command the regiments on frontal positions were asked to elect plenipotentiaries to conduct negotiations, but the army was completely demoralized by the substitution of elected privates for the regular officers. Addressing the Central Executive Committee of the Workmen's and Soldiers' Delegates on Nov. 25, Lenine alleged that Russia did not contemplate a separate peace with Germany, but sought to force the belligerent Governments to make a general peace and a democratic peace.

In the meantime elections for the Constituent Assembly were held. In Petrograd the Bolsheviki headed the poll with between 40 and 45 per cent. of the vote cast, and were in minority as against the combined forces of the Cadets and Social Revolutionaries. They were in a decided minority elsewhere in the country.

A development of Bolshevist policy was the publication by Trotzky, soon after he became Foreign Minister, of various confidential communications which had passed between the Russian Foreign Office and foreign Governments in the earlier years of the war. These revelations, although supporting the case against secret diplomacy, did not create the stir that was expected, because the general lines of secret understandings were already known, despite the absence up to then of the documentary proofs now produced by Trotzky.

Within nine months of the Czar's abdication the Russian revolution, which had begun as a successful attempt to destroy absolutism, had developed into a far more radical endeavor to create a new social order. Both in Russia and abroad the rise to power of Socialists who were determined to set up their own style of Government instanter, despite the peril from a powerful foreign foe established on Russian soil, caused indignant amazement and roused the bitterest of contro-

versies. The explanation offered by Socialists was that the ideas which were now exerting their influence had been proclaimed nearly seventy years before and had been disseminated by no propagandists more assiduously than the Russian revolutionists during their long years of repression and oppression. The Bolsheviki claimed to be Marxians, but behind the new movement which brought them into power were also traces of the influence of Bakunin, the founder of modern anarchism. It was not without significance that the only other faction which gave the Bolsheviki support was the left wing of the Social Revolutionary Party, led by Marie Spiridonova, who had some years before assassinated the Governor of a Russian province and who now wielded enormous influence among the poorer peasants. The Bolshevist leaders were not avowed anarchists, but the tendencies which had prevailed since the revolution in March, and which now became accentuated, showed distinct signs of an effort to dispense as far as possible with all government and all authority.

## BRITISH AFFAIRS

A turning point in British political history was marked by the reorganization of the Labor Party to strengthen its forces and take advantage of the forthcoming reform of the electoral system whereby the number of voters was about to be doubled. Hitherto the British Labor Party had been a sectional and rather narrow group. Now it aimed at becoming a national party. The Trade Union Congress, representing 4,500,000 workers, and the industrial co-operative societies, representing 3,500,000 members, decided to throw the whole of their strength behind the new political organization, which, allowing for duplication of membership, embraced at least two-fifths of the entire population of the United Kingdom. No country had ever before had such a large aggregation of working people enrolled under a single banner. The mere fact that the workers were now united in one powerful organization produced a deep impression in the minds of statesmen and public leaders, and there were some who already prophesied the advent of a Labor Government such as had for several years been the most striking feature of politics in Australia. But the first result which the new Labor Party gained was in regard to the statement of war aims by the existing Government.

While the Irish Convention was continuing its work of drafting an agreement which should settle the home rule question, the Sinn Feiners were busily pursuing their policy of irreconcilable opposition to the British connection. In October they held a convention at which a provisional Constitution aiming at an Irish republic was adopted and a program of secession drawn up. Evidence of preparations for a new armed rebellion forced the British Government to take precautionary measures, and had the further effect of rousing in Ulster the old antagonism, thereby making the solution of the home rule question once more very doubtful.

Among the nationalist movements to which the war had given fresh stimulus was that of the Jewish Zionists. For this branch of Jewish people the realization of their dreams would be found in the creation of a Jewish national State in the ancient land of Israel. As the British expedition in Palestine successfully wrested one area after another from the rule of the Turks, the Zionists renewed their representations to the British Government and were rejoiced to receive in reply the declaration of the British Foreign Minister that the Government viewed with favor the establishment of Palestine as a national home for the Jewish people and would use its best endeavors to facilitate the achievement of this object.

### FRENCH AFFAIRS

For months France had been afflicted by a curious and obscure disquiet, and it was not until the beginning of September that the world at large began to realize its characer. Louis J. Malvy, the Minister of the Interior, who owed his position in the Cabinet to the influence of Joseph Caillaux, the leader of the Radical Socialist Party, (which, however, was not a Socialist Party in the strict sense, but a popular progressive group,)

resigned his position to refute, he declared, charges made against him in connection with the alleged anti-patriotic activities of Miguel Almereyda, editor of the Bonnet Rouge. Leymarie, the head of the Secret Service, also retired. Then came the arrest of Paul Bolo, or Bolo Pacha, a financial adventurer, who was charged with treasonable activities and specifically with having received large sums of money from Germany, through the German Ambassador in the United States, for the purpose of obtaining control of leading French newspapers. The term "Boloism" thus became applied to all the activities associated with the names of Malvy, Bolo, and Caillaux, who also was subsequently indicted on charges of high treason.

The Ribot Government was severely censured for failing to suppress "Boloism" and for permitting Parliamentary interference with military plans, sometimes in the course of execution. Malvy's resignation, the first result of the attack on the Government, was only the prelude to the political crisis which led to the downfall of the Ribot Cabinet. After several days of uncertainty, during which Ribot endeavored to get together a new Government, but failed, Painlevé, the War Minister, received sufficient backing to form a Cabinet, assuming office as Premier on Sept. 13.

Painlevé's chief difficulty in carrying on the Government arose from the refusal of the Unified Socialists, under the leadership of Albert Thomas, to give him their support because they were not satisfied with the Government's war aims. Ribot had become Foreign Minister in the new Cabinet, and the Socialists distrusted him as an exponent of a policy of imperialism. Painlevé, to reassure the Socialists, in his first speech as Premier on Sept. 18, defined France's war aim in regard to Alsace-Lorraine as one of "disannexation" in contrast with Ribot's demands for direct annexation of the two provinces and territorial guarantees through the neutralization of adjoining German territory. Von Kühlmann, speaking in the Reichstag on Oct. 10, said that Germany could not in any form make concessions with regard to

Alsace-Lorraine and that the two provinces could never be the object of negotiations.

A few days later Ribot in the Chamber of Deputies precipitated a crisis by declaring that he had rejected an alleged German peace offer because it was a "trap." The Socialists and other parties of the Left and the Centre joined in demanding Ribot's resignation. No man, they said, had a right to describe as a "trap" what seemed a genuine peace offer.

Ribot was succeeded by J. Louis Barthou, a former Premier. Instead of adopting an attitude similar to that of Painlevé, as expressed in the "disannexation" formula, Barthou declared himself uncompromisingly in favor of the Ribot policy in regard to Alsace-Lorraine. On Nov. 13 another crisis arose and the Painlevé Cabinet fell, one of the reasons being Barthou's refusal to submit to the Foreign Affairs Committee of the Senate the document containing the alleged German peace offer. An almost equally important contributory cause of Painlevé's failure was his lack of a firm policy in dealing with "Boloism," which more than ever was agitating the public mind.

The new Premier was Georges Clemenceau, one of the most determined of "jusquauboutistes" or "bitterenders." He now took the lead in the attack on "Boloism," "defeatism," and the other secret influences which, patriotic Frenchmen were certain, were sapping the nation's energies and even infecting the fighting forces. With Stephen Pichon as Foreign Minister, he formed a Cabinet which the Socialists refused to join or support, but which obtained a strong enough backing in the Chamber to be able to carry on. In pledging himself to conduct the war to a victorious end, Clemenceau made it abundantly plain that there would be short shifts for pacifists and those engaged in treasonable or "semi-treasonable" activities.

## OTHER COUNTRIES

A mutiny in the German Navy, the story of which came out in debate in the Reichstag on Oct. 9, proved that, effectual as were the measures of the Ber-

lin Government to prevent the spread of revolutionary ideas, it was impossible to suppress the profound discontent and war-weariness of the people. According to the statement of Vice Admiral von Capelle, the Imperial Minister of Marine, the mutiny had taken place some weeks previously, but had been quickly quelled after three of the leaders had been executed. The Minister accused the Independent Socialists of having been responsible for the trouble and named specifically three Deputies—Vogtherr, Dittman, and Haase—as having been in conference with the ringleaders before the outbreak of the mutiny.

As a result of the disclosure the movement by the opposition to force the resignation of the Imperial Chancellor for failure to support a peace without annexations came to nothing, but a political crisis, brought about by the war party, rapidly developed, and on Oct. 24 Michaelis tendered his resignation as Chancellor to the Kaiser. Three days later Count von Hertling, the Bavarian Premier, was appointed to the vacant post, and various changes were made in the Ministry. The new Chancellor, who was 74 years of age, was an extreme Conservative, and his appointment signified no change in the essential policy of the German autocracy.

The supreme authority in Poland was transferred on Sept. 12 to a council of three Regents appointed by the German and Austro-Hungarian Emperors. The council was given legislative powers, but its decrees had to be countersigned by a Premier likewise appointed. The creation of a Council of Regents, which superseded the proclamation of Nov. 5, 1916, granting autonomy to Poland, was described as a temporary measure. After the war the Poles were promised a King and Parliament of their own. On Nov. 17 Professor Jan Kucharzevski, the historian, was appointed first Polish Premier.

New light was thrown on the intrigues of German diplomats by the act of the State Department of the United States in publishing on Sept. 8 a number of telegrams which had been sent in cipher by Count Luxburg, the German Chargé d'Affaires at Buenos Aires, to the Foreign Office in Berlin. These messages were dispatched by the Swedish Legation as their own official communications, addressed to the Stockholm Foreign Office. The startling revelation which the publication of the telegrams made was Count Luxburg's request that certain steamers should either be spared altogether by the submarines or sunk without leaving a trace, (" spurlos versenkt.") The effect of these revelations in Argentina was to rouse the deepest indignation against Germany. On Sept. 13 the Argentine Government handed Count Luxburg his passports and asked him to leave the country. This was followed by the Argentine Senate adopting on Sept. 19 a declaration to break off diplomatic relations with Germany. Meanwhile the Swedish Government announced that no further messages of any sort would be forwarded for Germany. In addition to other secret documents published by the United States Government were dispatches showing Count von Bernstorff's connection with the Bolo Pacha plot.

Following the lead of the United States, several more Latin-American republics aligned themselves against Germany. Costa Rica broke off diplomatic relations on Sept. 21, Peru on Oct. 6, Uruguay on Oct. 7, and Ecuador on Oct. 8. Brazil went the whole way by declaring war on Oct. 26. The attitude of Argentina was different. Notwithstanding a vote in both houses of the Argentine Congress in favor of breaking off diplomatic relations, President Irigoyen refused to depart from the policy of neutrality to which he had committed his Government. One of the causes of this action was the aggressive anti-war movement of the working classes, who paralyzed the country by a general strike on the railways and other obstructive measures. The Argentine workers were largely influenced by the French, Spanish, and Italian anarcho-syndicalist movements and were organized in sufficient strength to make themselves felt.

An international development of prime importance was the conclusion of an agreement between the United States and Japanese Governments in regard to the future of China. During September and October a Japanese Mission, headed by Viscount Ishii, held a number of conferences with the United States Government. Questions of Japan's co-operation with the Allies in regard to shipping and other matters were discussed, but the one tangible result of Viscount Ishii's visit was the signing on Nov. 2 of what was called the Ishii-Lansing Agreement. The primary point settled was the recognition by the United States of Japan's special interests in China. China, not having been consulted, protested vigorously against being thus disposed of. The final settlement of the question, however, could not be expected until the end of the war.

The absence of a thoroughly unified purpose on the part of the Allies, due to conflicting interests and, after the overthrow of the Kerensky Government, to the raising of issues which cross-cut the conflict between the national groupings, was the principal characteristic of the general diplomatic situation. In all countries forces varying in temper and size were at work for peace. In the United States, in Great Britain, and in Russia there was a growing demand for an exact statement of war aims and peace terms.

It was generally conceded that the leadership of the allied cause had passed into the hands of President Wilson. Without the assistance of America's millions of fighting men and vast material resources it was doubtful if the Allies could defeat Germany now that Russia was virtually out of the war. For that reason the United States acquired the right to define the objects for which the war should be continued. In addition to this material factor the United States exercised a great moral influence. As President Wilson, who was keenly alive to this aspect of the situation, repeated more than once, the United States had no gainful motive in the war.

The beginning of President Wilson's program of unifying allied aims in every direction, military, economic, and diplomatic, was seen in the sending of Colonel House at the head of a mission to consult with the allied Governments. The mission arrived in London on Nov. 7.

Meanwhile, the creation of a Supreme War Council, or Interallied Council, was being discussed at a conference of the British, French, and Italian Premiers, with their Chiefs of Staff, at Rapallo, near Genoa. The first act was to form an Interallied General Staff, consisting of Generals Cadorna, Foch, and Wilson. Premier Lloyd George, in a speech in Paris on Nov. 12, caused a stir by speaking with what he described as brutal frankness. The plight in which the Allies now found themselves, he said, was due to " national and professional traditions, questions of prestige, and susceptibilities," adding that the war had been " prolonged by particularism," and would be " shortened by solidarity."

The creation of the Supreme War Council and Lloyd George's speech aroused a storm of opposition in England on the presumption by the critics that it was a move to bring the commanders in the field under political control. But Lloyd George triumphed over his critics, and had the satisfaction of seeing made public a cablegram from President Wilson to Colonel House stating that the United States Government was emphatically of opinion that " unity of plan and control " was essential. By requesting Colonel House to attend the first meeting of the Supreme War Council, with General Bliss as military adviser, the President removed all doubts as to America's attitude toward the Rapallo plan.

The critical situation which was developing as the result of the rise to power of the Bolsheviki in Russia demanded unification of policy in regard to war aims and peace terms just as much as in regard to methods of conducting the war. Here again President Wilson, who had been both more alive and more sympathetic to the Russian Revolution, exercised a potent influence.

Turning now to the attitude of the Central Powers toward peace, we find that in Austria-Hungary there was a definite and widespread desire to end the war, and that between the Government and the people there was not such a sharp cleavage as in Germany, where the military party, flushed with the pride of conquest, was resolved to emerge from the war at the head of a greater Germany. The only peace the German autocracy was prepared to make was a victorious peace, and it left no stone unturned in this direction.

A German move for peace, made in September, 1917, was revealed through the publication of a secret diplomatic document by the Russian Bolshevist Foreign Minister, Trotzky, in the form of a telegram from the Russian Embassy in London, dated Oct. 6, which stated that the Spanish Ambassador in Berlin had been approached and asked to communicate Germany's desire to enter into peace negotiations. The allied Governments were accordingly informed, and Great Britain replied that it would receive any communication from Germany respecting peace and consider it in conjunction with the other allies. Germany denied that the move originated with it, but this denial was declared to be a " pure invention" by the British Foreign Minister. Nothing further came of it.

While the Governments and their spokesmen on both sides, as was seen in the German and Austro-Hungarian replies to Pope Benedict's peace proposals, and in the allied statesmen's comments on these replies, continued to pursue the familiar lines of argument, and while the movement for a clear statement of war aims gathered strength, as was seen, for example, in Lord Lansdowne's letter at the end of November, action was taken by the Bolshevist Government in Russia under the leadership of Lenine and Trotzky. The conclusion of an armistice on the eastern front as a preliminary to peace negotiations between Russia and the Central Powers opened an entirely new phase of the international situation.

# PROFESSOR PAUL PAINLEVE

Minister of War in the Ribot Cabinet and Designated as New Premier
of France
*(Photo Bain News Service)*

# THE DUKE OF AOSTA

Cousin of the King of Italy and Commander of One of the Italian
Armies Operating Against the Austrians
*(Photo Press Illustrating Service)*

# PERIOD XXXVII.

United States War Preparations—The Battle of the Julian Alps—Desperate Fighting of Canadians at Lens—The Scene of Carnage at Le Mort Homme—The Imperial Japanese Mission—Sweden's Unneutral Acts—The Belgian Prince U-Boat Crime—Spain and the World War—German War Losses—Russian Revolution—Three Years of Warfare in the Air—President Wilson's Reply to the Pope—German Chancellor on the Peace Note—The Socialists and the War—The Story of Kerensky's Life—A New Phase of the Balkan Question—Anti-Submarine Tactics—The Third Year of the Blockade—A War Sermon in Westminster Abbey—Italian Army's Spring Offensive—Disclosures of King Constantine's Relations with Germany—Germany After Three Years of War—The Austro-Germans and Islam—Indictment of Montenegro's King—Rumania Betrayed by Russia.

# CURRENT HISTORY CHRONICLED

## THE MONTH'S OUTSTANDING EVENTS

PORTENTOUS events marked the month ended Sept. 20, 1917. It was in that period that Russia was on the brink of civil war, which was avoided only by the quick action and firmness of Premier Kerensky and the Provisional Government; on Sept. 15 Kerensky proclaimed a republic, and the Constituent Assembly was summoned to meet in December.

In military affairs the most important event was the capture of Riga by the Germans, with the conquest of important sections of the rich provinces of Lithuania and Livonia, which the Germans assert they will permanently possess. On the western front the brilliant advance of the Italians in the Julian Alps was the outstanding feature, making the fall of Trieste seem probable and an invasion of the plains stretching to Vienna a possibility. The French made important gains in the Verdun section, restoring the line practically to what it was before the German advance in 1915. In Flanders there was continuous fighting, and there were some gains by the British in the Lens district; the sanguinary character of this fighting is shown by the casualty statements, which have been averaging for the British alone over 100,000 a month.

In political matters the most important occurrence was the disclosure by our State Department of German intrigues in Argentina and Mexico, in using the hospitality of the cables of the Swedish Legations to dispatch code messages of an offensively unneutral nature. In France the Ribot Ministry fell on account of lack of vigor, and Professor Painlevé, former War Minister, formed a new Cabinet which contained no Socialist members. In his initial statement to the Chamber the Premier announced a vigorous determination to fight until Alsace-Lorraine was restored to France, with indemnities; he was sustained by the Chamber on Sept. 19 by a vote of 378 to 1, the Socialists abstaining from the vote.

\* \* \*

## RUSSIAN REPUBLIC PROCLAIMED

THE Russian Republic was proclaimed Sept. 15, as follows:

General Korniloff's rebellion has been quelled. But great is the confusion caused thereby, and again great is the danger threatening the fate of the fatherland and its freedom.

Holding it necessary to put an end to the external indefiniteness of the State's organization, remembering the unanimous and rapturous approval of the republican idea expressed at the Moscow State Conference, the Provisional Government declares that the constitutional organization, according to which the Russian State is ruled, is a republican organization, and it hereby proclaims the Russian Republic.

(Signed)
Minister and President, KERENSKY.
Minister of Justice, YAROUDNI.

Russian matters preceding this proclamation are treated elsewhere, (Pages 63-72.) On Sept. 20 the Russian situation seemed greatly improved; the political tension had relaxed and a better spirit prevailed in army and navy than at any time since the revolution was launched.

\* \* \*

## FINANCING OUR WAR ACTIVITIES

A NARRATIVE of the remarkable achievements by the United States in the first six months after our war declaration appears on Pages 9-26. The gigantic nature of the nation's task is best demonstrated by the statement made to the House of Representatives on Sept. 14 by John J. Fitzgerald, Chairman of the Appropriations Committee, in Congress. He explained that the contemplated expenditures by our Government during the first year of the war, without reference to any unforeseen emergencies, would reach $18,208,228,085, of which $7,000,000,000 would be loaned to the Allies; this sum represents 23 per cent. of what all the other Governments had spent in three years. The revenue from taxes was estimated at a little over $4,000,000,000, the balance to be provided by bonds. On Sept. 18 Congress passed one war appropriation bill of $7,000,000,-000, the largest measure of its kind in history; this bill authorizes Government contracts for navy and artillery of $2,314,000,000, and gives the Shipping Board for new ships, plants, material, charters, construction, &c., $1,749,000,000. The bill carries $3,477,000,000 for the army alone.

\* \* \*

### THE KAISER AND ENGLAND

IN evidence that the feeling of hatred toward England in Germany had not subsided, Emperor William on Aug. 24, in an address to German battalions that had fought at the Flanders front, issued the following official statement:

> It is in God's hands when in His wisdom He will give us victory. He has taught our army a hard lesson, and now we are going to pass the examination. With the old German confidence in God, we shall show what we can do. The greater and mightier the problem, the more gladly we shall grapple with it and solve it. We shall fight and conquer until the enemy has had enough of these struggles.
>
> All Germans have realized who is the instigator of this war, and who is the chief enemy—England. Every one knows England is our most spiteful adversary. She spreads the hatred of Germany over the whole world, filling her allies with hatred and eagerness to fight. Thus every one at home knows what you know still better, that England is particularly the enemy to be struck down, however difficult it may be.
>
> Your relatives at home, who, too, have made great sacrifices, thank you through me. A difficult struggle lies ahead of us. England, proud of her stubborn resistance, believes in her invincibility, but you will show that you can achieve still greater things, for the prize of the war is the German people's freedom to live—freedom at sea and freedom at home. With God's help, we shall see the struggle through and be victorious.

\* \* \*

### BRITISH CASUALTIES IN FLANDERS

A STATEMENT issued by the British War Department shows that the Allies between April 9 and Aug. 22, 1917, captured 167,780 German and Austrian prisoners. Up to Aug. 22 Great Britain had captured 102,218 German prisoners and lost to Germany 43,000

British and East Indian prisoners. During August, 1917, the British losses were: Killed and died of wounds, 1,283 officers, 10,605 men; wounded, 3,671 officers, 39,025 men; missing, 310 officers, 2,774 men; total casualties, 5,264 officers, 52,404 men. The figures for April, May, June, and July, respectively, were:

|        | Officers. | Men.    |
|--------|-----------|---------|
| April  | 4,381     | 31,619  |
| May    | 5,991     | 107,075 |
| June   | 3,601     | 84,667  |
| July   | 2,490     | 68,858  |

The figures demonstrate the intensity of the fighting along the Flanders front during the five months since April, 1917, costing the British in casualties nearly 375,000 officers and men.

\* \* \*

CANADA'S draft law was given the final assent by the Justices of the Supreme Court Aug. 29, which was the final official sanction required to make it effective. It provides for raising 100,000 men and applies to males between 20 and 45 years of age; the first class is unmarried men between 20 and 34. All the predictions of dire civil conflicts to follow its enactment went amiss; Sir Wilfrid Laurier, who led the opposition, announced after the bill's final passage that " it was the duty of all loyal subjects to see that it was carried out harmoniously." The first call under the law is expected in early October.

\* \* \*

### THE DIRECTORY IN RUSSIA AND FRANCE

THE Russian revolution is following the French Revolution closely, so far as names go. Thus it has become the custom to speak of the " Constituent Assembly," where American usage would say " Constitutional Convention." And now we have the proposal to form a Directory of five, an Executive Committee to carry on the war, such as was established in France in 1795, (the Year III.) There is a marked difference: the French Directory was a committee chosen by the Legislature, which consisted of two houses. But in Russia even the Duma, the representative legislature which practically engineered the revolution, seems to have disappeared; this is the more striking because it was the Czar's intention to prorogue the Duma that precipitated the revolution. Though legally elected and endowed with authority, the Duma seems to exist only as a shadow, and the present Provisional Government has established itself without any election or legal organization whatever.

In 1795 the French Directory worked hard to prevent a restoration of the monarchy, and was even accused of falsifying election returns for this purpose. It was at this point that a young officer, Napoleon Bonaparte, fired the famous " whiff of grapeshot." Napoleon was rewarded with the command over the French armies in Italy in 1796; his splendid success there so strengthened him that in 1799 he was able to supersede the Directory, establishing a government of three Consuls, but retaining all real power in his own hands. In 1802 Bonaparte had himself elected Consul for life. In 1804 a vote of the nation declared him Emperor of the French, and he crowned himself at Paris, in the Pope's presence, as the successor of Charlemagne. How far the events which succeeded the Directory in France will be paralleled in Russia remains to be seen.

\* \* \*

## THE INVASION OF RUSSIA: 1917 AND 1812

HINDENBURG'S threat of an advance against the Russian capital and the presence of invaders on Russian soil in the Provinces of Kovno, Grodno, Volhynia, and Podolia inevitably recalls the last great invasion of Russia. The refusal of the Russian Emperor, Alexander I., to enforce the blockade of England led to that invasion, and in September Napoleon's army, which had numbered 500,000 when crossing the frontier, had reached Moscow, remaining there until the middle of October, although Moscow had been burned by the Russians. When the French retreat began the severe Russian Winter had already set in, and the sufferings of the retreating Grand Army have become an epic tradition. Only 20,000 of the invaders recrossed the Niemen.

Exactly the same conditions which resulted in the ruin of the Grand Army now face the Teuton invaders; with the difference that, while the invading army of Napoleon practically followed a single road to Moscow, thus simplifying the problems of supply, the Teuton armies will, apparently, be compelled to advance with a continuous, unbroken front nearly a thousand miles long if they try to carry out a great invasion. Such an advance, through a region of vast marshes and primeval forests, which extend for thousands of square miles immediately before the present Teuton lines, will without doubt involve enormous, perhaps insuperable, difficulties, now that the killing Russian Winter is beginning. The problem of supply will assume enormous proportions, since the Teuton army must be at least six times as large as the Grand Army of Napoleon. Even for motor trucks much of the country seems likely to be impassable. And the severity of Winter will last for the next six months.

\* \* \*

## THE ARGENTINE CIPHER AND OTHERS

THE intercepted Argentine and Mexican cipher dispatches are only the latest chapter in one of the world's great romances, the tale of secret messages sent between Kings and Ministers for thousands of years. One of the oldest examples of cipher is in Isaiah, vii., 6, " Let us set a King in the midst of Judah, even the son of Tabeal "; the last word being a cipher disguise for the name Remaliah. Another is in Jeremiah, xxv., 26, " the King of Sheshach " for the King of Babylon; the prophet's cipher consisted in using the second and twelfth letters from the end, instead of from the beginning, of the Hebrew alphabet—exactly the principle of substitute letters used today. In both these instances, dating from the eighth and seventh centuries before our era, the purpose was to conceal a perilous political secret.

Julius Caesar used a similar system, and cryptic writings were used by the Spartans, and by Ennius and Cicero. A group of political messages sent from England in the reign of Queen Mary by Giovanni Michael, the Venetian Ambassador, were based on a cipher so intricate that they have only recently been deciphered. Some time before Queen Mary's day Cardinal Wolsey, then at the

Court of Vienna, sent long cipher messages to Mary's father, the much-married Henry VIII. And seven centuries earlier the great founder of European nations, Charlemagne, wrote his dispatches in cipher.

But perhaps the high-water mark of secret writing was reached in the seventeenth century, when the Stuart Kings devoted much time and high ingenuity to crytography. Charles I. wrote long letters in cipher to his Queen, and also to his Ministers. After his defeat at Naseby in 1645 a large bundle of political documents in cipher, taken with his baggage, fell into the hands of the commanders of the Roundhead army. Some of these were deciphered at the time, one of them containing large concessions to Irish Roman Catholics; but one, at least, in a numerical cipher, was translated only as recently as 1858, more than 200 years after Naseby, by Wheatstone, who even devised a machine for the deciphering of cryptograms based on numbers. Another set of documents in cipher, of the same period, disclosed the Earl of Argyll's plot against James II. Yet another famous cipher document of the same time is the diary of the immortal Pepys, who perfected his system in 1660.

Francis Bacon in the same century applied his genius to the devising of ciphers, primarily " for the use of Princes " in political correspondence. Bacon says the three great requisites of ciphers are " that they be not laborious to write or read; that they be impossible to decipher, and, in some cases, that they be without suspicion." Applying this test to the Argentine cipher messages, it would seem that they comply with the first and last requirements: they seem to have been fairly easy to read, and, so far as the Swedish Minister, Baron Löwen, was concerned, they appear to have been wholly " without suspicion."

\* \* \*

### INTERNATIONAL SOCIALISM

THE ill-starred Stockholm Conference was the latest effort to revive the international, the worldwide federation of Socialists. The first attempt to organize the Socialists of all countries into one federation was made in London in 1847 by Karl Marx and his fellow-exiles. It was called the Communist League. It issued a manifesto just before the Revolution of 1848, but it was dissolved in 1852. The next attempt began through the visit of a number of French workmen to the London Exhibition of 1862, and called itself the International Association of Workingmen. It was not till 1866, however, that the first congress was held—in Geneva. The outbreak of the Franco-German war seems to have struck the deathblow of this international, for it never really recovered from the fact that owing to the war it was unable to hold a conference called in Paris. After the war its headquarters were removed to New York. It died in 1873.

No further attempts at the international fraternization of workingmen were made till 1889. The centenary of the French Revolution was being celebrated in Paris, and the French Socialist Parties called an International Socialist Congress. There were, as a fact, two Socialist Congresses — the Maixist and Possiblist. They combined later, and congresses were held at Brussels in 1891, Zurich in 1893, London in 1896, and Paris in 1900.

It was at the Paris Congress that the International Socialist Bureau was formed. Conditions of affiliation were drawn up, and were drawn to exclude anarchists, while including trade unions and other labor organizations. The conditions of affiliation are:

(1) All associations which adhere to the essential principles of socialism: Socialization of the means of production and distribution; international union and action of the workers; conquest of the public powers by the proletariat, organized as a class party.

(2) All the constituted organizations which accept the principle of a class struggle and recognize the necessity for political action (legislative and parliamentary) but do not participate directly in the political movement.

One of the duties of the bureau was to summon ordinary congresses at stated intervals and special congresses at times of international crises. In the present war nationalism proved stronger than internationalism even with Socialists, and until Stockholm was suggested there were no serious efforts to revive the International.

\* \* \*

### THE MONTH'S SHIPPING LOSSES

THE British Admiralty figures of merchant ships sunk by submarines or mines show a slight decrease for the last month. The record reads:

| | Over. 1,600 Tons. | Under 1,600 Tons. | Fishing Vessels. |
|---|---|---|---|
| Week ended Aug. 19... | 15 | 3 | 2 |
| Week ended Aug. 26... | 18 | 5 | 0 |
| Week ended Sept. 2.... | 20 | 3 | 0 |
| Week ended Sept. 9.... | 12 | 6 | 4 |
| Week ended Sept. 16... | 8 | 20 | 1 |
| Total for five weeks. | 73 | 37 | 7 |
| Total for previous four weeks. ............. | 74 | 10 | 4 |

French official figures for the three weeks ended Sept. 9 show the following sinkings: Over 1,600 tons, 7; under 1,600 tons, 6; fishing vessels, 2. One of the largest steamers recently lost was the Atlantic Transport liner Minnehaha, 13,-714 tons. The vessel was sunk off the coast of Ireland on Sept. 7, with a loss of forty-three lives. Since the war began she had made twenty-six voyages between America and England, carrying 16,000 tons on each trip. More exhaustive studies of submarine sinkings for the last eight months will be found on Pages 135 and 137.

\* \* \*

### THE WORLD AT WAR

OF the six continents—Europe, Asia, Africa, North and South America, and Australasia—Asia and Australasia are the most completely involved in the world war. Asia is completely implicated. The greater part of Asia is either British or Russian. Russian Siberia is in area equal to the whole of North America down to the Mexican border. Russia also has a large area further south, conquered by Russia from Mohammedan Princes, and generally known as Turkestan, Transcaspia, and so on.

The two powers which dominate nearly all the rest of Asia are China and Turkey, holding the eastern and western parts of the continent, as Russia and Britain hold the north and south. By a treaty of 1914, negotiated after the Chinese revolution, Tibet recognized China's suzerainty, and by a treaty signed in 1905 Afghanistan intrusted the management of its foreign affairs to England, a practical recognition of dependence. In Southeastern Asia, Annam is in the war, as belonging to France; Siam has recently declared war on her own account, while Japan, on the extreme verge of the Orient, has been in the war from the beginning. While Persia has not declared war, there has been much fighting on Persian soil, and the revolt of South Arabia brings that country also in, as the opponent of Turkey.

As nearly all Africa has been practically annexed by European powers, the whole continent is involved except the ancient empire of Abyssinia and unappropriated portions of the Libyan Desert. The fighting in Africa has been spread over a larger area than in any other continent, and has involved French, British, Belgians, Portuguese, and Germans. All North America, down to the Mexican line, is now belligerent; Mexico is neutral; Central and South America are more or less involved, but in a diplomatic rather than a military sense. In Europe six independent nations still remain neutral—Sweden, Norway, Denmark, (with Iceland and Greenland,) Holland, Switzerland, and Spain. Holland has large colonies in the East Indies and a foothold in Guiana, which are, therefore, out of the war.

\* \* \*

### POLISH LIBERTY POSTPONED

GERMANY and Austria, by a joint decree issued Sept. 15, transferred the supreme authority in Poland to a regency council of three members, appointed by the monarchs of the Central Empires. The council has legislative powers, but its decrees must be countersigned by a Premier, likewise to be appointed. This decree does not rescind but supersedes the proclamation of Nov. 5, 1916, granting autonomy to Poland. The Central Powers explain it as being a necessary measure during the continuance of the war. It was also announced that the Central Powers "would be obliged to occupy Polish soil during the war for the purpose of defending their eastern front."

In letters forecasting the new order the Emperors insist that this is simply a temporary measure, and that a Polish King and a Polish Parliament will sit at Warsaw after the war. The Polish armies raised originally as a national home organization were taken over by Austria just before the decrees were published; it is reported that they were sent to the Italian front. General Pilsudski, leader of the Polish Legion, was arrested by the Central Powers, and the Provisional State Council at Warsaw resigned in a body when the Polish troops were sent away.

\* \* \*

## POPE BENEDICT'S LETTER AND THE TEMPORAL POWER

IN quarters hostile both to Germany and the Vatican it has again and again been said that, in refraining from all protest against the violation of Belgium, the invasion of Serbia, and the numberless breaches of international law committed by the Teutons, Pope Benedict was obviously partial to Germany; and it was sometimes added that the Kaiser had promised to restore the temporal power of the Popes, as a reward for this partisanship. The temporal power, in this view, means, apparently, the restoration of the Papal States, which before 1860 extended across central Italy from the Tyrrhenian Sea to the Adriatic, and which from 1860 to 1870 were restricted to the western part of this area, with Rome as capital.

But there is another meaning of the term temporal power; and, in this sense, Pope Benedict's letter goes a long way to re-establishing it, or at least to asserting a claim for its exercise. For Pope Benedict offers himself as the arbiter between Kings, including not only those subject to the Church of Rome but the whole of Europe, and the Moslem Turkish Empire as well, to say nothing of the Hindu, Buddhist, and Shinto nations, India, Siam, China, and Japan, all now listed among the belligerents. This claim to be the arbiter between Kings

was gradually developed in the centuries which followed the alliance between the Pope and the Emperor, when Charlemagne was crowned at Rome on Christmas Day in the year 800. It was soon extended to include the right to make and dethrone Kings, while the Emperor, on his part, exercised the right to appoint Popes.

Thus the Emperor Henry III. appointed four German adherents successively to the Papal throne, while Henry IV. was practically deprived of the imperial throne and restored to it again, on the occasion of the memorable pilgrimage to Canossa, when he kneeled as a suppliant at the feet of Pope Gregory VII. In the same way King John of England, who in 1215 set his seal to Magna Charta, had previously been compelled to give up his kingdom by Pope Innocent III., receiving it again as a Papal fief. Perhaps the largest exercise of this power ever made was by Pope Alexander VI., who in 1493 divided the larger part of the world's oceans between Portugal and Spain, Portugal receiving all seas, with the lands they washed, to the east of a certain line, while Spain received everything to the west of it. This led to the establishment of Latin America, and the line of cleavage still exists, Brazil, to the east of the Pope's line, still speaking Portuguese, while the rest of South America, which lies to the west of the line, still speaks Spanish. Pope Benedict claims an equally extended jurisdiction, intervening in purely political questions of territories, annexations, indemnities, which affect every region of the globe.

\* \* \*

## TRIESTE, MIRAMAR, AND MAXIMILIAN

SOME four miles northwest of the port of Trieste, along the beautiful coast, on the jutting headland of Grignano, is Miramar, a charming and picturesque villa in the Norman style, built some sixty years ago by Maximilian, the ill-starred younger brother of the late Emperor Francis Joseph of Austria. Maximilian had great gifts and two hobbies—botany, which created the lovely gardens of Miramar, and naval tactics, which turned Trieste into the greatest naval base of the Austrian Empire. Maximilian, as a vigorous and able naval officer, had much to do with building up the Austrian fleet. He was, before the formation of United Italy, the Austrian Viceroy of Lombardy and Venetia, which Austria lost in 1859 and 1866. Maximilian then retired to Miramar with his wife Charlotte, daughter of Leopold I. of Belgium, the monarch chosen to rule over that small kingdom when Belgium was created and guaranteed as a neutral, inviolable State by the great European powers in 1831. At Miramar Maximilian received Mexican exiles, who asked him to go to Mexico and establish a monarchy. He at first refused, as both Francis Joseph and Napoleon III. were strongly opposed to the plan, and went instead on a botanizing trip to Brazil, then an empire. Later he allowed himself to be overpersuaded, went to Mexico, set up a monarchy, and was deposed and shot on June 19, 1867. This tragedy drove his wife insane, and Miramar became her prison-hospital. As the Italian and British monitors bombard Trieste, and as the Italian troops approach from the Carso on the north, the shells are likely to pass over the gardens and villa of Miramar.

* * *

### THE CORRESPONDENCE BETWEEN "WILLY" AND "NICKY"

THE highly sensational group of letters and telegrams recently printed in The New York Herald, between the two monarchs who signed themselves "Willy" and "Nicky," will stand, perhaps, as the last chapter in the monarchical diplomacy of the world in which Kings and Emperors, in the high-handed mediaeval fashion, disposed of peoples and nations without saying "by your leave." It is, perhaps, no secret that the treacherous proposal for a secret treaty between these two Emperors, forced by the masterful and magnetic "Willy" upon the weak-minded and weaker willed "Nicky," a treaty which involved the betrayal of France by Russia and the ruin of England by Germany and Russia acting in concert, was defeated by the resolute and far-seeing statesmanship of Count Witte, who became so well known to Americans at the time of the Peace of Portsmouth. On his return to Russia he discovered the treaty and, using the Berlin bankers as a lever, forced Kaiser Wilhelm to tear it up; but it appears that before it was destroyed Count Witte showed it to the famous international journalist and linguist, Dr. E. J. Dillon, who now vouches for its authenticity. The Willy-Nicky correspondence carries the world back to the days when nations and kingdoms were practically the private property of Kings and Emperors; when peoples and provinces were handed about as marriage dowries and were left in the wills of monarchs to their children. The granting of large regions of what are now the United States by Charles II. to his brother, the Duke of York, afterward James II., is an instance that comes home to us; and to that grant the largest city in the New World owes its name.

* * *

### CONSTITUTIONAL DEVELOPMENTS IN INDIA

THE world war, which is touching the British Empire at all points, is deeply affecting the development of India. In the House of Commons on Aug. 20 Samuel Montague, Secretary of State for India, made an important statement —the most important, perhaps, since the Imperial Government took over the administration of India from the old East India Company in 1858.

He laid down four principles which will be applied to the government of India. The first is that of increasing the employment of Indians in every branch of administration. The second promises the gradual development of self-governing institutions, with a view to the progressive realization of responsible government in India as an integral part of the British Empire. The third declares that progress in this policy can only be achieved by successive stages. The fourth lays stress on the point that the British Government must be the judge of the time and measure of each advance, and that they must be guided by the co-operation they receive from Indians, and by the extent to which it is found that confidence can be reposed in their sense of responsibility.

In the period since the Mutiny, 1857,

some progress has been made in the development of representative institutions in India. In 1909 the Indian Councils act established a Legislative Council for the whole of India, in which distinguished Indians representing all sections of the population take part. There are Indian members also in the Provincial Councils of Bombay, Madras, Bengal, and the other Provinces. There are elective District Boards, dealing, on the average, with populations of about a million each, whose members are predominantly Indians. Over 700 municipalities are also elective, and largely Indian in membership. So that, for the first time in the history of India, large sections of her population are receiving a practical training in representative self-government.

\* \* \*

### VAST TRADE IN EXPLOSIVES

THE wonderful development of the explosives manufacturing industry in the United States during the last four years is shown in a report issued by the Bureau of Mines, Department of the Interior. In the year 1913, which was a normal year, the exports reached $5,521,-077. The following year, in which the European war started, the exports reached $10,037,587; in 1915, $188,969,893; and in 1916, when the entire industry had been thoroughly organized, the total was $717,144,649. The total production of explosives in the United States during 1916, exclusive of exports, was 252,708 tons, an increase of 22,000 tons over the previous year.

\* \* \*

### THE RACE QUESTION IN FINLAND

FINLAND was joined to Russia by the Treaty of Frederikshavn, Sept. 17, 1809, as one of the results of the fraternization between Napoleon I. and Alexander I., which followed the Peace of Tilsit, July, 1807. France, it was agreed, should dominate Western Europe, while Russia might expand at the expense of Sweden and Turkey. Finland, taken from Sweden, is still governed under a Swedish Constitution dating from 1772, four years before the Declaration of Independence, though this Constitution has several times been amended. These amendments have given Finland a single Chamber of 200 members, elected by the vote of every citizen, man or woman, who is 24 years old. Finland, until March 15 of the present year, when Nicholas II. abdicated, was bound to Russia much as Hungary is bound to Austria, by the person of the sovereign, the Czar of Russia being also Grand Duke of Finland.

The present issue between Finland and Russia is whether the rights of the Czar, as Grand Duke of Finland, are inherited by the Provisional Government of Russia. In Finland, which has a population of three and a quarter millions, the Finns themselves number two and a half millions, while the Swedes number a third of a million. But the Swedes, though outnumbered eight to one by the Finns, are strongly intrenched, forming the landed aristocracy, and they are devoted to Sweden and Teutonic culture.

The Finns are one of the non-Aryan peoples, the most important of whom are the Turks and Magyars, (Hungarians,) both of whom represent successful invasions from Asia. To both Turks and Huns the Finns are related, forming a part of the group of North Asiatic peoples that stretch from Bering Strait across Siberia and northern Russia to the Gulf of Bothnia, which separates Finland from Sweden. In Northern Norway there is a small Finnish colony and a larger Lapp colony, numbering about 18,500, the Lapps being in all probability the last remnant of the oldest race in Europe, the race which was contemporary with the reindeer in France during and immediately after the glacial epoch, the race which hunted and painted the mammoth.

# Preparing to Fight Germany

## Military and Naval Progress of the United States in the First Six Months as a Belligerent

IT is now six months since the United States declared war on Germany, but as preparations for war had been begun immediately after the breaking of diplomatic relations, the period during which this country has developed its capacities as a belligerent is somewhat longer. A vast transformation of the whole nation's activities and modes of thought has been taking place, which at times it is difficult to perceive because of our very closeness to it. But we do know that in a comparatively short time the nation has multiplied its fighting forces tenfold, and under the direction of its captains of industry created the "army behind the army" on which military efficiency is dependent.

When the United States declared war against Germany, the strength of the regular army, including officers, was not quite 126,000, and that of the National Guard about 181,000, a nominal total of about 307,000. But the majority of these officers and men were not fit to take the field in a war such as is being now waged in Europe. In fact, it may be said that not a single unit was of immediate use, for the first troops sent to France with General Pershing are still undergoing training in the methods which have revolutionized the art of warfare. The Government's task was now to create practically a new army, an army trained in the light of the experience gained in Europe since August, 1914, and an army large enough to be of account in the desperate struggle with the unconquered millions led by the German war chiefs.

The regular army had to be increased to the full strength authorized by Congress. But voluntary enlistment proceeded slowly, and it was not until Aug. 9 that the 183,898 men required at the beginning of the recruiting campaign were obtained, thus bringing the regular army up to its full strength of 300,000 men. In March, a start had been made in mobilizing the National Guard, which even now is below its full strength, but enlistments have been fairly steady, and when the last units were drafted into Federal service on Aug. 5, the National Guard represented an addition of 350,000 men under arms. Here, then, were 650,-000 men who, in the course of a year, would gradually form the nucleus of the nation's armed forces on land.

### Training the New Officers

These men, in common with those secured by the selective draft law, however, would be useless without skilled leaders; and even more urgent than the need of raising armies was that of training officers. Special camps for this purpose were speedily established, and men, mainly belonging to the professional and educated classes, were selected to qualify for commissions. In August nearly 30,000 of these men qualified and were commissioned; while at the end of the month another 16,000 candidates were admitted to a second series of officers' training camps. By this time further enlistments in the regular army and National Guard, the calling into service of reservists and the assignment of duties to the new officers brought the total of the army up to more than 800,000, as is shown in the following statement, prepared by the Committee on Public Information from Government records:

On Sept. 6, 1917, there were in the regular army, National Guard and Reserve Corps of the army 72,828 officers and 741,053 enlisted men. In the navy there were 141,867 enlisted men, 41,473 Naval Reserves and 14,500 of the Naval Militia in the Federal service. There were 5,000 men in the Coast Guard and 6,500 in the Hospital Corps, making a total of 209,-340. The enlisted strength of the Marine Corps was 29,971; reserves in the services, 1,070; National Naval Volunteers,

704; retired men on active duty, 14. There were approximately 12,000 officers in the navy and 1,166 in the Marine Corps.

In other words, on that date the army had, including officers and enlisted men, 819,881, and the navy 254,265, making a total armed strength on that date of 1,-074,146 men, all of whom are volunteers. Prior to that time there was not a drafted soldier in a single training camp.

## For an Army of 2,300,000

Following this statement came the announcement of the War Department's plan for an army of 2,300,000 before the Summer of 1918. The first inkling of these plans was given when Secretary Baker testified on Sept. 7 that the United States Army would have a strength of 2,030,000 on Jan. 1, 1918. Then on Sept. 19, in asking Congress for emergency appropriations totaling $277,416,000, Secretary Baker stated that the money would be required to equip and supply an army of 2,300,000 men. This was the first official announcement made by the War Department concerning the number of Americans who will be prepared for service in France during the next year.

Announcement of the beginning of work on two more great army camps was made by the War Department on Sept. 7. These camps are at Newport News, Va., and Tenafly, N. J. " The camps are designated as concentration camps," an official announcement said, " and it is proposed to assemble and equip here, from time to time, troops that are awaiting orders. From these camps the troops may move to whatever locality is selected as the port of departure." Each of the new concentration camps will be capable of accommodating approximately 20,000 men, and will consist of from 800 to 1,000 buildings. The new camps will be rushed to completion by Nov. 1. Building of these camps on the seaboard is an indication that plans are rapidly maturing to send heavy reinforcements to Pershing's army in France.

This army of 2,000,000 will be made up of the 687,000 drafted men in the first levy, the National Guard expanded to 470,000 men, the regular army expanded to 450,000, auxiliary troops, including engineers and aviators, of 170,000; a

hospital corps of 140,000, and Quartermaster and other supply troops making up the remainder.

## About 70,000 Colored Troops

The problem presented by the large number of negro troops in the National Army was disposed of on Sept. 10 by the announcement of Secretary Baker that the rule of the regular army would be followed in their training, that is, they will be trained in separate organizations. There has, however, been no decision either on whether the negro troops are to be sent to France to fight in distinct units, as in brigades, or will be assigned to service by regiments. The call for negroes will be postponed, so that they will be called at a separate time, giving an opportunity to the officers of the camps to assemble the organizations of which they are a part substantially all at one time. They will not be the last called, but will be called separately. Of the 687,000 men called for as the first increment of the National Army, it is estimated that approximately 70,000 are negroes. In all, the army in France will need, it has been estimated, more than 100,000 men behind the lines for use along the roads and railways or on other special work. Negro troops will be largely employed in this way.

## Progress of the Draft Army

The progress in creating the National Army has been steady and without a hitch since the President signed the selective draft law on May 18. Over 9,500,000 young men were registered on June 5; the first quota of 687,000 men were drawn on July 20; the exemption boards then proceeded promptly with their work, and the first 30 per cent. of the first quota were ordered to report for duty on Sept. 5. On the day before the first drafted men were due in camp, parades and other celebrations were held in their honor throughout the country. The procession at Washington was led by President Wilson himself, with members of the Cabinet and of Congress and others following behind him.

President Wilson issued the following message of welcome to the soldiers of the National Army:

The White House,
Washington, D. C., Sept. 3, 1917.

To the Soldiers of the National Army:

You are undertaking a great duty. The heart of the whole country is with you.

Everything that you do will be watched with the deepest interest and with the deepest solicitude, not only by those who are near and dear to you, but by the whole nation besides. For this great war draws us all together, makes us all comrades and brothers, as all true Americans felt themselves to be when we first made good our national independence.

The eyes of all the world will be upon you, because you are in some special sense the soldiers of freedom. Let it be your pride, therefore, to show all men everywhere not only what good soldiers you are, but also what good men you are, keeping yourselves fit and straight in everything and pure and clean through and through.

Let us set for ourselves a standard so high that it will be a glory to live up to it, and then let us live up to it and add a new laurel to the crown of America.

My affectionate confidence goes with you in every battle and every test God keep and guide you!

WOODROW WILSON.

In a letter written to Thomas L. Chadbourne, Jr., of the Mayor's Committee on National Defense, New York City, the President declared he would like to be in the trenches. The letter follows:

The White House,
Washington, Aug. 30, 1917.

My Dear Mr. Chadbourne:

Please say to the men on Sept. 4 how entirely my heart is with them and how my thoughts will follow them across the sea, with confidence and also with genuine envy, for I should like to be with them on the fields and in the trenches where the real and final battle for the independence of the United States is to be fought, alongside the other peoples of the world, struggling, like ourselves, to make an end of those things which have threatened the integrity of their territory, the lives of their people, and the very character and independence of their Governments. Bid them godspeed for me from a very full heart. Cordially and sincerely yours,

WOODROW WILSON.

## Our Soldiers in France

The million men now under arms are at every stage of training, but of course those who are most nearly ready for actual fighting are the men who were sent under General Pershing to France in June, and whose training is being completed within sound of the big guns, just behind the front. The preparation of Pershing's army for its work in the trenches is being carried out largely under French guidance, though British instructors are also helping. French and British officers have also come to the United States to place their experience at the disposal of the War Department and of the officers who are to lead the new armies.

General Pershing on Sept. 1 moved his headquarters from Paris to a point nearer the American training camps. Discussing plans for the coming Winter, the General said that the American people must learn the meaning and value of patience, and not expect that the expeditionary forces landed in France can be rushed immediately to the front line trenches. When America does take her place in the line, shoulder to shoulder with the other allies, next year, she will be, General Pershing said, fully prepared to go through the Summer campaign and make the Germans feel the full weight of her military power.

The announcement was made on Sept. 12 that a large section of American field artillery had arrived in France, and that considerable progress had already been made in intensive training under the general supervision of the most expert French artillerists.

### Preparing the Aircraft Fleet

In no branch of modern warfare is skilled instruction more necessary than in the aerial service; and in both Europe and America our aviators are learning all they can from French and British experience. The United States has made one of its particular aims in the war the greatest possible achievement in aviation, and so that no obstacle should stand in the way, Congress voted the sum of $640,000,000 to be spent by the Aircraft Production Board in providing an enormous number of the most up-to-date and efficient flying machines. The appropriation was approved by President Wilson on July 24.

The Sheppard Bill legalizing the Aircraft Board was passed by the Senate

Sept. 12. Senator Sheppard of Texas, author of the bill, made this statement after its passage:

> The bill gives the present Aircraft Committee of the Council of National Defense a legal status and puts it under the joint control of the War and Navy Departments. All production contracts are subject to the control and approval of the Secretaries of War and Navy.
>
> The board is authorized to supervise and direct, under the requirements prescribed by the War and Navy Departments, the purchase, production, and manufacture of airship equipment and machinery, including purchase, lease, or construction of plants.
>
> The board will co-operate effectively with our allies in developing an aviation war program on a gigantic scale.

The bill provides that the personnel of the board shall consist of the Chief Signal Officer of the army, the Chief Constructor of the navy, and not more than seven other members, to be appointed by the President with consent of the Senate.

## The Liberty Aircraft Motor

What is regarded by American experts as the greatest military airplane motor yet built in the United States has been evolved by the combined efforts of American scientists, engineers, army officers, and Government officials. Secretary Baker on Sept. 12 announced that the Government had procured designs for such a motor and that it had been built and successfully tested. Secretary Baker's statement was issued after careful preparation of the material submitted to him by the Signal Corps and the Aviation Production Board. His statement follows in part:

> The United States aviation engine has passed its final tests. They were successful and gratifying. The new motor, designated by the Signal Service as the "Liberty Motor," is now the main reliance of the United States in the rapid production in large numbers of high-powered battleplanes for service in the war. In power, speed, serviceability, and minimum weight the new engine invites comparison with the best that the European war has produced.
>
> I regard the invention and rapid development of this engine as one of the really big accomplishments of the United States since its entry into the war. The engine was brought about through the co-operation of more than a score of engineers, who pooled their skill and trade secrets in the war emergency, working with the encouragement of the Aircraft Production Board, the War Department, and the Bureau of Standards. The story of the production of this engine is a remarkable one. Probably the war has produced no greater single achievement.
>
> An inspiring feature of this work was the aid rendered by consulting engineers and motor manufacturers who gave up their trade secrets under the emergency of war needs. Realizing that the new design would be a Government design and no firm or individual would reap selfish benefit because of its making, the motor manufacturers nevertheless practically revealed their trade secrets, and made available trade processes of great commercial value. These industries have also contributed the services of approximately 200 of their best draftsmen.
>
> While it is not deemed expedient to discuss in detail the performances and mechanics of the new motor, it may be said that standardization is a chief factor in the development of the Government's motor. Cylinders, pistons, and every other part of the motor have been standardized. They may be produced rapidly and economically by a great many factories operating under Government contracts. They may be as rapidly assembled, either by these plants or at a central assembly plant.
>
> The standardization of the new engine does not mean there will be no change in it during the war. There will be continuous experimentation as new types and improvements develop at the front and new ideas are born of the war emergency. If the engine can be improved, it will be improved, but as the motor stands today it is one of wonderful success and produced under dramatic circumstances. [*See also Page* 77.]

## What the Navy Has Done

The doings of the navy in the last six months are less obvious than of the land forces; but, relatively speaking, this branch of the United States defense service was at a much more advanced stage of preparation when America entered the war. The fleets had been mobilized before the declaration of hostilities. From the moment that President Wilson decided that he could by Executive act arm merchant vessels, the Navy Department had been busy arming and manning such ships as needed protection against the German submarines. Altogether, two hundred merchant vessels were supplied with gun crews and gunners in the first few months, and this number has been added to almost daily.

The Navy Department has rendered a great service to the British Admiralty by sending destroyers to the British Isles to help in the work of checking the ravages of the German submarines, and has taken over the cruiser patrol in the Western Atlantic all the way from Brazil to Newfoundland. Fuel and supply ships to serve the United States naval vessels in European waters have also been sent across the Atlantic so as to relieve the Allies of this service, and several small craft have been placed at the disposal of France. Two United States naval bases have been established on the French coast, as well as the one in the British Isles, from which the destroyers are operating against the German submarines. The navy has even gone to the aid of the Allies' aerial service by sending a hundred navy aviators to France. In addition to taking over the cruiser patrol of the coasts from Brazil to Newfoundland, the Navy Department has taken over the Coast Guard and Lighthouse Services.

To meet the demand for a larger personnel, two classes at Annapolis were graduated far ahead of their time, thus providing 380 new officers, while the enlisted strength of the navy has increased from 53,000 to over 120,000, and is gradually reaching the 150,000 maximum strength authorized by Congress.

Not the least important accomplishment of the navy has been its work in convoying Pershing's army to France. Under Admiral Gleaves this was so well carried out that neither a ship nor a single man has been lost. To sum up, it may be said that so far all the real burden of the war has fallen upon the navy, and that it has in no single case yet failed to live up to its traditions of the past or to the emergencies of the present.

War needs have caused the reorganization of the Atlantic fleet, which has been doubled in size and divided into two forces. This reorganization did not affect the division under Vice Admiral Sims, which is operating in European waters.

The naval vessels in which the greatest development has been taking place are those classed as destroyers. Secretary of the Navy Daniels conferred on Aug. 20 with representatives of twenty-five ship and engine builders for the purpose of providing the United States Navy with more destroyers than any other power. " Destroyers," he said, "are the one thing that a submarine fears." He indicated that the Navy Department would order all the destroyers the builders could produce. The sum of nearly $400,000,000 was mentioned as necessary to carry out this program. On Aug. 29, President Wilson approved the Navy Department's estimate of $350,000,000 for new destroyers. The main building program under the four-year plan will not be interfered with. Under the speeding-up régime a destroyer can be produced in about half the time it took before the war, that is, from ten to twelve months, instead of from eighteen to twenty months.

America had been rendering valuable medical aid in France and Belgium before becoming a belligerent. Work of the highest importance had been done by the American ambulances and hospitals organized by private effort; and when the war came these services were co-ordinated with new war medical activities. Special camps have been provided for thousands of civilian doctors for military service, and special hospitals built in the United States, while the number of medical units sent to France has been steadily increasing. The war has imposed a very severe strain upon the medical resources of the allied countries, so that one of the greatest services America has been able to offer to the Allies has been the prompt dispatch of doctors, nurses, and medical supplies.

[*Next month's issue will present the no less interesting story of what the United States has done on the economic side of the war.*]

# Army and Navy Training Camps

Thirty-two great training camps, each a city in itself, have been established and constructed for the drilling of the new recruits, and are now the chief centres of the nation's military activities. Besides these there are nine training camps for new officers, sixteen organization camps for the regular army, and similar centres for the drilling of aviators, medical officers, engineers, and Naval and Marine Corps.

The following table gives the names and other details of the National Guard mobilization camps, national army cantonments, regular army camps, second series of officers' training camps, medical, engineers', and aviation camps, army departments, and navy training camps and stations:

## National Guard Mobilization Camps

| Division or Branch of Service. | Name of Camp. | Location. | Commander. | Troops from. |
|---|---|---|---|---|
| Twenty-seventh Division | Camp Wadsworth | Calvert, six miles southwest of Spartanburg, S. C. | Maj. Gen. John F. O'Ryan | Guard from New York State. |
| Twenty-eighth Division | Camp Hancock | Wheeless, near Augusta, Ga. | Maj. Gen. Charles M. Clement | Guard from Pennsylvania. |
| Twenty-ninth Division | Camp McClellan | U. S. Military Reservation, near Anniston, Ala. | Maj. Gen. C. G. Morton | Guard from New Jersey, Delaware, Virginia, Maryland, and District of Columbia. |
| Thirtieth Division | Camp Sevier | Near Greenville, S. C. | Maj. Gen. J. F. Morrison | Guard from Tennessee, North Carolina, South Carolina and District of Columbia. |
| Thirty-first Division | Camp Wheeler | Seven miles from Macon, Ga. | Maj. Gen. F. J. Kernan | Guard from Georgia, Alabama, and Florida. |
| Thirty-second Division | Camp MacArthur | Waco, Texas | Maj. Gen. James Parker | Guard from Michigan and Wisconsin. |
| Thirty-third Division | Camp Logan | Five miles from Houston, Texas | Maj. Gen. George Bell, Jr. | Guard from Illinois. |
| Thirty-fourth Division | Camp Cody | Deming, New Mex. | Maj. Gen. A. P. Blocksom | Guard from Nebraska, Iowa, South Dakota, and Minnesota. |
| Thirty-fifth Division | Camp Doniphan | U. S. Military Reservation, Fort Sill, Okla. | Maj. Gen. W. M. Wright | Guard from Missouri and Kansas. |
| Thirty-sixth Division | Camp Bowie | Fort Worth, Texas | Maj. Gen. E. St. J. Greble | Guard from Texas and Oklahoma. |
| Thirty-seventh Division | Camp Sheridan | Three miles from Montgomery, Ala. | Maj. Gen. C. G. Treet | Guard from Ohio. |
| Thirty-eighth Division | Camp Shelby | Ten miles south of Hattiesburg, Miss. | Maj. Gen. W. H. Sage | Guard from Indiana, Kentucky, and West Virginia. |
| Thirty-ninth Division | Camp Beauregard | Five miles from Alexandria, La. | Maj. Gen. H. C. Hodges | Guard from Arkansas, Mississppi, and Louisiana. |
| Fortieth Division | Camp Kearny | Fifteen miles north of San Diego, Cal. | Maj. Gen. F. S. Strong | Guard from California, Utah, Arizona, New Mexico, and Colorado. |
| Forty-first Division | Camp Fremont | Near Charlotte, N. C. | Maj. Gen. H. Liggett | Guard from Washington, Oregon, Montana, Idaho, and Wyoming. |
| Forty-second ("Rainbow") Division | Camp Mills | Mineola, Long Island, N. Y. | Maj. Gen. William A. Mann | Guard units from 27 States. |

# PRESIDENT WILSON AND HIS CABINET

Front row (left to right): William C. Redfield, Robert Lansing, David F. Houston, President Wilson, William G. McAdoo, A. S. Burleson.  Back row (left to right): Josephus Daniels, William B. Wilson, Newton D. Baker, Thomas W. Gregory, Franklin K. Lane

*(Photo © Harris & Ewing)*

# THE ARCHBISHOP OF CANTERBURY

Accompanied by Field Marshal Lord Grenfell, the Primate Is Inspecting a Battalion Recruited From the Church Lads' Brigade

*(Photo © International Film Service)*

# National Army Cantonments

| Division or Branch of Service. | Name of Camp. | Location. | Commander. | Troops from. |
|---|---|---|---|---|
| Seventy-sixth Division | Camp Devens | Ayer, Mass. | Maj. Gen. H. F Hodges | Quotas from Maine, New Hampshire, Vermont, Massachusetts, Connecticut, Rhode Island, and New York. |
| Seventy-seventh Division | Camp Upton | Yaphank, Long Island, N. Y. | Maj. Gen. J. F. Bell | Quotas from New York, including New York City. |
| Seventy-eighth Division | Camp Dix | Wrightstown, N. J. | Maj. Gen. Chase W. Kennedy | Quotas from New Jersey, Delaware, and New York. |
| Seventy-ninth Division | Camp Meade | Admiral, Md. | Maj. Gen. J. E. Kuhn | Quotas from District of Columbia, Maryland, and Pennsylvania. |
| Eightieth Division | Camp Lee | Three miles from Petersburg, Va. | Maj. Gen. A. Cronkhite | Quotas from Virginia, West Virginia, and Pennsylvania. |
| Eighty-first Division | Camp Jackson | Five miles from Columbia, S. C. | Maj. Gen. F. H. French | Quotas from South Carolina, North Carolina, Florida, and Porto Rico. |
| Eighty-second Division | Camp Gordon | Thirteen miles northeast of Atlanta, Ga. | Maj. Gen. Eben Swift | Quotas from Georgia, Alabama, and Tennessee. |
| Eighty-third Division | Camp Sherman | Three miles from Chillicothe, Ohio | Maj. Gen. E. F. Glynn | Quotas from Ohio and Pennsylvania. |
| Eighty-fourth Division | Camp Taylor | Dumesnil, seven miles from Louisville, Ky. | Maj. Gen. H. C. Hale | Quotas from Kentucky, Indiana, and Illinois, |
| Eighty-fifth Division | Camp Custer | Four miles west of Battle Creek, Mich. | Maj. Gen. J. T. Dickman | Quotas from Michigan and Wisconsin. |
| Eighty-sixth Division | Camp Grant | Four miles from Rockford, Ill. | Maj. Gen. Thomas H. Barry | Quotas from Illinois. |
| Eighty-seventh Division | Camp Pike | Eight miles northwest of Little Rock, Ark. | Maj. Gen S. D. Sturgis | Quotas from Arkansas, Louisiana, Mississippi, and Alabama. |
| Eighty-eighth Division | Camp Dodge | Eleven miles north of Des Moines, Iowa | Maj. Gen. E. H. Plummer | Quotas from North Dakota, Minnesota, Iowa, and Illinois. |
| Eighty-ninth Division | Camp Funston | Four miles east of Fort Riley, Kan. | Maj. Gen. Leonard Wood | Quotas from Kansas, Missouri, South Dakota, Nebraska, Colorado, New Mexico, and Arizona. |
| Ninetieth Division | Camp Travis | Adjoining the U. S. Military Reservation at Fort Sam Houston, San Antonio, Texas | Maj. Gen. H. T. Allen | Quotas from Texas and Oklahoma. |
| Ninety-first Division | Camp Lewis | American Lake, sixteen miles south of Tacoma, Wash. | Maj. Gen H. A. Greene | Quotas from Alaska, Washington, Oregon, California, Idaho, Nevada, Montana, Wyoming, and Utah. |

## SIGNAL CORPS AVIATION CAMPS

| Location. | Field. | Squadrons. | Officers. | Enlisted Men. |
|---|---|---|---|---|
| Essington, Penn. | | 1 | 3 | 150 |
| Fairfield, Ohio | Wilbur Wright | 4 | 12 | 600 |
| Fort Sill, Okla. | | 1 | 3 | 150 |
| Mineola, Long Island, N. Y. | Hazelhurst | 2 | 6 | 300 |
| Mount Clemens, Mich. | | 2 | 6 | 300 |
| Rantoul, Ill. | Chanute | 2 | 6 | 300 |
| San Antonio, Texas | Camp Kelly | 8 | 24 | 1,200 |
| San Diego, Cal. | Rockwell | 2 | 6 | 300 |
| Total | | 22 | 66 | 3,300 |

# Officers' Training Camps

Second series: Aug. 27 to Nov. 26, 1917.
Total men admitted to all camps, 20,669.

Plattsburg Barracks, N. Y.—Commanding officer, Colonel Paul A. Wolf.

Fort Niagara, N. Y.—Commanding officer, Colonel J. W. Heavey.

Fort Myer, Va.—Commanding officer, Lieut. Col. C. W. Fenton.

Fort Oglethorpe, Ga.—Commanding officer, Colonel Herbert J. Slocum.

Fort Benjamin Harrison, Ind.—Commanding officer, Major Alvan C. Read.

Fort Sheridan, Ill.—Commanding officer, Lieut. Col. James A. Ryan.

Fort Snelling, Minn.—Commanding officer, Colonel J. D. Leitch.

Leon Springs, Texas—Commanding officer, Lieut. Col. J. D. L. Hartman.

Presidio of San Francisco, Cal.—Commanding officer, Lieut. Col. F. W. Sladen.

The regular army organization camps are located at:

Chickamauga National Park, Ga.
Douglas, Ariz.
El Paso, Texas.
Fort Benjamin Harrison, Ind.
Fort D. A. Russell, Wyo.
Fort Douglas, Utah.
Fort Ethan Allen, Vt.
Fort Myer, Va.
Fort Riley, Kan.
Fort Sam Houston, Texas.
Fort Sill, Okla.
Fort Snelling, Minn.
Gettysburg National Park, Penn.
Presidio of San Francisco, Cal.
San Antonio, Texas, (Camp Wilson.)
Vancouver Barracks, Wash.

## MEDICAL OFFICERS' TRAINING CAMPS

Allentown, Penn., 150 students, (Ambulance Corps.)

Fort Benjamin Harrison, Ind., 1,200 students.

Fort Des Moines, Iowa, 75 students, (colored.)

Fort Oglethorpe, Ga., 1,300 students.

Fort Riley, Kan., 900 students.

Total approximate number attending, 3,625 students.

## ENGINEER OFFICERS' TRAINING CAMPS

American University, Washington, D. C., 425 students.

Fort Leavenworth, Kan., 525 students.
Vancouver Barracks, Wash., 160 students.
Total, 1,110 students.

## DEPARTMENTS AND COMMANDERS

HEADQUARTERS, COAST ARTILLERY DISTRICTS, &c.

EASTERN DEPARTMENT.—Headquarters, Governors Island, N. Y.; commander, Brig. Gen. Eli P. Doyle, retired.

Middle Atlantic Coast Artillery District—Headquarters, Fort Totten, N. Y.

Panama Coast Artillery District—Headquarters, Ancon, Canal Zone.

NORTHEASTERN DEPARTMENT.—Headquarters, Boston, Mass.; commander, Brig. Gen. John A. Johnston.

North Atlantic Coast Artillery District—Headquarters, Boston, Mass.

CENTRAL DEPARTMENT.—Headquarters, Chicago, Ill.; commander, Major Gen. William H. Carter, retired.

SOUTHEASTERN DEPARTMENT.—Headquarters, Charleston, S. C.; commander, Major Gen. William P. Duvall, retired.

South Atlantic Coast Artillery District—Headquarters, Charleston, S. C.

SOUTHERN DEPARTMENT.—Headquarters, Fort Sam Houston, Texas; commander, Major Gen. John W. Ruckman.

WESTERN DEPARTMENT.—Headquarters, San Francisco, Cal.; commander, Major Gen. Arthur Murray, retired.

South Pacific Coast Artillery District—Headquarters, Fort Miley, Cal.

North Pacific Coast Artillery District—Headquarters, Seattle, Wash.

PHILIPPINE DEPARTMENT.—Headquarters, Manila, P. I.; commander, Major Gen. Charles J. Bailey.

HAWAIIAN DEPARTMENT.—Headquarters, Honolulu, Hawaii; commander, Major Gen. Frederick S. Strong.

## NAVY TRAINING CAMPS AND STATIONS

Philadelphia, (League Island;) Newport, R. I.; Cape May, N. J.; Charleston, S. C.; Pensacola, Fla.; Key West, Fla.; Mare Island, Cal.; Puget Sound, Wash., (Bremerton;) Hingham, Mass.; Norfolk, Va.; New Orleans, La.; San Diego, Cal.; New York Navy Yard; Great Lakes, Ill.; Pelham, N. Y.; Hampton Roads, Va., and Gulfport, Miss., (Winter.)

## MARINE CORPS TRAINING CAMPS

Port Royal, S. C.; Mare Island, Cal., and Quantico, Va.

# A Great American Mercantile Marine for the War Emergency

THE destruction of allied and neutral shipping since the war began in 1914 and the diversion by the Allies of an enormous amount of tonnage from normal trade channels had already, before the United States became a belligerent, forced this country to consider very seriously the problem of creating a mercantile marine of its own on a scale commensurate with its commerce. Ever since the civil war the United States has occupied a secondary position as a carrying nation. It has depended upon foreign ships for its ocean transportation, although for half a century efforts were repeatedly made to establish a mercantile marine.

The European war accentuated the problem. The Government was urged to take the matter in hand, and finally President Wilson secured the passing of legislation which authorized the appointment of a Shipping Board and the creation of a corporation to build ships. It was provided that the majority of the stock in this corporation should be held by the Government. Again there was delay, but our entry into the war hastened events, and on April 16, 1917, the Emergency Fleet Corporation was organized by the Shipping Board, and Major Gen. George W. Goethals, the engineer who built the Panama Canal, was appointed General Manager. Congress authorized the use of $50,000,000, and work was immediately begun to build a vast fleet of both steel and wooden ships to transport supplies to the Allies and thus frustrate the German submarine campaign. Contracts were awarded to various shipbuilding firms, and shipyards on both the Atlantic and Pacific Coasts began to hum with increased activity.

## Seizure of German Shipping

The first warlike act of the United States on entering the war was to seize all the German merchant ships laid up in the ports of the United States and its insular possessions. As many of these ships had been disabled by their crews, work was immediately begun to repair them. Early in June fourteen of the seized ships were assigned to the service of the Navy Department and renamed, while at the end of the same month President Wilson signed an executive order authorizing the Shipping Board to take " possession and title " of eighty-seven of the German-owned ships, representing 500,000 tons. The board secured from the President the broadest powers to repair, equip, man, operate, lease, or charter the vessels in any service for the United States or in any commerce, foreign or coastwise. These ships were in various ports on the Atlantic and Pacific and in insular ports. The directions referring to them did not affect the fourteen ships which had been taken over by the Navy Department. The eighty-seven ships were specified by name in the President's executive order.

On July 27 Secretary Daniels announced that the American flag had that day been hoisted on the great German liner Vaterland. He also stated that fifteen other German ships had been taken over by the Government and the work of fitting them out for transport service would be rapidly pushed to completion. The work on all these ships was begun some time previously by contract under the Shipping Board. The Navy Department had now taken over this work under its direction. Repairs to the Vaterland, which has been renamed the Leviathan, cost slightly less than $1,000,000. The Leviathan is the largest merchant vessel in the world. Subsequently other German ships were placed under the American flag.

The seized German ships represent the beginnings of the new American mercantile marine. But more important additions are being made by purchase and construction. Thus, Austro-Hungarian ships have been acquired by purchase, since a state of war thus far does not exist between the United States and

Austria-Hungary. International law permits the requisition of foreign tonnage if due compensation is paid to the owners. The first Austro-Hungarian ship thus acquired was the Martha Washington, 8,312 tons, which the Shipping Board announced would be requisitioned and turned over to the War Department for emergency service.

## The Shipbuilding Program

Major Gen. Goethals on July 13 outlined his shipbuilding program. He stated that contracts had then been awarded for 348 wooden ships, representing 1,218,000 tons and costing $174,000,000, and seventy-seven steel ships, representing 642,800 tons and costing $101,660,356. He added that negotiations were proceeding for another hundred wooden ships. Major Gen. Goethals then explained that he mainly relied on the construction of steel ships of standard pattern for getting the greatest amount of the most serviceable tonnage in the shortest time. Contracts were to be offered for the building of two plants (to be owned by the Government) for the construction of fabricated steel ships, to produce 400 ships, aggregating 2,500,000 tons, within eighteen to twenty-four months, and absorbing $550,000,000. Major Gen. Goethals also foreshadowed the commandeering of ships then in process of building for private account, aggregating more than 1,500,000 tons.

Disagreement between Major Gen. Goethals and the Shipping Board, of which William Denman was President, led to the resignation on July 20 of Major Gen. Goethals and the demand by President Wilson that Mr. Denman likewise resign. Edward N. Hurley, formerly Chairman of the Federal Trade Commission, was appointed President of the Shipping Board, and Rear Admiral W. L. Capps, Chief Constructor of the Navy, was designated General Manager of the Emergency Fleet Corporation. Bainbridge Colby of New York was also appointed a member of the Shipping Board.

The first important act of the Government after the reconstitution of the Shipping Board was the commandeering of all power-driven cargo-carrying and passenger vessels above 2,500 tons dead weight capacity under construction, and all materials, machinery, equipment, and outfit pertaining to such construction. The order was issued to the owners of shipyards on Aug. 3 by Admiral Capps in virtue of the authority delegated to the Emergency Fleet Corporation. Compensation, the order explained, would be paid at a later date. Thus, by a single stroke, the United States came into possession of over 1,500,000 tons of shipping in process of construction. Most of the 700 vessels commandeered were owned in Great Britain and Norway. When completed, these vessels will almost double America's steam tonnage in foreign trade.

With the submission of new estimates by the Shipping Board on Aug. 24 the Government's complete shipbuilding program was made public. It called for a total of 1,270 ships, of 7,968,000 tons, in addition to nearly 2,000,000 tons of shipping which was already under construction in American yards, and which had been commandeered by the Emergency Fleet Corporation. The program is to be carried out by the end of the fiscal year on June 30, 1918, and requires a new billion-dollar appropriation, thus bringing the total amount required for building, commandeering, and purchasing vessels up to two billions. The details of the program are shown in the following table:

### BUILDING PROGRAM

| | Number. | Tonnage. | Estimated Cost. |
|---|---|---|---|
| Ships contracted for | 433 | 1,919,200 | $285,000,000 |
| Ships ready to be contracted for when funds are available | 452 | 2,968,000 | 455,500,000 |
| Ships under negotiations | 237 | 1,281,400 | 194,000,000 |
| | | | $934,500,000 |
| Miscellaneous vessels | 150 | 1,800,000 | 300,000,000 |
| Organization and other miscellaneous expenses | | | 35,000,000 |
| Amount authorized by Congress June 6, 1917, ($300,000,000 appropriated) | | | 550,000,000 |
| Amount to be authorized for building program immediately in sight, making no allowance for changes in cost of labor and material | | | 719,500,000 |

COMMANDEERING PROGRAM

For commandeered ships, amount
required. ...................... $515,000,000
For commandeered ships, amount
authorized by Congress June 6,
1917 .......................... 250,000,000

Balance requiring authorization
by Congress ................. $265,000,000

PURCHASE PROGRAM

For vessels to be purchased other
than under construction or commandeered ................... 150,000,000

SUMMARY

Total amount, in round figures,
to be purchased in addition to
amounts already authorized:
For commandeered vessels...... 265,000,000
For construction of new vessels. 719,500,000
For purchase of new vessels.... 150,000,000

Grand total ................$1,134,500,000

Amounts desired to be appro-
priated for remainder of fiscal
year 1918:
For commandeered vessels...... $365,000,000
For building program.......... 400,000,000
For purchase of vessels........ 150,000,000

Total ....................... $915,000,000

## Three Great Shipyards

Contracts for the construction of three
great Government-owned shipbuilding
yards were awarded on Aug. 31 by the
Emergency Fleet Corporation to the
American International Corporation, the
Submarine Boat Corporation, and the
Merchants' Shipbuilding Company. After
the first ship is turned out from one of
these yards it will be possible to produce
one 5,000-ton steel vessel every two
working days.

On Sept. 7 it was announced that the
United States is to build a great fleet of
merchant vessels of from 10,000 to 12,000
tons, capable of attaining a speed of 16
knots or better. Contracts already entered into for ships of smaller capacity
and lower speed would be carried out, but
practically all of the millions which Congress had been asked for in addition to
the original appropriation of $500,000,-
000 for construction would be devoted to
the fast ships. At least 150 cargo ships
aggregating from 1,500,000 to 2,000,000
tons will be built under the new Shipping
Board plan, and not one of them will be
slower than 16 knots, while many of

them will be capable of 18 knots or more.
Careful investigations made by Chairman
Hurley of the Shipping Board and Secretary Redfield of the Department of Commerce showed that vessels capable of 16
knots or more were practically free from
successful submarine attack.

A question which is causing some perplexity was raised by the commandeering
of the ships building for British interests.
On one side it was proposed that they
should be retained by the United States
in spite of the objections of Great Britain, but it was pointed out on the other
hand that soon after the arrival of the
British War Mission in the United States
the British Government gave assurances
that it would not protest against the
commandeering of British vessels on
American stocks. Later there was an endeavor to put through an inter-allied
chartering agreement, which, in the view
of American officials, would have given
the United States hardly enough representation of power in the control of allied
shipping. For this reason the proposal
was rejected. Following this, Great
Britain is understood to have changed her
position on the question of commandeer
and to have demanded that the ships she
is building here be turned back to her on
their completion.

## The Chartering Commission

Another far-reaching development in
the control of the Shipping Board took
place on Sept. 6, when Mr. Hurley announced the formation of an American
Chartering Commission, with headquarters in New York, to have absolute power
over all charters of American ships or
by American shippers. The proposed
powers of the American Chartering
Commission are much broader than those
of the Inter-Allied Chartering Committee
in London. Mr. Hurley and the Shipping Committee of the Council of National Defense agreed upon a tentative
universal shipping rate to be enforced
on all Government shipments on American vessels. Close co-operation was also
arranged between the Embargo Administration Board and the Shipping Board to
insure the widest possible control of alien
tonnage.

The rounding off of the Shipping Board's jurisdiction was made manifest in the conclusion arrived at by the Exports Board and the Shipping Board that the United States has full authority to commandeer neutral tonnage tied up in American ports, as " war necessity." This decision affected 400,000 tons of neutral shipping, of which 250,000 was Dutch. An interesting point involved in this step was the revival of the ancient right of angary, which is recognized as part of international law and means the right to enforce transportation. All efforts to effect an agreement with the Allies for a general rate reduction in the Atlantic have so far proved ineffective, owing to the fact that Great Britain's method of shipping control has made it impossible for the British to co-operate in the Shipping Board plan. In regard to shipping on the Pacific, where Japan dominates the situation, negotiations were begun on the arrival of the Japanese War Mission headed by Viscount Ishii.

# Enemies Within the United States
## The Government's Treatment of Enemy Aliens. Spies, and Seditionists

THE large number of enemy aliens in the United States presents one of the many problems with which the Government has to deal. Technically, every German who has not taken out first papers and who, therefore, still owes allegiance to the Fatherland is an enemy alien; but, while the great majority of these aliens are naturally either sympathetic to German war aims, or at least unable to give their wholehearted support to the Allies, they are not a source of danger to the United States. Only a small section have given evidence of disaffection, or endeavored to cause trouble.

On the outbreak of war in 1914 the British Government interned all German subjects because it was difficult to know who were and who were not engaged in some form of espionage. Such a measure would be impracticable in the United States, and efforts have accordingly been limited to watching and arresting only those Germans whom there was some reason of suspecting as spies or agents of the German Government. This is the task of the Secret Service, and from the nature of its work it is impossible to give any idea of what has been done except where the arrest of Germans has actually been reported.

### Prisoners of War

The largest group of interned Germans consists of those who come under the heading of prisoners of war, as distinct from men suspected of espionage. Practically all these prisoners of war are officers and men who formed the crews of the German merchant vessels seized in American ports; and most of them were arrested in New York and sent in the first place to Ellis Island. The Government has leased a hotel and grounds at Hot Springs, N. C., and there established a detention camp, where several hundred German merchant officers and sailors are now accommodated in very comfortable quarters. Five hundred officers and a hundred sailors here enjoy their new-found leisure in a hundred acres of shaded lawn, and need not work unless they feel so inclined. As soon as new buildings are erected another six hundred men will be sent to Hot Springs.

The Germans at Hot Springs have caused no trouble, and do not seem inclined to do so. They are seafaring men and philosophic enough to enjoy their enforced holiday. They obey the few rules imposed on them. They answer roll call at 9 A. M. daily and take part in a fire drill. Then they are practically free within the grounds until taps sound at 11 P. M. They are practically on the "honor system" and are allowed to make rules for their own guidance through a number of committees. They work when they work and play when they play, idling but little. The chief officers have organized classes, and daily instruction is given to petty officers and common seamen in mathematics, navigation, and languages. Squads run through military setting-up exercises daily. Some of the men work for the Government, including fifty ship carpenters engaged in the construction of the new barracks, and others are employed as day laborers. The pay ranges from $20 to $30 a month. A number of the men work in the seven-acre tract, where a fine crop of vegetables is growing, and others find diversion in their own little garden plots. Agriculture appeals to most of the interned men.

By the riverside the officers have built a village of miniature rustic houses, using tree limbs and roots, stones, odds and ends of material found on the hotel grounds. One house has panels of old matting. A small church with a steeple is nearing completion. The prisoners are allowed to receive newspapers and other reading matter, and, subject to the station censorship, to write and receive letters. About thirty members of German officers' families have gone to the village of Hot Springs, and these the officers are privileged to receive for an hour each Sunday. They can see them as often as they wish, the families coming to the fence, but no conversation is allowed except during the Sunday hour. Few visitors are allowed to inspect the station, and they are not permitted to speak to the Germans except by way of salutation in passing. The Germans do not salute the Americans in charge, although they generally speak in salutation. The watchmen are not supposed to talk with them. The Germans are well fed on plain food—potatoes, beans, cabbage, turnips, and material for soups and stews. The United States furnishes the food at a cost of about 50 cents per man a day, and the German chefs cook it.

## Methods of Handling Prisoners

In the expectation that the progress of the war will throw on the United States the burden of looking after large numbers of prisoners, the War Department is completing plans for handling many thousands more. According to an official statement, all war prisoners, whether military or naval, will ultimately be placed in the custody of the War Department, and the Adjutant General of the army will have general control through five principal bureaus, namely:

1. A bureau of administration charged with the composition and personnel of the guards, the pay, rations, clothing, and transportation of them.

2. A bureau of employment in charge of the labor of prisoners, both within their places of internment and on Federal, State, and private projects without the prisons.

3. A bureau of religious and educational welfare, to which bureau all matters connected with religion, education, recreation, and the dealing with Red Cross and benevolent assistance will be conducted.

4. A bureau of inquiry charged with the custody of the records of war prisoners, and through which information concerning the prisoners will be transmitted to the enemy's Government and to the National Red Cross Society. This bureau is also charged with the forwarding of mail, money orders, and packages sent from the prisoners' home country for delivery to individual prisoners; and

5. A bureau of repatriation, charged with the final restoration of prisoners to their home country at the conclusion of hostilities.

## Three War Prison Barracks

The places of detention are known as war prison barracks and at present three such barracks have been established, located at Fort McPherson, Ga.; Fort Oglethorpe, Ga., and Fort Douglas, Utah. Each barracks is commanded by a Colonel of the regular army, assisted by a staff of officers similar to that of a commanding officer of an army post or camp.

The general regulations under which war prisoners are held were made the subject of a special article of the Fourth Hague Convention. In addition to this, the United States is bound by certain provisions of the Geneva Convention.

Officers who may be made prisoners are allowed, under the provisions of The Hague Convention, the pay of officers of the corresponding grade in the army of the captors' Government, and such is the present practice in the United States.

The enlisted men who are made prisoners are given the same medical attention, pay, clothing, and quarters as are allowed United States soldiers. The quarters authorized for war prisoners are similar to and constructed in accordance with the specifications governing the construction of cantonments used by the army of the United States. War prisoners are not confined in the sense of being placed in jails or prisons or penal institutions, but as it is necessary to limit their freedom of movement, the cantonments in which they are confined are surrounded by a wire fence. Within the limits of this fence prisoners are given liberty of action.

## Entire Religious Freedom

The Hague Convention requires that war prisoners shall enjoy complete liberty in the exercise of their religion. To provide for this, there is a chaplain of the regular army on the staff of the commandant of each war prison barracks, who has general supervision of the religious matters connected with the prison, and services are authorized for all prisoners so desiring where churches of special denominations are located in the vicinity of the places of internment. A representative of the International Committee of Young Men's Christian Associations is also accredited to each war prison barracks and, in conjunction with the barracks chaplain, assists in the athletic and social affairs of the prisoners. In the event of the death of a war prisoner, the same honors and respect are shown as in case of the death of an individual of corresponding rank in the United States Army.

The educational welfare of the prisoners is under the immediate control of the barracks chaplain, who is charged with the organization of courses of instruction as elected by the prisoners and who is aided in the work by the prisoners themselves. Later, vocational training will be introduced in each barrack to provide for prisoners who are without any trade or vocation, the qualified prisoners being used as instructors for the others.

Prisoners are entitled to send mail matter through international mails without postage. Mail matter for domestic destination is subject to postage, as is also all incoming mail, both outgoing and incoming mail being censored at the barracks.

As the number of prisoners increases, the Adjutant General will, under the authority granted him by Paragraph 6 of the Fourth Hague Convention, authorize the employment of these prisoners on work connected with the public service, for individuals, and upon their own account.

In arriving at the wages to be paid prisoners for these classes of work, the provisions of international law govern. When the work is for branches of the public service or for private persons, the conditions are settled in an agreement with military authorities. The wages of prisoners go toward improving their positions, and any balances remaining are paid them on their release, after deducting the cost of maintenance.

Complete records are kept of all sums disbursed for the care and upkeep of war prisoners, and at the close of hostilities reports of these disbursements are forwarded to the enemy Government for reimbursement.

## Some of Those Interned

Among the Germans who have been arrested—on the suspicion of being spies—by Secret Service agents of the Government are Carl Heynen, for years one of the most influential German agents in North America, and at one time German Consul General at Mexico City; P. A. Borgemeister, formerly a New York banker, but more recently confidential secretary to Dr. Heinrich Albert, late Financial Attaché of the German Embassy in Washington; Professor Jonathan Zenneck, an expert in wireless telegraphy, and Heinrich S. Ficke, auditor in New York City of the North German Lloyd Steamship Company, whose home on Staten Island commands a view of the ships entering and leaving New York Harbor. These and other suspects were connected either directly or indirectly with the German Government and great financial, industrial, and maritime concerns owned or controlled by

German interests. Most of the spy suspects are interned at Fort Oglethorpe, Georgia.

A Copenhagen dispatch, dated July 26, stated that more effective measures than were then in force for supervision of Scandinavian liners plying to the United States must be put into effect if the passage of numerous German agents and couriers and the transmission of intelligence by German spies in America were to be checked. It was said authoritatively that German passport-forging bureaus were equipping German agents in Scandinavia with fraudulent Scandinavian passports. These were copied from genuine originals in the same fashion as American passports had been counterfeited photographically by the Pass Bureau of the Admiralty. New names and descriptions are substituted occasionally, but sometimes the only change is to attach a new photograph of the ostensible holder. Every liner sailing to the United States carries 200 or 300 passengers, principally of Scandinavian nationality. There is little to prevent the Intelligence Department of the German Admiralty, now under the leadership of Captain Karl Boy-Ed, ex-Naval Attaché at Washington, from planting any desired number of agents, equipped apparently with genuine Scandinavian passports, among the passengers. Various attempts to recruit neutrals for courier and information missions to the United States had been reported more or less definitely. The Scandinavian police, the dispatch continued, also could tell a tale of unmasked Americans who were employed in the German Secret Service.

## Those Who Organize Sedition

Among the measures instituted by the United States Government is the prohibition of German residents from going within a certain distance of forts, armories, shipyards, piers, and other places where the presence of enemies or spies would be dangerous. Germans who can prove their good faith are allowed to go within the barred zones provided they have permits.

Another aspect of the enemy alien problem is the participation of Germans in movements of native origin, such as the stirring up of labor troubles, aiding anti-war agitation, and encouraging the activities of anarchist groups. As many of these movements were in existence before the United States entered the war and are local manifestations of a worldwide discontent with the existing social order, it is not always easy to draw the line between genuine reformers and pro-Germans; but to be on the safe side the Government has taken vigorous action in combating all movements opposed to the conduct of the war or tending to prevent enlistment and to destroy the fighting spirit in the nation. Under the Espionage act it is unlawful to discourage or oppose recruiting, and the Postmaster General has power to stop the mailing privilege of any publications which give voice to anti-war or anti-conscription views. About twenty Socialist and radical newspapers and magazines have been so dealt with.

A further development has been in connection with the German-language papers of the United States. Some of these newspapers have been, either by direct comment or by insinuation and satire, conducting an active campaign against the Government, and already several of them have been suppressed.

Considerable resentment has been expresssed by Socialists, radicals, and others against these measures on the ground that the Government is acting autocratically in abridging the freedom of the press and other rights guaranteed under the Constitution. Street meetings have also been prohibited or broken up; the headquarters of the Socialist Party in Chicago has been subjected to a domiciliary visit by Department of Justice agents, and papers seized; the home of Professor Scott Nearing, a radical writer on economics, has been similarly searched; and in every direction the Government has been vigorously endeavoring to suppress revolutionary and radical movements that are suspected of being seditious and treasonable.

The organization which has caused the greatest concern is the I. W. W., (the Industrial Workers of the World,) whose main tenet is the Syndicalist idea of dispossessing employers of their property and conducting the industries of the nation under the direct ownership and management of the workers themselves, organized in industrial unions, or guilds. The I. W. W. program, however, besides aiming at this form of industrial democracy, also approves methods of violence, which are due to anarchist influences, such as the destruction of property. This is the so-called plan of "sabotage," and it is this which has caused the Government to regard the I. W. W. as the most dangerous element in the community at the present time, and to suspect that the organization is being encouraged by German interests.

### Drafting Friendly Aliens

A resolution passed Congress on Sept. 13 authorizing the draft of all friendly aliens who have been in the country one year; those who claim exemption through treaty will be allowed ninety days to leave the country. It is estimated that this action will call approximately 1,275,000 men to the American colors; besides these there are 81,000 enemy aliens who under the resolution could be put to work related to the war, but not as soldiers. It is understood that Great Britain and France will take over their drafted nationals; the others would become part of the American forces.

On Sept. 19 a joint committee on the Trading With the Enemy act approved a clause stipulating that all papers printed in foreign languages, when criticising war measures, must file translation accompanied by an affidavit, with the Post Office of the city in which the publications are located.

Congress also enacted into law a measure carrying drastic regulations against any commercial intercourse in this country in which subjects of Germany may be financially concerned.

# Work of the American Red Cross
## Sketch of a Great Relief System

THE War Council of the Red Cross, with Henry P. Davison of J. P. Morgan & Co. as Chairman, was created May 10, 1917, by President Wilson to carry on the extraordinary relief work made necessary by the entrance of the United States into the European war. From May 10 to Aug. 31 this council appropriated for its work in the countries of the Allies the sum of $12,339,681. An elaborate report of the work of the American Red Cross, issued in September, contains many interesting details. The general objects of the work in France are described as follows:

1. To establish and maintain hospitals for soldiers in the American Army in France.
2. To establish and maintain canteens, rest houses, recreation huts and other means of supplying the American soldiers with such comforts and recreation as the army authorities may approve.
3. To establish and maintain in France canteens, rest houses, recreation huts, and other means of supplying comforts and recreation for the soldiers in the armies of our allies.
4. To distribute hospital equipment and supplies of all kinds to military hospitals for soldiers of the American or allied armies.
5. To engage in civilian relief, including:
   (a) The care and education of destitute children.
   (b) Care of mutilated soldiers.
   (c) Care of sick and disabled soldiers.
   (d) Relief work in the devastated areas of France and Belgium, such as furnishing to the inhabitants of these districts agricultural implements, household goods, foods, clothing, and such temporary shelter as will enable them to return to their homes.
   (e) To provide relief for and guard against the increase of tuberculosis.
6. To furnish relief for soldiers and civilians held as prisoners by the enemy and to give assistance to such civilians as are returned to France from time to time from the parts of Belgium and France held by the enemy.
7. To supply financial assistance to committees, societies, or individuals allied with the American Red Cross and carrying on relief work in Europe.

## Scope of Red Cross Work

Separate commissions of representative Americans, skilled in medical and administrative work, have been sent to Europe. The first commission, which went to France, is headed by Major Grayson. M. P. Murphy, Vice President of the Guaranty Trust Company of New York, has general supervision over the work of the American Red Cross in Europe, and its membership is composed of fourteen leading experts in special lines of work. Each of the other commissions has been selected along similar lines, and the work of all these commissions is either volunteer or is paid by private contributions.

"The effort," the report adds, "has been, in accordance with the expressed views of the President of the United States and of the civil and military authorities of France, to co-ordinate along helpful lines all relief work being done in France and America."

Concerning the scope of the Red Cross work in behalf of the United States Army the report says:

"The first and supreme object of American Red Cross care is our own army and navy. The American Army in France is received in large reception camps on the coast, and after several weeks of preliminary training the men are sent across the country to permanent training camps back of the firing lines. Along the route followed by the troops the Red Cross has established infirmaries and rest stations, each in charge of an American trained nurse with an American man to assist her.

"Additional infirmaries and rest stations will be established in the near future, and adequate buildings are also being erected wherever needed.

"Canteens are being established by the Red Cross at railway stations where American soldiers on reserve duty or on leave, and those returning to or from duty, may find rest and refreshment. Baths, food, games, and other comforts will be made available at these canteens.

"When American troops start for France the men are given comfort kits. Christmas parcels will be sent over later.

"The War Council has appropriated $100,000 for medical research work in France.

"To be able to do its work without delay, the Red Cross is establishing warehouses at different points of importance in the French theatre of war. An appropriation of $500,000 has been voted to establish this service and provide its first stock of supplies.

## Millions Spent for Supplies

"In response to a cable from the commission in France, the War Council appropriated $1,500,000 to purchase foodstuff to be sent to France.

"It has also appropriated $1,000,000 for the purchase of supplies in France; all for use in the hospital supply service.

"Near the firing line the Red Cross is establishing field canteens. Extending the work already begun by the French Red Cross, it will provide one of these canteens for every corps of the French army, and as well later for the American Army.

"To carry out these plans the War Council has made appropriations of about $700,000, which will establish the canteens and maintain them for about three months. Much of the equipment will be supplied by the French Army.

"A Red Cross transportation service, through the co-operation of the French, British, and Italian Governments, the United States Shipping Board, and the leading steamship and railroad companies, has been established to handle the vast quantities of medical and relief supplies now being shipped almost daily to France, Belgium, Serbia, Russia, and other belligerent countries.

"The Red Cross will have cargo space on every steamer chartered by the United States Shipping Board. Army transports also will carry Red Cross supplies.

"In advance of the fighting forces the United States sent to the European battlefields six base hospitals organized during the last year by the Red Cross—the first United States Army organization sent to Europe. These were sent at the request of the British Commission.

"More than a dozen base hospitals organized by the American Red Cross are now seeing active service in France, and others are rapidly being made ready for foreign service. Each of these base hospitals has a staff of 22 physicians, 2 dentists, 65 Red Cross nurses, and 150 enlisted men of the Army Medical Corps. Before war was declared, 26 of these units had been formed, and 47 are now ready for service. It costs at least $75,000 to equip a base hospital with beds, blankets, sterilizers, operating tables, tents, dental outfits, automobiles, and kitchens."

### 500,000 White Plague Victims

One of the most important undertakings of the Red Cross in France is to combat the tuberculosis peril. The report says that at the present time 500,000 persons are afflicted with tuberculosis as a direct result of the war, and that " scientific efforts to control the spread of the malady are not only of supreme concern to France herself but they are of great importance in making France healthy for our own troops." All work is being done under the general administration of the French Government and by French people.

For the relief of wounded and sick French soldiers and their families the American Red Cross has appropriated $1,000,000, and the organization has made plans to take care temporarily of the hundreds of thousands of destitute refugees in France. The report cites the French Ministry of the Interior as authority for the statement that these refugees number about 400,000, but adds that " there is reason to think that the number is much larger."

### Budget of Expenditures

The following summary, covering the financial part of the Red Cross' great undertakings, concludes the report:

The budget for expenditures in France to cover the period until Nov. 1, 1917, prepared by J. H. Perkins, Director of the Department of Military Affairs, Red Cross Commission in France, is for a total expenditure of $1,773,250. This covers work for the United States Army, surgical dressings, equipment and operation of diet kitchens, canteens, American Red Cross Motor Ambulance service, hospital expenses, &c.

The budget of the Department of Civilian Relief in France, prepared by Homer Folks, Director of the Red Cross Department of Civil Affairs in France, up to Nov. 1, 1917, calls for $2,190,353.

The budget of the Department of Administration in Paris, prepared by Carl Taylor, Director of Administration, up to Nov. 1, 1917, calls for $115,700.

The budget of the Planning Department, prepared by George B. Ford, Director, up to Nov. 1, 1917, calls for $3,890.

General appropriations have also been made, amounting in all to $10,692,601. They cover hospital supplies, foodstuffs, transportation supplies and motors, building material, machinery, medical research, child welfare work, clothing, American Ambulance Hospital expenses, nurses, &c.

Before appropriations are recommended by the French Commission they are carefully prepared by the Director of the particular department concerned. They are then considered by a Finance Committee, consisting of Major Murphy, Chairman; J. H. Perkins, H. H. Harjes, H. O. Beatty, Carl Taylor, Homer Folks, William Endicott, and Ralph Preston. Three of this committee constitute a quorum, and every appropriation reported must receive the consent of all present.

Most of those in charge, for the Red Cross, of the work in France are giving their own time and paying their own expenses. A special fund of $100,000 has also been privately contributed to meet expenses of members of the French Commission unable to pay their own way.

The appropriations made for use in Europe outside of France, covering drugs and medical supplies, relief funds, and expenses, are reported as follows:

| | |
|---|---|
| For Russia | $322,780.87 |
| For Rumania | 247,000.00 |
| For Italy | 210,000.00 |
| For Serbia | 222,500.00 |
| For England | 8,800.00 |
| For Armenia | 600,000.00 |
| Other appropriations | 36,000.00 |

The total appropriations by the War Council for Red Cross work in Europe are as follows:

| | |
|---|---|
| In France | $10,692,601.00 |
| Outside of France | 1,647,080.87 |
| Grand total | $12,339,681.87 |

Some of the European appropriations are to cover a full year, but the greater part, the report adds, will have been spent by November of this year.

# Progress of the War

## Recording Campaigns on All Fronts and Collateral Events From August 20 Up to and Including September 19, 1917

### UNITED STATES

President Wilson issued a proclamation forbidding exports to neutral countries without licenses.

The first contingent of drafted men for the National Army arrived at their cantonments Sept. 5. The second contingent was sent Sept. 18.

Pacifists held a meeting in Chicago under the auspices of the People's Council of America for Democracy and Terms of Peace.

Labor voiced its loyalty to the Government at the conference of the American Alliance for Labor and Democracy in Minneapolis.

President Wilson sent a reply to Pope Benedict's peace note, Aug. 27, rejecting the proposals and refusing to have any dealings with the present German autocracy.

### SUBMARINE BLOCKADE

According to British official statements, England's losses for the week ended Aug. 18, included fifteen vessels of over 1,600 tons; for the week ended Aug. 25, eighteen vessels; for the week ended Sept. 1, twenty; for the week ended Sept. 8, twelve. These included the Royal Mail Company's steamer Desna and the Leyland liner Devonian.

France lost between two and five ships of over 1,600 tons each week.

Norway lost twenty-one ships in August.

Four American members of the crew of the British schooner Minas Queen were lost when the ship was torpedoed.

The American steamer Susan was sunk.

Several American vessels, including the Westwego, were attacked by submarines off the coast of France on Sept. 5. In the battle which followed, one submarine was lost.

The Atlantic Transport liner Minnehaha was sunk on Sept 7, and fifty members of the crew were lost.

Statistics showed that 4,561,000 tons of shipping were sunk between Jan. 1 and Sept. 1.

Germany sent a note to Argentina promising to modify her blockade, giving Argentine food ships freedom of the seas. Argentina accepted an offer of indemnity for the sinking of the Toro and announced that she considered the incident closed. Soon after this, however, Secretary Lansing made public dispatches containing unneutral information for the German Government, sent in the Swedish code through the Swedish Legation in Buenos Aires in charge of Baron Lowen, by Count Luxburg, German Chargé d'Affaires at that capital. The Swedish Foreign Office decided not to recall Baron Lowen, declaring that he did not know the contents of the messages. The British Government asked Sweden for an explanation. Argentina dismissed the German Minister, recalled her Naval Attaché at Berlin, and demanded an explanation from Germany. An oral apology from the Under Secretary of the German Foreign Office to the Argentine Minister at Berlin was pronounced unsatisfactory. Germany sent a note to Sweden expressing regret for the disagreeable issues raised.

### CAMPAIGN IN EASTERN EUROPE

Aug. 22—Germans begin offensive between the Tirul marshes and the River Aa, penetrating Russian positions.

Aug. 23—Russians evacuate Riga.

Aug. 24—Germans reach the River Aa at some places on the Gulf of Riga.

Aug. 27—Germans take important positions east of Czernowitz and advance on the Riga front northwest of Jacobstadt.

Sept. 2—Germans cross the Diva River near Uxkul and push northward, and also advance toward Riga from the south.

Sept. 3—Germans occupy Riga.

Sept. 4—Russians retire northeast of Riga; Germans cut a nine-mile gap in their line.

Sept. 5—Russians in their retreat toward the northeast cross the Livonian River; forces east from Riga retire to Segevold, Lemberg, and Detesubrayd.

Sept. 10—Russians take the offensive in the region of Segevold, and force Germans back in a southerly direction.

Sept. 11—Russians begin an offensive in the southeast section of Bukowina.

Sept. 14—Russians on the Riga front capture Kronberg, Keitzen, Sisseral, and Peine.

### BALKAN CAMPAIGN

Aug. 24—Teutons repulse Russo-Rumanian attacks near Soveja, Rumania.

Aug. 29—Russian division abandons its position in the region of Fokshani.

Aug. 30—Teutons repulsed by Russians near Sochka.

Sept. 1—Rumanians ousted from hills northeast of Fokshani; Greek troops take part in raid in the Vardar sector.

Sept. 17—Italian troops move eastward through Albania and menace the Bulgarian right flank.

Sept. 18—Rumanians in the Suchitza Valley capture part of Teuton fortified positions near Varnitza.

## CAMPAIGN IN WESTERN EUROPE

Aug. 20—French break German lines north of Verdun on an eleven-mile front, gaining Avocourt Wood, Dead Man Hill, Talou Ridge, and the Corbeaux and Cumières Woods; British repulse German counter-attack north of Epehy.

Aug. 21—French capture the Côte de l'Oie, Regneville, and Samogneux; Canadians carry German positions on a mile front at Lens.

Aug. 22—British capture important strategic positions for a mile along the Ypres-Menin road, and penetrate German trenches further north.

Aug. 23—Canadians take important positions south of Lens.

Aug. 24—French capture Hill 304 on the Verdun front and advance one and one-quarter miles beyond it; British forced from the ground won on the Ypres-Menin road.

Aug. 25—French capture three fortified works near Béthincourt; British forced to give up ground captured near St. Quentin.

Aug. 26—French gain on a two and a half mile front east of the Meuse; British advance half a mile east of Hargicourt.

Aug. 30—British repulse German attacks on the Verdun front, and penetrate German positions in Champagne east of the Teton.

Sept. 1-3—French repulse German attacks between Cerny and Hurtebise.

Sept. 4—Canadians advance 250 yards on 600-yard front at Lens.

Sept. 6—French repulse violent attacks in the region of Cerny.

Sept. 7—British forced to relinquish positions gained north of Frezenburg.

Sept. 8—French launch new offensive on the right bank of the Meuse, occupying important positions on a front of about one and a half miles; Germans repulsed in Lorraine, east of Rheims, and north of Courcy.

Sept. 11—British on the Somme carry a German trench near Villeret and advance their line nearly a quarter of a mile.

Sept. 12—French in Champagne drive across two lines of German trenches, between St. Hilaire and St. Souplet, and enter the third line.

Sept. 14—Germans enter French trenches on a 500-yard front north of Caurières Wood.

Sept. 15—French retrieve losses north of Caurières Wood, but lose height near Chaume; British advance in Belgium east of Westhoek.

Sept. 18—Germans on the Champagne front, after a violent bombardment south of the Miette River, reach the French lines toward the Neufchatel Road; British improve their positions east of St. Julien and raid trenches in Inverness Copse.

## ITALIAN CAMPAIGN

Aug. 20—Italians cross the Isonzo River north of Gorizia.

Aug. 21—Italians capture defenses between Corite and Selo.

Aug. 22-24—Italians advance on the northern and southern wings of the Isonzo front in great drive on Trieste.

Aug. 25—Italians capture Monte Santo.

Aug. 27—Trieste civilians evacuate the city; Austrians evacuate Monte Santo.

Aug. 29—Italians gain complete control of the Bainsizza Plateau and enter the Chiapovano Valley.

Aug. 30—Italians surround Nakobil and attack the forest of Tarnovo.

Aug. 31—Italians consolidate their gains on the Bainsizza and Carso Plateaus, and make further gains on San Gabriele.

Sept. 1—German troops appear for the first time on the Carso front.

Sept. 2-3—Italians push on in the Brestovizza Valley.

Sept. 4—Italians capture Monte San Gabriele.

Sept. 5—Italians capture an Austrian position south of Ocrogio and repulse enemy attacks on the Carso Plateau from Castagnevizza to the sea.

Sept. 6-9—Monte San Gabriele changes hands several times.

Sept. 10—Turkish reinforcements thrown into the campaign along the Isonzo front.

Sept. 14—Italians gain the northwestern crest and the peak of Monte San Gabriele.

## AERIAL RECORD

On Aug. 22 Zeppelins raided Yorkshire, killing one man, and Gotha airplanes raided Dover, Margate, and Ramsgate, killing eleven persons and injuring thirteen. Eight German machines were brought down. Another raid was made on the east coast on Sept. 2, and on Sept. 3 bombs were dropped on the naval station at Chatham, killing 108 persons and wounding 92. The first moonlight raid over the London district occurred Sept. 4. Eleven persons were killed and sixty-two hurt.

The British bombarded Zeebrugge, Bruges, and many points back of the German lines in Belgium and Northern France.

The Germans attacked Calais and Dunkirk.

French aviators raided Stuttgart, Colmar, and bases near Metz.

British naval seaplanes dropped bombs on German destroyers along the Belgian coast, hitting one destroyer and sinking at least one trawler.

Italians raided Pola.

The Germans attacked Vandelaincourt Hospital on Aug. 22, killing ten wounded men, one woman nurse, and nineteen men nurses. Another attack on the same hospital was made on Sept. 6, when nineteen persons were killed and twenty-six injured. British-American hospitals on the French coast were attacked. One bomb fell on a Harvard hospital, killing four Americans and wounding ten others, and another fell on a St. Louis unit, killing one man.

## NAVAL MANOEUVRES

Italian floats mounted with huge, new guns, bombarded Trieste, while British monitors shelled the rear slopes of the Hermada. Italian and British monitors shelled Pola.

Four German mine sweepers were destroyed by British light craft off the coast of Jutland.

A German submarine bombarded Scarborough on Sept. 5, killing three persons and injuring five.

German submarines appeared in the Gulf of Riga, and shelled several places on the coast.

## RUSSIA

The National Conference was held at Moscow on Aug. 26.

A counter-revolutionary, monarchistic conspiracy to accomplish a coup d'état by arresting the Provisional Government was unearthed and many arrests were made in Moscow. Grand Duke Michael Alexandrovitch and Grand Duke Paul were arrested, together with Mlle. Margaret Hitrova and Mme. Liubov Hitrova. The Minister of Justice resigned after being upbraided by Kerensky for his failure to unearth the plot.

Several adherents of the old imperial régime, including Mlle. Virubova, were exiled and taken across the Swedish frontier.

General Soukhomlinoff, the former Minister of War, was placed on trial on a charge of treason and his wife on a charge of being an accomplice.

A Cabinet crisis arose as a result of the opposition of the Constitutional Democratic Ministers to the food program of M. Pieschehonoff and the land policy of M. Tchernoff, as well as to the attitude of the majority toward the Ukraine.

Premier Kerensky deposed General Korniloff and arrested his envoy, Vladimir Lvoff, following Korniloff's demand that all civil and military powers be turned over to him as Commander in Chief of the army. Korniloff responded to the order of dismissal by moving an army against Petrograd, where Kerensky proclaimed a state of siege. General Denikine, commander on the southwestern front, and the whole of his headquarters staff and General Erdelli were arrested. The Baltic fleet unanimously placed itself on the side of the Provisional Government. Kerensky became Commander in Chief of the army and General Alexeieff, Chief of General Staff.

General Krymoff, commander of the troops sent by Korniloff to capture Petrograd, was arrested and committed suicide. Korniloff himself was taken into custody.

The Bolshevikis gained control of the Petrograd Council of Deputies. This resulted in friction between the Constitutional Democrats and the Socialists in the Cabinet, followed by the withdrawal of all the Constitutional Democrats save one. A new Cabinet of five members was formed.

A republic was proclaimed by the Provisional Government on Sept. 14.

## MISCELLANEOUS

Louis J. Malvy, Minister of the Interior and Radical Socialist, quit the French Cabinet, and the head of the Secret Service, M. Leymarie, also gave up his post as a result of disclosures of alleged anti-patriotic activities on the part of Miguel Almereyda, editor of the Bonnet Rouge, and some of the directors of the paper. The Ribot Cabinet resigned, and Paul Painlevé, Minister of War, formed a new Ministry.

Because of the failure of efforts to induce the Poles to fight for Germany and Austria, the Central Powers decided to abandon their project with regard to the Kingdom of Poland as outlined in the joint proclamation of Nov. 5, 1916. They were reported to have planned a new partition, Germany to annex such parts of Russian Poland as she needed to rectify her strategic frontier, this including about one-tenth of the territory, and Austria to annex the remaining nine-tenths, uniting it with Galicia and proclaiming the whole the Kingdom of Poland, with a status similar to Hungary's, and with Emperor Charles as King. A decree published at Lublin and Warsaw on Sept. 12 transferred the supreme authority to a regency council of three members, appointed by the monarchs of the occupying powers.

# Military Events of the Month

## From August 18 to September 18, 1917

### By Walter Littlefield

AS last month's chronicle closed, the battle line from Flanders to the Adriatic seemed everywhere to be in movement. The British and French were again striking hard northeast of Ypres. The Canadians, already having cracked the carboniferous nut of Lens, appeared to be on the point of extracting the kernel. North of the Aisne and in Champagne the French were still checkmating the costly assault of the German Crown Prince. A bombardment at Verdun from the French side seemed to be puzzling military critics. The Italians were just launching their second great offensive of the year.

On the eastern front all was confusion and uncertainty—in the south the Rumanians and Russians were still gallantly contesting Moldavia with the Austrians, but further north the Russian military mutiny and the Teutonic obvious lack of men and munitions to take full advantage of it left the military situation there dominated by the question: Where will the Germans strike in order to obtain a maximum gain—strategic, political, or industrial—with the minimum extension of line?

In the course of the month three movements have developed and detached themselves from the foregoing mass until, by their intrinsic military importance, their sensational details, or their bearing upon the future, they have overshadowed all else. These are the great Italian offensive, which has changed the battle of the Isonzo into the battle of the Julian Alps; the occupation of Riga by the Germans, and the French expansion of their lines north of the town of Verdun, which, beginning as something of an enigma, like the great German assault on that place in 1916, is gradually assuming a strategic movement of definite progress and objective.

### Flanders Offensive Suspended

But first let us dismiss as briefly as possible the events which have suffered obscuration by comparison on the western front. Between Aug. 18 and 22 the British and French had consolidated their gains in Flanders northeast of Ypres on a three-mile front beyond St. Julien and Fortuyn, and had made a perceptible gain on the Ypres-Roulers road. The English alone had done the same on the road to Menin. These movements seemed a necessary preparation to an attempted envelopment of the Westhoek Ridge, which lies between.

Then, in the early days of September, occurred an event which caused the Allies in this region to suspend operations until they could discover its meaning. This was the German order to the civil populations of Thourout, Courtrai, and Roulers to take refuge in Ghent and Limbourg. Two explanations of this act have been advanced: First, that the Germans meditated a retreat to their fortified line, Scheldt-Ghent-Sas van Get; second, that they intended to flood the front of the Allies from Dixmude to Ypres by damming the Scheldt east of Ghent and turning its waters at that place up the Lys, which would also be dammed by the same obstruction, just as they had already flooded the country between Nieuport and Dixmude by means of the Yser and its canals.

To meet either emergency would require an entirely different line of action. It will be remembered that in both the Nieuport-Dixmude affair of 1915 and the German retreat to the Hindenburg line last Spring the Allies were taken by surprise. Now, Germany's advertised evacuation by the civil population of an area of 550 square miles in West Flanders is full of interesting possibilities.

At Lens, on the night of Aug. 21-22, both Germans and the Canadians exe-

THE NATIONAL ARMY CELEBRATION

President Wilson Leading the Parade at Washington, Sept. 4, 1917, in Honor of the Men Drafted From the District of Columbia
(Photo © Cinedinst from Underwood & Underwood)

DEPARTURE OF THE NEW YORK NATIONAL GUARD

The Crowd Outside the New York Public Library Bidding Farewell to the National Guard, August 30, 1917, Before Going Into Camp

(Photo Paul Thompson)

cuted simultaneous assaults—like the rushing together of two locomotives head on—and, as usual, the Canadians had the best of it. This coal city of closely packed dwellings has now become a citadel of reinforced concrete—possibly the strongest single position that has ever confronted the Allies on the western front. They have already entered some of the isolated quarters of the town, and have firmly established themselves on the north at the Cité St. Laurent and the Cité St. Edouard; on the west at Cité Jeanne d'Arc; on the south at Eleu or Leauvette. But between these suburbs and the concrete citadel lie the coal pits with their fathomless depths of ages and the mysteries of kultural strategy. Meanwhile, the struggle there has become a succession of avalanches of gas, burning oil, rifle and machine-gun fire, and hand-to-hand struggles in which the German loss seems all out of proportion to the military value of the place with its present industrial uselessness. Less of an enigma is the fact that the besiegers are cautious in their use of big howitzers and high explosive shells.

The remainder of this front through Champagne and the Argonne has witnessed a constant application of attrition—artillery duels, bombing, airplane combats, and raids carried out by the Allies—with particular emphasis on the St. Quentin sector, on the Aisne and in the Champagne. These three places and their relation as approaches to the great industrial city of Laon were sufficiently dwelt on last month. Toward the middle of September the British, by a series of small drives, had improved their positions amid the farms north of St. Quentin; on the Aisne and in Champagne the counter artillery bombardments of the French seemed to have gained dominance over those of the Crown Prince. The French raids, one of which in Champagne, between St. Hilaire and St. Souplet, on Sept. 12 swept over two of his trenches and established a line in the third, have accounted for many prisoners.

The wonders of the great Italian offensive begun on the night of Aug. 18-19

—scenic, strategic, and personal—will be found in a descriptive article elsewhere in this magazine. I shall merely try to conventionalize the stage of the great drama and record its acts and scenes.

Imagine a triangle erected on the forty-mile base extending from the Battery to Peekskill via Tarrytown, with its vertex at Boston. At forty miles on its northern side of 190 miles would fall Hartford; at forty-four miles on its southern side of 120 miles would fall Bridgeport. Place this triangle on a map of similar scale of the Austrian coastland, Carniola, Styria, and Lower Austria, with its base resting on Tolmino and Trieste, with Gorizia somewhere near Tarrytown, and Hartford would become the great Austrian fortress of Klagenfurt; Bridgeport, Laibach; while the vertex, Boston, would fall on Vienna. Superimpose the topography of Vermont and its Green Mountains, and we have a fair idea of the terrain over which the Italians are making their way, of the geographical obstacles which obstruct their path, and the remoteness of their objectives.

Their campaign of last year left them in the possession of Gorizia and its bridgeheads, but not of the heights, rising from 1,800 feet to 2,240 to the northeast and east of the town, and a foothold on the edge of the Carso Plateau, which is not unlike the approach to the Battery from Tarrytown, if only we imagine Manhattan Island strewn with volcanic heaps, some of them a thousand feet high.

No, the Hudson would not adequately represent the Isonzo, for between Peekskill (Tolmino) and Tarrytown (Gorizia) the river would have to become deep and swift and narrow and pass through gorges rising higher than the Palisades. On May 14 last, the Italians, in an attack which defied all rules of tactics, and almost the imagination of strategy, to say nothing of the forces of nature, crossed this gorge above Gorizia and won Monte Cucco, or Kuk, on the eastern bank of the river. In a sustained offensive of twenty-five days they developed their lines along this bank so as to include the Vodice Ridge and south to the steps of

Monte Santo; while on the Carso they
had mounted further on the plateau and
were within striking artillery distance of
the great volcanic mounds there —
Faitihrib, 1,200 feet; Castagnavizza,
with its protecting mound, 550 feet high;
Selo, backed by Starilokva, 580 feet, and
finally the great isolated mass of Hermada, with its varied summits rising
from 500 to 800 feet above the surrounding lowlands, across which they moved
until within mid-calibre range of Duino.
In these twenty-five days the Italians
captured 28,000 Austrians and had prob-

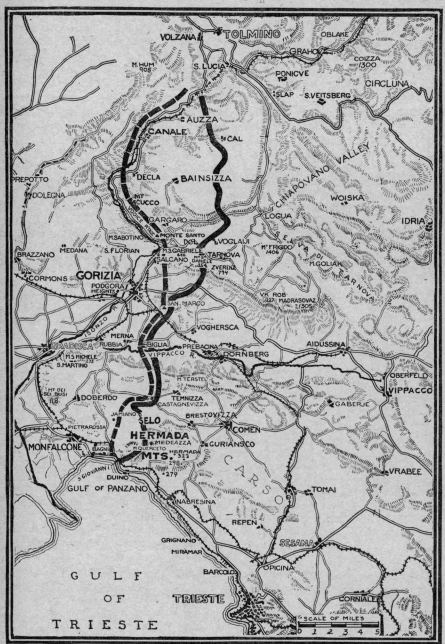

SCENE OF THE ITALIAN DRIVE IN THE JULIAN ALPS

ably rendered hors de combat over 100,-000.

## Italian Army's Achievement

Such was the situation when, on the night of Aug. 18, they began a second and still more spectacular offensive, the end of which is not yet. So far they have gained sixty-five square miles of territory. The Austrian casualties are calculated to be 150,000, over 35,000 of whom are known to be prisoners. The enemy has also lost an immense amount of war material, principally abandoned in the vast intrenched camps on Bainsizza or captured under convoy in the Chiapovano Valley, and over 2,000 cattle on the hoof.

But these figures give an inadequate idea of the vastness of the Italian achievement, its military and moral results, and its potentialities for the future. At the present moment it looms up the most important and longest sustained assault upon the enemy in his own territory since the war began.

For convenience it may be well to remember that four distinct forces, independent, yet each the complement of the other, are taking part: The Third Army, under General Cappello, in the north, on the Bainsizza Plateau, Monte Santo, Monte San Gabriele, and the approaches to San Daniele; the Second Army, under the Duke of Aosta, operating south to the sea, in the Valleys of Vippacco and Brestovizza, on the Carso, and before Hermada; the British and Italian monitors, which have bombarded Hermada and the Austrian ships and arsenals at Trieste and Pola; finally, the great Caproni aerial machines, which both on the battle line and over Trieste and Pola have ably aided the work of the soldiers and warships.

For weeks prior to Aug. 18 the Italians at sundown every night had by a great engineering feat diverted the water of the Isonzo above Anhovo, and had built in the shallow stream thus left ten-foot bridges, which were concealed from view when the water resumed its natural course each morning. On the eve of the crossing they supplemented these with four pontoon bridges laid while their searchlights blinded the eyes of the Aus-

trians on the opposite cliffs. These bridges extended from Anhovo up to Loga, a distance of four miles. That night the stream remained diverted and the army of Cappello crossed, while the Duke of Aosta performed a diversion on the Carso.

## On the Bainsizza Plateau

Thus a foothold on the northern part of the Bainsizza was gained, while simultaneously the right wing of Cappello's army descended upon the plateau from Monte Cucco and the Vodice and began to envelop Monte Santo and deploy into the Val Chiapovano. The Austrian army on the Bainsizza, threatened from three sides, made a rapid retreat to the ridge, 1,000 feet high, which bounds the eastern edge of the plateau from its sheer drop into the Chiapovano.

Bainsizza Santo Spirito—" The Windy Bath of the Holy Ghost "—is called a plateau merely because it forms an elevated foundation upon which rest isolated masses of rock, just like the Carso. It is fifteen miles north and south and ten east and west. The Austrians had turned it into a series of intrenched camps and had burrowed into the hills for machine-gun nests and mid-calibre emplacements. All the material there which fell to the Italians showed that the Austrians believed that their stay would be permanent, protected as they were on the front by the deep-gorged Isonzo and on the south by the mountains from Cucco to San Daniele.

On Aug. 24 the tricolor of Italy was flung to the breeze from the summit of Monte Santo. From this commanding height of 2,240 feet it was seen from Loga to the Hermada. On Sept. 1 Cappello had penetrated to a depth of seven and a half miles on a front of eleven over the Bainsizza, occupying all fortified positions and more than 40 villages and hamlets. On Sept. 14, after several repulses, the Italians established themselves upon Monte San Gabriele, which rises 1,700 feet above the Isonzo and dominates San Daniele by 300 feet.

Meanwhile the Duke of Aosta had been engaged in complementary manoeuvres in the south and with the object of enveloping the Hermada and clearing the Vippacco Valley and the approaches to Castagnavizza, and, on the low land in the extreme south, the marshes between San Giovanni and Duino.  On Sept. 5 he suffered severe counterattacks from Castagnavizza (Kostanjevica) on the lines Castagnavizza-Korite and Korite-Celle, but he captured Selo in the Brestovizza and the Duino railway tunnel. From Aug. 19 to 22 his " diversion " before Hermada was assisted by the Italian and British monitors, commanded by Admiral Thaon de Revel, which later bombarded the shipping and naval depots at Trieste and Pola.  On Aug. 29 a squadron of forty Caproni dropped more than 7,000 kilograms of bombs in the fortified woods of Panovizza.

## An Austrian War Council

All this time the Austrians were attempting to create distractions by making heavy attacks in the Trentino region and along the Carnic Alps.  Failing here, a council of war was called at Laibach on Sept. 7, presided over by Field Marshal Conrad von Hoetzendorf and attended by the commander on the Bainsizza front, General Boroevic, and the commander of the Carso, Field Marshal Koevess.  There it was determined to hold the eastern ridges of the Bainsizza and concentrate attacks against the Duke of Aosta.  Turkish and German reinforcements had already arrived on the front.  According to Austrian Staff reports, made known at Laibach, the Italians had been able to concentrate 5,000 guns on a three-mile front, against 1,000 of the Austrians.  On another front, half as long, 599 had been counted. These had discharged 91,500 projectiles of all calibres in fourteen hours.  It was found that the shells discharged from the Italian monitors, which are really floats of a design never before used in warfare, were greater in calibre than those ever before fired from a warship.

I will leave to the imagination all speculations in regard to what the envelopment of Tolmino, the occupation of

Klagenfurt or Laibach (Lubiana)—Laibach would, of course, isolate the entire Istrian peninsula, with Trieste, Pola, and Fiume—may mean, and to the supplies of guns and munitions from her allies which, it is authoritatively stated, would enable Italy to secure a decision against Austria.

San Gabriele doubtless dominates San Daniele, but beyond, on the way to Laibach, rises the great Ternova plateau to an altitude at Mount Goliak of 4,400 feet.  Still, the possession of San Gabriele should eventually make possible the outflanking of the Austrian positions on this plateau by way of the Chiapovano Valley on the northern side, and by the Laibach road at its southern base. With this accomplished, and with the removal of the danger of flanking which threatens the Duke of Asota's army on the Carso, the great Hermada might be carried by assault or " covered," and the road opened to Trieste.  The rest is all speculation, which invites poetry but dismays existing strategy.  Still, already by their bridging feats on the Isonzo the Italians have performed the impossible. They may do so again.

## The Fall of Riga

The dispatches which came from Petrograd between Aug. 22 and Sept. 15 were so clothed in political digressions that little was really learned of the causes which led directly to the fall of Riga on Sept. 2, or the subsequent military manoeuvres in that region.  It was taken for granted that the Germans had merely reached out their hand and grabbed the city from its mutinous garrison; that the Kaiser was inordinately pluming himself on a great military victory, which was really a political one of doubtful value; and that Petrograd might as well be surrendered in the same way and the Government withdrawn to Moscow.

This interpretation of the Petrograd dispatches is entirely wrong; the Germans fought hard for Riga, and won it by their superior artillery.  This half-German city is of little military value as long as the Russian fleet remains in being.  To be sure, three roads are laid open to the capital; but has Germany

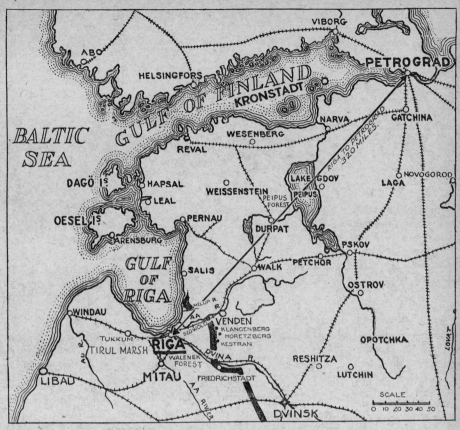

SCENE OF THE GERMAN ADVANCE INTO RUSSIA ON THE RIGA FRONT

the men to deploy over 300 miles, and at this time of year, with a Russian Winter approaching?

General P. A. Letchitzky, who, in the great Brusiloff offensive of 1916, had captured 115,000 Austrians from June 4 till June 12, was appointed to succeed General Klemlovsky in command of the northern armies on Aug. 15. It has not been revealed how he found the morale of officers and men on the Riga sector; but he has stated to the War Committee in Petrograd that the defenses west and south of the city—from the coast near Kemmern south up the Kurland River Aa and across the Tirul Marsh cut by the Mitau-Riga railway—were never bad, while the artillery southeast along the Dvina was outclassed in both calibre and number by the German guns recently brought up. At that time the Russians are believed to have been reduced on this

front, from Riga to Dvinsk, a matter of 160 miles, to barely 60,000. Klemlovsky's predecessor, the Russo-Bulgar General, Radko Demetrieff, had under him last Spring between 800,000 and 1,000,000 men.

Facing the depleted Russian line last month were the German Mitau detachment of eleven divisions and the First Reserve Army Corps 260,000 men, as far as Friedrichstadt, forty-five miles southeast of Riga—and thence the Eighth Army with four infantry and three cavalry divisions as far as Dvinsk. The German headquarters was at Shavli, fifty miles south of Mitau.

## Story of the Retreat

The story of what happened is soon told. On Aug. 22 the Germans began to advance from Kemmern, between the gulf and the Aa, drove in the Russian

MAP SHOWING GAINS OF THE FRENCH NEAR VERDUN, IN THE DIRECTION OF THE
GERMAN BASE AT METZ

cavalry outposts on the Tirul Marsh,
and bombarded the Russian positions on
the right bank of the Dvina north of
Dvinsk. On Sept. 2 they crossed the
Dvina near Uxkul, sixteen miles southeast of the city, and advanced up the
Mitau-Riga causeway. The advance
guard entered Riga that night.

On the same day, Sunday, Letchitzky
ordered the army to withdraw to the fortified line east of Lake Stint and up the
Jaegel, and then, on the 13th, to the line
River Nitzcope-Zegenhoff - Paush - Zege-
volt-Lupsala, further east.

According to the report of the Assistant Commissioner to the Council of
Workmen's and Soldiers' Delegates, the
troops withdrew fighting and inflicting

severe losses on the enemy; the breaking
of the front, the report said, was due to
the overwhelming superiority of the German artillery fire, which dominated and
put out of action the Russian batteries,
annihilated the Russian trenches, and
compelled the troops of the Guard, who
were half decimated, to fall back. After
the great German assault of November,
1915, which almost captured the city,
practically all the factories were removed
to the centre of Russia. In the last week
of August nearly all the heavy guns were
dismounted and sent to the rear.

Apparently Letchitzky gave up Riga
because he found it impossible of prolonged defense with the means at hand.
His retreat, however, has made the Ger-

mans stretch their line fifty miles. Already the Russians have begun to dent in its thin places, and up to Sept. 18 had advanced over a sector of seven miles.

### French Success at Verdun

On Aug. 20, after a silence of nine months, the magic word "Verdun" again thrilled the heart of France. On that date, after a bombardment of three days, the French went forward astride of the Meuse, taking, on an eleven-mile front, at a penetration of one and a quarter miles, all the fortifications between Avocourt and Bezonvaux, including the Avocourt Wood, Le Mort Homme, the Corbeaux and Cumières Woods, and Côte de Talou, Champneuville, Mormont Farm, and Hill 240, and over 4,000 prisoners. The next day, on a three-mile front and a penetration of one mile, they took the trenches between Cumières and Hill 240, with Regnéville on the left bank and Samogneux on the right, and the famous Côte de l'Oie, and over 5,000 prisoners.

On the 23d, 24th, and 26th other smashing blows were delivered and 10,000 more prisoners brought in from Hill 304, Camard Wood, the Fosses and Beaumont Woods, and the southern outskirts of Béthincourt. On Sept. 8 a movement was begun which was completed on the 9th to reduce the German isolated units in the sector of the Fosses and Caurières Woods.

A year ago the German maximum gain at Verdun was 120 square miles and the two permanent forts, Douaumont and Vaux; these were recovered respectively on Oct. 24 and Nov. 1, 1916; then on Dec. 15, 16, 17, and 18 Pétain, on the eve of his departure to take supreme command, developed a sudden offensive from west of Vacherauville east to the town of Vaux and north as far as Louvemont, which enveloped forty-five square miles of territory and 20,000 prisoners.

Nearly 100 square miles of the lost 120 have now been recovered. But that is not the point. The point is that the part recovered includes strategic positions which may have a bearing on another terrain which has been long silent —the front before Metz from St. Mihiel to the north of Nancy.

Between Verdun and Metz is the watershed of the Meuse-Moselle, part of which is called Plain of the Woevre. From the Plain of the Woevre Germany dominates the iron mines of the Basin de Briey, which, according to Herr Schrödter, the ironmaster of Düsseldorf, supply 80 per cent. of the steel for her armaments, and without which, still according to the same authority in a paper read to the Verein Deutscher Eisenhuttenlente, she could not carry on the war three months.

While this fact certainly illuminates the German offensive of a year ago, it may still be found useful in watching the progress of the French front on the western side of the Plain of the Woevre and its relation to the valley beyond.

## 300,000 Automobiles in Use in the War

There were approximately 300,000 automobiles in use on all the war fronts at the beginning of September, 1917, according to a compilation issued by the Japanese Government. This number did not include any of the motor transports about to be put in the field by the United States. The principal Entente belligerents had about 160,000 automobiles in use and the Central Powers 130,000. Those of the Entente were distributed as follows: England, 30,000, including 15,-000 for the conveyance of supplies; France, 80,000, including 25,000 for carrying supplies; Russia, 40,000, including 20,000 for carrying supplies; Italy, 10,000, including 5,000 for carrying supplies; Belgium, 10,300; Rumania, 1,700, and Serbia, 125.

The numbers of automobiles used for war service by the Central Powers were: Germany, 100,000, including 25,000 for conveyance of supplies; Austria-Hungary, 30,000, including 3,000 for carrying goods; Turkey, 750, including 50 for conveying goods, and Bulgaria, 300.

# The Battle of the Julian Alps

## Vivid Description of the Greatest Italian
## Offensive Since the Beginning of the War

[Special Cable. Copyrighted]

*By a Staff Correspondent of* THE NEW YORK TIMES

[See Map on Page 32]

*The enormous offensive began Aug. 18, 1917, by the Italian Army for possession of San Gabriele peak was still raging at the middle of September, with undiminished energy on the Italian side and desperate resistance on the Austrian side. Hardly any other battle of the war has been so costly on both sides. By Sept. 18 General Cadorna's forces had made a decisive conquest of the northwestern crest of San Gabriele and dominated the whole region from the Dol Hill and Gargaro basin. Wave after wave of Italian infantry swept up the slopes of San Gabriele, and the mountain was drenched in human blood; but victory remained with the Italians. The following description of an eyewitness was written on Sept. 13-15, and gives a wonderful panoramic view of the battle on the whole forty-mile front from Tolmino to Trieste:*

THE Italian front in Austria is the place of all places where war remains a dramatic spectacle. Here it can be followed by the eye even through a thousand cloud banks of breaking shrapnel. The artillery can actually look upon the objective for its shells. The observer can really gaze down into the trench lines, watch troops on the move, and catch the glimmer of sunshine on the bayonets in the Austrian posts many miles distant.

Here one really sees the war. * * * It is a real battle. I doubt if it is yet realized that it is now the biggest battle that has got into full swing upon any front during the entire war.

Up to now it has always been referred to as the battle of the Isonzo, but that name has become a misnomer because the Isonzo, excepting one little portion opposite Tolmino at the northern extremity of the offensive line, is now well within Italian possession. It might better be called the battle of the Julian Alps, for one by one the peaks, valleys, and tablelands of this gigantic range are coming behind the Italian lines.

The concept of the battle is Napoleonic —even more than that. The sheer audacity of it is what contributed to its initial success a few weeks ago. The retreat of the Austrians across the Bainsizza Plateau was almost a flight, partly because they could not believe the Italians would have the courage to try it.

Plateau is another misnomer for Bainsizza; there is nothing of a tableland in its composition. It is a vast, terribly rocky ground, with hills at least a thousand feet high and corresponding valleys. It is a plateau only in comparison to the peaks surrounding.

I will not follow in chronological order my witnessing of the battle of the Julian Alps, but rather I will show the progression of the line from the northern point of the offensive opposite Tolmino, to the Isonzo and Bainsizza, over Mount Santo and Mount St. Gabriele, across the Carso, in front of Hermada, and to the Adriatic. In seeing this battle the correspondent is free to choose his seats from the top gallery down to the reserved boxes beside the proscenium arch. Let us first go to the alley entrance and climb many flights to the second balcony, where I managed to find a seat in the middle of the front row.

From there, especially with good glasses, the view is splendid. It is the very top of Mount Zagradan—many thousands of feet above the sea, but not so high as the gigantic snow peaks beyond. On those snow peaks trenches are cut in the solid glacier. On Zagradan they are cut in the rock, but are always provided with coverings to prevent their being filled with snow. It is not a tremendously difficult climb; in fact, we went four-fifths of the way in an automobile, so wonderful and enduring are the Italian mountain roads.

In all that land there was no water when the Italians arrived. It is there now—everywhere. It is there because the Italians are the best engineers in the world. They have run pipe lines from the valleys up to every mountain crest.

## View of Conquered Mount Nero

I slipped into my seat in the middle front row and unhooked my glasses. The curtain had risen. The morning fogs had all gone and the midday sun made the air as clear as crystal. I have seen many things that are wonderful and beautiful, but I have never in my life seen such an amazing, breath-taking panorama as that spread before me. "Drink it in," my officer said, "and then I will tell you where we are." I drank it in, and then, following instructions, I fixed my glasses on a high peak far over to the left. The air was so clear that through the glasses it didn't seem more than half a mile away. It was Mount Nero. Its front, where I looked, seemed a sheer precipice of bare rock 8,000 feet from the valley to the cone-shaped summit, but out beyond toward higher snow peaks I could see a thin ridge connecting it, which proved that there was not so straight a drop on the other side. As I looked, my officer explained how Mount Nero was captured by the Alpini.

"You can't see our trenches there," he said, "because we hold the summit, and the trenches are on the other side. You see that sheer wall of rock facing us? Well, it was by going up that that our soldiers took Mount Nero. We had to have it. It is an important observatory —better than this one—for the Isonzo Valley. From there one can see almost to the Dolomites on the one side and almost to Laibach on the other.

"You see that long ridge connecting the peak with the mountains beyond? That is where we made a strong feint attack. We sent two columns along that ridge so that the Austrians thought that

was all we intended to do. But the third and principal column went up the precipice. They did it during one dark night. It was important that they should do it without a sound, as they were to take the summit from the rear by surprise. So they climbed up without rifles, which might have knocked against things and sent stones crashing down, and they went up in bare feet to avoid slipping and also to avoid sound. They carried only revolvers and hand grenades.

"They jumped on the Austrians just at dawn. But the Austrians, though surprised, were very strong. We quickly used up our revolvers and bombs and we took Mount Nero with our hands. I mean that the fight became so desperate that our Alpini literally conquered by fighting hand to hand, so that hundreds of Austrians were hurled bodily down that cliff to the valley over a mile below."

I meditated upon what I had been hearing. As I looked at that appalling cliff it seemed as though I had been reading some ghastly fiction. Then he told me to shift my glasses to the right along the ridge connecting Mount Nero with the Marnick—a lower peak, almost due north of Tolmino.

## Tolmino Spared by the Guns

"Going up the sides," he said, "you can see lines. Those are our roads. And down some distance from the summit you can see our trenches—a long, zigzag line in the white rock. Just under the crest runs another line. That is the Austrian trench."

My guide told me to keep following the trench lines with my glasses down far into the valley, where they disappeared under hills in the foreground. Then I studied the Isonzo as it wound its way about Tolmino.

That Austrian town was basking in an afternoon siesta. There wasn't a shot fired to disturb its tranquillity. I could see Austrian soldiers lounging in front of the barracks. I could see horses hitched to wagons standing in the village square and pedestrians moving slowly in and out of the shops. It was all within easy striking distance of hundreds of Italian guns, but an Italian shell has never yet been fired into Tolmino. Perhaps that will never happen. The Italians hope it will not be necessary and that Tolmino will fall in another way. They don't want to wipe it out in such a fashion as Gorizia.

I swept the glasses past the town, and further down the Isonzo on the far bank arose a sheer cliff, the top of which is the famous Bainsizza Plateau—the land of the Holy Ghost. The sun had shifted so that the entire Austrian side was bathed in brilliant light, while the Italian mountains were in the shade. This made everything still more visible, and far to the south I could see Mount Santo—the Holy Mountain—taken in this offensive. I could make out the crumbled remains of the shrine on its summit where at the beginning of the war Emperor Francis Joseph went to pray for the success of the Austrian arms. When the Italians took the mountain their regimental bands played in the ruins of that shrine, and the conductor was Toscanini.

Beyond Santo there seemed to be a volcano of smoke and fire, and above it all I could actually count the white puff balls in the sky that meant that shrapnel was exploding over Mount St. Gabriele, thirty miles away.

## On Bainsizza Plateau

The entire front of the present battle, which I call the battle of the Julian Alps, stretching from Tolmino to the Adriatic, is nearly forty miles — a greater distance than any other continuous offensive of the war. In that sector there are now grouped more soldiers of actual fighting units than have ever before comprised an " army of shock."

I crossed the land of the Holy Ghost (Bainsizza Plateau) on a road now being built by the Italians under Austrian shell fire. I don't know why they call it Holy Ghost Land. The Austrians named it that, and I didn't meet those Austrians to ask the reason. I saw some dead ones and prisoners, but I was too busy listening for that dread whine announcing the arrival of Austrian shells to waste time with questions. * * *

I could actually look into the trenches of Volnik, which is the furthest eastward point of the Italian lines in Austria, through glasses. I could see Italian soldiers in a trench shooting at Austrians in the trench beyond, which I could also see plainly. I always desire in following war operations to get to the interesting places first, wherever the going is possible; so I asked a General who was there to tell me the name of another person who, I learned, had preceded me. It was the inevitable Toscanini.

I began my ride over Holy Ghost Land by crossing the Isonzo at one of the famous fourteen bridges where the Italian attack began. The Isonzo, which is glacier water, and therefore always a most sinister green, is a torrent that runs through mountain gorges its entire length until it comes out into the plain at Gorizia. At some points this gorge rises sheer for thousands of feet, as between Santo and Sabotino, where it is so deep, dark, and narrow that one gets a deluded idea he can jump across, although the distance between crests is about half a mile.

## Barrier of Isonzo Gorges

As we approached the river coming down from Mount Zagradan in the north we could see it while we were miles away and far above it. The stream writhed along at a tremendous rate, exactly like a beautiful green snake, sometimes dark and dangerous, at other times a beautiful shimmer where a sun ray penetrated between the mountain peaks and crept into the valley. Through its entire course, except in the Gorizia plain, the gorge is so steep that at no point can one ever go down to the actual level of the water.

Even where pontoons were flung across in a single night, to permit the passage of the Italian Army, the river banks are perpendicular granite cliffs quite forty feet high. Then there comes a thin ledge where infantry can find safe footing and where the straight line from the water's edge changes to an incline leading to Bainsizza, another thousand feet up.

Months ago the Italians attempted to cross the river at some of these places, but were stopped by the Austrian fire. The troops who managed to climb that forty-foot precipice were slaughtered, and their bodies lay out on top of the ledge until they became skeletons.

The Italian trenches were just at the same level on the near side of the river. The lines of the Austrians were several hundred yards up an incline, looking almost straight down on the river—a series of perfect natural fortresses made of solid granite. They never expected the Italians to try again, or, if they did try, the Austrians believed it would be only a feint to cover operations further south in front of Hermada Mountain, which has barred the road to Trieste.

## Searchlights Blind Austrians

When the Italians did try again, and this time succeeded, it was the biggest scheme ever inaugurated by the silent wizard of the Italian armies—Cadorna. Its very audacity contributed to its success. When dawn followed the night of the crossing, the Austrians could scarcely believe their eyes. An army stood in front of them. On those bridges, constructed over that terrible gorge between darkness and dawn, an army corps had passed with scarcely the loss of a man.

And it was done chiefly by putting out the Austrians' eyes. On the hills opposite the Austrian positions, and at exactly the same level, the Italians had been concentrating searchlights for days. There seemed to be miles of them. On the night when the pontoons were to be thrown across they were turned full on the Austrians for the first time, dazzling them to such an extent that they could see nothing of the work going on under their noses and only a few hundred yards under at that. It was almost as near as if bridges were being thrown over Broadway while an enemy with preventive means was on top of the Times Building and searchlights were on the Hotel Knickerbocker.

Naturally, the Austrians must have known that something was going on. There was considerable firing, and one bridge was damaged. But for the most part the crossing of the Isonzo was a complete surprise.

While the searchlights streamed constantly overhead, the Italian engineers worked below in pitch dark. They had to drop their pontoon boats down that forty-foot wall on wooden skids, then join them across the rushing water, plank them over so that the troops could walk, and provide ladders for them to climb up the precipice on the Austrian side.

Time and again the current swept boats away before they were properly joined up. Frequently workers fell into the water and were carried instantly down. The constant cannonade helped the searchlights in fooling the enemy and kept the sound of the bridge-making from reaching the Austrians' ears.

In the morning, when the Austrians realized what had happened, they precipitated themselves backward a distance of more than seven miles to their positions beyond Volnik. What almost happened, instead of their successful retirement to Volnik, was the first surrender of an enemy army in this war.

When I arrived at the new footbridges I found the engineer corps still there making stone and concrete structures, over which artillery transports and my automobile could pass to the beginning of what is really Bainsizza. The Austrians had a fairly good road up behind their old lines to the top of a steep incline. There, where road making should be simpler than on the sides of mountains, their road trickled out into an ordinary Austrian path, and there I found what seemed to be thousands of Italian soldiers making a real military highway as quickly as possible.

We turned a curve suddenly and I saw in front an entire company of road builders lying flat on their faces squarely in our path. One of them yelled that the Austrians were sending over shrapnel. Another shouted at us to move on fast or turn back, warning us that waiting there was simply inviting a shell.

## A Race Under Shell Fire

An order was given and the company crawled to the side of the road. I began to think discretion was desirable and was about to say so when, like a shot, the car went forward. The chauffeur had decided where we were to go without waiting to hear from me. We were to go forward over a mile of open road, and we were to go at top speed.

The road from our speeding-up point was scarcely a road at all. It had been prospected as a road by Italian engineers only the night before, there had been blasting operations, and loads of crushed stone—they were blocks rather than ordinary stones—were strewn all along to make the going harder. Yet we did it somehow and always at top speed.

As I looked behind me, I counted five distinct upheavals in the road where shells had struck less than a minute after we had passed. The Austrians evidently had not expected to see an automobile, so they did not have the proper range. Later, after we left our car in a safe shelter, we saw shrapnel raining over that road for half an hour, in the vain hope that we might be going back. We had leaped through just in time and knew better than to go back—before dark—until the road was finished and properly screened, or until certain Austrian guns were silenced.

Every wounded man is carried by hand from Holy Ghost Land, and every bit of food and water is carried in by night, although water was being piped up even while we were there.

### Battle for San Gabriele

From Mount Santo (the Holy Mountain) one gets the greatest war spectacle in all the world—the fight for Mount San Gabriele. It is a stage box. The actors in the drama are so close that one can see the make-up and even watch the entrances and exits through the wings.

Mount Santo is an ideal looking mountain, for it rises 2,000 feet above the Gorizia plain and is so steep that the ascent seems like climbing a perpendicular wall. It is almost a sheer cliff on each side, and its summit rises like a church spire above everything surrounding except Sabotino, which is a mountain of its own level across the Isonzo half a mile away.

San Gabriele, which squats directly in front of Santo, is an ugly fat mountain of bare rock, the top of which is only 300 feet below the Holy Mountain's peak. That peak is the stage box so near the

tragedy that one could almost attract the performers' attention with tennis racket and balls.

Santo fell into Italian hands in much the same manner as many mountains fall—by being entirely surrounded and so compelled to surrender. Thus it became an observatory not only for the battle for San Gabriele, but for a near view of the operations clear across the Gorizia plain over the Carso to the sea. From there one understands more particularly the strategy that will eventually mean the fall of Trieste.

Although the long-drawn battle for San Gabriele is limited in action, the mountain being a salient in the Austrian line, there has never been anything except at Verdun so bloody and so terrible.

The climb up Santo is long and hard, but not dangerous in the daytime. At night it is another matter on account of the precipice. However, the Italians, according to their custom, are now hacking a fine wide road in its granite side, and in a few more weeks expect to use the road for automobiles and guns. At the very top there is a great pile of broken white marble.

### Where Francis Joseph Prayed

Up to a few months ago when the Italians concentrated their fire upon it, from Sabotino across the way these pieces were formed together into a sacred shrine where old Francis Joseph came to pray at the beginning of the war for the success of Austrian arms. The shrine faced west toward the old frontier. When the domineering Emperor was hauled up in a sedan chair to inaugurate thus the end of his tragic reign in a cataclysm of blood he prayed with arms spread out toward the smiling plains of Italy.

When the first shell burst through the stone portico of the shrine there stood revealed to the Italian observers a figure of the Virgin. Through the clear mountain air the observers on Sabotino could distinguish the colors of the frescoes about the Virgin's head. Another shell and both Virgin and frescoes crashed in fragments down the precipice facing Italy. To the Italian gunners it seemed an omen that the ill-luck of the House of Hapsburg would continue to the end and that by Italy would their ramshackle empire be split into pieces, only to be remolded in a better way.

And now that rubble pile of what was an emperor's shrine is a box seat from which to watch the Italian lines go forward on Austrian soil.

When first I looked down on the battle for San Gabriele I seemed to hang indirectly over the crater of a volcano. A matter of 40,000 Italian shells on a daily average are bursting over San Gabriele's crest. In addition are the Austrian shells, for the lines on San Gabriele are now so close that the topmost positions have been taken and retaken half a dozen times.

## A Rolling Sea of Smoke

At the moment of my arrival it seemed as if the artillery was outdoing itself for the final hours before dark. So for a few minutes I could see nothing but a rolling sea of smoke so near that I could almost smell it, while on an exact level with my eyes the puff balls of shrapnel sparked and exploded so rapidly that their detonations, rolling up mountain gorges, seemed to put the whole world a-tremble.

It all made me wonder whether we were still hanging on to our world. There was never fevered nightmare more appalling. No Hippodrome producer in his wildest imaginings ever pictured such a scene. Even Dante's Inferno was outclassed. It was veritably a hell on earth of which no pen can give the details.

Occasionally through the smoke waves we could see the bald, tortured surface of the crest. A shell would strike and we could see the sparks as a granite ledge was shivered and splintered in every direction. Caverns yawned up at us where the melinite bombs rebounded and spent their rage. Black lines zigzagged over the surface—crazy and grotesque. They were the trenches.

Sometimes we could see figures leaping upon the stone parapets. They were like damned souls. Another shell would blot out the sight, and when it cleared the figures would all be huddled and still—only black patches against the dirty gray of the rock.

I shifted my glasses to the breaking spray of shrapnel directly in front of me. There were the usual kinds of shrapnel, the white puff balls, and the ugly black clods. There was also a new kind, Austrian, that was yellow. The effect of all three together was marvelously beautiful. In that clear air, with the slanting sun rays and deep blue sky, when those three clouds of shrapnel would break simultaneously in about the same spot the colors spread out like a gigantic bouquet of flowers.

### Hermada and the Carso

I turned my glasses over Gorizia and the Carso to where the ugly turtle-backed Hermada Mountain has been blocking the road to Trieste. I had gone through Gorizia that morning, and had been duly and properly shelled. The Austrians fire constantly upon the town from Mount San Marco, a flat mud hill in front of the city, an ideal machine-gun nest that cannot be taken until it is flanked after the fall of San Gabriele. But Gorizia is only like every other captured city, and held no particular interest for me except just to say that I had been there.

I had also prowled over the Carso, that tableland of flint like our Bad Lands, which has caused more blindness among Italian soldiers than in any other army. The reason is that shells, hitting the Carso, so splinter the rock that quite as much damage is caused by splinters as by shells. Every trench is hewn from the solid rock. I often crouched in them to avoid pieces of rock that whistled through the air so far from the shell that I could not find the smoke of the explosion.

I glanced back to the inferno of San Gabriele. "But why spend so much time over this mountain," I asked the officer, "especially as you may say you have it?" He smiled. "You would be surprised to know how few men we have lost down there," he said, "and we are not occupied alone with San Gabriele. Meanwhile it has used up about fifteen Austrian divisions. * * * Most of those divisions are dead."

In the dying daylight I again fixed my glasses on the rocky slopes below. The artillery fire had lulled a little, so that we could see more clearly. All about the surface of the bald crest was dotted with black, grotesque shadows—shadows that did not move. There were the pieces of the fifteen Austrian divisions that were dead.

### Grandiose Display of Fireworks

Day fled quickly behind the higher mountains, and the evening fireworks began. Flares began to go up on all the surrounding hills, and were answered from mountain peaks miles away—rockets breaking in showers of stars that seemed to glimmer as far from the earth as the millions of real stars in the clear heavens.

We sat and watched, silent before the magnificent spectacle. The artillery was turned again upon San Gabriele. Shells crashed and exploded, striking lines of fire from the bare cliffs. The shrapnel hissed and screamed and screamed and broke in clouds of sparks.

For miles on every side the whole world seemed gone crazy. A thousand Japanese lanterns seemed to wave in a giddy whirl on the mountain peaks, then to break each into a dozen pieces and go out.

Sometimes sheds or motor caissons, struck by shells on far distant roads, would soar up in flames that lasted several minutes. In the valleys a million fireflies seemed to bob up and down in rhythmic air dance. Through every cleft and gorge the sound of cannon echoed and re-echoed as if a thousand valkyries were galloping madly from peak to peak,

while through all the infernal din there came the ceaseless barking of machine guns and sometimes the yells of men.

On San Gabriele itself we could see more plainly than by day. The explosions would sometimes light up spaces of rock for a distance of many yards. We could often catch glimpses of trenches and the shimmer of helmets and bayonets. Sometimes for brief moments between shifts in the smoke we could see troops climbing up the slopes between the zigzag black trench line clawing at the rocky ground. Once we saw men in the very act of falling backward in the bright light of an exploding shell.

Suddenly, quite suddenly, something happened. I scrambled to my feet and rubbed an unsteady hand over my eyes. My officer also got up quickly.

I had a strange feeling that a great power had suddenly come to watch and bid mankind to cease his struggles and be still.

For from behind a distant snow peak there had floated the splendid and majestic moon. All the flares and rockets seemed to fade away. The flashes of shrapnel and melinite died out before that effulgent glow of beautiful mellow light that softly draped and enfolded the entire gigantic scene.

Even the racket of the guns seemed to die down and the carnage to shrink.

It was the same cold, wonderful moon, but on that night it seemed like the eye of God from which there flowed too much light for armies to go on with their killing unashamed.

# The Desperate Fighting of the Canadians at Lens

## By Philip Gibbs

[War Correspondence From France, Aug. 23, 1917]

TO the south of Lene there is a slag heap overgrown with weeds, called the Green Crassier. It is clearly visible across the Souchez River beyond a broken bridge, and I have often seen it

from the lower slopes of Vimy. It was the scene of great fighting yesterday, for in the morning the Canadians, who are showing an indomitable spirit after ten days of most furious attacks and counterattacks, launched an assault upon it and seized the position.

Later in the day the enemy came back in strength, and after violent efforts succeeded in thrusting the Canadians off the crest of this old mound of cinders, though they still cling to the western side. It is another incident in the long series of fierce and bloody encounters which since the battle of Vimy on April 9 have surrounded the City of Lens and given to its streets and suburbs a sinister but historic fame.

The Canadians have fought here with astounding resolution. They have hurled themselves against fortress positions and by sheer courage have smashed their way through streets entangled with quickset hedges of steel, through houses alive with machine-gun fire, through trenches dug between concrete forts, through tunnels under red brick ruins sometimes too strong to be touched by shell fire, and through walls loopholed for rifle fire and hiding machine-gun emplacements designed to enfilade the Canadian way of advance.

Six German divisions have attacked them in turn and have been shattered against them. These are the Seventh and Eighth, the Fourth Guards Division, the Eleventh Reserve, the Two Hundred and Twentieth, and the First Guards Reserve Division. In addition to these six divisions some portions, at any rate, of the One Hundred and Eighty-fifth Division and of the Thirty-sixth Reserve Division have been engaged.

The total German strength used at Lens must well exceed fifty battalions, and the German losses may perhaps be estimated at between 12,000 and 15,000 men. The Canadians themselves have been hard pressed at times, but have endured the exhaustion of a great struggle with amazing strength of spirit, grimly and fiercely resolved to hold their gains unless overwhelmed by numbers in their advanced positions, as it has sometimes happened to them.

### City of Blood and Death

But it is no wonder that some of the men whom I met yesterday coming out of that city of blood and death looked like men who had suffered to the last limit of mental and bodily resistance. Their faces were haggard and drawn. Their eyes were heavy. Their skin was as gray as burnt ash. Some of them walked like drunken men, drunk with sheer fatigue, and as soon as they had reached their journey's end some of them sat under the walls of a mining village, with their chalky helmets tilted back, drugged by the need of sleep, but too tired even for that.

They were men of the battalions who three days ago came face to face with the enemy in No Man's Land, a stretch of barren, cratered earth between St. Emile and the northern streets of Lens, and fought him there until many dead lay strewn on both sides and their ammunition was exhausted. An officer of one of these battalions came out of a miner's cottage to talk to me. He was a very young man, with a thin, clean-shaven face, which gave him a boyish look. He was too weary to stand straight and too weary to talk more than a few jerky words. He leaned up against the wall of the miner's cottage and passed a hand over his face and eyes, and said: "I'm darned tired. It was a hell of a fight. We fought to a finish, and when we had no more bombs of our own we picked up 'Heine's' bombs and used those."

### They Call Him "Heine"

Heine — the Canadians call their enemy Heine and not Fritz—"was at least three times as strong as us, and we gave him hell. It was hand-to-hand fighting—rifles, bombs, bayonets, butt ends—any old way of killing a man— and we killed a lot. But he broke our left flank, and things were bloody in the centre. He had one of his strong points there, and swept us with machine guns.

"My fellows went straight for it, and a lot of them got wiped out. But we got on top of it, and through the wire, and held the trench beyond until Heine came down with swarms of bombers."

This young Canadian officer was stricken by the loss of many of his men— "the best crowd that any fellow could command"—and he had been through indescribable things under enormous shell fire, and he had had no sleep for days and nights, and could not sleep now for thinking of things. But he smiled grimly once or twice when he reckoned up the enemy's losses

The remembrance of the German dead he had seen seemed like strong wine to his soul. "We made 'em pay," was his summing up of the battle. The nightmare of it all was still heavy on him. and he spoke with a quiet fierceness about the enemy's losses and the things he had endured, in a way which would scare poor simple souls who think that war is a fine, picturesque business.

A senior officer of a battalion on the flank of his was a different type of man —like an English squire of the old style, with a fine smiling light in his eyes, in spite of all he had been through, and with a vivid way of speech that would not come fast enough to say splendid things about his men to describe the marvelous way in which they had fought in frightful conditions; to praise first one and then another for the things they had done, when things were at their worst.

He had been addressing some of the survivors of this battle when I came on him, and I saw them march away, straightening themselves up before this officer of theirs and proud because he was pleased with them. He thanked them for one thing above all, and that was for the gallant way in which, after all their fighting, they had gone out to fetch in their dead and wounded, so that not one wounded man lay out there to die or to be taken prisoner, and the dead were brought back for burial. He said a word, too, for "Heine," as they call him. The Germans had not sniped or machine-gunned the stretcher bearers, but had sent their own men out on the same mission, too. That was after the battle, and there was no surrendering while the fighting was on.

## Officer's Stirring Story

The officer's story of that was as wonderful as anything I have heard in this war. And the man himself was wonderful, for he had had no sleep for six days and nights, and had suffered the fearful strain of his responsibility for many men's lives, yet now when I met him straight from all that, he was bright-eyed, and his mind was as clear as a bell, and the emotion that surged through him was well controlled.

He described the things I have attempted to describe before the fortified streets and houses of Lens, which make it one great fortress tunneled from end to end with exits into concrete forts two yards thick in cement in the ruined cottages.

On the morning of our attack the enemy was expecting it, and within a minute and a half of our barrage put down his own barrage with terrific intensity. So there were the Canadians between two walls of high explosives, and it was within that inferno that they fought in the great death struggle. For the Canadians had already advanced toward the enemy's line, and in greater numbers— three times as great—he had advanced to ours, and the two forces met on the barren stretch of earth crossed by twisted trenches which for a time had been No Man's Land.

While the battalion on the left was heavily engaged, fighting with rifles and bombs until their ammunition gave out, and then with bayonets and butt ends, the battalion on the right was working southward and eastward to the northern outskirts of Lens. They came up at once against the fortress houses, from which machine-gun and rifle fire poured out.

The Canadians, in small parties, tried to surround these places, but many were swept down. Some of them rushed close to the walls of one house which was a bastion of the northern defense of Lens, and were so close that the machine guns through slits in the walls could not fire at them. They even established a post behind it and beyond it, quite isolated from the rest of their men, but clinging to their post all day.

The enemy dropped bombs upon them through the loopholes and sandbagged windows, fired rifle grenades at them, and tried to get machine guns at them, but there were always a few men left to hold the post, until at last, when the line withdrew elsewhere, they were recalled.

Before that night came there were

UNITED STATES TROOPS IN LONDON

American Soldiers, On Their Parade Through London, Crossing Westminster Bridge. The Imperial Parliament Buildings in the background

(Photo Central News)

BRITISH BIG GUNS AT WORK

A Remarkable Photograph From the Western Front of a Battery of Heavy Howitzers Pounding on the German Trenches

(*British Official Photo from Bain News Service*)

great German counterattacks. Masses of men carrying nothing but stick bombs, which they had slung around them, advanced down communication trenches and flung these things at the Canadians of the left battalion, who were fighting out in the open, and in another communication trench with the right battalion.

## Piled German Corpses

The enemy walked over the piled corpses of his own dead before he could drive back the Canadians, but by repeated storming parties he did at last force them to give way and retreat down the trench to gain the support of their comrades of the other battalion who had not been so hard pressed. These came to the rescue, and for a long time held the German grenadiers at bay.

The fighting was fierce and savage on both sides. A Canadian Major, with a revolver in one hand and a naked bayonet in the other, flung himself among the Prussians and killed those within reach of his fury. At one time he used the butt end of a rifle and clubbed them about the head. All through the day this officer was astounding in his reckless courage, and there were many young officers with him who fought to the death.

At last, weakened by their losses and with failing stores of ammunition, these two battalions were given the order to retire to a trench further back, and the survivors of the most desperate action in Canadian history withdrew, still fighting, and established blocks in the communication trenches down which the enemy was bombing, so that they could not pass those points to the line upon which here on the north of Lens the Canadians had fallen back.

Southward there had been no withdrawal, and other battalions had forced their way forward a good distance, shutting up that entrance to the city and getting down into the deep tunnels over which there howled the unceasing fire of the German heavies. Our own guns were hard at work, and I have already told how the Prussians were destroyed in the square of Lens by 12-inch shells and shrapnel.

## Lens Becomes a Deathtrap

*On Sept.* 17 *Mr. Gibbs recorded this later phase of the great fight for Lens:*

The Canadian and English troops during the five months of fighting have captured all the outer belt of these mining cities, and their artillery and the enemy's has left nothing of all the neat little houses and mine buildings but a wild orgy of ruin through which I walked yesterday on my way to Hill 70, which the Canadians took by a great assault a few weeks ago.

Lens itself is now no better than its outer suburbs. It is a town of battered houses without roofs and with broken walls leaning against rubbish heaps of brickwork and timber. The enemy sent out a wireless message that the English gunners were destroying French property by bombarding the city, and then made a deep belt of destruction by blowing up long blocks of streets.

After that the British guns completed the ruin, for there was a German garrison in every house, and in this kind of warfare there must be no tenderness of sentiment about bricks and mortar if the enemy is between the walls. So now in Lens the only cover for the Germans and their only chance of safety is below the ground in tunnels and cellars.

These are reinforced by concrete, and were built by the forced labor of civilians two years and more ago, when the city was menaced by a French attack. Into these tunnels the German garrisons of Lens make their way by night, and in them they live and die.

Many die in them, it is certain, for a tunnel is no more than a deathtrap when it is blocked at the entrance by the fall of houses or when it collapses by the bombardment of heavy shells, which pierce deep and explode with fearful effect. That has happened, as we know, in many parts of the German line, and recently on the French front whole companies of German soldiers were buried alive in deep caves. It is happening in Lens now, if the same effect is produced by the same power of artillery.

But death comes to the German soldiers

there in another way, without any noise and quite invisible and very horrible in its quietude. Many times lately the Canadians have filled the City of Lens with gas that kills and soaks down heavily into the dugouts and tunnels and stifles the men in their sleep before they have time to stretch out their hands for gas masks, or makes them die with their masks on if they fumble a second too long.

The enemy, who was first to use poison gas, should wish to God he had never betrayed his soul by such a thing, for it has come back upon him as a frightful retribution, and in Lens, in those deep, dark cellars below the ruins, the German soldiers must live in terror and be afraid to sleep.

Yesterday, when I went to that neighborhood, I saw four German soldiers who had come out into the open, preferring to risk death there rather than stay in their dungeon. They appeared for a minute around the corner of some brick stacks in Cité St. Auguste. It was strange to see them, as if they were visitors from another planet, for in this district of Lens on man shows his body above ground unless he is careless of quick death, and one may stare for days at empty houses and broken mine shafts and great black slag heaps without seeing any living thing.

# The Scene of Carnage at Le Mort Homme

*The most important victory of the French in August was the capture of the famous Le Mort Homme (Dead Man's Hill) and Hill 304, the two eminences which overlook Verdun, and around which for three years the bloodiest battles of the war have been fought. The capture of Le Mort Homme on Aug. 19, 1917, by the French is thus described by the official British military observer:*

FROM the Avocourt Wood, on the distant horizon in the west, for a stretch of thirteen or fourteen miles to a point well to the northeast of Verdun the whole series of ravines and ridges, one behind another, was a smoking furnace. The shelling was most furious on the west bank of the Meuse, beyond the bend hidden in the valley, especially on the summit of Le Mort Homme and the long level height of Hill 304. But on the right bank also, on the further side of Louvemont and toward Beaumont and on the Caures Wood beyond it, a nest of German batteries, the shell explosions followed one another so rapidly that the curtain of smoke hung steadily over the length and breadth of the positions which were being prepared for the advance as though it rose from a string of bonfires, instead of falling from the sky.

With every minute of the passing night the thunder of all those thousands of guns was getting more and more appalling. When the men went over the parapet and the French barrage began everything in the way of noise that had gone before was dwarfed and it was barely possible to hear even the whining of the shells traveling directly overhead. Every gun in every battery was working at red-hot speed with one continuous rattle and roar along the whole front. And with that hurricane of sound and fury the light began to dawn and a gray bank of mist grew out of the darkness ahead, so that we seemed to be looking down not upon land but on the sea rising up from our feet to meet the sky, as though France were actually defending her shores and hurling flame and iron at an invisible fleet.

Shortly after, when the splendid infantry had reached their first objective, that illusion had gone and the stronger light showed the crest of the ridge blurred by clouds of dust and smoke and the trench in which we were began to take shape, together with the smoke-bursts of the shells with which the enemy were trying to search out our batteries. One I saw fall almost on the top of a group of eight or nine men standing together in the trench. Two of them had their helmets knocked off by the shower of earth and stones it threw up, two were lighting cigarettes which were whisked out of their mouths, one was hit on the knee by a stone, and yet none of them got a scratch.

Then, as the sun began to shine, the air seemed suddenly to be alive with scores of airplanes and two long rows of balloons stretched far away into the distance. During the attack the observer in one of these balloons, which was unsuccessfully bombed by an enemy airman, had an extraordinary escape. He was so hard pressed, though his balloon was not destroyed, that he was obliged to fling himself out, and in his hurry he jumped on the wrong side, so that the parachute caught in the ropes of the basket and he was left suspended below it with his legs dangling in midair, unable to free himself till the men below had hauled him carefully down along with the balloon.

*A correspondent of The London Times, writing Aug. 23, 1917, thus describes the scenes about Le Mort Homme and the fearful ravages of the guns:*

As the sun rose in an almost cloudless sky, the night mists that cling to the flat valley of the Meuse and the scores of shallow valleys which run down into it melted away, and left the four rows of long ridges that are the defense of Verdun standing out bare and straight, one behind another, like so many lines of walls—Le Mort Homme and the Côte de l'Oie, on the west bank in the outer parallel. Inside them, on the east bank, in the loop of the river, the Côte de Talou and Hill 344. Inside, again, Froideterre and Thiaumont and Douaumont, and behind them Vaux and Souville and Belleville —those are the main alignments, and they are, of several others, the city's natural bulwarks.

Until you get on where no amount of camouflage would have enabled the French, before Le Mort Homme was taken, to move along in daytime, there are continuous canvas and brushwood screens and hangings of rush matting along both sides, and every twenty yards or so narrower strips of canvas are hung across overhead as well, like the flies in a theatre. You pass along

it feeling as if you were in a gallery or in a tunnel. But now that is all changed—a practical proof and symbol of the French advance.

In one way Le Mort Homme is different from most fields of battle. The upheaval of the surface is as complete as it is anywhere on the hills nearer Verdun, on the plateaus of the Chemin des Dames, or on the Somme. It is as complete and hideous and universal as the heart of the artilleryman could wish. Not a blade of grass, nothing but earth and stones and halk are to be seen. The shell holes overlap and break into each other over every foot of the two summits of which the hill is composed. The wire in front of what had been the enemy's front the French had wiped out. Nothing was left of the entanglement but a few twisted stanchions, and there was nothing to stop the advance of the French infantry when they made their charge but the rifles and grenades and machine guns of the German soldiers.

At least, that is what ought to have been the case. As a matter of fact, there were not, except in rare instances, even these. There was, of course, a barrage fire, which started, fortunately, a few minutes late, and there was a good show of gas shells. But the men who should have been in the way with weapons in their hands had either slipped off the hill before the attack or were hiding in the Bismarck Tunnel, eighty feet long, which burrows under the lower ground between the two crests, or in the more magnificent and commodious excavation, 800 feet long by 12 feet high and wide enough to take half a dozen men abreast, which runs from end to end of the further of the two crests, and is called after the more magnificent Crown Prince.

In this 150 Germans lie dead, killed by the effects of a well-aimed sixteen-inch shell, and from it 700 or 800 more officers and men were taken and sent to the rear as prisoners. The terrific bombardment had been too much for them and for those others who had already retired down to the valley off the little Forges Brook behind the hill. They could not face the music of those terrible guns any longer; their spirit was broken. The French batteries had not only swept away the wire from the path of the infantry; it had driven underground the men who were posted on the hill to defend it and to hold it at any cost.

It was this that made the difference between this battlefield and others I have seen. A few battered rifles and helmets and suits and grenades and tattered uniforms and other odds and ends of the ordinary battle wreckage were lying about among the shell holes, but not to anything like the extent that is bound to mark the scene of hard fighting. Hard fighting there was for the hard-bitten, keen, daring, lovable gars of the blue uniform, who swarmed over Le Mort Homme as they have over obstacle after obstacle thrown in their way by the invader in the long, cruel fight for their wives and their children and their homes. But that was later. The actual last taking of Le Mort Homme, the soil of which, in the many bitter fights that have been waged upon it, has become the soil of the tomb and the charnel house, was for them almost a walk-over, and those who are now on guard there are more than ever sure that the Boche is, and knows he is, a beaten man.

# The Imperial Japanese Mission
## Addresses by Viscount Ishii

THE Imperial Japanese Mission, after a reception of extraordinary cordiality in San Francisco, (described in these pages a month ago,) arrived in Washington on Aug. 22, 1917, by special train. The members included Viscount Kikujiro Ishii, Ambassador Extraordinary and Plenipotentiary; Vice Admiral Takeshita, Imperial Japanese Navy; Major Gen. Sugano, Commander Ando, and other diplomatic and military representatives of Japan.

The mission was received by President Wilson on the following day, when Viscount Ishii delivered his formal message from the Emperor of Japan, congratulating the President and people of the United States upon the chivalrous entry of this country into the European war. The speaker concluded with these words:

That America is now fighting on the side of Japan is a source of pride to his Majesty and to every Japanese. It is not the first time, I may be allowed to remind you, Mr. President, that this has happened. In 1900 I had the privilege of seeing with my own eyes the American and Japanese colors waving together when the allied troops, in the face of terrible difficulties, triumphantly relieved the besieged legations at Peking. I well remember the skill and courage with which the American civilians and soldiers co-operated in the defense. The resourceful bravery which those few Americans showed then American legions will show now.

The auspicious co-operation of the United States of America and Japan in the tremendous task of restoring the reign of mutual confidence and good-will among the nations of the earth cannot but draw us closer together. Our common efforts are directed to seeking an enduring peace, based on respect for the independence of the smallest and weakest States, on contempt for the arrogance of materialist force, on reverence for the pledged word. In the service of these common ideals our two countries must surely realize a far nearer friendship than before.

In his reply President Wilson expressed his pleasure at Japan's tribute, and added:

The present struggle is especially characterized by the development of the spirit of co-operation throughout the greater part of the world for the maintenance of the rights of nations and the liberties of individuals. I assure your Excellency that, standing as our countries now do, associated in this great struggle for the vindication of justice, there will be developed those closer ties of fellowship which must come from the mutual sacrifice of life and property. May the efforts now being exerted by an indignant humanity lead, at the proper time, to the complete establishment of justice and to a peace which will be both permanent and serene.

President Wilson entertained the members of the mission at a state dinner in the evening, and there followed several weeks of social and diplomatic activities for the visitors. In a statement to the press Viscount Ishii declared that the chief objects of his mission were to convey a friendly message from his Emperor and to arrange for the fuller co-operation of Japan with the United States in the prosecution of the war against Germany.

## Address at Washington's Tomb

On Sunday, Aug. 26, the members visited Washington's tomb at Mount Vernon as the guests of the Secretary of the Navy and Mrs. Daniels. After an address of welcome by Secretary Daniels the following speech was delivered by Viscount Ishii, whose command of pure English was thus early in evidence:

In the name of my gracious sovereign, the Emperor of Japan, and representing all the liberty-loving people who own his sway, I stand today in this sacred presence, not to eulogize the name of Washington, for that were presumption, but to offer the simple tribute of a people's reverence and love.

Washington was an American, but America, great as she is, powerful as she is, certain as she is of her splendid destiny, can lay no exclusive claim to this immortal name. Washington is now a citizen of the world; today he belongs to all mankind. And so men come here from the ends of the earth to honor his memory and to reiterate their faith in the principles to which his great life was devoted.

Japan claims entrance to this holy circle. She yields to none in reverence and respect; nor is there any gulf between the ancient East and the new-born West too deep and wide for the hearts and the understandings of her people to cross.

It is fitting, then, that men who love liberty and justice better than they love life, that men who know what honor is, should seek this shrine and here, in the presence of these sacred ashes, rededicate themselves to the service of humanity.

It is a fitting place, at this time, when all the world is filled with turmoil and suffering, for comrades in a holy cause to gather and here renew their fealty to a righteous purpose, firm in the determination that the struggle must go on until the world is free from menace and aggression.

Japan is proud to place herself beside her noble allies in this high resolve, and here, in the presence of these deathless ashes, she reaffirms her devotion to the cause and the principles for which they wage battle, fully determined to do her whole part in securing for the world the blessings of liberty, justice, and lasting peace.

As the representative of my people, then, I place this wreath upon the tomb of Washington with reverent hands; and in so doing it is my proud privilege to again pledge my country to those principles of right and justice which have given immortality to the name of Washington.

## Received by the Senate

The visitors were received with great ceremony by the United States Senate on Aug. 30. When they were escorted down the main aisle the entire audience arose, and the audience also arose before and after Viscount Ishii's address, and as the mission left the Chamber after shaking hands with Senators and Representatives.

In the absence of Vice President Marshall the address of welcome was made by Senator Saulsbury, who said:

Japan joins our great young nation in pledging anew a continuance of our old friendship which the troublemakers of the earth have tried so hard to interrupt. We now know how industriously insidious attempts have been made by the Prussian masters of the German people to bring about distrust and hatred in the world. The yellow peril was made in Germany, and Shantung was seized; the Slav peril was made in Germany, and Serbia was overwhelmed and Russia was invaded; but the thick-witted, smug, self-centred supermen of Germany, entering their last attempt at conquest, have roused a real peril—a real peril to themselves—and the free nations who believe in international honor, in the binding force of treaties, and in the pledged word are grimly, though so sorrowfully, engaged in creating, perfecting, and bringing to successful issue an alliance for the benefit of all earth's people, which will protect the rights of nations, small and great, and enable them to lead their lives in peace, and lead them unafraid.

### Viscount Ishii said in part:

I assure you, gentlemen, that the Japanese ideal of national life is, in its final analysis, not so very far removed from yours. We conceive of our nation as a vast family held together, not by the arbitary force of armed men, but by the force of a natural development. We shall call the common force that animates us a passion of loyalty to our Emperor and to our homes, as we shall call that of Americans a passion for liberty and of loyalty to their flag.

These two passions—passion of loyalty and passion for liberty—are they not really one? Is not the same control working in both cases—the intense desire to be true to our innermost selves and to the highest and best that has been revealed to us? You must be free to be Americans, and we must be free to be Japanese. But our common enemy is not content with this freedom for the nation or for the individual; he must force all the world to be German, too! * * *

Mr. President and gentlemen, whatever the critic half informed or the hired slanderer may say against us, in forming your judgment of Japan we ask you only to use those splendid abilities that guide this great nation. The criminal plotter against our good neighborhood takes advantage of the fact that, at this time of the world's crisis, many things must of necessity remain untold and unrecorded in the daily newspapers; but we are satisfied that we are doing our best. In this tremendous work, as we move together, shoulder to shoulder, to a certain victory, America and Japan must have many things in which the one can help the other. We have much in common and much to do in concert. That is the reason I have been sent, and that is the reason you have received me here today.

I have an earnest and abiding faith that this association of ours, this proving of ourselves in the highest, most sacred, and most trying of human activities, the armed vindication of right and justice, must bring us to a still closer concord and a deeper confidence one in the other, sealing for all time the bonds of cordial friendship between our two nations.

A similar address was delivered by Viscount Ishii before the House of Representatives on Sept. 5.

## Japanese at Perry's Tomb

Among the historic shrines visited by the Japanese Mission was the tomb of Commodore Perry at Newport, R. I., on Sept. 16. It was this American naval officer who had opened the Island Empire to Western civilization. The mission, headed by Viscount Ishii, entered the cemetery through a lane of apprentice seamen and Naval Reserves standing at present arms, while a band from the training station played the Japanese national hymn. A great crowd of soldiers, sailors, and civilians bared their heads in silence as Viscount Ishii stepped forward and placed on the tomb of the Commodore a large wreath made up in the colors of Japan, with white lilies and red gladiolas.

Retiring a few paces, the Viscount bowed profoundly before the tomb and resumed his place in the semicircle formed by other members of the mission and naval officers. One by one each member of the mission stepped forward silently and bowed low before the grave. As the last one paid his tribute, Bishop James De Wolf Perry of the Episcopal Diocese of Rhode Island offered a brief prayer.

Then the entire assembly stood at attention while the band once more played the Japanese national hymn and "The Star-Spangled Banner."

Speaking at a public reception in the Casino on the following day, Viscount Ishii paid this tribute to Japan's first American friend:

Newport is storied in the mind of every school child in Japan as the resting place of Commodore Matthew Perry. Not so long ago but that living men well remember and tell it to their grandchildren, Japan lived in isolation, well contented. One day there came a knocking at our door and, looking forth, we saw strange sights indeed. Fantastic folk in awesome ships with gruesome guns held out the hand of friendship, and thus came America and Commodore Perry to our shores.

These sixty years just passed must constitute one full chapter in the history of Japan. During all that time the Pacific Ocean, so illimitable then to us, has been growing more narrow daily. The East and the West, which stood aloof without a thing in common except their common humanity, have by that wonderful thread been drawn closer and even closer together until today we stand shoulder to shoulder as friends and allies defying the power of evil to destroy that splendid heritage which we are agreed to share as common heirs.

I am convinced that with the turning of the page and the opening of this new chapter of international history, and so through to the end of all time and all chapters, our good understanding will increase. The road between our homes will become more and more the beaten track of neighbors.

The visitors later were entertained in Boston, New York, and other cities, everywhere seeking to create closer ties between the two nations. The economic results of their conferences at Washington, though not made public, were believed to be of importance.

# Sweden's Unneutral Acts

## The Sending of the "Spurlos Versenkt" Dispatches to Germany Through Swedish Diplomats

THE Department of State of the United States on Sept. 8, 1917, startled the world by making public certain telegrams that had been sent in cipher to the Berlin Foreign Office—through the Stockholm Foreign Office—by the German Chargé at Buenos Aires, Argentina. Secretary Lansing's formal announcement was as follows:

*The Department of State has secured certain telegrams from Count Luxburg, German Charge d'Affaires at Buenos Aires, to the Foreign Office at Berlin, which, I regret to say, were dispatched from Buenos Aires by the Swedish Legation as their own official messages, addressed to the Stockholm Foreign Office. The following are translations of the German text:*

May 19, 1917. No. 32.

This Government has now released German and Austrian ships on which hitherto a guard had been placed. In consequence of the settlement of the Monte [Protegido] case there has been a great change in public feeling. Government will in future only clear Argentine ships as far as Las Palmas. I beg that the small steamers Oran and Guazo, 31st of January, [meaning which sailed 31st,] 300 tons, which are [now] nearing Bordeaux with a view to change the flag, may be spared if possible or else sunk without a trace being left, [" spurlos versenkt."]

LUXBURG.

July 3, 1917. No. 59.

I learn from a reliable source that the Acting Minister for Foreign Affairs, who is a notorious ass and Anglophile, declared in a secret session of the Senate that Argentina would demand from Berlin a promise not to sink more Argentine ships. If not agreed to, relations would be broken off. I recommend refusal and, if necessary, calling in the mediation of Spain. LUXBURG.

July 9, 1917. No. 64.

Without showing any tendency to make concessions, postpone reply to Argentine note until receipt of further reports. A change of Ministry is probable. As regards Argentine steamers, I recommend either compelling them to turn back, sinking them without leaving any traces, or letting them through. They are all quite small. LUXBURG.

### The Case of Herr Cronholm

This announcement by the American State Department was followed on Sept. 13 by another equally astonishing, as follows:

*The Department of State made public tonight the following translation of a letter, dated March 8, 1916, from the German Minister at Mexico City to Chancellor von Bethmann Hollweg:*

Imperial Legation, Mexico, to his Excellency the Imperial Chancellor:

Herr Folke Cronholm, the Swedish Chargé d'Affaires here, since his arrival here has not disguised his sympathy for Germany, and has entered into close relations with this legation. He is the only diplomat through whom information from a hostile camp can be obtained.

Moreover, he acts as intermediary for official diplomatic intercourse between this legation and your Excellency. In the course of this, he is obliged to go personally each time to the telegraph office, not seldom quite late at night, in order to hand in the telegrams.

Herr Cronholm was formerly at Peking and at Tokio, and was responsible for the preliminary arrangements which had to be made for the representation of his country in each case. Before he came out here he had been in charge of the Consulate General at Hamburg. Herr Cronholm has not got a Swedish but only a Chinese order at present.

I venture to submit to your Excellency the advisability of laying before his Majesty the Emperor the name of Herr Cronholm, with a view to the Crown Order of the Second Class being bestowed upon him. It would perhaps be desirable, in order not to excite the enemy's suspicion, to treat with secrecy the matter of the issue of the patents until the end of the war, should the decision be favorable to my suggestion. This would mean that the matter would be communicated to no one but the recipient and his Government, and even to them only under the seal of secrecy, while the publication of the bestowal of the decoration would be postponed until the end of the war.

I should be particularly grateful to your Excellency if I could be furnished with telegraphic news of the bestowal of the decoration, which I strongly recommend in view of the circumstances detailed above.                    VON ECKHARDT.

## Popular Indignation Aroused

The two publications created a profound sensation, especially in Argentina and other South American countries—also in Sweden. The telegrams from Count Luxburg containing the phrase " Spurlos versenkt " was the first official confirmation that this policy of destroying ships' crews was part of the general U-boat campaign.

When the news reached Buenos Aires there was first bewilderment, then dismay, followed by an outburst of anger at the Germans. Mobs gathered in the streets; the German centres of Buenos Aires were invaded, many shops were wrecked, the chief German clubhouse and leading German newspaper offices were burned. The mobs were quelled only after large bodies of troops had been employed. Demonstrations against Germans also occurred at Montevideo, Uruguay.

The Argentine Senate on Sept. 19 further evidenced its displeasure by passing, by a vote of 23 to 1, a declaration to break off relations with Germany. Popular feeling at Buenos Aires was strong for an immediate rupture.

The Swedish Minister at Buenos Aires, Baron Lowen, the day after the disclosure of the Luxburg dispatches made a simple disclaimer, declaring:

> I have not sent, nor caused to be sent, by the legation under my charge, any telegram from the German Legation. The news is a great and disagreeable surprise. I have cabled to my Government to clear up matters. In the United States they are very excitable.

Argentina was not slow in acting. On Sept. 13 Foreign Minister Pueyrredon sent the following note to Count Luxburg:

> Mr. Minister:
> You having ceased to be persona grata to the Argentine Government, that Government has decided to deliver to you your passports, which I transmit herewith by order of his Excellency the President of the nation.
> The introducer of embassies has instructions to assist you in your immediate departure from the territory of the republic. God keep you.      H. PUEYRREDON.

To Count Karl von Luxburg, Envoy Extraordinary and Minister Plenipotentiary of the German Empire.

The passport issued to Count Luxburg reads:

> Considering that his Excellency Count Karl Luxburg, Envoy Extraordinary and Minister Plenipotentiary of the German Empire, is leaving the Argentine Republic, the authorities of the republic are hereby requested to protect him in his passage to the frontier.
> Given at Buenos Aires, Sept. 12, 1917. Valid to the frontier.
>                               PUEYRREDON,
>               Minister of Foreign Affairs.

Count Luxburg, who is also Minister to Uruguay, asked safe conduct to Montevideo instead of returning to Berlin.

## Sweden's Official Statement

The Swedish Foreign Office, whose head is Admiral Lindman, Minister of Foreign Affairs, issued the following statement on Sept. 11:

> The Swedish Foreign Office has not received any account regarding the transmission of the telegrams mentioned in the statements of the Government of the United States, and the Swedish Government therefore is unable at present to determine what its position should be on the questions opened up by these statements.
> It is, however, accurate to say that just after the world war broke out the Swedish Foreign Minister expressed the opinion that he ought to transmit a German telegram concerning the civil population of Kiao-Chau, (the former German fortress in the Chinese peninsula of Shantung.)
> Statements to the same effect were made to the representatives of both belligerent groups without there being any question of Sweden taking over representation of any power's interests.
> As regards the United States, in particular, the United States Minister here has this year in certain special cases demanded and obtained permission to transmit letters to and from Turkey, and at a time when Turkey was not in a state of war with America and when Sweden had not yet taken over the protection of American interests.
> In the Summer of 1915 the wish was expressed from the British side that the transmission of telegrams between Germany and North America should cease. No formal demand was made, but notwithstanding this the Foreign Minister acceded to the wish. The Swedish Minister, who was cognizant of all the ne-

gotiations, was of the opinion that this was no bar to the continued transmission of telegrams to neutral States other than the United States and therefore to Argentina. Since then Sweden has continued to be the intermediary for communications between Germany and the Argentine.

The telegram mentioned in the American statement was written in code and in transmitting it the Swedish Minister was by that reason unable to recopy it. Whether its contents were as represented is a point which the first duty of the Swedish Government must be to confirm, and its next action must be to get an explanation from Germany if it be found that any misuse has taken place. Sweden will also, without regard to any reference made to her, take measures to prevent any repetition of the incident.

No application as to the cessation of the transmission of telegrams from Germany to the Argentine Republic has yet been made, either by the British or American Government, either now or at an earlier period.

The whole affair has only become known to the public through the press, but in spite of this the wishes, officially and semi-officially expressed by the interested parties, would immediately have been acceded to.

This statement was regarded as disingenuous, especially with reference to the transmission of letters to Turkey for the United States, for the reason that those dispatches were not in cipher, and their contents were open to the Turkish authorities to read.

The British authorities also criticised the statement. They held that it acknowledged a violation of the promise made to the British Government in 1916 to the effect that Sweden's practice of becoming an intermediary for the transmission of dispatches to Germany would cease.

In Sweden the disclosure was received with much indignation by the public, and it had the effect of winning for the opposition many new seats in the Chamber, an election being in progress at the time.

Germany gave the exposure no official recognition until Sept. 18, when the German Minister to Sweden formally expressed to the Swedish Government at Stockholm Germany's "keen regret for the embarrassments caused Sweden through the Buenos Aires telegram affair." The Swedish newspapers, both Government and Opposition, in their comments indicated that Germany's expression was not adequate, and the resentment which swept over the country at being made Germany's catspaw deepened. Up to Sept. 20 neither Germany nor Mexico had vouchsafed any official expression regarding the Mexican note, though Minister von Eckhardt issued a perfunctory denial of the charges, with the intimation that the letter was not genuine. Deep resentment was evidenced in official circles in England and France, especially against the rôle Sweden had assumed, but no official steps were taken. The Swedish Government, on Sept. 15, announced that no further messages of any sort would be forwarded for Germany from any point, with an intimation that the Government felt that it had been imposed upon and its courtesy abused by the character of the messages it had been called upon to transmit.

# The Belgian Prince U-Boat Crime

CONFIRMATION of the outrage committed by Germans at the time of the sinking of the Belgian Prince has been placed on record by G. Selenski, an able-bodied seaman who was Russian delegate to the International Conference of Seamen held at London to consider the U-boat crimes by Germany and Austria. Selenski is one of the three survivors of the Belgian Prince, which was attacked by a German submarine on July 31, 1917, when thirty-eight members of the crew were deliberately drowned after they had left their ship. His statement fully corroborates the affidavits—published in CURRENT HISTORY MAGAZINE for September (Page 406)—of the chief engineer and one of the sailors. Mr. Selenski's sworn statement is as follows:

"I signed at Liverpool on July 23, and sailed on the 24th. On July 31 the ship was torpedoed without warning, about

200 miles from the Irish coast. When the crew took to the boats the submarine hailed them to come alongside. They were then ordered to come on board the submarine. Five Germans who were in a small boat then smashed the lifeboats of the Belgian Prince with hatchets. The crew were then ordered to take off their lifebelts, and the lifebelts were taken down below in the submarine. The Captain was ordered down below also. The crew were on board the submarine for about an hour, on the foredeck, when, without any warning, the submarine submerged and left the crew to swim about, there being nothing in sight except the Belgian Prince, which had not sunk, but we could only just see her in the distance.

" I made up my mind to reach the ship, but I was endeavoring to save the third officer, and kept him afloat for half an hour, when he said, ' Oh, let me go now, and look after yourself.' I then swam to the ship and successfully reached her, after being in the water from 9 o'clock at night until 5 o'clock the next morning, Aug. 1. When I reached the ship there was the Jacob's ladder over the side, and I managed to get up this and boarded the ship. I was only aboard about half an hour when the submarine returned to the ship, and three or four Germans came on board and started to gather the clothes up out of the officers' quarters. All this time I was hiding at the after-end of the ship, but after the Germans had finished pilfering in the saloon they came toward the place where I was hiding, and there was nothing for me to do but jump over the stern again into the water.

" I then swam and held on to the rudder for half an hour, and then, as the submarine was coming away from the starboard side, I was compelled to swim to the port side to avoid them seeing me. The submarine then fired at the ship to make sure of sinking her, and eventually the ship started to settle down, and I was again compelled to swim about, and then the Germans noticed me and pointed their fingers at me, and were laughing and grinning also. I then swam to a dinghy which had floated off the ship, and, after struggling for about half an hour, I managed to get in the

boat; but prior to getting in the boat I picked up the ship's cat, which was floating about on a piece of timber, and took it in the boat with me.

" After about half an hour I was picked up by a patrol boat, and when I got on board the chief engineer and second cook were on board. I was then landed, and returned to Liverpool. I left the ship's cat with the crew of the patrol boat. I am now anxious to get away to sea again, and am waiting to know how long I shall have to wait before I can go. I was anxious to get back after I had been at home three days."

## Narrative of Ship's Cook

One of the two other survivors, William Snell, a negro, who was the second cook on the Belgian Prince, and who has returned to his home in Newport News, Va., gave the following detailed narrative to a New York newspaper:

The Belgian Prince left Philadelphia for Liverpool last June 24, with a cargo of ammunition and supplies, and reached Liverpool On July 15. There she reloaded with china clay and salt, and on July 27 started on her way back to America, Newport News being her objective point.

On July 31, at 8 o'clock in the evening, while I was in my cabin writing a letter, I heard an explosion, and soon after that another one. The first one was a shell which tore into the side of the vessel; the second one a shell which put our wireless apparatus out of commission. These details I learned afterward when I got on deck. But the moment I heard the noise I knew that we were being attacked, and I put on my lifebelt and ran to the deck.

Every man of the crew had been drilled and knew just what to do, and so there was no confusion. Three lifeboats were lowered and we were then ordered to gather alongside the submarine on the starboard side of the Belgian Prince. Machine guns on the deck of the U-boat were aimed at us and her crew also were armed with revolvers which covered us.

The commander, speaking very good English, ordered us to throw up our hands. We did so, and he then asked, " Where's the Captain?"

" Here I am," answered our Captain, and the commander told him to get aboard. The commander of the U-boat was a man of perhaps 27 years or so, smooth shaven and good-looking. At first he was rather pleasant, but this soon wore off, and he became extremely grouchy after awhile and frowned and seemed ready to kill every one of us.

"Where are your papers?" asked the commander. And after our Captain had given them to him he ordered our Captain to follow him below. A few minutes afterward the commander returned to the deck alone.

"Are there any gunners among you?" asked the commander. There were nine, but the first officer was afraid not only that the gunners would be put to death, but that all of us would have to suffer on account of them, so he said, "We had some, but they were all killed."

"Well, if there are no gunners among you," he said, "bring your boats alongside, and all hands come on deck."

Nine of the submarine's crew held revolvers at our faces while we were getting aboard. And we were then lined up forward of the conning tower. The commander also held a revolver in one hand, while with the other he searched us to see whether any of us had weapons in our clothes. When he got thorugh, he asked: "Has any one among you any kind of weapon?" To which all of us replied negatively, except that most of us had jack knives.

"Well, now take off your lifebelts," was his next order, "and lay them down on the deck." He seemed to take a greater dislike to some of us than to others, for he picked up some of the lifebelts and threw them into the sea.

Just then another officer of the U-boat spoke to the commander in German. I could not understand what he said. The one who spoke German appeared to be of higher rank than the commander, because as soon as he had finished talking the commander ordered his men to get into our two larger lifeboats and throw the oars overboard; then, after removing to his own vessel all the provisions and whisky and whatever other supplies we had, he himself removed the plugs, and the lifeboats immediately began filling with water. But they did not sink. I have heard it said since that the submarine crew used axes to destroy the lifeboats. I may have been too excited at the time to notice everything that was going on, but I hardly believe that this is true. In fact, one of our boats the Captain's boat—which had been run alongside the U-boat on the port side while the other two were on the starboard side, was not touched at all.

After the lifeboats had filled with water they were cut loose from the U-boat and they began drifting away.

The commander then pushed us forward away from the conning tower. Four Germans entered our Captain's boat and put off to the Belgian Prince, probably with bombs to blow up the vessel.

The next thing we knew the commander ducked into the conning tower, and closed the cap over it, and we of the Belgian

Prince were left alone on the submarine's deck. At almost the same moment we heard a whirring sound below, and presently the submarine started off at a lively clip. The Belgian Prince was soon left far behind. We must have gone about fourteen miles in the direction away from shore —the Irish coast was about 175 miles away— when I began feeling the water come up over my feet. Some of the others laughed and kept on chatting, and one of the men asked me for a cigarette. I told them I couldn't understand how they could take it so easy when it was plain that we were going to be drowned. Most of the men still laughed. They could not believe it possible that human beings could be fiendish enough to do such a thing.

When we were ordered to put our lifebelts on the deck I folded mine up before laying it down and then stood on it. Afterward I slipped it under my mackintosh; and now, when I saw that the submarine was getting lower and lower in the water, I slipped the lifebelt over my head and jumped into the water.

The reason I jumped was because I was afraid that when the submarine submerged the suction would drag us down to death. Scarcely had I struck out swimming and gotten a few yards away from the submarine before she went down with a peculiar sound, as if somebody had hit the surface of the water with a broad slat—something like a loud "whup."

The men began hollering, "Help! help!" It was awful. There we were, hundreds of miles from human help. The impossibility of obtaining help made the cries of the men so much more frightful. It was now about 9 o'clock and dark; still I could distinguish forms near me. They were men swimming, and among them nearest to me was a seaman I knew well but never knew his name. He, too, recognized me. "Cook," he said, "can you see her?" He meant the Belgian Prince, toward which we were swimming. I couldn't. It was too dark and beginning to become misty, and she was so far away.

"Let me rest my hands on you," the man pleaded. I feared for my own life and said, "No, I can't."

"Well, good-bye," he said, after a little while, "I can't go any further. Pray for me." And then I heard a gurgling sound and could not see him any more. We had been in the water more than half an hour. He was less than ten yards from me.

At 11 o'clock I could still see some men afloat. The water was calm on the surface, but the undercurrents were frightfully strong and gripped and pulled me around and around. The lifebelt undoubtedly saved me. I am a good swimmer and strong, but nobody without aid could last overnight in such a swirl of currents.

When daylight came I could see the Belgian Prince. She was still miles away. I saw the four men coming down from the vessel and enter the little boat. They were the four who had been sent from the submarine. I hollered, but when I was carried up on the crest of a swell and saw the submarine coming toward the little boat I stopped yelling and pretended to be dead. The water all around was strewn with bodies.

I could see three of the men get aboard the submarine. The fourth stayed in the little boat. The submarine submerged. Then I began hollering again, hoping the men would have pity and pick me up. Half an hour after this a British patrol boat came along and picked me up, and also the fellow in the boat. He proved to be George Selenski, an able seaman aboard the Belgian Prince. How he got into the boat is a puzzle to me. * * * The other man who was saved was Thomas Bowman, the chief engineer. He found a log of wood. He tried to save a young apprentice, but the poor lad died in Bowman's arms before rescue came.

# Spain and the World War
## By Manuel de J. Gálvan

[Mr. Gálvan is editor of Las Novedades, the oldest Spanish newspaper in the United States. He is connected by marriage with the leaders of the Conservative Party in Spain, and is related to one of the chief military commanders of the kingdom.]

TO convey to the readers of CURRENT HISTORY MAGAZINE a clear idea of the workings of Spanish public opinion during the world war and the tendencies and principles of politics that have influenced and swayed the Spanish people is by no means an easy task. To explain the causes of the successive political changes that have occurred in Spain would take more space than has been allotted to me; therefore I will simply relate the happenings in chronological order.

As a result of the "Bloody Week" in Barcelona in 1911, which culminated in the execution of Ferrer, Premier Maura had to resign; the Liberal leader, Mr. Moret, had declared his unwillingness and that of his party to co-operate in any way with the Government. Mr. Moret, the old statesman who had introduced English political methods into Spanish politics, then formed a Cabinet; but his lack of energy unfitted him to lead the young democracy of Spain, and after three months of weak rule there came a new Ministerial crisis. The Moret Ministry gave way to a more liberal Cabinet, headed by Mr. Canalejas, one of the most remarkable men that Spain has ever produced.

Mr. Canalejas, on being intrusted with the office of Premier, presented to Congress the program his party was to follow, and this program was destined to give new life to Spanish politics. One of the many great reforms advocated by the new Premier was the "Law of Associations," which was to make all religious organizations (outside of the five that enjoyed special privileges by virtue of the Concordat between the Spanish Government and the Holy See) liable to the civil laws and subject to the taxes imposed upon all other associations. This caused a battle royal in Parliament between the Liberal Party, which was supported by the Republican and Socialist elements, and the Conservative Party, supported by the Clergy and the old Carlist or Traditional Party.

The country was divided into two factions, and for the time being there were only two parties in Spain, one trying to deprive the religious orders of the special privileges permitting them to engage in industries and to own land without having to pay taxes, and the other party consisting of the monarchical, clerical, and conservative elements, trying by all means to maintain the old status, which violated the laws and permitted the clergy to hold, idle and unproductive, tracts of land that had been acquired as gifts, as well as to engage in manufacture without being subject to taxation. After many riotous outbreaks by the Conservatives against the Canalejas Government the liberal majority in Congress approved the law, and all attempts at disorder and destruction were quelled.

## Democratic Forces United

There were many more changes in the political status of the country. For the first time in the history of Spain the forces of democracy seemed to be blended in an effort to work wonders for the triumph of their principles, and the dynastic Liberal Party had the hearty support of even the Republicans, some of whose principal leaders were inclined to accept a position in the Cabinet, under the belief that it was possible to accomplish by evolution what had been impossible through force or revolutionary agitation.

When the Canalejas Government was assured of a long, peaceful reign and the reorganization of the old parties was almost accomplished the blow came. Mr. Canalejas was assassinated by an anarchist. Again disorder prevailed. The Liberal Party was split into two factions, one headed by Garcia Prieto, Marquis of Aluceunas, in charge of the portfolio of Estate, and the other by Count Romanones, also a member of the Cabinet, whose followers were the more advanced and educated of the Liberal Party. The Marquis of Aluceunas was temporarily appointed Premier, but very soon the Liberal majority in Congress appointed Count Romanones as Premier and charged him with the reorganization of the Cabinet.

Six months later the split in the ranks of the Liberal Party precipitated a new crisis, and the Conservatives came into power under the Premiership of Mr. Dato, a former lieutenant of Maura's. He was charged by the King to form a new Cabinet. He did not hesitate to do so, notwithstanding the fact that Maura was recognized leader of the party. The King considered it advisable not to appoint Maura, the old leader, as the Republicans and Socialists threatened to use force if necessary, in case Maura should head a Conservative Cabinet.

## Strict Neutrality Proclaimed

It was at that time that the great world war struck like a bolt from heaven. Premier Dato, after consulting all the political leaders of the country, proclaimed a policy of strict neutrality because it was the sincere wish of the public. Some Liberals expressed themselves in favor of Spain joining with the Entente Powers, but the overwhelming majority of Parliamentary leaders as well as the masses of the people gave unmistakable signs of favoring a policy of strict neutrality, so as to keep the country out of the terrible war and to keep their sons off the fields of battle. Mr. Dato, who personally favored that policy, took advantage of the wave of public feeling and held his country back from useless destruction.

An unprecedented era of prosperity and good feeling was the result of Spain's neutrality. All the products of the soil, all its manufactures, found a ready market in the allied countries. Small establishments grew into modern plants equipped with the latest machinery. Small villages attained in six months a degree of wealth and prosperity that they had never even thought of. But the thoughtless way in which merchants did business, exporting everything that was asked for by the allied countries, soon brought a scarcity of food products in the country. Prices soared to unusual heights, and the laboring classes found themselves unable to buy even the necessities of life. There were cases when people were unable to obtain food for money. The Government tried to prevent the exportation of foodstuffs by increasing the tariff, but this experiment was useless, as the merchants were able to export grain, cattle, and everything needed at home and still realize huge profits in France.

## Food Scarcity Causes Unrest

This situation created the present conditions. Premier Dato was accused of not having shown enough ability to cope with the situation, and had to resign. As Count Romanones, the Liberal leader, had made pro-ally declarations, the King hesitated to call him to form the new Cabinet until he had declared himself in favor of neutrality. This he did, and was appointed Premier.

This precipitated a new crisis. Conservative elements started a demonstration in favor of adhering to neutrality at all costs, while their leaders went around the country calling meetings in which they tried to awaken the ill-will of the people against the Entente Allies. They brought charges against England and France, whose policies in recent times, they declared, were consistently hostile to Spanish interests in Africa. The Gibraltar question was also brought up, and, on the whole, their work tended to range the sympathy of the people with the Central Empires.

The Liberals of the country found themselves in a very difficult position, because, pledged to a policy of absolute neutrality, they could not oppose the campaign of the Conservatives, started primarily and apparently on behalf of neutrality. Notwithstanding this, the Republican Party decided to oppose the Conservative propaganda, and started a campaign to enlighten the masses. The leaders endeavored to bring before the people the advantages of a policy favorable to the cause of the Entente Allies.

### An Era of Strikes

Meanwhile, although the food situation was alleviated, the laborers found that their salaries were not enough to bring any comforts and that they earned scarcely enough to live. Very soon their discontent was shown in the organization of strikes, the most important of which was that of the railroad employes, who demanded higher wages. The Government was compelled to intervene, and the railroad companies agreed to meet the demands of the workers. Instead of calming the disorder, this resulted in the organization of more strikes, and as the men's claims were just they had to be granted; but the increase in salaries agreed to by the employers was not proportionate to the new economic conditions. The Government took measures to import grain, but the restrictions imposed by the British blockade and, on the other hand, the submarine war made it impossible to overcome the scarcity of food.

The pressure brought to bear on the Government by the diplomatic representatives of the Entente Allies, as well as the ruthless campaign of the German submarines, which had sunk several Spanish vessels while they were sailing within Spanish territorial waters, con-

vinced Premier Romanones of the necessity of joining the Entente Allies in the great war against autocracy. He issued a strong note of protest to the German Government, submitted his ideas to the King, provoked a crisis, and, as a majority of the Liberal Party was in favor of peace, the result was his resignation. Mr.

EDUARDO DATO
*Premier of Spain*

Garcia Prieto, Marquis of Alhucemas, the other prominent leader of the Liberal Party, undertook to form a new Cabinet pledged to maintain the policy of neutrality.

### The Army Threatens Revolt

During this period the Republican and Socialist Parties had been waging a campaign in favor of a more democratic government, and they took advantage of the existing state of affairs to incite the people to revolution. The army, which up to this time had maintained the most strict discipline, seeing that the country was on the verge of a revolution, tried to exert its influence in favor of some needed reforms. The artillery corps and the engineers had organized commissions to present to the Government all claims pertaining to their particular arm of the service, and the infantry in the same manner proceeded to organize its claims.

In the first place, the soldiers' pay, on account of the high cost of food, was insufficient for the obtaining of proper rations. There had been great favoritism shown in the promotion of officers, and the commissions were organized to do away with all this injustice.

The Government was made aware of this movement, initiated in Catalonia, and the Minister of War ordered General Alfau, Military Governor of the province, to arrest the officers connected with it. General Alfau carried out the order, but presented his resignation as Governor and went to Madrid to protest against the unwise and unjust order, since the infantry was doing nothing more or less than the other arms of the service had done when they organized commissions.

General Marina was sent to Barcelona to succeed General Alfau, but on arriving there he found that the temper of the army was such that to insist on punishing the officers who had been arrested on the order of the Minister of War would provoke an open revolt. All the other branches of the military unit joined in manifestations in favor of the movement of the infantry, and the whole army became so threatening that the Government hastened to comply with the demands, beginning with the dismissal of General Aguilera, the Minister of War, on the charge that he had been the cause of all the discontent of the army. The example set by the army was followed by all military units of the nation, and even the clergy organized "juntas" to attend to its own welfare.

## Uprisings in Catalonia

The King called into power the Conservative Party, and Premier Dato formed a Cabinet to cope with the situation. As the Congress was in recess, some of the Catalonian Congressmen requested of Premier Dato a decree which would allow them to convene. This the Premier refused, but the Catalonians attempted to convene, and they called an extraordinary legislature in the name of the majority of the representatives. The Government officials surrounded the building in which they were to meet and prevented them from so doing.

While all this was going on in high political circles the Republicans and Socialists, emboldened by the military unrest and by the general discontent of the masses, started a revolutionary campaign which culminated in uprisings in Catalonia, Valencia, and Viscaya. In Barcelona the trouble started with a strike of the railway employes. The military authorities lent the aid of the police to the companies in order that they might run their cars with strikebreakers, and this brought about clashes between the police and the strikers. In a very short time the whole city was in arms, and it was necessary for the military authorities to send troops to disarm the rebels, who had already built barricades in different parts of the city.

For six days there was street fighting of such nature that the troops in some places were compelled to use artillery fire against the houses in which the rebels had their headquarters. According to official reports, the number of dead on the rebel side reached thirty-three, with sixty-six wounded, and the number of civilian dead is placed at 115, with 680 wounded.

In Valencia there was a similar uprising, and it has been impossible to obtain the exact number of dead and wounded, although it is said that there were more than five hundred casualties. In Bilbao, Province of Viscaya, the uprising was frankly republican. Two days of fierce fighting took place between the army and the populace.

## Pro-German and Other Elements

The complexity of the situation in Spain is caused primarily by the economical conditions brought about by the war. The laboring classes know that the country is enjoying an era of unprecedented prosperity, that the middle and upper classes are becoming richer by leaps and bounds, that the Spanish peseta is at a premium above all other money, and, notwithstanding, they are not able to share in this wealth as do the other classes that are enriched at the cost of their labor.

At the same time the international situation exerts a great influence in dividing public opinion into two clear factions. The conservative elements are without exception pro-German, and so are the army, the clergy, and a majority of the Liberal Party, while the Republicans and the Socialists, with a minority of the Liberal Party, are pro-ally. The masses are neutral, because they have been acquainted with the havoc and destruction that would be caused should Spain enter this war. Therefore they would gladly join in any uprising directed against Spain's participation in the war.

The King up to the present time has maintained strict neutrality, although his personal sympathies are believed to be pro-ally. His tolerance of all political opinions, his marked tendency to deal leniently with political offenses and conspiracies, and his courage, generosity, and charitable traits have made him very popular with all classes. The Republicans know and readily acknowledge that the Spanish people are not advanced enough to be able to establish an orderly republican Government, because the radical elements predominate and the anarchists take advantage of any uprising to commit revolting acts of vandalism. This is recognized by the majority of the thinking class, although the forces of democracy begin to chafe under the constitutional monarchy, no matter how liberal in form and in practice it may be. At the same time, there is uneasiness and discontent among all classes, with a gradual disintegration of the old political parties, and this might at any time produce a national crisis that would change the whole political structure of the Spanish Peninsula.

# German War Losses

THE man power of Germany in September, 1917, with the war casualties, was estimated by experts at the French Army Headquarters last month as follows:

Fixed formations on the various fronts, employed on lines of communication, and stationed in the interior, 5,500,000.

Divisions undergoing formation and men in depots, 600,000.

Losses in killed, permanently disabled, and prisoners, 4,000,000; wounded under treatment in hospitals, 500,000. Total, 10,600,000.

The following figures account for all men called for service up to the present.

Trained men mobilized immediately on the outbreak of the war, 4,500,000.

Untrained ersatz (compensatory) reservists called out, August, 1914, to February, 1915, 800,000.

Class of 1914 recruits called out November, 1914, to January, 1915, 450,000.

First ban of untrained Landsturm called out at the beginning of 1915, 1,100,000.

Class 1915, called out May-July, 1915, 450,000.

Remainder of untrained Landsturm called out the same month, 150,000.

Class of 1916, called out September-November, 1915, 450,000.

Contingent of hitherto exempted men called out in October, 1915, 300,000.

Second contingent exempted men called out early in 1916, 200,000.

Second ban Landsturm early in 1916, 450,000.

Class of 1917, called out March-November, 1916, 450,000.

Third contingent exempted men late in 1916, 300,000.

Class of 1918, called out November, 1916, to March, 1917, 450,000.

Class of 1919, called out in part in 1917, 300,000.

Additional exempted men, 1917, 150,000. Total, 11,500,000.

The discrepancy in the figures is accounted for by the omission of the mail units. The total mobilizable male resources of Germany since the beginning of hostilities, including the yearly classes of recruits up to 1920, number about 14,000,000. Those called up number 10,-600,000. The remainder are accounted for as follows:

The remaining part of the class 1919 awaiting call, 150,000; class of 1920 still uncalled, 450,000; men employed as indispensable in industries and administrations, 500,000; men abroad unable to reach Germany, 200,000; men entirely exempted owing to physical disability, 2,100,000.

Recruits of the 1920 class cannot be called legally until they attain their seventeenth birthday.

# Russia's Escape From Civil War

## The Moscow Conference and General Korniloff's Attempt to Overthrow the Kerensky Government

RUSSIA during the month ended Sept. 15, 1917, went through the most dramatic and trying period since the revolution was launched. This experience, in the judgment of competent observers, left the Provisional Government stronger, inspired new confidence in the permanency of the revolution, blasted the hopes of the reactionaries and monarchists, and dispelled definitely all fear that Russia would make a separate peace with the Central Powers.

The first theatric setting to the thrilling chapters which Russia is furnishing to modern history was the extraordinary conference which sat as a National Assembly at Moscow, the ancient capital. The extreme gravity of the country's position at the front and throughout the vast domain impelled Premier Kerensky to convoke, without waiting for a constituent assembly, an "Extraordinary National Council" to meet at Moscow on Aug. 26, 1917. At this conference the lines of cleavage, which later led to General Korniloff's rebellion, became clearly defined.

The conference consisted of 2,500 delegates, as follows: 188 members of the four Dumas, 100 representatives of the peasants, 229 representatives of the Councils of Workmen's and Soldiers' Delegates of all Russia, 147 delegates of the municipalities, 113 representatives of the Union of Zemstvos and towns, 150 representatives of industrial organizations and banks, 313 representatives of co-operative organizations and 176 of professional unions.

### Kerensky's Speech at Moscow

Premier Kerensky opened the conference with a speech of great length, in which he reviewed the general situation, saying in part:

Those who think the moment has come to overthrow the revolutionary power with bayonets are making a mistake. Let them take care, for our authority is supported by the boundless confidence of the people and by millions of soldiers who are defending us against the German invasion.

Citizens, the State is passing through a period of mortal danger. I do not say more, for you all understand. You see it, for each of you experiences it, in a different way. You all know the task incumbent upon you for the struggle against a powerful, implacable, and organized enemy demands great sacrifices, self-denial, deep love of our country, and the forgetting of domestic quarrels. Unfortunately, not all who are able are willing to offer all this on the altar of their country, ruined by war, and they thus render the critical situation of our country more serious every day.

In our political life this process of disorganization is worse, even causing certain nationalities living in Russia to seek their salvation, not in close union with the mother country, but in separatist aspirations. On top of all this come the shameful events at the front, when Russian troops, forgetting their duty to their country, gave way without resistance to the pressure of the enemy, thus forging for their people fresh chains of despotism. We fell so low because we could not free ourselves from the fatal inheritance of the old régime which we hated but obeyed because we feared it. Therefore now, when power rests on liberty, not on bayonets, we are transported with delight, although there is some hereditary distrust of this new power.

Those who once trembled before the government of autocrats now boldly march against the Government with arms in hand. But let them remember that our patience has its limits, and that those who go beyond them will have to settle with a Government which will make them remember the time of Czarism. We shall be implacable, because we are convinced that supreme power alone can assure the salvation of the country. That is why I shall oppose energetically all attempts to take advantage of Russia's national misfortunes, and whatever ultimatum is presented, I shall subject it to the supreme power and to myself, its head.

### Not a Time for Decadence

The Premier declared that the destructive period of the revolution had passed and that the time had come to consolidate the conquests of the revolution. He continued:

> For this reason we ask you, citizens, whether you feel within your hearts the indispensable sacred fire for the attainment of this object, whether you represent, here in Moscow, the national strength which is necessary to assure the prosperity of the country or will give the world and us another picture of decadence?
>
> A little time ago we indignantly replied to a proposal to conclude a separate peace. A few days ago we witnessed another attempt, equally base, directly against our allies. The latter rejected it with equal indignation, and in the name of the great Russian people I say to our allies that it was the only reply we expected of them.

Notwithstanding the none too friendly attitude toward the mother country of certain nationalities of the Russian State, M. Kerensky continued, the Russian democracy would give them all it promised through the Provisional Government and all that the Constituent Assembly might yet decide to grant. But when the limit of tolerance was passed, or where there was a desire to take advantage of the nation's difficulties in order to violate the free will of Russia, they would cry "Hands off!" The Premier said the Government would prevent by force reopening of the dissolved Diet in Finland and that he hoped the country would approve this decision. His statement was cheered.

"The Government will endeavor," the Premier went on, "to protect the army " against the subversive influences which " deprived soldiers of all sense of mili- " tary duty and will struggle energetical- " ly against the Maximalists, against all " attempts by them to corrupt discipline."

## Difficulties of Finance

M. Avskentieff, Minister of the Interior, and M. Prokopovitch, Minister of Trade and Industry, followed M. Kerensky.

The first year of the war, said M. Prokopovitch, cost Russia 5,300,000,000 rubles, the second year 11,200,000,000 rubles, the third year already 18,000,000,-000 rubles, while the total revenue for 1913 was 16,000,000,000.

Regarding the question of food, he said that the country's position was extremely difficult. There was actual scarcity in several provinces and a mini-

mum in Petrograd and Moscow. He was endeavoring to nurse such industries as remained, and he considered it necessary to control the profits of manufactures in order to prevent them from becoming rich at the expense of the populace.

Vice Premier Nekrasoff told the conference how expenses had increased during the war. He said that in 1914 about 219,000,000 rubles of paper currency had been put in circulation, 223,000,000 in 1915, and 290,000,000 in 1916; that in the first two months of 1917 there had been issued 846,000,000, and from March onward the issue averaged 832,000,000 rubles monthly.

The budget, said M. Nekrasoff, was in a profoundly abnormal condition because it had placed on one side the cost of the war, and thus, in effect, there were two budgets, one giving a false impression of prosperity, and the other concealing the germs of financial catastrophe.

### Expending Enormous Sums

The Vice Premier admitted that the new régime was costing the country much more than the old, and that the new administrative bodies were absorbing enormous sums, the Food Committee, for instance. He said the financial difficulties were largely due to the extraordinary increase in the pay of workers, and instanced the Putiloff factory, the workers of which alone had been paid this year 90,000,000 rubles. Another source of difficulty was the small amount of revenue from taxation, excise charges and other sources. Direct taxation could not keep pace with the State's expenses, and indirect taxation was becoming a necessity.

Continuing, M. Nekrasoff enumerated a series of measures which would strengthen the financial position of the country, including various monopolies, especially on sugar, tea, and matches. He emphatically denied reports that the Government was contemplating confiscation of private possessions of landed property. It would never, he said, embark on such a dangerous adventure, believing firmly that the citizens of the country would do their duty.

General Korniloff, the Commander in

Chief of the Army, addressed the second sitting of the conference. This address, in the light of his subsequent revolt, is especially significant.

General Korniloff said the death penalty, restoration of which he had asked, together with other measures, constituted only a small part of what was necessary in an army stricken with the terrible evils of disorganization and insubordination. In the present month soldiers had killed four regimental commanders and other officers, and ceased these outrages only when they were threatened with being shot. Quite recently one of the regiments of Siberian Rifles, which had fought so splendidly at the beginning of the revolution, abandoned its positions on the Riga front. Nothing except an order to exterminate the entire regiment availed to cause it to return to its positions. The commander continued:

> Thus we are implacably fighting anarchy in the army. Undoubtedly it will finally be repressed, but the danger of fresh débâcles is weighing constantly on the country.
>
> The situation on the front is bad. We have lost the whole of Galicia, the whole of Bukowina, and all the fruits of our recent victories. At several points the enemy has crossed our frontier and is threatening our fertile southern provinces. He is endeavoring to destroy the Rumanian Army and is knocking at the gates of Riga. If our army does not hold the shore of the Gulf of Riga the road to Petrograd will be opened wide.
>
> The old régime bequeathed to Russia an army which, despite all the defects in its organization, nevertheless was animated by a fighting spirit and was ready for sacrifices. The whole series of measures taken by those who are completely foreign to the spirit and needs of the army has transformed it into a collection of individual groups which have lost all sense of duty and only tremble for their own personal safety.
>
> If Russia wishes to be saved the army must be regenerated at any cost. We must immediately take measures such as I have referred to, which have been approved in their entirety by the acting Minister of War.

### Reform Measures Adopted

General Korniloff then outlined the most important of these measures, in addition to restoration of the death penalty, which are: First, restoration of discipline in the army by the strengthening of the authority of officers and noncommissioned officers; second, improvement of the financial position of officers, who have been in a very difficult position in the recent military operations; third, restriction of the functions of regimental committees, which, although managing economic affairs of the regiments, must not be permitted to have any part in decisions regarding military operations or the appointment of leaders. He continued:

> The strength of every army depends upon conditions in the district in its rear. The blood which will inevitably flow during the restoration period may be shed in vain if the army, having been reorganized and prepared for battle, remains without reinforcements and fresh supplies of projectiles and equipment. I therefore think it indispensable that the measures taken at the front should also be applied in the rear.

The commander went on to say that according to information at his disposal the condition of the railways was such that by November the army would not receive any more supplies. In support of his statement he quoted a telegram from the Commander in Chief of the southwestern front, saying that the shortage of bread and biscuit on this front amounted almost to famine. General Korniloff then read figures relating to the production of war materials, which he said had fallen, compared with the period from October, 1916, to January, 1917, by 60 per cent. for guns and shells and 80 per cent. for airplanes.

"If this state of affairs continues," he added, "the Russian armies will find "themselves in the same state as in the "Spring of 1915, at the time of the re-"treat in Poland, Galicia, and the Car-"pathians."

He expressed his firm belief that the measures which he proposed would immediately be put into execution.

"I believe," he said, "that the genius and the reason of the Russian people will save the country. I believe in a brilliant future for our army. I believe its ancient glory will be restored."

When General Korniloff concluded his speech there were prolonged cheers from every side except the Extreme Left, where several members of the soldiers' and workmen's organization remained silent.

General Korniloff immediately left the hall and proceeded to a train, which took him to headquarters.

### Firm Stand of Cossacks

General Kaledines, leader of the Don Cossacks, representing the Council of Cossacks, mounted the tribune and read a resolution passed by the Cossacks demanding above everything, for the salvation of the country, the continuation of the war until complete victory was attained, in close union with the Allies. General Kaledines proposed, with the same end in view, the following measures:

First, placing the army outside of politics; second, the suppression of regimental committees and councils and the restriction of the functions of those which may be maintained with a purely economic mission; third, revision of the declaration of soldiers' rights; fourth, reinforcing discipline by strong measures and by the application of those measures to the districts in the rear; fifth, restoration of the rights of commanders to inflict punishment.

In presenting his views General Kaledines defied the extreme radicals. " Who " saved you from the Bolsheviki on the " 14th of July?" he asked contemptuously. " We Cossacks have been free " men. We are not made drunk by new- " found liberties and are unblinded by " party or program. We tell you plainly " and categorically, remove yourselves " from the place which you have neither " the ability nor the courage to fill and " let better men than yourselves step in, " or take the consequences of your folly."

The reading of the resolution was punctuated by cheers from the Right and by some protests from the Left.

Vladimir Naboukoff, a prominent Social-Democrat, speaking in the name of the first Duma, declared the country aimed at the establishment of a strong and independent power, uninfluenced by political parties, a power which, based on democratic principles, would establish obedience to the law, civil liberty, and personal security. The speaker emphasized the absolute necessity of the independence of the high command of the army from every private influence.

N. C. Tcheidse, President of the Council of Workmen's and Soldiers' Delegates, who was received with frenzied applause by the Left and with cries of " Long live the leader of the Russian revolution!" read a statement pointing out that only the active support of the revolutionary democracy would make possible the regeneration of the army and the country and the salvation of Russia.

" The democracy," he said, " cannot be " detached from the revolutionary coun- " try, and nothing but power based on " support of the countless masses of the " people can save the country from its " critical position and give the victory " over our enemies without and within."

M. Tcheidse declared the unified revolutionary democracy recognized that the vital interests of the country and the revolution demanded the application of the following measures:

First, in the domain of food supplies, the Government, pursuing a firm policy, should maintain a monopoly of cereals and a policy of fixed prices for agricultural products.

Second, in the domain of commerce and industry, the defense of the country and the supplies of munitions demanded more radical measures for the regulation of transport and the increase of the productivity of industry.

Third, the finances required the rigorous application of laws dealing with the income tax and war profits, besides other reforms, such as the introduction of succession duties and of taxes on articles of luxury corresponding to their increase in value, with other fiscal measures. As regards loans, the Government should take strong measures to make all bear their full share.

Fourth, agrarian reforms should be introduced to prevent all usurpation of land, whether by individuals or groups of individuals or societies.

Fifth, regarding the organization of the army, the respective rights and duties of the army commanders, commission and army organizations should be defined.

Regarding the question of nationality, the Government should pass an act granting to all nationalities the right of deciding their lot, upon agreement, in the Constituent Assembly.

M. Tcheidse concluded with an appeal for support for the Provisional Government, which he said should be invested with full and complete powers.

### Alexeieff on Army's Disintegration

During the third day's session the most important address was made by General

Alexeieff, former Commander of Chief. He drew contrasts between the army of the old régime, poorly equipped with mechanical resources but strong in warlike spirit, and the present army, well supplied with food and arms but completely poisoned and enfeebled by ill-interpreted and ill-applied doctrines which have been put forward, notably in the famous Order of the Day No. 1. These doctrines, he declared, had split the army into two opposite camps, officers and soldiers, which have become almost irreconcilable.

Speaking of the committees elected by the soldiers of the various units, General Alexeieff said they were useful to the army from an economic standpoint, but were fatal to discipline of the troops. None the less subversive was the influence of Government commissaries, whose appointment, he asserted, created an extremely dangerous quality of power.

The General maintained that after publication by the Government of the declaration of the rights of soldiers all respect toward leaders disappeared, the officers becoming veritable martyrs and having to pay very dearly for the offensive of Aug. 1 and the subsequent retreat. The General cited some remarkable illustrations of this. On one occasion, he said, when an attack was being launched the force which advanced was made up of twenty-eight officers, twenty non-commissioned officers, and two soldiers. All the others looked on coldly while these heroes perished.

The General declared it would be impossible to carry on the war to a victorious conclusion unless the strongest possible efforts were made by the Provisional Government and by the troops themselves to reanimate and regenerate the army.

## Warning by Kerensky

In closing the conference Premier Kerensky spoke as though he had a premonition of an impending revolt. He said:

The Provisional Government will stand on guard over the revolution. It will suffer no counter-revolutionary attempts, whatever be their source, for the Provisional Government is the incarnated will of the whole Russian people. It does not regret having convoked the conference at Moscow, which, although it has not yielded practical results, has allowed all Russian citizens to say frankly what they think necessary for the State.

Premier Kerensky then spoke of the services rendered to the country by the revolutionary democracy, which, he observed, took power at a terrible moment in the life of the State.

"Whoever endeavors to wrest their conquests from the people," he concluded, "will never succeed, for they have now become public property."

## Message From President Wilson

At the first session of the conference the following cablegram was received from President Wilson and read amid great applause:

President of the National Council Assembly, Moscow:

I take the liberty to send to the members of the great council now meeting in Moscow the cordial greetings of their friends, the people of the United States, to express their confidence in the ultimate triumph of ideals of democracy and self-government against all enemies within and without, and to give their renewed assurance of every material and moral assistance they can extend to the Government of Russia in the promotion of the common cause in which the two nations are unselfishly united.

WOODROW WILSON.

## Results of the Conference

The conference, while it took no definite action, being invested with no authority, served to bring out clearly a distinct line of cleavage between the radical or socialistic element, represented by Kerensky and the controlling factors of the Provisional Government, on the one hand, and the conservatives or bourgeoisie, represented by the Generals in the field—in the persons of Generals Korniloff, Alexeieff, Denikene —with the Constitutional Democrats and industrial and financial conservatives, on the other. In fact, it was this division that was apparent shortly after the revolution was proclaimed, and that had its first manifestation in the resignation of Professor Milukoff from the Cabinet, the resignation of General Brusiloff in the field, and the breakup of the first and second Cabinets. It was the fundamental difference between socialism and conservatism, though both factions were resolutely opposed to a separate peace and enthusiastic and implacable enemies of the old order.

So acute had become the division between the two elements that when the Moscow conference was convened serious trouble from the extreme radicals was apprehended, as they looked askance at the conference as a conservative movement.

In view of alarmist rumors of impending riotous demonstrations the Military Governor of Moscow took precautions against disorders of all descriptions, and the council threatened to show a rigor in this respect unknown even in ante-revolutionary days. The building in which the council met was surrounded by a close chain of soldiers, with officers every few yards, the soldiers being picked men from regiments of the Signal Corps or cadets training for officers. The chambers under the building were occupied by soldiers with fixed bayonets.

The interior of the Opera House was decorated elaborately, the foot bridge connecting the auditorium with the stage being hung with festoons of revolutionary red. Interspersed among the members of the council were to be seen characteristic Russian types, including Tartars in peaked caps, white-robed Mullahs from the Volga, Georgians robed in cloth of gold cassocks, and dignitaries of the Greek Orthodox Church, who had arrived for an Ecumenical Church Congress.

There was a general strike in Moscow the day the conference met, as a protest by the radicals, but there was little or no disorder, and business resumed its normal functions the next day.

## *The Fall of Riga*

Immediately on the heels of the Moscow conference it was clear that the Germans had determined to take advantage of Russia's political chaos and of the consequent demoralization of Russia's armies. Pressure was resumed on all fronts, and the Russians steadily retired, many regiments making no show of re-

sistance. Only slight advances were made in the Rumanian region, but great German progress was made in Livonia, on the northern part of the front, where the main pressure was brought to bear.

On Aug. 31 it was evident that the Germans were preparing an advance on Riga, the most important Russian Baltic port. The first evidence of this was a series of raids by forty German bomb carriers and battle planes on various islands in the Gulf of Riga and at the entrance to the Gulf of Finland. German troops crossed the Dvina southeast of Riga on Sept. 2, and a German offensive was opened in the region of Mitau, southwest of Riga. On Sept. 3 it was officially announced that Riga had surrendered. Its fall was announced by Berlin as follows:

After careful preparation German divisions on Sunday morning crossed the Dvina on both sides of Uxkull. The infantry crossing was preceded by a heavy bombardment by artillery and mine-throwers. A footing was gained on the northern bank of the river after a short fight. Where the Russians offered resistance they were driven back by vigorous attacks. The movements of our troops are in progress and are proceeding according to our plans.

The enemy gave up his positions west of the Dvina owing to our advance. Our divisions are moving forward there also, while fighting with the Russian rear guard. Dense columns of every kind are making their way hastily in a north-easterly direction along the roads leading out of Riga. Burning villages and farms mark the routes taken by the retreating west wing of the Twelfth Russian Army.

The following was the announcement from Petrograd:

On account of the threatening situation an order has been given for the abandonment of Riga. Some Russian detachments voluntarily left their positions and are retiring toward the north.

The German offensive on this front began Saturday by an attack on the Russian Uxkull position, following artillery preparation which lasted several hours. The Russian troops defending the Dvina River withdrew and the Germans succeeded in throwing two bridges across the Dvina and passing to the eastern bank.

The Russian infantry, in spite of the brilliant action of the artillery, which destroyed one of the enemy bridges, could not stop the German thrust, and the enemy, taking advantage of this, rapidly developed his success and began an advance northward. Russian counterattacks against him were unsuccessful.

The fall of Riga created great enthusiasm throughout Germany. Church bells were rung, thanksgiving services were held, the cities were bedecked with flags, and everywhere it was proclaimed as a great triumph. Lieut. Gen. Baron von Ardenne asserted that the taking of Riga was " a first-class warlike deed." He stated that the main defense of the city was an army of 150,000 men, and that the line was broken after heroic fighting. The Pan-Germans seized the opportunity to proclaim again the invincibility of the German arms, and the newspapers all over the country declared that Riga was German at heart and would forever remain as part of the German Empire.

### The Kaiser's Congratulations

The Kaiser extolled the capture of the city in the following address to the Eighth German Army:

Riga is free.

When the news ran through all the districts of Germany, a storm of jubilation and enthusiasm arose everywhere in the Fatherland and in the foremost trenches in the enemy country.

This town, founded by the spirit of the old German Hanseatic League, with a German history and which always has endeavored to maintain its German origin, has gone through heavy times. By the German Army, in which are incorporated all the German tribes, this town again is liberated from long oppression.

The operation, which by the command of the supreme army commander and under the direction of Prince Leopold of Bavaria was begun and undertaken with confidence in the efficiency of the troops which in over three years of war have so brilliantly stood the test, has been carried through by all arms more quickly and more energetically than was expected, and was a surprise to the enemy. A crushing blow hit him, so he lost his bridgehead.

The liberation of Riga is the deed of the Eighth Army and its well-tried commander. It again has proved that our steel-hard will to victory will defend us, no matter how long the war lasts, but such blows as the battle of Riga increase the prospects that the end will come soon. They add to the glory of our arms and give fresh laurels to the troops participating.

Therefore I express to you my thanks for the brilliant feat of arms, the Fatherland's thanks, and the enthusiastic thanks of the people, who stand behind you watching your deeds, but who also create and labor with their hands and till the fields to give us our daily bread. The present harvest, now well brought in, will feed us.

Also in this respect the Lord of Creation has granted our prayers, and by His daily bread protected this army and your people at home against distress. Therefore, happen what may, and no matter how long it may last, on, then, upon the enemy with joyful hearts and iron will to victory over all the enemies of Germany.

### The Effect in Russia

The loss of Riga intensified the political excitement in Russia and produced a profound crisis. Conspiracies and plots by monarchists were unearthed. Grand Duke Michael Alexandrovitch, brother of the former Czar; his wife, the Countess Pohlen, and the Grand Duke Paul and his wife were taken into custody on Sept. 5, also other Grand Dukes and their families in different parts of the country. General Gurko, formerly commander of the southwestern front, was charged with treason and exiled. The wave of unrest spread throughout the country. Petrograd was apprehensive over the approach of the Germans, and large numbers of people left the city. The Provisional Government was charged with responsibility for collapse of the army on account of lack of discipline and weakness in dealing with the extreme radicals.

### General Korniloff's Revolt

It was on Sept. 9 that the storm broke, and General Korniloff, the Commander in Chief of the Russian Armies, raised the flag of revolt against the Provisional Government. The story is thus related by the most authentic correspondents:

At 1 o'clock Saturday afternoon, after Premier Kerensky had inspected a deputation of Russian soldiers from the Balkans, Deputy Lvoff of the Duma called him by telephone and demanded an interview, declaring that his mission was of great importance.

M. Kerensky at first refused to receive M. Lvoff, but later in the afternoon did receive him, whereupon Lvoff declared that he had come as General Korniloff's plenipotentiary in order to demand the surrender of all power into Korniloff's hands. M. Lvoff said that this demand did not emanate from Korniloff only, but was supported by a "group of political workers," meaning an organization of Duma members, Moscow industrial interests, and other conservatives, which had played the rôle of opposition at the national conference at Moscow.

This group, said M. Lvoff, did not object to Kerensky personally, but demanded that he transfer the portifolio of war to M. Savinkoff, Assistant Minister of War, who all along had supported Korniloff's demands. M. Lvoff added:

"If you agree, we invite you to come to headquarters and meet General Korniloff, giving you a solemn guarantee that you will not be arrested."

Premier Kerensky replied that he was amazed, and described Korniloff's ultimatum as an act of effrontery and treason so incredible that he was unable to believe his ears. Therefore he resolved first to communicate with General Korniloff direct. In an exchange of telegrams Korniloff confirmed fully to the Premier his demands.

M. Kerensky then announced to M. Lvoff that the Provisional Government would not consent to such demands and would take every possible step to crush Korniloff's criminal conspiracy. Lvoff was then placed under arrest and subjected to a severe examination, during which he gave the details of the conspiracy and the names of the prominent men involved.

## Kerensky's Vigorous Action

Premier Kerensky acted with resolution and celerity. He immediately deposed the Commander in Chief as a traitor, arrested his envoy, Vladimir Lvoff, proclaimed a state of siege in Petrograd and vicinity, and appointed as chief of all the armies of Russia General Klembovsky, commander on the Riga front, after General Lokomsky had refused to take the post.

General Korniloff responded to the order of dismissal by moving an army against the capital.

Late on Sept. 10 Kerensky issued a proclamation, addressed to the army, the fleet, and the nation, and also to the committees of the army at the front, outlining the attempted coup of General Korniloff, through Vladimir Nicolaievitch Lvoff, and the measures that had been taken as a result. Regarding General Lokomsky, the Premier said:

The Chief of Staff, General Lokomsky, also proved a traitor. He refused to carry out the Provisional Government's order to assume command of the armies in view of General Korniloff's dismissal, indicating to the Provisional Government the possibility of civil war on the front, the opening up of the front to the Germans, and the conclusion of a separate peace. The Government is in full agreement with the executive of the Workmen's and Soldiers' Delegates for taking measures for the crushing of the counter-revolutionary plot instituted by traitors to their fatherland.

After announcing the dismissal of Korniloff and stating that he would be punished for treachery, the proclamation adds:

Against Korniloff's attempts to direct individual military detachments to Petrograd most decisive measures have been taken.

The proclamation referred to the statement of the Workmen's and Soldiers' Delegates, suggesting that the army and navy ignore commands issued by Generals Korniloff and Lokomsky, and added:

All of the army organizations should give the Government and the executive of the workmen and soldiers decisive co-operation and support in their struggle against counter-revolution. The conspiracy has no deep roots among the commanding force of the army. It is necessary to preserve full calm and firmness and to use every exertion in the struggle with the external enemy. All events and measures taken by army organizations should be indicated to the workmen's and soldiers' organization.

## Soldiers' and Peasants' Proclamation

The text of the communication of the workmen's and soldiers' and peasants' organizations "To the army at the front, to the Naval Committee, and the army generally," in which all are urged to rally around them, not only the mass of soldiers, but those in command of the army, in support of the Provisional Government, says:

General Korniloff, having put himself at the head of a military counter-revolutionary conspiracy, has moved troops toward Petrograd. His purpose is the deposition of the Provisional Government and the seizure of its powers. The troops directed to Petrograd have been deceived into believing that they are sent to crush a conspiracy of the Maximalists, which is nonexistent in reality.

The communication then tells of Korniloff's dismissal and declares him a traitor, and adds:

The problem of the Army Committee is to maintain the Provisional Government, to frustrate the criminal designs of General Korniloff, and to apply all measures to prevent his conspiracy from reflecting itself disastrously on the stability of the front.

The message concluded with a request that none of the orders of Korniloff should be carried out, or "those of the traitors who have adhered themselves to him." It admonished those to whom it was addressed to carry out quickly and punctually all the demands of the central committees and the Provisional Government, to explain to all the soldiers, especially among the wavering detachments, "the true meaning of Korniloff's plot," to take all measures of precaution necessary, and to secure "a bond with us by instituting control over all transmitting apparatus," and, finally, "to explain in what measure you can demonstrate your support of the Provisional Government by armed force."

## Message to America

The Premier also issued the following notice to the American people the same day:

The situation with respect to the conflict between the Provisional Government and the revolting Commander in Chief is more serious than we earlier contemplated, and it is impossible to predict what developments may ensue in the next few hours. But as regards the fundamental position there is no doubt. The fundamental position is that the Petrograd Supreme Government is absolutely unanimous in favor of all decisive measures which we have prepared and are preparing against the present attempts by a military rebel, in alliance with the reactionary elements of the country, to exploit the fatherland's internal troubles in order to effect a counter-revolution, with the design of robbing the Russian people of their hard-won liberties.

So much for the Government. Regarding the nation I declare that I have no doubt whatever that the mass of the population is behind the Government in its new fight for freedom; and, that being so, I have no doubt whatever about the triumph of our cause. In that triumph I have absolute and unqualified faith.

## Proclamations by Korniloff

General Korniloff issued two proclamations, the circulation of which was prohibited. The first, dated at Mohilev, denounced Premier Kerensky's description of Vladimir Lvoff's mission as untrue and declared that Korniloff did not send Lvoff to Kerensky, but that Kerensky first sent Lvoff to him with the aim to create trouble.

Russian men, [continues the proclamation,] our great fatherland is perishing. The Government under pressure of the Bolsheviki majority of the councils is acting in full accord with the plans of the German General Staff. Overwhelming consciousness of the impending ruin of the fatherland compels me in this menacing moment to summon all Russian men to save perishing Russia. All in whose breasts beat Russian hearts, all who believe in God, let them flock to the temple and pray God to perform a great miracle— a miracle of saving the fatherland.

I, General Korniloff, son of a peasant and Cossack, declare to all that I require nothing personally, nothing except the salvation of mighty Russia, and I swear to lead the nation by the road of victory over the foe to a constituent assembly, through which the nation will decide its own fate and choose the organization of its own political life. But I shall never betray Russia into the hands of its traditional foe—the German race—or make the Russian people the slaves of Germany. I prefer to die on the field of honor and battle rather than to witness the shame and infamy of Russian land.

Russian people! In your own hands rests the fate of your country.

(Signed) KORNILOFF.

## Collapse of the Revolt

Events moved rapidly on the 11th and 12th. Premier Kerensky, with the approval of the Provisional Government, declared martial law in Moscow as well as in Petrograd; he assumed the functions of Commander in Chief and tendered the position of Chief of Staff to General Alexeieff. Meanwhile an Executive Committee of five, known as the Provisional Military Committee, took complete control of affairs, and military measures were taken to defend Petrograd and resist the rebels. On the 12th, from expressions of loyalty which came to the Provisional Government from the Workmen's and Soldiers' Delegates, from the Constitutional Democrats, from the Bolshiviki, (Extremists,) the Ukrainians, Finns, and distinguished Generals, it was clear that the Korniloff revolt had failed to receive the expected support. Nevertheless Korniloff with several battalions advanced toward Petrograd, and on Sept. 12 occupied Gotchina, thirty miles southwest of the capital, but there was no bloodshed.

Meanwhile, on the night of the 13th General Alexeieff, the most distinguished of the Generals of the former régime, who had been friendly to the revolution, was won over by the Provisional Government. Upon word from him to Korniloff demanding the latter's unconditional surrender, the revolt collapsed, and Korniloff's troops deserted him. One division, composed of Georgians and Caucasians, most of whom were Moslems, stated that in following General Korniloff toward Petrograd they were under the impression it was to quell an outbreak by the radicals. They were sent home to the Caucasus with the promise that they would not be called upon to serve against their coreligionists, the Turks.

The collapse of the Korniloff revolt was complete. The Provisional Government was reconstituted on stronger lines, with a view to the strict enforcement of rigid discipline in both army and navy.

Colonel Verskovsky, former commander of the Moscow military district, was appointed Acting Minister of War. Admiral Dmitri Nicolaievitch Verdervski, a well-known writer on naval technical questions and former commander of the Baltic Fleet, was made Minister of Marine. General Teplovest was named Commander of the military district of Petrograd, and M. Paltchinski, former Assistant Minister of Trade, Military Governor General of Petrograd. Generals Russky and Dragomiroff were appointed respectively Commanders in Chief of the northern and southwestern fronts. General Russky previously had been in charge of the Russian armies on the northern front. He was removed from the command in May of the present year, but remained a member of the Council of War.

# A German Officer Explains the Marne Retreat

*Lieut. Gen. Baron von Freytag-Loringhoven, who is now Deputy Chief of the German General Staff, recently published a review of the operations in the west in August, 1914, which contained this comment on the battle of the Marne:*

We were too weak to force our way through on the Marne. Troops for the threatened east had already been withdrawn, and others were tied up by Antwerp and Maubeuge. Moreover, our enemies had already a superiority of about 750,000 in numbers. We had to protect our eastern frontier, while the French were being strengthened by the English and Belgians. Enormous results had been achieved before we began the retreat from the Marne, and that fact must never be forgotten. Although we did not succeed, and in the circumstances hardly could succeed, in overthrowing France, that is only additional proof that our bold enveloping advance through Belgium alone gave us the possibility of carrying on the war for years on enemy soil, and of keeping Germany secure.

Today it almost looks as if many people had become terrified at the great deeds of our army at the beginning of the war. What else is it, when people keep on insisting anxiously and apologetically upon the fact that we intend nothing but mere defense? The state of the battle area in Northern France and Belgium shows how our frontier territories would look if we had confined ourselves to mere defense—quite apart from the fact that this defense would long ago have had to be conducted in the interior of Germany, even if it were possible at all.

The German people ought to rejoice in the memory of our first victories in the west, thinking in gratitude of its sons whose bodies rest in Belgium and France, and thinking gratefully of its Kaiser and the army

# The Lessons of Three Years of Warfare in the Air

*The material for this article was given to the writer by a leading American practical scientist who has intimate knowledge of the subject*

AFTER three years of warfare it is now admitted that aircraft have not fulfilled the prophecies made at the beginning of the war. Great changes have been brought about by the use of airplanes, but it cannot be said that they have become a determining factor in the grand tactics of the present war. The appeal to the imagination was strong—the possibilities of war waged from the air seemed endless. Armies at once were endowed with eyes far aloft in the air, and great fleets of aircraft were to follow, able to shower destruction on their helpless prey below, making useless all armies with earth-bound equipment.

The armies with eyes in the air have become realities, but the destructive fleets of aircraft have not been evolved. The Zeppelins have not proved of any offensive military value, and no airplane has yet been devised that can carry its fuel with weight of armament or explosives sufficient for a serious bombardment.

The United States has recently made a huge appropriation for aircraft, and already it is being urged, by experts abroad and in this country, that this is the opportunity to change the types of airplanes and thus make our great numbers of aircraft an active offensive force. In this case, as in many other forms of war material, the United States is fortunate in having the lessons of the war available before building the new American aircraft, and the lessons of the war plainly show that the present types of airplanes are lacking in offensive power.

On the other sustaining element, the water, it is realized that the problem of designing a warship is controlled by the three balanced factors of speed, armor, and guns. Whatever increase is given to any one factor of these three is taken away from one or both of the others. The same inexorable law applies to the warships of the air, but in the airplanes both the Entente and Teutonic allies have made speed of such preponderating importance that their machines have almost no powers of offensive. The airplanes destroy one another—and so far this has had no great effect on either side—but they are not able to destroy anything else to the extent of getting real military results. Even for the short flights, the raids over the Channel against England, the Germans have only attained a hurried, badly directed dropping of bombs, which has done very little military harm, and which has shown none of the elements necessary for an offensive against military works.

## Everything Sacrificed for Speed

This obsession for speed at the cost of offensive power is explained by the conditions of airplane development at the outbreak of the war. For some years in Europe airplanes had been given a great vogue. In fact, flying had become a popular sport, and the public mind had been thrilled by the feats of aviators, of which the basis was speed. The military aviators were influenced by this, and naturally the military machines were developed along the same lines. This neglect of the offensive in airplanes is also explained in Germany by confidence in the Zeppelins for the offense, as these lighter-than-air dirigibles were highly thought of by German military experts before the war. Similar dirigibles were also relied upon to some extent in the other European countries, and this may also have drawn away attention from the airplane as a weapon of offense.

Consequently, the airplane of extreme speed was the natural choice of both sides at the outbreak of the war, and from the similarity of types, with all the aviators of the same school, the advantages for each side were the same.

Here was a strange case of the first extensive use of a new element in war— in that it merely added a like amount to each side of the equation. Each side used the new weapon in practically the same way, and the airplane soon became a part of the fixed conditions of warfare, without either side gaining anything from its use. Other advanced developments, the howitzer artillery, intrenching tactics, barrier fire, the submarine, &c., have won tactical results; but the most revolutionary force of all has remained practically equal on each side of the battle front.

If either army had possessed airplanes when the other army had none, or if there had been for either side an overwhelming superiority against which the enemy planes could not exist, or if one side had developed a real offensive in airplanes, it would have been a different story. But, with conditions as described, the airplanes became scouts and artillery spotters for the opposing armies—and such they have remained, giving an element of practically equal military value to each side.

### Raids Without Tactical Effect

The attempt to use the Zeppelins for offense failed because of their vulnerability. There have been desultory attempts at raiding with airplanes. None of these has scored an important military success. The German airplane raids across the Channel have had every condition in their favor. The distance is short and comparatively free from danger of hostile attacks, giving airplanes the least possible necessity to consume fuel. Yet, even in the latest attacks, where attempts were made to use a number of airplanes in concert, the Germans were not able to cause much damage in a military sense. Each raid was a scurry over England, and there has been no evidence of ability to devise a real bombardment. The new type of German biplane is supposed to be designed for bombardment, but the same desire for high speed has restricted its offensive power.

Such raids by the Allies have been more exposed to enemy attacks, and have been handicapped by the necessity of carrying greater amounts of fuel; in consequence the results have been even less than in the German Channel raids. Lately there have been some attempts to use airplanes in attacks, to co-operate with infantry after artillery bombardments, but it cannot be said that they have accomplished anything of tactical value. In fact, looking at the airplane from the point of view of results in the military offensive, its tactical value may be truly called negligible after three years of warfare.

Consequently, to arrive at the present real tactical value of the airplane in the war, it is necessary to consider it as a scout and director of artillery. To measure this value we should first of all realize the great advances in the development of the anti-aircraft gun. At the beginning of the war a machine a few hundred feet in the air was comparatively safe. Now safety from these guns has become a matter of thousands of feet— in fact, less than 10,000 feet in the air is considered a dangerous range. The last raid over London was at 15,000 feet.

### Unreliable as Artillery Aid

The war had not lasted many months before the unreliability of the fast airplane as a spotter for artillery was plainly shown by the great numbers of captive balloons that appeared all along the lines on the western front. The advantages of these quietly moored posts of observation were soon evident—with their definite portions of terrain to observe, and their telephonic communication with the artillery below. The gun-directing value of the airplane also decreased as the enormous increase came in the use of heavy artillery. A bombardment is no longer sending a flight of shells at a particular spot, but it is the delivery of great numbers of shells over a defined area of many hundred square yards. The barrier fire is now more a matter of carefully time-scheduled alternations of gun-fire and advances than the result of signaled observations.

As the fast airplane was gradually forced higher into the air by the anti-aircraft guns, its observations necessarily became less and less reliable. Details became blurred, especially after the development of "camouflage" concealments. The present phase of scouting from airplanes is photographing the terrain with long tele-cameras. Here again the airplane is now at a disadvantage. The clearly cut trenches were easily recorded by the camera, although it was hard to judge of the number of men in them. But this year a great part of the German front is no longer a row of trenches. Many of the enemy's lines are now holes and pits irregularly scattered about, with ferro-concrete barrel-like turrets ("pill-boxes") which can be pushed up for offense or flattened level with the ground. This arrangement has decreased the area of injury and increased the area necessary for an effective bombardment. It has also lessened the value even of photographic observation from the air, as will be readily understood when it is realized how little the forms and shapes of such defenses show against the contour of the terrain. This inherent lack of visibility has been assisted by every kind of camouflage that could be devised. In consequence photographs taken from the air have become of less value.

## Failure as Air Scouts

At the beginning of the war it was too hastily assumed that aircraft as scouts meant the end of surprises on any great scale in warfare. It was natural enough to think that, with scouts in the air, manoeuvres of large bodies of troops could not be concealed from an enemy. Yet this has not proved to be the case in actual warfare. On the eastern fronts there have been overwhelming concentrations of superior forces against Generals who apparently had no idea that anything of the kind was happening; but in these campaigns it is not fair to assume that there were always aircraft available as scouts. On the western front it has been a different thing. Here the armies have been all the time intrenched against one another, making the most difficult conditions for such manoeuvres under any circumstances, and there have been swarms of airplanes of each side in the air.

Yet, with these theoretically prohibitive conditions, there have been, among many surprises, two of the greatest of such manoeuvres by large bodies of troops in military history. In February, 1916, the Germans were able to concentrate hundreds of thousands of men and hundreds of guns against a sector north of Verdun, and to blow the French out of their trenches—with the French Generals confessedly unable to tell where the attack was to be made. In March, 1917, Hindenburg on the Arras salient of over fifty miles was able to withdraw safely to positions far in the rear all his men, material, and guns, without giving any information of this great movement to the aircraft of the Allies.

That these two great manoeuvres should not have been detected seems incredible—but such is the fact. Although at times there has been a great deal of talk of "supremacy in the air," it must not be thought that, in either instance, the allied machines had been driven from the air—no such condition existed. The failure of the allied airplanes to observe them is explained by the conditions already described and by the Germans' taking advantage of darkness and unfavorable weather for the transfers. It must also be remembered that there is a constant stream of transport service going back and forth behind each modern position, under cover of which reinforcements can be sent forward and withdrawals can be made.

## Aircraft Forces Evenly Balanced

The dramatic battles in the air between the planes have filled much space in the public eye, and have made some of our people think that the war is being fought principally by fearless aviators. But, to get at the real value of this phase of the war in the air, it is only necessary to ask, What tactical results have been accomplished by these fights? The answer cannot be evaded, that, while aviators have been having an exciting time among themselves, these battles have won little military result for either side. Neither side has driven its enemy from the air nor established a superiority that would cripple the enemy air scouts. It has been a matter of give and take, leaving the same equality in aircraft for both sides.

In Great Britain before the war there had not been any such craze for aviation as on the Continent. Consequently, at the outbreak of the war there was a strong party in the British service who favored types of less speed. This might have resulted in a more useful type of airplane; but the naval element and the influence of the Admiralty were in favor of great speed in aircraft, and this made the British build the Continental type of fast airplane, to which they have adhered, as have the other European builders.

The feeling among the British naval men was that high speed in their airplanes, as in their battle cruisers, gave them a distinct advantage, like the weather gauge—a choice of position. In warships there has been a healthy reaction against speed in favor of power. In the air the argument for choice of position in manoeuvring over the land was even more unsound, because, while at sea areas of water are of no value and can be yielded at will, on land terrain cannot be yielded in the same way, as a gain of terrain is usually the objective.

### Use of Aircraft at Sea

Over the sea the present aircraft are of use somewhat as over the land. It will readily be understood that they can observe greater areas of sea surface under favorable conditions; but it must also be realized that unfavorable weather conditions are more frequent at sea. One additional great disadvantage on the sea is the inability of the present airplane to navigate. When out of sight of the land, or of its ship, it is lost. There are some hopes of overcoming this drawback, but at present in this respect the lighter-than-air dirigible has a great advantage over the airplane. In fact, the most useful task of the Zeppelin or other dirigible seems to be that of an observer at sea. Captive balloons have also been shown to be of value at sea, and they are in use in the different navies.

At first it was hoped that aircraft would be of great use in detecting submerged U-boats, but experience has proved that only in a flat calm can the submarine be seen at any distance under the surface. The slightest ripple conceals the U-boat. But for observing large areas of water, and marking the appearance of the U-boat on the surface, the airplane and the dirigible are of real value.

The torpedoplane, which is now so often referred to in the press, is a machine built to carry and launch a torpedo. Of course, this means a real offensive weapon, but it must be kept in mind that the machine is thus restricted to one form of attack, and that conditions for such an attack must be perfect to insure success. It is difficult to see any wide use for this type of machine in the present situation on land and sea.

On the sea superior speed is a great advantage when a single warship is matched against another—but this advantage is lessened when a number of warships are supporting one another in formation. In the same way an individual airplane of superior speed has a great advantage over its enemy. The faster plane can choose its own position, and attack the "blind spots" of its slower antagonist. That is, it can take positions where the crew of the slower airplane cannot well use their gunfire—attacking the tail, for instance. But this advantage disappears against a number of slower airplanes in supporting formation, especially if, as a result of a sacrifice of excessive speed, the slower airplanes are more stable gun platforms and better armed.

### Airplanes in Massed Attacks

An airplane is peculiarly adapted to hitting a two-dimension target, if it has enough ammunition, and if the attack is not a haphazard scurry at high speed as at present. The attack of a squadron of well-armed airplanes, all working together, would be a very different thing, with systematized co-operation in finding, sighting, signaling back, &c. It would no longer be a matter of chance shots, but of real damage in a military sense. Although there have been attempts at something of the kind on a small scale, there have not yet been any co-ordinated massed formations, or any concerted tactical use of squadrons of airplanes in great numbers. There were not more than twenty-two in any of the raids on London, and six seems to be the usual number when a squadron is sent up from behind the allied lines on the west front. It is natural that a tactical use of airplanes in numbers has not been developed because of the present lack of offensive power.

From the foregoing it will be seen that the present status of the airplane in war is practically that of an equal weapon for each side used in the same way—that the reason for this equality is the fact that both sides have made speed the great factor, and speed used in the same way. Consequently, the following is the problem that the United States faces when entering the war in the air: Three years of development of this new element of warfare by the other nations have made aircraft an equal weapon—and an equal weapon is no weapon at all. After all this effort resulting in a stalemate, is there any chance that our nation will be able to make this new weapon a deciding factor in the grand tactics of the war?

The United States is again face to face with first principles and must consider the elements of speed, armor, and armament. It is obvious that the airplane is so vulnerable in its extended planes that a heavy weight of armor is useless. In fact, there does not seem to be any sense of having armor except to protect the bodies of the airmen and the tanks of fuel from gunfire below them. This reduces the problem to the question of finding the proper balance between speed and armament that will give airplanes offensive power and make them suitable for tactical use in fleets.

## Possibilities of " Liberty Motor "

That the United States has already made great progress in the solution of this problem is shown by the statement given out Sept. 13, 1917, by Secretary of War Baker, regarding the invention of a new standardized motor for aircraft. The United States has not followed European types of engines, but has in a wonderfully short time developed an engine standardized in the most recent efficiency of American industries. Of course, no details have been given, but a standardized engine means in itself that extreme individual speed has been abandoned. The following are extracts from Secretary Baker's statement:

One of the first problems which confronted the War Department and the Aircraft Production Board after the declaration of hostilities was to produce quickly a dependable aviation motor. Two courses were open. One was to encourage manufacturers to develop their own types; the other to bring the best of all types together and develop a standard. The necessity for speed and quantity production resulted in a choice of the latter course and a standard motor became our engineering objective.

An inspiring feature of this work was the aid rendered by consulting engineers and motor manufacturers, who gave up their trade secrets under the emergency of war needs. Realizing that the new design would be a Government design and no firm or individual would reap selfish benefit because of its making, the motor manufacturers, nevertheless, patriotically revealed their trade secrets and made available trade processes of great commercial value. These industries have also contributed the services of approximately 200 of their best draftsmen.

Parts of the first engine were turned out at twelve different factories, located all the way from Connecticut to California. When the parts were assembled the adjustment was perfect and the performance of the engine was wonderfully gratifying.

Thirty days after the assembling of the first engine preliminary tests justified the Government in formally accepting the engine as the best aircraft engine produced in any country. The final tests confirmed our faith in the new motor.

British and French machines as a rule are not adapted to American manufacturing methods. They are highly specialized machines, requiring much hand work from mechanics, who are, in fact, artisans.

The standardized United States aviation engine, produced under Government supervision, is expected to solve the problem of building high-class, powerful, and yet comparatively delicate aviation engines by American machine methods—the same standardized methods which revolutionized the automobile industry in this country.

With the completion of the final tests of the motor—tests which satisfied and gratified both expert engineers and army officers—progress already has been made toward organizing industry for the manufacture of the new machines, and deliveries will begin within a comparatively short time.

With this new engine American military aviation may be expected to enter a new epoch.

# The First American Flag on the French Front

[Published by arrangement with the Revue Bleue, Paris. Written by the Rev. S. N. Watson. and translated for CURRENT HISTORY MAGAZINE]

UNDER the burning skies of August, 1914, there was seen in the streets of Paris a procession of soldiers of the Foreign Legion. Over the heads of one of the groups floated the Stars and Stripes. The soldiers who formed this American group belonged to the Second Regiment of the Foreign Legion, and their devotion to France and to liberty had impelled them to enlist. Their flag was the first American flag on the French front. Some one had offered them this flag here in Paris, where the group was formed. They took it with them to Rouen, where they had their first camp. When Rouen was threatened by the enemy this regiment was sent to Toulouse. Returning from Toulouse to Paris for active service at the front, its members draped the starry banner over the side of the cattle car in which they were riding; and, arrived at the front, they always found a place of honor for their idolized flag. When they slept at night, or when they went "over the top" in an assault, one man or another always carried it with him.

At last came the moment when the United States took its place in the war. The little group of American volunteers was dispersed. Three were dead, one was grievously wounded, one was a prisoner in Germany. Of one of those now dead it is reported that he lay three days in his bed without saying a word and that suddenly he seized the flag and waved it, crying "I'm an American!" and expired.

One of the survivors sent the flag to the rector of the American Church in Paris, asking him to offer it to the French Government. The rector willingly accepted the task. He wrote to the Minister of War, telling of the request of his compatriots, and received this cordial reply:

I accept with pleasure, in the name of the French Army, this glorious emblem, for which General Niox, Governor of the Invalides, has reserved a beautiful place in the Hall of Honor of the Musée de l'Armée. This flag will thus remain a striking witness of the devotion to France displayed by the American volunteers who, from the beginning of the war, came to fight in the ranks of our army for right and civilization.

The day set for giving over the flag was the Fourth of July. The first detachment of American troops arrived in Paris to take part in the ceremony, which was held in the Court of Honor of the Hôtel des Invalides. The sky was overcast, the air deliciously cool; the galleries were crowded, and the walls of that old building, which have seen so many glorious spectacles, formed a remarkable background. All had been arranged in perfect taste by the Military Governor of Paris and his staff. In the centre of the court were the President of the French Republic, the Minister of War, Marshal Joffre, and other French notables, grouped about the American Ambassador and General Pershing. Before them were ranged three American groups, followed by a French band. Then came the bearers of emblems.

The music enters first, then the American troops advance, marching with a rolling gait like that of sailors. One immediately recognizes the effect of their training on the prairies. They are clean and fresh, but evidently rugged chaps. Then come these old territorials in their muddy and faded uniforms, just as they have grown dear to Parisians, whether French or foreign. How those old poilus were applauded, how proud Paris was of them when they took their place, marching with the same quick, confident, staccato step as in that fateful month of August, 1914!

The American band played " The Mar-

# COMMANDERS OF THE NEW DIVISIONS

**GENERAL JOHN O'RYAN**
Twenty-seventh Division at Spartanburg, S. C.
*(Photo © Paul Thompson)*

**GENERAL WILLIAM A. MANN**
Forty-second Division at Mineola, N. Y.
*(Photo Central News)*

**GENERAL JAMES PARKER**
Thirty-second Division at Waco, Tex.
*(Photo Press Illustrating Service)*

**GENERAL F. J. KERNAN**
Thirty-first Division at Macon, Ga.
*(Photo © Harris & Ewing)*

# COMMANDERS OF THE NEW DIVISIONS

**GENERAL EBEN SWIFT**
Eighty-second Division at Atlanta, Ga.
*(Photo © Harris & Ewing)*

**GENERAL HENRY T. ALLEN**
Ninetieth Division at San Antonio, Tex.
*(Photo © Harris & Ewing)*

**GENERAL F. S. STRONG**
Fortieth Division at San Diego, Cal.
*(Photo © Harris & Ewing)*

**GENERAL F. H. FRENCH**
Eighty-first Division at Columbia, S. C.
*(Photo © Harris & Ewing)*

seillaise." The French band played " The Star-Spangled Banner." Then General Pershing was presented with a guidon on behalf of the descendants of the soldiers who fought by the side of Washington and Lafayette in the American War of Independence, and also with a flag ornamented with lace made by the women of Du Puy.

Now comes the moment to honor the legionaries. The great army has taken their place; the pioneers of liberty are retiring. The rector of the American Church advances, accompanied by Charles Carroll, who carries the flag. Both are descended from old American families, and the rector first addresses General Pershing, saying:

> It is my privilege, my dear General, to present this flag to France on behalf of the first of our soldiers who came here to serve her, our American legionaries, who, through love of France and of liberty, enlisted in the French Army in 1914. They have been proud to give all that they had to give, and we are proud of them. They have been the forerunners of this great American army which is arriving now with you at its head, and they hand over to you the work so bravely begun. Now your new banner replaces their battle-torn flag, but theirs is intrusted to their beloved France to keep forever in this national sanctuary in the heart of France, the Museum of the Invalides.

Then turning to the noble veteran, General Niox, who stood on the right with his artillery officers, the rector addressed these words to him:

> My dear General: It is my great privilege today to act as the representative of my fellow-countrymen in bringing you this flag, their flag, which they have so greatly loved. They loved it even unto death, and they loved it for what it represents. Its sky of blue, in which float the eternal stars, represents the infinite, the absolute, the dwelling place of infrangible justice. These white stripes are the emblem of truth which never changes, and these stripes of red are the rivers of blood which the lovers of justice and truth have always shed freely to protect them and secure them to the children of tomorrow.
>
> What a prophet this flag has been, the first American flag that has floated over

the heads of those who were fighting on the soil of France for the ideals which the banner represents, and which are the life and soul of France! It was not permitted to our gallant boys of the Foreign Legion to carry their flag openly, like the colors of a commander when he leads his soldiers to the charge, but they carried it just the same; one after the other, they carried this flag wrapped about their bodies as a belt—a life-preserver for the soul; one after the other, they were wounded—some were killed—and it was in this way that the American flag received its first baptism of blood in this conflict where now it has its recognized place.

This flag has been the prophet of what has come to pass, now that the great Republic beyond the sea is physically taking the place which it has always held in spirit. We are rendering a service to the comrades who died for France when we ask you to accept this emblem for which they gave their lives. It is also an inspiration to the living to be worthy of those pioneers who preceded them on the road that leads to eternal liberty and the redemption of justice.

Accompanying the flag is a neat bronze plaque with this inscription:

DRAPEAU

PORTE PAR LES

VOLONTAIRES AMERICAINS

DU 2E REGIMENT DE LA LEGION ETRANGERE

| | |
|---|---|
| *C. R. Phelizot | F. W. Zinn |
| Edward Morlae | P. Olinger |
| J. W. Ganson | R. Soubiron |
| D. W. King | W. Thaw |
| J. J. Casey | H. Chatcoff |
| F. Wilson | Charles Trinkard |
| G. Casmèze | R. Scanlon |
| F. Capdeville | W. B. Hall |
| Dr. Van Vorst | **J. J. Bach |
| *P. A. Rockwell | **Dennis Dowd |
| K. Y. Rockwell | George Delpeuch |
| Edgar Bauligny | F. Landreaux |
| Charles Sweeny | |

*Dead. **Prisoners.

In the heart of Paris, which is the heart of France, now rests the first American flag borne on the French front in this great war. It is surrounded by walls of stone, insensible to this honor; but the memory of those who carried that flag yonder where it received its first baptism of blood will be cherished in the hearts of all of us, Americans and Frenchmen alike, and will have a place there forever.

# Destruction of St. Quentin Cathedral

A CORRESPONDENT of the Havas Agency, an association similar to The American Associated Press, telegraphed the following from Paris on Aug. 17, 1917:

Yesterday evening at nightfall French lines were perceived approaching at places to within a kilometer of the suburbs of St. Quentin. The cathedral was surrounded with smoke. Soon flames burst forth, and the fire increased in intensity. Toward midnight the imposing building, dominating the plain with its lofty mass, disappeared in the flames, the sinister light of which was seen for nearly twenty miles around. It is impossible to ascertain the causes of the fire. The Germans will not be able to assert that the fire was started by French shells, for, since St. Quentin has been in proximity to our lines, not a French projectile has fallen on the town. This afternoon the cathedral is still surrounded with smoke. The whole superstructure which formed the lofty roof has disappeared. The apse has completely fallen in. It appears that the four walls, blackened by the flames, and forming as it were the sinister carcass of what was one of our finest churches, has alone survived, with the towers breached, jagged, and reddened by fire. The conflagration, having devoured everything, is now appeased, but thick smoke still ascends in front of the cathedral, appearing to rise from the town quarter.

The London Post commented on the foregoing by citing an illustration of the German idea of culture, as follows:

The unfortunate city of St. Quentin affords two instances of the character of the German's services to culture. In a recent number of the Woche, Lieutenant Hofmann describes a museum which has been established by the German army in the fortress town of Maubeuge in France as a place of intellectual repose for German officers far from the excitement of war, and as a witness to Germany's consideration for culture in the occupied provinces of our ally.

This museum, once a third-class shop, the "Pauvre Diable," on the Place du Marché, Maubeuge, consists of the most important works of art taken from St. Quentin and its neighborhood, an enterprise carried out by Lieutenant Baron de Hadeln, art historian, and Lieutenant Keller, a Berlin architect. The writer gives a very graphic account of the contents of this "place of distraction." From the vestibule to the first floor of the house the walls are covered with tapestry, representing the most brilliant specimens of the best periods of the art of the Beauvais and Gobelins factories. One room is transformed into an empire salon, and its red damask hangings give the fullest value to Canova's marble bust of Napoleon. There are paintings, bronzes, and furniture from the Goulincourt Castle, and the Louis Philippe salon has splendid French and Oriental carpets, soft and restful, where "the boot of the German rests with joy." The curtains are of yellow silk, chairs are gayly decorated, and the porcelain and pictures are good.

The Cathedral of St. Quentin could not be removed to Maubeuge to save it from the "French artillery," so the Germans themselves have destroyed it by fire. But they first removed from the doomed building a Gothic statue of St. Quentin, the patron of the town, and from the same basilica were taken a charming "Madonna" and precious stained glass windows.

The most valuable works in the museum at Maubeuge are the wonderful pastels of Quentin La Tour, who was a native of his name town. These portraits of famous French men and women of the eighteenth century were the glory of St. Quentin, and are, as Lieutenant Hofmann says, "the most delicate flowers of a refined art," more than eighty in number, yet, he continues, "I did not experience the least fatigue in contemplating them." Then he goes on eloquently, "these priceless works of art have been placed here [in Maubeuge] safe from the ravages of war. The German spirit and German force ever know how to safeguard the intellectual patrimony common to all nations." But as a Frenchman remarks: "The world would better appreciate this eloquent eulogy of the services Germany renders to 'culture' if it were not recorded every day in the communiqués: 'La Ville de Reims a reçu 1,600 obus.'" and he could now add, "if we were not aware of the dastardly destruction of the Cathedral of St. Quentin."

# President's Reply to the Pope

## Text of Historic Peace Communication
## That Caused a Sensation in Germany

*The peace proposal of Pope Benedict, which was sent to all the belligerent powers under date of Aug. 1, 1917, and which appeared in the September issue of* CURRENT HISTORY MAGAZINE, *was answered by President Wilson on Aug. 27 through Secretary of State Lansing. The American reply was universally accepted by the Entente nations as expressing their sentiments on the subject. Its outstanding feature was an indirect message to the German people to the effect that no peace was possible with their present " irresponsible " Government. The debate precipitated in Germany and elsewhere by this message is summarized below. Following is the full text of the reply to the Pope:*

WASHINGTON, D C.,
Aug. 27, 1917.

*To His Holiness Benedictus XV., Pope:*

*In acknowledgment of the communication of your Holiness to the belligerent peoples, dated Aug. 1, 1917, the President of the United States requests me to transmit the following reply:*

EVERY heart that has not been blinded and hardened by this terrible war must be touched by this moving appeal of his Holiness the Pope, must feel the dignity and force of the humane and generous motives which prompted it, and must fervently wish that we might take the path of peace he so persuasively points out. But it would be folly to take it if it does not in fact lead to the goal he proposes. Our response must be based upon the stern facts and upon nothing else. It is not a mere cessation of arms he desires; it is a stable and enduring peace. The agony must not be gone through with again, and it must be a matter of very sober judgment what will insure us against it.

His Holiness in substance proposes that we return to the status quo ante bellum, and that then there be a general condonation, disarmament, and a concert of nations based upon an acceptance of the principle of arbitration; that by a similar concert freedom of the seas be established; and that the territorial claims of France and Italy, the perplexing problems of the Balkan States, and the restitution of Poland be left to such conciliatory adjustments as may be possible in the new temper of such a peace, due regard being paid to the aspirations of the peoples whose political fortunes and affiliations will be involved.

It is manifest that no part of this program can be successfully carried out unless the restitution of the status quo ante furnishes a firm and satisfactory basis for it. The object of this war is to deliver the free peoples of the world from the menace and the actual power of a vast military establishment controlled by an irresponsible Government which, having secretly planned to dominate the world, proceeded to carry the plan out without regard either to the sacred obligations of treaty or the long-established practices and long-cherished principles of international action and honor; which chose its own time for the war; delivered its blow fiercely and suddenly; stopped at no barrier either of law or of mercy; swept a whole continent within the tide of blood—not the blood of soldiers only, but the blood of innocent women and children also and of the helpless poor; and now stands balked but not defeated, the enemy of four-fifths of the world. This power is not the German people. It is the ruthless master of the German people. It is no business of ours how that great people came under its control or submitted with temporary zest to the domination of its purpose; but it is our business to see to it that the history of the rest of the world is no longer left to its handling.

To deal with such a power by way of peace upon the plan proposed by his Holiness the Pope would, so far as we can see, involve a recuperation of its strength and a renewal of its policy; would make it necessary to create a permanent hostile combination of nations against the German people, who are its instruments; and would result in abandoning the new-born Russia to the intrigue, the manifold subtile interference, and the certain counter-revolution which would be attempted by all the malign influences to which the German Government has of late accustomed the world. Can peace be based upon a restitution of its power or upon any word of honor it could pledge in a treaty of settlement and accommodation?

Responsible statesmen must now everywhere see, if they never saw before, that no peace can rest securely upon political or economic restrictions meant to benefit some nations and cripple or embarrass others, upon vindictive action of any sort, or any kind of revenge or deliberate injury. The American people have suffered intolerable wrongs at the hands of the Imperial German Government, but they desire no reprisals upon the German people, who have themselves suffered all things in this war, which they did not choose. They believe that peace should rest upon the rights of peoples, not the rights of Governments—the rights of peoples great or small, weak or powerful— their equal right to freedom and security and self-government and to a participation upon fair terms in the economic opportunities of the world, the German people of course included if they will accept equality and not seek domination.

The test, therefore, of every plan of peace is this: Is it based upon the faith of all the peoples involved or merely upon the word of an ambitious and intriguing Government, on the one hand, and of a group of free peoples on the other? This is the test which goes to the root of the matter; and it is the test which must be applied.

The purposes of the United States in this war are known to the whole world, to every people to whom the truth has been permitted to come. They do not need to be stated again. We seek no material advantage of any kind. We believe that the intolerable wrongs done in this war by the furious and brutal power of the Imperial German Government ought to be repaired, but not at the expense of the sovereignty of any people—rather a vindication of the sovereignty both of those that are weak and of those that are strong. Punitive damages, the dismemberment of empires, the establishment of selfish and exclusive economic leagues, we deem inexpedient and in the end worse than futile, no proper basis for a peace of any kind, least of all for an enduring peace. That must be based upon justice and fairness and the common rights of mankind.

We cannot take the word of the present rulers of Germany as a guarantee of anything that is to endure, unless explicitly supported by such conclusive evidence of the will and purpose of the German people themselves as the other peoples of the world would be justified in accepting. Without such guarantees treaties of settlement, agreements for disarmament, covenants to set up arbitration in the place of force, territorial adjustments, reconstitutions of small nations, if made with the German Government, no man, no nation could now depend on. We must await some new evidence of the purposes of the great peoples of the Central Powers. God grant it may be given soon and in a way to restore the confidence of all peoples everywhere in the faith of nations and the possibility of a covenanted peace.

ROBERT LANSING,
Secretary of State of the United States of America.

# Comment of the Nations on the President's Reply

THE reply of the President to the Pope's peace note received enthusiastic approval throughout the United States and was unreservedly indorsed by all the influential newspapers and authorized spokesmen of the allied nations; it produced a profound impression in Germany and Austria, and was sympathetically received by all the elements of the neutral nations except those with pronounced pro-German leanings. Semi-official news from the Vatican indicated that the Pope was disappointed.

## German-Americans Approve

The German-American view was expressed by the New-Yorker Staats-Zeitung in a rather favorable comment by the editor in chief in these words:

The President's note to the Pope has met with the hearty approval of all Americans. It appeals to German-Americans particularly because it dispels the mist which has heretofore hung over our participation in the war. It tells the American people plainly what they are contending for, and what they are not contending for—a reply long delayed to a question which we have been waiting to have answered.

And it appeals to those of us who have not forgotten the history hickoryed into us before the "sacred right of lying" was enthroned in the world.

The German-language press in this country was frankly opposed to our entrance into the war—so long as we could honorably keep out of it. Once in the war, however, a determination to support the Government occupied its editorial policies. While others have been snapping at the heels of the Administration—yelping their little seditious words of advice—destroying that unity of mind which is necessary to team work—we have presented a solid front of support. We have spoken for—and to—that potential element of the American Nation which springs from Germany—always in the past a friend of America, and now unfortunately compelled to be in arms against her.

We, German-Americans, appreciate the President's note perhaps more fully than others can. We read in it a message from ourselves to our friends across the waters—a message which could not have been better indited by a German himself, whose escape from "local atmosphere" had made him a citizen of the world. We find in the President's words an appreciation of the true worth of that great people from which we are descended—a willingness to extend to them the hand of friendship utterly lacking in the tone of our associated statesmen.

The President has at last given the American people a program about which there can be no dissension, no question, and no disagreement.

The German people would be grievously misled if they were made to believe that Americans of German descent would support any but their own Government, carrying out its constitutional duties. They would be grievously misled if by designing intrigants at home or abroad they were to be convinced that Germans abroad are not solicitous that they, too, should participate in the advantages of democracy—a democracy in fact as well as in name, which the latter have come to esteem.

The President has not only left the way open to the German people to peace. He has gone much further. He has leveled away its chief obstacles. He has repudiated the language of Old World spokesmen. He has spoken as the New World would speak.

The appearance of Woodrow Wilson as spokesman of her enemies cannot pass in Germany as a matter of no concern.

What the President said in his reply to his Holiness the Pope as to peace is what the American people would say with one voice, were a nation capable of individual articulation. The President expressed therein what all Americans feel—and especially German-Americans—a hope and a longing that through his words the German Nation may progress to that early and enduring peace which the world so sadly needs.

## The English Press

The following were characteristic comments by the leading London newspapers:

### The Daily News:

If the President's reply is a merciless indictment of the infamies of Prussian militarism, it is equally a passionate appeal to the German people to repudiate the evil system that has enslaved them and uses them to enslave the world. The distinction which Mr. Wilson has insisted on throughout between the people and the system is now stated with matchless force.

### The London Post:

At the end of three years of unspeakable strain and anxiety, it is an inestimable service to the Allies to find such leadership as this—strong, clear-sighted, inflexible, inspiring new courage and faith, shaming the faint-hearted, and silencing the perverse and the disaffected.

With a directness and a cogency which cannot be too much admired, President Wilson gives to the Pope's peace proposals the only answer which those who are not ready to capitulate to Germany could give.

Certain extremely quoted persons in this country have recently been plaintively demanding to know what we were fighting for. Others have been contending that it is necessary for British delegates to confer with the enemy at Stockholm in order that our aims might be understood. Both claims are sufficiently disposed of in President Wilson's latest note. What we are fighting for is to defeat Germany—the one condition precedent to any tolerable peace.

### The London Times:

The theoretical distinction [between the German people and their rulers] is sound enough, but we cannot help thinking that up to the present it has proved to be quite negligible in practice. Wilson is right in a sense when he says that the German people " did not choose the war." They did not choose it, because, under the Bismarckian Constitution, they have no choice at all in such high matters, but they accepted it with enthusiasm. They have given it throughout their active support. Their representatives have voted with unanimity supplies for its continuance.

## French Comment

### The Paris Temps:

The sentiment which inspires the entire note, just as it inspires the entire French policy, is the conviction that we cannot treat with the German Government at present.

The President of the United States in his patient negotiations regarding submarine warfare had the same experience as France in ten years of discussion of Moroccan questions, and has drawn the same conclusion. Nothing would be gained by signing tomorrow a new " scrap of paper." It would not conduce to world peace. It would merely give the Prussian General Staff time to prepare for new aggression.

That surely was not the end which the Pope proposed. He said the fundamental point must be the substitution of the moral force of right for the material force of arms, but Mr. Wilson has seen clearly and explained clearly that negotiation as suggested by the Holy Father would end in an entirely different result. In Germany it would give to the Imperial Government a renewal of strength. Outside of Germany it would compel persons who desire to remain free to create a permanent league against the German danger. It would result, in fact, in consolidating Prussian militarism and in perpetuating a régime of armed peace.

It is not to achieve this that the United States entered the war. It is not for this that we are fighting. President Wilson wants a real peace, one which will do away with the causes of war. His doctrine is logical from one end to the other. It is because he wants a pacific Germany that he rejects the idea of inclosing it within a wall. It is because he counts upon the opening of the eyes of the German people that he refuses to treat with the Hohenzollern autocracy. He has confidence in the future. He believes his idea can be imposed even on the enemy.

We join the President in this pious hope, but this hope will not be realized unless the United States perseveres indefatigably in the battle for victory of the right. The calmness with which Mr. Wilson contemplates future peace corresponds with the energy with which he will continue to conduct the war. That is the comforting impression left by reading his note. More than ever we have faith in his untiring firmness.

### L'Humanite, Paris:

President Wilson's language is that of lofty reason, which ignores cupidity and hatred. It may make itself heard by the German people, whom it asks to repair the evil they have done and then to take their place among the other nations without their rights or existence being menaced.

It is to the German people that President Wilson has made reply in answering the Pope. If the Pope has been only the mouthpiece of the Central Powers, President Wilson's reply was the most direct and the wisest it was possible to make. If the German people want peace they know just on what conditions it can be obtained.

## Italian Comment

### The Tribuna, Rome:

President Wilson has put forward the great struggle between might and right in such a decisive way that it is impossible to wave it away by sleight of hand. * * * That struggle must end in the absolute triumph of right without limitations and reserve, and that triumph cannot be obtained by ambiguous conciliations or subtle compromises with those who habitually violate the rights of others, and who, with their haughtiness not yet tamed by the condemnation of the world and inevitable defeat, continue such violations.

## The Corriere della Sera, Milan:

President Wilson's answer sets forth the fundamental reasons why the allied powers cannot consider the Pope's proposals. The era of treaties made for breaking is past. Europe must emerge from this red inundation as another Europe. The Pope is in a neutral position which will not and can not be changed. He has a right and a duty to seek peace. This position is understood and respected by the Allies.

## The Giornale d'Italia:

President Wilson once more has interpreted the voice of millions who are ready to suffer in order to assure peace to future generations. His marvelous patience and charity in dealing with past tergiversations of the German Government made it his natural right to be the first to voice on this occasion, with grave, measured speech, the sentiments of all humanity oppressed by the Teuton threat, proving that the same principles that induced the head of Catholic Christianity to invoke peace are those which induced and obliged America to enter the war.

## Its Effect in Germany

German official and newspaper comment on the reply was passionate and bitter, the only important newspaper exception being the Socialist organ *Vorwärts*. In discussing the President's demand that peace must be negotiated by the German people, this newspaper said:

The German people are fighting this severest of all fights, not for the rights of certain families or for a distinct form of government, but for their own existence. For that reason the Socialists supported national defense, and for no other reason. The thought were unbearable that those out there are fighting, not for the maintenance of the empire, but for the preservation of conditions not worthy to be upheld. It would be unbearable to think that a single mother's son fell, not for the rights of the people, but for the privileges of certain persons.

Take the world map and look at one country after another. Everywhere the decision in political questions lies in the hands of persons chosen by the people. It is so everywhere else; why can it not be so with us?

After more than three years of war a great power says to us that it must be so with us, if we wish to reach peace. Perhaps that is not more than a pretext, but if so, it is so cleverly chosen that we cannot meet it with words but with deeds. The Government of a country at war with us has a perfect right to demand that for the conditions under which peace is to be concluded the people themselves shall be the guarantee. We cannot be persuaded that the German people, the most active and educated in the world, are not fit for that form of government under which other people have grown great.

The opinions of Vorwärts provoked violent criticism by the Pan-German and annexationist press. The general tone of the press throughout Germany and Austria was bitter, resentful, and extremely abusive of the President.

This comment of the *Berlin Lokal-Anzeiger* was characteristic:

President Wilson declines the Pope's mediation with the same mass of swollen phrases with which he has already satiated the German peoples. We are told that the war is not being waged against the German Nation, but against their "masters."

The absolute mendacity of Mr. Wilson's phraseology becomes apparent when his dictum as to the rights of nations which are capable of shaping their own destinies is opposed to the wish of the German people to be governed by these very "masters." Mr. Wilson, therefore, does not intend to give us our liberty, but to deprive us of liberty to arrive at our own decisions.

For that matter, this whole mass of words has as its sole purpose the expression of the intention to prolong the war at any price. In this resolve Mr. Wilson, who is fighting for the freedom of mankind, orders peace meetings dispersed and pacifists arrested.

This war has exposed in its nakedness much that is low and contemptible; its remaining task was to exhibit a hero like this coldly calculating mathematician, whom a singular fate in a momentous hour has given the power over one hundred millions of people.

The *Cologne Gazette*, regarded as semi-official, said:

Every word of President Wilson's note is grotesque nonsense. The climax of all the nonsense is that the German people are groaning under a cruel Government. Has not the entire German people, rich and poor, Socialist and Conservative, continually repeated that it stands firm for the Emperor and the empire? The solution of the puzzle is that Mr. Wilson wants to persevere with the war. America's business world needs the war at this conjuncture. America's future needs the big army that is just in the making.

Mr. Wilson hopes for disunity in Germany, and therefore offers the German people peace at the cost of the German Government's fall. This trick is too transparent. The German people may be relied upon to range themselves more firmly around the Emperor against this hypocrite.

## The Austrian View

The Vienna Reichspost received the following communication, which was accepted as the official view regarding the Pope's peace note:

The Pope's note, which aimed at a just and durable peace, is in absolute harmony with the aims of the monarchy. As to concrete proposals, Austria is willing to evacuate occupied territories and renounce all claims to indemnities once the exhortations of the Pope regarding grad-

ual disarmament, the establishment of international arbitration and the full freedom of the seas, composing the guarantees necessary for the world's peace, are carried into effect, but under this last condition must be understood all the consequences deducible from the Pope's proposals—namely, that the naval bases of Great Britain at Gibraltar and Malta and near the Suez Canal shall disappear, as also the occupation of Avlona by Italy.

As to the questions regarding Austro-Italian territories, Italy has not the least right to territory which Austria has possessed for a century, and the autonomous population of Southern Tyrol and the populations of Istria, Dalmatia, and the littoral are opposed to union with Italy.

# How the German Chancellor Presented the Peace Note

DR. MICHAELIS, the German Chancellor, presented the peace note of the Pope to the Main Committee of the Reichstag on Aug. 21, 1917. He first read a long and absolutely confident telegram from Field Marshal Hindenburg, and referred to the war aims of Germany's enemies as being groundless as ever, and as again disclosing the existence of secret arrangements. He then said:

" It is easily to be understood that in view of the attitude of our enemies the German Press maintains that it is impossible for us to make fresh peace proposals."

Here the Chancellor quoted the Vorwärts of Aug. 19, as follows:

At no moment of the war has it been as clear as it is now that the responsibility for the prolongation of the war rests alone with our enemies. Their answer to our outstretched hand was a smashing blow with the fist. At this moment there is for us only one possibility, that is, to defend ourselves and our skin.

" I think," continued Dr. Michaelis, " that this is the general feeling of our people. It is in such a situation as this that I now submit to you the peace demonstration contained in the Pope's note. The contents I believe are known to all of you. The fundamental ideas advanced therein correspond with the position which the Pope takes up in accord with his whole personality and

his charge as the head of the Catholic Christendom.

## Pope's Attitude Welcomed

" The Pope places in the foreground his conviction that the moral force of right should replace the material force of arms. On this foundation he develops his proposals for arbitration and disarmament. I cannot take up any definite position with regard to the material tenor of the proposals, or go into any detail regarding them until an agreement has been reached with our allies. It is only possible for me to explain my views in quite general terms, and I might do this in two directions.

" I repudiate the suggestion that the Pope's proposal was inspired by the Central Powers. I affirm that the Pope's proposal, as made known through the press, was due to his spontaneous decision as head of the Roman Catholic Church. If I must make any reservation in regard to details, I can say at once that it corresponds to the attitude we have often made known and to our policy since Dec. 12 last, that we are sympathetically inclined toward every attempt to inspire thoughts of peace among the nations amid the misery of the war, and that we especially welcome the action of the Pope, which, in my opinion, is based on a sincere desire for impartiality and justice. The note was not the result of our initiative, but was put forward on the spontaneous initiative of the Pope.

" We greet with sympathy the Pope's efforts by a lasting peace to put an end to the war of nations. In regard to the answer to the note we are communicating with our allies, and the negotiations have not yet been brought to an end. For the present I am unable to enter upon a closer discussion of material points in the Pope's note, but I am ready to discuss the matter further with the committee until our answer is ready. I express the hope that our common labor may bring us near to the desire which we all have at heart, namely, an honorable peace for the Fatherland."

### The Debate

In the debate that ensued Socialist speakers welcomed the action of the Pope, as, they declared, they would welcome any steps which might bring about peace, and more especially because good results were expected of it.

The Liberal Party declared its agreement with the Chancellor in his sympathetic interpretation of the Pope's action, and associated itself with the Chancellor's remarks upon it. Centre speakers likewise associated themselves with the Chancellor's remarks. They said they regarded the action of the Pope, whose impartiality was known throughout the world, as extraordinarily valuable progress toward the peace which was so ardently desired by all nations. The party expressed the hope that this historic act, supported by the most lofty ideals, would meet with full success.

National Liberal speakers declared that they were not yet able to examine closely the material contents of the Pope's note, but could associate themselves with the words of the Chancellor. The Conservative Party also associated itself with the remarks of Dr. Michaelis, but reserved its attitude as to details.

The German group especially welcomed the firm declaration of the Chancellor that the note had emanated spontaneously from the Pope, without any instigation by the Central Empires. The party re-garded the Pope's action as more sympathetic than the previous attempt at mediation by President Wilson.

Independent Socialists regretted that previous speakers had expressed only general sympathy with the note without entering into discussion. The Reichstag must not renounce its influence on the matter of drafting the reply.

### Pan-German Resolutions

A campaign was launched early in September by Pan-Germans to have the leading cities of the empire, through their commercial and industrial bodies, answer the President's note by a fresh appeal for loyalty to the Kaiser. This was done by such leading cities as Hamburg, Bremen, Leipsic, Stettin, and others.

The Hamburg Chamber of Commerce passed the following resolution on Sept. 4:

With indignation we protest against the hypocritical criticism by President Wilson, who at present governs the United States with autocratic power. We shall not tolerate any interference by hostile Governments with the interior affairs of Germany.

We strongly reject the repeated attempts to hold Germany responsible for the war, which is in gross contradiction to incontrovertible facts, and we shall most decidedly oppose efforts by the enemy to create dissension between the German people and the German Government.

The whole German people are firmly determined to fight to a victorious ,end for the preservation of the German Empire, embodied in Kaiserdom, and for the removal of the arbitrary despotism exerted by England over the free seas. These rights can only be enforced against the onslaught of our enemies by the united power of our army and navy, which have sworn allegiance to the German Kaiser, and will remain loyal to their oath against a whole world of greedy enemies.

Similar resolutions were passed by the Chamber of Commerce at Bremen, which sent the following telegram to the Kaiser:

Bremen merchants raise an indignant protest against President Wilson's hypocritical reply to the Pope, in which he professes to combat the German Government in order to drive the American people, with whom Germany never had a quarrel, into a war which they reject. It is an impudent and brazen attempt to sow dissensions between the German Government and the people, while by British arbitrariness our noncombatants, children and women, are cut off from all outside supplies in order to exhaust the nation by hunger.

This attempt can only fill with indignation and contempt German merchants who have had the opportunity in foreign lands to compare German with foreign conditions. In this hour Bremen merchants pledge themselves to unalterable allegiance to your Majesty, wearer of the imperial crown, as the empire's guardian,

rewon after centuries of long struggles by the united German people in 1871. They again declare their unalterable confidence and belief in a victorious outcome of this righteous war of defense.

In the course of his speech the President of the Chamber, Herr Fabrius, said no other enemy utterance had evoked such wrath in every German heart as President Wilson's note, in which the most sacred rights of the German Nation were assailed.

# Democratic Agitation in Germany

ALL reports from Germany during the first two weeks of September indicated deep political unrest and violent agitation among the various political factions. The Main Committee of the Reichstag was in session late in August and adjourned Aug. 29, until the assembling of the Reichstag late in September. Upon adjournment it was announced that a motion by the Social Democrats and Independent Socialists recommending abolition of martial law failed of acceptance.

Resolutions presented by the majority parties calling for abrogation of the political censorship and containing recommendations for modification of other censorial restrictions were adopted, as was a recommendation of the coalition parties for nullification of an order of the Federal Council, dated Aug. 3, subjecting motion pictures to rigid censorship.

All reports regarding the sessions of this committee indicated that there was extreme tension and bitter disagreements and debates, but no official reports of the proceedings were given out.

One speech of Chancellor Michaelis at a session of the committee was given out Aug. 23. He was quoted as follows:

As regards our enemies, their number has increased since the adjournment of the Reichstag by three, namely, Siam, Liberia, and China. These countries have no convincing reason for enmity against us. They acted solely under pressure of the Entente and the United States, the latter having great influence over Liberia and China. We have made it clear to these countries that we shall bring them

to account for the damage done under international law to German interests.

After referring to the solidarity of Germany and her allies, the Chancellor read a telegram from Field Marshal von Hindenburg saying that the military situation was more favorable for Germany than ever. The Chancellor added:

Our success on land corresponds with our success on the sea. In the month of July, according to the latest reports received, 811,000 tons of shipping were sunk. When we take into consideration our results on the one hand and the failures of our enemies on the other, it appears to be incomprehensible that our enemies show no disposition to prepare the way for consideration of terms of peace, not to mention peace which includes renunciation.

I was able to show recently by information regarding a Franco-Russian secret treaty what far-reaching war aims France had and how England supported French desires for German land. Only recently a member of the British Cabinet declared that there would be no peace until the German armies had been thrown across the Rhine. I am now able to show that further arrangements were made by the enemy regarding their war aims, some of the details of which were already made known to the committee on an earlier occasion. I proceed in chronological order:

On Sept. 7, 1914, the enemy coalition decided only to conclude a joint peace. On March 4, 1915, Russia made the following peace demands, of which England approved by note on March 12 and France by note of the same date, namely: Russia to receive Constantinople, with the European shore of the strait; the southern part of Thrace as far as the Enos-midia line, the islands in the Sea of Marmora, the islands of Imbros and Tenedos, and, on the Asia Minor side, the peninsula between the Black Sea, the Bosporus, and the Gulf of Ismailia as far as the River Sakarieh in the east.

This basis was laid down, and the negotiations continued their course in 1915-16. In the course of them Russia obtained the promise of the Armenian vilayets of Trebizond and Kurdistan, and Messina and the Hinterland, extending northward as far as Sivas and Kharput. England's share was to be Mesopotamia, and the rest of Turkey in Asia was to be divided into English and French spheres of interest.

Palestine was to be internationalized, and the other districts inhabited by the Turks and Arabs, including Arabia proper and the holy places of Islam, were to be formed into a special federation of States under British suzerainty.

When Italy entered the war she demanded her share of the booty. Fresh negotiations were opened, which in nowise pointed at renunciations. I think we shall have further details about them, which will be published later.

With such far-reaching enemy war aims it may be understood why Mr. Balfour lately stated that he did not consider it advisable to make a detailed statement on the war policy of the Government. Those are the bottom facts as they appear to us at the present moment, when we visage the possibility of concluding peace.

# The British Official View

THE first British official expression on the subject of the Pope's peace note was uttered by Lord Robert Cecil of the War Cabinet, Minister of Blockade. In a statement issued Aug. 31, 1917, and regarded as expressing the British official view, he said:

The President's note is a magnificent occurrence. It thrilled us all over here, and the opinions which I heard expressed by representatives of allied countries were equally warm and appreciative. I am certain that none of the allies would be able to improve upon it, and I am not certain that none of the allies would be necessary.

There does not appear to me to be anything inconsistent as between the President's note and the economic policy of the Allies declared at the Paris conference. The resolutions of the Allies were purely defensive measures, and in no way aggressive.

They had in view the necessity for restoring the economic life of the Allies and protecting ourselves against any aggressive and militarist commercial policy which might be pursued by our enemies after the war. German schemes for driving their allies into a Central European commercial bloc show that such a policy is a real danger. We do, indeed, hold that in this struggle economic considerations are as vital as purely military and naval measures. We have to maintain and foster the economic strength of those who are fighting the Central Powers quite as much as we have to organize our armies and navies.

We Allies also believe that we are right in attacking the economic strength of our enemies with every legitimate weapon at our command. That is why we rejoice at the vigorous policy which the United States is pursuing in regard to exports and other matters. Depend upon it, there is no more potent weapon with which to bring home to Germany the folly and wickedness of her militarist leaders than to show her that war does not pay even in the strictest commercial sense.

Germans are fond of boasting of their war maps and pointing to the territories which they have overrun. They forget that in the pursuit of their militarist policy and their contempt for all international law and the rights of noncombatants and neutrals, they have arrayed against themselves forces whose commercial and financial resources are immeasurably greater than their own.

Hardly a week passes without some indication that even those nations which still remain neutral are getting to the end of their patience. It is scarcely extravagant to say that if the war goes on many months longer the Central Powers will find literally the whole of the rest of the world arrayed in arms against them.

That is a state of things which gives rise to two observations. In the first place, it shows that in the modern world military force is not everything; that even if the German armies were really as successful and invincible as the Kaiser and his Generals boast, the future of Germany would still be increasingly dark. The second observation is more full of hope. It indicates, perhaps, the real solution of the greater world problem of the day, namely, how we can take precautions to prevent future wars. The great difficulty of all schemes for leagues of nations and the like has been to find an effective sanction against nations determined to break the peace.

I will not now discuss at length the difficulties of joint armed action, but every one who has studied the question knows they are very great. It may be, however, that a league of nations, properly furnished with machinery to enforce the financial, commercial, and economic isolation of any nation determined to force its will upon the world by mere violence, would be a real safeguard for the peace of the world. In any case that is a subject that may well be studied by those sincerely anxious to put an end to the present system of international anarchy.

# American Labor on War and Peace

THE American Alliance for Labor and Democracy met at Minneapolis Sept. 6. It represented the leading labor associations of the United States, and was presided over by Samuel Gompers, President of the American Federation of Labor. Resolutions were unanimously adopted condemning the efforts of pacifists who were claiming to represent labor organizations. The war aims of the United States were presented in the following resolutions, unanimously adopted:

Since the United States entered the war the President has upon three notable occasions clearly and explicitly set forth the American aim, the objects which must be attained by any peace to which the United States can agree. We refer especially to the war message of April 2, 1917, the note to Russia on May 26, and the reply to his Holiness the Pope, dated Aug. 27, 1917. The war objects stated by the President in these historic documents were as follows:

1. Recognition of the rights and liberties of small nations.

2. Recognition of the principle that government derives its just power from the consent of the governed.

3. Reparation for wrongs done and the erection of adequate safeguards to prevent their being committed again.

4. No indemnities except as payment for manifest wrongs.

5. No people to be forced under sovereignty under which it does not wish to live.

6. No territory to change hands except for the purpose of securing those who inhabit it a fair chance of life and liberty.

7. No readjustments of power except such as will tend to secure the future peace of the world and the future welfare and happiness of its people.

8. A genuine and practical co-operation of the free peoples of the world in some common covenant that will combine their forces to secure peace and justice in the dealings of nations with one another.

The resolution then points how, in his Russian note and again in his address at Washington on June 14, President Wilson gave a solemn warning against the sort of peace desired by the German military power, and how, in his note to the Government of Russia on May 26, he stated that America was "fighting for no advantage or selfish object of her own, but for the liberation of peoples everywhere from the aggressions of autocratic force." The resolution concludes:

We, the men and women of the trade union and Socialist movements of America, organized into the American Alliance for Labor and Democracy, in submitting this record to our fellow-citizens, assert that in all history no Government has ever stated its aims on entering a war, or while such war was being fought, with anything approaching the definiteness, clarity, and candor revealed by these utterances. We assert, moreover, that in all essential particulars the aims thus set forth are entirely consistent with the great ideals of democracy and internationalism, for which the American labor movement has always stood and which are fundamental to its being.

We rejoice at the fact that we are thus solemnly committed to the principle of the complete autonomy and independence of nations. Only upon the basis of this generous nationalism can anything like a great and worthy internationalism be established. We rejoice, too, that this nation is thus solemnly pledged not only to refrain from attempting to extend its own dominion over any other nation or people, but to use its great influence to the end that no nation shall " attempt to extend its policy over any other nation or people."

We approve unreservedly the distinction drawn by the President between the German people and their Government, and we believe that by insisting that peace cannot be made with the Hohenzollern dynasty, but only with a democratized Germany, the President of the United States has, as befits his great station, rendered noble service to the cause of international democracy.

# Who Was Responsible for the War?

## Statement by Dr. Michaelis

DR. GEORG MICHAELIS, the German Chancellor, issued a statement Sept. 5 in regard to alleged disclosures at the trial in Petrograd for high treason of General Soukhomlinoff, former Minister of War. The Chancellor sought to prove, from certain testimony in that trial, that Russia was responsible for beginning the war. He said:

The statements of the former Russian War Minister and the former Chief of the General Staff (General Januschkevitch) are of the greatest importance. They are calculated completely to destroy the legend of Germany's guilt in starting the war, and they will force European opinion, if the reports are allowed to be published abroad, to revise its judgment on Germany.

The moment at which these disclosures were made is the more favorable, as we have just had knowledge of the American reply to the Pope's note urging peace. In Secretary Lansing's answer the German Government is described as an irresponsible Government which secretly planned to dominate the world, which chose its own time for the war, and cruelly and suddenly executed its plan; which did not heed legal barriers or truthfulness, which flooded a great continent with the blood, not only of soldiers but of innocent women and children, the helpless and the poor.

When adopting these accusations from the Entente factory of calumnies, the American Government obviously had no knowledge of the course of the proceedings against General Soukhomlinoff. Otherwise its judgment would certainly have been quite different.

### Blames the Czar's Advisers

It certainly is now established irrefutably that it was not Germany which chose the time for the war, but the military party surrounding the Czar, who was under the influence of France and England. It is well known that the German Emperor, who, before the war, clearly, and on every occasion, expressed his own desire and that of the German people for peace, especially regarding Russia, was surprised by the events which occurred during his pleasure trip to Scandinavian waters. Up to the last moment, in the exchange of telegrams with the Emperor of Russia and the King of England, he made the most earnest and fervent attempts in the interest of peace.

The importance of the new disclosures is that the Czar, who had to decide as to war or peace, in fact came to the conviction, from the German Emperor's efforts, that Germany did not desire war. The consequence of this conviction was his positive order to cancel the Russian mobilization, but a couple of criminals, who belied the Czar, disregarded the order and thwarted its execution.

A consequence of the Emperor's efforts also was the Czar's order to General Januschkevitch to give the German Ambassador, Count von Pourtales, assurances of Russia's desire for peace. The execution of this order was frustrated by M. Sazonoff, (then Russian Foreign Minister,) who obviously feared that the German Ambassador, who hitherto had done good service in the interest of peace, could perhaps take further effective steps for prevention of the threatening war.

### Says Allies Incited Russia

Who was behind all these men? They certainly did not of their own accord plan to drive the great power of Russia, then Europe, and finally the whole world into a war of unparalleled terribleness.

I need not remind you of the relations between General Soukhomlinoff and the French group of Chauvinists, M. Poincaré and his associates. It is well known that the election of M. Poincaré to the Presidency was a sign of an aggressive Franco-Russian alliance against Germany, and that General Soukhomlinoff was ordered to Paris to play the Presidency of the French Republic into M. Poincaré's hands. At that time in Paris General Soukhomlinoff made a statement about the Russian Army and the alterations of Russian plans for mobilization, while shortly before the war he provokingly repeated well-known articles in the Bourse Gazette (of Petrograd) about Russia's preparedness. A long time previous aggressive plans against Germany were prepared by an influential political group in France, England, and Russia.

Regarding English influence at Petrograd during the critical days July 29 and 30, (1914,) I only need to refer to a telegram of the Reuter correspondent at Petrograd and to the well-known report of the Belgian Chargé d'Affaires, de l'Escaille, which clearly show that the certainty of English support strengthened the determination for war of the leading men of Russia.

### Alleges Attempt to Dupe Germany

While Russia thus prepared an aggressive war, and secretly mobilized not only against Austria-Hungary but against Germany, attempts were made to mislead and betray Germany in order to gain time for Russia to move her troops to the frontiers. The word of honor of General Januschkevitch will live in history, as Major von Eggeling, who at that time was the German Military Attaché at Petrograd, telegraphed the word of honor of the Chief of the Russian General Staff and expressly referred to his statement that until July 29 in the afternoon no order of any kind for mobilization had been given.

General Januschkevitch declared to the German Military Attaché that the reassuring statements of General Soukhomlinoff of July 27 regarding the eventual Russian intentions as to mobilization were still good. Despite this, General Januschkevitch had in his pocket the prepared mobilization order. Germany was to be duped with a proposal of arbitration at The Hague Court while Russia busily continued to bring her army to a war footing for the attack which had been planned.

In this connection the importance of the Czar's telegram to Emperor William, which was dispatched July 30 at 1:20 o'clock in the afternoon, and which announced the general mobilization of the Russian Army, is evident. This mobilization, according to the Czar's well-known ukase of 1912, meant war against Germany, and was intended to maintain the deception that the military measures which were in force were solely ordered for reasons of defense against Austrian preparations.

The Czar's telegram also announced the visit of General Tatischtscheff with a letter to Emperor William. Where was Tatischtscheff? Can it be possible that General Soukhomlinoff and General Januschkevitch and their accomplices prevented his departure, or was the announcement of his mission only intended deceitfully to lull Germany into security?

### Hegemony of Europe

Germany was obliged to enter a most serious fight for the defense of her existence because she was threatened by her neighbors, France and Russia, which were eager for booty and power, which wanted to destroy her, and which were urged on by the island empire beyond the Channel because England was of the opinion that it was a fight for the hegemony of Europe, as Viscount Grey, formerly British Foreign Secretary, once said.

England did not like to see contested this hegemony, which she believed was menaced. For this reason she supported Germany's hostile neighbors in their policy which aimed at war. Neither the German Government nor the German people, which are unshakably devoted to their imperial leader, were at that time or at any other time filled with the lust of power or conquest, as has been falsely ascribed.

If the contrary had been true, then Germany would certainly not have allowed (to pass?) the opportunity which more than once was offered, in the years which elapsed between the last war with France and the outbreak of today's world war, to begin the war under less difficult conditions. In that period of European history were moments when England and others were paralyzed by warlike complications, outside of European. Despite these facts, our hands did not seize the sword which, as Mr. Lloyd George once admitted, we were forced to keep sharp, owing to Germany's menaced position in the heart of Europe.

Nothing else but the mischievous will of the criminal enemy war agitators forced us into the sanguinary defensive war for life and freedom. No American note can alter this historical truth, which now again is confirmed by General Soukhomlinoff and General Januschkevitch, nor can the American note shake our firm determination to fight in loyal harmony between the crown and the people for our war aims, namely, maintenance of our rights to Germany's integrity, freedom, and a future of assured peaceful development, for which our heroes have now been fighting and bleeding for more than three years.

### Charged With Suppression

On Sept. 7 the Russian newspapers reached Copenhagen with details of the testimony to which the Chancellor had referred, and it appeared that he had suppressed or overlooked important parts of it in arriving at his conclusions as expressed above.

Accounts of the trial published in the Novoe Vremya of Petrograd showed that in the attempt to prove that Russia was responsible for beginning the war the Germans either deliberately suppressed or omitted important parts of the testimony given by General Januschkevitch, ex-Chief of the Russian General Staff.

In its report of the trial the semi-official German news agency omitted in its entirety a passage regarding an interview between General Januschkevitch and the German Military Attaché in Petrograd. It appears from the Novoe Vremya that General Januschkevitch testified precise reports had been received that German mobilization already was secretly in progress. The Russian Staff knew that this could be done, under the German law, without formal proclamation, whereas in Russia a public manifesto from the Emperor was necessary.

On the following day, according to the testimony given, a dispatch was received from the Russian Ambassador at Berlin confirming the previous information that the German mobilization was in progress. The Emperor then expressed his thanks to General Januschkevitch for not having revoked the mobilization order.

## The Guns in Sussex

### By SIR ARTHUR CONAN DOYLE

Light green of grass and richer green of bush
　　Slope upwards to the darkest green of fir;
How still! How deathly still! And yet the hush
　　Shivers and trembles with some subtle stir,
Some far-off throbbing, like a muffled drum
　　Beaten in broken rhythm oversea,
To play the last funereal march of some
　　Who die today that Europe may be free.

The deep-blue heaven, curving from the green,
　　Spans with its shimmering arch the flowery zone;
In all God's earth there is no gentler scene,
　　And yet I hear that awesome monotone.
Above the circling midge's piping, shrill,
　　And the long droning of the questing bee,
Above all sultry Summer sounds, it still
　　Mutters its ceaseless menaces to me.

And as I listen all the garden fair
　　Darkens to plains of misery and death,
And looking past the roses I see there
　　Those sordid furrows, with the rising breath
Of all things foul and black. My heart is hot
　　Within me as I view it, and I cry,
" Better the misery of these men's lot
　　Than all the peace that comes to such as I! "

And strange that in the pauses of the sound
　　I hear the children's laughter as they roam,
And then their mother calls, and all around
　　Rise up the gentle murmurs of a home.
But still I gaze afar, and at the sight
　　My whole soul softens to its heartfelt prayer,
" Spirit of Justice, Thou for whom they fight,
　　Ah, turn, in mercy, to our lads out there!

" The froward peoples have deserved Thy wrath,
　　And on them is the Judgment as of old.
But if they wandered from the hallowed path,
　　Yet is their retribution manifold.
Behold all Europe, writhing on the rack,
　　The sins of fathers grinding down the sons,
How long, O Lord! " He sends no answer back,
　　But still I hear the mutter of the guns.

# The Socialists and the War

## Labor Conference in London

THE British Labor Party conference on Aug. 21, 1917, decided by the narrow margin of 3,000 votes, in a total of 1,234,000 ayes to 1,231,-000 noes, to send delegates to the Stockholm conference. Its previous vote to send delegates had been 1,846,000 ayes to 550,000 noes. It was this earlier action that had caused the break in the English Cabinet and forced the retirement of Arthur Henderson. The close vote on Aug. 21, notwithstanding the ardent appeals for affirmative action by Mr. Henderson, was regarded as a victory for the opposition, and the Stockholm conference was regarded from that moment as doomed. Such, indeed, proved to be the fact, for a few days later the conference was called off to an indefinite date and Mr. Henderson himself withdrew his support; the English labor vote in its favor was subsequently recast and was found to be overwhelmingly against representation.

An effort was made late in August to revive the International in England by an inter-allied Socialist conference of the Entente nations.

The United States was not represented at the conference, and one South African delegate was the only representative of the British overseas dominions. Delegates from pacifist bodies were in the majority. Seventy delegates, representing Great Britain, Belgium, Russia, France, Portugal, Greece, South Africa, and Italy, were present. More than half of them were British, representing various sections of the Socialist and Labor Parties. The Trade Union Congress, representing the bulk of British labor, had only eight delegates in attendance, and the Labor Party twelve.

The conference considered the reports of two commissions, one appointed to deal with the general question of the International Socialist Conference at Stockholm and the other to consider and report on the drafts of peace terms submitted by the various Socialist parties. The commission on the Stockholm conference decided by a majority to recommend that all sections of the Socialist and labor organizations should be represented at that gathering, and voiced a protest against the decision of the British Government to refuse passports to delegates.

The Belgians made a united protest against attendance at the Stockholm conference. They, with their supporters from other countries, decided that Emile Vandervelde, Belgian Minister of Munitions, should move, and that Camille Huysmans, Secretary to the International Socialist Congress, should second an amendment to the committee report, to the effect that the Socialists of Entente countries should not be represented at Stockholm. This amendment was defeated.

It having been decided that the conference must be unanimous before any action could be taken, this protest of the Belgians and others left the matter where it was before the London conference met.

### Declaration By the Delegates

A declaration signed by the Belgian, British, French, Greek, and Italian representatives at the conference in London, where, it is declared, the Socialists of the allied countries reaffirmed their faith in the principles proclaimed at their first reunion, was published Sept. 2 by Humanité, the Socialist organ.

The European conflict, says the declaration, began through the antagonism of the capitalistic group, through imperialistic policies and the deliberate aggression of Germany toward its neighbors. This aggression, it is asserted, still menaces the existence of nationalities and faith in international treaties. More than ever, continues the declaration, the Socialists, after three years of war, believe that the victory of German imperialism would spell defeat and the elimination of democracy and liberty from the

# CONTROLLERS OF AMERICAN SHIPPING

**WILLIAM C. REDFIELD**
Secretary of Commerce
*(Photo by Pack)*

**EDWIN N. HURLEY**
President of the Shipping Board
*(Photo © Harris & Ewing)*

**ADMIRAL W. L. CAPPS**
Manager of Emergency Fleet Corporation
*(© Harris & Ewing from Paul Thompson.)*

**BAINBRIDGE COLBY**
Member of the Shipping Board
*(Photo Davis & Sanford)*

# BUSINESS MEN AIDING THE GOVERNMENT

**BERNARD M. BARUCH**
Chairman of Central Buying Commission
*(Photo © Underwood & Underwood)*

**ROBERT S. BROOKINGS**
Member of the War Industries Board
*(© Harris & Ewing from Paul Thompson.)*

**HARRY A. GARFIELD**
Fuel Controller

**ROBERT S. LOVETT**
Member of the War Industries Board
*(Photo by the Misses Selby)*

world. The Russian revolution is alluded to as not having succeeded in coordinating the popular energies against the militarism of the Central Powers, while the great American democracy has had to enter the conflict to impose the recognition of right upon the brutal domination of the Central Empires.

It is to combat definitely this evil influence of imperialism, the document proceeds, that the allied nations must pursue vigorously their military efforts and show clearly what are their war aims and their peace conditions, for a stable peace must be founded upon right. The Socialists find the best guarantee of this kind of peace in the principles affirmed by the Russian revolutionists, with certain exceptions, namely, that peace without contributions must not exclude just reparation for damages and peace without annexation must not exclude dis-annexation of territories conquered by force.

### Belgium Must Be Indemnified

The right of peoples to govern themselves can only be brought about by a society of nations founded upon international law and strong enough to resist all Governments which might attempt to violate that law, the argument runs. The Socialists, accordingly, desire Belgium to be restored and indemnified for the violation of her neutrality; they want Serbia and Rumania re-established in independence and economic life and the Polish question settled in conformity with a Polish plebiscite and with the complete restoration of Poland in its original independence in view. They desire the same principles applied to all Europe, from Alsace-Lorraine to the Balkans, including Trieste and the Trentino, so that each shall be nationally reunited with the country to which its inhabitants desire to belong.

The Socialists say they feel it an essential duty to oppose every offer to transform a war of right and defense into one of conquest, which might bring about new conflicts. The peace they desire, a just and durable peace, is not possible, according to their profound conviction, until all the peoples enjoy democratic institutions which shall guarantee them against dynastic ambitions and the political and economic designs of hegemonies, castes, and ruling classes.

The Socialists express themselves as convinced that the peoples of Germany and Austria cannot achieve their desired peace until they have discarded their present irresponsible Governments for democratic régimes, which shall include the downfall of militarism.

The declaration concludes with the statement that this must be the last of all wars, but adds the reminder that this can be achieved only if the Socialists of all parties work for the creation of a pacific Federation of the United States of Europe and the World, which shall assure the liberty of the peoples and the unity, independence, and autonomy of the nations.

An incomplete conference of international Socialists opened at Stockholm Sept. 5, 1917. The German delegates present were Georg Ledebour, Social Democratic leader; Hugo Haase, leader of the Socialist minority in the Reichstag, and Arthur Stadthagen, Social Democratic member of the Reichstag. There were also present Russian, Rumanian, Finnish, and Scandinavian delegates. It was announced on Sept. 7 that the conference originally proposed would be postponed for two months, but it was generally recognized that the movement had ended in a fiasco. This was confirmed on Sept. 13, when it was announced that on account of the complications in Sweden over the exposure at Buenos Aires the conference, if called again, would not meet in Sweden.

# A German Socialist on the Reichstag Resolutions

EDUARD BERNSTEIN, minority Socialist leader and member of the Reichstag for Breslau, contributed an article to Die Neue Zeit, a German Socialist weekly, Aug. 3, 1917, in which he assailed the Reichstag peace resolutions. In the course of his article he quoted from the July 19 speech of Hugo Haase, leader of the Independent Social Democrats:

"'The statement regarding the beginning of the war is historically untenable,' Herr Haase said, * * * 'and the same verdict must be passed upon the new Chancellor's version of those events. We do not forget Austria's ultimatum to Serbia, Austria's mobilization against Russia, nor the councils held here in Berlin July 5, 1914, nor the activities of Tirpitz and von Falkenhayn in those critical days.' And after revealing the confused and equivocal nature of the Reichstag peace program, our colleague said: 'The resolution ends in a bellicose blare of trumpets (in schmetternde Kriegsfanfaren) and lashes the people into war-fury once more.' In truth, could any man read the closing words of the resolution as an invitation to peace? * * *

"The words 'Right to Development' contain the whole controversy between Socialism and Chauvinism, and can be used by the Jingo parties—not only Herr Michaelis, but Count Westarp and Herr Dietrich Schäfer and all the Ueberannexionisten — to cover their war aims. There is but one word that can draw a clear line between peace and imperialism * * * it is the right of self-determination for all peoples. That word is missing in the Reichstag's pronouncement. Not only is it missing, but its place is taken by phrases which leave the door open to all kinds of veiled annexations, economic and other; and instead of clinching the matter by a demand for international free trade, the Reichstag demands the 'freedom of the seas.' Listen to Haase on that:

"'What do you mean by "the freedom of the seas"? Before the war our fleet, in its brilliant expansion, sailed proudly and unhindered on every sea, and in peace its "freedom" was secure. * * * How do you propose to achieve this result in war? A Socialist world would be a world without war, where this problem could not arise. But as long as there are wars the freedom of the seas in war will belong to the strongest power. Where is your guarantee against that? There is but one way: the way of general disarmament and the abolition of capture at sea.'

## Reaction at the Helm

"The demand made in the threefold declaration of the pacifists closed with the sentence: 'Unless the Reichstag insists on disarmament as part of a general peace program, its ostensible intentions will assuredly—and justifiably—be misinterpreted abroad.' The reception of the report of July 19 abroad proves the justice of these words. * * * At first a profound impression was made, and all over Europe men breathed more freely. * * * In Germany and in every country a change was wrought under our very eyes * * * even the fiercest anti-German writers changed their tone a little * * * and everywhere men began to see light through the darkness of war. * * * But these hopes were utterly destroyed by the issue of the Ministerial crisis. Bethmann Hollweg fell, not before the new Block, (Centre, People's Party, and majority Socialists,) but before the sweeping attack of the Right, reinforced by all the elements of reaction in German society. He went, followed by the tears of the Left. * * * Bethmann fell before the onset of reaction. Tied hand and foot by his entourage—those serried ranks of reactionaries whose voice always has the last word in our affairs—he was powerless to make progress. And Michaelis * * *? He steps into office with the benediction of these gentlemen, hailed as the trusted agent of Hindenburg and Ludendorff, and his speech bears the hallmark of the approval of the High Command. * * * The army has won; and, politically, we know what 'the army' means. The manner in which the crisis has been solved is a manoeuvre * * * and even if half a dozen parliamentarians were made Ministers, the essence of the system remains absolutely unchanged. * * * We are not one inch nearer a parliamentary régime.

"Dr. Michaelis is not a parliamentary Chancellor * * * he is the hope of the stern, unbending Tories * * * and his declaration that German war aims could be realized within the limits of the majority resolution was but an empty favor (ein Blumensträusschen) thrown to the new bloc, which only made the resolution itself ring the more hollow. It is depressing to realize this, and we cannot be surprised that the promised jubilation fell flat. Let us acknowledge that the bourgeois parties have progressed in adopting the policy of the resolution * * * but we must also confess, with pain, that for Social Democrats it is a miserable compromise. Coalitions always lead to compromise, and, as is well known, I am not an uncompromising opponent of political coalitions. But this coalition means, not compromise, but the betrayal of our Socialist faith and the desertion of well-tried Socialist comrades. It throws doubt on the good faith of the German people. * * *

## The Real Enemy of Peace

"In the Chancellor's speech, security and guarantees figure largely. * * * Security is, in this war, the greatest of all questions; it appears in every speech of friend and foe alike * * * but it can only be found in a radical change of the State systems and in the uprooting of militarism. One accident or another may bring hostilities to an end * * * but there can be no enduring peace between the nations as long as militarism holds sway. And one of the causes which has given this question such prominence has been the capitulation of German Socialists to militarism. * * *

"The formation of the bloc with the Centre and the People's Party does not alter this, but rather emphasizes it * * * for the framers of the resolution have shown their anxiety not to arraign German militarism. * * * Here, if nowhere else, we had to say No! And in saying it we run no risk of being misunderstood, for our attitude is clearly defined in the memorial which Haase gave to the Dutch-Scandinavian Peace Committee on our behalf, and in the resolution which the Independent Socialists tabled in the Reichstag in the following form:

The Reichstag seeks a peace without annexations of any kind or indemnities, based on the right of self-determination of all peoples.

It demands the restoration of Belgium and compensation for all the wrongs done to her.

The Reichstag demands the immediate initiation of peace negotiations on the basis of this program: an international agreement for general disarmament, freedom of international trade as well as unrestricted international intercourse; an international agreement for the protection of workmen from exploitation; recognition of the equal rights for all the inhabitants of any State, irrespective of sex, race, speech or religion; protection of national minorities; an international tribunal for compulsory arbitration.

For the execution of this peace program and for the attainment of peace, the immediate raising of the state of siege is the most urgent prerequisite. Equally indispensable is the complete democratization of the whole constitution and government of the Empire and its constituent States, which can only find a final and sure issue in the creation of the social republic.

"Let any one compare the true mind of socialism, thus clearly and succinctly set forth, with the Reichstag resolution and then bethink himself how differently German Social Democracy would stand before the world today, how much nearer it would have come to an understanding with the Socialist-Labor Parties of other countries, and thus to the end of the war, if the resolution I have just quoted had been backed by the united force of all its representatives, one hundred strong, in the German Reichstag."

# Creating Belgium's New Army

### By General Leclercq

*Military Attaché of the Belgian Legation*

THE problem of recruiting for the Belgian Army is a very complex and difficult one, inasmuch as the enemy holds more than 95 per cent. of our territory and keeps in close confinement about 80 per cent. of the Belgian population.

When, for instance, a young man, residing in Charleroi, attempts to join the Belgian Army, he meets with almost insuperable difficulties. Every man of military age residing in the occupied part of Belgium must register at the kommandantur every three or four days, and his failure to do so instantly reveals his absence. Once he is gone he can only travel during the night, in a northerly direction, and he is obliged to avoid all cities and towns, as he could not explain his presence there; he must live on what he can obtain en route or on whatever food he has been able to take with him.

After ten days he reaches the vicinity of the Belgo-Dutch frontier; this boundary is barred by a triple net of barbed wire, through which runs at regular intervals a high-tension electric current; moreover, the border is closely guarded by German sentries and frequent patrols.

The ingenious ways and means resorted to by some Belgian youths to attempt to overcome all these obstacles cannot be revealed here; but a great number of young men have unfortunately either been shot by the enemy, electrocuted on the wires, or made prisoners, and, as is known, the fate of a prisoner in Germany is far from happy.

If the young Belgian has succeeded in escaping into Holland he has still to cross the North Sea to England; here new dangers confront him—the German submarines are particularly numerous in these waters and sometimes succeed in stopping and searching ships.

Such are the reasons why the main contingents of recruits cannot be obtained from the occupied territory. They are composed of Belgians who were residing abroad before the war or who took refuge in foreign countries at the beginning of the campaign and enlisted in the army as soon as they reached the age of 18.

When they fulfill certain prescribed conditions of age and ability they may choose their service, but the majority are assigned to the infantry. There are about fifteen instruction camps for recruits; the training period covers from four to six months and is, of course, very strenuous. As soon as the new recruit is considered sufficiently trained he is sent to the depot of the army division to which he is assigned and whence he will join his regiment at the front.

The twofold difficulty of recruiting and organizing the instruction camps outside of the country, however, did not prevent the numerical strength of the army from continuing to increase in spite of the enormous loss of one-third of its force in the heavy battles at Liége, Namur, Antwerp, and along the Yser.

At present the fighting forces of the Belgian Army may be estimated at from 200,000 to 220,000 men.

## How Officers Are Trained

The immediate need of subordinate officers has necessitated the opening of instruction camps for auxiliary sub-Lieutenants, (Centres d'Instruction de sous-Lieutenants auxiliaires, or C. I. S. L. A.). The different arms have their separate instruction camps, so there are special courses for infantry, artillery, cavalry, and engineering corps. They are spread all over the northwest of France. Young men who possess a complete high school education, who have had six months' active service at the front, and are recommended by their superiors in rank, can be admitted to the course. This training, which is very arduous, covers a period of four months.

The following details, for instance, explain the working of the instruction camps for the cavalry: This school was started in April, 1915, and is located in an agricultural domain, comprising a castle, a farm, and various auxiliary buildings suitable to house some hundred men and a like number of horses. There is also some low-lying ground that is used as a field for exercising. The country, being well wooded, rough, and hilly, offers all the requisites to train future officers to all the daring risks of horsemanship necessary to cavalry reconnoitring. The horses are mostly of American origin, of light build and thoroughbred.

The military students rise at 5 A. M.; a daily drill of about one hour in vaulting makes them so supple that the majority forthwith succeed in jumping four horses standing abreast. Drill is mostly done in the open air. The candidate has to ride horseback from six to eight hours daily, going through riding exercises connected with the school of cavalrymen, and must specialize in the study of reconnoitring as required of a cavalry officer. The students must jump all obstacles in the way of streams, ditches, steep banks, &c.

Four hours a day the candidate devotes himself to theory, and as the cavalryman does nearly as much trench service as the infantryman the students are instructed in the principles of soldier training and are initiated in the technics required for tirailleurs, sentries, and trench diggers.

At the end of the drill the entire company travels 150 miles, in four stages, to reach the special instruction camps for gunners and grenadiers, (grenade throwers.) They also visit a training depot of the French Army specially designed for the study of suffocating gases and the means of fighting such gases.

When they leave the school these young men are appointed Adjutants, then Auxiliary Sub-Lieutenants, and are classified according to their record of service, their abilities, and their merits.

The training camps for infantry are conducted on the same principles. Each drill is first an experiment, leading to the regulation which the instructor wants to demonstrate, and the subsequent exercises explain these regulations. Each candidate has to keep a notebook and enter therein the kind of work done each day and the instructions received while engaged in such work.

### Schools for Specialists

Besides these general instruction camps, there are also schools for all special services which had to be created to comply with the needs of actual warfare. The handling of the machine gun is studied at Criel. This school possesses machine guns of all types used not only with the Belgian Army but also in the enemy countries. This makes it possible for the gunners to use every captured gun against those from whom it was taken.

The period of instruction extends over four weeks, and is continued in the units. It includes the study of the gun, its mechanism and its use in various fields and under all possible circumstances. How to assign a location, how to reach it under cover, how to conceal the location of guns and gunners from the enemy—all this forms part of the instructions. Nearly all noncommissioned and aspirant officers have gone through the Criel School.

There are also two schools for "grenadiers." Out of every company a noncommissioned officer is chosen and sent to this school; when he returns he becomes instructor in this particular line in his company; he trains special squads for this work, but each man is taught all principles and knows how to operate the gun. Such exercises take place one afternoon each week.

### School of Camouflage

There is also a school of masquerading, ("camouflage,") where the ways and means are taught to conceal what actually exists and to stimulate what does not exist. At present it is possible to approach in broad daylight on ordinary ground within sixty feet of an observing enemy. Batteries are concealed, false batteries are placed in position, observation posts are erected within a few yards from the enemy trenches.

# Belgium's Starving Women and Children

## Statement by Baron Moncheur

*Baron Moncheur, head of the Belgian Mission to the United States, gave to a representative of* THE NEW YORK TIMES *at the beginning of September, 1917, the following sketch of the increasing wretchedness of his people:*

BELGIUM only yesterday was one of the principal centres of human activity. Today the silence of death reigns over its mines and its factories. Belgium has become for its inhabitants merely a cage whose bars are formed of German bayonets. The enemy has robbed us of everything—money, provisions, raw material, and machinery. All commerce was destroyed and our factories put out of business. Consequently our workmen were thrown out of employment. I mention the causes of stagnation so that the resulting misery of our poor, famished people might be better comprehended.

Here in America just now one hears a great deal about the hardships the men must undergo on the fighting line—in the trenches. It is all very true that modern warfare is more terrible than any conception of wars formed in the human mind before. But the soldier has a far better time of it in this war than do the wretched householders who remain at home. A man on the firing line has the force of mental excitement as a kind of diversion, and he is removed from the scene of responsibility. He knows that his country is raising money to keep him at least moderately well fed. He doesn't feel the nag of hunger beneath his shirt, and after he becomes accustomed to it he finds it is rather healthful to sleep in the open air. Of course, it is a terrible thought that haunts him day and night, that he doesn't know which moment may be his last. His lot is not easy.

But, come away from the trenches; go into the homes of the common people, and even the homes of the hitherto moderately rich, if you would find the real sorrow of Europe today. And all the sorrow of the war seems to be focused with dreadful stress upon poor little Belgium. Just imagine a nation on half rations of food. If one person gets enough to eat, some other person is bound to starve. You well-fed Americans can with difficulty draw the mental picture of a nation on one-half ration. I mean that a person is only getting to eat one-half the amount of food theoretically necessary to keep an idle man alive.

Those of our men who can find work to do often give out on account of insufficient nourishment. Physical resistance to sickness has been greatly diminished by reason of this state of semi-starvation, and the mortality rate has become enormously increased. I have seen statistics indicating that the mortality rate for the first three months of 1917 among workmen was three and a half times greater than the average rate for the same period in previous years. Every day the bread line becomes longer and longer. One of the agents of the Commission for Relief reports that in a certain district of Belgium applicants for the daily soup ration increased from 60,000 to 400,000 in two months.

A short time ago a member of the Commission for Relief visited a town of 1,000 population and singled out a number of homes of the working people at random. This investigation showed:

1. That the people were living almost exclusively on the rations of the Commission for Relief, with little or no nourishment in the way of native foodstuffs.

2. That the ration from the Relief Commission was often eaten in advance by many families, so that the semi-weekly bread ration would not last until the next one came around. In this way thousands would go for more than one day a week without food in the house.

3. That as a general rule two scant meals a day were eaten, and the families went to bed without supper early in the evening to shun the pangs of hunger.

4. That the women and older children (not admitted to the soupe scolaire)

suffered especially because they were obliged to give a part of their daily bread ration to the father, who required this to give him strength for his daily work.

5. That the workingmen were in an emaciated and greatly weakened condition because their work was using up their bodies faster than their scant food supply could replace this spent energy.

This same agent of the Relief Commission reported conditions as being so bad in this particular locality that even the German soldiers were often so moved with pity as to divide their own limited rations with the hungry little children about them.

It was found that workmen were going to their posts of duty with almost empty dinner pails, a part and sometimes the whole of their midday meal consisting of sliced rababaga, the Belgian cattle beet. These workmen had fallen off in weight amazingly during the first three months of the present year, anywhere from ten to forty pounds. A general strike was declared last April, the workmen simply saying to their employers that they had not the physical strength to work any longer. There were no differences between the workmen and their employers, no disputes to be settled, but just a condition of incapacity to do the work required because of being half starved.

About twenty of the wives of these workmen appeared before the representatives of the Relief Commission to plead the cause of the families of all the laborers of the province. They were led by a woman whose face indicated that she was intelligent and accustomed to better times in the past. This woman broke down in trying to voice the sufferings of 300,000 persons in the province, and it was found that she was on the verge of starvation. To all such persons and such delegations the agents of the Relief Commission could only say that they were doing their best and would try to do better in the future. The daily ration allowed consisted of bread, 300 grams; rice, peas, or beans, 16 grams; bacon and lard, 13 grams; herrings, coffee, and so on, very small quantities; soupe populaire, 1 liter;

sugar, (native,) 20 grams; butter, (native,) 3 grams. This ration furnishes a total of 1,130 calories a day in point of food value, which is scarcely half enough to keep an idle man alive.

It is needless to talk of the prices of foodstuffs in Belgium. To know that they are prohibitive is sufficient. I was informed just before I was leaving that practically no meat was available. In London, Paris, and Rome they have what they call meatless days. In Belgium every day is a meatless day. I was told that the cheapest grade of half-spoiled veal, which was about all the meat that ever found its way into Belgium, was selling for 7 francs per kilo, which means about 70 cents a pound. Cold-storage eggs were selling at 50 centimes each, or about $1.20 a dozen. Milk was hard to get at 70 centimes per liter. In fact, in the rural districts the cows had nearly all been killed for food. Many a baby has died in Belgian cities for lack of milk, which used to come from the country near by. Butter was beyond the reach of all except the wealthy, going at about $1.75 a pound. Potatoes were selling at around 15 cents a pound. Carrots were 13 cents a pound. But what is the use of talking about the prices of food commodities where the consumer has no money with which to purchase food?

It has been carefully figured out by the Commission for Relief that as long as the imported ration is as small as it has been the last few months the demand for native food will be such that it cannot, at the outside, satisfy more than 5,000,000, and these authorities, who have the situation so well in hand, plainly show that the remaining 2,000,000 people must depend solely upon the ration of the Relief Commission—or just one-half enough to support life.

In spite of all efforts on the part of the Germans to turn these suffering Belgians against England and her allies, and to cause them to lose faith in American charity, I rejoice to say that my people have not been fooled. They know where their friends are, and they feel the deepest gratitude to the people of the United States for their unfailing friendship and kindness.

# The Story of Kerensky's Life

## Told by One of His Russian Friends

V. V. Kiryakoff, a Russian journalist, recently contributed this glowing sketch of Kerensky to the Niva of Petrograd, from which it has been translated for CURRENT HISTORY MAGAZINE.

"* * * Him as her first love,
The heart of Russia cannot forget."

WHO is not familiar with the name of Alexander Federovich Kerensky, first citizen of free Russia, first national tribune Socialist, first national Minister of Justice, Minister of Truth and Honesty? From day to day now they are writing about A. F. Kerensky in the newspapers and journals of all the world; congratulatory telegrams are flying to him from all parts of Russia and Europe; delegations from Russia and foreign parts greet in his person the revolutionary Russian Nation, which was created by the mild, honest, kindly revolution. Thousands of people attribute to him the joy of their present free organization and their escape from the dark past of oppression.

In a word, there is now no more popular man, no name more famous than that of Alexander Federovich Kerensky. It has become with us and abroad, so to say, a title of honor, a symbol of the great, beneficent Russian revolution.

Why are all hearts drawn to Kerensky? Why is all attention centred upon his words and actions? Why has the passionate heart of the great Russian revolution made precisely him its first, unforgettable love? It is about this that I wish now to tell.

### Kerensky's Early Youth

Not long ago I heard on a street car such a conversation as this:

"How do you explain Russia's warm love for A. F. Kerensky?"

"It is by mutuality: Russia loves the one who already for a long time has passionately loved Russia, loved her honorably, as sons do, with real love."

And that is the truth. He has loved Russia passionately, with a son's love, first of all on account of her sufferings, which for long centuries were inflicted by her hereditary tormentors, the auto-cratic Czars and their doglike guardsmen. He loved warmly with a brother's love the whole working nation because of that groan which for centuries was rising not only "over the great Russian river," but over all the great Russian land.

That "song like a groan," Alexander Federovich first heard in his cradle by the great Russian river. He was born on the Volga, in Simbirsk, in the memorable year 1881. His father, Fedor Michaelovich, was director of the Simbirsk Gymnasium. The first breath of A. F. Kerensky (he was born on April 22) nearly coincides with the last breath of the great fighters for Russia's freedom—the national martyrs, Sophia Perovsky, Timothy Michaelov, Andrei Zhelyaboff, Kibalchich, and Riskoff—who were hanged by order of Alexander III. in Semenovsky Square.

The first childish recollections of Kerensky, then a boy of 6, according to his own words, were a perplexed remembrance of the silent terror which seized Simbirsk when the city learned of the punishment of the son of a local director of the public school, a student, Alexander Illitch Ulyanoff, for participating in the attempt of the last national martyrs to kill Czar Alexander III., (March 1, 1887,) then already entirely crushed under the elephant's burden of his autocracy over unhappy Russia.

The first school recollection of Kerensky is about his comrades, mates in childish plays, children of the working people, left by the Czar Alexander outside the gymnasium's threshold. "Peasants! and they are creeping into the gymnasium to learn!" exclaimed the Czar in 1887, when told that one of the political prisoners was an assistant of a peasant's son who was teaching in the gymnasium. And the Czar's serf, at that time Minister of Education, more truly a minister of darkness, Count Delyanov, prohibited the taking into the gymnasium of peasants and citizens' children, "kitchen children." Such were the first days of schooling which the "father Czar" gave to his little subject, A. F. Kerensky.

Entirely different was the schooling which the mother Volga gave him. The Volga carried to the child not only the "song like a groan," but free songs about the beloved national hero, Stenka Razin, whose famous rock is found in the vicinity of Simbirsk. Who knows whether there was not burned into the childish soul of the future first citizen of free Russia the words of the national song:

If there is in Russia even one person,
Who with people's falsehood is not acquainted,
Who has not oppressed the muzhick,
Who loves freedom as his dear mother,
And in her name is struggling,
Let that one boldly go to enter that rock,
Let him to it lay down a keen ear,
And the great cliff, all that Stephan thought,
All that, will repeat to him.
—From "The Rock of Stenka Razin."

## Kerensky's Gymnasium Years

In the year 1889 Kerensky's father was transferred from Simbirsk to Tashkent. With him went also "Sasha Kerensky," as his companions in Tashkent Gymnasium called him. The kindly epithet from the pupils tells better than all the long descriptions how they loved him. In youthful mischievousness and pranks and in "warlike actions" against disliked or ridiculous teachers, as in the joint reading and development circles, he was everywhere and always, to persons of his own age, Sasha Kerensky.

Tashkent is the gate to Siberia. The groaning of the political strugglers for free Russia, who were languishing at that time in the galleys or in exile, were near now, and more audible. Sasha Kerensky's ear, attentive to the people's sufferings, with pain took in all the stories about the unendurable situation of the nation's friends martyred by the Czar's prison officials in Siberia's "places of destruction." Punishment and whisperings go upon much freer tongues there than in Central Russia.

What George Kennan has since related to us in his famous book about Siberia, still earlier was written in "heart's blood and in the fluid of the nerves" on the impressible soul of A. F. Kerensky and printed in his youthful marrow.

From all that we have read, heard, and seen of the living outline of Sasha Kerensky the Creator fashioned in him the outline of the whole everlasting picture of the sub-voluntary life of the entire Russian Nation—the laborious, patient, innocent, all-enduring, all-forgiving, much-suffering Russian Nation. And he loved it, that Russian Nation, with all his first passion, an early youth's love, penetrated with deep respect for the first strugglers for the freedom and happiness of the nation.

## Student Years at Petrograd

In 1899 Kerensky finished at Tashkent Gymnasium and entered the Petrograd University under the Law Faculty. The years 1899 and 1900 in our fatherland's life were broken up. The second famine seized the eastern part of Russia and revolutionized the people's thought, placing before them the questions of evolution and revolution.

The last ten years of the nineteenth century ran by under the sign of cultural-educational work on behalf of the nation. National books, national newspapers, national reading rooms, national theatres, even national operas, behold the line, sanctioned by law, along which at that time went the activities of the Russian intellect and especially of Russian youth.

Political non-legalized activity traveled along the same paths. It was the day of "The Group of Free Labor," G. V. Plechanov, Axelred and Viera Zasulich; the organization, under N. Lenin, of the Russian Social Democratic Party; the organization of the Social Revolutionary Party, with the zealous participation of Gershuny and of the "Grandmother of the Russian Revolution," E. K. Breshko-Breshkovsky. Both of these non-legalized political currents maintained themselves on the icy surface of legalized social life. Under the form of legalized literary Marxism, there were Peter

Struve, Bogucharsky-Jakovloff, and others, (" Novoe Slovo " and " Nachalo,") and under legalized nationalism there were N. K. Michaelovsky, V. G. Korolenko, V. V., (Vorontzoff,) and others, (" Russkoe Bogatstvo.")

The legally permitted literary struggle of the two fundamental political and social currents awakened the youth and likewise divided them into two political camps.

The workingmen's circles, at first " economists " and later " politicals "; peasant circles, at first " social educationals " and later the " political revolutionaries "; circles of " national rights " among the revolutionary formations of the intellectuals—these were the first watercourses of the non-legalized revolutionary work in Russia at the end of the last century.

Among these currents of social and national thought Kerensky formed his political convictions. Love of the nation and of the unfortunate people was always growing and broadening in his honest breast. That love pushed him into the party which is nearest to the nation, the party of the peasantry and the workingmen, the party which has written on its flag, " Land and liberty for the whole working nation! By struggle you will obtain your rights! "—the party of the " social revolutionists."

About 1904, the year of Kerensky's finishing with the Law Faculty of Petrograd University, the social revolutionists had already definitely come together in a compact body and sent forth the heroic political martyrs, Karpovich, Balmashoff, Egor Sazonoff, and others. These men took upon their own shoulders the heavy task of freeing their fatherland from the Czar's life-guardsmen, the tyrants of the nation, the Ministers Bogolyepoff, Sipyagin, and Pleve.

## The Revolution of 1905-06

All his time which was free from studious occupations and social activities A. F. Kerensky spent with the family of L. Baranovsky, a brother of the Tashkent General, Baranovsky. He married Olga Llvovna, the daughter of L. Baranovsky, in the year 1904.

After finishing with the university Kerensky turned entirely to social and political activity. The social revolutionists already had a solid organization in Petrograd. To one of its party groups Kerensky united himself, presently paying for this by arrest and imprisonment.

Events in the meanwhile were developing. After the " punishing " of V. K. Pleve by the social revolutionists on July 25, 1904, and of the Grand Duke Sergei Alexanderovich, Feb. 5, 1905, the Government went backward. There appeared a manifesto on Feb. 18, 1905, about attracting into the Government people clothed with the nation's confidence. About the 6th there was an announcement about the establishment of local councilors, as they were called, the " Bulginsky " Duma, but it did not satisfy a single class of the population. Then this period ended, Oct. 17, 1905, in the granting of a Constitution, with freedom and a legislative Duma.

The First Duma met on April 27, 1906. That Duma was the " nation's wrath." The nation had finally met the Government, and expressed to it directly and frankly its thoughts about land and freedom. In answer to this the Czar and his Government dissolved the First Duma.

The calling of the Second Governmental Duma was set for February, 1907. All the parties, already fully organized, hastily began to prepare. A. F. Kerensky took an active part in the elections. At that time the party of social revolutionists gave up the idea of " boycotting " the Duma and announced an " entrance " into it.

In Petrograd was formed a circle of " Land and Liberty," occupied in preparing for the election of " S. Rs." (social revolutionists) to the Second Governmental Duma. In this organization Kerensky was a zealous member. I recall his young, thin figure—lively, active, always burning with internal fire. About him at that time they were saying: " Always in the vanguard with bared breast." His strong speeches burned with the fire of feeling. His characteristically fluent words always astonished with their directness, precision, and quickness; his tactical suggestions carried with them the stamp of Governmental wisdom.

## The Period of Reaction

The Second Duma was scorched in the fire of reaction and espionage. Many of the social democrats and social revolutionists went into prison, into exile, to the galleys, and to the scaffold.

On June 3, 1907, a new election law was published, creating a Third Governmental Duma of the nobles. Reaction was violent. Officialism took vengeance on the nation and the nation's friends for the late defeat, and it struck hard. The courts were flooded with political prosecutions; the prisons were filled with arrested men and women. To Siberia and to the galleys long processions were dragged. The executioners could not get through with their hangings.

A. F. Kerensky took up the defense of his friends in the party. Having connected himself with one of the most famous members of the bar, and occupying himself solely with judicial work, which he carried on so successfully as to promise him a very high rank in the law, Kerensky turned aside from all this to throw himself into the defense of " politicals " without distinction of party, but most frequently of all on behalf of " S. Rs."

Out of all the numerous political trials of the period of reaction the one in which Kerensky shone most brilliantly was that of the Dashnaktzutiuns, a socialistic Armenian party closely allied to the social revolutionists. In this trial the Czar's investigators and judges manufactured false documents. When in 1913 began the famous Beiliss trial, Kerensky offered his advocacy to set forth that matter; and for the bringing out cf a resolution of protest he was sentenced by the Government to one month in prison. However, the Government at that time did not succeed in locking him up, for he was already a member of the Fourth Duma.

The shooting down of the workingmen in the Lena gold mines of the Lena Association caused such suffering in the soul of Kerensky that he decided to go himself to Lena and investigate the entire matter. As a result he not only laid the case before the Duma but gave out a separate pamphlet, " Truth About Lena " —which was immediately confiscated by the Government.

## Kerensky as a Deputy

At the time of the elections for the Fourth Duma, in the 300th year of the House of Romanoff, the socialist political parties almost entirely disappeared from the stage. Their members were scattered like dust; some languished in the galleys, in the prisons, and in exile; some ran across the frontiers; some resorted to living in huts and went into common day labor.

The Socialist Revolutionary Party, inasmuch as it was most dangerous to the Government, was visited with the heaviest penalties. The Government sought to thrust a knife into its very heart. What the Czar's executioners could not do was accomplished by his spies—Azeef and his followers.

To go to the Fourth Duma under the flag of social revolution was impossible. The situation required conspiracy, the painting of the outside with " protective coloring." Thus arose the " Workingmen," the " labor group." The labor group played the rôle of protective color also in the First Duma for all social revolutionists who did not want to be subjected to party discipline in the matter of " boycotting " the First Duma.

A boycott of the First Duma was announced by the social revolutionists because that party considered it necessary to call, not a Duma, but a Constitutional Assembly. Now the labor group had to play the rôle of protective coloring not only for those already emancipated from party discipline, but for those actual members of the party who had decided to serve as a speaking trumpet of the national will in the Fourth Duma.

However, that unavoidable ruse of political warfare was seen through by the Czar's Government, and besides Kerensky not a single " S. R." went into the Governmental Duma. Kerensky got into the Fourth Duma from a small town, Volsk, of the Province of Saratov, from the Second Dictrict of the city electors.

The Government's spies did not succeed in getting evidence against Kerensky, so that the formal fact of his election was declared in accordance with strict law.

### Shadowed Everywhere by Spies

The Czar's Government decided upon a contest with the nation's friends, who were consequently the Government's sworn enemies, and the means used were the usual ones—its spies. Every step of Kerensky was known to the Police Department: when and where he went, or had gone, how much time he spent, with whom he went out, what he spoke about, what he had done, &c. Because of his liveliness of character and quickness of movement he received from the Police Department the characterizing nickname of "Quick One." The Police Department penetrated by its spies almost into Kerensky's very family. Kerensky took into his family a well-recommended young man, a certain Mitya Alimoff. According to Kerensky's own statement, Alimoff became a "great pet," that is, he was caressed and encouraged and helped in every thing he could do or be, and was sent to study at the Petrograd Psycho-Nerve Institute. Here that Mitya Alimoff was by the Secret Service Department taken as its dirty weapon. It is unknown when or how the unfortunate youth fell into the clutches of the Secret Service; it is only known that he sold Kerensky for 20 rubles a month.

When Kerensky learned of this, his grief was boundless. "If you only knew how I pity Mitya," said Kerensky to me. "Indeed, it is not his fault. He is young and inexperienced. It is the fault of these who ruined him. It is the fault of that accursed old rotten organization."

When Mitya Alimoff was arrested by the Saratoff Central Committee as a provocator, not long afterward, there was sent to the address of A. F. Kerensky, already Minister of Justice, a telegram: "Shoot, he has confessed." Kerensky immediately answered the Saratoff Committee with an official telegram to this effect: "If it is possible, liberate Alimoff. He will find his judge in his own conscience."

The labor group organization of the Fourth Duma moved Kerensky up to the rôle of a leader of that faction. I shall not dwell upon his five years' activity in that capacity. I will say only that there was not one question concerning the rights of the people to "land and liberty" which remained unilluminated by Kerensky in the Duma Tribune. Passionate, convincing speeches of the nation's friend, to my regret, reached the nation only in the form of extracts or simply continuous wide empty spaces. They sometimes compelled even the open enemies of the nation, such as Makaroff II. and Zamislovsky, to think.

Read or merely turn over the pages of the little book, "Activity of the Faction of the Labor Group in the Fourth Governmental Duma," prohibited and excluded from circulation by the Czar's Government, and you will see how firmly and passionately Kerensky was fighting for the rights of the entire laboring people, especially for the peasantry.

In July, 1915, on Kerensky's initiative, there was called at Petrograd, in his rooms, a conference of the representatives of the national currents—labor, national socialists, old and young social revolutionists—for the purpose of working out a general tactical platform for an active political struggle with the old administration. At that conference Kerensky stepped forth with brilliant speeches about the pressing necessity of the unity of all national currents and of the regeneration of the party of social revolutionists, and about the working up of a program of the party in connection with Russia's political and economic situation.

### As a Lecturer and Writer

Closely connected with Petrograd, Kerensky, however, did not limit his activity merely to the capital. All vacations of the Duma he usually spent in traveling the provinces, Moscow, Saratoff, Samar, Kazan, Charkov, Volsk, Tashkent, Lena, Samarkand, &c. Where, indeed, was not the "Quick One" making work for the department of police spies?

In every place where he was, if the smoldering coals of partisan political work did not at once break into flame, yet all this began to burn in the hearts

and minds of "sedimentary" workingmen, awakening in them a common party
consciousness, drawing them to a new
nearness to the nation, to work for its
happiness.

I remember in October, 1915, at Samar
they received from Kerensky a telegram:
" I shall come the 29th, arrange a lecture.
Theme:' Military Session of the Duma.' "

The information was spread. Whispers
started. They arranged with those "responsible." They got permission. An old
comrade, Joseph Abramovich Tzadikoff,
arranged the financial part of the lecture.

The "Quick One" arrived. He flew
everywhere. With jokes and stories of
Petrograd he awakened and sprinkled
every one with living water. On the
second day came the lecture. The Olympic Theatre was packed with people—
workingmen, peasants, intellectuals. A
warm, passionate speech was poured
forth like a stream during the course of
two hours. The situation of the country
became clear, clear to painfulness and
sorrow. " Oh, how well I have spent this
day! " cried Tzadikoff, returning from
the lecture and lying down on his bed.
Inside of an hour he died of ruptured
heart. Kerensky had given him the last
joy of his life, joy before dying, originat-
ing in the ideal heights of the soul.

I remember another October at the
same Samar, the October of 1916. Again
a telegram from Kerensky and again the
same contents. * * * The second
part of the lecture was presented by
Kerensky with such an uplift that the
auditorium fairly shook with thunders of
applause. Especially good were the concluding, almost prophetic, words of the
lecturer. I recollect them very well.

" But on the change of all that old
order," said Kerensky, "or rather disorder, will soon follow a new order. It
will bring to us democracy, unified
economic life, and democracy is already
coming. * * * I already clearly hear
the steps of the nation. Prepare to meet
it. Prepare to go with it, foot with foot
and hand in hand."

Coming out of the Olympic those who
had attended the lecture did not go away,
but stayed waiting Kerensky's exit. The
youths consulted together to arrange an
ovation for him; but he withdrew unnoticed from the building. The huge
crowd, dammed up in two streets, did not
depart for half an hour. The alarmed
police sent out a strong detachment of
mounted guards, but they were unnecessary. On finding that Kerensky had
already gone, the crowd peacefully departed.

If it is added that the whole gross
proceeds of the lecture were given by
Kerensky to the publication of the national journal of Samar, the News, closed
down by the administration afterward at
the fifth number, and to the help of
political exiles, it is hardly necessary to
say that Kerensky's lectures were one of
the abounding means for freeing the
nation from age-long political and social
oppression.

Such a burning activity did not permit
him to occupy himself diligently with
literature; yet he wrote some brilliant
articles on political themes. So, for example, in 1905-6 he worked for the journal
Burovyestnik. I especially recollect one
of his articles, in which he brought out
the thought that an election to the Constituent Assembly ought to be held among
the soldiers still to be found in Siberia
after the war with Japan. Kerensky's
book, " Truth About Lena," appeared as
an intense cry of a heart sickened by the
workingmen's situation. In recent years
Kerensky's articles on political questions
appeared in the national journals,
Zavyety and Severneya Zapisky.

## On the Eve of Revolution

It is a psychic peculiarity of Kerensky
that he has a " feeling in the nerves " for
political events, which often amounts to
prophetic foresight—what is called intui-
tion, sometimes called the " sixth sense."
This faculty of presentiment was shown
in Kerensky's speeches in the Duma delivered several months before the revolution. Thus, in the session of Oct. 16,
1916, Kerensky said:

Gentlemen, now you yourselves see that
all which it is possible to say about a
Government, and which it is possible to
allege against a Government, all is said.
We have heard not from the mouths of
those on the left, not from Russian liberals, but from mouths of Octobrists and
Conservatives, a declaration that the Gov-

ernment is " ruining the country," that it " appears to be treasonable "; that Russia's " future existence is threatened by a collapse of the Government." But what kind of deduction is to be made from these words? * * * If, say, the representative of the left wing of the Octobrists, S. I. Shidlovsky, were to say to us: " I am not a revolutionist, I denounce revolutionary methods," then truly Shidlovsky might be compared to Molière's hero, who in perplexity and astonishment one beautiful day found out that he had " said something in prose." Indeed, the proceeding in which S. I. Shidlovsky participated is revolutionary. * * * You, gentlemen, to the present time under the word " revolution " understand some kind of anti-Governmental activity, destroying the Government, when all the histories unite in saying that revolution is a method and sole means for saving Government—that it is the most strenuous moment of a struggle with a Government which is ruining a country. A revolutionary process is an objective process, and I will remind you that in the year 1789, in France, there was a Count Mirabeau who did not suspect for a very long time that he was one of the greatest factors of a revolution, and an anti-dynastic one. [Speech interrupted by the President of the Duma.] * * * I want to say, gentlemen, that there will come a question, not about words, but about activities and methods of struggle. And once for all, gentlemen, understand that you, heroes of Molière, are participating in such a turn of Russia's history as is called " a revolutionary proceeding." * * *

Feeling the approach of the revolution, Kerensky energetically brought to light the revolutionary consciousness of the Duma and pushed it forward into revolutionary procedure. At another time he said:

Indeed, the Government is sitting on the very tip of the soldiers' bayonets. When at such moments they say, " We are fighting by lawful means," we are fighting by the " articles of the law," then I ask, with entire sincerity and without polemics, do you not yourselves feel that you have no weapon in your hands, because those lawful means, those laws, are on the other side? Acting along " the lawful path," you are like Don Quixote when he was fighting windmills. They leave to you that " lawful method "; it hinders no one. * * * If those in power use the lawful apparatus of government only for the purpose of doing violence to the country, only in order to bring it to ruin, it is the citizen's duty not to submit to that law.

However, the Duma did not recognize the revolutionary process; it still resisted itself. The President interrupted Kerensky. In the hall arose an unimaginable noise. The protest against Kerensky threatened to remove him from his chair by force. The proceedings broke up. Soon the Duma was prorogued to Feb. 14, 1917.

On the next day after the opening of that session—on Feb. 15, 1917—Kerensky stepped forward with his first historical, already clearly revolutionary, speech, beginning:

I agree with the thesis of the last speaker, the member of the Duma, Milukoff, that we are entering upon a critical period of the three years' fight; but permit me to be not too much of an optimist, and to show you that effort and that duty which ought to lie upon the entire nation—and upon you also—a great deal more seriously. The crisis, gentlemen, upon which we are entering, perhaps have already entered, is continuing not merely in Russia. No, all Europe is choking itself in blood, which is poured forth generously in huge rivers now for the third year. * * * Can you, gentlemen, holding in your hands your country's destiny, and answering for that blood, can you say that you have done all, that you have exerted all your efforts, not with enthusiasm and pathos of words from that chair, but that you have manifested likewise all efforts of political activity and political will? Were you able, recognizing your responsibility, to take on yourselves a personal risk in struggles with that old system which is ruining the country? [Milukoff, from his place: " We have done more than you."]

I speak, gentlemen, not for the purpose of entering into a partisan discussion. I recognize also frankly—because this moment is absolutely to be accounted for, and we ought to speak only the truth— I recognize, gentlemen, that we representatives of democracy could not always fulfill our duty to the finish; but we were always at the height of understanding our historical problems as they stood before us. I do not wish to enter into quarrels or a party fight. I wish, gentlemen, that this, our session, and these days, may pass in the full consciousness of the greatest sufferings and the greatest responsibility which soon will fall upon us and upon everybody, without differences over our political convictions. I would like in these last moments, before the great event of the years, that we should look to the end and to the immediate future, and in these last times ask ourselves, can we really do something, not in order to reach Constantinople, not in order to divide Europe by the map, but in order to save the national inheritance, an heirloom from the past which has fallen into our hands? * * *

If you will forget that you are sitting within the walls of the Tavrick Palace, where the authentic voice of life comes to you muffled, where the pain and suffering of the nation loom large in a repelling and broken light; if you will recall real life; if you will look on that which surrounded you two weeks ago, when you were preparing to come here, you will understand, gentlemen, that the country already is in chaos, that we are living through a disturbance such as has never in historical times happened in the life of our fatherland, one compared with which the year 1613 seems like children's tales. Before you, gentlemen, is the very same picture through which France survived in the time of the great Revolution. Gentlemen, that chaos stares you in the face, and I ask you, have you a consciousness and feeling of political responsibility in this historical moment, so as to subject your individual and class social interests to the interest of the Government? I say to you that you have not yet that consciousness.

But look, gentlemen, look in that chaos at what the Government did. They tell us "the administration is at fault," the administration officials who like shadows come and go in these places, (pointing to the Government benches.) But did you frankly ask yourselves the question in all its breadth and depth, Who are those who bring here these "shadows"? Will these marionettes answer, those who came here for the purpose of going away? Where, then, is that real Government, where are those people who, as the facts show, are leading us into ruin? You found them; you said from here openly and directly: "Not you, you dwarfs, who, even in such a historical moment, place your personal interest in advance of the Government's interest; not you, but your masters." The master must be found. Where is he—the one who sends these officials here? * * *

And if you recall the history of the Government for these three years you will remember, gentlemen, how much has been said here about "dark forces," and how those speeches about dark forces created a league of the young naïve visionaries with the political adventurers—and Rasputin did not stand forth as that "dark force." Did we then enter upon a new era of Russian life? No, it remained entirely as it was. They send new Rasputins here, and they will have them in numbers without end. Rasputin was changed for Protopopoff, and Protopopoff for Rittich.

But you, then, when you spoke about "dark forces," did not lead into error; you did not lead the nation into side paths, you did not remove the responsibility of those who sought to be responsible for these weak ciphers of officials, obedient playthings, who were ruined, paying with their blood for other's sins. * * * I, gentlemen, can speak freely on this point because you know that I, in my political convictions, share the opinion of the party which placed frankly on its flag the possibility of terror, the possibility of armed struggle with special representatives of the Government. I belong to the party which openly recognized the necessity of killing tyrants. We were the remnants—

At this point Kerensky's speech was interrupted by the President of the Duma, who said:

Duma Member Kerensky, I beg you, in laying down the program of your party, not to give foundation for affirming that the Governmental Duma can grant any invitation to anything similar to that about which you are speaking.

### Kerensky replied to this:

I speak about what was done in classic times by the citizen Brutus, and along with this I reject here these means of obscuring human consciousness, and of turning the people's indignation toward that which is worthless and away from the few who are guilty as regards the people.

### Final words permitted to be spoken by Kerensky, were:

How is it possible to cover up one's inactivity in discharging one's duty by a pretext of the requirement of law? Your enemies are not observing the law; they openly laugh at the entire country, and are jeering at you. They destroy the law every day! With lawbreakers there is only one path, the path of physical removal. Think, gentlemen, think, and then will you not come with me to the one conclusion—that sometimes a gangrenous disease, which may destroy its victim inside of two weeks, must, as in my own case not long ago, be healed by an immediate surgical operation, so that the patient may be regenerated to newness of strength and life!

These significant words were shouted angrily by Kerensky at the entire Duma three weeks before the outbreak of the revolution.

# General Korniloff's Untiring Energy

GENERAL KORNILOFF, whose clash with Kerensky has thrown both men into a new flash of limelight, is described as equally admirable in force and character. An Englishwoman who met him in the early days of the war, and who has known many officers of nearly every nation, recently wrote:

" I have never encountered a Russian or an officer with such a personality as General Laurence Korniloff. When first I knew him he was unknown to the world—a simple General of a Siberian infantry division. Yet even then I was conscious of a certain awe—not of the man himself, but of the latent power in him. An iron will and an iron frame; an incarnation of the best war spirit plus a tender heart. Such is the man upon whom all Russia leans today, and whose shoulders are broad enough and strong enough even for so great a burden."

M. Breshko-Breshkovsky, the Russian journalist, has told in the Paris Matin some little known facts about General Korniloff, obtained from personal contact. He says:

" Discussing the situation at Petrograd and recalling the days when he commanded the garrison in the capital, Korniloff spoke of the historic scene when he had to read the decree of the Provisional Government to the Czarina Alexandra. The General had hesitated slightly at the time, and this had rather puzzled those around him.

" He explained it to me in a curious way. ' When I saw the angry, sullen face of the ex-Czarina I was suddenly reminded of the first visit I had paid her in the same palace after my escape from Austria. I painted the horrible fate of our prisoners and implored her to intervene for their protection. But while I talked her face grew dark, stern, suspicious, and she finally dismissed me abruptly and very coldly. And now here I was again face to face with her and reading the Government decree to her!

" ' For a moment she seemed so forlorn and beaten that I was ready to stop, but then again I thought of the cold, inaccessible Empress, the German woman who would hear nothing about the sufferings of our prisoners, and I forced her to listen to every syllable.'

" General Korniloff's career is one long list of incredibly brave deeds and untiring energy. Of all the officers in the Russian Army, he had the fewest friends to ' push ' him. The son of a poor Siberian Cossack, Korniloff at 13 years of age was keeping goats on the steppes and had not learned to read. Yet at 16, after solitary and unaided study, he passed brilliantly into the cadet school. Thence he passed out first on the list into the staff college. His knowledge is remarkable. He speaks fifteen languages and has made a special study of Oriental tongues.

" Everything about the man abounds with energy. He has the build of an athlete, and neither his severe wounds nor the fearful privations of prison camps have left any mark upon him. Every one knows how he escaped from Austria, but people forget the amazing thoroughness with which he carried it out. Finding it impossible to get away from the building where he was confined, he had the will power to abstain from food for fifteen days, and when, almost a skeleton, he was removed to the hospital as a dying man, he allowed himself only three days to rest before making his escape.

" With all this Korniloff is steady, cool and clear-sighted. A fortnight ago I happened to be with him at Kolomea when the Austrian lines were broken by the Eighth Army, and Halicz and Kalush captured, and he was receiving enthusiastic congratulations. Korniloff alone remained skeptical, for he alone knew the real condition of his troops. He said to me, ' With another army it would be possible to march in triumph to Lvoff (Lemberg,) but with this one, when the shock battalions have all been in action and depleted, I am at the mercy of any counterattack the enemy may make.'

" Korniloff said practically the same

thing again later. 'An army in which each company calls a meeting to settle whether it shall or shall not take the offensive is no longer an army.'

"But I knew by the way he spoke that he had accepted his difficult task with the intention of reforming these enormous masses of men into a true army."

# A New Phase of the Balkan Question

## By Milivoy S. Stanoyevich, M. L.
### University of California

A NEW phase of the Balkan question appears in the Declaration of Yugoslav Independence heralded at Corfu on July 20, 1917, when, at a meeting of the Serbian Government and the South Slav Committee of London, a new State was practically formed. [This proclamation was published in September CURRENT HISTORY MAGAZINE, pp. 431-432.] Being the result of long dreamed of aspirations, this step is noteworthy in two respects. It has none of the puerility of the previous attempts of the Serbo-Croatian coalition to unite Dalmatia with Croatia, (1905,) when by the adoption of the resolution at Fiume, on Oct. 2, the Croats formulated a program for securing freedom and unity through union with the Hungarian " Coalition Party," and on Oct. 16 the Serbs at Zara agreed with them in creating an identical platform. Furthermore, the Declaration of Yugoslav Independence just proclaimed at Corfu seems to have the approval of the powers; at least one is inclined to believe so in view of the contemporary amity of the Balkan conference in Paris and London, (May 28 and July 25, 1917.)

The birth of democracy in Russia, sounding the keynote of future Balkan aspirations, was an indication of a bond of strength between North and South Slavs. Unity of South Slavs has long been the program of the future for the Balkans; this has been recognized with ever-increasing clearness by the Balkan people since the beginning of the great war. Recalling figuratively the " Illyria " of Napoleon's idea in the opening days of the nineteenth century, this program seems reasonable. It is the unification of a certain part of the Balkan people on the basis of homogeneity of language and ethnographical characteristics. Narrowly speaking, it is unification of Serbs, Croats, and Slovenes, but broadly speaking the lands include Serbia and Montenegro, Bosnia and Herzegovina, Dalmatia and the Dalmatian Archipelago, Croatia and Slavonia, including Reika (Fiume) and the Medjumurje, (the country between the Rivers Mur and Drave,) Baranja, Bachka and Banat, Istria, the Quarnero Isles and Trieste, the Slovene lands, i. e., Carniola, Southern Carinthia, Southern Styria, and the adjoining districts in Southwestern Hungary.

Practical steps toward Southern Slav amalgamation have been looked for as the outcome of the plans undertaken by the Yugoslav Committee, formed in London in 1915, with branches in North and South America. While propaganda was carried forward by this body, Serbia played the part of the South Slav Piedmont on the battlefield in efforts to weld together a new composite State—Yugoslavia.

And now in the third Summer of war comes the declaration of the formation of the new State. This proposed State is to be a kingdom ruled by the reigning house of Serbia, the Karageorgeviches, dominated by a Parliament elected from the three component peoples; it is maintained that this kingdom shall be composed of those lands where now live the Serbians, Croats, and Slovenes in large and compact masses, and that the Orthodox, Catholic, and Mohammedan religions are to be professed accordingly as the citizens prefer. Matters of unification concern the creation of a flag and a coat of arms, the adjustment of the Julian and Gregorian calendars, and the resolution to hold to the equal and respective uses of the two scripts, Cyrillic and Latin.

The Magna Charta of this State, unlike the Berlin Treaty of 1878, proclaims unity instead of disruption in the Balkans.

It remains to be seen what will result from this new political organization, which must have international affiliations. Naturally the voice of Austria-Hungary, should she survive to acclaim her views, will oppose the loss of Croatia, Dalmatia, Bosnia-Herzegovina, and the trade of the Adriatic. As for the subject powers, the other smaller Slavic States, Poland, Bohemia, &c., it is hoped that they will lay aside jealousy and view with hopeful eyes this emergency of a sister power. And Greece, guarding the portal of the south in the peninsula, will also be called upon to grasp friendly instead of inimical hands, as she so disastrously did with Serbia in the beginning of the war, for, backed by the Entente Allies, Greece cannot but comply with their policy. And that the proclamation of Yugoslavia accords with the sanction of England, France, and Russia is seen in the docile attitude with which Italy seems to be putting up with claims which must in some measure shut her out from complete domination of the Adriatic Sea. Together with the official visits of Italy's Premier with England's and Serbia's Premiers, and the renewed Italian offensive at Trieste, it seems likely that into the clauses of the new Yugoslav Declaration of Independence (especially Clause Ninth) can be read some adjustment of a problem which still holds the seeds for a new Balkan imbroglio.

## The Name of France

By HENRY VAN DYKE

[Read by the author at the Lafayette Day celebration in the City Hall, New York, Sept. 6, 1917]

Give us a name to fill the mind
With the shining thoughts that lead mankind;
The glory of learning, the joy of art—
A name that tells of the splendid part
In the long, long toil and the strenuous fight
Of the human race to win its way
From the ancient darkness into the day
Of Freedom, Brotherhood, Equal Right—
A name like a star, a name of light—
   I give you FRANCE!

Give us a name to stir the blood
With a warmer glow and a swifter flood—
A name like the sound of a trumpet, clear,
And silver-sweet, and iron strong,
That calls three million men to their feet,
Ready to march, and steady to meet
The foes who threaten that name with wrong—
A name that rings like a battle-song—
   I give you FRANCE!

Give us a name to move the heart
With the strength that noble griefs impart—
A name that speaks of the blood outpoured
To save mankind from the sway of the sword—
A name that calls on the world to share
In the burden of sacrificial strife
When the cause at stake is the world's free life
And the rule of the people everywhere—
A name like a vow, a name like a prayer—
   I give you FRANCE!

# Military Operations of the War

## By Major Edwin W. Dayton

*Inspector General, National Guard, State of New York; Secretary, New York Army and Navy Club*

## VIII.—The Great German Attack on Verdun

AS the Autumn of 1915 faded into the chill of Winter the great armies on the western front repaired the losses incurred in the hard campaigns in Champagne and at Loos, Halluch, and Vimy. Terrific blows had been struck and the enemy had suffered severe losses in casualties and prisoners, but while the fortified lines had been forced back slightly the Germans had successfully withstood all allied efforts to break through. The German reserves had proved sufficient, and there certainly was need on all sides for reinforcements of men and replenishment of supplies. The supplies of both men and shells were promptly furnished, however, and there were several hard battles in Champagne and Artois in November. Early in the month a German counteroffensive in Champagne met with considerable success, and further north a continuous battle raged among the intricate subterranean fortifications of the "Labyrinth" in Artois. A number of German divisions had been brought to the west from Russia, and the Teuton forces were ample for all defensive requirements, and even sufficient to warrant occasional attacks on a fairly important scale.

Lord Derby's recruiting campaign had produced a large number of recruits in England, and there was an important change in command at the front, where on Dec. 15 Sir Douglas Haig became Commander in Chief following the resignation of Sir John French. Both British and Canadians were active in raids upon enemy trenches near Neuve Chapelle and before Armentières, while a German attack on the British lines was repulsed after a smart engagement. Despite the difficulty of midwinter mountain warfare there was a prolonged struggle on the Hartmanns-Weilerkopf,

where the fortunes of war favored first the Germans and then the French. No other part of the whole battle front has remained so nearly stationary throughout the whole war to date as the lines in the Vosges. The battles at the end of 1915 left the situation much as it had been and as it still remains.

### German Attack on Verdun

When 1916 dawned, the Germans were claiming that the war was won and the Allies were answering that the real fighting had not yet begun. It was evident that the Allies were stronger in both men and munitions, and that consequently another great allied offensive was to be anticipated in the Spring of the new year. The characteristic German method of meeting such a situation was to launch a great attack at a point distant from the sector in which the Allies were mobilizing men and guns for their new effort. It was quite certain that both French and British would prefer to strike again above the Aisne, and therefore the Germans chose an important place considerably to the south for attack.

Verdun was selected for the effort. If captured it might unlock a road via St. Menehould to Paris, and if seriously menaced it was sufficiently important to compel France to hurry reinforcements from the north even though the transfer of troops might disrupt all plans for a great offensive in the Spring. Germany had certainly not forgotten the defeats which crushed the efforts to reach Paris in the Summer of 1914, but doubtless every artillerist was impatient to see the great forts about Verdun crumble under the fire of the siege howitzers as had the steel and concrete defenses in Belgium and Northern France. The walls which had withstood the rush in August,

1914, were walls of Belgian, French, and British flesh and blood. The Germans hoped that the French at Verdun would rely more upon the elaborate system of forts while the bulk of their infantry and field artillery were gathered toward the north.

The zone of operations lying between

GERMAN CROWN PRINCE

the salient at St. Mihiel and the wooded Argonne was under the general command of the Crown Prince, and a success there would be to his credit. Certainly his military reputation needed some stimulation, for his only successes had been negative. He had held his sector, but had failed always to win any worthwhile advance.

Verdun lies directly upon the main highway into France from Metz, and therefore was most convenient for an assault based upon that great German military depot. The city on the banks of the Meuse is surrounded by the Côtes de Meuse, which, rising on an average some 250 to 300 feet above the floor of the valley, provide an ideal terrain for the military engineer. The eastern face of the hills overlooking the Woevre was studded with elaborate old-style forts at Douaumont, Vaux, Tavannes, Moulainville, with several other forts protecting the southern approaches along the more

southern road to Metz through Manheules.

The west side of the river was amply protected by an almost equally elaborate system of forts on a front of more than eight miles along the hills west of a line from Charny to Duguy. Altogether the circle of forts measured about thirty miles, and before the war included the best type of Brialmont permanent steel and concrete defenses with heavy guns mounted in disappearing turrets. When the French engineers learned how little reliance might be placed upon these devices, General Sarrail, who held Verdun against the Crown Prince in the first months of the war, began the construction of a far-flung line of intrenchments and obstacles beyond the line of forts. It was Sarrail who defeated the attempt of the Crown Prince to reach south from the Argonne and by joining forces with von Strautz at St. Mihiel inclose Verdun.

The early failure of those efforts may have influenced the decision to make the new effort directly against the east face of the position, a plan which had the advantage of the most direct and abundant lines of communication with the base at Metz. However, I believed in 1915 and still hold that this was a decided error of judgment. The men and munitions expended on the east side of the Meuse would have been more wisely spent in a drive south through Varunes and the Forest of Hesse to the Verdun-St. Menehould railway line. The French defenses on this front were strongly held, but attacks such as were hurled against Douaumont in the first week of the great attack might have won advantages on the west side of the river sufficient to interrupt the flow of reinforcements to the besieged city on the east bank. It was in the end the failure to stop the constant reinforcement of the garrison that made the whole German effort a failure. A quickly successful attack on the east side might have succeeded in rolling the French forces on that side of the Meuse back against a river whose bridges could in such an event have been smashed by artillery fire. The Meuse, swollen by Winter rains, achieves a width of a thousand yards at

Verdun. Such a success would have been a great victory, but nothing experienced in the campaigns of 1915 warranted a belief that the French infantry could be rushed in any such fashion.

The French had, in the Winter of 1914, under Sarrail, prepared a plan which provided means for a defense of Verdun by a force of 250,000 men. Motor and railway transport arrangements were devised on a scale adequate in prospect and ample when actually called upon. France possessed in Sarrail a fine soldier and a great organizer, and was fortunate to have had him stationed just where his courage and genius were most needed; but apparently not all of his defensive measures were in good order when the storm broke.

### Beginning of the Great Attack

About the middle of February, 1916, when General Herr was in command of the Verdun garrison, the Germans began a bombardment on a wide front, but, although enough heavy shells fell in the town of Verdun to induce the civil officials to send away the last of the populace, there was nothing to indicate a serious attack. It was on the morning of Feb. 21 that the real bombardment began. Soon after 7 o'clock the most furious storm of shellfire that had ever been known was poured upon the French first-line positions, which were, in a few minutes, torn to pieces by a hurricane of four and seven inch projectiles, with a number of big thirteen-inch Austrian shells added. At midday the German infantry advanced, and with almost no opposition took what had been the French first line in the Bois d'Haumont and the Bois des Caures, wooded heights on the right bank of the river, about six miles above Verdun. The French infantry, holding this outer line, had been a small force and fell back to the prepared second line, which, however, was not as well developed as it should have been.

At this stage the German assault moved with mathematical precision, and the artillery attack, after wiping out the first positions, was lifted to a barrage fire, which blocked any reinforcements from coming up to the help of the detachments under attack. When the German infantry moved forward the columns were preceded by strong reconnoitring patrols, followed by bomb throwers and engineer detachments to prepare the new positions for the occupation of the strong forces about to take them over. Late in the afternoon two

GENERAL SARRAIL

battalions of Chasseurs under Lieut. Col. Driant, the Deputy from Nancy, made a counterattack, which won back some of the positions on the wooded heights.

At daybreak on Tuesday, the German guns poured shrapnel, high explosives, and tear shells upon the French lines, and in the woods close to Brabant liquid fire was used. By night the village of Haumont was taken as well as Beaumont, where in stubborn rear-guard fighting the brave Driant and many of his chasseurs met a glorious death. That night the French retired to Samogneux and a line to the east through Herbebois and Ornes, but the German artillery and infantry were still too powerful to be checked, and on the 23d and 24th, the French lines had to fall back from Ornes to Bezonvaux and from Samogneux to Hill 344 and Mormont Farm. The Germans were attacking with an infantry force estimated at not less than 225,000 bayonets, and the corps included the famous Third Corps of Brandenburg. The Crown Prince had for this great operation the active assistance of Marshal von Haeseler as well as von Strautz. The strategy was credited to von Falkenhayn.

By the morning of Friday, the 25th, the Germans were pressing forward to attack the thoroughly prepared positions on a line through Vacherauville, the Côte du Poivre, Louvemont, Les Chambrettes Farm, the Woods of La Vauche, and Hardaumont to Vaux. Several brigades of fresh infantry had arrived on this new French front, but by this time the Germans had concentrated on this small sector of less than five miles eighteen divisions. In the middle of that snowy afternoon the Germans took Louvemont, and about the same time they delivered a terrific attack on Douaumont, the highest point among the hills east of the Meuse. The German infantry suffered enormous losses in the repeated attacks upon Douaumont, where the Third Regiment of French Zouaves made a splendid defense.

### Germans Take Fort Douaumont

By this time the gravity of the situation was apparent, and General de Castelnau, who had taken over the French command, was reinforced by the brilliant young hero of the Champagne campaign, General Pétain. In four days the Germans had forced the French lines back four miles, and on the evening when Pétain arrived the Twenty-fourth Regiment of Brandenburgers fought their way into the ruins of old Fort Douaumont. The next morning, Saturday, the 26th, Pétain hurled the Twentieth Corps of Nancy, under General Balfourier, upon the enemy and succeeded in driving him back with the exception of a small group of Brandenburgers who persisted in holding on among the ruins of Fort Douaumont.

Meanwhile the German attacks on Pepper Hill had failed and the French held on at the village of Douaumont, some six hundred yards northwest of the fort. On Sunday, the 27th, and Monday, the 28th, there were heavy snow and hard fighting, during which two divisions of

Brandenburgers renewed the assault on Douaumont. The battle extended somewhat toward the south, and other German corps began to attack from the Woevre in an effort to turn the flank of the positions on the heights which the French infantry were defending so stubbornly. On this front a Bavarian corps took part of the village of Manheulles, north of Les Eparges, but could make no further progress.

In the first week of March the Germans opened a new attack on the west side of the Meuse. Here a high ridge was the key to the whole outer scheme of defenses, just as on the opposite side of the Meuse the Poivre Heights and Douaumont were all important key positions. On the west side it was a hill called Le Mort Homme, and a somewhat higher hill designated as Hill 304, both positions mutually supporting and situated on either side of the Béthincourt-Esnes road. The Forges brook cuts a way across the ridge from south to north and so separates these hilltops.

The Germans, while preparing for the attacks west of the Meuse, renewed their efforts on the east and succeeded in entering the village of Douaumont. On March 6 two German divisions began the attacks on the west of the river and captured Forges and Regneville, as well as a valuable hillcrest (265) just west of Regneville. The following day Fresnes fell, and the enemy won a redoubt in Hardaumont Wood. At midnight of March 8-9 a force of Brandenburg and Posen regiments entered Vaux only to be bayonetted out by a vigorous French counterattack. The assault was repeated in a tremendous battle which lasted all of March 9, but although the Brandenburgers fought until annihilated, they failed to win.

On March 10 and 11, having been heavily reinforced by new troops, the Germans continued the effort and finally forced their way into the ruins of what had been the eastern end of the town of Vaux. The heroic defense of Vaux was as vital to the salvation of Verdun as that across the river on Poivre Heights.

The battle continued to swing back

and forth across the Meuse as the Germans delivered fresh assaults first on one series of heights and then on the other, with occasionally an extension of their efforts along the Woevre front. On March 14 a great attack was begun against Le Mort Homme by a force of about 25,000 infantry, in five great suc-

GENERAL HENRI PETAIN

cessive waves. It won a spur on Le Mort Homme, but not the main hill itself, although that was announced at the time. Another great attack on March 16 was defeated by the French, who clung to these vital hill defenses with unparalleled determination. Renewed German efforts to enlarge their grip on Vaux suffered defeat, and the total German losses by this time were appalling. It seems to be well established that the Third Brandenburg Corps, which entered the battle in February over 20,000 strong, lost by March 10, in about ten days' fighting, more than its total original strength. Although the huge casualties of the first battles were quickly replaced by reserves, this fine corps was practically wiped out by the struggles against the French intrenched positions, and their losses are said to have totaled 22,000 men killed, wounded, and missing.

Of course, the French, too, lost heavily, but Pétain adhered to the plan of holding the front lines with the smallest possible number of men, and his losses were not great except in the desperate counterattacks necessary to recapture important lost positions such as Douaumont and Le Mort Homme.

### Crown Prince's Efforts Fail

By the middle of March it is quite certain the Germans had used on this battle front of not over thirty miles' extent fully half a million men, and although both men and munitions had been spent with prodigal freedom, no success had crowned their almost superhuman efforts. The French had been pushed back closer to the inner line defenses, and it was by this time evident that the German staff would persist to the last in this major offensive unless the Allies could create a diversion by launching some great counteroffensive further to the north.

While huge reinforcements had come to the Verdun front from the German armies in Russia and the Balkans, the lines from Flanders to the Argonne had been maintained in full strength in constant anticipation that the British would strike hard somewhere on the north. The counteroffensive was for some reason long delayed and France continued to bleed at Verdun until dangerously close to collapse before the diversion was actually made. By March 20 the German artillery, which had been firing heavily for some days, concentrated a terrific fire on the Avocourt-Malancourt sector lying to the west of Hill 304. Bavarians and Württembergers won a footing in Avocourt Wood, where they dug in elaborately. The battle on this front raged on for days with the Germans gradually winning ground on the lower spurs to the west of Hill 304, but on March 29 General Pétain delivered a powerful counterattack which somewhat relieved the dangerous pressure at Avocourt, where the Germans were driven out of a redoubt in the woods. Further north the Germans continued to attack Malancourt, and after numerous repulses won part of the village on the last day of March. Pétain withdrew the remnant of the garrison from Malancourt and Haucourt to Hill 304, having

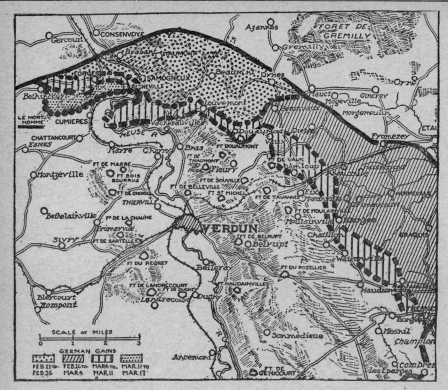

MAP SHOWING THE GERMAN GAINS IN THE BATTLE OF VERDUN—ALL LOST
IN A FEW DAYS A YEAR LATER

sold the little towns at a very high price, since they were only outlying posts for the hill positions a mile to the south.

Meanwhile, the Germans east of the Meuse, after a week of bitter fighting, fought their way into the outskirts of Vaux, and in the first days of April drove powerful columns in Caillette Wood and Hardaumont Wood, west and north of Vaux. These successes seriously threatened the French communications behind Fort Douaumont. On April 3 General Mangin's division made a magnificent counterattack and recaptured most of the lost ground in Caillette Wood and around the pond on the west of Vaux. The ravines between the town and the wood were choked with German and French dead, as the result of one of the bloodiest conflicts in the whole long siege.

### A Triumph for France

On the west sector the Germans continued to attack in great force, and gradually won their way along the Haucourt - Béthincourt - Cumières line. By April 8 the French had yielded ground on the west front of about six miles to a depth of about one mile in the series of heavy battles since the middle of March.

On Sunday, April 9, the Germans delivered another tremendous assault on a wide front, intending to crush in the French lines on Le Mort Homme and Hill 304. They attacked Avocourt Wood and Crow Wood in heavy formations without success, but on the flank at the riverside won a footing in Cumières. On Le Mort Homme, the Germans got into some of the first-line trenches, but were held by the heroic defense of the 151st Regiment of the Line with the 8th and 16th Battalions of Chasseurs. This great assault persisted for several days and a little headway was made by German storming columns in a ravine on the southeast face of Poivre Heights, but by April 10 the effort wore out and the great siege subsided temporarily, although heavy bombardments continued to alternate with infantry charges. By the middle of April French counter-attacks grew much more frequent.

If the casualties at Verdun in the two months' fighting are reckoned at 300,000, it will probably be fair to assume that of this total not more than one-third were French. Never in all the history of French military glory has there been a brighter chapter than that written at Verdun. Every poilu in the ranks chanted "You Shall Not Pass," and died gladly to confirm the interdiction. Superficial military critics had long credited the French soldier with brilliant adaptability for attack, but had denied him credit for ability to "stand the gaff" on a long, hard defense. The armies under Maud'huy in Arras, de Castelnau before Nancy, and Pétain at Verdun have forever disproved that slander.

Verdun was a veritable hell in February, March, and April, 1916, but the French held it against artillery and infantry attacks of unparalleled intensity and persistence. An astonishing revelation was the preservation of the élan for attack which suffered no loss of enthusiasm by the long periods of dogged defense. From the gallant eloquence of Driant to his Chasseurs facing death in Caures Wood to the gasping phrase "Passeront-pas" of the humble private giving his life on Le Mort Homme, there seemed never to have been a moment when cheerful sacrifice of life itself could not be relied upon.

The great German armies went down to defeat before a greater foe at Verdun, but, heroic and competent as the French were, there came a time in the Spring when the Germans succeeded in pushing dangerously close to the beleaguered city on the northeast front. They were slowly but steadily crushing in the defenses on this front, and had in May and June taken Fort Vaux, the strongly fortified positions at Thiaumont Farm, Douaumont, and were within three short miles of Verdun. Across the river they had Cumières and Le Mort Homme and were eating their way into Hill 304. Then the great storm to the north broke as French and British together hurled themselves against the German lines above the Somme. The Germans were compelled to shift all available reserves to that hard-pressed sector through the Summer months, and so the great effort to take Verdun rested. There have been many hard battles on both sides of the river since then, but the French have gradually pushed the invader back from his hard-won positions in the Vaux sector. The most serious of the later German attacks have been in the region of Hill 304, which remains a massive barrier to their progress on the west front.

## Serbia Overwhelmed

Serbia had been the superficial cause of the worldwide war and for two years was remarkably successful in avoiding any serious castigation. The early Austrian efforts to invade the little Balkan State had been defeated and the menace of mighty Russia on the east had prevented any renewal of Austrian efforts to avenge the murders at Serajevo in June, 1914.

Early in the Autumn of 1915 Bulgaria joined the middle Europe alliance, and thus a dangerous new foe close at hand loomed up on the Serbian horizon. Field Marshal von Mackensen appeared across the Danube opposite Belgrade in command of a new German-Austrian army. A fortnight later French and British divisions were landing at Saloniki. The stage seemed set for a great allied campaign in co-operation with the Serbs to turn back the new invasion from the north and at the same time punish the Bulgars for joining the Teuton cause. The French under Sarrail were the first to land at the Greek port, and they pushed out northward at once to prevent the Bulgars from seizing the Iron Gate, the narrow gorge on the Vardar, 90 miles above the base, the only pass through which rail communication with Northern Serbia could be maintained. By the end of October Sarrail's men were 75 miles up the Vardar above Krivolak and General Mahon's Tenth British Division had come up to Lake Doiran, where they guarded the French right flank from any possible Bulgar attack.

About the middle of September Austrian batteries began to bombard Belgrade, but it was not until Oct. 3 that the heavy bombardment with great guns began. A few days later the Teuton armies crossed both the Save and Danube rivers, and on the 8th the Germans were in part of Belgrade; by the morning of the 9th the army of von Kovess had captured all of the capital. Other columns pressed forward across the rivers, and by Oct. 11 the Germans had deployed on a front of 100 miles from Shabatz to Graditza.

As soon as the Germans were safely over the river frontiers, the Bulgars formally declared war—on Oct. 12—and a few days later von Kovess drove the Serbs from the positions south of Belgrade to which they had retreated after the town fell. Raiding Bulgar cavalry cut the railway at Vrania, (Vranja,) and the Serbian town of Egri Palanka was taken by a Bulgarian army. Veles fell on Oct. 20 and Uskub was lost on the 22d. At the latter point the meeting of the river valleys along which the railways run produces a traffic centre which practically controls all the travel routes of Central and Southern Serbia.

The principal Serbian armies in the north were now cut off, a disaster which might have been averted if the Allies from Saloniki had been a little earlier on their job of keeping the Bulgars away from the Vardar Valley.

### Serbia's Fate Sealed

On Oct. 26 a column from the army of von Gallwitz crossed the Danube at Orsova and on the same day both Negotin and Prahovo were captured by Bulgarians, who seized large quantities of supplies sent up the river for the Serbs. By the end of the month the Austrians and Bulgars had joined hands and the fate of that part of Serbia which lay below the Rumanian frontier was sealed. On Oct. 30 the Germans reached Kragujevatz, the Serbian arsenal, and the North Serbian army had been driven back toward Nish. Another force held the hills north of Monastir. Nish fell on Nov. 6, and after a heroic resistance at Katchanik the last of the northern army began a terrible retreat toward Montenegro.

At Babuna Pass, above Prilep, a Serb force of about 5,000 men fought bravely to stem the tide of invasion, but, finding that no help could be expected from the Allies, this heroic remnant finally retreated toward the Albanian frontier.

While the Serbs were struggling to hold the Babuna Pass a strong French column, trying to join hands, got to within ten miles of the pass, but, meeting powerful Bulgar forces, was compelled to abandon the effort and retreat to an intrenched camp at Kavadar. So ended the hope that the Allies would succor the Serbs. The remnants of the armies which had fought to save the fatherland were soon struggling over the wild mountain roads toward the west. By the end of November, 1915, practically all of Serbia was in the hands of the enemy, and early in December the French began to retreat from Serbia into Northern Greece. In the first week of December the Austro-Germans took Monastir and the Bulgarians began to attack the British positions near Lake Doiran. After a not very stubborn defense both French and British armies fell back before the Bulgarians and retreated behind the field fortifications, which had been prepared on an extensive scale outside Saloniki. The Greeks, making some virtue of necessity, handed the seaport over to the Allies, who soon found themselves in a state of siege behind the fortifications along the hills outside the city.

# Anti-Submarine Tactics

## By Lieut. Commander Charles C. Gill

### United States Navy

Lieut. Commander Gill has been in active service in the United States Navy fourteen years, part of which time he was a member of the Faculty at the United States Naval Academy. He is the author of numerous articles on naval topics. The article here presented was written after a voyage through the war zone in the expedition commanded by Admiral Gleaves, and it is published with the special sanction of the Secretary of the Navy and the Admiral of the Fleet.

IF we can believe the spokesmen of the Prussian Government, Germany is depending upon her submarine navy so to cripple the ocean trade supplying men, food, and munitions to allied armies as to compel the acceptance of peace terms pleasing to the present leader of the German Nation.

Hindenburg has announced that it is only necessary for the German armies to hold their own on land while the U-boats at sea decide the war in Germany's favor.

It is strange that Germany's first soldiers should point out that the submarine, the only naval weapon able to evade the allied blockade, promises a respite and a hope that the German armies cannot give, even though the latter have been successful on all fronts and have conquered entire countries. Thus does Germany acknowledge the principle so well taught by the distinguished American naval officer, Admiral Mahan, that in all great wars between commercial nations land power is ancillary to sea power.

The answer of the United States to this Hindenburg announcement is characteristic and may be phrased somewhat as follows: The American Army will help hammer the Prussian lines while the American Navy defeats the U-boat.

As the war now enters upon its last stage there can be no doubt as to the final result. The end is in sight, and, as in past wars, so in this one, the force of sea power is slowly but surely shaping the issues. As the arteries of sea-borne commerce to the Teutonic Powers are more and more effectually blocked, and as the U-boat terror subsides while new strength and vigor from America, Africa, and Asia are transported more and more

easily to France, England, and Italy— the realization will slowly but surely be forced home that Pan-Germanism has been defeated and that Germany must give up the evil policies she has fought so desperately to defend and propagate.

It was Germany's unscrupulous methods of using her U-boats against commerce that precipitated war with the United States, and now it is the obvious mission of the American Navy to overcome this submarine menace in the Atlantic. As soon as this mission is accomplished and the U-boat campaign is demonstrated a failure, it may be assumed that Germany will stand ready to yield pretensions as a victor.

Secrecy is important in the development of certain kinds of anti-submarine tactics. Mention cannot be made of new devices, because to forewarn the enemy is to forearm him. But no harm will result from an outline discussion of the older though still effective methods of submarine defense which are now well known to the enemy. On the other hand, a clearer understanding of the question will stimulate interest in the wider development and practice of common-sense methods against the submarine. These may contribute quite as much to the ultimate defeat of the U-boat as highly scientific inventions.

In order to understand anti-submarine tactics it is necessary to know something of the tactical characteristics of the craft against which these countermeasures are directed. Of course, any very recent developments are not known, but there is no evidence at hand that radical advance has lately been made in U-boat construction.

The cruising radius of the larger submarines is about 6,000 miles when steaming on the surface at a slow speed of six to ten knots. The newer boats are reported to have a maximum speed of eighteen knots, but economy of fuel is so important, and the consumption is so much greater for high speeds, that submarines use the economical slower speeds except perhaps for short spurts. It is obvious that submarines operating from distant bases cannot well afford to chase merchantmen unless they happen to be slow ones. Their usual procedure is to lie in wait along the trade routes and attack the ships which run up to them.

### Limitations of Submarines

Submarines, after cruising a certain distance while submerged, are compelled to come to the surface to recharge their batteries. Here again the maximum submerged speed of about fourteen knots for the newer boats and about ten knots for the older types is extremely uneconomical. For example, approximately speaking, the average submarine when submerged can go four to five hours at ten knots, a total distance of about forty miles; or ten hours at about seven knots, a total distance of seventy miles; or thirty-six hours at about four knots, a total distance of 144 miles; or seventy-two hours at steerage way, (about two and one-half knots,) a total distance of 180 miles. It also has been rumored that the most recent U-boats can go as far as 250 miles at a stretch without coming to the surface. But when the limit is reached, whatever it may be, the submarine must stop and wait for an opportunity to come to the surface to recharge batteries.

It follows, then, that anti-submarine tactics which force the enemy to go comparatively long distances at high speeds tend to limit their activities. It is reported that when the prospects are such as to promise considerable uneconomical cruising, either on the surface or submerged, submarine commanders usually abandon the attack.

It may be mentioned here that it is extremely hard to control merchantmen and compel them to practice simple anti-submarine tactics—such as steering zig-zag courses—calculated to embarrass the submarine in the accomplishment of its purpose. It is difficult for seamen who for years have navigated the usual lanes to understand and carry out instructions intended to safeguard them from a foe they cannot see. When the tangible proof of the enemy's presence arrives it is too late. Utmost vigilance is necessary at all times, and to get this requires a strict discipline which does not exist on board the majority of trading ships. The percentage of torpedoed ships is not sufficiently high to spur the crews to great exertions.

There are many influences inclining the individuals on board ships passing through the war zone to the opinion that getting safely by is largely a question of luck. There seems to be more or less prevalent a sort of fatalistic attitude toward the submarine, or the gambler's attitude of taking a chance against being torpedoed, with a resulting laxity in the observance of safeguarding measures. Whatever be the cause of this indifference to the practice of simple anti-submarine tactics of evasion, there is plenty of evidence that many a ship has played into the hands of the U-boat either by failure to carry out instructions, or by a poor lookout system, or by neglect to steer zigzag courses before sighting the submarine, or by stupid seamanship after sighting it. This is unfortunate, but not surprising. The nature of the submarine enemy is such that to combat it successfully requires a personnel of a high order of intelligence, well trained and well disciplined.

### How Torpedoes Operate

The armament of the U-boats consists of both guns and torpedoes. The hull of the newer types is protected to some extent by armor, but is still so vulnerable that few U-boats will risk a gun engagement with a well-armed enemy. As nearly all ships are now armed, the torpedo has become the principal weapon of attack.

The general characteristics of the torpedo are now pretty well known. It is a highly scientific mechanism consisting of many intricate parts ingeniously assembled in a metal shell about twelve to twenty feet long, twenty-one inches in diameter, weighing about one ton, and valued in this country at about $6,000. In appearance a torpedo somewhat resembles a small, elongated auto-submarine. It has horizontal and vertical rudders which can be so adjusted, in conjunction with an automatic steering device, as to make the torpedo keep at a certain depth and either travel straight or in a curve. The torpedo is propelled by a screw driven by an automatic compressed air engine, capable of giving a speed as high as thirty-six knots. By the act of launching from the tube a starting lever is tripped, which causes the propelling mechanism to go ahead at full speed. The head of the torpedo carries a powerful bursting charge. The object of submarine tactics is to detonate this high explosive against the underwater body of the target ship.

To accomplish this object the submarine commander has to make preliminary observations through his periscope, estimate the course, speed, and distance of the enemy, manoeuvre his boat to a favorable position, make the necessary firing adjustments, aim the torpedo, and then launch it.

It is obvious that the closer the target the better the chances of scoring a hit. Torpedoes are rarely fired by submarines at greater ranges than one thousand yards because the percentage of hits at longer ranges is comparatively small. Glancing hits, moreover, are not often effective. When the target ship is end on, the torpedo, even when correctly aimed to hit, frequently glances off without exploding, (bow wave and wake currents assist this deflection), or if it does explode fails to do much damage. Torpedoes are so expensive, the supply is so limited, and the U-boats themselves are so precious that every effort is made to avoid risk of failure and destruction.

## U-Boat's Method of Attack

It is thus seen that submarine tactics are not altogether simple. If the target ship is fast, steers zigzag courses, keeps a bright lookout, carries guns, and is also attended by escort ships specially equipped for destroying submarines, the difficulties in the way of successful attack are considerably increased.

The problem facing the U-boat Captain may be summarized as follows:

Keeping in mind the importance of safeguarding his own ship and also the necessity of economizing in both fuel and torpedoes, he first studies the situation and if he is in a favorable position ahead of his quarry, he decides to attack. Assuming that the approaching vessel is armed, he submerges before there is likelihood of discovery. He then observes at more or less frequent intervals through his periscope, takes bearings of the approaching target ship, and estimates her course, distance, and speed. His purpose is to avoid discovery and at the same time to manoeuvre into a favorable position for launching at about one thousand yards' range a torpedo so aimed and adjusted as to strike the enemy ship at an angle of incidence to her fore and aft line greater than thirty degrees.

## Critical Moment of Attack

There are, of course, any number of variations in the methods of making a submarine attack, but as an illustration, suppose a U-boat submerged and approaching from a bow bearing at a speed of six knots toward a target ship advancing at twelve knots. With fairly good glasses a periscope can be distinguished with reasonable certainty in comparatively smooth water by an alert lookout at 3,000 to 4,000 yards.

As the ship can probably escape by manoeuvring if the periscope is seen before the torpedo is fired, it follows that the critical time for both the attacker and the attacked is during the interval of approach from the range of 4,000 yards to the firing range of about 1,000 yards. This interval will last approximately from seven to ten minutes, depending upon the angle of approach and upon how accurately the submarine judges the course of the target ship. Beginning at 4,000 yards the submarine can be expected to show about one foot of periscope and observe for a period of about thirty seconds. After this four or five successive observations will probably be taken at intervals of about one minute, the period of time that the periscope is exposed diminishing gradually to ten or twelve seconds.

### Periscope Almost Under Water

In the meanwhile the submarine will have closed to about 2,000 yards, and from now on only a few inches of periscope will be exposed, but at more frequent intervals, about every thirty seconds, and the length of time the periscope is shown will decrease to from ten to five seconds.

At about one thousand yards the firing exposure will be made, and this will probably be for about twenty-five seconds in order to assure a well-aimed torpedo.

The above procedure is not absolute—some submarine commanders show more periscope in attacking and others less—but it may be taken as typical. This means that from the time the submarine can be seen to the time the torpedo is fired about ten minutes elapse, during which there are about fifteen exposures of the periscope for gradually diminishing periods of time, ranging from thirty seconds down to five seconds, except the last exposure for firing, which lasts about twenty-five seconds.

There has been some talk of a German invention designed to enable a submarine to make a successful approach and attack without showing any periscope. It is improbable that any such device is in general use at present.

### Tactics Used Against U-Boats

Anti-submarine tactics comprise both methods to destroy enemy submarines and methods to evade their attack. Of course, the primary objective is to destroy the enemy ships, but, since it is easier for the larger vessels, transports, and merchantmen to evade the attack, every effort should be made by the transports and merchantmen to develop tactics of evasion while the fighting navy is developing tactics to destroy. Cordial understanding and co-operation, therefore, between the fighting navy and the merchant navy are of first impor-

tance in the successful development and practice of anti-submarine tactics.

The means within the ship of frustrating submarine attack are the lookout, the manoeuvre, and the gun.

An efficient lookout system is essential. A ship can usually avoid attack if the submarine or even the torpedo is sighted when still far enough away to permit a change of course before the torpedo can travel the intervening distance. Safety depends upon " seeing," and an alert lookout by gaining 200 or 300 yards in sighting a periscope may avert destruction. The need for a system of intensively trained and organized lookouts is too often neglected.

Zigzag tactics make attack difficult. Also a quick manoeuvre the instant a periscope or torpedo is sighted will often save the ship. Alert seamanship is, therefore, a main reliance of capital ships in avoiding submarine attack.

The gun is chiefly useful to compel a submarine to keep submerged. The presence of the gun is important to embarrass the attack; but to hit a periscope is difficult, and even if a lucky hit is scored no serious damage is done, as spare periscopes are carried by all U-boats.

### Skilled Work of Destroyers

Tactics aiming to destroy the submarine can be best used by the destroyers and other small craft specially equipped for this work. Nets and other devices which have proved useful against the smaller type of submarine in comparatively restricted areas are not effective against the larger seagoing U-boats. Under-water weapons such as bombs and plunging shell are needed to attack an under-water enemy.

Plunging shell are somewhat similar in their operation to bombs. It may be supposed that such shell kept falling just short of a periscope by a well directed gunfire and fused to burst both on contact and at a certain depth make it very uncomfortable for an attacking submarine.

The seagoing destroyer appears to be the best type of anti-submarine craft so far developed. It combines abilities to scout, to escort, and to destroy.

Seagoing craft of all descriptions approaching the characteristics of the destroyers and capable of carrying guns and bombs are useful. Yachts, fast tugs, and other comparatively small vessels capable of keeping the sea and making reasonable speed can all do good work in the war zone.

Torpedo boats and the smaller submarine chasers and patrol boats, though not so useful as more seaworthy vessels, are still of value for operating nearer the shore. Mine sweepers also are needed.

Seaplanes, dirigibles, (Blimps,) and kite balloons make good scouts because of the large areas they can cover. Weather conditions are seldom such that submarines entirely submerged can be seen by aircraft, but this does not make the latter less valuable for detecting periscopes and submarines awash or on the surface. Also air craft mark the spot where a periscope is sighted and so assist destroyers and patrols in the effective use of their bombs.

Cruisers and converted cruisers are needed for distant convoy work, to carry seaplanes, to carry kite balloons, and also for various administrative and mothership duties.

An anti-submarine force, therefore, includes cruisers, converted cruisers, destroyers, submarines, torpedo boats, patrol craft, mine sweepers, sea planes, dirigibles, and kite balloons, all supplied in as large numbers as can be obtained.

## Submarines Now More Wary

As has already been remarked, the details of new equipment and new methods employed in anti-submarine tactics cannot be made public. It is better to let the U-boats find these out at their own cost. But as they learn of the increasing number and variety of schemes used to destroy them they realize that the chances against them have increased. This in itself is a restraint, which makes the U-boats more wary and consequently less effective. At best there is not much comfort or security in a long submarine cruise. The prospect of dying like a rat in a trap is not pleasant, whether because of accident, or shipwreck, or hostile attack. The strain of constant guard against the devices of an alert enemy must tell on even the strongest nerves. Any method or. contrivance which increases the anxieties and difficulties of the U-boats is thus helpful in checking their activities, and may contribute in unexpected ways to their destruction.

The nature of the U-boat makes trickery conspicuous in German submarine tactics, and. it is fitting that countertricks should prove effective against them. But, as plunging shell, bombs, and other suitable weapons are developed, it is probable that the allied navies will find simple and direct anti-submarine tactics best. History has shown that in the majority of naval campaigns direct methods usually triumph over those which rely upon deceit. It is not unreasonable to suppose that merchantmen of the near future may be so equipped as to make them auxiliary naval submarine hunters; and as tactics to destroy supplant tactics to evade, trade routes will gradually be cleared of this, literally speaking, snake of the sea.

The submarine menace is very real, and people are beginning to appreciate the facts and figures which show it to be the all-important problem of the war. But the United States Navy, if squarely ranged against this menace, will answer it. Anti-submarine tactics are being developed right along, and, while the U-boat as a lawless commerce destroyer was unforeseen and countermeasures consequently not prepared during previous years of peace, still to assume that it will not be successfully met is unjust to the navy, which is upholding traditions handed down from John Paul Jones, from Decatur, and from Farragut. It is safe to conjecture that as soon as Uncle Sam's seamen get fairly started on the work in hand they will prove more than a match for this German underwater navy which hides and strikes and runs away.

# German Seamen's Defense of U-Boats

## Reply of British Seamen

A NEW and significant chapter of war history has recently been written by the organized sailors of the belligerent countries, in the form of a report prepared by the German Seamen's Union with a view to justifying the U-boat warfare; and of an equally formal and much more scathing answer by the British seamen, who have suffered from that warfare. At the same time an international conference of merchant seamen met at London and voted for the withdrawal of all the sailors' unions of allied and neutral countries from the international union hitherto controlled by a Central Council in Germany.

The International Transport Workers' Federation has its Central Council in Berlin. Under date of March 8, 1917, this council sent a " German Report Upon the U-boat Warfare," along with a circular letter to the seamen's unions of neutral lands. The letter said in part:

The consequences of the German U-boat warfare for the neutral States, and particularly for their seafaring population, stand forth particularly prominently, and therefore all the more conspicuously. In consequence of impulses reaching the I. T. U.'s Central Council, either by direct or by indirect route, from America, England, and other lands, we regard it as necessary and as a duty to seek to describe the situation which the U-boat warfare has created above all for the seamen of the neutral lands. For this purpose we have encouraged the officers of the German Seamen's organization to give an objective account of the causes and the aims of the German U-boat warfare. This is now to hand.

### The German Seamen's Report

Following is the full text of the report referred to above:

The question of the blame for the world war we will here leave on one side. This question would lead to a conscious taking of sides, which we desire to avoid in this context.

The causes of the war lie, according to the German view, mainly in the sphere of economics, and thereby both the intensity of this world war and its form as a war of economics and of trade are conditioned. It is also, moreover, these economic causes of the war which have placed the war by sea in the foreground before all other events of the war.

At the commencement of the war Germany and the neutrals pinned their hopes upon the respecting by all parties of international and maritime rights as fixed at The Hague Convention and by the Declarations of Paris and London. If these had been correctly observed in the sea warfare, the seamen of all States would have seen their interests kept in view to such extent as was necessary.

England preferred to take up a one-sided standpoint which regarded only its own interests. It either interpreted all the rules for the sea war to its own advantage in a one-sided way, limited them in arbitrary fashion, or else discarded them altogether. It was nothing else than arbitrariness on the part of England when it subsequently tried to replace the international rights of sea warfare that they themselves had discarded by rules that served only their own interests.

England's bad example was followed by its allies. Their motto at the present day is: "No consideration for the German people, arbitrariness toward the neutrals, and egoism in the achievement of their own interests and aims."

The freedom of the seas was destroyed, Germany and its allies were cut off from contact with the world, and the possibilities of neutral navigation were greatly limited. England certainly had no unqualified command of the sea, but nevertheless did violence to international navigation. And protests from the neutral States, whether sharp or mild, were simply ignored by England and France whenever they found it good to do so. Every new German or neutral protest only stirred England to new arbitrary acts and to an intensification of its terrorizing measures.

### The Reprisal Excuse

In this way Germany not only obtained the theoretic right, but was also practically compelled and obliged to adopt reprisals—i. e., to take preventive measures for its self-defense. Germany's intensification of the war by sea was caused by the aforesaid English actions.

When Germany, in face of this situation, resorted to U-boat warfare, this was because that was the most dangerous weapon that could be employed against England. From the technical point of view it was a novelty, behind which lay no practical experiences, and which, therefore, stood outside all international rul-

# SMASHING WIRE ENTANGLEMENTS

The Effect of Trench Mortar Shells on Barbed Wire Entanglements, Which
Are Cleared Out of the Way Before an Infantry Charge
*(Canadian Official Photo from American Press Association)*

# FRENCH TRAIN RIDDLED BY BULLETS

A French Railway Train Which Has Come Under the Fire of Machine
Guns, So Badly Damaged as to Be of No Further Use
*(French Official Photo from Pictorial Press)*

The Church of Alexander III., One of the Most Interesting Pieces of Architecture in the City Now Occupied by the Germans

ings. No doubts can be entertained as to the legitimacy and justifiability of its employment.

Germany employs this sharp weapon because pressure always calls forth counterpressure. Meanwhile, even in its U-boat warfare, it has shown respect for human and humanitarian principles, not only as against the neutrals, but also as against its enemies. Isolated mistakes of German U-boat commanders have certainly increased the difficulties of neutral navigation, but Germany has acceded in every well-founded and just case to the claims for compensation put forward.

To all this England reacted merely by intensifying the war of starvation against German civil population, with a renewed provocation of neutral navigation, the freedom and independence of which it curtailed more and more, and the safety of which likewise became more and more threatened. Eloquent pieces of testimony to this are England's misuse of flags and the systematic arming of trading vessels intended to serve peaceful ends.

The unfavorable effects and hard consequences of the German U-boat warfare upon neutral navigation as well, can not, and ought not, to be contested; they are clear and evident, but must be put down to the account of England. England and its allies have pressed the neutral ships into their service, have induced neutral ships' Captains not to regard German rules of sea warfare and official warnings. In spite of this, Germany has shown comprehension for all neutral protests, and has been conciliatory in facilitating, as far as possible, the task of neutral navigation, so far as it did not carry contraband exclusively in the English interest or in the interest of England's allies, or so far as it was not serviceable to them in other ways.

Germany went yet further, and sought to bring the sea warfare, by the mediation of the United States, back to the international rules. England was to grant the freedom of the seas and to abandon its war of starvation against the civil population of Germany and its allies; in return, the U-boat warfare was to be restricted to its original purposes.

England did not merely refuse this generous German offer, but replied with new arbitrary acts, and took even sterner measures against the neutral States of Europe, in particular against Holland, Norway, Sweden, and Denmark.

## England's Starvation Policy

In conflict with all the principles of international right and humanity, England makes the greatest efforts, without distinction of sex and age, to drive the non-combatant German civil population into starvation, in order, in this way, indirect-ly to bring Germany to her knees in a military sense. In this intention England does not shrink back from a starvation policy against the neutral peoples—a fact which emerges with clearness from its repeated limitations of imports and its continual confiscations of neutral cargoes. The seamen in the neutral lands ought, further, to remember what consequences this English arbitrariness and violence have invoked upon the neutral lands and their navigation.

In December, 1916, came the well-intentioned German offer of peace, the acceptance of which would have put an end to the U-boat warfare. At the command of England and on an English initiative the German peace offer was rejected harshly and without ceremony, and upon its rejection followed an intensified closing of the North Sea, which had as its final effect a blockade of a part of the Danish and Dutch coasts. To this were added a sharp English control of neutral shipping, a greater intensity in plunderings of the post on the English and French sides, increased seizures of neutral ships, refusal to supply bunker coal, &c. One provocation against Germany followed upon the other.

Germany was thus confronted with the problem: Is it possible to put a speedy end to England's unexampled conduct for the advantage of the German people, of their allies, and of the neutral lands? Germany answered this question in the affirmative by proclaiming, on Jan. 31, a rigorous U-boat warfare as the consequence of the eternal English challenges. Germany announced an intensification of the blockade of England and its allies by sea, but conceded, in spite of the widening of the blockade area, certain necessary exceptions for the neutrals, at the same time threatening to sink every vessel which, in spite of warnings, entered the blockade area. Once again pressure called forth pressure, severity was answered with severity, and extremes met; with this exception, that Germany benevolently showed consideration for the neutral States and their interests, a consideration unknown to and in no way adopted by England.

## Germany's Purpose Explained

The purpose of the intensified German U-boat warfare is not to destroy wares of all kinds and to sink ships, in particular neutral ships; still less does it lie in the intention of the Germans to destroy neutral seamen's lives. The intention is rather to bring to a standstill all navigation to the ports of England and its allies; in other words, to cut off these lands entirely from all imports and exports by sea.

Against this England and its allies find prepared for them only the same fate, in an economic aspect, which England, from the beginning of the war, was firmly determined to inflict upon millions of German citizens, old people, women and children, as well as, let it not be forgotten, the neutral peoples.

The task before us is to make this English blow, as brutal as it is inexcusable from an international point of view, recoil in its effects upon England itself, in order that in this way England may be made the readier for peace, and this not only in the German interest, but also in that of the neutrals.

The intensified U-boat warfare admits, in spite of all this, of a dangerless sea-traffic between the peoples of the Old and of the New World, and concedes further a similarly unhindered and dangerless traffic by sea between the Scandinavian lands and Germany.

What Germany now expects from the neutral maritime States is the following: They must fall in with Germany's published and extended closure of the seas against England and its allies, in the same degree as they hitherto respected the corresponding measures adopted by England or its allies. All that is required of them, accordingly, is to be fair.

Germany is waging this intensified U-boat warfare only as a measure of self-defense, above all, against England. England is now itself to feel the methods which it hitherto has applied with brutal ruthlessness to other peoples, also to such as now stand in a hostile or unfriendly relation to Germany.

The German U-boat warfare is intended to, and certainly will, shorten the war in general, i. e., will hasten to bring about the peace for which all peoples long. To that extent it serves also the interests of the neutral States. In any case, its chief aims demand an objective consideration, in particular from the workmen in the neutral lands. And these its chief aims ought also to be adopted to making it easier and more tolerable for seamen in the neutral lands to bear the temporary inconveniences that it carries with it.

### Safety in Submission of Neutrals

A strict observance of the rules laid down by Germany for German U-boat warfare signifies the surest protection for neutral goods and human lives, and means the saving of neutral ships as cultural assets after the war, an object of the greatest interest, both to Germany and to the neutral lands.

England, in consequence of the U-boat warfare, oversteps all bounds in its terroristic measures against the navigation of the neutral lands with the aim of forcing them into the service of themselves and their allies. England wishes in this way to escape from the extended sea blockade at the cost of the neutrals, as well as from its economic consequences, and so to protect and spare its own ships at the cost of the mercantile navies of the neutrals. Such a policy is traditional with England.

Will and can the neutral navigation and the neutral shippers pay this tribute to England? Upon the answer, affirmative or negative, to this question depend the consequences of the intensified German U-boat warfare to the neutral shippers and the neutral seamen.

If this tribute is paid to England it may bring about material advantages to the shippers in the shape of larger profits. But it would expose neutral lives and property to extreme dangers and to certain destruction. A refusal of the tribute demanded by England might condemn the neutral shipping to a partial inactivity and occasion material losses to shippers and seamen, but would protect neutral lives and neutral property and render them safe for the future.

It is from this point of view that the navigation interests, and above all the seamen, ought to consider the question and to draw thence their conclusions as to the effect upon themselves.

For them the question is one of self-help for their own protection and self-preservation. The future will show whether the instinct of self-preservation, in particular among seamen, is stronger than England's powers of persuasion and its advocates of all kinds in the neutral lands.

## The British Seamen's Reply

The following is the text of the " Reply of the Organized Seamen of the British Mercantile Marine to the account published by the German Seamen's Organization as to the Causes and the Aims of the German ' U ' boat Warfare." It was prepared by Charles P. Hopkins and was made public in London on Aug. 20, 1917:

1. The German seamen, after significantly refusing to discuss the question of the blame for the commencement of the war, state that the causes of it lie, according to the German view, mainly in the sphere of economics.

With regard to this it may be observed that the event which led to the crisis from which this war proceeded was the wholly unjustifiable demand made by Austria, with Germany's connivance, upon Serbia by the presentation of the Austrian ultimatum, the acceptance of which was inconsistent with the continuance of Serbia as an independent power. Is is possible that economic reasons may have prompted this step on the part of the Central Powers, but, whatever the reasons, they can hardly justify their action in deliberately bringing about a crisis which they knew and, to all appearances, hoped would result in a world war for which, as the military events of the first few months showed, they had been so patiently and thoroughly preparing. Great Britain, on the other hand, can hardly be accused of entering the war for economic reasons, any more than her allies can. The British Government during the crisis before the declaration of war did all that was possible to avert war, or, failing that, to localize the conflict. Their efforts were vain, because good-will was absent on the side of the Central Powers.

Up to almost the last moment the British Government refused to pledge itself to come to the assistance of France, and it was only the violation of Belgium which finally turned the scale on the side of British participation—a violation by Germany of a treaty which she was pledged to observe. Even the Germans recognized the wrong they did in Belgium at the outbreak of war, although they have since tried to explain it away. It should not be forgotten that the German Chancellor, speaking in the Reichstag on Aug. 4, 1914, stated, in referring to the violation of the neutrality of Belgium and Luxemburg: "The wrong — I speak openly—the wrong we thereby commit we will try to make good as soon as our military aims have been attained."

2. The German seamen maintain that Germany pinned her hopes at the commencement of the war upon the respect by all parties of international and maritime rights.

What are the facts? At the very commencement of the war the Germans engaged in the indiscriminate laying of mines upon trade routes in defiance of all the rules of international law, and to the common danger of neutrals as well as belligerents. This disregard by Germany not only of international law at sea, but of the elementary dictates of humanity, has been constantly maintained throughout the war both on land and at sea. It will suffice to mention such incidents as the sacking of Louvain and the torpedoing of the Lusitania and many other passenger ships; the poisoning of wells; the forced deportations from Belgium; the shooting of Miss Cavell and Captain Fryatt; the torpedoing of hospital ships, and the numerous cases in which the U-boat commanders have deliberately fired upon the crews of merchant ships after they had taken to the boats.

### Reprisal Claim Refuted

3. But the chief point made by the German seamen is that the submarine warfare is justified as a measure of reprisal against the British blockade of Germany.

The Germans maintain that it is illegal to cut off the food supplies of an enemy country.

This is a curious contention, because one of the avowed objects of the submarine blockade when it was first started was that it was to cut off all supplies from this country. Moreover, did not the Germans in the war of 1870 starve the City of Paris, both the civilian population as well as the garrison? Further, German statesmen themselves have on various occasions laid down the principle that to stop the food supply of the civil population is as natural and legitimate a method of bringing pressure to bear on an enemy country as it is upon the defenses of a besieged town. This view is upheld on the authority of both Prince Bismarck and Count Caprivi.

It is thus quite evident that the British blockade is neither contrary to international law nor to the views held by German statesmen; but, quite apart from this, it is quite impossible for the Germans to justify submarine warfare as a measure of reprisal against Great Britain for the simple fact that submarine warfare was instituted before the passing of the Order in Council of March 11, 1915, which instituted the blockade.

The following list of incidents in chronological order should suffice to dispose of this plea:

September, 1914.—The Dutch vessel Maria, from California to Dublin and Belfast, with grain for the civil population, was sunk by the German cruiser Karlsrhue.

Oct. 26, 1914.—The Admiral Gantéaume, with 2,000 unarmed refugees, sunk by a German submarine.

December, 1914.—Admiral Tirpitz foreshadowed the adoption of the submarine campaign.

Jan. 27, 1915.—The American ship William B. Frye, with wheat from Seattle to Queenstown, was sunk by the German auxiliary cruiser Kronprinz Wilhelm.

Feb. 4, 1915.—The declaration by the German Government of their intention to institute a general submarine blockade of Great Britain and Ireland with the avowed purpose of cutting off all supplies from those islands. This blockade was put into effect officially on Feb. 18, 1915, although, as a matter of fact, a merchant ship had been sunk by a German submarine at the end of January.

It was not until March 11, 1915, that the present measures against German trade were put in force by Great Britain.

Before the enforcement of those measures, it will thus be seen the Germans had destroyed cargoes of foodstuffs coming to the civilian population of this country; had declared their intention of instituting a system of submarine outrage, and had actually submarined merchant vessels without warning. And yet they now try to justify their submarine blockade as a measure of reprisal!

### An Insincere Excuse

4. The German seamen seek to make out a case that the intensified submarine warfare was brought about owing to the refusal of the Allies to accept the German so-called peace proposals at the end of 1916, and that it was only when those proposals had been taken at their proper value by the Allies as an unnecessary attempt to place the blame of the war on the Entente Powers that Germany reluctantly instituted unrestricted submarine warfare.

It is sufficient, in answer to this, to refer to what the German Chancellor said in the Reichstag when announcing the adoption of unrestricted submarine warfare. He said that as soon as he himself, in agreement with the Supreme Army Command, reached the conviction that ruthless U-boat warfare would bring Germany nearer to victorious peace, then the unrestricted U-boat warfare would be started. He continued as follows:

" This moment has now arrived. Last " Autumn the time was not yet ripe; but " today the moment has come when, with " the greatest prospect of success, we can " undertake this enterprise. We must " therefore not wait any longer. Where " has there been a change? In the first " place, the most important fact of all is " that the number of our submarines has " very considerably increased as compared " with last Spring, and thereby a firm " basis has been created for success."

Does this not prove conclusively that it was not any scruple or any respect for international law or neutral rights that prevented unrestricted submarine warfare from being adopted earlier, but merely the lack of means to carry it out?

Another reason given by the Germans to justify unrestricted U-boat warfare is that Great Britain refused to grant Germany the " freedom of the seas." Apparently the German idea of warfare is that Germany should be free to exercise to the full her land-power, but that the Allies should not be free to exercse their sea-power, which they have always used with humanity and respect for neutrals, in striking distinction to German methods.

Finally, the German seamen claim that they have been more considerate to neutrals than the Allies, that they have placed fewer hindrances in the way of neutral trade, and that all they desire is that neutrals will be fair to them and will respect their measures equally with the British measures. To this it may be asked how many neutral lives have the Germans sacrificed at sea, and how many have the Allies? The answer to the first question shows an appalling disregard of innocent neutral lives on the part of the Germans, whereas, so far as is known, no neutral has lost his life at sea owing to the armed forces of the allied Governments.

### Treatment of Neutrals at Sea

With regard to the restrictions on neutral trade all that Great Britain has asked is that neutral countries do not serve as bases of supply to the enemy, a request at once natural and in accordance with the spirit of international law. Neutral countries have received freely the supplies necessary for their home consumption. It is true that neutral ships as the price of receiving British coal have been required to comply with certain conditions laid down by the British Government; but as the coal in question is British property and there is no obligation at all on Great Britain to supply this commodity, of which she herself and her allies stand in great need, it is clear that she is rightly entitled to demand some service from the people to whom she supplies this product.

The Germans, on the other hand, have placed a restriction on neutral trade, which is wholly unjustifiable, by proclaiming a danger zone, in which all ships are sunk at sight, whether trading with an enemy country or engaged in purely neutral trade. For instance, a ship like the Bloemersdyke, a neutral ship carrying a neutral cargo to a neutral country, was sunk by the Germans, as well as many vessels carrying relief for Belgium, which they have destroyed in defiance of all their pledges. There is this great difference between the German danger zone and the British blockade: The latter is a justifiable use of sea power, gained by the command of the sea, and is carried out with due respect for neutral lives and neutral property. Neutrals are at liberty to contest the action taken in the prize court. The German measure, on the other hand, is the mere arbitrary declaration of a danger zone over an extent of sea where they have no real control, but is merely a zone in which they say that indiscriminate murder by submarines is permissible. There is no respect for neutral lives or for neutral property. In fact, the Germans hope, by a system of barefaced murder, to force neutral shipping to abandon the traffic which German sea power, exercised in a legitimate manner, is powerless to prevent. The Germans may seek to justify their policy, but the judgment of the world has already been formed, and nation after nation joins the ranks of Germany's opponents, to fight side by side with the free peoples of the earth against the military despotism which is the avowed enemy of democracy and freedom.

### Drastic Action by Seamen

An international conference of seamen and firemen of allied and neutral countries met in London in August to consider the crimes committed by commanders and crews of U-boats. Havelock Wilson presided. In the session of Aug. 18, 1917, the conference passed resolutions demanding reparation and recommending withdrawal of the various national seamen's unions from the International Transport Workers' Federation and the formation of a new organization by sailors of allied and neutral nations. Delegates were present from France, Italy, Denmark, Norway, Sweden, Australia, and other countries. The following resolution was unanimously adopted:

That this international conference composed of all sections of seafarers employed in merchant ships of allied and neutral nations hereby expresses our sense of horror and indignation at the brutal crimes perpetrated by the commanders and crews of submarines belonging to the Central Powers, of suffering entailed not so much on ourselves as on our wives and children, and we hereby pledge ourselves to support any action calculated to put an end to the present measures adopted by the commanders and crews of those submarines.

The French delegate moved a resolution declaring " that reparation must be " made by the Austro-Germans for their " inhuman conduct of submarine war- " fare, and until such reparation be made " the seafarers represented at this con- " ference declare that they will hold the " Austro-German seafarers equally re- " sponsible with the authorities for such " conduct, and reserve to themselves the " right to take such action on the con- " clusion of the war as may be deemed " best to enforce the views expressed in " the resolution." The Scandinavian delegate seconded, and the resolution was unanimously adopted. There was also passed unanimously a resolution put by the Scandinavian representatives that " all delegates present recommend to " their organizations to withdraw from " the International Workers' Federation, " and that an International Federation " Executive be elected by those repre- " senting the seafarers' unions belonging " to allied and neutral countries."

Mr. Moore of the Imperial Merchant Service Guild then moved a resolution that " this International Conference " pledges itself that, unless the present

" methods of Austro-German submarine " warfare do cease, we will refuse in " the future to sail in any ships carry- " ing seamen of the Central Powers." This was carried with cheers.

## Firing on Lifeboats

The conference also drew up the following list of authenticated cases in which enemy submarines fired upon helpless men in small boats after they had left their ships:

(1) Kildare, British steamship. Sunk by submarine April 12, 1917. While boats were pulling clear of ship shells came over them and then a submarine was seen on the surface. She fired from ten to fifteen shells at the boats, killing an A.B.

(2) John W. Pearn, British steamship. Sunk by submarine May 1, 1917. Submarine fired two shots at boat which was pulling away.

(3) Vulcana, British steamship. Sunk by submarine March 7, 1917. After boat had got out, she capsized in the heavy swell running, and had to be righted. Firing was continued by the submarine until boat was clear.

(4) Belgian Price, British steamship. Sunk by submarine July 31, 1917. Lifeboats not fired on, but broken up and survivors thrown into the sea after being placed on outside of submarine, which submerged, leaving them to their fate, after also depriving them of lifebelts.

(5) Westminster, British steamship. Sunk by submarine Dec. 14, 1916. Survivors took to boats and were shelled by submarine, Captain and chief officer being killed.

(6) Eavestone, British steamship. Sunk by submarine Feb. 3, 1917. Submarine turned her gun on boats, firing three shrapnel shells and striking both boats. Third shell killed master, steward, donkeyman, and two A.B.'s; severely wounded second officer.

(7) Addah, British steamship. Sunk by submarine June 15, 1917. Submarine opened fire on master's boat, killing eight men, and after boat had been sunk and men were swimming in the water submarine shelled them with shrapnel.

(8) Umaria, British steamship. Sunk by submarine May 26, 1917. Submarine fired on boat, injuring all occupants.

(9) Vanland, Swedish steamship. Attacked by submarine July 23, 1917. As lifeboat was making for shore, submarine continued to fire on master and crew with machine gun, wounding the second mate.

(10) Baltic, Swedish steamship. Sunk by submarine June 27, 1917. Boats fired on for about an hour after crew abandoned ship.

(11) Freden, Danish steamship. Sunk by submarine May 22, 1917. Lifeboat damaged, and several of crew wounded

while trying to mend it; one Frenchman killed, others severely wounded.

(12) Hestia, Dutch steamship. Sunk by submarine March 30, 1917. One boat fired on by submarine and sunk, six Dutchmen and seven Chinamen being killed.

# Fighting Hostile Submarines

## Sketch of the Methods Used by the French and Italian Navies in the Mediterranean

Pierre Mille, a staff correspondent of the Paris Temps, recently made an extended visit to the French fleet. On his return he wrote the article which is here translated for CURRENT HISTORY MAGAZINE.

NAVIGATION on the surface has two enemies—the mine and the submarine. There are several types of mines, differing in diameter, priming, and explosives. But in general every mine consists of three parts: the mine itself, which should explode at first contact with an object that strikes it; the weight that anchors it at a certain spot and keeps it from drifting, and the cable that connects the anchor and the mine, maintaining it in a position about ten feet below the surface. The use of mines that are not fixed to the bottom is forbidden by The Hague Convention, but that has not hindered the Germans from using them.

Every day new mines are discovered, evidently set in place a short time before. They have been sown either by neutral fishing vessels owned by the enemy or by enemy ships disguised as neutrals; or, again, by special submarines built for that purpose. These submarines lay mines along the coast as a fish lays eggs—happily in smaller numbers. The mine is even more destructive than the torpedo. One has been known to cut a ship in two—even a warship—as if it had been done with a pair of shears.

A mine-laying submarine has no torpedoes, but nothing hinders it from having guns. Besides, we are only at the beginning, perhaps only the early dawn, of the use of submarines. At present only great surface vessels are capable of assuring mastery of the high seas; the proof is that we are holding that

mastery. But it is almost certain that in the future the submarine will be so perfected that even the armored cruisers will be forced to descend and operate under the water. * * * But that is the future; the Germans began the war ten years too soon. In spite of all their efforts, and of an energetic will to succeed, they cannot, in the midst of war, lacking time and materials, bring about this great revolution. For the present submarine navigation is full of difficulties, which prevent the new weapon from producing its maximum effect.

### Fuel for Thirty Days

It is not impossible that enemy underseas craft in the Mediterranean have been able at times to get supplies of fuel oil on the coasts of certain neutrals or on certain islands, but they have no imperative need to do so. They carry enough to run thirty days, and they need only to go from a German port to Pola or Cattaro in order to find what they need without asking a favor of anybody, leaving those ports then to "work" regularly in the Mediterranean, and remaining at sea for a month without need of new supplies. The real service that unscrupulous neutrals can render them is to furnish information as to the routes taken by ships they wish to sink and to furnish them with fresh vegetables and meats.

The question of fresh food is very important, in fact, for the submarine crews, whose work is hard and exhausting. Life on board the underseas craft of the Entente is still more difficult than that on the German submersibles. The reason is simple. Our submarines have only one task—to sink U-boats; they have no surface vessels to sink. They are obliged, therefore, in this hunt to operate almost entirely under water. This produces an incessant nerve tension for our crews and makes it practically impossible for them to eat anything but preserved foods. They have, indeed, a little electric stove for cooking, but it is seldom used, because it consumes electricity. On the contrary, when an enemy submarine has struck its blow it can retire—the ocean is large. It comes to the surface, like the porpoises and turtles; it sleeps, it rests. And the men do their cooking on deck with kerosene, or even with coal. With coal! One can scarcely imagine such luxury.

## Three Kinds of Peril

Except for this advantage, the enemy submarine is in no better position than ours. Like the flying fishes—though it cannot fly—it has to fear attack on the surface, under water, and in the air above. On the surface its enemy is the torpedo boat; beneath, it is the net and the submarine. It may even chance to hit a mine—sometimes a mine laid by its friends—which destroys it just the same. Above, its enemy is the seaplane, a voracious hawk. When the submarine comes to the surface it never knows what may fall upon its head.

"My dear fellow," I heard the commander of one of our submarines say to a friend at dinner, "I came to the surface, and what do you think I saw? An Austrian seaplane 300 yards above my nose!"

"And then?"

"Then I bent my back to receive the hailstorm. Well, the enemy did not see me, or perhaps he was as much disconcerted as I. * * * I had time to dive, but it was a close call!"

Enemy submarines are no better off amid these perils than are our own. That is why, if we had enough submarines, patrol boats, convoy ships, hydroaeroplanes, life would become almost absolutely impossible for the German and Austrian U-boats. From now on their existence will be painful. They must have perfectly trained crews and particularly energetic and intelligent commanders. It should be noted that the enemy's successful submarine attacks are almost always by the same units, the same commanders.

## How Mines Are Destroyed

The boats that destroy mines are trawlers—ordinary patrol trawlers, or net layers, and dredge trawlers. The former are content to discover the mines and report their whereabouts. The dredge trawlers tow a sort of giant shears, which cut the buoy ropes of the mines and bring them to the surface, where they are made to explode.

This is not the only work of the trawlers. They not only lay the steel nets, but also watch them. They are sentinels, scouts, hunters of submarines and mines. Officers of the navy and of merchantmen, with our coastwise fishermen, take part in this constant patrol work. Nowhere will you see finer men or more accomplished sailors. Perpetual heroism, stubborn and weatherbeaten, reigns on those cockleshell craft. During the eight months of the stormy season the men can seldom do any cooking on board: the high waves sweep the deck from stem to stern and extinguish the fires. The men then eat canned foods, as do those on the submarines.

On the torpedo boats, the destroyers, and the pleasure yachts requisitioned for war service the hardships are much the same, the work is as constant and hard, and the patience is of the same heroic sort. These vessels never rest. It is their thankless and dangerous task to pursue submarines, fight them, and convoy merchant ships. Convoying is only a last resort: if there were enough torpedo boats the patrols would suffice to purge the sea of the submarine peril. But there are not yet enough of these vessels—there never will be enough. All efforts ought now to be concentrated upon the building of light fighting ships, as hitherto they have been concentrated on the manufacture of heavy artillery.

I have not, however, completed the enumeration of the means of defense.

There is the drifter, the trawler that drags a net behind it, fishing for ·submarines as they used to fish for mackerel. For months and months it drifts with the winds and currents, scouring the sea, its net always in the water, never stopping, almost never going into port. Its crews are Frenchmen, mostly Bretons; and with them, too, are English fishermen from the North Sea and rough and fearless sailors recruited from waters as far away as the Pacific. Each crew of nine men is composed, as nearly as possible, of a single family—father, sons, uncles, and nephews. But it may happen that the father is placed under the orders of the son; it is a question of professional aptitude.

The monotony of their quest, which may be fruitless for months on end, dulls the brains of these men separated as they are from the rest of the world; their eyes take on a look of emptiness or of wildness; they have half forgotten the use of language, and sometimes, as if drunk with solitude and hypnotized with mirages, they conjure up strange visions and find diversion in them. But it also happens sometimes that their sombre and silent watch is rewarded: they have at various times had the fierce joy of feeling a submarine shudder in their net. In that case they drop an enormous bomb through the water upon their prey, a bomb capable of tearing the hull to pieces even if it explodes sixty yards ·away. The danger to themselves is almost as great as to the submarine. It often means their own shipwreck. If they escape, in proud silence they hoist to the maintop the death's-head flag of the old buccaneers.

## The Guns of Flanders

### By A. W. K., London

Boom! Boom!
Can't you sense it? Can't you feel it? Can't you hear it?
'Tis the drumming of the guns,
Boom! B'room!
Don't you hear it? Can you bear it? Don't you fear it?
'Tis the thudding of the guns.
Patient, peeving, laughing, weeping,
Scheming, dreaming, waking, sleeping;
Youth and age; flippant, sage;
Guilty, just; none but must
Feel the hum come
When our sons' guns
Give tongue and dun the Hun runs.
Ah! the guns!

Crack! Whup!
Did you speak us? Do you teach us or beseech us?
We're the guns, the Flanders guns.
Crash! Crump!
Do you ask us of our task, us in our mask, us
Demon guns, hounders of Huns?
You sit and moon. We'll fume and boom.
We'll croon the tune of hell-hounds' doom.
Point and bark! Recoil and hark!
On the mark! Stiff and stark
Are the Huns' sons
When our gun tongues
Dun doom upon the Hun runs.
Oh! we're guns!

# The Third Year of the Blockade

## Review by a British Expert

*Archibald Hurd, The London Telegraph's noted naval writer, is the author of the following survey of blockade activities and submarine warfare of the year ended Aug. 4, 1917:*

THE military blockade has been supplemented by the commercial blockade since March 11, 1915. During the past year, owing to the entrance of the United States into the war, with the support of practically all the other countries on the American Continent, the blockade has been rendered complete. In an economic sense Germany is now passing into a comatose condition. For over three years she has obtained only exiguous supplies overseas, either directly or through neighboring countries. Now that traffic is being stopped. Three years ago the blockade operated on two lines—the Dover-Calais line to the south and the Scotland-Iceland line to the north, with a branch toward Norway. The work of the naval patrols was supplemented by a number of ingenious compacts concluded by the Foreign Office with Denmark, Norway, and Holland, on the one hand, and American traders on the other. The constriction by these means was being tightened without antagonizing American or other interests when the United States abandoned her neutrality.

Now the area of blockade has been extended; its furthest limit is to be traced in the ports of the American Continent, where ships and cargoes are scrutinized and, in order that it may be made more effective, a severe rationing system is being imposed upon those nations which have the misfortune to be Germany's neighbors.

Submarine piracy brings Germany no relief from the pressure of the blockade; it hastens rather the process of economic exhaustion and weakens her military effort, for she has only a certain amount of labor and material to employ on land or sea. This development on the part of Germany was not foreseen by the naval authorities of this country or any other country. In the first place, reliance was put on the dictates of humanity and the law of nations; in the second place, the sea going capacity and military value of the submarine were underestimated. Germany has utilized the submarine because it is the only type of man-of-war which she can trust outside her mine-protected areas, except at increasing risk. When the campaign opened, a large number of submarines had been constructed and manned; they were suddenly released on the trade routes in the confident expectation that they would produce a coup, sinking so many merchant ships that within a few weeks this country, humiliated and terrified, would seek for peace; Germany knew that without uninterrupted sea communications the armies overseas could not be supported and the civil population of these islands and of the Allies could not fight. We now have the Admiralty's figures for five complete months:

| | Sunk by Mine or Submarine. | | | | |
|---|---|---|---|---|---|
| | 1,600 Tons Under Gross 1,600 Tons | | Total | Unsuccess- fully | Total At- |
| Record for— | or Over. | Gross. | Sunk. | Attacked. | tacked. |
| March ........ | 65 | 27 | 92 | 59 | 151 |
| Weekly aver.. | 16.25 | 6.75 | 23.0 | 14.75 | 37.75 |
| April ........ | 132 | 52 | 184 | 101 | 285 |
| Weekly aver.. | 26.2 | 10.4 | 36.8 | 20.2 | 57.0 |
| May .......... | 89 | 41 | 130 | 94 | 224 |
| Weekly aver.. | 17.8 | 8.2 | 26.0 | 18.8 | 44.8 |
| June .......... | 85 | 24 | 109 | 90 | 199 |
| Weekly aver.. | 21.25 | 6.0 | 27.25 | 22.5 | 49.75 |
| July .......... | 65 | 13 | 78 | 48 | 126 |
| Weekly aver.. | 13.25 | 3.25 | 19.5 | 12.0 | 31.5 |
| Weekly average for 5 months. | 19.8 | 7.1 | 26.9 | 17.8 | 44.7 |

There are elements in this examination of the Admiralty returns of the last five months which must be discouraging to the Germans and encouraging to us. The basis upon which the campaign was undertaken was that it would offer to Germany the absolute assurance of an early peace in accordance with her wishes—in short, save her from another Winter of warfare. Preparations for the campaign had been made over a period of two years. The engine-making and shipbuilding resources of Germany had been concentrated on the construction of submarines, and a large training school had been established for officers and men. According to official statements made in Berlin, arrangements had been made for sending to sea an increasing number of submarines from February onward. By the Summer the campaign was to reach its maximum, and Germany was to reap immediate advantage from the operations of increased numbers of submarines acting during the long Summer days when visibility is good.

What has happened? It is impossible to draw elaborate and detailed conclusions from the Admiralty figures. In the first place we are presented with a statement of the number of " targets "—that is, ships of all nationalities entering or leaving British ports. On the other hand, we learn only the number of British vessels sunk by submarines or mines, and to this is appended a statement of the number of British vessels unsuccessfully attacked by the means of submarines alone, since it is impossible, of course, to tabulate the number of ships which do not strike mines, for that would reduce the return to an absurdity. But certain definite conclusions are revealed by the analysis which has been made above.

The average weekly sinkings, which amounted to as much as 36.8 in April, have since fallen to 19.5—a reduction by nearly a half. At the same time, the number of vessels attacked unsuccessfully has dropped from 20.2 to 12 in July, again furnishing satisfactory evidence of the failure of the enemy submarines. Whether that be due to the increased arming of British merchant ships, to the growing efficiency of the British offensive measures, or to the inability of the Germans to maintain as many submarines at sea as was the case in April—owing to losses or other causes—it is impossible to say. The only conclusion to be formed is that owing to one or other of these causes, or all the causes in combination, the losses of ships by mine and submarine are about half what they were in April, and that there has been an appreciable decline in the number of merchantmen attacked.

Let the position be clearly understood. On the one hand, the race between the two blockades has not been decided in favor of the submarine, and it is established beyond question that, even though the depredations continue on the average of the last five months, a long period must elapse before this country would be forced to succumb, even though in the meantime little success attended improved efforts to combat the submarine and make good the losses of merchant shipping. Can Germany hold out? Even if our losses continue at the present rate to the end of the year, they will not be decisive.

But the continuance of those losses must prove a grave embarrassment and a source of weakness, because the number of ships remaining at our disposal is limited, and there are about 40,000,000 people to be fed and supplied with raw materials for work, apart from the needs of the navy and army, which under the conditions of war are stupendous, representing millions of tons annually of sea transport, and the demands of our allies for shipping are large. Our naval and military operations make an irresistible prior claim on tonnage, and consequently every ship which is sunk involves a reduction in the carrying power at the disposal of the civilian population. That is the position.

In a normal year we turn out, in addition to men-of-war, nearly 2,000,000 tons of merchant shipping. Under war conditions we can, if labor and material are supplied, increase that output by 50 or 100 per cent. Everything depends upon our putting into the shipbuilding campaign all the energy at our command, irrespective of all other claims, not excluding those of the army. Without adequate supplies of merchant shipping neither the army nor the navy can maintain the struggle, and the nation must be undone.

The naval year has been marked by no naval battle, and few incidents which will find a place in the history of this world war. Destroyers have made " tip and run " raids to the coast in the darkness from time to time; on one occasion they broke through into the Channel, but failed to interrupt the army's communications. No single one of those incidents was of the slightest military importance, though, unfortunately, loss of life resulted.

The fourth year of naval war opens with the British fleet commanding the seas with a success which was never anticipated in the years before the war. It is on the offensive every day and all the day, as well as by night, as the Germans have learned to their cost. Our vast naval engine somewhat resembles a fan. In August of 1914, we hardly realized its size and its strength as it lay hidden, far more completely than today, behind the fog of war. With the progress of hostilities it has been spread out, until today it covers the oceans of the world. There is no sea in which a British squadron is not on service; vast auxiliary forces numbering not far short of 3,000 keels, have come into existence, each vessel deftly fitting into the general scheme.

The fan has gradually been opened out. The base, on which the effective strength of the outspreading stems depends, consists of the grand fleet, with its battleships, its battle cruisers, its light cruisers, its destroyers, its submarines, and its great assembly of auxiliary craft. The outer squadrons on duty in the English Channel and Atlantic, in the White Sea and the Bay of Biscay, off Gibraltar and in the Mediterranean, in the Red Sea and in the Persian Gulf, off the Cape of Good Hope and the east Coast of Africa, in the East Indies, the Pacific and the Indian Ocean, constitute the stems of the naval fan, the intervals between which are filled in with destroyers, patrol vessels, monitors, mine sweepers, and other complementary craft. There has never been an organization comparable to that which today supports our every war effort. Its virtue lies, not in the ships of steel or wood, but in the men. A third year of war has tested the seamen of our age as the seamen of the last great war were never tested.

# Submarine Sinkings in Eight Months

## Total Ship Tonnage of 4,561,000 Sunk Since the Beginning of Germany's Intensified U-Boat Campaign

### By Charles H. Grasty

*War Correspondent of The New York Times*
[Copyrighted]

London, Sept. 9, 1917.

FOLLOWING, in terms of tonnage, are the monthly sinkings by German submarines from January to August, inclusive, the figures being for the Allies and neutrals in the aggregate, but not including raider losses and ships damaged or beached but not sunk. The weekly averages are given for purposes of comparison:

| Month. | Total Tonnage. | Sunk Weekly. |
|---|---|---|
| January (four weeks) | 333,000 | 83,000 |
| February (four weeks) | 479,000 | 120,000 |
| March (five weeks) | 600,000 | 120,000 |
| April (four weeks) | 788,000 | 197,000 |
| May (four weeks) | 549,000 | 137,000 |
| June (five weeks) | 758,000 | 152,000 |
| July (four weeks) | 463,000 | 116,000 |
| August (five weeks) | 591,000 | 118,000 |
| Total | 4,561,000 | ...... |

Against the loss of about four and a half million tons in eight months new construction is estimated at less than a million tons, leaving the net loss to allied and neutral shipping at about three and a half million tons. The loss to American shipping is said to have been less than one-half of 1 per cent.

While the decline in the shipping loss in July and August was substantial, it cannot be regarded as satisfactory, and the situation continues to call for the kind of activity demanded by a great emergency. America's opportunity for service lies more immediately and urgently in the direction of putting down the submarine menace than even in sending soldiers to France, all-important as that is. In fact, these two matters are inseparably connected.

As submarine attack and defense are reduced to a business, a good deal of mystery surrounding the war under water is clearing up and commonplace facts are becoming known. The popular mind pictures the waters off the British coast as swarming with submarines. It is a matter of general knowledge in naval circles now that the number of German submarines in the Atlantic Ocean never exceeds twenty and that the number operating in the North Atlantic off the British coast does not exceed ten. These figures do not include submarines engaged exclusively in mine laying.

It is estimated in the best British naval circles that Germany has not built as many as 300 submarines altogether, and that about 150 of all conditions are in existence today.

The U-boat is of very delicate mechanism and needs frequent repairing, which, in the main, explains the small number operating in the Atlantic and elsewhere. Most of the boats are being repaired or replenished constantly and out of commission.

Still another reason is the difficulty in getting crews and keeping them going. The work is so hard and the dangers are so constant that officers and crews peter out. After a few months the men lose their appetite and cannot sleep.

The internal arrangements of a submarine are such as to make life on one of them extremely trying. Plumbing fixtures, kitchens, and eating facilities are jumbled together, and ventilation is necessarily bad. It is very difficult to maintain whole crews in service.

Another difficulty, and one constantly increasing, is the shortage of material for torpedoes. Wild shots are much more frequent than formerly.

The multiplication of destroyers has greatly increased the nerve-racking character of submarine duty. U-boat navigators are deathly afraid of the destroyers, with their speed, guns, and depth bombs. The presence of destroyers and other patrol boats in force in the English Channel explains the immunity of transports which have carried millions of soldiers back and forth between France and England without serious loss.

## Cannot Raid in Fleets

Another submarine weakness which impedes operation and shakes the nerves of U-boat men is the blindness of their craft. When submerged they cannot see, and there have been many collisions. For this reason they cannot operate in companies, which furnishes still another explanation of the small number utilized.

As is well known, the submarine, when submerged, must keep in motion, as it cannot otherwise maintain its equilibrium. When it stops it is liable to " up-end."

It is clear, therefore, that the submarine campaign, as it now stands, is one depending upon hysterical courage. Germany lashed herself into a spasm-like fury in the early months of last Winter, and the peak of her effort was reached in April, when the sinkings aggregated about 200,000 tons a week. In order to accomplish this extraordinary result extraordinary means were used which it was impossible to sustain in subsequent months. The comparatively low figures of July and August represent, to some extent, the reaction from the high pitch of energy in April.

There is much gratified comment here on the action of Washington in placing increased orders for the construction of destroyers, and the period subsequent to Jan. 1, 1918, is looked forward to confidently. The next four months are necessarily to be a time of anxiety, and America is relied upon fully to employ her superb energy and resourcefulness in protecting allied interests during that dangerous period.

The principle of the convoy system has been soundly established by the experience of the last few months. Naval authorities hold that it is clear that shipping can be protected by escorting vessels. It is only a matter of having enough cruisers and destroyers. With an adequate number of these vessels the destruction of shipping can be reduced to the point of new construction, and whenever that is done Germany will bite the dust.

# Ambassador Page's Plymouth Address

## An Eloquent Statement of War Aims and Mutual Relations of Britain and America

Walter Hines Page, the United States Ambassador to Great Britain, delivered a speech at Plymouth, England, on Aug. 4, 1917, which moved the great gathering in the Guildhall to enthusiasm and was later printed in full in the London papers. The most striking portions are here presented as worthy of permanent record.

I AM glad to stand in this town and at the beginning of this new era in the life of our race to pledge the unwavering fellowship of free men across the sea—the sea that once separated us, but that now unites us. I pay homage here to the immortal memory of those sturdy men who sailed from this harbor nearly three hundred years ago and carried to the making of our New World that love of freedom which now impels us to come to the defense of the imperiled freedom of the world. The idealism of the Republic rests on their unconquerable spirit, which we keep yet, thank God, when a high duty calls us. In memory of them, and in the comradeship of this righteous war, whose awful shadow will darken the world till we win it, I greet you as kinsmen.

We are met on the most tragic anniversary in history. It is not a day to celebrate for its own sake. What we shall be glad to celebrate will be the day of victory and its anniversary ever afterward. But, before we achieve victory, it is fit that we meet on this dire anniversary to fortify our purpose, if it need fortifying, and to pledge ourselves that the brave men who have died shall not have died in vain and to reassert our purpose to finish the task, even if it exhaust the vast resources and take all the valiant lives of the Allies in Europe and of the Republic across the sea. For what would the future of the human race be worth if the deliberate and calculated barbarism of our enemies overrun the earth? The supreme gift of free government, which this brave island gave to the world, and to which all free lands chiefly owe their freedom, would be swept away. Let the darkness of death overtake us now rather than that the darkness of tyranny should sweep over the whole world of free men.

No American can come to Plymouth without thinking of the going of the English from these shores to the new land, where they set up a new freedom and laid the foundations of the most prosperous and hopeful community on the earth. In the course of time those New World communities fell apart from political allegiance to the old land. But they fell apart from the old land only in political allegiance. If we had need to discuss this political divergence, I should maintain that political separation was as well for you as it was necessary for us, and that by reason of it human freedom has been further advanced and a new chapter in free men's growth opened throughout the English-speaking world.

### Race Which Endured

The American Revolution was a civil war fought on each side by men of the same race. And this civil war was fought in the Colonial Assemblies and in Parliament as well as on the battlefields in America, and it was won in the Colonial Assemblies and in Parliament as well as on the battlefields in America, for from that day on you have regarded colonies as free and equal communities with the mother country. This civil war naturally left a trail of distrust, the greater because of the long distance between us by sail. But, when the first steamship came over the ocean, and still more when the cable bound us together, a new union began to come about. But in the meantime the American community had developed in its own way, and we had become so fixed and different in our conventions and ways of life that we could not easily come back to your conventions and ways of life if we would. In fact, there is no other test that the British people have had—no test that any people has ever had—which proved its great qualities so well as the British settlement and management of America. Here were men in a new land, cut off from close contact with their kinsmen at home, who took their political affairs in their own management, and thereafter were without guidance or support from their more numerous kinsmen left behind.

How did the race stand such a test? No other migrating race has stood such a test so well; and those first English colonists have now grown, by natural increase and by numerous adoptions, into a people which today include more English-speaking white men than the whole British Empire. They have not only outgrown in numbers all the British elsewhere, but they have kept what may be called the faith of the race. They have kept the racial and national characteristics. They have kept British law, British freedom, British Parliaments, British character.

I am not boasting of my own land; I am only reciting how your race has endured and survived separation from you and your land. Our foundations were British; our political structure is British, with variations; our social structure is British—also with important variations; more important still, our standards of character and of honor and of duty are your standards; and life and freedom have the same meaning to us that they have to you. These are the essential things, and in these we have always been one.

And now the day of our supreme test and of the heroic mood is come. There is now a race reason why we should have a complete understanding; and such a complete understanding has come. You will, I hope, pardon me for even alluding to our old differences; for they are now long-forgotten, far-off things. I allude to them only to clear the way. It is not the going of the Pilgrims nor the falling away of the colonies that we now celebrate, but rather the coming of American warships, which symbolize the new union of the two peoples that this fierce assault on our civilization has revealed afresh. Politically two peoples, in all high aims and in the love of freedom we are one, and must now remain at one forever.

## Differences Swept Away

This war has swept away incidental differences between us as a harrow smoothes a field. Not only are our warships come. Our troopships, too, have landed an army on the soil of our brave ally, where the enemy yet keeps the wavering line of an invader, and more warships will come and more troopships, million-laden, if need be, till that line is forever broken and till the submarines are withdrawn or are forever submerged. There is coming the greatest victory for free government that was ever won, and the day of this victory which we are both fighting for may turn out to be the most important date in our history, or perhaps in all history. And the necessity to win it has cleared the air as no other event in modern times has cleared it; and but for the millions of brave lives it has cost, this clearing of the air would richly repay all that the war will cost. It has revealed the future of the world to us not as conquerors, but as preservers of its peace. The free, peace-loving nations will have no more of this colossal, armed, and ordered pillage; and no combination of the peace-loving nations can be made effective without both branches of the English-speaking peoples. This empire and the great Republic must then be the main guardians of civilization hereafter, the conscious and leagued guardians of the world.

It is this that the war has revealed to us. It is not a task of our seeking. But it is a task that we will, with the other free peoples of the world, gladly undertake. To undertake it, our comradeship must become perpetual, and our task is to see to it that it be not broken nor even strained—our task and our children's task after us. It is, of course, the function of Governments to keep friendly nations in proper relations to one another; and both our nations fortunately can and do trust both our Governments to do that. Through all the difficulties and differences that arose between our two

Governments during the early stages of the war, there was no rupture of friendly dealing. When the full story of these years of delicate relations comes to be told it will be seen that mutual toleration and forbearance played a far larger part than a rigid insistence on disputed points. Such differences as we had were differences between friends. I am sure that I may say with propriety that the two distinguished British statesmen who were his Majesty's Chief Foreign Secretaries during this period showed a spirit in their dealings with the United States Government that put the whole English-speaking world in their debt; and I am sure that they would say the same for the Government of the United States.

### Mutual Knowledge

But while, fortunately, our two Governments may be fully trusted to bind us together, Governments come and Governments go. Far more important than any particular Government is the temper and action of public opinion in free countries such as ours. The complete and permanent union in all large aims of our two nations, generation after generation, must, therefore, rest on the broad base of a friendly and informed public opinion in both countries. If this argument be sound it leads us—every one of us—to a high duty. The lasting friendship of two democratic nations must rest on the sympathetic knowledge that the people of each nation have of the other—even upon the personal friendships of large numbers of people one with another. Personal friendships make a friendly public opinion. It is, therefore, the highest political duty that Britons and Americans can have to build up personal knowledge of one another and personal friendships.

[Here Mr. Page urged the use of new textbooks in the schools of both England and America—simple and interesting books that should teach the youth of each nation to appreciate the qualities of the other. He concluded:]

Most valuable of all the activities that lead to a permanent sympathy is our present fellowship in war. American fighting units are come and very many more will come. They all work side by side with your men and with the French. And most of these, of course, are young men, and, like your young men, the flower of our race. Now these are forming companionships that nothing can sever. Men who go forth to die together, if fate so will it, understand one another as long as they survive. Beside the comradeship of arms, formed where death comes swift and frequently, other companionships seem weak. For men's naked souls are then bared to one another. In this extremest trial that man ever underwent anywhere at any time the high emotions and the guns are at work; everything else of life is still or pushed out of consciousness. And men who come together then are forever inseparable. Already there's many a corner of a foreign land that is forever England; and presently there'll be many a corner of a foreign land that is an American grave also.

Those that die and those that live will hereafter alike so bind our two peoples in mutual understanding that any disturber of that understanding will but play the poor part of a sacrilegious fool.

# A New Covenant Between the Great English-Speaking Nations

*This noteworthy editorial article appeared in The London Telegraph on Aug. 16, 1917, under the title, " A New Covenant ":*

FOR the first time in history, a body of American troops marched through the streets of London yesterday. They made their way to Buckingham Palace, where King George received the salute; they were greeted by the Prime Minister and other members of the War Cabinet, a meeting of that body being adjourned for the purpose, and they were acclaimed by thousands of sightseers, representing not merely the capital of the empire, but the empire itself. If ever there was an imperial city, it is the London of today, with Canadian, Australian, New Zealand, South African, and other oversea troops thronging its streets, enjoying leave from the rigors of duty, and in our midst a score and more official representatives of the great dominions. London has become the nerve centre of a vast organization which draws its strength from every sea and every clime, and finds its inspiration in the confidence that, as a result of this war, the cause of freedom will be firmly established. It was this London, with a sprinkling of Belgian, French, and Italian residents, which yesterday cheered the advance guard of the great American Army.

The scenes presented during the march of these fine, muscular, athletic men from the other side of the Atlantic—typical of American manhood—must convince their fellow-countrymen that the significance of their intervention in this titanic struggle is fully realized. Washington once declared, with all that pride which distinguished him, even though realizing that he was merely " a member of an infant empire," that " these United States shall one day have a weight in the scale of Europe." That day has dawned; the new expansion was made evident in the streets of London yesterday, when citizens of the dominions, in unison with representatives of these islands, raised their voices to welcome the valiant soldiers who in no long time will be fighting under " Old Glory " on the battlefields of the Continent.

What did it all mean? The Monroe Doctrine, which was framed to protect the peoples of the New World from the evils pressing down the Old, has been superseded, or rather extended; the soldiers whom we greeted yesterday with sincere appreciation and admiration represent a new principle—the unity of the English-speaking world in defense of the inalienable rights which the common forefathers of the two races handed down to their successors as a priceless heritage. The American soldiers were the outward and visible sign of a new covenant.

Mr. Gerard has revealed the violent division of opinion which occurred in Germany last Spring as to the importance of American intervention. When the submarine issue was being discussed, the apostles of organized force, Marshal von Hindenburg, Grand Admiral von Tirpitz, and their entourages professed a contempt for the United States—a mere democracy. Dr. Bethmann Hollweg and a few civilians were doubtful whether piracy was worth the risk it involved. As we have long known, the hesitations of the latter were swept aside; the submarine was accepted as " offering the best and only means of a speedy, victorious ending of the war." In three months, at the latest, it was declared, England would be suing for peace; the other allies would be left without support to collapse; and the dreaded fourth Winter campaign, which the Germans were determined, if possible, to avoid, need not be faced. In those circumstances what the United States, unprepared to use her power in a European struggle, said or did was of little consequence. She had a fleet, it was true, but her army was even smaller than the " contemptible British Army "; her people were undisciplined, and would refuse to bear the military yoke which the British had accepted. In that way the Germans, in desperate straits, consoled themselves.

The awakening has begun. General Pershing and the fine body of officers and men under his orders in France are working the conversion; the march through London yesterday will assist the movement; those thirty-two great training camps in the United States, each bearing the name of a military hero of the American people—Lee, Sherman, Jackson, Grant, Sheridan, Funston, McClellan, MacArthur, Cody, and others—will complete the work. The foundations are being laid in the deep-rooted sentiments of the American people of a great

# CZAR OF RUSSIA AS A PRISONER

Nikolai Romanoff Photographed in the Grounds of the Palace at
Tsarskoe Selo, Where He Was a Prisoner Before Being Sent to Siberia
*(Central News Photo)*

# RUSSIAN GIRL SOLDIERS

Girls With Close-Cropped Hair Who Joined the " Battalion of Death"
*(Photo American Press Association.)*

Service Caps Being Distributed to the Girl Soldiers
*(Photo © International Film Service)*

national army. Do the Germans wonder what its strength will be? They will learn—they have already learned—that two million men are to be placed in the field. Are they curious as to the fighting value of those troops? Could they have seen the soldiers who were acclaimed in London yesterday they would have gained some conception of the character of this new force which, in due course, in spite of piracy, will cross the Atlantic. The submarine, instead of proving their salvation, will be their undoing, bringing to nothing all those dreams of dominion by land and sea in which, a little over three years ago, they freely indulged.

Over sixty years ago Mazzini looked to the United States to save Europe; he thought he heard a voice from the other side of the water declaring, " We will no longer give Cain's answer to God, Who has made us free; we will not allow foreign armies to suppress the aspirations which we hold sacred, the ideas which may enlighten us. Let every people be free to live its own life. To maintain this liberty, we are ready to intervene by word of mouth—if need be, by the sword." Those hopes were not fulfilled in his experience. But, though he could not fix the hour or day of their realization, he had the vision. " There is something great in this idea of an Anglo-American alliance. * * * The laying of the first stone of that religious temple of humanity which we all foresee is a labor well worthy the co-operation of the two worlds." The soldiers who marched through London were heralds proclaiming by their presence and martial bearing that, in the fine words of Julia Ward Howe's Battle Hymn:

> He is trampling out the vintage where the
>     grapes of wrath are stored;
> He has loosed the fateful lightning of his
>     terrible, swift sword.

The Germans, unconsciously employing the submarine as the agent of world destiny, are drawing the civilized peoples of the world within a union the members of which have sworn that Prussianism, and all that it represents of misery, servitude, suffering, and death, shall be crushed.

# A War Sermon in Westminster Abbey
## By the Archbishop of Canterbury

London's principal religious service at the opening of the fourth year of war was held in Westminster Abbey, and was attended by the King. The Archbishop of Canterbury, the Most Rev. Randall Thomas Davidson, preached from the text, " Seeing we are compassed about with so great a cloud of witnesses * * * let us run with patience the race that is set before us," (Hebrews xii., I.) Recalling the fact that he had stood in the same pulpit on Aug. 2, 1914, the Primate said:

THREE years ago! It seems like ten. Some of us find it hardly possible to "think ourselves back" into the prewar days or revivify in vision the sunny homes, the radiant hopes that then were ours. Then came the first weeks and months of war. To most people it is becoming increasingly difficult to feel again the glowing impulse which throbbed in every fibre of British manhood as we gave ourselves in serious purpose to the high emprise whereto, as we unhesitatingly believed then—as we unswervingly believe still—we were called by every obligation to which an honorable man must rise. We are no more doubtful of it now than we were in those August weeks three years ago, but the long, long strain does tell upon nerve and muscle; and a stiffened upper lip and a sternly firm endurance must in some measure replace the comparative buoyancy and spring with which in those first eager days we deliberately faced the dread ordeal of a vast world war. At this anniversary time we pause and take stock of the three years' outcome. Face it squarely at its grimmest and its saddest; try to belittle nothing, to exaggerate nothing.

Is it all worth while? Does the issue which shone out so clearly in those first days hold good? If we could have foreseen in all their wide ghastliness these three years of human strife and devastation, should we have acted as we did? Would we reverse it now if we could? Ask that question up and down the land and the answer from almost every thoughtful man and woman would roll back overwhelmingly: " We were right then. We are right now." Horrible as it all is, and was, we could do no other. And yet, God knoweth, it is not quite easy to keep the earlier, the more sharply cut issue clear and pure and unconfused. So much has happened to blur and besmirch it. We are very human, and in fields so vast and in conditions so unlooked for there has been abundant room for mistake or for vacillation; for weakness or for cross-counsels; for rash experiment or for overcaution. Human passion and vengefulness, righteous wrath, and sometimes unrighteous wrath, have flared up. The picture has lost the cleanness of its first color, and has become scratched and blotched. Yet there the plain facts are, if we look for them and get back to them. There did come an issue in the world's story, and we could not and did not evade it. That definite issue of " right and wrong," of honor and dishonor, has been no whit impaired, and through the confusion we can get back to it if we will. So getting back to it, as it is well we should, we find ourselves in touch with what is highest and purest in our country's history, and the knowledge nerves us to the patience which is so difficult and yet so necessary now.

My friends, can we not, in this building, of all places in our land, transfer that injunction straight and plainly to ourselves? Respice—Circumspice. Here beneath our feet lie the bones of scores of the men who, in nine centuries of change and chance, have upheld in and for our country, high witness to the principle of loyalty to truth, of stainless honor, of dauntless courage, of tireless patience. Their forms look down on us in marble from the walls. Their example —the example of that cloud of witnesses —is at once a reassurance and an inspiration to the weakest hearted and the most wayward of us all. There is no

epoch, there is scarcely a great episode, in English history but has its representative among these great witnesses. In this transept, to quote Macaulay's stirring words, " Chatham seems still, with eagle face and outstretched arm, to bid England be of good cheer." Over the western door his yet more illustrious son seems once again to " pour forth the lofty language of inextinguishable hope." So we might run on. Take modern times only, Johnson, Wilberforce, Gladstone, Salisbury, and many more have each of them a message for today. And their witness, after all, is one.

And now upon us, the men and women of this generation in the world's life, the duty, the privilege has at a supreme crisis been laid of upholding, on our country's, our empire's part, the principles of good faith and honor; and, as it seems to us, of liberty and of ultimate peace. We are not alone. Our great allies have, in their own way and with us, the same grave task to fulfill. Notably we thank God for the incoming on our side of the great Republic of the Western World. That fellowship, arriving when it did, is the surest human witness that could be borne to the greatness of our cause. It knits a strong and sacred bond which is to outlast these tempestuous years and to weld our peoples in imperishable brotherliness of service for the welfare of the world.

To us, then, is intrusted a great, a consecrated task. How are we going to do it? Only the merest handful among the people of a great country have the opportunity of showing what we call heroism in its large, conspicuous sense. Nay, it is the veriest handful even in the fleets upon the sea and the armies in the field. But the power of witness and the power of patience belong emphatically to us all; the power in each man of witness to something, to some cause, perhaps to some one that he feels to be higher than himself.

To those men among the shell-swept trenches or on the black and hissing sea the call comes. It has perhaps no special peremptoriness from one hour to another. But it is there. It rings out and rings on, in ears that are open to it, and for answering it aright those men need not courage only, but the more difficult thing—patience, cheery patience in face of hourly dangers and discomforts, perhaps for days or weeks on end, and then, when the actual moment is reached, the flash and rush of dauntless bravery. It has been a revelation to us all. It bids us revise our estimate of many whom we knew and loved, nay, it bids us revise our estimate of what we all of us can do. As a keen thinker wrote a few weeks ago, " It changes the whole aspect of the world, even to a man whose life is advanced and his character somewhat set, when the men who were his intimate friends are proved to have had in them, not merely the ordinary virtues and pleasantnesses of common life, but something high and resplendent which one associates with the stories of old saints or heroes—still more when there is burned into him the unforgettable knowledge that men whom he loved have died for him."

The thoughts and prayers and thanksgivings of not a few of us are centred upon some unobtrusive, perhaps unknown, grave on the banks of the Yser or the Somme, or under the cliffs of Gallipoli, and the proudly sad thanksgiving that we offer breathes fellowship and hope. " Seeing that we are compassed about with so great a cloud of witnesses, let us—us too—run with patience." We, too, can. We will.

" With patience." Am I not speaking the mind of every one of us if I say that is just what we find hardest? The horribleness of growing accustomed week after week, month after month, for three long years, to the sad sights and sounds and tidings of the same dread tramp and toll and tribute of persistent war—O God! we exclaim, that the veriest cataclysm of battle might come if only it meant the end, and if only the victory for which we pray and agonize were won.

There lies our test. It is to steel us to the long patience that we need the help of the cloud of witnesses. They witness, to what? To Him Whose ways are not as our ways, and Who gives the power to endure as well as the power to strike.

They did witness, they do witness, to that. They have proved it true. We believe, with every fibre of our being, that there is in these mighty things a right and a wrong. We have a cause given us to uphold, and—if we may reverently borrow a very sacred phrase—we are " straitened until it be accomplished." Meantime, every offering of what we are or have, every output of self-denial for others' sake, every setting aside of personal likings, or interest, or gain on behalf of what is given us, as a people, to do is, in St. Paul's words, our " reasonable service," our service deliberately rendered for what, in our souls, we believe to be for truth and liberty among men. There is something in the heart of each one of us which answers to that call. There is an "inner man" which lies ready for any summons, any offering which may be asked of it. It is often untested, unemployed, because of our hard inattention to the voice of conscience, which is in truth the Voice of God:

I have a temple I do not
Visit, a heart I have forgot;
A self that I have never met,
A secret shrine—and yet, and yet—

This sanctuary of my soul
Unwitting I keep white and whole,
Unlatched and lit, if Thou shouldst care
To enter or to tarry there.

With parted lips and outstretched hands
And listening ears Thy servant stands;
Call Thou early, call Thou late,
To Thy great service dedicate.

" To Thy great service dedicate." That lifts our thoughts and prayers away from present strifes and battlings, and swings us out into the larger vision of what is to be the outcome of it all. It is to that ultimate issue that we are really " dedicate." The three years have cost us much. They have perhaps taught us even more. We have seen, we do see, not perils only, but failures and weaknesses and sins, which, in the rush of new conditions and in the perplexities of untried paths, have too easily beset us. We Christians belong here and now to a city which hath foundations deeper than those of earthly kingdoms—a city whose Builder and Maker is God.

# Italian Army's Spring Offensive

## Official Narrative of Operations of General Cadorna's Forces From March to June, 1917

THE following account of the operations of the Royal Italian Army under General Luigi Cadorna on the various Alpine fronts has been issued by the Italian General Staff at General Headquarters:

The long period of inactivity in war operations, imposed by the Winter and protracted to the end of April by the inclemency of the weather, was a period of fruitful preparation for the army. The higher military authorities, seconded by the firm support of the Government and with the entire energies of the nation at their disposal, directed their attention to further development in the organization of the army, enlarging and strengthening its units. The supply service was perfected and every effort was made to insure an incessant production of all kinds of war material and to adapting the most recent scientific inventions to the actual system of warfare.

New regiments were formed and grouped under higher units organically complete in their subsidiary services. Powerful artillery was cast and distributed. The number of machine guns was largely increased. At the same time the intensified production of ammunition enabled the staff to create large stocks of reserve, so indispensable for carrying out effectively any offensive action on a large scale and for having to resist an eventual strong offensive on the part of the enemy.

The engineer corp service was greatly increased, as also the production of technical appliances of warfare, of which, as the present war has proved, an army cannot be too freely supplied.

Aviation was greatly developed. The output of machines was intensified and everything was done to render them more powerful, so that this arm, which had given such brilliant results, might be able to carry out offensive and reconnoitring work with greater facility.

With these various forms of activity, so different taken singly but co-ordinated with one aim in view, the Italian Army, war-hardened by experience and encouraged by the results of the past, prepared to face its third Spring in war.

### Battle on the Julian Front

Toward the end of Winter the General Staff, being aware of a big concentration of Austro-German forces on the Trentino front, a sure sign of a coming offensive action, had already organized every means for adequately meeting the situation, and was conscientiously able to address words of faith and strength to the nation. But, as at the beginning of April the enemy's preparations were seen to be slackening, the General Staff decided to take the initiative in the operation.

The plans of the General Staff for the Spring offensive were as follows: First of all, to engage the enemy on all the front from Tolmino to the sea in an intense artillery action, which would leave him doubtful as to the real direction of the decisive attacks; then to attack on the right wing to the north of Gorizia, and, lastly, to strike cut on the Carso.

On the Trentino front a big array of forces and artillery, ready for an offensive, had placed the Italians in the position of being able to face an attack of the enemy, had the interrupted preparations for his offensive been resumed.

### Attack on the Middle Isonzo

The first phase of the action, the objective of which was the heights to the left of the Isonzo from Globna to the Salcano defile, was intrusted to the General Staff of the Gorizia Army. This operation was to be carried out by means of a heavy frontal attack on the massif mentioned, supported on the right by a strong assault on the Gorizia hills and masked on the left by a demonstrative action, including the fording of the Isonzo, between Loga and Bodrez, as a menace to the rear of the Austrian positions on the Bansizza-S. Spirito Plateau.

A vigorous demonstrative action, which was to contribute to the success, had to be effected by the Third Army on the southern edge of the Carso.

The operations were begun on May 12 with careful artillery preparation.

The bombardment reached its maximum intensity and violence on the morning of May 14. About midday the Italian infantry began their advance from Plava and Gorizia. During the first assault Hill 383, east of Plava, (Poggio Montanari,) was carried by the Udine Brigade (Ninety-fifth and Ninety-sixth Infantry Regiments,) while the Firenze Brigade, (127th and 128th Infantry Regiments,) braving with magnificent valor the terrible fire of the enemy, succeeded in reaching the spur of Hill 535 on Mount Cucco. At the same time the Avellino Brigade (231st and 232d Infantry Regiments) with great élan rushed the Zagora barrier, partially occupying the strong points of Zagomila; the 230th Infantry (Campobasso Brigade) climbed the slopes of Mount Santo, and by evening penetrated the convent thereon; and to the east of Gorizia the Messina Brigade (Ninety-third and Ninety-fourth Regiments) carried the strongly fortified Hill 174, north of Tivoli.

On the other portions of the front the pressure was strong, but met everywhere by the stubborn resistance of the enemy, who forced the Italian troops to engage in a heavy struggle.

### Forcing a River Passage

During the night of the 15th a detachment of two battalions (Thirty-seventh " Bersaglieri " and the Cervino " Alpini ") and subsidiary parties surprised the Austrians completely, forced the passage across the Isonzo between Loga and Bodrez, organizing themselves in an improvised bridgehead to the left of the river.

At dawn on the 15th the attack on the heights was continued with renewed vigor. In this way the summit 611 on Mount Cucco and Hill 524 on the Vodice were carried, in the face of most violent attacks of the Austrians, who also stormed Hill 174, but ineffectually.

As the occupation on Mount Santo could not be maintained, the Italians had to withdraw their lines to a position under the summit.

The days following, until the 22d, may be considered as being devoted to the organization and the consolidation of the conquests begun on the 14th and 15th. They were days of fighting of unheard of violence and of undying glory for the Italian troops. Subject to most furious fire and numberless counter-attacks, the positions reached were extended. The success was increased by the occupation of Hill 363, (east of Plava,) the hamlets Globna and Palliova, and a firm hold was obtained on the whole mountainous ridge which, culminating in Mount Cucco, separates the Isonzo from the deep valley which branches out in front of Anhovo. Some advantageous points were reached on Hill 126 at Grazigna, (east of Gorizia.)

Once the demonstrative manoeuvre had been accomplished, the bridgehead of Bodrez was abandoned on the 18th; the withdrawal was carried out by surprise as the occupation had been, though the enemy, alarmed, had already brought numerous battalions against the small Italian detachment.

While the operations on the Isonzo heights were taking place, the demonstrative action further south, on the outskirts of the Carso, intrusted to the Third Army, was being carried out.

For several consecutive days the enemy was closely engaged and the Italian troops were even able to progress temporarily northeast of Dosso Faiti and on Hill 126, south of Vippacco.

Altogether these days secured for the Italians the possession of most of the rocky bastion of Mount Cucco and Mount Santo, beyond the Isonzo, and allowed them to advance their lines from Hill 363, over the eastern versant of Mount Cucco, over Hills 592 and 652 on the Vodice, on the saddle of Hill 503, and from this point to the western slopes of Mount Santo as far as the old line facing on the Isonzo the spur of S. Valentino.

The success of this first stage of the Italian offensive was crowned by the taking of 7,113 prisoners, including 163 officers, 18 guns, a great number of bomb-throwers and machine guns, and a large quantity of war material.

### The Austrian Diversion

No sooner had the Italian attack on the heights to the left of the Isonzo become delineated than the Austrians attempted a diversion on the Trentino front to lighten the pressure of the Italians and misguide their attention.

The action was carried out from May 19 to 22 by means of most violent concentration of fire on the Italian positions in Val Sugana and on the Asiago Plateau and several infantry attacks to the west of Lake Garda and in the Adige Valley.

During the night of the 21st the " Dente del Pasubio " (the Tooth of the Pasubio) was attacked in force, but the Austrians were repulsed with severe losses. Another furious attack was delivered on the 22d with big forces on the Italian positions on the Piccolo Colbricon in Travignolo Valley. This attack, after a small initial success, ended in the complete rout of the Austrians, who left a good number of prisoners in the hands of the Italians and hundreds of dead in front of the latter's defenses.

### On the Carso Plateau

The attempts to divert the attention of the Italians had no other effect for the Austrians than that of causing themselves new losses without succeeding in modifying the decision of the Italian General Staff, who, as soon as preparations were completed, ordered the second phase of the action to be begun on the Carso.

On May 23, from 6 A. M. to 4 P. M., all the artillery of the Third Army shelled with great violence the enemy's positions, which had been partially destroyed by previous bombardments and always kept under fire to prevent their being put into working order again. At 4 o'clock in the afternoon the infantry began the attack.

On the left wing, according to the plans of the General Staff, the action, though it was to be only demonstrative, was conducted with great firmness and skill, and the not easy task was carried out by engaging the Austrians east of Mount Vucognacco, on Hills 378 and 363, and in the neighborhood of Castagnavizza.

The troops at the centre and on the right carried the Austrian intrenchments close to the Italian lines, the Bologna Brigade (Thirty-ninth and Fortieth Regiments) meanwhile spreading out in the sector south of the Castagnavizza-Boscomalo road, and, going round the last-named village to the south-west, they advanced past Lucati and captured Jamiano, Hills 92, 97, 77, 58, Bagni, (east of the Adria Works,) and Hill 21.

One hundred and thirty airplanes, including a group of the Royal Navy seaplanes, took part in the battle.

The Austrians, who at first had replied very weakly to the destructive fire of the Italians, reserving all the force of their artillery to stop the attack of the infantry, were surprised by the rapid advance, and only toward evening began a violent reaction with persistent counterattacks and heavy bombardments. But the Italians gained the day, as is proved by the number of prisoners captured —over 9,000, including 300 officers.

### Monitors Take a Hand

The battle was furiously resumed the next day (May 24) and extended to the sea, two monitors shelling the Austrian positions on the coast. The left of the Third Army continued to act as a pivot, exerting great pressure on the Austrians and meeting their counterattacks with the Barletta Brigade, (137th and 138th Regiments,) while the centre prosecuted the operation of isolating and capturing the Boscomalo salient, and succeeded with the Padova Brigade (117th and 118th Regiments) and Mantova Brigade (113th and 114th Regiments) in reaching the slopes of Hills 235 and 241, in the vicinity of Fornaza, and in pushing forward toward Hill 219, northeast of Komarje. The right wing— Bergamo Brigade, (25th and 26th Regiments,) Toscana Brigade, (77th and 78th Regiments,) Arezzo Brigade, (225th and 226th Regiments,) and the Second Bersaglieri Brigade, (7th and 8th Regiments)—continuing the frontal attack brilliantly begun the day before, reached and closed on the enemy line at Flondar.

On the 25th, while the left wing, fulfilling its task, provoked a heavy barrage fire and succeeded also in carrying some elements of the Austrian trenches, the centre completed the capture of the Boscomalo salient and reached the following line approximately— Hill 202, southeast of Boscomalo, to Hill 251, south of Castagnavizza, and the right wing (Seventh Army Corps) broke through the Flondar line about south of the Jamiano-Brestovizza road, some detachments being pushed forward as far as the heights between Flondar-Medeazza and S. Giovanni.

The attempts of the enemy to arrest the advance were on this day and on the following ones desperate—most violent shelling, counterattacks in force without consideration for losses, and bombardments by airplanes flying very low—but the Italian advance proceeded vigorously.

On the 26th of May, while the left wing, overstepping by its impetus the mandate received, maintained for some time a position

beyond the village of Castagnavizza, the centre completed the occupation of Hill 241 and went forward on Hill 219, and the right wing advanced on the hills west of Medeazza and

THE ISONZO FRONT, WHERE ITALY IS FIGHTING FOR TRIESTE

reached the mouth of the Timavo River. On the 27th, fighting slackened on the left; at the centre the Italians still advanced, completing the occupation of Hill 219, (Fornaza,) while the right wing occupied the trenches east of Komarje and the village of S. Giovanni.

On the 28th some parties of the Forty-fifth Division, to the extreme right, went beyond the Timavo as far as Hill 28, but, however, they were not able to maintain themselves there.

On the succeeding days, until the 31st, the positions captured were extended, rectified, and strengthened under the protection of the artillery, which neutralized the Austrian fire concentrated on these positions.

## Vigorous Counterattacks

While the Italian manoeuvre was becoming manifest on the Carso and the action bid fair to be heavy, the Austrians attempted with every means to distract the Italian forces and diminish the pressure on his part of the front by redoubling their counterattacks on the positions, left of the Isonzo, which had been captured during the first phase of the battle by the Second Army Corps. The efforts of the Austrians were mainly directed against the Vodice, their object being to retake it in order to justify the official silence as to its having been lost and on account of the particular importance of its position with regard to Mount Santo.

The attacks of the Austrians were met with as much vigor by the Italian troops, for in order to contribute to the action on the Carso and to systemize their own position as was necessary, they also engaged between the 23d and the 27th in a series of fights, some very furious, in the area of Hill 363, Vodice, Mount Santo, Hill 126, slopes of S. Marco. This fighing had the effect of considerably bettering the position of the Italians on the slopes of Hill 363 and on the eastern versant of the Vodice and somewhat on the northern slopes of Mount S. Marco, (the area comprised was Hill 174 east, Diruta House, Du Pini House, Dosso del Palo.)

The most furious fighting which took place in these days was, on the 24th, during the Austrian attacks on the Italian lines from Hill 363 (Plava) to the Vodice, at Tivoli, at Grazigna, and on the Faiti; on the 25th, again on Hill 174 (Tivoli) and on the Vodice; on the 26th, at the head of the Palliova Valley; and on the 27th on Hill 126, east of Grazigna.

On the 28th the Austrians, employing big forces, were able to reach the summit of the Vodice, but were at once driven back. On the same day they again attacked Hills 126 and 127, but without success. On the 29th and 31st three consecutive attacks were repulsed by the Fifty-third Division.

The persistency of these attacks, the considerable number of forces employed by the Austrians, and the intense movement of troops in the rear, all go to prove that the manoeuvre of the Gorizia Army was successful in drawing the Austrians toward it, thus favoring the operations taking place on the Carso.

The tangible results of the second phase of the battle were 16,568 prisoners, including 441 officers, 20 guns, a large number of machine guns and trench mortars. The Italian line from Castagnavizza to the sea was advanced from one to four kilometers, and a

threatening and formidable series of Austrian intrenchments were destroyed, thus leaving more breathing room for the future operations of the Italians.

The total number of prisoners taken from the 14th to the 28th was 23,681, including 604 officers; 38 guns, including 13 of medium calibre, 148 machine guns, 27 trench mortars, besides a considerable quantity of rifles and war material.

## The Austrian Counteroffensive

There is no doubt that the Austrians, foreseeing the Italian offensive or intending to carry one out themselves, had taken advantage of the favorable situation on the Russian front and ordered a concentration of troops and war material behind their lines East of the Isonzo.

The Italians during their offensive had had tangible proof of the presence of new Austrian artillery. As the reinforcements had arrived too late or in too limited a number to stop the Italian advance, the Austrians employed them in a counterattack, which was favored by their knowledge of the ground and by the fact that the Italian defenses in the new positions had not had time enough to be sufficiently consolidated.

The big effort which the Austrians intended to make on the Carso was preceded by strong demonstrative actions. On the 1st of June, while a violent artillery fire was directed on the Faiti, infantry attacks were begun on Hills 174, (Tivoli,) 126, (Grazigna,) and 652, (Vodice.) On the 2d the bombardment of the Faiti became more violent, and on the 3d the fire was intensified along the whole front from Mount S. Marco to Flondar. The Italian artillery replied effectively and held the infantry in check.

On the 4th of June the Austrians began the general attack, between Mount S. Marco and the sea, which lasted without interruption for three days of hard struggle sustained by Italian troops in difficult conditions, on positions still partly demolished by the previous actions or else recently captured and not yet organized enough for defensive purposes.

The attack was at first temporarily successful on the Italian left, firmly held and violently repulsed in the centre, and on the right was at first held with difficulty, but afterward completely stopped.

During the night of the 3d to 4th of June the new positions occupied by the Italians on the northern slopes of Mount S. Marco were violently attacked, and the Austrians succeeded in gaining a foothold, but a heavy counterattack at once dislodged them. The Austrians at dawn on the 4th penetrated the destroyed defenses on Dosso Faiti, but détachments of the Tevere Brigade (215th and 216th Regiments) and the 251st Regiment, (Massa Carrara Brigade,) with a violent counterattack lasting all day, succeeded the same night in driving them back.

The positions between Versic and Jamiano

were the scene of a struggle of extreme violence. The troops of the Sixty-first Division, the gallant soldiers of the Grenadier Brigade of Sardegna, (First and Second Regiments,) the Siena, (Thirty-first and Thirty-second Regiments,) and Bari (139th and 140th Regiments) Brigades, engaging in frequent hand-to-hand struggles, by a stubborn defense and by delivering several counterattacks, succeeded in getting the better of the enemy, who, suffering very severe losses, was forced to abandon the attack.

These positions, the real key to the line reached during the recent offensive on the Carso, and which gloriously withstood wave after wave of furious enemy assaults, remained firmly in the possession of the Italians.

## Italians Retire, Fighting Fiercely

To the right, south of Jamiano, where detachments pushed well forward had been obliged to halt, the Italian fire had come to a standstill. The position was not an advantageous one from a tactical point of view, and the short time which elapsed between the Italian offensive and the Austrian action had not given the Italians the opportunity to modify these conditions to their advantage. It was therefore necessary to retire, not so much for the onset of the Austrians, as to withdraw the line from the destructive effects of the artillery. The ground abandoned by the Italians was a strip from 200 to 800 meters on a front of slightly more than two kilometers. It was the only advantage gained in what the enemy intended to be a complete recovery from the reverse suffered during the second half of May. A further 585 prisoners, including thirty officers, were taken during this defensive fighting.

The positive results of the Italian offensive during the Spring were conspicuous, as has been said, for the tactical objectives arrived at, and they were no less important for the damage inflicted on the Austrians. Besides the 24,260 prisoners, (including 634 officers,) it is calculated that at least 100,000 men were placed hors de combat. No obstacle and no force was able to arrest the Italian infantry, which fought tirelessly on difficult ground during continuous attacks and counterattacks for eighteen days without interruption and without rest.

The co-operation of siege, field, and mountain artillery was most effective. Some batteries did not hesitate to advance with the infantry to the line of fire. Ten British batteries of medium calibre and the Royal Navy artillery contributed most efficiently. The trench mortar batteries and machine-gun companies greatly distinguished themselves, the former in destroying enemy entanglements and trenches, the latter in accompanying the infantry in the assaults and in strenuously defending the positions attacked. Though the cavalry was not employed in its particular tactical task, it contributed largely with officers and soldiers to the forming of trench mortar batteries and machine-gun companies, paying its tribute of blood. The aviators, with great valor, did most useful reconnoitring and offensive work. All the special sections of the engineers distinguished themselves by working calmly under fire and fighting, when necessary, side by side with the infantry. The sappers, telegraphists, bridging, mining, and train companies, the balloon sections, and the aerial cableway sections all contributed to the success. Excellent work was done by the Royal Army Medical Corps, Red Cross, and Military Order of Malta services and by the supply, motor-car, and railway services.

## Action on the Trentino Front

The Austrians had not had time to recover from their reverse on the Isonzo when the energy of the Italian troops obliged them to defend themselves on the Asiago Plateau. Notwithstanding the advantage of their defensive positions, which nearly everywhere dominated the Italian ones, the Austrians were here obliged to constantly change the position of their troops to the points threatened by the intense bombardments and infantry raids of the Italians, who dealt them a series of reverses, which, according to reliable information, had a demoralizing effect on their capacity for resistance,

In the more southern part of the sector the Fifty-second Division, with its " Alpini " and " Bersaglieri " units and the Piemonte Brigade, (Third and Fourth Regiments,) in close co-operation with the artillery of all calibres, were gradually able to capture and hold against numberless counterattacks the Agnella Pass and the massif of Mount Ortigara, the summit of which is 2,105 meters (6,904 feet) high, (June 10-19.)

Altogether 1,500 prisoners, including 85 officers, were captured.

Besides these operations of strategic importance, many other minor tactical actions took place in various other parts of the front, and are the best proof of the fighting spirit of the Italian troops and their aptitude in overcoming the difficulties of mountain warfare, which requires besides high military qualities also patient and tiring work. In this way the successful explosion of a mine on the Colbricon permitted the Italians to extend their occupation, and repeated enemy counterattacks were repulsed, April 13, 14, and 18. On April 22 an advanced post was recaptured and most of the garrison made prisoner near the Tre Cime Shelter Hut, (Drei Zinnen Hütte,) at the head of the Rienza. During the night of April 23 Austrian raids were repulsed on the Zugna, (Adige Valley,) in the Campovedil (High Cordevole) and Gabrie (west of Tolmino) areas, while an Italian detachment occupied by surprise an advance post near Castagnavizza, capturing the defenders.

An immense mine was exploded by the Austrians on the Piccolo Lagazuoi (Rio Costeana) on the night of May 23, causing a big landslip, which, however, did but little damage, at once made good by the Italian defenses.

The Italians, on their part, during the night of June 22, exploded a powerful mine under the Austrian positions on Hill 2668, on the southern edge of the Piccolo Legazuci, destroying all the enemy garrison and establishing themselves on the summit itself.

During the second half of May and at the beginning of June some " Alpini " parties, by boldly scaling the heights, succeeded in occupying several dominant points at the head of the Zebrù Valley, (Ortler,) and on June 15, with the help of skiier sections, the Corno di Cavento, the key to the defense of the Fumo and Genova Valleys, was captured.

### Aerial Activity

During this period of the offensive the Italian airmen took a conspicuous part in brilliant air fighting, in patient and continuous reconnoitring flights, and in successful bombing raids.

Thirty-five Austrian machines were brought down in air fights or by anti-aircraft guns.

Large quantities of explosives were several times dropped on the Austrian railway lines and on their points of assemblage at Volcia Draga, Rifemberga, Opcina, S. Daniele, (Branizza,) S. Lucia, (Tolmino,) in the Adige and Brenta Valleys, and on the Asiago Plateau.

The Vipacco Valley, where Austrian troops and hutments were massed, and where there was intense convoy and artillery traffic, was bombed day and night by airships and airplanes with successful results.

Veritable air battles took place on May 23 over the Austrian lines at Medeazza and Flondar, and on June 19 during the fighting in the Mount Ortigara area. During these battles reconnoitring airplanes preceded in the vanguard to discover the enemy guns, the big battle-planes followed closely, dropping immense quantities of explosives on the enemy's trenches, and even flying low enough to attack with their machine guns, while chasing-planes effectively carried out their work of protection by engaging the numerous enemy machines which attempted to repulse them.

The Italian Army has thus victoriously entered on its third year of war, proving by its great increase in material and continued progress in organization that it is ably seconded by an incessant display of physical and moral energy on the part of the entire nation in arms, which, conscious of the value of the work done and of its own strength, has perfect faith in the final victory.

[*The story of Italy's Summer campaign of 1917 appears in the earlier pages of this issue of* CURRENT HISTORY MAGAZINE.]

# July, 1914

### By EDWARD SHILLITO

In that lost world always it is July,
    Always July that ends the peaceful times!
Life snapped for us, when from the rain-cleansed sky
    Fell soft the scent of limes.

Still hangs that world, like kingdoms in the tales,
    Told in an Orient forest with quiv'ring breath,
Where at a wizard's nod all warm life fails,
    And there's no life nor death.

Sundered from us it shines: upon the brink
    Of precipice, cut sheer by giant hands,
Above the chaos where we strive and sink,
    And rise again it stands.

Lost world, no daring feet can scale those heights;
    No word of ours to life can quicken thee;
Thy silver mornings—thy untroubled nights,
    Our eyes may never see.

But always in the flood-tide of the year
    You, who were with us in that last July,
Will cross to our new world; you we shall hear,
    And see you, till we die.

# Disclosures of King Constantine's Relations With Germany

A WHITE BOOK, containing the Greco-Serbian Treaty, and documents relating thereto and to the Germano-Bulgarian incursion into Eastern Macedonia, was distributed to the Deputies of the French Chamber on Aug. 17, 1917.

The documents establish that there existed an agreement between the Athens Government and the Central Powers. It first appears in a telegram from General Bairas to the General Staff, stating that a Bulgarian Major had a meeting with a Greek officer and declared that, in virtue of an agreement between General von Mackensen and the Athens Government, an occupation extending to two kilometers within the Greek frontier, provided it was a strategical necessity, was allowed at any point, and that consequently the heights surrounding Lechovo had been occupied. The following day General Yanakitsas, the Minister of War, telegraphed to the commander of the Kavalla Army Corps that it had only agreed that the Germano-Bulgarians could advance to the frontier line, but under no circumstances must doubt be cast on the Bulgarian officers' good faith, nor should force be used, as the maintenance of friendly relations was desired.

Then comes a letter from Count von Mirbach, the German Minister, to M. Skouloudis, the Premier, stating that, in view of the movements of the Allies' troops, the Germano-Bulgars were compelled to enter Greek territory in order to insure free transit through Rupel Pass. Count von Mirbach formally declared that this was a purely military necessity, that Greek sovereignty would be respected, and that the population would be well treated. Similar assurances were given by M. Passaroff, the Bulgarian Minister.

## Charges Against Premier

At this juncture M. Skouloudis sent protests to the Entente Powers, and it is charged that this was done to deceive them. A few days later M. Skouloudis made a statement to Parliament regarding the occupation of Rupel Pass, in which, it is charged, he misrepresented the facts.

Another document is the following telegram from the Greek Minister in Berlin, addressed to M. Skouloudis:

> Have reason believe we must keep in view probability Germano-Bulgar advance into Rupel Pass.

Other documents from a German source certify the existence of an agreement regarding Fort Rupel, and furnish evidence of understandings with the Bulgars.

Reports were received from Greek diplomatists and provincial authorities concerning Bulgarian atrocities against Greeks, with a view to the annihilation of the Greek element in Eastern Macedonia, but these reports were shelved.

The documents include a telegram from the Greek Minister at Bucharest to M. Gounaris, stating that he had been informed by a British colleague that, according to sure information, Germany had categorically assured the Sofia Government that Greek neutrality had been definitely insured, even in the event of a Bulgarian attack against Serbia. On receipt of this telegram M. Gounaris addressed a telegraphic circular to all Greek Legations, communicating the Bucharest telegram, and requesting them to state if an opportunity offered

> that a Bulgarian attack against Serbia could not leave Greece indifferent, and that the only result of a Turco-Bulgarian agreement would be the further cementing of the ties uniting those countries.

M. Gounaris's subsequent attitude showed that this telegram was issued for effect only, and was not acted upon.

## Telegram to the Kaiser

Telegrams exchanged between the Kaiser and King Constantine when Great Britain declared war on Germany reveal the attitude of the King. Replying to the Kaiser's telegram recalling reasons why Greece should stand by Germany's side, King Constantine telegraphed, through the Berlin Legation:

The Emperor knows that my personal sympathies and political opinions draw me toward him, and I shall never forget that it is to him we owe Kavalla. After mature consideration, however, I fail to understand how I could serve his purpose by the immediate mobilization of my army. The Anglo-French fleets rule the Mediterranean, and would destroy our warships and merchant navy. They would occupy our islands and would prevent the concentration of my army, which can only be effected by sea, there being no railways. Without being able to render him any service we would disappear from the map.

Consequently I am of opinion that circumstances impose on us neutrality which can be profitable to him, considering that I engage not to harm his friends and my neighbors, so long as they do not harm our local Balkan interests.

The Greek Minister in Berlin sent a dispatch to King Constantine, the principal passage in which is: "Von Jagow has told me that he thinks the Emperor will understand the necessity expressed by your Majesty of maintaining neutrality for the present. Von Jagow repeated to me the advice he had formerly given, to come as speedily as possible to an understanding with Sofia and Constantinople, adding that Serbia today constituted the 'skin of the bear.'"

## New King's Throne Speech

An Athens dispatch of Aug. 4, 1917, gave the following text of the speech which the young King Alexander made from the throne after taking the oath to the Constitution in the Chamber of Deputies:

It is with sincere joy that I address this first greeting to the representatives of the nation. You know the events which brought about some months ago the division of the Hellenic State, but the benevolent solicitude of the protecting powers of Greece succeeded, without sacrifices or an internal struggle, in reconstituting the national unity by the re-establishment of liberal institutions. The conditions upon which the transmission of the royal power was effected have clearly shown the path to be followed in the future. They render necessary the appeal to the national sovereignty, so as to revise and consolidate at the same time as the throne a form of government established on the basis demanded by the popular will, to decide in

the most precise fashion the extent of the sovereign rights of the people as well as the extent of the royal authority as defined by the Constitution, by giving it the democratic character which is the desire of the dynasty. "The royal power resides in the love of the people," but foreign events did not permit the immediate convocation of the National Assembly, and that is why, in order to inaugurate the new constitutional era which we are entering, we have repealed the decree which by a violation of the Constitution dissolved the Chamber, and have convoked this Chamber for its regular second session.

Gentlemen, I am glad to inform you that my Government, faithful to national tradition, has already given its foreign policy the orientation approved by the people at the elections of May 31 and ratified by the Chamber. After two glorious wars Greece desired peace, of which she had great need, in order to retrieve her sacrifices and to regain her strength with a view to reorganizing the State recently enlarged, and to render it capable of accomplishing its great civilizing mission in the East. Greece was therefore grieved to see a new war break out which would result in a general conflagration, setting against one another two worlds, two civilizations, and two opposed conceptions of nationalities and of humanity. Indeed, it would have been sufficient for little Greece to remember her traditions, her history, and her duty in order not to hesitate spontaneously to offer her feeble forces to that group in the conflict whose war aim was to defend the rights of nationalities and the liberty of peoples.

### The Hereditary Enemy

But more imperious obligations called Greece into the same camp, and she has therefore now adopted an attitude which duty and honor imposed upon her toward the brave and chivalrous ally—the defense of the rights of Hellenism and the debt of gratitude contracted for her original liberation and for the protection which she has always enjoyed. If it had been given to the entire nation to follow as soon as possible such a policy, it would more rapidly and more effectively have assured the defense of the country against the hereditary enemy. Part of the Greek Army has fortunately had occasion to prove at the front its value and morale by heroic acts, thanks to which Greece has been able to regain the esteem of the allied armies and foreign public opinion, and her prestige, until then so deeply sullied, and to avoid the national catastrophes which were threatening her. The heroism and self-sacrifice of the troops at the front are a most happy augury for the ultimate fate of the struggle undertaken by united Greece, for they are evidence of the fine pride and gallantry of the Hellenic Army.

Faithful to this policy, my Government has already recalled the representatives of Greece from the capitals of the enemy countries. The first result of this policy has been the decision taken at the last conference in Paris to re-establish in its integrity the sovereignty of the State by the abolition of all the controls recently imposed, and by the evacuation of the Epirus and the other regions occupied by the Allies. Greece is justly proud to have found in this conference the same consideration as her powerful protectors and allies. My Government will submit to you the legislative measures necessitated by the needs of the war, convinced that it will have your whole support, but the country has other needs than these as the result of the existence of a state of war. * * *

I appeal to your unanimous aid in studying the measures indicated in the present circumstances as regards the economical situation of the State and the country. Gentlemen, never has the country passed through a more serious period. Greece has to defend her territory against barbarous aggressors. But if in the trials of the past Greece has been able, thanks to the civilizing strength of the morale of the race, to have overcome the conquerors and to rise free amidst the ruins, today it is quite a different matter. The present cataclysm will decide the definite fate of Helenism, which, if lost, will never be restored. I am convinced that to accomplish the great and difficult task which the country has undertaken it will have assistance equal to the danger of which you are aware. I am also certain that the self-sacrifice of the Hellenic people will rise to the heights demanded by the struggle to which we have been called by the supreme care of our national defense, and for which I wish success by invoking the Divine assistance.

### Monarchy on Final Trial

Premier Venizelos made a definite statement on Aug. 25 regarding the pos-

sibility of a Greek republic. It was delivered in the Chamber of Deputies at Athens, and was elicited by a speech of George Cafantaris, Chairman of the delegation which recently visited America, who said he was deeply impressed with what he had observed of republican institutions in the United States. He moved the Government's draft of the reply to the throne speech, but closed with a strong expression in favor of the establishment of a Greek republic.

M. Venizelos promptly made a short declaration to the effect that the views of M. Cafantaris did not represent the Government's position. He said he had often told the former King Constantine that the nations of the world were gradually approaching the idea of abolishing the institution of kingship and it depended upon the existing Kings themselves to hasten or postpone this inevitable consummation. Unfortunately, Constantine's policy had been such as to deal a mortal blow to the idea of a monarchy, and many Greeks who formerly opposed a republic now admitted its advisability in principle, though he considered it still premature.

" The Government, nevertheless," continued the Premier, " is of the opinion that it is our duty to give the monarchy another trial. This, of course, is a final trial, but I am sure that the Greek people and the coming Constituent Assembly will be disposed to render possible the continuation of our present system of democracy presided over by a King."

This statement was received with prolonged applause, as clearly defining the Government's position on the recent growing tendency toward a republic.

# Germany After Three Years of War

## Short Rations and Unshod Feet

A HOLLAND goldsmith who lived four years at Hagen, in Germany, arrived at Amsterdam early in August, 1917, having fled the country on account of the intolerable food conditions. He stated that a great change had come over the financial position of pensioned servants of the State as the war proceeded. He knew cases of men who had pensions of 96 marks a month which were reduced at first to 64 and then to 32 marks. The Government paid premiums to artillerists for used-up shells. Later, instead of paying money for them, it awarded the men war loan stock, and men were given three days' leave for subscribing 1,000 marks to the war loan.

He said that the food was deplorable. He had to rise at 6:30, when he was given a cup of coffee and two slices of bread; the coffee was made out of hips and haws. The bread, for some reason, was always covered with sawdust. Some of the Germans ate sawdust and all. He always kept his two slices of bread until breakfast, at 9 o'clock, when he had another cup of coffee. At 1:30 he went to his boarding house for dinner. There were twelve boarders, including some Swiss, a Walloon, and several Germans.

### Meagre Fare at Dinner

The table was laid for dinner, but nothing to eat was placed upon it until a tureen of soup was brought in, which was immediately pounced upon by one of the Germans, a fat man, who always took the first helping, being careful to remove such fat as might be floating on the top and a good share of the solid residue which had settled at the bottom. His fellow-guests resented this very much, and ultimately a rule was established that the guests should be served first in rotation, each thus getting a chance of securing some of such fat as there was in the soup, the ingredients of which were never known to those who consumed it.

After the soup portions of cooked green vegetables were served. These were followed sometimes by portions of potatoes. At 4:30 two slices of bread were served out with blood sausage, (black pudding,) and at 7:30 the men got their supper, consisting of another kind of soup, served boiling hot. If not taken very hot it would have been uneatable. This insufficient diet naturally sent the clients further afield for food. They went " hamstering " on their own account. " Hamstering," indeed, said the Hollander, " is the great occupation in Germany in the present time. Every one ' hamsters '—that is, every one obtains stores of provisions by clandestine means."

Latterly great care had been taken by the municipalities to husband the resources of gas, the only way in which the people were able to get their food cooked being by having it at stated hours when gas was available. Not only gas but other things were sometimes " cut off." At the time of an air raid on Düsseldorf the postal service was " cut off." A similar measure was adopted at Essen at the time of an air raid. At that time the principal railway station was shut off from the public and men coming to their work in the morning were obliged to leave the trains two miles from the station.

The shortage of leather induced the professors of Hagen to set the example of going barefoot. One of the professors appeared one day in his classroom without shoes or stockings. Others followed his example, and after a while the pupils presented themselves at the schools unshod. The professor's enthusiasm only lasted about three weeks, but the boys continued to go barefoot.

By degrees all the men were called up for military service and their places were taken by boys and women. The supply of food became so short that demonstrations were made and at Hagen 2,500 men and women presented themselves at the Town Hall demanding food. The demand of the people was only satisfied by their being given seed potatoes.

## Women as Railway Guards

Another returned traveler from Germany made the following statement regarding the employment of women:

"The number of women railway guards increases steadily. In very many cases they are badly acquainted with their duties, and have no better answer to give than: 'Es tut mir leid, mein Herr; ich fahre die Strecke selbst zum ersten Mal,' ('I'm sorry, Sir; it's the first time I've done this journey myself.') One sees women employed on railways not only as guards, as formerly, but as brakemen and artisans. Once at a railway junction I saw a whole crowd standing together. They wore long, thick overcoats for the nights, which were then still cool, their hair brushed back under the regulation caps, the bag with tools and other necessaries over the shoulder. Where a number of male colleagues was mingled with the group, it was hardly possible to distinguish between them. There was no distinction in the matter of uniform, and only in the case of the women one noticed peeping out under the heavy overcoats smaller feet less stoutly shod than those of the men. I must say that these women compelled my respect, for they seemed burly and healthy and not unhappy at finding themselves in the position they now occupy.

"One already hears anxiety expressed concerning the future of these women workers. On the one hand, the women have become independent and will be less amenable to the ordinary requirements of family life. On the other, it is believed that the opportunity of employment will be small after the war, so that those who are obliged to continue to provide for their own subsistence will hardly be able to maintain themselves. Moral deterioration will be the inevitable consequence of this state of things. There is already much complaint about the moral conduct of the women workers. I was told that in Westphalia, where prisoners of war and women work together in the mines, the most deplorable condition of things prevails."

## Scarcity of Small Change

A correspondent who recently returned from Germany reported a great shortage of small change. There is much put into circulation, but it disappears again immediately. No one can say precisely where it remains, but it is suspected that the agricultural population bury it in the earth in order not to have to change it for paper.

Regarding the attitude of the German people toward the war, this traveler wrote as follows in August, 1917:

"Germany is tired of the war—there is no question about that. In spite of themselves the Germans long ardently for peace. One hears nothing more of the lust of conquest; but I must say that I have never heard anybody in Germany say, 'We must give it up.' I do not know what the people imagine will be the end of the war, and I believe they do not know themselves. They are depressed, and how can it be otherwise with the frightful losses that they have suffered? I know cases of young men who are the sole survivors of the class with which they left school. There is not a municipal, police, or railway office where one does not see bending over a desk a woman in black who has lost her breadwinner and who must now provide a precarious subsistence for herself. I have never heard terms of reproach associated with the name of the Kaiser, any more than with those of the statesmen of lower rank, although a general democratic, if not socialistic, spirit has penetrated the people. I have heard dignified men of high position say that all this fuss about Princes must be done away with after the war—that the times would not admit of so much money being wasted in this way any more. The worst is expected of the demands which the people, especially the soldiers returning from the field, will make after the war.

"There is no question of the prevalence of a revolutionary spirit in Germany, but that there is sometimes tension here and there is a fact. Popular entertainments are given regularly in all towns, to which the people can go without payment. We have returned to the days of old Rome—rather less bread but more circuses. The late Spring, which made an early harvest impossible, caused much disappointment. One often heard it said with emphasis, ' No, we cannot go through another Winter.' "

# The Austro-Germans and Islam
## French Official Report on the Remarkable War Propaganda of Germany in Moslem Countries

*We translate herewith for readers of* CURRENT HISTORY MAGAZINE *the most interesting portions of a report made to the French Chamber by Louis Marin, Deputy from Nancy, on the French Mission to Arabia:*

FROM the very beginning of the war the Germans have been developing a world wide propaganda that has proved formidable in its wealth of material resources, its ingenuity, its variety of methods, and the regularity of its operations. Pamphlets in all the languages of Europe and Asia have been scattered with a profusion that staggers the imagination. Holland, the Scandinavian countries, Spain, the United States, and South America were first inundated; then came the turn of Africa and Asia, though with less success, despite the power to pass well guarded frontiers.

The Allies, it is true, replied to this frantic propaganda, but all too tardily; and whatever their efforts in this line, it may fairly be said that in quantity of output the Germans surpassed them " as much as a 420 shell surpasses a 75." Tracts, brochures, manuals, maps, documents of every sort, journals, dispatches, calendars, stage dramas, songs, films, the German propaganda has laid every imaginable form under contribution. Enormous sums have been spent in editing and distributing this matter gratis to all who would read it.

The Germans did not limit themselves to sowing their ideas among the neutrals and among the malcontents and dupes in enemy countries; with the same methodical industry they cultivated among their own people and those of their allies a faith in invincible Germany, which was about to draw inestimable profits from certain victory. For this purpose alone almost 25,000 volumes in German, not counting fugitive sheets and small tracts, were published. A quarterly catalogue entitled " Die Deutsche Kriegsliteratur: Teildruck aus dem Register zu Heinrichs's Halbjahrs-Katalog," (German War Bibliography: A Separate Edition of the Table of Contents of the Semiannual Catalogue of the Heinrichs Press, Leipsic,) contain about 15,000 titles of books devoted solely to the events of 1915, Germany's certain and sweeping victory, the origins of the war, the laws of war, the organization of German commerce after the war, German war humor, correspondence from the front, war dispatches, &c. To this deluge of print must be added the manuals at arms, books of prayer, songs, military instruction, hygiene, guides in all languages, to obtain any idea of the systematic poisoning of public opinion throughout the whole world undertaken by the Prussian Generals and their staff of learned doctors.

### Propaganda in the Orient

A war machine so well equipped naturally reserved some of its best products for the Mohammedan subjects of the Entente and for Oriental neutrals who were not sufficiently Germanophile. The former especially engaged its attention; a Mohammedan revolt would deprive the Allies of dreaded native soldiers, and compel the use of numerous troops to suppress uprisings far from the front. No intrigues were left untried in the effort to make this magnificent double stroke succeed.

As the seas were controlled by the Allies, it was through Spain, Turkey, San

Francisco, and the Philippines that the Germans dispatched their venomous literature to South Africa, East Asia, and the far Orient. In Spain, indeed, the propaganda is still carried on almost in broad daylight, despite the benevolent neutrality of the Government toward the Entente. It is under the patronage of Prince Ratibor, the German Ambassador at Madrid, and recruits its agents from the Germans who have long been residents there, or from recent refugees and men interned in Spain. Its operations are centralized at Barcelona and are directed in that city by Mr. Hofer, a printer and typefounder. It possesses a wireless telegraph outfit, a press, and a publicity staff to furnish Spanish newspapers and magazines with reading matter, photographs, and cuts favorable to the cause of the Central Empires.

From Barcelona, Cadiz, Almeria, thanks to the agents of the German Navy League and the North German Lloyd, there were shipped by trickery on neutral vessels—chiefly Dutch and Spanish—tracts in Arabic, Turkish, Persian, Hindustani, Bengali, Punjabi, Malay, Chinese, Annamite, Siamese, almost all printed at Berlin, some in Switzerland or even in Spain, to preach revolt to the natives against their English, French, Russian, and even Dutch oppressors, and to sound the praises of invincible Germany, born protector of Islam and of the Mohammedans of all the world.

To this work there was added, in order to "instruct the Orient in world politics," a bi-monthly review in German, whose title, translated, reads: New Orient: Bi-Monthly Edition of the Correspondence of the Bureau of Oriental Information. (Published at Berlin.) This deals especially in questions of Asiatic policy which are considered thorny for the Entente, such as "Anglo-Russian Rivalry in Persia," "Siam and France," "The Condition of British India," &c. The Allies can at least find in it interesting facts regarding the present functioning of the Turkish Government. The Osmanischer Lloyd, edited by Dr. Uebelhör, appears to be devoted more especially to keeping up the morale and confidence of Germans living in Constantinople.

To stir up trouble in British India,

emissaries went there from Turkey, through Persia and Afghanistan, to denounce, in the name of the Sultan, the so-called crimes of England against Islam. They incited the native Moslems to revolt against Great Britain, to refuse their aid against the Sultan and his faithful ally, "Hadji William," whose resounding pilgrimage to Jerusalem they could recall, and who, descended from a sister of Mohammed, was pretending to be a Christian in order to keep his power over his brave people, but always with the desire and certitude of turning soon to the faith of the Prophet. While awaiting that glorious day the Mohammedans should join with the Hindus and seize the present extraordinary opportunity to free themselves from the British yoke.

To these seeds piously sown in the ignorant crowd the Germans added, for the educated classes, curious brochures in Hindustani, Punjabi, Bengali, all ably edited and well presented typographically, and all denouncing the injustices and crimes of Great Britain, at the same time pointing to England's inevitable defeat under Germany's blows. Similar brochures in the Malay language urged the Malays of the Straits Settlements to revolt against the rule of the infidel and obey the Caliph at Constantinople.

In Persia it was a matter of casting odium upon both Englishmen and Russians, and of talking much more of Mohammed than of the Caliph at Constantinople, thus suiting the sentiments of the Shi'ite Mussulmans. Tracts in the purest Persian denounced the land greed of England and Russia, and extolled the benefits which the Shah and his empire could derive from German protection.

Pamphlets in Oriental Turkish and in Azerian Turkish for the benefit of Russian Mussulmans unveiled to them the crimes alleged to have been committed by their masters in East Prussia, and urged their duty to revolt against the empire of the Czars and make common cause with the Turco-Germans.

It is not only among the Malays and the Islamized Tiams of French Indo-China, and among the Chinese Mussulmans that Germany has tried to stir up trouble. Her activities are seen even more clearly in the recent uprisings, wholly Islamic in character, among the native Malays and Javanese of the Dutch West Indies.

South Africa, a granary and military nursery for the Allies, has attracted the special attention of the Germans, as it was certain to do. Unable to approach it by way of the north or the ocean, which was guarded by the allied fleets, they attempted to penetrate to it by way of the northeast. Through Abyssinia they sent money, munitions, and some Turkish officers—not to mention considerable presents to the Senussi tribesmen, who were in revolt on the western edge of Egypt—to arouse the Sudan and foster resistance to the Italians in Tripoli. The suppression of these revolts is now practically complete.

The same thing was done in Tunisia, where the mass of the population, like its princes, remained perfectly loyal to France despite the secret excitations of a few fanatics and the egoistic rantings of a few young Tunisians. In Algeria and Morocco the Arabs and Berbers enlisted in crowds under the French flag, and their heroic deeds at the front are well known. Yet the propaganda for these two countries had been prepared with almost excessive care by the Germans; not being able to approach the natives from the south, it was through Spain and Spanish Morocco that they tried to contaminate them. From Madrid, from Seville, from Malaga, there issued with tireless activity during the whole year of 1915 and a great part of 1916 a stream of tracts in Arabic—some in Maghrebin characters, others in Berber—all edited with rare art and impudence for the purpose of inciting the Algerians, and especially the Moroccans, to throw us into the sea. Thanks to our squadrons and to the close watch of our frontiers instituted by General Lyautey few of these appeals " to the noble inhabitants

of Chaouia" against the " infamous French " reached their destination, and none produced any effect.

Such was the nature of these reservoirs of intellectual poison gas, labeled " Made in Germany." One of our most noted Oriental scholars, M. Cabaton, professor in the School of Oriental Languages, has patiently gathered a large collection of them and translated them with care in their most minute variations. [Here follow twelve pages of titles of German tracts.] They have a double aim: to excite the hatred and scorn of the Mohammedans against the European powers, whose crimes against Moslem subjects and whose repeated defeats in the present war are exploited; and to excite admiration for Germany, protector and friend of Islam, rich and victorious among the nations of the earth.

The conclusion is inevitable: all the Mohammedans in the world, downtrodden by Allies or neutrals, ought, under pain of being remiss in their religious duties, to join in the Jehad, the holy war proclaimed by the Sultan at Constantinople, Caliph and Commander of the Faithful. They are assured of final success, thanks to the support of invincible Germany.

It is undeniable that the German propaganda aiming to arouse against the Allies all their Mussulman subjects was organized on a grandiose and methodical plan and pursued with tireless energy from the beginning of the war. It was a large undertaking, and it appears to have failed utterly.

Its failure seems due principally to the fact that it was bookish, though addressed to Oriental peoples who pay little attention to reading; therein lay its grave psychological error. Its insistence in lauding Germany to the skies, with its too evident exaggeration of statistics, also helped to render it suspect, even among the Mussulmans most inclined to listen to it.

# Turkey's Heavy Hand in Syria

## Fate of the Lebanon

*Syria, from Damascus to Aleppo, is suffering in divers and terrible ways from the war. The majority of the population is said to be in sympathy with the anti-Turkish revolt in Arabia, and on July 6, 1917, Al Hussein ibn Ali, the new King of the Hedjaz, entered Southern Syria with troops and took possession of the little town of Akaba, pushing on beyond Ma'an, the Ma'on of the Old Testament. Jerusalem has long been threatened by the British expedition from Egypt. Natives of Syria, especially the Christians, are dying by thousands from starvation and disease. The Turkish Government has taken various and drastic measures to meet the double peril to its tottering power. Among other things, it has abolished the last of the old liberties of Lebanon, as related in the following article by K. T. Khairallah, a native Syrian, which is translated from the Temps of Paris:*

TURKEY, profiting from the war's complications, has just wiped out the last vestiges of the autonomy of the Lebanon. The Temps of July 25, 1917, has announced the suppression of the elective Grand Council and the nomination of Turkish Governors in Batrou and Zahle.

Since 1861, thanks to an international convention, the vilayet of Lebanon possessed a statute which guaranteed its autonomy. That convention, entered into on June 9 of that year by Turkey and the great powers—Great Britain, France, Russia, Austria-Hungary, and Prussia—was modified in 1864, received the additional signature of Italy on July 27, 1868, and has since been renewed six times.

In 1915, under cover of military necessity, Turkey violated Article 14 of that convention when she invaded Lebanon territory with 40,000 soldiers. The Lebanon, disarmed by the very terms of the international agreement, saw its militia dispersed, its high functionaries sent into exile, and had at last to resign itself to seeing a Turkish Governor, designated by Turkey, taking the place of the ruler who had been recognized by the great powers. It was only two years afterward, at the beginning of 1917, that the Government at Constantinople tried to justify this violation. By a note addressed to its German and Austrian allies it denounced the Treaties of Paris and Berlin, and concluded by announcing the abolition of Lebanon's autonomy. "It was under pressure of the French Government," the note declared, "that that autonomy was created."

To justify its violations the Turkish Government has systematically garbled historical truth. The initiative of France in 1860 did not tend to create an autonomous government in the Lebanon, since that existed already; but to make it respected by those who were interested in destroying it. The great powers and Turkey herself at that time bore witness to "a state of fact." Ever since 1516, the year of the Ottoman entry into Syria, the Lebanon had not ceased to be governed by its independent emirs. If the civil war of 1860 caused its liberties to be restricted, the powers guaranteed to it in return certain economic advantages represented by dues which Turkey paid regularly until 1876. Since then she has not kept her bargain, and her debt to the Lebanon now amounts to many millions of francs.

After the last protocol of Dec. 23, 1912, the people of the Lebanon protested. A petition signed by more than 300,000 persons was addressed to the great powers and presented on Dec. 17, 1913, by my colleague Skandar Ammun and myself, to the French Government. To put an end to the unsolved question, the Government at Constantinople found it simpler to take possession of the Lebanon.

The people of that vilayet, who are in a most lamentable state, are incapable of making their rights respected. Lebanonians living abroad, acting through their political committees in Cairo, in New York, in Sao Paulo, in Buenos Aires, and elsewhere, have addressed protests to all the powers in behalf of their country's liberty. Their eyes naturally turn toward the Allies, who are fighting for justice and the liberation of oppressed peoples. They call attention to the extermination with which their country is threatened, and their right to freedom from the yoke which since 1861 has oppressed them.

Yonder on the sunny hills of Lebanon, facing the Mediterranean waves, lived a little nation, industrious and pacific. For three years a thick veil has hidden from the eyes of the world the atrocities and nameless horrors which it has endured. What remains of it, now that famine, epidemic, and the "justice" of the Turk have wreaked their will upon it? At least let the ashes of the dead, of those who were our dear ones, rest in ground freed from all servitude!

# The Dogs of War
## By H. Wood
*Staff Writer of The Exchange Telegraph*

DOGS have now become of such a general and important use in the entire French Army that it is no longer possible to supply the demand. Although numerous societies throughout France for the breeding of dogs send large and regular quotas to the armies, and although every dog pound in France contributes every cur that comes its way, thousands of dogs are still needed. For the numerous duties that have been developed dogs, regardless of race, color, or previous condition of servitude, can be utilized. The only qualification necessary is that of an average dog's intelligence, which is sufficient to permit its being trained for one of the regular services now assigned to the canine tribe in the French Army.

A dog kennel (and by kennel is meant an establishment large enough for the training of hundreds of dogs) is now just as much the regular equipment of every French army as are its kitchens, its automobile trains, or its munition caissons. The kennel for each army is usually situated in the front line, where the army is fighting. As fast as dogs can be secured and trained they are sent down to the front for active participation in the fighting.

Like everything else in the present great struggle, the rôle of the dog has changed and developed to an extent never before dreamed of. Previously war dogs had been trained only for two general purposes—that of carrying aid to the wounded and that of accompanying patrols for the purpose of scenting out the enemy. The Belgians had added one rôle of their own, owing to the development of dog transportation in the country— namely, that of dog teams for drawing machine guns. While these original rôles are still preserved to a certain extent in the present struggle, the new tasks that have been developed for dogs are vastly more numerous and important. Two of these rôles—those of "liaison" dogs and sentinel dogs—can almost be said to have attained a degree of supreme importance. The "liaison" dogs, or those that carry messages from the first-line fighting troops to the commanding officers in the rear, have perhaps the most dangerous and the most useful rôle.

One of the greatest problems developed by the present war—and one that has not yet been successfully solved by any army—is that of keeping up communication between the force attacking and the artillery and commanding posts in the rear. The terrible barrages of artillery fire with which the enemy seeks to cut off and prevent such communication explain the difficulty of the problem—a difficulty that is only equaled by the supreme necessity of a solution. The principal methods up to date have been only ground and surface telephones, (that are laid as fast as the troops advance,) wireless telegraphy, airplanes, and foot runners. Recently the Germans have tried a system of inclosing the message in a shell and shooting it from a trench mortar through the French barrage to the rear. None of these has completely solved the problem, any more than has the use of dogs by the French, but the latter are nevertheless rendering the most extraordinary service.

Thousands of dogs are found that have an aptitude for this task. They are given a special training, even down to accustoming them to shell and barrage fire. Once they are given the message to carry to the rear it is seldom if ever that they fail to arrive with it, unless first killed either by shell or machine-gun fire. Hundreds of these dogs have fallen and are still falling victims on the field of honor; but when it is considered that every dog thus killed saves the life of a soldier who would have otherwise been obliged to carry the message rearward, it is readily seen that their deaths are not in vain.

Many dogs that fail to show an aptitude for " liaison " work develop into excellent sentinels. The aptitude for this is not so easily developed as might be imagined, owing to the fact that the most valuable services must be rendered at night. Hundreds of dogs that prove first-class sentinels during the day might become nervous, fidgety, and excitable under night conditions at the front. The dogs, however, that arrive at the perfection required take their place on the top of the trench alongside the gun barrel of their master, detect every patrol or every individual soldier that attempts to approach the barbed-wire entanglements in front, and lets his master know in a quiet way, without even tipping off to the enemy, that his approach has been discovered.

Although these new rôles have superseded to a large extent the original one of carrying aid to the wounded on the battlefield, dogs are still being trained and used in this work. One of the veterans along this line, who is named " Dick," and who won the Croix de Guerre at Verdun, where his master was killed and himself badly wounded, has just recovered sufficiently to go back into service. He has been attached to a section of the American Ambulance. Another one of these early Red Cross types, who also won the Croix de Guerre, but who was too badly wounded ever to be able to return to service, is being used in a unique way. He has the task of monitor at the Army Dog Hospital at Neuilly, and sees to it that refractory dogs become docile and obedient. If compulsory education for dogs produces the same general increase in intelligence that it is supposed to for humans, the canine population of France, with the close of the war, should be the centre of dog intelligence of the entire world.

## Breaking News of War Casualties

The Australian Commonwealth Government has a humane and considerate method of informing relatives when soldiers lay down their lives on the battlefield. When the military authorities in Melbourne receive word that a soldier has been killed they send a wire to the priest or minister in the town where the nearest relatives to the man reside, and the message, which is addressed to the clergyman, is couched in the following terms:

It is officially reported that Sergeant Billjim, No. 1234, Twenty-sixth Battalion, was killed in action on Jan. 27. Please inform Mr. and Mrs. Billjim (father and mother) and convey to them our deep regret, also the sympathy of their Majesties the King and Queen and the Commonwealth Government in the loss that they and the army have sustained by the death of this gallant soldier.

The clergyman immediately conveys the sad intelligence, and in a few days the Premier, as head of the State, sends a letter which varies according to the different States. That sent by Crawford Vaughan, Premier of South Australia, who autographs every document, reads as follows:

Dear Mr. and Mrs. Billjim: On behalf of the Government of South Australia, I desire to convey to you an expression of sympathy in the loss of your dear son who, it has been officially reported, was killed in action whilst serving with the Imperial Forces in France.

The heroic deeds of those who have fallen in fighting for their Empire will never be forgotten, for it is realized that a man can render no greater service than to lay down his life in the cause of liberty, justice, and civilization.

[Signature.]

# Indictment of Montenegro's King

## Documents Indicating That His Intrigues With Austria Have Forfeited His People's Confidence

This noteworthy article, which appeared anonymously in The New Europe, sheds some new light upon the mysterious collapse of Montenegro in the Autumn of 1915, and indicates that King Nicholas has forfeited the confidence of his people. The author writes from the Jugoslav viewpoint, being an advocate of a great South Slavic State centring about Serbia; but after making allowance for this bias, the evidence presented is sufficient to show that the exiled King has placed himself under "a moral boycott on the part of all Montenegrins of any political standing." King Nicholas and his family are in France.

THE great war has placed the dynastic principle on its trial. In our own country and in Italy the royal houses have indentified themselves, even more closely than before the war, with the aspirations of their peoples, while in Belgium and Serbia King Albert and Prince Alexander have become the symbols of democratic kingship. But, by an irony of fate, our greatest and our smallest ally present us with the reverse of the medal. The world knows how the House of Romanoff came to an end; and, in the present article, we give our readers a glimpse of the dynastic straits to which King Nicholas has reduced himself and his family by a long course of intrigue.

Mystery still surrounds the collapse of Montenegro in the Autumn of 1915; but it is now known that the King's third son, Prince Peter, had a secret meeting at Budva in Dalmatia in May of that year with the former Austro-Hungarian Military Attaché, Colonel Hupka; that telephonic communication was at times maintained between Cetinje and Cattaro; that by the King's orders the Montenegrin Army remained absolutely inactive for many months, and that General Jankovitch, the Serbian General, sent to Cetinje at the Czar's instance, and his successor, Colonel Peshitch, were hampered at every turn; that an agent of Prince Danilo negotiated in Switzerland with an agent of the Central Powers for a separate peace during the Bulgarian onslaught; that Prince Peter, on his father's orders, withdrew the Montenegrin troops from the key position of Mount Lovtchen at the critical moment and allowed the Austrians to enter almost unopposed; and that the King, disregarding the unanimous resolution of his Parliament to fight to the end, telegraphed to the Emperor Francis Joseph and Baron Burián. It was only the invading Austrian General's excessive conditions, and the stern attitude of his own officers, that finally determined King Nicholas to retire to Medua and so to Italy—the bulk of his army having meanwhile been caught helplessly in a trap. But, as is well known, Prince Mirko was left behind to reinsure Montenegro with the Central Powers.

Once established in France, King Nicholas sought to retrieve his fortunes by offering the post of Premier to Mr. Andrew Radovitch, whose record as a patriot and a democrat is known to every Southern Slav. Subsequent events are related below.

### Admonished by a Patriot

On Aug. 18, 1916, Mr. Radovitch presented a memorandum to King Nicholas in the following terms:

The events now taking place in the various theatres of war provide me, as a devoted subject, with the occasion for drawing your Majesty's attention to the future destinies of our country. There is no longer any doubt as to the complete victory of our allies, which will lead to the final fall of the Turkish Empire in Europe, the defeat of Austria-Hungary, and the liberation and union of the Serbian people. More than any other people, it has paid with its blood for its deliverance, which will probably be followed by that of the Croats and Slovenes, who, in agreement with the Serbs, aim at creating a Jugoslav State. This idea represents the ideal of a whole people. * * * He who seeks to combat the movement will sooner or later be vanquished, for he will find himself confronted by a torrent which carries away everything in its path.

It is conceivable that, solely out of regard for the august person of your Majesty, Montenegro might be re-established, while the other Jugoslav territories formed a State under the sceptre of the Karageorgevitch. In the most favorable circumstances Montenegro would expand in Herzegovina as far as the Narenta, and would form, with Rugusa, the Bocche di Cattaro, and Skutari, a State of about a million inhabitants. The country is peopled by the most energetic elements to be found among the Serbs, but as its richness does not correspond to the spirit and enterprise of the people, discontent has sprung up, and from day to day the desire for union with its brethren of prosperous Serbia and Bosnia increases.

After this war it will be very difficult to govern in all countries. Democracy will become dangerous, and will shatter like a torrent all obstacles in its way. The statesmen will be faced by the heavy task of guiding it prudently, in order to prevent overthrow and upheaval. There is no doubt that the events which took place in our country before and after the catastrophe will render Montenegro more difficult to govern than any other State; to this must be added the recent internment of the Montenegrins, and the famine to which a large part of our unhappy population will inevitably succumb. At the best, financial union will have to be followed by military and political union with Serbia or the Jugoslav State. But despite this imperious necessity, excited spirits in the two Serb States will leave no means untried to produce union, so that they would become the theatre of every kind of intrigue, such as our common enemies would encourage. Instead of the peace and well-being so amply merited by the Serbian people after so many sacrifices, discord and trouble would prevail.

### Abdication Tactfully Suggested

The issue of such a situation can easily be foreseen, especially *after the reign of your Majesty*. You would find it impossible to accept the exorbitant demands of democracy, and would end, amid discontent, a reign which, especially during the first forty-five years, has been rich in glory. Recent events, however, need to be effaced by a striking act such as would worthily crown your Majesty's reign.

Montenegro has, for many centuries, been the intrepid champion of Serbian liberty and the Slav vanguard toward the West. The day when, with God's help, the Jugoslav lands are liberated, this task will have been gloriously achieved. Your Majesty's great ancestor, the greatest of Serbian poets, the Prince Bishop of Montenegro, Peter Petrovitch-

Njegosh, offered to the Ban Jelashitch, a Croat and a Catholic, to place himself at the head of the Jugoslav State. Your predecessor, Prince Danilo, placed his throne at the disposal of Prince Michael, solely in order to realize union of the Serbs.

Your Majesty in your youth gave free play to your patriotic sentiments in the hymn, "Onamo, Onamo," so dear to all Serbs, and in your works, "The Empress of the Balkans" and "The Poet and the Vila." Your Majesty has kindled the national conscience of our people and inspired it with the sacred idea of realizing the solemn vow of every Serb. The happy moment has come for your Majesty to realize this dream, and to leave behind you one of the proudest names in Serbian history. * * *

Your Majesty should become the champion of a strong and compact Jugoslav State, in which the Serbs, Croats, and Slovenes would enter, and, perhaps, later on, even the Bulgars, as an autonomous unit. This State should be formed on the model of Italy, with equality of all its members. The Croats are nearer to the Serbs than were the Piedmontese to the Neapolitans; both are more akin to the Slovenes than the Piedmontese to the Sicilians. Until a common code has been drawn up the various provinces must retain their present legislation. The differences between them will soon be smoothed over, as in Italy. The roughness of the Serbs of Serbia and Montenegro will be toned down by the culture and love of order of the Serbs, Croats, and Slovenes of the Hapsburg monarchy. The Croats cannot wish for an independent Croatia, since it would be under the tutelage of Hungary. * * *

### For Union of Southern Slavs

The memorandum goes on to point out that union must be followed by the fusion of the two Serb dynasties, which is rendered easier by the fact that the Prince Regent of Serbia is also the grandson of King Nicholas. It is therefore suggested that Kings Nicholas and Peter should both abdicate in favor of Prince Alexander, and that the succession to the throne of the united State should be assigned after him to Prince Danilo of Montenegro, and then alternately to the heirs of the two dynasties. The proper procedure would, it is added, be for King Nicholas and his heir to notify to the Czar their acceptance of these proposals, and then to conclude a formal treaty to that effect with the Serbian Government. The Montenegrin people would, after the war, be given an opportunity of ratifying the decision on a basis of universal suffrage. " There is not a Serb and in general not a Slav who would not welcome with enthusiasm so momentous a step on the part of your Majesty, who, in the history of the Serbian people, would become the rival in glory of the Emperor Dushan. * * * "

These proposals were received with apparent approval by King Nicholas last Summer, but the actual decision was continually postponed. At last Mr. Radovitch, finding that a visit paid by the King to Italy in the Autumn had increased his tendency to evade the issue, presented a second memorandum on Jan. 11, 1917, couched in even more explicit terms than the first. The essential passage in this document runs as follows:

From the fall of the Serbian Empire [1389] to the present day, the ideal of the whole Serbian people has been union. Whenever this has appeared possible, we have seen Serbian monarchs who were ready to make sacrifices for the sake of unity. Never since Kosovo have we been so near to the realization of this ideal. * * *

If, unhappily, Montenegro is not capable, at this decisive moment, of offering effective aid in the struggle to realize an ideal which it has held for five centuries, your Majesty and your Government have none the less the duty to do all that is possible in this direction. * * * But it is clear that the most difficult question to regulate is the dynastic question, which alone—at least, in the view of us Serbs—could interfere with the idea of unification.

Dynasties which only considered their own private interests might evoke difficulties, and would, by doing so, incur grave responsibility. Holding as I do the view that this is the only road to safety and union for all Serbs and even Jugoslavs, I take the liberty of begging your Majesty to send an autograph letter to H. M. the Emperor of Russia, declaring your willingness to take, as soon as possible, the necessary measures for reaching an accord with the Sovereign and Government of the kingdom of our brothers of Serbia, and also with the representatives of the other Jugoslav countries, in order to decide our unification and lay its foundations.

### Attitude of New Cabinet

Mr. Radovitch's proposals were declined by King Nicholas, on the pretext that the time was not yet ripe, and accordingly the Cabinet resigned. The Czar signified his disapproval of the King's separatist intrigue by conferring upon Mr. Radovitch the Order of the White Eagle. He was succeeded as Premier by General Matanovitch, while Foreign Affairs were intrusted to Mr. Tomanovitch, the son of a former Premier, and Finance to Mr. Ilitch, a Serb advocate from Croatia, and only recently a Montenegrin subject. It might have been expected that men who owed their position entirely to the King's personal favor could be relied upon to fulfill his behests, but there are limits beyond which men of honor cannot be induced to go. Annoyed at the activity of the Montenegrin Committee of Union, founded by Mr. Radovitch and other prominent exiles, the King insisted that his Government should address a note to the Allies, disavowing the committee and declaring that " the Montenegrins continue to regard the Montenegrin Government as the sole representative of their interests." To this demand General Matanovitch refused the assent of his Government in the following terms:

The alliance gives us rights, but also imposes upon us duties. * * * The principle of nationality is the basis of our struggle against the Central Empires, the formula for solving the future constellation of Europe. * * * We unhappily are unable to fulfill our military duties, but we can and are bound to, remain inalienably faithful to the great principle for which our best sons have shed their blood. To accept this note, which officially proclaims separatism *pur et simple* for one part of our people, would be to disavow the alliance, to break the last thread which binds us to it, and force on a rupture of diplomatic relations.

The demobilization of the Montenegrin Army in January, 1916, lost us the friendship of Great Britain and aroused the suspicions of the other Allies, and even of our Serbian brethren. The political catastrophe which would be the infallible result of this note would mean the definite ruin of our country.

The reasons which serve as basis for the Government's policy are as follows: The *status quo* is no longer possible in the Balkans. The national conscience is awake and expanding in all sections of our nation. *The idea of union has become the faith, the religion, of the masses.* This faith has been created through the centuries by thousands of national martyrs. * * * Today it only depends upon the attitude and skill of our popular representatives whether our national problem is to be solved by normal and legal means. For the separation of any section of our people would necessarily, as an anti-national reaction, lead to a revolution such as might efface the traces of the past.

General Matanovitch concluded by laying great stress upon the need for "a sincere and profound entente with Serbia," and for identifying the Montenegrin dynasty with the national ideal.

## Another Cabinet Crisis

Not merely did this memorandum fail to evoke any satisfactory reply, but a fresh crisis was produced by King Nicholas's action in telegraphing on May 24 to the King of Italy in the following terms:

> I am happy to learn of the glorious successes obtained by your heroic army, to which my admiration and enthusiasm go out. Greeting with all my heart its supreme chief, I hope that this same hand which is liberating Italian lands will soon be stretched out toward my unhappy mountaineers.

The compliments to Italian prowess, altogether unexceptionable in themselves, were interpreted by the whole of Slav public opinion, and unquestionably intended by the King himself as a direct slight to Serbia and a peculiarly insidious bid for Italy's aid in frustrating Jugoslav unity. Fortunately, the record of King Nicholas is sufficiently well known in Rome to make the Consulta chary of giving more than a perfunctory support to the inveterate Balkan intriguer. His action, however, rendered a Cabinet crisis inevitable, and on June 5 General Matanovitch addressed a fresh memorandum to the King, explaining his reasons for accepting office last Winter and for now resigning.

> The solution put forward by the late Premier, in favor of the union of the dynasties and alternative reign, seemed to me very complicated, unrealizable, and calculated to give rise to serious consequences. At that time I agreed with the opportunists, believing that this great work would have to be realized in the most advantageous way possible and with the least possible injury to existing historical foundations. For the rest, I was in entire agreement with my predecessors. The great events which are shaking the world open a new era in human history. Our

people is also ingulfed in the chaos of events. * * * Montenegro could not escape the general movement; and on the day when the barriers separating it for centuries from its blood brothers—and particularly from Serbia—had fallen, the problem of reconstructing the Serbian State had arisen of itself. The new situation demanded a new form of State; separatism, being in conflict with the spirit of the age, became impossible for the future.

The Government, he continued, accepted office on the understanding that a project of union should be prepared, ready to submit to Parliament for approval after the restoration of peace. More than once he asked the King's permission to proceed with the draft, but met first with evasion and on May 15 with a definite refusal. He wrote:

> The annoying consequences of this have robbed us of the little prestige which was left to us: For your Majesty's refusal could only be interpreted in competent quarters as hesitation to pronounce openly on a question of international policy which divides the world into two opposite camps. *Besides, your Majesty has seen fit to raise great and delicate political questions whose solution was contrary not only to the spirit of the Government program, but also to the Constitution of Montenegro.*

The telegram to the King of Italy, the Premier concluded, was a denial of the Jugoslav ideal, such as the Government could not ignore, the more so as its dispatch without the knowledge of the Government was quite unconstitutional. General Matanovitch and his colleagues thus saw no alternative but to resign.

## Abdication Openly Demanded

Mr. Ilitch went even further. In his letter of resignation he flatly accused the King of acting "in flagrant contradiction to the program of the Government," and added that in his opinion "the action of T. R. H. the Princes is not in accord with the interests of the royal house, with the obligations toward the Allies, and with the well-being and ideal of the nation." He even expressed the fear that "the end may be a collapse of the dynasty's prestige," and concluded by demanding in so many words that "the Petrovitch dynasty should abdicate in favor of H. M. the King of Serbia," as "the sole conceivable means of avoiding a catastrophe." He not unnaturally added that his letter might be treated as an act of resignation.

This dramatic action may be taken as a moral boycott against the dynasty on the part of all Montenegrins of any political standing. The new Premier, Mr. Eugene Popovitch, an old man of 72, is a native of Dalmatia, but has for most of his life been an Italian subject, and was for many years Montenegrin Consul General in Rome. If he is scarcely known to his nominal compatriots, his colleagues are entirely unknown and sub-ordinate officials, who have never played any political rôle and are mere creatures of the King. The most striking proof of the discredit which he has brought upon himself is the refusal of the Allies to admit his representative to the recent conference in Paris.

Disregarding all hints, King Nicholas was unwise enough to give to the press a statement to the effect that Mr. Popovitch was the Montenegrin delegate to the conference, who none the less remained outside.

# Rumania Betrayed by Russia

## Secret Documents of the Czar's Government Reveal Cause of One of the War's Great Tragedies

The National Review of London, edited by L. J. Maxse, recently published an important article, of which the most significant portion is printed below:

TODAY, thanks to the upheaval at Petrograd, many documents destined to remain forever hidden among the secret archives have come to light. The explanations they furnish are as unexpected as they are valuable. Public opinion, ignorant of the truth, had accepted the most natural explanation and had attributed the two capital faults to the Government of Bucharest; but now, to the general stupefaction and indignation, it became evident that, far from being guilty of carelessness and want of foresight, Rumania was the victim of a terrible plot hatched in Berlin in concert with the men of the old régime at Petrograd, enemies of the cause they were called upon to defend.

Irrefutable evidence shows that the date of the declaration of war and the plan of campaign were forced upon Rumania by the Government of Petrograd, presided over by Messrs. Stürmer and Protopopoff. It is superabundantly proved that these men, who came up against the gentle obstinacy of Nicholas II. every time they tried to convince him of the necessity of concluding "a separate peace," had no other object in view than to put their country into the position of being forced to do so.

The check of the Rumanian intervention, on which many fine hopes were founded, seemed to serve their purpose to perfection. It has been proved now that the offensive of Brusiloff had come to a full stop at the beginning of August. And, still more, his armies were running the risk of being outflanked. Arrested at the passes which debouched into the Hungarian plain by the army of Koewess, General Brusiloff had been obliged to turn the front of his armies to the northwest—toward Lemberg—thus exposing his flank to the divisions which Hindenburg was bringing up against him.

### Plan of Petrograd Plotters

A complete defeat of the Russian armies, for which they would have been responsible to the Emperor, to Russia, and to the Allies, would not have suited these men. The defeat of Rumania, which they could impute to the inefficiency of her army, would lead equally to the same end, without compromising their personal prestige. At any price it was necessary to turn away from the Galician front the storm which was threatening.

So the plan they conceived was put

into execution. On July 1 the Imperial Government sent to the Rumanian Government the now famous ultimatum, the brutality of which is equaled only by its perfidy. It was the first document of a correspondence with which the revelations of General Iliesco in the Matin have made us acquainted—revelations completed by the publication of Count Czernin's last report in the Austrian Red Book and loyally confirmed by the men of the new régime in Russia. Nothing is more distressing than the reading of this correspondence. On one side the constant reminders of promises, the despairing remonstrances; on the other the haughty, sometimes even injurious, tone, the feigned assurance. "Now or never," says the Russian ultimatum which forced Rumania into the war, "for it must not be hoped that we shall again permit the Rumanian Army later on to make a military promenade and enter Austro-Hungarian territory in triumph."

It was impossible for the Rumanian General Staff to resist the imperious orders of their powerful neighbor, especially as at that moment no help could be hoped for from England or France, both distant and both entirely absorbed by the battle of the Somme. Despite their heroic efforts and their daily successes, the British and French armies had not yet succeeded in their principal object, the relief of Verdun, against which Hindenburg was at that moment preparing his last attack with formidable forces. It was impossible to hope that, under these circumstances, France and England would oppose the wishes of the Russian Government, especially as they were expressed in terms which left no other alternative than to advise the Rumanian General Staff to come to an understanding with the Russian command. France gave a last proof of her solicitude for Rumania in pledging herself to come to her help by a general offensive of the Saloniki army, which should begin eight days before the date of the entry of Rumania into the campaign.

## Sarrail's Army Checkmated

The desire of France to help this new ally was so sincere that M. Briand, then President of the Council, breaking all precedents, went so far as to announce in the Chamber the projected offensive of the Orient forces. The treason which unfortunately surrounded this army on all sides rendered it impossible for General Sarrail to carry out this plan at the opportune moment. Warned by the pro-Germans of Athens of the impending attack, the Bulgarian Army made the first move, and, attacking on both flanks, obliged General Sarrail to regroup his forces, which paralyzed his movements. Thus the Rumanian General Staff remained alone to face the Government of Petrograd.

Obliged to yield to the Russian ultimatum and to declare war on the day fixed in it, they asked the Russian higher command for their co-operation in the plan of campaign worked out by them, showing how impossible it would be, with the sixteen divisions, which represented the whole army, lacking heavy artillery, completely unprovided with machine guns, to cover the 600 kilometers of the Danubian front and at the same time attack on the 700-kilometer front of Transylvania. They proposed taking possession of the bridgeheads of Rustchuk and Sistov in order to guard against a passage of the Danube. To hold in check the 200,000 Bulgars, reinforced by several Turkish divisions, whom the Rumanian General Staff knew to be concentrated against the Dobrudja front, they asked for the help of seven or eight Russian divisions. Thus assured against all danger on the southern front, they might, in liaison with the left wing of Brusiloff's army, invade Transylvania with some chance of success. Before all, they insisted on the delivery of 400 machine guns which the Russian Government had promised to hold in readiness on the frontier, so as to be able to deliver them the day Rumania should declare war.

## Rumania Forced Into a Trap

The answers of Messrs. Stürmer and Protopopoff to these proposals left Rumania no longer any doubts as to the extent of the sacrifce demanded of her. They were opposed to all operations on the Danube, declaring that they had been categorically assured that the Bulgarians would lay down their arms. They took entire responsibility for it. On no account were hostilities to be directed against them. For the same reason they judged it absolutely useless to comply with the request for seven or eight divisions: "Who is threatening the Dobrudja front?" said a message coming from the Russian higher command. And when the Rumanian General Staff insisted on certain information, according to which about eight Bulgaro-Turkish divisions were advancing toward this front, a new message arrived, which said that two divisions might be put at their disposal. These indeed arrived. One of them was composed of Serbian, Croatian, and Czech prisoners belonging to Austrian regiments captured in Galicia. As to the machine guns, not one could be procured, and it was only later that M. Protopopoff confessed that he had not been able to deliver them because they had been placed on the roofs of the houses in Petrograd to put down the threatening revolution.

These messages were well calculated to dispel the last illusions of the Rumanian Government. It is hard to conceive that they could have been blind enough to believe that, with their sole resources— sixteen divisions, summarily armed— they would succeed not only in conquering vast extents of territory, but also in keeping them, when they could already hear the tread of the Bulgaro-Turkish armies, reinforced by three German divisions under Marshal Mackensen, advancing toward the Danube, and when, in the north, an army of élite, with material of crushing superiority, was preparing, under the command of Falkenhayn, for a crushing counteroffensive.

## A Tragic Alternative

The Rumanians were thus placed before the tragic alternative of risking the fight under conditions in which defeat— with all its terrible consequences—was nearly certain, or of resisting the Russian ultimatum and, in this case, giving up all hopes of the union and emancipation of the race, resigning themselves to become to Germany what the Asiatic monarchies of old were to the Roman Empire. They chose the first alternative, trusting to the honor of the British and French Governments that they would take account of the immense sacrifice Rumania was making.

The beginning of the campaign could seem brilliant to those who judge only by appearances, but the fears expressed as to the bad faith of the Bulgarians were not long in being realized, and the Russian assurances on this subject speedily proved fallacious; the Dobrudja was attacked by large forces. This part of the immense front of 1,300 kilometers had now to be defended, and the divisions called back from Transylvania, where, at the first bound, sweeping before them the Hungarian troops, they had reached Sibin.

The Second, Fifth, Tenth, and Fifteenth Divisions, withdrawn in haste and sent, under the command of General Averesco, to the Dobrudja, retrieved the situation by a brilliant success, thus avenging the check of Turtukai. But by this the Transylvanian campaign was compromised. For the last time the Rumanian Government made a moving appeal to their ally, enumerating in detail the strength of the enemy and showing that only the immediate dispatch of considerable reinforcements could give hope of resisting the two armies with which Falkenhayn and Mackensen proposed inclosing Rumania as in a vise. How was it possible, indeed, for the Rumanian Army, left to its own resources, to resist thirty-seven divisions, with a superior armament, twenty of which belonged to the élite of the German Army, when a great power like Italy, whose army had given proof of such brilliant qualities, had nearly yielded to the attack of thirty-three divisions composed exclusively of Austro-Hungarians? But M. Stürmer could now hardly stop in the disastrous course he had taken. He confined himself to prescribing a regrouping of the Rumanian forces still left to themselves.

## Gallant but Hopeless Fight

From the end of September, with all the energy of despair, the army retreated step by step, defending the passage of each river; first the Jiul, where, after a magnificent effort, it succeeded in retrieving the situation by destroying the Eleventh Bavarian Division, killing or capturing down to the last man—next the Alt, and finally the Arges, the last rampart defending Bucharest. At this moment, in December, two Russian divisions, the first since the two divisions sent to the Dobrudja, arrived to take part in the defense of the capital. But in this battle, which for three days remained undecided, their part was null, for even there they did not arrive in time. The left wing of the Rumanian Army being turned, the divisions which had, under General Averesco, bravely held out on the line Predeal-Bucharest were obliged to beat a retreat and take up a last stand on the line Galatz-Focsani, thus abandoning with the capital all the rich Wallachian plain.

The Rumanian Government gave a last proof of their spirit of sacrifice in destroying, before they retreated, everything that could possibly serve for the revictualing of the enemy. Besides the cereals, of which the Germans found only very small quantities, all the splendid modern plant of the rich petroleum industry was systematically destroyed. An Anglo-Rumanian commission was intrusted with the task of setting fire to the petroleum wells, which cover a vast region on the southern slope of the Carpathians. The sight of the flames and the columns of smoke, which plunged whole territories into darkness; the regiments defiling mute and gloomy, the populations fleeing terror-stricken before the blackness spreading like a cloud which the midday sun could not pierce, have left on the memory of all those who witnessed this grand but terrible spectacle an impression which will never fade. Thus the expected sacrifice was accomplished.

Of the 620,000 soldiers who, on Aug. 28, had marched at the given signal, and in whom Rumania had placed the hope of the realization of her ancient dream, only a third remained to continue the struggle along the line of the Sereth. Well over 200,000 men were killed or wounded, about 100,000 had been taken prisoner in the different places where they had been surrounded through the junction of the armies of Falkenhayn and Mackensen.

### Rumania and Verdun

The year 1916 ended in disaster for Rumania, but she had the satisfaction of knowing that her sacrifice had not been in vain, and that these successes of the Kaiser's troops had been largely made up for elsewhere. For by drawing down on herself the thirty-seven divisions of élite which would otherwise have been employed on other fronts, she had saved the armies of Letchitsky and Brusiloff from a counteroffensive which had caused the gravest anxiety. She could also claim with pride that she had not been quite a stranger to the fullness of the successes of her allies on the Somme and the Ancre, and that she had contributed to the definite and complete check of the Germans in the battle of Verdun—a battle second in importance only to that of the Marne—and the name of which will predominate in the history of the war in 1916.

Let us hope that the military conferences of the Allies intrusted with the conduct of the war will decide to use the new army of half a million of men which Rumania has organized in a way more profitable to the complete and definite victory of the Allies.

# THE EUROPEAN WAR AS SEEN BY CARTOONISTS

[Italian Cartoon]

## Undiminished Power

—*From Il 420, Florence.*

GERMANY: "They say we are exhausted.  We are as great as ever."

# The Other Danger

—*From Nebelspalter, Zurich.*

When Europe lies bleeding and dying, look out for the hyenas of the East [the yellow races of Asia.]

[Spanish Cartoon]

# The New Don Quixote

—From *Iberia, Barcelona.*

"Don Quixote has become a Yankee."

[Words of Jaime Brossa, at a Spanish banquet given to the French Minister of Fine Arts.]

# Eye to Eye

—*From The Chicago Herald.*

**The Dark Ages face to face with the New World.**

# American Peace Arguments

*—From The Chicago Herald.*

View looking west from Berlin.

# Comic Relief

MICHAELIS'S PRETENSIONS

—*From The Passing Show, London.*

The new German Chancellor amuses the Entente.

# Johnny Yank

—*From The Sydney Bulletin.*

" Waal, boys, guess there's room for me in here somewhere! "
[American troops landed in France on June 28, 1917]

# The Potsdam Sphinx Found Out

—*From The Passing Show, London.*

THE GERMAN PEOPLE: "O Majesty! Your riddle of victories on every front has remained unsolved for three years, but now we know the answer—the utter defeat of Germany and the doom of the Hohenzollern!"

# The Kaiser System

A fine chance the German people have to start something!

—*Ohio State Journal.*

# Civilization in 1917

" Death and hunger, murder and lies upon earth, peace and good-will toward the devil."

—*From Nebelspalter, Zurich.*

# Anti-Germ-an Poison Mask

—From The Sunday Evening Telegram, London.

The most suitable costume for members of civilized nations who have personal dealings with the people of German race in future.

# The Missing Word

—From News of The World, London.

PREMIER LLOYD GEORGE: "Say 'Restoration,' you son of a gun, 'R-restoration!'"

# American Intervention

—*From L'Asino, Rome.*

GERMAN MILITARISM: "I hear a noise!"

# Agriculture in Russia

—*From Novy Satirikon, Petrograd.*

LANDLORD: "Why do you stand on one foot?"

PEASANT: "Because I can't put the other down without trespassing on your property."

# The Entente Jewel, Consistency

—*From Kladderadatsch, Berlin.*

CHORUS OF THE ALLIES: "We will never negotiate with an autocratic Government—never!"

VOICE OF NICHOLAS (above): "And those fellows once called me brother!"

# The Rainbow

—*From The New York Times.*

America's hosts are coming, a thousand thousand strong.

# Tremble, Germany !

—*From Lustige Blaetter, Berlin.*

The U-boat is doomed!  China's invincible fleet is going to eat it up.

# Lightening the Load

—*From the Nieuwe Amsterdammer, Amsterdam.*

VON BETHMANN (casting class privilege overboard): "It must go, Majesty, or it will cost you your crown."

## Reading the Stars

—*Manchester Union.*

## He Wants an "Honorable Peace!"

—*Manchester Union.*

## The Cross Bearer

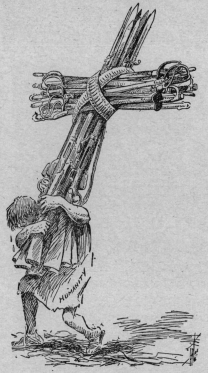

—*Los Angeles Times.*

## The Bankrupt

—*Dayton News.*

## William: "Shake and I'll Forgive All"

—*Baltimore American.*

## She Will Not Trust Him

—*Baltimore American.*

WILLIAM: "See, I prepare the way with my cloak!"
PEACE: "Yes, that's all it is!"

## The Bird Will Not Be Fooled

—*Baltimore American.*

## The Italian Renaissance

—*Baltimore American.*

[Russian Cartoon]

# Labor and Capital in Russia

—*From Novy Satirikon, Petrograd.*

LABOR: "I used to dream of shedding the blood of the bourgeois. I now delight in making him shed something else."

# Holland Shut Out From Commerce by England and Germany

—*From De Amsterdammer, Amsterdam.*

"Our relations with all foreign powers remain friendly."
[Speech from the Dutch Throne.]

*(Photo Harris & Ewing)*

One of the Posters Used to Advertise the Second Issue of United States War Bonds.

General Tasker H. Bliss, New Chief of Staff in the United States Army, (at left,) and
Major Gen. Hugh L. Scott, His Predecessor, (at right.)

# PERIOD XXXVIII.

Haig's Hammer Strokes in Flanders—Mobilizing Our Industries for War—Worldwide Embargo Against Germany—Financing America's War Needs—Latin America and the War—Germany's Waning Man Power —Slang and Slogans of War in France—A Boy's Last Letter to His Mother—How Greece Prolonged the War —The Socialist Parties of Russia—Revelations of German Plots—German Peace Propaganda—Poland's Standard on the Field of Battle—The Rise and Fall of the Fortress —Joffre and Hindenburg—How Lorraine was Saved in 1914—Lord Haldane's Mission to Germany—Secret Diplomacy of Two Autocrats—How Turkey Joined the Germans—Germany and the Armenian Atrocities—The Appalling Plight of Serbia—The Attempted Restoration of the Manchus—The War Record of the British Dependencies.

# CURRENT HISTORY CHRONICLED

### THE MONTH'S CHIEF DEVELOPMENTS

OCTOBER, 1917, witnessed a series of furious British drives in Flanders almost without a parallel in history. The result was a gain of a sector on the more elevated land lying east of Ypres. This gave the allied troops a strategic advantage in the disposition of their forces, which will be of great value in further thrusts; these are clearly in contemplation throughout the Winter. The French gave important assistance on the left flank, where they hold a small sector. There was almost continuous fighting along the Meuse, in the Verdun sector, without any material change in the lines. On the Austro-Italian front in the Julian Alps the gains made by the Italians on the Bainsizza Plateau were held; toward the end of October it was reported that forty new divisions of Germans and Austrians were being moved from the Russian front to resist the Italians. The Russians suffered a severe disaster by the loss of important islands in the Baltic, which gave the Germans control of that sea, to the imminent peril of the naval bases of Reval, Viborg, and Kronstadt, and with a serious possibility of a naval offensive against Petrograd itself. It was announced on Oct. 19 that on account of the imminence of German control of the Gulf of Riga the Russian Government was preparing to transfer the capital from Petrograd to Moscow. The British scored an important success in Mesopotamia by the capture of a small Turkish army northwest of Bagdad, making secure their occupation of that city.

The political situation developed important phases during the month. Exposures of the treachery of German diplomats in the United States and in Argentina brought several Latin-American States to the side of the Allies. The internal situation in Germany was profoundly disturbed by a growing opposition to the new Chancellor, the disclosure of a mutinous feeling in the German Navy, and the grave shortage in food and fuel, which was becoming more acute on account of the rigid embargo on all cargoes to European neutrals.

The war preparations in the United States proceeded with almost feverish speed, on a scale of magnitude heretofore unknown in history; it was reported toward the end of October that over 100,000 American troops were already in France and that fully 500,000 would be there by Spring. The Second Liberty Loan campaign was vigorously prosecuted, and two billions had been subscribed by Oct. 20.

\* \* \*

### GOVERNMENT INSURANCE FOR SOLDIERS

THE Soldiers Insurance bill, as finally adopted, makes all officers and men and women in both branches of the service eligible; the policies range from $1,000 to $10,000, and the age limit is 15 to 65. The premium is based on age: a man of 30 on a $1,000 policy pays 69 cents a month, &c. The policy is payable in monthly installments to the insured, if wholly disabled, and to the heirs at his death. The premiums are payable monthly and will be deducted from pay unless instructed to contrary; failure to pay within 31 days after a premium is due forfeits the policy, but insured may be reinstated within 6 months. The following persons may be named as beneficiaries: Husband, wife, child, both legitimate and illegitimate; adopted child, grandchild, father, mother, grandparents, step-parents, brother, sister, of the half as well as whole blood.

\* \* \*

### A HISTORIC SESSION OF CONGRESS

ONE of the most memorable sessions of the United States Congress was that which ended on Oct. 6, 1917. This, the first session of the Sixty-fifth Congress, began by special call on April 2, and the same evening heard President Wilson's address recommending a declaration of war. More legislation of the most far-reaching order was passed than in any previous session, while the appropriations ran to billions of dollars. This session will be historical as definitely marking the great transformation of the Republic, with its early ideas of avoiding entangling alliances, into a mighty world power fully and frankly recognizing that its interests are as wide as humanity itself. No one has been better aware of this development of the nation than President Wilson, as can be gathered from several of his utterances before circumstances drove him to the conclusion that the United States could no longer remain a neutral. And not the least interesting feature of the session has been the extraordinary ascendancy which the President established over Congress, receiving authority for practically every war measure he demanded, and successfully resisting those he deemed inadvisable.

\* \* \*

### BELGIUM'S FIGHTING STRENGTH

THE Belgian Army on Oct. 17, 1917, consisted of the following: One hundred and twenty thousand men on the 25-mile Belgian firing line; back of the line, 100,000 more Belgian troops in training or reserve; back of these, a fully equipped munitions system and base and transport organization. In Belgian munition factories, in France or England, operated by Belgian managers and worked by Belgian women, children, and wounded men, a large part of the supplies for the army are produced. As Belgium can no longer levy taxes in her own territory, she has been financed by loans from Britain, France, and the United States, which is lending her $7,500,000 a month. In Africa the Belgian flag waves over the Congo territory and a Belgian army of 43,000 natives, commanded by Belgian officers, has conquered from Germany 180,000 square miles. At the outbreak of the war Belgium had only 30,000 regulars and 150,000 national guardsmen.

\* \* \*

### FORMER RUSSIAN OFFICIALS IN PRISON

IN the Troubetskoi Bastion of the Fortress of St. Peter and St. Paul at Petrograd, where for two centuries have been immured regicides, nihilists, bomb throwers, and victims of autocratic tyranny, are now interned eight conspicuous Russian figures, viz.: General Rennenkampff, who carries a black record for his tyranny and injustice toward the 1906 revolutionists; M. Bieletsky, former Direcor of Police and accomplice of agents provocateur; the reactionary former Minister of the Interior, M. Makaroff, who caused the election of a burglar to the Duma to act as a spy; former Minister of Justice J. Tscheglovitoff, whom the late Count Witte characterized as the "most clever, most corrupt man in Europe"; Prince Alexander Dolgorukoff, the cavalry commander seized last month as a supporter of General Korniloff; General Voyeikoff, the former Emperor's palace commandant, and, finally, Alexander Protopopoff, once classed as a patriotic member of the Duma, next an oppressive Minister of the Interior, and last the ally and slave of Rasputin.

\* \* \*

### BRITAIN'S RELIANCE UPON THE UNITED STATES

AT a dinner tendered to Congressman Medill McCormick in London, Sept. 12, Mr. Bonar Law, Chancellor of the Exchequer, acting as representative of the Prime Minister, referred to the entrance of the United States into the war in these words:

I see it constantly stated in German newspapers that that is the last hope of the Allies. We do rely upon the Americans, and with good reason, for I, as Chancellor of the Exchequer, am ready to say now what I should have been very sorry to admit six months ago, that without the aid of the United States the financial position of the Allies would have been in a very disastrous situation today. We have reason to be grateful for the readiness of the help which has been given by our allies on the other side of the water in this respect. But, though we rely upon the United States, that does not mean that we are ceasing our own efforts.

Nothing that has been said by Mr. McCormick in his very eloquent speech gave me so much pleasure as the statement coming from an observer from the outside of what the United Kingdom has done in this war. I think that it is a record of which not only we who have seen it have reason to be proud, but a record upon which those who come after us will dwell as the brightest page in the long history of the British Empire. I know of no previous war in which this country has been engaged where on the whole the people have supported right and left, thick and thin, the vigorous prosecution of the struggle. On all previous occasions, as, indeed, now, there were parties—there have been peace parties—but never before in our history has the voice of faction been so little heard as in the great struggle in which we now are engaged.

\* \* \*

## JAPAN'S FINANCIAL AID TO THE ALLIES

THE announcement that the Russian Provisional Government had obtained a credit of 66,667,000 yen (about $33,333,500) in Japan through the sale of that amount of treasury bills to the Japanese Government was made in a cablegram received on Oct. 8 by Akira Den, financial commissioner of the Japanese Government in New York. The issue bears interest at 6 per cent. and runs for one year. Japan took the Russian securities at par. The proceeds will be used by Russia in paying for munitions of war bought in Japan. The willingness of Japan to grant this loan arose partly from confidence in the new régime in Russia and partly as a consequence of the United States embargo on gold exports. Japan had recently been a heavy importer of gold, much of it being used to meet Russian obligations in Japan. When the gold embargo became effective, Japan found it advantageous to grant new credits to Russia. According to official figures, Japan has loaned the allied Governments approximately 500,000,000 yen (about $250,000,000) since the war began. A total of 221,667,000 yen in Russian Treasury bills has been sold in Japan. The British Government has sold 100,000,000 yen of Exchequer bonds to the Japanese, and a total of 76,000,000 yen of French Treasury bills has also been sold in Japan. Of these loans the British Exchequer bonds, amounting to 100,000,000 yen, were paid in American money.

\* \* \*

## SOME INSTANCES OF INTERNATIONAL TREACHERY

THE questionable activities of Bernstorff and Luxburg have had their historic parallels. Bethmann Hollweg's was not the first "scrap of paper." A noteworthy instance is that which Bismarck brazenly related of himself, in telling how he tricked Napoleon III. into war in 1870. There was a question of putting a Hohenzollern on the throne of Spain. France protested. The French envoy at Ems had an interview with the King of Prussia, afterward Kaiser Wilhelm I. of Germany. The King's secretary telegraphed an account of the interview to Bismarck, his Prime Minister, on July 13, 1870. Moltke was with Bismarck, deeply despondent; Bismarck, talking of the German sense of honor, deliberately altered the telegram, turning it, as Moltke said, from a parley into a challenge, and gave it to the press. It instantly aroused France and brought on the war. Bismarck explains his motives: "It is important that we should be the ones attacked!" The story is told at length, with the telegram as sent, and as falsified, in "Bismarck the Man and Statesman."

A notable act of treachery was committed by Austria, one among many, at the time of the Crimean war, 1854. Nicholas I. of Russia, in part through sympathy for the oppressed Slavs in Hungary, sent an army, in 1849, to crush Kossuth's Magyar republic and save the power of the Hapsburgs. Five years later, when Russia was in danger, Austria cynically refused to help her and secretly aided Russia's enemies.

The violation of the Pragmatic Sanction is a historic case of perfidy. Prussia had consented, by that agreement, to support the succession of an Austrian Princess, Maria Theresa. But no sooner did she come to the throne, on the death of her father, Emperor Charles VI., than Frederick II. of Prussia, "Old Fritz in the Elysian Fields," as his successor recently called him, broke his oath and seized the Austrian province of Silesia, thus plunging the world into war. In the matter of the Danish Duchies, Schleswig and Holstein, Bismarck was guilty of signal treachery toward both Denmark and Austria, for, while both Austria and Denmark had certain claims to the Duchies, Prussia, which seized them after two predatory wars, had no real rights there.

### OESEL AND DAGOE ISLANDS

ON Oct. 15 it was announced from Petrograd that German forces had two days previously landed on Oesel and Dagö Islands, at the northeast end of the Gulf of Riga, after bombarding the land forts, and had silenced the Russian batteries and occupied Arensburg, the capital of Oesel. This action really put Oesel and Dagö on the map, bringing them into prominence for the first time since the twenty years' war between Charles XII. of Sweden, and Peter the Great, the maker of modern Russia. This long war, in which Peter deliberately set himself to learn Charles's strategy by being beaten by him, was closed by the Treaty of Nystad, on Sept. 10, 1721, which gave the two islands, with the contiguous mainland, to Russia. They had belonged to Sweden since 1645; for nearly a century before that date, namely, since 1559, they had belonged to Denmark.

Russia is so large, and the maps of Russia are consequently on so small a scale, that these two islands are almost invisible on a general map of the Russian Empire. But Oesel is of considerable size, about 1,000 square miles, or as large as the State of Rhode Island; Dagö is one-third as large, or 364 square miles. Their distance from Petrograd is about equal to the distance from New York to Washington. Arensburg, famous for its sea bathing, has monuments of both the Swedish and the Russian occupations, and also a large Lutheran church. It has 5,000 inhabitants, Oesel having in all about 62,000 inhabitants, while Dagö has 16,000. Both islands are flat, formed —like Nantucket and Martha's Vineyard —largely of glacial drift dotted with erratic boulders and glacial lakes; but Oesel has high chalk cliffs on the northern coast. Large areas of both islands are covered by pine forests, but considerable areas bear good crops of grain, flax, hemp, and roots. Oesel is also famous for a breed of small, very hardy horses.

The population in both islands is predominantly Esthonian, akin to the Finns, and many of the old national customs and traditions of the Esthonians, with their national dress, are preserved, untouched by Swedish or Russian influence. The climate of the islands is healthy, and milder than the mainland, and Arensburg, on the south shore of Oesel, is a Summer resort for the people of Riga.

* * *

### THE CAUSES OF HOLLAND'S NEUTRALITY

HOLLAND is ostensibly neutral, because she has so much to fear from both sides. She refrains from hostility to Germany for three reasons: sympathy, pecuniary advantage, and the dread of a German invasion. The Court is strongly pro-German; Queen Wilhelmina, whose mother was a Princess of Waldeck, married, in 1901, Prince Henry of Mecklenburg-Schwerin. They have one daughter, Princess Juliana Louise Emma Marie Wilhelmina, the heir to the crown of the Netherlands. Self-interest further holds Holland to Germany; she has made immense sums by selling food to the German army and civil population, creating a new class, nicknamed "goulash barons." She is further in dread of German invasion; it has been notorious for many months that Germany has strong forces on the Dutch frontier, ready to strike; and, while the Dutch army is mobilized, there are no strong fortresses, though Holland could defend a part of her territory by cutting the dikes and flooding a large area, leaving North and South Holland, with parts of Zeeland and Utrecht, practically impregnable. But this would mean the ruin and desolation of a great part of her territory.

Holland has equally strong reasons for not declaring war on the Entente. Her immense colonies, in both the Eastern and the Western Hemisphere, lie open to attack by the English fleet. These colonies amount to about 740,000 square miles, with a population of nearly 50,000,-000 in the Dutch East Indies; with Dutch Guiana, or Surinam, in South America, in area 46,000 square miles, but very sparsely populated, having about two inhabitants to the square mile. Dutch Guiana has already been twice in English hands—during the Napoleonic wars—but most of it was restored to Holland in 1814 and 1815. There are also the islands of which Curaçao is the chief, in area 400 square miles, with a dense population of 56,000. During the Napoleonic wars, England's sea power completely dominated the then immense colonial empire of Holland. British Guiana, South Africa, and the Dutch East Indies were all taken by England at that time, though the greater part of the East Indies was later restored to Holland; England, however, holding the Straits Settlements, with Singapore.

The fear of losing the still vast remnant of a much vaster colonial empire effectually prevents Holland from making common cause with Germany and declaring war against England and her allies. There is also the deep-rooted patriotism of the Netherlanders, who know that, once on Germany's side, they would practically cease to be an independent nation.

* * *

## POLAND'S NEW CONSTITUTION

BY a decree issued Sept. 15, 1917, that part of Poland which was taken from Russia has been granted by the Emperors of Germany and Austria a new Constitution. This new Constitution is distinguished from the former by two things: 1. It gives part of Poland a full State apparatus—a Council of Regency of three Persons to fulfill the functions of a King, a Ministry, and a Council of State. 2. It gives also this new Polish Government certain legislative powers. The former Council of State was merely a consultative body.

The legislative powers of the new body can only make laws within the restricted domain assigned to it by the German and Austrian Governments, and even within this domain the Governor General has the right of veto if he protests within fourteen days. This Government is not allowed to have any voice whatever in foreign affairs. The most important State functions are kept in the hands of the German authorities.

The new Government does not have national sovereignty, as it is nominated by Germany and Austria, and it can exercise only local self-government.

* * *

## ALSACE AND LORRAINE IN THE WAR

IT is stated on good authority that more than 30,000 men of Alsace and Lorraine have fought under the French flag; five Generals from the lost prov-

inces have been killed in action while fighting for France, to wit: Generals Sibille, Dupuy, Dion, Trumelet-Faber, and Stirn. Since the beginning of hostilities German courts-martial sitting in the annexed provinces have inflicted sentences totaling five thousand years' imprisonment on citizens of Alsace and Lorraine, whose offense has been the expression of opinions favorable to France.

Since Alsace and Lorraine were annexed by Germany in 1871 until the outbreak of the war in 1914 no fewer than 500,000 of the inhabitants of the provinces, according to official figures, have migrated to France. Immediately after the declaration of war, three years ago, every one of real Alsatian or Lorraine origin who could find a way to do so made a hurried departure over the frontier line. Hundreds of those remaining, owing to their inability to leave in time, were at once seized as suspects and sent to prison or internment camps, where they have been kept in confinement for three years.

* * *

## SOUTH AMERICA IN TWO WORLD WARS

THE general alignment of the South American nations against Germany in the present world war brings to mind that it was the last world war, a century ago, which brought these Latin republics into existence. The beginning was made when Napoleon's invasion of Spain and Portugal drove the Portuguese royal house to its great colony in Brazil, in 1807; there its members continued to reign, though as an independent empire, until Nov. 15, 1889, when Dom Pedro II. was compelled to abdicate. The second step was taken when Simon Bolivar, who had studied Spanish tyranny in Madrid, revolution in Paris, and democracy in the United States, joined the insurrection at Caracas in April, 1810. On May 25, 1810, the people of the Argentine rose against Spanish rule, declaring their independence on July 9, 1816. Chile declared its independence in September, 1810. Paraguay followed in 1811. In the House of Commons Canning took up the cause of the new republics, declaring that he " had called a new world into existence, to redress the balance of the old"; that "France may get Spain, but she will not get the Spanish colonies." Great Britain then formally recognized the Empire of Brazil and the republics of Mexico and Colombia. In 1832, after civil war, Colombia was divided into three independent States — Colombia, Venezuela, and Ecuador. Peru became independent in 1821, and on Dec. 2, 1823, Monroe made the celebrated declaration which completed the work of recognition begun by Canning. In 1825 Bolivia and Uruguay came into separate existence; the latter had belonged to Brazil. Thus it was the French invasion of the peninsula, with the consequent weakening of the Spanish monarchy, which gave the South American nations their chance to spring into independent life. England first recognized and supported them, as an act of hostility to Napoleon. The United States, thirteen years later, confirmed and completed that recognition.

* * *

## SWEDISH PRO-GERMANISM AND BERNADOTTE

THE marked German sympathies of the Swedish Court are a legitimate heritage from the founder of the present dynasty, Marshal Bernadotte, one of Napoleon's most famous warriors, who deserted him and went over to Prussia. Bernadotte had been jealous of Bonaparte from the beginning; and when the great Corsican was named First Consul, Bernadotte, the ambitious son of a Pau lawyer, became openly hostile, and took part in a plot to overthrow the dictator. This was in 1802.

After the French Nation, by an almost unanimous plébescite, had confirmed Napoleon in power, an outward reconciliation took place between the two men, and Bernadotte was given the command of considerable armies. In 1809 he was in command of a mixed force in Jutland. At that time, Gustavus IV. of Sweden, who, a few months earlier, had ceded Finland to Alexander I. of Russia, had made himself so unpopular that he was compelled to abdicate, being succeeded by the aged and childless Charles XIII. The leaders of Sweden offered the succession of the throne, with the title of Crown Prince, to Bernadotte, who went through the form of asking Napoleon's consent.

This renewed the old quarrel between them, and when the retreat from Moscow laid Napoleon open to attack, the new Crown Prince of Sweden was found among the enemies of the French Emperor. He fought on the Prussian side against Napoleon at Dennewitz and Leipsic, and hoped to be named King of France on Napoleon's first abdication and exile to Elba. He was disappointed, but five years later, in 1818, the aged Charles XIII. died, and Bernadotte succeeded to the crown of Sweden, living until 1844, when he died at the age of eighty. He reigned under the title of Charles XIV., and King Gustav V., the present King of Sweden, is his great-grandson, the dynasty being called the House of Ponte Corvo, from the Duchy conferred upon Bernadotte by Napoleon.

* * *

## THE PROBLEM OF MODERN CHINA

EVER since the great epoch of State Socialism in the Sung dynasty, China has been the weakest of great nations. So completely was the Middle Kingdom enfeebled by the pacifism of that Socialist period, that for the greater part of the intervening period, the Chinese have been ruled by foreign conquerors, first the Mongols and later the Manchus, with the native dynasty of the Mings between. Ever since the conquest by the Manchus, in 1644, China has been a land of contradictions, at once the most democratic and the most autocratic country in the world. The saying that "the voice of the people is the voice of God" has existed in China for 3,000 years. There is no hereditary nobility, if we except the descendants of the sage, Confucius, who are held in especial honor. All Government posts are filled, and have for many centuries been filled, by open examinations, based on a study of the national literature, and no Government official has ever had the power to pass his position on to his children. The sense of equality is, perhaps, greater and has always been greater in China than in any other land. Yet, for all their democracy of feeling, the Chinese have been governed by an absolute autocracy, the military autocracy of the conquering Manchus, whose fighting men have garrisoned all the fortified cities of China. So, while China has had an army it has been, since 1644, a foreign army; the Chinese themselves have not been trained to arms. In all probability the desire to remedy this age-long weakness, to give China a strong national army, has been one of the controlling motives which have decided China to enter the world war; for a strong national army would mean a new lease of life to the oldest and most numerous of nations, a nation which has survived from the days of the ancient Chaldeans and the Egypt of the Pharaohs.

\* \* \*

### MOTHERLAND VS. DOMINIONS

THE British Government refutes the story that large numbers of trained soldiers fit for service are kept in idleness in the United Kingdom while the troops from the Dominions are at the front. In an official statement it is explained that of every six British soldiers fighting at the front, at least five were recruited in the United Kingdom. With reference to casualties, the statistics show that the percentage has been higher among the troops from the United Kingdom than among the Dominion troops. The figures in the four series of battles on the Somme, around Arras, Ypres and at Messines Ridge are as follows:

DIVISIONS ENGAGED

|  | Motherland. | | Dominions. |
|---|---|---|---|
| Somme | 5 | to | 1 |
| Arras | 3½ | to | 1 |
| Ypres | 7 | to | 1 |
| Messines | 2 | to | 1 |

CASUALTIES PER DIVISION

|  | Motherland. | | Dominions. |
|---|---|---|---|
| Somme | 5 | to | 4 |
| Arras | 7 | to | 6 |
| Ypres | 5 | to | 1 |
| Messines | 11 | to | 13 |

\* \* \*

### WHAT ITALY HAS DONE

GENERAL GIARDINO, Italian Minister of War, reviews Italy's efforts in part as follows:

With regard to the theatre of war, our front, which measures four hundred and six miles, is about equal to those of the French, English, and Belgian armies combined, and, even if a large part of this is

mountainous, that does not permit of greatly decreasing the density of the troops in consequence of the outline of the frontier and the immediate neighborhood of regions of capital importance for us, rendering it absolutely indispensable for us to be everywhere perfectly secure.

Indeed, the frontier line among the high mountains has required greater labors for the construction of roads, lodgings for the troops, fortifications, &c., and has called for a greater intensification of services than would have been needed in the plains.

Altitudes of over 10,000 feet have been reached not only by mountain artillery but also by field guns, and even by numerous siege batteries, so it will be obvious what an enormous expenditure of labor is required for the construction of roads and shelters under such conditions and for supplying the tens of thousands of quadrupeds needed, and for the transport on men's shoulders of all that is essential in order to live and fight at heights which cannot be reached even by mules.

For all this admirable effort Italy has mobilized twenty-six classes, that is to say, over 4,200,000 men, who have been almost entirely employed as fighting units to keep up the numbers required and replace losses. In the last splendid action she succeeded in breaking through the enemy's line in a section of capital strategic importance despite the Austrians' more favorable position, and thus striking a blow the vigor of which is proved by its repercussion on the entire group of enemy nations.

\* \* \*

### FAMOUS COMMANDERS TRIED FOR TREASON

THE trial and sentence of General Soukhomlinoff, who was Minister of War in Russia when the great war broke out, bears many resemblances to the trials of two famous commanders—the Englishman, Admiral Byng, and the Frenchman, Marshal Bazaine. When Frederick the Great of Prussia, turning the Pragmatic Sanction into a scrap of paper, robbed Maria Theresa of a part of her inheritance, England and France took opposite sides in the quarrel, which developed into the Seven Years' War, and thus led to the great struggle between France and England, in America and India. Admiral Byng was, in 1756, in command of the English Channel Fleet. Minorca was threatened by a French force from Toulon, and Byng was sent to drive back the French and relieve the garrison of Fort St. Philip, the chief stronghold in Minorca. He sailed, expecting defeat and already determined to give up the attempt, if there was any considerable resistance. He fought a losing battle against the French, and sailed home after only four days. Public opinion in England universally condemned him. He was tried for treason and shot on March 14, 1757, within a few weeks of Clive's great victory at Plassey, in Bengal.

The distinguished French General, Marshal Bazaine, had commanded the French forces of Napoleon in Mexico, during the short and tragic reign of Emperor Maximilian, younger brother of the late Francis Joseph of Austria; in Mexico, Bazaine had been involved in many intrigues, and was even accused of trying to gain the crown of Mexico, largely to please his young Mexican wife. On his return to France he was given high command by Napoleon III., and led a French army of 140,000 at the beginning of the Franco-Prussian war. His movements were incredibly slow and indecisive, and he finally took refuge in the fortress of Metz, where he began a treasonable correspondence with the Prussians, many details of which have never been completely cleared up. To Bismarck he proposed " to save France from herself." Marshal MacMahon was on his way to relieve Metz when he was surrounded and disastrously beaten at Sedan, and shortly after Bazaine surrendered with his whole army. It is said that, had he held out only a week longer, the French could have defeated the weak German force on the Loire and marched to the relief of Paris. Bazaine returned from Prussian captivity, and in 1873 was put on trial, condemned, first to death, and later to exile for life. He was sent to the Island of Sainte Marguerite, close to Cannes, but escaped, first to Italy and later to Madrid, where Alfonso XII. of Spain welcomed and honored him. Marshal Bazaine died in 1888.

Concerning Soukhomlinoff, while it seems certain that he was guilty of grave dereliction of duty in the matter of military secrecy, his friends assert that in many ways he was a model War Minister. Bark, the Russian Minister of Finance, testified, in the Petit Parisien, that the Russian mobilization at the beginning of August, 1914, " went off with a regularity which surpassed all expectation," and many critics defend the view of Soukhomlinoff, that modern fortresses are an element of weakness rather than of strength, being effectively superseded by temporary trenches.

\* \* \*

STATISTICS furnished by the French and British authorities to the American-British-French-Belgian Permanent Blind Relief War Fund show that there are in England, France, and Belgium more than 3,000 soldiers who have been totally blinded in the war and nearly 25,000 blinded in one eye, a large proportion of whom will eventually lose the sight of the other as the result of shock or of the wounds themselves. In addition, there are in France alone nearly 200 who, besides losing both eyes, have also suffered, by explosions or amputation, the loss of both arms or both legs, or a leg and a hand, and in many cases have been rendered stone deaf.

\* \* \*

KUHARA FUSANOSUKE, head of the Kuhara Mining Company, one of the richest men of Japan, will erect a gigantic shipbuilding enterprise, to rival the great industrial City of Essen. He will acquire 1,500,000 tsubo of land, and there establish an industrial city, with a population of 200,000. Over thirty separate workshops are to be built, and nearly 35,000 workmen will be employed.

\* \* \*

IN the six months ended Sept. 30, 1917, the revenue income of the United Kingdom was $1,276,110,200, an increase over the corresponding six months of 1916 of about $500,000,000, of which $280,000,000 was excess profits tax, $75,000,000 property and income tax. The total annual revenue of the United Kingdom is now over $2,600,000,000; the expenditure chargeable against revenue is at the rate of $12,000,000,000 per annum.

# Military Events of the Month
## From September 18 to October 18, 1917
### By Walter Littlefield

## The Battle of Flanders

AFTER a pause of more than a month the battle of Flanders, which is rapidly losing its designation as the third battle of Ypres, has been renewed by the Allies with redoubled fury. Meanwhile, they had evidently solved to their satisfaction the problem set them by the Germans early in September, when the civil population of several towns of the Flanders plain were ordered to leave their homes. Between the 20th of September and the middle of October the periodic assaults made on the front southeast, east, and northeast of Ypres forced into the enemy's lines a new salient of far greater proportions than that eliminated last Summer.

German military critics believe that it reveals a desire on the part of the Allies to gain the coast, where the submarine bases of Ostend and Zeebrugge are in operation, and where intervening dunes conceal the aerodromes whence attacks are made upon England. English and French critics rather favor the idea of an encircling movement of Lille from the north. According to the military results themselves, either objective—or both— would be logical. The complete occupation of the high ground, the so-called Passchendaele Ridge, which runs like a series of mounds northeast, would command the lowlands to the coast, almost parallel to it, twenty-odd miles away. The possession of the road to Menin with the town itself would seriously threaten Lille or at least deprive it of one of its most important railway connections.

In detail the engagements of the month have been characterized by the "tank" vs. the concrete "pill box," and by counterattacks broken up by the low-altitude fire of swarms of Anglo-French aviators. The losses to the enemy are known to have been prodigious, while those of the Allies have been comparatively light— demonstrating the thorough artillery preparation before attack, and the varied and ingenious methods of throwing back counterattacks.

Field Marshal Sir Douglas Haig opened the ball on Sept. 20, with many and sundry extras on Sept. 26. These efforts appeared to have for their objective the control of the Ypres-Menin road. Then came similar and well-defined operations further north along the ridge, in which he was assisted by the French of Pétain—Oct. 4, 9, and 12. Most of the attacks were begun at sunrise, and before noon had usually reached their objectives, and, not infrequently, consolidated the positions won.

Meanwhile, formidable and almost daily naval and aerial attacks were being launched against Ostend and Zeebrugge, and aerial attacks against the aerodromes of the dunes. On Sept. 22 a German counterattack from the air over Ostend resulted in the loss of three enemy seaplanes; on the night of Sept. 27 British naval aircraft raided the Zeebrugge lock-gates, submarine docks, and the aerodromes at St. Denis-Westrem, Goutrode, and Houttave. On Sept. 30 the photographs of a similar raid revealed well-defined loss to the enemy. All these raids seemingly lend color to the dictum of the German critics that the coast is the main objective of the battle of Flanders.

### Fighting for Polygon Wood

The attack of Sept. 20 began precisely at 5:40 A. M. on an eight-mile front, between the Ypres-Comines Canal and the Ypres-Staden Railway. The North Country regiments carried Inverness Copse; the Australians, Glencorse Wood and Nonne Boshen; the Scottish and South African brigades, Potsdam,

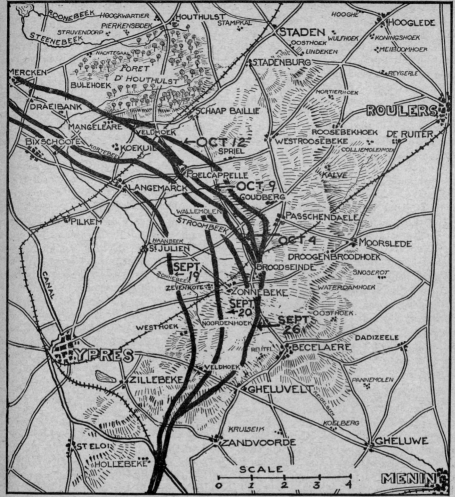

MAP SHOWING BRITISH GAINS IN FLANDERS, STROKE BY STROKE, GIVING THEM
CONTROL OF THE HIGH GROUND KNOWN AS PASSCHENDAELE RIDGE

Vampir, and Borry Farms; the West Lancashire Territorials, Iberian Farm and the concrete pile known as Gallipoli. All these points were reached in the élan of the attack. Then, on the right, the English county troops proceeded with sharply contested advance to their final objectives in the woods north of the Ypres-Comines Canal and in the neighborhood of Tower Hamlets; in the centre the North Country and Australian battalions fought on for over a mile, enveloping the southern hamlet of Veldhoek and the western portion of Polygon Wood. This was the greatest penetration. All was done according to

schedule, almost on schedule time. Before the morning was over a number of local German counterattacks had been broken up and the British troops were resting.

On the 22d strong German counterattacks were launched and repulsed, save on a small section on the right. These repulses were principally accomplished by the low-altitude firing of the British airmen, some 300 machines being engaged. Three days later the Germans won a temporary gain on Passchendaele Ridge near Polygon Wood.

Then on the 26th came the second smashing drive on a six-mile front with from a half mile to a mile depth. South of the Ypres-Menin road the English home troops completed the capture of the Tower Hamlets Spur, and gained their objective—the German concrete works on its further slope. In the centre some companies of Argyll and Sutherland Highlanders met with a stubborn resistance, so that the assault further north was carried into the afternoon, with the Australians clearing the remainder of Polygon Wood and the English, Scottish, and Welsh battalions accomplishing their remote objective—Zonnebeke, a mile away. On the extreme left the North Midland and London Territorials reached their objectives on both sides of the Wieltje-Gravenstafel and St. Julien-Gravenstafel roads. This advance reached half a mile through a maze of fortified farms and concrete redoubts.

Almost simultaneously the Germans had launched seven heavy counterattacks, which, carried into the following day, nevertheless left the British in full possession of their objectives—with light losses to them but with heavy losses to the enemy.

### British Win Main Ridge

The attack of Oct. 4 began at 10:35 on a front of over eight miles from south of Tower Hamlets to the Ypres-Staden Railway, north of Langemarck. It gave the British possession of the main ridge up to 1,000 yards north of Broodseinde. The weather prevented further advance, as it doubtless did counterattacks on the part of the enemy, although a few were attempted in the afternoon southeast of Polygon Wood. In this attack the French protected the British right. Evidently a more formidable drive had been prepared; as it was, the British losses were light, and the German heavy, including, since Sept. 20, 10,000 prisoners.

The main strength of the two subsequent attacks—Oct. 9 and Oct. 12—was also directed over the Passchendaele Ridge. Meanwhile, it was learned from prisoners that the attack of the 4th had anticipated a fierce German assault by half an hour, during which time the barrage fire of the British had unconsciously wrecked five divisions of the Germans,

massed for the advance which never took place.

On the 9th the operations extended over a front of ten miles. The French, on the north, pierced the German positions to a depth of a mile and a quarter, capturing the villages of St. Jean de Mangelaere and a northern hamlet of Veldhoek, with numerous intervening concrete redoubts. The British drove to a depth of a mile and a half, going beyond Poelcapelle. This operation put the English and French within long-range gunshot of Roulers and gave them the principal heights of the ridge commanding the plain of Flanders.

With the advance of the 9th it became geographically, if not strategically, obvious that another drive of similar magnitude would unlock the German front from Bixschoote to the sea. Such a drive, however, did not at once occur. The three hours' assault in the early morning of the 12th, succeeded by a consolidation of positions on the 13th, brought the Allies on a six-mile front to within 500 yards of the town of Passchendaele. Rain then brought operations temporarily to a standstill.

### Results of Five Engagements

The foregoing five engagements have carried the Allies to the Ypres-Roulers road on the northeast, and to the neighborhood of Passchendaele, a distance of a little over three miles; they have gained nearly a mile to the southeast over the Ypres-Menin road; the area covered includes about twenty-three square miles. Their losses have been comparatively light, according to official bulletins and reports of eyewitnesses, while those of the Germans, particularly when their attempted offensives have been prematurely assailed and in their counterattacks, have been correspondingly large. Indeed, the slaughter of the Germans surprised in mass formations has been compared to their most fatal days before Verdun.

The second stage of the month's fighting in Flanders, over the commanding Passchendaele Ridge, has been compared by some critics to the decisive battle of the Marne. It is hardly that, but rather the occupation of commanding positions, from which such a decisive battle may be developed.

The ground occupied by the Allies has revealed several interesting things, uncovered several German secrets. More and more are the Germans abandoning their patent and marvelously perfected system of trenches for purposes of defense; more and more are they relying on the concrete redoubt, called the " pill box," which is easily observed by the French and British airmen, and almost as easily blown to pieces by accuracy of their artillery fire—the survivors are left to the " tanks." Again, it has been observed that three out of five of the German shells thrown fail to explode. An examination of them has revealed poor substitutes for metal caps and priming. Many of their high explosive shells detonate without great concussion, and in a cloud of black smoke, like the burning of common gunpowder. Individual initiative on the part of officers below the rank of Colonel is becoming very rare. Small detachments group for surrender, rarely for a last stand. All this eloquently betrays the waning morale of the enemy.

## Germans Control Gulf of Riga

When the Germans occupied Riga in the first week of September it was obvious that this port could be of little use to them unless they also controlled the waters of the Gulf of Riga, on the eastern shores of which troops might be disembarked for a land investment of the Russian naval base of Reval. For, although it was quite out of the question to expect Germany, with her depleted man power, to deploy through the 300-odd miles necessary to reach Petrograd, yet the same object might be attained by the Gulf of Finland if only the protected ports of the southern shore could be eliminated. Landing parties, not necessarily permanent, would be required to attack these ports from the shore side, and work along the coast under the guns of warships. But where could these detachments find a base as long as the Russians controlled the Gulf of Riga?

The Russian fleet, on account of the revolution, was believed to be at a low grade of resistance, yet weeks passed without a move being made by the German fleet to secure the gulf. The reason is now believed to be the mutiny at Wilhelmshaven, the first news of which was revealed by Admiral von Capelle, the German Minister of Marine, in the Reichstag on Oct. 9.

From German naval refugees in Switzerland it has subsequently been learned that the mutiny was much more serious than officially reported—it embraced not only Wilhelmshaven but the Baltic base of Kiel. At both places storehouses were wrecked and supplies destroyed, and 12,000 men on board twenty-five ships were involved in an actual revolt against the Kaiser. The first outbreak began as far back as July 30; the second, principally at Kiel, was on Sept. 2—the very day on which the German advance guard rode through Riga.

### Two Islands Captured

The mutiny, however, merely postponed what was both a strategic and a tactical necessity if the occupation of Riga was to be anything more than a political gesture. On Oct. 8 a strong German naval force was observed off the Danish Island of Bornholm, sailing east-by-north. Two days later German motor boats appeared in the Gulf of Riga, and were dispersed by the shore batteries. Evidently their observations were to the effect that an entrance to the gulf could not be forced through the defended waters between Oesel Island and Cape Domesnees—a mined channel twenty miles wide—for on Oct. 13 German detachments under the protection of the guns of warships were landed on the shore of the Gulf of Tagalah, a northern inlet of Oesel Island, and near the village of Serro on the southern shore of Dagö Island. By Oct. 15, Arensburg, the chief city of Oesel, was in the possession of the invaders, and the garrisons of both islands were fleeing to the mainland eastward. (The islands have together an area about equal to Rhode Island, and a population of 50,000.) On Oct. 18 the Russian Admiralty reported the loss of the battleship Slava, 13,516 tons, in defending the gulf.

Thus, what Germany attempted to do in August and September, 1915, when

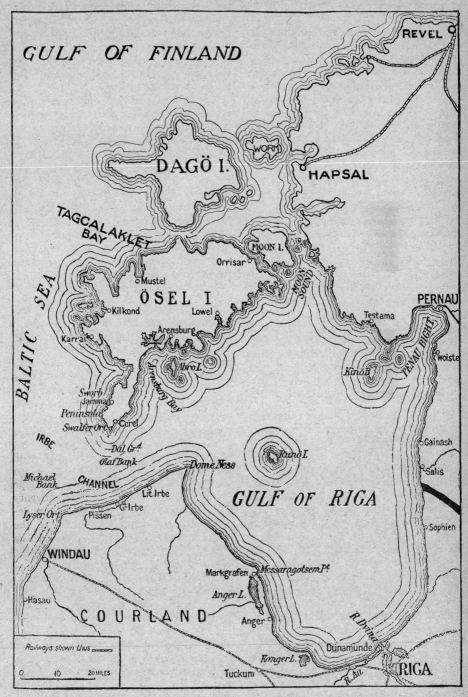

RUSSIAN ISLANDS CAPTURED BY GERMAN FORCES, GIVING THEM CONTROL OF
THE GULF OF RIGA

she landed a force on Cape Domesnees, only to be destroyed a few days later, and then fought a naval battle off Oesel, in which the Russians claimed to have sunk five light cruisers and torpedo boats and to have seriously damaged the old battleships Wittelsbach and Kaiser Friedrich, she now accomplished.

### German Gains in Russia

Complementary to these engagements the Germans have made gains beyond Riga, but with severe losses. On Sept. 21 they captured Jacobstadt, on the Dvina, together with positions on a twenty-six-mile front to a depth of six miles—still, however, on the western, or left, bank of the river. Jacobstadt, according to Berlin advices, furnished the victors with rich booty. Evidently as a preparation for the naval manoeuvres, German airmen soon after raided fortified positions on the Gulf of Riga, in an attempt to ascertain the location and strength of the Russian fleet.

The German operations indicate Reval as the objective. Reval would, indeed, be a prize. It is the capital of Esthonia, and is on the Bay of Reval, an arm of the Gulf of Finland, 200 miles west-southwest of Petrograd. Just before the war, when the Czar's naval authorities discontinued their attempts to make Libau (occupied by the Germans on May 8, 1915) a naval base on account of the shifting ground of the harbor and the poor natural defenses, they had the alternative of choosing Reval or Riga. The latter was finally deemed too remote from the Baltic, and Reval was chosen, and was in a fair state of preparation when the war began. Northeast, at a distance of seventy miles, is Hanga, the most southwesterly point of Finland. A triple range of mines connects the two ports, thus forming the first line of sea defenses of both Helsingfors, the capital of Finland, and of Petrograd.

### British in Asiatic Turkey

Owing to the lack of co-operation on the part of the Russians in Asia Minor and Persia, the position of Sir Edmund Allenby on the borders of Palestine and of Sir Stanley Maude in Mesopotamia had become delicate, to say the least. Meanwhile the Turks and their masters, taking advantage of the passivity of Russia, had amassed in the Aleppo region, which commands each front, respectively by the Damascus-Medina railway extension and by the Bagdad Railway and caravan trail extension, a large number of divisions, which had been formally promised actual German support in the way of troops. The work of training proceeding at Aleppo, however, was slow. There was dissatisfaction with the German high command, and the Pashas, Enver, Talaat, and Djemal, were in disagreement with each other and with the German authority present. Food was plentiful, but the rails taken from the French Syrian lines were found insufficient to complete the Bagdad Railway, and the rolling stock had gradually rotted or rusted away under the sun of the desert or the moisture of the oases.

Three recent events have served at least to lessen the delicate position in which Maude and Allenby had been lying all Summer. The potential energy of these events, however, invites both exaggeration and disparagement—exaggeration on account of the geographical situation, disparagement because the control of Turkey in Asia forms, for both Wilhelmstrasse and Ballplatz, a most vital post-bellum asset.

### Capture of Ramadie

On Sept. 30 a British official dispatch announced that the Anglo-Indian Army, under Sir Stanley Maude, operating in Mesopotamia, had captured the town of Ramadie on the Euphrates, and with it the entire army of Ahmed Bey. This achievement, preceded by a storming of Mushaid Ridge, in which Maude's superiority of artillery and of mobile cavalry manifested itself, had occurred on Sept. 29. On Oct. 5, the Russian Army Headquarters announced that the Caucasian army had taken by assault the village of Nereman, in the Kikatsh-Amadia sector.

Ahmed Bey's division at Ramadie was destined no doubt to advance down the Euphrates and thereby seriously threaten Maude's left flank, if not cut his communications below Kut-el-Amara. They waited for reinforcements from Aleppo, and their waiting was fatal. Maude, with

# COMMANDERS OF NATIONAL GUARD DIVISIONS

**MAJOR GEN. GEORGE BELL, JR.**
Thirty-third Division at Houston, Tex.
*(Photo Press Illustrated Service)*

**MAJOR GEN. HENRY C. HODGES**
Thirty-ninth Division at Alexandria, La.
*(© Harris & Ewing)*

**MAJOR GEN. E. ST. J. GREBLE**
Thirty-sixth Division at Forth Worth, Tex.
*(Central News Photo Service)*

**MAJOR GEN. W. M. WRIGHT**
Thirty-fifth Division at Fort Sill, Okla.
*(© Harris & Ewing)*

# COMMANDERS OF NATIONAL ARMY DIVISIONS

**MAJOR GEN. HARRY F. HODGES**
Seventy-sixth Division at Ayer, Mass.
(© Harris & Ewing)

**MAJOR GEN. J. E. KUHN**
Seventy-ninth Division at Admiral, Md.
(© Harris & Ewing)

**MAJOR GEN. ADELBERT CRONKHITE**
Eightieth Division at Petersburg, Va.

**MAJOR GEN. C. W. KENNEDY**
Seventy-eighth Division at Wrightstown, N. J.

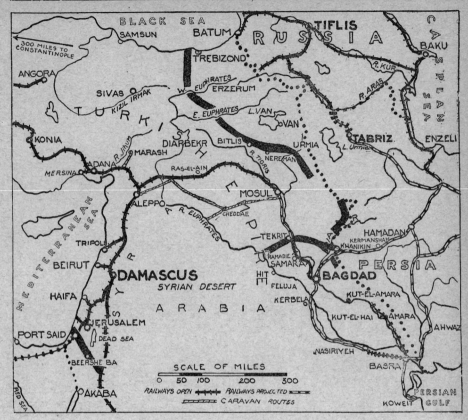

MAP SHOWING BRITISH AND RUSSIAN POSITIONS IN ASIATIC TURKEY, OCT. 18, 1917
[The name of Gaza, southwest of Jerusalem, omitted from map by oversight.]

the climatic conditions lifted, moved with rapidity and won a surprise. Attacking the advanced positions on Mushaid Ridge at dawn of Sept. 28, after a night march, he quickly secured them, fought a severe battle during the day, carried the main positions, and then so disposed his troops that the enemy had no avenue of escape. It was a fine, finished piece of work.

Ramadie is about 130 miles south and a little east of Mosul; Nereman is 50 miles north of Mosul; Mosul is the southern terminal of the Bagdad Railway feverishly completed by German engineers since the Spring of 1916, from Ras-el-Ain. The southern section proceeding north from Bagdad had been completed as far as Tekrit. Between Tekrit and Mosul on the Tigris there is an unfinished section of about 90 miles. Anglo-Indian detachments occupied Tekrit last April— the last act of the campaign before the

torrid season set in which made manoeuvres impossible.

Thus with the opening of the new campaign we see Mosul, the largest and most important inland city now in Turkish possession, apparently menaced, while almost simultaneously comes the news from the British-Egyptian army at Gaza, before Jerusalem, 550 miles across the Arabian Desert west of Bagdad, that it has been joined by Arab detachments coming north from the new Arabian kingdom of Hedjaz (the Red Sea littoral) over the Damascus-Medina Railway.

### Facts of the Situation

Mosul is now menaced by three armies, and the presence of an Arab force at Gaza shows the restoration of the Damascus-Medina Railway as far north as that place. By this railway, therefore, the Arab reinforcements who have long been drilled and supplied by the British authorities on the Red Sea littoral may be measurably increased, or heavy artillery may be sent via the railway south to the extreme end of the peninsula, where the British naval station at Aden has been invested by Ali Said Pasha with the Thirty-ninth Turkish Division since July, 1915. Ali is not strong enough to attack Aden by assault and has his camp just out of range of the warships in the harbor. Since the revolt of the Grand Shereef of Mecca, now the King of Hedjaz, his communication with the north has been cut off, and the Arab tribes with him are only awaiting reinforcements from Hedjaz and a cryptic summons from Sir James Bell— "The lion is hungry"—to turn against him.

Following the surrender of Kut-el-Amara by General Townshend in April, 1916, after a five months' siege, the Germans believed that the British power in Mesopotamia had been crushed and it only remained for the Turks to give it the coup de grace. They discovered their mistake when, eight months later, Major Gen. Sir Frederick Stanley Maude, with a new Anglo-Indian army, reopened the campaign from below Kut. This he recaptured on Feb. 24, 1917. He occupied Bagdad, the ancient city of the Caliphs, on March 11; annihilated the Eighteenth Turkish Army Corps at Islabulet, near Samara, on April 18, and the Thirteenth on the 30th in the gorge of Shatt-el-Adam, in the Jebel Hamrin Hills. These victories, with outposts at Tekrit, had opened the war north to Mosul when the fighting season closed.

### Russians in Asia Minor

A word should be said about the Russians in this region, so that the influence of the revolution at Petrograd on them may not be misunderstood. A difference must be made between the Russian army in Persia and that operating from the Caucasian front, which has just captured Nereman. The former, composed of conscripts from the great industrial cities of Western Russia, early felt the influence of the revolution. They captured Khanikin, on the Persian frontier, on April 4, but surrendered it on the 15th of the fol-

lowing July. They still hold the high ground on the left bank of the Diala, but their ambitious dream of reaching Bagdad before the British has been reduced to a protection of Sir Stanley Maude's right flank. They also have to keep order in the Russian sphere of influence in Persia.

It is different with the Army of the Caucasus. This is composed of Kuban and Terek Cossacks and native Caucasians, who have hated the Turk for generations, who have never forgotten the surrender of hard-won Erzerum in 1878, and who regard the revolution merely as a means better to reinforce their campaign. They have vast stores of supplies at reconquered Erzerum, at Trebizond, and at Bitlis, and the propaganda of political agitators for peace has no influence among them.

In the race between the Russian Persian army and the Anglo-Indian army for Bagdad the latter won, but with the Army of the Caucasus as his rival for Mosul Sir Stanley Maude has a more formidable and persistent antagonist.

Many interesting things are certain to unfold themselves in the next few months in Asiatic Turkey, but before taking the defeat of the Turkish armies there as a foregone conclusion it should not be forgotten that the German Kaiser paid a visit to Constantinople in the middle of October, and with him came Field Marshal von Falkenhayn and several score of German officers. One may be sure that the All-Highest will not see his long-cherished dream for Egypt and the Berlin-Bagdad route to the Persian Gulf vanish without a prodigious effort to have it realized.

### Events on Other Fronts

The Italians, as the month closes, are still slowly but surely pushing the Austrians from the remaining slopes of Monte San Gabriele, repelling counterattacks there, on the Carso, and along the rapidly freezing defiles of the Trentino. On Sept. 28-29 the troops of General Cappello, by a sudden drive, captured two elevated positions south of Podlaca and southeast of Madoni on the Bainsizza Plateau—possibly as the first step toward entering the Chiapovano Valley behind Monte San Gabriele and San Daniele.

In the Verdun sector, on the western front, the Germans have been making prodigious efforts to keep the French from gaining more ground—efforts which have every appearance of possessing a potential offensive were they not broken up by well-directed artillery fire. This was the case north of the Bois de Chaume on Sept. 24, and again at the same place on Oct. 10.

The same story might be told of the sectors further west—on the Aisne and in Champagne—where the German Crown Prince's heavy artillery preparations for assault invariably turn into duels in which his own guns are silenced and his subsequent advance of infantry shattered with a loss of men that is rapidly reaching the number he sacrificed at Verdun. Further west still, the concrete citadel of Lens, with its subterranean nests, continues to withstand the pressure of the Scots, Canadians, and Welsh.

# Haig's Hammer Strokes in Flanders
## Vivid Description of Some of the Historic Battles During September and October, 1917
### By Philip Gibbs
[CABLED TO THE NEW YORK TIMES. COPYRIGHTED.]

*The British offensive in Flanders, which began on July 31, 1917, continued intermittently all through August, September, and October. On Oct. 16 Premier Lloyd George sent the following telegram of appreciation to Field Marshal Sir Douglas Haig:*

*The War Cabinet desires to congratulate you and the troops under your command upon the achievements of the British armies in Flanders in the great battle which has been raging since July 31. Starting from a position in which every advantage rested with the enemy and hampered and delayed from time to time by the most unfavorable weather, you and your men have nevertheless continuously driven the enemy back with such skill, courage, and pertinacity as have commanded the grateful admiration of the peoples of the British Empire and filled the enemy with alarm. I am personally glad to be the means of transmitting this message to you and your gallant troops, and I desire to take this opportunity of renewing my assurance of confidence in your leadership and in the devotion of those whom you command.*

## Battle for the High Woodlands
[SEPTEMBER 20]

THE ground over which the British swept this morning [Sept. 20] was assaulted again and again by troops who ignored their losses and attacked with the most desperate and glorious courage, yet failed to hold what they had gained for a time, because their final goal was attained with weakened forces, after most fierce and bloody fighting. The empire knows who those men were—old English county regiments, who never fought more gallantly; Scots, who only let go of their forward positions under overwhelming pressure and annihilating fire; Irish divisions, who suffered the supreme ordeal and earned new and undying honors, by the way they endured the fire of many guns for many days.

As long as history lasts the name of these woods, from which most of the trees have been swept, and of these bogs and marshes which lie about them will be linked with the memory of those brave battalions who fought through them again and again. They are not less to be honored than those who, with the same courage, just as splendidly fought through them again over the same tracks, past the same deathtraps, and achieved success by different methods, by learning from what the first men had suffered.

Abandoning the old trench system,

which we could knock to pieces with artillery, the enemy made his forward positions without any definite line and built a great number of concrete blockhouses so arranged in depth that they defended one another by enfilading fire, and so strong that nothing but a direct hit from one of our heavier shells would damage them; and a direct hit is very difficult to make on a small mark like one of those concrete houses, holding about ten to twenty men at a minimum and fifty to sixty in their largest.

These little garrisons were mostly machine gunners and picked men, especially trained for outpost work, and could inflict great damage on an advancing battalion, so that the forward lines passing through and beyond them would be spent and weak. Then behind, in reserve, lay the German shock troops, specially trained also for the counterattacks which were launched with strong striking forces against our advanced lines after all their struggle and loss.

## The Formidable Blockhouses

Those blockhouses proved formidable things—hard nuts to crack, as the soldiers said who came up against them. There were scores of them, whose names will be remembered through a lifetime by the men of many battalions, and they cost the lives of many brave men.

Beck House and Bairy Farm belong to Irish history. Wurst Farm and Winnipeg, Bremen Redoubt, and Gallipoli, the Iberian and Delta Farms, are strongholds around which many desperate little battles, led by young subalterns or sergeants, took place on the last day of July and on many days since.

English and Scots have taken turns in attacking and defending such places as Fitz Clarence Farm, Northampton Farm, and Black Watch Corner, in the dreadful region in Inverness Copse, and Glencorse Wood. Today the hard nut of the concrete blockhouse has been cracked by a new method of attack and by a new assault planned with great forethought and achieved so far with high success.

All through the night the British heavy guns were slogging, and through the dark, wet mist there was the blurred light of their flashes. Before dawn a high wind was raging at thirty miles an hour across Flanders, and the heaving, water-clogged clouds were only 400 feet above the earth. How could the airmen see? When the attack began they could not see. Even when they flew as low as 200 feet they could see nothing but the smoke, which clung low to the battlefield, and could only guess the whereabouts of the German batteries.

## Swarm of British Aircraft

The sky over the salient was a strange vision, and I have seen nothing like it since the war began. It was filled with little black specks like midges, but each midge was a British airplane flying over the German lines. The Germans tried to clear the air of them, and the anti-aircraft guns were firing wildly, so that all about them were puffs of black shrapnel. Behind, closely clustered, were the British kite balloons, like snow clouds where they were caught by the light staring down over the battle and in wide semicircles about the salient.

The British heavy guns were firing hammer strokes, followed by the shrill cry of traveling shells, making a barrage before the troops and having blockhouses for their targets, and building walls of flying steel between the Germans and the attacking troops.

In the near distance were the strafed woods of old battlegrounds, like Wychtshaete Ridge and Messines, with their naked gallows trees all blurred in the mist.

The troops had lain out all night in the rain before the attack at something before 6 o'clock. They were wet through to the skin, but it is curious that some of them, whom I saw today, were surprised to hear that it had been raining hard; they had other things to think about. But some of them did not think at all. Tired out in mind and body under the big nervous strain which is there, though they may be unconscious of it, they slept.

## Appalling Barrage Fire

The barrage ahead of our men was terrific, the most appalling fence of shells that had ever been placed before advancing troops in this war. All the men describe it as wonderful. " Beautiful " is a word they use, too, because they know what it means in safety to them.

In the direction of the Polygon Wood the plan of attack seems to have worked like clockwork. The assaulting troops moved forward behind the barrage, stage by stage, through Westhoek and Nonneboschen and across Hannebeke stream on their left with hardly a check, in spite of the German blockhouses scattered over this country. In those blockhouses small garrisons of picked troops had been demoralized, as any human beings would be by the enormous shellfire which had been flung around them. Some, but not all, it seems, of the blockhouses had been smashed, and in those still standing the German machine gunners got their weapons to work with a burst or two of fire, but then, seeing the British troops on them, they were seized with fear and made signs of surrender.

## The Battle About Cameron House

### [SEPTEMBER 25]

Increasing their barrage fire to great intensity yesterday, [Sept. 25,] the Germans flung it down in Glencorse Wood and Inverness Copse, fired large numbers of heavy, long-range shells over Westhoek Ridge, Observatory Ridge, and Hooge, and concentrated most fiercely on the ground about Cameron House, Black Watch Corner, and Tower Hamlets.

At 6 o'clock in the morning, supported by this terrific fire, they launched their first attack on the British troops around Cameron House, and, owing to their losses, the British were obliged to fall back some little way in order to reorganize for an assault to recapture their positions. These fought through some awful hours, and several of their units did heroic things to safeguard their lines, which for a time were threatened.

While they were fighting in this way, the Australians, on the high ground this side of Polygon Wood race track and the mound which is called the Butte, also had to repel some fierce attacks which opened on them soon after 8 o'clock in the morning. The enemy was unable to pierce their line and fell back from this first attempt with great losses in dead and wounded. This attack was followed by a second thrust at midday, which met the same fate. At 2 o'clock in the afternoon the Australians sent some men to help the troops on their right, who were passing through a greater ordeal owing to the storm of fire over them and the continued pressure of the enemy's storm troops, who were persistent, throughout the afternoon, in spite of the trails of dead left in their tracks.

It was a serious anxiety on the eve of a new battle, but it failed to frustrate the British attack. All the area through which the enemy was trying to bring up his troops was made hideous by artillery fire and the work of the Royal Flying Corps. It was a clear, moonlight night, with hardly a breath of air blowing, and all the countryside was made visible by the moon's rays, which silvered the roofs of all the villages and made every road like a white tape. The British planes went out over the enemy's lines, laden with bombs, and patrolled up and down the tracks and made some thirty attacks upon the enemy's transport and his marching columns. All his lines of approach were kept under continual fire by guns of heavy calibre, and for miles around shells swept the points which marching men would have to pass, so that their way was hellish.

The British aircraft went out and flew very low and dropped bombs wherever the observers saw men moving through the luminous mists of night. Behind the British lines air patrols guarded the countryside. On the battlefield there was no unusual gunfire for several hours after dark. The guns on both sides kept up the usual night bombardment in slow, sullen strokes, but, at least on the Australian front, it was not until about 4:45 o'clock in the morning that the enemy opened a heavy barrage on Glencorse Wood. The Australian troops were already massed beyond that ground for the attack which was due soon.

Our new form of barrage is the most frightful combination of high explosives and shrapnel that has yet appeared in the war, and it rolled backward and forward about them so that the garrisons huddled inside until our men slipped behind them and thrust rifles or bombs through the machine-gun loopholes, if the Germans had not previously escaped to the shell craters around where they might have more chance.

Here I might say that the Germans have already modified their methods of holding blockhouses. While only a few men remain inside, the rest of the garrison is distributed in shell holes on each side, with machine guns in organized craters. Some of these Germans were found by our men, and though many of them had been killed by our gunfire,

others remained shooting and sniping until they were routed out.

The worst part of the ground on this line of attack was around the blockhouse called Boston Farm, where there is a swamp so impassable that some British soldiers who tried to make their way through it had to work around and up toward Hill 40. Here they came under machine-gun fire, and although some of them forced their way up the slope of the knoll on which the inn had stood, they did not quite reach the crest. Meanwhile some of our other troops, attacking around about Zonnebeke, where the ground was swept by machine-gun bullets, seized the ruins of the church and the outskirts of the station yard.

## The Shambles About Inverness Copse
### [SEPTEMBER 30-OCTOBER 2]

When I went over the ground of Inverness Copse and Glencorse Wood a few days ago there were more dead than I had ever seen before on one battleground. They were strewn around blockhouses, lying in the foul water of swamps and shell holes, in dugouts broken by the British fire and half buried in the heaved earth. It is like that over a wide stretch of country, and behind that ground which the British have taken and hold there is other ground, miles back, over which the German dead are scattered like Autumn leaves. For the British gunners have no limit to their ammunition now, and their shells go in ceaseless flights over the enemy's lines to smash their human targets.

This morning again the German infantry was assembled three times and sent forward into the shambles—three times for attacks on each side of that Ypres-Menin road which strikes through this country of death. Polygon Heights was their goal, but the men up there are ready and strong for any hostile advance. With machine-gun and rifle fire and the pounding of "heavies" these morning attacks have been beaten off.

Imagination fails to picture the scenes out there behind the German lines—the agony of those men who, like the Poles among them, have no desire to fight, and

only terror of the fury of shellfire into which they are ordered like poor beasts for slaughter and sacrifice. Lines scribbled in German notebooks and found on the battlefield give glimpses of this human anguish and of the blood and filth through which these men move. Here is one such note by an unknown German officer:

If it were not for the men who have been spared me on this fierce day and are lying around me and looking at me timidly, I should shed hot and bitter tears over the terrors that have menaced me during these hours. On the morning of Sept. 18 a dugout containing seventeen men was shot to pieces over our heads. I am the only one who withstood the maddening bombardment of three days and still survives. You cannot imagine the frightful mental torments I underwent in those few hours. After crawling out through the bleeding remnants of my comrades and the smoke and débris and wandering and fleeing in the midst of raging artillery fire in search of refuge, I am now awaiting death at any moment. You do not know what Flanders means. Flanders means endless endurance; Flanders means blood and scraps of human bodies; Flanders means heroic courage and faithfulness even unto death.

### Fight For Polygon Wood

" I was on the last position three-quarters of an hour before the barrage passed," said a young officer. He spoke the words as if telling something rather commonplace, but he knew I knew the meaning of what he said—a frightful and extraordinary thing; for with his platoon he had gone ahead of the storm of fire and had to wait until it reached and then passed them. Some of their losses were because of that, and yet they might have been greater if they had been slower, because the enemy was caught before he could guess they were near.

Some ran toward their own lines with their hands up, shouting "Kamerad!" believing that they were running toward the British. They were so unready for the attack that the snipers had the safety clips on their rifle barrels, and others were without ammunition.

The way to the last objective was easy, on the whole, and the Germans were on the run with the British after them. The hardest time came afterward, as it nearly always comes, when the ground gained had to be held for three more days and nights without the excitement of attack and under heavy fire. That is when the courage of the men is most tried, as this battalion found. The enemy had time to pull themselves together, the German

gunners adapted their range to the new positions and shelled fiercely across the ways of approach and scattered 5.9s everywhere.

It was riflefire for the British men all the time. They had not troubled to bring up a great many bombs, for the rifle has come into its own again, now that the old trench warfare is gone for a time or for all time. So, with rifle and machine-gun fire they broke down the German counterattacks and caught parties of Germans, who showed themselves on the slopes of Passchendaele Ridge, and sniped incessantly. They used up a prodigious quantity of small-arms ammunition, and the carriers risked their lives every step of the way to get it up to them. They fired 30,000 rounds and then 16,000 more.

There was one officer who spent all his time sniping from a little patch of ground that had once been a garden. He lay behind the heaped ruin and used his field-glasses to watch the slopes of rising ground on his left where human ants were crawling. Every now and then he fired and picked off an ant until his score reached fifty.

## The Capture of Passchendaele Ridge
### [OCTOBER 4]

It has been a strange and terrible battle—terrible, I mean, in its great conflict of guns and men—and the enemy, if all goes as well with the British as it is now going, may have to remember it as a turning point in the history of this war —a point that has turned against him with a sharp and deadly edge. For realizing his great peril if the British strengthened their hold on Passchendaele Ridge, and knowing that they intended to do so, (all the signs showed him that, and all our pressure on these positions,) he prepared an attack against them in great strength in order to regain the ground he lost on Sept. 26, or, if not that, then so to damage them that their advance would be checked until the weather choked them in mud again.

His small counterattacks, or rather his local counterattacks—for they were not weak—had failed; even his persistent

hammering at the right wing by Cameron House, below Polygon Wood, had failed to bite deeply into the British line, though for a time, on Sept. 25, it had been a cause of anxiety to them and made the battle next day more difficult and critical. But these attacks had failed in their purpose, and now the German high command decided for a big blow, which was to be delivered at 7 o'clock this morning.

It was a day and an hour too late. The British battle was fixed for an hour before his, and so it happened that the British troops, in order to follow their own barrage, had to pass through that of the Germans, which fell upon them before they leaped up to the assault; and it happened also, most terribly for the enemy, that the British were not stopped, but went through that zone of shells without disorder, and on the other side, behind their own barrage, swept over the German assault troops and annihilated their plan of attack.

The Germans did not attack. Their defense even was broken. As the British lines of fire crept forward they reached and broke the second and third waves of men who had been ordered to attack and caught them in their support and reserve positions. One can only guess what the slaughter has been. Five German divisions were involved in it.

## Scene Behind the Lines

Preparations on a big scale were started as soon as the last battle was fought and won. No words of mine can give more than a hint of what those preparations meant in the scene of war. Everywhere there has been a fever of work—Tommies, Chinkies, and colored men piling up mountains of ammunition to feed the guns. Under shellfire bracketing the loads on which they worked, the engineers carried on.

Tracks were put down, new lengths of " duckboard " laid, and new rails. The enemy's shells came howling over to search out all this work, which had been observed by airplanes, and at night flocks of the latter came out in the light of the moon to drop bombs on the men and the works. Now and again they made lucky hits—got a dump and sent it flaming up in a great torch, killed horses in the wagon lines laboring up with transport laid out a group of men, smashed a train or truck—but the work went on, never checked, never stopping in its steady flow of energy up to the lines, and the valor of all these laborers was great and steady in preparing for today. Knowing the purpose of it all filled one with a kind of fear—it was so prodigious, so vastly schemed.

I passed a dump yesterday, and again today, in the waste ground on the old battlefield near Ypres, and saw the shells for the field batteries being unloaded. There were thousands of them, brand new from the British factories, all bright and glistening and laid out in piles. The guns were greedy; here was food for their monstrous appetite.

This morning, when the men rose from the shell holes and battered trenches and fields of upheaved earth to make this great attack, the rain fell still, but softly, so that the ground was only sticky and sludgy, but not a bog. Rain was glistening on their steel helmets, and the faces of the fighting men were wet when they went forward. They had passed already through a great ordeal, and some of them—a few here and there—could not rise to go with their comrades, they lay dead on the ground.

## Germans Try New Tactics

Along the lines of these thousands of men the stretcher bearers were already busy in the dark, because the enemy put over a heavy barrage at 5:30, and elsewhere later—the prelude to the attack he had planned. His old methods of defense and counterattack had broken down in two battles. The spell of the " pill box," which had worked well for a time, was broken so utterly that those concrete blockhouses were feared as deathtraps by the men who had held them.

The German high command hurried to prepare a new plan, guessing that of the British, and moved their guns to be ready for the next attack, registered on their own trenches, which they knew they might lose. The barrage which the Germans sent over was the beginning of a new plan. It failed because of the great courage of the British troops, first of all, and because the German infantry attack was timed an hour too late. If it had come two hours earlier it might have led to the undoing of Haig's men— might, at least, have prevented anything like a real victory today; but the fortune of war was on the side of the British, and the wheel turned around to crush the enemy.

The main force of his attack, which was to have been made by the Fourth Guards Division, with two others, I am told, in support, was ready to assault the centre of the British battle front in the direction of Polygon Wood and down from Broodseinde Crossroads. It was the British, however, who fought the German assault divisions at Broodseinde Crossroads and took many prisoners from them before they had time to advance very far. The enemy's shelling had been heavy about the ground of Inverness Copse and Glencorse Wood, where a week or so ago I saw frightful heaps of German dead, and spread over a wide area of the British line of battle along Polygon Wood Heights and the low ground in front of Zonnebeke. The men tell me that it did not do them as much harm as they expected. The shells plunged deep in the soft ground, bursting upward in tall columns, and their killing effect was not widespread. Many of them also missed the British waves altogether.

So, half an hour later, the British attacking troops went away behind their own barrage, which was enormous and annihilating. Wet mist lay heavily over the field, and it was almost dark except for a pale glimmer behind the rain clouds, which brightened as each quarter hour passed, with the men tramping forward slowly to their first objective.

### Terrible Battle Picture

The shell craters on the German side were linked together here and there to form a kind of trench system, but many of these had been blown out by other shellbursts, and German soldiers lay dead in them. From others men and boys —many boys of 18—rose with arms upstretched, as white in the face as dead men, but living and afraid. Across these frightful fields men came running toward the British line. They did not come to fight, but to escape from the shellfire which tossed up the earth about them, and to surrender. Many of them were streaming with blood, wounded about the head and face, or with broken and bleeding arms. So I saw them early this morning when they came down the tracks which led away from that long line of flaming gunfire.

The scene of the battle in those early hours was a great and terrible picture. It will be etched as long as life lasts on the minds of the men who saw it. The ruins of Ypres were vague and blurred in the mist as I passed them on the way up, but as the moments passed the ragged stump of the Cloth Hall, the wild wreckage of the asylum, and the fretted outline of all this chaos of masonry which was so fair a city once crept out in the light which flashed redly and passed.

So it was all the long way to the old German lines. Bits of villages still stand, enough to show that buildings were once there, and isolated ruins of barns and farmhouses lie in heaps of timber and brickwork about great piles of greenish sandbags and battered earthworks.

### Hundreds of Guns Volleying

The British guns were everywhere in the low, concealing mist, so that one could not walk anywhere to avoid the blast of their fire. They made a fury of fire. Flashes leaped from them, with only a pause of a second or two while they were reloaded. There was never a moment within my own range of vision when hundreds of great guns were not firing together. They were eating up the shells which I had seen going up to them, and the roads and fields across which I walked were littered with shells. The wet mist was like one great damp fire with ten miles or more of smoke rising in white vapor, through which tongues of flame leaped up stirred by some fierce wind.

The noise was terrifying in its violence. Passing one of those big-bellied howitzers was to me an agony. It rose like a beast stretching out its neck, and there came from it a roar which almost split one's eardrums and shook one's body with the long tremor of the concussion. These things were all firing at their hardest pace, and the earth was shaken with their blasts of fire. The enemy was answering, but with no great threat to the British guns. His shells came whining and howling through all this greater noise and burst with a crash on either side of the mule tracks and over the bits of ruin near by and in the fields on each side of the paths down which German prisoners came staggering with their wounded.

Fresh shell holes, enormously deep and thickly grouped, showed that the German guns had plastered this ground fiercely, but later in the morning their shelling eased off, and the guns had other work to do over there, where the British infantry was advancing—other work, unless the guns lay smashed with their teams lying dead around them, killed by the British counterbattery work with high explosives and gas; for in the night the British smothered the Germans with gas and tried to keep them quiet for this battle and all others.

## Like a Ridge of Volcanoes

We went eastward and mounted a pile of rubbish and timber, all blown into shapelessness and reeking with foul odors, and from that shelter looked across to Passchendaele Ridge and Hill 40, on the west of Zonnebeke and the line of the ridge that goes round to Polygon Wood. It was all blurred, but clearly through the gloom were seen the white and yellow cloudbursts of the British shellfire and the flame of the shellbursts.

It was the most terrible bombardment I had ever seen, and I saw the fire of the Somme and of Vimy and Arras and Messines. Those were not like this, great as they were in frightfulness. The whole of Passchendaele crest was like a series of volcanoes belching up pillars of earth and fire.

" It seemed to us," said man after man who came down from those slopes, " as if no mortal man could live in it. Yet there were many who lived, despite all the dead."

I saw the living men. Below the big pile of timber and muck on which I stood was a winding path, with other tracks on each side of it between deep shell craters, and down those ways came batches of prisoners and the trail of the British walking wounded. It was a tragic sight, in spite of its proof of the victory and valor of the British and the spirit of the British wounded, who bore pain with stoic patience and said, when I spoke to them, " It's been a good day; we're doing fine, I think."

## The Procession of Wounded

The Germans were haggard and white-faced men, thin and worn, and weary and frightened, many of them. The greater number were wounded. Some of them had masks of dry blood on their faces and some of them wet blood all down their tunics. They held broken arms, from which the sleeves had been cut away, and hobbled painfully on wounded legs.

It was a procession down that winding path which a painter should have seen, to put down a true picture of one side of war. Shoulder-high, the stretcher bearers, swaying a little to the swing of the stretchers, carried the German and British wounded. I saw a German officer on one of the stretchers. He had a cloak over him and his head drooped over the side of the pole. I think he was already dead. Another man died as they carried him. His head flopped first to one side and then to the other, and then his body was shaken with a great rigor and he lay still. A young soldier had been blinded. All the top of his face was covered with a bloody rag, and he walked stiffly, with an Englishman on either side of him, guiding his footsteps over the rough ground. They passed and passed, these men—platoons of Germans marching together with one or two British soldiers with fixed bayonets beside them, and single figures, not guarded at all, but making their way slowly and painfully across the fields in the same direction as the British wounded. There were many boys among them—boys with shaven heads, without caps or helmets; wizened white-faced boys, whose shrapnel helmets were like extinguishers, and lazy boys, with great spectacles on their noses.

But they were not in the majority. Most of the men I saw—and I saw hundreds of them—were men between 20 and 30, and big, strong, and tough. After this battle their skin was gray, and their eyes stared out of deep sockets. They shrank when some of their own shells came overhead and burst near them on the way down to safety, and they looked with dazed eyes at the English soldiers and at the ambulances and wagons further on. It had been a great defeat for them, and they did not hide their despair. They did not fight stubbornly for the most part, but ran one way or the other as soon as the British barrage passed and revealed their assailants. The British gunfire had overwhelmed them.

In the blockhouses were groups of men who gasped out words of surrender. Here and there they refused to come out till bombs burst outside their steel doors, and here and there they got machine guns to work and checked the British advance for a time, as at Joist Farm, on the right of the attack, and at a château near Polderhoek, where there had been severe fighting. There was heavy machine-gun fire from a fortified ruined farm to the north of Broodseinde, and again from Kronprinz Farm, on the extreme left. The enemy also put down a heavy machine-gun barrage from positions around Passchendaele, but nothing has stopped the British seriously so far. They swept up and beyond Cravenstavel and Abraham Heights, went through and past the ruins of Zonnebeke Village, and with great heroism gained the high ground about Broodseinde, a dominating position giving observation of all the enemy country.

## The Desolation Around Ypres
### [OCTOBER 7]

It rained hard yesterday, giving an unforgettable demonstration of the nature of the difficulties which the British troops have encountered in many of their recent operations. Within a few hours the entire country had been turned into a mass of deep, clinging mud, through which one made his way with the greatest effort. A stream known as Honnebeke, which is one of the many little waterways that cover not only this section but most of the battle zone, was surrounded by a veritable morass. It would be impossible to cross it at many places.

Shell holes had rapidly filled with water, and ponds were to be seen in which a score of men might easily drown if they were unfortunate enough to fall down the slippery sides. Often a small pool of water covered a considerable shell hole.

A wounded man was being brought back from Broodseinde Ridge. It took four sturdy stretcher bearers to carry him, and they were floundering miserably at every step. It must have taken them several hours to negotiate their journey.

It seemed inconceivable that men could work, much less fight, over such filthy ground; yet the British soldiers and officers were carryng on steadily yesterday their operations. And in recent days they have often fought over just such territory as this.

Nowhere on the western front has the war printed more cruel marks of devastation than in the wide zone east of Ypres, where such fierce and sanguinary fighting has been proceeding at intervals since the British launched their initial attack.

This whole region, much of which in peace times was prosperous farming country, has been turned by the artillery fire into a desolate waste of vast and deep shell craters, which are so close together that in innumerable cases they interlock. Farmhouses have been pulverized and plowed under in the ruthless sweep of the shells, and village sites are marked by little portions of walls where churches or other big buildings once stood.

Cottages are buried beneath heaps of turned-up earth, and there is scarcely a vestige of grass or other green thing to be seen in miles of tramping. Trees have been smashed into matchwood, and their roots turned up in grotesque shapes to add to the sinister aspect of the country. Here and there, where little forests stood, the hardier trees have clung to their birthright, but their branches have been shorn from their trunks.

## The Battle for Houltulst Wood
### [OCTOBER 9]

The French yesterday gained about 1,200 yards of ground in two strides, captured hundreds of prisoners, many machine guns and two field guns, and killed large numbers of the enemy in this attack and in the bombardments which preceded it.

The allied troops are within a few hundred yards of that forest of which Marlborough spoke when he said, "Whoever holds Houltulst Forest holds Flanders," and have gone forward about 1,500 yards in depth along a line beyond Poelcapelle, across the Ypres-Cheluvelt road.

The enemy again suffered great losses. Two new divisions, which had just been brought into line, the 227th, straight from Rheims, getting into line at 3 o'clock this morning, while the 195th arrived from Russia, have received a fearful baptism of fire, and at least three other divisions have been hard hit and have given many prisoners from their raids into British hands.

It was a black and dreadful night. The wind howled and raged across Flanders with long, sinister wailings as it gathered speed and raced over the fields. The heavy stormclouds, hiding the moon and stars, broke and a deluge came down, drenching the British soldiers who marched along the roads and tracks, making ponds about them where they stood. It was cold, with the coldness cutting the men with the sharp sword of the wind, and there was no glimmer of light in the darkness.

To those who know the craterland of battlefields and with light kit or no kit have gone stumbling through it, picking their way between shell holes in the daylight, taking hours to travel a mile or two, it might have seemed impossible that great bodies of troops could go forward in an assault over such a country and win success in such conditions. That they did so is one more proof that the British troops have in them the heroic spirit which is above the normal laws of life. This battle seems to me as wonderful as anything the British have done since the Highlanders and the naval division captured Beaumont Hamel in the mud and fog. It was more wonderful even than that, because on a greater scale and in more foul weather.

## Men Plastered with Clay

This morning I have been among men who lay out last night before the attack which followed the first gleams of dawn today, and who staggered and stumbled up to take part in the attack. These men I met had come back wounded. Only in the worst days of the Somme have I seen such figures. They were plastered from head to foot in wet mud, their hands and faces being covered with clay like the hands and faces of dead men.

They had tied bits of sacking round their legs, and this was stuck on them with clots of mud. Their belts and tunics were covered with thick wet slime. They were soaked to the skin and their hair was stiff with clay.

They looked to me like men who had been buried alive and had been dug out again. And when I spoke to them I found that some of them had been buried alive and unburied while they still had life. They told me this simply as if it were the normal thing. Others, without being flung down by a shellburst or buried in a crater, fell up to their waists in shell holes and up to their armpits and sank in water and mud.

A little group of men whom I knew had to make their way up to join in their unit's attack in the dawn. It was at dusk that this handful of men set out on the way up to the battle line, and it was only a few miles they had to go, but it took them eleven hours to go that distance, and they did not get to the journey's end until half an hour before they had to attack. * * * They had no food all that time. "I would have given my left arm for a drop of hot drink," said one of them. "I was 'fair perished' with the cold."

They went over to the attack, these troops who were cold and hungry and exhausted after a dreadful night, and they gained their objective and routed the enemy and sent back many prisoners.

There were a number of German blockhouses in front of them beyond Abraham Heights and Gravenstafel. On their left there was a blockhouse called Peter Pan, though no little Mother Wendy would tell stories to her boys there.

## German Troops Heavily Massed

Beyond that little house of death were Wolf Copse and Wolf Farm, from which the fire of German machine guns came swishing in streams of bullets. There was no yard of ground without a shell hole, they were linked together like the holes in honeycomb, and German troops were very thick because of their new methods of defense—very dense in the support lines, though the front line was more lightly held, the men being scattered about in these craters.

Large numbers were killed and wounded when the British barrage stormed over them, but numbers crouching in the old craters were left alive, and as the barrage passed they rose and came streaming over in small batches with their hands high. They came to meet the British, hoping for mercy.

Many prisoners were made before the first objective was reached, and after that by harder fighting some of the men in the shell holes, wet like the British and cold like them, decided to keep fighting and fired rifles as the British struggled forward. Not all the prisoners who were taken came down behind the British lines. The enemy was barraging the ground heavily, and many of their own men were killed and some of the British stretcher bearers as they came down with the wounded.

Up in the leafless and shattered trees on the battlefield were Germans with machine guns and German riflemen, who sniped the British as they passed. Many of these were shot up in trees and came crashing down.

Up on the left of the attack, where the British linked up with the French, Germans were taken prisoner in great numbers, officers as well as men. The hostile bombardment was not so heavy as on the right, so that the casualties seem to have been light there.

In spite of the frightful ground, all the objectives were taken, so that the allied line was drawn close to Houltulst Forest.

### Heroic Work of Lancashires

The brunt of the fighting fell in the centre upon the troops of the North Country, the hard, tough men of Lancashire and Yorkshire, and it was the Lancashires' day especially, because of these third-line territorial battalions of Manchesters and East Lancashires and the Lancashire Fusiliers, with other Lancashire comrades. There were some among them who went over the bags, as they call it, for the first time, and who fought in one of the hardest battles that has ever been faced by British troops.

The night march of some of these men who went up to attack at dawn seems to me, who have written many records of brave acts during three years of war, one of the most heroic episodes in all this time. It was a march which in dry, fine weather would have been done easily enough in less than three hours by men as good as these, but it took eleven hours for these Lancashire men to get up their support line; and then, worn out by fatigue that was physical pain, wet to the skin, cold as death, hungry and all clotted about with mud, they lay in the water of the shell holes for a little while until their officers said: "Turn out, boys!" And they went forward through heavy fire and over the same kind of ground and fought the enemy with his machine guns and beat him—until they lay outside their last objective and kept off counterattacks by the few machine guns that still remained unclogged and the rifles that somehow they had kept dry. Nothing better than that has been done, and Lancashire should thrill to the tale of it, because her sons were its heroes.

At night the lightly wounded men who tried to get back had a desperate time trying to find their way. Some of them walked away to the German lines and were up to the barbed wire before they found out their mistake. It was difficult to get any sense of direction in the darkness, but the German flares helped them. They rose with a very bright light flooding the swamps of No Man's Land with a white glare and revealing the tragedy of the battlefield, where many bodies lay still in the bogs, for many Germans had been killed.

Before the darkness the German airplanes came over, as it were, in dense flocks. One Lancashire boy declared that he counted thirty-seven as he lay looking up to the sky from a shell hole, and they flew low to see where the British had made their line.

For many days splendid and chivalrous work has been done on this part of the ground by the stretcher bearers. Out of 250 laboring in these fields over 100 were hit, and all of them took the utmost risk to rescue their fallen comrades in the fighting lines. The sappers and pioneers, the transport men and gunners, fought not against an enemy from Germany, but against one more difficult to defeat, and that was the mud, which made all their work misery and hampered them over every yard of ground; but for many hours, in light and darkness, they worked their way forward, making new tracks, struggling up with wagons and mules, keeping communications open with the front line and the troops in support.

## The Battle in the Mud

### [OCTOBER 12]

The British troops went forward again today, further up the slopes of Passchendaele Ridge, striking northeast toward the village of Passchendaele itself, which I saw this morning looming through the mist and white smoke of shellfire, with its ruins like the battlements of a mediaeval castle perched high on the crest.

A clear line was made for the barrage which would be fired by the British guns this morning, but some troops had still to go up, and some men had to march through the night as those Lancashire men had marched up three nights before. They had the same grim adventure; they, too, fell into shell holes, groped their way forward blindly in the wild downpour of rain, lugged each other out of bogs, floundered through mud and shellfire from 5 in the evening until a few minutes only before it was time to attack.

The enemy was busy with his guns all night to catch any of the British who might be on the move. He flung down a heavy barrage round about Zonnebeke, but by good chance it missed one group of men thereabout and scarcely touched any of the others in that neighborhood. But his heavy shells were scattered over a wide area and came howling through the darkness and exploding with great upheavals of wet earth. Small parties of men dodged them as best they could and pitched into shell holes five feet deep in water when they threatened instant death.

Then gas shells came whining, with their queer little puffs, unlike the exploding roar of the bigger shells, and the wet wind was filled with poisonous vapor, smarting to the eyes and skin, so that some of the men had to put on gas masks.

The march up to the battle line might have shaken the nerves of most men, might even have unmanned and weakened them, by the fainting sickness of fear, but it only made the British angry to the point of wild rage.

"To hell with them!" said some of them. "We won't spare them when we go over; we will make them pay for this night."

They used savage and flaming words, cursing the enemy, the weather, the shellfire, and the foulness of it all. I know the state of the ground, for I went over this crater land this morning to look at the flame of fire below Passchendaele spur.

I had no heavy kit, like the fighting men, but I fell on the greasy "duckboards," as they fell, and rolled into the slime, as they had rolled.

The rain beat a tattoo on one's steel helmet. Every shell hole was brimful of brown or greenish water. Moisture rose from the earth in a fog. The British guns were firing everywhere through the mist and thrust sharp little swords of flame through its darkness, and all the battlefields bellowed with the noise of the guns.

I walked through battery positions; past enormous howitzers which at twenty paces' distance shook one's bones with the concussion of their blasts; past long-muzzled high-velocities whose shells, after the first sharp hammer stroke, went whinnying away with the high, fluttering note of death; past big-bellied 4.2s and monsters firing lyddite shells in clouds of yellow smoke.

### A Grim Picture

Before me, stretching away round Houthulst Forest, big and dark and grim with its close-growing trees, was Passchendaele Ridge, the long, hummocky slopes for which the British were fighting, and their barrage fire crept up it, and the infernal shellfire rising in white columns was on top of it, hiding the broken houses there until later in the morning, when the rain ceased a little and the sky was streaked with blue, and out of the wet gloom Passchendaele appeared with its houses still standing, though all in ruins.

There were queer effects when the sun broke through. Its rays ran down the wet trunks and forked naked branches of dead trees with a curious, dazzling whiteness, and all the swamps were glinting with light on their foul waters; and the pack mules, winding along the tracks, slithering and staggering through the slime, had four golden bars on either side of them when the sun shone on their 18-pounder shells.

There was something more ghastly in this flood of white light over the dead ground of the battlefields, revealing all the litter of human conflict around the captured German " pill boxes," than when it was all under black stormclouds.

# The Nations at War

BY the action of Peru and Uruguay in breaking off relations with Germany, the number of nations now in that stage of belligerency is seven, while eighteen others are now at war with Germany and her allies. The following summary and dates are from the Official Bulletin:

*At war with Germany or her allies:*
Serbia, Russia, France, Great Britain, Montenegro, Japan, Belgium, Italy, San Marino, Portugal, Rumania, Greece, Cuba, Panama, Siam, Liberia, China, and the United States.

*Diplomatic relations broken with Germany:*
Brazil, Bolivia, Haiti, Honduras, Nicaragua, Peru, Uruguay.

*Declarations of war made:*
Austria vs. Belgium, Aug. 28, 1914.
Austria vs. Montenegro, Aug. 9, 1914.
Austria vs. Russia, Aug. 6, 1914.
Austria vs. Serbia, July 28, 1914.
Bulgaria vs. Serbia, Oct. 14, 1915.
China vs. Austria, Aug. 14, 1917.
China vs. Germany, Aug. 14, 1917.
Cuba vs. Germany, April 7, 1917.
France vs. Austria, Aug. 12, 1914.
France vs. Bulgaria, Oct. 18, 1915.
France vs. Germany, Aug. 3, 1914.
Germany vs. France, Aug. 3, 1914.
Germany vs. Portugal, March 9, 1916.
Germany vs. Russia, Aug. 1, 1914.
Great Britain vs. Bulgaria, Oct. 16, 1915.
Great Britain vs. Austria, Aug. 12, 1914.
Great Britain vs. Germany, Aug. 5, 1914.
Great Britain vs. Turkey, Nov. 5, 1914.
Greece (Provisional Government) vs. Bulgaria, Nov. 28, 1916.
Greece (Provisional Government) vs. Germany, Nov. 28, 1916.
Greece vs. Bulgaria, July 2, 1917.
Greece vs. Germany, July 2, 1917.
Italy vs. Austria, Aug. 21, 1915.
Italy vs. Bulgaria, Oct. 19, 1914.
Italy vs. Germany, Aug. 28, 1916.
Japan vs. Germany, Aug. 23, 1914.
Liberia vs. Germany, Aug. 4, 1917.
Montenegro vs. Austria, Aug. 10, 1914.
Panama vs. Germany, April 7, 1917.
Rumania vs. Austria, Aug. 27, 1916.
Serbia vs. Turkey, Dec. 2, 1914.
Siam vs. Austria, July 21, 1917.
Siam vs. Germany, July 21, 1917.
Turkey vs. Allies, Nov. 23, 1914.
Turkey vs. Rumania, Aug. 29, 1916.
United States vs. Germany, April 6, 1917.

# Progress of the War

### Recording Campaigns on All Fronts and Collateral Events From September 19 Up to and Including October 18, 1917

## UNITED STATES

Congress adjourned on Oct. 6, after passing measures appropriating $21,000,000,000 for war purposes, and enacting the War Revenue bill, which provided for the raising of $2,700,000,000 by taxation.

The campaign for the second Liberty Loan—an issue of $3,000,000,000—opened Oct. 1. President Wilson appointed Oct. 24 Liberty Loan Day.

Colonel Edward M. House was appointed by the President to gather data that would be needed by American envoys to the peace conference.

A proclamation governing the distribution and licensing of foodstuffs was issued by the President on Oct. 10.

The Trading with the Enemy act, which was passed by Congress, was put into effect by an order issued by President Wilson on Oct. 14. It provided for the supervision of all exports and imports, for the use of enemy patents, for a strict censorship of news, and for licensing of foreign-language publications. The Exports Administrative Board was replaced by the War Trade Board.

## SUBMARINE BLOCKADE

The American steamships Lewis Luckenbach and Platuria were sunk. An American destroyer was torpedoed by a German submarine in European waters on Oct. 16. A petty officer was killed and five men were injured. The vessel was disabled, but managed to reach port.

England's losses for the week ended Sept. 23 included thirteen vessels of over 1,600 tons; for the week ended Sept. 30, eleven; for the week ended Oct. 7, fourteen, and for the week ended Oct. 14, eighteen. A British destroyer was sunk at the entrance to the English Channel on Sept. 23. The cruiser Drake was destroyed, and an officer and eighteen men were killed. Fifty-six lives were lost when the cruiser Champagne was sunk.

French and Italian losses averaged two or three vessels of over 1,600 tons each week. The French munitions steamer Medie was torpedoed in the Mediterranean on Sept. 23, and 250 lives were lost.

Norway lost nineteen ships in September.

The Chinese ship Glenogie was sunk.

The Argentine Senate voted for a break with Germany on Sept. 19, and on Sept. 22 the Government sent an ultimatum to Berlin demanding an explanation of the behavior of Count Luxburg and a repetition of the promise made concerning Argentine shpiping. On Sept. 23, just as the Chamber of Deputies was preparing to vote for a break in relations, a message was received from Berlin repudiating Luxburg. The Chamber voted on Sept. 25 to sever relations, but President Irigoyen refused to act.

Costa Rica severed relations with Germany.

Peru sent an ultimatum to Germany on Sept. 26, demanding that satisfaction be given for the sinking of the bark Lorton. On Oct. 5 the Senate and Chamber voted to sever diplomatic relations, and the German Minister was given his passports on Oct. 6.

Ecuador announced that Dr. Perl, the German Minister to Peru and Ecuador, would not be received by the Ecuadorian Government.

Uruguay severed relations with Germany Oct. 7, and waived her neutrality rules in favor of the Allies.

## CAMPAIGN IN EASTERN EUROPE

Sept. 22—Germans capture Jacobstadt, together with positions on a front of 26 miles, six miles deep, on the west bank of the Dvina River.

Sept. 24—Russians occupy German positions in the Silzeme sector.

Sept. 25—Russians repulse attacks on positions south of the Pskov-Riga highroad.

Oct. 1—Russians advance in the Riga region, pushing the foe back in the Spitals Farm sector.

Oct. 13—Germans land troops on the coast of the Gulf of Tagalab, and on Oesel and Dagö Islands; garrison of Oesel fights the invaders.

Oct. 14—Germans occupy the whole northern and eastern part of Oesel Island, but fail in attempt to seize Moon Island.

Oct. 15—German forces occupy Orensburg on Oesel Island.

Oct. 16—Germans extend their gains on Oesel Island and institute an offensive against the Svorb peninsula.

Oct. 17—Germans take the entire island of Oesel and crush Russian force on Svorb peninsula; Russians frustrate their attempt to throw a bridge across the Dvina River.

Oct. 18—Germans capture Moon Island.

## CAMPAIGN IN WESTERN EUROPE

Sept. 20—British penetrate German line on eight-mile front along the Ypres-Menin road to a depth of more than a mile and capture the villages of Velahoek and Zevenkote; French repulse attacks southeast of Cernay.

UNITED STATES NAVAL ENCAMPMENT AT NEWPORT

(© Press Illustrated Service)

Men of the United States Navy, Stationed at Newport, R. I., Marching to Church to Hear a Sermon by Dr. Manning of Trinity Church, New York City

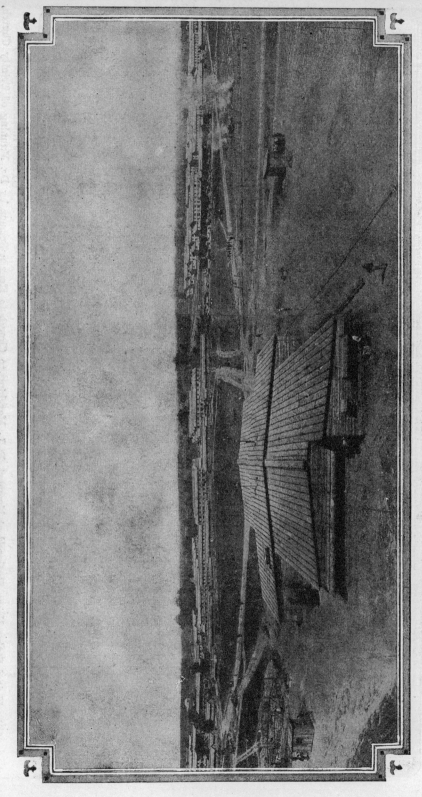

A TYPICAL CANTONMENT OF THE NATIONAL ARMY

General View of Camp Dix, Where New Jersey's Drafted Men Are Being Trained for Service in the National Army

(© *Underwood & Underwood*)

Sept. 21—British thrust Germans from their last strong point northeast of Langemarck and consolidate their gains; Germans in Champagne lose heavily in unsuccessful attack on Mont Haut.

Sept. 22—German counterattacks south of the Ypres-Menin Road repulsed.

Sept. 24—French repulse German attacks north of Bezonvauz and near Beaumont.

Sept. 26—British pierce German line on a four-mile front in the Zonnebeke region.

Sept. 27-28—British repulse seven fierce counterattacks east of Ypres.

Sept. 30—British break up German offensive near Tower Hamlets.

Oct. 1-3—Germans fail in attempt to drive British from new positions east of Ypres.

Oct. 4—British advance on an eight-mile front from north of Langemarck to a point south of Tower Hamlets, winning the crest of the Passchendaele Heights.

Oct. 5—French repulse surprise attacks on the Aisne, in Champagne, and in Upper Alsace.

Oct. 9—British drive Germans from their last positions in Poelcapelle and push on for nearly two miles to the northwest; French pierce German positions to a depth of a mile and a quarter on a mile and a half front, capturing St. Jean de Mangelaers and Veldhoek.

Oct. 10—French gain more ground toward Houthulst Forest; Germans northeast of Verdun reach advanced French lines near the Bois de Chaume.

Oct. 13—British advance southwest of Passchendaele Village and take part of Houthulst Wood.

Oct. 15—Germans bombard British positions south of Broodseinde.

## ITALIAN CAMPAIGN

Sept. 23—Italians repulse Austrian attacks on the Bainsizza Plateau in the region of Kal and west of Volnik.

Sept. 24—Italians repulse Austrian counterattacks in Marmolada region.

Sept. 29—Italians gain ground by surprise attacks above Gorizia.

Sept. 30—Italians capture high ground south of Podlaca and southeast of Madoni, in new drive on the Bainsizza Plateau.

Oct. 3—Italians repulse attacks on the western slopes of San Gabriele.

Oct. 15—Heavy fighting on the Julian front; Italians make successful attack on the southern slopes of Monte Rombon.

## CAMPAIGN IN ASIA MINOR

Sept. 28—British capture Mushaid Ridge and occupy Ramadie on the Euphrates, taking prisoner Ahmed Bey, the Turkish commander, and his staff.

Oct. 4—Arabs, in revolt against the Turks, have effected a junction with the British in southern Palestine and control the Hedjaz Railway as far north as Maan.

Oct. 5—Russians in the Kikatsh-Amadia sector of the Caucasian front take the village of Nereman, 50 miles north of Mosul; British advance up the Tigris.

Oct. 11—Turks repulsed by Russians southwest of Erzingan.

## BALKAN CAMPAIGN

Sept. 19—Rumanians attack Austro-German positions south of Grozechti.

Oct. 6—Russians on the Rumanian front check attack near Radautz; Bulgarians take Russian positions north of the Buzeu River, but lose them by counterattacks.

Oct. 15—Scottish troops raid Homondos on the Struma front.

## AERIAL RECORD

German aviators bombarded London and the southeast coast of England on Sept. 24. Fifteen persons were killed and seventy injured. The next night another raid was made on London, and seven persons were killed and twenty-six injured. Two German machines were brought down in a raid on Sept. 29; eleven persons were killed and eighty-two injured. Nine persons were killed in a raid on Sept. 30. On Oct. 1 four squadrons of German machines made the strongest air attack yet made on coast towns; ten persons were killed and thirty-eight injured.

British naval airmen bombarded Ostend, Zeebrugge, and other Belgian coast towns, and dropped bombs on German bases back of the Flanders line.

The French raided German bases from Lorraine to Belgium, and bombarded Frankfort-am-Main, Stuttgart, Treves, Coblenz, and Baden.

The Germans made several air raids in the Baltic, in the region of the Gulf of Riga.

## NAVAL RECORD

British warships bombarded German naval works at Ostend on Sept. 22.

The presence of two German raiders in the South Pacific Ocean, manned by the crew of the German raider Seeadler, was announced by the Navy Department, and allied warships scoured the seas to find them.

The Italians captured an Austrian destroyer in the Adriatic Sea.

German warships silenced Russian batteries on Oesel and Dagö Islands as their troops landed on Oct. 13. In an engagement between Russian and German naval forces on Oct. 14, in Soeia Sound, two German torpedoboats were sunk and two damaged. One Russian torpedo boat was sunk. On Oct. 18 the Germans seized Moon Island, trapping the Russian battleships in the Gulf of Riga, and sinking the battleship Slava.

## RUSSIA

General Alexeieff resigned as Chief of the General Staff. Premier Kerensky appointed General Tcheremisoff to succeed him.

General Soukhomlinoff, former Minister of War, was sentenced to hard labor for life after conviction on the charges of high treason, abuse of confidence, and fraud. His wife was acquitted.

M. Terestchenko resigned as Foreign Minister in the Cabinet of Five.

The Congress of Non-Slav Nationalities met in Kiev and passed a resolution declaring that Russia must be a federal democratic republic.

A revolution occurred in Turkestan against the Government at Petrograd.

The Democratic Congress was held in Petrograd. It declared in favor of a coalition Government, with the bourgeois element excluded, and opposed coalition with the entire Constitutional Democratic Party.

Kerensky formed a coalition Ministry, including four Constitutional Democrats.

## MISCELLANEOUS

Austria-Hungary and Germany replied to the Pope's peace proposal, accepting his offer as a basis for the beginning of negotiations, but avoiding any suggestion of definite concessions. It has been reported that Germany sent a supplementary note offering to give up Belgium for trade and military guarantees on condition that Belgium maintain administrative separation of the Flanders and Walloon districts.

France has been investigating reports of acts of treason. Louis J. Malvy, former Minister of the Interior, was accused by Leon Daudet of betraying secrets to Germany. Deputy Louis Turmel was arrested on a charge of trading with the enemy. Bolo Pasha was arrested as a spy, and revelations concerning his efforts in the United States to buy control of the French press in the interests of a separate peace with Germany were made public. In this plot, former Ambassador von Bernstorff was found to be involved.

Great Britain declared an absolute embargo on the northern neutrals to stop the sending of supplies into Germany, and cut off all commercial cable communication with Holland until the Netherlands Government should place an absolute restriction on the transit of war materials through Holland from Germany to Belgium. In retaliation, Holland stopped all ships to England.

Vice Admiral Capelle announced in the German Reichstag on Oct. 9 that a plot had been discovered in the navy to paralyze the fleet so as to force the Government to make peace. A mutiny occurred on warships at Wilhelmshaven. Three men were shot and over a hundred sentenced to prison. The blame was put on the Socialists. Capelle resigned on Oct. 12. On Oct. 18 another mutiny was reported among sailors at Ostend who refused to go on board submarines, and serious mutinies occurred in the Austrian Navy at the Pola and Fiume bases because of bad food conditions and inhuman treatment by officers.

The Emperors of Germany and Austria-Hungary named a Council of Regency for Poland.

The Swedish Minister at Washington asked the aid of the United States in obtaining the release of official mail held by the British Embassy in Washington.

# A Homesick Soldier's Letters

A French soldier, René des Touches, tells in his " Pages of Glory and Suffering " a little story that actually happened. In his regiment at the front there was a brave little fellow who was depressed because he never received any letters. Every day the " vaguemestre," or baggage officer, brought mail for others—letters from wives, sweethearts, and friends—and while the fortunate poilus retired in silence to devour the precious words from home, the lonely man endured new pangs of homesickness. But one day a letter—a real letter, delightfully long—came for this man, who had been born in one of the invaded provinces; and that was the beginning of a regular correspondence, soon, alas! cut short by his death in a gallant charge. Before dying, he had had the joy of thinking that some one back yonder, far from the front, had thought of him. The little story ends with these words: " Now, it was the good baggage officer, who, seeing the desolation in the eyes of the lonely man, had written those letters."

# Mobilizing Our Industries for War

## Story of the Wonderful Transformation Which the First Six Months of War Have Produced in American Industrial and Commercial Life

THE development of highly technical methods of waging war, especially as regards the vast quantities of supplies which are required for armies of millions of men, but which can be produced only by a great and efficient industrial system, has given the United States a unique opportunity of demonstrating its power and resourcefulness in the creation of what has been called "the army behind the army."

Six months have now passed since the United States entered the war, and, although there had been comparatively little preparation, a great transformation has already taken place in industry, trade, and finance. Governmental functions have been enormously extended, but there has been no interference with private enterprise such as this suggests, because the business men of the nation have voluntarily come forward to co-operate with the Government or relieve the Government of many heavy burdens by taking control themselves of the new war administration which has been brought into existence at Washington alongside the political organization we know as the United States Government.

### Council of National Defense

The central body of this new war administration, the directing authority of the nation's industrial mobilization, is the Council of National Defense, which was appointed by President Wilson before the United States went to war, when he realized that sooner or later the nation would be forced to fight. The council, however, was not an entirely new creation, but the result of a development which had begun with the preparedness movement. The business men of America had seen Great Britain go through a year or more of confusion in readjusting the activities of a highly developed industrial nation to the needs of modern warfare, so that when the United States

joined the Allies there were at least the beginnings of organization. Moreover, America had already become a great munition manufacturing country, and in this respect was in a much more favorable position in April, 1917, than Great Britain in August, 1914. As the months went on and the belief grew that there was more than a possibility of the United States not being able to keep out of the war, manufacturers and business organizers awoke to the fact that military preparedness was valueless without industrial preparedness; and from the time of the sinking of the Lusitania onward the question of economic mobilization began to be studied with increasing seriousness.

The Navy Department took one of the first steps toward linking up the nation's fighting forces more closely with the industrial system. The Naval Consulting Board was established, and to it eleven engineering and other scientific societies were invited to send two representatives each. This meant that the scientists, inventors, and technical experts of the nation were now definitely enlisted to use their brains for the security of the nation. The next thing to do was to enlist the actual controllers and organizers of production.

This was done by forming a Committee on Industrial Preparedness, under the Chairmanship of Howard E. Coffin, engineer, automobile manufacturer, and one of the nation's captains of industry. The committee undertook and carried through a very remarkable piece of work by making a complete survey of the whole industrial capacity of the United States for the purposes of war. Over 29,000 factories and plants furnished full information regarding their equipment, output, the number and skill of their workmen, and an estimate of what they could produce in the way of munitions or other warlike material if called upon to do so.

The information thus obtained was collated in proper form, and from that time onward the Committee on Industrial Preparedness knew how to turn the industrial activities to their most effective use in case of war.

The Council of National Defense was the direct result of the Committee on Industrial Preparedness, and was appointed by President Wilson to take the place of the latter when he realized that sooner or later the nation might be at war. The council was made up of the Secretaries of War, the Navy, the Interior, Commerce, and Agriculture, and an Advisory Commission of seven nonofficial citizens, namely, Howard E. Coffin, Daniel Willard, a railroad President; Julius Rosenwald, head of the nation's greatest mail-order business; Bernard Baruch, a leading figure in Wall Street; Hollis Godfrey, engineer and technicologist; Samuel Gompers, President of the American Federatiton of Labor, and Franklin Martin, representing the medical profession.

Under the Council of National Defense there has gradually grown up a large number of boards and subsidiary committees, each manned by experts and business men, and each charged with some special duty in utilizing the economic resources of the nation for war purposes. In addition there are various new Governmental bodies which are responsible for the carrying out of legislative enactments or exercising powers conferred upon them by the President, such as the Food Administration Board and the Shipping Board.

## War Industries Board

Originally, the most important body under the Council of National Defense was the General Munitions Board, with Frank A. Scott as Chairman. But at the end of July it was reorganized as the War Industries Board, with Mr. Scott again at the head, and consisting of only seven members, all practically selected by President Wilson himself, and all responsible to him through the Council of National Defense.

Associated with Mr. Scott on the board are Lieut. Col. Palmer E. Pierce, representing the army; Rear Admiral Frank F. Fletcher, representing the navy;

Bernard M. Baruch, Robert S. Brookings, Robert S. Lovett, and Hugh Frayne.

The change became necessary because volunteer workers in the war service of the Government were buying from themselves as producers and selling to themselves as agents of the Government. The fact that they had no power to buy or to fix prices, but only to recommend where things might be bought and to suggest prices, was generally lost sight of by those who feared the dangers of graft, but even the appearance of the possibility of graft has been done away with by the scrapping of the old Munitions Board and the creation of the new Board of War Industries. The Council of Defense, in the statement announcing the organization of the new board, said that this action "makes clear that there is a total dissociation of the industrial committees from the actual arrangement of purchases in behalf of the Government."

The War Industries Board is also an improvement in the greater power it has of recommending prices. Under the old régime it was only possible for the Munitions Board to suggest a price for a specific purchase at the request of the War or Navy Department, that suggestion having no official weight in the matter of the next purchase of the same commodity by the same department. Now the War Industries Board may suggest a price that will hold until it sees fit to modify it because of economic changes.

Under the old board there was some effort to determine priority of supplying needs of this or that department for any given necessity, but the machinery was quite inadequate. It has now been perfected by the new board. The appointment of Hugh Frayne, the labor union organizer, as one of the seven, gives the workingmen of the country fuller representation in the vital war organizations. The War Industries Board may be summed up as the American equivalent of the British and French Munitions Ministers, with the difference that its head does not occupy a place in the Cabinet.

Mr. Scott, describing the functions of the War Industries Board, said:

It is absolutely essential for co-ordinating our industries and putting them behind our military forces in the most effective manner. Furthermore, it is one of the chief duties of such an organization not only to obtain the available supply on the best terms, but to develop a greater supply, for which there is present lack of producing facilities. We must foresee the military necessities for a long time to come, and see that provision is made for them in advance, for the sake of the army and navy and for the sake of normal industry.

As an illustration we will take a manufacturer with a forge who has never made gun forgings, but who has the facilities to do so. That manufacturer must be persuaded to devote his plant to serving the country's new need. And so on through all forms of industry from which war supplies are obtained.

The best example of what may be obtained for the Government and of what waste the Government may be protected from by co-ordination is offered by the tangible, simple case of buying cotton duck for the army and navy. The Quartermaster's Department of the army uses duck for tentage; the Ordnance Department uses it for haversacks and kit carriers; the Medical Department uses it for hospital cots; the Signal Corps uses duck in aviation supplies. The need of this commodity in the navy is about as widespread. In peace times each one of these sub-departments buys its own supply of duck without reference to what another department is doing or paying to get the same commodity. But with the beginning of war the needs of every one of these separate departments become so vast, not only in the matter of cotton duck, but for guns and ammunition and vehicles and raw materials and all other supplies, that their independent and separate buying would be fatal. They would bid against each other in a rapidly rising market, and an incidental evil would be that the lesser need might get supplied before the greater need. It was to prevent all this that the General Munitions Board was hurriedly put together at the outset of the war, and it is to prevent it still more effectively as well as to accomplish other things that the new board has been created.

It was announced on Oct. 8 that war service committees representing the several industries furnishing war supplies to the Government were to be organized to take the place of the subordinate advisory committees of the Council of National Defense. The new committees will have no official connection with the Council of Defense, but serve the Government as consulting agents after the manner of the existing committees. This arrangement abolishes the technical dual function so far exercised by several members of the Council of National Defense organization, which made it possible for them to represent the Government and their own concerns in the same transaction. "We have realized that there were "technical objections to the organization of these subordinate committees "for some time," said Walter S. Gifford, Director of the Council of National Defense. "Section 3 of the Food bill, "which expressly forbids Government officials to participate in the negotiation of contracts in which they are interested, really put into the statutes a "policy which we had been following "since the organization of these committees. In no case has one of these "committees ever reported or recommended directly to the purchasing officers of the Government. It has been "our policy to have the committee recommendations pass first through the "hands of a disinterested committee of "the council, which has in many cases "rejected the original recommendations."

From the industries represented by the committees the Defense Council will select experts to serve as advisers to the War Industries Board. These men will be required to sever their business connections that there may be no question of their eligibility to act for the Government in dealing with sellers. Twenty-two members of the advisory committees of the council, Director Gifford said, had offered their resignations out of a membership of more than 300, but in no case had these been accepted. The resigned members were continuing to serve the council in an advisory capacity.

### Spending Ten Billion Dollars

The buying activities of the War Industries Board are under the supervision of a subsidiary committee, consisting of ex-Judge Robert S. Lovett, (head of the Union Pacific Railroad,) Robert S. Brookings, and Bernard M. Baruch, who, in the course of America's first year in the war, are handling orders for more than ten billion dollars. Mr. Baruch's duty is to watch over the supply of metals and other raw materials, both for the United States and for the allied Governments. In the buying of steel he is assisted by J. Leonard Replogle, President of the American Vanadium Company, head of the Wharton Steel Company, and one of the ablest organizers in the steel business, while the copper buyer is Eugene Meyer, Jr., a well-known Stock Exchange man. Judge Lovett's work is to decide questions of priority in the distribution of orders among producers and the apportionment of deliveries. On priority matters affecting steel he has the assistance of Mr. Replogle. Mr. Brookings deals with finished products. Herbert C. Hoover, the Food Administrator, acts with the buying committee in all matters pertaining to foodstuffs.

### Buying for Other Nations

Further importance attaches to the buying committee because of its co-operation with the war missions which the allied Governments have sent to the United States. Formal agreements were signed on Aug. 24, 1917, by the Secretary of the Treasury, with the approval of the President, on behalf of the United States, and by Lord Northcliffe, special representative of the British Government; M. Jusserand, the French Ambassador, and M. Bakhmeteff, the Russian Ambassador, for the creation of a commission, with headquarters at Washington, through which all purchases made by the allied Governments must proceed. The agreements named Messrs. Baruch, Lovett, and Brookings as the commission who were selected as members of the War Industries Board to co-ordinate the purchases of the United States with those of the allied powers. The Italian, Belgian, and Serbian diplomatic representatives at Washington subsequently signed agreements to make all purchases through the buying commission.

The necessity of making the buying commission of the War Industries Board act in a similar capacity for the Allies arose from the many disadvantages resulting from the competitive buying of belligerent countries in the United States. France, for example, has been buying copper in very large amounts in this country at a price far in excess of that likely to be paid by the United States under existing agreements with the copper syndicate. Similar instances were also found in the matter of buying wheat and meat supplies. In some cases it was found that agents of the allied countries had combed the Western markets for grain months in advance of any efforts of American buyers and had large quantities of materials stored awaiting favorable conditions of shipment, while prices went upward in consequence of the steadily increasing scarcity of certain staples.

### War Prices for the Allies

The War Industries Board and its Central Purchasing Commission began now to put into effect the policy outlined in the statement issued by the board on Aug. 8, in the course which it was said:

In the purchase of war materials in this country our allies shall be charged no more than our own Government has to pay. Guns and ammunition employed against our enemy are for our benefit as much when used by our allies as when used by our own men; and it is obviously unjust to require our allies when fighting our battles to pay our own people more than our own Government pays for the materials necessary to carry on the war. A mere statement of the proposition seems enough; and we are confident that our manufacturers, who have so patriotically responded thus far to the calls of our Government in this emergency, will readily accept this policy.

But this policy has two important limitations. First, it is to be reciprocal. The Allies must henceforth apply the same principle in dealing with their own producers and in selling to us and in selling to each other. Second, the arrangement must be limited to war materials in order to protect our own industry. We must not allow raw materials sold by our producers at prices patriotically conceded to our Government and its allies for war purposes to be diverted to industry and trade abroad which may come in competition with our own manufacturers and producers. Measures will be taken by the board for the best possible assurance that materials sold at a concession in price for war purposes shall be applied only to war purposes.

In fixing the prices to be paid by the Governments we shall allow a reasonable profit, but shall deny the extortion now exacted for many commodities of prime necessity.

The war makes enormous drafts upon many raw materials absolutely necessary to the industrial life of the nation and to the ordinary existence of the people. This has resulted in the bidding up of prices for what is left of many materials of prime necessity in manufacture to a point obviously out of all relation to the cost of production, and involving unconscionable profits on our national resources, and the consequence is that the cost to the public of all the articles in the manufacture of which such materials enter has reached a level never before known.

The determination of production costs —and hence of prices—comes largely within the sphere of the Federal Trade Commission, which was in existence before the United States went to war. It had power to take over coal supplies, and, if necessary, resell to the consumer. But in this respect its functions were handed over to a new administrative body, to which reference will presently be made. The Federal Trade Commission has undertaken a national food survey, an investigation into flour milling conditions, and other tasks of discovering the extent of supplies and costs of production, with a view to fixing prices. President Wilson has depended largely upon the commission for information of this nature in connection with his measures to regulate prices.

## Fixing Prices of Steel

An interesting example of how prices have been fixed is seen in the case of steel. When the war began in 1914 the steel producers were getting $14 for pig iron, $23 for steel bars, and $22.80 for plates. Two years later these prices had risen to $24, $49.60, and $56.40; but until a few weeks ago they were still higher— $58, $110, and $160, that is, from four to seven times higher. The profits earned by the iron and steel producing companies eclipsed almost anything else in the industrial history of the country. In accordance with his repeated declarations against profiteering, President Wilson took steps to reduce prices of steel for the Government, for the Allies, and for the public to a more reasonable level. On Sept. 21 representatives of the big steel interests, including Judge E. H. Gary and J. A. Farrell of the United States Steel Corporation and President Grace and Charles M. Schwab of the Bethlehem Steel Company, were summoned to Wash-

ington to confer with the War Industries Board. The result was a voluntary agreement under which prices were cut one-half or more. According to an official statement the savings amounted to from 40 to 70 per cent. The agreement, as approved by the President, became effective immediately, but is subject to revision on Jan. 1, 1918. The following was the schedule of prices contained in the official statement issued on Sept. 24:

| Commodity. | Price Basis. | Agreed Upon. | Recent Price. | Reduction. Am't. | P.C. |
|---|---|---|---|---|---|
| Iron ore: | | | | | |
| Lower Lake ports | *$5.05 | *$5.05 | .... | .. | |
| Coke: | | | | | |
| Connellsville | .... | †6.00 | †16.00 | $10.00 | 62.5 |
| Pig iron | .......... | *33.00 | *58.00 | 25.00 | 43.1 |
| Steel bars: | | | | | |
| Pittsb'h, Chicago. | ‡2.90 | ‡5.50 | 2.60 | 47.3 | |
| Shapes: | | | | | |
| Pittsb'h, Chicago | ‡3.00 | ‡6.00 | 3.00 | 50.0 | |
| Plates: | | | | | |
| Pittsb'h, Chicago | ‡3.25 | ‡11.00 | 7.75 | 70.5 | |

*Gross tons. †Net tons. ‡Hundredweight.

It was stipulated that there should be no reduction in the present rate of wages; that these prices should be made to the public and to the Allies as well as to the Government; and that the steel men pledged themselves to exert every effort necessary to keep up the production to the maximum of the past, so long as the war lasts.

It was stated by some who fought for radical reductions that the United States Steel Corporation could produce plates at from $34 to $36 a net ton. While $65 steel will represent a large profit, much of this will enter the Government coffers by means of war taxes. It is understood that the prices contained in the agreement will not affect existing contracts, at least where war work is involved. The United States Shipping Board, through its Emergency Fleet Corporation, has been paying $50 a ton on account for steel plates, pending the announcement of the Government price. On all its work the $65 price for plates will be paid, and, as it involves something like 2,000,000 tons in the next year, this will mean an increase of approximately $30,000,000 over the tentative payments agreed upon. The Navy Department has been paying, under agreement with the steel industry, $58 a ton for plates. This price will be maintained for the contracts already entered into, and the navy will then join the other Governmental agencies, the Allies, and the public in paying $65 for its plates.

### Private Purchasers Must Wait

Coincident with the announcement of the agreement, Judge Lovett, as Chairman of the Priority Board, issued a statement placing the distribution of iron and steel under absolute control by license. Preference is given to the War and Navy Departments and the Emergency Fleet Corporation of the United States Shipping Board. Next comes the supply for the needs of the Allies. Private interests not engaged in war work must wait until the last before obtaining supplies. It was also announced that the constitution of Judge Lovett's Priority Board was now complete, the other members appointed being Major Gen. J. B. Aleshire, George Armsby, Rear Admiral N. E. Mason, Edwin B. Parker, J. Leonard Replogle, and Rear Admiral A. V. Zane.

The price of copper has been fixed at 23½ cents a pound. Previously to this the Government carried through one of its first transactions as buyer for the Allies by purchasing 77,600,000 pounds of copper at 25 cents a pound.

### Coal Prices

Coal has also been brought under the jurisdiction of the Government. President Wilson, on Aug. 23, signed an executive order appointing Dr. Harry A. Garfield, President of Williams College, to the position of Fuel Administrator. This was done under the authority conferred upon the President by the act of Aug. 10, which provides for the control of the distribution of food products and fuel. He had, on Aug. 21, fixed a scale of prices for bituminous coal, ranging from about $2 to $3 a ton, according to district and grade; and on the day he named Dr. Garfield as Fuel Administrator he fixed the prices of anthracite coal at the mine from $4 to $5.30 a ton, according to grade, and set forth the conditions under which jobbers would be permitted to operate. The regulation of the retail trade in both bituminous and anthracite coal was left to Dr. Garfield, with authority to use drastic means to protect the consumer from exploitation. The conditions under which the dealers are to sell coal are being formulated by the Fuel Administrator in co-operation with the Federal Trade Commission. To save the coal situation in the Northwest Dr. Garfield issued an order on Oct 1 stopping temporarily the shipment of coal into Canada from the lake ports. In this way it was hoped to divert a large quantity to the Northwest, where the need for immediate supplies was being acutely felt.

The coal prices fixed by the Government were contested by the mine operators, and a diminution of output has followed, with some disorganization of the industry.

## All Railroads United in One System

The war has had a remarkable effect upon the management of the railroads. Here there has been practically no intervention by the Government, and yet, almost at a stroke, the railroads were placed under centralized control as soon as the nation was at war. The vastness of this enterprise may be appreciated when it is stated that the number of railroads thus merged into one great national system was 693, operating 262,000 miles of track, using 2,326,987 freight cars, employing 1,750,000 persons, and owned by 1,500,000 security holders.

The initiation of this great step in industrial mobilization took place at a meeting at Washington on April 11, 1917, when fifty railroad Presidents representing the transportation business of the entire country responded to the appeal of Secretary Lane and Daniel Willard, Chairman of the Advisory Commission of the National Defense Council, by deciding to co-operate and eliminate all competitive activities. The President appointed a commission of five of the most experienced railroad officers in the country, with plenary powers to establish policies for any or all of the railroads of the country. Independent companies for the time being abdicated their independent functions and intrusted their operations to the direction of this committee, with the single purpose of obtaining for the nation a maximum of transportation efficiency.

The fundamental feature of the arrangement is that instead of the Government assuming any responsibility, as has been done in Great Britain, for the operation of the railroads under wartime conditions, that responsibility is placed upon railroad officers.

The Railroads' War Board, presided over by Daniel Willard, is part of the Council of National Defense and works through an Executive Committee, of which Fairfax Harrison is chief, with Robert S. Lovett as director of priority shipments.

## Achievements of Railroad Board

In a statement issued on Sept. 9 the board reviewed its achievements during the first five months of its existence:

The voluntary act of the 693 railroads of this country in merging their competitive activities for the period of the war and uniting in one continental system has not only made the transportation problem presented by the war less cumbersome to handle, but surer of satisfactory solution.

In addition to welding into one loyal army each and every one of the 1,750,000 persons employed by the railroads, the co-ordination of the nation's carriers has made possible the most intensive use of every locomotive, every freight car, every mile of track, and every piece of railroad equipment in the country. It has also facilitated the securing of invaluable co-operation from the shippers and the general public.

Skilled and experienced railroad men have been sent to every cantonment to assist the constructing Quartermaster there in the movement of all supplies necessary to the erection and maintenance of these military cities. A trained executive has also been stationed in the Washington Headquarters of the Supervising Constructing Quartermaster, so that every car needed in the transportation of Government supplies might be made available when needed. As a result of these co-operative activities, the movement of thousands of carloads of lumber and other supplies has been accomplished practically without a hitch.

In addition, at the request of the Government, plans have been perfected whereby 1,000,000 men will be moved from nearly 5,000 different points to the thirty-two training camps for the National Army and National Guard by Oct. 20.

Among some of the things accomplished by the board in the first four months of its existence have been the organizing of special equipment for hospital and troop train service, the standardization of settlements between the Government and the railroads, eliminating a large volume of correspondence and red tape, and the creation of a special committee on express transportation, to co-ordinate the work of the companies with the general problem of transportation.

Car shortage has been reduced 70 per cent. On April 30 the so-called car shortage amounted to 148,627; on June 30 these figures had been cut to 77,144; on Aug. 1 the excess of unfilled car requisitions over idle cars amounted to only 33,776.

In May freight transportation service rendered by about 75 per cent. of Class 1 roads—earnings of $1,000,000 or more—was 16.1 per cent. in excess of the service rendered in 1916. In that year, which was one of unusual activity, the freight service rendered by the carriers was 24 per cent. in excess of that rendered in 1915.

Approximately 20,000,000 miles of train service a year has been saved by the elimination of all passenger trains not essential to the most pressing needs of the country. Freight congestion at many important points has been averted by promptly moving empty cars from one railroad to another, irrespective of ownership. Through the pooling of lake coal and lake ore a saving of 52,000 cars in moving these commodities alone has been achieved. A further saving of 133,000 cars has been made possible by the pooling of tidewater coal.

By regulating the movement of grain for export, the number of cars ordinarily required for this service has been reduced, despite an abnormal export increase this year, 75,682,028 bushels of wheat, corn, barley, and oats being shipped to the Allies from May 1 to July 14. Although the figures on the intensive loading of freight cars are not complete, a sufficient number of reports have been received from the twenty-seven local committees of the War Board to show that commercial bodies and individual shippers in all parts of the country are giving hearty co-operation to the railroads' campaign to make one car do the work of two.

# Progress in Solving the Shipping Problem

The creation of an American mercantile marine was described in the October issue of this magazine, (pp. 17-20.) During the month that has since elapsed further important developments have taken place. A revised table showing the shipping facilities upon which the United States and the Allies may depend during the next year or two was issued by the Shipping Board on Sept. 26, 1917. It shows that the Government has under construction in deadweight tonnage, including 400 vessels of foreign ownership which were requisitioned on the stocks, approximately 1,036 cargo vessels of 5,924,700 tons capacity. These vessels have actually been contracted for; some of them were due to be off the stocks before the end of November, 1917, and most of the remainder before the end of 1918. A table prepared by the Shipping Board showed the world's available tonnage in the early part of September, 1917, to be as follows:

| United Kingdom— | Atlantic | Pacific |
|---|---|---|
| Liners ................. | 4,860,000 | 650,000 |
| Tramps ................ | 8,540,000 | 450,000 |
| Norway ................. | 1,800,000 | 50,000 |
| Sweden ................. | 860,000 | ...... |
| Denmark ................ | 690,000 | ...... |
| Holland ................ | 1,200,000 | 275,000 |
| United States .......... | 2,000,000 | 400,000 |
| France ................. | 1,600,000 | 220,000 |
| Italy .................. | 1,250,000 | 70,000 |
| Greece ................. | 470,000 | ...... |
| Spain .................. | 750,000 | ...... |
| Portugal ............... | 150,000 | 50,000 |
| Russia ................. | 350,000 | 200,000 |
| Belgium ................ | 280,000 | ...... |
| South America .......... | 600,000 | 200,000 |
| China .................. | ....... | 35,000 |
| Japan .................. | 100,000 | 1,900,000 |
| Total .................. | 25,500,000 | 5,500,000 |

Vessels on inland waterways and in the Baltic are estimated at 6,000,000 tons gross; coastwise shipping at 6,000,000 tons, and enemy shipping at approximately 5,000,000 tons. These are not accounted for in the table. The tabulated figures are of peculiar interest as bearing upon the world's ability to fight the submarine menace successfully.

## Work of Shipping Board

An important statement was also issued on Sept. 26 by the Shipping Board regarding its program, which was revised by Chairman Hurley and Rear Admiral Capps, General Manager of the Emergency Fleet Corporation. It read in part:

During the past two months the Emergency Fleet Corporation has awarded contracts for 118 wooden vessels, of 3,500 tons deadweight capacity each, to twenty-seven different shipyards. There had previously been awarded contracts for 235 wooden vessels of similar type to the above, and for fifty-eight vessels of composite construction, thereby making a total award to date of 411 wooden and composite vessels of an aggregate deadweight tonnage of 1,460,900. During the past two months the designs for machinery have been completed for the manufacture of engines, boilers, and other articles of equipment for these vessels, for which the facilities available of machine shops and boiler works throughout the country have been availed of. Specifications have been prepared and negotiations outlined and initiated for the assembly and installation of machinery in wooden vessels, the most of which have been, or are being, constructed as " hulls only." Great difficulty has been experienced on the Atlantic coast in obtaining suitable lumber for these ships.

Since Aug. 1 there have been awarded contracts for 155 steel cargo vessels of 1,076,800 deadweight tonnage, distributed among six shipyards. The most important of these contracts are for vessels of the so-called fabricated type, and special shipyards are being prepared for them. Contracts for the boilers, machinery, and steel construction of these vessels have already been placed, and the contractors are actively at work in the preparation of the sites for the assembling of the ships. Previous to Aug. 1 seventy steel cargo vessels of 587,000 tons total deadweight capacity had been contracted for. These vessels were distributed among ten shipyards. Therefore, at the present time the total number of steel vessels under construction for the United States is 225, with a total aggregate deadweight tonnage of 1,603,800.

By proclamation of Aug. 3, 1917, the fleet corporation requisitioned all vessels under construction in the shipyards of the United States of 2,500 tons deadweight capacity and above. The total deadweight tonnage under construction thus acquired, and on which orders have been issued to proceed with maximum expedition, exceeds 2,000,000 tons deadweight. There are now under construction for the Emergency Fleet Corporation:

| Type of Vessels. | Number of Vessels. | Total Deadweight Tonnage. |
|---|---|---|
| Wood | 353 | 1,253,900 |
| Composite | 58 | 207,000 |
| Steel | 225 | 1,663,000 |
| Requistioned vessels | 400 | 2,800,000 |
| Grand total | 1,036 | 5,924,700 |

In addition to the above, Congress, in a pending bill, is authorizing the construction of additional vessels whose total deadweight capacity will be nearly 5,000,000 tons. Plants for the major portion of these additional vessels are now in course of preparation, and many of them will be of special types adapted to particular necessities of war. With the passage of the pending bill the Congress will have authorized $1,799,000,000 for the Shipping Board and the Emergency Fleet Corporation.

The statement said that 150,000 additional workers were required in the shipyards to insure full production.

### Merchant Vessels Commandeered

The requisitioning by the Shipping Board of every American merchant vessel of more than 2,500 tons deadweight capacity available for ocean service was announced on Sept. 27. The date fixed for the order to become effective was Oct. 15. A certain number of ships have already been taken over for the army and navy, and of those now requisitioned all except those actually used in Government service are being turned back to their owners for operation on Government account, subject at all times to any disposition the Shipping Board may direct.

Simultaneously with the announcement regarding this step, the charter rates were made public. These rates cut sharply into those formerly charged by American owners for carrying Government supplies. The chartering is under the direction of the Shipping Board's Chartering Commission, to the Chairmanship of which Welding Ring of New York has been appointed. The commission's headquarters are in New York City, and the new rates apply for the present only to the Atlantic. An important side of the commission's work is the solving of the situation created by the act of the British shipping authorities in insisting upon American shipowners securing their approval of transatlantic charters. With the establishment of a United States Governmental agency, a system of co-operation between the American and allied shipping authorities comes into existence for the best employment of ocean transportation facilities, to the satisfaction of both the Governments concerned and the shipowners.

### British View of Emergency

The necessity that the United States should put forth every effort to increase the number of oceangoing ships was emphasized in a statement made on Sept. 28 by the British Controller of Shipping, in the course of which he said:

The question the United States must face is whether, on the basis of the shipbuilding preparations she is now making, it will be possible for her to send any substantial force to France next Spring without such a drain on the world's shipping as will subtract just as much from the fighting strength of the other allies as her own forces will add.

The loss of shipping since the beginning of the ruthless U-boat war is now roughly equal to the total losses prior to that time. By next Spring Germany may be expected to destroy 200 vessels in excess of what are built in the meantime. Next Spring this year's harvest will be largely exhausted and the need of supplying Italy, France, and Great Britain will be largely increased. At the same moment the United States will need a large increase in vessels to transport its army and to maintain it.

What must be the program of the United States? It must be large enough to outbuild submarine destruction. Even if this means the building of 6,000,000 tons a year, which is three times the best the British have done, and five or six times what the United States has previously done, this is not impossible if the United States puts into it an effort comparable with the efforts the Allies put into creating their armies, navies, and munitions. To build 6,000,000 tons of shipping would require about 3,500,000 tons of steel, or less than 10 per cent. of her output. It would take not more than 500,000 men, the majority unskilled.

The task thus outlined is small compared with the effort put forth by the principal belligerents in other directions. Great Britain, for example, increased her army from 250,000 to over 5,000,000. She added 250,000 men to her navy and trebled it in size, while in munitions the British effort, whether measured in money, men, or material, has been greater than what is needed for an adequate American shipbuilding program. It would be the most incongruous thing in the history of warfare if the war, in which such immensely greater strength has been exerted in other directions, should have the issue decided by failure to solve the problem of building 6,000,000 tons of shipping a year in a country with such vast resources as the United States.

### The Shortage of Vessels

The predicament of the French Government in not being able to secure ships to convey large quantities of army supplies which were ready to be sent from America was described in a Washington dispatch of Oct. 3. Some of this enormous tonnage had been lying on American piers for more than a year, and the congestion, it was said, was increasing. Supplies ordered and paid for by the French Government were being sent by rail to the seaboard almost every day, but very little was getting across the Atlantic. The statement went on to say that after months of fruitless negotiations with the Shipping Board the French War Commission to the United States had applied to Secretary Baker for ships, and if that move failed an appeal to the President direct would be made. The Shipping Board's reply to the French Commission was that it could not move French material as well as supplies for the American expeditionary force in France. The urgency of the French demand arose from the fact that the supplies included steel for shells and nitrates to make explosives.

Japanese help in solving the shipping problem was the main question discussed by Viscount Ishii, head of the War Mission to the United States, and Secretary Lansing. Following Viscount Ishii's departure, a statement from a Japanese source showed that Japan could not furnish more ships. That nation, it was said, felt that it was already doing its share in the war and was providing its full quota of ships. One-third of Japan's total oceangoing tonnage is in European waters. This amounts to 300,000 tons. Japanese ships have also been sunk by the German submarines. Business in Japan is suffering from the scarcity of ships to carry goods between the Americas and Japan. At the same time efforts are being made to carry on the peacetime trade of England in the Indian Ocean and in the Pacific, between India, Australia, and Britain's other possessions, as well as China. Japan has also been the carrier for Russia between the United States and Vladivostok. Japanese industries are suffering from a great shortage of steel plates, especially her shipbuilding industry, for they are dependent now upon the United States for steel.

A way out of the difficulty—a way which would supply Japan with steel and divert Japanese ships to the Atlantic—was subsequently said to have been discovered as the result of further negotiations on the basis of reciprocal service.

## Exports Under a Drastic System of Control

No less far-reaching than any of the other war measures sanctioned by Congress during the special session is the large and varied group of regulations dealing with exports. The two acts of Congress which make possible this drastic system of Government control of our foreign commerce are known respectively as the Espionage act, approved June 15, and the Trading with the Enemy act, approved Oct. 6. Both cover a wider range of subjects than their titles indicate. The Espionage act was passed " to punish acts of interference with foreign relations, the neutrality and the foreign commerce of the United States, to punish espionage, and better enforce

the criminal laws of the United States, and for other purposes." Among the other purposes is to deal with the publication of seditious matter. The Trading with the Enemy act covers several of the same subjects as the Espionage act and extends powers already granted under that act.

Turning to the executive side, we find that in regard to foreign commerce a new and powerful arm of the Government has been created, first under the name of the Exports Administrative Board, and subsequently in its present form as the War Trade Board, with Vance McCormick in both cases as Chairman. The Board's first task was to enforce the section in the espionage law "making certain exports in time of war unlawful." Since the law became effective in June the President has issued a number of proclamations; but soon after the enactment of the Trading with the Enemy act on Oct 6, a new Executive order, issued on Oct. 14, reorganized practically the whole system on a much wider and more drastic basis.

### The War Trade Board

The War Trade Board consists of Vance McCormick, Chairman, representing the Secretary of State; Dr. Alonzo E. Taylor, representing the Secretary of Agriculture; Thomas D. Jones, representing the Secretary of Commerce; Beaver White, representing the Food Administrator; Frank C. Munson, representing the Shipping Board, and a representative of the Secretary of the Treasury. All but the Treasury representative were members of the Exports Administrative Board, whose work is now being done by the Bureau of Exports of the War Trade Board. The name of the Exports Council was changed to War Trade Council, with the Secretary of the Treasury and Chairman Hurley of the Shipping Board added to its membership, the Secretaries of State, Agriculture and Commerce and the Food Administrator. This body acts in an advisory capacity to the President and the War Trade Board.

An official statement accompanying the President's order explains that previous proclamations forbidding the export of various articles without a license are continued in full force and effect, but new licenses are now granted by the War Trade Board instead of by the Exports Administrative Board.

## The Trading With the Enemy Act

The Trading with the Enemy act makes it unlawful, under severe penalties, to trade without a license with any person who there is probable cause to believe is an enemy or ally of an enemy. The act provides that "trade" shall be deemed to mean:

(a) To pay, satisfy, compromise, or give security for the payment or satisfaction of any debt or obligation.

(b) To draw, accept, pay, present for acceptance or payment, or indorse any negotiable instrument or chose in action.

(c) To enter into, carry on, complete, or perform any contract, agreement, or obligation.

(d) To buy or sell, loan or extend credit, trade in, deal with, exchange, transmit, transfer, assign, or otherwise dispose of or receive any form of property.

(e) To have any form of business or commercial communication or intercourse with.

### Enemies Defined

Any person, no matter of what nationality, who resides within the territory of the German Empire or the territory of any of its allies or that occupied by their military forces is expressly made an "enemy" or "ally of enemy" by the act. Even citizens of the United States who have elected to remain within such territory are "enemies" or "allies of an enemy" within the provisions of the act. Further, any person not residing in the United States, of whatever nationality and wherever he resides, who is doing business within such territory is placed within the definition of "enemy" or "ally of enemy." So also is any corporation created by Germany or its allies. So also is any corporation created by any other nation than the United States and doing business within such territory. Further, for the purpose of this act, the Government of any nation with which the United States is at war or the ally of such nation is an "enemy" or "ally of enemy," and the act makes no restriction as to where the officer, official, agent, or agency may be located.

It is equally unlawful to trade with any person who is acting for an enemy, and it makes no difference what the nationality or what the residence of such person may be. On the other hand, in dealing with subjects of Germany who are resident in the United States, the mere fact of their nationality does not make them "enemies" within the meaning of this act.

The Trading with the Enemy act,

however, gives power to the President to grant licenses to trade with the enemy. The exercise of this power has been delegated by the President to the War Trade Board.

### Enemies in Domestic Trade

The Trading with the Enemy act provides that a person who is " an enemy" or " ally of enemy," doing business within the United States, may apply for a license to continue to do business in the United States. The main application of these provisions will be to German or ally of German concerns which are doing business in the United States through branch houses or agents. Insurance companies were previously dealt with in the President's proclamation of July 13, 1917. It is not necessary, however, for a German subject or the subject of an ally of Germany who is resident in this country to apply for a license unless for some other reason he falls within the definition of " enemy " or " ally of enemy." No change of name by an enemy is permitted except by license.

The Trading with the Enemy act prohibits and imposes severe penalties on communicating with the enemy, but licenses may be granted for relief from the various communications.

The act contains various provisions as to the application for patents by citizens of the United States in enemy countries during the war, and for the use in the United States by citizens of the United States of enemy-held patents during the war, and also for the suspension of information as to certain patent applications made in the United States, secrecy as to which is necessary for military reasons. The Federal Trade Commission deals with all these matters.

### Seizing Enemy Property

Among the most important and far-reaching of the provisions of the Trading with the Enemy act are those dealing with the taking over by the United States Government of the custody and control of " enemy " property within the United States.

Any person in the United States holding any property for an " enemy " must report the fact to the Alien Property Custodian. The Alien Property Custodian may require a transfer to himself of any property held for or on behalf of an " enemy " or the payment of any money owed to an " enemy " by a person in the United States. Any person in the United States so holding any property or so owning any money may transfer such property or pay such money to the Alien Property Custodian with his consent.

### Control Over Foreign Exchange

The President by his Executive order committed to the Secretary of the Treasury the executive administration of the broad powers conferred by the act as to the prohibition and regulation of transfer between the United States and foreign countries of coin, currency, bullion, credits, and securities. The Secretary of the Treasury, with the assistance of the Federal Reserve Banks, passes on applications for leave to export bullion, coin, and currency.

The President created a Censorship Board to administer regulations as to the censorship of cable, telegraph, and mail communications between the United States and foreign countries. This board is composed of representatives of the Postmaster General, of the Secretary of War, of the Secretary of the Navy, of the War Trade Board, and of the Chairman of the Committee on Public Information.

The Trading with the Enemy act provides that every paper printed in a foreign language shall furnish translations to the Postmaster General of the matter concerning the war printed by it, unless a permit to omit doing so is granted to it.

The act provides that it shall be unlawful for any person without a license to transport or attempt to transport into or from the United States, or for any American vessel to transport in any part of the world any citizen of an enemy or ally of an enemy nation. The administration of this provision is vested in the State Department.

Collectors of Customs are given the right to refuse clearance to vessels which are transporting cargo in violation of the provisions of the Trading with the Enemy act. Power to review such refusal of clearance by the Collector is vested in the Secretary of Commerce.

# The Press Under Post Office Censorship

Although Congress emphatically refused to permit the establishment of a press censorship when the Espionage bill was under discussion, far-reaching powers have been conferred upon the Postmaster General by a clause in the Trading with the Enemy act. The section in question reads:

Any print, newspaper, or publication in any foreign language which does not conform to the provisions of this section is hereby declared to be non-mailable, and it shall be unlawful for any person, firm, corporation, or association to transport, carry, or otherwise publish or distribute the same, *or to transport, carry, or otherwise publish or distribute any matter which is made non-mailable by the provisions of the act relating to espionage, approved June 15, 1917.*

Section 3 of the Espionage act, referred to in this clause as defining non-mailable matter, reads:

Whoever, when the United States is at war, shall willfully make or convey false reports or false statements, with intent to interfere with the operation or success of the military or naval forces of the United States or to promote the success of its enemies; and whoever, when the United States is at war, shall willfully cause or attempt to cause insubordination, disloyalty, mutiny, or refusal of duty, in the military or naval forces of the United States, or shall willfully obstruct the recruiting or enlistment service of the United States, to the injury of the service or of the United States, shall be punished by a fine of not more than $10,000 or imprisonment for not more than twenty years, or both.

The chief opponent of press control by the Postmaster General was Senator Norris of Nebraska, who pointed out that the new provision took away from a publisher his right to fight an order in the courts until after it was useless to fight; that it vested in the Postmaster General—an administrative officer of the Government—the power to adjudge a publisher guilty in advance of trial by any judicial tribunal, and to destroy his business through a mere edict. The Postmaster General had already put out of business thirty-eight or forty publications, under the provisions of the Espionage act, and not one of these publishers had been arrested for violation of

that act. Yet, Senator Norris contended, if the Postmaster General was within his right every one of these men was guilty of a crime, and should be punished by imprisonment.

## Statement by Mr. Burleson

Publications need not fear suppression under the new censorship provision, Postmaster General Burleson explained in an interview on Oct. 9, unless they transgress the bounds of legitimate criticism of the President, the Administration, the army, the navy, or the conduct of the war. Mr. Burleson continued:

We shall take great care not to let criticism which is personally or politically offensive to the Administration affect our action. But if newspapers go so far as to impugn the motives of the Government, and thus encourage insubordination, they will be dealt with severely.

For instance, papers may not say that the Government is controlled by Wall Street or munition manufacturers, or any other special interests. Publication of any news calculated to urge the people to violate law would be considered grounds for drastic action. We will not tolerate campaigns against conscription, enlistments, sale of securities, or revenue collections. We will not permit the publication or circulation of anything hampering the war's prosecution or attacking improperly our allies.

Mr. Burleson explained that the policy of the foreign-language newspapers would be judged by their past utterances and not by newly announced intentions. "We have files of these papers, and "whether we license them or not depends "on our inspection of the files," he said. German-language newspapers not licensed would be required to publish English translations. No Socialist paper would be barred from the mails, Mr. Burleson said, unless it contained treasonable or seditious matter. "The trou-"ble," he added, "is that most Socialist "papers do contain this matter."

That Socialist newspapers did oppose the war was admitted by Morris Hillquit, when he appeared at the hearing at the Post Office Department in Washington on Oct. 15 on behalf of The New York Call, which had been summoned to show cause why it should not be deprived of its mail privileges.

### President Wilson's Attitude

President Wilson's views are indicated in a letter to Max Eastman, editor of The Masses, a Socialist magazine which has been declared non-mailable. The President wrote:

I think that a time of war must be regarded as wholly exceptional, and that it is legitimate to regard things which would in ordinary circumstances be innocent as very dangerous to the public welfare, but

the line is manifestly exceedingly hard to draw, and I cannot say that I have any confidence that I know how to draw it.

I can only say that a line must be drawn, and that we are trying, it may be clumsily, but genuinely, to draw it without fear or favor or prejudice.

Many Socialist and pacifist publications have already been barred from the mails and some have in consequence ceased to exist, the most important of such defunct papers being The American Socialist, published from the headquarters of the Socialist Party.

# Food Administration at Work

The establishment of a new Government department to regulate and control food supplies during the war was recorded in the September number of CURRENT HISTORY MAGAZINE, (pp. 389-392.) Since then the Food Administration, under Herbert C. Hoover, has taken important steps in the direction of regulating prices and placing distribution upon a more economical basis.

The basic price of the 1917 wheat crop was fixed by President Wilson on Aug. 30 at $2.20 a bushel, as recommended by the Price Fixing Commission, headed by Dr. H. A. Garfield. The price was based on Chicago delivery and was the figure at which the Food Administration decided to buy supplies of what is known as No. 1 Northern Spring wheat for the United States and its allies. It was estimated that under the schedule of prices flour could be produced at about $9 a barrel and that there ought accordingly to be a slight decrease in the price of bread. The $2.20 basis was 20 cents higher than that named for the 1918 crop in the Food Control act. In concluding his statement, President Wilson said:

Mr. Hoover, at his express wish, has taken no part in the deliberations of the committee on whose recommendation I determine the Government's fair price, nor has he in any way intimated an opinion regarding that price.

### Government Buying Wheat

The Government, through the $50,000,-000 United States Grain Corporation of the Food Administration, made its first appearance in the wheat market on Sept. 5, and the principle of Government control had its first application in regard to foodstuffs. Government agents at the central zone offices throughout the country went into the market at the opening of the business day and took possession of the wheat in elevators and terminals, buying at the basic price of $2.20 a bushel. From that day onward every bushel of wheat in the country has passed and continues to pass through the Grain Corporation from the elevators and terminals to the mills. The Government is buying only on warehouse receipts, and no contracts are made for future delivery. The men who went into the market for the first time on Sept. 5 found everything ready for their coming, and, it is said, there was no friction nor the slipping of a single cog when the machinery of the Federal control started. The wheat was sold at an advance of 1 per cent., to cover the cost of handling. Not a single fraction of a cent goes into the profit side of the books of the Food Administration. The control of the Food Administration over prices begins in the elevators and ends with the sale of flour at a 25-cent-a-barrel profit by the millers. The food law allows millers to keep only a thirty-day stock on hand, a measure to prevent hoarding.

To save the millions of bushels of grain used annually in the manufacture of whisky, the provision of the Food Control act which prohibits the making or importation of distilled liquors was made effective on Sept. 8. Of the 100,-000,000 bushels of grain which formerly

AMERICAN TROOPS IN TRAINING "SOMEWHERE IN FRANCE"

Men of the American Expeditionary Force Learning the Art of Throwing Hand Grenades, at Their Training Camp in France

UNITED STATES SOLDIERS WEARING STEEL HELMETS

The Fact That the Men of the American Army in France Are Beginning to Wear Steel Helmets Is Another Evidence of Their Becoming Part of the Fighting Forces of the Grand Alliance

went to the distilleries each year, it is calculated that about 40,000,000 were used to make whisky and other distilled liquors. A large number of small distilleries were forced to close down as the result of the prohibition, but others producing alcohol for commercial and medicinal uses continued in operation. The whisky drinker is not likely to be deprived of his drink for some time yet, however, because it is estimated that about 230,000,000 gallons had accumulated in the bonded warehouses, liquor stores, and saloons. This is enough to provide for two years' average consumption.

## Reducing Sugar Consumption

The sugar industry was taken over by the Government on Sept. 15, when the President issued a proclamation placing all branches of the business under a strict licensing system as from Oct. 1. This action was taken to enforce agreements entered into by the Food Administrator and the beet and cane sugar men. Mr. Hoover fixed the price at $7.25 a hundredweight for beet sugar at refining centres. A saving of many millions of dollars to the country's consumers is anticipated as a result of the new system.

The necessity of economy in the use of sugar was urged by Mr. Hoover in a statement issued on Sept. 23 apropos of a request from the French Government for supplies. The statement read:

We have received a request from the French Government that we allow them to export from the United States 100,000 tons of sugar during the next month, and probably more at a later period. Our own situation is that we have just sufficient sugar to maintain our normal consumption until the first of January, when the new West Indian crop becomes available to all.

Our consumption is at the rate of ninety pounds per person per year—a little under four ounces per day per person. The French people are on a ration of sugar equal to only twenty-one pounds per annum per person—or at the rate of less than one ounce per day per person—a little more than the weight of a silver dollar each day. The English and Italian rations are also not over one ounce per day.

The French people will be entirely without sugar for over two months if we refuse to part with enough from our stocks to keep them supplied with even this small allowance, as it is not available from any other quarter.

Sugar even to a greater amount than the French ration is a human necessity. If our people will reduce by one-third their purchases and consumption of candy and of sugar for other uses than preserving fruit, which we do not wish to interfere with, we can save the French situation.

## Controlling All Foodstuffs

The most sweeping measure of food regulation was that enacted by President Wilson on Oct. 10 when he issued a proclamation setting forth the terms under which the Food Administration, after Nov. 1, would control the manufacture, storage, importation, and distribution of practically all of the essential foodstuffs. The proclamation provided that a license, issued under rules and regulations governing the conduct of the business of the licensee, must be secured on or before Nov. 1 by individuals and corporations with certain exceptions. The proclamation concluded with a warning that any violation of the regulations would be subjected to the penalties provided for in the Food Control act.

# America's Military Progress During the Month

THE new armies of the United States are not being subjected to rush and hustle, but are growing into effective fighting forces in a thoroughly purposeful manner, so that when they make their appearance on the firing line they will be capable of a maximum of effort. The regular army on Oct. 12, 1917, had to its credit 226,918 new enlistments, that is, over 43,000 more than the number originally required to bring it up to war strength. On the other hand, as certain National Guard divisions had not reached full strength, their ranks had to be filled up from the men drafted into the National Army. Orders were accordingly issued by the War Department on Oct. 13 for the transfer of about 75,400 drafted men to bring six National Guard divisions up to war strength. The orders also involved the transfer of about 55,000 drafted men from Eastern and Middle Western cantonments to Camps Gordon and Pike. Altogether about 130,400 men were redistributed and regrouped to fill up tactical units. About 250,000 men of the draft army had not yet been mobilized because the cantonments were not ready in every particular.

The training work mapped out by the War Department for National Guard and National Army divisions before they are regarded as ready for duty abroad is based on a sixteen weeks' course of the most intensive kind of work in the open, varied with lectures by American and allied officers who are experts in modern warfare. Great stress is laid upon the necessity for night training. Trench raiding, scouting, trench building, and operations of all kinds which may be called for in actual combat are duplicated at the camps through the night hours. Target practice runs through the entire course, and the schedules call for forty hours' training each week. A striking feature of the program is the fact that practically the entire period of sixteen weeks is devoted to training individuals, platoons, and companies. Brigade, divisional, and even regimental exercises are reserved for a later period with some minor exceptions during the last weeks

Details of the Government system of insuring members of the nation's fighting forces were made public on Oct. 14 by the War Risk Insurance Bureau of the Treasury Department. The insurance law is applicable to the entire military and naval establishment of the United States, including army, navy, Marine Corps, Coast Guard, Naval Reserves, nurses, and all others serving with the army and navy. Provision is made for family allowances, for re-education of wounded and cripples, and for compensation in case of death or injury.

The specimen contract made public by the Secretary of the Treasury is based on age 25 and is for $5,000. The premium is $3.30 a month. The insurance is payable in installments of $28.75 per month in case of death or total disability.

The table given for a $5,000 policy begins with a monthly premium of $3.15 at the ages of 15, 16, and 17 years, increases to $3.20 a month for the ages of 18, 19, and 20; to $3.25 a month for the ages of 21, 22, and 23; with progressive increases for ages above those given. The minimum amount of insurance is $1,000, the maximum $10,000. The monthly premium for a $10,000 policy at age 25 is only $6.60.

President Wilson on Oct. 8 signed commissions as Generals for Major Gen. Tasker H. Bliss, who has succeeded Major Gen. Hugh L. Scott as army Chief of Staff, and for Major Gen. John J. Pershing, commanding the American forces in France. Though both officers have equal rank, General Bliss takes precedence by virtue of his position as the directing head of the entire army organization. The new grade carries a salary of $10,000 a year, an increase of $2,000 over the pay of Major General. Only four other officers of the United States Army have held the rank and title of General. They were Washington, Grant, Sherman, and Sheridan. The grade of Lieutenant General also was revived by Congress, the rank to be given commanders of army corps. Besides the new commissions for Generals Bliss and Pershing, the President signed commissions of army bureau chiefs to be Major Generals and commissions of many new Brigadier Generals whose nominations were confirmed by the Senate in the closing hours of the special session of Congress.

More than 100,000 American officers and soldiers are now in France under General Pershing's command. Training is proceeding to the utmost satisfaction of the military authorities.

## Increased Activity of the Navy

Reports from Admiral Sims, the American naval commander in Europe, show that every type of naval craft from small launches to powerful warships is now included in his force. The most recent additions were Coast Guard cutters and fishing vessels for mine-sweeping work. American naval vessels, including destroyers, are doing convoy work in the Mediterranean as well as in and near British and French waters.

Mr. Daniels, Secretary of the Navy, on

Oct. 9 awarded contracts to five shipbuilding companies for the construction of $350,000,000 worth of destroyers. This is the biggest contract for vessels of this type ever awarded by any Government. With the award of these contracts the war construction program of the American Navy was brought to a total of 787 vessels, including all types, from superdreadnoughts to submarine chasers. The total cost of the program is estimated at $1,150,400,000.

# Worldwide Embargo Against Germany

## Neighboring Neutrals Affected

THE first step toward an embargo was the issue of the President's proclamation on July 9 prohibiting exports of coal, food, grains, meats, steel, and other products except by license. In an explanatory statement the President said that his purpose was " the amelioration of food conditions which have arisen or are likely to arise in our own country before new crops are harvested." But in his next proclamation, dated Aug. 27, the President had a further object in view, namely, to prevent neutral nations from re-exporting foods into Germany from the United States. Those neutrals were no longer to get supplies which " either directly or indirectly " might be made the " occasion of benefit to the enemy." Sweeping in its terms, the proclamation placed under control of the Export Council all articles of commerce, so far as the neutrals of Europe were concerned. The President, in a supplemental statement, pointed out that it was obviously necessary to exercise a closer supervision of trade with these Governments than with others. Coin, bullion, currency, and evidences of debt were included in the restricted list affecting the European neutrals and enemy countries. This was to prevent money going to neutrals upon whom Germany, offering coal and other essential supplies in return, made demands for gold.

Enemy countries and European neutrals adjacent to Germany and its allies were treated in a separate section of the proclamation. Another section directed that certain commodities be added to the list of articles already under export control to all countries of the world, including the allies of America. The most notable of these were cotton, sugar, and lumber.

### Strict Rationing of Neutrals

The fact that the President treated the position of the European neutrals, such as the Scandinavian countries, Holland, Spain, and Switzerland, in a separate section, and cut off from them, except under special license, practically every commodity from the United States, was regarded here as the initiation of a policy of strict rationing on a basis that would leave for Germany no hope of help from those quarters.

An embargo on the exportation of coin, bullion, and currency, except by license of the Secretary of the Treasury, by advice of the Federal Reserve Board, was proclaimed by President Wilson on Sept. 7. This step was made necessary by heavy withdrawals of gold by Japan, Mexico, and Spain. For some time previously Treasury and Reserve Board officials had been viewing with concern the tendency of gold to flow away from the United States, a movement which started with the financing of the Allies. Within the five weeks' period ended Aug. 17 exports totaled $73,000,000, or more than four times the total of imports. The movement had been too recent, however, to affect substantially the great volume of gold in this country. The stock was then $3,000,000,000, of which approximately 40 per cent. had been imported since January, 1915. Imports of gold during the current year were more than

$538,000,000. Exports were estimated to have approximated $300,000,000, or more than twice as much as the volume exported altogether in 1916. Much of this gold went to Japan, which had a balance of trade against the United States, and recently exportations to Spain had assumed large proportions.

## Arrangement with Canada

The Exports Administrative Board, co-operating with the Canadian Food Controller, announced on Sept. 14 that at the request of the United States Food Administrator all exports of wheat, wheat flour, butter, and sugar to Canada and Newfoundland would require an individual license for each shipment. The purpose of the order, it was explained, was to provide means of closer co-operation between the American and Canadian Food Administrators and to put the United States in position to conserve its supplies if shortages appear likely. Shipments of food in small quantities, however, were permitted to both Canada and Mexico. Dr. H. A. Garfield, the Fuel Administrator, requested the Exports Administrative Board to permit no more coal to be shipped from the country except under license restrictions, and asked that no licenses be granted unless they were approved by the Fuel Administration.

## Tightening the Food Embargo

To tighten up restrictions previously made the Exports Administrative Board published on Sept. 16 a conservation list which included wheat, wheat flour, sugar, steel, iron, and many materials needed for the manufacture of explosives, announcing at the same time that the export of these commodities would be " practically prohibited " for the present. The ruling was accepted generally as definite notice to most of the northern neutrals of Europe that for some time to come they would have to get along without American wheat, and that at no time during the war period would shipments be made to them except on the strictest rationing basis, and only after obtaining satisfactory guarantees.

A modification of previous orders was made by the board on Oct. 2, when it issued a long list of American commodities which it was decided might be exported to other nations, with the exception of Germany, her allies, and the neutral countries contiguous to Germany, without obtaining a license. There were about 600 articles in the list. The decision did not affect wheat and other vital cereals, the more important shipbuilding steel, meats, sugar, raw cotton, concentrated fodder, coal, fuel oils, and other products looked upon as essential to this nation's welfare. Neither did it disturb the complete embargo declared against Holland, Sweden, Norway, and Denmark, the nations accused of helping to feed Germany.

The London Gazette of Oct. 2 printed a p oclamation by the British Government prohibiting the exportation to Sweden, Norway, Denmark, and the Netherlands of all articles, except printed matter of all descriptions and personal effects accompanied by their owners. The action in this worldwide embargo was taken at the instance of the United States, which insisted that Great Britain so modify its regulations as to prevent nullification of the American embargo.

## Ban on Bunker Coal

A final step to prevent Germany, or northern neutrals of Europe, from obtaining products of the United States, Canada, Mexico, or any of the South American nations that might aid the enemy, was taken on Oct. 4 by the Exports Administrative Board, by placing a ban upon bunker coal. In an official statement it was asserted that the United States had failed to obtain the definite information it had asked of northern neutrals concerning their actual needs for home consumption, and the status of the traffic in which they had engaged with the Central Powers. It was stated further that the Administration had adopted as definite the policy that it would in no way contribute to trade with these neutrals which " will undoubtedly accrue to the benefit of the enemy."

The ban on bunker coal was adopted with the approval of all the Allies. It followed closely Great Britain's declaration of a complete embargo against the Northern European neutrals, which was designed to strengthen the embargo already put into force by the United States. Latin-American countries were now the only nations left in the world in which Germany had a chance to obtain foodstuffs and other necessaries through the border countries. With this source cut off, allied statesmen felt that the ring around Germany was drawn so tightly that the economic pressure, reinforcing the Allies' ever-growing military superiority, would make the German people see their cause is hopeless.

## Plight of European Neutrals

The American embargo was viewed with considerable alarm and no little resentment by the neutral nations of Northern Europe. The prohibition of exports and the withholding of bunker coal licenses resulted in the complete paralysis of Dutch and Scandinavian shipping in the transatlantic trade. Passenger and freight vessels to the number of 136, representing 750,000 gross tons and worth $150,000,000, were detained for many weeks in Atlantic ports, most of them in New York Harbor. Included in the total were fifty Dutch freighters, which were loaded with wheat in August, fifty-three Norwegian freighters, besides Danish and Swedish vessels. Some of them were tied up as early as July. As has already been mentioned, the reason for holding up these vessels arose from the determination of the United States Government to prevent supplies reaching Germany through contiguous neutral countries. According to a statement, dated Aug. 20, by the Intelligence Bureau of Diplomatic Information of one of the allied Governments, the excess in 1916 of Dutch food imports over home consumption was sufficient to provision 1,200,000 soldiers for one year.

An agreement entered into between Holland and Germany, fixing the percentage of exports from the Netherlands to the Central Powers, was, according to an announcement on Sept. 29, refused recognition by the United States, and a translation of documents bearing upon the agreement, which had come into the possession of the Government, was made public. The negotiations, which took place in September, 1916, showed that Germany demanded:

At least 75 per cent. of the total exports of butter.

At least 66 2-3 per cent. of the total exports of export cheese.

At least as much pig meat and sausage as was exported to other countries, including exports for the relief of sufferers in Belgium.

At least the same amount of live cattle or meats as was exported to other countries.

At least 75 per cent. of the total export of vegetables.

At least 75 per cent. of the total exports of fruit and marmalade.

At least 75 per cent. of the total exports of fresh and preserved chickens' and ducks' eggs.

At least half the total exports of flax.

To enforce these demands Germany threatened to cut off exports of coal into Holland, thereby causing the closing down of factories and the absence of heat in the houses of many of the people. Holland was thus still in the crossfire of embargoes on essentials coming from both belligerent groups. A further step toward bringing pressure to bear upon Holland was the refusal of the United States Government to permit Dutch ships to leave America unless they guaranteed to return to the jurisdiction of the United States. The Nederland Steamship Company, on Oct. 9, announced that it had acquiesced in the American conditions for granting bunkering facilities, which provide that the company's vessels for every voyage between Java and the United States should make a return voyage with cargoes exclusively American or partly Canadian.

The most drastic action by the United States was foreshadowed at this time by the statement in New York shipping circles that if America's allies were badly in need of supplies through lack of tonnage the United States Government probably would sequester Dutch steamships in American ports for the period of the war and afterward pay for them whatever sum a court awarded. The Dutch steamship companies in Holland did not wish to charter the vessels to the United States Government because they said the tonnage was needed to take foodstuffs to Holland. At this writing (Oct. 18) the fate of these ships has not been decided.

# Financing America's War Needs

## Appropriations of Sixteen Billions

RECORD-BREAKING appropriations were made during the special session of Congress to finance the nation's war program. Beginning with a general deficiency appropriation bill for $163,000,000, of which $100,000,000 was to be spent on national security and defense, Congress gradually piled up liabilities for over eleven billion dollars. Actually, the amount of the appropriations, made for the fiscal year ending June 30, 1918, was $16,901,966,814, but of this sum $7,000,000,000 represents loans to the Allies, which are repayable. The following table shows how appropriations are distributed:

| | |
|---|---:|
| Expenses incident to the Sixty-fifth Congress, first session | $68,020.00 |
| Loans to the Allies under act of April 24, 1917 | 3,000,000,000.00 |
| Expenses of preparation and issue of bonds and certificates of indebtedness under act of April 24, 1917 | 7,063,945.46 |
| Bureau of War Risk Insurance, cost of insuring vessels and their cargoes, &c. | 45,150,000.00 |
| Urgent deficiency act for the military and naval establishments | 3,281,094,541.60 |
| Increase of signal corps of the army, including purchase, operation, &c., of airships | 640,000,000.00 |
| Expenses under act to encourage production, conserve the supply, and control distribution of food products and fuel | 162,500,000.00 |
| Expenses under the act to stimulate agriculture and facilitate the distribution of agricultural products | 11,346,400.00 |
| Additional loans to the Allies under act of Sept. 24, 1917. | 4,000,000,000.00 |
| Expenses of preparation and issue of bonds, certificates of indebtedness, and war-saving certificates | 21,377,890.92 |
| Expenses under the act establishing a military and naval family allowance, compensation, and insurance fund for the benefit of soldiers and sailors and their families | 176,250,000.00 |
| Expenses under the act to define, regulate, and punish trading with the enemy. | 450,000.00 |
| Urgent deficiency act for the fiscal year 1918 and prior years, on account of war expenses | 5,356,666,016.93 |
| Interest on bonds and certificates (estimated) | 200,000,000.00 |
| | |
| Total appropriations, Sixty-fifth Congress, first session | $16,901,966,814.91 |

To this total must be added the appropriation made during the second session of the Sixty-fourth Congress, amounting to $1,977,210,200, and the following contract authorizations for the fiscal year ending June 30, 1918:

| | |
|---|---:|
| Fortification | $5,250,000.00 |
| Naval | 86,145,532.00 |
| Sundry civil | 900,000.00 |
| Urgent deficiency appropriation act of June 24, 1917 | 16,550,000.00 |
| Urgent deficiency appropriation act of October, 1917 | 2,401,458,393.50 |
| Act to authorize the construction of a building for the use of the Treasury Department | 1,250,000.00 |
| | |
| Total contract author'z'ns. | $2,511,553,925.50 |

We thus get the following aggregates:

| | |
|---|---:|
| Appropriations, Sixty-fourth Congress, second session | $1,977,210.200.05 |
| Appropriations, Sixty-fifth Congress, first session | 16,901,966,814.91 |
| Contract authorizations, fiscal year 1918 | 2,511,553,925.50 |
| | |
| Grand total | $21,390,730,940.46 |

By deducting the $7,000,000,000 lent to the Allies, we find that the cost of the war and the ordinary expenses of the Government for the year amount to $14,390,730,940.

These expenditures are being met from three sources: (1) Revenues under existing laws and Post Office receipts, (2) new taxation, (3) and loans. Under the first two heads the total revenue is estimated at $4,193,370,000, of which $2,500,000,000 will come from the war taxation measures passed during the special session. An act of Congress of Sept. 24, 1917, authorizes an additional issue of bonds of $3,538,945,460, thus leaving $3,906,861,554 which is covered neither by taxation nor by loans, and which will have to be provided for during the next session of Congress.

Senator Smoot in an analysis of the Government's finances shows that the United States is raising 36 per cent. of its expenditure by direct taxation, while the percentage raised by direct taxation in other countries after three years are the following: Great Britain, 26; France, 14½; Germany, nearly 15, and Canada, 8.

## Drastic Income Taxation

The War Revenue bill was the last important measure disposed of by Congress before the conclusion of the special session. It had been under discussion nearly four months and imposes taxation on a drastic and comprehensive scale. An additional tax and a surtax are levied on the incomes of all married men over $2,000 a year and on those of unmarried men over $1,000 a year. Grouping together the old tax, the new tax, and the surtax, the levy on a number of typical incomes of married men will work out as follows:

| | | | |
|---|---|---|---|
| $3,000 | $20 | $15,000 | $730 |
| 4,000 | 40 | 20,000 | 1,180 |
| 5,000 | 80 | 25,000 | 1,780 |
| 6,000 | 130 | 50,000 | 5,180 |
| 7,000 | 180 | 100,000 | 16,280 |
| 8,000 | 235 | 500,000 | 192,680 |
| 9,000 | 295 | 1,000,000 | 475,180 |
| 10,000 | 355 | | |

The most striking feature of the new taxation is the levy on profits. A graduated tax of from 20 to 60 per cent. on excess profits of corporations, partnerships, and individuals will be levied on a basis of invested capital, as compared with invested capital of the three years 1911-1913. The graduated excess profit rates are 20 per cent. of excess profits not in excess of 15 per cent. of the invested capital for the taxable year; 25 per cent. on profits in excess of 15 per cent. and not over 20 per cent. of such capital; 35 per cent. on excess over 20 and under 25 per cent. of capital; 45 per cent. on over 25 per cent. and under 33 per cent. of capital, and a maximum of 60 per cent. on profits in excess of 33 per cent. of such capital.

The War Revenue act also contains new imposts on tobacco, liquor, insurance, transportation, amusements, (theatre tickets, &c.,) and club dues, cosmetics, perfumes, and proprietary medicines, and increases postal rates. Letters, except drop letters, will require three cents postage; while increases are made on second-class mail matter, the latter not to go into effect until July, 1918, and thereafter in an annual progressive scale.

## Second Liberty Loan

Secretary McAdoo announced on Sept. 27 the terms and details of the second issue of Liberty Loan bonds. The announcement read in part:

With the approval of the President, I have determined to offer on Oct. 1, 1917, three billion or more dollars of United States of America 4 per cent. convertible gold bonds, due on Nov. 15, 1942, and subject to redemption at the option of the United States at par and accrued interest on and after Nov. 15, 1927. The bonds will bear interest from Nov. 15, 1917.

The exact amount of bonds to be issued under this offering will depend on the amount of subscriptions received. It is, of course, to be expected that subscriptions considerably in excess of $3,000,000,-000 will be received, and in that event the right is reserved to allot bonds in excess of $3,000,000,000 to the extent of not over one-half of the sum by which the subscriptions received exceed $3,000,000,000. In other words, if subscriptions to the extent of $5,000,000,000 are filed $4,000,000,-000 of bonds may be allotted.

The bonds will be offered as before at par and accrued interest and will be in denominations of $50 and multiples thereof.

The bonds shall be exempt, both as to principal and interest, from all taxation now or hereafter imposed by the United States, any State, or any of the possessions of the United States, or by any local taxing authority, except (a) estate or inheritance taxes, and (b) graduated additional income taxes, commonly known as surtaxes, and excess profits and war profits taxes, now or hereafter imposed by the United States, upon the income or profits of individuals, partnerships, associations, or corporations. The interest on an amount of bonds and certificates authorized by said act, the principal of which does not exceed in the aggregate $5,000, owned by any individual, partnership, association, or corporation, shall be exempt from the taxes provided for in clause (b) above.

If a new issue at a higher rate of interest is offered, holders of these bonds will have the right to convert.

### A Financier's War Service

Frank A. Vanderlip, President of the National City Bank of New York, the largest national bank in the United States, entered the service of the Government on Sept. 25 for the purpose of floating the $2,000,000,000 certificates of indebtedness authorized by Congress on April 24 in addition to the $5,000,000,000 of war bonds then authorized to provide $3,000,000,000 to be loaned to the Allies and $2,000,000,000 to be employed in our own projects of military preparedness. Mr. Vanderlip's salary is one dollar a year. He is spending four days a week at Washington, and while absent from New York is keeping in touch with his office in the National City Bank continually by telephone. As Assistant Secretary of the Treasury under Secretary Gage, Mr. Vanderlip had direct charge of placing on the market the bonds required to build up the United States Army and Navy, especially for the Spanish war. For several months Russell C. Leffinwell, a banking lawyer of New York and one of Mr. Vanderlip's aids in the conduct of the National City Bank, has had an office in the Treasury Department Building, where he has been a constant adviser of Secretary McAdoo in shaping the terms and conditions of the first two issues of war bonds. Mr. Leffinwell remains on duty in the Treasury Department, and is co-operating with Mr. Vanderlip in the work of selling not only the certificates of indebtedness, but the bonds of the Second Liberty Loan. In answering Secretary McAdoo's request for his aid Mr. Vanderlip surrendered for the period of the war not only active direction of his office as President of the National City Bank, but his active connections with the American International Corporation and the International Mercantile Marine Company, in both of which he was an influential factor.

# Latin America and the War

## Many Republics, Following the Lead of the United States, Have Broken With Germany

COSTA RICA formally severed diplomatic relations with Germany Sept. 21, 1917. Passports were handed to the diplomatic and Consular representatives of Germany at San José, and the Costa Rican delegation and Consuls of Germany were recalled. President Tinico is reported to have discovered that German residents had joined with the former President, Gonzalès, in conspiring against the Government. German residents at Costa Rican ports were interned.

On Oct. 6 the Peruvian Government handed his passports to Dr. Perl, the German Minister, the Peruvian Congress by a vote of 105 to 6 having passed a resolution presented by the Minister of Foreign Affairs providing for a rupture of diplomatic relations. Prior to this action efforts were made to blow up the interned German steamships in the harbor of Callao, the seaport of Lima; it was believed that the Germans attempted to wreck the vessels to prevent their falling into the hands of the Allies. On Oct. 10 the British and United States Governments were notified by the Peruvian Foreign Office that the use of Peruvian ports was extended to their war vessels. This action opened to the Allies practically the entire coast of South America without the usual restrictions of neutrality—except the ports of Argentina and Colombia.

The Republic of Ecuador, on Oct. 8, took a step tantamount to a severance of relations with Germany by announcing that the German Minister, Dr. Perl, who had been handed his passports by Peru, would not be officially received by the Ecuadorean Government in case he attempted to come to Quito.

Uruguay officially broke relations with Germany on Oct. 7 by decree of the President, and all functionaries of the republic were ordered to withdraw from German territory. The Chamber of Deputies voted in favor of the rupture by 74 to 23. The President of Uruguay previously—on June 20—had issued an order announcing that "no American country which, in defense of its own rights, should find itself in a state of war with nations of other continents, will be treated as a belligerent." President Viera, in his message to the Parliament, declared that the Uruguayan Government had not received any direct offense from Germany, but that it was necessary to espouse the cause of the defenders of justice, democracy, and small nationalities.

Uruguay, with other neutrals, has been a sufferer from Germany's U-boat warfare and other actions in disregard of international rights. In a note to the United States Government on April 14 the Montevideo Government said it did not recognize Germany's unrestricted warfare, and did recognize that the action of the United States in declaring war was a proper answer to Germany's actions.

Uruguay, on May 1, sent a note to London and Paris, asking for information as to the sinking of the Gorizia, a Uruguayan ship, and later made a protest to Germany. In May it joined in the suggestion for concentrated action by South American countries toward Germany. On Sept. 14 the Uruguayan Government, in a note to Argentina, approved the action of the Buenos Aires Government in handing his passports to Count von Luxburg.

The following German ships interned at Montevideo were seized by the Uruguayan Government:

| Vessel. | Gross Tonnage. | When Built. | Owners. |
|---|---|---|---|
| Bahia | 4,817 | 1898 | H. Süd-Amerika |
| Harzburg | 4,677 | 1907 | Hansa Line |
| Mera | 4,797 | 1901 | Kosmos Line |
| Polynesia | 6,022 | 1904 | Hamburg-Amerika |
| Salatis | 4,764 | 1906 | Kosmos Line |
| Silvia | 6,580 | 1900 | Hamburg-Amerika |
| Thuringia | 6,152 | 1904 | Hamburg-Amerika |
| Wiegand | 4,849 | 1911 | Roland Line |

Total ton'ge. 42,658

President Irigoyen of Argentina up to Oct. 18 had succeeded in maintaining his country's neutrality, notwithstanding the vote of both houses of Congress in favor of a rupture in relations. The Argentine Foreign Minister announced on Oct. 9 that relations with Germany would not be broken so long as Germany fulfills its latest pledge, made early in October, "to recognize the Argentine flag and respect the nation and people." Feeling ran high throughout Argentina, and the country was almost in a state of civil war owing to bitter conflicts between the pro-war and neutrality factions. A nationwide strike on the railways was a serious cause of disturbance and produced a crisis which was not allayed until the demands of the strikers were practically granted.

The action of Uruguay and the hesitation of Argentina created some friction between the two republics, which was aggravated by the following statement, said to have been made by the Foreign Minister of Uruguay, in urging the Uruguayan Congress to break off relations with Germany:

Uruguay, as a small nation between two great ones, must seek a balance of force to resist the possible hegemony of Argentina, with which nation we still have questions which are not settled definitely. This balance consists in bringing closer together Brazil and the States of our connection with the great States of the present conflict so that it will make impossible an attack on Uruguayan sovereignty without an immediate reverberation throughout the American Continent.

The unsettled questions between Uruguay and Argentina concern the River Plate. Argentina asserts that the river belongs to her, while Uruguay insists that she owns half of it. The dispute involves the ownership of the important island of Martin Garcia, now held by Argentina.

South American nations that have broken relations with Germany are Brazil, Peru, Bolivia, Paraguay, and Uruguay. The Central American Governments breaking with Germany are Guatemala, Nicaragua, Costa Rica, and Honduras. Panama and Cuba declared war on Germany on April 7, the day following the American declaration. Haiti broke relations with Germany in June.

The Pan-American nations that have not yet severed diplomatic relations are Colombia, Venezuela, Ecuador, Chile, Argentina, Salvador, and Mexico. As stated above, however, Ecuador has practically ruptured relations.

# Submarine Sinkings of the Month

DURING the month ended Oct. 14, 1917, there was apparently a diminution in the losses of ships sunk by German submarines and mines. The British Admiralty record shows the following:

| | Over 1,600 Tons. | Under 1,600 Tons. | Fishing Vessels. |
|---|---|---|---|
| Week ended Sept. 23.. | 13 | 2 | 2 |
| Week ended Sept. 30.. | 11 | 2 | .. |
| Week ended Oct. 7.... | 14 | 2 | 3 |
| Week ended Oct 14... | 12 | 6 | 1 |
| Total for four weeks | 50 | 12 | 6 |
| Total for previous four weeks ...... | 58 | 34 | 5 |

The record for the week ended Sept. 30 was the lowest since the U-boat war was proclaimed. During the week ended Oct. 7 British shipyards launched more tonnage than the Germans sank. French Admiralty figures showed that for the two weeks ended Sept. 30 the losses were: Over 1,600 tons, 12; under 1,600 tons, 10; fishing vessels, 6. During the week ended Oct. 14 Italy lost four steamers of over 1,600 tons each. During the month of September Norway lost nineteen merchant ships representing 30,800 tons. Twenty Norwegian sailors were killed and seventeen reported missing.

The most disastrous sinking was that of the French munitions steamer Medie, 4,470 tons, which was torpedoed in the Mediterranean on Sept. 23. The number of lives lost was 250 out of the 500 members of the crew and passengers, including sailors and prisoners of war. The explosion of the torpedo detonated the munitions in the ship's cargo. Five officers and fifty-one men were lost when the British armed mercantile cruiser Champagne was torpedoed and sunk.

Charles H. Grasty, in a cable dispatch dated London, Oct. 6, to THE NEW YORK TIMES, said that it looked as if the September total of losses had dropped as low as 350,000 tons, or a weekly average of less than 90,000. The actual figures for the first two weeks included the allied and neutral as well as British losses. The average compares with a weekly average of nearly 130,000 tons for the eight months from January to August, inclusive, these also being the losses for the Allies and neutrals. Adding the September figures to those given in CURRENT HISTORY MAGAZINE in October, Page 137, the total amount of shipping lost during the first nine months of 1917 amounts approximately to 4,911,000 tons.

The most hopeful sign of the slackening of the German submarine campaign was seen in the announcement on Oct. 6 of reduced premiums by the United States War Risk Insurance Bureau. The official statement said that the reduction of insurance rates from 6½ to 5 per cent. for American vessels and cargoes traversing the war zone was made "because of the decrease in the risks."

The British cruiser Drake, 14,100 tons, was, according to an Admiralty announcement, torpedoed and sunk off the north coast of Ireland on Oct. 2. One officer and eighteen men were killed by the explosion. The remainder of the ship's company was saved. The Drake was well known to vessels entering and leaving New York Harbor during the first eighteen months of the war, for she overhauled many and examined their papers. In January, 1916, she was refitted at the Bermuda naval dockyard and went in search of the German raider Möwe.

# Germany's Waning Man Power

## Some Significant Figures

A STUDY of the official vital statistics of England and Germany reveals the fact that the war has had a much more disastrous effect on the birth rate of Germany than on that of England. The comparison is between the German cities of Berlin, Hamburg, Leipsic, Munich, Dresden, Cologne, and Breslau, with a combined population of 6,000,000, and the English cities of London, Birmingham, Liverpool, Manchester, and Sheffield, with a population of over 7,000,000. The effects of the war on the numbers of births may be seen in the following table, which relates to the first six months of each year specified:

|  | Births in the Above-Named German Towns. | Births in the Above-Named English Towns. |
|---|---|---|
| 1913 (first half)...... | 65,090 | 96,939 |
| 1915 ................. | 57,596 | 94,252 |
| 1916 ................. | 39,552 | 88,186 |
| 1917 ................. | 34,370 | 78,426 |

The direct effects of the war on births could not be felt until about April, 1915, and these figures do not reveal the actual loss of three years of war. But up to the end of last June these German towns had lost on the 1913 standard by the deficit in births a number practically equal to the whole of the births for that year, while the loss in the English towns was rather less than one-third of that amount.

If the loss in 6,000,000 population averages 60,000 a year, in the German Empire the loss in three years was nearly 2,000,000 potential lives. A German authority, Karl Doorman, gives the round figures of births in the German Empire for the years 1915 and 1916, and these show a loss on the 1913 scale of 1,165,000 up to the end of 1916. The percentage of decrease for the whole empire as shown by Doorman is on the 1913 scale 22.4 per cent. in 1915 and 40 per cent. in 1916. For the seven towns which have been chosen the decrease for the first half of 1916 is 39.2 per cent., a lower rate than that for the whole empire for that year and one that is sufficiently near to the empire rate to warrant regarding it as substantially accurate as an index to the whole of the country. Applying the same method to the figures for the English towns, the potential loss in England and Wales for the same period is about 300,000.

It is stated further that the deaths in Germany independent of the losses in the field since the beginning of 1915 have exceeded the births by 600,000; hence the total population of the country, including the soldiers everywhere, is less today by 600,000 plus the deaths in the field, which are estimated at 2,000,000, making 2,600,000 total decrease. In England, on the contrary, the births yet exceed the deaths, estimated at an excess of 600,000 in the three years, which counterbalances the deaths in the field, so that England's total population as yet shows no actual loss.

The Chief of the German General Staff, General Ludendorff, issued an order early in September, 1917, in which he betrayed the necessity of economizing "human material." The order was as follows:

Chief of the German General Staff to the Armies Afield:

The consumption of munitions has remained constantly very high recently on the fighting fronts, in spite of the fact that the combative activity has generally diminished. In particular, consumption of shells for mortar and heavy field howitzers is much greater than production. This is serious. However, the superior direction of the army cannot issue a new general order for a further restriction in the consumption of munitions, because our losses on all the fighting fronts continue to be very high, and would become even higher if further general instructions were made.

Economy in men is even more important than economy in munitions. It is necessary to try and obtain an improvement on these two points. To this end it is necessary to use as carefully as is possible the munitions according to the order previously given on repeated occasions, and, on the other hand, to regulate the tactics of our methods of fighting according to the regulations given and the circumstances, so as to diminish our losses.

According to orders which we have seen and according to the complaints of the troops, it is no longer in doubt that we persist in our old ways of seeing things, and that we continue along these lines on certain occasions. These are in first-line positions—too severe fighting for the possession of ground, even a trench element which is of little tactical value, without importance and even disadvantageous to be defended; hasty counterattacks without information from the artillery; the too dense occupation of the first lines; the keeping too close of large reserves in the open when no attack is planned; too much artillery fire against positions where there is no enemy, such as destructive cannonading of empty trenches; useless barrage fire and cannonading, especially during the night, when there is not sufficient information for regulating the fire.

(Signed)    LUDENDORFF.

It was announced on Oct. 16 that Germany had called to the colors all eligible men under 47 years of age and was keeping in the ranks men aged 49.

H. Warner Allen, the Government correspondent at the French front, made a study late in September of the German man power. He estimated the German mobilization as follows:

### 1914

| | |
|---|---|
| Trained men | 4,500,000 |
| Ersatz-Reserve | 800,000 |
| 1914 contingent | 450,000 |

### 1915

| | |
|---|---|
| Landsturm first ban | 1,100,000 |
| 1915 contingent | 450,000 |
| Remainder first ban Landsturm | 150,000 |
| 1916 contingent | 450,000 |
| Combed out from " unfit " | 300,000 |

### 1916

| | |
|---|---|
| Combed out from " unfit " | 200,000 |
| Second ban Landsturm untr'd | 450,000 |
| 1917 contingent | 450,000 |
| Combed out from " unfit " | 300,000 |
| 1918 contingent | 450,000 |

### 1917

| | |
|---|---|
| Combed out | 150,000 |
| Part of 1919 contingent | 300,000 |

| | |
|---|---|
| Total | 10,500,000 |

To this total of 10,500,000 must be added the remaining men of the 1919 contingent and the 1920 contingent, together estimated at 700,000 men, making in all 11,200,000. The remaining 2,800,000 men required to make up the total of 14,000,000, given as the grand total of German man power, are to be accounted for as follows:

| | |
|---|---|
| Men of military age employed in indispensable occupations in Germany, originally 750,000, now, as result of combing out. | 500,000 |
| Men of military age abroad | 200,000 |
| Permanently unfit | 2,100,000 |
| Total | 2,800,000 |

The German casualty lists up to July 31, 1917, give the following losses:

| | |
|---|---|
| Killed | 1,158,601 |
| Wounded | 2,922,320 |
| Missing | 710,454 |
| Total | 4,791,375 |

It is believed that these figures are considerably within the mark, and that the permanent losses in the German Army in the three years are rather in excess of than below 4,000,000. The Allies' conclusion as to the actual German man power at the middle of September, 1917, was as follows:

| | |
|---|---|
| Men actually employed in the army on the front, behind the lines, and in the interior | 5,500,000 |
| Men incorporated and shortly available, forces left over from divisions in course of formation, and men in dépôts | 600,000 |
| Remainder of 1919 contingent and 1920 contingent | 700,000 |
| Permanent losses | 4,000,000 |
| Men in treatment in hospital | 500,000 |
| Germans abroad | 200,000 |
| Permanently unfit | 2,100,000 |
| Men required in interior for life of country | 500,000 |
| Total | 14,100,000 |

# Mutiny in the German Navy

IN a debate in the German Reichstag, Oct. 9, Vice Admiral von Capelle, the German Minister of Marine, revealed the fact that a mutiny had occurred in the German Navy some weeks before, but that it had been quickly quelled and three of the leaders had been executed. He gave only meagre details, but made the direct accusation that the Independent Socialists were responsible for the uprising by influencing the sailors through their propaganda; he named specifically three Deputies, Vogtherr, Dittman, and Haase, as having been in conference with the leaders of the mutiny before the outbreak. The disclosure created great excitement and met with indignant denials from the accused. The Chancellor sustained von Capelle and corroborated his accusations.

As a result of the disclosure the movement by the opposition to force the resignation of the Chancellor for failure to support the peace plans of the "no annexationists" failed. Two days later it was announced that von Capelle had resigned, but this was not confirmed up to Oct. 18. The Reichstag adjourned until December, with the political pot seething and a general impression that the days of Chancellor Michaelis were numbered. He was criticised for lack of firmness and was charged with failure to develop definite leadership over any of the conflicting groups.

A former Lieutenant in the German Navy, Rudolph Glatfelder, made public Oct. 16 a circumstantial story of the mutiny, which he declared he personally witnessed and participated in. Earlier in the war he had been exchanged by the Russians as an incapacitated prisoner, having been captured from the German cruiser Magdeburg at the bombardment of the Russian port, Libau, Aug. 4, 1914, in which engagement he lost an eye. In Germany he joined the Social Democrat group, known as the Marxian Internationalists, who have resorted to I. W. W. tactics to strike a blow for German democracy.

He stated that the mutiny was originated by a group of German revolutionists operating in Switzerland. In May, 1917, 149 revolutionary spies, of whom 85 were women, had been sent to German naval stations to foment the disaffection among the sailors. Glatfelder said he was the head of a group that operated at Wilhelmshaven. He asserted that there was located there a hospital with 20,000 patients, known as "repulsive cases," mere human remnants, whom the authorities kept there in concealment, leaving their families under the impression that they were at the front; he said there were fully 200,000 such repulsive casualties in the empire.

The dead, he added, are buried at sea; as many as 700 have been dropped overboard in one day from the "death ferry." Late in June the crew of a "death ferry" shouted defiantly that the victims were unwilling sacrifices and "would have damned their souls before offering them to the Kaiser." A serious riot ensued; the Captain and four of the crew were overpowered and thrown into the sea; the officiating parson aboard was shot. The crew was overpowered at length, tried, and executed.

This was the beginning. On July 30 8,000 sailors were assembled on the parade ground at Wilhelmshaven to listen to speeches upholding the policy of the Government in the war to offset the socialistic propaganda. As they marched by the platform the Admiral in charge asserted that one of the marching marines had sarcastically smiled at him, whereupon one of the naval officers jumped from the stand and struck the marine in the face with his gloved fist. At once the 8,000 sailors and marines turned on the officers present like wolves and literally tore their bodies into shreds, killing fifty or more. A bloody riot followed; one of the forts took sides with the mutineers and engaged in a bombardment with the ten other coastal forts. The rioters meanwhile began their work of destruction, and in a few hours had blown up four large uncompleted warships in the harbor and burned two Zeppelins, besides warehouses, sheds, wharves, &c. Before the mutineers could reach their ships many of them were mowed down by machine guns. They were at length overpowered by the loyal troops, who were summoned in tens of thousands, and the ringleaders were tried and executed.

It was announced on Oct. 16 that the three Deputies who were accused of fomenting trouble would be prosecuted in the criminal courts.

# Slang and Slogans of War in France

## By Arthur H. Warner

[Mr. Warner's article, which was contributed to THE NEW YORK TIMES of Oct. 7, 1917, furnishes interesting sidelights on the history of the war in France]

AS a resident of France from the beginning of the war until a few months ago there stand out in my memory four war cries, each marking an epoch in the development of the French spirit. They are:

" France d'abord! " (France first!)

" Jusqu'au bout! " (Unto the end!)

" Coute que coute! " (Cost what it may!)

" On les aura! " (We will get them!)

How that first watchword, " France first! " comes back to one as expressing the spirit of the Summer of 1914, the period of mobilization and upheaval. It appeared in the newspapers, it was printed on stationery, it was on every lip; and, more important, it was in every heart in those early days of danger.

Everything unessential had to give way. Resolutely and gladly the country subjected itself to a policy of elimination. Museums and theatres were closed at once. Expensive shops and luxurious hotels found that they belonged to a life that had ceased to exist, and, one by one, they shut their doors. The sale of absinthe was prohibited, and the cafés of Paris were closed at 8 P. M.

France lived in those days in a state of patriotic exaltation akin to religious frenzy. Dancing and music were suppressed by public accord. One could not even sing or play the piano behind closed doors in one's own home unless it was the " Marseillaise " or some other patriotic air.

Then came the Autumn, with the news of the human toll France had paid in the retreat from the border and the glorious stand at the Marne. Came, too, the numbing realization that the war, which had been counted on to end by Christmas, must be fought through the Winter. The patriotic exaltation that had carried France through the early weeks was gone, but in its place grew a sterner, deeper courage. It found expression in two words, made dynamic by use in a message to the people of Paris by General Gallieni. Called upon to serve as Military Governor of the capital when the Germans were just outside its gates, General Gallieni responded:

" I have received the mandate to defend Paris against the invader. This mandate I will fulfill jusqu'au bout! "

" Unto the end! " The soldiers repeated it through gritted teeth as they settled down to hold, from the North Sea to the Vosges, a line of trenches which during that first Winter were little more than drainage canals (which did not drain) and were as yet inadequately provided with heat or shelter.

" Unto the end! " The civilians repeated it as they faced the gigantic problem of sustaining their soldiers and organizing the country for a protracted war.

Spring found the line still firm and the Entente Allies beginning an offensive which, it was then hoped, would sweep the Germans from France.

A new phrase began to appear in the press—" Coute que coute! " (Cost what it may!) It became a watchword. Better pay any price and get through with it. A grim and heroic resolution, but it proved impossible of realization. What had been looked forward to as the great offensive had to be slowed down to await better artillery, more ammunition.

A year later another slogan came into prominence. The defeat of German ambitions at Verdun, and the proof during the Summer of 1916 that at last the Entente Allies had an offensive which could advance against German intrenchments, gave rise to a new sentiment. France had always been hopeful. She now became confident. To voice this new-born attitude she began to popularize a soldier saying of which General Pétain had made use in an order to the troops at Verdun. " On les aura! " (We will get them!) became the most widespread slogan of the war.

In addition to watchwords which have been associated with passing epochs of the war, there are others, serious and amusing, in which popular philosophy has been crystallized. One of these owes its origin to a drawing by the cartoonist Forain, published early in the conflict, in which a soldier in the trenches is represented as saying to another, " If only they hold out! "

" Who ? " asks his companion.

" The civilians! " is the answer.

" If only they hold out! " (" Pourvu qu'ils tiennent! ") is quoted again and again by persons writing on the war, and each succeeding month adds to its weight in revealing the importance, in a modern struggle of any length, of the effort and spirit of the civilians.

Artists have found inspiration in another phrase, " Arise, ye dead! " (" Debout, les morts! ") The story is that a trench held by French soldiers was entered from one end by Germans, making a surprise attack. A dozen of the French fell, dead or wounded, in the fighting, and the rest, believing themselves outnumbered, finally fled. As the Germans advanced to take possession of the trench one of the men, lying prone before them, rose to his knees in a supreme effort, grasped some hand grenades, and, hurling them at the enemy, shouted to his companions stretched on the ground about him, " Arise, ye dead! "

Several among the wounded responded to the heroic cry, and the Germans, frightened at this almost supernatural occurrence, fell back, though not before the Frenchman who initiated the attack had been killed.

Turning from the heroic to the commonplace, one must not forget to mention the ubiquitous phrase, " C'est la guerre," a standing comment and excuse in France since the war. Sometimes it expresses a philosophical recognition of conditions. Sometimes it is an attempt to cover up personal shortcomings. If you complain to your groceryman that his prices are too high, he shrugs his shoulders and replies, " It's the war." If you scold your laundry woman for dropping a sploch of ink on your best shirt, she falls back on the same efficient excuse. " It's the war."

Then there is " Taisez-vous! Méfiez-vous! Les oreilles ennemies vous écoutent," which may be translated, " Don't talk! Be on your guard! The ears of the enemy hear you." This was placarded all over France as a warning. It is not certain that it accomplished any good in that direction, but it has furnished a deal of amusement and taken its place among the sayings of the war.

The slang of the war comes next to the slogans as interpretative of the psychology of the conflict. The word to which first place should be given from this standpoint is " embusqué." It means literally " in ambush " or " in hiding," but since the war the word has been popularized as a noun to describe men who have been mobilized, but have made use of influential friends to get them a billet well away from the firing line.

The contempt which the French feel for that type of man may be judged from the fact that to call a man an embusqué is the supreme insult. A woman was recently fined for calling a policeman an embusqué, even in the heat of argument.

At the other end of the pole from the embusqué is the poilu. The explanation has been set forth that poilu, or hairy, as a nickname for the French fighting man is not due to the fact that he is without benefit of barber, but goes back to the time when there existed a body of soldiers who wore hats of hair, from which they came to be known as poilus. As they attained a reputation for great bravery and hardihood, the name came to mean a supersoldier.

Whatever be the historical derivation of the word, it is certain that the average Frenchman uses the term in its literal sense to indicate one whose beard is unshaven and whose hair is unshorn— in other words, a man who has been long enough at the front to become acclimated. The word did not come into general use until some months after the war began. The slang term for a private of the line at the outset of the conflict was piou-piou.

The respect, almost reverence, attached to the word " poilu " in France today undoubtedly helps many a soldier to bear the grime and the discomfort of the war. It may sometimes lead to an unnecessary exaggeration of them. A clean, new uniform, for instance, is an object of suspicion. The wearer is likely to be taken for that most odious of all creatures, an embusqué.

A French soldier is also spoken of as a "blue," (bleu,) appropriate in view of the color of the new army uniform. The young soldier, who has been called up since the war began, is a "bluet," (bleuet,) and the familiar blue corn flower has become his emblem. Another and older term for one of these youngsters is a Marie-Louise. Strictly speaking, he is a recruit called up ahead of the usual time, but, of course, this is the case in respect to all the new classes mobilized during the present war. The word goes back to the marriage of Napoleon with Marie Louise of Austria in 1810, when France had exhausted her men and was calling up boys for the army.

When a "bluet," or Marie-Louise, first takes the field, he is naturally the object of much good-natured chaff from the veterans. Pierre Falké, a French illustrator, has made a drawing of a smooth-faced youngster arriving at the front, where he is greeted by an underofficer, with a beard like a hedgehog's back, who says, sternly, "It's understood now that if by tomorrow you haven't a mustache, I'll give you four days' imprisonment."

The war seems to have made of the average soldier a philosopher and a fatalist, who jests at danger and radiates cheerfulness, but there are occasions when he does not live up to this part. One of them is when, on leave from the trenches, he reaches the last day of his holiday and must return to the front. Then he loses his smile and his banter, and in soldier slang has the cafard. Literally, the word means cockroach.

The source of that word boche, an abbreviation of alboche or alleboche, has been a subject of discussion in France since the war brought the term into prominence. The most plausible explanation seems to be that, in French slang, it is not an infrequent device to substitute boche or oche for the final syllable of a word, with a view to treating it in a trivial or disdainful way, and that alleboche has been thus made from allemand, the recognized word for German.

The spirit of jest and raillery which animates the soldier at the front is expressed in the prevailing description of a shell as a marmite, which in normal life is a pot for cooking stew, and, by extension, the stew itself. Bullets are "prunes," (pruneaux.) A soldier refers to his bayonet affectionately as his "Rosalie," or, more slightingly, as a "fork" or "toothpick." A machine gun is sometimes a moulin à café, or coffee grinder, and on other occasions a machine à découdre, that is, a machine to unsew, or an "unsewing machine."

Of course, the French soldier is continually christening by new names the familiar objects of his daily life. The beef with which he is served is known as "monkey," (singe,) while wine passes under a number of names, the commonest of which is pinard. The poets of the trenches know how to praise their pinard with all the enthusiasm, if not with the genius, of Omar Khayyám.

# A Boy's Last Letter to His Mother
## Story of an 18-Year-Old Hero From Perugia

SOON after Italy's declaration of war, in May, 1915, Enzo Valentini, a boy of 18 in the Perugia high school, son of the Mayor of that city, wrote to his mother this noble letter, containing his last will and testament:

"Little mother, in a few days I am going to leave for the front. For your dear sake I am writing this farewell, which you will read only if I die. Let it also be my adieu to papa, to my brothers, to all those who loved me in this world. Because in life my heart, in its love and gratitude to you, has always given you its best thoughts, it is to you also that I desire to make known my last wishes.

"You know the joys of my life have been poetry, art, and science. * * * Many persons have loved me. To each of them you will give in remembrance of me some trifle that was mine and that you will yourself choose from the things that you care for least. I wish that they, too, should possess something of the friend who has vanished, to rise like the flame above the clouds, above the flesh, *et ultra,* (you remember my motto?) into the sun, into the soul of the universe. * * * You will therefore find herewith a list of names.

"Try, if you can, not to weep for me too much. Think that, even though I do not return, I am not dead. My body, the less important part of me, suffers, wears out, and dies; but not myself—I the soul, cannot die, because I come from God and must return to God. I was created for happiness and through the joy that underlies all suffering I must return to the happiness eternal. If I have been a little time the prisoner of my body, I am none the less eternal. My death is a liberation, the beginning of the true life, the return to the Infinite.

"So do not weep for me. If you think of the immortal beauty of the ideas to which my soul has willingly sacrificed my body, you will not weep. But if your mother heart weeps, let the tears flow: a mother's tears will always be sacred. May God keep account of them: they will be the stars of his crown. * * *

"Be strong, little mother. From the beyond your son says good-bye to you, to papa, to the brothers, to all those who loved him—your son who has given his body to fight those who wished to extinguish the light of the world."

The story of the rare spirit that penned the foregoing lines has been told by the young man's lyceum teacher, Francesco Picco, in a brochure ("Breviario di guerra di uno studente," Turin, Paravia, 1917) containing long extracts from the young soldier's notes and letters. "Brilliantly cultivated," says the teacher, "young Valentini also possessed, along with a clear call for the natural sciences, certain wonderful artistic gifts. He had made a collection of insects, and won public approval by an exhibit of his pastels and aquarelles. His style, flexible and expressive, was already formed. But he instantly abandoned his pen, his pencils, and his brushes and left for the war, filled with a sincere and joyous enthusiasm. He volunteered as a common soldier and was soon away in the Alps.

"The longer I stay here," he wrote, "the more I love the mountains. Their spell is slower than that of the sea, but it is deeper and more lasting. Every hour that passes, every cloud, every morning mist clothes the Alps in new beauty so great that even the rudest of our brave soldiers, peasants though they be, pause to look; it may be only an instant, but it is enough to prove that the soul never forgets its celestial origin, even if it be imprisoned in the roughest shell. The days follow each other calmly, uniformly serene. It seems as if the Autumn ought never to end. The divine solemnity of the nights is inexpressible, especially now that the moon fills them with soft enchantment. There are hours in the day when everything is so saturated with light, and when the silence is so profound that the light seems to cease, letting the silence blaze forth into the immense harmony." (Sept. 20.) "At nightfall," he wrote later, "when the fires redden the vast blue in the direction of the barracks, we get under way. At 10 o'clock I reach my tent, dead with fatigue, and happy, convinced that the world is beautiful."

Such was the life of Enzo Valentini at the front from the middle of July to the latter half of October, 1915. "I have not yet been in battle," he wrote to his teacher, but by the time the letter had been read he had fallen mortally wounded. His company, entering the trenches Oct. 17, had taken part in the ceaseless combats that raged about the Col di Lana. In the afternoon of the 22d came the assault upon the Sano di Mezzodi. When the turn of his platoon came, "beautiful and full of audacity, he was the first to dash from the trench, drawing after him all who hesitated," and making the mountains ring with the old Italian war cry of liberty, "Savoia! Italia!"

He ran far forward without being touched by the infernal hail from the Austrian guns, paused to embrace his friend, Lieutenant Mayo, and then, still leading the charge, fell pierced by five shrapnel bullets. His comrades carried him back, dying, to a grotto, where surgeons dressed his wounds. The Lieutenant who helped to carry him, concludes his narrative thus:

"We laid him down on a litter before the grotto, amid the great rocks, under the sombre vault of the sky, his face upturned to the stars. He was a little depressed, asked for a drink, and fainted; they carried him to the operating room and I never saw him again. I have been told that they carried him down the side of Mount Mesola to "his" little lake, and that he sleeps there in death. But for us he is still living in the glory of his youth, there on the Alps, waving his cap with an edelweiss flower in it, and crying, 'Savoia!'"

# For Women Who Write to Soldiers
## Words of Advice from Marcel Prévost
### Member of the French Academy

*This appeal to the women of France, from the pen of one of the foremost living French writers, recently appeared on the front page of the Bulletin des Armées, the official organ of the French Army, from which it has been translated for* Current History Magazine:

MY anxious sisters, the women of France, it is to you that I address myself; I wish that these very simple lines may come to you at the moment when you are beginning a letter to the loved one at the front * * * particularly if he is your son, your brother, your husband, your father, and if, therefore, the letter you are going to write is to carry to him the odor of the fireside, the fragrance of the home.

Women of France, I see you as if I were sitting by your side. The old white-haired mother, the young wife whose swift, healthy blood colors her cheeks, the young girl obstinately secret over the anguish of her heart, the schoolgirl whose childhood has been ripened too soon by war. * * * And I see, too, the table, a thing of art or a piece of kitchen furniture; the ink bottle, an antique gem or a humble bit of spattered glass; the paper from a peddler's cart, ruled off in naïve squares, or the beautiful sheets of tinted vellum, marked with a monogram; the rude pencil or the elegant pen. * * * I see these accessories of the letter to be written, and I see her who is about to write it. Will she kindly listen to me before tracing a line?

Frenchwoman, what are you going to write to the soldier who is bound to you by ties of blood, by ties of love, and for whom your letter will be both something of yourself and something of the home? Oh! I know what comes first by instinct, before everything else—I know the words that are inclosed in the first drop of ink or in the extreme point of your lead pencil: "How long the time is, and how I yearn to see you again!" That is what is burning in your thoughts and in your fingers. When you shall have written that, it seems to you that you will be a little comforted. Then your instinct will prompt you to depict the cruel void in the home left by the absent one, all that is going not so well, or not going at all, since he departed, all that weighs heavily upon the lives of women when the men are far away. To tell of these tears and troubles, is this not to remind him how indispensable he is, how much reason you have to miss him and to love him?

Finally, having described with all the troubled warmth of your heart what a desert you are living in, your instinct will impel you to conclude with a new and more ardent lament over this calamity of war, which leaves you so lonely—a long, heartrending, desolating wail, like that of a faithful dog that has been abandoned.

That is what you wish to write, is it

not? Well, that is just what should not be written if you do not wish to harm him who is to receive the letter and who loves you.

It is for him, not for you, that the letter ought to be written. It is not to solace you, but to help him to live his hard life. His life is dangerous almost without cessation, and when it does cease to be dangerous it often becomes more dreary. Almost everything around him conspires to use up his spirit and ruin his resistance. The thing to do is to send him strength, if you can; in any case, it is a sin to breathe weakness into him.

What then? Should one lie to him?

No, women of France, the poilu wants no lies. Tell him the truth, but truth that is comforting; the little, happy things of the day and place, the winning of a school medal by the child, the fine health of the old folks, the solution of a problem that had worried you, the thriving appearance of a certain crop. A letter that begins with good news is like a visitor who smiles from the moment of entering the door. Afterward there will be time to tell the less comforting truths, but only the necessary ones, those which must be known without delay, which cannot wait for the home furlough. The rule is this: Never to tell the soldier at the front anything that will sadden him and that he does not need to know. To take away, without absolute necessity, a little of his courage is as bad as if you took away some of his blood.

Above all, avoid vague rumors, good or bad, which are based on nothing, and which are almost always harmful. At the time of the German attack on Verdun there were women who wrote from the distant Dordogne or from Brittany: "They say Verdun is going to be taken." What madness! They were writing that to the men who, in the ravines of Le Mort Homme, were driving back the barbarians with hand grenades! It was criminal, but it was also great foolishness. In like manner when the Paris factory girls, under the paternal eye of agents, sang gayly through the streets, "We want our twenty cents and the English vacation week," there were women in the provinces who wrote to the poilus on the strength of burlesque tittle-tattle, "They say there is revolution in Paris." What a sinister fantasy! I may add that false "good news," such as "They say that the war is soon going to end," is scarcely less silly or injurious. What sadness, what deceptions have been promoted in this way, with the best of intentions, from behind the lines to the front, between two beings who love each other!

Women, tell the soldier only things that are certain.

The letter is finished, the information about events, people, the home, family affairs is given with sincerity, yet with the wish to omit nothing that is comforting, to defer as much as possible all disquieting news that can wait, and to abstain from all vague predictions, good or bad. With what shall you close?

Above all, I insist, not with this evident and sterile prayer: "Ah, that this may end soon, and that you may return!" Your soldier knows very well that you long for that, but if you must say it to him again, that is not the best way to do it. You should put it in some such form as this:

"The home and household are waiting for you, and are thinking only of you; but we, who are suffering less than you, wish to equal your patience and courage, for we know that peace can come only through patience and courage. All the rest is empty words. The home and the household are waiting for you; you continue to be everything here, the same as before, more than before. We are trying to keep it prosperous and inviting for the day of your return. Our hearts are more loving and tender than ever for you, and every hour of separation makes you more precious to us."

Say that—you will say it much better than I—and then drop the letter in the post box. You will thus have the joy of thinking that, thanks to it, the man who receives it will have a little comfort. He will read and reread its pages, each time feeling himself more secure, and when evening comes he will sleep more calmly. Think how, if your letter robbed him of rest or even spoiled one hour of sleep—

that precious sleep which is broken into by the inclemencies of the weather, by the noises, the alarms, the whole formid- able nightmare of war—how sad and wrong it would be! Wouldn't you feel remorse, women of France?

# How Greece Prolonged the War

## Acts of Pro-German Cabinets Under King Constantine Revealed Before Commission of Inquiry

A COMMISSION of inquiry is investigating the acts of the pro-German Cabinets of Skouloudis, Professor Lambros, and other members of the Cabinets which served German interests in Greece until the abdication of King Constantine. The former Greek Minister at Sofia, Naoum, in his evidence showed that when Greece mobilized in 1915 a panic arose in Sofia; the Bulgarian newspapers quieted the excitement by announcing that the King of Greece was opposed to the proceeding and would force the resignation of Venizelos, and it developed that the Bulgarian Foreign Office was informed of this from Athens several days before it occurred, thus proving the close relation between the Greek Court and the German interests.

In an address before the Greek Chamber, late in August, M. Venizelos laid bare the treachery of the ex-King to the Allies. He related how the King, after giving him permission to proceed with a declaration of friendliness to the Entente early in September, 1914, changed his mind and refused to sanction any proceedings against Turkey. He told of negotiations which followed with Bulgaria, and how the attitude of the latter changed when $100,000,000 was received from Berlin and Vienna, showing that she was leagued with the Central Powers.

### Greece and Gallipoli

Subsequently he proposed to the King to aid the Entente with an expeditionary force against the Dardenelles. The King gave his approval, but it was again frustrated by the pro-German staff and withdrawn. He asserted that if Greece had acted when he urged intervention, Greek troops would have been in Constantinople within a fortnight, as the Gallipoli Peninsula was at that time practically defenseless.

M. Venizelos read out at this point a number of dispatches from the Greek representative at Constantinople in confirmation of the statement that the Turks had been preparing to evacuate the city. Proceeding, he insisted that he had been right in wishing to send the Greek Army to Gallipoli, and explained in detail the advantages to Greece that would accrue from the occupation and internationalization of the Dardanelles. Turkey, he argued, would have been destroyed, Russia would have had her food supplies by sea, would have been able to export her grain, and would have escaped the enemy's offensive of the Spring of 1916. Bulgaria, seeing the Greek and Franco-British armies on her rear, would probably not have dared to intervene; while the prestige of Greece would have been augmented, for, thanks to her efforts, Germany would have lost the East, and the war would have been ended one year earlier.

He told of the election in the Spring of 1916, when his party won 184 seats against a combined opposition of 123; yet the Gounaris Cabinet, which had been repudiated, held on ten weeks longer, and it was not until Aug. 10, 1916, that the King again sent for him— and then " it was not with the intention of co-operating sincerely with me," he added, " but in order to plot against me."

M. Venizelos told how he gave new assurances of help to Serbia, and reported the King as saying: " I do not wish to go to the help of Serbia because Germany will be victorious, and I do not wish to be defeated." M. Venizelos, in reply, put before the King the strategical arguments and other considerations which weighed in favor of an immediate attack on the Bulgarians, whose morale was shattered, who were in possession of only 400 rounds of ammunition per gun, and who would need a considerable time to replenish their supplies. " If we prevented the crushing of Serbia," he had said to the King, " within thirty days we should get to Sofia; in any case, we should get to a point beyond which the Austro-German advance for technical reasons would be impossible."

To all these arguments the King's only reply continued to be: " I do not wish to intervene; we shall be beaten by Germany." The Prime Minister then told the King that he had not the right to enter into divergence for the second time from the leader of the majority of the nation; it would be a better course for the King, he declared, to decree the abolition of the Government. The King replied: " For national affairs I am responsible before God." M. Venizelos then offered his resignation, but the King obliged him to remain in power in order to deal with the mobilization. King Constantine then gave his consent to a request being made to the Allies for the 150,000 men whom Greece was to have furnished to Serbia in accordance with the treaty. M. Venizelos had no sooner relinquished office than the King changed his mind, but the step had already been taken, and in due course the Franco-British troops landed at Saloniki. The Zaimis Cabinet did not protest against the landing. " If at this point I did not become a revolutionary," declared M. Venizelos, " it was because a civil war would have been provoked, and Bulgaria would have profited by the occasion to invade Greece."

Returning to the subject of the treaty with Serbia, M. Venizelos declared that M. Zaimis would be known to history as the man who had broken the word of Greece, and recalled how the resignation of M. Zaimis had been brought about by the insulting attitude adopted toward the Chamber by the Minister for War, this event being followed by the formation of the Skouloudis-Gounaris Cabinet, which

was responsible for the shameful treachery of the surrender of Fort Rupel.

The latest dispatches from Athens confirm the fact that a new army of 300,000 will now be mobilized by Greece as soon as the equipment can be supplied by the Allies. The plan of the Allies in the Balkans is said to be to advance upon Sofia, capital of Bulgaria, and thus to cut off communications between Germany and Turkey. Germany is said to be drawing great quantities of supplies, especially oil and wheat, from Turkey, and this traffic cannot be interrupted until the line is cut by the international army now operating in Macedonia. The 300,000 men Greece will add to the Anglo-French troops will give the Allies a preponderance of strength which is expected to overcome the enemy in that theatre of the war.

It is stated that the mobilization by the former King Constantine emptied the warehouses and used up all military stores and equipment, leaving available for military employment only the 80,000 troops raised by the Provisional Government of Venizelos at Saloniki, who are now fighting side by side with the Anglo-French army in Macedonia.

### Greek Minister at Washington

Georges Roussos, the new Greek Minister to the United States, presented his credentials on Sept. 21, and in the course of his address to President Wilson, said:

Greece, my country, is just emerging from an exceptionally grave crisis. It overcame it because of the Hellenic people's devotion to the democratic principles which have always been theirs, and because of the assistance which the protecting powers graciously extended to them.

As soon as the Hellenic people were free masters of their own destinies they unconditionally performed the duty they had incessantly proclaimed as theirs; they took sides with the noble and generous nations that are striving to secure for the world an era of justice and true freedom. Among those nations the United States is one of the most spirited in the pursuit of that end. Through you, as its authorized spokesman, Mr. President, it has uttered words which startled mankind and proclaimed principles that have for once and all established the sanctity of the purposes it aims to achieve. The weak, the oppressed, all now live in the certainty that their liberties will be restored.

In his reply President Wilson said:

You state that the main object of your mission is to draw closer the ties of traditional friendship which bind Greece to the United States. I receive this statement with the same pleasure that I accept your credentials, and, in turn, beg to assure you that I shall be always willing and ready heartily to co-operate with you in striving to give substantial reality to those Divine ideals of right, liberty, and justice by which both Greece and the United States of America seem to be guided.

I was more than gratified when the supremacy of democracy was proclaimed throughout Greece by the action of your Government in casting in its destiny with the United States and the allied powers of Europe in the great conflict in which they are engaged for the preservation of civilization and the realization of the rights of the weak and oppressed. I thank you for your feeling of unity with the United States in this noble and righteous cause.

## " Good-bye, Soldier Boys! "

*This striking statement of why the United States is at war with Germany appeared as an editorial article in The Oakland (Cal.) Enquirer when Oakland's first contribution to the army that fights for freedom of the seas marched away into history. After a reference to the civil war veterans who fought on land and ocean, the article continues:*

The lads that go now, high hearted as were they, go to bleed and do and die in a war that is fought under water, on the surface, and in the air above. They go to face the clouds of poisonous gas and the barrage of fire. They go in the face of all these, to give blow for blow, to pit American wits, initiative, and courage against these qualities in the servants of imperial ambition.

They go to do more. They go to prove that they are the soldiers of a great Republic whose people are civilized. They go to write it into history that humanity, mercy, and justice have their place in war as in peace. They go to victory, in which the despoilers of the homes of noncombatants shall be punished, the monsters who deflower women shall die wretchedly, the inhuman wretches who condemn noncombatants to slavery shall pass under the rod. They go to compel the Huns who have violated all law, divine and human, to drain to the dregs the bitter cup of sorrow they have pressed to the lips of the weak and the innocent.

They go, God's own avengers of the unspeakable suffering of the people of Belgium, Northern France, Poland, Serbia, Rumania, and Armenia. As they march, unseen in the clear air above them are the spirits of the American mothers and babies that perished in the roaring sea, murdered in the Lusitania. They go to cleanse the earth of the men who began by violating treaties and have progressed by violating the common promptings of humanity which have been held sacred even by the red Indians of America and the black tribes of Africa.

They are the armed guards of American honor, of the covenants of Almighty God. On this great mission we send them with every blessing, with every ascription of honor. They go to prove that this great Republic is great not only in material things, in its proud cities, its far-flung fields, and its laden orchards and purpling vineyards, but great in the ineffable things of the spirit, in the courage of its people and its purpose to fling high and far the banners of the best civilization created by man.

Good-bye, boys, acquit yourselves like men!

# The Month's Developments in Russia

## A Coalition Cabinet and an Advisory Parliament Formed
## The Korniloff Affair—Soukhomlinoff's Conviction

RUSSIA'S internal politics during the month ended Oct. 16, 1917, assumed a form which could be called stable if compared to the welter from which they emerged after the so-called Korniloff revolt. Of the many assemblies and conferences convoked since that period, the nearest approach to a representative body was the Democratic Congress, which met at Moscow Sept. 27. It contained 1,200 delegates coming from all over Russia. The presiding officers were five representatives of the Workmen's and Soldiers' Delegates, five each from town Zemstvos, and two each from other groups. N. C. Tscheidse, President of the Council of Soldiers and Workmen, opened the conference, and was followed by M. Avskentieff, President of the Peasants' Delegates.

The congress was summoned by the Workmen's and Soldiers' Central Council. It was assumed to be under the control of the ultra-Socialists; the extreme radicals, or Bolsheviki, thought they would be able to sway the convention to their program of extreme measures, and to seize the reins of power. But the congress, while radical in its demands, did not go to extremes. Premier Kerensky consented to address the body. He was sympathetically heard by the more moderate groups, and exercised a profound influence over the attitude and acts of the convention.

After several days' sessions it became apparent that more moderate counsels were in the ascendency. A Coalition Cabinet, in which the Constitutional Democrats should participate, was favorably discussed. The Congress adopted a resolution providing for a preliminary Parliament, which is to have a consultative and not a legislative function, and which is to consist of 231 members, of whom 110 represent the Zemstvos and towns. The Congress, by a vote of 839 to 106, passed a resolution declaring for this Parliament, but at the same time demanded that no step be taken toward naming a Coalition Cabinet without its sanction.

### Coalition Cabinet Named

Premier Kerensky on the same day again exhibited his iron resolution by practically defying the Congress and naming a real Coalition Cabinet, as follows:

Premier, A. F. KERENSKY.
Minister of Foreign Affairs, M. I. TERESTCHENKO.
Minister of Interior, M. NIKITIN.
Minister of Agriculture, M. AVSKENTIEFF.
Minister of Labor, M. GVOZDEFF.
Minister of Supplies, M. PROKOPOVITCH.
Minister of Finance, M. BERNATZKY.
Minister of Religion, M. KARTASHEFF.
Minister of Public Welfare, M. KISHKIN.
Minister of Trade and Industry, A. I. KONOVALOFF.
State Controller, M. SMYRNOFF.
Minister of Justice, M. MALYANTOVITCH.
Minister of Education, M. SALASKIN.
President of the Ecumenical Council, M. TRETYAKOFF.
Minister of War, General VERKHOVSKY.
Minister of Marine, ADMIRAL VERDERVSKI.
Minister of Ways and Communications, M. LIVEREVSKY.

The Constitutional Democratic Party, against which the Democratic Congress was in opposition, is represented by Kishkin, Konovaloff, and Smyrnoff. The portfolios of Foreign Affairs, War, Marine, and Interior remain unchanged.

In addition to carrying out an active foreign policy, the new Government declared that the serious internal difficulty of Russia was due chiefly to the Korniloff rebellion. The New Government pledged that its business acts would be on the basis of agreements between representatives of the bourgeoisie, the tax-paying element, and the revolutionary democracy. It pointed out that the success of such a program is possible only if the nation is united. The Government's statement in conclusion said that it had three principal aims:

To raise the fighting power of the army and navy.

To bring order to the country by fighting anarchy.

To call the Constituent Assembly as soon as possible.

The Cabinet is determined to ignore as far as possible the activities of the Workmen's and Soldiers' Delegates and centre its efforts in gaining the support of the armies.

### Functions of the New Parliament

The new Parliament, which is called the " Temporary Council of the Russian Republic," was accepted by the new Coalition Government as an advisory body, and will be organized by the Government. It will consist of 120 delegates, from all groups and all parts of the country, and will have the right to interpellate the Government, which must reply. The Government, however, will not be responsible to the Parliament. This body will remain until the Constituent Assembly acts. The Constituent Assembly has been called to assemble in December; it will consist of 730 delegates, to be elected by popular vote. The military in all parts of Russia will take part in the election of delegates under the same conditions as civilians.

The new Government seems to have met popular approval except among the extreme Radicals, or Bolsheviki; but the impression has gained ground that this group is losing its influence. The situation was complicated in the early days of October by a strike on all railway lines for higher wages; there was a complete tieup, but after a few days the matter was settled. The political situation in the country at this writing (Oct. 16) is more promising than a month ago, but the Government is still seriously beset by the pernicious activities of the Bolsheviki, who are outspoken in their hostility. The month has been marked by general unrest, accompanied by some loss of faith in the revolution by the masses on ac-count of the jarring political factions and by a serious increase in disorders. A revolt broke out in Turkestan early in October, and a state of war was declared in that province. General Korovnitchenko, the commander at Kazan, (Eastern European Russia,) was given troops, with orders to suppress the revolt.

### Island Surrendered to Germans

A much more serious occurrence was the taking of Oesel Island, in the Gulf of Riga, by the Germans. This is believed to foreshadow an attack on Reval, endangering Kronstadt and Petrograd. The German forces, which landed on Oesel Island, under the cover of ninety war vessels, had occupied up to Oct. 16 practically the whole of the island. German torpedo boats penetrated the inner waters between the islands of Oesel and Dagö, and in repeated engagements pressed back the Russian naval forces into the Moonsund. The Germans were thus about to gain full control of the Gulf of Riga, threating the Russian capital itself. A further exodus of civilians from Petrograd was reported to be in progress on Oct. 16.

Premier Kerensky, in an urgent appeal to the Baltic fleet to defend the fatherland " in this hour of trial," divulged the fact that the garrison of Kronstadt, the chief fortress and military port of Russia and the station of the Baltic fleet, twenty miles west of Petrograd, by its attitude already had weakened the defensive resources of the fortress. Eight dreadnoughts, a dozen light cruisers, forty torpedo boats, and thirty mine sweepers participated in the German landing on Oesel Island.

### New Light on Korniloff Affair

Later revelations at the end of September and early in October strengthened the belief that the so-called revolt of General Korniloff was attributable to a blunder of Lvoff and others who served as emissaries between the General and the Premier. A copy of the Order of the Day issued by General Korniloff on Sept. 10 explains in detail how the error arose. It appears that the Provisional Government was apprehensive of a serious Bolsheviki uprising, and asked Korniloff, as Generalissimo, to place at its disposal several divisions of troops. He gave the orders, feeling that the revolt should be summarily suppressed, and that a strong Government of a few should be formed at once to save the country. His statement continues as follows:

Later there came to me Vladimir Lvoff, speaking on behalf of Kerensky, and asked me to state my views as to the best method of organizing the new Government. I replied that I considered the only solution lay in the establishment of a dictatorship and the proclamation of martial law. By dictatorship I did not mean a one-man dictatorship, inasmuch as I had pointed out the necessity of my participation in the Government. I let it be known in making this decision that I considered and still consider any return to the old régime an utter impossibility. The task of the new Government should be devoted exclusively to saving the country.

Later I exchanged telegrams with Kerensky, who asked if I would confirm what I had said. As I could not entertain the idea that an emissary sent me by the Provisional Government could distort the sense of my conversation, I replied that I did confirm my words fully and again invited Kerensky and Savinkoff to come to Stavka, as I could not answer for their safety if they remained in Petrograd. It is evident from the foregoing that my proceedings were in full accord with the Provisional Government, and I had every reason to believe that the Ministry was not playing a double game.

I learned to the contrary when I received a telegram saying that I immediately must hand over my supreme command. I conferred by telegraph with the Ministry of War and learned that Savinkoff not only had repudiated the proposals made by me, but even disavowed the fact of their having been made. Considering that further hesitation presented fatal dangers, and moreover as the orders issued could not be countermanded, I decided, with a full appreciation of the weight of my responsibility, not to hand over the supreme command, hoping that I might save my country and the Russian people from the imminent danger of enslavement by the Germans.

General Chablovsky, President of the commission of inquiry into the Korniloff affair, returned to Petrograd Oct. 15, and in an interview declared that he did not see in the actions of General Korniloff and the other accused officers any character of high treason. It was proved, he said, that General Korniloff throughout the movement committed no act of a nature to weaken the fighting front. General Chablovsky expressed the opinion that General Korniloff could be sentenced only under Article 100, dealing with attempts against the established régime and involving the penalty of life imprisonment.

## Conviction of Soukhomlinoff

The trial of General Soukhomlinoff, former Minister of War, accused of high treason, ended with his conviction on Sept. 26, 1917. He was sentenced to hard labor for life on the charges of high treason, abuse of confidence, and fraud. Mme. Soukhomlinoff was acquitted.

The jury deliberated seven hours and announced that they had arrived at a verdict of guilty on twelve of the thirteen counts preferred against Soukhomlinoff. A verdict of not guilty on the first charge, accusing him of inaction and inertia during the war with the object of assisting the enemy by weakening the Russian armed forces, was rendered.

General Soukhomlinoff received the verdict calmly, but his wife burst into tears. The jury found no extenuating circumstances, and the Prosecutor demanded the highest penalty, imprisonment for life at hard labor.

General Soukhomlinoff delivered the concluding speech with signs of great emotion. He affirmed that he had always been an ardent reformer and did more for the army than his predecessors had done in thirty years. Instead of the expected 3,000,000 soldiers, he pointed out, there had been mobilized before the beginning of active operations from 5,-000,000 to 6,000,000, and now there were from 10,000,000 to 15,000,000. The Germans, he declared, had lavished praise on his successful mobilization. With a flourish of his arms, Soukhomlinoff exclaimed:

" If I had lacked the self-sacrifice to abandon a splendid post at Kiev to go to that penitentiary, the War Office, I should never be here."

Soukhomlinoff lamented that of all the statesmen who could bear witness to his reforms, the chief of them, Stolypin, was now in his grave.

At the trial the chief accusers were Rodzianko, President of the Duma; Dr. Milukoff, the leader of the revolution, and Gutchkoff, first War Minister after the revolution. M. Rodzianko declared that General Soukhomlinoff's conduct had seriously alarmed the Duma a long time before the war, for it clearly saw his criminal slowness in the organization of the Russian Army. The ex-Minister, M. Rodzianko asserted, did not love the Duma, and showed his contempt for it. When the situation at the front became threatening, owing to the lack of shells, and the Duma sounded the alarm and appealed to the patriotism of the workers, General Soukhomlinoff at first feigned a great interest in the question, but soon afterward he began to oppose a systematic resistance to the efforts of the Deputies. This resistance made worse and complicated still more the terrible situation of the army, which found itself under the necessity of fighting without arms. In March, 1915, the Grand Duke Nicholas declared that the continuation of the war in these conditions was becoming impossible. "I then went," M.

Rodzianko continued, "to Galicia, and what I saw there filled me with terror. I affirm that the responsibility for the enormous losses which we suffered during the retreat entirely falls upon General Soukhomlinoff. The Committee of Defense which was specially created to investigate the activities of the ex-War Minister at once established his culpability. I then appealed to the ex-Czar, and persuaded him to convoke the Duma and to dismiss Soukhomlinoff."

The prosecution, in summing up the evidence, declared that when the investigation of General Soukhomlinoff's affairs began there was no thought that the charges would include spy work and treason. The evidence, however, he declared, led constantly to the close connection of General Soukhomlinoff and his wife with Colonel Maisoidof and other notorious spies.

The Prosecutor said the evidence proved that General Soukhomlinoff carelessly permitted war plans to lie about his house, especially in his wife's boudoir, where an Austrian agent had easy access to them.

# General Russky's Account of the Czar's Abdication

*Nicholas II. signed the notice of abdication at Pskof on March 15, 1917. One account of the event, given by Deputy V. V. Shulgin, (also spelled Choulgine,) was printed in the July issue of this magazine. Another and fuller story of the episode, as related by General Nicholas V. Russky, the chief representative of the Russian Army in this act of the revolution, is here placed on record. It has been translated for* CURRENT HISTORY MAGAZINE *from the original article, which appeared in the* Russkaya Volya *a few days after the incident.*

AT the time of abdicating the throne, the Czar made no attempt to send soldiers to quell the revolution, for the simple reason that I proposed his retirement at a moment when his situation was already beyond remedy. I learned on March 10 that he was preparing to return to Tsarskoe Selo. I was surprised, therefore, to receive a telegram that night stating that the Czar's train was scheduled from Bologoe through Dno to Pskof. It was to arrive there at 8 o'clock in the evening of the 14th.

I drove up to the station to meet him, and ordered that his arrival should take place unnoticed. The train came at 8. From the Czar's first words I was convinced that he was in the hands of fate. Nicholas usually said little, and on this occasion he was even more curt and economical of words. Events had not only agitated him, but also made him angry. He never dreamed of adopting repressive measures against the revolution, however; on the contrary, at 2 o'clock that night he sent for me and said: "I have decided to submit and to give the people a responsible Ministry. What is your opinion?"

A manifesto concerning a responsible Ministry lay already signed upon the table. I knew that this compromise came too late, and that it would fail, but I had no intention of expressing my opinion, because I had no direct instructions from the Executive Committee, nor even simple news of what was taking place. Therefore I proposed to talk by telephone immediately with Rodzianko.

I succeeded in getting Rodzianko on the line at Petrograd in the office of the Chief of Staff only after 3 o'clock at night. That conversation of ours lasted more than two hours. Rodzianko gave me all the details of the quick turn of events, and definitely told me that the only way for the Czar was manifestly to abdicate the throne. Following my talk with Rodzianko, I immediately transmitted this fact to Alexeieff and to the commanding officers at the front.

At 10 o'clock in the morning I went to the Czar with a report of my conversations. Guarding against lack of confidence in my words, I asked to have with me an officer of my general staff, Danieloff, and a commissary officer, General Savich, who would support me in my persistent advice to the Czar to abdicate for the sake of Russia's welfare and of victory over the enemy. At that time I already had answers from General Alexeieff, the Grand Duke Nicholas, General Brusiloff, and General Evert, who all unitedly recognized the necessity of abdication.

The Czar listened to my report and stated that he was ready to abdicate the throne, but would desire to do this in presence of Rodzianko, as the latter had promised to come to Pskof. However, Rodzianko had given no indication of a desire to come. On the contrary, in my night conversation with him over the wire he had definitely said that he could by no means leave Petrograd, and that he did not wish to do so.

We left the Czar with the expectation of decisive action on his part. After luncheon, at 3 o'clock, the Czar called me in and stated that the instrument of his abdication was already signed, and that he abdicated in favor of his son. He handed me a telegram, signed by him, concerning his abdication; I put it into my pocket and went out, intending to dispatch it from my office. Quite unexpectedly, at the office I found a telegram from Gutchkoff and Shulgin, containing the information that they had left Petrograd for Pskof at 3:35 P. M. On receiving that telegram I refrained from publishing the document in regard to abdication, and went back to the Czar. He evidently was quite glad to hear that these commissioners were on their way, hoping that their coming to me was evidence of some change in the situation.

The commissioners' train for some reason was late, arriving about 10 at night. The Czar waited with impatient expectation. I personally kept away from him when he hastened to meet and speak with them, but during the whole time old Fredericks [Count Fredericks, the Court Chamberlain] never left him alone.

At the moment of the commissioners' arrival I was in my railway carriage. Disregarding my order that on the arrival of the commissioners they should first be brought to me, one of the Generals got them first, met them, and took them straight to the Czar. When I came into the Czar's car, A. I. Gutchkoff was reporting to him in detail concerning the late events. A specially strong impression was made upon Nicholas II. by the news that his personal guard had gone over to the rebel army. That fact struck him so forcibly that he did not listen attentively to the further report of Gutchkoff.

The rest we all know. At the Czar's question, "What is to be done now?" Gutchkoff, in a tone permitting of only one decision, said, "You must abdicate the throne."

The Czar quietly listened to the commissioners of the Executive Committee. After a long pause he answered:

"Very well. I have already signed the act of abdication in favor of my son, but now I have come to the conclusion that my son's health is not strong enough. I do not wish to part from him. Therefore

I have decided to make over the throne to Michael Alexandrovich."

The commissioners made no reply. The Czar retired with Fredericks into a neighboring car to compose a new document of abdication. For ten minutes a heavy silence reigned. Finally Fredericks appeared with a typewritten act of abdication which the Czar had signed. The commissioners asked Fredericks to countersign the signature. With the assent of the Czar, Fredericks attached his signature. There are two copies of the act of abdication, one of which is kept by me; the other I gave to Gutchkoff, taking his receipt for it.

Thus in the course of twenty-four hours Nicholas II. signed in succession three acts: at 2 o'clock at night the 2d (15th) of March, a manifesto concerning the granting of a responsible Ministry; at 3 o'clock in the daytime an abdication in favor if his son Alexis, and finally at 10 o'clock at night the abdication in favor of Michael Alexandrovich.

.The arrival of the Czar at Pskof was known to all, but a surprising coolness and indifference to that fact prevailed among the inhabitants and soldiers. The Czar often walked entirely alone upon the station platform, and none of the public gave attention to him. He spent his time exclusively in company of several Generals of his suite who accompanied him.

Inside of half an hour after the delivery of the act of abdication and the departure of the Executive Committee of the commissioners the Czar's private train was routed through Dvinsk to Stanka, and on March 4 (17) at 6 o'clock in the evening I received a telegram from Stanka announcing his arrival there.

[In conclusion General Russky exhibited Nicholas's signed act of abdication. This is a closely written telegram blank, on which a typewriting machine has inscribed the famous text of the abdication. Nicholas's signature, which is in pencil, has been covered with lacquer, but Fredericks's countersignature, which is in ink,

has not been so covered. Further details on this part of the historic episode have been given by V. V. Shulgin, one of the two commissioners above named, as follows:]

When we had read and approved the Czar's abdication, it seems to me that there followed a clasping of hands, as if of a hearty character. However, at that time I was undoubtedly agitated, and may be mistaken. It is possible this did not happen. I recall that when at last I looked at my watch, it was 11:48. Therefore it is necessary to think that all these events of huge historical importance took place between 11 and 12 o'clock in the night of March 2-3, (15-16, new style.) I recollect that when this happened a thought flashed through my mind of how well it was that it came on March 2, and not on March 1. After that we said good-bye. It seems to me that there was no bad feeling on either side at that moment. In my soul there was rather pity toward the person who in that moment was redeeming his mistakes. Noble thoughts illuminated his resignation of power.

From external appearances, the Czar was entirely tranquil, and friendly rather than cold. I forgot to say that General Russky and I agreed that there should be two copies of the act signed by the maker's own hand, for the purpose of preserving it, since in the stormy situation at Petrograd, where we were taking it, it could easily be lost. In that situation the first signed act on the small pages ought to remain with General Russky. We then carried in the second copy, also written with a typewriter, but on large-sized sheets. The signature of the Czar, in the same way, on the right hand, was done with a pencil, and on the left side with a pen, and the Court Minister, Fredericks, countersigned it. On receiving this copy, which was intrusted to our care by General Russky, we, that is, Gutchkoff and myself, gave a receipt. That copy we brought to Petrograd and succeeded in giving it over into safe hands. There were moments when the document brought danger.

# The Socialist Parties of Russia

## What the Various Factions Stand For

AT the close of the nineteenth century the peasants of Russia formed a radical democratic organization, whose activities, naturally, remained clandestine. After the revolutionary events of 1904-5 there were created—or, rather, they officially declared their existence—certain peasant societies that were very important by reason of the number of their members. At the head of these bodies was the All-Russian Peasant Union, and, after the creation of the Duma, the Group of Toil. The programs of both were very much alike. While the Peasant Union, however, concentrated its energies upon organizing the peasants in a compact body with a view to seizing the lands of the nobles and distributing them among the peasants, the Group of Toil became the Parliamentary representative of the rural democracy. After the elections for the First Duma the committees of Deputies from the Group of Toil, in fact, took the place of the All-Russian Peasant Union, which had been broken up by Governmental repression after the defeat of the revolutionaries.

Kerensky, the present Premier, originally belonged to the Group of Toil, but his later activities in the Duma caused him to be classed with the moderates in the Social Revolutionary Party.

The program of the Group of Toil, established by the "populist intellectuals," proclaimed "the right of all citizens to the land, the suppression of private ownership of real estate, and the creation of a national estate of public lands." All persons desirous of cultivating the soil were to receive from this public estate allotments not exceeding the "norm of labor," that is, the amount of land which the user could cultivate with his own hands and those of his family, "without paid help." These allotments were to be given only for use, not for possession.

The Socialists in the towns, almost all factory workmen, combated the program of the Group of Toil from the beginning. They reproached it with putting an obstacle in the way of all development of farm production, and declared that it rendered impossible the organization of great enterprises employing machinery and salaried workmen, creating not an equality of wealth, but an equality of poverty.

### The Social Revolutionaries

The Social Revolutionary Party has numerous points of contact with the Group of Toil. Its Duma members, almost all men with the viewpoint of peasants, formerly figured in the Group of Toil, for the Social Revolutionary Party, which was not solidly organized before the Czar's abdication, had never been recognized by the Government.

On the agrarian question the Social Revolutionaries espouse the struggle against the bourgeois principle of property, taking their stand upon the communistic principle, upon Russian peasant traditions, and upon the opinion, very general among the people, that the land belongs to no one and that the right to enjoy its use is acquired only by working on it. This party also is fighting for the socialization of the land and for its exclusion from commercial exchange. Like the Group of Toil, they have faith in the realization of agrarian socialism; they establish an absolute antithesis between the middle-class principle of capitalistic society and the peasants' traditions of communistic life. They do not regard the *mir* and the whole organization of the rural Russian commune as a survival of the past, constituting a form inferior to the capitalistic system, but look upon it as the very foundation upon which to realize their ideal.

This conception has always been violently combated by the Social Democrats, who are convinced Marxists, believing that Russia cannot arrive at socialism save by the path of capitalism, the path followed by all other countries of Europe; that the socialization of the means and tools of production on the farms will be possible only when conditions favorable to socialization shall exist in all the other domains of social economy; when production shall be strongly centralized, the differentiation of classes very marked, and labor freed from capital.

The principal leaders of the Social Revolutionary Party are Kerensky, the present Premier; Tchernoff, former Minister of Agriculture; Peshekhonoff, Food Administrator; Miakotine, Boukanoff, Avtsentieff, Savinkoff, (Robchine.) Since the revolution they have founded two newspapers, the Dielo Naroda at Petrograd and the Zemlia i Volia at Moscow.

## The Social Democrats

The Social Democratic Party, very strongly organized, has as its adherents the working population of the great industrial centres and almost all the students. Its origin goes back to the end of the nineteenth century, when Russian industry began to experience a great expansion. The noted Russian Socialist, Plekhanoff, an adept in the theories of Marx, founded at Geneva in 1884 the Association for the Liberation of the Working Class, out of which came the first propagandists of socialistic ideas in Russia. These created in the Russian villages the most important of the secret societies that kept up communications with the central committee at Geneva.

As the existence of trade union organizations was then impossible, the leaders instituted a purely revolutionary propaganda. Owing to the general discontent with the autocratic régime, this propaganda was welcomed even by the liberal bourgeoisie, who were willing for the moment to sacrifice their class interests for the sake of triumphing in their political aims. The revolutionary movement of 1904-5 and the general strike which broke out in October, 1905, and which ultimately caused the promulgation of the constitutional manifesto of Oct. 30, 1905, were the work of this party. The leaders are divided into two factions, as follows:

## Bolsheviki and Mensheviki

The Bolsheviki, or Maximalists, form the Left or radical wing of the Social Democratic Party, which is largely the party of the proletariat. The party split in 1906, and the ultra radicals, led by Nikolai Lenine, were then in the majority, or "bolshinstvo," and hence got the name Bolsheviki, which meant the majority faction. Today the Bolsheviki are also known as Maximalists, Leninites, Extremists, Zimmerwaldians, and Internationalists. They are opposed to offensive warfare, they want an immediate general peace, and seek to establish immediately the rule of the proletariat, the division of land, and the dispossession of the property classes. They are enemies of the present Provisional Government, even with a Constitution, and a large faction is extremely anarchistic in its views. They reject on principle any co-operation with legal organizations, and regard revolutionary action as alone effective. Nevertheless, two of their chiefs, Skobeleff and Tseretelli, by force of circumstances, accepted places in the Government, the former as Minister of Labor, the latter as Minister of the Interior. Their other leaders are Tscheidze, Lenine, Tschenkeli. Their organs, created since the revolution, are the Social Democrat at Moscow and the Pravda (Truth) at Petrograd, and Gorki's review, Novaia Zhisn, (New Life.)

The Mensheviki, or Minimalists, comprise the Right, or moderate elements of the proletarian Social Democratic Party. In the split of 1906 they were in the "menshinstvo," or minority, and became known as the Mensheviki or minority party. In contrast to the Bolsheviki, the Mensheviki believe in a compromise with the middle class, in the fullest prosecution of the war, and in gradual socialistic reforms. Though enemies of the present régime and not averse to revolutionary action, they admit the possibility of utilizing for their ends all the existing organizations — co-operative societies, trade unions, mutual aid funds, Parliamentary activity—and are declared advocates of the participation of workingmen in the War Industries Committees, among which have been created groups of workingmen with an autonomous or-organization. The chief leaders of the Minimalists or Mensheviki are Plekhanoff, Burtseff, Deutsch, Alexinsky. Their organs created since the revolution are—at Petrograd, the Rabotchaia Gazeta (Workingmen's Journal) and the Edinstvo, (Unity,) edited by Plekhanoff; at Moscow, the Vpered, (Forward!)

But the Bolsheviki are not all in the Social Democratic Party. The Social Revolutionary Party, which consists chiefly of peasants, also has its Bolsheviki and Mensheviki factions. The Bolsheviki are the radical extremists of the party, who in the Summer of 1917 adopted the name Bolsheviki because they were largely in harmony with Lenine on the issues of the day. The Social Revolutionary Party is at present the strongest of Russia's socialistic organizations. The leader of its Bolsheviki is Gotz, and apparently also Victor Tchernoff, ex-Minister of Agriculture and an almost fanatical believer in the doctrine of communal ownership of all the land by the peasantry, to be distributed among them immediately.

There are also the Mensheviki of the Social Revolutionary Party, moderates, and the most nationalistic of the Socialist factions. Their leaders are Kerensky, Avtsentieff, "Babushka" Breshkorakaya. Like the Mensheviki of the Social Democratic Party, they favor a coalition Government, a compromise with the bourgeoisie, and active warfare against the enemy.

## The Constitutional Democrats

To complete the tale of parties and factions, there should be a mention of the Constitutional Democrats, or Cadets, though they do not belong under the head of Socialists. The popular appellation "Cadets" is built of the initials of the party's real name, Constitutional Democrats. The leader of the party is Paul Milukoff, ex-Minister of Foreign Affairs. The Constitutional Democrats comprise all the bourgeois elements of the nation, the business and industrial interests as well as the landed and professional classes. They are sometimes called Progressives or Liberals. They stand for conservatism, nationalism, fullest prose-

cution of the war in co-operation with the Allies, and for the postponement of all internal reform till after the war. They are the solid and stable element of the country, and were in control at the time of the first organization of the Provisional Government, but have since been thrust into the background by the more radical and aggressive factions of the Socialist parties.

To sum up, the Group of Toil is a purely parliamentary organization composed of peasant Deputies, whose program is closely akin to that of the Constitutional Democrats, except on the agrarian question, where they hold absolutely to the principle of communistic ownership of the land. Russians do not consider this a really socialistic party.

The Revolutionary Socialists and the Social Democrats, on the contrary, are two purely socialistic parties, whose rivalry has long divided the intellectual youth of Russia into two warring camps. But theoretically, save on the agrarian question, both have a program almost always in common—a democratic republic, universal suffrage for both sexes, substitution of militia for the regular army, election of Judges, suppression of indirect taxes, an eight-hour day. The revolution, moreover, has brought about profound changes in the Socialist parties; it is noticeable that in recent events the Social Democratic Minimalists have almost always allied themselves with the moderate Social Revolutionaries to fight against the wild schemes of the Social Democratic Maximalists. In the Democratic Congress held at Petrograd at the beginning of October, 1917, the Cadets were absent, having boycotted the meeting, and the struggle over the question of a Coalition Government was wholly between the Bolsheviki of the two socialistic parties and the Mensheviki of the same two parties.

It may be added that the Soviet, or Council of Workmen's and Soldiers' Delegates, which has done much to create the present state of chaos, is an irregular, self-constituted body made up largely of peasants, workmen, and soldiers belonging to the two great Socialist parties, which represent the majority of the masses of the nation.

# Air Raids and Reprisals

## Thirty-four Attacks on London, Killing 865 and Wounding 2,500, Goad England to a Change of Policy

WAR in the air reached much greater ferocity in September and October, 1917, than ever before, and extensive preparations were begun by all the belligerents to speed up the manufacture of airplanes and to give this arm of the service a far greater importance than in the past.

During the full moon period between Sept. 24 and Oct. 1 there were six important air raids on London; 52 men, women and children were killed outright and 258 wounded. No material damage to military or munition establishments was inflicted; the only result accomplished was to arouse among the English people such a clamorous demand for reprisals that Premier Lloyd George announced to a crowd of poor people in the southwest district of London on Oct. 3:

"We will give it all back to them, and we will give it soon. We shall bomb Germany with compound interest."

### General Smuts on Reprisals

On the same day Lieut. Gen. Smuts, speaking with the authority of a member of the War Cabinet, said the Government had been reluctantly forced by recent air raids on London and other English cities to apply the maxim of "an eye for an eye and a tooth for a tooth" and to carry out an air offensive on an unprecedented scale against German cities. General Smuts declared that the national temper instead of weakening was hardening under the strain of these terrors and abominations. He continued:

If the Germans understood the psychology of this people, they would have no doubt about the results. Cowards become more cowardly under threat of danger, but brave men and women only become more determined. And the people of London after these raids are thinking less of peace than ever before.

But the Germans never have understood the psychology of their enemies, and so they will continue to blunder to the end of the chapter. It is wrong to think that we hitherto have had no means of carrying our aerial warfare into the enemy country. I already have said that ever since the battle of the Somme we have had a clear military superiority in the air, and on a small scale we could have followed that up by bombing enemy centres as the enemy bombed London and other places in this country. But we felt that we should prepare for an air offensive on a large scale, and we were also anxious to avoid adding further horrors to a war already the most cruel in the history of the world.

But we are dealing with an enemy whose culture has not carried him beyond the rudiments of the Mosaic law, and to whom you can only apply the maxim of "an eye for an eye and a tooth for a tooth." On that principle we are now most reluctantly forced to apply to him the bombing policy which he has applied to us. I am afraid we no longer have any choice in the matter.

Last month our naval and military airplanes dropped 207 tons of bombs behind the lines of the enemy. In the same period he dropped four and one-half tons of bombs on London. In that month we bombed him on twenty-three days and on nineteen nights, chiefly attacking his airdromes, and, as the figures show, damaging his machines and pitting his airdromes with shell holes. We also bombed his billets, trains, transport and railway stations, causing him the heaviest losses.

### Another Chapter of Horrors

Allow me to emphasize two points which I hope will be borne in mind when it is ultimately found that my words are not bluff, but serious and far-reaching in their import.

First, we did not begin this business of bombing industrial and populous districts. The enemy began the practice, just as he began the use of poison gas and other contraventions of international law. And we have been most reluctantly forced to follow suit after a long delay, which severely tried the patience of the British public.

Secondly, I look upon these developments of the arts of war as utterly bad and immoral, and while I do not fear them if, as in the present case, they are forced on us, yet I should infinitely prefer that both sides should desert such cruel practices. We shall do our best to avoid German abominations, and in our air offensive against military and industrial

MAKING THE SECOND LIBERTY LOAN A SUCCESS

(Photo Paul Thompson)

A Great Demonstration, in Connection with the Second Liberty Loan Campaign, Outside the City Hall, New York City

IN HONOR OF THE AMERICAN RED CROSS

(Photo Paul Thompson)

The Great Farewell Parade in New York City of the American Red Cross Women and Men Who Are Serving in Hospitals Abroad

centres of the enemy we shall use every endeavor to spare, as far as is humanly possible, the innocent and defenseless who in the past enjoyed the protection of international law.

*It is almost unbearable to think that another chapter of horrors must be added to the awful story, but we can only plead that it has not been our doing, and the blame must rest on an enemy who apparently recognizes no laws, human or Divine; who knows no pity or restraint, who sang te deums over the sinking of the Lusitania and to whom the maiming and slaughter of women and children appear legitimate means of warfare.*

In the face of such abominations it is not for us to meekly fold our hands. We can only fight to the uttermost for the ideals of a more human civilization, which we trust and feel convinced will triumph in the end.

Early in October France began a series of air raids on German cities in reprisal for raids on the French cities of Bar-le-Duc and Dunkirk. Bombs were dropped upon Stuttgart, Frankfort-on-the-Main, Rastatt, Baden Baden, Dortmund, Türingen, and other cities.

## Air Raids on London

German aircraft raided England thirty-four times between Jan. 19, 1915, and Oct. 1, 1917, killing outright 865 men, women, and children, and wounding over 2,500. The list of the principal raids is as follows:

| 1915 | Killed | Injured |
|---|---|---|
| Jan. 19 | 4 | .. |
| May 31 | 6 | .. |
| June 6 | 24 | .. |
| June 15 | 16 | .. |
| Aug. 9 | 14 | .. |
| Aug. 12 | 6 | .. |
| Aug. 17 | 10 | .. |
| Sept. 7 | 13 | .. |
| Sept. 8 | 20 | .. |
| Oct. 13 | 56 | 144 |
| 1916 | | |
| Jan. 31 | 61 | 101 |
| March 15 | 12 | 33 |
| March 31 | 43 | 66 |
| April 1 | 16 | 100 |
| May 2 | 36 | .. |
| Aug. 9 | 6 | 17 |
| Aug. 24 | 8 | 36 |
| Sept. 2 | 2 | 13 |
| Sept. 23 | 38 | 125 |
| Sept. 24 | 36 | 27 |
| 1917 | | |
| May 24 | 76 | 174 |
| June 5 | 2 | 29 |
| June 13 | 97 | 439 |
| July 4 | 11 | 36 |

| 1917 | Killed | Injured |
|---|---|---|
| July 7 | 37 | 141 |
| July 22 | 11 | 26 |
| Aug. 12 | 32 | 43 |
| Aug. 22 | 11 | 13 |
| Sept. 3 | 108 | 92 |
| Sept. 24 | 15 | 70 |
| Sept. 25 | 7 | 26 |
| Sept. 28 | 11 | 82 |
| Sept. 30 | 9 | 42 |
| Oct. 1 | 10 | 38 |

## Scenes During a Raid

The scenes in London during an air raid are full of thrilling interest. Three years' experience with such perils have hardened the public, and panic no longer is shown. A correspondent thus describes the scenes during the raid of Sept. 26 on London:

"The lesson of the advisability of seeking cover quickly has obviously been taken to heart, and the great majority of people sought the nearest available shelter directly the louder sound of the guns indicated the closer approach of the raiders. Tube stations were favorite resorts in the fortunate neighborhoods where they were to be found, and crowds of people were grateful to the railwaymen, policemen, and "specials" who shepherded them to the safe depths.

"Every station was packed with orderly crowds. At first the booking-office floors, the first to be reached from the street level, proved the most popular sections of the stations, but as the firing came nearer people sought the more secure protection of the platforms and corridors.

"Churches also were opened to the public for shelter, and here large numbers sought refuge, particularly at those which were known to have crypts and underground spaces. In some cases a red lamp burning outside warned the public that shelter could be found within. Public buildings of all kinds which were stout enough to offer some resistance to possible bombs had open doors, and caretakers and others of the staffs in many of the great blocks of offices and business premises were also quick in their offers to share their greater safety with any who sought it.

"For some time the buses and taxicabs continued to run, although there was a noticeable air of hurry about those speeding westward from the more exposed areas in the east. In a few cases drivers refused to stop to pick up would-be passengers. In several instances there were passages of arms between drivers and the more considerate conductresses.

" As the firing grew heavier, however, and the flash of the bursting shells could be seen clearly in the neighborhood, drivers and fares of both taxis and buses left the vehicles to seek shelter, and soon the main streets presented a curious appearance, with few pedestrians, and with long rows of lightless and deserted vehicles lined up by the curbs. But within two or three minutes only of the last reports, drivers and conductresses were again mounting the buses, and there was no lack of passengers to accompany them on the resumed journeys.

" Before the raid the police were out with ' Take cover ' notices, some cycling through the streets and others patrolling with the placards, a number of which were attached to the posts of central refuges.

" There was no surprise, no scare, no panic. Folk had told each other what might be expected on a moonlight night, and they took the handiest cover with cheery confidence in its effectiveness. Tube subways were specially useful. Men, women, and children—not many children, by the way—flocked down the steps to these places, and quietly waited until danger was over. Men read their evening papers; city girls who had been working late became absorbed in their favorite novels, with which they beguile traveling time in tram and train; and the woman inclined to be tearful or nervous was reassured by comforting words from her neighbors."

## Tragedy at a Hotel

Another correspondent describes the effect of a bomb falling in front of a hotel as follows:

" A number of guests are reported to have gathered in the porch to watch the progress of the raid. A bomb dropped close to the main entrance, almost on the pavement, killing several of those who stood near. The concussion of the explosion was terrific. Three porters of the hotel, two of whom were just going off duty, and all of whom were outside the building, were killed instantly. Three other people, it is said, who were in the roadway also were killed outright, and a gentleman and a lady who were standing in a doorway opposite also were killed.

" Great bravery was shown by a number of persons in this hotel, and one man who was badly injured himself was most assiduous in helping others. A doctor, whose head was cut, and hastily bandaged, performed his humane work with great energy. Several persons were passing at the time, and eight of the passers-by are stated to be among the injured, bringing the total, with those who suffered in the hotel, up to fifteen. The bomb made a hole in the roadway some four feet deep, the force of the explosion blowing out all the windows in front of the building, even to the sixth story, and shattering the glass in most of the houses on either side of the street for several hundred yards.

" In another area one bomb dropped on a six-floor tenement house, totally destroying the upper portions of the building. A lad of 15 years lost his life under very pathetic circumstances. When the alarm was given, the people in the tenements ran into the cellar of a neighboring public house, which had been thrown open by the proprietor. This lad was in safety in the cellar, when he rushed back into the danger zone to join his aged grandfather, who was bedridden in the tenement. He had just arrived when the bomb dropped. A beam fell and struck him on the temple, apparently killing him instantly. He was found lying underneath the beam. His grandfather was seriously injured, and was taken in an ambulance to the hospital."

## In a Narrow Street

The havoc wrought by one airplane in a narrow street is thus described:

" The noise of gunfire was the first warning which the people of the district received, and but for the fact that sufficient time passed before the sudden terror of the bombing to enable the majority of the inhabitants to take shelter, the casualty list must have been far larger than it actually was. The airplane flew in an oblique direction across the many intersecting streets, and bombs were dropped at distances of about two hundred yards apart.

" The first bomb fell in a street. A moment later the second crashed into the side of another road with destructive effect. A great hole was scooped out in the ground. The fronts of two-story houses opposite were partially shattered, and in most of the other houses in the street glass was smashed, woodwork hurled inward, and the contents of rooms displaced.

" A girl was just entering the doorway of a house near the explosion and she was killed instantly. On the other side of the street a man standing in his doorway was terribly wounded about the upper part of his body, and another man who was leaning against the front garden fence also received severe injuries. Nearly all the other people in this street were under cover, and they escaped physical harm. A man and his wife, who were just going into the cellar when the bomb exploded, were flung headlong down the steps.

" The third bomb fell in a back garden against a party wall between two streets, and it dug a huge crater in the soft earth. The backs of two houses were partially blown in, but fortunately the inhabitants had left two minutes earlier to take shelter in a neighbor's house, in which the only damage was broken glass. Other houses were less seriously damaged, and because the tenants had taken shelter in the centre of the buildings only one girl was seriously injured.

" The fourth bomb caused more material damage, but nearly all the people in the street had left their little houses to find refuge in a school building forty or fifty yards away. The bomb fell in a back yard near the middle of a row of houses, and the rooms just opposite were almost completely wrecked. If any one had been within he could not conceivably have escaped unhurt. All along the street, on both sides, windows and doorways were blown out, and a bank and a jeweler's shop were damaged.

" The special volunteer policemen, who have been assisting the regular police since the beginning of the war, in emergencies, are receiving shrapnel helmets for protection during air raids. These helmets are similar to those worn in the trenches and hereafter will be a common sight in London. Soldiers on leave and ambulance drivers only have heretofore used them during raids."

## Effects of the Raids

The change of opinion in England from composure over the raids to a demand for reprisals is traceable to a realization that while the material damage from raids is negligible, they did succeed in diverting considerable pressure which otherwise would have been felt on the battle fronts. By the employment of some fifty machines and at the most two hundred men, including aviators and mechanics, the enemy has forced England to detach several hundred valuable guns and several thousand men, including skilled gunners, for home defense, and also a large number of machinists, searchlights with operating staffs and other experts. The number of men and the amount of material devoted to this offensive are small compared with the men and material these attacks compel England to maintain for the defensive.

Local and suburban travel has been largely at a standstill during these periods, and all classes of night work have been interfered with, while the day work has been curtailed that clerks and workmen might get to their homes from offices, factories and shops before the expected raids began. Ten thousand persons who are not compelled to remain in London have moved to country resorts at a large aggregate expense, and the late afternoon trains have been packed with the nightly exodus. Many poor families have camped in suburban parks and commons.

## Death of Guynemer

Captain Georges Guynemer, officially credited with destroying fifty-three German airplanes, known as " King of the Aces," (an " ace " is an aviator who has brought down five enemy aircraft,) met his death shortly after leaving Dunkirk Sept. 11. He was only 23 years old, son of a manufacturer who had been a Captain in the French Army. He was rejected as a private on account of frail health five times and at length was allowed to enlist as a student aviator. Three weeks after he received his pilot's license in January, 1916, he brought down his fifth enemy airplane, and thereafter every few days some new heroic feat was credited to him. His most spectacular feat, for which he was made a Lieutenant and decorated with the Cross of War, was on Sept. 29 last year, when he rose in the air to defend a comrade of his escadrille who had been attacked by five German Fokkers.

At a height of more than 10,000 feet Captain Guynemer shot and dropped two of the Germans within thirty seconds of each other. He then pursued the three others, and in two minutes had shot down his third enemy machine. He was pursuing the remaining two Fokkers when an enemy shell exploded under his airplane and tore away one wing.

" I felt myself dropping," he said later. " It was 10,000 feet to the earth, and, like a flash, I saw my funeral with my saddened comrades marching behind the gun carriage to the cemetery. But I pulled and pushed every lever I had, but nothing would check my terrific descent.

" Five thousand feet from the earth the wrecked machine began to turn somersaults, but I was strapped into the seat. I do not know what it was, but something happened and I felt the speed descent lessen. But suddenly there was a tremendous crash and when I recovered my senses I had been taken from the wreckage and was all right."

Three times Captain Guynemer was wounded in battle, but each time slightly. In one day he was officially credited with shooting down four enemy aeroplanes, which was the record, as was his feat of dropping the three Fokkers in two minutes and thirty seconds when he himself dropped 10,000 feet.

Aside from that fall, the nearest he was to death, he always believed, was when his machine was disabled by shell fire and it fell with him in No Man's Land, between the French and German trenches. The Germans opened a galling machine-gun fire to prevent his escape, but the French went " over the top "

and in a sanguinary hand-to-hand conflict he was rescued.

Captain Guynemer was always alone in his airplane. He used the lighest craft that would carry sufficient gasoline and a machine gun with ammunition. To him gasoline and ammunition were more valuable than a gunner. The machine gun was attached to the top of the airplane, directly above his head, and was so arranged that when he pulled a lever the gun would be discharged. As the gun was fast to the airplane, he had to point his airplane at the enemy. Sights were arranged in front of him, so that when the enemy came within the sights he pulled the gun lever and it would begin firing.

For his exploits in the air Captain Guynemer won the Cross of the Legion of Honor, the Military Medal, the War Cross and nearly every other honor his grateful country could bestow.

## How He Met His Death

Guynemer's last fight is described by a comrade, who is quoted by Excelsior as follows:

" Guynemer sighted five machines of the Albatross type D-3. Without hesitating he bore down on them. At that moment enemy patrolling machines, soaring at a great height, appeared suddenly and fell upon Guynemer.

" There were forty enemy machines in the air at this time, including Count von Richthofen and his circus division of machines, painted in diagonal blue and white stripes. Toward Guynemer's right some Belgian machines hove in sight, but it was too late.

" Guynemer must have been hit. His machine dropped gently toward the earth and I lost track of it. All that I can say is that the machine was not on fire."

### Airplane Activity

The French War Ministry announced on Oct. 12 that in September French aviators destroyed sixty-seven German airplanes and two observation balloons, forced eighty machines to land badly damaged, and made 1,099 bombing raids in which more than 165 tons of explosives were dropped within the German lines.

In September the allied aviators of the

French, British, Italian, and Russian armies dropped more than 500 tons of explosives upon enemy camps and cities. Several of the most noted German aces were killed in aerial combats.

The United States has appropriated $640,000,000 for the construction of aircraft, and contracts for more than 20,000 airplanes have been let.

### German Figures

The Berliner Tageblatt, with the caution that its figures are not "absolutely trustworthy," gives the following statement of air warfare:

|  | Airplanes Shot Down. | |
|---|---|---|
|  | German. | Enemy. |
| 1914 ..................... | — | 9 |
| 1915 ..................... | 91 | 131 |
| 1916 ..................... | 221 | 784 |
| 1917 (to end of July) .... | 370 | 1,374 |

From Aug. 1, 1914, to July 31, 1915, 72 enemy airplanes were shot down, of which 39 fell into German hands; from Aug. 1, 1915, to July 31, 1916, 455 enemy airplanes were shot down, of which 267 fell into German hands; from Aug. 1, 1916, to July 31, 1917, "about" 1,771 enemy airplanes were shot down, of which 776 fell into German hands.

In 1915 two enemy captive balloons, so far as is known, were shot down; in 1916, 42; in 1917 to Aug. 1, 142. Three enemy airships were also shot down.

Total aircraft shot down from Aug. 1, 1914, to Aug. 1, 1917, about 2,298 enemy and 682 German airplanes, 186 enemy captive balloons, and 3 airships.

The London Times took strong exception to these figures, replying as follows:

The Paris Matin, whose authority is at least as high on the one side as that of the Berliner Tageblatt is on the other, stated on Jan. 1, 1917, that the French brought down 450 German machines in 1916 and the British 250. This figure of 700 compares with the German admission of 221. There is confirmation of this unofficial estimate in the table compiled from the statements in the official communiqués of British and French Headquarters which appeared in The Times of Dec. 5, 1916, and which showed that, for the six months June to November in that year, 666 German machines were brought, shot, or driven down by the Allies. If we take the year 1917 as it is calculated by the Tageblatt—Aug. 1, 1916, to July 31, 1917—the official British and French figures show that 2,076 German machines were sent down—1,325 by the British, 751 by the French. It is not pretended that all these were destroyed, but if we take, merely for May, June, and July, those which were officially stated to have crashed, to have been destroyed, brought down in flames, shot down by gunfire, or captured, we get, instead of the Tageblatt's figure of 370 for the whole year, 523 for three months.

—*Dallas News.*
### Who Can Blame Him?

# Revelations of German Plots

## Von Igel's Captured Papers Disclose Bernstorff's Illegal Intrigues in the United States

*The State Department at Washington in late September and early October, 1917, made public through the Committee on Public Information a series of secret German papers which had been captured a year and a half earlier from Wolf von Igel, German propaganda agent, and which reveals portions of the vast system of criminal plots carried on in this country with the knowledge and active assistance of Count von Bernstorff, the German Ambassador at Washington. The narrative printed below is based on that of the Official Bulletin.*

A T the time in the Fall of 1914 when the German plots against Canada were fomenting in this country there was established at 60 Wall Street, New York, an "advertising" office presided over by a large, suave man of Teutonic aspect named Wolf von Igel. There were two peculiar features about this office. One was that it was frequented during two years of singularly quiet and unbusinesslike existence chiefly by Germans who had nothing whatsoever to do with advertising. The other was a large safe, bearing the insignia of the German Imperial Government.

To this office there came one morning in April, 1916, while von Igel was preparing a mass of papers which he had taken from the safe for transfer to the German Embassy in Washington, four United States Secret Service agents from the Department of Justice, who made their way past the guardians always on duty, put von Igel under arrest, and undertook to seize the papers. The German was powerful and brave. With the aid of one associate he stubbornly fought the officers, striving to rescue the papers, to close the safe, to get to the telephone and communicate with his superiors. Revolvers were drawn by the Secret Service men. They produced no effect upon the intrepid von Igel.

" This is German territory," he shouted. " Shoot me and you will bring on war."

## German Embassy Protests

There was no shooting. But after a protracted struggle the defenders were overpowered and the papers seized. The German Embassy at once entered its protest. These were official papers. They were sacrosanct. The diplomatic prerogative of a friendly nation had been overridden and the person of its representative insulted. To this the State Department replied that the invaded premises at 60 Wall Street were described in the contract as a private business office for the carrying on of advertising, and that von Igel had not been formally accredited as a German representative.

When the papers were examined by the Department of Justice the reason for von Igel's determined fight became apparent. Here, in the form of letters, telegrams, notations, checks, receipts, ledgers, cashbooks, cipher codes, lists of spies, and other memoranda and records were found indications—in some instances of the vaguest nature, in others of the most damning conclusiveness—that the German Imperial Government, through its representatives in a then friendly nation, was concerned with—

Violation of the laws of the United States.

Destruction of lives and property in merchant vessels on the high seas.

Irish revolutionary plots against Great Britain.

Fomenting ill-feeling against the United States in Mexico.

Subornation of American writers and lecturers.

Financing of propaganda.

Maintenance of a spy system under the guise of a commercial investigation bureau.

Subsidizing of a bureau for the purpose of stirring up labor troubles in munition plants.

The bomb industry and other related activities.

### German Ambassador Alarmed

From the moment of the seizure of these papers Count von Bernstorff realized that his position was in danger; but the revelation of their contents was delayed, and his activities continued, as shown by telegrams that come into the later phases of the present story.

During the early stages of the war Bernstorff contented himself with the establishment of a great secret service in this country, coupled with a machine for propagating anti-British sentiment. When the United States and Great Britain were involved in dispute over British methods of seizing American shipping bound for Germany, Bernstorff by every means possible focused attention upon the injustice of the allied cause. When this policy failed, Bernstorff, acting by agents throughout the country, sought to cripple American industry which was helping the allied war machine. During this period he carefully avoided becoming directly involved in the crimes. He established von Papen, Boy-Ed, Wolf von Igel, and Dr. Albert in New York, where they kept far enough from him to clear his official skirts. Then von Igel became the leader of the dynamite men working with Boy-Ed and von Papen. Finally von Igel was caught red-handed. Bernstorff was invited by Secretary Lansing to go to the State Department and claim such papers as he regarded as official, but he did not go, knowing that they incriminated the embassy itself.

### Placing Bombs on Vessels

One of the most significant papers in the von Igel collection is a letter of July 20, 1915, written upon the stationery of the Bureau of Investigation. This innocent-pretending agency was at the outset the secret service of the Hamburg-American Steamship Company. Under Paul König, its manager, it became an adjunct to the German diplomatic secret service. " XXX " is the secret designation of König, who is now under indictments on criminal charges in connection with his " diplomatic " work, and is interned at Fort Oglethorpe. The person represented by the figure " 7000 " is Captain von Papen, former Military Attaché

of the German Embassy and the practical executive of its underground system. The document describes the subterfuges of " XXX " (König) so that he might not be identified by the mysterious —— when they met. " XXX " states that money was to be drawn for the payment of $150 to the unnamed person, under peculiar precautions, through " Check No. 146 on the Riggs National Bank, Washington, dated July 16, payable to ——, signed ——, amount $150. No reason was given as to why the payment was made," says the report.

Several days after the payment the recipient called at the " passenger office of the —— Line " and made a statement, which is thus embodied in the XXX report:

> My name is ——. I have an office at the —— building, but I do not care to state my local address. I intend to cause serious damage to vessels of the Allies leaving ports of the United States by placing bombs, which I am making myself, on board. These bombs resemble ordinary lumps of coal, and I am planning to have them concealed in the coal to be laden on steamers of the Allies.

### Brought Sample Bomb

Finally XXX states that " the caller " brought with him a sample bomb, " such as has been described to you by the subscriber," and asks for the instructions.

The document is lettered at the foot, " O. R. to 7000," indicating that the secret agent known as " O. R." had transmitted it to von Papen.

Now for the proof, direct and unescapable. Check 146 on the Riggs National Bank has been traced and added to the Secret Service collection. It is payable to König and signed by von Papen. Therefore, von Papen stands convicted, on the evidence of a report claimed as an official document by the Germans, of paying money to a plotter designing to blow up merchant ships sailing from the Port of New York.

Three members of the gang of plotters who received thousands of dollars for distributing the bombs which sank thirty ships carrying munitions to the Allies in 1915 were arrested in New York Oct. 10, 1917, and are now held for trial. The evidence against them was found in von Igel's papers.

Compare the foregoing facts with the following authorized statement from Berlin, transmitted by wireless for publication in THE NEW YORK TIMES in December, 1915:

> The German Government has, naturally, never knowingly accepted the support of any person, group of persons, society, or organization seeking to promote the cause of Germany in the United States by illegal acts, by counsel of violence, by contravention of law, or by any means whatever that could offend the American people in the pride of their own authority.

## Making Trouble in Factories

Closely related to and to some extent under the guidance of von Igel was the German and Austro-Hungarian Labor Information and Relief Bureau, with central headquarters at 136 Liberty Street, New York City, and branches in Cleveland, Detroit, Bridgeport, Pittsburgh, Philadelphia, and Chicago. The head of the enterprise was Hans Liebau, from whom it took its familiarly accepted name of the "Liebau Employment Agency." During the trying days which followed the arrest of the Welland Canal conspirators it was unwaveringly asserted that the Liebau concern was a bona fide employment agency and nothing else, with no object other than to secure positions for German, Austrian, or Hungarian workmen seeking employment. That was for publication only. In von Igel's papers the truth appears, brought out by the refusal of the Austro-Hungarian Embassy to continue its subsidies to the bureau.

That the Austro-Hungarian Embassy had taken official cognizance of the bureau previously, however, is disclosed in the letter written by the Ambassador to the Austro-Hungarian Minister for Foreign Affairs, which was found in the possession of James F. J. Archibald by the British authorities Aug. 30, 1915. In this letter the Ambassador stated:

> It is my impression that we can disorganize and hold up for months, if not entirely prevent, the manufacture of munitions in Bethlehem and the Middle West, which, in the opinion of the German Military Attaché, is of importance and amply outweighs the comparatively small expenditure of money involved; but even if the strikes do not come off, it is probable that we should extort, under pressure of cir-

cumstances, more favorable conditions of labor for our poor, downtrodden fellow-countrymen. So far as German workmen are found in the skilled hands, means of leaving will be provided immediately for them. Besides this, a private German employment office has been established which provides employment for persons who have voluntarily given up their places, and it is already working well. We shall also join in, and the widest support is assured us.

## Letter to Count Bernstorff

The following representations on behalf of the bureau's efficiency were made, under date of March 24, 1916, in a letter to the German Ambassador, von Bernstorff:

> Engineers and persons in the better class of positions, and who had means of their own, were persuaded by the propaganda of the bureau to leave war material factories.

The report comments with unconcealed amusement upon the fact that munitions concerns innocently wrote the bureau for workmen (which, of course, were not furnished) and continues in reviewing later conditions in the munitions industry:

> The commercial employment bureaus of the country have no supply of unemployed technicians. * * * Many disturbances and suspensions which war material factories have had to suffer, and which it was not always possible to remove quickly, but which on the contrary often lead to long strikes, may be attributed to the energetic propaganda of the employment bureau.

Von Igel's close connection with the enterprise is indicated by a number of items. For example, there is the notation that H. Hanson had established a Liebau branch office in Detroit, and an entry of £12 paid to Dr. Max Niven, Chicago, in February, 1916, for the "labour fund," and an inquiry, addressed by a bureau official to von Igel, asking whether the Bosch Magneto Works manufactured fuses for shells, the bureau having evidently been applied to for workmen for the Bosch plant. A reply in the negative stated that the company is "universally known for its friendly attitude toward Germans."

Several lines of communication between the German Diplomatic Service and the Irish revolutionary movement are indicated in the captured documents. John Devoy of New York City, now editor of The Gaelic American, was one of the active agents of this connection. Significant entries appear here and there; references to messages from the German Embassy at Washington and the German Consulate at New York; mention of a secret code to be employed in communicating with him and of a " cipher Devoy "; also a notation, the details of which remain undiscovered, concerning " communication re manufacture hand grenades." Devoy it was who acted, for a time at least, as go-between for the German Secret Service dealings with Sir Roger Casement, executed by the British for treason. There are several references to money and messages for Sir Roger Casement, or, more briefly, " R. C.," and one record of a check for $1,000 for Casement, evidently handled by Devoy.

Devoy's intimate connection with the German cause is disclosed in two letters to Ambassador von Bernstorff, the text of which follows:

New York, April 8, 1916.
The following communication from confidential man John Devoy was duly transmitted:
" Letter dated March 22, delayed by censor, seems conclusive that first messenger arrived safe with proposal to send supplies and that cable was suppressed. Second also safe. Third, with change of plans, due about April 15."
John Devoy further requests that the following telegram be dispatched to Sir Roger Casement:
" No letter now possible. All funds sent home. Sister and M.'s family well."
Should Sir Roger be absent or ill, then J. D. requests that the telegram be delivered to John Montieth.
(Signed) K. N. St.
To His Excellency the Imperial Ambassador, Count von Bernstorff, Washington, D. C.
New York, April 15, 1916.
Herewith inclosed a —— report received by us today from John Devoy. Kindly order further steps to be taken.
The important parts of the report were sent there today per telegram. (S. copy.)
(Signed) K. N. St.
To the Imperial Ambassador, Count von Bernstorff, Washington, D. C.

Though this incriminating evidence was in its possession, the Department of Justice has refuted the charge that it told the British Government of the Irish revolutionary plot and Casement's part in it. Department of Justice officials admit that the papers relating to Casement were sent to Washington the night before Casement's arrest was reported, but they were not received by the Attorney General until the afternoon of the day upon which the British authorities picked up the Irish leader, and were not presented to the State Department until 7 o'clock that evening. Meanwhile, Casement had spent several hours in an Irish prison.

## Justice Cohalan Involved

It is not improbable that the signature at the bottom of the extraordinary message which follows is in the " cipher Devoy " referred to in the von Igel papers. New York Supreme Court Justice Daniel F. Cohalan has long been prominent in Irish-American circles. The communication as translated into von Igel's record is typewritten, line for line, below a cipher, except for the signature, which remains untranslated from the original cipher figures. It is dated New York, April 17, 1916, numbered 335-16, and inscribed at the top " Very Secret."

No. 335-16.
Very secret.
New York, April 17, 1916.
Judge Cohalan requests the transmission of the following remarks:
" The revolution in Ireland can only be successful if supported from Germany, otherwise England will be able to suppress it, even though it be only after hard struggles. Therefore help is necessary. This should consist, primarily, of aerial attacks in England and a diversion of the fleet simultaneously with Irish revolution. Then, if possible, a landing of troops, arms, and ammunition in Ireland, and possibly some officers from Zeppelins. This would enable the Irish ports be closed against England and the establishment of stations for submarines on the Irish coast and the cutting off of the supply of food for England. The services of the revolution may therefore decide the war."
He asks that a telegram to this effect be sent to Berlin.
5132 8167 0230.
To His Excellency Count von Bernstorff, Imperial Ambassador, Washington, D. C.

Along this same line is a code message by wireless to Banker Max Moebius, Oberwallstrasse, Berlin, which is interesting chiefly as showing the code method of important communications practiced by the German official plotters in the United States. The code translation was found with a copy of the message among the von Igel papers. The original is a dispatch in German, which, translated into English, sounds like an innocent business transaction, viz.:

> National Germania insurance contract certainly promised. Executor is evidently satisfied with proposition. Necessary steps have been taken.    HENRY NEUMAN.

But it is not so innocent and harmless as it looks, for what the message really means is this: "The Irish agree to the proposition."

## Plots in Canada

Canada was also the object of solicitous interest on the part of Germany's representatives in the United States, as is startlingly proved in the plot to blow up the Welland Canal. Another lesser but not unpromising enterprise against Canada was foregone by von Igel because the volunteer plotter was too old, "though he has the best good will," and also because of his known connection with the Gaelic-American and Indian revolutionists. Such is the indorsement upon the letter signed only "X" by one who thus sets forth his qualifications for fomenting disorders in Quebec:

> As Honorary President of the first Independence Club started in Montreal about the time of the Boer war, and of which the Hon. Honoré Mercier, now Minister for Colonization in the Government of the Province of Quebec, was one of the Vice Presidents and later President, I am well known among the members and journalists of that organization. * * * There is now in place of the Independence Club a secret society based upon its principles, aiming at the total separation of Canada from the British Empire. * * * It includes all the former members of the Independence Club and men high in Canadian political life. The adherents are, for the most part, French and Irish Canadians.

## Mexican Intrigues

The information carefully and extensively set forth in the secret documents of German officialdom was something wide of the facts. For example, a long memorandum on March 1, 1916, transmitted by the secret agent Captain

Böhm, dealing with the Mexican crisis, appears to have been largely the work of some fervid and projective imagination. The memorandum purports to outline President Wilson's expected message to Congress. It predicts that the President will attribute Mexico's anti-American activities directly to German money and incitement; that he will call upon Congress to support him in radical measures, (the prophet even attempts to paraphrase the language to be employed in the message,) and that Congress will indorse the President's stand, following which upward of 150 German spies and *agents provocateurs* were to be arrested and the Ambassadors of the Central Powers to receive their passports. For all this Captain Böhm's authority is thus indicated over his own signature:

> The foregoing memorandum has just been given me by an acquaintance returning from Washington. This acquaintance is a skillful journalist who has good connections. I cannot vouch for his reliability, but I know he hates the present Administration and fights it. His informant is a former Secretary of the American Embassy in Rome, now in Washington.

Captain Böhm himself was too loose of tongue for the good of his service, as would appear from a report by the German Military Information Bureau, dated March 21, 1916. Captain Böhm decided to leave "after the reports received here were submitted to him, to the effect that members of the press were informed as to his personality and the purpose of his being here. Too great confidence in the silence of his henchmen, especially the members of the American Truth Society, * * * was probably the cause of his becoming quickly known here."

Thus the American Truth Society, which has so strenuously denied its pro-German associations, figures as indirectly linked up with Germany's secret representative. This society is still extant, and Jeremiah A. O'Leary, its moving spirit, is now editor of Bull, recently shut out from the mails for publishing seditious matter.

Of more direct military interest to the United States is an espionage enterprise hinted at in a secret code message of April 11, 1916, signed "13232, 46729,

"46919," addressing von Igel to this effect:

> Herewith respectfully send extract regarding troops stationed California and armament coast fortifications.

## Magazine Writers Involved

Journalists, lecturers, and publishers were liberally employed by von Igel and his associates for the purposes of German propaganda. Among those are two magazine writers and war correspondents, James F. J. Archibald, now in Washington, and Edwin Emerson, said to be in Africa. The following curious entry appears in von Igel's official records:

PURE WAR EXPENSES

Edwin Emerson .................... $1,000
Fair Play (Mr. Braun) .......... $2,000
Fair Play ( "    "  ) ........... $1,500
Marcus Braun ..................... $1,000
J. Archibald ..................... $5,000

Concerning the identity of the last entry, says the Official Bulletin, there might be room for doubt but for a signed receipt from J. F. J. Archibald acknowledging the sum of $5,000 from the German Embassy. What return Archibald ever made in service is not clear, except that certain war correspondence for which he contracted with New York newspapers was so obviously prejudiced on the side of the Central Powers that they declined to accept it.

Fair Play appears to have received in all $4,500 in the course of a few months in 1915. Marcus Braun figures as its editor.

All these, it must be remembered, are but a small portion of one German agent's records. They represent but one chamber, as it were, in an enormous and complicated maze of underground plotting. Other entries appear too vague to indicate anything more definite than some connection with or interest in enterprises already notorious—payments to the Welland Canal conspiracy; references to the Maverick and the Annie Larsen, blockade runners; side lights on Japanese propaganda, Mexican plots and Canadian lines of secret information; even hints that officers high in the military service of the United States were being improperly used for German military enterprises.

How far the plot goes will probably never be known. The spider, von Igel, had scuttled away to his own refuge in Germany. His nest is destroyed. But the strands of the web that he wove may still stretch over many parts of the United States.

## Bernstorff Himself a Plotter

The most sensational of the revelations of German plotting in the United States was made by Secretary Lansing on Sept. 21, when he published without comment a secret telegram written by Ambassador Bernstorff himself and asking his Government for $50,000 to be used in influencing Congress. This was not one of the papers taken from von Igel, but was of much later date, and Mr. Lansing stated that the cablegram had not been sent to Germany through the State Department, leaving it to be implied that it went by way of some neutral legation. The text of the Bernstorff message to the Berlin Foreign Office, which is dated Jan. 22, 1917, is as follows:

> *I request authority to pay out up to $50,000, (fifty thousand dollars,) in order, as on former occasions, to influence Congress through the organization you know of, which can perhaps prevent war.*
>
> *I am beginning in the meantime to act accordingly.*
>
> *In the above circumstances a public official German declaration in favor of Ireland is highly desirable, in order to gain the support of Irish influence here.*

Von Bernstorff's effort to use money "to influence Congress" caused a sensation among members of the Senate and House. Congressman Heflin of Alabama increased the excitement by declaring in the House that he could name "thirteen or fourteen members who had acted suspiciously." Congressman Howard of Georgia asserted that he "believed that he could point to certain persons who got some of it"—the money to which Count von Bernstorff referred in his cable message to the Berlin Foreign Office.

Three days later, on Sept. 24, the subject led to the most turbulent session the House of Representatives had seen since the struggle to overthrow Speaker Cannon in 1911. Representative Norton of North Dakota called to account Representative Heflin of Alabama and Representative Howard of Georgia for insinuating that members of Congress had profited by German intrigue. Two resolutions of inquiry, one by Representative Norton and the other by Representative Fordney of Michigan, were introduced and sent to the Rules Committee. The first resolution called upon both Representative Howard and Representative Heflin to make good, and the second mentioned only Representative Heflin.

Before a full membership, while the galleries were crowded with spectators, Representative Heflin stood up under the hoots and jeers and heckling of practically the entire House. When called upon time and again to name the men who had received money from Germany he evaded the question. In the succeeding days the storm abated, when it became apparent that Mr. Heflin's suspicions were without solid basis, and that Ambassador Bernstorff evidently had expected not to bribe Congressmen with $50,000, but to keep up a propaganda of letters and telegrams for influencing them.

## Motive of Bernstorff's Request

Secretary Lansing later made public the fact that when Count Bernstorff, who is now the German Ambassador to Turkey, asked his Government for $50,000 to influence the American Congress last January the Ambassador was already aware that Germany was about to resume ruthless submarine warfare. The request for the money was sent on Jan. 22, 1917. Secretary Lansing said that on or before Jan. 19 the Ambassador had read the order from Dr. Zimmermann, German Minister for Foreign Affairs, directing Admiral von Eckhardt, the Minister in Mexico, to arrange an alliance between the Japanese and Mexican Governments to attack the United States and alienate American territory. In that order von Eckhardt was informed that on Feb. 1 Germany would begin unrestricted submarine warfare. Bernstorff knew this from the Zimmermann message, and he wanted the corruption fund to endeavor to stay the inevitable resentment of the American Government. The evidence indicates that the money was used largely through pretended pacifist societies and individuals who were working secretly or openly for Germany's cause.

## Promoted Sabotage Plots

Further disclosures made by the State Department on Oct. 10 revealed the fact that the German Government, through its Ambassador, was engaged in acts of war against the United States fifteen months before this country entered the conflict. Secretary Lansing gave out three messages exchanged either by cable or wireless between the Berlin Foreign Office and General Staff on the one hand and Count Bernstorff, the German Ambassador in Washington, on the other. Count Bernstorff is directly implicated by these messages in German official plans to injure the United States.

The first of the three messages is dated Jan. 3, 1916. The American Government entered the war on April 6, 1917. This message is in the form of directions to Count Bernstorff from Dr. Zimmermann, who retired recently from the office of Minister for Foreign Affairs, to arrange to destroy the Canadian Pacific Railway. Germany was at war with Great Britain and her colonies, and the only concern of the United States in this particular phase of the matter would be that the German Ambassador in Washington was being used to further plots involving a nation with which the American Government was on friendly terms. But in the two subsequent messages, one dated Jan. 26, 1916, and the other Sept. 15, 1916, violations of the law of nations directed against the United States were ordered. Secretary Lansing's statement was made in this form:

*The Secretary of State publishes the following two telegrams from the German Foreign Office to Count Bernstorff in January, 1916:*

Jan. 3. (Secret.) General Staff desires energetic action in regard to proposed destruction of Canadian Pacific Railway at several points with a view to complete and protracted interruption of traffic. Captain Boehm, who is known on your side and is shortly returning, has been given instructions. Inform the Military Attaché and provide the necessary funds.
(Signed,)    ZIMMERMANN.

Jan. 26. For Military Attaché.
You can obtain particulars as to persons suitable for carrying on sabotage
in the United States and Canada from
the following persons: 1. Joseph Mac-
Garrity, Philadelphia, Penn.; 2. John
P. Keating, Michigan Avenue, Chicago;
3. Jeremiah O'Leary, 16 Park Row, New
York.

One and two are absolutely reliable
and discreet. No. 3 is reliable but not
always discreet. These persons were indicated by Sir Roger Casement. In the
United States sabotage can be carried
out on every kind of factory for supplying munitions of war. Railway embank-
ments and bridges must not be touched.
Embassy must in no circumstance be compromised. Similar precautions must be
taken in regard to Irish pro-German propaganda.

(Signed.) REPRESENTATIVE
OF GENERAL STAFF.

*The following telegram from Count
Bernstorff to the Foreign Office in Berlin
was sent in September, 1916:*

Sept. 15. With reference to report A.
N. two hundred and sixty-six of May
tenth, nineteen sixteen. The embargo
conferee in regard to whose earlier fruitful co-operation Dr. Hale can give information, is just about to enter upon
a vigorous campaign to secure a majority
in both houses of Congress favorable to
Germany, and request further support.
There is no possibility of our being compromised. Request telegraphic reply.

The State Department preserved
silence as to where it had obtained the
German official secret correspondence in
this and similar cases. State Secretary
Lansing merely said that the last three
messages had not been sent to Berlin under cover of the United States diplomatic code, thus leaving it to be implied
that communications had been carried on
between Bernstorff and his Government
through the medium of some neutral
embassy at Washington.

## One "Former Occasion"

It is now possible to reconstruct the
history of one of the "former occasions"
on which Bernstorff had tried to influence Congress by the use of German
money. In 1915 he had worked through
the organization that called itself
Labor's National Peace Council. When
his agent, Rintelen, was exposed, ending
that organization's usefulness, he substituted the American Embargo Conference. This tool he began to employ
effectively in November, 1915, and only

President Wilson's determined action
prevented it from actually controlling
certain legislation. Its task was to
formulate and direct a trumped-up sentiment in favor of an embargo on munitions, and against the right of American
citizens to travel on British ships. How
near it came to succeeding was recorded
in these pages at the time.

The conference met in November, the
date evidently being planned by Bernstorff with a view to the meeting of
Congress in December. The outcry it
created was so effective that on Dec.
13, 1915, Senator Kenyon of Iowa introduced a resolution forbidding Americans
to take passage on ships carrying munitions.

On Jan. 10, 1916, Senator Gore introduced his first resolution forbidding
the sale of contraband to England as
long as she persisted in her blockade.
On Jan. 20 Senator Hoke Smith demanded an embargo, and favored a
truculent attitude toward England.

On Feb. 3 The Providence Journal exposed the origin of the American Embargo Conference, declaring that it was
" planned and brought into existence by
" Count Johann von Bernstorff at Wash-
" ington and financed directly from the
" office of Dr. Heinrich Albert, the fiscal
" agent of the German Government in
" New York City," and that it had " taken
" up the work of the so-called Labor's
" National Peace Council." Yet on Feb.
22 the Congressmen who were unconsciously playing Bernstorff's game went
so far as to use their various embargo
resolutions to frighten the President,
and the next day the House Committee on
Foreign Affairs served notice that unless
the President warned Americans off
armed ships within twenty-four hours
the House would pass the Gore resolution.
On Feb. 24 the President wrote Senator
Stone, Chairman of that committee, declaring, " I cannot consent to any abridg-
ment of the rights of American citizens
in any respect." On Feb. 25 The Providence Journal disclosed the fact that the
whole plot had been formulated by Bernstorff, and that two weeks before messages had been sent to pro-German newspapers directing them to publish articles

preparing the minds of their readers for it.

Nevertheless, on the same day Speaker Clark and Representative Kitchin told the President that the Gore resolution would pass by at least 2 to 1. The President forced the issue, and when the Gore resolution came to a vote on March 3 it was defeated in the Senate by a vote of 68 to 14. The McLemore resolution was

defeated four days later in the House by 276 to 142. This is the history of one "former occasion," when Count Bernstorff had used German money to hoodwink Congress. With a paper organization created and financed by him under orders from Berlin he had fooled and tricked Congress into believing that the noise it made was the voice of the American people.

# Activities of Bolo Pasha as German Agent

THE most amazing instance thus far discovered of the German Government's lavish waste of the German people's money for useless intrigues in other countries is that revealed after the arrest of Paul Bolo, alias Bolo Pasha, in Paris, Sept. 29, 1917. Bolo had long been under suspicion and had been temporarily under arrest several weeks before, but only upon receipt of important evidence from the United States was he imprisoned without bail. He is a Frenchman, born at Marseilles, and, according to an article in the Paris Matin, is a brother of an eloquent French prelate of that name. He has had an adventurous career in various countries, including Egypt, and at the beginning of the war he was penniless; but when in Switzerland in March, 1915, he met Abbas Hilmi, former Khédive of Egypt, and apparently concluded an arrangement by which he was to receive $2,500,000 to be used in influencing the French press in favor of a German peace. The plan was approved by Gottlieb von Jagow, German Foreign Minister, who was to pay the money partly through the ex-Khédive and partly through Swiss and American banks.

In accordance with this arrangement $1,000,000 was paid by roundabout methods through Swiss banks, to avert suspicion. Abbas Hilmi and an associate are said to have collected $50,000 as a commission. After that time Bolo Pasha and Abbas Hilmi seemed to have fallen out, for their relations ceased. At the time of his arrest Bolo was said to have received $8,000,000 from Germany, of which $2,500,000 had been

traced to the Deutsche Bank. Large portions of this sum were said to have been paid through an American channel. The actual facts, now proved by the documents, go far toward confirming those original estimates.

Bolo arrived in New York on Feb. 22, 1916, and left on March 17 following. He had rooms at the Plaza Hotel, and was careful not to be seen in public with German agents. He saw Bernstorff secretly in Washington.

When the French Government got an inkling of his traitorous activities it appealed to Governor Whitman of New York for evidence, and ten days' work by Merton E. Lewis, the Attorney General of the State, assisted by an expert accountant, resulted in sensational disclosures which were made public on the evening of Oct. 3. The evidence, which included photographic reproductions of many telltale checks, letters, and telegrams, revealed the fact that Count Bernstorff, then German Ambassador at Washington, had eagerly fallen in with Bolo's proposition to betray France by corrupting the press in favor of a premature peace and had advanced him the enormous sum of $1,683,500 to finance the plot. The State Department and Ambassador Jusserand examined the evidence and attested its genuineness.

Many banks had been used to confuse and hide the transaction, but the persons and agencies who figured knowingly in it are Bolo Pasha, Ambassador von Bernstorff, and two bankers—Hugo Schmidt, former New York agent of the Deutsche Bank of Berlin, who acted as Bernstorff's financial agent, and Adolph Pavenstedt, former head of the New York banking house of G. Amsinck & Co.

## Disposal of the Money

Of the mass of documents exhibited by Attorney General Lewis, the most important was a letter written by Bolo Pasha to the New York City branch of the Royal Bank of Canada on March 14, 1916, three days before he sailed to return to France. That letter reads:

New York, March 14, 1916.
The Royal Bank of Canada, New York, N. Y.

Gentlemen: You will receive from Messrs. G. Amsinck & Co. deposits for the credit of my account with you, which deposits will reach the aggregate amount of about $1,700,000, which I wish you to utilize in the following manner:

First—Immediately on receipt of the first amount on account of this sum pay to Messrs. J. P. Morgan & Co., New York City, the sum of $170,068.03, to be placed to the credit of the account with them of Senator Charles Humbert, Paris.

Second—Establish on your books a credit of $5,000, good until the 31st of May, in favor of Jules Bois, Biltmore Hotel, this amount to be utilized by him at the debit of my account according to his needs, and the unused balance to be returned to me.

Third—Transfer to the credit of my wife, Mme. Bolo, with agency T of Comptoir National d'Escompte de Paris a sum of about $524,000, to be debited to my account as such transfers are made by you at best rate and by small amounts.

Fourth—You will hold, subject to my instructions, when all payments are complete, a balance of not less than $1,000,000.
Yours truly,          BOLO PASHA.

That is how the $1,683,500, which was the exact amount Bernstorff ordered Schmidt to place at the service of Bolo, came into the latter's actual possession.

## Text of Bernstorff's Dispatches.

Direct evidence that Count Bernstorff was the master mind behind the plot on this side of the Atlantic came to light in five dispatches that were made public by Secretary Lansing on Oct. 5. These messages were exchanged in the Spring of 1916:

*The Department of State communicates to the press the following telegrams bearing upon the case of Bolo Pasha, exchanged between Count von Bernstorff and Herr von Jagow, German Minister of Foreign Affairs.*

Number 679, Feb. 26. I have received direct information from an entirely trustworthy source concerning a political action in one of the enemy countries which would bring peace. One of the leading political personalities of the country in question is seeking a loan of one million seven hundred thousand dollars in New York, for which security will be given. I was forbidden to give his name in writing. The affair seems to me to be of the greatest possible importance. Can the money be provided at once in New York? That the intermediary will keep the matter secret is entirely certain. Request answer by telegram. A verbal report will follow as soon as a trustworthy person can be found to bring it to Germany.    BERNSTORFF.

Number 150, Feb. 29.    Answer to telegram Number 679. Agree to the loan, but only if peace action seems to you a really serious project, as the provision of money in New York is for us at present extraordinarily difficult. If the enemy country is Russia have nothing to do with the business, as the sum of money is too small to have any serious effect in that country. So, too, in the case of Italy, where it would not be worth while to spend so much.    JAGOW.

Number 685, March 5.    Please instruct Deutsche Bank to hold nine million marks at disposal of Hugo Schmidt. The affair is very promising. Further particulars follow.    BERNSTORFF.

Number 692, March 20.   With reference to telegram Number 685, please advise our Minister in Berne that some one will call on him who will give him the passport Sanct Regis and who wishes to establish relations with the Foreign Office. Intermediary further requests that influence may be brought to bear upon our press to pass over the change in the inner political situation in France so far as possible in silence, in order that things may not be spoiled by German approval.    BERNSTORFF.

Number 206, May 31.    The person announced in Telegram 692 of March 20 has not yet reported himself at the legation at Berne. Is there any more news on your side of Bolo?    JAGOW.

## French Senator Involved

In France the most sensational feature of the case was Bolo's payment of $170,000 to Senator Charles Humbert, owner of Le Journal. The money was in part payment for 1,100 bonds of that newspaper. Senator Humbert immediately came out with a statement to prove that he was entirely unaware of the treasonable purpose of the purchaser. He gave facts showing that Bolo Pasha had used his contract with Le Journal to extract money from Germany. On Oct. 12 a French military court inquiring into the case appointed a sequestrator for the money advanced to Senator Humbert. It amounted in all to $1,200,000, and was handed over to the care of the Deposit and Consignment Office, a section of the Ministry of Finance.

Whatever the total number of millions extracted from the German Government by Bolo Pasha, the utter futility of the expenditure, so far as Germany is concerned, must remain one of the most striking features of the case.

# The Disease Germ Plot at Bucharest

CLOSE upon the heels of the von Igel intrigues a new chapter of German criminality was revealed on Sept. 23 by Secretary Lansing's publication of the documents relating to the plot of German diplomatic agents to use deadly microbes and powerful explosives against Rumania at a time when friendly relations still existed between the two countries. As CURRENT HISTORY MAGAZINE published this dark chapter of German diplomacy in its April issue, (page 72,) translating it from unofficial French sources, and as the documents now vouched for by the United States Government are substantially the same as those then presented, this case will be treated here only in a brief summary.

The evidence given out by the State Department shows that before Rumania had declared war against Austria-Hungary, and was observing strict neutrality, German official agents clandestinely introduced into Bucharest, the capital of Rumania, packages containing explosives powerful enough to wreck public works, and vials containing deadly microbes destined to infect domestic animals and susceptible of provoking terrible epidemics among the human population of the country. The vials contained anthrax microbes and the bacilli of glanders.

The box of disease germs bore the seal of the German Consulate at Kronstadt. In the inside of this box, above a layer of cotton wool, this typewritten note in German was found:

Inclosed 4 small bottles for horses and 4 for cattle. Utilization as formerly stipulated. Each phial suffices for 200 head. If possible, to be administered directly into the animals' mouths, otherwise into their fodder. We ask for a small report about successes obtained there, and in case of good results the presence for one day of M. K. would be required.

After its discovery of the plot the Rumanian Government called in William Whiting Andrews, the Chargé d'Affaires of the American Legation at Bucharest, who witnessed the digging up of the boxes of explosives and the packages containing the vials of microbes from the grounds of the German Legation, to which they had been secretly moved from the German Consulate in Bucharest on the eve of Rumania's declaration of war.

Just before Rumania broke relations they were removed to the legation. Some of the objects were even taken to the German Legation after the American Legation at Bucharest had taken over the protection of German interests.

Dr. Bernhardt, former confidential agent of the German Minister, and servants of the German Legation confessed that this had been done. In this respect, the action of Germany's agent was a deliberate abuse of the protection which the United States Government was giving to German interests in Bucharest. At that time the United States was at peace with Germany and had agreed to take charge of Germany's legation in the Rumanian capital.

" The protection of the United States was in this manner shamefully abused and exploited," says the official report of Chargé d'Affaires Andrews to the State Department.

# BARON VON KUEHLMANN

The German Foreign Secretary, Who Was Chosen to Replace Herr von Zimmermann.
Von Kuehlmann Was Formerly at the German Embassy in London

# COUNT OTTOCAR VON CZERNIN

The Austro-Hungarian Minister of Foreign Affairs and Head of the Government of the Dual Monarchy

# German Peace Propaganda

## Replies of Central Empires to the Pope's Appeal
## Speeches of Government Leaders on Both Sides

*President Wilson's reply to the peace proposals of Pope Benedict was printed in the October issue of* CURRENT HISTORY MAGAZINE. *No replies were made by the Entente Powers, but it was semi-officially announced by Great Britain, France, Italy, and Russia, that President Wilson's answer expressed in letter and spirit their attitude. The official replies of Germany and Austria-Hungary were made public on Sept. 22, 1917. The full text of the German note, as transmitted by Chancellor Michaelis to Cardinal Gasparri, Papal Secretary of State, is given below:*

## Text of Germany's Reply to the Pope

HERR CARDINAL: Your Eminence has been good enough, together with your letter of Aug. 2, to transmit to the Kaiser and King, my most gracious master, the note of his Holiness the Pope, in which his Holiness, filled with grief at the devastations of the world war, makes an emphatic peace appeal to the heads of the belligerent peoples. The Kaiser-King has deigned to acquaint me with your Eminence's letter and to intrust the reply to me.

His Majesty has been following for a considerable time with high respect and sincere gratitude his Holiness' efforts, in a spirit of true impartiality, to alleviate as far as possible the sufferings of the war and to hasten the end of hostilities. The Kaiser sees in the latest step of his Holiness fresh proof of his noble and humane feelings, and cherishes a lively desire that, for the benefit of the entire world, the Papal appeal may meet with success.

The effort of Pope Benedict is to pave the way to an understanding among all peoples, and might more surely reckon on a sympathetic reception and the whole-hearted support from his Majesty, seeing that the Kaiser since taking over the Government has regarded it as his principal and most sacred task to preserve the blessings of peace for the German people and the world.

In his first speech from the throne at the opening of the German Reichstag on June 25, 1888, the Kaiser promised that his love of the German Army and his position toward it should never lead him into temptation to cut short the benefits of peace unless war were a necessity, forced upon us by an attack on the empire or its allies. The German Army should safeguard peace for us, and should peace, nevertheless, be broken, it would be in a position to win it with honor. The Kaiser has, by his acts, fulfilled the promise he then made in twenty-six years of happy rule, despite provocations and temptations.

In the crisis which led to the present world conflagration his Majesty's efforts were up to the last moment directed toward settling the conflict by peaceful means. After the war had broken out, against his wish and desire, the Kaiser, in conjunction with his high allies, was the first solemnly to declare his readiness to enter into peace negotiations. The German people support his Majesty in his keen desire for peace.

Germany sought within her national frontier the free development of her spiritual and material possessions, and outside the imperial territory unhindered competition with nations enjoying equal rights and equal esteem. The free play of forces in the world in peaceable wrestling with one another would lead to the highest perfecting of the noblest human possessions. A disastrous concatenation of events in the year 1914 absolutely broke off all hopeful course of development and transformed Europe into a bloody battle arena.

Appreciating the importance of his Holinesss' declaration, the Imperial Government has not failed to submit the suggestion contained therein to earnest and scrupulous examination. Special measures, which the Government has taken in closest contact with representatives of the German people, for discussing and answering the questions raised, prove how earnestly it desires, in accordance with his Holiness' desires, and the peace resolution of the Reichstag on July 19, to find a practical basis for a just and lasting peace.

The Imperial Government greets with special sympathy the leading idea of the peace appeal wherein his Holiness clearly expresses the conviction that in the future the material power of arms must be superseded by the moral power of right. We are also convinced that the sick body of human society can only be healed by fortifying its moral strength of right. From this would follow, according to his Holiness' view, the simultaneous diminution of the armed forces of all States and the institution of obligatory arbitration for international disputes.

We share his Holiness' view that definite rules and a certain safeguard for a simultaneous and reciprocal limitation of armaments on land, on sea, and in the air, as well as for the true freedom of the community and high seas, are the things in treating which—the new spirit that in the future should prevail in international relations—should find first hopeful expression. The task would then of itself arise to decide international differences of opinion, not by the use of armed forces, but by peaceful methods, especially by arbitration, whose high peace-producing effect we together with his Holiness fully recognize.

The Imperial Government will in this respect support every proposal compatible with the vital interest of the German Empire and people.

Germany, owing to her geographical situation and economic requirements, has to rely on peaceful intercourse with her neighbors and with distant countries. No people, therefore, has more reason than the German people to wish that instead of universal hatred and battle, a conciliatory fraternal spirit should prevail between nations.

If the nations are guided by this spirit it will be recognized to their advantage that the important thing is to lay more stress upon what unites them in their relations. They will also succeed in settling individual points of conflict which are still undecided, in such a way that conditions of existence will be created which will be satisfactory to every nation, and thereby a repetition of this great world catastrophe would appear impossible.

Only on this condition can a lasting peace be founded which would promote an intellectual rapprochement and a return to the economic prosperity of human society.

This serious and sincere conviction encourages our confidence that our enemies also may see a suitable basis in the ideas submitted by his Holiness for approaching nearer to the preparation of future peace under conditions corresponding to a spirit of reasonableness and to the situation in Europe.

# Reply of the Austrian Emperor
## (*Official translation.*)

Holy Father: With due veneration and deep emotion we take cognizance of the new representations which your Holiness, in fulfillment of the holy office intrusted to you by God, makes to us and the heads of the other belligerent States, with the noble intention of leading the heavily tried nations to a unity that will restore peace to them.

With a thankful heart we receive this fresh gift of fatherly care which you, Holy Father, always bestow on all peoples without distinction, and from the depth of our heart we greet the moving exhortation which your Holiness has addressed to the Governments of the belligerent peoples.

During this cruel war we have always looked up to your Holiness as to the highest personage, who, in virtue of his mission, which reaches beyond earthly things, and, thanks to the high conception of his duties laid upon him, stands high above the belligerent peoples, and who, inaccessible to all influence, was able to find a way which may lead to the realization of our own desire for peace, lasting and honorable for all parties.

Since-ascending the throne of our ancestors, and fully conscious of the responsibility which we bear before God and men for the fate of the Austro-Hungarian Monarchy, we have never lost sight of the high aim of restoring to our peoples, as speedily as possible, the blessings of peace. Soon after our accession to the throne it was vouchsafed to us, in common with our allies, to undertake a step which had been considered and prepared by our exalted predecessor, Francis Joseph, to pave the way for a lasting and honorable peace.

We gave expression to this desire in a speech from the throne delivered at the opening of the Austrian Reichstag, thereby showing that we are striving after a peace that shall free the future life of the nation from rancor and a thirst for revenge, and that shall secure them for generations to come from the employment of armed forces. Our joint Government has in the meantime not failed in repeated and emphatic declarations, which could be heard by all the world, to give expression to our own will and that of the Austro-Hungarian peoples to prepare an end to bloodshed by a peace such as your Holiness has in mind.

Happy in the thought that our desires from the first were directed toward the same object which your Holiness today characterizes as one we should strive for, we have taken into close consideration the concrete and practical suggestion of your Holiness and have come to the following conclusions:

With deep-rooted conviction we agree to the leading idea of your Holiness that the future arrangement of the world must be based on the elimination of armed forces and on the moral force of right and on the rule of international justice and legality.

We, too, are imbued with the hope that a strengthening of the sense of right would morally regenerate humanity. We support, therefore, your Holiness' view that the negotiations between the belligerents should and could lead to an understanding by which, with the creation of appropriate guarantees, armaments on land and sea and in the air might be reduced simultaneously, reciprocally and gradually to a fixed limit, and whereby the high seas, which rightly belong to all the nations of the earth, may be freed from domination or paramountcy, and be opened equally for the use of all.

Fully conscious of the importance of the promotion of peace on the method proposed by your Holiness, namely, to submit international disputes to compulsory arbitration, we are also prepared to enter into negotiations regarding this proposal.

If, as we most heartily desire, agreements should be arrived at between the belligerents which would realize this sublime idea and thereby give security to the Austro-Hungarian Monarchy for its unhampered future development, it can then not be difficult to find a satisfactory solution of the other questions which still remain to be settled between the belligerents in a spirit of justice, and of a reasonable consideration of the conditions for existence of both parties.

If the nations of the earth were to enter, with a desirable peace, into negotiations with one another in the sense of your Holiness' proposals, then peace could blossom forth from them. The nations could attain complete freedom of movement on the high seas, heavy material burdens could be taken from them, and new sources of prosperity opened to them.

Guided by a spirit of moderation and conciliation, we see in the proposals of your Holiness a suitable basis for initiating negotiations with a view to preparing a peace, just to all and lasting, and we earnestly hope our present enemies may be animated by the same ideas. In this spirit we beg that the Almighty may bless the work of peace begun by your Holiness.

## The World's Comments on Austro-German Notes

It was announced by Vatican officials that the replies of the Central Powers were disappointing in that there were no specific references to evacuation or restoration. A story gained circulation later to the effect that the notes had been altered at the last moment—that the Pan-Germans had eliminated all references to Belgium and to disavowal of indemnities and annexations.

The comment of the newspapers in the various countries was colored by their own bias. Allied and American newspapers almost without exception treated the replies with disdain and characterized them as a further demonstration of Teutonic duplicity and hypocrisy; this was likewise the official view among the Allies. The German-Austrian press regarded the notes as further evidence of the peaceful intentions of the Central Powers, and declared that they were sufficiently specific, though some radical German newspapers spoke otherwise. The Catholic press in Holland manifested a sympathetic attitude, and asserted that the course of peace was advanced by the replies, but this view prevailed nowhere else.

The Austrian Premier, Dr. von Seydler, on the reassembling of the Reichstag, Sept. 25, referred to the Papal note in these terms:

We believe that agreements can be attained, which under proper guarantees might enable armaments to be gradually and simultaneously reduced, among other things by the introduction on this basis of obligatory arbitration for international disputes.

Our readiness to arrive at an agreement with our enemies on these bases is absolutely serious and sincere and is inspired by the consciousness of our strength. But if our enemies are not prepared to take the proffered hand we will continue our defensive war to the utmost.

Believing that a strong Austria, insuring contentment of all races, is the best guarantee of a lasting peace, we are striving to reform the Constitution, and the Government resolutely condemns the mistaken view held by certain parties that Austria's salvation is to be hoped for from Austria's enemies.

The German Chancellor, in a speech to the Main Committee of the Reichstag Sept. 28, answered the critics of Germany's reply in these words:

The German reply to the Pope's note met with the approval of our friends and allies, while a majority of our enemies have given it an obviously embarrassed reception. It is difficult to understand how any one acquainted with the international situation and international usages could believe that we ever would be in such a position as, through a one-sided public statement on important questions which are indissolubly bound up with the entire complex of questions which must be discussed at the peace negotiations to bind ourselves to a solution to our own prejudice.

Any such public statement at the present time could only have a confusing effect and injure German interests. We should not come a step nearer peace, but it would contribute certainly to a prolongation of the war. I must at present decline to specify our war aims and bind the hands of our negotiators.

In conclusion the Chancellor attacked President Wilson's reply to the Pope's note:

The President's attempt to sow dissension between the people and the Government of Germany has no prospects of success. His note has had the opposite effect from what he desired and has bound us more firmly together in a stern resolve to oppose resolutely and energetically all foreign interference.

## Germany's Peace Ultimatum: "Breakdown of Europe"

Dr. Richard von Kühlmann, Secretary for Foreign Affairs, also on Sept. 28 addressed the Main Committee of the Reichstag on the Pope's proposals, saying in part:

This courageous initiative of the Pope will mark an epoch in the history of this tremendous battle of nations and will appear as an unfading page in the annals of Vatican diplomacy. The Pope threw the word "peace" into the turmoil of battle at a time when events threatened to transform Europe into a place of bloodstained ruins.

The German people and the German Government, whose consciousness of their strength and internal security always made it easy for them to emphasize their willingness to conclude an honorable peace, have reason to welcome gratefully the initiative of the Curia, which made it possible for them to set forth again their national policy in a clear, unambiguous manner. I say intentionally "national policy," as I hope and believe the reply of the German Government, both as regards its form and contents, embodies the de-

sires of an overwhelming majority of the Germans.

The principles of the reply to the Papal note as presented by the Government appear acceptable to the representatives of all the parties. Consequently I believe I can say with full right that all attempts of the enemy to drive a wedge between the German people and the German Government on the question of the basis of our foreign policy and by the propagation of the fiction that the German people do not stand behind the Kaiser and the Imperial Chancellor will be repulsed in the most crushing manner by the support given to this document. * * *

Dr. von Kühlmann declared that the breakdown of European civilization would leave every nation weaker and poorer, no matter to what combination it might belong. He continued:

When the young power, Germany, nearly fifty years ago entered the circle of old powers she was greeted by nobody with great enthusiasm; but these fifty years have proved more than abundantly that the new power brought strength to the whole of Europe. If today our enemies believe that they are able to turn back the course of history and bring into existence again a weak formation of federated States alongside a Prussia which has been subjected to deadly mutilation, these are only delusions, which are hardly pardonable in the case of political theorists, and must be ruinous in the case of responsible statesmen.

As long as our enemies base themselves on fiction—the more clever ones among them do not believe in it—the time may come in which the German Nation, doing penance in sackcloth and ashes, and beating its breast in sorrow, may grovel under the yoke of despicable demands.

We shall have to continue to speak by the sword. It may not be easy to show the truth plainly to the nations of the Entente, which have been incited by legends invented at the beginning of the war, but how otherwise is the new spirit to come into existence? This is an indispensable condition if we are to arrive at a termination of the present struggle of the nations.

The German people are firmly convinced that they are conducting a just war. From this conviction they draw strength cheerfully to meet the great sacrifices which the times demand.

## Definite Refusal to Discuss Alsace-Lorraine

Foreign Secretary von Kühlmann on Oct. 10, at a plenary sitting of the Reichstag, became more definite in expressing Germany's war aims. He said that the attitude of the Entente Powers gave no prospect that the Pope's proposal would be successful, notwithstanding the agreement of the Central Powers "to collaborate not only in the termination of the present conflict but in the reconstruction of a Europe nearly ruined." He continued as follows:

The great question prolonging the struggle is not the future of Belgium, but that of Alsace-Lorraine. Great Britain, according to our information, has pledged herself to France that she will continue the fight for the conquest of Alsace-Lorraine both politically and with her armies so long as France desires to adhere to the program of regaining those provinces. This being the actual situation, I think it proper to give a clear and firm statement of our attitude, since, curiously enough, there still seems to be a misconception in this respect among our enemies, and even among our neutral friends.

*There is but one answer to the question, "Can Germany in any form make concessions with regard to Alsace-Lorraine?" That answer is "No." So long as one German hand can hold a gun the integrity of the territory handed down to us as a glorious inheritance by our forefathers can never be the object of negotiations or concessions.*

When it seemed expedient to France to accept the formula "without annexations" the French resorted to the transparent trick of bashfully covering up with the word "disannexation" what is in reality a barefaced and forceful conquest. The trick is really too clumsy to be worthy of repute. Now, except for France's demand for Alsace-Lorraine, there is absolutely no impediment to peace, no question which could not be solved by negotiations or a settlement in such a way as to render superfluous the further sacrifice of blood.

Our enemies heretofore have been careful not to reveal their real war aims. What they have told the world is a maximum program, which can only be realized after the complete military defeat of the Central Powers.

The German Government has never answered this program because we believe in dealing with real sober facts. Our answer to our opponents' assertions that they cannot obtain a clear conception of our intentions is our reply to the Pope, and the parliamentary discussions in connection with this. They leave no doubt in the mind of any one who wishes to understand the essential principles of our peace program.

## Reiterated by the Chancellor

Chancellor Michaelis, in his address at the same session, Sept. 10, supported the attitude of the Foreign Secretary in these words:

The German Nation will stand together as one man unshakable, and persevere in the fight until its right and the right of our allies to existence and development are assured. In its unity the German Empire is invincible.

We must continue to persevere until the German Empire, on the Continent and overseas, establishes its position. Further, we must strive to see that the armed alliance of our enemies does not grow into an economic offensive alliance.

We can in this sense achieve a peace which guarantees the peasant the reward of his land; which gives the worker merited recompense; which creates a market for industries and supplies the foundation for social progress; which gives our ships the possibility on a free voyage of entering ports and taking on coal all over the world. A peace of the widest economic and cultural development, a real peace. This peace we can attain within these limits.

*As long as our enemies confront us with demands which appear unacceptable to every single German, as long as our opponents wish to interfere with our frontier posts, as long as they demand that we shall yield a piece of German soil, as long as they pursue the idea of driving a wedge between the German people and its Emperor, so long shall we with folded arms refuse the hand of peace.*

We can wait. Time is working for us. Until our enemies perceive that they must reduce their claims, so long must the cannon speak and the U-boats do their work. Our peace will yet come.

## Lloyd George's Answer

Premier Lloyd George answered Baron Kühlmann on Oct. 11 in an address at London, as follows:

I cannot think of any statement more calculated to prolong the war than the assertion of the German Foreign Secretary, von Kühlmann, that Germany would never contemplate the making of concessions to France respecting Alsace-Lorraine. *However long the war lasts, England intends to stand by her gallant ally, France, until she redeems her oppressed children from the degradation of a foreign yoke.* This means that the country must husband its resources, and, when demands were put forward for improvements here and there, my answer is: "Concentrate upon victory."

## Former Premier Asquith, the same day, referring to the same subject, said:

German diplomacy is not celebrated for deftness, but even in its annals it will be difficult to find a more clumsy or more transparent manoeuvre than this maladroit attempt to sow discord between ourselves and our French allies. Von

Kühlmann relegates the Belgian question to a secondary position. I have formally asked whether Germany was ready to restore Belgium in the only real sense acceptible to the Allies, but I have received no answer, and von Kühlmann, who can be boisterously definite and precise concerning Alsace-Lorraine, preserves regarding Belgium an unbroken, but significant, silence.

The first speech of Dr. von Kühlmann was not sympathetically received by the Vatican, and was a disappointment, as he was expected to indicate concrete conditions, while on the contrary it unveiled a warlike spirit in the German governing party, in direct opposition to the attitude assumed by the Pope in his proposal.

Following these speeches a warm debate ensued in the German Reichstag, and for a while it was thought the peace advocates would overthrow the Government, but a disavowal by the Chancellor that the Government was acting in collusion with the Pan-German faction to the exclusion of other political parties, and the disclosures regarding the naval mutiny which involved the independent Socialists, put the peace advocates on the defensive and strengthened materially the militarists.

# Austria-Hungary Explains Her Demands

Count Czernin, the Austro-Hungarian Minister of Foreign Affairs, on Oct. 3 delivered an address at Budapest which created considerable stir among the belligerent nations and was regarded as evidence of a growing and acute necessity of peace. He said in part:

The millions who are fighting in the trenches or behind the lines wish to know why and for what they are fighting. They have a right to learn why peace, which the entire world desires, has not yet come. When I was appointed to my post I utilized the first opportunity openly to declare that we did not want to oppress any one, but that on the other hand we would not suffer any oppression, and that we were prepared to enter upon peace negotiations as soon as our enemies accepted the standpoint of peace by agreement.

Count Czernin said a plain statement of war aims was indispensable. He explained the conversion of the Central Powers to the doctrine of disarmament by declaring that armaments were necessary until the world was convinced that Austria-Hungary was not a dying State, subject to dismemberment. In conclusion, Count Czernin threatened that unless peace without annexations or indemnities were immediately accepted it would be necessary for Austria-Hungary to revise its program and seek compensation for further costs of the war. He said:

This war taught us that we must reckon on a great increase in former armaments. With unrestricted armaments the nations would be compelled to increase everything tenfold and the military estimates of the great powers would amount to billions.

That is impossible. It would mean complete ruin. To return to the armament status of 1914 would be a great reduction, but there would be no meaning in not going further and actually disarming. Hence complete disarmament is the only issue from the difficulty.

Gigantic fleets will have no further purpose when the nations of the world guarantee the freedom of the seas, and land armies will be reduced to the level required for the maintenance of internal order. Every State will have to give up something of its independence for the purpose of insuring the world peace.

Probably the present generation will not live to see the completion of this great pacific movement. It can only be realized slowly, but I consider it our duty to place ourselves at the head of the movement to do everything humanly possible to accelerate its materialization.

## Disarmament on High Seas

Strongly emphasizing the necessity for naval disarmament on the high seas, Count Czernin said:

I purposely say the high seas, for I do not extend the idea to narrow seas, and I freely admit that for sea communications special rules and regulations must obtain. With these factors made clear every ground for territorial guarantees disappears.

This is the basic idea of the beautiful and sublime note which the Pope addressed to the whole world. If this basis is accepted by our enemies we can renounce the enlargement of the Austro-Hungarian Monarchy, always provided that the enemy completely evacuate our territory.

Count Czernin then came to the final principle which he said it was necessary to observe to insure the free and pacific development of the world, namely, economic freedom. He said economic war must absolutely be eliminated from every future arrangement.

Before we conclude peace we must have the positive certainty that our present opponents have relinquished the idea of economic war. These, gentlemen, are the basic principles of the new world order, as they present themselves to my mind, and they are all founded on all-around disarmament.

The question of indemnities which the Entente is always advancing assumes remarkable completion when one considers the devastation their armies have wrought in Galicia, Bukowina, Tyrol, the Isonzo, East Prussia, in Turkish territories, and the German colonies. Does the Entente intend to compensate us for all this, or is it so completely mistaken in its judgment of our psychology that it hopes for a one-sided indemnification?

We do not seek strength in big words, but in our glorious armies, the firmness of our alliances, the steadfastness of our people and the wisdom of our war aims. We do not demand a Utopia. We can neither be bent nor destroyed. Conscious of our power and clear as to what we must attain, we go our ways.

Saying that he had been blamed both at home and in unfriendly countries for plain speaking with regard to the Austro-Hungarian peace terms, Count Czernin proceeded:

In broad outline our program for the reestablishment of order in the world has been laid down in our reply to the Pope's note. It may appear to be inconceivable to any people that the Central Powers desire to make renunciation with respect to military armaments, but the war has produced new facts, conditions, and conceptions which have shaken the foundation of European politics as they previously existed.

Especially has the idea crumbled which held that Austria-Hungary was a moribund State. It was the dogma of impending dissolution of the monarchy which made our position in Europe difficult. By proving ourselves in this war thoroughly sound, and, at least, equal to the others, we destroyed the hopes that we could be overthrown by force of arms.

Now that this proof has been given, we are in a position simultaneously with our allies to lay aside arms and regulate future conflicts by arbitration. * * *

We have from the beginning stated our aim and adhered to it. But let no one cherish the delusion that this pacific and moderate program of ours can and will hold good forever. If our enemies compel us to continue the war we shall be obliged to revise our program and demand compensation.

I speak for the present moment, because I am convinced that world peace can now come on the basis which I have set forth. If the war, however, continues we reserve for ourselves a free hand. I am absolutely convinced that our position a year hence will be incomparably better than today. But I would consider it a crime to carry on the war for any material or territorial advantages for a single day longer than is necessary for the integrity of the monarchy and our future safety.

If our enemies refuse to listen and compel us to continue this murder, then we reserve the right to revise our terms. I am not very optimistic of the disposition of the Entente to conclude peace by agreement on the above basis. An overwhelming majority of the entire world wants peace by agreement, but some few men are preventing it.

We shall in this case pursue our way with sang froid and steady nerves. We know that we can hold out at the front and at home. Our hour will come, and with it a sure guarantee of the free and peaceful development of Austria-Hungary.

# The British Viewpoint

The British viewpoint of peace was expressed by former Premier Herbert H. Asquith in an address at Leeds Sept. 26, under the auspices of the War Aims Committee. He described the German reply to the Papal note as teeming with "nebulous and unctuous generalities," but giving no indication that Germany would take any practical steps to open the road to a real and lasting peace. He asked:

Is there any reason to think that Germany has learned the lesson of the inevitable consequences of international spoliation? Is there in the Chancellor's dispatch or in any recent authoritative declaration of the German Government any indication that it is prepared not only to repeat the crime of '71, but to take any practical steps which alone can open the road to a real and lasting peace?

Is Germany ready to restore what she then took from France? Is she ready to give Belgium complete independence, political and economic, without fetters or reservations, and with as complete an indemnity as any merely material compensation can provide for the devastation of her territory, the sufferings of her people? A definite reply to these questions would be worth a whole column of pious platitudes.

## German Barbarity an Obstacle

Alluding to the necessity of destroying Prussian militarism, Mr. Asquith referred to the American revelations of the German machinations in Bucharest as fresh proof of the brutality and callousness with which Germany had waged war. [This exposure is treated elsewhere.] He said that nothing had aroused more worldwide surprise and consternation than the fact that the German Nation applauded with fervor the most barbarous transgressions of the German Government.

It shows [he said] from what unmeasured perils, from what a setback to the whole machinery of civilization mankind has been delivered, now that the Allies have shattered forever the dreams of German hegemony.

## War Aims

Passing to the subject of war aims, he said:

We are fighting for two aims, one immediate, the other ulterior. The first is, not the restoration of the status quo, not a revival of what formerly was called the balance of power, but the substitution for the one and the other of an international system under which both great and small States can be assured of a stable foundation and independent development.

I assume, as a matter of course, the evacuation by the enemy of the occupied territories of France and Russia. I have already referred to Alsace-Lorraine and Belgium. But wherever you turn in Central and Eastern Europe you see territorial arrangements which are purely artificial in their origin, which offend the interests and wishes of the populations concerned and which remain seedplots of potential war.

There are the just claims of Italy, Rumania, and Serbia. There is Poland, concerning which, I believe, all our people heartily indorse the wise and generous words of President Wilson. The cases of Greece and the Southern Slavs must also not be forgotten, and what is required is the permanent liquidation of all these dangerous accounts.

Coming to the second aspect of an enduring peace, Mr. Asquith said:

We must banish once for all from our catalogue of maxims the time-worn fallacy that if you wish for peace you must make ready for war.

I am not a sentimentalist, and do not expect the sudden regeneration of mankind, when in the world's war offices the lion will lie down with the lamb and international relations become a perpetual love feast. I fear that even the youngest of us will not live to get more than a distant and imaginative glimpse of that beatific vision, but, speaking not as a Utopian or dreamy idealist, I assert that we are waging not only war for peace but war against war, and for the first time in history we may make an advance to the realization of an ideal, to which great men of action in the past, such, for instance, as Henry IV. of France, who was not visionary but a practical statesman, have been groping their way.

You will not at first, perhaps not for a long time, be able to dispense with coercion, military or economic, against the disloyal and recalcitrant, but we may well hope that the positive law, with its forcible restraints, may gradually recede into the background and sovereign authority be recognized to rest in the common sense of mankind.

It is impossible to believe that this universal upheaval will not leave abiding traces in the industrial and economic worlds. When the storm has passed over must we not, after such common discipline which has spared no class in society, see things that concern our daily lives and our relations to one another in a new and truer perspective than was ever possible before? In the meantime we must keep our powder dry.

Mr. Asquith said that peace could not be found in a cessation of active hostilities, followed by a process of territorial bargaining to be embodied ultimately in paper protocols and pacts and left there at the mercy of a chapter of accidents, which had wisely been called " the Bible of fools." He added:

Still less can you find peace worthy of the name in any arrangement imposed by victor or vanquished which ignores the principles of right and sets at defiance the historic traditions, aspirations, and liberties of the peoples affected. Such so-called treaties contain within themselves their own death warrant and simply provide fertile breeding ground for future wars.

We have a crucial example of the folly and futility of such a transaction in the treaty of 1871. That act of high-handed, short-sighted violence, against which Europe ought to have protested, is the primary cause of the race in armaments, which proceeded at an ever-accelerated pace for forty years before the outbreak of this war.

Mr. Asquith said that both Bismarck and von Moltke foresaw the evil conse-quences of the treaty, von Moltke assert-ing that Germany must be armed to the teeth for fifty years to keep the prov-inces won in six months.

## America's View Expressed Through the League of National Unity

President Wilson's attitude toward the German peace agitation, as expressed in his reply to the Pope, was reiterated Oct. 8 at Washington in an address by him at the White House to the newly or-ganized League of National Unity. The President gave his indorsement to the purposes of the league in an address em-phasizing the need of team play by the forces of American thought and opinion. He expressed the belief that American public opinion, although understanding the war's causes and principles, needed guidance to remember that the war should end only when Germany was beaten and Germany's rule of autocracy and might superseded by the ideals of democracy. The President gave warning that it should not be forgotten that Ger-man success would mean not only pre-vention of the spread of democracy, but possibly the suppression of that already existing.

The aims of the new league are " to " create a medium through which loyal " Americans of all classes, sections, " creeds, and parties can give expression " to the fundamental purpose of the " United States to carry on to a success-" ful conclusion this new war for the in-" dependence of America and for the " preservation of democratic institutions " and the vindication of the basic princi-" ples of humanity." The league's initial announcement continues:

In this crisis the unity of the Amer-ican people must not be impaired by the voices of dissension, of sedition. Agita-tion for a premature peace is seditious when its object is to weaken the determi-nation of America to see the war through to a conclusive vindication of the princi-ples for which we have taken arms.

The war we are waging is a war against war and its sacrifices must not be nulli-fied by any truce or armistice that means no more than a breathing spell for the enemy.

We believe in the wise purpose of the President not to negotiate a peace with any irresponsible and autocratic dynasty.

We approve the action of the National Government in dispatching an expedion-ary force to the land of Lafayette and Rochambeau. Either we fight the enemy on foreign soil, shoulder to shoulder with comrades in arms, or we fight on our soil, backs against our homes, and alone.

While this war lasts, the cause of the Allies is our cause, their defeat our defeat, and concert of action and unity in spirit between them and us is essential to final victory. We therefore deprecate the ex-aggeration of old national prejudices— often stimulated by German propaganda— and nothing is more important than the clear understanding that those who in this crisis attack our present allies, attack America.

We are organized in the interests of a national accord that rises high above any previous division of party, race, creed, and circumstance.

We believe that this is the critical and fateful hour for America and for civili-zation. To lose now is to lose for many generations. The peril is great and re-quires our highest endeavors. If defeat comes to us through any weakness, Ger-many, whose purposes for worldwide do-minion are now revealed, might draw to itself, as a magnet does the filings, the residuum of world power, and this would affect the standing and the independence of America.

We not only accept but heartily approve the decision reached by the President and Congress of the United States to declare war against the common enemy of the free nations, and as loyal citizens of the United States we pledge to the President and the Government our undivided sup-port to the very end.

The Honorary Chairmen of the league are Cardinal Gibbons, Frank Mason North, Federal Council of the Churches of Christ of America, and Theodore N. Vail, President American Telephone and Telegraph Company. The Vice Chair-men are Samuel Gompers, President American Federation of Labor; Charles

A. Barrett, President Farmers' Educational and Co-operative Union of America, and George Pope, President National

Association of Manufacturers. Director, Ralph M. Easley, Chairman National Civic Federation.

# Premier Painlevé on Alsace-Lorraine and the Only Peace France Will Accept

*The following official declaration in the Chamber on Sept. 18, representing the views of the French Government, expresses the minimum aims of France and discloses the irreconcilable attitude of France and Germany with respect to Alsace-Lorraine. The statements on this subject made in the Reichstag by the German Chancellor and Foreign Minister, as given elsewhere, are in direct opposition to those of France, making Alsace-Lorraine the present storm centre of the issues of the war. M. Painlevé said:*

No enemy manoeuvre, no individual weaknesses can turn France from her unshakable determination. That determination she draws from the purest traditions of our race—those generous principles of liberty which the Revolution sowed among the peoples and which today bring together the civilized universe against German imperialism. If France pursues this war it is neither for conquest nor vengeance. It is to defend her own liberty, her independence, and at the same time the liberty and independence of the world. Her claims are those of right; they are even independent of the issue of battles. She proclaimed them solemnly in 1871 when she was beaten. She proclaims them today when she is making the aggressor feel the weight of her arms.

The disannexation of Alsace-Lorraine, reparation for the damage and ruin wrought by the enemy, and a peace which shall not be a peace of constraint or violence, containing in itself the germ of future wars, but a just peace, in which no people, whether strong or weak, shall be oppressed, a peace in which effective guarantees shall protect the society of nations against all aggression on the part of one among them—these are the noble war aims of France, if one can speak of war aims when it is a question of a nation which, during forty-four years, despite her open wounds, has done everything in order to spare humanity the horrors of war.

As long as these aims are not reached France will continue to fight. To prolong the war one day more than necessary would indeed be to commit the greatest crime in history, but to stop it a day too

soon would be to deliver France into the most degrading servitude, to a moral and material misery from which nothing would ever deliver her.

That is what each soldier in our trenches, each worker, each peasant in his factory or in his furrow, knows. It is that which causes the indissoluble union of the country through all its trials; it is that which is the secret of that discipline in liberty which victoriously combats the ferocious brutality of German discipline. This discipline, springing from reason and mutual confidence, previous Governments have maintained for three years of war, and the present Government has no conception of any other.

But it is not only the will of the country that must be directed to this single aim of the war. We must direct to it also all our material forces. National defense is an entity which is not to be split up into fragments. Men, munitions, supply, transport, are all problems to which isolated solutions cannot be supplied, for they are interdependent. We can only cope with them by means of a vast effort of co-ordination and synthesis which, comparing the various needs and possibilities, will be able to secure the increase of production, the imposition of indispensable restrictions, the stoppage of speculation and of the rise in prices by putting at the disposal of the nation herself all the resources which she commands.

It is a difficult program that the Government will set itself to carry out, making private interests yield to the general interest, but it is aware of the fact that it is the nation itself in its conscious spirit of patriotism that can make the effort which shall count for most when the safety of the country is at stake. Who, then, would hesitate to impose on himself the necessary sacrifices, trying enough, but so light compared with the sufferings of our soldiers?

This necessary co-ordination of the forces of the country is no less imperative between the Allies, fighting together yesterday or today, brought together by the same holy cause. It is necessary that they act as though they constituted a single nation, a single army, and a single front for the defeat of the one would be the defeat of all, just as the victory of the one will be the victory of all. All must equally contribute of their men, their arms, and their money. On this condition only the superiority of their resources, still too scattered, will become crushing. Such a policy will allow France, without completely exhausting herself, to meet at once her economic needs and guard her frontiers. Since August, 1914, the French Army has been the invincible shield of civilization. Her blood has been shed in torrents. It is necessary for the happy issue of the war that she should keep to the end the plenitude of her vigor.

The problems of war, however absorbing they may be, ought not to make us unmindful of after-war problems which otherwise might take us by surprise. The period which will follow the conclusion of hostilities must be prepared for a long while in advance, and with as much minute care as mobilization itself. To restore the reconquered districts; to prepare an extensive program of public works which will multiply our industrial forces and regulate the return to normal life by avoiding crises of unemployment for the demobilized men; greatly to increase the production and credit of France; to associate the nation in the working of new industries; to prepare for the transformation to peace conditions of munition factories; to establish our fiscal system on just, bold, and well-thought-out taxes; to carry out loyally the recent reforms introduced into the relations between workmen and employers, so as to adapt these to practical conditions and to make them part of our social life—these are some of the dominating ideas which should guide the development of our ardent democracy. When, after these hard years of suffering, our soldiers return to their homes, to these conquerors who will have made right triumph among the nations, no one will grudge either gratitude or justice.

## Written on Going Into Action

### By ERNEST GARSIDE BLACK

[The author is one of the many Canadian college men at the front in France. He is a graduate of McMaster University, Toronto.]

O God of Battles, now that time has come
　Which in the pregnant months in camp has been
The goal of everything, my hope, my fear,
　The peril of the thing as yet unseen.

That fear and wounds and death may pass me by,
　Is not the boon, O Lord, for which I pray,
For having put the rim within my lips,
　I do not ask to put the cup away.

But grant the heart that Thou hast given me
　May in the hour of peril never fail,
And that my will to serve and do my part
　May ever o'er my will to live prevail.

Thou knowest, Lord, my soul doth not fear death,
　Although my body craves to live its span;
Help me to grapple with my body's fear,
　And grant, O Lord, that I may play the man.

The Somme, Oct. 1, 1916.

# Poland's Standard Again on the Field of Battle

## By Waclaw Perkowski

AFTER a long absence from the field of battle—an interval of fifty-four years—the Polish standard, the white eagle on the red field, again appears on the battle line in the fight "for our liberty and yours." In the west, the Government of France has given its consent to the organization of an autonomous Polish Army; and in the east the Provisional Government of free Russia has followed suit. At last Poland takes her place in this war beside the allied powers as a nation fighting for her rights, for her independence, and for the reunion of all her territories in one Polish State in accordance with the military program of the Allies. She fights against the Central Powers, which, being today at war with the whole civilized world, are at the same time the sole oppressors of the Polish Nation.

In France the Poles had long worked to rouse the Government to the justice of consenting to the organization of a Polish Army; and on June 4, 1917, the following report, signed by the President of the Council of Ministers, (now the Minister of Foreign Affairs, Alexander Ribot,) and the Minister of War, (Paul Painlevé,) was submitted to the President of the French Republic:

> The number of Poles already taking part in the struggle for the rights and liberty of peoples or capable of enrolling in the service of the cause of the Allies is sufficiently high to justify their union into one distinct corps. On the other hand, the intentions of the allied Governments, and in particular of the Russian Provisional Government, on the subject of the restoration of the Polish State could not be affirmed better than by permitting the Poles to fight everywhere under their national colors. Finally, we consider that France must hold it an honor to concur in the formation and development of a future Polish Army. The affinities that unite our two races and the affection the Poles have never ceased to testify to our country impose on us a moral obligation to participate in that touching and glorious mission. If you share this point of view, we have the honor to ask you to affix your signature to the annexed decree.

### Decree Creating Polish Army

The decree, which was signed by Raymond Poincaré, President of the French Republic, at Paris, on June 4, reads as follows:

> Article 1. There is created in France, for the duration of the war, an autonomous Polish Army, placed under the orders of the French High Command and fighting under the Polish colors.
>
> Art. 2. The raising and maintenance of the Polish Army are assured by the French Government.
>
> Art. 3. The arrangements in force in the French Army concerning the organization, grades, administration, and military justice are applicable to the Polish Army.
>
> Art. 4. The Polish Army shall be recruited (1) from among the Poles now serving in the French Army; (2) from among the Poles of other origin admitted to pass into the ranks of the Polish Army in France or to contract a voluntary engagement for the duration of the war under the standard of the Polish Army.
>
> Art. 5. Further Ministerial instructions will regulate the application of the present decree.
>
> Art. 6. The President of the Council of Ministers, the Minister of Foreign Affairs, and the Minister of War are charged, each in what concerns him, to the execution of the present decree, which shall be published in the Official Journal of the French Republic and inserted in the Bulletin des lois, (Bulletin of Laws.)

For the formation of this Polish Army the Minister of War immediately created a Franco-Polish Military Mission, under the leadership of General Louis Archinard. The Government has authorized all Poles, even those who are French citizens and are serving in the French Army, to enlist in this new force, and it is seeking agreements with the other allies under which all Poles serving in their armies will be enabled to join the Polish Army.*

---

*Working in the United States in the interests of the Polish Army in France has been

## Basis of the French Decree

In order to understand the political basis of the French decree calling to life the Polish Army, it is worth while to quote a few words from the appeal of the well-known Polish publicist and novelist, Waclaw Gasiorowski, addressed to the French in his Polonia of Paris on May 12:

> The Polish question has obtained in the last months a complete and radical solution. There has been proclaimed the independence of Poland and the reunion in one State of all her territories. Poland, free and independent, will rise again in the plenitude of her former might and power. And yet dissatisfaction again has seized the Poles. But, before your lips open to condemn us, before you turn away from us and from our importunate reclamations, before you fetch a sigh with pious commisseration because of " the want of moderation of which the Poles give proof," listen to us.
>
> Yes, Poland will be unified and independent; but, meanwhile, a new census of aliens has been decreed here in France; and we shall again be carried on the lists as Germans, Austrians, and Russians—nothing but that!
>
> What, in short, do we Poles in the camp of the Allies desire? We desire that Poland may figure among the peoples that are fighting for the rights of man. We desire that the standard of the White Eagle should float beside the colors of those who have guaranteed us the liberation of our fatherland. We desire that our independence should be realized, that the unification of our territories should become an accomplished fact. We do not want to be impassive witnesses of this great struggle; we want to take part in it, we claim the rights that by just title belong to us as members of the Polish Nation.
>
> Let our fatherland, invaded by the enemy, at length learn that without waiting for any international pacts, accords, and

treaties, the Polish colors are already flying under the protective wing of the Entente. Let it know that the work of the restoration of Poland has already been initiated; that we Poles have at length been recognized as well here, in France, as in America, in England, in Russia, and in Italy, as free citizens of free and unified Poland.

Upon the publication of the decree by President Poincaré for the formation of the Polish Army in France, the same writer said in the Polonia:

> The days of our impotence have ended! The holiest longings of those who would fight for the independence, for the reunion of the fatherland torn to pieces, have been realized. The idea of a self-active, national Polish Army in France has turned to fact. We greet this fact with tears of joy; we greet it as the recompense for our unwavering faith in the indissolubility of the ties of fraternity uniting Poland and France for ages; we greet it as the dawn of our resurrection to liberty, to power, to rebirth. * * *
>
> The Polish Army in France will be an "autonomous" army, or a national Polish Army. This army will stand under the Polish standard, will have the Polish command, Polish uniforms, Polish officers, and will take the oath to unified and independent Poland. * * * This army will be created on democratic principles worthy of the traditions of our chief, the immortal Kosciusko, worthy of the republican land in which it has been conceived. The emblem of the White Eagle will shed its rays on all alike; it will respect the citizen in the soldier, and measure privileges by personal merit.
>
> The Polish Army in France will be the symbol of our fatherland, one and inseparable forever. * * * Like the sun, which dries up the puddles after the heavy shower of the night, so the Polish Army will absorb all that over which till now there has weighed the curse of vassalage, the subjection to different States, the wandering over the world, the misery of our people. The Polish Army in France will reunite in its ranks, in the first place, all those who here, in the west, are scattered in different regiments, divisions, and armies. These hosts will form a base; and about this kernel there will group itself an energetic, numerically large, morally powerful, nationally incorruptible force called to play a part of great reach in the history of our country. Such will be the Polish Army in France!

## Polish Army in Russia

In Russia the principle of the independence of Poland necessitated the constitution of a Polish Army completely autonomous, commanded by Polish offi-

---

a mission composed of Waclaw Gasiorowski, Prince Stanislaus Poniatowski, and others, and Henry Franklin Bouillon, who was recently called back to France to enter the new Cabinet of his friend Prime Minister Painlevé. The campaign to recruit Poles in this country for the Polish Army training in France has been indorsed by the United States War Department, according to a dispatch from Washington of Oct. 6. Polish-Americans subject to draft and those with dependents will not be accepted. Recruits will be trained at a camp already established by Polish interests near Niagara-on-the-Lake, Ontario.

cers, and fighting under the Polish national standard. In view of the proclamation by the Russian Provisional Government of an independent and unified Poland and of the appointment of the Liquidation Commission, which is to liquidate all the interests of Poland with Russia, the cause of a separate Polish Army in Russia and the exclusion of the Polish troops from the general Russian Army had to come by the very force of events. Almost immediately upon the proclamation to the Poles by the Provisional Government of free Russia a meeting of Polish soldiers in the Russian Army was held in Minsk, at which resolutions were adopted calling for the creation of an autonomous Polish Army. The idea of creating a Polish Army out of the Poles " dispersed in the sea of Russian troops " took root very quickly in the Polish community in Russia. Letters began to pour in numerously to the Polish papers in Russia from Polish officers and soldiers, and expression was given to this by all organizations of military. Poles called to life in various parts of Russia by the example of the Polish Military Union, which arose in Moscow on April 11 and declared for the creation of a Polish Army. On June 13 a Congress of Delegates of Military Poles in session in Petrograd resolved, by an overwhelming majority, that the Government of free Russia should without delay proceed to the reunion of the military Poles scattered over the vast territories of the Russian State in a distinct military unit under Polish leaders and a Russian commander in chief.

The Russians themselves early accounted for the necessity of realizing this urgent problem; and the Congress of Delegates of Russian Workmen and Soldiers, held at Minsk, decided upon the formation of a Polish Army. At length, on July 17, the Russian Chief General Staff ordered that the Polish soldiers desiring to enter the Polish Army should be grouped in separate divisions and sent where the Polish Army is forming—the Government had permitted the Poles to create a distinct Polish Army with its own staff and under the supreme command of a Russian commander. Up to the middle of July there had enlisted in this Polish Army 320,000 soldiers, and the number increased after the promulgation of the order of the General Staff of July 17.

## Motives of the Movement

What motives governed the organizers of the Polish Army in Russia is shown by the organ of the Division of Polish Officers and Soldiers, the Polish Wiadomosci Wojskowe (Military Intelligence) of Kiov, when it says:

A united Poland the Central Powers will not give us voluntarily, because the restoration of the Grand Duchy of Posen, Silesia, and West Prussia is the overthrow of the Prussian State. It is a matter here of a struggle for life or death. The breed of Teutonic knights lording it over our land will not cede our liberty voluntarily. Therefore, we bind our hopes to the victory of the Entente, in whose triumph we believe sacredly. The Entente sets forth the standard of liberty and self-determination of nations, under which we stand as a people; and displaying the standard of an independent and unified Poland, it unites the whole Polish Nation, without regard to the cordons that at present separate us. For these two standards, the common and the Polish, raised by the Entente, we want to fight and will fight faithfully to our last drop of blood. Therefore, we recognize the Polish Army as the symbol of Polish Statehood and as an indispensable factor in the ranks of the Entente coalition in the conquest of the independence and unification of Poland, which is possible only after the abolition of Prussian militarism.

## To Raise 500,000 Men

The cadres of the Polish Army in Russia are already complete, and all that remains is to exclude the Poles from the Russian Army. Of lack of trained material for the Polish Army there can be no complaint, for the Poles in the Russian Army have always been reckoned as numbering between 800,000 and 1,-000,000. Competent persons affirm that the distinct Polish Army in Russia can reach 500,000 men. In the Russian Army there are a great many very capable Polish officers, but very few superior officers. The reason for this, says the Paris Polonia, is that twenty-five years ago there was promulgated a secret order that interdicted, save in exceptional cases, the nomination of Poles to grades superior to that of Captain; and at that time the higher military schools were also closed to the Poles.

Three hundred Polish officers taken by Russia from Austria early informed the Council of the Polish Military Union in the Moscow garrison that they were willing to enter the Polish Army, and declared that the 3,000 Polish officers of the Austrian Army in Russian captivity would undoubtedly fulfill their national duty.

The Polish standards bearing the slogan " For Our Liberty and Yours " captured from the Poles by the Russians in the revolution of 1830-31, and held since that time in the Kremlin at Moscow, were delivered with due solemnity on April 21 on the order of the Russian Minister of War and the Russian Premier by the commandant of the Moscow troops to Alexander Lednicki, the Presi-

dent of the Liquidation Commission, (one of the tasks of which is the preserving of the national property which is now being restored to the Polish Nation;) and were conveyed with great honors to Kiov, where they were deposited with reverence in the Church of St. Alexander under guard of the Division of Polish Rifles.

" If the Poles create their separate " army, which in union with the Russian " Army will expel the Germans, there " must come the recognition of this mili- " tant unit by all the Allies. But an " army without a Government, separate " and directing that army, cannot exist," observes the Polish Dziennik Zwiazkowy (Alliance Daily) of Chicago. " Conse- " quently, there must also come the " recognition of a legitimate Govern- " ment of united and independent Poland, " which, by the nature of things, must " rise beyond the bounds of Poland."

## Paderewski's Appeal to His Countrymen

The National Department of the Polish Central Relief Committee of Chicago, whose Chairman is I. J. Paderewski, the pianist, issued an appeal on Oct. 6, 1917, calling upon unnaturalized Poles in the United States to enlist under the Polish standard. The document is in part as follows:

Providence has decreed that on the centennial of the death of Thaddeus Kosciusko there arises a Polish national army upon the Continent where he so valiantly fought for freedom. France has given life to this army and has offered her aid and support. France does not require the sacrifice of Polish blood. She can prevail without our humble aid. Over 5,000,-000 men now fight in her defense.

France, the leader of civilization, like Poland, a frequent defender of the oppressed, is concerned chiefly that in this struggle of light against darkness, right against might, democracy against autocracy, all liberty-loving peoples may participate.

Larger and smaller nations are already engaged, and now the United States of America has joined France and her allies. Should, in this struggle for the freedom

of nations, the Polish colors be missing it would be shameful.

Conscious of our sacred duty to the motherland, conscious of our obligations to America, we have long waited for this opportunity, with a full sense of our responsibility before God, the nation, and our own consciences. Today, having received assurances of protection, having received a favorable declaration by the United States Government that enlistment into the Polish Army of all those who are not legally subject to draft in the United States Army shall not be opposed, we call to you from the bottom of our hearts and challenge you to the ranks, to army, to battle, to the trenches, to a great and glorious struggle for the protection of threatened humanity, for the wrongs suffered by Poland.

Go, so the world may know that in your breast the knightly valor of your forefathers has not been stilled; that the fearless bravery of the Poles of old has not vanished.

Go, to give testimony that the American Pole is a worthy heir to the glory of Polish arms.

On the same day the United States had authorized this separate recruiting for the Polish Army.

# The Rise and Fall of the Formal Fortress

## By Thomas G. Frothingham

### Member of Military Historical Society of Massachusetts

*" Still the most reliable fortress for a country is a good and well-commanded army and a well-educated, brave, and intelligent population."*—Viollet le Duc.

ONE great proved fact in the present war has been the uselessness of the formal fortress in the military result. Formal fortresses had been made important factors in the pre-war military calculations, because of the imaginary strength that had been assigned to them. In reality they were an empty threat. Yet this threat so influenced the plans of the German Great General Staff that the invasion of France was deliberately planned through neutral Belgium rather than through the French fortresses.*

The result was that the initial German superiority was frittered away in Belgium, and the surprise of the all-conquering Teutonic howitzer artillery was wasted on outlying fortresses. To this extent the French fortresses had an important tactical effect upon the military results of the war without firing a shot, but this was the end of their value in warfare. In the few short weeks before the battle of the Marne the uselessness of formal fortresses had become so self-evident that they were replaced by Petersburg intrenchments, and the lesson learned in four years of our civil war was at last grasped by European military experts.

The progress of the art of formal fortification is as interesting as the end of such fortresses has been dramatic and astounding. The formal fortress had its beginning in the primitive need to protect families and goods. From the first herding together in places easy of defense to the elaborated systems of European military science, the different phases of the formal fortress reflect the conditions of the times as well as any landmarks in history.

## Viollet le Duc's Great Work

A great master of the art of fortification has left a record of this progress of a formal fortress from its first primitive form to the typical fortress of his day. Viollet le Duc was a great architect of the Second Empire, and to this talent he " added the highest qualifications of the military engineer."** His book is now little known except to military students, but in his " Histoire d'une Forteresse " he has described with great vividness the growth of a French fortress from the first occupation of a stronghold in the tribal migrations.

For obvious military reasons Viollet le Duc did not select any definite fortress, but he described a typical site, and traced the development of a typical fortress of his day. This will be followed to his conclusion, (1875,) but his final proposed system of fortification is so like Verdun, the fortress most in the public mind in this war, that, in continuing the story of the fortress to its final stage the actual conditions at Verdun will be described.

In Figure 1 is shown the first refuge chosen by the tribal migration of a fair-haired Northern race in France, an elevated promontory on a river among wooded hills. The occupation of this place by the strangers was peaceful, and many of the inhabitants of the surrounding country joined them in their settlement; but, as these Gauls prospered, forays were made upon them and they were much harried and plundered. At length the elders of the tribe ordered the " Oppidum " built, as shown on the plan.

This was a rampart of logs and earth with a parapet of stakes fixed by osier bands and pierced with loopholes. The

---

*" The Moltke of 1870," &c. CURRENT HISTORY, February, 1917.

**Bucknall.

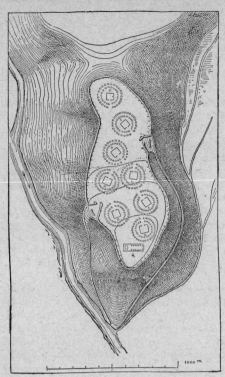

FIG. 1—THE OPPIDUM

after a costly invasion, when the Oppidum was only saved by bringing in fighting men from another tribe, the warriors arrogated for themselves the control of the Oppidum and demanded contributions from the inhabitants in return for their protection. The people were forced to agree to give one day's labor in four and one-fourth of their crops and cattle to their defenders; and, as time went on, these became hereditary rights, resulting in the rule of the chiefs and their warriors in the Gallic Cités.

FIG. 2—THE GALLIC CITE, 58 B. C.

rampart encircled the crown of the promontory, and, helped by the slope, made a strong defense against an assault. The inclosure was approached by two roads that circled the plateau, exposed to missiles of the defenders from the ramparts. The two gates were also well defended. Within were tribal houses, as shown in the plan, and the Némède, the Druid inclosed temple, (A.) This Oppidum was the first phase of the formal fortress, and it will be observed that in the Némède was the beginning of what was later to be the keep or citadel.

At first there was no regular garrison of the Oppidum. It was guarded in turn by the young men, who relieved one another every twenty-four hours, and it was a refuge from attacks for the people. But in the fourth century B. C. many of the Gauls had been engaged in foreign wars, and a warrior class began to grow up among them. Raids and wars increased among the tribes, and the trained warriors were needed more and more to defend the Oppidum. Finally,

### Forts in Caesar's Time

The Gallic Cité was the second stage of the formal fortress. (Figure 2.) It will be seen that the Cité is the Oppidum, made much stronger for defense. The ramparts had been reinforced with stone and towers had been built along the ramparts, as shown in the plan. The town straggled along the slopes of the promontory, and a part of it was on the other side of the river, which was crossed by a stone bridge. It will be seen that the bridge was protected by a tête de pont, which was also built of stone.

The rule of the Chiefs and the warrior caste, which had been created by the defenders of the Oppidum, had become absolute and their tax upon the people had become a vested right; yet the inhabitants themselves were more prosperous, because the contributions levied upon them by the Chief were not as oppressive as losses from plundering invaders. This was the condition of the fortress at the time of Caesar's Gallic wars. The Chief of the Cité, like other Gallic chieftains, had aided the Helvetii, and a punitive expedition was sent against him by the Roman General.

The Chief defied this army, and the Cité promptly received a lesson in the besieging tactics of the day from the Romans, who were very skillful in reducing fortresses. The Roman legate first invested all approaches of the place, and prepared for an assault upon the Cité by cutting a great quantity of wood on the northern plateau and bringing it in front of the northern ramparts.

With this wood and earth he threw up a typical Roman agger, a mound of logs and earth, opposite the ramparts of the besieged. Approaching this the Romans built two covered galleries and a movable tower. This last they rolled to the top of the agger against the rampart, and by attacking from the tower won the main defenses of the Cité.

The Chief of the Cité, with his surviving warriors, took refuge in the stronghold beyond the Némède (A) in the southern end of the Cité. This the Roman legate easily carried, by filling the ditch with faggots and earth, and advancing his legionaries under linked shields, (a testudo,) and the fortress of 58 B. C. had succumbed to the advanced siege methods of the day.

### Permanent Roman Camp

After his final victory over the Gauls at Alesia (52 B. C.) Caesar gave orders for the establishment of a permanent Roman camp on the site of the Cité; and this was the next stage in the progress of the fortress. (Figure 3.) It will

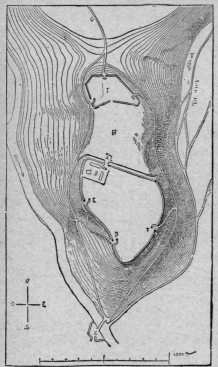

FIG. 3—THE PERMANENT ROMAN CAMP

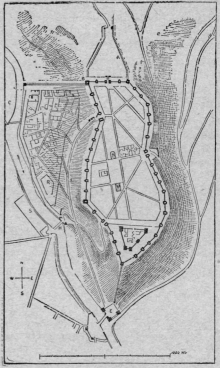

FIG. 4—THE GALLO-ROMAN CITE

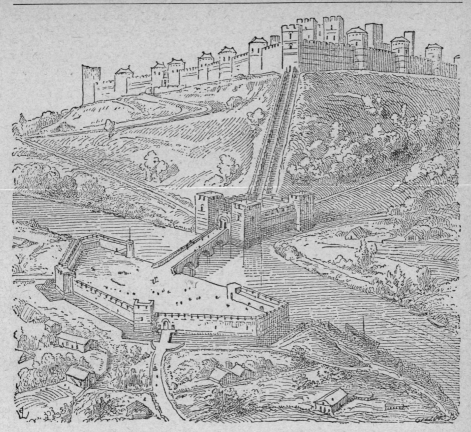

FIG. 5—THE GALLO-ROMAN CITE AS FORTIFIED BY THE ROMAN EMPEROR JULIAN, A. D. 359

be seen that the town was blotted out, and that on the site of the Cité was built this stern fortified camp, which was a charge upon the people to keep in repair, and to be always ready for the use of the Roman Legions. After generations, when the surrounding country had become tranquil, the Roman Camp became a Roman Colony, enjoying peace and prosperity for three centuries.

In 359 A. D. the Roman Emperor Julian found it again necessary to fortify the place against the Germans, and the formal fortress entered another stage of its existence as a Gallo-Roman Cité. (Figure 4.)

Julian had then about him Byzantine engineers, the most skilled in the world in fortifying places. They began by removing the houses that had been built on the slopes of the plateau in times of peace, thus restoring all the military ad-

vantage of the slope, as in the Roman Camp. The ramparts were of well-founded masonry with stone towers. The northern exposed front was made longer, with a fosse and palisades, and a vallum and outwork, (A.) The gates, tête de pont, &c., were protected by strong towers, and the Cité thus fortified (Figure 5) was able to defy the barbarians, who did not know how to undertake the siege of a well-defended place.

In the twelfth century the fortress had become a feudal castle, (Figure 6,) and in 1180 the Baron decided to greatly strengthen its defenses. He sent for a master of the works—a native of Troyes, whom he had known in Palestine—and together they devised the stronghold shown in Figure 7.

This great increase in the strength of the Castle aroused the jealousy of the Baron's over-lord, the Duke of Burgundy,

FIG. 7—BIRDSEYE VIEW OF THE FEUDAL CASTLE, 1180 A. D.

who seized upon a pretext for a quarrel, and moved to attack the Castle with his army. The Baron prepared for defense, but sent a secret message for help to King Philip Augustus of France. The siege that followed used all the resources of that most picturesque age of warfare, and it is interesting to record as the last test of the fortress before the use of gunpowder.

The Baron had only 1,800 men and he could not hope to defend the whole pla-

teau, but only the castle. This the Duke completely invested, closing the bridges and building an intrenchment or contravallation across the plateau north of the castle. On each end of this contravallation the besiegers built a wooden tower. The Baron, who had brought the secret of Greek fire from the East, promptly destroyed one of these towers in the night by hurling Greek fire from his largest trebuchet, following this with a sortie of the garrison, which inflicted

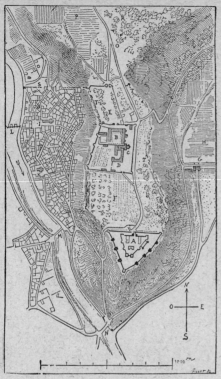

FIG. 6—THE FEUDAL CASTLE

great loss in the confusion caused by the fire.

The besiegers retaliated by bringing up trebuchets and mangonels, which forced the garrison to give up the barbican. The besiegers then brought up a cat, a movable wooden gallery, under which they mined the wall and battered it down with a bossom, gaining the outer court after days of bloody fighting.

The besieged had destroyed a huge new movable tower with their Greek fire —thus giving the old fortress revenge for the Roman movable tower which had captured it over 1,200 years before—and the garrison was still holding out manfully after more than forty days of siege, when the place was relieved by the approach of the French King's army.

### The Coming of Gunpowder

In the next 200 years the fortress had been compelled to face new conditions. (Figure 8.) A new force had appeared, and the first awkward attempts to defend against artillery with artillery were in

evidence. But it also must be remembered that the first artillery imitated the trebouchet of the mediaeval siege, and for attack and defense there was not yet any change in methods brought about by the new weapon.

The masonry walls were much more massive, and, as will be seen in the plan, new strong towers had been built projecting from the walls. These were devised with great pains and misdirected ingenuity to contain the new artillery. Clumsy as were the resultant works, these artillery towers were the ancestors of the bastion.

In a month's siege, sustained by the fortress at this stage by the army of Louis XI. of France, (1478,) the artillery of both parties is thus described:

|  | Bombards. | Veuglaires, Spiroles. |
|---|---|---|
| Attack on the northern boulevard | 4 | 2 |
| Battery on the slopes of the eastern hills | 2 | 4 |
| Before the tête du pont | | 4 |
| On the western slopes of the plateau commanding the lower town | | 2 |
| Park of reserve | 6 | 12 |
| Total | 12 | 24 |

The artillery of the besieged consisted of:

|  | Bombards. | Culverins. |
|---|---|---|
| On the platforms of the three great northern towers | 3 | 3 |
| In the casemated batteries of these towers | | 6 |
| On the earthwork in front of the northern boulevard | | 2 |
| On the northern boulevard | 1 | 2 |
| On the boulevards B, C, H, I, K. | 5 | 5 |
| On the cavalier commanding the bridge | 1 | 2 |
| Reserve in the abbey and the castle | 4 | 8 |
| Totals | 14 | 28 |

Pathetically feeble as this array seems today for the attack and defense of a first-class fortress, these cannon were the most formidable artillery of their time. It is also shown on a scale plan that the first long-distance bombardment was opened at less than 250 meters, and it is stated that certain guns were to be reserved for use at close quarters! Consequently, it is no surprise to learn that

FIG. 8—THE FIRST DEFENSES AGAINST
ARTILLERY

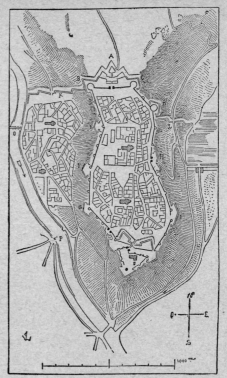

FIG. 9—THE BASTIONS OF BAR-LE-DUC

this siege was almost a repetition of the siege of the feudal castle, with these primitive cannon taking the place of the stone-throwing machines.

These cannon threw large stones, some of them of 200 pounds weight, and, though they caused greater losses to the besiegers, they also were more destructive to masonry defenses at close quarters, and they made it easier to undermine the walls. The northern outwork, the boulevard at D in the plan, was first reduced, then the tower and northern rampart at E were battered in, and the last refuge of the garrison at A was surrendered twenty-seven days after the first investment.

### Artillery and the Bastion

In the seventeenth century engineers were beginning to learn the use of the new artillery arm. It became evident that, against this more powerful machine, the weakness of a formal fortress lay in allowing the enemy to get near

enough to breach the walls. The next phase of the fortress, (Figure 9,) designed by Bar-le-Duc in the reign of Henry IV., marked the appearance of the bastion instead of the artillery tower, which greatly increased the area of defensive artillery. On the north the boulevard and towers had been replaced by bastions, and by this means the enemy was forced to begin operations at 1,000 yards. It is hard to realize that in those days 1,000 yards was not an effective range for artillery.

In 1636 these defenses successfully resisted an attempt to besiege them by the Imperialist troops, using trench approaches, which afterward became so highly developed in siege warfare. But the fortress was well commanded, and the attacking army, badly led and ill-disciplined, was ordered to raise the siege after four weeks of useless effort.

The next stage of the fortress (Figure 10) shows the highest development of the bastion by the great French en-

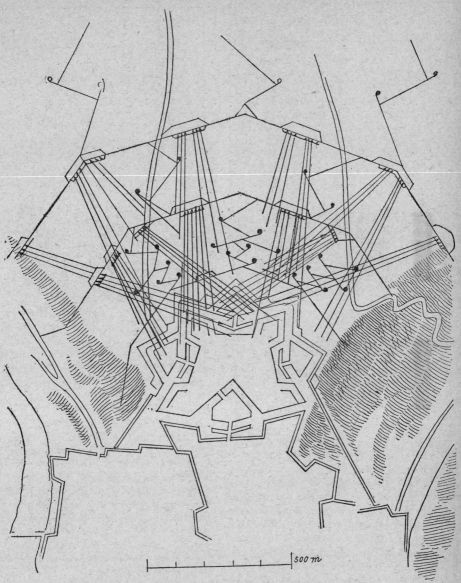

FIG. 11—THE SCIENTIFIC ATTACK ON VAUBAN DEFENSES

gineer, Vauban, who dominated the schools of fortification far into the nineteenth century. It will be seen at once how greatly the area of the artillery fire of the fortress was increased.

Figure 11 is a plan of the recognized attack on these Vauban works, which became the standard of European sieges. The trench approaches, placing of batteries, and successive advances to the first, second, and third parallels are plainly shown. Following these approaches the final stage of a siege was still a breach and an assault, as in the attack on the feudal castle. These defenses and these prescribed methods of attack became accepted elements in warfare, and each fortress had its assigned strength and well defined amount of force and time necessary to reduce it.

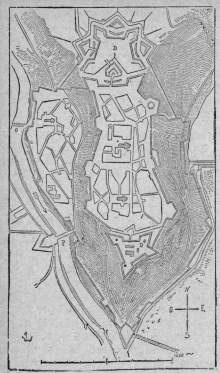

FIG. 10—VAUBAN'S DEFENSES

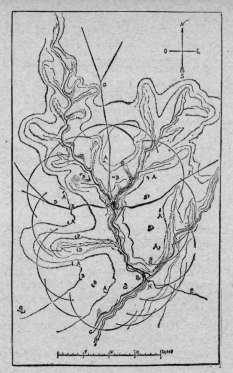

FIG. 12—THE ENCEINTE AND CHAIN OF
FORTS

The siege of Sebastopol (1854) first upset all these accepted methods. This was a weak fortress, and it was thought that it would fall "after a short cannonade."* It unexpectedly withstood a siege of 349 days because the great Russian engineer, Todleben, made a bold use of "improvised defenses."†

### Chain of External Forts

Of course these defenses approached the recent solution of the problem of fortification; but this was obscured by criticism of the attack, just as the actual solution at Petersburg, ten years later, was ignored in the first mistaken criticism of our civil war. At first there was so strong an impression abroad of a war of undisciplined mobs fighting against one another that the real results of the civil war in finding the best weapons and methods were not realized until the present war.

The rifled gun had so greatly increased

* Hamley.
† Sir George Clarke.

the range of artillery that, even in the formal European schools, it became evident that the bastion should be pushed forward and made an outwork of the fortress. This was the origin of the later plan of the chain of external forts. Viollet le Duc, among others, had urged this upon the French Emperor, but in the atrophy and official demoralization of the Second Empire little was done, and the French fortresses were an easy prey in the war of 1870. The Germans reduced most of the French fortresses at their leisure by bombardment. Verdun, which was then of the type of fortress shown in Figure 10, a bastioned enceinte with a Vauban citadel, fell after forty-three days.

Figure 12 shows Viollet le Duc's final scheme for the formal fortress, the enceinte and surrounding chain of forts and batteries. It will be seen at once that this was the plan of Verdun at the outbreak of the present war. But something more than this arrangement of forts had given to the fortress the reputation of strength that scared away the first German attack in 1914.

### Revolution Due to Howitzers

What made the empty threat effective was the artificial value that had been assigned to the new use of concrete and steel in the construction of the formal fortresses. So highly were these recent fortresses esteemed, as an adjunct of defending armies, that the German Great General Staff had not been able to realize the tremendous power over them of their howitzer artillery. So revolutionary was this weapon that it is not strange its effectiveness was not considered sufficient to upset all the calculations of years.

Only as recently as 1907 Sir Edward Clarke, the leading British expert, had declared that "the idea of breaching hidden casements by planting shells successively on a few square yards of area may evidently be dismissed as futile." Yet this is exactly what the Teutonic howitzer artillery has accomplished against all formal fortresses attacked by it. Every steel and concrete fort has proved to be a pent-house of destruction after a few of these deadly shells have been dropped upon it. At once this became so evident, from the experience of Liége, Namur, &c., that in September, 1914, Verdun and the other French fortresses were intrenched, and became merely sectors of the Petersburg intrenchments which are now strung along the western front.

The chains of forts have been dismantled, and at the battle of Verdun in 1916 Verdun was no longer a fortress. It was nothing but the name of a system of trenches. Yet the name in the French mind meant the prestige of France, and for its defense they made the desperate stand that beat back the German attacks. The position in itself was of no more value than any other system of trenches.

It will be remembered that Fort Douaumont and Fort Vaux were no longer forts, but merely places in the lines of trenches. The great guns are no longer mounted in definite places. They are now scattered about on railway and caterpillar mounts, with every device of concealment and camouflage. The terrain is now a labyrinth of pits and trenches, with nothing left of the formal fortress. The whole structure of twenty-five hundred years has been overthrown in a few months.

## What France Is Doing for Serbians

France, torn as it is by war, is supporting and giving refuge to 200,000 Belgians, furnishing them with the same kind of quarters as those allotted to French refugees from occupied territory; it has likewise gathered in many Serbians driven from their homes by the invader, and has set about preparing for the restoration of their unhappy kingdom by giving to Serbian youth the education best suited to the needs of national renaissance. A treaty signed at Corfu on Nov. 9, 1916, which the French Parliament has ratified, gives an official organization to this fraternal enterprise. It regulates the distribution of the young men among the universities and French normal schools, and arranges for the Serbian Government's nomination of Serbian professors to teach the literature, language, and history of their country. The treaty also provides for instruction of French students by these Serbian professors, exempts a certain number of Serbian students from the educational laws, and appropriates funds for their maintenance. This treaty is valid for three years and can be renewed for similar periods by tacit continuation.

# Military Operations of the War

### By Major Edwin W. Dayton
*Inspector General, N. G. N. Y.; Secretary, New York Army and Navy Club*

## IX.—The Battle of the Somme

THE opening of 1916 was an anxious period for the Allies. France had held fast at Verdun against the most terrific attacks, but gradually the assailants pressed in closer, until at the end of May it seemed that even the heroic devotion of that marvelous defense must succumb. The world began to fear that England for some reason was unable to create the much-needed diversion in the north. Contemporary writers are contending that the Allies deliberately delayed their northern offensive in order to compel the enemy to maintain strong armies along the whole front to meet the attack which every one knew was soon to come.

It seemed that their well-known superiority over the Germans in both men and munitions ought to have made it possible to make strong feints at several places, in addition to launching a real attack on a great scale. Verdun, although an important link in the frontier defenses, was not, after all, a place whose loss would have been fatal to France. The moral effect, however, of a German success at Verdun might have been a serious matter. Such a result would have renewed Teuton hopes, and would certainly have disheartened many of the neutrals weary of waiting to see the Germans defeated. Whatever the real reasons may have been, it is safe to say that the Allies delayed their northern attack to the very last moment if the diversion was intended to save Verdun. When they did strike, however, their attack was on a scale both in extent of front and duration of effort far beyond anything they had previously undertaken on the western front.

A remarkable feature was the great part played by the French, who proved their ability to develop a major offensive on a wide front while continuing to hold the defenses at Verdun with forces strong enough for frequent counterattacks. The vitality of the French after the trying defense of Verdun was one of the surprises of the war.

The weeks immediately preceding the great attack in Picardy seemed full of promise for the Allies. In June Italy had checked the dangerous Austrian attack on the Trentino, and in the first week of the same month Brusiloff began the attack on Galicia and Bukowina which threatened to crush Austria.

The struggle had raged steadily in Flanders and Artois through two hard years. Whenever the thunder of guns quieted elsewhere in Europe, Asia, or Africa, attention always returned to Ypres, Loos, Souchez, Vimy, Hulluch, and the Labyrinth, where the war gods never ceased to gather their steady toll of British, French, and German lives. A little further to the south lay Picardy, the Santerre, a sobriquet reminiscent of the old wars, when the fair fields were the sang terre of a hundred bloody campaigns. But since the Autumn of 1914, when Castelnau and Maud'huy had won the race for the coast by extending and covering the allied left flank, the lines which congealed then into the intrenched positions in Picardy had been the quietest of all.

### Germans in the Ascendency

London had been whispering for months about the "great push" which was to come, but all through the Spring there was very little activity along the British front, except for mine explosions and tunneling, mingled with small trench raids. In April, May, and June there were a number of brilliant small exploits, but mostly distinguished as sharp counterstrokes recovering trenches which the Germans had stormed. There was a noticeable lack of initial attack, and the best that could be done appeared to be the prevention of any large permanent gain by the enemy. If the gage of military supremacy was to be the ability to maintain the initiative it had to be confessed that the decision would rest with the Germans. The great attacks were theirs in Russia, the Balkans, and at Verdun, while in the east their defenses had been much more than negative successes in Gallipoli and Mesopotamia. Only in Armenia had victory rested with the Allies when the Russians took Erzerum and Trebizond. In June the Italians just managed to stop the Austrian attack in the Trentino.

It was high time for the Allies to force the rôle of the defense upon the Germans. The saving of Verdun was an immediate and obvious necessity, but demonstration of an ability to maintain a successful aggressive campaign against the enemy was a greater and more important need. The situation was realized and the Winter and Spring had been used to perfect the equipment necessary for a great offensive. Both England and France poured men and munitions into the sector north of the Somme, where the enemies faced each other on a wide curve running from the river east of Maricourt and west of Mametz, Fricourt, La Boiselle, Ovillers, Thiepval, Beaumont, Hamel, Serre, Gommecourt, and Monchy to the railway from Bapaume to Arras.

Above Thiepval the Ancre crossed the battle front, flowing south to join the Somme back of the French front. As the battle developed into its later stages the shallow valley of this little river was the scene of long, hard battles about Grandcourt, Pys, and Miraumont. South of the Somme, just before the great battle opened, the Germans scored some gains at Frise and Dompierre, which indicated their appreciation of the fact that a storm was brewing whose force they desired to judge by reconnoissance in the region where they doubtless anticipated it would break.

Earlier in the Spring they felt out the French positions in the region of Roye and Albert, but the perfection of their fortifications in the chalk hills of Picardy made the Germans confident that any allied effort there was doomed to certain failure. They had not been idle while

the fighting paused for long months in this region, for they had eagerly seized the opportunity to convert every hill and village into a scientific fortification provided with intricate approaches and numerous supports. The hill villages were

GENERAL SIR HENRY RAWLINSON

real fortresses, with deep-sunk refuges for the garrisons in time of bombardment, and artfully concealed machine-gun nests only to be disclosed when attacking infantry presented a worth-while target.

### General Haig's Preparations

While the Germans were digging in, General Sir Douglas Haig was improving roads, building military railways, dugouts, field hospitals, and magazines. More than a hundred pumping plants were installed to provide an adequate supply of water from many new wells, and when the engineers were not boring wells they were driving mines under the enemy's front line works. General Sir Henry Rawlinson commanded the troops assigned for the attack, with his left flank below Gommecourt and his right in touch with the French above Maricourt. On this front of less than fifteen miles the British had five corps, with a reserve army lying ready behind. The co-operating French army, (the Sixth,) formerly that of Castelnau, was commanded by General Fayolle, and comprised three corps of war-tried veterans, including the famous Twentieth, which at Verdun had won great fame in Douaumont and Avocourt.

While these great armies, with their enormous artillery equipment, were being assembled it was essential that the German air scouts should be prevented from discovering the location of the concentration. Apparently the allied airmen won the control of the air in Picardy, for the Germans were for some weeks brushed out of the sky over that area. Through the latter part of June both British and French batteries began to bombard the enemy lines along the whole front, through Picardy, Artois, and Flanders, and it is believed that the enemy was led to expect the attack much further north than the Somme sector, probably somewhere between Albert and Arras. Rain in the last week of June delayed the operations for several days, but more than seventy trench raids were made, in addition to a number of gas attacks and mine explosions.

As the battle was planned, the British objective was the high ground between the Ancre and the Somme, through Thiepval, Longueval, and Ginchy, in the direction of Combles. The French were to attack below Combles and across the Somme. As the northern part of the British objective was commanded by the enemy positions on the further side of the Ancre, it became necessary to increase the scope of the British assaults by extending the attack to include Gommecourt, five miles above Beaumont Hamel.

## Beginning of the Great Battle

At 7:15 on the morning of July 1, 1916, the bombardment reached the utmost fury. At half after the hour there was a pause for a few seconds, and then the bombardment shifted to a barrage, and on a front of twenty-five miles the allied infantry leaped from their trenches and rushed to the attack.

The immediate objective of the British infantry (six divisions) was the high

ground bisected by the Ancre, and despite the utmost gallantry these brave troops were doomed to a costly defeat. The fortified villages of Thiepval, Beaumont Hamel, Serre, and Gommecourt had withstood the hurricane of shell fire and remained practically impregnable. The extraordinarily deep shelters for both men and machine guns enabled the garrisons to return to the surface when the assault developed in time to sweep the advancing lines with rifle and machine-gun fire. Back of the villages the German artillery had excellent observation posts on high ground, and the ranges were figured with mathematical precision. Just before the assault the heavy German guns fired a cloud of six and eight inch high explosive shells into the British front line trenches, and their shrapnel barrage moved with the troops as they advanced.

At Beaumont Hamel a mine which had been seven months digging was exploded under an enemy redoubt, which was blown to pieces with all the ground about it. Nevertheless the German battalions showed splendid morale by immediately getting their automatic rifles and machine guns into effective action.

The British regiments advanced in many successive lines, and in spite of terrible losses some detachments penetrated deep into certain parts of the enemy positions. None, however, were able to hold the ground gained, and by nightfall the remnants of those splendid divisions were back in the old British trenches. Of the groups which fought their way into the German lines nearly a thousand were captured by the enemy, and even on the next day some others succeeded in fighting their way back.

Further south, where perhaps the Germans had not anticipated the attack, real successes were scored. Mametz and Montauban were taken, as well as the outlying defenses of La Boiselle. Fricourt was seriously threatened, and below Thiepval the Leipsic redoubt fell into the hands of the British, which proved a great point of vantage in the later operations. On July 2, about noon, another division was hurled at Fricourt, and that well-nigh impregnable fortress was taken.

On the first day the marvelous French infantry charged with characteristic speed and effect, which won complete success. They gained the outer defenses of Curlu and Hardecourt on the 1st, and completed the captures on the 2d of July. South of the Somme the French succeeded in surprising the Germans and captured Dompierre, Becquincourt, and Bussu, as well as Fay.

## Results of the Opening Phase

In summing up the results of the opening phase of the great battle of the Somme, we may say that the Allies captured German first-line positions from Mametz to Fay on a front of about fourteen miles, with 6,000 prisoners and a large quantity of guns and stores. In the northern sector, where the enemy had anticipated an attack, the ground won could not be held because every position was rendered untenable by the perfect arrangement of secondary and flanking defense works. There the great battle resolved itself into a long series of siege operations, much like the German attacks at Verdun, only much more successful.

In the southern area of the battlefield on Sunday, July 2, the French followed up their initial successes by capturing Curlu, Frise, Mereaucourt Wood, and the powerfully fortified village of Herbecourt. At some places south of the river they broke through the German second-line positions, besides gaining the command of the railway from Combles to Péronne, and their advanced positions were not more than four miles from the latter city. For a short time it seemed as though a quick success might carry the French into Péronne and the British on to Bapaume by the southern approaches, but the arrival of strong German reserves, as well as the great losses incurred by the British in the northern sector, combined to defer the realization of those hopes for long months.

On July 3 and 4 the British infantry fought desperately and won La Boiselle, after suffering severe losses. Thiepval resisted all efforts to capture it, and although Contalmaison was stormed on July 7 it was recaptured by the Third Prussian Guard Division, (the "Cock-

chafers,") who lost 700 prisoners when the village was first taken by the British. In heavy rain progress was made east of La Boiselle along the Bapaume road, and part of Leipsic redoubt was captured. Hard battles raged about several small wooded positions, and after several days of heavy battling Contalmaison was again stormed, and on July 10 captured, after bitter house-to-house fighting. On Sunday, July 16, Ovillers was taken, with 2 surviving officers and 124 soldiers of the Guards.

Through the early days of the month battles were fought for Fricourt Wood, Mametz Wood, Trones Wood, and it was not until July 12 that the British infantry fought their way through Mametz Wood so as to face the German second line positions. Even then neither side could claim Trones Wood.

Meanwhile the French, continuing to fight splendidly along the line of the river, after taking Belloy-en-Santerre, forced their way into part of Estrées and defeated numerous counterattacks. On Sunday, the 9th, Fayolles men took Biaches and were only a mile from Péronne. In less than two weeks' continuous fighting the French forced their way through to the German third-line positions on a front of approximately ten miles, capturing 85 guns, 12,000 men, and 236 officers.

## Haig's Drive on Bastille Day

On Bastille Day (July 14) General Haig celebrated the great French fête day by a grand attack on a front from a point below Pozières to Longueval and Delville Wood, approximately four miles. Soon after 3 o'clock in the morning the Third and Fifteenth Corps attacked after a tremendous bombardment, and in the darkness before dawn reached the German positions with almost no loss. This attack was everywhere successful, and by evening the British occupied the whole of the German second line between Longueval and Bazentin-le-Petit. Trones Wood had been cleared, most of Longueval captured, and the British infantry had pushed up the road to within less than six miles of Bapaume. Cavalry had been brought close up the night before, to be ready in case an opening might be

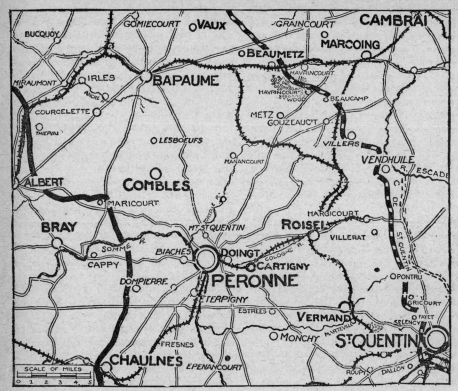

MAIN AREA OVER WHICH THE BATTLE OF THE SOMME WAS FOUGHT

made toward the rear, through which the mounted men might ride to their long-hoped-for opportunity. That hope was not realized, for no break in the enemy line resulted, such was the perfection of his interior lines of defense.

In Trones Wood 170 men of the Royal West Kents were found surrounded by the enemy, but holding on grimly to a valuable point of vantage gained in the night attack. In the early evening of the 14th a troop of Dragoon Guards and a troop of Deccan Horse made their way up a shallow valley and intrenched in a cornfield at a point where they were able to cover the flank of the infantry attacking the formidable enemy positions in High Wood. The fight for this fortified wood continued on the 15th, but strong counterattacks by a German division compelled the British troops to abandon this very difficult position.

### The Fight for Delville Wood

A hard battle raged for two weeks about Longueval and Delville Wood, east of the little town. The British fought their way into the woods without great trouble, but found it impossible to retain the ground gained because of the machine-gun fire from powerful field works near by. The fight for this wood was among the deadliest episodes of the whole Somme battle. The South African brigade fought desperately for a foothold for several days, but finally was relieved, after suffering enormous losses. One splendid battalion, after losing all its officers, repulsed a powerful attack by a crack Brandenburg division; the long battle in this wood was as glorious for the South African troops as Ypres for Canadians or Gallipoli for Australians. Delville Wood was not completely conquered until the last week in August.

On July 16 Ovillers was captured, also Waterlot Farm, a strong fortification southeast of Longueval. Four days later the British renewed the assault upon

High Wood, and made considerable progress in that very difficult sector. The furthest corner of this wood was defended by a division of the Magdeburg Corps with the utmost bravery, and it required two months of hard fighting to finally wrest the last trench from its stubborn defenders.

At midnight on July 23 a bitter struggle began about Thiepval, and an Anzac division of Australians fought again as they had the year before against the Turks in Gallipoli. It was not, however, until the 26th that General Haig was able to announce the capture of this fortified town, to which the Germans clung with heroic tenacity. In the last days of July the capture of Longueval was completed, and hard fighting in Delville Wood won some gains. The Germans repulsed an attack on Guillemont, and as the month ended they defeated powerful attacks at Pozières, although they could not prevent the Australians from gaining a position on the edge of their intrenchments after furious hand-to-hand fighting.

On Aug. 4, at 9 in the evening, the Australians rushed the fortified windmill on the crest of the ridge northeast of Pozières, and won as well the German second-line trenches. A counterattack with liquid fire temporarily dislodged them from a small section; but even that was again taken, and in the following week, in spite of very heavy losses, these splendid British soldiers drove their attack still further into the Teuton lines about Pozières and in the direction of Mouquet Farm, a strong fortification commanding the northwest approach to Pozières and the highway from Albert to Bapaume. The troops who won these successes at great cost continued to suffer heavily from a deadly flanking fire from the German fortifications at Thiepval and heavy batteries further to the north and northeast.

## The Situation in August

Before the middle of August the French had conquered all the German positions south of the Somme, and on the 12th, in a perfectly planned assault on a front of fully four miles, penetrated German positions to an average depth of about 1,200 yards. This advance aimed straight at the main road from Péronne to Bapaume, reached the edge of Maurepas, and below that town cut well across the Maurepas-Cléry road. Still further south they won the Monacu Farm position and drove the enemy fully 700 yards beyond. A few days later they linked up their left flank with the British right north of Maurepas.

In the middle of August the British continued to fight hard at Pozières, High Wood, and Guillemont in heroic efforts to win better protection for the left flank of forces holding the trenches won earlier in the month. Gradually gains were reported northwest of Pozières and in the region of Bazentin le Petit and Martinpuich. About the same time the Germans were compelled to yield some ground near Mouquet Farm and Ginchy. At 8 A. M. on Aug. 18 two British battalions charged suddenly and captured the powerful Leipsic redoubt, south of Thiepval. This attack was so well planned that plenty of machine guns were immediately available to repulse the enemy's counterattack. Elsewhere that day progress was won close to Martinpuich and Longueval, but after capturing the stone quarry close to Guillemont this strong fortification was lost in a counterattack.

The French, co-operating with great success, carried part of Maurepas and stormed a hill position southeast of the town, which was defended by a division of the Prussian Guard newly arrived on the battle line. Although the whole of the First Guard Corps of Prussians was now confronting the French between Maurepas and the Somme, the wonderful poilus yielded never an inch of ground once recovered from the invaders.

On Sunday, Aug. 20, after a severe bombardment the Germans recaptured some trenches lately lost to the British near High Wood and Mouquet Farm, but failed to hold their own when in turn counterattacked. Several days later the Germans repeated their efforts at Guillemont, but failed, and on the 24th the British carried in a fine attack the Hindenburg trench, an outlying defense of Thiepval, and on the same day the French completed the conquest of Maurepas and kept touch with the British between that town and Guillemont, thus continuing their drive toward Combles. Five German attacks were repulsed on the last day of August by a battalion of the Sussex regiment, between Ginchy and High Wood.

Sunday, Sept. 3, saw the next great concerted attack by the Allies. British and Australian troops took but could not hold High Wood, Ginchy, and Falfemont Farm, a mile southeast of Guillemont. The Prussian Guards opposing them proved themselves foes worthy of the best soldier traditions in courage and tenacity. A number of positions were won and held east of Mouquet Farm.

### Fighting for Their Own Homes

Further to the south the French First Corps, recruited from the northeast of France, and consequently fighting to redeem their own homes, attacked gloriously in the sector from the Somme to Maurepas, where they stormed and held the villages of Le Forest and Cléry. Above Le Forest the French drove their attack to a point above the crossroads on the southern edge of Combles.

The Irish Guards captured Guillemont, the strong fortified village in the second line of the German defenses, which had withstood every previous attack. This British success a mile and a half west of Combles helped consolidate the splendid French victories south of the town, although the loss of Falfemont Farm left the Prussians in a salient between the heads of the allied advance. On Sept. 4, however, the British made some new progress near the farm, and, pressing on at night in heavy rain, they gained Leuze Wood and all of the farm position, thus getting within a thousand yards of Combles on the west and northwest.

At the same time a new French army— General Micheler's Tenth Army—attacked the Germans south of the Somme, and in one sudden rush on a front of three miles carried the German first line from Chilly to Vermandovillers and took several thousand prisoners. The next day the French attacked on both sides of the Somme, and won a number of woodland trenches and the ridges between Bouchavesnes and Cléry, as well as the village of Omiécourt.

The Germans made a number of powerful counterattacks on Sept. 7 and 8 along the whole front, but failed completely in the face of the greatly superior allied artillery. On Sept. 9 the Irish regiments which took Guillemont captured Ginchy, but a number of other attacks broke down, notably one aimed at a field fort called the Quadrilateral, east of Ginchy. Nevertheless, the Allies were pressing hard upon Combles, north of the Somme, and the new French army south of the river was less than half a mile from Chaulnes, an important centre of roads and communications. The Chaulnes-Roye railway was cut and the Germans seemed quite unable to halt this new French force, which was so greatly extending the scope of the attack on the German line.

### Thiepval a Hard Problem

It was evident that renewed efforts must be made by the British to drive the enemy back in the region from Thiepval north, where the Germans had defeated all efforts to dislodge them. Unless that could be done there would be a dangerous exposure of the left flank of forces pushing on toward Bapaume beyond Pozières and Longueval. The danger of salients is a lesson well taught in this war.

As the Germans lost ground in July and August, they busied themselves with new lines of defense back of what was the third line in their original scheme. This new line assumed the characteristic form of the later German defenses, in which prominence is given to powerful field forts mutually supporting rather than continuous lines of intrenchments. Thiepval was a notable example, and the Germans made every effort to similarly fortify Courcelette, Martinpuich, Flers, Lesboeufs, and Morval. This series of defenses was particularly interesting to the student of fortification, because it followed the plan which was so successful in Champagne in the Autumn of 1915. It will be remembered that the field works which stopped the French then were on the reverse side of the hills and so close under them that the entanglements and trenches were practically uninjured by the preliminary bombardment.

SNAPSHOT OF RUSSIAN SOLDIERS IN DISORDERLY RETREAT

*(Central News Photo Service)*

A Scene During the Russian Retreat in Galicia. The Headlong Flight Seen in This Photograph Was Caused by the Cry, "The German Cavalry Have Broken Through."

GERMANS CAPTURED IN THE BATTLE OF FLANDERS

*(British Official Photo from Western Hemisphere Union)*

A Large Haul of German Soldiers Captured by the British During the Great Battle in Flanders. The Prisoners Are Being Marched to the Railroad

So here these villages lay on the reverse side of the main ridge, hidden from view except to aerial scouts. In addition the Germans fortified Gueudecourt, Le Sars, Encourt l'Abbaye, on a still further interior line, with an additional back stop along the Péronne-Bapaume road in the region of Le Transloy and Sailly-Saillisel. All these must be reduced before Bapaume could be taken, but again allied hopes were running high.

## When Rumania Entered

In the end of August Rumania entered the war on the allied side, an event hailed by all who longed for the defeat of the Teutons as a sure factor toward the accomplishment of that end. Brusiloff's successes were so impressive, and at that time looked so permanent, that Rumania felt it needful to get in at once if she was to be reckoned among the victors, for just then Sarrail seemed ready to contribute toward a conclusion by sweeping up through the Balkans. In the light of what soon happened to Russia and Rumania, it seems difficult now to remember that a great majority of the onlookers held strongly to these opinions. The first of September, 1916, looked as though it might be the beginning of the end, for in addition to all the hoped-for things in the east, it had been proved that in the west the French and British had men, guns, and munitions sufficient to push the German out of his most skillfully designed defenses.

In the Somme battle the German higher command had used the finest troops at their command, but Prussians, Brandenburgers, Bavarians had all been compelled to yield ground. Most important was their inability to recover any of the ground. Pushing them back was a sure, although slow and very costly, process. Of course, the hope under the surface everywhere was that their defense somewhere would crack and permit a great manoeuvre battle on the open field. The immediate objective of all this welter of blood and treasure was the quite unimportant town of Bapaume, in front of the British, and Péronne, facing the French. Many miles back from those places lay the points of real importance—

Lille, Douai, Cambrai, St. Quentin. That was (and is) a line of French cities where the Tricolor must float again before the days of the German on French soil could begin to be numbered. It is hard to realize that the battle of the Somme, one of the hardest in all history, was an attack upon an outer line of defenses only. However, as the Allies were definitely committed to the plan of pushing the German front back rather than attempting to roll his line up from a flank, it was evident that the work of the Summer must be continued with grim determination.

## Coming of the "Tanks"

For the renewal of the struggle Britain brought up the corps d'élite of the army. Old regulars, Guards, and new army men, although of different designations, were all by now war-tried veterans with proud histories of hard fighting. Australians, New Zealanders, and the men of Newfoundland contributed famous units to fight side by side with Scotch and Irish regiments.

For the new offensive a new weapon appeared, officially called "Machine Gun Corps, Heavy Section," but soon to become widely known by their frolicsome nickname, "tanks." Looked upon as an experiment, the British had faith enough in their possibilities to make a very considerable number of these heavily armored vehicles, propelled on caterpillar wheels by powerful motors, and armed with machine guns. The German Secret Service seems to have known of their preparation long before the British troops on the firing line had ever seen one, and when the "tanks" got into action they met a new armor-piercing bullet especially intended to stop them. The story now widely told is that a certain lovely woman spy in Paris and elsewhere gleaned the knowledge from an indiscreet officer of the "tank" service who fell under the influence of her wiles.

Nevertheless, the huge leviathan-like creatures waddle over the battlefields, crushing entanglements, straddling trenches, and rumbling up the streets of battle-torn villages, always spitting showers of machine-gun bullets and often adding a material terror for those facing them in the trenches. Of course, the optimistic accounts of widespread terror and panic created by their appearance were gross exaggerations. If all that was claimed had been true, there would have been nothing for the British infantry to do but gather up herds of frightened Germans and shepherd them back to the prison pens.

### Combles and Thiepval

By the middle of September all arrangements had been perfected, and on the night of the 14th the Fifth Army began by storming the Hohenzollern Trench and a redoubt called the " Wunderwerk," southeast of Thiepval. For three days the British bombardment had continued, and at 6 o'clock on the morning of the 15th it developed into absolute fury. A few minutes later the British infantry were over their parapets, with the queer mottled tanks, spitting fire, rumbling along with them. That afternoon the Canadians carried Courcelette, and it was a proud day for French Canadians to help win back some of the ancient motherland. The Scotch stormed Martinpuich, a position of great strength. After a terrific battle the London territorials finally cleared the Bavarians out of High Wood, although their losses were very heavy. The New Zealanders took Flers. On the right flank the Germans in the Quadrilateral and Bouleaux Wood defeated the best efforts of the Guards brigades, assisted by an old regular division and London territorials.

As a whole the day was a great triumph for the British. Of the twenty-four tanks which crossed the German line seventeen kept in action all day and were undoubtedly a great help in attacking machine-gun nests and concealed trench refuges. The allied air service at this time seemed distinctly to master the Germans and contributed greatly to the efficiency of the British artillery fire. Among the long list of casualties, England's Prime Minister mourned his son, Lieutenant Raymond Asquith of the Grenadier Guards.

When the British charged, the French were never idle, and on the 13th Fayolle's men stormed Bouchavesnes and took more than 2,000 prisoners. On the 14th they took a fortified farm southeast of Combles, and on the 17th and 18th below the Somme these splendid fighting men won Vermandovillers, Berny, and Deniécourt. In the next few days both British and French withstood hard counterattacks, and on the 18th the British finally won the Quadrilateral, after stern, close fighting.

At high noon on Sept. 25 another great attack began. The guards this time triumphed and took Lesboeufs and a regular division stormed Morval, on the road north of Combles. The French captured Raucourt, east of Combles, and thus nearly completed the circle about that strongly fortified place. On the 26th the British were masters of Gueudecourt, and the French stormed Fregicourt and Combles.

Further to the north, Thiepval, that long-sought fortification, was finally captured by two divisions of the new army. Mouquet Farm and Zollern redoubt were also won. September was a month of great triumph for the Allies on the Somme. With October bad weather came, and heavy gales with drenching rain greatly delayed projected attacks, as the country roads became almost impassable for transport and communications.

### Last Phases of the Battle

Early in October some ground was gained beyond Le Sars along the Albert-Bapaume highway. Then for a month a wearisome struggle went on up the slopes of Warlencourt, where the Germans had installed their machine guns with great skill. On Nov. 5 the British gained the crest, but were driven out that night by a newly arrived German Guard division.

After Thiepval was taken, it was still needful to face strong nearby defenses above the village, where two redoubts, Stuff and Zollern, were not reduced for some weeks. Late in October both were finally captured, with the top of the ridge between Upper Ancre and Courcelette. The French in this Autumn fighting took Saint Pierre Vaast Wood, and on Oct. 8 won a way across the Bapaume-Péronne road. In turn they won Ablaincourt and the approaches to Chaulnes. About the middle of October

Fayolle took Sailly-Saillisel after a series of hard battles, but the Germans regained Sailly at the end of the month.

In the middle of November, when the frost had stiffened the roads, the British renewed the attack against the high ground above the Ancre, where the Germans held fast at Serre, Beaumont Hamel, and Beaucourt, with a powerful position in the rear at Pusieux-du-Mort. Hard fighting followed at all of these places, and especially about Beaucourt, but the British would not be denied a firm grip on these essential heights commanding Bapaume, and by the time the Winter storms ended the battle of the Somme they were well established east of Beaucourt and above Grandcourt.

Five months of fighting had won back only a rather narrow strip of French soil, but one in which the enemy had exhausted every defensive device. The ground was ready for greater things in the next year, and the battle of the Somme had sealed the fate of the great German offensive at Verdun.

# Harry Lauder at the Front

*This poignant story, told by Dr. George Adams, describes a visit made by Harry Lauder, the singer and comedian, to his son's grave in France:*

THE men went wild with enthusiasm and joy wherever he went. One day I was taking Harry to see the grave of his only child, Captain John Lauder of the Argyll and Sutherland Highlanders, as fine a lad as ever wore a kilt, and as good and brave a son as ever a father had.

As we were motoring swiftly along we turned into the town of Albert and the first sharp glance at the cathedral showed the falling Madonna and Child. While we lingered a bunch of soldiers came marching through dusty and tired. Lauder asked the officer to halt his men for a rest and he would sing to them. I could see that they were loath to believe it was the real Lauder until he began to sing. Then the doubts vanished and they abandoned themselves to the full enjoyment of this very unexpected pleasure. When the singing began the audience would number about 200; at the finish of it easily more than 2,000 soldiers cheered him on his way.

It was a strange send-off on the way that led to a grave—the grave of a father's fondest hopes—but so it was. A little way up the Bapaume road the car stopped and we clambered the embankment and away over the shell-torn field of Courcelette. Here and there we passed a little cross which marked the grave of some unknown hero; all that was written was "A British Soldier."

He spoke in a low voice of the hope-hungry hearts behind all those at home. Now we climbed a little ridge, and here a cemetery, and in the first row facing the battlefield was the cross on Lauder's boy's resting place.

The father leaned over the grave to read what was written there. He knelt down, indeed he lay upon the grave and clutched it, the while his body shook with the grief he felt. When the storm had spent itself he rose and prayed: " O God, that I could have but one request. It would be that I might embrace my laddie just this once and thank him for what he has done for his country and humanity."

That was all, not a word of bitterness or complaint. On the way down the hill I suggested gently that the stress of such an hour made further song that day impossible. But Lauder's heart is big and British. Turning to me with a flash in his eye he said, " George, I must be brave; my boy is watching and all the other boys are waiting. I will sing to them this afternoon though my heart break!" Off we went again to another division of Scottish troops.

There within the hour he sang again the sweet old songs of love and home and country, bringing all very near, and helping the men to realize the deeper what victory for the enemy would mean.

# Joffre and Hindenburg: Their Methods and Battles

## A Study by Gabriel Hanotaux
### Member of the French Academy

*M. Hanotaux, the historian and former Foreign Minister of France, has prepared a series of important articles on the early battles of the war, in some cases citing facts and documents not generally known. The following, translated for CURRENT HISTORY MAGAZINE, comprises interesting portions of M. Hanotaux's studies, including a luminous explanation of the battle of Tannenberg. First comes an analysis of the French retreat from Charleroi to the Marne, (August, 1914,) in which appears this sketch of General Joffre.*

EYEWITNESSES have related that in those hours of secret anguish, when he alone could know how great was the peril, General Joffre remained his accustomed self, attentive, studious, busy, confident. His anxiety was apparent only in his greater application. With half-closed eyes he concentrated his mind, and words addressed to him found him silent.

The virtues of Joffre are, in the moral realm, calmness, and, in the intellectual realm, equilibrium. Such is his nature, in which reflection aids instinct: when he does not feel sure, he seeks. He feels every modification in the balance of forces, and, moving himself, so to speak, as a counterpoise, he revises his plans, re-forms the lines, and is not satisfied until he has restored stability.

In the terrible crisis in which he found himself, when the enemy had suddenly thrown to the west of him forces heavier than those which he could oppose to them, his first movement on learning the facts was to seek for a new equilibrium. Even before the enemy movement was completed he intervened. Not a moment did he delay in mending the raveled woof, in repairing the torn situation: he cut his cloth to sew it anew.

Many a commander would have been stubborn. Fighting foot by foot is a resource that tempts soldiers, if merely for its heroism. But Joffre realized that to stop his armies, even for battle, was to risk their destruction. Before all, they must escape in order to get a fresh hold.

He saw and acted at the same time—clear vision and promptness. Joffre in adversity revealed himself to himself and to the country. His figure then appeared as it will remain in history, grave, strong, and resolute. France found a man, a chief, a captain.

## Joffre's Note to His Armies

[The historian goes on to retrace the measures taken by General Joffre to regain the initiative, citing this important official note, which contains all the essentials of a new tactic adapted to the circumstances. The comments in brackets are those of M. Hanotaux:]

General Headquarters, Aug. 24, 1914.

It appears from what we have learned through the fighting up to the present day that our attacks are not executed with a close combination of infantry and artillery. Every operation of a whole army should consist of a series of actions in detail aiming at the conquest of points of support. [Is this not a whole tactical philosophy?]

Every time that one wishes to capture a vital position it is necessary to attack with the artillery, to hold back the infantry, and to send it to the assault only at a distance which makes it certain that the objective can be attained. [From that time forth there were no more attacks without artillery preparation.]

Every time that it has been attempted to throw the infantry into the attack from too great a distance, before the artillery has made its action felt, the infantry has fallen under the fire of machine guns and has suffered losses that could have been avoided. [A measured criticism of the gravest of the errors that led to the first reverses. We have here the " binding together of the different arms " and their subordination to the end in view, not to more or less systematic theories.]

When a vital position is taken it should be organized immediately, trenches dug, the artillery brought up in order to checkmate all counterattacks of the enemy. [The use of intrenchments, the employment of artillery to organize the ground won; trench warfare has made its appearance.]

The infantry seems not to understand the necessity of organizing itself in battle for long endurance. [The idea of the tactics of the long breath and even of a company organized for duration is substituted for the earlier idea of a war of movement and spirited offensive. Joffre appears as he is, a genius of stability.]

Throwing into line numerous and dense units, it immediately exposes them to the fire of the enemy, which decimates them, summarily stops their offensive, and often leaves them at the mercy of a counterattack. [Here already we have the grave danger of the counterattack. Now the counterattack, as the future will show, is the whole of this war.]

It is by means of a line of riflemen suficiently spaced and continually supported [how much in two words!] that the infantry, sustained by the artillery, should lead the battle, holding on in this way until the moment when the assault can be judiciously delivered. [A reminder of the most beautiful French quality, judgment, discretion.]

The German cavalry divisions always go into action preceded by a few battalions in automobiles. Thus far the main bodies of their cavalry have never let themselves be approached by our cavalry. They travel behind their infantry, and from there send out cavalry detachments [patrols and reconnoitring parties] that seek the support of their infantry as soon as they are attacked. Our cavalry pursues these detachments and strikes against positions solidly held. [An exact picture of the tactics introduced by the German cavalry—also a lesson.] Our cavalry divisions should always have infantry support to strengthen them and increase their offensive powers.

The horses also should have time to eat and sleep; without that the cavalry will be worn out prematurely before having been employed.

*The General Commanding in Chief.*
J. JOFFRE.

[Upon the basis of this note there followed a regrouping of the French armies and the preparation of the offensive that saved France at the Marne. In another article M. Hanotaux continues:]

I have tried to indicate the origins of the battle of the Marne. It is admitted henceforth that what constitutes Joffre's glory is to have been able to parry the German plan of encirclement, based on the doctrines of von Schlieffen; to have parried it on the right by his army of the east, which stopped the enemy before the forest opening at Charmes, and, on the left, by his decision to transport a part of his troops from the east to the west in such fashion as to seize the mastery of events on the Ourcq and throw the Germans back upon the Aisne.

These gifts were won for history, but in order to appreciate all their value I wish now to try to compare the events that took place on the eastern front at the moment when those just referred to were taking place on the western front.

As we shall see, the German military chiefs applied the doctrines of von Schlieffen there also; but there they won success with them. The campaign in East Prussia presents a positive proof that fully confirms the negative proof of the battle on the French frontier.

### The Russians in Prussia

Two Russian armies had invaded East Prussia; one, commanded by Rennenkampf, followed the great railway that binds Petrograd to Berlin by way of Gumbinnen, Insterburg, Allenstein, Eylau, on toward Thorn on the Vistula. While besieging or masking Königsburg, Elbing, Danzig, it counted upon occupying East Prussia and there awaiting the success of the general manoeuvre aimed against Austria by the Grand Duke Nicholas.

The other Russian army came from Warsaw and the banks of the Narew. It advanced from south to north in order to march, like the other, upon the Vistula in the direction of Danzig, there to join Rennenkampf's army and clear the way to Berlin.

The preliminary mission intrusted to the two armies of the north was singularly facilitated by the fact that Germany, not foreseeing so rapid a mobilization of the first Russian armies, had left on that frontier only three active army corps and some reserve formations. The two Russian armies—separately weaker than the German army—would be much stronger than it when once united. Unfortunately, they were not in close communication with each other, being separated by the almost impenetrable region of the Masurian Lakes.

The first commander of the German army, von Prittwitz, advanced on the frontier before Rennenkampf; he was beaten at Gumbinnen on Aug. 20. Rennenkampf advanced as far as Insterburg on the railway north of the Masurian Lakes; he installed his army in East Prussia and threatened Königsberg. Meanwhile Samsonoff, coming from the Narew, was debouching to the southwest of the lakes and skirting them with the object of joining Rennenkampf near Osterode-Eylau.

The German army, which was still facing Rennenkampf near Gumbinnen, saw its communications menaced by this advance of Samsonoff. It beat a precipitate retreat, and von Prittwitz believed he had no choice but to retire behind the Vistula. The population was fleeing as far as Berlin.

There was a great sensation in the headquarters of the German General Staff, which had staked everything on the western front, and which at that moment (Aug. 20-22) still had some painful fighting to do at Charleroi, in the Ardennes, and on the Lorraine frontier, so that it did not feel any too sure of victory.

## The Coming of Hindenburg

It was in this hour of peril that a dispatch, dated at Namur, went to seek at Hanover in a tavern where he was smoking his pipe and drinking his habitual bock an old, retired General, Hindenburg, and named him at one stroke the commander of the army on the eastern front. For his second in command they gave him Ludendorff, who, leaving Namur with all necessary instructions, came to seek him at Hanover. The two men took the train together in the night of Aug. 22, studying their maps on the journey, formulating their plan, and writing their orders.

Far from thinking of retiring behind the Vistula, Hindenburg and Ludendorff decided to resume the offensive against the Russian armies, attacking them separately while they were still divided by the Masurian Lakes. Hindenburg first turned his attention to Samsonoff's army, which had come from Warsaw and the Narew, and which most directly menaced his communications. Samsonoff was an impetuous man; having excellent troops, he was full of confidence, and was marching straight ahead; he was just the man to fall headforemost into the trap that his enemy was setting for him.

This was the trap: Hindenburg had arranged his troops in a vast semicircle formed by the lines of hills on each side of Allenstein, the one toward Usdau on the west and the other toward Willenberg on the east. The Twenty-second German Army Corps, at the entrance of the semicircle, at Soldau, on the railway from Warsaw, received an order to engage Samsonoff's army, and to retreat while fighting, thus luring it as far as possible into the curve of the German lines. At the proper moment the two sectors of the semicircle were to close in upon Samsonoff, envelop and crush him; it was Schlieffen's manoeuvre, the extension of the front and the action of both wings.

Samsonoff entered the semicircle in pursuit of the Twenty-second German Corps, the Twenty-second fell back, Samsonoff followed, forcing it westward, and finally establishing his headquarters at Allenstein. He believed he had won a victory. His right, finding no enemy forces before it, extended itself northward and reached the Petrograd-Berlin railway near Rastenburg.

## Samsonoff's Army Trapped

The position of Samsonoff may be compared to that of the classic runner, with his right hand stretched high in the air toward Rennenkampf, the body in full career, but the left foot delaying in the rear toward Usdau. It was exactly at this moment when Samsonoff was hurling himself forward, that Hindenburg, beginning the real manoeuvre, seized him by that left foot. A German force, coming partly from Thorn, and reinforced by all the units available, appeared at Usdau and threw itself against the communicating lines of Samsonoff in the direction of Soldau.

Samsonoff failed to grasp the meaning of this movement, and went on pursuing his idea of breaking the German front at the middle. He hurled himself against the Hohenstein-Tannenberg lines, which Hindenburg had garnished with his heavy guns and his best troops. The latter withstood the shock of Samsonoff's desperate assaults, which were renewed for three days—Aug. 26-29.

Meanwhile Hindenburg's extreme right wing continued its turning movement, gained the first advantage at Usdau, and marched next upon Soldau with the object of closing the door on Samsonoff at that point. In the other direction Mackensen, who held the eastern sector

of the semicircle, turned Samsonoff's flank on the east, defeated his right wing, and pushed on toward Willenberg, the other door. Without pausing in the pursuit he turned toward Samsonoff's main force, which was still fighting desperately in the direction of Hohenstein-Tannenberg, and fell upon its rear. It was the same as if von Hausen had succeeded in his Meuse manoeuvre on the western front and had fallen upon the rear of Lanrezac at Charleroi.

### The Battle of Tannenberg

Apparently at that moment Samsonoff

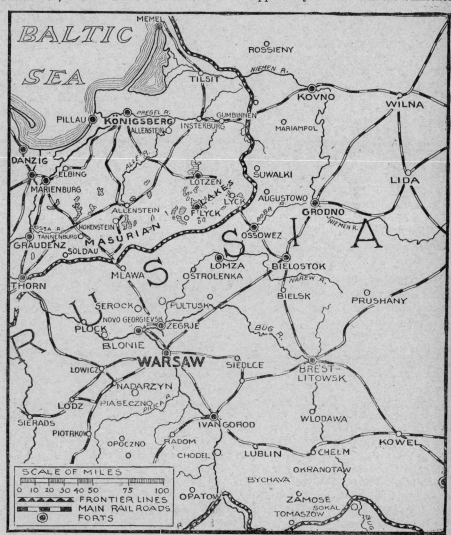

SCENE OF THE BATTLES OF TANNENBERG AND THE MASURIAN LAKES

realized what was happening. He tried to snatch himself out of the trap; he evacuated Allenstein in haste and rushed toward Soldau to open a way toward the Narew and Warsaw. It was too late. Hindenburg's right wing had entered Soldau. The doors of escape were closed one after the other. In the swamps and network of little lakes Samsonoff's army was surrounded. It fought heroically, a hopeless fight. Even surrender, if it had been desired, was impossible. After the incredible efforts of five whole days of battle there remained only the shattered fragments of a great army, strewn about in the trackless maze of swamp lands; troops wandering through the woods, units mixed in a hopeless mob, cannon mired in the stagnant water, regiments formed from soldiers of all arms, the most vigorous débris gathered up by the most energetic officers in order to break through the circle by charging at random!

Some divisions got through. Others clung in rags to the thickets of thorn trees, or wandered in circles, completely lost. Samsonoff did not wish to survive the disaster; he placed himself in the first ranks and was killed by a shell, which also struck his Chief of Staff. Thus ended what the German historians call emphatically " the greatest battle of destruction in history." They all give the credit to the strategic teachings of Schlieffen. I have before me a German brochure explaining the battle of Tannenberg with diagrams; its title is " From Hannibal to Hindenburg," and it contains this sentence: " It was Schlieffen who before his death dictated the whole plan of the great war against France and Russia."

## Battle of Masurian Lakes

For reasons that have not been explained Rennenkampf had remained motionless at Insterberg while Samsonoff was getting himself crushed at Tannenberg, two marches away. On hearing the news he felt the danger that now menaced himself. He adopted measures against it, but measures directly inverse to those of Samsonoff, and, in a different way, no less unwise. Samsonoff had attacked headlong and without manoeu-vring. Rennenkampf resolved to defend himself where he was. He supported his right on the sea at Libau, his left on the Masurian Lakes at Lötzen; he fortified his centre on the Berlin-Petrograd railway, along which he expected Hindenburg to approach. He threw up earthworks all around him, and made of the space between Allenburg and Lötzen an enormous redoubt, in which were crowded four army corps. Thus prepared and equipped, in a position that seemed to him impregnable, he waited.

At only one point he thought of a sort of countermanoeuvre. Orders were given that fresh troops from Grodno should advance along Hindenburg's flank in the direction of Lyck, and should fall upon the German right wing in case it tried to debouch to the east of the Masurian Lakes.

Hindenburg, in spite of the difference of situation, undertook to repeat against Rennenkampf the manoeuvre that had just succeeded against Samsonoff. It is always the great idea of Schlieffen. The battle began on Sept. 6 and coincided exactly with the French battle of the Marne. Hindenburg had received from the western front two corps, the Eleventh and Guard Reserve, besides a division of cavalry. Thus he took all the reserves that the interior could furnish, and he threw every man of them into the battle. The troops went into the conflict wearied by terrible marches, but, thrilled by the triumph of Tannenberg, they had faith in their victory.

Hindenburg began with a feint. On his left the Königsberg garrison, reinforced by the sea route, made a sortie and threatened to cut off Rennenkampf in the direction of Tilsit. But the real attack was made on the right the next day, Sept. 7. Mackensen, von der Goltz, von Morgen, von François debouched by all the roads from the Masurian Lakes, advanced upon Lötzen, Gross Gablick, Goldhap, and undertook to cut off Rennenkampf from the Russian frontier. It was the manoeuvre of encirclement. The German right wing, ceaselessly reinforced, fought a series of terrible battles that lasted four days.

Here appeared the happy results of

the somewhat tardy manoeuvre which Rennenkampf had improvised; the fresh troops, the Third Siberian Corps and the rest debouched from Grodno. There followed an hour of anguish for Hindenburg, which sufficed to save Rennenkampf. The latter, assailed on both flanks and at the centre, did not do as Samsonoff had done; he did not become stubborn. Profiting from the hour of hesitation produced by the manoeuvre on his left, he retreated. His centre had been subjected to terrible assaults; he had lost his foothold at Allenburg, Gerdauen, Gumbinnen. He was barely in time. His army regained the frontier after a most painful retreat.

Here Hinderburg's success was incomplete. Schlieffen's system provides only for absolute crushing. Rennenkampf escaped. I cannot give the details of the military operations—they can be found in my "History of the War." But the point I am making is in the comparison of the operations on the west and east fronts. Samsonoff took the offensive without manoeuvring, Rennenkampf stood on the defensive almost without manoeuvres, while Joffre, who knew his business, was manoeuvring all the time. He took the Schlieffen system on its weak side, that of rash extension of front. The Germans, held back first at the breach at Charmes, were finally beaten on the Marne.

Thus was obtained the greatest reversal of fortune, perhaps, that history has ever seen. The Yser, Verdun, the Somme, are the daughters of that initial thought. The battles of Tannenberg and the Masurian Lakes throw light for us on the battle of the Marne. The Schlieffen system succeeded on the one hand and failed on the other. The manoeuvre of Joffre was one of the most beautiful intellectual operations of military genius in all time; it is a magnificent expression of French genius.

# How Lorraine Was Saved in 1914
## Told by Maurice Barrès
### Of the French Academy

*Among the valuable historical sketches called forth in France by the third anniversary of the Marne was one contributed by Maurice Barrès to L'Echo de Paris, describing the little-known battle in which General Castelnau hurled back the German invasion east of Verdun, two weeks before the Marne battle. The essential portions of the article are here translated for* CURRENT HISTORY MAGAZINE.

OUR enemies could believe themselves masters of the world in August, 1914. With what proud confidence they advanced after Sarreburg, after Morhange, after Charleroi! And yet they were stopped so hard and so definitely that they never tried to seize Paris, or Nancy, or the passage of the Moselle. Let us recall those days of our extreme peril and understand by what virtues of our soldiers and commanders, by what complete unity of the French people, we obtained that miracle of victory.

Visiting Lorraine to help my fellow-countrymen celebrate at Rozelieures, at Gerbéviller, at Mesnil-sur-Belvitte, the great deeds done by the armies of Castelnau and Dubail, I traversed daily the scene of the "battle of Charmes," which others call the battle of Borville or the battle of Rozelieures. Aug. 25, 1914, the culminating point, decisive of a long battle which was itself the pivot of all the manoeuvres of the Marne, was a day of immense importance. It assured the safety of Lorraine and of France. * * *

The gratitude of Lorraine and of France ought to be inscribed upon the school of Pont Saint Vincent, where General Castelnau—working amid the absolute confidence of his army and of the people, because of his knowledge of Lorraine and his admirable character, seconded and supported by a General Staff whose chief was General Anthoine—directed the battles of Charmes and of the Grand Couronné. It was on Aug. 22, one hour after noon, that Castelnau came to establish his headquarters in that modest structure, now venerable. Whence did he come?

On Aug. 19, 20, and 21 the armies of Dubail and Castelnau had fought at Sarreburg and Morhange—fought without success. Nevertheless, the Germans, who had suffered heavy losses in those battles, made no attempt to cut off our line of retreat. They had lost contact. Our two armies fought during their retreat by a combined movement in which the two commanders helped each other. I hope some day to be able to tell the story of General Dubail as he stood in the City Hall of Rambervillers and directed the victorious resistance of his troops and of the Twenty-first Corps.

From the Blandan Barracks at Nancy on Aug. 20 General Castelnau had, under pressure of necessity, taken all precautions to assure the defense of Nancy and to permit his main forces to establish themselves behind the Meurthe and the fortified front of the Grand Couronné. His wish was not to give battle until after all the army corps were completely remade. The country people described the scene to me along the routes of march—the columns finding their way, the isolated men regrouping themselves, the trains, the parks of artillery, the convoys winding along the left bank of the Meurthe. Recovery of contact with the Germans took place on the 22d; they had received reinforcements, and our rear guards and cavalry sought to check them and understand their direction.

Would there be time to finish the preparations on the heights of the Grand Couronné? And on the heights of Saffrais, of Belchamp, of Borville, where the work was dragging? Could the armies stop up the hole just in front of the forest opening at Charmes, that is to say, at one of the decisive points between Castelnau's right and Dubail's army? Would there be troops enough to guard that thirty-seven-mile front from Sainte Geneviève to Dorville? Those expected from the Alps—released

by Italy's assurances—could they arrive for the decisive hour?

All those problems were thought out and controlled by Castelnau in the little schoolhouse of Pont Saint Vincent, where, hour by hour, depending upon his air scouts and cavalry, he knew or divined what the enemy was doing or intended to do, leaving his maps only to walk back and forth with hands behind him, or to throw himself for a few hours fully dressed upon a couch in a corner of the room, surrounded by his staff.

On the evening of the 23d, and still more in the night of the 24th, he emerged rom his keenest anguish, being convinced that he could stop the retreat, that his troops were in condition to fight. All his positions were ready and solidly held. To guard against every contingency, the destruction of the bridges over the Moselle and lower Meurthe was arranged for—even down in the forest opening of Neufchâteau—and the fort of Bourlemont was armed and reoccupied. In the region of Lenoncourt he got together a strong group which he held ready with all the available forces of the Twentieth Corps to execute a powerful counterattack.

Where will the shock come? The first part of the morning of Aug. 24 passes in the expectation of an assault by the Germans on the Rembêtant, that is to say upon Nancy, but behold! at 8 o'clock from all directions comes the information to Pont Saint Vincent that two German army corps are marching southward in all haste toward Charmes.

In place of attacking Castelnau on the heights, the Germans evidently have taken for their objective the possession of the bridgeheads on the Moselle. They are going to be able, in the neighboring woods of Charmes, to approach the river without being seen or touched. Even before reaching it they will seize, on the right bank, the line Vesoul-Epinal-Nancy, which at this moment has become one of the great arteries in which flow the life and hope of France. Ten miles further on, at Tantonville, on the left bank, is another artery no less active, the line of Chalindrey - Mirecourt - Nancy, which brings to the Grand Couronné night and day the means for its resistance. Beyond lie Neufchâteau, Chaumont, the death of all our hopes.

In his haste Prince Rupprecht of Bavaria refuses to believe that Castelnau and Dubail have been able to re-establish themselves; he executes before them "the manoeuvre of scorn," as von Kluck was to do a little later before Gallieni and Maunoury; he does not try to join battle with them, but to outstrip them on their lines of communication. He rushes forward, he pushes his columns along, thus laying his flank open to the blows of the Grand Couronné.

Instantly Castelnau profits by this imprudence of pride. He orders an offensive upon the flank and rear of the enemy columns, yet a limited offensive, without engaging his principal force, without relinquishing the support of his positions, which he continues to reinforce for the reception of any attack. And at the same time (about 10 o'clock in the morning) his cavalry corps, which is commanded by General Conneau, and which includes the famous regiments from Lunéville, pushed by the Germans in the direction of Charmes, makes a stubborn stand on the crest of Morviller, on the Naquée Farm and in the Jointois Wood, inflicts serious losses with its artillery, and, finally, in the evening, falls back in good order upon Dorville, thus assuring the union of Castelnau and Dubail and stopping up the neck of the bottle in the direction of the Moselle.

Borville! In the evening of the 24th, in the little schoolhouse of Pont Saint Vincent, General Castelnau, bending over the map of these regions, which, as a former resident of Nancy and a Lorrainer at heart he knows marvelously, repeats ceaselessly the name of that obscure village. Borville! His thought returns continually to that plateau—military students say that peak—a plateau in two parts, the Haut du Mont and the Bormont, which dominates the country, and upon which he wishes to establish his strongest artillery before daybreak.

During the whole night of the 24th, a night that is heavy and starless, the cavalry batteries of the Sixteenth Corps, all that could be called in time, are hurrying up that mountainside. We are going to see them, during the day of the 25th, hurling their thunderbolts from morning till night upon the German advance, barring its passage, making it vacillate, driving it back and saving the Moselle.

Elsewhere the troops from the Alps, freed by Italy, have arrived at the rear of the Charmes front.

# To the Students of Liége

## (August 1914)

### By BERNARD FREEMAN TROTTER

[The author of this poem, a Canadian and a graduate of McMaster University, Toronto, was killed at the front in France, June, 1917.]

In old Liége, when those dark tidings came
  Of German honor callously forsworn
  And the red menace that should bring the scorn
Of ages on the Kaiser's name and shame
  And crown their city with a deathless fame,
    The students wrote, they say, that Summer morn
    For their degrees, then joined the hope forlorn
Of Liberty, and passed in blood and flame.

O valiant souls! who loved not Duty less
  Than Honor, whom no fears could move to shirk
  The common task, no tyrant's threat subdue
When Right and Freedom called in their distress—
    Not vain your sacrifice nor lost your work;
    The World's free heart beats high because of you!

# Lord Haldane's Mission to Germany

## Important Official Conversations at Berlin in 1906 and 1912 Bearing on Issues of the War

RICHARD BURDON HALDANE, now Viscount Haldane, was British Secretary for War under the Premiership of Sir Henry Campbell-Bannerman, and in September, 1906, he accepted an invitation from the German Kaiser to visit Berlin at the time of the military manoeuvres. He was working in close connection with Sir Edward Grey, then Foreign Minister, with whom, in December, 1905, he had begun the international discussions which led to the entente with France regarding military assistance in case France should be invaded.

Before his trip to Berlin he had conversed with the French General Staff. The idea of these conversations was that, if Germany attacked France, Great Britain should help with an expeditionary force to hold the French frontier opposite Belgium. Haldane was convinced that assistance could not be given within a reasonable time, and bent all his thoughts toward organization for extreme rapidity in mobilization and transport, which meant complete reorganization of the British Army. The system then established served as the effective basis for British military operations when war came eight years later.

Emperor William read a speech which Haldane had made to Germans in London, and invited him to attend the German Army manoeuvres. At Berlin the British War Secretary and his two assistants were allowed, at their request, to make a thorough study of the German War Office and its system. Afterward Haldane took part in several important official conversations on questions bearing upon the possibilities of just such a war as has since broken out. The British Government has never given the text of these conversations to the public, but they have been seen in printed form by men in Government positions, and on Sept. 1, 1917, The Manchester Guardian published an article containing interesting portions of them. According to the writer of this article, Lieut. Gen. von Moltke, Chief of the German General Staff, in a conversation asked Haldane to put whatever questions he liked.

" In that case," replied Haldane, " I shall call for the plans for an invasion of England."

Von Moltke replied, " We have not one in the building," to which Haldane, looking out of the window toward the Admiralty, said, " Perhaps they are there." Von Moltke admitted that they were there, and that they were very good plans, too.

### The Bagdad Railway

The article gives for the first time details of Emperor William's negotiations of the Bagdad Railway agreement. While visiting Windsor Castle in November, 1907, Emperor William took Haldane aside the first evening of his visit and said how sorry he was there was so much friction over the Bagdad Railway.

" My answer was we wanted a gate to protect India from troops coming down the new railway," said Haldane.

Asked what he meant by a gate, Haldane replied that he meant control of the furthest off section of the railway—the one nearest the Persian Gulf. To this Emperor William replied:

" I will give you the gate."

The Foreign Office regarded the negotiations favorably, but it was considered necessary to bring in France and Russia, whose interests also were involved. A conference in Berlin of the four powers was arranged with the support of Emperor William, but it was defeated at Berlin on the ground that an agreement about the Bagdad Railway was no business of Russia's.

This, says the article, was the first and clearest indication of two facts about German foreign policy—that the Emperor was not quite master in his own house and that official Berlin was divided into two parties, one anxious for a working agreement between England, France, and Germany, and another, not yet avowedly a war party, regarding all these attempts as hopeless or dangerous, or both. Then, and for some time afterward, Emperor William belonged to the first party and genuinely was anxious for friendly relations with England. The Crown Prince, with Admiral von Tirpitz and the General Staff, and probably Prince von Bülow, belonged definitely to the second.

The party division became much sharper, and later was persisted in by Germany even after the war began. Haldane had German sympathizers in the same sense that Emperor William had English sympathizers, who believed it was for the good of the world that England and Germany should come to an understanding. The key to Haldane's whole policy was, while preparing against the eventual triumph of the anti-English party, to strengthen as far as possible those in Germany disposed to be friendly.

## Haldane at Berlin in 1912

Viscount Haldane visited Berlin in the Spring of 1912, not to negotiate a treaty, but under instructions by Sir Edward Grey to discuss affairs freely and refer everything to the Cabinet. This visit was much more significant from the international point of view. It was after Agadir, when Germany realized for the first time that England meant to stand by France. It was brought home to the Kaiser by Mr. Lloyd George's statement at the Mansion House, as coming from the well-known pacifist of the time. The message was all the more significant, coming from him. But what really disturbed the Kaiser was the fact that Lord Haldane had mobilized—that is, he had had everything ready, and had but to touch the button to concentrate the troops. The Kaiser knew more about the mobilization scheme than English people did, and he did not like it. What he did not know was that the First Lord of the Admiralty at the time (Mr. McKenna) objected to providing transports to carry the expeditionary force to France. He

was in favor of military isolation. Mr. McKenna's opposition to the expeditionary force was the reason why he was moved from the Admiralty and Mr. Churchill put in his place. Mr. Churchill completed the transport arrangements in close co-operation with the War Office. Something like a joint staff was created.

The subjects of conversation at Berlin in 1912 were the general European situation and the German shipbuilding program in consequence of the growth and power of Germany as the head of the Triple Alliance. Naturally, there had been other powers which tended to approximate thereto, but there was no reason why the Triple Alliance and what was called the Triple Entente should not be friendly.

Viscount Haldane assured Dr. von Bethmann Hollweg, who seemed skeptical, that Great Britain had no agreement with France and Russia except as had been published. Great Britain's military preparations were not hostile. Referring to Morocco, Viscount Haldane said that if Germany had intended to attack France and destroy her capacity to defend herself Great Britain would have had such an interest in the result that she could not have stood by and seen it done.

## Chancellor Makes Proposition

Dr. von Bethmann Hollweg proposed as a formula that neither England nor Germany should enter into any combination against the other. Substantially the following conversation ensued:

Haldane—I don't like that way of putting it. Suppose Germany joined in an attack on Paris, or Belgium, or Portugal, which we are bound by our treaty obligations to defend.

The Chancellor, (satirically)—Or Holland.

Haldane—I am not clear about the treaty situation in regard to Holland, but supposing Germany were to pounce upon France and proceed to dismember her? England surely could not stand idly by.

The Chancellor—Yes, I suppose what you say is fatal to my formula.

Haldane—What about an undertaking against aggressive or unprovoked attack and against all combinations and plans directed to that end?

The Chancellor—But how can you

define what is meant by aggressive and unprovoked attack?

Haldane—How many grains make a heap? But one knows a heap when one sees one.

Haldane asked what good was an agreement if Germany was going to increase her battleships and force England to do the same. England, he said, certainly would have to lay down two keels to Germany's one.

Dr. von Bethmann Hollweg was anxious to meet Haldane, says the writer in The Manchester Guardian, but evidently was nervous about what the Admiralty would say. The next day the question was discussed at luncheon with Emperor William, Admiral von Tirpitz, and Dr. von Bethmann Hollweg.

Haldane made the point that an agreement would be bones without flesh if Germany went on with her new fleet. The Emperor was visibly disturbed at the suggestion that there could be no political agreement worth having unless there was an agreement about German shipbuilding.

Admiral von Tirpitz said it was hard for Germany to make any admission about Great Britain's two-power standard. Haldane said the initiative was with Germany. The conversation resulted in the dropping of one battleship from Germany's program. Count zu Reventlow in his book asserted that three were dropped.

### Tentative Agreement Reached

The next day the conversation between the Chancellor and Haldane resulted in a provisional approval of Haldane's formula for the entente, with the addition of three important articles. These were:

If either side became entangled in a war in which it could not be said to be the aggressor the other would observe benevolent neutrality and try to localize the conflict.

The neutrality should not apply where there were no reconcilable existing contracts. The contracting powers were to do all in their power to prevent differences between them and other powers.

The Chancellor offered England an exceptional position in the railway between Bagdad and Basra. Haldane asked for the controlling position. Germany was to recognize England's political interests in the Persian Gulf and Southern Persia and to help England get from Turkey a concession for an extension of the railway from Basra to Koweit. Germany asked certain territorial changes in Africa.

The article says that the proposed settlement was, on the whole, favorable to England, except that Turkey was drifting into the position of a dependency of Germany. Dr. von Bethmann Hollweg would have yielded on the naval difficulty for the sake of an agreement in the Near East, but Admiral von Tirpitz had his way for the sake of a few ships which have been of no value to Germany in the war.

The article concludes:

"Haldane tried by every means consistent with Great Britain's interest and honorable obligations to strengthen the hands of the moderates in Germany, while his enemies have strengthened the hands of the extremists and supplied them with arguments that England, despite her fair professions, was the real enemy.

"Considering the political forces at work, the war may have been inevitable, but those who tried to make headway against the current have no reason to regret their endeavor."

# Secret Diplomacy of Two Autocrats

## The Kaiser-Czar Correspondence

SIXTY-FIVE telegrams exchanged by the German Kaiser and the Czar of Russia in 1904-07 were discovered in the Czar's secret archives at Petrograd, where a correspondent of The New York Herald obtained and published them. The documents had been unknown even to the Russian Ministers of State, and the world would probably never have learned of their existence but for the sudden deposing of the Czar. They are vouched for by Vladimir Burtseff and M. Schegoloff, who have charge of the imperial Russian archives, and any lingering doubt of their authenticity was removed on Sept. 8 by the publication of a German semi-official communiqué in the Rhenish Westphalian Gazette and other Government organs in the following terms:

> There was an exchange of telegrams between the Kaiser and the Czar in 1904 and 1905 with the object of defeating English pressure and maintaining peace. The exchange arose from the fact that Britain at that time put difficulties in the way of provisioning and coaling the Russian fleet on an Eastern voyage by German supply ships. The Kaiser's proposal for common action was met by the Czar with a far-reaching proposal for a treaty.
>
> Probably the publication of this correspondence at the present moment will produce an appearance of autocratic action to support President Wilson's message to the Pope, but it should be realized that at that time the Czar held an autocratic position and the Kaiser would have been guilty of grave dereliction of duty if he had not exercised his personal influence with him. It is a great pity that the Kaiser's efforts failed, for otherwise the world might have been spared the present war.

### Plot to Isolate England

The correspondence was carried on in English, and was so intimate that the two sovereigns signed themselves "Willy" and "Nicky." The period was that of the Russo-Japanese war, and the Kaiser made many suggestions as to how to conduct it. His chief object, however, was the formation of a triple alliance, consisting of Germany, Russia, and France, for the isolation of England. With this end in view, as the telegrams reveal, he made strenuous efforts to get the Czar to sign a secret treaty with him, which was to be unknown to Russia's ally, France, until after it was completed; then France would confront a *fait accompli* and would have to join. It appears that such a treaty was actually signed by both Emperors, but was afterward torn up when Count Witte discovered its existence.

But the real significance of the Willy-Nicky correspondence, as one commentator remarks, was neither in the Kaiser's disposition to meddle everywhere, nor in the Czar's weak willingness to betray France, but in the proof that two autocrats could thus plot in secret to dispose of vast national and international interests, very much in the spirit of two sovereigns planning to give each other a new uniform or decoration. Nowhere appeared an intimation that there was a Government to be consulted. The whole affair was kept from the knowledge of Chancellors and Foreign Ministers.

### Paris and the British Fleet

The text of the principal telegram from the Kaiser to the Czar is as follows:

Berlin, Oct. 27, 1904.

For some time the English press has been threatening Germany that she must on no account allow coals to be sent to the Baltic fleet, now on its way out. It is not impossible that the Japanese and British Governments may launch joint protests against our coaling your ships, coupled with a summons to stop further work. The result aimed at by such a threat of war would be the absolute immobility of your fleet and its inability to proceed for want of fuel.

This new danger would have to be faced in common by Russia and Germany together, who would both have to remind your ally France of the obligations she took over in the treaty of the dual alliance with you in the event of a *casus foederis* arising. It is out of the question that France on such invitation would try to shirk her implicit duty toward her ally. Though Delcassé is Anglophile and would be enraged, he would be wise enough to understand that the British fleet is utterly unable to save Paris.

In this way a powerful combination of the three strongest Continental powers would be formed, to attack which the Anglo-Saxon group would think twice. Before acting you ought not to forget to order new ships, so as to be ready with some of them when the war is over. They will be excellent persuaders during the peace negotiations. Our private firms would be most glad to receive contracts.

## The Dogger Bank Incident

In the night of Oct. 21, 1904, Russia's Baltic fleet, on its way to Japanese waters, sighted what its excited officers believed to be two Japanese torpedo boats in the North Sea near the Dogger Bank, and opened fire on them—with the result that they sank one British trawler, killing two fishermen and wounding six. The Czar's next telegram to the Kaiser shows how the incident played into Germany's hands, so far as the desired anti-British treaty was concerned:

St. Petersburg, Oct. 28, 1904.
Of course, you know the first details of the North Sea incident from our Admiral's telegram. Naturally, it completely alters the situation. I have no words to express my indignation with England's conduct. I agree fully with your complaints about England's behavior concerning the coaling of our ships by German steamers. Whereas she understands the rules of keeping neutrality in her own fashion, it is certainly high time to put a stop to this.

The only way, as you say, would be that Germany, Russia, and France should at once unite upon arrangements to abolish English and Japanese arrogance and insolence. Would you like to lay down and frame the outlines of such a treaty? As soon as it is accepted by us France is bound to join her ally.

In acknowledging the draft of the Treaty, the Czar telegraphed to the Kaiser as follows:

St. Petersburg, Nov. 23, 1904.
Before signing the last draft I think it advisable to let the French see it. So long as it is unsigned one can make small modifications in the text. I ask your agreement to my acquainting the Government of France with this project, and upon getting their answer I shall at once let you know by telegraph.

## Hoodwinking France

Then the Czar changed his mind about showing the treaty to France. On Nov. 26, 1904, the Kaiser telegraphed to the Czar as follows:

You have given me new proof of your perfect loyalty by deciding not to inform France without my consent. It is my firm conviction that it would be absolutely dangerous to inform France before we have both signed the treaty. It would have an effect diametrically opposed to our wishes. It is only the absolute and sure knowledge that we are both bound by the treaty to lend each other mutual help that will bring France to press upon England to remain quiet and keep the peace for fear of France's position being jeopardized.

Should, however, France know that a Russo-German treaty is only projected and still unsigned, she will immediately give short notice to her friend, if not secret ally, England, to whom she is bound by the entente cordiale, and inform her immediately. The outcome of such information would doubtless be an instantaneous attack by the two allied powers, England and Japan, on Germany, in Europe as well as in Asia. Their enormous maritime superiority would soon make short work of my small fleet, and Germany would be temporarily crippled.

This would upset the scales of the equilibrium of the world to our mutual harm, and, later on, when you begin your peace negotiations, would throw you alone on the tender mercies of Japan and her jubilant and overwhelming friends. It was my special wish, and, as I understood it, your intention, too, to maintain and strengthen this endangered equilibrium of the world through an express agreement between Russia, Germany, and France. That is only possible if your treaty becomes a fact before the previous information of France leads to catastrophe.

On the following day the Kaiser telegraphed to the Czar as follows:

Berlin, Nov. 27, 1904.
Today again serious news has reached me from Port Said and Cape Town. There is now no time to be lost. No third power must hear even a whisper about our intentions before we conclude the convention about the coaling business. The consequences otherwise would be most dangerous. I, of course, place full reliance on your loyalty.

## The Czar Nicholas replied on Nov. 28, 1904:

I fully agree that both our Governments must now come to a permanent under-

# RUINS OF LA COULOTTE, CAPTURED BY CANADIANS

*(Canadian Official Photo from Western Newspaper Union)*

All That Was Left of the French Village of La Coulotte, Near Lens, When It Was Captured by the Canadians After Fierce Fighting

IN THE CRATER ZONE ON THE WESTERN FRONT

*(Canadian Official Photo)*

Shellholes Filled With Water After Heavy Rains Have Been One of the Causes of Numerous Transportation Difficulties During the British Offensive

standing. You may fully rely on my loyalty and my wish to arrive at a speedy settlement of this serious question.

## The Secret Treaty Signed

During the following year the telegraphic correspondence continued at intervals, ranging over various international questions of the hour. Russia had been beaten and the peace negotiations were in progress at Portsmouth, N. H., but the Kaiser continued to offer advice to his pliable friend, seeking always to make capital for himself at the expense of France and England. The telegram which indicates that the Willy-Nicky treaty was actually signed, though never revealed to France, was sent by the Kaiser at the end of September:

> Gluchburgostsee, Sept. 29, 1905.
>
> The working of treaty does not—as we agreed at Bioerkö—collide with the Franco-Russian alliance, provided, of course, the latter is not aimed directly at my country. On the other hand, the obligations of Russia toward France can only go so far as France merits them through her behavior. Your ally has notoriously left you in the lurch during the whole war, whereas Germany helped you in every way as far as it could without infringing the laws of neutrality. That puts Russia morally also under obligations to us; do ut des.
>
> Meanwhile the indiscretions of Delcassé have shown the world that though France is your ally she nevertheless made an agreement with England and was on the verge of surprising Germany, with British help, in the middle of peace, while I was doing my best to you and your country, her ally. This is an experiment which she must not repeat again and against a repetition of which I must expect you to guard me. I fully agree with you that it will cost time, labor, and patience to induce France to join us both, but the reasonable people will in future make themselves heard and felt. Our Moroccan business is regulated to entire satisfaction, so that the air is free for better understanding between us. Our treaty is a very good base to build upon. We joined hands and signed before God, who heard our vows. I therefore think that the treaty can well come into existence.
>
> But if you wish any changes in the words or clauses or provisions for the future or different emergencies—as, for instance, the absolute refusal of France, which is improbable—I gladly await any proposals you will think fit to lay before me. Till these have been laid before me and are agreed upon the treaty must be adhered to by us as it is. The whole of your influential press, Nowosti, Nowie Wremja, Russj, &c., have since a fortnight become violently anti-German and pro-British. Partly they are bought by heavy sums of British money, no doubt. Still it makes my people very chary and does great harm to the relations newly growing between our countries. All these occurrences show that times are troubled and that we must have clear courses to steer; the treaty we signed is a means of keeping straight, without interfering with your alliance as such. What is signed is signed, and God is our testator. I shall await your proposals. Best love to Alix.
>
> WILLY.

The exchange of telegrams continued intermittently until Aug. 2, 1907, but more briefly and with less cordiality on the Kaiser's part after the failure of his proposed triple alliance against Great Britain. The full story of how Count Witte, the Russian statesman, using the Berlin bankers as a lever, compelled the abandonment of the project still remains to be revealed when the German Kaiser's secret archives some day come to light.

# How Turkey Joined the Germans

## A Question of the Date Raised by a Secret Telegram From Berlin to King Constantine

TURKEY did not declare war against any of the Allies until Nov. 5, 1914, three months after the beginning of the great conflict. During that time the Entente Powers accepted Turkey's protestations of neutrality and sought to enlist Turkish sympathies on their side. Was Turkey deceiving the Allies all that time? The question is raised by the publication of a secret telegram in the Greek White Book, which was laid before the Chamber of Deputies at Athens on Aug. 18, 1917. The telegram is from M. Theotokis, the Greek Minister at Berlin, and is dated Aug. 4, 1914. On that day the Kaiser summoned Theotokis to an audience, read a telegram just received from King Constantine, and instructed the Greek Minister to reply as follows:

> The Emperor informs me that an alliance has this day been concluded between Germany and Turkey. Bulgaria and Rumania also are taking their stand alongside Germany. German warships in the Mediterranean are to join the Turkish fleet and act with it. By this action the King of the Hellenes will see that all the Balkan States have joined Germany in the struggle against Slavism.
>
> The Kaiser asks you to mobilize your army, place yourself at his side, and march with him hand-in-hand against Slavism and the common enemy. If Greece does not side with Germany there will be a complete breach between Greece and the empire.

The Emperor added: " What I ask to-day is the execution of what the two sovereigns have often discussed."

The next day Theotokis again telegraphed Constantine, saying Jagow had confirmed under seal of absolute secrecy the conclusion of an alliance between Germany and Turkey. Theotokis added that his impression was that the Emperor would not object to seeing Greece extend her territory at the cost of Serbia.

The London Times, always critical of the Asquith Government, accepts this " mortifying disclosure " at its face value, holding that King Constantine and his Ministers knew of the German-Turkish alliance before Great Britain had even entered the war, whereas the Allies negotiated three months with Turkey while Turkey was already the sworn ally of Germany. "The Turks had actually to attack them before they would awaken to it," says The Times. " Our Ambassador at Constantinople was himself in England when the alliance was made, and seems to have returned to Constantinople with general instructions to work with the Turkish 'moderates,' though the Turkish Government, as we now know, was already committed against us. So late as Oct. 12 his anxiety was lest we should do anything which the Turks might interpret as aggressive, and thus weaken the resistance which these moderates were offering to Enver."

A diplomatic correspondent of The Westminster Gazette, however, presents an entirely different view, and in doing so reveals so much inside knowledge that the main portions of his article are here reproduced:

> May it be pointed out that the so-called "documentary evidence" consists of the bare word of the Kaiser and his Foreign Secretary, speaking to a notably pro-German Greek Minister, with the avowed purpose of dragging Greece into the war on the side of Germany? May it be further suggested that what was at that date an obvious lie as regards Rumania and Bulgaria was possibly not an unimpeachable truth as regards Turkey, and that when this statement is confronted with the actual facts, such as eyewitnesses recorded them in Constantinople, the very different impression is created that the public is put in the presence, not of any sensational disclosure of diplomatic secrets, but of a characteristic instance of the constant Prussian practice of using falsehood and misrepresentation as tools in diplomacy.
>
> As soon as the news of the German declarations of war reached Constantinople, a council of Ministers was summoned at the Porte to discuss the situation. In the course of that council the Minister

of War, Enver Pasha, moved a resolution that Turkey should immediately side with Germany. He found himself alone in his opinion, all the Ministers without exception declaring themselves against the proposal. Unfortunately, when Enver, as a subsidiary motion, proposed a partial mobilization, which he qualified as the pure precautionary measure which neutral neighbors always take, this was granted, and thus his personal power was dangerously enhanced.

That Enver Pasha henceforward became more and more troublesome, bullied his colleagues, and never ceased to advocate an alliance with Germany, there is not the slightest doubt. But there is also no doubt whatever that the Turkish dynasty, the great majority of the Turkish Cabinet, including the Grand Vizier, were steadfastly opposed to Turkey joining in the war, putting forward the reason that Turkey was already half ruined through the successive Tripoli and Balkan wars, and in the utmost need of rest and peace.

The Germans exerted all their cunning to help Enver. During the whole of August, 1914, they kept boldly asserting that Rumania had concluded an alliance with Germany and was ready to attack the Russians; in September, 1914, they asserted that the centre of the French Army had been broken through, the two wings routed, and France definitely put out of fighting condition. Even those tempting falsehoods did not prove persuasive. Not only did Enver fail to engineer a majority for war in the Turkish Cabinet, but some of his most important colleagues, the Grand Vizier included, openly declared that if ever such a majority was found they would immediately resign.

This lasted till the end of October, 1914, when the "coup" of the Black Sea was performed, that sudden aggression on the Russian harbors of Odessa and Theodosia by Turkish cruisers under command of German naval officers, which involved Turkey in the war. There is every reason to believe that it was accomplished by the Germans in understanding with Enver, because they realized that nothing but an unexpected and irretrievable accomplished fact could actually drive Turkey into that war alliance which they so ardently desired. With the exception of Enver, probably of the Minister of the Interior, Talaat Bey, and of the President of the Council of State, Halil Bey, and possibly of the Minister of Marine, Djemal Pasha, all the members of the Turkish Cabinet were taken by surprise, formally disapproved of war, sent a deputation to the French Embassy, begged

that the allied Ambassadors would not leave Constantinople, and offered apologies and an indemnity to Russia. They were told that either all the Germans must go—that is, all German naval and military instructors—or the Ambassadors would go themselves.

The Turkish Cabinet then begged that the mediation of America and Italy, still neutral, might be accepted, and that the Ambassadors would not leave. This was also rejected, and the Ambassadors left. Thereupon four Cabinet Ministers immediately resigned: Djavid Bey, Mahmoud Pasha, Oskan Effendi, and Boustani Effendi. The Grand Vizier declared that war was a "criminal folly," but was prevailed upon to remain in office by urgent and most likely threatening appeals to his patriotism. The aged and bodily and mentally weak Sultan was practically irresponsible. The Crown Prince Youssouf Izeddin Effendi, receiving in audience of departure a personal friend of allied allegiance, commissioned him to convey to M. Poincaré and to Sir Edward Grey the expression of his deep sorrow and of his sympathy with the Allies.

The presumption is that, on Aug. 4, the Kaiser was trying to drag in Greece by the inducement and threat of a Turkish alliance, as he since tried to drag in Turkey by the inducement and threat of a Rumanian alliance, and, most likely, was endeavoring to drag in Bulgaria by the inducement and threat of a Greek alliance. It is quite possible that on Aug. 4 some secret undertaking was given by Enver, acting personally, to Liman von Sanders or to Wangenheim. But between a secret personal understanding with a Minister, and an alliance concluded with the Cabinet of which that Minister is a member, there is always, in constitutional practice, and in the facts of the case there is especially, such an abyss of difference that, before pronouncing against the keen and able diplomatists who fought to the last a hard fight in Constantinople, it were perhaps advisable to await more conclusive evidence than the obviously interested and palpably dubious assertions of Kaiser Wilhelm and Herr von Jagow.

The sudden death of the Turkish heir apparent, Prince Youssouf Izeddin, in the Spring of 1916, is generally believed to have been due to his anti-German attitude. Though the official reports ascribed his death to suicide, the Prince's friends declared he had been assassinated. The facts discussed in the foregoing article seem to have a direct bearing upon his fate.

# Germany and the Armenian Atrocities

## Cowardice of the Policy That Permitted and Abetted the Crime Denounced by a German

*Dr. Harry Stürmer, a former German army officer and war correspondent, has written a book entitled " Two Years in Constantinople," in which he describes the cruelties with which the Turks almost exterminated the Armenians, while German diplomats and military leaders looked on without a protest. Writing from Switzerland, Dr. Stürmer denounces the German Government and tells the story of how the sight of the Armenians' sufferings changed his life.*

I HAVE spoken to Armenians who said to me: " Formerly Sultan Abdul Hamid massacred us from time to time by thousands. At stated intervals, in regular pogroms, we were turned over to the knives of the Kurds, and certainly suffered terribly. After that the Young Turks, at Adana, in 1909, showed they, too, could shed the blood of thousands of us. But since our present sufferings, rest assured we look with longing back upon the massacres perpetrated under the old régime. Now we have to complain not of a definite number of murdered people; now our whole race is slowly but surely being exterminated by the chauvinistic hatred of an apparently civilized, apparently modern, but, for that very reason, terribly dangerous Government. Now they are taking our women and children, who die on those long wearisome trips on foot that they have to make while being deported, or in the concentration camps without anything to eat. The few pitiful survivors of our people in the villages and cities of the interior, where the local authorities eagerly carry out the Central Government's orders, are then forcibly converted to Islamism, and our young girls are put into harems and houses of prostitution.

" Now that the Young Turks find themselves bleeding white in a disastrous war, they are trying to right the balance of the races and permanently establish themselves as the predominant element in the country. That is why these are not merely abortive outbreaks, but calculated political measures against our people; and therefore we can hope for

no mercy. Since Germany, weak and conscienceless, permits our extermination, if the war lasts much longer the Armenian people will simply cease to exist. And so we now look back with regret to Abdul Hamid's times, terrible as they were."

Was there ever any more terrific tragedy in the history of a race? And this was a race quite free of all illusions of nationalism, cognizant that it would be helpless crowded in between two great nations. The Armenians had felt no real impulse toward Russia until the Young Turks, whose comrades they had been in revolt against Abdul Hamid, foully betrayed them. They had been completely loyal to their Osmanli citizenship, more so than any other element of the empire, with the exception of the Turks themselves.

### Torture of a Victim

I believe I have in these few paragraphs sufficiently characterized the spirit animating this policy of extermination, as well as its results. I only wish to put in evidence one more incident, which affected me most because it was a matter of personal experience.

One Summer's day in 1916, at about noon, my wife went alone to the Grand Rue de Pera to do some shopping. We lived only a few steps from Galata Seraï, and daily could see the troops of unhappy Armenians enter the police station under escort of the gendarmes. Eventually you get hardened even to such sad sights and come to regard them not as individual but as political misfortunes. But this time my wife returned after a few minutes, all a-tremble. She hadn't been able to go on. As she passed the "Caracol" she heard the sound of some one being tortured, muffled groans as of some animal in agony, half dead of pain. "An Armenian," was what a person standing at the entrance of the building told her.

At that moment the crowd was, driven away by a policeman.

"If such things can be done in the bright light of day in the busiest part of the European city of Pera, then I wonder what they do to the poor Armenians in the uncivilized districts of the interior?" asked my wife. "If the Turks behave like wild beasts here in the capital, so that a woman can't go into the main street without meeting with this kind of terrible shock, then I can't go on living in this fearsome country."

Then she gave utterance to her boundless indignation at what, for more than a year, she had seen whenever we went out on to the streets: "You are brutes, contemptible brutes, you Germans, to allow the Turks to do this. You have the country absolutely in hand. Cowardly brutes you are, and I'm never going to set foot in your accursed land again."

At the moment when my wife, in her sorrow, indignation, and disgust at such cowardice, broke out into tears and flung at me her curse against my country, at that moment I mentally tore the ties that bound me to Germany. Truly, I had known enough for a long time.

### German Assurances Distrusted

I remembered the conversations I had had with gentlemen from the German Embassy in Constantinople, and also with the American Ambassador, Morgenthau, about the Armenian question. I had never believed in the assurances, given out by the German Embassy, that it, the German Embassy, had done everything possible to stop the murderous persecutions of harmless Armenians, a long distance away from the front, who, from their very nature and social position, were in no position to meddle with political matters. I equally distrusted the German Embassy's assertion that it had done all it could to prevent the deported women and children—deported, no doubt, for that very purpose—from being al-

lowed to perish. On the contrary, I gathered the impression that the German Government's conduct in the Armenian matter was controlled by a mixture of motives—on the one hand, cowardice and lack of conscience; on the other, by shortsighted stupidity.

The American Ambassador, who warmly espoused the Armenian cause, naturally preserved a good deal of reserve when talking to a German journalist like myself, and would not give his real opinion of the conduct of his German colleague. Nevertheless, in my many conversations with this sympathetic person, who has done so much for humanity in Turkey, I heard nothing which would tend to destroy my impression of the German Embassy's conduct, and yet I gave some indication of my impression during my conversations with Mr. Morgenthau.

Germany's attitude gave evidence of the most shameless cowardice, I have said. We certainly had sufficient control of the Turkish Government in military, financial, and political matters to be able at least to force it to observe the most elementary rules of humanity. Enver, no less than Talaat, chiefly responsible for the Armenian persecutions in his capacity as Minister of the Interior and practical dictator, would have had no choice but to follow Germany unconditionally, once the alliance and war were entered into. They would have accepted an order to stop the Armenian massacres with gnashing of teeth, but unquestioningly, nevertheless. * * * I had been witness of the plight of a German lady, married to an Armenian deported en bloc with many others, who came daily to the embassy antechamber, weeping and asking for help. Yet the embassy always turned a deaf ear to her plea.

Even the Turks laughed at us for this boundless exhibition of cowardice; they said that the Russian Government, in spite of the abrogation of the capitulations, would, in Germany's position, surely have made a serious affair if the same thing had happened to a poor Russian Jew. Turks generally, in spite of their accustomed formal amiability, let me feel their contempt for our boundless lack of backbone. * * *

## German Diplomats Blamed

I can't help imagining that, in spite of pretty official speeches, which I often heard at the German Embassy about the Armenian problem, the diplomats at bottom had very little interest in the salvation of this people. How do I come to make such a frightful charge? I was often at the German Embassy when the Armenian Patriarch, after some particularly terrible attack upon his people, came with tears in his eyes, and begged for help. And I never could discern anything in the excited hurryings hither and thither of our diplomats except anxiety to preserve German prestige and wounded vanity, but never a worry for the fate of the Armenian people. I time and again heard from German lips from all sorts of individuals, from the lowest to the highest, expressions of hatred, based on absolute misunderstanding of the facts, against the Armenians, unconsidered repetitions of the official Turkish publications.

And, unfortunately, the fact has been established by nurses and doctors returning from the interior that German officers, more eager than some of the Turkish officials of local districts, who hated to carry out the instructions of the Committee of Union and Progress, lightheartedly took part in the extermination and expulsion of the Armenians. A well-known instance, and one sufficiently established by proof, was that of two traveling German officers who came to a little village in further Asia Minor, where some Armenians had taken refuge in the interior of a house, refusing to be driven away like animals. Guns had been placed in position to drive them out of their shelter. But no Turks were to be found with the courage to carry out orders and fire on women and children. These German officers, then, without any orders, took up the matter as a sporting affair, and seized the occasion to show their skill in artillery practice. Certainly such shameful occurrences were not taking place daily, but they exactly fit in with the spirit which inspired the utterances of dozens of highly educated, highly placed Germans—not military people—with regard to the Armenians.

Just such a case, however, of criminal interference by military persons, in the interior of Anatolia, was officially brought to the attention of the embassy. At that time Count Wolff-Metternich happened to be the German Ambassador, a man who, in spite of his years, and in contrast to Freiherr von Wangenheim, victim of a weak and criminal optimism and pro-Turk blindness, now and then dared to oppose the Turkish Government. In the present instance he reported the matter to Germany; whereupon this very crime which he reported was made the pretext for his dismissal.  * * *

## Policy Called Stupid

And, finally, it was a shortsighted piece of stupidity on the part of our officials to stand by and witness the extermination of the Armenians without raising a finger to interfere. For the rising tide of Turkish chauvinism eventually had to be faced by our Government. Nobody with any foresight at all could have had a moment's doubt, after the Summer of 1915, that Turkey would only stick to us as long as she absolutely needed our military and financial help; that there would be no room for us in a completely victorious entirely Turkish Turkey; that we wouldn't even have a commercial chance. Nevertheless, we allowed a large element of the population, 1,500,000 souls, to be wiped out; an element which was progressive, possessed of a European outlook, intellectually adaptable, without a spark of chauvinism or fanaticism, disposed to be our friend. We simply didn't worry at all about this people, which is bound, eventually, to recover from its fearful misfortunes, and will hereafter be our deadliest enemy, instead of, as formerly, sincerely in sympathy with German aims.

The mixture of " consciencelessness," cowardice, and blindness displayed by our Government in the Armenian matter, alone would suffice to undermine the loyalty of any thinking human being who believes in humanity and civilization. Not every German will light-heartedly, like those diplomats of Pera, face the shame of having history note that the refinedly cruel extermination of a civilized and worthy people coincided with the period of Germany's hegemony in Turkey.

I frequently reported home to my newspaper matter concerning the Armenian persecutions and the fact that they were due to a guiding spirit of bestial Young Turk chauvinism. The Foreign Office followed these reports with interest. But I never saw any evidence in my newspaper that my expositions of the situation were bearing fruit.

Finally, at the time my wife, in such dramatic fashion, flung her curse in Germany's teeth, I resolved no longer to represent my newspaper. I have to thank the sufferings of those poor massacred and tortured Armenians for my spiritual and moral-political enfranchisement.

# Armenians Killed With Axes by Turks

## Harrowing Account by President of Anatolia College

THE slaughter of all the Armenian Faculty members of Anatolia College, Marsovan, Northern Asia Minor, with 1,200 others, by Turkish peasants, whose pay for the work was the privilege of stripping the clothing off their victims' bodies, was described by the Rev. George E. White, President of the college, upon his return to the United States in the Autumn of 1917. The massacres were committed at night by order of the Turkish Government, he said, the Armenians being sent out in lots of a hundred or two hundred to their doom and their bodies rolled into prepared burial trenches.

"One group of our college boys asked permission to sing before they died and they sang 'Nearer, My God, to Thee,' then they were struck down," Dr. White said. The number of Armenians who have been massacred is estimated by the American Committee for Armenian and Syrian Relief in New York City at from 500,000 to 1,000,000, while there are a million still living in need of immediate aid. Dr. White, who is now living in Minneapolis, was ordered to leave Marsovan by the Turkish Government. He was formerly pastor of the Congregational Church in Waverley, Iowa.

"The situation for Armenia," he said, "became excessively acute in the Spring of 1915, when the Turks determined to eliminate the Armenian question by eliminating the Armenians. The Armenian questions arise from political and religious causes.

"On the pretext of searching for deserting soldiers, concealed bombs, weapons, seditious literature or revolutionists, the Turkish officers arrested about 1,200 Armenian men at Marsovan, accompanying their investigations by horrible brutalities. There was no revolutionary activity in our region whatever. The men were sent out in lots of one or two hundred in night 'deportations' to the mountains, where trenches had been prepared. Coarse peasants, who were employed to do what was done, said it was a 'pity to waste bullets,' and they used axes.

"Then the Turks turned on the women and children, the old men and little boys. Scores of oxcarts were gathered, and in the early dawn as they passed the squeaking of their wheels left memories that make the blood curdle even now. Thousands of women and children were swept away. Where? Nowhere. No destination was stated or intended. Why? Simply because they were Armenians and Christians and were in the hands of the Turks.

"Girls and young women were snatched away at every turn on the journey. The girls sold at Marsovan for from $2 to $4 each. I know, because I heard the conversation of men engaged in the traffic. I know because I was able to ransom three girls at the price of $4.40.

"The misery, the agony, the suffering were beyond power of words to express, almost beyond the power of hearts to conceive. In bereavement, thirst, hunger, loneliness, hopelessness, the groups were swept on and on along roads which had no destination.

"I received word from Ambassador Morgenthau that our premises would not be interfered with. Next morning the Chief of Police came with armed men and demanded surrender of all Armenians connected with the college, girls' school, and hospital. We claimed the right to control our grounds as American citizens. More than two hours we held them at bay. They brought more armed men. They again demanded surrender of the Armenians. I refused. They challenged me for resisting the Turkish Government. They said any one who did so was liable to immediate execution.

"They broke open our gates, brought in ox carts, and asked where the Armenians were. I refused to tell. They went through the buildings, smashing down the doors. Then our Armenian friends, feeling that further attempt on our part to save them would bring more harm probably than good, came forth, professed themselves loyal Turkish subjects, and offered to do what was required.

"An oxcart was assigned each family, with a meagre supply of food, bedding, and clothing. The mother sat on the load with her children about her, the father prepared to walk beside the cart. I offered prayer, and then the sad procession, carrying seventy-two persons from the college and hospital, moved away.

"These teachers were men of character, education, ability, and usefulness, several of them representing the fine type of graduates from American or European universities. The company went in safety for about fifty miles. Then the men were separated from the women, their hands were bound behind their backs, and they were led away. The eight Armenian members of the staff of instruction of Anatolia College were among the slain. The women and children were moved on and on. No one knows where, and no one knows how many of them are still living.

"The Government officers plowed the Armenian cemetery in Marsovan and sowed it with grain as a symbol that no Armenian should live or die to be buried there. No Armenian student or teacher was left to Anatolia College, and of the Protestant congregation in the city of 950 souls more than 900, with their pastors, were swept away. It was a Government movement throughout—a movement against the Armenian people.

"These things are typical of what took place through the six provinces of the Turkish Empire known as Armenia. The Armenians are the Yankees of the East —the merchants, manufacturers, capitalists, artisans, and among the best of the farmers. One-quarter of a million people succeeded in escaping into Russian Caucasus, and among them American representatives have done wonderful work in caring for the sick, giving bread to the hungry, clothing the naked, caring for orphans. Probably a million more went to Syria and Mesopotamia, where they have been dependent upon American relief, which is helping this worthy people to pull through alive."

# The Appalling Plight of Serbia
## A Chapter of Balkan Atrocities

DETAILS of the terrible plight of the surviving population in Serbia have penetrated the veil of silence in sufficient numbers to establish the certainty that in the Autumn of 1917 the unfortunate nation is rapidly perishing of starvation and cruelty. The story of atrocities extends back to the very beginning of Bulgar-Teutonic occupation. Dr. Anthony Anthanasiados, a physician formerly in the service of the Serbian Government, furnished The London Times with the following narrative from Serbian Field Headquarters:

When the Serbian Army retreated in the Autumn of 1915 I was at my headquarters at Prishmina and decided to stay there. Bulgarian cavalry entered the town Nov. 11, followed by German and Austrian infantry. The first day the troops behaved well. On the morrow, seeing that 'the shops remained closed, the troops plundered them bare. The Germans led in the pillage.

The violence was not confined to the shops, but private dwellings, too, were looted. The houses then were torn down and the wood was used for fuel. Several forcible contributions were levied upon the town, provisions being seized whenever they were not forthcoming on demand. The Germans took all the beds from the Serbian hospitals, turning adrift the occupants, even those suffering from severe wounds. These beds they sent to Austria.

Soon the invaders began to intern townsfolk, principally school teachers and priests, of whom not one was left at liberty. The Turkish residents had been rejoicing before the arrival of the allies of Turkey, but they soon had cause to regret their attitude. One Turkish notable told me his people were exasperated beyond endurance by the dishonoring of their women at the hands of the Bulgars and Austro-Germans. German officers were among the criminals. Often the Turkish citizens were compelled to be the spectators of such scenes.

Finally I was able to leave and arrived at Belgrade, where I found conditions similar. The houses had been pillaged and many trainloads of loot sent to Austria. I was forced to proceed to Nish, where I became acquainted with several Bulgarians whom I attended in my professional capacity. One of them, Dr. Tendas, related that he caused twenty-four Serbian professors to be brought to a certain orchard, where, with his own hands, he brained them all. I overheard another Bulgarian telling quite calmly how he had killed two priests and two school teachers. All this was done with the object of eradicating the Serbian population.

## A Lieutenant's Experience

The Serbian Legation in London issued in September, 1917, a harrowing account of the sufferings of the Serbian people as related by Vidak Koprivitsa, a Lieutenant in the Serbian Combined Division, who, as an invalid, was recently exchanged by the Austro-Hungarian authorities, and is now in a hospital in France.

Lieutenant Koprivitsa, writing to Serbian friends in England, says that he was taken prisoner along with other seriously wounded Serbian officers in the advance of the Austrians on Vrntsi. The enemy immediately conducted a search of all houses in all the villages and towns of this district and requisitioned all available food, leaving only half a pound of flour per head. Some days afterward the wounded officers who had been left on the road between Kralyevo and Bashka were brought into the hospital in which Lieutenant Koprivitsa was lying. They told terrible stories of what they had seen on the journey; the road was strewn with corpses of fugitives who had been killed by the Germans by the side of their carts and wagons. The Germans had done their horrid work to the cries of little children and the wailing of their mothers.

The German General who visited the town asked Prince Lopkovitch why he had not yet erected the gallows. The Austrians quickly took the hint and put up gallows in all the larger towns and villages, and pictures showing people hanging on them were soon circulated and distributed among the population. From Vrntsi the Lieutenant and his fellow-sufferers were removed to Keczkemet, and some months later to a town called Briks, where was an internment camp for Russians. After a stay of five days at Briks they were removed to Heinrichsgrun, where in the earlier days of 1916 there had been 30,000 Serbian soldiers and 200 Serbian officers. In this camp the misery was appalling. At first from twenty-five to thirty persons were dying daily, and the number grew rapidly. Many of the unhappy Serbian soldiers found their graves there through starvation, disease, and hard labor in the mines. Officers as well as soldiers were barefooted and in rags—mere ghosts of men.

## The Camp of Death

The wounded men were given some wretched wash, which went by the name of soup. The "bread" they could hardly swallow, it was so bitter. It was made out of horse chestnuts, acorns, and potato peelings. The officers in the hospitals four times a week received as a special favor about a quarter of a pound of horseflesh and some rye bread. The huts were deadly places, and the nights were bitterly cold, not only because of the wretched shelter, but owing to the lack of covering. There were 3,000 men affected by tuberculosis who were absolutely without care or attention. Heinrichsgrun was just a Serbian cemetery, rows of graves being continually added with due regularity as fresh batches of prisoners came in. Here died more than 20,000 victims. The complaints and cries for help of the dying men directed to the Serbian Red Cross and to the Spanish Ambassador in Vienna brought no response.

In August, 1916, Bulgarian officers visited this camp and began to pick out as " recruits " those men who hailed from the territories in Serbia occupied by the armies of King Ferdinand. At the beginning of September, 1916, the Lieutenant was removed to Aschach, where 150 officers 'and 25,000 soldiers were crowded together. Here there reigned the same grim horrors. From this camp, as well as from others, the Austrians carried away Serbian soldiers to the Italian front in order that they might work on the construction of fortifications and in trench digging. In these camps are placed along with the prisoners of war interned civilians—women, old men, and children —a great many children between 10 and 12 years of age. The Lieutenant saw with his own eyes these wretched boys and girls picking up scraps of food from the drain-courses.

## Letter Written in Blood

A letter in possession of the Serbian authorities, written by a Serbian who had barely escaped hanging by the Bulgarian authorities, was published in the Paris newspapers in August, 1917. It revealed the fact that there had been a futile attempt at insurrection in April, 1917, followed by even greater cruelties than those which had provoked it. The writer was a refugee in the mountains, and the letter, written with his own blood for ink, was smuggled out by a Serbian sentry. It advises all Serbians to kill themselves rather than submit to capture; it tells of the forcible deportation of thousands of children to Constantinople; of the frightful tortures inflicted upon prisoners before they are

executed by the Bulgarians, such as hanging by the tongue; of gibbets erected everywhere to dispose of Serbian prisoners of war, especially of insurrectionists.

The names of both sender and recipient have been suppressed for obvious reasons, but both are on file in the Serbian archives with the original of the letter, which runs in part as follows:

I escaped April 25 from the Bulgarian prison where I was incarcerated with twenty comrades after having been surrounded and captured in the revolt near ——. I was taken, put in prison and condemned to be hanged, but during the night my friend —— arrived with a band in Prokouplie, killed the sentinels and rescued me. In consequence I was able to reach the mountains. There are more than 5,000 of us insurgents. Nearly all of the other mountains are filled with insurgents.

The Bulgarians had summoned all the male population between the ages of 16 and 65 in order to incorporate them in the army and send them immediately to the front. At the same time they had gathered together all the young people between 13 and 16 and had sent them to Constantinople. It was this vandal process of these monstrous Mongols that provoked the revolt.

The unfortunate mothers, exasperated by the cries of their children as they were carried off by force, attacked the Bulgarians with stones. This was a genuine revolt, to which the Bulgarians replied with gibbets to which they hanged women and children. Finally the people, exhausted and revolting, threw themselves upon the Bulgarian depots. Men and women carried off arms and ammunition, first to Prokouplie, then to Leskovatz, Lebane, Vrania, Viassotintze, Zayetchar, Kniajevatz, Pojarevatz, and the villages. Meanwhile two Bulgarian divisions arrived, and a bloody battle developed; we should have been able to defeat the Bulgarians as we had defeated the Germans if they had not used a cowardly strategy to prevent us from attacking them; they forced the women and children to march in front of their ranks. Unable to fire upon our own people, we withdrew as far as Korvingrad, where a new battle began and where the Hungarians attacked us from behind. We made an opening and took refuge in the mountains. Since I was dead from fatigue I was taken prisoner, and with a dozen other insurgents was condemned to be hanged. Waiting while the gibbet was prepared, we were incarcerated in the prison of Prokouplie, but one of our bands killed the garrison and rescued us.

So here I am in the mountain of ——. It may be that when you read these lines I shall no longer be among the living, but the insurrection cannot be snuffed out so easily, for the Bulgarians are proceeding systematically to exterminate our nation. On the 25th of April they placed aboard trains at Belotintze 8,000 children between the ages of 12 and 15, bound for Constantinople. Many of the children jumped from the cars along the way, and found death in that manner.

### Victims of Exploitation

The Serbian Government on Aug. 29, 1917, issued a protest to the world against the treatment of Serbia by the Austrian and Bulgarian authorities. Referring to the economic exploitation of the occupied territory the protest said:

They (the Austrians and Bulgarians) change the laws on taxation and customs; they introduce new monopolies, abolish the moratorium; force the inhabitants to subscribe to their war loans and make donations to their Red Cross. From an economic standpoint they consider the regions occupied as definitely acquired by them.

The evident aim of their economic administration is to bring about the ruin of the inhabitants of the country under occupation. They have crushed with new taxation a people which was economically exhausted, and have forced on them new customs duties and fresh monopolies. They are extorting more than 100,000,000 crowns from this people for debts due to Austrians and Germans and in addition several million crowns for subscription to war loans. Serbian money (the only money in which our population could make its payments) has been arbitrarily reduced to one-half its value.

At the same time the Serbian Government gave notice that at the peace negotiations after the war Serbia would demand indemnities both for the Serbian State and for individuals.

### Serbs Robbed of Harvests

According to a statement issued on Sept. 4, 1917, by the Serbian Press Bureau in London, the Austrians, Germans, and Bulgarians carried off all of this year's harvests in Serbia, depriving the surviving families of food. Meat, lard, butter, and spices are altogether unobtainable. Most families have only one loaf of bread a week. There is virtually no milk in Serbia, and thousands of women and children whose men folk perished in the war are doomed to starve. According to this report, 80,000 Serbian prisoners have perished in Austria and Hungary.

The Journal de Génève, published in Switzerland, commenting upon Lord Robert Cecil's assurance of Serbia's ultimate liberation, grimly remarks that there may be no Serbs left alive to benefit by reparations and restitutions unless something is done in the meantime to save them. It continues:

Nobody knows the exact returns of the Serbian losses, but, according to the most optimistic estimates, one-fourth of the population has already perished owing to the war, to epidemics, to want of food, and to privations of all kinds. If we consider only the men, and more especially those of the educated classes, the proportion is even far greater. On account of this the birth rate will decrease for years, and of what value for the population will be the children who have lived or are born under the influence of such physiological distress? * * * Serbia is not being supplied with food, and her fate is therefore many times worse than that of Belgium.

The Americans and the Swiss gave her some help last year, but this work of charity is now interrupted because the Americans have themselves entered the war, and no longer have access to Serbia, and because Switzerland, being rationed, no longer disposes of foodstuffs for export, and is no longer permitted to procure them elsewhere to convey them to the necessitous Serbs, although she could do it in perfect safety, thanks to the facilities granted her by the Austro-Hungarian Government.

The same applies to the Serbian prisoners in the German and Austrian camps; there the last representatives of the flower of the manhood of the Serbian population are dying by inches. In Geneva one has seen several convoys of repatriated Serbs, all tubercular or scrofulous in consequence of their long privations and insufficient food.

### Some Terrible Figures

Under the title "The Agony of Serbia" an article appeared in the September issue of Justice, signed by Kosta Novakovitch, Secretary of the Serbian Trade Unions in France and editor of the Journal Ouvrier of Belgrade, containing the following figures and statements:

As to Serbia itself, the state of things is more hopeless than ever. The official statistics are published in several Austro-Hungarian journals and fully in the Official Journal at Belgrade, the Belgradske Novine. There it was stated that the Serbian population in the territories occupied by Austria-Hungary a year ago was only 2,218,027. The population normally would have been 3,170,000. There is, therefore, a reduction of 951,973, or 28.2 per cent. The male population has been reduced by 38.3 per cent. In some towns this percentage is much greater. At Belgrade it is 65.6 per cent.; at Chebatz 47.6 per cent. There are now in Serbia 144 women to 100 men. At Belgrade even the female population has gone down by 21.6 per cent.

In the Segedi Naplo of Aug. 2, 1917, the Secretary of the Chamber of Commerce at Segedine states that the difference between the official Serbian statistics of 1910 and the returns now made by the Bulgarians in the territories they occupy is 300,000. The same authority states that all the males from 18 to 60 are away from their homes. In 1910 the population of Serbia was 4,300,000. It is now reduced by 1,352,000. Then there are the massacres committed by the Bulgarian military authorities after a revolt of the Serbian people against enforced recruiting. The revolt was crushed in blood. Those left were deported. This fact is admitted by the Bulgarian War Minister in the document sent to the Bulgarian Headquarters, (No. 763, May 20, 1917, Sofia.)

Dr. Otokar Ribar, the Austrian Reichsrat Deputy, declared in the Vienna Parliament on June 26 last: " Serbia will be saved, but there will no longer be Serbs." He said these words when protesting against the greatest crime committed in this war, the deportation of 30,000 Serbian women, children, and men from the departments of Vranje, Nish, and Pirot, and their internment in Asia Minor. Fugitives relate that, among those 30,000, there were 8,000 women and young girls delivered over to the Turks. Of these a great number courted death by throwing themselves out of the trains conveying them to Asia Minor. War prisoners and those interned are suffering actual martyrdom. They are ravaged by hunger and disease. Their number decreases daily. The deaths are put by all at 60,000, by some as high as 80,000. After the retreat from Serbia, and during the reconstitution of the Serbian Army, quite 20 per cent. died at Corfu. Our losses on the Saloniki front have been about 50 per cent. of the Serbian forces which have taken part in the operations of General Sarrail's armies.

Imagine, then, the state of mind of those surviving in France and near Saloniki who receive every day letters from their families remaining in Serbia appealing for bread, and money to buy bread; requests, too, from prisoners and those interned, who cry: " Send us bread, or you will not see us again alive." Unfortunately, very little is done to help our population. The Swiss Central Committee at Geneva sent provisions to the value of something over £11,000 in 1916. Seven hundred thousand kilogs. of maize were brought from Rumania, but of this quantity only 200,000 kilogs. have been milled. The American Committee has sent twenty-two wagons of provisions, clothing, and boots. This is all for last year. From last October our Government began to send regularly £6,000 a month for the entire population of Serbia. What is this among 2,000,000 people?

## Starvation in Montenegro

The following statement was duly sworn and attested before the American Consul at Bordeaux by a native of Montenegro, who, as an American subject, was able to leave that country before war was declared by the United States:

I, Sabonovic John, American citizen, of Montenegrin origin, was born in Montenegro March 13, 1886, at Grahovo, Montenegro, and I went to the U. S. 1906, where I stayer until 1914, when I returned to Montenegro in April to get my wife at Cettinje, staying there for three years until 2 May, 1917. During this time I visited Grahovo on 26 April, 1917, when I saw 182 persons, women, children, &c., die in twelve days because of lack of food, there being no food in the country whatever except a mixture of grass and millet, and not enough of that. The people have eaten up all the dogs, &c., they can find; Nicksich city is like this, also Drobnjoci, Piva, and Kelasin, and all the people are in the same conditon, rich as well as poor, as money will not buy food.

I believe there are certainly 200 people a day dying of famine in the country. The Austrian authorities allow each person in Cettinje to buy 10 " dek " of cornmeal a day, (a handful about,) so the situation there is a little better than in the rest of the country, where no such food can be bought. I believe that there are but two battalions of Austrian soldiers, one in Cettinje and the other spread around the country, in all Montenegro, and about 20,-000 in Albania, Scutari, and Droc, which are all I know of.

The soldiers treat the population badly, making all the men work on the roads, and if from fatigue or thirst a man stops work to rest or drink he is shot on the spot. Work is about ten or twelve hours a day, and pay of 2 kronen paper a day. A person in 1916 (there is no food now) would buy something to sell, food, &c., and soldiers would take it without money.

They treat the people better in Cettinje than other places, but everywhere the people are too poor and badly nourished to try to revolt. The Austrian soldiers in the country are perhaps more badly nourished than the people, and I have seen in the same villages above mentioned myself, from March until May 2, 1917, 200 soldiers, Austrians, die of starvation in Cettinje alone. The men on the front are a' little better than those in the interior, but there they are also dying of starvation, as from time to time soldiers return from the front in starved condition.

The Governor of Montenegro, von Webber, who stays at Cettinje in the King's house, is a civilian, and does not try to misuse the people, the reason the condition of the population in the capital is better than that in the rest of the country, perhaps. I believe that from 10,000 to 15,000 persons have died of starvation in Montenegro. I am sure that the Austrians can get no food, as they are dying, and also the soldiers talk to the population and tell them that they know the war cannot last more than a month or two more, as we ourselves can get nothing to eat.

All the country is in the same impoverished, starving, and subject condition, the only city a little better than the others being Cettinje, above stated.

I hereby certify that the above statements are all true and correct to my best knowledge, and that I actually saw and know the things which I have related above.

# What Is Meant by "Freedom of the Seas"

*F. Sefton Delmer, late English Lecturer in Berlin University, recently gave a London paper the following account of a lecture delivered by Count zu Reventlow and never reported in the German press:*

During my recent stay in Berlin I heard the words "Freiheit der Meere" bandied about often-enough, and reams of newspaper sermons were preached on the text. In a Socratic vein I asked various Germans of my acquaintance what the expression really meant, but I could never get a satisfactory answer.

In England the man in the street takes the term to mean freedom for the Germans to coal at our ports in times of peace and to run in and out of our harbors in the same uncontrolled fashion as before the war. The jurist, on the other hand, says that the term can evidently not apply to times of peace, but can only mean that the German wishes us to forfeit our right of search and blockade in time of war.

Count zu Reventlow, however, at a great public meeting in March, 1917, in the Berlin Philharmonic Hall, gave quite a different interpretation, and as everything he said that evening had been memorized from a carefully censored manuscript, not a word of which he would have been allowed to utter unless his explanation had been in harmony with the ideas of the Government, I think I am justified in calling the following definition the official one:

"What do we Germans understand by "the freedom of the seas?" he said. "Of course we do not mean by it that "free use of the sea which is the com- "mon privilege of all nations in times of "peace, the right to the open highways "of international trade. That sort of "freedom of the sea we had before the "war. What we understand today by "this doctrine is that Germany should "possess such maritime territories and "such naval bases that at the outbreak "of a war we should be able, with our "navy ready, reasonably to guarantee "ourselves the command of the seas. We "want such a jumping-off place for our "navy as would give us a fair chance of "dominating the seas and of being free "of the seas during a war. [Cheers.] "The inalienable possession of the Bel- "gian seaboard is therefore a matter of "life and death to us, and the man is a "traitor who would faint-heartedly re- "linquish this coast to England. Our "aim must be not only to keep what our "arms have already won on this coast, "but sooner or later to extend our sea- "board to the south of the Strait of "Calais."

# The Attempted Restoration of the Manchus in China

### By W. Reginald Wheeler

*Professor of English in the Christian College at Hangchow, China*

Professor Wheeler is an American, a graduate of Yale, with a degree from Harvard as well. He is at present the head of the English department of Hangchow Christian College.

ON July 1, 1917, in the sixth year of the Chinese Republic, Chang Hsun, a provincial Governor and a "war lord" of the most extreme type, proclaimed from Peking that he had overthrown the existing Government and had restored the Manchus to the throne. On July 4 practically the entire country voiced its "declaration of independence" from this Manchu Government; on July 14 the victorious republican Generals entered the capital. This opposition and this victory of the Chinese republicans took place on the independence days of the American and the French republics; the coincidence is both significant and symbolical, and the story of the struggle is one of vital interest to republicans of both Orient and Occident.

The apparent cause of the breakup of the republican Government was the disagreement over the declaration of war against Germany; other issues involved a contest between the President and Premier, and the Parliament and Military Governors. But, fundamentally, the present situation is the outcome of the struggle which has been going on ever since the establishment of the republic; the contest between monarchists and republicans; between militarists and democrats. As C. T. Wang, Vice President of the Senate and a graduate of Yale, has put it: "The real issues are: Shall there "be government by law or by force? "Shall the will of the people as expressed through the Assembly prevail, "or that of a privileged few? Shall the "military forces of the nation be used to "uphold the country, or to uphold certain "individual Generals? Upon these issues "the country and the free and democratic "nations of the West should be called "upon to pass judgment." These issues made this situation in Asia a part of the great world situation into which America has entered as one of the champions of freedom and law.

## China and Germany

The account of China's relation with Germany since the latter's submarine declaration on Feb. 1 is rather complicated. On Feb. 4 the American Minister, Dr. Reinsch, notified the Foreign Minister that his Government had already severed relations with Germany, and requested the Chinese Government to follow the United States in its protest. Peking responded, and on Feb. 9 formally protested to Germany. The note concluded with a declaration of its intention of severing diplomatic relations if the protest were ineffectual. The immediate answer of Germany was to torpedo the French ship Atlas in the Mediterranean on which were over 700 Chinese laborers. On the evening of March 10 the German Government definitely replied, but on that very afternoon Parliament had empowered the Government to break with Germany.

The rupture occurred on March 14 at noon; the German Minister and his staff were handed their passports, and German interests were turned over to the Dutch Legation. The mildness of Germany's note of March 10 was rather a surprise to inhabitants of China, who remembered the seizure of Tsing-tau in 1898, and the appropriation of Shantung as the result of the murder of two German missionaries, and the ruthlessness of the German troops at the time of the Boxer uprising. A leading Chinese lawyer commented thus on the change of attitude:

The troops under Count Waldersee, leaving Germany for the relief of Peking, were instructed by the War Lord to grant no quarter to the Chinese; on the other hand, the latter were to be so disciplined that they would never dare look a German in the face again. The whirligig of time brings its own revenge, and today, after the lapse of scarcely seventeen years, we hear the Vossische Zeitung commenting on the diplomatic rupture between China and Germany, lamenting that even so weak a State as the Far Eastern republic dares look defiantly at the German Nation!

The breaking off of relations with Germany brought to light the state of discord which had existed for some time between the Premier, Tuan Chi-jui, and the President, Li Yuan-hung. The former is a military leader and has been trained in the Manchu type of government. The latter is a real republican in spirit and has insisted that every act of the State be carried out according to the existing Constitution. The Premier desired to break off relations without consulting Parliament; the President insisted on the latter step, and after Tuan had threatened to resign, and had actually left the capital for Tientsin, the President persuaded him to return and to present the question to Parliament. This was done with the result already indicated.

## China's Distrust of Japan

Having taken two steps, the next move was to declare war. Here, however, appeared many difficulties. It is hard for a foreigner to judge Chinese public opinion, but after a trip through the coast cities and 800 miles into the interior as far as Chang-sha, the following factors seem to me to be involved:

The Chinese sympathize as a whole with the professed aims of the Allies, but they cannot reconcile with those aims the action of one of the allied nations—Japan. In the Orient, in Chinese eyes, Japan has stood for all that Germany, as depicted by its worst enemies, stands for. Japan's action in Korea, including the Korean conspiracy, and its present Government there; the taking of Tsing-tau in the Fall of 1914 and its retention after having publicly declared an opposite purpose; in 1915 the serving of the Twenty-one Demands, especially Group V.; and last Fall the demands following the Cheng Chiatung affair in Manchuria—all these acts in Chinese eyes cannot be reconciled with the oft-repeated declaration that the Allies are fighting for the rights of small or weak nations and that each nation may shape its own Government and destiny. The present Terauchi Government professes to be friendly to China, but the Chinese feel that such a friendly attitude now cannot be reciprocated, unless reparation and restitution are made for the acts of the past. This is the program of the Allies in Europe: the Chinese cannot understand why such a program should not be applied in Asia. Accordingly there is a feeling of distrust, fear, and hatred in Chinese hearts for Japan that can hardly be overstated. And that is the chief obstacle to its belief in the aims of the Allies.

Other factors are a realization that their own military power is slight, and a fear of "losing face" by comparison with the Allies; the fear that food prices will increase; the devotion to peace, which is deep rooted in the nation; and finally the policy of "proud isolation," which until recent years has marked all China's relations with other nations. It is a long step for a people ruled for centuries by an alien dynasty to attempt republican self-government; it is an almost incredible act for China as a whole to grasp the present world situation and to take its proper place in relation to it.

## Other Factors Against War

Added to these main factors are minor ones: the fact that Germany, despite its harsh treatment in the past, has energetically and nicely carried on a propaganda in the East, supplying military aids and arms to the Chinese Army, and sending out Consuls and diplomatic officers who are scholars in Chinese literature and philosophy with sufficient funds to entertain Chinese officials as they like to be entertained; on the other hand, the Allies have at various times, perhaps unconsciously, offended the Chinese. The opium trade, carried on by citizens of the British Empire; the recent Lao-Hsi-Hai affair in the North, where French officials attempted to appropriate property which the Chinese thought was theirs; the advice of the

American adviser, Dr. Goodnow, to return to the monarchy; the ineffectual enforcement of the " open door " treaty, which practically all the Allies, including Japan, have signed—all these facts have tended to produce a pessimism in the minds of Chinese regarding idealistic words which seem to be unbacked by deeds. This pessimism seems to be shared by many of the younger, foreign-educated leaders in regard to the favorable outcome of the conference at the close of the war—to many it seemed immaterial whether or not China should have a voice in that council. A final complication was the struggle between the military party and the democrats, each fearing to have the other gain the power which would accrue to it if it were in control when war was declared.

Despite all these difficulties, it seemed fairly certain that the " third step " would be taken in due time. Thus, on April 16, following the detention of the Chinese Minister at Berlin, the Peking Gazette, the most influential of the papers published by the Chinese, requested an early decision. But at this point the Premier thought fit to summon a council of Military Governors and their representatives to hasten the decision of the country, and the ultimate consequences were disastrous.

The outline of events was somewhat as follows: The conference met April 25. After much arguing and exhorting, the majority of the conference were won over to the view of the Premier. But signs of opposition on the part of the Parliament against the Premier and his supporters began to develop. There was also the feeling that the Premier had promised certain returns from the Allies, such as increase of the Chinese customs duties, and relief from the Boxer indemnity, but that on account of the opposition of Japan, and for other reasons, these returns could not be secured.

### Parliament Threatened by Mobs

On May 1, however, the Cabinet passed the vote for war without asking conditions or returns, and on May 7 the President, through the Cabinet, sent a formal request to Parliament to approve of this declaration. Parliament delayed, and

then, on May 10, an attempt was made to force it into a decision by a mob which gathered outside the National Assembly and threatened the members of both houses. There seems to be little doubt that some official of the Government had incited and promised protection to the mob, as it collected at 10 o'clock in the morning, and was not dispersed until 11 at night, when the report was circulated that a Japanese journalist had been killed. The Peking Gazette openly accused the Premier of being behind the riot. Telegrams from all parts of the country poured in protesting against this attempted coercing of Parliament; all the Ministers of Tuan's Cabinet resigned, leaving him standing alone.

On May 18, the Peking Gazette, edited by Eugene Chen, a Chinese born and educated in England and a British subject, a brave opponent of Yuan Shih-kai and his monarchical schemes, and a stanch supporter of the republic, published an article entitled " Selling China," in which it accused the Premier of being willing to conclude with the Japanese Government an agreement which much resembled Group V. of the Twenty-one Demands of 1915. That night Mr. Chen was arrested, and later, without any fair trial, he was sentenced to four months' imprisonment. The case stirred up much comment, and finally, as a result of the intercession of C. T. Wang and others, on June 4, the President pardoned him.

### Military Governors Revolt

In the meanwhile events were marching swiftly. The contest between militants and democrats was clearcut. Demands were made for Tuan's retirement from the Premiership; his military friends on the other hand urged his remaining in office. On May 19 the decision was reached in Parliament that there was a majority for war, but that the question would not be decided while Tuan was Premier. The Military Governors left on May 21 amid much speculation and some fear as to their future action. Before going they sent a petition to the President, indirectly attacking Parliament, by criticising the Constitu-

UNITED STATES SOLDIERS GUARDING THE LEGATION AT PEKING

tion which it had practically finished and asking that Parliament be dissolved if the Constitution were not corrected. The three points to which they objected were:

(1) When the House of Representatives passes a vote of lack of confidence in the Cabinet Ministers, the President shall either dismiss the Cabinet or dissolve the House of Representatives, but the said House must not be dissolved without the approval of the Senate. (The French system.)

(2) The President can appoint the Premier without the countersignature of the Cabinet Ministers.

(3) Any resolution passed by both houses shall have the same force as law.

Obviously these three points give more power to the President and to Parliament than an autocratic Premier and his supporters would desire. The answer to this petition was an increased demand for the retirement of Tuan and the formation of a new Cabinet. The Premier refusing to resign on May 23, the President dismissed him from office. Wu Ting-fang was appointed acting Premier, and there was a feeling of relief. Li Ching-hsi, nephew of Li Hung Chang, was nominated on May 25 for Premier, and on May 28 his nomination was passed by the House of Representatives, 388 to 56, and next day by the

Senate, 166 to 25. On May 30, C. T. Wang, Chairman of the Committee for Writing the Permanent Constitution, published a statement saying that the second reading was practically finished and reviewing the chief points of interest in the new document ready for promulgation.

The Chinese ship of state seemed to have weathered another of its many storms. But suddenly rumor came from Anwhei that General Ni Shih-ching had declared independence, and that he was backed by most of the other Northern Generals and Governors, who, as Putnam Weale put it, looked upon Parliament and any Constitution it might work out as " damnable Western nonsense, the real, essential, vital, decisive instrument of Government in their eyes being not even a responsible Cabinet, but a camarilla behind that Cabinet which would typify and resume all those older forces in the country belonging to the empire and essentially militaristic and dictatorial in their character." This declaration of result was received without approval by the people of the country. I talked with men from many sections of the country and they all agreed that the Military Governors had no definite ideal or purpose except their own glory and power.

## The President's Answer

All waited for the President to speak. His answer to this defiance came in no uncertain tones and was received by patriots with enthusiasm. Would that he had maintained the same stand throughout the ensuing events! Some of the more important passages in his message were:

It is a great surprise to me that high provincial officials could have been misled by such rumors into taking arbitrary steps without considering the correctness or otherwise of the same. * * * You accuse the Cabinet of violating law, yet, with the assistance of a military force, you endeavor to disobey the orders of the Government. The only goal such acts can lead to is partition of the country like the five Chi and making the country a protectorate like Korea; in which case both restoration of the monarchy and the establishment of the republic will be an idle dream. You may not care for the black records that will be written against you in history, but you ought certainly to realize your own fate. * * *

I am an old man. Like the beanstalk under the leaf I have always been watching for any possibility of not seeing and understanding aright. Yea, I walk day and night as if treading on thin ice. I welcome all for giving me advice and even admonition. If it will benefit the country I am ready to apologize.

But if it be your aim to shake the foundations of the country and provoke internal war, I declare that I am not afraid to die for the country. I have passed through the fire of trial and have exhausted my strength and energy from the beginning to the end for the republic. I have nothing to be ashamed of. I will under no circumstance watch my country sink into perdition, still less subject myself to become a slave to another race.

Of such acts I wash my hands in front of all the elders of the country. These are sincere words from my true heart and will be carried out into deeds.

                          LI YUAN-HUNG.
May 31, 1917.

## Southern Provinces Loyal

Following the declaration of independence of the northern provinces, most of the southern ones declared their opposition to this stand. They were led by Yunnan, Kweichow, Kwantung, and Kwangsi, who originally opposed the monarchical movement of Yuan Shih-kai

last year. Some of the loyal Generals' telegrams were hotly worded. From Tang Chi-yao, Governor of Yunnan:

Chi-yao is unpolished in thoughts and ignorant of the ways of partisanship or factionism. All he cares and knows about is to protect the republic and be loyal to it. If any one should be daring enough to endanger the Chief Executive or Parliament, I vow I shall not live with him under the same sky. I shall mount my steed the moment order is received from the President to do so.

## From a General in Kwantung:

The reason why the rebels have risen against the Government is that they are fighting for their own posts and for money. That is why their views are so divergent and their acts so ill-balanced. It is hoped the President will be firm to the very last and give no ear either to threat or inducement. This is the time for us to sweep away the remnants of the monarchist curse and reform the administration. With my head leaning against the spear I wait for the order to strike and I will not hesitate even if I should return to my native place a corpse wrapped up in horse-skin!

## Friendly Warning from America

The military party nevertheless met at Tientsin and elected Hsu Shih-chang, Generalissimo. But soon signs of dissension appeared among them. On June 7 was made public a friendly warning from America. The American Minister, Dr. Reinsch, transmitted the following message to Dr. Wu Ting-fang, the Minister of Foreign Affairs:

The Government of the United States learns with the most profound regret of the dissension in China and desires to express the most sincere desire that tranquillity and political co-ordination may be forthwith re-established.

The entry of China into war with Germany—or the continuance of the status quo of her relations with that Government—are matters of secondary consideration.

The principal necessity for China is to resume and continue her political entity, to proceed along the road of national development on which she has made such marked progress.

With the form of government in China, or the personnel which administers that government, the United States has an interest only in so far as its friendship impels it to be of service to China. But in the maintenance of China by one central united and alone responsible government, the United States is deeply interested, and now expresses the very sincere hope that China, in her own interest and in that of the world, will immediately set aside her factional political disputes, and that all parties and persons will work for the re-establishment of a co-ordinate government and the assumption of that place among the powers of the world to which China is so justly entitled, but the full attainment of which is impossible in the midst of internal discord.

This was welcomed by Chinese as a pledge to support the Central Government. By the Japanese it was received with varying degrees of disapprobation and suspicion, the chief grievance being that Japan had not been consulted beforehand.

### The President Weakens

On June 9 an ultimatum was sent from Tientsin either by Chang Hsun or by Li Ching-hsi, threatening to attack Peking if Parliament was not dissolved. The President was isolated and members of Parliament and other democrats could not reach him. Rumor reported that he was about to give in and dissolve Parliament. The British adviser to the Chinese Government advised him not to do so. The Japanese adviser gave the opposite counsel. Wu Ting-fang, Acting Premier, refused to sign the mandate. Finally, on June 12, the mandate was issued, countersigned by General Chiang Chao-tsung, commander of the Peking gendarmerie. The next day an explanation was made by President Li in which he admitted he was forced to issue the mandate against his will, but that he did it to save Peking and the country from war and destruction. He declared he would resign as soon as opportunity came.

On June 15 Chang Hsun arrived in Peking with Li Ching-hsi. Eight of the provinces that week canceled their independence, stating that their desire for the dissolution of Parliament had been satisfied. The members of Parliament made their way, many of them in disguise, to Shanghai and there held meetings and sent out manifestoes. Affairs were apparently at a standstill with the country thus divided when the great coup d'état was carried out by Chang Hsun. Affairs thereupon moved swiftly.

On June 30 Kang Yu-wei, a known advocate of the monarchy, arrived in Peking. He had traveled incognito from Shanghai. His first visit was to Chang Hsun. On July 1 at 4 A. M. Chang Hsun and his suite called on the Manchu boy Emperor and informed him of his restoration, and seated him on the throne. President Li Yuan-hung was requested to resign, but refused. He was then practically held prisoner. Numerous imperial edicts were issued, countersigned by " Chang Hsun, member of the Privy Council."

On July 3 Feng Kuo-chang repudiated any connection with the restoration, his name having appeared in the edicts as one of the petitioners. The Military Governor of Canton issued proclamations that the Cantonese would fight to maintain the republic. Many similar messages were sent by other provinces. Japanese troops proceeded to the Forbidden City, took President Li Yuanhung out of the custody of Chang Hsun's men and escorted him to the Japanese Legation. On July 4 the President issued a pledge to fight for the republic. On July 5 hostilities broke out at Lang Fang on the Peking-Tientsin railway. General Tsao Kun arrived at Liuliho with 10,000 troops en route to Peking. The diplomatic body notified the Peking authorities that the Procotol of 1901 providing for open railway communication between Shanhaikwan and Peking must be observed. On July 5 trains out of Peking were packed to overflowing with Chinese fleeing to Tientsin. A special train with a foreign detachment was stopped at Lang Fang by a republican General, who requested the passengers to turn back, as Chang Hsun's troops had torn up the tracks a mile further on.

By this time the entire country, with the exception of three provinces, had declared its opposition to the Manchu movement. Tuan Chi-jui came out of his retirement, offering to take command of the republican army. Liang Chi-chao, who was such a force against Yuan Shih-kai, denounced the whole movement.

### The Battle at Peking

The republican troops advanced upon Peking, and on July 7 American, Japanese, and British soldiers arrived at the capital, after having been detained at

Fengtai, where firing between the opposing Chinese forces was in progress; several bullets struck the train, and a Japanese postman was injured. An airplane later dropped a bomb over Fengtai station and wrecked the shed. Chang Hsun's troops at Paoma Chang retired inside the capital without fighting and concentrated at the Temple of Heaven. Another airplane flew over the Forbidden City and dropped bombs. Chang Hsun, on July 8, resigned, but the abdication of the Emperor was not published, his protector holding out for favorable terms.

Vice President Feng Kuo-chang assumed the office of Acting President at Nanking, which was declared the capital of the Provincial Government. Dr. Wu Ting-fang arrived in Shanghai with the seal of the Ministry of Foreign Affairs, although on July 9 the Premier announced that he was dismissed from office. Several Ministers of the Manchu Cabinet on this day were captured while attempting to escape. Chang Hsun refusing to surrender and 50,000 republican troops having surrounded Peking, on July 12, at 4 A. M., the attack was begun in earnest. The battle continued nine hours. Several foreigners were wounded; fire broke out in the Forbidden City; Chang Hsun took refuge in the Dutch Legation, and the republican flag was raised over the Forbidden City. Several thousand of Chang Hsun's troops surrendered and were disarmed and sent back to Hsu-chowfu.

On July 13 Chang Hsun's troops offered to surrender their arms upon payment of $80,000. General Tuan Chi-jui accepted the offer by telegraph and arranged for a temporary loan from the Yokohama Special Bank to make the payment. Chang Hsun's internment came about by his visit to the Legation Quarter, which is neutral territory. He was trying to arrange for mediation. On July 14 Tuan Chi arrived in Peking. President Li left the Japanese Legation for his private residence. On July 15 Tuan Chi-jui assumed the office of Premier, though the southern provinces showed opposition to him. On July 16 Li Yuan-hung entered the Peking French Hospital. Dr. Sun Yat-sen and his party arrived in Canton from Swatow. In an interview he stated it was desirable that the southwestern provinces should be joined together for the restoration of the Provisional Constitution. On July 17 President Li, in a telegram to the provinces, refused to resume office. Mandates were issued appointing Wang Ta-hsieh Minister for Foreign Affairs, and Premier Tuan Chi-jui concurrently Minister of War. The Chin-Pu-Tang Party at Tientsin voted to support the Tuan Government. Acting President Feng Kuo-chang expressed his willingness to succeed Li Yuan-hung.

The present situation still has possibilities of dissension, with the Parliamentarians backed by the southern provinces, and the Kuo-Ming-Tang, or Progressive, Party, opposed to Tuan Chi-jui, and the Chin-Pu-Tang, or Conservative, Party backed by the military Governors. But it has been proved, as one eminent journalist has affirmed, that the monarchy is " stone-dead." The Yuan Shih-kai dynasty lasted eighty-two days, Chang Hsun's lasted eight, and there is no question of the advance of public opinion and popular feeling in this regard.

## Duty of the United States

To those who live in the Orient it seems that America is facing both a duty and a danger in this situation of China and Japan—a situation in which a great people is trying to work out a stable republic, with another people by its side avowedly imperialistic in policy and ready to take advantage of any weakness of its neighbor. The duty is to see that the slogan, " The world must be made safe for democracy," is not restricted merely to the Western Hemisphere. The danger is that, if Japan is allowed to control and use China's resources for its own purposes, the battle against militarism must again be waged in the East as it has been fought in the West.

To reveal the Chinese attitude in this regard I will quote, in conclusion, from the recent utterances of Chinese statesmen and competent foreign critics. Dr. Wu Ting-fang, formerly Minister to the United States, and recently Chinese Secretary of Foreign Affairs, speaking at a tiffin given in his honor by the American University Club on July 13, said:

The war in Europe is being fought to put an end to Prussian militarism; and I want the Americans here to understand that China's present troubles are due to exactly the same causes. We are engaged in a struggle between democracy and militarism. Between 55 and 60 per cent. of the taxes of China are now going to support militarism in China. This must be changed, but the change must be gradual. I ask Americans to be patient and give China a chance. Democracy will triumph. Please be patient with us. Study China and try us from our own point of view instead of your own.

I hope to see the day when the Stars and Stripes and the fire-color flag of China will be intertwined in an everlasting friendship. These nations believe in universal brotherhood; in the rights of the people of small nations to manage their own affairs, as outlined by the great American President in his war declaration. I make this statement with hostility to no nation.

### Hon. C. T. Wang, Vice President of the Chinese Senate, spoke in the same vein:

With the strongly ingrained love for democracy and the firm belief in the necessity of subordinating military authority under the civil, in the character of our people, we do not hesitate for a minute to affirm that in China, just as it is in free and democratic nations of the world, constitutionalism shall prevail over militarism. We, like the Entente Allies, have time on our side. We shall have to make the same sacrifices for the final victory of constitutionalism and democracy as they are making in their titanic struggle on the battlefield of Europe. Let us resolve that we will.

In an address delivered before the semi-centennial anniversary of The New York Nation, Dr. Wellington Koo, Minister to the United States from China, said in part:

In the first place, the people of the Far East feel that in any reconstruction which may take place after the war the Far East should be included; that the problems of the Far East should receive due consideration. * * * In the second place, the reflective minds of the Far East feel that not only the problems of the Far East should be given full consideration,

but also the voice of the Far East should be freely heard at the council board of nations. There is, in the third place, yet another thought which is quickening the hearts of a very large portion of the people in the Far East, particularly of the people in China, and that is, that in any reconstruction to take place hereafter, the base of the foundation should be built upon justice, international justice. The people of the Far East in general feel that every act of aggression, wherever arising, should be a matter of concern, not only of the victim and oppressed, but should also be of serious interest to the world at large; for every act of aggression and oppression, unchecked and uncondemned, is sure to react to the detriment of the international society.

Here between China and the United States, for instance, we have a concrete example of how two nations, always basing their mutual intercourse on justice, could get along in cordial relationship and in perfect understanding; more than a century of trade intercourse, eighty-seven years of missionary work, seven decades of diplomatic relations, and nearly half a century of educational co-operation, have all been characterized by a sustained feeling of friendliness and cordiality, so that Chinese and Americans, wherever they meet, can always talk to each other without hidden thoughts and with perfect confidence in the good-will of each toward the other. There is no suspicion or friction between them. The two countries are living in a happy state of friendship that grows from day to day. What two countries have done can be accomplished by the world at large.

The definite assistance which America could give China was described by C. T. Wang, in an article published July 28, in Shanghai. I knew Mr. Wang at Yale. He has had wide acquaintance with American affairs, and in China has stood for all that is best in its Christian and national life. His article deserves careful reading by American friends of China:

In this vital struggle, where shall America, the champion of democracy, stand? We entirely agree with Mr. Milliard in his views expressed through the editorial columns of his paper [Milliard's Review] on July 28, which we will reproduce here for emphasis:

" A primary requisite is that, as between reversion to an archaic monarchy, " or the retention of a military oligarchy, " or a graduated advance toward genuine " republicanism, the influence of the " United States ought to be thrown " definitely to bring about the latter alter- " native. If this leads to quasi-interfer-

" ence with Chinese politics, then that
" responsibility must be faced. It is becom-
" ing rather ridiculous, at a time when
" America is engaged in a world war,
" when the whole life of the American
" people is being readjusted to meet these
" war conditions, and with the avowed
" principal object of saving democratic
" principles of Government from being
" smothered by autocratic militarism,
" that the power and influence of the
" United States should be applied in one
" place abroad, and should not be applied
" in another place abroad; that direct
" American assistance should be accorded
" to some nations that are trying to cast
" off the yoke of autocracy, and be de-
" nied to other nations that are making
" the same effort."

At any rate, neither France nor Great
Britain, we take it, would raise any
objection to America giving substantial
aid to China. By process of elimination
Japan is the only power left whose attitude is doubtful. Will she object or will
she not, if the United States renews her
open-door policy? If she objects and
does not wish China to grow strong and
united and to establish and develop liberal
and democratic institutions, then, as Mr.
Milliard has well put it: " It is very im-
" portant for China to know it, and for
" the United States to know it." In view
of the repeated assurance given both by
the Japanese Minister of Foreign Affairs
and the Japanese press, we are rather
persuaded to believe that if the United
States renews the open-door policy at this
juncture Japan is likely to fall in with
it.

Besides political assistance, America is

also in an excellent position to aid China
financially, of which she stands so much
in need.

A third way in which America can help
China is to bring China a sufficient number of experts who can aid China to
establish and develop large industrial
plants and factories and to train and
bring up a large force of native industrial
and technical leaders.

Mr. T. F. Milliard, the foremost journalist and authority on matters in the
Far East, on July 21 voiced his idea of
America's duty very clearly. With it I
will close:

Yes, it is very inconvenient for democracy, at the time when the issue of a
world war is narrowing down to a test
of the fate of democracy, to have two
great nations like Russia and China trying republicanism for the first time, and
under precarious conditions; for the difficulties of Russia approximate the internal difficulties of China with republicanism. But just because the local and
general conditions are rather unfavorable,
and further because of the linking of these
experiments with the cause of democracy
throughout the world by reason of the
war, it becomes virtually impossible for
the United States to remain a mere spec-
tator of the course of events in Russia
and China. Action to hearten, encourage,
and support Russia already has been
taken by the United States Government.
Action to hearten, encourage, and support China in her effort to maintain a republic ought to be devised and undertaken without delay.

# The Surrender of Chang Hsun's Army

*A correspondent of The London Times,
writing from Peking on July 17, 1917,
gave this account of the brief battle that
ended the dream of Manchu restoration:*

PEKING has a population of a
million souls, two-thirds of whom
are contained within the three-
mile square of the Tartar City and the
other third within its southern attach-
ment, the Chinese City. When 30,000
or 40,000 soldiers choose to fight a
battle within so restricted an area it
is plain that the inhabitants thereof
must taste of the bitterness of death,
even though they may happily survive
the ordeal. If Peking huddled itself
indoors on the night of Wednesday,

June 11, there was reason for it.
Chang Hsun had refused to surrender,
and the republicans were coming to
smoke him out. The Legation Guards
and the foreign volunteers were standing by. Foreigners resident outside the
Legation quarter were coming in. The
streets were filled with police pledged
to prevent looting and to protect civilians. In the very dead of night the
dread thing began to happen. At the
various gates battalion after battalion
poured in and filled the streets. Guns
were laboriously dragged up the ramps
and mounted on the walls. Chang
Hsun made no attempt to hold the
entrances. He let the enemy close in

upon him on all sides. Despite his reputation as a filibuster, he is a child in the art of war.

The roar of guns waked me while dawn was yet below the horizon. As I tumbled into my clothes I could hear the quivering treble of machine guns and musketry competing with the bass of the artillery. It was no affair of outposts, but a royal bombardment with all arms. The quarter-mile along the Austrian glacis was not pleasant walking, for many bullets near the end of their flight sighed past, some thudding into the walls of the adjacent houses and a few spurting up dust on the road before me. Never a soul to be seen except the police crouching at the corners, feverishly anxious for my company. In the telegraph office I found the whole staff strung up to concert pitch and all the wires down; that is not a witticism, but the melancholy truth. My intention of apprising the world of what was happening almost before it had happened was defeated because of those broken wires. Meanwhile the din was terrific and spent bullets were clattering in the veranda. I climbed to the roof, and there, high above the rest of Peking, I was able to survey the fairest of scenes.

Nothing in sight moved, yet the whole city reverberated to the continuous thunder of a heavy bombardment. Guns posted in the west were shelling a corner of the Imperial City close at hand, where Chang Hsun had his residence, with his men camped round him. His guns were replying in that direction, and firing eastward almost over my head. I could hear the rushing of the projectiles, as it were, screwing their way through a resisting medium. Bullets thinly wailed in the air above, and some thumped disagreeably into the iron roof rising behind me. One with a nasty scrunch took a corner of a brick out of a chimney beside me. There came a new sound, a droning as of a monster bee, rising and falling to the ear, as it reached one through the instable air. Into the blue above sailed an airplane, slowly and persistently pursuing its way. It was heading for Chang Hsun's corner, and I

eagerly watched until there streaked down from it a bomb upon which the sun momentarily gleamed. A roar, and a sudden rising cloud, showed that there had happened somewhere below what is a commonplace to you at home.

Chang Hsun had let himself be divided, half in the Temple of Heaven, half in the Imperial City, within which, in the Purple Forbidden Palace, the little Emperor, his empire hopelessly in the dust, crouched in terror. The two forces were separately attacked in overwhelming numbers, and, despite the handicap on the attackers so to manage that the Legation Quarter and the Manchu Palaces and the swarming, uncomplaining herd of the people might suffer as little as possible, the battle was soon won. The Temple of Heaven was surrounded and commanded by artillery. Rushing in the teeth of machine guns proved dangerous to life, and the besieging General sent men under the white flag to propose terms. The besieged agreed to capitulate, and to surrender their arms on payment of three months' wages, the money to be delivered before nightfall. Visitors later in the day inspecting the scene found royalists and republicans fraternizing, and disputing amicably over their tea as to who were the real winners.

At the Imperial City the attackers captured the eastern gate, and with that in their possession were able to scale the walls and to drive the defenders into the maze of lanes in rear. On the western side Chang Hsun's men were pressed back into the outer courtyard of the Forbidden City. At this juncture Chang Hsun realized the silence around the Temple of Heaven, and, conceiving the game up, went off to the Legation Quarter to ask for mediation. Meanwhile his men, now located where they were difficult to get at without damage to the palaces, kept up a desultory fire that made a noble noise, but constituted no real defense. When they were advised that their leader was detained in the Legation Quarter they surrendered gladly—to the police. Foreign visitors were on the spot to see, almost before the few dead were cold. Two of Chang Hsun's wounded had had their heads cut off. One man had been electrocuted by a falling wire. The telephone wires streamed from the posts like a woman's hair hung out to dry. Chang Hsun's luxurious house was a burned-out shell. His armored motor car had been pierced by many bullets, and the horses of his bodyguard, tethered to a wall, were strung up by the necks in fantastic positions, dead as mutton.

Now that all is over we know that the total for both sides, and including Chinese and foreign civilians and the legation guards on duty, is 25 killed and 45 wounded.

# Japan's New Pledge Regarding China

## Statement by Viscount Ishii

CHINA'S suspicions of Japanese aggression, mentioned in the foregoing article by Professor Wheeler, were the subject of an official denial by Viscount Ishii, head of the Japanese Imperial Mission to the United States. In the course of a noteworthy address delivered in New York on Sept. 30, 1917, at the Mayor's banquet in his honor, the Mikado's official spokesman assured his audience that the doors of both Japan and China were always open to Americans, and continued:

In spite of all the effort to make you believe that Japan as she grew stronger was always trying to close the door, I tell you that there never has been an hour when our common sense or our sense of our own responsibility failed us. Why close our door in violation of our pledges, or endeavor to close our neighbor's door, when we are in honor bound to protect it?

The opportunity for you to trade in Japan or China has never been an equal opportunity in its literal sense. As you went far afield and brought us knowledge of the West, taught us how to grow and how to trade, so we, as we gained wisdom, knowledge, and strength, went into other fields to trade and to learn. We went to China, where the door was open to us as to you, and we have always realized that there nature gave us an advantage. There was no need—there is no need—to close that door on you, because we welcome your fair and honest competition in the markets everywhere. We are trading there where we have a natural advantage, and where, unless we are very stupid or very inactive, we are bound to succeed, and we are trading here where your advantage is equally and naturally as great.

I am persuaded that the grumblings and the whisperings about a door closed in China by the Japanese against America did not come from the broad and generous heart of the enterprising American in New York or elsewhere, but are the result of ten years of an enemy's effort to create prejudice and distrust. Gentlemen, I assure you that a closed door in China has never been and never will be the policy of my Government. The door is open, the field is there. We welcome co-operation and competition, all tending to the betterment of the equal opportunity.

But this propaganda of ill-will has by no means stopped with the persistent cry of "closed door." Much has been written about Japan's policy toward China as being one that sought only the aggrandizement of Japan and the confusion, disruption, or oppression of our neighbor. Here again let me reassure you. The policy of Japan with regard to China has always been the same. We want good government, which means peace, security, and development of opportunity in China. The slightest disturbance in China immediately reacts upon Japan. Our trade there is large and increasing; it is valuable to us, and China is our friendly neighbor—with vast and increasing potentialities for trade.

Circumstances for which we were in no sense responsible gave us certain rights on Chinese territory, but at no time in the past and at no time in the future did we or will we seek to take territory from China or to despoil China of her rights. We wish to be and to always continue to be the sincere friend and helper of our neighbor, for we are more interested than any one else except China in good government there, only we must at all times, for self-protection, prevent other nations from doing what we have no right to do.

We will not only not seek to assail the integrity or the sovereignty of China, but will eventually be prepared to defend and maintain the same integrity and independence of China against any aggressor. For we know that our own landmarks would be threatened by any outside invasion or interference in China.

For many years our common enemy has been the worst enemy of China. Since the outbreak of the war in Europe, China has been a hotbed of German intrigue, and in all of this China has perhaps been the greatest sufferer. I cannot give you the positive proofs about the German in the Far East as you have had them placed before you by the alert authorities in Washington, but I can give you as my conviction that the German in China is responsible for most of the unfortunate occurrences and the malicious widespread misinformation scattered throughout the world for the purpose of impairing the relations of the countries concerned in China and securing the downfall of China to Germany's advantage.

When Japan or America appeared to make progress in China we always have had sinister rumor of oppression or the false suggestion of a policy directed against the integrity of that country; boycotts which have cost you first of all and then us ill-spared millions; revolution, disturbances, and civil war have prevented a development by which China, first of all, and her honest friends might profit.

The Pacific Ocean is our common highway. It is guarded, and the highway has been swept by our ships of the pirates of the seas, so that our countries' trade may continue and our intercourse be uninterrupted. We guard the Pacific Ocean together with our ships, but more than this, and better than the ships or the men or the guns, is the assurance of the notes exchanged between your Secretary of State, Elihu Root, and our Ambassador Takahira, in 1908, in which it was mutually agreed and "formally resolved to respect the territorial possessions belonging to each other in the region of the Pacific Ocean." Gentlemen, Japan is satisfied with this. Are you? If so, there is no Pacific Ocean question between us. We will co-operate. We will help and we will hold, each of us, what is guaranteed under that agreement.

This notable utterance was characterized by some newspapers as the declaration of a Monroe Doctrine for Asia. In a speech to New York press representatives, two days later, Viscount Ishii said this was inaccurate, and went on to emphasize and clarify his meaning by this further statement:

In a speech delivered on Saturday night I made particular reference to the policy of Japan with regard to China. This reference took the form of a repetition of the pledge and promise that Japan would not violate the political independence or territorial integrity of China; would at all times regard the high principle of the open door and equal opportunity. Now I find that this utterance of mine is taken as the enunciation of a "Monroe Doctrine in Asia." I want to make it very clear to you that the application of the term "Monroe Doctrine" to this policy and principle, voluntarily outlined and pledged by me, is inaccurate.

There is this fundamental difference between the "Monroe Doctrine" of the United States as to Central and South America and the enunciation of Japan's attitude toward China. In the first there is on the part of the United States no engagement or promise, while in the other Japan voluntarily announces that Japan will herself engage not to violate the political or territorial integrity of her neighbor, and to observe the principle of the open door and equal opportunity, asking at the same time other nations to respect these principles.

Therefore, gentlemen, you will mark the wide difference and agree with me, I am sure, that the use of the term is somewhat loose and misleading. I ask you to note this with no suggestion that I can or any one else does question the policy or attitude of your country, which we well know will always deal fairly and honorably with other nations.

Ex-President Taft, who was one of the speakers at the Mayor's banquet, referred in these words to the agreement made with Japan by President Roosevelt:

In Mr. Roosevelt's Administration what was called a "gentlemen's agreement" was made with Japan, and in my Administration the treaty then existing was succeeded by another treaty into which was incorporated that same "gentlemen's agreement," and it is only the truth of history to say that that agreement by the gentlemen of Japan has been kept as gentlemen keep agreements.

# China's Treatment of Enemy Aliens

*K. K. Kawakami, a correspondent of The New York Evening Post, wrote from Tientsin on Aug. 17, 1917:*

THIS is a memorable day for China. For the first time since Western powers established exterritoriality within her borders, China has ordered two European nations to give up that privilege, at least for the time being. Today 300 Chinese police invaded the German and Austrian settlements in Tientsin, and raised the flag of the Republic of China where till yesterday flew the ensigns of the Governments at Berlin and Vienna. The subjects of the Central Powers, some 300 in number, have accepted the inevitable in a matter-of-fact fashion and have surrendered themselves to the jurisdiction of the Chinese authorities.

The German settlement here measures 650 acres, and that of Austria-Hungary 184 acres. The idea of foreign settlements with exterritorial rights originated with the British and the French, who, as early as 1860, secured 950 acres and 250 acres, respectively, for the purpose of establishing in China an imperium in imperio. In 1900, Germany, Japan, Russia, Austria, Italy, and Belgium followed suit. Last year France, by an exhibition of force, succeeded in adding a large area to her original settlement.

Germany's only other settlement in China is that in Hankow, with an area of 506,000 square yards. It is the largest of all foreign concessions in that city, and was established in 1895. This has also been taken over by the Chinese authorities.

Perhaps the greatest source of German influence has been the Deutsche-Asiatische Bank, with its head office at Shanghai and its branches at Tientsin, Peking, Hankow, Canton, Tsing-tao, and Tsinan-fu. Organized in 1889, the bank has been the financing agent in China for the German Government. Among its chief investments, amounting to some hundred million dollars, are: (1) Loan to the Chinese Government for military reform; (2) part of Anglo-German loan to the Chinese Government; (3) part of second Anglo-German loan to the Chinese Government; (4) loan for currency reform; (5) part of five-power loan to China; (6) Hu-kwan Railway bond; (7) Tientsin-Pukow Railway bond; (8) second Tientsin-Pukow Railway bond.

When Chinese officials seized the office of the Deutsche-Asiatische Bank, it was found that the funds had been disposed of, only a pittance remaining in the coffers of each office. As the bank is obviously an organ of the German Government, its investments in China, as well as its property, are likely to be confiscated. The following regulations, just issued by the Chinese Government, indicate the course of action it will take in disposing of the interests of the bank:

(1.) All moneys deposited in the said bank by the German Government or Government institutions shall be confiscated.

(2.) Apart from whatever property or moneys in the said bank which are to be confiscated, the employes of the said bank shall liquidate all other accounts and hand to the Government officials a detailed statement thereof, so that the Government may appoint special officials to seal such property in order that it may be adequately protected.

(3.) All loans made to the Chinese Government by the said bank shall no longer be binding on the Chinese Government in case the concessions or rights secured on such loans are controlled by the German Government. In case such rights or concessions are exercised by German civilians, they should be held in abeyance until after the war, and until diplomatic relations between the two countries have been revised.

(4.) No payments shall be made on deposits in the said bank by enemy subjects.

At this moment there are at Shanghai six German merchant vessels, with a total tonnage of 15,431, and three Austrian vessels, aggregating 9,491 tons. At Swatow are four German ships, totaling 6,203, and at Amoy one German ship of 1,770 tons. All in all, fourteen vessels, of 32,895 tons, have been seized by the Chinese Government.

Of German employes of the Chinese Government, there are 126, not including German teachers employed in various

Chinese schools. These have already been dismissed, with their salaries paid up to the end of this month. As for German teachers in schools maintained by the Central or Provisional Governments, they will be permitted to remain in their respective posts as long as they live quietly and keep aloof from politics.

While the Britishers and Frenchmen in this part of the world are jubilant over China's entry into the war, they are dissatisfied with China's decision not to expel or intern all Germans, civilians as well as others, but simply to register them with a view to securing their orderly, peaceful conduct. Roughly estimated, there are about 2,000 Germans in all China—500 in Shanghai, 400 in Hankow, 300 in Tientsin, 200 each in Tsing-tao, and Tsinan-fu, 100 in Peking, and the rest scattered in different parts of the country.

# The War Record of the British Dependencies

THE British dependencies, that is, the various crown colonies and protectorates, which are distinct from the self-governing colonies, or dominions, have a war record which, if not so conspicuous as that of the other sections of the British Empire, is none the less remarkable in view of their resources.

The British West Indies have a male population of about 1,040,000 in all, of whom some 150,000 are East Indian coolies. The proportion of Europeans varies from 1 per cent. to 5 per cent. Practically every available man went to England to join the army, as is shown by the impossibility of finding European officers for the West Indian contingents. From the negro population, in addition to the two battalions of the old regular West India Regiment, there have been raised contingents forming the British West Indies Regiment, which is drawn from all the West Indian colonies, and is now a very considerable force. There are also local defense forces.

Europeans also returned to England from the Eastern colonies in large numbers to join the new army. Ceylon sent a contingent 230 strong in November, 1914, and has since sent smaller parties home to enlist. In Malaya, which has sent home a very large number of Europeans to join the army, commissions have now been appointed on the lines of the tribunals at home, to decide between volunteers for service and their employers, and similar action is being taken in Hongkong. In spite of the fact that there have been a rising in the Straits Settlements and very serious riots in Ceylon, these colonies have released their standing garrisons by raising local volunteer forces, and have made, or are making, service compulsory for Europeans. Hongkong did not require compulsion, because every fit man volunteered.

Fiji, out of a total white population of about 4,000, has sent contingents to the British Army of 141 men, besides which about 280 men have joined the Australian or New Zealand expeditionary forces, or have enlisted in England.

Of the smaller non-African colonies Bermuda, out of a population of 6,700 Europeans, has contributed a company to a British regiment and a force of field and garrison artillery from the colored population, besides providing a militia regiment for the garrison. The Falkland Islands and St. Helena have raised volunteer regiments for garrison duty.

The British forces which operated in Togoland and the Cameroons were almost entirely natives of West Africa, and the campaign which ended in the conquest of the Northern Cameroons was carried out by the Nigerian regiment of the West African frontier force. Nigerian troops have been sent to East Africa, and a large number of carriers (for whom there is an urgent demand) are continually going. It is impossible to reduce the garrisons in West Africa below a certain number, as the possibility of local trouble is always present. The number of officers and noncommissioned officers who have had experience with West African troops is limited, and to meet the shortage a large number of officials and other civilians with West African experience have been given temporary commissions. Native marine ratings have been recruited in Nigeria for service in Mesopotamia.

The conquest of Togoland, so far as the British share in that achievement is concerned, was carried out singlehanded by the Gold Coast; while the colonies of the Gambia, Sierra Leone, and the Gold Coast all sent contingents to assist in the operations in the Cameroons, (1914-16.) Since then the Gold Coast has sent nearly all its standing military force to East Africa to assist in the operations against the Germans, and the Gambia has sent the whole of the military force that it maintains to the same theatre. The standing military forces of Sierra Leone are being utilized as a garrison for Sierra Leone and the Gambia; other companies have been lent to Nigeria. On the other hand, Sierra Leone is now raising large numbers of carriers for service in East Africa.

Most of the Europeans in these colonies are Government officials (including military officers) and employes of trading and mining firms. As regards the latter class, many have returned to England for service with the army, and others have been drawn upon to accompany combatant troops and carriers to East Africa, or for service with the local garrisons. The East Africa Protectorate was one of the first parts of the empire to adopt the principle of compulsory service. As far as settlers of military age are concerned, more than two-thirds are on military service, while of the European officials some 40 per cent. have joined the colors. In Uganda and Ny-

asaland, although the European population is smaller, every available European of military age is on military service. Although the native populations are large, the tribes that are warlike and suitable for fighting material are comparatively scarce. The local native force (other than police) of the three protectorates of East Africa, Uganda, and Nyasaland, is known as the King's African Rifles. They are being fully employed in the operations against German East Africa. In addition, some irregular native troops have been raised in the East Africa Protectorate and Uganda for the local operations, and an immense number of carriers have been recruited. Zanzibar, which was formerly dependent for its garrison on the East Africa Protectorate, has now raised a defense force of its own, and provides for its own safety.

Rhodesia has provided a regiment which participated in the campaign against German Southwest Africa; and another Rhodesian contingent, nearly 1,000 strong, partly recruited in the Union of South Africa, was sent to East Africa, and has been employed in the operations. The Northern Rhodesia police and volunteer forces, and a native Matabele regiment, in addition to several thousand carriers, are also now engaged in the operations against German East Africa from the south, under Brig. Gen. Northey. Moreover, considerable numbers of Rhodesians have gone independently to England and joined British regiments. In a few of the colonies it is " impossible to raise a unit of any military value." In such a case all that can be done is to raise " labor battalions " as and when the military authorities require.

# THE EUROPEAN WAR AS SEEN BY CARTOONISTS

[English Cartoon]

## Growing Weaker

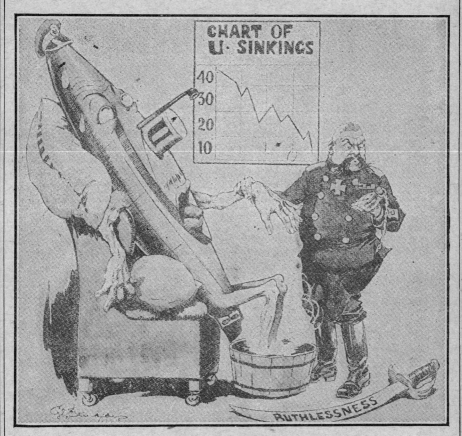

—*From The Passing Show, London.*

The doctor is trying to keep up hope.

# Kerensky

—© *Le Rire, Paris.*

It needs a strong grip to drive a chariot of State with such a team.

# The Art of Camouflage

—© *Le Rire, Paris.*

" And to think that before the war I was doing miniatures ! "

# The Russian Napoleon

*—From Kladderadatsch, Berlin.*

KERENSKY: "This is very unpleasant! My Napoleonic career seems likely to *begin* with the burning of Moscow."

# Between the Devil and the Deep Sea

—*From Iberia, Barcelona.*

Chancellor Michaelis has to choose between "Disastrous Peace" and "Disastrous War." Which will he take?

# Two Views of Freedom

The people led by Freedom—and

*From Nebelspalter, Zurich.*

The people after they have been led by Freedom.

# Forced to Re-tire

—*From The People, London.*

# A Blighted Troth

—*From The Sunday Evening Telegram, London.*

PRESIDENT WILSON: "Sakes alive! D'you think I'd advise any Old World to hang its chances of peace on the word of a blighter like that?—only chance is to hang hi-m!!"

# "What Will You Give for Her?"

—From The New York World.

Germany wants "peace by negotiation."

# Post-Bellum Honors

ERECTED TO
THE DISCREDITABLE MEMORY OF
THE MAN WHO, DURING THE GREAT
FIGHT IN DEFENSE OF OUR LIBERTY,
WENT ABOUT ASKING,
"WHAT ARE WE FIGHTING FOR?"

*—From The Halifax Herald.*

A statue to be erected after the war.

# Time as England's Ally

—*From Kladderadatsch, Berlin.*

"She takes such long steps, Tommy—we can't keep up."

# Why We Are Fighting

For the Freedom of the Seas.

For the Republic to Which We Owe
Our National Life.

That Conquest Shall Not Enslave
Democracy.

That Might Shall Not Enslave Right.

—*Robert Carter in Philadelphia Press.*

# More Power

*—From The New York Times.*

**Getting ready for a long run.**

# Why We Are at War

—From The Chicago Herald.

# "Drink Up, and Let's Go"

—From The Chicago Herald.

# No Joking Matter

—*From The Philadelphia Press.*

THE KAISER: "Don't laugh, son. That's the man who ruined the royalty business."

# Kindred Spirits

—*Rochester Union and Advertiser.*

But the greatest of these is William Hohenzollern.

# Easier Said Than Done

—*From The Passing Show, London.*

THE PRESIDENT: "Here is the road to democracy and you will find rest and peace when you reach the top."

GERMAN PEOPLE: "But that armed man bars the way!"

THE PRESIDENT: "Well, just throw him on one side."

[President Wilson's reply to the Pope's Peace Manifesto was to the effect that no negotiations could proceed until the German people adopted democratic institutions and removed their present rulers.]

## Wilhelm: "Do Your Worst— This War May Be Our Last"

## "Ach, That Dog, Now He Wants the Moon!"

—Portland Oregonian.

—Baltimore American.

## The Blow Almost Killed Father

## Eventually, So Why Not Now?

—Washington Star.

—St. Joseph News-Press.

## German Diplomacy

—*Chicago Herald.*

## " I'll Give Up Belgium, See!"

—*St. Louis Post-Dispatch.*

## William Apologizes

—*Birmingham Age-Herald.*

## The End of the Trail

—*Charleston News and Courier.*

## Only Yesterday 'Twas But a Speck on the Horizon

—Dayton News.

## Argentina Proves That Republics Are Ungrateful

—Dayton News.

## They Want the Case Dismissed

—Dallas News.

## Next!

—Dallas News.

## Another Failure—The Stockholm Peace Conference

The game refused to be lured into the trap by the bright light. —*From the Amsterdammer, Amsterdam.*

# COUNT GEORG VON HERTLING

The New Imperial Chancellor of Germany in Succession to
Dr. Michaelis.
*(Photo International Film Service.)*

# VITTORIO ORLANDO

Who Has Succeeded Bosselli as Premier of Italy. Orlando Was
Formerly Minister of the Interior.

# PERIOD XXXIX.

American Troops' First Fight in Europe—Austro-German Invasion of Italy—The Battle of Flanders—French Victory at Chemin des Dames—Russia's Radicals in Revolt—United States Army 1,800,000 Strong—The Supreme War Council—Brazil at War with Germany—President Wilson's Labor Address—Effect of the United States in the War—Germany's Political Changes—French War Economies—Zeppelins in a New Raid Meet Disaster—What the Belgian Army is Doing—The Armed Merchantman—The Kaiser's Responsibility—The Systematic Exploitation of Belgium—A Chapter of German Atrocities—The Reorganization of Rumania—Australasia's Record in the War—The English in India—In the War Prisons of Eastern Siberia—A Historic Peace Conference—Armed and Armored Automobiles in the War—Japanese-American Agreement Regarding China.

# WAR COUNCIL TRIUMPHS

## Lloyd George Wins Parliament to the Allied Council Plan by Notable Speech

*Premier Lloyd George delivered a notable speech in Parliament on the evening of Nov. 19, 1917, in defense of the plan to establish a Supreme War Council, in which Great Britain, France, Italy, and the United States should jointly participate. Earlier details of this important change of allied methods appear on Pages 434-436 of this issue. It had been announced previously that former Premier Herbert H. Asquith would be the spokesman for the opposition, and the debate was looked forward to as the most serious attack on Lloyd George since his accession to power. The New York Times received the full text of the speech of the Premier by special cable, and consequently it is inserted in this issue of the magazine as a special supplement, the regular forms of the December issue having been closed.*

MR. ASQUITH in opening the discussion said that in war responsibility for what was done and what was left undone rested on the shoulders of the Government of the day. It was the business of the advisers of the Government to give counsel as to the best means whereby the policy of the Government could be brought to a successful issue.

It was of vital importance in war that there should be frequent and intimate consultations among the statesmen of the Allies and as complete co-ordination as circumstances permitted. Germany had the advantage that the policy of all the Governments of that alliance was decided by a central authority; Austria and Turkey had no voice in either policy or strategy.

"It is urgent," continued Mr. Asquith, "that the Allies develop by all the means possible the machinery for complete consultation, communication, and co-ordination. We should welcome any scheme or arrangement which would provide for more frequent communication between the General Staffs, supplemented by the appointment of liaison officers of high rank."

### Against Interfering with Staffs

He would deprecate, however, said Mr. Asquith, the setting up of any organization that would interfere with the responsibility of the General Staffs to their Governments, or derogate in any way from the authority and legitimate responsibility of each of the allied staffs to its own people.

Dealing with the Premier's speech in Paris, (part of which is printed on Page 435,) Mr. Asquith strongly emphasized that there was no mention of the navy, while in many aspects of the war the navy dominated strategical considerations. It suggested unity of control and meant unity of command, but he did not desire to read any such purpose into the Premier's statement. He asked whether the advisory staff officer would have a separate staff and what would happen if his staff and the General Staff were not in agreement. Which would give way or decide the question?

Sir Edward Carson, interrupting: "The War Cabinet."

Mr. Asquith said that the object of the debate was to dispel certain misapprehensions which had been excited, not so much by the scheme as by the Paris speech. Referring to that speech, he went on to say that while he would continue to eschew all unnecessary controversy, he would be failing in his duty if he were to pass it by.

The Premier had selected four cases in criticism of the allied strategy—two, Serbia and Rumania, in which he himself and Mr. Lloyd George had in their respective capacities equal responsibility, and two, Russia and Italy, which belonged to this year. Mr. Lloyd George's view regarding Serbia was not the view taken by any military authority of weight in this country, he asserted.

The proposition that there was only one front was perfectly sound, and one of the corollaries was that you might render the best service to any ally at one end of the line by exerting the maximum effort at the other end of the line. It was a sacred trust of the Allies to see that the future freedom and security of Serbia and Rumania were adequately assured.

Mr. Asquith went over the Premier's references in his Paris speech to Russia and Italy and asked what the Premier meant by "we." He suggested a doubt whether a council at Versailles last March would have affected the Russian situation. He also asked whether it was not a fact that up to the eve of the German attack General Cadorna was full of confidence and serenity and gave assurances that he would triumph over it.

"Lloyd George regaled the good people of Paris," he added, "with irrelevant rhetoric."

Mr. Asquith doubted whether any allied council would have interfered with the successful offensives in the west in favor of more attractive adventures elsewhere. He concluded:

"We have no reason to be ashamed of our contribution to the war. We have kept the seas free. We have expanded our army into seventy divisions, and we have placed our arsenals and credit at the disposal of our allies, and so we will go on to the end."

## Premier Lloyd George's Address

*The full text of the Premier's speech in reply is as follows:*

"My right honorable friend's speech divided itself naturally into two parts. The first dealt with a practical, and therefore most important, question, and the other dealt with the question of the presentment of the case. With regard to the first he examined our proposals in a calm and dispassionate way, and I hope I shall follow his example.

"I shall first deal with one or two criticisms which he offered upon the question as to whether it is desirable to secure greater unity of control and, if so, whether we have adopted the right method of securing that unity. That is far more important than anything else which has taken place in Paris or elsewhere.

"I am glad my right honorable friend made my task very much easier by practically accepting the principle upon which we based our action. He admits there is need for greater co-operation and co-ordination.

"I don't think he has denied that the mere machinery which was adopted when he was Prime Minister and which I subsequently adopted, the machinery of conferences and consultations between the Allies, has not proved all that was necessary. What he does deny—and I shall come to that later—is that, although the present machinery is inadequate, he does not accept my proposition that the Allies have suffered substantially in consequence. On that ground I shall join issue with him later on.

### Suffered from Defects of System

" I think we have suffered grievously, as I explicitly said in Paris, through no fault of any individual or any staff, but owing to defects of the system. That is why I thought the time had come to make a complete change in the method of co-ordinating our position.

" As my right honorable friend has said, the enemy had the advantage in the possession of interior lines. That is the reason why we should do our best to overcome that advantage by co-ordinating our effort.

" This is not the first time that Germany has won through the lack of co-ordination on the part of allies. In the time of Frederick the Great, in spite of an overwhelming mass of material and men against him, his important success was attributable in the main to the fact that the allied powers did not co-ordinate their efforts. It is essential that we should avoid the mistakes of the past, either in this campaign or elsewhere.

" May I just say that any criticism which I have directed against the past in proposing this change in our method of securing common action was not directed against any staff or any Commander in Chief either in this or any other country. It is the business of the Commander in Chief to look after his own particular front. It is not his business to survey the whole field of operations in Europe, Asia, and Africa. It is quite as much as he can do to look after

his own particular front. I made no attack upon General Sir Douglas Haig, Sir William Robertson, or any other army chiefs.

### First Proposed by Kitchener

" Who was it first suggested this idea of co-ordination? I see there is a suggestion (my right honorable friend has not made himself responsible for it, but it has been freely stated outside) that this scheme is part of the civilian attempt to interfere with soldiers.

" Who was the first to suggest it? It was Lord Kitchener in 1915, and he proposed it in almost the very same terms in which I recommended it in Paris. That was in 1915, and I say that if his advice had been followed—I admit there were difficulties then and that it's easier to-day—if it had been carried out at the time by the Allies, I say without hesitation that we should have been further forward in the war by now. But here again I am not criticising anybody. After all, the Allies are taught by the difficulties and disasters which come through lack of common action.

" The second time it was proposed was in July of this year. A meeting of the chiefs of the allied staff in Great Britain, France, and Italy passed a resolution urging the necessity of unity of action on the western front by the promoting of an interallied military organization, which would study and prepare for the rapid movement of troops from one theatre to another.

" Therefore, when it is suggested that there is a device on the part of civilians to get control of strategy, I am glad of this opportunity of quoting the authority of three great soldiers as proof that its initiative and suggestion came in the first instance not from politicians.

" Now I come to the second point. Having argued that it is desirable to get some sort of control at the front, working in co-ordination, what is the best method of doing it? We examined three alternative proposals. The first, put forward in responsible quarters, was the appointment of a generalissimo for the whole of the allied forces. I was utterly opposed to that suggestion. For reasons which it would not be desirable to dicuss here it would be attended with the greatest difficulty.

### America for Going Further

" Another suggestion which found favor not only in France but, I observe, also in America, was that the committee should have greater power than we proposed to confer upon it. Therefore the idea of America is not that we have gone too far but that we have not gone far enough. There are reasons why I think that it would be undesirable to set up a separate authority unless we are driven to it by the failure of the present experiment, for the success of which goodwill and co-operation on the part of all concerned are essential. Soldiers will represent all allied countries. They will be assisted by technical advisers, drawn from all the allied armies, which will help the various Governments to co-ordinate their plans.

" That is the present proposal. What are its advantages? The first is that the information which is at the disposal of each of the allied States will be at the disposal of a central council. The second advantage of the new council is that it will be a permanent body. Under the old system there was only one meeting a year between the allied staffs. That meeting was held for the purpose of surveying the strategy to be pursued on thousands of miles of front, on which millions of men were engaged. It was utterly impossible.

" Therefore, I say, an essential part of this scheme, if it is to achieve its object, is that it should be permanent.

### Must Survey the Whole Field

" It will be the duty of this central body to survey the whole field and not merely a part. It may be said that each General Staff does that at present. Well, in a sense they are bound to consider not only their own front but other fronts as well, but it is a secondary matter. They naturally do not devote the same study to it. There is always delicacy on the part of any General Staff to criticise another General.

" With regard to the Italian front it is very difficult to give answers about these matters without saying something which will hurt, perhaps, our ally. My right honorable friend asked me questions about what General Cadorna has said, and I am not sure that I can answer him. I don't want to be pressed about it. I would rather not, because there is a great deal to be said about that and a good deal to be said about our view about the position of the Italian Army that is much more important from the point of view of our country, but it was a view we could not press. We were not responsible for the Italian front.

" The advantage of the central council is that we would have the right to press the things we knew, suspected, or believed about the Italian front as much as about our own. The Italian Government knew something about it, but naturally Sir William Robertson would not go on pressing things about another front beyond a certain point. We got to the consideration of them, but it was too late.

" That is one of the difficulties of the old system, but it must come to an end if you are going to insure victory. The Italian front is important to our front, and whatever happens there affects the operations on ours.

"That is why we have come to the conclusion that the mere machinery of liaison officers which we had, that the occasional meeting of Ministers and Chiefs of Staffs once or twice a year, is utterly inadequate, utterly inefficient for the purpose of securing real co-ordination, and that you must have a permanent body constantly watching these things, constantly advising upon them, and constantly reporting on them to the Government whether as to the French, Italian, or Russian front.

"With regard to the navy, I can assure my right honorable friend that representation of the navy is not an afterthought; it is essential that all information regarding naval operations should be known to these military advisers. That is a different thing to the establishment of a naval council and to co-ordinating naval strategy. A good deal can be said for that. We are suffering from lack of it now, anybody who knows what is happening in the Mediterranean could tell that. There is a great deal to be said for a similar council dealing with naval strategy to that which is set up for military considerations. But that is a very different thing.

"My right honorable friend asked whether the new council would have its own expert staff or would it be dependent on information supplied by the individual staffs. You cannot set up there a rival intelligence department. It would be utterly impracticable and thoroughly mischievous. We have about the best Intelligence Department probably in Europe, and one of the most distinguished soldiers in the army at the head of it. The only staff you require there is a staff necessary to co-ordinate the information which comes from the various staffs. The final decision must remain with the Government. That is the case now. There will be no change after this has been done.

### Paris Speech Was Deliberate

"My honorable friend challenged some things I said in Paris. Let me say at once about the speech, that I considered it carefully. It is suggested that I was assisted by Mr. Churchill. That speech was written and handed over to be interpreted before I saw the right honorable gentleman. I never altered a comma of it, and he never knew what I was going to say until he heard me at that particular meeting.

"Naturally, this has been worked up into a web of intrigue. If that speech was wrong, I cannot plead any impulse and that it was something I said on the moment. I had considered it, and I did it for a deliberate purpose.

"I have seen resolutions for unity and for co-ordination. Where are they? You might as well throw them straight away into the waste-paper basket. Lord Kitchener tried it on Jan. 28, 1915. I have seen other schemes by M. Briand and my right honorable friend. Somehow or other they all came to nought because naturally you get the disinclination of independent bodies to merge their individualities in a sort of common organization. It is inevitable, and I was afraid that this would end in the same way.

"We went to Rapallo with a document —a carefully prepared document. It was passed by the Cabinet before I left, but I was afraid of this. There was a beautifully drafted document prepared by the Allies at two or three conferences. Nothing happened—simply an announcement in the papers that at last we had found some means of co-ordination.

"There had been too much of that,

and I made up my mind to take the risks, and I took them, to arouse public sentiment, not here merely, but in France, in Italy, and in America, to get public sentiment behind us, to see that this document became an act.

"It is not easy to arouse public opinion. I may know nothing of military strategy, but I do know something of political strategy. And to convince and to get public opinion interested in a proposal and to convince them of the desirability of it is an essential part of political strategy. That is why I did it, and it has done it. [Loud cheers.] I determined to deliver a disagreeable speech that would force everybody to talk about this scheme, and they have talked about it.

"The result is that America is in, Italy is in, France is in, Britain is in, and public opinion is in, and that is vital.

"The suggestion is made that I am blaming my own country, but I am not.

"My right honorable friend instanced the illustrations of Serbia, Rumania, Russia, and Italy. But France was just as responsible for them as we were, but no more. Italy was surely responsible. It was not a pleasant thing for Italy or for me to remind them that they had lost 2,500 guns. It was more pleasant to say that we had captured a kilometer than to say to Italy that she had lost 200,000 prisoners. It was disagreeable all around, but it was necessary in order to give force to the movement.

"The field is north, south, east, and west. Our business is to bring pressure on the enemy from every point of the compass, and inflict hurt on him where you can.

"That is our argument and that is why we want a central council—a council which will examine the whole field of operations, and not merely a part of it, with the advice of England and her Generals to be given when it is required, and the advice of others to be given to us.

"We need every brain, we need all the experience, we need all the help, and they need it, and their need is greater than ours at the present moment. We want victory, and we will get it, but I don't want the whole burden of winning to fall on Great Britain; and I want, therefore, an interallied council, so to order the whole field of battle that the whole resources of the Allies shall be thrown into the conflict, in order to bring pressure to bear on the enemy.

## Could Have Saved Serbia

"With regard to Serbia, if our troops who were sent there had been sent six weeks earlier, we should not have had the Balkan tragedy. I do not withdraw a single syllable I have said. I do not say this because of what my right honorable friend has said, but because of what his friends have been saying. Really, when I see it said in certain quarters, 'hands off the army,' it makes me feel as if I am crossing the Channel in a torpedoboat destroyer on a choppy sea.

"I will lay down two propositions and I defy any man to challenge them. The first is that no soldiers in any war have had their strategical dispositions less interfered with by politicians. There has not been a single battalion or gun moved this year except on the advice of the General Staff. Not a single attack has been ordered in any part of the battlefield except on the advice of the General Staff, and there has not been a single attack not ordered.

"The whole campaign of this year has been the result of the advice of soldiers. Never in the whole history of war in this country have soldiers got more consistent and more substantial backing from politicians than they have in this war. I do not mean a backing of speeches; I mean a backing of guns, ammunition, transport, shipping, railways, supplies, and men. Speeches are no substitute for shells.

"I have only twice during this war acted against the advice of soldiers. The first was in the gun program. I laid down a program in advance of the advice of soldiers and against it. I was told then that I was extravagant and that the program would not be necessary. There is no soldier today who will not say that I was right.

"The second time I acted against the advice of soldiers was in the appointment of a civilian to reorganize the railways behind the lines, and I am proud to have done it. There is not a soldier now who will not say that he is grateful that I pressed my advice in spite of the attacks in the press that I was interfering with the soldiers.

"Apart from the great and matchless valor of our troops—and in spite of everything that has been said, no man has used warmer or more deepfelt words of gratitude and admiration for them than I have—apart from that, and the skill in the disposition of our soldiers, what are the two most conspicuous features in the great attacks in Flanders? The first is the overwhelming mass of artillery and ammunition; the second is the fact that the whole supplies are running right into the firing line by arrangements made by my right honorable friend, the First Lord of the Admiralty.

"I am not going here to define what the function of a politician is and what the function of a soldier, but do not make any mistake. You want both policy and strategy. They are inextricably interwoven.

"These are things which belong pure-

ly to the sphere of the soldier, and the politician who meddles in them is mischievous. He is meddling with something which requires years of training. There is also the sphere which is purely political, and the soldier who meddles in that is just as mischievous as the politician who meddles in strategy. Every one thinks he can edit a newspaper and become a statesman without any training or experience.

"Every one says 'I could show these politicians how to do things.' I should just like to see some of these gentlemen here for five or ten minutes. We would show them that even politics is an art that requires experience.

### Must Work Together

"But there is a vast sphere in war which is partly political and partly military. Supplies, transport, shipping, the distribution of man power, diplomacy, and the morale of the people—all these things are political, even more than they are military, and to divide people into politicians and soldiers in war is unscientific. What you want is the co-operation of both. Let them work together. The men who would try to separate them and foster disunion among them are traitors to their country. We have got to go on, and that is why I am looking forward to co-operation between not merely civilians and soldiers, but between allies and allies.

"Here let me utter one word of warning. When I see paragraphs by people who write recklessly without knowing the mischief they are doing, I think they are doing this in order to put us and our armies on bad terms with France, fostering suspicion of France. Why, Germany is lavishing money to create suspicion, distrust, and jealousy of England in France, Italy, Russia, and America. There is one country where they have conspicuously failed to move a single peasant to anything but heartfelt gratitude for what this country has done, and that country is France.

"Are we to tolerate men in this country who, for purely political or personal reasons, are disseminating distrust and jealousy of France in the hearts of Englishmen? I say we ought to stop this business.

"Since I have been in this war I have striven to get, not merely co-operation between the Allies, but friendship, good-will, and comradeship. I have done my best to make these people our friends. That is the secret of our success.

"It is essential that you should have this perfect good-will. The idea that poor France—trampled upon, with so many of her sons lost to her forever, with her richest provinces torn from her —should want anything except emancipation from this deadly menace that has threatened her for fifty years is false. That is all she seeks, and I hope, whatever happens to this controversy, that at any rate they will keep their hands and tongues and pens from trying to foster suspicion, jealousy, and distrust between France and ourselves.

### Unity the Way to Victory

"It is better to tell the people what is going on, and I have no anxiety that would modify for one moment my confidence.

"There were two fears, two things that could defeat us.

"There was the submarine menace. If that had wrenched from us the freedom of the seas, then, indeed, our hopes would be shattered. But of the subma-

rine I have no longer any fear. We are on its track, and I am glad to tell the House that on Saturday we destroyed five of these pests of the seas.

"The only other thing is lack of unity. Unity is the only sure way to victory— a victory that will bring peace and healing to a world which is bleeding to death."

### Other Speeches

Admiral Sir Hedworth Meux followed the Premier. He maintained that the scheme the Premier had explained was very different from that outlined in his Paris speech.

Commander Wedgwood characterized the Premier's speech as largely camouflage, and a lamentable descent from his Paris utterance. The council, he said, ought to possess executive powers. If anybody had come to see the Premier's funeral he had found a very wakeful corpse.

Sir Edward Carson confirmed the full approval and confidence of the Cabinet in the document the Premier took to Rapallo and declared that there would be no whittling down, but that the agreement would be rigidly adhered to as one of the most sacred documents formulated by the Allies during the war. If there were a divergency of views on the central council, he said, the Government would take the problem back to its own staffs, and it would be decided by those at home.

The Premier's success in winning Parliament to the plan and his complete triumph over his critics were emphasized by the fact that the debate was closed with the withdrawal of the motion for adjournment, without a division.

# CURRENT HISTORY CHRONICLED

## THE MONTH'S GREAT EVENTS

NOVEMBER, 1917, the forty-first month of the war, witnessed the high tide of momentous occurrences, chief of which were the following: The disastrous retirement of the Italian armies; the rebellion of the Reds in Russia, followed by civic and military demoralization throughout that country; the rapid acquisition from the Turks of Palestine by British troops; the strategic gains in Flanders and along the Aisne and Ailette by the Anglo-French forces; the first baptism of fire received by American troops in European trenches; the sensational overthrow of the Painlevé Cabinet, and the coming into supreme power of the picturesque Georges Clemenceau; finally, the decision of Great Britain, France, and Italy to form a Supreme War Council for co-ordination of effort, a project which the United States Government has unqualifiedly indorsed. On Nov. 19 the news from Italy indicated that the Austro-German invasion had met strong resistance along the River Piave, and there was hope among the Allies that the threatened fall of Venice might be averted; but the situation was recognized to be so very grave that Venice was practically evacuated and her most precious art treasures removed. Russia was in a ferment of civil war between the various radical and moderate factions, and as a military factor in the war was completely eliminated. These disturbing features were partially offset on the allied side by the capture from the Turks of large portions of Palestine, and by the serious dents that were made in the Hindenburg-Seigfried line in France by the French and English, presaging a further German retirement to a new line of defense. Politically the chief event was the formation of a new Cabinet in France headed by the dominant militant figure of the republic, Georges Clemenceau, indicating fresh access of vigor to that country; Italy and Germany also changed Premiers, and Lloyd George triumphed over his foes by the indorsement of his plan for a Supreme War Council uniting Italy, France, Great Britain, and the United States into one efficient central consultative body.

\* \* \*

## CHANGE OF MINISTRY IN FRANCE

THE Painlevé Ministry, after sixty days' existence, was forced to resign on Nov. 13, following its defeat in the Chamber of Deputies by a vote of 277 to 186; the Socialists refused to support the Government. The Cabinet was weak at the start on account of lack of assurances of support from the unified Socialists, who objected to the retention of former Premier Ribot in the new Ministry. It survived through sixty precarious days because the Socialists, while not giving it support, abstained from casting their votes in opposition. The crisis came on the night of Nov. 13 in a debate over the Government's lack of firmness and definiteness in dealing with the Bolo Pasha scandals.

A new Cabinet, headed by Georges Clemenceau, was completed within forty-eight hours after the fall of Painlevé, which marks a new speed record. In addition to the Premiership, Clemenceau took the War Portfolio. Stephen Pichon was made Foreign Secretary; he held the same portfolio in 1910, and is known as a relentless advocate of the recovery of Alsace-Lorraine. All the members are regarded as uncompromising fighters, and have opposed all previous War Ministries on the ground that these were open to suspicion of weakness or temporizing. Jules Pams, the new Minister of the Interior, was the Presidential candidate of the Radical Left in 1913.

The new Cabinet represents a concentration of the Republican groups and excludes Conservatives, Socialists, and Royalists. The new Premier is well known to Americans. He taught school in Connecticut in his youth, and married an American. He was Prime Minister from 1906 to 1909, and in recent years has been one of the most audacious and fearless critics of any Government or official whom he suspected of timidity or indecision in prosecuting the war.

\* \* \*

### JERUSALEM IN THE WAR

THE world's sense of reverence is shocked by the thought that Jerusalem, so long a holy city, equally for Hebrew, Christian, and Moslem, may be involved in the destruction of the war. Yet no city on earth has been more constantly involved in war, more frequently destroyed and rebuilt. Indeed, from the outset it was a city of war. Judah attacked it; David captured it, made its stronghold still stronger, and transferred his capital thither from Hebron. He built a palace and tabernacle of wood on the holy hill, which his son, Solomon, turned into splendid stone. Under Solomon's son, the magnificent rhetorician Rehoboam, the city of David began to wane, and presently felt the disasters of the capitivities—only to be rebuilt and restored.

Alexander the Great, conquering Palestine, spared Jerusalem, but its walls were razed by Ptolemy I. in the year 320 B. C., to be rebuilt by Simon a century later. The walls were again destroyed, and the city burned by Antiochus Epiphanes, to be rebuilt three years later by Judas Maccabeus, who strengthened David's original hill fortress on Zion. The walls were again razed by the Greeks, to be rebuilt by Jonathan, and Herod turned the old city into a magnificent capital and commercial centre. Pompey besieged the Temple hill in the year 65 B. C., and once more destroyed the walls, which were again restored by Antipater, but in the year 37 before our era, the Romans carried the city by storm.

Titus again captured Jerusalem, in the year 70 A. D., and cut down and destroyed the fruit trees. Jerusalem was rebuilt by Hadrian, taken, in the year 614, by Chosroes; in the year 637 the Caliph Omar captured it, and since that date it has been, for the most part, under Moslem rule. The Turks took Jerusalem in 1076, ten years after William of Normandy conquered England. In 1099 the Crusaders took the city. Saladin re-captured it in 1187, and, five years later, built the walls which were razed again in 1219. The Crusaders held it again in 1228, but only for fifteen years. In 1517 the Osmanli Turks captured Jerusalem, and Suleiman the Magnificent built the present walls in 1542. Jerusalem has been fought over for 3,000 years.

\* \* \*

### DECLINE IN DRUNKENNESS IN ENGLAND AND SCOTLAND

THE official report of convictions for drunkenness between 1909 and August, 1917, in England and Wales shows the following weekly averages: 1909, 3,090; 1914, 3,388; 1916, 1,544; 1917, (8½ months,) 929. Convictions for drunkenness have fallen off very considerably in consequence of the no-treating order. This order was issued on Oct. 11, 1915, and for the seven weeks following— to Nov. 28, when it became operative— the number of convictions recorded weekly in London was 792. In the four weeks of January, 1916, there were 592 cases, and the following month 616, after which a fluctuating decrease took place till last December, when the weekly average rose to 735. From that date each month of this year showed a decrease, till July last, when there were 310 convictions, compared with 261 in June; but in the following four weeks, which ended on Aug. 12, the number stood at 295.

In 1914 the weekly average in Birmingham was 72, but in the first six months after the date of the no-treating order it fell to 23, while in June of this year it was as low as 9, rising, however, to an average of 17 in August last. Liverpool had 236 cases a week in 1914, and for six months after the order the number was 121; it was 91 in January, and ended with 57 in August. In Manchester the 1915 average was 83, and after the order came into operation on Feb. 14, 1916, a remarkable decrease took place. The last return shows that there was an average of 21 in August, but in June it was as low as 18. Sheffield's average was 28 in 1914, 3 in June, 1917, 7 in August.

In Scotland the weekly average for four weeks in 1915 before the orders was 1,485; in 1916 after the orders it was 947, and in 1917 the last return was 583. The average in Edinburgh has fallen from 158 in 1914 to 60 in 1917; in Glasgow from 461 in 1914 to 178 in 1917, and in Inverness from 13 to 1.

\* \* \*

## IN THE STREETS OF ASKALON

FOR the second time in history the armies of England have captured Askalon, "the city of holm oaks." It was taken before by Richard I., the Lion-hearted, in 1191, from the chivalrous Saladin, and the English rebuilt the town and restored the fortifications. But Sultan Bibars captured it in 1270, and completed the work of destruction by filling up the ancient harbor. In older days, the Egyptians, Greeks, and Romans successively held this famous city; and in still earlier days it loomed large in the wars between Israel and the Philistines.

About the year 1425 before our era, immediately after the death of Joshua, "Judah took Gaza with the coast thereof, and Askalon with the coast thereof, and Ekron with the coast thereof," exactly on the lines of General Allenby's present advance; these three, with Ashdod and Gath, form the famous "five cities of the Philistines." Askalon stands out again in the great love-story of Samson. It was the source of his famous riddle, "Out of the eater came forth meat, and out of the strong came forth sweetness," which the hero revealed to his beloved "daughter of the Philistines," after she had wept for seven days. In revenge for her betrayal of the answer, Samson "went down to Askalon and slew thirty men of them and took their spoil, and gave change of garments unto them which expounded the riddle"; but Samson's wife was given to his companion.

The prophet Jeremiah fulminated against "the Kings of the land of the Philistines and Askalon: Drink ye, and be drunken, and fall and rise no more, because of the sword which I will send among you." And again: "Baldness is come upon Gaza; Askalon is cut off with the remnant of their valley. \* \* \* How can the sword of the Lord be quiet, seeing that the Lord hath given it a charge against Askalon?" But even more magnificent is the burst of poetry in David's lament for Saul and Jonathan: "The beauty of Israel is slain upon thy high places; how are the mighty fallen! Tell it not in Gath, publish it not in the streets of Askalon; lest the daughters of the Philistines rejoice, lest the daughters of the uncircumcised triumph."

\* \* \*

## VENICE AND THE GERMANS

IT is one of the curious cyclic returns of history that Venice was originally founded as a place of refuge from the Huns, in the year 452, when Attila sacked the rich city of Aquileia, not far from where Trieste now stands. The isles of the lagoon were occupied by refugees, and this population was constantly increased as the barbarians strengthened their hold on Northern Italy. Byzantine influence was soon felt, beginning with the sixth century and the reign of Justinian, when the Venetians fought beside Belisarius against the Goths. From that time Venice was a part of the Eastern Empire, linked with Constantinople, the new Rome.

The Popes, joining hands with the northern invaders, fought against Venice, which turned to Byzantium for aid. Thus it came that the great Byzantine Cathedral of St. Mark was built in Venice. A sea victory over the Dalmatian pirates made Venice mistress of the Adriatic about the year 1,000, since when the "wedding of the sea" has been celebrated, for this was the beginning of Venetian sea power. In the sixteenth century the Pope and the Emperor (Maximilian) again joined hands against Venice; later, her enemies were the Pope and Spain. From the period of the Crusades, with their expeditions by sea to the Levant, Venice became a great Oriental power, holding, among other rich possessions, both Crete and Cyprus, and, in virtue of a treaty with the Turks, holding the monopoly of the trade with India across the Isthmus of Suez.

But the discovery of the sea route round the Cape of Good Hope to India dealt a blow at this monopoly, and the power of Venice began to wane. After fighting Austria on the present Italian battlefields, Napoleon Bonaparte in 1797, by the treaty of Campo Formio, gave

Venice to Austria; from that time until 1815 it belonged alternately to Austria and France. Thereafter, until 1866, it was held by Austria—that is, until fifty-one years ago. In that year the defeat of Austria at Sadowa by Prussia and at Custozza by Italy broke Austria's power, and Venetia, with Venice as its capital, was added to united Italy.

\* \* \*

### THE LEGEND OF BRAZIL

BRAZIL'S entry into the world war adds to the belligerent territory an area of three and a quarter million square miles, practically equal to that of the United States; a territory extremely rich, though still sparsely populated. Before Columbus made the landfall of San Salvador, Portuguese navigators had explored and annexed the Azores, Canaries, and Cape Verde Islands in the wide Atlantic, and had put in a claim to the regions about and beyond these islands. This claim was indorsed by Pope Alexander VI. in 1493 and, when the most easterly part of the coast of South America was discovered, it fell to Portugal in virtue of this claim and decision, and Portuguese it has remained ever since, though long independent. Brazil is, in fact, the only American nation whose official tongue is Portuguese. It might well have been called New Portugal, as Central America was called New Spain, and as a more northerly region was called New England. But it received a far more ancient name, which goes back to the days of pagan Ireland and the dawn of Celtic literature; for in the oldest Irish legends, Brasil or Brazil was the name of the western paradise beyond the sunset, to which the souls of departed heroes went, and where the souls of the living sometimes visited them in dreams. Brendan, the early Irish navigator, who without doubt made an extensive voyage in the Atlantic Ocean, was said to have visited this enchanted isle, as other Irish travelers unquestionably reached Iceland. The tradition of his visit was handed down and accepted as authentic; so much so that on the Venetian map of Andrea Bianco, of the year 1436, the Isle of Brasil is marked, well out in the Atlantic Ocean. It was, therefore, on the maps and charts of the early voyagers of the time of Columbus; and, when the eastern extension of South America was in due course discovered, it was identified with the once enchanted Isle of Brazil, and the name has remained to this day.

\* \* \*

### THE FUTURE OF PALESTINE

THE declaration of the British Foreign Secretary, Mr. Balfour, that "the "Government views with favor the estab-"lishment of Palestine as a national home "for the Jewish people, and will use its "best endeavors to facilitate the achieve-"ment of this object," will, when realized, mark the greatest change in the status of Palestine since the days of Alexander the Great. Palestine may once more become a "land flowing with milk and honey," as in the days of the grape clusters of Eshcol. During the centuries of conquest and foreign dominion much of Palestine has been almost a desolate waste, exceedingly far from a land of plenty. The reason is quite simple: The almost complete destruction of trees on the porous limestone hills had allowed the plentiful Spring rains to rush down the hillsides in destructive torrents instead of remaining as a reservoir of fertility; exactly the same thing as turned the Italian Carso, also porous limestone, into a desolation. And the terraced grain fields on the slopes have fallen into ruin.

The first problem, therefore, for the hill country is a complete afforestation scheme, which should, within twenty years, restore the ancient luxuriance; especially a complete replanting of vines and olives, widely destroyed by the Romans, is needed. But below the hills, along the shore of the Mediterranean, there is a wide strip of very fertile land, on which extensive agricultural colonies have been planted in recent years, and have greatly prospered, raising large quantities of excellent cereals, cotton, and fruit. In the year before the war Jaffa exported oranges, unequaled for flavor, to the value of $1,600,000, and the whole coast region could easily be turned into a fruit garden rivaling Southern

California. The formation of the hills, largely chalk and limestone, gives little hope of mineral wealth, but sheep and Angora goats could be successfully raised on the uplands, and, by extensive tree planting, to conserve the water of the Spring rains, the cultivated belt could be greatly extended, restoring the old fertility.

* * *

### THE ORIGIN OF THE COSSACKS

THE name Cossack, or, more correctly, Kazák, accented on the second syllable, is not Russian but Tartar. It dates from the great invasion of the Tartar hordes—"horde" being the Tartar name for an army—set in motion by the genius of Genghis Kahn at the beginning of the thirteenth century, a movement of expansion which resulted in the conquest of nearly all Asia and much of Europe. The title Kazák, a horseman, was shortly adopted by the mounted soldiers of the free communities which were formed in the border country, (called the Ukraine, from the Russian word "krai," a border,) which lay between the Moscow principality and the Black Sea, and stretched westward to the Carpathians, the scene of "Fire and Sword" and "The Deluge." These self-governing communities had their strongholds on the reefs and islands of the Dnieper and the other rivers that traverse the southern plain; and the ceaseless wars with the Tartars and Turks developed a caste of mounted warriors among them who came to be known as the Kazáks. In the reign of the Czar Alexis, the father of Peter the Great, the southern communities elected to join their fortunes with Russia, the Kazáks reserving their organization and privileges. Mazeppa, under Peter the Great, tried, at the end of his long life, to break this union. He was, therefore, the father of the "Ukraine" movement.

There are, perhaps, a quarter of a million Cossacks in the Russian Army, preserving their old military training, holding their land by military tenure, and still keeping and exercising the right to elect their own Hetman, or supreme leader. They are the strongest and most united force in Russia today. It was said that the Provisional Government intended to destroy their privileges and organization, merging them in the regular army, and to their resentment at this certain present developments are in all probability to be traced.

* * *

### TWO SINKING EPISODES IN THE NORTH SEA

GERMAN fast cruisers on Oct. 18 attacked a convoy in the North Sea, between the Shetland Islands and the Norway coast. Two British destroyers— the Mary Rose and the Strongbow—also five Norwegian, one Danish, and three Swedish merchant vessels, were sunk. Eighty-eight officers and sailors were lost when the destroyers went down; 150 passengers and sailors perished with the merchantmen. The official British statement of the raid says of the Germans:

> Anxious to make good their escape before the British forces could interrupt them, no effort was made to rescue the crews of the sunken British destroyers, and the Germans left the doomed merchant ships while these were still sinking, thus enabling the British patrol craft, which arrived shortly afterward, to rescue some thirty Norwegians and others, regarding whom the details are not yet known. The German Navy by this act once more and further degraded itself by disregard of the historic chivalry of the sea.

One correspondent says that the details of the butchery of the crew of the merchantmen pass description. Two women on one ship waved a piece of white cloth which was perfectly visible. They were silenced by a volley from the German cruisers.

The Norwegian newspapers bitterly denounced the raid as "a murderous attack." Norway addressed the German authorities on the subject, expressing "concern" over the raid on neutral vessels, but no other known steps were taken.

The British Admiralty on Nov. 3 announced the sinking by British destroyers in the Cattegat waters of a disguised German raider, the Crocodile, 1,000 tons; an auxiliary cruiser, the Marie, 3,000 tons, and ten armed trawlers. In contrast with the action of the Germans, the report of Captain Lauterbach of the

Marie states that the British destroyers ceased firing as soon as the vessel burst into flames, and began rescuing the crew. The British succeeded in saving thirty Germans.

\* \* \*

### THE RICHES OF LORRAINE

FRANCE'S demand for the restoration of Alsace-Lorraine is strengthened by the revelation by the German Under Secretary of War of the enslavement of the girls of the provinces: " Eight and a half per cent. of the girls are less than seventeen years of age; one-half of them have been subjected by force to work at the front." But, as well as the moral reason, there are economic reasons why France will demand the two provinces. They contain a large part of her national wealth; on them Germany has not only built up her immense prosperity, but has cast cannon to wage the present war. Without these resources, she could not have carried on the world war for six months; for of the 2,800,000,000 tons of iron ore within Germany's present boundaries, 2,000,000,000 tons, or five-sevenths, are in Lorraine. Germany's vast iron industry was practically built up with the iron of Lorraine. Further, Germany yearly exported enormous quantities of Lorraine iron ore.

Of incalculable value also are the deposits of potash in Alsace, which have been operated only during the last eight years. The beds at the foot of Hartmanns-Weilerkopf, the scene of many battles in the present war, are estimated to contain more than 3,000,000,000 tons of pure potash, valued at about $35,000,-000,000. As potash is one of the most valuable plant foods, the meaning of this is plain. It means potential food for the whole world. The return to France of the provinces will, therefore, mean an incalculable enrichment of France. It will further mean that Germany will be, to that extent, the less able to prepare for or wage future wars.

\* \* \*

### PRESIDENT WILSON'S FIRMNESS

PRESIDENT WILSON'S determination to prosecute the war to a victorious finish was expressed in two telegrams sent on Nov. 16. In one to the King of the Belgians on his fête day the President said:

> For the people of the United States I take this occasion to renew expressions of deep sympathy for the sufferings which Belgium has endured under the willful, cruel, and barbaric force of a disappointed Prussian autocracy.
>
> The people of the United States were never more in earnest than in their determination to prosecute to a successful conclusion this war against that power and to secure for the future obedience to the laws of nations and respect for the rights of humanity.

To a loyalty conference representing six Northwestern States in session at St. Paul, Minn., he telegraphed as follows:

> You have come together as the representatives of that Western empire in which the sons of all sections of America and the stocks of all the nations of Europe have made the prairie and the forest the home of a new race and the temple of a new faith. The time has come when that home must be protected and that faith affirmed in deeds. Sacrifice and service must come from every class, every profession, every party, every race, every creed, every section.
>
> This is not a banker's war or a farmer's war or a manufacturer's war or a laboring man's war—it is a war for every straight-out American, whether our flag be his by birth or by adoption. We are today a nation in arms, and we must fight and farm, mine and manufacture, conserve food and fuel, save and spend, to the one common purpose.
>
> It is to the great Northwest that the nation looks, as once before in critical days, for that steadiness of purpose and firmness of determination which shall see this struggle through to a decision that shall make the masters of Germany rue the day they unmasked their purpose and challenged our Republic.

\* \* \*

### BRITISH BATTLE LOSSES

MR. BAKER, our Secretary of War, made a public statement on Nov. 10 that " up to about June 1 the losses of the British expeditionary forces in deaths in action and deaths from wounds were about 7 per cent. of the total of all the men sent to France since the beginning of the war." He added that the percentage now is still less, owing to improved tactics and allied superiority in artillery.

The charge that England is not bearing its full share of the fighting done by British armies was effectively answered by Premier Lloyd George on Oct. 29, when he stated that in round numbers 75 per cent. of the British Empire's contribution in men had come from England, and 75 per cent. of the loss had fallen on England. He added that Scotland had done its share and Ireland had made a distinguished contribution, while in voluntary recruiting Wales had beaten the record by a shade. The dominions had contributed between 700,000 and 800,000 men in the total of about 5,000,000 British soldiers under arms.

The Westminster Gazette has gone into the matter of percentages more in detail, stating that between July 31 and Oct. 6, 1917, the British troops engaged in the battles in France were divided as follows:

English ...70 per cent.   Scottish .. 8 per cent.
Overseas ..16 per cent.   Irish ..... 3 per cent.

The casualty proportions are:

English ...76 per cent.   Scottish ..10 per cent.
Overseas .. 8 per cent.   Irish ..... 6 per cent.

An official summary of Australian casualties from the beginning of the war to July 28, 1917, shows the following:

| | |
|---|---:|
| Dead | 28,547 |
| Wounded | 43,238 |
| Missing | 4,056 |
| Sick | 27,207 |
| Prisoners of war | 2,143 |
| Unspecified | 248 |
| Total | 105,439 |

The number listed as wounded does not include those who have recovered and returned to the front. The total number of officers and men sent from Australia up to June 30, 1917, was 306,227, so that casualties accounted for one in three. There were between 50,000 and 60,000 recruits in training, the total number of volunteers who had enlisted in the Australian imperial force having reached over 362,000.

* * *

BELGIAN RELIEF WORK SINCE OUR
ENTRY INTO THE WAR

THE American Commission for Relief in Belgium is continuing its activities on as great a scale as at any time before this country went into the war, and this work is not curtailed by the withdrawal of the American representatives from Belgium. For the present the loans from the American Government, which are made monthly, have sufficed to meet the requirements of the commission under the limitations as to shipping, but the commission still receives contributions for specific charities and is transmitting considerable sums to many individuals from contributors in America. The commission, which has offices in New York, London, and Rotterdam, purchases food for the occupied areas, ships it to Holland, and transships it at Rotterdam for the occupied territory, where it is taken in charge by the Dutch and Spanish representatives of the commission and handled as it was handled before by the Americans. Since the end of April, 1917, the Relief Commission has shipped from America 240,000 tons of foodstuffs. The commission apprehends that with the increasing cost of food and the increasing needs of the exhausted territories occupied by the enemy it is likely that further general appeals will have to be made to the public.

* * *

AT the annual meeting of the American Society of Naval Architects and Marine Engineers, held in New York on Nov. 16, President Powell of the Bethlehem steel works stated that the American output of merchant tonnage in 1917 would be 750,000. He expressed the belief that it would be 3,000,000 tons in 1918. Secretary of the Navy Daniels announced that the shipyards would complete more destroyers in the eighteen months ending with February, 1919, than the country was able to build in twenty-five years before the war.

* * *

IT was officially announced in Parliament on Nov. 15 that since July 1, 1916, the British had captured from the Turks 30,197 prisoners and 186 guns, and from the Germans on the western front 101,534 prisoners and 519 guns. The approximate square mileage in territory conquered or reconquered by the British in the same time was 128,000. The total number of prisoners captured on all fronts since the beginning of the war was 166,000, while the captured guns numbered 800.

# American Troops' First Fight in Europe

## An Officer's Tribute to Our Soldier Dead, First to Give Their Lives in Battle on French Soil

THE first announcement that American troops had been under fire in Europe was contained in a dispatch dated Oct. 27, 1917, which stated that "on the morning of a recent day somewhere in France" the artillery had fired the first shot; that the same evening the helmeted infantry had marched into the trenches, and that there had since been intermittent artillery fighting.

This news, however, did not mean that the American expeditionary force had begun to participate in the execution of the Allies' military plans, but only that the culminating phase of the training had begun. The sector chosen for this work was the quietest on the western front.

The Americans shelled German gun positions and troops, the enemy sending back shell for shell. The first shell case was sent to President Wilson. The shot was fired by a red-haired gunner as his comrades in the ranks and the assembled officers cheered. Later, a luncheon in the field was attended by the American and French artillerists, in celebration of the first American contact with the enemy. The gun used in firing the first shot was one of the famous French 75s. On the second day the French shelled a German battery position, which was located by sound, and the enemy replied vigorously, projectiles falling close to the Americans, who joined in the artillery duel. All the troops were relieved after a certain period by others. Thus the American expeditionary forces were initiated into actual war conditions.

### Americans Greeted on Arrival

As the first American troops entered the trenches, under cover of night, they received an enthusiastic welcome from the French, despite the necessity for the utmost quietness. Every American was shaken by the hand, some were hugged, and even kissed on both cheeks.

Greetings being over, the Americans settled down, and at daylight, under low-hung, dripping clouds, they got their first view of the German lines, stretching away in the rolling terrain. It rained day after day, and the Americans had a substantial first taste of mud.

Although the officers were certain that the Germans knew the Americans were opposite them, there was no special activity. One American battery observed and scattered a marching enemy group with shellfire. Desultory and intermittent shelling, characteristic of the sector, continued, the Germans sending over projectiles every now and then and the American and French batteries firing back shot for shot. There was no infantry firing of any consequence.

The first expedition of the Americans into No Man's Land followed a couple of nights later. After penetrating into the wilderness of barbed wire and shell craters, they returned without a scratch. Accompanied by French troops, they clambered from the trenches up the scaling ladders, equipped with hand grenades, rifles, revolvers, and trench knives, their steel helmets strapped tightly beneath their chins. Headed by the squad leader, they set off on tiptoe until they reached their own barbed wire, along which they felt in the darkness until they found the prepared gap. Then they stepped through, actually into No Man's Land.

The Americans wriggled along on their stomachs, revolvers in hand, and did a workmanlike job as coolly as if a night patrol in No Man's Land was a regular thing. When the last man whispered down the line, "All done," or its French equivalent, "Tout fait," the patrol crept back as silently as it had come, stopping now and then when any noise was heard.

The first battalions of Americans in

the trenches were relieved by others, according to a dispatch dated Nov. 1. Casualties were negligible, the only one reported being an officer, who was wounded in the leg by shrapnel on Oct. 28.

## First American Casualties

A German War Office bulletin on Nov. 3 reported that "at the Rhine-Marne Canal, as the result of a reconnoitring thrust, North American soldiers were brought is as prisoners." Confirmation of this was contained in the official statement issued in Washington.

The War Department has received a dispatch from the Commanding General of the American expeditionary forces, which stated that before daylight Nov. 3 a salient occupied for instruction by a company of American infantry was raided by Germans.

The enemy put down a heavy barrage fire, cutting off the salient from the rest of the men.

Our losses were three killed, five wounded, and twelve captured or missing. [A revised list showed that the wounded were eleven and the missing the same number.]

The enemy's loss is not known. One wounded German was taken prisoner.

The raid was carried out against members of the second contingent entering the trenches for training. These men had been in only a few days.

Before dawn the Germans began shelling vigorously the barbed-wire front of the trenches, dropping many high explosives of large calibre. A heavy artillery fire was then directed so as to cover all the adjacent territory, including the passage leading up to the trenches, thereby forming a most effective barrage in the rear as well as in the front.

Lieutenant William H. McLaughlin, in charge of the detachment of Americans, started back to the communicating trenches to his immediate superior for orders. The barrage knocked him down, but he picked himself up and started off again. He was knocked down a second time, but, determined to reach his objective, got up again. A third time he was knocked down and badly shell-shocked, and was put out of action.

Soon afterward the Germans, to the number, according to the report, of 210, rushed through the breaches and wire entanglements on each side of the salient, their general objective barrage in the forefield having lifted for a moment.

The Germans went into the trenches at several points. They met with stout resistance. Pistols, grenades, knives, and bayonets were freely used.

## First to Fall in Battle

For many minutes there was considerable confusion in the trenches, the Germans stalking the Americans and the Americans stalking the Germans. In one part of the trench an American private engaged two Germans with the bayonet. That was the last seen of him until after the raid, when a dead American was found on the spot. Another was killed by a blow on the head with a rifle butt from above.

Some of the Americans apparently did not realize at the beginning of the attack just what was going on. One of the wounded, a private, said:

"I was standing in a communicating trench waiting for orders. I heard a noise back of me and looked around in time to see a German fire in my direction. I felt a bullet hit my arm."

The Germans left the trench as soon as possible, taking their dead and wounded with them. An inspection showed, however, that they had abandoned three rifles, a number of knives and helmets.

The three men killed—the first Americans actually to fall in battle in this war—were:

GRESHAM, JAMES B., (Corporal,) of Evansville, Ind.

ENRIGHT, THOMAS F., (private,) of Pittsburgh, Penn.

HAY, MERLE D., (private,) of Glidden, Iowa.

## French Tribute to the Dead

The burial of these three men took place on Nov. 6. With a guard of French infantrymen in their picturesque uniforms of red and horizon blue standing on one side and a detachment of American soldiers on the other, the flag-wrapped caskets were lowered into the grave as a bugler blew "taps" and the batteries at the front fired minute guns. As the minute guns went off the French officer, commanding the division in this section, paid tribute to the fallen Americans. His words, which were punctuated by the roar of the guns and the whistle of shells, touched both the French and Americans. In conclusion the French officer said:

In the name of the —th division, in the name of the French Army, and in the name of France I bid farewell to Private Enright, Private Gresham, and Private Hay of the American Army.

Of their own free will they had left a prosperous and happy country to come over here. They knew war was continuing in Europe; they knew that the forces fighting for honor, love of justice, and civilization were still checked by the long-prepared forces serving the powers of brutal domination, oppression, and barbarity. They knew that efforts were still necessary. They wished to give us their generous hearts, and they have not forgotten óld historical memories, while others forget more recent ones.

They ignored nothing of the circumstances, and nothing had been concealed from them—neither the length and hardships of war, nor the violence of battle, nor the dreadfulness of new weapons, nor the perfidy of the foe. Nothing stopped them. They accepted the hard and strenuous life; they crossed the ocean at great peril; they took their places on the front by our side, and they have fallen facing the foe in a hard and desperate hand-to-hand fight. Honor to them. Their families, friends, and fellow-citizens will be proud when they learn of their deaths.

Men! These graves, the first to be dug in our national soil, and but a short distance from the enemy, are as a mark of the mighty land we and our allies firmly cling to in the common task, confirming the will of the people and the army of the United States to fight with us to a finish, ready to sacrifice as long as is necessary until final victory for the most noble of causes, that of the liberty of nations, the weak as well as the mighty. Thus the deaths of these humble soldiers appear to us with extraordinary grandeur. We will, therefore, ask that the mortal remains of these young men be left here, left with us forever. We inscribe on the tombs, " Here lie the first soldiers of the Republic of the United States to fall on the soil of France for liberty and justice." The passerby will stop and uncover his head. Travelers and men of heart will go out of their way to come here to pay their respective tributes.

Private Enright, Private Gresham, Private Hay! In the name of France I thank you. God receive your souls. Farewell!

## Wounded and Missing

The official list of wounded and missing in this first battle of American troops on European soil was as follows:

### WOUNDED

McLAUGHLIN, WILLIAM H., (First Lieutenant;) W. R. McLaughlin, Coltec, Ark.

GIVENS, HOMER, (Corporal;) father, William F. Givens, Cloverdale, Ala.

GRIGSBY, WILLIAM P., (private;) mother, Mrs. Lizzie Grigsby, 1,278 Willow Avenue, Louisville, Ky.

DEIFER, LOUIS A., (private;) Mrs. Katherine Deifer, Box 48, Route 6, Sullivan, Ind.

FANN, PAUL W., (private;) George W. Fann, Sarona, Wis.

WESLEY, GEORGE, (private;) Miss Margarette Welch, 623 Eighth Street, Dayton, Ky.

SMITH, LESTER C., (private;) R. A. Smith, R. F. D. 5, Concord, N. C.

SMITH, JOHN J., (private;) brother, F. D. Smith, Box 82, Ludington, Mich.

HOPKINS, CHARLES J., (private;) brother, James W. Hopkins, Stanton, Texas.

BOX, GEORGE L., (private;) father, James L. Box, 700 North Grady Street, Altus, Okla.

ORR, CHARLES L., (private;) mother, Mrs. Sarah Regnell, R. F. D. 5, Lyons, Kan.

### MISSING

HALYBURTON, EDGAR M., (Sergeant;) father, George B. Halyburton, Stoney Point, N. C.

MULHALL, NICHOLAS L., (Corporal;) mother, Mrs. Bridget Mulhall, 189 Ninth Street, Jersey City, N. J.

GALLAGHER, DANIEL B., (private;) father, Neil Gallagher, Blocton, Ala.

McDOUGAL, FRANK E., (private;) father, R. L. McDougal, 822 East First Street, Maryville, Mo.

GRIMSLEY, CLYDE I., (private;) Frank Grimsley, Stockton, Kan.

DECKER, HOIT D., (private;) W. F. Decker, Vincennes, Ind.

LESTER, JOHN P., (private;) father, William Lester, Tutwater, (probably error for Tutwiler,) Miss.

GODFREY, HERSHEL, (private;) father, William C. Oberst, 109 North Ridgway Avenue, Chicago, Ill.

LAUGHMAN, HARRY R., (private;) Ada R. Laughman, 461 Oakwood Boulevard, Chicago, Ill.

HAINES, EDWIN H., (private;) mother, Mrs. Elizabeth Haines, Route 4, Woodward, Okla.

KENDALL, VERNON M., (private;) father, Sam Kendall, R. F. D. 2, Roll, Okla.

## Location of the Event

The reading of the German and American reports together indicated that the raid took place in the region of the Vosges Mountains, close to the point where the canal connecting the Marne with the Rhine crosses the border between France and Lorraine. This route runs from Nancy via Saarburg and Zabern to the City of Strassburg. The region where the first contact between the Americans and the Germans was established had not figured in extensive fighting since the earlier days of the war. It was through this region, as well as from the direction of Belfort, toward the south, that the French pushed their lines toward Strassburg, only to be driven back into the Vosges Mountains very soon afterward by the Germans.

During the night of Nov. 6 and the following day the German guns rained shells of various calibres on the American positions. So thickly did they come at one time in the early hours of the morning that it was thought another barrage was about to be placed for a second raid on the American trenches. But none developed. The American artillery gave the Germans back shell for shell, pounding the enemy battery positions and breaking shrapnel over their trenches. All the time the rain had continued, and vast seas of mud extended in every direction. At some points the water running down the mountainous hills flowed into the dugouts, the occupants being forced to pump out repeatedly in order that the dugouts might remain tenable.

The second fatal contact of American troops with Germans was announced Nov. 15. A group of Americans was in a shack in the reserve when the Germans began shelling heavily. The officers ordered the men to a dugout, but before they could get there a big shell dropped on the position and exploded, killing and wounding several soldiers. The American gunners concentrated their fire on the communicating trenches of the enemy, and it is thought that their shells caused casualties and considerable damage.

# The American Army in France

## By Laurence Jerrold

### Special War Correspondent of The London Telegraph

THE first American troops landed in France in June. I saw them land, and when I recollected this the other day [written Sept. 26, 1917] I was amazed at what I saw. The American troops in their billets, their camps, their training grounds, their rifle and gun practice grounds near the front, are already absolutely at home. The French villagers have adopted now a broken Franco-American language—sister tongue, though different, to the now classic Anglo-French spoken for three years from Calais downward. The American troops have made themselves at home, have settled all their arrangements with businesslike finality, and are out to do their job thoroughly. Their bases near the front seemed to me already definitely organized. They are settled in villages, where they disturb the villagers by aggressive sanitation. They have abolished all dunghills, to the old farmers' amazement and alarm. They have purified the water, cleaned up the streets, cottages, and farmyards. The villagers, at first terrified by these wild measures, are now reconciled, and every little village grocery sells American matches, American tobacco, American groceries, sterilized milk, "canned goods," American mustard, and everything American except American whisky. For at the messes, where I was received with open arms as an ally of today and forever—no American officer makes any doubt about that—cold American purified water and French coffee with American sterilized milk are the only drinks. Villages of France have become American, and American café au lait, colored cars, and motor bikes with sidecars tear all over the country, driven by university boys turned "chauffeurs."

### Practicing Under Barrage Fire

Our new allies are learning from us both—from us old allies, English and French. I first saw a French division in horizon blue teach the new American Army, in khaki and wearing British trench helmets, what a modern battle is like. It was a moving sight. It was poignant, really, when one heard that the French division had just come back from Verdun and was enacting over again in play what it had just done in terrible and glorious earnest. The American Staff stood on a knoll watching, with the French Staff explaining. On the edge of the hill to the left of the staff the new American Army watched. Further to the left the French troops came on. Every " poilu " among them had just come from the real thing. He grinned as he played at war this time, and one felt how he must enjoy playing at it now. But he played very well and earnestly. The whole thing was done as one has before watched it being done under less reassuring circumstances for one's self.

The lines advanced in open formation, then stopped for the barrage fire to be pushed forward. Flares were sent up to signal to the artillery. There was another step forward under barrage fire, another (sham) barrage fire, more flares and rockets, the horizon-blue line crept cautiously round to take the first trenches, the machine-gun parties came up. One more barrage fire and more signals, then the boche trenches below us were taken.

### Americans Quick to Learn

It was all exactly as it would have been in real war. The French Colonel of Artillery, straight from action, explained it to the American Generals, General S. and General D., (who has just won the French Military Cross at Verdun.) The American troops understood and appreciated keenly. Who would not? These play-actors in the hollow at our feet had just come from the real tragedy, and had fought and won, but had paid the price of victory.

The American soldier (officers told me) understands the manoeuvre well. The officers find that their men are quick at grasping individual field work, i. e., make admirable noncommissioned officers with initiative, enterprise, and intelligence. French officers, many of whom speak English perfectly, while several American officers I met speak very good French, give enthusiastic and intelligent assistance. French and Americans are not much alike in method or by temperament. I heard a French officer describing a battle with perfect technical accuracy, but also with dramatic expressiveness and with the literary sense. An American officer immediately translated the French into American, and it was American—short, sharp, almost crackling with crisp Americanisms. It was the same battle described, but the difference in the descriptions was delightful to note. Differences are nothing. The French are keen to teach, the Americans, if possible, keener still to learn, and each understands the other thoroughly to a common end.

### Pupils and Instructors

British instructors and American pupils understand each other equally well. I never was more amused, pleased, cheered, and bucked up than by watching British Sergeant instructors training American officer cadets. Imagine a typical British Sergeant, with three years of war behind him and with seven or more years of British military training before that, spending every ounce of his energy, every particle of his keenness, and every word of his vocabulary teaching young Americans what they will have to do in a few months' time, and the young Americans using every muscle of their body, all their alertness, and all their keenness, too, to make themselves ready for the fight that all are yearning to be in.

Parties of American officer cadets, (including young Lieutenant ——,) dug line upon line of sham trenches, killed dummy boches on the way, dashed through four lines of trenches, dug themselves in at the last, and began instant rapid fire at more boche targets. " Advance! " said the Sergeant. A second later " Go! " and the young chaps leaped out. " Kill 'em sweet and clean! Clean killing is what we want!" shouted the Sergeant. The young Americans were at the dummies, and each dug his dummy with a wild "Yah!" or college yell or scream. "Go on!" roared the Sergeant; "there are more boches beyond. Clean killing is what we want." And the Americans charged at several more lines of dummies before they leaped into the front trench and began firing.

All over the countryside in these splendid sweeping valleys and green woods, the American army is training with furious zest.

To drive or walk in woods and fields is almost as dangerous as visiting front-line trenches. In every field, around every knoll, the American army is blazing away with rifles, guns, and machine guns.

# Military Events of the Month
## From October 18 to November 18, 1917
### By Walter Littlefield

## Story of the Great Battle for Venice

IN following their policy of holding their strongest and nearest enemies and of attacking their weakest and most remote—with Russia rendered inactive, Serbia overwhelmed, and Rumania fought to a standstill—it was logical that the Germans should next select Italy. Here success might place Austria's most formidable enemy hors de combat and open the back door into France.

The Austrians had tried to do this in May and June, 1916. They had attacked Italy's historically and geographically weakest front at its strongest point, and had reached out over the Sette Comuni beyond Asiago, twenty miles from the Trentino frontier. Their object was to reach Vicenza, and thence Verona. From these points they could develop positions east and west—east along the system of railways which fed the Italian army on the Isonzo front, thereby isolating that army; west through the old quadrilateral, Mantua, Peschiera, Verona, and Legnago, absorbing the industrial centre of the peninsula and paving the way to a peace at Rome, if not an approach to the back door of France.

But the Italians, diverting 500,000 men who had been training on the plains between Milan and Turin and were on their way to the Isonzo front, were able to flank the Austrian position on the Sette Comuni, from Primolano, in the Val Sugana, on the northeast, and from the Val Astico on the southwest. So the Austrians were rolled up back into the Trentino with the loss of over 80,000 men.

But the supplies which had carried Cadorna so far beyond the Isonzo last September were not sufficient to complete his work. In his last exploit he had left the front across the slopes of Monte Nero exposed at Plezzo and at Tolmino; the Bainsizza front, at the Idria, on the north, and at Monte San Gabriele and Monte San Daniele, on the south. Here Germany, with six Austro-German divisions and then thirteen of forty-seven released from the Russian front, struck. The invaders were in command of General von Below, who had been decorated by the Kaiser in Courland and in Macedonia; under him were von Krobatin at Plezzo, von Krass at Tolmino; von Henriquez, ready to cut in through the Vippacco, and Wurm in charge on the Carso. Several divisions of the Austrian troops of Generals Boroevic and Koevess had been elbowed out of the way by the Germans. Field Marshal Conrad von Hoetzendorf was no longer in command. It was a thoroughly German outfit and had been prepared in the usual thorough German fashion.

For nearly a year the Italian troops on the Plezzo-Tolmino front had not been replaced. They had begun to fraternize with the Austrians there. The latter showed them forged copies of Italian papers containing stories of revolts in Naples and Genoa and of British mercenaries there firing upon starving women and children. The Socialist Camorra of Ferri, the pacifist Camorra of Giolitti also got in their fine work of destroying the morale of these isolated, war-weary soldiers.

Then the attack came. The front smashed in the north was bent down through the valleys of the Natisone and the Judrio until it became necessary to escape from the Bainsizza, from Gorizia, from Vippacco, and from the Carso.

### Defenses of Veneto

The region of Veneto is defended from the east and north by five natural lines of defense—the right banks of the Tagliamento, of the Livenza, of the Piave, of the Brenta, of the Adige—and two of these have been rendered stronger by art. In the Spring of 1915, when Italy expected to declare war on Austria simultaneously with rupturing the Triple Alliance Treaty, she had fortified the Tagliamento line and intended to retreat to it. But on account of Giolitti's plottings she did not then declare war. Meanwhile, the Austrians removed between 200,000 and 300,000 men from the frontier for work against the Russians in Galicia. Thus the Tagliamento line was not used. Later the western bank of the Piave was fortified with practice trenches.

By the time the retreating armies had reached the Piave a natural contraction had taken place in the north—from the Val Sugana. It was not until then that the Germans made a sudden drive from the Trentino and reached Asiago—the extreme point of the Austrian invasion in June, 1916, but now no longer threatened from the Val Sugana. Asiago, on the plateau of the Sette Comuni, is on the left-rear flank of both the Piave and the Brenta lines, and on the right-rear flank of the Italian Army before Rovereto, along the Val Terragnolo and across the Lago di Garda. Thus the last resort

of the Regione di Veneto is the Adige, which flows through the Trentino into Italy, along the side of the Quadrilateral through the Province of Verona and separating the Province of Padua from that of Rovigo, thence into the Adriatic just south of the mouth of the Brenta and the Lagoon of Venice.

The military details which have brought the Italian armies to the Piave and the Germans to threaten their rear from the Sette Comuni run chronologically as follows:

### The Battle in Detail

On Sunday, Oct. 21, the artillery of the enemy began a bombardment on carefully selected positions of the Plezzo-Tolmino front and from the slopes of the Idria upon the northern flank of the Italian loop on the Bainsizza. By the 24th it had become apparent that the bombardment was being performed principally by German guns, under cover of which the enemy had broken through the first-line trenches at Plezzo and just south of Tolmino had crossed to the west bank of the Isonzo, under the protection of the bridgehead of Monte Santa Maria and Monte Santa Lucia. From these two points the enemy was able to converge along the Isonzo south and north upon Caporetto, to cut off the Italian detachments retreating from the Monte Nero region, and to open the way down the Natisone and the Judrio. Thus threatened in their rear the principal divisions of the Second Army under General Capello, on the Bainsizza, and those of the Third under the Duke of Aosta, on the Carso, began to retreat.

Thus by the 26th the enemy had advanced beyond Caporetto, crossing the frontier to the valley of the Natisone, while further south he had gone beyond Ronzina by descending the Val Judrio, and had forced some 30,000 Italians, mostly road builders, however, to surrender. About 250 guns of position, principally 6-inch and 8-inch howitzers of old pattern, had to be abandoned. The next day Berlin reported that the number of prisoners had reached 60,000 and the number of captured guns over 500. On the morning of that day Ger-

# THE UNITED STATES WAR MISSION

**COL. EDWARD M. HOUSE**
Special Ambassador.
*(Photo Press Illus. Service.)*

**BAINBRIDGE COLBY**
Member of the Shipping Board.
*(Photo Davis & Sanford.)*

**VANCE McCORMICK**
Chairman of the War Trade Board.
*(Photo by Bain News Service.)*

**OSCAR T. CROSBY**
Assistant Secretary of the
Treasury.
*(© Harris & Ewing.)*

# CIVILIANS ACTIVE IN WAR WORK

JUDGE C. H. LINDLEY
Head of the Legal Department of
the Food Administration.
(© *Harris & Ewing.*)

FRANK A. VANDERLIP
President National City Bank of
New York, Serving as Treasury
Adviser.
(© *Harris & Ewing.*)

A. MITCHELL PALMER
Custodian of Alien Property.
(© *Harris & Ewing.*)

CHARLES R. PAGE
Member of the United States
Shipping Board.
(© *Harris & Ewing.*)

man troops by a violent series of assaults had secured possession of Monte Matajur, from which they were able to dominate the Italian retreat down the Natisone and the Judrio.

Meanwhile, the Italians, who had attempted to consolidate a new line between Monte Matajur and Auzza on the Isonzo, had to give way. The retreat of the Second Army from the Bainsizza and the slopes of Monte San Gabriele and Monte Santo, lying south, and from Monte Cucco, west, became almost a rout across the improvised bridges of the Isonzo and through Gorizia, which the enemy artillery from the abandoned positions was rapidly leveling with the ground. On the 28th Berlin reported the occupation of Cividale, on the Natisone, the railway approach to the Italian General Headquarters at Udine, ten miles to the southwest. In the centre the Austrians, sweeping across the Bainsizza and down the slopes of the mountains already mentioned, had occupied Gorizia and were threatening the Duke of Aosta's left flank.

Here on the 29th the Austrians met with a stubborn resistance along the Vippacco, which undoubtedly saved from destruction the Third Army now in more rapid retreat to the southwest of Gorizia. On the Gorizia-Udine railway, Cormons, the first town in Austria occupied by the Italians at the beginning of the war, was recaptured, thereby turning the flank of a detachment that was attempting to make a stand before Udine.

A glance at the map will show that the advance of the Germans had now reached a point which threatened the rear of the Fourth Italian Army, which, from the beginning of the war, had been guarding the passes which led from Carinthia into the Regione of Veneto across the frontier barrier of 100 miles of the Carnic Alps. Consequently, this army began to abandon its positions at the Ploecken Pass and similar places, seeking the protection of the valleys which carried streams into the upper Piave and Tagliamento Rivers.

On Oct. 24 Udine was taken by the Fourteenth German Army. This brought the enemy within sixteen miles of the centre of the Tagliamento on its lower (southern) course. This river, which rises in the district of Carnia a few miles east of Pieva di Cadore, in the Venetian Alps, first flows eastward, through deep-cut, sheltered gorges, a rapid and narrow stream, by Ampezzo and Tolmezzo, for about forty miles, and then, turning abruptly southward, it traverses, through many broad and some shallow channels, the plains and then the marshes of the Province of Udine, and empties into the Adriatic opposite the Bay of Trieste. In its middle course this river had been strongly fortified, in anticipation of a retreat from the frontier, if Italy, as has already been pointed out, had made war on Austria on May 5, 1915, instead of eighteen days later. Then, however, there would have been no Fourth Army to take care of retreating from the Carnic and Venetian Alps, and the Second and Third Armies would have been strongly intrenched, with guns of position. Now all was different; there were few guns of position and all three armies were in full retreat.

By Nov. 1 the enemy had reached the middle of the Tagliamento line, while in the south, being confronted by no bridgeheads, he had crossed the lower reaches of the river south of Codroipo. Over the plains of Udine the Second and Third Armies were fighting gallant rearguard engagements.

It was all in vain. The Tagliamento line could not be held. There was no adequate artillery to protect what had once been formidable bridgeheads at Latisana and other places. And by, literally, hundreds of isolated encircling movements detachments of the enemy had increased the number of his prisoners to 180,000 and his number of captured guns to 1,500—so the Berlin report stated on Nov. 1. It was small satisfaction that just 120 years before Napoleon had beaten the Austrians on the same ground. But Napoleon was leading an offensive army; Napoleon was a master of artillery and had the guns. Cadorna was conducting a retreat; he was not a master of artillery, he had few guns, and —he was not Napoleon.

The Teutonic hosts swept on, crossing the Tagliamento at fifty places, princi-

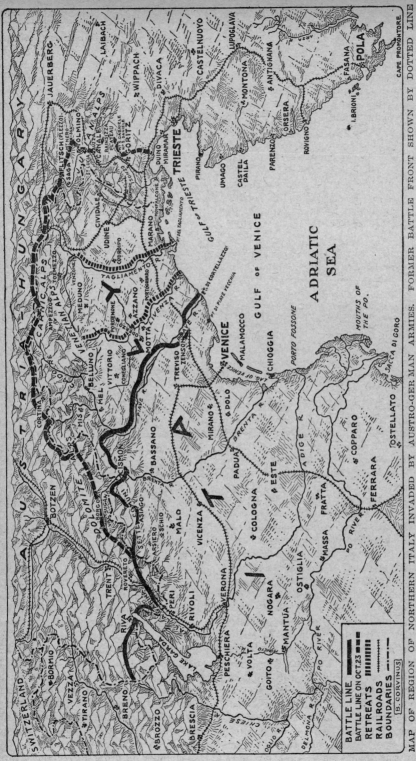

MAP OF REGION OF NORTHERN ITALY INVADED BY AUSTRO-GERMAN ARMIES. FORMER BATTLE FRONT SHOWN BY DOTTED LINE ON THE EAST; PRESENT FRONT BY BLACK LINE NORTH OF VENICE. (NOV. 18, 1917)

pally at Tolmezzo and Pinzano. The next line was the Livenza. This river promised fewer positions for resistance. But at the Piave, from ten to twenty miles further west, the situation was different. There the right bank was protected by the most modern and approved practice trenches constructed by " rookies " before they had been allowed to go to the battle line. And behind the Piave the Second and Third Armies were being reformed. But from the north the Fourth Army was in ever-increasing retreat through the Venetian Alps, while in the northwest the First Army, with its right thereby exposed, was beginning to leave its hard-won Dolomite terrain and stubbornly held passes in the Cadore. The Trentine Cortina had been given up; the fortifications of Comelico, Santo Stefano, Lorenzago, and Piave di Cadore surrendered.

By skillful manoeuvres on the Tagliamento the invaders had captured by Nov. 8 an additional 17,000 prisoners, making a quarter of a million in all; the number of guns taken was 2,300.

At this period a change was made in the Italian High Command: General Diaz took the place of Cadorna, and was to be assisted by Generals Badoglio and Giardino. There was also formed for the conduct of the war a triune General Staff, with General Foch, Chief of Staff of the French War Office; General Sir Henry Hughes Wilson of the British General Staff, and General Cadorna. French and British reinforcements were hourly arriving in Italy, and with adequate heavy artillery, but it was deemed inexpedient to risk them at the Piave line, possibly not even at the Brenta. The Piave line was, therefore, left to the Italians to defend alone with such batteries of British mid-calibre guns as had successfully made their retreat with the Duke of Aosta's army from the Carso.

And now on Nov. 10 the full scope of German strategy was revealed by the descent of an Austrian detachment from the Trentino to Asiago, twenty miles southeast from the frontier, eight miles west of the Brenta, and twenty miles west of the upper Piave, thus not only threatening the left rear of the retreating armies, but the right rear of the First Army holding the line before Rovereto along the Val Terragnola and across the Val Lagarina, through which the Adige flows from the Trentino down to Verona and the plains of Western Veneto.

## Second Phase of the Battle

Thus the great battle for Venice entered upon its second phase. On the 11th Austro-German forces operating from the Cadore captured the city of Belluno on the upper Piave, and from Asiago worked eastward on the Sette Comuni and from the Val Sugana southward. On the Sette Comuni they captured the advanced Italian posts on Gallio and Monte Serragh, (1,116 meters high;) on the Piave they took by storm the Vidor bridgehead, where the Italian troops on the heights of Valdobbiadene had made a gallant stand. On the western bank of the lower Piave the Italian line was beginning to stiffen, but was not sufficiently consolidated to prevent the enemy on the 13th from crossing near Zenson, nineteen miles from Venice, and taking a bridgehead further up the stream at Monte San Dona. In the Sette Comuni they wrested Monte Langara from its defenders, but failed to pierce the line Monte Gallio-Longara-Meletta di Gallio.

The next day the enemy attempted to divide the Italian forces on the upper Piave by occupying Feltre and Pirmolano, and to the west of the Lago di Garda they made ineffective attempts to drive the Italians from their positions on the Lago Ledro. On the 15th there were intensified attacks on the Sette Comuni extending eastward to the Piave below Feltre, and here the Italians withdrew from Monte Tomatico to a stronger position. On the southern reaches of the Piave the Italian floats with huge naval guns, which had been so effective in clearing the southern approaches to the Carso in August, aided the army in consolidating its positions on the western bank. Further aid was given by the engineers, who opened the flood-gates erected when the course of the Piave was changed in order to reclaim a large terrain south of San Dona and to prevent

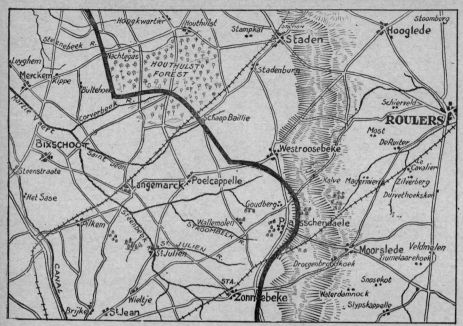

FLANDERS FRONT AFTER BRITISH CAPTURE OF PASSCHENDAELE

sudden risings in the lagoons of Venice. Thus a triangle formed by the Piave and the Sile (the old mouth of the Piave) with its vertex at Musile was suddenly placed under water, enveloping the enemy, who had crossed the river at Grisolera, four miles from the coast.

Through Nov. 17 and 18 the Austro-German invaders were trying in vain to develop their position at Asiago by desperate attacks both west and east of the Lago di Garda; east of Asiago, from their positions on the Brenta in the Val Sugana; from Feltre down the Piave. Further down the Piave at several places they effected crossings, only to be enveloped or forced back to the left bank. While these assaults were rapidly assuming the appearance, in the ruthless sacrifice of men, of the German Crown Prince's conduct at Verdun and on the Aisne, General Diaz was making no mention of the employment in the defensive of French and British troops.

### Battle of Flanders Resumed

On the western front the battle of Flanders has been renewed, developing, not southeast of Ypres along the road which leads to Menin, but along the Ypres-Roulers road to the northeast, embracing the village of Passchendaele, more strategic, fortified farms and " pillboxes " on the ridge of that name, along the Ypres-Staden railway, and north through the outskirts of the Forest of Houthulst, and still further north until it included the Merckem Peninsula, which lies a short walk south of Dixmude. Owing to the weather, these advances, which are gradually enveloping West Flanders, were not accompanied by the naval and air raids upon the submarine bases of Zeebrugge and Ostend which emphasized the advance over the Passchendaele Ridge a month ago; but the enemy airdromes on the dunes have been bombed, particularly Varssenaere and the Thourout railway junction.

### Passchendaele Captured

Early in the morning of Oct. 22 the British, with the French troops co-operating on their left, secured strategic positions on both sides of the Ypres-Staden railway, while the French secured the southern defenses of Houthulst Forest and a number of fortified farms. On the 26th the British took the German positions at Bellevue Spur and Wolf Copse,

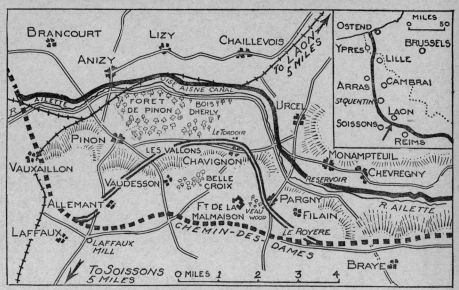

WHERE THE FRENCH FORCED THE GERMANS TO RETIRE FROM THE CHEMIN DES
DAMES: DOTTED LINE, FRENCH FRONT BEFORE THE ADVANCE; DOUBLE
LINE, EXTENT OF FRENCH THRUST; HEAVY BLACK
LINE, EXTENT OF GERMAN RETREAT

west of Passchendaele, and Polderhoeck Château, north of Gheluvelt; the French, the village of Draeibank, Papagoed Wood, and a number of fortified farms. On the following day the British extended their positions west and south of Passchendaele, while the French, advancing on both sides of the Bixschoote-Dixmude road, captured the villages of Aschhoop, Kippe, and Mercken, and more fortified farms.

The strategy of these moves is perfectly apparent—both obvious and irresistible: for on the 28th French troops, with the Belgians operating on their left, advanced across the morasses two miles south of Dixmude and captured the terrain known as the Mercken Peninsula, a strip of land formed by canals on the north, west, and south. Two days later, after that period of diverting raids further south, the British with the Canadians in the van made a sudden advance from their positions on Bellevue Spur and Wolf Copse, reached out and took most of the defenses of Passchendaele, and then retired to their old positions in the face of overwhelming German reinforcements, which were slaughtered by a barrage covering the retirement. Then,

after a week of bombardment, the Canadians tried it again, this time sweeping clear through Passchendaele to positions 800 yards beyond. From the 7th until the 14th there were heavy German counterattacks, but this time the Canadian line beyond Passchendaele did not budge. The Germans lost heavily.

### Petain at Chemin des Dames

After the battle of the Marne the Germans strongly intrenched themselves along the ridge of the Chemin des Dames, between the Ailette and the River Aisne; part of the ridge was wrested from them last May and June, but up to the present engagement the net result of the whole series of operations of the French was that they had managed to secure the enemy's points of observation over the valley of the Aisne east and west without themselves winning a line from which they could command the valley of the Ailette to the north over the historic plateau crowned by the cathedral of Laon.

The Germans, although having lost their observation posts commanding the Aisne, believed their positions south of the Ailette would withstand any amount of bombing. As early as Oct. 17 Pétain began searching out these positions hidden in quarry caverns, sometimes with six-inch and sometimes with eight-inch guns. Having ascertained these positions by their return fire, on the 20th he added some batteries of fifteen and sixteen inch, and for three days he thundered away at intervals with these monster tubes until the rocks crumbled before the detonation of high explosives and the quarry caverns lay exposed. The breaches thus made were observed by the airmen overhead and then into them were poured a steady stream of shrapnel from the famous French " 75s " in their hitherto silent hiding places near the front line. When all was ready, the enemy experienced another exhibition of the " Pétain touch," which is becoming as traditional on land as the " Nelson touch " has been for a century and more on sea.

### Taking of Malmaison Fort

At precisely 5:15, amid the mist and rain of the morning of Oct. 23, the French infantry rushed forward with splendid élan and carried Malmaison Fort, in the centre, and the villages of Allemant and Vaudesson on the left. They attacked on a six-mile front, and their penetration was two miles. They were supported by a highly concentrated barrage of 16-inch shells and by squadrons of newly devised " tanks." Before them melted away the Second and Fifth Guard Divisions, based on Leuilly and Cornell, and flanked west and east by the Thirteenth Division, south of Chivy, and the Forty-seventh Division of the Reserve, south of Vorges. Nor did the Fourteenth and Twenty-first Divisions supporting these troops have a chance, for before they could be used the French advance had torn to tatters their carefully prepared strategy—to attack right and left. The French captured 10,-000 prisoners and seventy heavy guns and a huge amount of supplies.

The next day the French reached the Oise-Aisne Canal, capturing 2,000 additional prisoners and fifty more heavy guns. From the 26th to the 30th, by consolidating their positions, they captured another thousand prisoners and forty more heavy guns.

Meanwhile, the French aviators had noticed signs of preparations for a German retreat. A retreat was inevitable; as the positions of the enemy south of the Ailette, on the Oise-Aisne Canal, and the western ridge of the Chemin des Dames, could now be enfiladed from the west and east. The only question was: What would be the scope of the retreat? Would it be a mere local retirement beyond the Ailette and the canal, or would it include the entire triangle protecting Laon, from a line running from Craonne and its plateaux on the west to the St. Quentin salient on the north, thus obliterating the Laon elbow?

### The German Retreat

The French were prepared for either eventuality, but the Germans, on the night of Nov. 1, chose the former, withdrawing beyond the Ailette and abandoning the western elevations on the Chemin des Dames, with the French close at their heels, until the enemy reached his prepared positions on the northern side of the Ailette Valley.

The French assault, beginning on Oct. 23, and the German retreat of Nov. 1 regained about forty square miles of French territory in the Department of the Aisne. French military critics declare that the more extended withdrawal on the part of the enemy was abandoned at the last moment through his inability to remove his heavy guns, and, at the same time, protect his rear.

In analyzing the advance of the French southwest of Laon and the subsequent falling back of the Germans across the Ailette, they foresaw early in the month a rectifying of the German front from Verdun southwest along the frontier in front of Nancy and Lunéville, with possibly the voluntary retirement of the enemy from the St. Mihiel triangular salient which embraces the Plain of the Woevre between the Meuse and the Moselle—a wedge between Verdun and Metz. A retirement on this part of the line is believed to be imminent, not only because the Germans north and northeast of Verdun have lost most of their strategic positions, but because, in case of a drive of the Allies over the frontier into Lorraine, the movement of reinforcements from the west would be handicapped. So far, however, the month has produced nothing but violent artillery duels at Chaume Wood, Verdun front, to bear out the prophecy.

## Around Riga

Last month we left operations around the Gulf of Riga in a condition which seemed to foreshadow an attack by sea and land upon the Russian naval base at Reval and opposite, upon the coast of Finland, with a possible naval demonstration before Petrograd. The bulk of the Russian Baltic fleet of some twenty ships, having lost the battleship Slava and some small craft, was apparently locked up in that part of Moon Sound which lies between Dagö and Oesel Islands and the mainland by a strong German fleet of fifty, which, according to Russian reports, had lost six light units in combat and had been crippled to the extent of sixteen. On Oct. 21 the German expedition reached the mainland, effecting a landing at Werder and operating from Moon Island, which lies north of the sound. Meanwhile the Russian ships supposed to have been effectually trapped in the sound escaped.

The Kaiser, who had just returned to Berlin from his visit to his ally the Sultan at Constantinople, highly praised the Riga operation as proving the " preparedness of my navy," and there were criticisms of the British Admiralty in the London press for not having sent a fleet to engage the enemy in the Baltic—criticisms which were met by the reply that the channels leading from the Skagerrak to the Baltic were too dangerous to penetrate, particularly as their waters, commanded by Denmark and Sweden, might at any time be rendered unneutral by a German coup.

Henceforth, the operations in the Riga region and, indeed, throughout the entire eastern front became influenced by two widely different events: The desperate call of Austria for troops to defend her territory along the Julian Alps from the Italians and the attempted coup d'etat of the Bolsheviki against the Provisional Government as represented by Kerensky at Petrograd, which began on Nov. 6. The first of these events, which is essentially

military, caused a shortening of the Teuton lines by consolidation in the rear to the east of the City of Riga by a withdrawal toward the Skuli-Lemberg line in the south, and by a postponement of the development of the expedition against the mainland east of the Gulf of Riga. The consequences elsewhere, on the Austro-Italian front, have already been treated of. The second of the events is largely political, although fraught with the ebb and flow of civil war, and with it this review has no particular concern, except to say that so paralyzed had become the Russian forces at the front that the withdrawal of forty-seven Teuton divisions hence offered no particular inspiration to renew hostilities.

## The Holy City Invested

As these pages are going to press, one of the most romantic campaigns of the war is being developed upon the plains of Palestine. The Holy City is invested from three sides, and, although it may be days, even weeks, before the particulars of the campaign come to hand—the meagre bulletins of the British War Office have made known bare facts—famous Biblical sites have fallen before the advance of the British-Egyptian army and the Turks have lost over 20,000 men, nearly half of whom have been registered as prisoners.

In my last review, with the aid of a map of Asiatic Turkey, the season's opening activities of the Anglo-Indian army in Mesopotamia were recorded and their strategic relationship was shown with the Russian Caucasus army in the north and with the British-Egyptian army away in the west, in Palestine, and some emphasis was laid on the Turkish army concentrated at Aleppo, the junction of the Bagdad and Damascus-Medina railways, under the command of the German Field Marshal Mackensen, erroneously announced in the cable dispatches to be leading the Austro-German forces in Italy.

The Aleppo army has not yet come upon the scene but, save for the fact that the Anglo-Indian Army on Nov. 6 occupied Tekrit, on the Tigris, ninety-seven miles northwest of Bagdad—the

SCENE OF BRITISH ADVANCE IN PALESTINE FROM GAZA TO JAFFA, WITH JERUSALEM
THREATENED

Turks retiring from thirty to fifty miles north in the direction of Mosul—the army in Palestine has consistently claimed the attention of the month. For, not only has the British-Egyptian army operating there under the direction of General Allenby captured or destroyed over 20,000 Turks and won a formidable strategic point on the Abushusheh Ridge commanding Jerusalem from the northwest, but almost every step of the invading armies has revived Old Testament memories.

### The Changed Situation

Moreover, Allenby's victories have served to allay the fear that had been augmenting since last Spring, and guardedly referred to in a former review, that possibly all was not well with the army in Palestine. A moment may now be taken to explain the causes of this fear:

On March 29 the British War Office announced that on the 26th and 27th inst. heavy losses had been inflicted on the Turks, who had lost 900 prisoners, a few miles south of Gaza. The next day the Turks, in a bulletin issued from Constantinople, claimed a " brilliant victory," and on April 2 the British War Office, in a further report, announced that on March 26 an attempt " to capture Gaza by a coup de main " had failed and that on the 27th a Turkish attack had been " repulsed, with heavy losses," while on March 28 " our infantry was withdrawn to the Wadi Ghuzzeh."

And so the situation stood, with uncomfortable rumors about Mackensen's activities at Aleppo, until the good news of this month.

On Oct. 31, after a night's march, Allenby's army made a sudden attack upon Beersheba, and before the sunset had occupied the city, taking 1,800 prisoners. Thus did the British-Egyptian army enter the " Promised Land "—extending from Beersheba, forty miles southwest of Jerusalem, to Dan, about 100 miles north of the Holy City—" from Dan to Beersheba."

The next to fall was Gaza, three miles

from the sea, on the 6th. Gaza was the city whose gates Samson is said to have carried away, (Judges XVI., 3.) It has an Assyrian, Median, and Egyptian history as well as a Jewish. The Crusaders found it a heap of ruins in the twelfth century, but in 1799 Napoleon found it sufficiently restored to merit investment.

## Victorious March to Jaffa

Following the fall of Gaza with 1,900 casualties to the Turks a series of minor engagements took place—the mounted troops cleared the way through Jemameh and Huj, French and British warships cannonaded the Turkish lines of communication near the coast, and aircraft bombed their bases. By Nov. 9 the whole Turkish Army was moving rapidly northward, leaving the coastal railhead at Beit Hanun in Allenby's hands.

Four hundred prisoners and ten guns had been picked up on his victorious way to Askalon on the coast and he estimated the enemy's casualties to date at 10,000, exclusive of prisoners.

By Nov. 15 the junction point of the Beersheba-Damascus railway was taken from the Turks with the loss of 1,500 prisoners and several pieces of artillery. Continuing his drive, Allenby then pushed on from the Surar (Brook Kedron) northward to the Jaffa-Jerusalem railway, and then swept eastward along the railroad to its junction with the Beersheba-Damascus line, only twelve miles from the Holy City.

By the 15th the British-Egyptian army had reached a line from Er Ramleh and Ludd to a point three miles south of Jaffa, the port of Jerusalem. The next day they seized the Abushusheh Ridge, five miles southeast of Ramleh. Here 431 Turks were killed and 360 surrendered. Ramleh is on the Jaffa-Jerusalem railway, twenty-two miles northwest of the Holy City. On the 16th the British War Office reported that the number of prisoners verified since Oct. 31 exceeded 9,000. On Nov. 17 Jaffa was occupied by Australian and New Zealand mounted troops without opposition.

## Americans at the Front

On Oct. 27 it was officially announced that the American troops in France had begun to finish their intensive training in the trenches " of a quiet sector on the French front." Less than a week later, just as the Germans were completing their retreat across the Ailette, they announced the capture of some American patrols on the front of the Marne Canal, which connects the Rhine with the Marne via Toul and Nancy. Since then a number of raiding parties have had their adventures in No Man's Land on this front; casualties have been received and inflicted under French tuition. There have been artillery duels, and Americans have been killed by German shells.

Following the loss by torpedoing of an American destroyer on Oct. 16 and the transport Antilles on the 17th, homeward bound, came the news of the sinking on Nov. 5 by the same means of the converted yacht Alcedo. In the first case one man was lost; in the second, seventy men were reported missing; in the third, twenty.

Other events of more or less military importance have been the destruction of four Zeppelins in France as they were returning from a raid on England, on the night of Oct. 19-20; the destruction of nine neutral vessels and two British destroyers by a couple of German cruisers, between the Shetland Islands and the coast of Norway, on Oct. 17; the bombardment of the outlying depots of Metz within a radius of twenty-five miles of the fortress, on Oct. 29; the destruction of a German cruiser and ten patrol ships by British destroyers in the Cattegat, on Nov. 2, and a clash between British and German light squadrons off Heligoland, the results of which, on Nov. 18, had not been officially reported.

# Austro-German Invasion of Italy

## Sudden Blow That Drove Cadorna's Armies
## Back to the Piave River and Threatened Venice

[See Map on Page 395]

THE world was startled in the closing days of October, 1917, by the news that Austro-German armies had burst through the Italian front in the Julian Alps and along the Isonzo and were sweeping southwestward into the Venetian Plain. The retreating Italians fought heroically, trying to stop the enemy flood in each successive valley as they fell back, but in vain, until they finally checked the invaders at the Piave River. At the present writing—Nov. 19—the precarious Piave line still holds, but the Austro-Germans are almost within firing distance of Venice.

The story of this Italian disaster, with the loss of more than 250,000 prisoners and 2,300 guns in the first week, will require time to fill in some of its tragic details, including those of its causes. The outstanding fact is that on Oct. 24 a sudden attack by German and Austrian infantry in the Julian Alps resulted in their capturing the Italian positions near Plezzo and Tolmino and in the northern portion of the Bainsizza Plateau. The Plezzo-Tolmino sector was held by the Italian Second Army, under General Capello, and at least one unit of that army failed to resist—threw away its arms and fled, or surrendered without fighting. At this point the enemy burst through, threatening the rear of the Third Army, on the south, and forcing the hasty retirement of the whole Italian force along the seventy miles of hard-won front from the Carnic Alps to the sea.

The Italian War Office in its bulletin next day charged certain units of its own troops with "cowardice," and, though the word was afterward modified, General Cadorna summed up the cause of the initial break in this terse sentence: "The violence of the enemy's attack and inadequate resistance broke our left wing on the Julian front." The "inadequate resistance" has been explained as follows:

"Opposite the Second Italian Army the Austrians had placed regiments composed largely of Socialists, and these utilized the war-weariness of opponents similarly infected to convince the latter that an end of the fighting would come if the soldiers on both sides should refuse to kill each other any longer. Fraternization followed, and an exchange of promises to do no more shooting. Then the demoralized — and demoralizing — Austrian division was withdrawn, and in its place were put German shock troops. These it was that almost unopposed smashed through the Italian line and began the flanking movement of which the results have been so disastrous to Italy."

### Story of the Retreat

Glimpses of the great retreat of the next two weeks are afforded by the eyewitness narratives of several press correspondents caught in the swirl of its movements. It was an orderly retreat, often masterly in its strategy and always illumined by the heroism of the men who fought the rearguard actions, sacrificing themselves in order to delay the enemy and give their own armies time to withdraw. Perceval Gibbon, who was at Udine, the Italian headquarters, when it was evacuated, wrote on Nov. 1:

"It was on Oct. 27 that the news arrived that a retirement had been decided upon. I had telegraphed the previous day regarding the events which culminated in the enemy's occupation of Caporetto, a little village on the upper Isonzo, where a great series of dams had been constructed by which, if need were, Cadorna could have drained the Isonzo dry by nightfall. On Friday his columns were driving northwest against Monte Stol and southwest along the Natison Valley and toward Tarcento. Further east and south, along the Isonzo Valley, Italian troops were fighting desperately. Guns which had been lost were being retaken by hand-to-hand fighting with the bayonet among batteries, and on Monte Nero the heroic Alpini, isolated from the rest of the army and hard pressed by the Germans, were holding out victoriously, sending messages by carrier pigeon announcing that they would continue to maintain their positions to the death.

"On Saturday night I spoke to the Major commanding one of those superb battalions. He had been wounded and had been rushed out on an ambulance under fire just before the roads were cut. He was desperate for nothing but an opportunity to get back to his battalion, but a breach in the line toward Caporetto made his heroism vain. The Germans were already actually in the rear of certain sectors, and by Saturday night the retreat had been begun.

## Poison Shells Harass the Retreat

" The withdrawal from the front line was a manoeuvre of infinite difficulty, which a touch of panic would have converted into the ruin of the army. The enemy maintained his terrific fire upon the Italian communications, so that the troops withdrew into the tornado of shells of every kind that makes a hell of war. Gas shells loosed vapors that haunted the roads invisibly; acid shells set the men suddenly gasping and strangling; tear-producing shells half blinded them. Nothing could have brought them help but the dozen rearguard actions roaring and flaming at their heels and superb and long-confirmed discipline.

" While they withdrew, a force of those splendid desperadoes who volunteer for rearguard fighting smashed its way up to Liga and delivered attacks which cleared the army's feet on that sector.

" Further south the Duke of Aosta's Third Army was giving proof of fine soldiership. It answered the ponderous enemy attack upon Selo on the Carso by a counterattack which actually carried its line forward to Stari Lokva and which under any other circumstances would have given it a permanent gain of ground; but its business now was to withdraw its retirement under unceasing pressure over the terrible ground of the Carso, made more terrible by the

blinding rain which thrashed down throughout Saturday. With the Isonzo to cross and the infinitely delicate and perilous operation of the rearguard action to carry out, it was a feat which no defeated army could have attempted. It was one of the great achievements of the war. The British artillerymen, who bore a part in the action, saved all their guns.

## Udine Is Left Empty

" During Saturday the civilians of the threatened districts of Udine and its adjoining villages began their flight westward. The little City of Udine poured itself along the great level highway which runs westward toward the cities of the plain, and by Sunday morning the poor little town with its shuttered shops and vacant streets, wherein one's footfall echoed forlornly through the deep arcades which shade its sidewalks, had taken on the air of a cemetery.

"I walked to each of the city gates in turn. There were forgotten dogs sitting at the locked doors of abandoned houses, whining feebly. A terrified cat inside a window grating cowered and shivered in the station whence the last train had departed. A little group of walking wounded who had arrived too late were sitting on the platform waiting for some one to counsel them. Near the Aquileia Gate a row of great warehouses and factories belonging to the Department of Munitions had been set on fire and was burning with tremendous clear, red flames, which waved hundreds of feet high in the wet and rainy air.

"Toward noon it was evidently time to leave. I think I was the last civilian to go. I took a last look around from the summit of Castle Hill. Rain squalls inhabited the wide landscape like a population. Roads seemed to crawl and writhe with their dense westward traffic, and from Cividale, where the army had set fire to military depots, there arose great spires of flame and smoke. In Udine no chimney smoked. The little Palazzo, the most dreamily beautiful thing in Northern Italy, showed no flag; only under its columned loggia the frescoes of Pordenone glowed in their immortal colors.

" Warsaw, Vilna, Bucharest—I knew and loved them all; and now little Udine, so meek, so comely in its surrender to the pest that infests Europe. My own way rearward was by the great road which runs through Codroipo, Pordenone, and Treviso. It was a river running bank-high with the population of the retreat—vehicles four abreast crawling at the pace of the slowest; guns and caissons, private motor cars and donkey carts, soldiers on foot, and all that infinitely pitiable débris of war, the weary women and crying children whom Germany has made homeless. It is these last who give to every retreat its air of tragedy and disaster."

### Tragedy of the Refugees

Another correspondent, Ward Price, describes the scene thus:

" When the population of Udine heard rumors of disaster they began to leave the city, finally departing in crowds, even children being harnessed to truckloads of furniture. Great tractors got the guns across the long bridge one at a time, finally only one being left to continue the fire upon the enemy from the east bank.

" Scenes along the road were like a Gustave Doré conception of the day of judgment. Explosions and fires constantly took place at the rear and lighted up the terrible scene. The correspondent boarded a train which made fifteen miles in thirty-one hours, and then got out and went forward afoot. Soldiers and civilians were afraid to stop marching lest their legs swell. It was remarkable the small amount of harm the Austrian airplanes did to the dense columns along the roads.

" A gap has been made between the Second Italian Army and the Third, which is falling back in superior order to the south. Into the gap the Austrians pushed detachments of troops dressed in Italian uniforms which mingled with the retreating army and suddenly opened fire to the right and left with machine guns. At the same time Austrian field guns, mounted on armored motor cars, began shelling the refugees from the rear."

### Fall of Gorizia and Udine

The Berlin War Office on Oct. 27 made conspicuous announcement that the Italian drive was " under the personal supreme leadership " of Emperor Charles of Austria, and later named General Otto von Below and General Alexander von Krobatin as the commanders of the two Austro-German armies engaged. On Oct. 28 they took Gorizia, for which Italy had made great sacrifices a year ago, and Cividale, which the Italians left in flames. On the 30th, six days after the first attack, Udine, the General Italian Headquarters, was in the hands of the enemy. The Italians burned all bridges and towns behind them, leaving a trail of flames. By Nov. 1 they had passed behind the Tagliamento River, burning the last bridgeheads as the enemy came up in force on the east bank. The Tagliamento line, however, could be held only a few days.

" The safe retirement to the Tagliamento," wrote a correspondent, " was due to the unexampled heroism of large bodies of Italians of such spirit as the Alpini on Monte Nero, who refused to surrender, and the regiments of Bersaglieri at Monte Maggiore, who perished to the last man rather than yield ground. It was because of such resistance in the face of overwhelming forces of enemy artillery and infantry that the civil population was able to retire. It was owing to the valor of Italian aviators, combating the Austro-German army of the air, that fleeing women, children, and old men who crowded the roads were not struck down by bursting bombs."

### Abandoning the Tagliamento

The whole Tagliamento line had to be abandoned by Nov. 6, but the retirement was glorified by a score of heroic fights, as the troops of the rearguard brought the enemy again and again to a standstill and secured safely for the main armies as they established new lines on the Piave. Perceval Gibbon wrote on Nov. 9:

" Yesterday there was intense action along the Livenza from the foothills of the Carnic Alps to the foothills and water meadows of Motta, where the river broadens toward marshes and lagoons. The front here runs close to that other quaint and beautiful little City of Conegliano, another of those antique and characteristically Italian nests of prosperity and national life which are dotted so thickly over the battlefields of the last few days.

" One cannot but believe that the sight of the fields and cities, the contact with the mere soil of Italy has had its influence upon the fighting forces in its stimulus of burning patriotism. The men to whose defection on Oct. 24 Cadorna attributed his disaster were members of an army corps who were beyond their borders, fighting on Austrian soil. The mystery of why they failed has yet to be cleared up, and will make a strange chapter of war history.

" Now the armies are yielding up Italian soil, and where at some point they gain a success they must not profit by it, but fall back and again are leaving miles of Venetia, the fairest and ripest land on earth, to the traditional enemy.

" The Duke of Aosta's Third Army proved its discipline and skill in the first phases of the retreat from the Carso. It is still on the south of the line, driving back and back and turning to fight at each stage in the road."

The Italian forces by Nov. 10 were on the west bank of the Piave River, and the Austro-Germans were facing them across that stream from Susegana, in the foothills of the Alps, to the Adriatic. The whole Italian line, besides, was in danger of being flanked from the north, for the enemy had captured Asiago, a stronghold on the Trentino front, twenty miles west of the Piave. It had fallen after desperate street fighting. Belluno and Vidor had already passed into the hands of the enemy. Feltre, west of the upper Piave, followed on the 14th. The fate of the whole Piave line, and of Venice and Padua with it, thus hung in the balance.

## Heroic Work of the Motor Cars

A thrilling phase of the retreat was the part played by the Italian armored motor cars, each of which has three quick-firers in its turrets. The duty to which these cars was assigned was to hold the bridges from the Tagliamento to the Piave River until the cavalry rearguards had passed across, and then to burn the bridges behind them. The commander and a number of his men were seen by The Associated Press correspondent at their camp, where they recounted their experiences as though they were every-day occurrences.

Huge cars resembling tanks stood about at the camp, showing the scars received in the recent ordeal. They have heavily armored bodies. There is a steel door, and for observation purposes two small openings are provided. The two turrets above revolve, the upper one having one quick-firer, the lower two.

The orders were to " hold to the death " the bridges at Sacile, Polcenigo, Santa Lucia, and San Giovanni until the Bersaglieri and cavalry had crossed. That they succeeded is shown by the fact that all the rearguards made their way over the bridges, that all the bridges were burned, and that the section returned, leaving only one damaged machine with the enemy, although eighteen of the forty cars were in such crippled condition that it was necessary to abandon them after the bridges were burned.

## Dramatic Encounters

The machines were divided, ten being stationed at each of the four bridgeheads. After seeing their own rearguards safely across, they awaited the approach of the enemy advance guards, even staying in some cases until the cars were surrounded by hostile patrols, which were then mowed down by the batteries of quick-firers.

At the San Giovanni bridge one car took its station during the night midway across the bridge. Early in the morning it was ordered to surrender by a German car which bore the imperial crest and carried a German Captain and two Lieutenants. Instead of surrendering, two Italian Captains and four gunners suddenly opened the steel door and sprang out with carbines. The German Captain and one Lieutenant were killed. The other Lieutenant and the German car were captured and brought back.

At the Sacile bridge the cars had orders to hold for three hours, but they held for thirty-two hours. At Santa Lucia the commander ordered one of his machines to advance against an enemy patrol which was dangerously near. The car was rushed forward, sweeping the enemy from its double turrets, but when this mission was accomplished and the car was turned back, it was found that the bridge was on fire. The only way was to cross this burning bridge. The car was steered straight over the smoking structure, while the burning planks creaked under its huge weight. It crossed safely, and is one of the cars brought back.

### Drowning Out the Enemy

When the Austro-Germans began to cross the low delta at the mouth of the Piave, less than twenty miles from Venice, Italian engineers cut the dikes that held in the Piave and Sile Rivers and inundated the whole region. The flood was loosed on Nov. 15 at the point where the enemy had succeeded in crossing the Piave—near Grisolera—and in a few hours the inundated territory included a triangle about twelve miles on each side, with its apex at Dona di Piave. A correspondent gave this account of it:

" The water effectively holds the enemy at most exposed points and for fifteen miles on the west bank of the Piave. The flooded area is about seventy square miles, and the water is a foot to five feet deep and twelve miles in width at some points, making the district impossible of occupation or movement by enemy troops. The enemy clings to the west bank at Zenson, but is crowded into a small U-shaped position and relying on batteries across the river to keep the Italians back. Austro-German efforts to bring over large forces by pontoons have not succeeded, according to latest reports, either at Zenson or at points further north, where the invaders are feeling their way in an effort to get across.

" The lower floors of the houses in such villages as Piave Vecchia are under

water, and the campanili stick up from the mud-hued level of the flood like strange immense water plants; and here in the silence of the floods the enemy is

REGION INUNDATED BY THE ITALIANS
AT THE MOUTH OF THE PIAVE
TO SAVE VENICE

moving in boats and squelshing over mud islands. Peasants, awaiting rescue from the inundation, see him arrive with feelings much like those of shipwrecked people who hail a passing sail and find it is a pirate craft."

Thus the battle raged within hearing of Venice, while the inhabitants fled by thousands and tens of thousands, so that by Nov. 18 there were less than 20,000 people left in the city. The number of refugees from the invaded districts who were in need of food was estimated at 400,000 by the Red Cross officers at Rome. The Italian front, which had been nearly 450 miles long, was little more than 180, and threatened at every point. Allied troops from France and England were hastening to Italy's aid by thousands as fast as steam could carry them, and the United States had given $230,000,000 credit and rushed ships and supplies—all to the sound of fierce gun duels on the Piave front, and with each day adding to the ruins of a beautiful land.

# The Battle of Flanders

## Story of the Desperate British Onslaughts That Won Passchendaele Ridge

PASSCHENDAELE RIDGE, the chief objective of the British in their offensive in Flanders, for the possession of which hundreds of thousands of men fought desperately for weeks, passed entirely into the hands of the British on Nov. 10, 1917, when the last dominating point was captured by assault and the German lines were pierced half a mile. In evidence of the titanic character of the struggle for the ridge it was announced Nov. 16 that data in possession of the British staff showed that Crown Prince Rupprecht of Bavaria in two months had exhausted ninety-one German divisions (nearly 1,365,000 men) in defending vainly the Passchendaele Ridge and in fruitless counterattacks.

In a similar period of about two months the Germans, during the battle of the Somme, used eighty-six divisions, (1,-290,000 men.)

The British losses in the assaults are not given, but the weekly casualty reports since August have varied from 18,000 to a little under 25,000, the latter number being approached in the two weeks preceding the capture of the ridge.

### Description by an Eyewitness

Philip Gibbs thus describes the first success of the Canadians on Nov. 6, when they fought their way over the ruins of the village and into the ground beyond:

"What is Passchendaele? As I saw it this morning through the smoke of gunfire and the mist, it was just one ruin. Only the ruin of its church, a black mass of slaughtered masonry and nothing else, not even a house, was left standing. Because of its position as the crown of the ridge, that crest seemed to many men to be the prize for which all these battles of Flanders had been fought, and to get to this place and the slopes and ridges on the way to it, not only for its own sake, but for what it would bring with it, great numbers of our most gallant men have

given their blood. Thousands, scores of thousands, of British soldiers of our own home stock and from overseas have gone through fire and water, the fire of frightful bombardments, the water of swamps, and of shellholes in which they have plunged and waded.

"To defend the ridge and Passchendaele, the crest of it, the enemy had massed a great number of guns, an incredible number of machine guns, and many of his finest divisions. To check our progress he had devised new systems of defense and built his concrete blockhouses in formation at every crossroad and in every bit of village or farmhouse. Our men had to attack that chain of forts through girdles of machine-gun fire, and, after paying a great price in life, mastered it.

"The weather fought for the enemy again and again on the days of our attacks, and the horrors of the mud and bogs in 'crater land' extending over a wide sweep of country belong to the grimmest remembrances of every soldier who has fought in this battle of Flanders.

### Enormous German Losses

"The enemy may brush aside our advance as the taking of a mud patch, but to resist he at one time or another put nearly a hundred divisions into this arena of blood, and the defense cost him a vast sum of loss in dead and wounded. I saw his dead in Inverness Copse and Glencorse Wood. Over all this ground the young manhood of Germany has spent itself. It was not for worthless ground that so many of them died and suffered agonies or fought desperately and came back again in massed counterattacks that were swept to pieces by our guns and our rifle fire.

"True, Passchendaele is but a pinprick on a fair-sized map, but so that we should not take it the enemy has spent much of his man power and his gun power without stint, and there flowed up to his guns tides of shells almost as great as the tides that flowed up to our guns. Throughout these months he has never ceased by day or night to pour out hurricanes of fire over all these fields in the hope of smashing our progress.

"A few days ago orders were issued to his troops in the name of Hindenburg that Passchendaele must be held at all costs, and, if lost, must be recaptured at all costs.

### Victorious Canadians

"The Canadians have had more luck than the English, New Zealand, and Australian troops who have fought battles on the way up with the most heroic endeavor, and not a man in the army will begrudge them the honor they have gained, not easily nor without the usual price of victory, which is some men's death and many men's pain.

"For several days the enemy had endeavored to thrust us back from the positions we held around Crest Farm and on the left beyond Paddebeeke, where all the ground is a morass. The Naval Brigade, which fought there on the last days of last month, had a very hard and tragic time. It was grim stoicism in holding on to the exposed outposts—small groups of men under great shell fire—which enabled the Canadians this morning to attack from a good position.

"A special tribute is due to two companies of British infantry, which, with Canadian guides, worked through a large plantation, drove a wedge into the enemy territory and held it against all attempts to dislodge them. Heavy German counterattacks had been made during the last few days to drive us off Crest Farm and Meetcheele spur, but they only made a slight lodgment near Crest Farm and were thrust back with great loss. Meanwhile there was the usual vast activity on our side in making tracks, carrying railroads a few hundred yards nearer, hauling forward heavy guns out of the slough in which they deeply sank, and carrying up stores of ammunition and supplies for men and guns. All this work by pioneers, engineers, transports, men, and infantry was done under an infernal fire and in deep mud and filth.

### Awful Ordeal by Night

"Last night the enemy increased his fire as if he guessed his time was at hand. All night he flung down harassing barrages and scattered shells from his heavies and used gas shells to search out our batteries. He tried hard by means of every devilish thing in war to prevent the assembly of the Canadians, lying out in shell craters and in deep slime and mud under this fire. Though there were anxious hours and a great strain upon officers and men, and casualties here and there, the spirit of the men was not broken, and in a wonderful way they escaped great losses.

"The weather was moist and soft last night, with a stiff wind blowing. The weather prophets in the evening had shaken their heads gloomily and said, 'It will rain beyond all doubt,' but luck was with our troops, for the sun rose in a clear sky. There was great beauty in the sky at daybreak, and I thought of the sun of Austerlitz and hoped it might presage victory for our men.

As I saw Passchendaele this morning, the long ridge to which the village gives its name appeared black and grim below the clouds right around to Polygon Wood and the height of Broodseinde. Below the ridge all our field guns were firing, and the light of their flashes ran up and down like jack o' lanterns with flaming torches.

"Far behind me were our heavy guns, and their shells traveled overhead with a great beating of wind. In the sky around was the savage whine of German shells and all below Passchendaele Ridge monstrous shells were flinging up masses of earth and water. Now and then fires were lighted and blazed, and then went out in the west smoke."

### A Futile Counterattack

Various strong efforts were made by the Germans to retake the main position after its capture by the British on Nov. 10. The most determined was on Nov. 14, which is thus described by Mr. Gibbs:

"The enemy's troops were massed in the neighborhood of Wesroosebeke, and advanced under the protection of a violent barrage from the crossroads north

# GENERAL VON BELOW

German Commander in Chief on the Italian Front.
*(Photo Press Illustrating Service.)*

# GENERAL ALEXANDER VON KROBATIN

Former Austro-Hungarian War Minister, and Commander of the
Austrian Army in the Drive Against the Italians.
*(Photo Bain News Service.)*

of Passchendaele. Our men sent up S O S signals, and our guns at once opened fire upon the enemy's assembly places and tracks with intense and destructive concentration. Our machine gunners also swept the ground of approach with streams of bullets and scythed down the ranks of German storm troops. Their foremost waves seem to have been shattered, and only small bodies were able to approach our trenches, where they were repulsed after violent fighting.

"This attack did not come as a surprise. It is clear from what our prisoners have said that the German command was seriously chagrined by the loss of Passchendaele, and by the failure of immediate action to recapture it. The importance of this crest of the ridge, giving observation over the low country beyond, makes the German higher command deeply anxious to regain it, even at a great sacrifice of life.

" For some days past the Germans have been shelling all our ground, not only on the ridge itself, but also around Frezenburg and Inverness Copse, and all the roads beyond Ypres with great ferocity. At night, after intense counterbattery firing with high explosives, they have used gas shells against our guns. They have also brought up high-level guns and directed them against Ypres and other places behind our lines.

" They have some advantage in artillery over our positions at Passchendaele, owing to the distribution of their guns, which can enfilade the crest from two sides, but their infantry cannot make any counterattack without assembling on a narrow neck of ground north of Passchendaele village, where they are likely to be caught again, as yesterday, by our bombardment. For both sides the place is still a caldron, and the firing about it is very fierce.

" It is not easy to induce the German soldiers to come out in counterattacks, judging from the words of an officer who is a prisoner. The men are in a mutinous spirit against the continual slaughter in their ranks, and even the officers themselves have in recent battles run back and taken cover in dugouts, leaving their companies to noncommissioned officers. That, however, is the demoralization of men already nerve broken by shelling, and may not be true of the fresh divisions brought up for new attacks."

# French Victory at Chemin des Dames

## Culmination of a Bitter Struggle That Ended in a German Withdrawal on the Aisne Front

*The French on Oct. 23, 1917, delivered a smashing blow about seven miles northeast of Soissons on a six-mile front, and advanced to a depth of more than two miles at one point. More than 8,000 prisoners were taken in the fierce onslaught, besides 70 heavy guns, 80 machine guns, and 30 mine throwers. The attack began at 5:15 A. M. in rain and mist, and lasted less than six hours. A correspondent describes the advance as follows:*

THE battle opened before dawn along a nine-kilometer front, from the northeast of Laffaux, about the neighborhood of Vauxaillon, to La Royère Farm. Amid inky darkness the French troops left their trenches, and, with a terrific barrage fire from the most powerful concentration of French guns ever gathered on such a short front preceding them, they made their way toward, into, and over the first German positions, sweeping all resistance aside.

Altogether, six German infantry divisions were aligned, facing the French attacking forces, but none of them was able to withstand the onslaught. The advance continued like clockwork.

Several squadrons of tanks participated in the battle and aided the advancing infantry. It was by means of these most modern war implements that the Filain Farm was captured.

The battlefield bears no resemblance to battlefields anywhere else. The ground all around is broken with steep hills rising from deep valleys. The crest on which the fight occurred was vital for the Germans, and they held to it tenaciously.

Most of the prisoners taken were caught in quarries. One group, composed of 400 men, was led out to surrender by a German soldier, who spoke Franch, and assured his comrades that they need not fear bad treatment from their captors, despite the assertions currently made to them by their officers that the French massacred prisoners. Another batch of prisoners fell into the hands of the French just as they alighted from motor trucks, in which they had been hurried to the battlefield as reinforcements.

The losses of the Germans were extremely heavy, as was testified to by the heaps of dead found beneath the ruins of quarries, which crumbled under the French bombardment.

### Brilliant Work of Aviators

During the attack the aviation service rendered immense service for the French commander, working under the most unfavorable conditions for flying, namely, mists, heavy clouds, and strong winds. The airmen flew over the infantry when they were making the attack, and when they saw the German infantry assembling for a counterattack they advanced toward the enemy at an altitude of less than 100 yards, showered machine-gun bullets upon him, and brought about a dispersal of the assemblage.

Several French machines flew over the Laon railroad station and attacked arriving troop trains. Some of the machines accompanying the infantry columns kept so low that they were obliged to shorten the antennae of their wireless apparatus. All the airplanes participating in the battle were riddled with bullets. One of them fell blazing among the French troops. The pilot was uninjured and ran to the nearest battalion.

The attack took three main lines. Striking out from both sides of the mill of Laffaux toward Allemant village, the French had to deal with the Fourteenth Division—Westphalian troops—who suffered heavily in last year's fighting before Verdun. The largest proportion of prisoners was captured in this sector, where the turning point of the Hindenburg defense system has been smashed.

The centre of the assault lay northward from the Mennejean Farm across the Laon highroad. This sector was defended by the Twenty-second Guard Division. The most important of all was the sector on the French right, extending from La Royère Farm at Malmaison Fort, the capture of which was the great event of a brilliant day. It was defended by the Fifth Guard Division, the fort itself being held by elements of the Grenadier Guards.

On the left flank of the attack the enemy had in line the Thirty-seventh Division, and on the right the Forty-seventh Reserve, so that this front of exceptional strength was defended by six divisions.

## Positions of Vital Value

The position on this part of the Aisne heights had remained since the successful French offensive of April and May one of a dreadfully unstable equilibrium. The German command had lost much, but not everything, and for several months had used lavishly its human material in the hope of tightening its hold upon what remained to it of this important barrier—the southern corner of the Hindenburg line. Mennejean, La Royère, and Pantheon farms, among other points, became positions of vital significance.

The French held their own and the French command throughout the late Summer was steadily preparing one of those powerful and wonderfully organized efforts which give the cleanest success at the lowest cost. Passing up and down the Aisne this Autumn we have seen railways multiplied and new camps springing up in field and forests. All these preparations could not escape the eyes of the boche. The enemy knew the death challenge was being uttered once more, and had plenty of time to bring up reinforcements and otherwise to make ready.

## Labyrinths of Malmaison

The old fort of Malmaison was declassed long before the war, but it has been of immense use to the enemy as an observatory. Against such an attack as today's its glacis had been cleared, its shell reconstructed and furnished with machine-gun posts, and connected with a labyrinth of caves and tunnels running back to the northern edges of the plateau and so to the German rear.

This underground system of defenses illustrates a characteristic of the field, which distinguishes this from other offensives. The hills are honeycombed with limestone caves, grottoes, and tunnels. Nature began the work and engineers have extended it.

The fight was bound to be, therefore, to an abnormal degree, an artillery battle. To attempt to rush an intricate fortress like the Malmaison plateau before at least such works as had been detected by air scouts had been destroyed would have been to doom many gallant men to death. The spur of the plateau west of that on which the farm stands was known to be traversed by a tunnel called after the neighboring farm Mont Parnasse. The tunnel was large enough to shelter a whole brigade. On our side there were also tunnels and caves in which reserves awaited the moment of action.

Our victory definitely ruins the German hope of holding on to the Chemin des Dames. The positions which stopped our pursuit after the Marne in September, 1914, and limited our progress in April—these are now in our possession. It is impossible to overestimate the value of this local success in awaiting the hour of decisive victory.

## Chemin des Dames Abandoned

In consequence of the thrust of Oct. 23, which was followed immediately by further desperate advances, the German hold on the Chemin des Dames became untenable, and this whole sector was evacuated by the enemy on Nov. 1. The retirement was along a fifteen-mile front to the Ailette River, and involved the surrender of forty square miles of territory. The Germans here lost 12,000 prisoners, including 1,000 from the Prussian Guard, with 200 cannon, 700 Maxims, and 200 trench mortars.

The Chemin des Dames is—or rather

was—a road over the ridge that dominates the valley of the Aisne and the Ailette Valley, and its importance was taken advantage of by Napoleon in 1814 in operations that led to the battle of Craonne. The Germans had been in control of the Chemin des Dames since September, 1914, when, after the failure of the thrust toward Paris, the Teuton armies were turned back by Joffre in the battle of the Marne. They clung to this position desperately, and the French never lost sight of the value of the recapture of the intrenched line along this road.

## The Battlefield Described

G. H. Perris, the war correspondent, wrote on Nov. 4 regarding the scene of this French victory:

It is one of the bloodiest battlefields of the war, comparable to the hills before Verdun and the Flanders ridges. Its conquest is an unsurpassed story of heroic persistence, commenced in the middle of April under the commandership in chief of General Nivelle. This was completed after more than six months of ceaseless fighting under General Pétain.

The first offensive carried the French well on to the summit of the Aisne Hills. Then a deadly duel began. The enemy, whether by choice or necessity, never attempted a general offensive, but during the next three months delivered nearly forty local attacks with large bodies of shock troops and great concentration of artillery.

At the end of July I gave reasons for believing that he had then lost at least 100,000 men in these savage but fruitless assaults. They did not cease, but died down somewhat until last month, when there was a recrudescence of the conflict.

Meanwhile Pétain had been preparing one of his characteristic blows, the main features of which are a limited front strategically chosen, and an overwhelming artillery power and organization of attack so minute as almost to preclude failure in any part. We now see the results. Less than half of the front of the Aisne Hills was attacked, but the success in this field is so complete that the enemy has had to abandon the whole of it.

## Result of the Battle

This battle, in the judgment of THE NEW YORK TIMES military critic at Washington, was one of the most decisive of the war. The sector penetrated was part of the so-called Siegfried line. He wrote on Nov. 4 as follows:

The French on Nov. 5 were four miles nearer Laon. The distances from the new French positions in the Chemin des Dames region to Laon are: From Corbeny, 11 miles; from Craonne, 11 miles; from Ailles, 8½ miles; from Cerny, 8 miles; from Courtecon, 7½ miles, and from the fort at Malmaison, 8 miles. These points swing around, in the order named, from Corbeny on the east to Malmaison on the west of the Cemin des Dames, and the air line distance along the Chemin des Dames ridge from Corbeny to Malmaison is 13½ miles. This is the front from which the artillery of the new French positions on the Chemin des Dames ridge will converge their fire on the eminences of the Fort Montberault ridge.

All operations in the Aisne sector are considered of the greatest importance by the French, not only because of the effort they have been making for months to penetrate the Siegfried line, but because it was along the line of Laon-Soissons that the Germans hoped to be able to reach Paris. The battle front during the last Summer, in the region of Anizy-le-Château, 8.69 miles southwest of Laon, was the nearest to the German line on the western point to Paris. There has been a great bend of the line toward Paris, in the region between St. Quentin and Rheims, and Laon was the pivot of the circle and the base from which the Germans supplied every man and gun in their line around the masif of St. Gobain and the Chemin des Dames.

The Crown Prince of Germany has clung stubbornly to his very elaborate and complicated sets of trenches and gun positions in this region. So long as he held both St. Gobain and the Chemin des Dames, Laon and the valleys lying beyond to the northeastward were safe. Once the French are in possession of these two masifs of hills, and of Laon, whose evacuation would then be forced, it would be necessary for the German forces to relinquish the St. Gobain masif and give up the valley to the north, northeast, and east of Laon.

# Progress of the War

## Recording Campaigns on All Fronts and Collateral Events From October 19 Up to and Including November 18, 1917

### UNITED STATES

Sunday, Oct. 28, was observed as a day of prayer for the triumph of American arms, in compliance with President Wilson's proclamation.

Plans were made for seizing approximately $1,000,000,000 worth of German-owned money and other property subject to confiscation by the Government under the Trading with the Enemy act.

The Second Liberty Loan campaign closed Oct. 27. Subscriptions amounted to $4,617,-532,300.

The Emergency Fleet Corporation of the United States Shipping Board was reorganized in order to speed up the work of construction, and Charles A. Piez was placed in supreme charge.

An American Congressional delegation visited unofficially the western allied countries and the battle fronts.

New selective draft regulations were issued, canceling all exemptions and discharges, and repealing all preceding regulations.

Announcement was made on Nov. 7 that Colonel Edward M. House had arrived in England at the head of an American commission to take part in a series of war conferences. He received a message from President Wilson stating that the Government of the United States considered unity of plan and control between all the Allies and the United States essential to success, and asking him to attend the first meeting of the Supreme War Council, with General Tasker H. Bliss as military adviser.

Official announcement was made on Oct. 27 that American troops were in the first-line trenches on the French front. On Nov. 3 three Americans were killed, eleven wounded, and eleven reported missing after a German raid on a salient on the Marne-Rhine Canal. Further casualties occurred on Nov. 15 and Nov. 16 in the shelling of American trenches and in firing on patrols.

### SUBMARINE BLOCKADE

The American army transport Antilles was sunk Oct. 17, while homeward bound, and sixty-seven men, including sixteen soldiers, were lost. The transport Finland was attacked on Oct. 28 while homeward bound. Nine men were killed, but the ship was able to return to a European port. Twenty-one men were killed when the patrol boat Alcedor was sunk on Nov. 6. The steamer J. L. Luckenbach, after a four-hours' battle with a submarine, was saved by the arrival of a destroyer.

Two naval gunners and several members of the crew were wounded. The D. N. Luckenbach was sunk off the coast of France on Oct. 27, and five members of the crew were lost. A steamer carrying four American Congressmen to Europe was attacked off the coast of Wales on Oct. 27, but was saved by the work of the naval gunners. Seventeen men were lost when the steamship Rochester was sunk on Nov. 2.

England's losses for the week ended Oct. 20 included seventeen ships of over 1,600 tons, for the week ended Oct. 27 fourteen, for the week ended Nov. 3 eight, and for the week ended Nov. 10 one. The British cruiser Orama was sunk Oct. 19.

French and Italian shipping losses averaged about two ships of over 1,600 tons weekly.

Danish losses in 1916 included forty-six steamers and twenty-eight sailing vessels.

Norway lost nineteen ships in October, including the Leander. Forty-eight Norwegian seamen were killed.

On Oct. 25 President Braz of Brazil sent a message to Congress announcing that the steamship Macau had been torpedoed in the Bay of Biscay, and declaring that it was impossible to avoid noting the state of war that Germany had imposed on Brazil. On Oct. 26 Congress voted the declaration of war. The Germans set on fire and sank the German gunboat Eber in the harbor of Bahia after the Brazilian Government had ordered its seizure. German uprisings occurred in Southern Brazil, and on Nov. 3 President Braz sent to Congress recommendations for reprisals against German aggressions. The Chamber of Deputies voted these measures and also voted a state of siege.

### CAMPAIGN IN EASTERN EUROPE

Oct. 19—Germans land troops on Dagö Island; Russians begin to evacuate Reval.

Oct. 22—Germans land troops on the Werder Peninsula, driving back the defending troops and occupying part of the peninsula.

Oct. 23—Russians repulse second attempt of the Germans to land on the Esthonian coast; Germans withdraw toward the Skuli-Lemberg line.

Oct. 24—Germans shorten their line between the Gulf of Riga and the Dvina River, giving up advanced posts.

Oct. 25—Germans retreat fifteen miles on the Riga front, near the Pskoff highroad and in the sector of the Little Jaegel River; civilians begin to evacuate Kronstadt;

German forces fail in attempt to land on the Werder Peninsula.

Oct. 26—Germans withdraw as far as the Riga-Orel railway; Russians repulse attacks on the Werder coast of Esthonia.

Oct. 27—Withdrawal of German troops on the Riga front continues; Russians follow them as far as the Annehof sector without getting in touch with them.

Oct. 29—Germans withdraw from the Werder Peninsula.

Nov. 3-4—Russians fraternize with Germans in the Dvinsk region.

Nov. 10—Report that Germans have entered Helsingfors.

## CAMPAIGN IN WESTERN EUROPE

Oct. 19—Germans direct heavy artillery fire against Zonnebeke and British positions near the Manin Road.

Oct. 21—French repulse German attacks west of Mont Carnillet, on both banks of the Meuse, and in the La Chapelette sector.

Oct. 22—British capture valuable positions southeast of Poelcappelle.

Oct. 23—French smash through German lines on the Aisne, about seven miles northeast of Soissons, on a six-mile front, piercing them to a depth of more than two miles and capturing Malmaison Fort and four villages; Germans force British from a farm in Houthulst Forest.

Oct. 25—French continue their advance on the Aisne, capturing Pinon and Pargny Filain; British repulse German attacks south of Houthulst Forest.

Oct. 26—British take positions west of Passchendaele, including Bellevue Spur; French capture Draeibank, Papagoed Wood, and several fortified farms south of Houthulst Forest, and advance on the Aisne, taking Filain.

Oct. 27—Announcement made that American troops are in the trenches.

Oct. 28—Allies in Flanders capture the entire Mercken Peninsula.

Oct. 29—Germans repulsed by the French near Chaume and Courrières Wood.

Oct. 30—British capture Passchendaele Village, but are driven out.

Nov. 2—Germans retreat from the hilly portion of the Chemin des Dames.

Nov. 3—French advance to take ground evacuated by Germans on the Chemin des Dames and take entire district between the Oise Canal and Corbeny as far as the south bank of the Ailette River; three Americans killed, eleven wounded, and eleven missing in raid on salient on the Marne-Rhine Canal.

Nov. 4—French advance along the Ailette River; Laon reported evacuated by civilians.

Nov. 6—Canadians take Passchendaele and push on 800 yards beyond the town.

Nov. 8—French resume activity in Upper Alsace, in the Sundgau district.

Nov. 9—Germans attack Verdun positions, but are repulsed by the French at Chaume

Wood; French in Alsace carry out successful raid near Seppois.

Nov. 10—British complete conquest of Passchendaele Ridge.

Nov. 14—Americans ambush a large German patrol in No Man's Land, killing or wounding a number of the enemy; Germans repulsed at Passchendaele.

Nov. 15—More American casualties reported as result of shelling of American trenches; Belgians repulse raid north of Bixschoote; British check German patrols in Menin Road.

Nov. 16—Germans repulse French forces which worked their way across the Ailette River into the German advanced line; more casualties among American troops.

Nov. 17—British carry out a successful operation northwest of Passchendaele, on the Goeberg spur and force Germans to give up Vocation Farm.

## ITALIAN CAMPAIGN

Oct. 23—Italians repulse strong attacks in the Cadore region at Monte Plana.

Oct. 24—Austro-German offensive begun; Italian positions near Flitsch and Tolmino and in the northern part of the Bainsizza Plateau captured.

Oct. 25—Teutons extend their gains on the Isonzo in the region of the Santa Maria and Santa Lucia bridgeheads.

Oct. 26—Teutons advance beyond Karfreit and Ronzina on the Isonzo River; Italians begin to evacuate the Bainsizza Plateau.

Oct. 27—Austro-German forces press on through the spurs of the Julian Alps, taking the heights of Stol and Mount Matajur; second Italian army defeated.

Oct. 28—Teutons take Gorizia and Cividale and press forward from the Julian Alps to the sea; Monte Santo captured.

Oct. 29—Italian Isonzo front collapses; Third Army fails to check Teutons' advance between the Wippach River and the Adriatic Sea and retreats toward the sea; Teutons take Cormons; Second Italian Army retreats toward the Tagliamento River.

Oct. 30—Teutons occupy Udine and press on toward the Tagliamento River; Italians cut bridges to delay advance; Italians yield on Carnia front near Ploecken.

Oct. 31—New Austrian army under General von Krobatin moves southwestward from the Carnic Alps and attacks Gemona; Germans push on southeastward from Udine.

Nov. 1—Austro-German forces penetrate Italian rearguard positions to the east of the lower Tagliamento, capturing bridgehead positions at Dignano, Codroipo, and Latisana; Anglo-French reinforcements reach the Italian eastern front.

Nov. 2—Italians abandon the eastern bank of the Tagliamento River from the Fella Valley to the Adriatic Sea; fighting takes place on the middle and lower sectors of the river.

Nov. 4—Italians repulse heavy Teuton attacks

on advanced posts in the Daone and Giu-
mella Valleys.

Nov. 5—Austro-German troops cross the middle Tagliamento River.

Nov. 6—Italians abandon the entire Tagliamento line; Austro-Germans occupy positions on a ninety-three-mile front in the
Carnic Alps and the Dolomites from the
Bella Valley to the Colbricon.

Nov. 7—Austro-Germans reach the line of
the Livenza River.

Nov. 8—Teutons cross the Livenza River and
capture a General and 17,000 troops in
outflanking operations on the Tagliamento.

Nov. 9—Teutons advance toward the Piave
River; General Cadorna replaced by General Armando Diaz as first in command of
Italian armies; Interallied Military Council formed.

Nov. 10—Teutons take Asiago; Italians yield
the east bank of the Piave River from
Susegana to the Adriatic Sea, burning
bridges in their retreat.

Nov. 11—Teutons take Belluno and the Vidor
bridgehead and win ground in the Sette
Comuni and the Sugana Valley; Italians
retake positions on Gallio and Monte
Serragh.

Nov. 12—Austro-Germans cut off retreating
Italian forces in the upper Piave and
Cordevole Valleys and advance down the
Piave to Feltre.

Nov. 13—Teutons establish themselves on the
western bank of the Piave, near Zenson,
take Fonzaso and two mountain fortifications between the Sugana and Cismone
Valleys, and Monte Longara in the Sette
Comuni.

Nov. 14—Teutons occupy Primolano and
Feltre and cross the Piave River near the
Adriatic Sea; Italians foil surprise attack
at their rear, near Lake Garda; art treasures removed from Venice.

Nov. 15—Italians repulse Teuton attempts to
cross the Piave River, but abandon advanced posts at Monte Tomatico.

Nov. 16—Italians open the floodgates of the
Piave and Sile Rivers in an attempt to
save Venice; Teuton attacks from Asiago
to the Piave River checked.

Nov. 17—Teutons cross the Piave River at
two points, but are driven back; Prasso-
lan captured.

Nov. 18—Italians repulse Teuton attempts to
cross the Piave, and expel Germans who
crossed near Fagore; Teutons withdraw
slightly between the Brenta and the Piave.

## CAMPAIGN IN ASIA MINOR

Oct. 20—British begin enveloping movement
northeast of Bagdad and drive Turkish
forces in the vicinity of Kizil-Robat
across the Diala River.

Oct. 25—Russians drive Turks from the valley of Moerivan and advance to the southeastern bank of Lake Zeribar.

Nov. 1—British take Beersheba.

Nov. 3—British attack Gaza.

Nov. 4—British advance up the Tigris and
capture Turkish positions twenty miles
north of Samara.

Nov. 5—British pursue Turks north of Beersheba; Russians capture first-line Turkish trenches in the Kalkit-Tchiflik sector
in Asia Minor; British occupy Tekrit,
ninety-seven miles northwest of Bagdad.

Nov. 7—British take Gaza and advance north
of Beersheba, capturing Khuweilfeh.

Nov. 8—British mounted troops advancing
through Jemameh and Huj reach the
south bank of the Wady Hesu, establish
contact with forces advancing from Gaza;
northern bank of the Wady Hesu and
Herbieh, and Turkish coastal railhead at
Beit Hanun captured; entire Turkish
Army retreats toward the north.

Nov. 10—British take Askalon.

Nov. 13—Turkish forces attempting to take
new positions on the Wadi-Supereir driven
back five miles to the Wadi-Surar, eight
miles south of Jaffa; British take Mes-
miyeh, Katrah, and Mughar.

Nov. 15—British seize junction point of the
Beersheba-Damascus railroad with the
line to Jerusalem.

Nov. 16—British reach a line from Er Ramle
and Ludd to a point three miles south of
Jaffa.

Nov. 17—Turks prepare to take a stand north
of Jaffa.

Nov. 18—British take Jaffa.

## BALKAN CAMPAIGN

Oct. 22—Germans in Macedonia wrest some
hill positions from the French.

Oct. 26—British take four Bulgarian towns
on the northeastern shore of Lake Tahinos.

Nov. 13—Italians repulse attacks at the bend
of the Cerna River and Hill 1,050.

## AERIAL RECORD

Thirteen Zeppelins raided the eastern and
northeastern counties of England at midnight, Oct. 19. Thirty-four persons were
killed and fifty-six injured. The Zeppelins
were attacked on their return voyage by
French airmen and four machines were
destroyed and three captured. The L-49
was brought down intact, the first one to
be captured thus in the war. In a raid
on the southeast coast of England on
Oct. 31, only three out of thirty German
machines succeeded in reaching London.
Eight persons were killed and twenty-one
injured.

The British dropped bombs on many German
bases in Flanders, including Ghent, Zeebrugge, Bruges, and Vlissighems. Saarbrucken was raided and six tons of explosives dropped on the Beirbach works.

Thirty civilians were killed in a German raid
on Dunkirk on Oct. 27.

The British raided Pirmasens and Kaiser-
lauten, in Bavaria, on Nov. 1.

British naval aviators, in a raid over the
Gallipoli Peninsula and Constantinople,
hit the Turkish War Office and the Turkish warship Sultan Selim, formerly the

Goeben, causing an explosion on the Goeben.

## NAVAL RECORD

Two German raiders attacked a convoy in the North Sea on Oct. 17, and sank five Norwegian vessels, one Danish, and three Swedish, and two of the British escorting destroyers, the Mary Rose and the Strongbow. One hundred and fifty lives were lost. Norway sent a protest to Germany.

The Russian fleet was driven into the inner waters of Moon Sound behind a barrier of mines planted by German submarines. German submarines appeared in the Gulf of Finland. On Oct. 21 six German torpedo boats were sunk, and two dreadnoughts, one cruiser, six torperdo boats, and one transport were put out of action in the fighting in and near the Gulf of Riga. The German fleet bombarded positions on the western coast of the gulf.

A German warship was sunk by a mine in the sound, off the coast of Sweden, on Nov. 1.

On Nov. 3 British forces in the Cattegat sank the German auxiliary cruiser Marie of Flensburg and ten German patrol boats, including the Crocodile.

An electrically controlled German boat was destroyed off the Belgian coast on Nov. 3 by British patrol vessels which it attacked. The British Admiralty announced that this was the fourth boat of its kind to be destroyed.

A British destroyer and a small monitor which were operating in conjunction with the British army in Palestine were destroyed by German submarines, according to reports made public on Nov. 14.

On Nov. 17 British light forces sank one German light cruiser and crippled another, off the coast of Heligoland.

## RUSSIA

Armed naval detachments, under orders of the Maximalist Revolutionary Committee, occupied State buildings in Petrograd on Nov. 7. Premier Kerensky placed soldiers on guard, and declared the Workmen's and Soldier's Committee an illegal organization. On Nov. 8 the Bolsheviki, headed by Nikolai Lenine and Leon Trotzky, seized Petrograd, and announced their purpose to seek an immediate democratic peace, to turn the land over to the peasantry, and to convoke the Constituent Assembly. On Nov. 9 the Revolutionary Committee took over all the Government offices in Moscow, and Lenine in a speech before the Workmen's and Soldier's Congress in Petrograd announced a plan for a three months' armistice, during which elected representatives of all nations should settle the terms of peace. Various other plans for handing the Government over to the people were announced. The All-Russian Council of Workmen's and Soldiers' Delegates named a Bolsheviki

Cabinet and adjourned. Lenine was appointed Premier and Trotzky Foreign Minister. Clashes occurred between the Kerensky and Bolsheviki forces, with varying reports as to the outcome, and on Nov. 14, after the defeat of his forces between Tsarskoe Selo and Pulkova, Kerensky fled. General Dukhonin assumed the post of Commander in Chief of the loyalist forces. The Bolsheviki forces entered Petrograd Nov. 15, and were reported in control of Moscow. A split in the Lenine Cabinet occurred on Nov. 17, and several Ministers and five central committeemen resigned.

## MISCELLANEOUS

As the result of an acute political crisis Dr. Georg Michaelis placed his resignation as Chancellor in the hands of the Kaiser on Oct. 24. Social, economic, and political tasks were transferred from the Minister of the Interior to the new Imperial Department of Economics. Vice Chancellor Helfferich was relieved of the administration of the Department of the Interior, and Under Secretary of the Interior Wallraf was appointed Minister of the Interior. Under Secretary of State Rudolph Schwander was appointed head of the Imperial Department of Economics. On Oct. 27 the resignation of Michaelis was formally announced, and Count von Hertling, the Bavarian Premier, was named Chancellor and Prime Minister of Prussia. Helfferich resigned as Vice Chancellor and Frederick von Payer was named to succeed him.

The French Cabinet, headed by Paul Painlevé, offered to resign on Oct. 22, but President Poincaré refused to accept the resignation on the ground that the Chamber of Deputies had voted confidence in the Ministry. Painlevé therefore named J. Louis Bartho as Minister of Foreign Affairs to replace Alexander Ribot. On Nov. 13 the entire Cabinet resigned, following its defeat in the Chamber after a debate on the Allied War Council and other matters. The Socialists refused to support the Government. Georges Clemenceau formed a new Cabinet, in which Radicals predominated.

The Bosselli Cabinet resigned after the failure of a vote of confidence in the Italian Chamber of Deputies, on Oct. 26. Vittorio Orlando formed a new Ministry. General Cadorna was replaced by General Armando Diaz, on Nov. 8, as head of the armies in the field.

As a result of conferences in Italy the Interallied War Council was formed on Nov. 9. It is composed of the Premiers of Italy, England, and France, a member of each Government, and a military representative of each country. These latter members are General Cadorna, General Wilson, and General Foch. Professor Jan Kucharzevski was appointed Premier of Poland.

BOLSHEVIKI LEADERS AT A FUNERAL: NIKOLAI LENINE, THE RADICAL "PREMIER," IS
THE BEARDED MAN ON THE EXTREME RIGHT, AND LEON TROTZKY,
"FOREIGN MINISTER," IS NEXT TO HIM

# Russia's Radicals in Revolt

## A Revolution Within a Revolution Brings
## Civil War and Chaos to the New Republic

RUSSIA was in the throes of civil war when these pages of CUR-RENT HISTORY MAGAZINE were written, Nov. 20, 1917. Armed insurrection against the Provisional Government and Premier Kerensky had been precipitated on Nov. 7 by the radical socialistic elements, known as the Bolsheviki or Maximalists. The revolt was under the direction of a committee of the Workmen's and Soldiers' Delegates, headed by Leon Trotzky, President of the Central Executive Committee of the Petrograd Council, and Nikolai Lenine, a revolutionary agitator of the extreme radicals. The revolutionists at Petrograd organized themselves into a Maximalist Revolutionary Committee. They first seized the offices of the telegraph and telephone companies and occupied the State Bank and Marie Palace, where the Preliminary Parliament had suspended its sittings in view of the situation.

There had been earlier intimations that the outbreak was threatened; in fact, it had been openly asserted by the Bolsheviki leaders late in October that the Kerensky Government had lost the confidence of the real Russian revolutionaries and would be displaced by the Maximalists. Premier Kerensky realized the seriousness of the threat, but took no vigorous steps to frustrate the uprising, probably for fear of precipitating the crisis.

### Kerensky's Strange Interview

The Premier issued a statement on Nov. 1 through The Associated Press to all the newspapers of the Entente and Central Powers which produced grave concern over Russian affairs. It conveyed an intimation that he had almost despaired of restoring civil law in the distracted country. In this statement, which proved to be his last official public utterance before his overthrow, he said that Russia was worn out by the long strain, but that it was ridiculous to say the country was out of the war.

The Premier referred to the years in which Russia had fought her campaigns alone, with no such assistance as has been extended to France by Great Britain and now by America. He said he felt that help was needed urgently, and that Russia asked it as her right. The Premier urged that the United States give aid, in the form of money and supplies, and appealed to the world not to lose faith in the Russian revolution.

"Russia has fought consistently since

"the beginning," he said. "She saved "France and England from disaster "early in the war. She is worn out by "the strain and claims as her right that "the Allies now shoulder the burden."

The correspondent called attention to the report that Russia was out of the war, and asked the Premier for a frank statement of facts.

"Is Russia out of the war?" Premier Kerensky repeated the words and laughed. "That," he answered, "is a "ridiculous question. Russia is taking "an enormous part in the war. One has "only to remember history. Russia be- "gan the war for the Allies. While she "was already fighting, England was only "preparing and America was only ob- "serving. Russia at the beginning bore "the whole brunt of the fighting, thereby "saving Great Britain and France."

### Produces Grave Concern

The statement of the Premier produced grave concern. The authorities at London, Paris, and Washington were disposed to excuse the utterance as a plea for forbearance and sympathy from the Allies. At London, Dr. Pares, Professor of Russian History and head of the School of Russian Studies in the University of Liverpool, said:

The extent of the sacrifices which Russia has already made is not and can not be realized here until the full statistics of Russia's losses are published. I may say that in July, 1915, after only one year of war, I knew on the authority of the Russian War Office that the Russian losses to that date amounted to 3,800,000 men.

### Story of the Revolt

The story of the rebellion which resulted in the overthrow of the Provisional Government, plunging the country into civil war and producing a state of chaos in civil and military matters throughout the vast domain, had not been officially narrated up to Nov. 20; the details which appeared from day to day were fragmentary and contradictory. In fact, after Nov. 8, when the first meagre details were given of the seizing of the State Buildings at Petrograd by the Bolsheviki, no further authentic news came out of Russia for ten days, and the rumors that did reach the outside world through indirect channels were contradictory.

On Nov. 6 the Revolutionary Military Committee of the Workmen's and Soldiers' Delegates demanded the right to control all orders of the General Staff in the Petrograd district, which was refused. Thereupon the committee announced that it had appointed special Commissioners to undertake the direction of the military, and invited the troops to observe only orders signed by the committee. Machine-gun detachments moved to the Workmen's and Soldiers' headquarters.

Premier Kerensky appealed to the Preliminary Parliament for a vote of confidence, and while the measure carried by a bare majority of 123 to 102, twenty-six members abstained from voting, and many refused to attend the sitting. It was thus clear that Kerensky could not rely upon the Parliament.

### Rebels Seize Petrograd

The blow fell on Nov. 7. The garrison at Petrograd espoused the cause of the Maximalists, and complete control of the city was seized with comparatively little fighting. The Provisional Government troops holding the bridges over the Neva and various other points were quickly overpowered, save at the Winter Palace, the chief guardians of which were the Women's Battalion. The latter surrendered before the actual battle began, but the military cadets remained true to the Provisional Government and held the palace for several hours. The Bolsheviki brought up armored cars and the cruiser Aurora and turned the guns of the Fort of St. Peter and St. Paul upon the palace before its defenders would surrender.

Prior to the attack the Workmen's and Soldiers' leaders sent the Provisional Government an ultimatum demanding its surrender and allowing twenty minutes' grace. The Government replied indirectly, refusing to recognize the Military Committee.

### A Bolsheviki Proclamation

That evening the Military Revolutionary Committee issued the following proclamation:

To the Army Committees of the Active Army and to all Councils of Workmen's *and Soldiers' Delegates and to the Garrison and Proletariat of Petrograd:*

We have deposed the Government of Kerensky, which rose against the revolution and the people. The change which resulted in the deposition of the Provisional Government was accomplished without bloodshed.

The Petrograd Council of Workmen's and Soldiers' Delegates solemnly welcomes the accomplished change and proclaims the authority of the Military Revolutionary Committee until the creation of a Government by the Workmen's and Soldiers' Delegates.

Announcing this to the army at the front, the Revolutionary Committee calls upon the revolutionary soldiers to watch closely the conduct of the men in command. Officers who do not join the accomplished revolution immediately and openly must be arrested at once as enemies.

The Petrograd Council of Workmen's and Soldiers' Delegates considers this to be the program of the new authority:

First—The offer of an immediate democratic peace.

Second—The immediate handing over of large proprietarial lands to the peasants.

Third—The transmission of all authority to the Council of Workmen's and Soldiers' Delegates.

Fourth—The honest convocation of a Constitutional Assembly.

The national revolutionary army must not permit uncertain military detachments to leave the front for Petrograd. They should use persuasion, but where this fails they must oppose any such action on the part of these detachments by force without mercy.

The present order must be read immediately to all military detachments in all arms. The suppression of this order from the rank and file by army organizations is equivalent to a great crime against the revolution and will be punished by all the strength of the revolutionary law.

Soldiers! For peace, for bread, for land, and for the power of the people! (Signed)

THE MILITARY REVOLUTIONARY COMMITTEE.

## Demands of the Leaders

The Petrograd Council of Workmen's and Soldiers' Delegates held a meeting at which M. Trotzky made his declaration that the Government no longer existed; that some of the Ministers had been arrested, and that the preliminary Parliament had been dissolved. He introduced Nikolai Lenine as "an old comrade whom we welcome back."

Lenine, who was received with prolonged cheers, said:

"Now we have a revolution. The "peasants and workmen control the Gov-"ernment. This is only a preliminary "step toward a similar revolution every-"where."

He outlined the three problems now before the Russian democracy. First, immediate conclusion of the war, for which purpose the new Government must propose an armistice to the belligerents; second, the handing over of the land to the peasants; third, settlement of the economic crisis.

The Congress of the Councils of Workmen's and Soldiers' Delegates of all Russia, which opened Nov. 7, issued the three following proclamations on the 8th:

*To All Provincial Councils of Workmen's and Soldiers' and Peasants' Delegates:*

All power lies in the Workmen's and Soldiers' Delegates. Government commissaries are relieved of their functions. Presidents of the Workmen's and Soldiers' Delegates are to communicate direct with the Revolutionary Government. All members of agricultural committees who have been arrested are to be set at liberty immediately and the commissioners who arrested them are in turn to be arrested.

The second proclamation reads as follows:

The death penalty re-established at the front by Premier Kerensky is abolished and complete freedom for political propaganda has been established at the front. All revolutionary soldiers and officers who have been arrested for complicity in so-called political crimes are to be set at liberty immediately.

The third proclamation says:

Former Ministers Konovaloff, Kishkin, Terestchenko, Malyanovitch, Nikitin, and others have been arrested by the Revolutionary Committee.

M. Kerensky has taken flight and all military bodies have been empowered to take all possible measures to arrest Kerensky and bring him back to Petrograd. All complicity with Kerensky will be dealt with as high treason.

## When the Die Was Cast

The story of the revolt, as told by a correspondent, states that the Petrograd Soviet held a meeting on the night of Nov. 6, when the political situation had been discussed in the light of Kerensky's threats a few hours earlier in the Democratic Council. The Bolsheviki leaders were still hesitating as to the wisdom of a demonstration. The minority parties apparently took it for granted that an armed demonstration was improbable.

At 3 o'clock on the morning of the 7th unanimity was reached, as a result of a series of reports received from garrison units expressing readiness to accept orders from the Military Revolutionary Committee. It was decided to strike. The Provisional Government forthwith was declared nonexistent.

At 4:30 o'clock the first detachment left the Soviet headquarters and descended upon the Government Bank, in accordance with the plan prepared by the committee. The whole success of the Bolsheviki coup turned upon this plan of campaign. The promoters were naturally unwilling to divulge details, but Smolny Institute (Bolsheviki headquarters) gossip declared that its authors were three hitherto unheard-of youths, and dwelt lovingly on the completeness of the details. Petrograd awoke on Nov. 7 and went about its normal business, and only toward midday was it realized, except in the centre, that the old Government had been painlessly replaced. Some hundreds of young men of the officers' training corps and the women soldiers formed the sole defense of the Provisional Government. These encircled and garrisoned the Winter Palace, and were themselves surrounded by garrison troops.

The cruiser Aurora arrived from Kronstadt and took up a position on the Neva opposite the Winter Palace. In the afternoon the cruiser fired a blank shot as a warning to the palace inmates. This started a slight panic, and a party of sailors landing for pourparlers was fired on, one being killed and one wounded. This apparently was the most serious case of bloodshed on Wednesday.

In the afternoon the Nevsky Prospekt was cleared of traffic, and machine guns and quick-firers were placed at the principal crossings throughout the city. Perfect quiet was maintained.

Another correspondent estimates the casualties among the defenders of the Winter Palace on Nov. 7 at about thirty killed and wounded.

## Bolsheviki Peace Plan

The Workmen's and Soldiers' Congress at Petrograd passed the following peace resolutions on Nov. 10:

The Government considers a peace to be democratic and equitable, which is aspired to by a majority of the working classes of all the belligerent countries, worn out and ruined by war—the peace which the Russian workmen called for on the fall of the monarchy. It should be an immediate peace, without annexation, (that is to say, without usurpation of foreign territory and without violent conquest of nationalities,) and without indemnities.

The Russian Government proposes to all belligerents to make this peace immediately, declaring themselves ready without delay to carry out all the conditions of this peace through plenipotentiaries of all countries and nations.

By annexation or usurpation of territory the Government means, in accordance with the sense of justice of democracy in general and of the working classes in particular, any annexation to a great and powerful State of a weak nationality without the consent of that nationality and independently of its degree of civilization and its geographical situation in Europe or across the ocean.

If any population be kept by force under the control of any State, and if, contrary to its will, expressed in the press or in national assembly, or to decisions of parties, or in opposition to rebellions and uprisings against an oppressor, the population is refused the right of universal suffrage, of driving out an army of occupation and organizing its own political régime, such a state of things is annexation or violent usurpation. The Government considers that the active carrying on of the war in order to share weak nationalities which have been conquered between rich and powerful nations is a great crime against humanity.

Accordingly, the Government solemnly proclaims its decision to sign peace terms which will bring this war to an end on the conditions mentioned above, which are equitable for all the nationalities.

It suggests an immediate armistice of three months that the representatives of " all the nations in the war or its victims " may participate in the negotiations, and declares that a conference of all the nations of the world should be convoked to give final approval to the peace terms drafted.

The German Kaiser announced Nov. 20 that he would not treat with the Bolsheviki Government.

## The Bolsheviki Cabinet

The following Cabinet was named by the All-Russian Congress of Workmen's and Soldiers' Delegates on Nov. 9 to serve until the Constituent Assembly should meet:

Premier—NIKOLAI LENINE.

Foreign Minister—LEON TROTZKY.

Minister of the Interior—M. RICKOFF.

Minister of Finance—M. SVORTZOFF.

Minister of Agriculture—M. MILIUTIN.

Minister of Labor—M. SHLIAPNI-KOFF.

Committee on War and Marine—M. OV-SIANNIKOFF, M. KRYLENKO, and M. BIBENKO.

Minister of Commerce—M. NOGIN.

Minister of Education—M. LUNA-CHARSKY.

Minister of Justice—M. OPPOKOV.

Minister of Supplies—M. THEODORO-VITCH.

Minister of Posts and Telegraphs—M. AVILOFF.

Minister of Affairs of Nationality (a new post in charge of the affairs of the different nationalities within Russia)—M. DZHUGASHVILI.

Minister of Communications—M. RIAZ-ANOFF.

The Cabinet members are all Bolsheviki, and are supported by the Left and the Social Revolutionist Pary, the other parties having withdrawn from the Workmen's and Soldiers' Congress. Bibenko is a Kronstadt sailor, while Shliapnikoff is a laborer.

Lenine, like most of the prominent Russian agitators, had to use an alias in his revolutionary activity. His real name is Vladimir Ilyitch Uulyanoff; he was born of a noble family at Simbirsk, on the Volga, about 1870.

Leon Trotzky, the chief coadjutor of Lenine in the rebellion, had been living in New York City three months when the Czar was overthrown, but had previously been expelled from Germany, France, Switzerland, and Spain. The real name of this Maximalist leader is Leber Braunstein, and he was born in a town in the Russian Government of Kherson, near the Black Sea.

## Kerensky Defeated

The news following the uprising was conflicting; it was not until Nov. 18 that the real facts were procurable. When the insurrection occurred, Kerensky succeeded in escaping from Petrograd, but the other members of his Cabinet were arrested, though subsequently released. Kerensky succeeded in persuading about 2,000 Cossacks, several hundred military cadets, and a contingent of artillery to fight under his banner. He advanced toward Petrograd, but his forces were greatly outnumbered by the Bolsheviki. The forces met near Tsarskoe Selo, a few miles beyond Petrograd; here the Kerensky troops met defeat, and the leader was reported to be in flight.

At Moscow, after desultory fighting, the Government troops were defeated and the entire city passed into the control of the Bolsheviki; it was reported that 3,000 persons were slain in the street fighting.

News from all parts of Russia on Nov. 19 indicated that the Kerensky Government had everywhere collapsed. Conditions were chaotic. It was reported that the Bolsheviki had quarreled and several members of the Cabinet had resigned. Ukraine had again declared its independence; the Finnish Socialists had dissolved the sitting Diet and reconvened the previous Socialist Diet, which in turn declared Finland to be an independent republic. It was reported that General Kaledines, the hetman of the Cossacks, had declared against the Bolsheviki, and was organizing an army to save the country. News from the front was disquieting, it being reported that the army was without rations. The whole country was reported to be in revolt, with no central authority. The American Ambassador at Petrograd on the 19th asked for a special train to carry out of the city the 200 Americans there, and the Americans at Moscow were preparing to depart.

The only hope of the distracted country lay in the inability of the revolutionists to fulfil their promises. It was believed that the masses would soon realize the illusory dreams of the radicals, and turn en masse to the moderates, from whose number some strong man would emerge to save the country from complete anarchy and preserve for the nation its new democratic institutions. In many quarters on Nov. 20 it was believed that General Kaledines and the Cossacks might yet save the situation.

# United States Army 1,800,000 Strong

FIGURES published in Washington on Nov. 7, 1917, showed that the United States Army was then over 1,800,000 strong, distributed as follows:

| | |
|---|---:|
| National (draft) army | 616,820 |
| National Guard called into Federal service | 469,000 |
| Regular army | 370,000 |
| Special branches | 200,000 |
| Reserves | 80,000 |
| Officers | 80,000 |
| | |
| Total | 1,815,820 |

The most important step to increase still further and organize on a better basis the fighting forces of the nation was initiated by the War Department's plan to examine by means of a questionnaire and classify the remaining nine million young men registered under the Conscription act, but not yet called for service. President Wilson on Nov. 10 issued as a foreword to the new regulations an appeal for assistance in the work of classification. It read, in part:

> The task of selecting and mobilizing the first contingent of the national army is nearing completion. The swiftness with which the machinery for its execution had to be assembled left room for adjustment and improvement. New regulations putting these improvements into effect are, therefore, being published today. There is no change in the essential obligation of men subject to selection. The first draft must stand unaffected by the provisions of the new regulations. They can be given no retroactive effect.
>
> The time has come for a more perfect organization of our man power. The selective principle must be carried to its logical conclusion. We must make a complete inventory of the qualifications of all registrants in order to determine, as to each man not already selected for duty with the colors, the place in the military, industrial or agricultural ranks of the nation of which his experience and training can best be made to serve the common good. This project involves an inquiry by the selection boards into the domestic, industrial, and educational qualifications of nearly 10,000,000 men.

The President fixed sixty days as the period within which the work should be accomplished, and called upon all citizens to help in getting it done quickly and efficiently.

## First Two Classes of Registrants

The first two classes from which the 9,000,000 men registered for military duty are to be drawn are as follows:

### CLASS I.

(A) Single man without dependent relatives.

(B) Married man, with or without children, or father of motherless children, who has habitually failed to support his family.

(C) Married man dependent on wife for support.

(D) Married man, with or without children, or father of motherless children, man not usefully engaged, family supported by income independent of his labor.

(E) Unskilled farm laborer.

(F) Unskilled industrial laborer. Registrant by or in respect of whom no deferred classification is claimed or made. Registrant who fails to submit questionnaire and in respect of whom no deferred classification is claimed or made.

All registrants not included in any other division in this schedule.

### CLASS II.

(A) Married man with children or father of motherless children, where such wife or children or such motherless children are not mainly dependent upon his labor for support for the reason that there are other reasonably certain sources of adequate support, (excluding earnings or possible earnings from the labor of the wife,) available, and that the removal of the registrant will not deprive such dependents of support.

(D) Married man, without children, whose wife, although the registrant is engaged in a useful occupation, is not mainly dependent upon his labor for support for the reason that the wife is skilled in some special class of work which she is physically able to perform and in which she is employed, or in which there is an immediate opening for her under conditions that will enable her to support herself decently and without suffering or hardship.

(C) Necessary skilled farm laborer in necessary agricultural enterprise.

Best available estimates indicated that the first of the five classes would include more than 2,000,000 men subject for duty with the colors before any man in any other class would be called.

### The Officers' Training Camps

The Secretary of War on Nov. 13 announced a reversal of the policy he had previously adopted in regard to holding in reserve the officers graduated from training camps. When Secretary Baker first notified the Adjutant General that only officers would be assigned to active duty where vacancies existed, it was estimated that fully 8,000, or half of the number expected to be commissioned in the camps, would be placed on the reserve list. There were so many vigorous protests against this plan that Secretary Baker decided to revert to the original plan of the Army General Staff and officers in charge of training camps.

There were about 19,000 students in the second series of officers' training camps, which closed on Nov. 27. The opening of the third series was fixed for Jan. 5, 1918.

To balance the divisions of the national army and National Guard and meet the special requirements of the expeditionary forces in France, the Engineer Corps has been expanded since March 1 from 2,100 men to 95,000 men. There are now 408 officers on active duty and more than 5,000 reserve officers, compared with 256 officers eight months ago, and an additional 1,200 reserve officers about to graduate. The active force now includes nine railroad regiments and one forestry regiment as part of the national army, while seventeen pioneer regiments authorized with the national army are in process of formation. Additional National Guard units, equivalent to about seven regiments, have been called into the Federal service and their reorganization into seventeen pioneer engineer regiments for the seventeen divisions of the National Guard troops is well under way. Organizing of troops for special service, such as lumber supply, road construction, camouflage service, gas and flame work, mining work, mapping, &c., also has been undertaken by the engineers.

Major Gen. John Biddle, it was announced on Oct. 28, had been appointed Assistant Chief of the Army General Staff. General Biddle was formerly President of the War College, and is one of the ablest engineers in the army. The General is a native of Michigan, and was born Feb. 2, 1859. During the Spanish-American war he served as Lieutenant Colonel, Chief of Engineers.

# The Spirit of the National Army Camps

*Christopher Morley, writing to* THE NEW YORK TIMES *under date of Oct. 24, 1917, gave this stirring description of a typical training camp:*

LAST night two other civilians and I watched the 311th Regiment of Infantry at Camp Dix, (Wrightstown, N. J.,) pass in review before its Colonel. In the cool, sober twilight of Autumn, the ranks of khaki blended magically into the dun background of woodland and corn stubble. The regimental band, organized less than two weeks ago, played " The Star-Spangled Banner " in a way that brought our heels together. Any man watching those long lines of men who a month or so ago were professors, barbers, plumbers, and clerks realizes the marvelous combination of discipline, understanding, and clear business sense that is behind the national army. No man calls it the draft army after seeing the men in action. These men are becoming volunteers in the full sense of the word.

Through three rich, splendid October days I wandered about Camp Dix, in an ever-increasing wonder, humility, and admiration. Here is taking place something so marvelous, so portentous for our nation, so vast a democratic experiment, that one watches it with a tingle of consecration. Every little squad, learning the manual of arms, seems to be touched with a vivid, splendid light, when one thinks of the royal purpose and cause that have brought these men together.

I speak in full knowledge of the sadness of broken human ties that lies behind the eyes of every conscripted man.

I do not forget the mistakes that have been made—men with several dependents taken from home in an agony of apprehension about their families. Thousands of these men are ignorant, unlettered, asking no more of life than bread and butter; great causes and the shock of democracy and autocracy have no meaning to them. Hundreds know no word of English. But so marvelous is the spirit of the camp, so quickly do the men outgrow their homesickness and sense of strangeness, that after two or three weeks most of them would not go home if they could.

A visit to one of the cantonments is unforgettable. The greatness of this superb effort to raise an army that will be truly national—drawn from every rank of the nation, every man playing the part for which he is best fitted—floods the heart with fire and pride. These molten pools of manhood have been poured into the crucible. The dross is being purged, the hardening metal tempered and welded. The finished weapon will be terrible in edge and onset. I think it will be the finest army the world has ever seen, because it is a true cross-section of a nation. To witness a national soul coming to birth in these men makes one a better citizen. There is no sight in America today that can compare with it. If only excursion trains for pacifists could be sent to all the camps!

I speak only of Camp Dix, the only cantonment I have seen, but I doubt not the others are the same. At Camp Dix I have talked to men ranging from the General in command down to the humblest and most homesick private. I have messed with the privates, with quartermaster officers, and at the beautiful old farmhouse occupied by the staff officers. Throughout all ranks the spirit is the same. These men are out to do a big job, in no spirit of heroics or swank, but soberly, advisedly, with intent to see it through. I thought down there of the French title of " Mr. Britling," which is " M. Britling commence a voir clair." We may well begin to see clearly when our army chiefs tackle the business in hand in such splendid fashion as is evidenced at Camp Dix. We may have been slow in starting, but, under heaven! we are building this army in the right way.

Typical of the whole cantonment was an experience I had while walking with one of the staff Captains, who was showing me round. A mile or so from one end of the camp I heard wild strains of music issuing from a clump of woods. I asked what this meant. He took me over and showed me the school for buglers, where a dozen men, under a Sergeant of the regular army, were learning their notes. Not one of them had had a bugle n his hand more than a week. They were allowed only two hours a day for practice, but the Sergeant assured us that he was very proud of their progress. As we walked away they burst gallantly into the mess call—their favorite melody, and the one they play best!

In that spirit the national army is going about its task. Men who a month ago had no conception of citizenship, no pride of country, and even only a smattering of English, now show a fine and mettlesome temper that is perfectly astounding. The singing initiated by the Y. M. C. A. is a potent factor in arousing this lusty esprit du corps. One of the first and finest things done by the association at Camp Dix was to start the men singing, under Stanley Hawkins, who is a genius at song leadership. Nothing sticks so thrillingly in the memory as the sound of those hundreds of voices roaring their favorite choruses. If you could hear them sing, you would know that all is well with the national army. Here is one of their new favorites:

Good-bye, Maw! Good-bye, Paw!
Good-bye, mule, with yer old hee-haw!
I may not know what this war's about,
But you bet, oy gosh, I'll soon find out;
And O my sweetheart, don't you fear,
I'll bring you a King fer a souvenir:
I'll bring you a Turk and a Kaiser, too.
An' that's about all one feller can do!

No comment on the cantonments would be complete without some mention of the superb work the Y. M. C. A. is doing for the men. There are sixty-four Y. M. C. A. men at Camp Dix, serving the soldiers in every possible way; there are nine big buildings, each intended to serve 5,000 soldiers; also a headquarters build-

# GENERAL J. C. SMUTS

South African Statesman and Soldier, Who Has Become a Leading
Military Authority in England.

# LEADERS IN BRITISH WAR ACTIVITIES

**LORD READING**

Lord Chief Justice of England and
Financial Adviser to the British
Mission in America.

*(© Harris & Ewing.)*

**GEORGE N. BARNES**

Labor Leader and Member of the
British War Cabinet.

**GEN. SIR H. C. O. PLUMER**

Commander of the Second British
Army on the Western Front.

*(Photo Bain News Service.)*

**COLONEL E. D. SWINTON**

The British Officer Who Is Generally Recognized as the Inventor
of the "Tank."

*(© Harris & Ewing.)*

ing, an auditorium seating 3,000, and a clubroom for officers. In these buildings the men can read, write letters home, (the Y. M. C. A. gives away 1,000,000 sheets of note paper every month at Camp Dix,) buy stamps and postal cards, hear music, join classes in English and French, Bible classes, and enjoy some kind of healthy entertainment every night. There is no finer sight in America than one of those Y. M. C. A. buildings packed with these new nephews of Uncle Sam.

Imagine a long room built of fresh, clean timbers; lit by electric light, a high platform at one end, flags of all the Allies hanging from the rafters. The benches are crowded with men; over 500 in the room altogether. Perhaps it is movie night; into the vivid bar of light thrown by the machine curls the strong, warm reek of hundreds of pipes and cigarettes. And as the film runs to an end the lights flash on, some one sits down at the piano, and the men thunder the chorus of one of their best chansons:

Old Uncle Sammy, he needs the infantree.
He needs artilleree, he needs the cavalree.
When he gets them, we'll all go to
　　Germany.
God help Kaiser Bill!

From the bottom of my heart, I beg every man and woman who can do so to visit one of the cantonments. One comes away twenty times enriched in citizenship, in patriotism, in understanding of what this great Republic means.

# The United States as Shipowner

THE commandeering by the United States Shipping Board of all steamers of more than 2,500 tons was effected on Oct. 15. The approximate number of vessels affected was 500, aggregating about 2,000,000 tons. Bainbridge Colby, the member of the Shipping Board who was in charge of putting the new system into operation, said that the requisitioning would not make any material difference in the present movement of ships. He added:

We are turning the ships back to the owners to operate them on Government account, under the sams system as in England. We will not disturb them until there is a concrete case of need. Our purpose is to unify the control of all these ships available for ocean traffic. We have fixed a requisition rate, based on a fair appraisal, which replaces the speculative, hectic bidding for tonnage under the old private charters. The rates are considerably under the prevalent high rates.

Edward F. Carry of Chicago became the Shipping Board's director of operations for the purpose of unifying the control of ocean traffic.

Tremendous efforts have been made to speed up the Government's shipbuilding program, so as to complete the million tons fixed to be ready by March 1, 1918. The Shipping Board has initiated plans to get twenty-four hours of service a day out of all shipyards in place of the single eight-hour shift, or to get at least two shifts. The main difficulty has been to secure enough labor, both skilled and unskilled, to supply all the shipyards. More than 300,000 additional workers were reported on Oct. 26 as necessary for the construction of tonnage needed at once. At that date the steel shipbuilding program was reported to be twenty vessels behind schedule.

## Contract for Seventy Ships

The largest single order placed by the Emergency Fleet Corporation was announced on Nov. 4. This was the contract for seventy 8,000-ton vessels, to be built within twelve months, at a cost of $100,000,000, which was awarded to the American International Corporation, operating the great Government fabricating yard at Hog Island, on the Delaware River, in close association with the American Bridge Company. The American International Corporation previously had a contract for fifty 7,500-ton vessels at a cost of $50,000,000.

Further reorganization of the Emergency Fleet Corporation went into effect on Nov. 12 as part of the effort to produce 6,000,000 tons of ships by the end of 1918. One of the most important changes put Charles A. Piez, a Chicago engineer, recently elected Vice President of the Fleet Corporation, in charge of the actual construction of the vessels, and placed in his hands the many problems confronted in obtaining materials and a more complete spirit of co-operation with the builders. Mr. Piez took over a good deal of the work hitherto done by Rear Admiral Capps, General Manager of the corporation, who still remained the chief executive officer. James Heyworth of Chicago, one of the large contractors of the country, was chosen to specialize on the work of building wooden ships, contracts for 310 of which have been let. He replaced Rear Admiral F. T. Bowles, retired. Judge John Barton Payne was appointed head of the legal department of the corporation.

Irving T. Bush, founder and head of the Bush Terminal Company of New York, on Nov. 5 accepted the position of chief executive officer of the New York Port War Board, created to mobilize every facility of both the New York and New Jersey sides of the port in the interest of war maritime efficiency. The New York Port War Board was created in a conference held in New York City on Nov. 3, which was attended by Secretary Baker and Generals Baker, Shanks, and Abbott.

### Ships from Neutral Nations

The shipping resources of the Allies received a valuable addition by the agreement, announced on Nov. 13, under which the United States secured over 400,000 tons of ships belonging to the Northern European neutral nations and Japan. The European neutrals finally agreed to turn over to the United States and the Allies ships in exchange for foodstuffs that only America could supply. Japan was asked to sell to the United State a large amount of tonnage in the Pacific in exchange for steel ship plates which the Japanese were anxious to obtain to complete their merchant shipbuilding program. Many of the ships acquired from neutrals were assigned to routes between American ports and South America, each releasing an American or British vessel for service through the war zone.

In its negotiations the United States dealt in a different manner with each, Norway, Sweden, Holland, and Denmark. A large part of the Norwegian merchant marine, most of which is owned in Great Britain, already is in the allied service. The Dutch insisted that none of their vessels be put into service that would take them through the war zone. Most of the Dutch ships turned over were assigned to transport to the United States wheat from Argentina and Australia and sugar from Java.

These agreements helped to ease the situation created by the determination of the United States to embargo any and all supplies which might be sent through neutral countries into Germany. The War Trade Board, exercising the powers granted to it under the Trading with the Enemy act, ended Germany's last hope of drawing, through indirect channels, on American resources by issuing on Oct. 15 its form of agreement, which all shippers must sign.

The first export license was issued to Captain Raoul Amundsen, the explorer, for foodstuffs, fuel, and oil needed for his expedition to the north pole.

# Food Control and Lower Prices

THE Food Administration, headed by Herbert C. Hoover, has further extended the area of its control during the last month. A slight downward tendency in food prices is said to be in part due to the closer grip which the Food Administration is getting on producers and distributers

President Wilson and Mr. Hoover on Nov. 1 officially approved rules and regulations governing licenses under Presidential proclamations affecting dealers and handlers of twenty staple food commodities. Retailers doing a gross business of more than $100,000 annually must take out licenses, as well as all whole-

salers, manufacturers, and other distributers of the foodstuffs specified in the
President's proclamations.   More than
40,000 applications had already been received on Nov. 1.

Beginning Nov. 3, all direct trading of
American millers, exporters, and blend-
ers of flour with European countries was
prohibited, according to an announcement made at the offices of the United
States Food Administration's Milling
Division in New York City.  The business
was taken over by the Food Administration.  The change was considered necessary to control and centralize the exports
of flour to neutral countries in Europe,
and also to regulate the quantities of
flour forwarded to these countries, so as
to provide for the minimum quantity of
that actually required.

President Wilson's proclamation putting the baking industry under license
was made public on Nov. 12, and steps
were taken by the Food Administration
to organize machinery for the enforcement of the regulations.  All bakeries,
consuming ten barrels of flour or more
a month, are brought under these regulations, and are requested to apply for information so that they may adjust plants
to the use of the standard weights and
formula adopted for " war bread."  The
proclamation covers the baking of cake,
crackers, biscuits, pastry, and other products, and applies not only to bakers but
also to hotels, restaurants, and clubs
where bread or other products of their
own baking are served.  Heads of house-
holds who do home baking are called
upon by the Food Administration to
watch carefully the formulas and other

instructions issued from time to time and
co-operate voluntarily.

The first article in which the American people experienced a shortage was
sugar.  Mr. Hoover appealed again on
Oct. 19 for a reduced consumption of
sugar, so that France and other allied
countries might not suffer more severely.
The present shortage, he said, was
brought about by the great increase in
exports over normal times.  The widespread publicity given to the temporary
shortage of sugar started a rush on the
retail grocery stores in New York and
other Eastern States.   Unscrupulous
dealers seized the opportunity to raise
prices, in some cases to 20 cents a pound,
although the wholesale price of refined
granulated sugar was being held at just
under 8½ cents a pound.  The retail price
had been planned to remain at about 9½
cents.  Mr. Hoover dealt with the situation by arranging to obtain 200,000,000
pounds of raw sugar from Louisiana producers.  This transaction involved $13,-
000,000.

One family out of every three in the
United States had already pledged support to the Food Administration's plan
for voluntary food conservation, according to reports received up to Nov. 6,
showing that the total enrollment for
the country was 7,406,544.  More than
90 per cent. of the country's better class
hotels had signed pledges and the others
were coming into line.  Although the
movement for a meatless Tuesday and a
wheatless Wednesday was not started
until late in September, it had been generally accepted by public eating houses
everywhere.

# The Second Liberty Loan

SUBSCRIPTIONS for the 4 per cent.
bonds of the Second Liberty Loan
closed on Oct. 27, 1917, and amounted
to $4,617,532,300, or 54 per cent. more
than the amount asked.  The bonds ultimately allotted to subscribers totaled
$3,808,766,150, or $808,766,150 above the
amount sought.  The number of subscribers had never been equaled in history,

the total being 9,400,000.  The subscriptions less than $50,000 were distributed
among 9,306,000 persons.  The largest
individual subscription was $50,000,000,
made by the Du Pont Powder Company
of Wilmington, Del.  The subscriptions
ranging from $50 to $50,000 aggregated
$2,488,469,350.

The First Liberty Loan subscriptions

had totaled $3,035,000,000, an oversubscription of practically 50 per cent., with more than 4,000,000 subscribers

The second loan campaign was conducted with great earnestness and brought forth many spectacular demonstrations throughout the country. Parades, mass meetings, curbstone assemblies, and similar gatherings were the distinguishing features, and the personal canvasses by all financial and civic agencies were animated, earnest, and well nigh universal. The Government expressed deep satisfaction over the success of the loan.

Every Federal Reserve district in the country took its full quota, proving that the response was national. The total subscriptions in New York City were $1,550,453,450.

### Other Financial Matters

Up to Nov. 8 the official credits and advances by the United States to the Allies were as follows:

|  | Credits. | Advances. |
|---|---|---|
| Great Britain... | $1,860,000,000 | $1,475,000,000 |
| France | 1,130,000,000 | 850,000,000 |
| Russia | 450,000,000 | 191,400,000 |
| Italy | 500,000,000 | 265,000,000 |
| Belgium | 58,400,000 | 54,500,000 |
| Serbia | 3,000,000 | 3,000,000 |
| Total | $4,001,400,000 | $2,838,900,000 |

The expenditures by the United States Government in October exceeded $1,000,-000,000, of which $470,200,000 went to the Allies, $133,934,862 for redemption of loan certificates, $395,296,200 for the Army and Navy Shipping Board, aircraft, Food Administration, and maintenance of the ordinary Governmental activities.

The daily expenditures of the British Government in the three months ended Sept. 22 were $32,070,000. The House of Commons on Oct. 30 voted $2,000,-000,000 new credit, bringing the total British loans for 1917 to $9,500,000,000 and the total since the beginning of the war to $28,460,000,000.

The British Chancellor stated on Oct. 30 that the German Reichstag had voted a total credit since the war started of $23,500,000,000, but this did not include advances to Germany's allies nor the expenditure for separation allowances, both of which are included in great Britain's total, and which in Germany reached $6,630,000,000; hence the actual expenditures of Great Britain since the war began, according to the Chancellor, were $8,500,000,000 less than Germany's.

Petrograd announced Nov. 1 a subscription of $2,000,000,000 to Russia's second liberty loan.

# Gibraltar Offered to Spain by Germany

Count Romanones, former Premier of Spain, made the following statement in an interview granted to the Madrid correspondent of the Roma Tribuna early in September, 1917:

It has been said that a victory of the Central Empires would give Spain great advantages and would enable her after the conclusion of the war to become one of the great powers of Europe. Why should I conceal from you the fact that this tempting mirage has been skillfully and insistently displayed before the eyes of the Spanish people? Morocco, Gibraltar, and Portugal were the gifts which were offered to Spain.

No. Let us leave similar reasonings to the deluded and to those who cannot see that the present immense conflict will end in the triumph of the peoples which stand for social and political liberty.

# U-Boat Sinkings of the Month

## Decrease in Merchant Marine Losses—First American Naval Vessels Torpedoed by the Enemy

A STEADY decrease in the number of British ships sunk by submarines suggests that the German U-boat campaign has passed the zenith of its success. The latest British Admiralty records show the following losses:

|  | Over 1,600 Tons. | Under 1,600 Tons. | Fish'g Vessels. |
|---|---|---|---|
| Week ended Oct. 21, 1917.. | 17 | 8 | 0 |
| Week ended Oct. 28...... | 14 | 4 | 0 |
| Week ended Nov. 4....... | 8 | 4 | 0 |
| Week ended Nov. 11....... | 1 | 5 | 1 |
| Total for four weeks... | 40 | 21 | 1 |
| Total previous four weeks. | 50 | 12 | 6 |

During the same four weeks French losses were five steamers of over 1,600 tons and three under 1,600 tons; while Italian losses were five over 1,600 tons, four under 1,600 tons, and five sailing vessels. During the month of October nineteen Norwegian vessels, aggregating 34,577 tons, and forty-eight Norwegian seamen were lost.

According to statistics published by the Danish Ministry of Commerce, the Danish merchant fleet during 1916 lost forty-six steamers, of which thirty-eight were destroyed through war accidents, and twenty-eight sailing vessels under 200 tons were lost, of which nineteen were lost through war accidents. German U-boats destroyed twenty-seven steamers and Austrian submarines four steamers. In 1915 the losses were only twelve steamers, representing a value of six million crowns, ($1,608,000.)

## Statement by Sir Eric Geddes

A comprehensive review of the submarine situation was made on Nov. 1 by Sir Eric Geddes, the new First Lord of the Admiralty, in his maiden speech as a member of the House of Commons. He said:

I have studied from a variety of sources the statements made from time to time by the enemy as to tonnage and position, and have come to the definite conclusion that not only does he not know what is being sunk, but that he would like very much, indeed, to know what is being sunk regularly month by month or week by week, or even exactly for a period.

However great the loss of mercantile tonnage is, we cannot at this stage of the war pick any one item to deduce therefrom that the war, even any phase of the war, is going well or badly.

The general situation regarding submarine warfare can best be demonstrated by the following figures: Since the beginning of the war between 40 and 50 per cent. of the German submarines operating in the North Sea, the Atlantic, and the Arctic Ocean have been sunk. During the last quarter the enemy has lost as many submarines as during the whole of 1916.

As regards the sinkings of British merchant tonnage by submarines, the German official figures for August are 808,-000 tons of all nationalities. They sank a little more than half of that for all nationalities.

For September their official figures are 679,000 tons. They sank far less than one-third of that amount of British tonnage, and less than one-third of that amount of all nationalities.

The number of German submarines which do not return is increasing. Since April, the highest month for British losses, they have steadily decreased, and latterly to a marked degree. September was the most satisfactory month; October was only slightly worse, and better by 30 per cent. than any other month since unrestricted submarine warfare began. The net reduction in tonnage in the last four months is 30 per cent. less than anticipated in the estimate prepared for the Cabinet early in July.

The total net reduction since the beginning of the war from all causes in British tonnage on the official register in ships over 1,600 tons is under 2,500,000 of tons gross, or 14 per cent.

Summarized, the submarine warfare amounts to this: Our defensive measures have during the last seven months proved so efficacious that in spite of the increased number of ships which are passing through the danger zone, there has been steady reduction in the damage done by the enemy submarines. In the meantime

UNITED STATES PATROL SHIP ALCEDO, SUNK BY A GERMAN SUBMARINE, WITH
LOSS OF TWENTY-ONE LIVES

we are sinking enemy submarines to an increasing extent. Our offensive measures are improving and will still more improve and multiply.

But, on the other hand, the Germans are building submarines faster than they have hitherto done, and they have not yet attained their maximum strength. It appears to me, therefore, that the submarine warfare, as elsewhere, is becoming a test of determination and ingenuity between the two contending forces.

At the outbreak of the war Germany possessed over 5,000,000 tons shipping. Today nearly half of it has been sunk or is in the hands of ourselves or our allies. She has a 50 per cent. reduction to our 14 per cent.

It had been asked, Geddes proceeded, whether Great Britain was building merchant tonnage at a sufficient rate to replace the sinkings. In reply he said that the new national yards now being built would be ready in six months, and continued:

The output of merchant tonnage for the first nine months of 1917 is 123 per cent. higher than the total output for the whole of 1915. Standard vessels have been ordered representing nearly 1,000,000 gross tons. More than half of these are under construction.

According to the First Lord there were now 235 large drydocks in the British Isles where merchantmen could be repaired.

The German Admiralty issued a reply

to Geddes's speech, asserting that he had omitted Mediterranean sinkings and that his figures were in net tonnage while those of the German Government were in gross tonnage; but the British Admiralty contradicted both assertions and supported the statement as above recorded.

The First Lord of the Admiralty had occasion again on Nov. 16 to speak on submarine sinkings before the House of Commons. He said that the favorable figures of the week should not be taken as indicating the end of the submarine menace. He reminded his hearers that the Germans were still building U-boats faster than the Allies were destroying them, and that mercantile marine tonnage was not being maintained. He added that economy in everything which was seaborne continued to be of vital importance, and that all work which could be diverted from other fields to the shipyards would have a direct bearing on the winning of the war.

### Sinking of the Antilles

During the month several American vessels have been lost. The steamer Antilles, an army transport, was torpedoed on Oct. 17 while returning to America and under convoy of American patrol vessels. Out of about 237 on board 167 persons were saved. These included all the army and navy officers. The 70 missing men included army and navy enlisted men, three engineer officers of the ship, and merchant seamen. The Antilles was a merchant vessel of the Southern Pacific Line hailing from Philadelphia, which had been taken over by the navy and fitted out especially for army transport service. She carried a naval armed guard on board. The disaster—the first of the kind since the American Government began its enormous task of shipping its army of more than a million men to France—marks the heaviest toll of American lives taken in submarine warfare since the destruction of the Lusitania. Not only was the Antilles the first American army transport to be lost in the present war, but so far as official records have been disclosed she is the first vessel convoyed by American patrol ships that has been lost.

## Attack on the Cassin

The United States destroyer Cassin (Commander Walter H. Vernou) had a narrow escape from destruction in an encounter with a German submarine in the war zone on Oct. 16. While the vessel was on her patrol station a submarine was sighted on the surface about five miles distant. The Cassin immediately proceeded at full speed toward the submarine. She searched the area for about thirty minutes, when Commander Vernou sighted a torpedo running at high speed near the surface about 400 yards away, headed to strike the Cassin amidships. He rang for emergency full speed ahead on both engines, put the rudder hard over, and was just clear of the torpedo's course when it broached on the surface, turned sharply toward the vessel, and struck the stern of the Cassin. Fortunately only one engine was disabled, thereby permitting the destroyer to re-

main under way, circling in search of the submarine. After about an hour the submarine exposed its conning tower long enough for the Cassin to fire four shots. The Cassin continued the search until dark, when, having been joined by other British and American patrol vessels, she was taken safely into port.

The Navy Department announced on Nov. 1 that the transport Finland, 12,806 tons, had been torpedoed while returning from foreign water, but that the damage to the ship was so slight that she returned to port under her own steam. Like the Antilles the Finland was under escort of naval convoy, and in each instance no sign of torpedo or submarine was seen. Three naval gunners, four merchant seamen, and two enlisted army men lost their lives.

## The Alcedo and Others

The Alcedo, a patrol boat, was torpedoed and sunk by a German submarine early in the morning of Nov. 5, with the loss of one officer and twenty men. Before the war the Alcedo was a steam yacht belonging to George W. C. Drexel of Philadelphia. This was the first American fighting ship to go down since the war began.

On Oct. 30 the picket boat of the U. S. S. Michigan foundered. Apparently, the Navy Department announcement said, the entire crew were lost. The finding of the bodies of three of the crew and the failure to find any other trace of the boat or its occupants led the department to believe that all were drowned.

The American steamer Rochester, 2,551 tons, was torpedoed and sunk on Nov. 2. Seventeen men lost their lives, including six enlisted men of the navy who were serving as armed guards. The survivors endured terrible hardships for many days before they reached land.

# The Supreme War Council

## A Step Toward Allied Unity, and the Storm Raised by Mr. Lloyd George's Explanation

A CONFERENCE of the Premiers of Italy, France, and Great Britain, with their Chiefs of Staff, held at Rapallo, near Genoa, on Nov. 9, 1917, resulted in the creation of an inter-allied strategic board — to be known as the Supreme War Council—for the more efficient co-ordination of the Entente military energies and a more vigorous prosecution of the war along definite and unified lines. The following were in attendance: The British Premier, David Lloyd George; the French Premier, Paul Painlevé; the Italian Premier, Vittorio Orlando; Lieut. Gen. Sir William Robertson, Chief of the Imperial Staff at British Army headquarters; Major Gen. Sir Henry Hughes Wilson; General Smuts, formerly the British Commander in South Africa; the Italian Foreign Minister, Baron Sonnino; the French Minister of Missions Abroad, Henry Franklin-Bouillon; General Foch, Chief of Staff of the French War Ministry, and their staffs.

The first act of the Supreme War Council was to create an Interallied General Staff consisting of General Cadorna, representing Italy; General Foch, Chief of Staff of the French Ministry, and General Wilson, sub-chief of the British General Staff. General Cadorna relinquished his place at the head of the Italian forces and accepted this position. He was replaced as Commander in Chief of the Italian armies by General Armando Diaz, with General Badoglio as second in command and General Giardino third.

### Text of the Agreement

The agreement of the three powers is as follows:

First.—With a view to better co-ordination of the military action on the western front, a Supreme War Council is composed of the Prime Minister and a member of the Government of each of the great powers whose armies are fighting on that front, the extension of the scope of the council to other fronts to be reserved for discussion with the other great powers.

Second.—The Supreme War Council has for its mission to watch over the general conduct of the war. It prepares recommendations for the consideration of the Governments and keeps itself informed of their execution and reports thereon to the respective Governments.

Third.—The General Staff and military commands of the armies of each power charged with the conduct of the military operations remain responsible to their respective Governments.

Fourth.—General war plans drawn by competent military authorities are submitted to the Supreme War Council, which under high authority of Government insures its concordance and submits, if need be, any necessary changes.

Fifth.—Each power delegates to the Supreme War Council one permanent military representative, whose exclusive function is to act as technical adviser to the council.

Sixth.—Military representatives receive from the Government and the competent military authorities of their country all proposals, information, and documents relating to the conduct of the war.

Seventh.—The military representatives watch day by day the situation of the forces and the means of all kinds of which the Allies and enemy armies dispose.

Eighth.—The Supreme War Council meets normally at Versailles, where the permanent military representatives and staffs are established. They may meet at other places according to circumstances. Meetings of the Supreme War Council take place at least once a month.

### Blunders of the Entente

In an address at a luncheon given in Paris on Nov. 12 by Premier Painlevé, David Lloyd George discussed the plan—now known as the Rapallo plan—for centralized direction of allied activities against the enemy. In this speech he made a number of frank avowals which created a profound stir. He said in part:

Unfortunately we did not have time to consult the United States or Russia before creating this council. The Italian disaster necessitated action without delay to repair it. This made it indispensable to commence right now with the powers whose forces may be employed on the Italian front. But, in order to assure the complete success of this great experiment, which I believe is essential to the victory of our cause, it will be necessary that all our great allies be represented in the deliberations. I am persuaded that we shall obtain the consent of these two great countries and their co-operation in the work of the interallied council.

Mr. Lloyd George talked of the reasons for not taking the step earlier. He referred to "timidities and susceptibilities" when it came to treating questions on any front not commanded by Generals taking part in the interallied consultations. The Allies had committed a great fault, he said, in not assisting Serbia adequately in holding her line. The result was that the Central Empires broke the blockade and procured men and supplies from the east, without which Germany would have been unable to maintain the force of her armies. He continued:

Why was this unbelievable fault committed? The reply is simple. It was because no one in particular was charged with guarding the Balkan gate. The united front had not become a reality. France and England were absorbed by other problems in other regions. Italy thought only of the Carso. Russia was mounting guard over a frontier of a thousand miles, and, even without that, she could not have passed through to have helped Serbia, because Rumania was neutral.

It is true that we sent troops to Saloniki to succor Serbia, but, as always, they were sent too late. Half the men who fell in the vain effort to pierce the western front in September that same year would have saved Serbia, saved the Balkans, and completed the blockade of Germany.

You may say this is an old story. I grant you that it was simply the first chapter of a series that has continued to the present hour; 1915 was the year of the Serbian tragedy; 1916 was the year of the Rumanian tragedy, which was a repetition of the Serbian story almost without change. This is unbelievable, when you think of the consequences to the Allies' cause of the Rumanian defeat. Opulent wheatfields and rich petroleum wells passed to the enemy and Germany was able to escape us.

Through the harvest of 1917 the siege of the Central Powers was raised once more, and the horrible war was once more

prolonged. That would not have happened had there existed some central authority, charged with meditating upon the problem of the war for the entire theatre of the war.

## "A War Condemned to Disaster"

After reviewing the Italian campaign the Premier said:

As far as I am concerned, I had arrived at the conclusion that if nothing was changed I could no longer accept the responsibility for the direction of a war condemned to disaster from lack of unity. Italy's misfortune may still save the alliance, because without it I do not think that even today we would have created a veritable superior council.

National and professional traditions, questions of prestige and susceptibilities, all conspired to render our best decisions vain. No one in particular bore the blame. The guilt was in the natural difficulty of obtaining of so many nations, of so many independent organizations, that they should amalgamate all their individual particularities to act together as if they were but one people.

## Mr. Lloyd George said later:

I have spoken today with a frankness that is perhaps brutal—at the risk of being ill-understood here and elsewhere, and not, perhaps, without risk of giving a temporary encouragement to the enemy; but now that we have established this council it is for us to see that the unity it represents be a fact and not an appearance.

The war has been prolonged by particularism. It will be shortened by solidarity. If the effort to organize our united action becomes a reality, I have no doubt as to the issue of the war. The weight of men and material and of moral factors in every sense of the word is on our side. I say it, no matter what may happen to Russia, or in Russia. A revolutionary Russia can never be anything but a menace to Hohenzollernism.

But even if we are obliged to despair of Russia, my faith in the final triumph of the cause of the Allies remains unshakable.

## French Premier's Indorsement

Premier Painlevé, in his speech at the luncheon, remarked:

A single front, a single army, a single nation—that is the program requisite for future victory. If after forty months of war, after all the lessons the war has taught us, the Allies were not capable of that sacred international union, then, in spite of their sacrifices, they would not be worthy of victory.

In discussing the manner of accomplishment of this fusion, M. Painlevé said:

The enemies' alliance realized unity of effort by brutal discipline, one of the peoples among them having mastered the others and rendered them serviceable. But we are free peoples. We do not admit of subjection to other peoples in time of war. That independence is at the same time a source of strength and weakness— of strength because there is a capacity for resistance which is unknown to subject peoples, and of weakness because it renders more difficult co-ordination of military operations. To reconcile this independence with the need for unity of direction which is required to achieve an efficacious war policy will be the work of the Interallied War Committee and of the Superior War Council just created by the Allies.

## Strong Opposition Rises

The creation of the Supreme War Council and the reasons so bluntly expressed by the British Premier aroused a storm of opposition in England on the presumption by the critics that it was a movement to bring the commanders in the field under political control.

Premier Lloyd George, in the House of Commons on Nov. 14, further elucidated the plan in reply to questions by former Premier Asquith. The Premier, after reading the text of the agreement to the House, said:

From the foregoing it will be clear that the council will have no executive power, and that final decisions in the matter of strategy and the distribution and movements of the various armies in the field will rest with the several Governments of the Allies; there will therefore be no operations department attached to the council. The permanent military representatives will derive from the existing intelligence departments of the Allies all information necessary in order to enable them to submit advice to the Supreme Allied Council.

The object of the Allies has been to set up a central body charged with the duty of continuously surveying the field of operations as a whole by the light of information derived from all the fronts and from all the Governments and staffs, and of co-ordinating the plans prepared by the different General Staffs, and, if necessary, of making proposals of their own for the better conduct of the war.

A political storm raged over the matter for several days in England, the chief criticism being that there was danger of the military chiefs being subordinated to political control. It was soon officially announced that the United States authorities approved of the Rapallo plan.

## New Italian Army Leaders

General Armando Diaz, General Cadorna's successor as Commander in Chief of the Italian Armies, is a Neapolitan, 56 years of age. He was educated in the military college at Naples and in the celebrated military academy at Turin. He laid the foundation of his reputation in the Abyssinian campaign, and built it up during the Libyan war, in which he was wounded, and the plan of campaign of which was largely of his own devising. He was promoted to the command of the Twenty-third Army Corps on the Isonzo, after brilliant successes achieved in his leadership of a division operating on the Carso.

General Badoglio, who, with General Giardino, former Minister of War, succeeds General Porro in the sub-chieftaincy, is a native of Piedmont and is 40 years of age. He also won distinction in Italy's campaign in Africa. In his rapid course through all the grades of the military hierarchy he received no fewer than three promotions for merit in actual warfare. General Foch, who is the dominant figure of the Interallied General Staff, is a hero of the battle of the Marne, is 66 years old, and was detached from active service last April, to be made French Chief of Staff. He has enjoyed a brilliant reputation as one of the foremost strategists in the French Army. He spent his early years in Metz. After the Franco-Prussian war he went to Paris and devoted himself to preparing for the next war with Germany, which he confidently believed was inevitable.

During the battle of the Marne, General Foch held the centre of the French line with 120,000 men and was opposed by 200,000 Germans, including the famous Prussian Guards. Both his wings were driven back, and then Foch launched a terrific attack against the German centre, which was successful and forced the whole German line into a general retreat.

# Colonel House's Mission to the Allies

AMERICAN Commissioners to consult with the Allies arrived at London Nov. 7, 1917. Neither the appointment nor the departure of the commission had been disclosed until its arrival was announced. Colonel E. M. House of New York, a personal friend of President Wilson, is the Chairman; the other members are Admiral Benson, Chief of Naval Operations; General Bliss, Chief of the General Staff; a representative of the Treasury in the person of Assistant Secretary Crosby; Vance C. McCormick, Chairman of the War Trade Board; Bainbridge Colby of the Shipping Board, Dr. Alonzo E. Taylor of the Food Administration, and Thomas Nelson Perkins, representing the Priority Board.

Secretary of State Lansing's announcement of the creation of the commission, published on the day of its arrival at London, stated that the object of the conferences which the envoys were to hold was " a more complete co-ordination " of the activities of the various nations " engaged in the conflict and a more com- " prehensive understanding of their re- " spective needs, in order that the joint " efforts of the cobelligerents may attain " the highest war efficiency." He continued:

While a definite program has not been adopted, it may be assumed that the subjects to be discussed will embrace not only those pertaining to military and naval operations, but also the financial, commercial, economic, and other phases of the present situation which are of vital importance to the successful prosecution of the war.

The United States in the employment of its man power and material resources desires to use them to the greatest advantage against Germany. It has been no easy problem to determine how they can be used most effectively, since the independent presentation of requirements by the allied Governments has been more or less conflicting on account of each Government's appreciation of its own wants, which are naturally given greater importance than the wants of other Governments. By a general survey of the whole situation and a free discussion of the needs of all, the approaching conference will undoubtedly be able to give to the demands of the several Governments their true per-

spective and proper place in the general plan for the conduct of the war.

Though the resources of this country are vast and though there is every purpose to devote them all, if need be, to winning the war, they are not without limit. But even if they were greater they should be used to the highest advantage in attaining the supreme object for which we are fighting. This can only be done by a full and frank discussion of the plans and needs of the various belligerents.

It is the earnest wish of this Government to employ its military and naval forces and its resources and energies where they will give the greatest returns in advancing the common cause. The exchange of views which will take place at the conference and the conclusions which will be reached will be of the highest value in preventing waste of energy and in bringing into harmony the activities of the nations which have been unavoidably acting in a measure independently.

In looking forward to the assembling of the conference it cannot be too strongly emphasized that it is a war conference, and nothing else, devoted to devising ways and means to intensify the efforts of the belligerents against Germany by complete co-operation under a general plan and thus bring the conflict to a speedy and satisfactory conclusion.

The last sentence of Secretary Lansing's statement disposed effectively of the rumor that the commission would consider peace propositions.

The commission was met by the British Foreign Minister, Arthur J. Balfour, and was cordially greeted by the British authorities. It was announced from London on Nov. 16 that the work of the commission was proceeding satisfactorily, and that the members were " well satisfied with the spirit in which they had been met by their ' opposite members ' in the fields they had to cover, and all reported good progress." The statement further added:

The pending arrangements, which will carry the co-operation of the American and British Governments to a fuller stage than in the past, could hardly have been reached at an earlier juncture. The United States Government will have, when the work of the commission is concluded, as it will be soon, all the material by which to determine the exact manner in which it can best contribute to the common cause of the Allies. It will have a clear perception of the different needs and will be in a position to supply them without wasteful dispersion of energy. The investigations which the members of the commission have had made have confirmed their opinion that the resources of the Allies, supported by America, will prove adequate to meet all needs in all directions—men, money, shipping, food, appliances, and material of every kind.

President Wilson made public on Nov. 18 a cablegram he had sent to Colonel House, in which he stated emphatically that the United States Government con-

siders "unity of plan and control" between all the Allies and the United States essential; he asked Colonel House to attend the first meeting of the Supreme War Council with General Tasker H. Bliss as military adviser. The President's action was understood to remove all doubts as to this Government's attitude toward the Interallied Council. It impressed upon the opposition factions in England and France the fact that the United States gave the Rapallo plan its unqualified indorsement.

# Russia's Financial Plight

Fresh proof of the serious plight of Russian finance was given in the speeches delivered at the Moscow conference, where it was asserted that in the three years of war Russia had expended 45 to 50 per cent. of the material resources of the people. Imports were only 16 per cent. of the volume required, and a commodity famine had been caused at a time when production had declined 50 per cent.

M. Nekrasoff, the Minister of Finance, said that the State purse was empty. The unfavorable factors of the pre-revolutionary period could not be deemed the sole cause of bad conditions, he said, for the activity of the revolutionary period had been the more prodigal. For the revolutionary period from March 1 to July 16, 1917, credit notes had been issued for 832,000,000 rubles; in 1914 the amount was 219,000,000 rubles; in 1915, 223,000,000 rubles; in 1916, 290,000,000 rubles, and from Jan. 1 to March 1, 1917, 420,000,000 rubles.

The United States Government up to the Lenine revolt had advanced a total credit of $325,000,000 to Russia, of which sum $190,900,000 was in actual cash. When Kerensky issued his interview (referred to on Page 420) Nov. 1, the United States responded immediately by placing $31,000,000 to the credit of the Russian Government.

General Dessino, representative of the Russian Army with the British, early in November gave the following information of the number of Austro-German troops on the Russian frontiers:

> Four German infantry divisions and three Austrian infantry divisions had been withdrawn from Rumania and Galicia immediately prior to the attack on the Italian front. At the same time a few German divisions have been transported from the French front.

> The total mass of enemy troops which is being maintained at present against the Russian armies is: Eighty-six infantry and ten cavalry German divisions, thirty-three infantry and eleven cavalry Austrian divisions, and seven Turkish and Bulgarian infantry divisions, making a total of 147 divisions.

An authority possessed of exact information concerning the Russian military situation said:

> Only seven German divisions have been withdrawn from the Russian front for use against Italy. There was a moment, however, when the last Russian offensive against the enemy conducted by General Brusiloff produced a critical situation and compelled Germany to rush eighteen divisions to the Russian front to arrest the Russian advance.

> The Germans have not seen fit to recall these troops. The conditions on the Riga front are such that the Germans are facing the necessity of falling back, and this certainly is not proof of the collapse of the Russian Army.

# Brazil at War With Germany

## Significant Reply to the Pope

BRAZIL declared war on Germany Oct. 26, 1917, and President Braz sanctioned the act by official proclamation. The vote of the Chamber of Deputies in favor of the war declaration was 149 to 1; in the Senate it was unanimous. The Germans, in anticipation of the action of the Brazilian authorities, set on fire and sank the German gunboat Eber at Rio Janeiro, a vessel of 984 tons. A few days later German submarines in the Atlantic sank two Brazilian ships, the Acary and the Guaniba, which had formerly belonged to Germany.

President Wilson on Oct. 30 cabled as follows to the President of Brazil:

> Allow me, speaking for the people and the Government of the United States, to say with what genuine pleasure and heartfelt welcome we hail the association with ourselves and the other nations united in war with Germany of the great republic of Brazil. Her action in this time of crisis binds even closer the bonds of friendship which already united the two republics.

The Chamber on Nov. 7 adopted the following measures of reprisal against Germany. They had been recommended by the President:

> Annulment of contracts for public works entered into with Germans.
> Prohibition of new land concessions to German subjects.
> Control of German banks, eventual annulment of their license, and the extension of these measures to German commercial firms.
> Prohibition of the transfer of ownership of German properties.
> The internment of German subjects.

A few days after the declaration of war strikes were reported throughout Southern Brazil, said to be due to Germans. The German population in three States of Southern Brazil is as follows:

| | Total Population. | Germans. |
|---|---|---|
| Rio Grande do Sul | 1,682,736 | 200,000 |
| Parana | 554,934 | 180,000 |
| Santa Catharina | 463,997 | 85,000 |

The Brazilian Army on Nov. 8 was concentrated in the State of Rio Grande do Sul for strike duty, and plans were inaugurated to increase the army to 100,000 by conscription, including men between the ages of 17 and 30.

Shortly after Brazil entered the war Secretary Lansing at Washington made public two dispatches which had been sent through the Swedish Minister at Buenos Aires by Count Luxburg, the German Chargé d'Affaires of the Argentine Legation. They revealed a plot to violate the Monroe Doctrine by consolidating the German settlements in Brazil. The text of the telegrams was as follows:

> No. 63. July 7, 1917.—Our attitude toward Brazil has created the impression here that our easy-going good nature can be counted on. This is dangerous in South America, where the people under thin veneer are Indians. A submarine squadron with full powers to me might probably still save the situation. I request instructions as to whether after a rupture of relations legation is to start for home or to remove to Paraguay or possibly Chile. The Naval Attaché will doubtless go to Santiago de Chile.
>
> LUXBURG.

> No. 89. Aug. 4, 1917.—I am convinced that we shall be able to carry through our principal political aims in South America, the maintenance of open market in Argentina and the reorganization of South Brazil equally well whether with or against Argentina. Please cultivate friendship with Chile. The announcement of the visit of a submarine squadron to salute the President would even now exercise decisive influence on the situation in South America. Prospect excellent for wheat harvest in December.
>
> LUXBURG.

These dispatches had been made known to the Brazilian authorities prior to their declaration of war against Germany.

### Reply to Pope's Peace Note

Brazil's views of the only manner in which durable peace may be obtained were set forth in the Government's reply to the peace proposal made last August by Pope Benedict. The note, which was made public on Nov. 14, is signed by the Brazilian Minister of Foreign Affairs, Dr. Nilo Peçanha, and is addressed to the Brazilian Minister at the Holy See. It explains that the President of the republic had not personally replied to the Pope's peace proposals because only now is Brazil in a state of war. The note follows:

The Brazilian Nation, which has never engaged in a war of conquest, but has consistently advocated arbitration as the solution for external conflicts in the constitution of the republic, and has no grievances and sufferings past or present to revenge; which has solved with serenity all questions regarding territorial limits, and with a precise knowledge of what belongs to her and an accurate acquaintance with the extent of her vast territory; which, thanks to the labor not only of her own sons, anxious to prove themselves worthy of so rich a patrimony, but of that of all foreigners whom our hospitality has assimilated; this nation, your Excellency can assure his Holiness, would have remained apart from the conflict in Europe in spite of the sympathy of public opinion for the Allies' liberal cause had Germany not extended the war to America and thereby prevented intertrading between all neutral countries.

Without renouncing her obligations as an American nation, this country could not fail to assume the position of a belligerent as a last resource, without hatred or any interest other than the defense of our flag and our fundamental rights.

Happily today the republics of the New World are more or less allied in their rights, but all, equally menaced in their liberties and their sovereignty, draw closer the bonds of the solidarity which formerly was merely geographic, economic, and historic, and which the necessities of self-defense and national independence now make political as well.

For such reasons Brazil can no longer maintain her isolated attitude, and now, in close solidarity as she must be and really is with the nations on whose side she has ranged herself, she can even speak as an individual entity.

No Brazilian heart can receive without emotion the eloquent appeal of his Holiness in the name of the Almighty to the belligerents in the cause of peace. Though no State religion has been adopted by Brazil, and all creeds are equally free, none the less Brazil is the third Catholic country of the world, and has maintained unbroken for centuries relations with the Government of the Holy See. Brazil, therefore, recognizes the generous motives that inspired the appeal of his Holiness asking that by disarmament and arbitration and the establishing of a régime in which the brute force of armies shall give way to the force of moral law, the restoration of France and Italy should be granted, and the Balkan problem and the restitution of liberty to Poland be considered.

Only the countries most deeply interested in these questions can judge if the honor of their arms has been saved in this war, or if these modifications of the political map of Europe are likely to restore tranquillity.

So long as the political and military organization that suspended living law the world over and suppressed spiritual conquests supposed to be established beyond question—so long as this power continues to abuse the alleviating functions of war and to destroy the Christian spirit that inspired the society of nations, only these nations can say whether confidence in treaties has disappeared and whether any other force excepting some new spirit of order can be accepted as a guarantee of peace.

Through the sufferings and the disillusions to which the war has given rise a new and better world will be born, as it were, of liberty, and in this way a lasting peace may be established without political or economic restrictions, and all countries be allowed a place in the sun with equal rights and an interchange of ideas and values in merchandise on an ample basis of justice and equity.

The Colombian Senate on Oct. 20 adopted a resolution protesting against German submarine warfare.

# President Wilson's Labor Address

## Survey of the War Situation in a Noteworthy Speech Before the Federation of Labor

*President Wilson, at the invitation of the Executive Committee of the American Federation of Labor, delivered the following address before the annual convention of that body in Buffalo, N. Y., Nov. 12, 1917. An immediate effect of the speech was seen in the action of the labor leaders next day in calling off all strikes involving Government work. After a few preliminary sentences President Wilson said:*

I AM introduced to you as the President of the United States, and yet I would be pleased if you would put the thought of the office into the background and regard me as one of your fellow-citizens who had come here to speak, not the words of authority, but the words of counsel, the words which men should speak to one another who wish to be frank in a moment more critical perhaps than the history of the world has ever yet known, a moment when it is every man's duty to forget himself, to forget his own interests, to fill himself with the nobility of a great national and world conception, and act upon a new platform elevated above the ordinary affairs of life, elevated to where men have views of the long destiny of mankind.

I think that in order to realize just what this moment of counsel is it is very desirable that we should remind ourselves just how this war came about and just what it is for. You can explain most wars very simply, but the explanation of this is not so simple. Its roots run deep into all the obscure soils of history, and in my view this is the last decisive issue between the old principles of power and the new principles of freedom.

### Germany Before the War

The war was started by Germany. Her authorities deny that they started it. But I am willing to let the statement I have just made await the verdict of history. And the thing that needs to be explained is why Germany started the war. Remember what the position of Germany in the world was—as enviable a position as any nation has ever occupied. The whole world stood at admiration of her wonderful intellectual and material achievements, and all the intellectual men of the world went to school to her. As a university man, I have been surrounded by men trained in Germany, men who had resorted to Germany because nowhere else could they get such thorough and searching training, particularly in the principles of science and the principles that underlie modern material achievements.

Her men of science had made her industries perhaps the most competent industries in the world, and the label "Made in Germany" was a guarantee of good workmanship and of sound material. She had access to all the markets of the world, and every other man who traded in those markets feared Germany because of her effective and almost irresistible competition.

She had a place in the sun. Why was she not satisfied? What more did she want? There was nothing in the world of peace that she did not already have, and have in abundance.

### Monopoly Methods Employed

We boast of the extraordinary pace of American advancement. We show with pride the statistics of the increase of our industries and of the population of our cities. Well, these statistics did not match the recent statistics of Germany. Her old cities took on youth, grew faster than any American cities ever grew; her old industries opened their eyes and saw a new world and went out for its conquest; and yet the authorities of Germany were not satisfied.

You have one part of the answer to the

question why she was not satisfied in her methods of competition. There is no important industry in Germany upon which the Government has not laid its hands to direct it and, when necessity arise, control it.

You have only to ask any man whom you meet who is familiar with the conditions that prevailed before the war in the matter of international competition to find out the methods of competition which the German manufacturers and exporters used under the patronage and support of the Government of Germany. You will find that they were the same sorts of competition that we have tried to prevent by law within our own borders. If they could not sell their goods cheaper than we could sell ours, at a profit to themselves, they could get a subsidy from the Government which made it possible to sell them cheaper anyhow; and the conditions of competition were thus controlled in large measure by the German Government itself.

### Aimed to Dominate World's Labor

But that did not satisfy the German Government. All the while there was lying behind its thought, in its dreams of the future, a political control which would enable it in the long run to dominate the labor and the industry of the world. It was not content with success by superior achievement; it wanted success by authority.

I suppose very few of you have thought much about the Berlin-to-Bagdad Railway. The Berlin-to-Bagdad Railway was constructed in order to run the threat of force down the flank of the industrial undertakings of half a dozen other countries, so that when German competition came in it would not be resisted too far—because there was always the possibility of getting German armies into the heart of that country quicker than any other armies could be got there.

Look at the map of Europe now. Germany, in thrusting upon us again and again the discussion of peace, talks about what? Talks about Belgium, talks about Northern France, talks about Alsace-Lorraine. Well, those are deeply interesting subjects to us and to them, but they are not talking about the heart of the matter.

Take the map and look at it. Germany has absolute control of Austria-Hungary, practical control of the Balkan States, control of Turkey, control of Asia Minor. I saw a map in which the whole thing was printed in appropriate black the other day, and the black stretched all the way from Hamburg to Bagdad—the bulk of the German power inserted into the heart of the world. If she can keep that, she has kept all that her dreams contemplated when the war began. If she can keep that, her power can disturb the world as long as she keeps it, always provided—for I feel bound to put this proviso in—always provided the present influences that control the German Government continue to control it.

I believe that the spirit of freedom can get into the hearts of Germans and find as fine a welcome there as it can find in any other hearts. But the spirit of freedom does not suit the plans of the Pan Germans. Power cannot be used with concentrated force against free peoples if it is used by a free people.

### Allusion to Austria-Hungary

You know how many intimations come to us from one of the Central Powers that it is more anxious for peace than the chief Central Power; and you know that it means that the people in that Central Power know that if the war ends as it stands they will, in effect, themselves be vassals of Germany, notwithstanding that their populations are compounded with all the people of that part of the world, and nowithstanding the fact that they do not wish, in their pride and proper spirit of nationality, to be so absorbed and dominated.

Germany is determined that the political power of the world shall belong to her. There have been such ambitions before. They have been in part realized. But never before have those ambitions been based upon so exact and precise and scientific a plan of domination.

May I not say that it is amazing to me that any group of people should be so ill-informed as to suppose, as some groups in Russia apparently suppose, that any reforms planned in the interest of the people can live in the presence of a Germany powerful enough to undermine or overthrow them by intrigue or force? Any body of free men that compounds with the present German Government is compounding for its own destruction. But that is not the whole of the story. Any man in America, or anywhere else, who supposes that the free industry and enterprise of the world can continue if the Pan-German plan is achieved and German power fastened upon the world is as fatuous as the dreamers of Russia.

What I am opposed to is not the feeling of the pacifists, but their stupidity. My heart is with them, but my mind has a contempt for them. I want peace, but I know how to get it, and they do not.

You will notice that I sent a friend of mine, Colonel House, to Europe who is as great a lover of peace as any man in the world, but I did not send him on a peace mission. I sent him to take part in a conference as to how the war was to be won, and he knows, as I know, that that is the way to get peace if you want it for more than a few minutes.

## Nobody Must Block the Way

All of this is a preface to the conference that I referred to with regard to what we are going to do. If we are true friends of freedom—our own or anybody else's—we will see that the power of this country, the productivity of this country, is raised to its absolute maximum and that absolutely nobody is allowed to stand in the way of it.

When I say that nobody is allowed to stand in the way, I don't mean that they shall be prevented by the power of the Government, but by the power of the American spirit. Our duty, if we are to do this great thing and show America to be what we believe her to be, the greatest hope and energy of the world—then we must stand together night and day until the job is finished.

While we are fighting for freedom, we must see, among other things, that labor is free; and that means a number of interesting things. It means not only that we must do what we have declared our purpose to do, see that the conditions of labor are not rendered more onerous

by the war—but also that we shall see to it that the instrumentalities by which the conditions of labor are improved are not blocked or checked. That we must do. That has been the matter about which I have taken pleasure in conferring from time to time with your President, Mr. Gompers. And, if I may be permitted to do so, I want to express my admiration of his patriotic courage, his large vision, and his statesmanlike sense of what is to be done. I like to lay my mind alongside of a mind that knows how to pull in harness. The horses that kick over the traces will have to be put in a corral.

## Capitalists Are Included

Now to "stand together" means that nobody must interrupt the processes of our energy, if the interruption can possibly be avoided without the absolute invasion of freedom. To put it concretely, that means this: Nobody has a right to stop the processes of labor until all the methods of conciliation and settlement have been exhausted; and I might as well say right here that I am not talking to you alone. You sometimes stop the courses of labor, but there are others who do the same. And I believe that I am speaking of my own experience not only, but of the experience of others, when I say that you are reasonable in a larger number of cases than the capitalists.

I am not saying these things to them personally yet, because I haven't had a chance. But they have to be said, not in any spirit of criticism. But in order to clear the atmosphere and come down to business, everybody on both sides has got to transact business, and the settlement is never imposible when both sides want to do the square and right thing. Moreover, a settlement is always hard to avoid when the parties can be brought face to face. * * *

We are all of the same clay and spirit, and we can get together if we desire to get together. Therefore, my counsel to you is this: Let us show ourselves Americans by showing that we do not want to go off in separate camps or groups by ourselves, but that we want to co-operate with all other classes and all other groups in a common enterprise, which is to release the spirit of the world from bondage.

### Manifestations of Mob Spirit

I would be willing to set that up as the final test of an American. That is the meaning of democracy. I have been very much distressed, my fellow-citizens, by some of the things that have happened recently. The mob spirit is displaying itself here and there in this country. I have no sympathy with what some men are saying, but I have no sympathy with the men that take their punishment into their own hands, and I want to say to every man who does join such a mob that I do not recognize him as worthy of the free institutions of the United States.

There are some organizations in this country whose object is anarchy and the destruction of law, but I would not meet their efforts by making myself a partner in destroying the law. I despise and hate their purposes as much as any man, but I respect the ancient processes of justice and I would be too proud not to see them done justice, however wrong they are. And so I want to utter my earnest protest against any manifestation of the spirit of lawlessness anywhere or in any cause.

Why, gentlemen, look what it means: We claim to be the greatest democratic people in the world, and democracy means, first of all, that we can govern ourselves. If our men have not self-control, then they are not capable of that great thing which we call democratic government. A man who takes the law into his hands is not the right man to co-operate in any form of or development of law and institutions. And some of the processes by which the struggle between capital and labor is carried on are processes that come very near to taking the law into your own hands. I do not mean for a moment to compare them with what I have just been speaking of, but I want you to see that they are mere graduations of the manifestations of the unwillingness to co-operate.

### New Instrumentalities

And the fundamental lesson of the whole situation is that we must not only take common counsel, but that we must yield to and obey common counsel. Not all of the instrumentalities for this are at hand. I am hopeful that in the very near future new instrumentalities may be organized by which we can see to it that various things that are now going on shall not go on. There are various processes of the dilution of labor, and the unnecessary substitution of labor, and bidding in distant markets, and unfairly upsetting the whole competition of labor, which ought not to go on—I mean now on the part of employers—and we must interject into this some instrumentality of co-operation by which the fair thing will be done all around. I am hopeful that some such instrumentalities may be devised, but, whether they are or not, we must use those that we have. * * *

# Organized Labor on War Issues

THE annual report of the Executive Council of the American Federation of Labor, submitted at the federation's convention in Buffalo, Nov. 12, 1917, showed organized labor in the United States to be in substantial accord with the war aims of the Government. It demanded a representation of wage earners at the peace conference when the war ends, and opposed all "vindictive" indemnities. The text of the report is in part as follows:

It is an imperative duty from which there is no escape that wage earners, as well as all other citizens of this Republic, support our Government in its righteous effort to defend principles of humanity and to establish democracy in international relations. Because we desire permanent peace, it is our duty to fight and sacrifice until these purposes can be achieved.

When nations can send representatives to negotiate peace terms in accord with this concept, we maintain that the basic provisions of the peace treaty should be formulated with regard to the rights and welfare of the men, women, and children constituting the nations, rather than the

Governments of the nations. The Government should be only an instrumentality of the people, instead of dominating and actuating their lives. This terrific war must wipe out all vestiges of the old concept that the nation belongs to the ruler or Government.

We hold that the same principles should apply to relations between nations, and that secret diplomacy should be replaced by diplomatic representatives responsible to their own people and received by either the Parliament of the country to which they are accredited or by a representative of the people, responsible to them.

Working people have never been properly represented in diplomatic affairs. The future must be constructed upon broader lines than the past. We insist, therefore, that the Government of the United States provide adequate and direct representatives of wage earners among the plenipotentiaries sent to the Peace Congress, and urge upon the labor movements of other countries to take like action.

After outlining the principles upon which peace should be negotiated, the report offers a suggestion for reconstruction of labor conditions:

We suggest that all prejudice and partisan spirit can best be eliminated by reconstructing international labor relations and thus bring to new problems and a new era activity and co-operation unhampered and unperverted by former alliances or old feuds. The basis of reconstruction should be the trade union movements of the various countries. We recommend that an international labor conference of representatives of the trade union movements of all countries be held at the same time and place as the World Peace Congress, that labor may be in touch with plans under consideration and may have the benefit of information and counsel of those participating in the congress. * * *

In our own country there is evident in every kind of war work the necessity for some national agencies for better adjusting the supply of workers. We are entering a period where there must be greater economy in the use of the man power of our country. A central, efficient employment agency with its branches is plainly necessary in performing the gigantic task that is now before the Emergency Fleet Corporation and in the necessary work of production of war supplies.

With the withdrawal of hundreds of thousands of men for military purposes there is necessity for readjustment in the industrial field. Effective employment agencies, under the control of the Department of Labor, co-operating with local agencies and associations, would be an invaluable adjunct to our war machinery. Such agencies will also be keenly needed in the transition period that will follow the declaration of peace and the work of demobilization.

Since the war began, the report says, the American labor movement has secured the best agreements with the Government that have been secured in any warring country. "The agreements established a new period in the industrial world," says the report, "a period in which the Government has sanctioned standards based upon principles of human welfare and has substituted these standards for the old system under which profits were paramount."

Concerning the much-discussed suggestion for the conscription of labor, the report says:

Immediately after the declaration of war by the United States Government an agitation was commenced for the purpose of organizing what was to be known as an "Industrial Reserve." It was proposed that men in industry should become part of a semi-military organization to be directed and controlled by our military establishment, to the end that those employed in industry could be shifted from one location to another. Because of its military feature, the proposition was opposed by the officers of the American Federation of Labor.

In the light of the experience gleaned in foreign countries now engaged in war, it appears that the shifting of workers has not only been necessary but vital to the carrying on of the great conflict. Several plans have been proposed, but none thus far has been accepted as a proper solution of the problem. If the war continues for any considerable period, this question will have to be met. The primary agency necessary for dealing with proper adjustment of workers is a national employment bureau, equipped to give workers information of employment opportunities and employers information of available and suitable workers. It is one of the necessary and essential activities of the war that certain industries on occasions are called upon to materially increase production, and, in this event, some plan must be inaugurated to meet the needs of the Government.

The report recognizes the possibility that war conditions may bring about a "more general advent" of women in industry. Demand is made that equal pay be given for equal work without regard to sex.

# Effect of the United States in the War

## By Arnold Bennett

By Arrangement With The London Chronicle

IF you pessimistically doubt whether the United States will ever be able to exercise her admitted power in the European arena, consider how all pessimistic prognostications about the United States have been falsified. (Incidentally, do not forget that she is already exercising that power, in the economics and on the seas of the European arena.) It was said that President Wilson did not mean what he wrote to Germany. He did mean what he wrote. It was said that he would lose the Presidency. He did not lose the Presidency. It was said that he could not unite the nation. He did unite the nation. It was said that the nation would not go to war on a scale commensurate with its strength. It has gone to war in the grand manner. It was said that the selective draft law would be a failure, and would occasion riots. It did not occasion riots, and it was not a failure; on the contrary, it enrolled 10,000,000 men in one day. It was said that the $2,000,000,000 loan would be a failure. The $2,000,000,000 loan was greatly oversubscribed, by over three million people, and the bulk of it was subscribed in small sums. (And recollect that the rate of interest is only 3½ per cent., which, allowing for the fact that interest on capital rules appreciably higher in the United States than in Western Europe, is the equivalent of at most 3 per cent. here.)

### The Expeditionary Force

Finally, it was said, and is said, that the United States will not succeed in transporting her army to the field of war. Events have not yet contradicted this particular pessimism, but that they will do so I have not the slightest doubt. The means of transporting the army are being prepared concurrently with the army itself, and that army will duly arrive—unless Germany falters earlier— and when it arrives it will satisfactorily account for itself. Self-satisfaction alone —and the American people have higher motives than that—would compel the United States "to do its damnedest" in this war. The United States is on its mettle; it has to prove its quality to Europe, and it will do so. The speeches of all American leaders of opinion show a complete grasp of the moral issues of the war, a complete adherence to those democratic principles which a strong party in Britain still refuses to accept, and a complete determination to achieve the definite triumph of those principles. And if the general conduct of the nation shows anything, it shows that the nation and the leaders are in admirable unity.

But, highly as I value the physical contribution which the United States is making and will make to the war, I value still more highly the moral contribution which she will make to the collective common sense of the belligerents when the peace congress at last meets. The thought that our statesmen now in power will represent the British Commonwealth at the peace congress is humiliating and positively disquieting to a very large proportion of Britons, myself among the number. I will say nothing about allied countries except that I doubt if they will display more sagacity in the matter of peace terms than our own Government is likely to show.

### The Lesson of 1870

The fact is that the suggested allied peace terms agreed upon by the Allies, and untimely revealed to the world at Petrograd in the early part of this year, showed that the Allies had learned little from history, and that especially they had not learned the great lesson of 1870. The peace terms thus disclosed could not possibly have resulted in a permanent peace. Far from that, they had in them the seeds of permanent discord, since they repeated the very mistake made by Prussia in 1870 and by other military oligarchies in all ages. One of the worst items in the terms was denied by M. Ribot, but in a dubious formula which was nearly as unsatisfactory as the thing it tried to contradict.

Before the entry of the United States into the war the democrats of all allied countries were in a quandary. They wanted, and rightly wanted, a military victory over Germany; but they feared that a military victory over Germany would mean a militaristic peace with all the anti-democratic and reactionary and fatal consequences of a militaristic peace. And that this fear was reasonably justified there can be no doubt. The entry of the United States into the war has liberated democrats from their quandary. They can now desire a military victory without any dread of a militaristic peace which would permanently antagonize Germany and give the German military scoundrels a new hold over the duped German people. They can do this, because the United States, when peace comes, will be the strongest and the least exhausted partner among the Allies, and the United States will not consent to a militaristic peace. The United States is led by an extremely powerful and an unusually far-seeing individuality, and the opinions of President Wilson about the principles of peace are known, and he is committed to them.

All this does not imply that I look on the United States as Paradise and the citizens of the United States as paragons of political wisdom far superior to ourselves. I do not. The United States has much to learn, and to learn even from us. It suffers from many faults, (some of which have been indicated—of course, with keen approval—by Lord Northcliffe in his article.) But it does happen that in the universal acceptance of certain great ax-

ioms of democracy, the United States, like Australia and New Zealand, is further advanced in the evolution of political opinion than we are. The influence of the United States will be employed against all vicious European vested interests, and agaist the natural but unwise promptings of revenge, and against any insidious indirectness of speech or act. And I rank this future moral work of hers above her purely military work.

## When Peace Is Signed

And the participation of the United States will react favorably upon affairs not merely beyond the war, but beyond the peace treaty. It is agreed by all expert authorities that after the peace treaty has been signed the supply of the raw materials of the world will have to be regulated for a long time by some international board—whatever happens to the hoped-for league of nations. The doings of that board will form the very basis of world reconstruction. Now the standing of the United States on the board will be much surer, and her action is likely to be much fairer, as an ex-belligerent, than they would have been had she remained neutral. The fact that she has fought side by side with the Allies cannot fail to affect her attitude and mold her conduct. The sympathy between Britain and herself will be notably deepened, and the force of the democratic ideals of all the English-speaking peoples thus combined will be increased accordingly. For all kinds of reasons the English-speaking peoples, if they remain together in good faith, will be in a position to work wonders in the huge affair of reconstruction. For example, they control between them the world's supply of gold, rubber, wool, cotton, copper, and tin.

London, Sept. 19, 1917.

# Clothing and Food Control in the Central Empires

GERMANY has pursued a steadily progressive policy of restriction in order to conserve the clothing supply of the country. The adoption of a more rigid embargo by the United States is still further reducing the supply of textile materials and will necessitate further restrictive measures.

By military order, dated Feb. 1, 1916, the entire textile industry and a great part of the clothing industry were placed under State control and stocks were requisitioned at prices fixed, in case of dispute, by an Imperial Arbitration Office. Besides clothing suitable for the army, navy, civil service, or for prisoners of war, these requisitions involved blankets, bedding material, and other household linen, handkerchiefs, &c. The issue of uniforms to many railway employes was at the same time stopped. By an order of Feb. 25, 1916, it was made a penal offense to advertise or hold any kind of stocktaking or bargain sales, and an appeal was made to the patriotism of German women to maintain a simplicity of dress "more in keeping with the seriousness of the times." Later in the Spring of 1916 the Ministry of War gave its approval to an order fixing a maximum length of material to be employed in making each article of dress for women and children.

## Clothing Bought Only by Permit

By a Federal order dated June 10, 1916, the Government added clothing to the large list of articles subjected to rationing in Germany, and a system of clothing tickets was accordingly introduced. It was laid down as a principle that while there could be no standard of consumption applicable to all classes of the population, it was possible to establish the minimum requirements of individual classes, and local authorities were enjoined to grant permits for as much clothing as might be considered a minimum for each class. As a rule people were not to be permitted to go beyond 20 per cent. of their normal requirements. Persons applying for permits for the first time were to be questioned as to the details of their wardrobe, and only if they were found not to possess an adequate stock of clothing could the permit be issued. Well-to-do people were to be directed to purchase articles of luxury (which were embargo free) rather than goods which were in general demand. Before long it was found that the differentiation between rich and poor in the matter of facilities for buying clothes was causing bitterness.

A stocktaking of the country's clothing supplies in the Autumn of 1916 showed that still greater economy would have to be enforced, and consequently a long list of further articles was brought under the ticket system. At the end of 1916 Government control was extended to second-hand clothing and underwear. Under an order issued on Christmas Day ordinary trade in second-hand clothing, linen, and footwear was put an end to, and the old-clothes business was transferred to the local authorities. Second-hand clothing could only be sold by these authorities against a permit. In February, 1917, there was fresh evidence of the progressive exhaustion of the stocks of clothing materials and clothing in Germany. Purchase permits for underwear and stockings were only obtainable with great difficulty, not more than two pairs of stockings being allowed to any one person in three months. The well-to-do were appealed to officially through the press to deliver up every article of clothing and footwear which they possibly could spare.

## Clothing Materials Requisitioned

By an order dated March 22, 1917, a general requisition of clothing and clothing materials for civilian use was instituted. On April 2 a series of drastic regulations prescribed the absolute maximum of wearing apparel of all kinds for men, women, and children and babies, and the local authorities were prohibited from issuing purchase permits to any person already in possession of the authorized maximum. Simultaneously new regulations were issued prescribing in minute detail the amount of material that might be used in any garment or article of household linen; and proprietors of hotels, boarding houses, &c., were warned that they could not be allowed to purchase fresh bed and table linen. In May, 1917, the public were officially enjoined to use paper fabrics for shrouds, while the use of shoes and stockings for burials was forbidden. At the same time the Government started relief measures on a large scale by the issue of standard clothing to the poor. It would seem that much of the clothing now worn throughout Germany, including military uniforms, is made from materials diluted in varying degrees with substitutes such as paper yarn and cellulose, the warmth and wearing properties of which are doubtful as compared with materials spun, woven, or knitted wholly from wool and cotton.

## Women's Hair for Straps

The great spinning district of Alsace is almost without employment, for there is no material. New goods are made wholly or in part of wood-pulp paper. The manufacturers use ring-spinning machines or twisting machines, not mules. The paper is cut into strips from three-sixteenths to half an inch wide, and by their new method they make thread from this paper which can be woven into cloth. Workmen's blouses and children's clothes are the commonest fabrics of this kind, while at Leipsic Fair were shown women's dresses made of the paper material. But it is also impregnated for use as sacking, tent cloth, and sandbag material. Latterly there is a certain falling off of the import of raw material from Sweden even for this "substitute," and everything capable of being pulped is being commandeered by the Government.

Alsace also furnishes what a traveler calls the weirdest female product of this war—girls wearing red caps with the inscription, "I have given my hair for the Fatherland." Women's hair is very high in price for it is woven into straps which are employed as driving-bands for machinery. It is even rumored (so serious is the leather shortage) that hair will be "commandeered" early next year, and that women will have to sacrifice it to the Fatherland.

## The Weekly Food Ration

The grain situation in October, 1917, was such that the German Government could give no definite assurance that the bread supply would last until the next harvest, even with the greatly reduced ration then in use. It was stated by authoritative observers that the existing bread ration could be maintained only by the use of substitutes further affecting the quality of the bread. Flour was and is milled to 94 per cent. of the grain. Bread and potatoes are the bulk of the ration, and the potato crop is much smaller than was expected. It was stated in October that the meat allowance would almost certainly have to be decreased; infants' milk had already been reduced, and milk and butter would soon be obtainable in still scantier amounts.

Information concerning the weekly ration allowed the German people and the civilian population in the occupied portions of Belgium and France was received and made public in October by the United States Food Administration. The published statement, beginning with the German ration per person per week, was as follows:

Flour, 3.45 pounds; potatoes, 7.05 pounds; cereals, (oats, beans, and peas,) 7 ounces; meat, 8.8 ounces; sugar, 3 ounces; butter and margarine, 2.8 ounces, and other fats, 2.8 ounces.

Stated in terms of American housekeeping these items amount to sufficient flour to bake 4½ pounds of bread; one-half peck of potatoes; a cupful of beans, peas, and oatmeal; one-half pound of meat; 12 dominoes of sugar; 6 individual patties of butter, and an equal amount of other fats.

For the population of that portion of Northern France occupied by the Germans the allowance is as follows:

Sufficient flour for 5 pounds of bread; one-fifth peck of potatoes; one cupful of cereals; 12 1-3 ounces of bacon and lard, and 10 dominoes of sugar.

Here meat, butter, and margarine are all replaced by bacon and lard. The allowances of flour and cereals are slightly increased, but the allowance of potatoes is less than half the German ration, while that of sugar is also reduced even below the meagre German allowance.

The ration for the civilian population of the occupied portion of Belgium is similar to that of Northern France, except bacon and lard are replaced by meat and butter.

The German ration, compared with the ration used as standard for purposes of comparison by the Food Administration, shows that in body building protein the Germans have 0.41 of a pound and the standard ration 1.08 pounds. In fats the German ration contains 0.43 of a pound, as compared with standard 0.7 pound. In carbohydrates the German ration contains 4.17 pounds, as compared to 9.9 pounds for the standard ration. In total calories the German ration aggregates 10,542, as compared to 24,000 in the standard ration.

The standard ration is regarded as sufficient only for a person in a sedentary occupation or one involving relatively slight physical labor, and yet it provides two and one-half times as much body-building protein and nearly twice as much fat and nearly two and one-half times as much carbohydrates as the German ration.

### American Woman's Experience

Miss Ellen Worfolk, an American woman who has lived in Berlin ten years, landed at an American port on Nov. 6, 1917, and described war conditions in Germany as follows:

Food is scarce in Germany and people are getting very thin. I became so weak through the lack of proper nourishment that I had to apply for a milk card, and was placed on the same diet as the babies, which resulted in an improvement in my health. The death rate among infants is not so great as reported in the newspapers outside Germany, and in fact is not much higher than it was before the war. The reason for this is that the fresh milk is given to babies and old people, and healthy persons under 45 cannot obtain any milk for their tea or coffee. The people have two ounces of butter and an ounce of margarine per week doled out by the Government, and sometimes they can buy a little extra butter at $3 a pound. The sugar allowance is one pound and a half a month and 75 cents a pound for any that can be obtained from the grocers.

There is no white bread in Germany. The average German eats war bread, which is dark in color and not very palatable, and there is another kind called whole-wheat bread, which is bought by the wealthy classes, but it has very little wheat in it. Half a pound of meat a week is allowed to each person. When there were no potatoes last Spring the Government served out a pound of meat per person. The people were also encouraged to make marmalade for use instead of butter and had an extra ration of one pound and a half of sugar served out to them.

Women are now employed in operating transit facilities all over Germany and the deaths and accidents have increased from 200 to 500 per cent. In regard to accidents on elevators the increase was partly due to the fact that when cables were worn out they were replaced by ropes of an inferior grade. Most people walk up and down stairs now in Berlin and other cities.

Clothing is poor and must be purchased on a ticket. Cotton goods have almost entirely disappeared from the stores. Men are allowed one suit of clothes, with an extra pair of trousers, a year, and the women one house gown and two other dresses a year. There is a great deal of mourning to be seen in the streets of Berlin, in spite of the official suggestion that it should not be worn. The Emperor cannot prevent the German people mourning their dead.

### Famine Prices in Austria

Lieutenant Alberto Virgili, a Roman officer who escaped from the prison camp at Haismacher, Hungary, tells of seeing Serbian and Russian prisoners raking through rubbish heaps and eating the refuse they found. They were literally starving, having no friends at home, as the Italian prisoners have, to feed them by parcel post. The situation in Austria-Hungary, as described to a New York World correspondent by Lieutenant Virgili, may be summarized as follows:

Olive oil costs $8 a pint. Butter and soap are not to be had. The Austrian authorities try all known ways to get food through Italian prisoners, who are fed exclusively on the parcel post packets their families send them.

The civil population of Austria get a weekly ration of one pound of bread and are supposed to make up the deficiency by means of potatoes, which cost 50 cents a pound; dried beans, formerly much used in making soups, are $1 a pound, and corn flour is scarce at $3 a kilo, (somewhat over two pounds.)

For millionaires and invalids who can afford to make the sacrifice, a few Viennese bakers are still selling famous long rolls weighing two pounds, made of white flour from Hungary, at $2 each. A few fortunate storekeepers still have some white flour which was bought in Hungary at the beginning of the war, but this costs $5 a pound.

Coffee is as rare as diamonds. Whoever happens to have any can easily sell it to the rich at $50 a pound. Then the buyer gives a party and everybody talks about it for a week afterward. A poor woman in Trieste hoarded twenty pounds of coffee. A rich Vienna woman journeyed twelve hours to Trieste and bought it all for $800.

A man's ready-made suit of shoddy costs from $100 to $150 even in the small cities, where labor is cheap. Boots and shoes cost from $30 to $50 a pair. They are made of substitutes for leather. A pair of cotton socks costs, if real cotton, $1.

Yet not one of the escaped prisoners, exchanged officers, and refugees with whom the correspondent talked sees any prospect of a revolution in Austria. The key to this seems to lie in the fact that no young men are left in the villages and smaller cities. It is true that the women revolted in Vienna, Prague, and Gratz, but the Moslem troops fired upon them, killing several hundred.

The army is tolerably well fed, and the people, disciplined to obedience for centuries, are in the main devoted to the house of Hapsburg, which is less an imperial house than an institution. The Austrian people are encouraged by frequent promises of revolution in Italy and France.

# Germany's Political Changes

## Count von Hertling Succeeds Dr. Michaelis
## as Chancellor—Liberals Claim a Victory

DR. GEORG MICHAELIS, who had held the portfolio of Imperial Chancellor of Germany since July 14, 1917, placed his resignation in the hands of the Kaiser on Oct. 24, 1917. The resignation was accepted, and Count Georg F. von Hertling, who was occupying the position of Prime Minister of Bavaria, was named as his successor, though Dr. Michaelis temporarily retained the office of Prime Minister of Prussia. The resignation of Michaelis was due to his lack of sympathy with the majority groups of the Reichstag and his suspected attitude of opposition to broadened Parliamentary powers. It was charged that he was not candid in his declarations respecting the Reichstag peace proposals and showed a partiality to the extreme Pan-German annexationists.

Count von Hertling consulted with various groups before he accepted the portfolio, which fact was hailed by the liberal leaders as the dawn of a new day in Parliamentary reform; also as the first real evidence of the democratization of German institutions. This view, however, was vehemently attacked by elements of the liberal press.

The Emperor sent the following autograph letter to the retiring Chancellor:

I am unable to deny the weight of the reasons for your resignation, and I have by decree complied with your request for release from the offices of Chancellor, President of the State Ministry, and Minister of Foreign Affairs.

In difficult times you, with self-sacrifice and readiness, responded to my call and performed useful service in the highest offices of the empire, the State, and the Fatherland. I cannot forego expressing to you my thanks and my acknowledgment of your faithful, untiring labor.

As a token of my esteem I confer upon you the Chain of the Grand Cross of the Order of the Red Eagle. The decoration goes herewith.

Hoping you will continue gladly to place your proved powers at the service of the Fatherland, I remain, your well-disposed Emperor-King, WILHELM.

Count von Hertling is 74 years old. He was the Bavarian Premier for five and a half years. In the past he was always regarded as extremely conservative and opposed to Parliamentary reforms. He was opposed to the idea that a Chancellor should be responsible to Parliament. On Oct. 10, in the Bavarian lower house, in discussing the question of the " disannexation " of Alsace-Lorraine, he expressed himself unmistakably in favor of the division of this imperial territory, suggested last Spring, between Prussia and Bavaria.

" Of the sacrifice of this German terri- " tory," he said, " there can be no talk. " In the question of Alsace-Lorraine, Ba- " varia must represent not Bavarian but " German views. According to Bavarian " views, the union of Alsace with South " Germany and of Lorraine with Prussia " would be expedient, but the idea of au- " tonomy is a great mistake, and would " not produce any reconciliation with " France.

" It is not yet time," he also said, " for Germany to make any declaration " with regard to her pawn, Belgium. In " all the circumstances she must take " care to obtain political and economic " guarantees against the future hostility " of Belgium, but we must proceed with " moderation and with consideration for " the wishes of the Belgian people."

Count von Hertling was born in Darmstadt in 1843. He studied at Münster, Munich, Berlin, and in Italy, and in 1882 became a Professor of Philosophy at Bonn. He served in the Reichstag from 1875 to 1890 and from 1896 to 1898. In 1912 he was made Bavarian Minister of Foreign Affairs and Prime Minister.

Among his works are " Matter and Form and Aristotle's Definition of the Soul," " The Limits of the Mechanistic Interpretation of Nature," " John Locke and the Cambridge School," " The Principles of Catholicism and Science," and a study of Albertus Magnus.

Friederich von Payer, a progressive leader, was designated as German Vice Chancellor, succeeding Dr. Karl Helfferich, who was particularly obnoxious to the liberals. Herr Friedberg, national liberal leader, was made Vice President of the Prussian Ministry. The resignation of Admiral von Capelle as Minister of Marine was not accepted.

The fact that both the new Chancellor and the Foreign Minister, von Kühlmann, are leaders in Catholic circles has left the impression that their appointment presages closer relationship between Germany and the policies of Austria-Hungary and the Vatican.

# French War Economies

A WAR correspondent tells of the remarkable results of the measures adopted by the French military authorities to prevent waste. At the beginning of the war there was inevitably a terrible waste in clothing. Today everything—old uniforms, old boots, old socks, down to the merest rags—is turned to some purpose. To this end large establishments have been organized in various centres, where thousands of hands are employed, to deal in each case with the waste from one particular army. A typical example of these establishments is to be found at Orléans. Here, on the one hand, fresh uniforms and clothing are warehoused and distributed among the troops, and, on the other hand, all the old clothing sent back from the front is renovated and transformed.

For the heavier work reservists of the oldest contingents, assisted by prisoners of war, are employed. The great bulk of the labor, however, is done by women and children, whose wages render them independent of other assistance. Over 6,000 women and children are employed at this one establishment in Orléans, and of these 4,500 are able to work in their own homes. During August no less than $85,000 was paid out in wages.

Two hundred and thirty different articles of clothing and equipment are dealt with in this factory, and each day a train of thirty trucks, which in Winter is increased to forty-five, arrives loaded with the soiled linen, torn and worn-out clothes of the army. The linen is washed, repaired, and returned. The clothes are sorted and disinfected. Boots still worth mending are repaired. Those that are not are taken to pieces, and any sound leather that remains is used to form the uppers of the wooden-soled trench boots. Fragments of leather are converted into bootlaces, and waste pieces not utilizable for other purposes are transformed into buttons for prisoners of war. Five hundred good pairs of boots leave the workshops every day.

Whenever possible uniforms are mended and cleaned until they look like new. Repairs to soldiers' overcoats alone represent a saving to the country of between $2,500 and $3,000 a day. Uniforms that are past repair are unpicked and the woolen cloth utilized for many purposes, the smallest fragments being used to make the little round collar badges which distinguish the different companies in the battalion. All cotton waste is sent to the explosives factories. Socks, buttons, blankets, and sheepskin coats are all sorted and renewed. There is even a workship for dealing with metal objects, such as helmets, water bottles, and the like.

Every day 2,000 cartridge pouches are turned out as good as new at a cost of a few centimes, as against 4 francs for the new article. The repairing of sheepskins alone shows a daily saving of $1,600. Each day 8,000 pairs of slippers are made from pieces of old clothes, representing a value of $3,200, while 300 knapsacks, which would cost 24 francs each if bought new, are turned out every day at a cost of 60 centimes each.

There is a special workshop for women who have from time to time an unoccupied hour, though they are unable to give up the whole of their time. They can come into this workshop at any time they like and can work as long as they like. They are paid so much an hour, and are paid on the spot.

# War Museums in France

BOTH the French and the British are establishing temporary war museums near the front in France, preparatory to the creation of a great permanent war museum after the struggle is over. They illustrate the variety of implements in modern warfare and emphasize episodes in the immediate present which, no doubt, will be invested with reverence for the future historian.

In one of the temporary museums back of the British front may be seen the carved oak table from shelled Arras used by Sir Douglas Haig at his headquarters throughout the battle of the Somme. There are other memorials of Sir Douglas Haig. There is the First Corps headquarters flag which he carried in the Mons retreat, his first flag as commander of the First Army, and souvenirs of the Marne and the early Belgian campaigns. There is a British Red Ensign from Verdun, the gift of the commandant of the citadel, which was suspended in that fortress during the German attack last year; the Union Jack which the Warwicks brought into Péronne and placed in the Grand Place, together with their crest and motto painted on a wooden panel. There are several other flags of great interest—of which one must not forget to mention the first tanks flag— the first Portuguese flag in the trenches, the first American flag to fly in France after the declaration of war by the President, on the Hotel de Ville, Paris. There are German flags, too, as, for instance, a large one unearthed in the Hotel de Ville at Péronne, another from Beaumont Hamel. But, in the matter of flags, the pride of place is naturally assigned to the great Union Jack unfurled in the early days of August, 1914, from the Hotel de Ville at Boulogne, to greet Great Britain's arriving troops, the first modern British banner to be officially flown in France.

After flags come captured guns. But there is here only room for the smaller engines of war, such as trench mortars, minenwerfer, and granatenwerfer, with a few machine guns damaged in battle. There is a great, ungainly minenwerfer, captured at Vimy by the Canadians, and other pieces taken by the Scottish Rifles, the Royal Engineers, and other units in special circumstances of valor. There are dozens of enemy rifles, inscribed with the names of villages in the Somme or Arras region where hand-to-hand conflicts were waged.

"One could write a long chapter on these rifles alone," says an English reporter, "from the first brought back from a dead German in the great retreat to one wrenched from the hands of a Bavarian giant at St. Julien only the other day—not until he had slain several of our men. German material is here in profusion—shells of every calibre, shellcases and basket carriers, flammenwerfer, bombs, axes, knives, pistols, wirecutters, and a unique collection of trench clubs, including one with a flexible handle and a heavy steel head positively devilish in its ingenuity. There are also to be seen a series of gas alarm gongs, a German field telephone with a history, and a German bicycle on which an adventurous

obche rode up to our lines at the Menin Gates, Ypres. Scattered through this museum are life-size figures attired in enemy uniforms and modeled and colored by a Colonel who is also a Royal Academician. In one case the head and body armor has been scoured and burnished so that the white steel glitters and makes the figure look like a representation of a mediaeval warrior. Over his shoulders he carries a crossbow which discharged grenades in the Winter of 1914-15, and behind him is one of our own catapults which saw service at Neuve Chapelle.

"Then there are the enemy proclamations on the walls, enemy prints depicting our soldiers, enemy maps captured on the battlefields and sometimes stained with blood, German officers' notebooks and sketchbooks, German trench signs and street signs—one bears the legend, 'Nach Verdun,' another 'Nach Vimy'—sometimes portentous, occasionally poetical."

# John Galsworthy's Pen Picture of War Victims in France

*The English novelist John Galsworthy, in the course of his labors for the French Wounded Emergency Fund, wrote to an American friend this description of the pitiful struggle of the people whose homes have been destroyed by the war:*

ON our way home from Noyon we passed through a small place completely destroyed, and to our surprise saw an old woman bending over a washtub. We got out of the car and picked our way through high grass, barbed wire, and stones. The poor old body—70 years old—had crept back seven weeks before to look for her home, and, finding it in ruins, had taken up quarters in the next-door cottage, where one room was watertight, and in which she had a few things the soldiers billeted in a near hamlet had given her. She was the sole occupant of the place, and began to cry bitterly directly we spoke to her. She had taken a door from another ruined house and propped it up against the one she had adopted, which had

none. Of course there was no glass in the windows, and the stone flooring was entirely broken up.

She had planted a few potatoes, carrots, and beans, which were coming up. She could neither read nor write, and had heard no news of her only relatives— a son and his wife—he a soldier in the hospital.

Saucepans, cups, knives, or plates did not exist. She made her little fire on a few bricks with bits of wood out of the dugouts and trenches near by.

In her garden with a mass of barbed wire and weeds were growing some currants and gooseberries, which she insisted on picking for us, and her poor old brown face quite cheered up when we told her we would come back with some things and give her a helping hand to tidy up her little hovel.

We visited Omiecourt—there is nobody living there at present, but plenty longing to come back if somebody will help them.

We also investigated Hynecourt-le-Petit, where we found ten people, (population before the war 150,) three of them men. One, a dark-brown, cheery old peasant, was the Mayor! They had all been driven out by the Germans a year ago, and his wife and child were still unheard of. They ran from the ruins, dragging their children and greeting us with outstretched arms. One room in that place was watertight—and in it they were all sleeping; some on wooden beds made with trench wood, covered with hay, and some on the floor.

And so the story runs everywhere. Practically the whole population of this desert, who have trickled back by twos and threes since the Germans drove them out and burned their villages, is without living accommodation.

To enable the land to bear crops next year the peasants must return to these destroyed villages this Winter. There are perhaps from two to thirty houses or rooms in each village, according to its size and condition, which can be temporarily repaired if help can be secured. The Government (French) can do nothing at present. The first thing to do is to make a few watertight rooms with tarpaulin roofing, and there must be garden and farm tools, (all burned by the Germans,) cement, cooking utensils, clothing, beds, bedding, (all ruthlessly destroyed by the Germans,) food and farmyard stock, such as chickens and rabbits, in order that the former inhabitants may return.

There is nothing but the bricks and the dust left behind by the Germans. You see small children playing among all this, and until these were clothed by outside help many of them were found naked immediately after the Germans retreated.

Of this huge scar on the face of France we are asked to heal a tiny portion and to make again a living thing out of death; to give back some sort of future to a few hundreds of poor souls utterly deprived.

One can only grasp it in terms of our own countryside. Each one knows some country village; let him or her think of that without a tree, without a wall standing, with every means of livelihood cut off, without beasts or birds, save the rats and the crows; a mass of rubble and rusty wire, deep holes, and unexploded shells.

Let him imagine that this goes on mile after mile, village after village, county after county. Let him fancy the villagers he knows—little shop-folk, cobbler, postman, blacksmith, laborers, their wives, daughters, mothers, the children he sees daily going to school—all killed, captives, or dispersed, bereaved of each other, robbed and ruined, without a place to set foot, shelter from the night, stick, stone, or penny left, as naked of subsistence as the day they were born.

Let him picture the old folk, fit only for care of others, living like that old woman near Noyon! Broken homes, broken hearts, broken lives! There are hundreds of these villages out there, thousands upon thousands of homeless, hopeless, ruined folk.

## Bronze Plaques to Mark the Sites of German Atrocities

The devastated City of Senlis, which was partly burned by the Germans, commemorated the third anniversary of the event by attaching to its walls three large bronze plaques, one of which bears this inscription:

On Sept. 2, 1914, by order, the German soldiers, with torches and incendiary bombs, set fire to the City of Senlis. One hundred and ten houses were entirely destroyed.

Another is erected near the hospital against which the Germans turned their guns:

On Sept. 2, 1914, after having, in contempt of all law and humanity, thrown before their troops many innocent civilians, women and little children, the Germans turned their machine guns upon the hospital, riddling with bullets the rooms crowded with sick and wounded. On that day German bullets killed fifteen members of the civil population, and no gesture of protest or defense was offered to justify this barbarism.

The third plaque, set in the wall of the City Hall above the door, reads thus:

On Sept. 2, 1914, in City Hall Square, at 3 o'clock in the afternoon, the Germans of von Kluck dragged out the Mayor of Senlis, Eugene Odent, aged 59 years, and, after a day of torture, shot him in the evening in the woods of Chamant. With

him six unfortunate workmen were taken as hostages and assassinated.

Léon Bourgeois, the Minister of Labor, presided at the exercises that attended the erection of these accusing inscriptions, the first of many with which the Ligue Antiallemande has undertaken to mark the sites of German atrocities in France.

# Desolation in the French War Zone
## Described by Sir Edward Carson
### Member of the British Cabinet

*Sir Edward Carson, former First Lord of the Admiralty, after a visit to the war zone in France on Sept. 26, 1917, thus vividly described his impressions:*

WRITTEN accounts of the front convey but a small idea of the extent of the territory covered by a ruthless hive of industry wholly devoted to the purposes of war. The ceaseless movement in every direction of countless machines and vehicles of every conceivable description, the immense numbers of men busy at all sorts of occupations, as in a great industrial centre which densely covers mile after mile at long distances from the actual fighting, give a first impression of an almost chaotic variety of activity, until one remembers that behind it all is a directing mind which coordinates everything toward the accomplishment of a single preconceived purpose. It is thus realized how interdependent are all the parts of this stupendous war machine—how each separate wheel, bolt, piston, and pin plays an essential part in the whole, from which it could not be abstracted without crippling the work in hand. One thus sees spread out before one's eyes a picture of our national effort converted into tangible results, and one grasps how literally true it is that the man at home in the workshop, the shipyard, and the mine is the comrade and fellow-worker of the soldier in the trench.

Just as no written account gives a true notion of the magnificent work our men are doing in Flanders and in France, so, too, no written account can enable one

to conceive the frightful devastation that has been wrought by the Germans. You may read of defiled and ruined churches, of crumbled villages, of destroyed woods, of deserted fields pitted with waterlogged shell holes, but not the most vivid imagination can picture the reality which these phrases try to describe. Even when one stands on the ground itself, among thistles knee-deep and stretching in every direction as far as sight, aided by field glasses, can reach, and when one tries to thread one's way between holes, the smallest of which would hold a taxicab and the largest a church, it is difficult to believe that what looks like a vast expanse of rough moor or fen, covered with every conceivable kind of litter and filth, and without a sign of human habitation or human care, was, until the coming of the Hun, a rich plateau of wheat and rye, of beet and potatoes, of hops and apples and plums, with bright little clusters of gardened cottages, of which it is now difficult even to find a trace by searching among the rank weeds for the lime and brick dust that alone mark the site of former prosperous village life. My one regret is that this abominable desolation cannot be witnessed by every Englishman, if there be any such, who for one moment tolerates the idea of a peace without full reparation. This wilderness cannot, at all events for some generations to come, be made to blossom again like the rose. It will probably be afforested, if it can be sufficiently leveled even for such use.

What is to become of its former inhabitants no one knows. Many families have disappeared altogether. The men have been killed; the women who survived have been deported. In other cases they are refugees to other parts of France, where they have managed to find some sort of subsistence, and where they will probably remain permanently. Occasionally some owners are allowed to make a temporary return to search for possessions buried, perhaps, in garden or orchard, but which are but rarely to be found, since it is almost impossible to determine even the site of any particular plot of ground now merged in the surrounding wilderness. Germany has suffered none of this terrible devastation, and has had the advantage of carrying on this destructive work on the soil of Belgium and France along the western front.

No reparation can ever make good what Germany's crime against humanity has destroyed; but no one can witness the work of the Hun without vowing that the reparation shall be as complete as France and her allies can exact from the despoiler.

# Treachery of King Constantine and His Queen

THE pro-German activities of ex-King Constantine and his German wife—the Kaiser's sister— were revealed by the discovery of secret documents in the Palace at Athens. Among the telegrams given out Nov. 4, 1917, was the following, dated Nov. 23, 1916, by the Queen to her brother Wilhelm:

> By a miracle we are unhurt. The Allies bombarded the palace for three hours with the French fleet, which opened fire without warning. We took refuge in the cellars.
>
> There was lively street fighting today, revolutionaries firing from houses on the army and people, who fought magnificently. It was a great victory against four great powers, whose troops fled before the Greeks and withdrew, escorted by Greek soldiers.
>
> There is great anxiety as to the demands which the Entente will make, but we are prepared for anything. Please tell us when the army of Macedonia will be sufficiently strong to take the offensive definitely.

Emperor William replied to his sister as follows:

> I thank you cordially for your telegram, which has caused me deep emotion. I know the dangers through which you and Tino have passed. I admire your courage at this difficult time.
>
> I also note with pleasure the magnificent attitude of the army and their loyalty to the royal house. May God deliver you from your horrible position.

The Entente once more has shown its hand, and nothing remains for Tino to do but to take open action against these brutes. The intervention of Tino, with his forces co-operating against Sarrail's western flank, would bring about a decision in Macedonia and the liberation of poor Greece. Tino knows that.

A dispatch from King Constantine dated Jan. 21, 1916, was as follows:

> The King of Greece pledges his word to the German Emperor that in no circumstances shall any soldier or native be employed by the royal Government against the German troops or their allies. Greece consents to the use of the Drama-Seres Railway by Germany and her allies.

Another telegram, dated two days later, explains that the journeys of Prince Nicholas and Prince Andre to Petrograd and London had no political character. It says the visits were intended " to draw closer the bonds which existed between the royal house of Greece and the Courts of London and Petrograd—bonds which of late have very much relaxed." In later telegrams King Constantine bewailed that he could not do what he wanted to do because of Entente pressure and the blockade.

A Commission of Inquiry appointed by the Greek Chamber reported that official documents proved the following charges against all the members of the Skouloudis-Gounaris Cabinet except Admiral Coundouriotis:

1. That they assumed office, though not possessing the confidence of the nation, and dissolved the chamber unconstitutionally for the purpose of forcing the personal policy of the Crown upon the nation.

2. That they usurped the legislative power by promulgating, by unconstitutional decree, laws for the increase of the pay of army, navy, and gendarmerie officers.

3. That they contracted two secret loans in Germany without recording them in the public accounts, and without the knowledge or consent of Parliament.

4. That they dishonored the treaty with Serbia and committed numbers of acts tending to assist the Germans and Bulgarians as against the allied forces.

5. That they surrendered to the Germans and Bulgarians, voluntarily and by prearrangement, Fort Rupel and Eastern Macedonia, with a whole army corps and large quantities of arms, munitions, and supplies.

6. That they supported and protected in every possible way the pro-German propaganda managed by Baron Schenck, which included the corruption of the press, spending 6,000,000 drachmas ($1,200,000) in one year alone.

7. That they employed violent and unlawful means to intimidate public opinion, and repeatedly violated the constitutional right of assembly.

8. That without any military necessity they prolonged the state of mobilization of the army for nine months, when they had no intention of making war, and thereby inflicted enormous economic losses upon the country.

9. That they carried on systematic propaganda in the amy, during the mobilization, in order to poison the minds of citizens against Liberal policy, and in favor of the Crown's personal policy, thereby destroying the fighting spirit of the nation.

10. That, in order to win the votes of the Mussulman electorate in Macedonia at the elections, they surrendered to the Mussulman landowners the large estates which the State held as security for the restitution of Greek property which had been seized by the Ottoman Government.

All the accused are under arrest.

# Zeppelins in a New Raid Meet Disaster
## Dramatic Aerial Events of the Month

JUST when it had been taken for granted that the Germans would use no more Zeppelins in their air raids on England, one of the most determined attacks was made. This was on the night of Oct. 19, 1917. At least eleven airships took part in the attack. On their return journey across France five were lost, including one captured complete and undamaged at Bourbonneles-Bains.

The casualties in all districts of England visited by the raiders were twenty-seven killed and fifty-three injured. An aerial torpedo which fell in London killed eight children of one family. Altogether it destroyed three houses, with a loss of fourteen lives, thus almost wiping out two whole families. Those who were not killed were seriously injured.

The raiding Zeppelins were chased all the way across France by airplane squadrons, aided by anti-aircraft guns. At least five failed to escape, namely:

1. L-44, destroyed at St. Clement, near Lunéville. All the crew perished.

2. L-45, brought down at Mison, near Gap in the High Alps, forty-eight miles south-southeast of Grenoble. Destroyed by crew, who were all captured.

3. L-49, forced down near Bourbonne-les-Bains and captured with its crew.

4. Official number unstated, brought down between Gap and Sisteron, (in the High Alps.) Set on fire by crew, who were captured.

5. Official number unstated, chased by French aviators near Fréjus, (Toulon district,) and believed to have drifted out over the Mediterranean and fallen into the sea during the night.

Of the eventual fate of L-50, which came down at Dammartin, in the Haute Marne Department, and reascended after jettisoning some of her crew and one of her gondolas, nothing definite is known. Two other Zeppelins were not accounted for in any way, and they may have escaped across the French frontier via Switzerland.

Members of the captured crews said that the original squadron of raiders numbered twelve vessels, which started from three separate ports. The failure of the expedition, according to one of the chief officers of the French Army aero-

THE AMERICAN EXPEDITIONARY FORCE

United States Troops Marching Through a Village Near Their Training Camp in France.
(Photo Pays de France.)

THE LIBERTY LOAN PARADE IN PHILADELPHIA

The Famous Liberty Bell Was Carried on a Float in the Parade for the Second Liberty Loan.
(*Photo International Film Service.*)

nautical service, was due partly to atmospheric conditions and partly to bad working of the wireless apparatus. The officer added:

The wireless stations in Germany, on which these vessels depend for their guidance—because no means have yet been found for calculating drift, and the compass seems practically useless without that—seem not to have been working well. We know that the L-49, brought down at Bourbonne, had a breakdown of its wireless motor and so could not possibly get the usual guidance. It had been completely lost for hours. These monsters have been built, so far as land raids are concerned, to reach and remain at a great height and to cover a long distance. The German Government has still so much faith in them that it is turning out two per month. They are 650 feet long, 116 feet high, and have a capacity of 183,000 cubic feet.

Since anti-aircraft guns can now do good practice at a height of three or four miles, they must commonly remain above this level. At this height their own bombs cannot be aimed at a precise objective, and the raiders are helpless before bad weather.

As to the cost and trouble of their construction, I have made a curious little calculation which shows that for the goldbeaters' skin, forming with a cotton lining the envelope of the ballonets of a single Zeppelin, the intestines of 300,000 cattle are needed. There are various ingenious details in the construction. Between the eighteen ballonets contained by the envelope a number of chimneys are set to carry out at the top any leakage of gas. A passage within the envelope contains the ballast, petrol bombs, and several beds. There are four cars. The front one carries the commander, most of the crew, the wireless machinery, and one of the five motors. The vessel can normally make forty-five to sixty miles an hour. All the instruments are well made. The ballast bombs and other packages are marked with luminous numbers at night. To get from one car to another is an awkward journey, as you must pass up a rope ladder and through the interior passage.

The L-49 has two vertical rudders and two lateral planes for rising and falling. It has two machine guns, but no upper platform. It carried eighteen men and two tons of bombs. It had reached a height of 7,000 meters (four and one-quarter miles) over London and had then encountered not only a strong north wind but a temperature falling as low as 33 degrees below zero centigrade. The men had frozen hands and became half stupefied with the cold. The water ballast froze, although a certain amount of alcohol had been mixed with it to prevent this happening. Although there is an arrangement to raise the radiators within the protection of the cars, their water also froze. The compass was in good condition, but, in the circumstances, was useless.

Six tons of bombs were dropped by British aviators on the Burbach works west of Saarbrucken, Rhenish Prussia, on the night of Oct. 24. Four German airdromes also were attacked, forty-five heavy bombs having been dropped and direct hits made on a group of hangars, On Oct. 30 French bombing escadrilles dropped large quantities of explosives in the Metz region, while the British continued to make raids on munition plants in Rhenish Prussia.

Seven hundred and four airplanes and seaplanes were brought or driven down on the western front—including the Belgian coast sector—during September. This is a higher total by nearly 300 than was reached in the preceding month, and compares with 467 in July, 713 in May, and 717 in April of this year. The German airplanes and seaplanes which fell to British and French airmen and gunners numbered 462. According to a statement issued by the German War Office on Nov. 12, the Entente losses in October were 244 airplanes and nine balloons.

One of the most notable of recent air raids was that made by a fleet of fourteen Italian machines on Oct. 10 against Cattaro, one of the principal Austrian naval bases. The airplanes started together from near Milan, flew to the Apennines in a gale and arrived in a body near Rome. There they rested awhile and then flew to their taking-off camp on the Adriatic shore and thence to Dalmatia and Montenegro and home. The squadron afterward flew together something like 1,000 miles without failure on the part of any machine or any hitch. The poet, d'Annunzio, who took part in the raid and received his fourth medal for valor since the beginning of the war, described the expedition in the following characteristic language:

In my opinion it was the most extraordinary ever attempted by airplanes fitted for flying overland. We crossed the sea with little aid from the compass, making more than 250 miles without any landmark.

The flight was more enjoyable than any other I have made because of its character of adventure. It was a true and proper adventure of Ulysses. As we sighted the enemy's coast line each one of us felt a mysterious emotion which we shall never forget. The minutes consumed in recognizing places through the mist and the treacherous brilliance of the moon are for me among the most lyric of my memories. I would not exchange for any other remembrance of joy the emotion I felt in recognizing the points of Arza and Ostro. We felt in ourselves a subtle, silent cheerfulness such as must sometimes have been that of Ulysses, while we struck the enemy in his sleep.

The uncertain play of his signal lights, [referring to the signals which the Austrians flashed, as they supposed, to one of their own flying squadrons, and which pointed out their targets to the Italians,] made us laugh homerically in our seats. I turned toward my pilots and received their beautiful, youthful hilarity through their strange masks.

What shall I say of our return, of the moment when we discovered in the mist the thin line of our coast? It was like the ravishment of love.

# What the Belgian Army Is Doing

## Told by Emile Cammaerts

*Emile Cammaerts, the Belgian poet, who is one of The London Telegraph's special contributors, visited the Yser front in October, 1917, and recorded his impressions in this spirited article:*

I HAD not seen the Belgian front for three years. It was in December, 1914, on the morrow of the battle of the Yser, a vision of mud and rain, and a thousand hardships cheerfully borne. The work of re-equipment had scarcely started. Many things were still wanting, and some units looked, in their medley of uniforms, like irregular bands of brigands. A few farms could be seen emerging from the floods, like islets from the sea, and the men had to wade knee-deep to reach their advance posts. Everything was gray, misty, silent, and mysterious—a desert haunted by an army of ghosts. The thousands of dead whom we had just lost made their presence felt, and there was a pervading reek in the air.

To visit the Belgian trenches as they are today, with the vivid memories of what they used to be, is to step from dream into reality, from the trial of sacrifice into the hope of an early reward. The bright weather which we enjoyed still increased the contrast. We moved in a world of colors where the warm tones of khaki and of the screens of " camouflage " blended in strange harmony with the blue of the sky and the vivid red of some freshly wrecked brick wall. The floods were much lower, covered with rustling reeds, alive with water hens and sea gulls. Around Dixmude, Ramscapelle, and Nieuport shells were bursting incessantly. Field guns were barking away close by, and the voices of many heavies could now be heard on our side. From time to time some long-distance shells whizzed overhead. Every detail of the scene brought the same message of life, struggle, and readiness, from the sturdy helmeted infantryman going to his rest camp after a spell in the trenches, to the well-organized defenses in every village close to the front, to the narrow footbridges leading to the advance posts in the floods where Belgians and Germans confront each other every night in an amphibious war full of surprises and thrilling incidents.

For even in the sector of the floods the front held by the Belgian Army has never ceased to be lively. With the exception of the counterattack of Steenstraete, during the second battle of Ypres, no operation on a large scale has been made since 1914, but the artillery duel has never stopped for more than a few days, and there is not one night when some bombing expedition or some advance post raid does not take place. Those who would go to the Belgian front with the preconceived idea that nothing happens in that quarter might be sorely disillusioned. They might, for instance, undergo the same experience as the Italian aide de camp who, while accompanying King Victor Emmanuel and King Albert in their recent tour of inspection, found himself unexpectedly half buried by a shell. It would be a great mistake to judge the work of the Belgian Army, or, for the matter of that, of any army, from the extremely concise and guarded utterances of the official " communiqués."

## A Contrast in Types

There is a small cemetery close to the church of Adinkerke, near Furnes, where the peasants and fishermen who lived in that village used to find a peaceful rest after a long and busy life. Here, among the civilians, close to the iron paling, is the simple tomb of our great national poet, Emile Verhaeren. The cemetery has been enlarged to make room for some of the boys whom Belgium has lost since the battle of the Yser. Only those who died of wounds in the neighboring hospitals are buried here, and similar cemeteries can be found closer to the front and in the rear as far as Calais. I have walked through these rows of graves, standing close together, and read there many familiar names on many simple crosses. Rich men, poor men, students, and laborers, some who fought since Liège, others who had come from the occupied provinces. Every tomb bears a number, and before I had reached the end of the last row I counted 2,000 of them. There are, indeed, many more things happening than the official communiqués allow us to dream of.

I have just said that the tomb of Verhaeren is at Adinkerke, but his body is no longer there. Owing to the frequent German air raids to which the village has been subjected lately, the poet's friends have had the coffin transported to a safer place, if any place can be called " safe " in independent Belgium. For there is not a town, not a village, in this region which has not received some German shell or bomb. Furnes itself, which used to be King Albert's headquarters, has had to be abandoned, not only by the soldiers, but even by the charitable British ladies who used to comfort and help the wounded and the destitute civilians. The picturesque old market place, once a scene of great animation, is now deserted, and the grass is growing between its cobblestones. A few of the old Spanish gables stand crooked at a dangerous angle, and one house only is still inhabited by an old lady and her daughter, who keep a small café. The four or five soldiers and civilians who are allowed to remain in the town gather there, after their day's work, to drink a glass of beer and play a game of cards, for the Belgian instinct of companionship is hard to kill.

I had the opportunity of talking with the old lady who presides over this peaceful assembly. She told me that she had only just come back from a " holiday " she had been obliged to take in France after the last raid, and she confessed to me that this war had been a great worry to her: " Oui, Monsieur, cette guerre, c'est bien ennuyeux." The day before I had met at Arras a Frenchwoman who had kept her little shop open throughout the bombardment. She was very neatly dressed, and, with a bright smile, explained that she had been congratulated by the " préfet." " Oui, m'sieu," she declared, " j'suis une martyre d'Arras." There you have the two types of Flemish and French temperament in a nutshell. They express themselves differently, but they act in the same way.

## Brave Englishwomen

From the top of the clockhouse of Furnes, amid a cloud of frightened, cawing crows, you could see the whole country spread before you like a map in the evening light. Nieuport was clouded with bursting shells, and the straight line of the Belgian front could clearly be seen along the Yser floods as far as Caeskerke, and further on beyond Dixmude and Loo, where the enemy line stands so close to our own that in calm weather the faintest whisper can be heard on either side, and is invariably followed by a hail of hand grenades. Straight before us we could see Ramscapelle, which we had not been able to visit owing to a heavy bombardment, and Pervyse, where we had called on two English ladies who established there a first-aid station in 1914, and have remained faithfully at their post.

Some change also had occurred there. The " miss," as they are called, have had to leave their old home owing to the visitation of a German shell, and to take up new quarters at the end of the village, on the ground floor of a red-tiled cottage. The first floor has disappeared, but the roof has been skillfully repaired and lowered so that the house looks more or less like a little boy who has tried on his father's hat. If I did not fear to be indiscreet, I should also mention that one of these ladies—who, needless to say, remains a " miss " for the soldiers—has married a Belgian officer, and is now Mme. la Baronne de T. There is not a corner of this Belgian front at Furnes, La Panne, Adinkerke, or Pervyse where Belgian heroism has not been comforted by English kindness, and where the smile of some Englishwoman has not alleviated the sufferings of some Belgian soldier.

On my way back on the boat, as luck would have it, I met a Belgian officer on leave, to whom I expressed my admiration for the transformation which had occurred during these last years, and how happy I felt to see the Belgian Army re-equipped and stronger in men and material than it had ever been before. This was his answer:

Yes, we have worked a good deal, but there is something much more amazing than these physical improvements; it is the fact that the men, after so many months of patient waiting, have kept up their spirits. When Londoners see our soldiers coming on leave without their trench equipment and in fresh uniforms they do not realize the hard life which they are leading in Flanders. If, instead of enjoying this bright weather, you had experienced a spell of slush and rain you would have gathered a very different impression.

You are, of course, aware that it is nowhere possible to dig one's self in in this part of Flanders, so that everywhere our trenches must be built up with sandbags. That means, of course, that the least bombardment upsets your defense works and obliges the men to repair them constantly.

A spell of rain after dry weather is nearly as bad, and you can see your parapet melting and slipping away before your eyes. Then there is the " camouflage," those screens of reeds which you find so picturesque. Do you realize that these reeds must be cut at night in the floods and carried in bundles to the roads? When they are dried they are strung together and fixed by wires to poles ten feet high. And there are miles and miles of roads to be screened. You must never forget that there is no division of work in the Belgian Army, no shock troops, no fatigue parties. We cannot afford that. The same man fills sandbags one day and joins in a raid the next, after a three-mile walk. I once weighed one of my men's greatcoats after such a night march through the clay, mud, and the rain. It weighed over fifty pounds.

Quite apart from the fact that the soldiers are cut off from their people, and that a few only hear from them from time to time, there is the tedious monotony of pursuing the same work amid the same difficulties. In every other army some shifting of troops is possible. We are still marking time on the same spot. Many men would gladly risk their lives for a change of surroundings. As it is, the only trouble we have with them is in trying to avoid useless losses. Only a few days ago I lost two men who, in spite of strict orders, were foolhardy enough to play cards on their parapet close to the German lines. And if by chance they kill a rabbit or any other game they will not wait until the evening to go and fetch it in full view of the snipers. There will be only one difficulty about an advance, to keep them from rushing into their own barrage. * * * But, of course, it cannot be helped. We must remain on Belgian soil around the King. * * *

## The King's Self-denial

I had passed, a few hours earlier, before the simple house in which King Albert lives with the Queen, surrounded by a few aides de camp, and I had endeavored to imagine the monotonous round of his daily work; his visit to headquarters, where, helped by his Chief of Staff, General Rucquoy, he examines all the measures dealing with the main administration and direction of the Belgian Army; then some inspection either in the rear or toward the front lines, where so many soldiers have met him more than once in dangerous corners and bad weather, by day and night.

Once a week King Albert presides over a council of Ministers, taking his large share of responsibilities in the work of reconstruction which is already confronting his Government. He keeps himself informed not only of the least incident happening in the army, but of all the news which might reach him from occupied Belgium. And this incessant work and worry is only relieved, from time to time, by a short visit to the British or French front in France. With the exception of a few days spent with her children abroad, Queen Elizabeth has remained at the side of her husband, and, thanks to her influence and active work, the Belgian field ambulances and hospitals are now among the best on the western front.

Some people have regretted that King Albert should never leave the zone of danger; others have wondered why, if not for himself, at least for the sake of his people, he would never consent to gather, in Paris, London, or New York, the fruits of his worldwide popularity. * * * His glory may shine for the world, but he ignores it. He has refused to reap the crop which he has sown in anguish before the joy of victory has ripened it. With the humblest of his soldiers he prefers to wait patiently until the day of deliverance crowns his efforts. He is much too simple and unaffected to make a vow of reserve and silence, but, with a sure instinct, he has chosen the best way of disarming criticism and preserving to the last his people's loyalty, his soldiers' affection, and his friends' confidence.

### Lesson of the Yser

There is a great lesson to be learned on the Yser, whether you speak to the men in their dugouts, to the civilians in the wrecked houses, or to the General at headquarters. The soldier will tell you " that he is longing to go forward, since he is tired of remaining where he is, and there is nowhere else to go in Belgium "; the civilian admits that the war is a nuisance, but that " there is no place like home," even if the shells are dropping close to it; and the General will explain to you that the most difficult part of his work is not so much giving the right orders as " oiling the machine in order to see them properly carried out." In this last strip of free Belgium, where cabbages grow against the trenches, close to the flowered tombs of three years ago, common sense has become heroic and heroism has become matter of fact. Inspiration does not alight on men's brows like a bird sent from heaven, it crowns their heads like the solid steel helmets worn by the soldiers, and protects them against bullets sent from hell.

## Artillery Fire for a Canary Bird

How one little canary bird caused consternation among an entire division of British troops and brought down upon its own head a hurricane of rifle fire and finally point-blank shell fire, is told by Dr. Robert Davis, recently arrived in the United States to lecture at the Officers' Training Camps on the activities of the Red Cross in Europe.

For more than a month on a northern sector of the line the British had been secretly mining beneath the German trenches. The work was almost complete. During the operations several canary birds were, as usual, kept in the excavations to warn the workers of the presence of fire damp, which is fatal to the birds. One little songster, however, escaped from its job, flew into the middle of No Man's Land, and, alighting on a bush, began to sing.

Consternation reigned in the British lines. If the bird should be discovered by the Germans the work of weeks would go for nought, as the enemy could easily interpret the meaning of its presence, and prepare to combat the sapping operations. The infantry was immediately ordered to open fire on the canary to destroy it. But it seemed to bear a charmed life. Even the sharpshooters failed to bring it down as it hopped from twig to twig. Finally the artillery had to be called on. A trench gun with a well-timed shell blew the bird and the bush and the song into nothingness.

# The Armed Merchantman

## By Thomas G. Frothingham

*Member of Military Historical Society of Massachusetts and of the United States Naval Institute*

THE armed merchantman originated from the necessity of the first peaceful traders upon the seas to defend their lives against pirates. Yet, after piracy had become extinct, taking away any use for arms in the pursuit of commerce, it has remained for the twentieth century to produce a Government that has deliberately reverted to the tactics of the pirate—and this has again made the armed merchantman a necessity to defend the lives of passengers and crew.

The first daring Phoenicians who made ventures on the Mediterranean were not by any means peaceful traders, and they were armed as a matter of course. These earliest merchants knew that their customers were often ready to acquire their merchandise by force without any payment—and it must also be stated that many of the earliest trading ships carried away with them the customers as well as the goods. But in a short time it became evident that the best way to secure permanent trade did not consist in knocking on the head the visiting trader and his crew. On the other hand, there was not a warm welcome for the return of a trading ship which on its last visit had carried away its customers into slavery. These quickly learned lessons became the basis of commerce, which has proved the greatest factor in the intercourse of nations, and of which the essential element has been peaceful fair dealing.

Even in the time of Solomon, a thousand years before the Christian era, when Tyre was the great commercial port of the world, there was an established code of ethics in trading over the seas. Such commerce became a potent influence in the spread of civilization, and the merchants of the different countries united in regulation and protection of peaceful traffic.

In contrast to these merchants pursuing their trade, those traders who still resorted to predatory methods became outlawed. They were repulsed from the ports of trade, and they resorted to attacks on peaceful trading ships to plunder their cargoes. Even in ancient times these raiders became known as pirates— and against them the peaceful merchantmen armed themselves.

### Mediterranean Pirates—and Pompey

With the commerce of the Mediterranean under the control of the Phoenicians, who extended their voyages beyond the Pillars of Hercules, the pirates were never a seriously disturbing element. But after the destruction by Rome of Carthage, the successor of Tyre, piracy increased to alarming proportions. The Romans, to whom the control of the Mediterranean had passed, were not instinctively a maritime nation, and commerce on the seas was only an auxiliary of their dominion on the land.

Finding great profit from raids on peaceful commerce, these pirates were recruited from all the various nations of the Mediterranean, and there grew up organized pirate communities, whose strongholds were Crete and Cilicia. These pirates finally had the audacity to plunder the grain ships destined for Rome; and this at last aroused the dormant power inherent in the S. P. Q. R.

In 67 B. C., Pompey was given three years' unlimited command (Lex Gabinia) over the Mediterranean and its coasts for fifty miles inland. Using these powers rightly, Pompey, by a concerted campaign, accomplished results that would be considered extraordinary even in these days of enlarged figures. Plutarch's straightforward account of this war is such a statement of great achievement that it should be quoted:

However, Pompey, in pursuance of his charge, divided all the seas and the whole Mediterranean into thirteen parts, allotting a squadron to each, under the command of his officers; and having thus dispersed his power into all quarters, and encompassed the pirates everywhere, they began to fall into his hands by whole shoals, which he seized and brought into his harbors. As for those that withdrew themselves betimes, or otherwise escaped his general chase, they all made to Cilicia, where they hid themselves as in their hives; against whom Pompey now proceeded in person with sixty of his best ships, not, however, until he had first scoured and cleared all the seas near Rome, the Tyrrhenian, and the African, and all the waters of Sardinia, Corsica, and Sicily; all which he performed in the space of forty days, by his own indefatigabale industry and the zeal of his lieutenants.

The results of this wonderful campaign were: Three thousand vessels captured, 10,000 pirates put to death, 20,000 captives settled in the interior, the destruction of all the pirates' strongholds, and the freeing of all the Mediterranean from piracy. After this drastic treatment, as long as Roman domination endured, the merchantman only needed to arm against skulking foes in the Mediterranean; but this armed protection had to be increased in voyages beyond the Pillars of Hercules. In the outlying seas dangerous raiders were still to be encountered.

## Powerful Moorish Pirates

As the Roman power waned, and after the last remnants of the Roman Empire were destroyed by the downfall of Constantinople, piracy was revived. The Moors had conquered the northern coasts of Africa, and, although they had been expelled from Spain, they maintained strongholds in Tripoli, Tunis, Algiers, Morocco, &c., and these ports became nests of the most dangerous pirates the world has ever seen. Again it was necessary for merchantmen to arm for defense in the world's greatest area of commerce, the Mediterranean Sea.

Until the middle of the seventeenth century there was some semblance of a government of these regions by Turkish Pashas, but after this time the African ports were frankly piratical communities, living on plunder and from the sale and ransom of captives. The number of Europeans held for ransom and sold into slavery was astonishing—and more astonishing was the fact that some of the powers of Europe indulged these pirates and used them as a means of injuring their rivals. Great nations actually paid tribute to these Moorish pirates for immunity for their ships, a disgraceful subservience almost unbelievable in these days.

Our young nation early in its history broke away from this custom, and in the Tripolitan war (1801-05) and by the expedition against Algiers under Decatur (1815) asserted the right of American ships to pursue their commerce without submitting to tribute.

After the peace of 1815, when there was no longer any need for European powers to use the Moorish pirates against their enemies, conditions in the Mediterranean much improved, and the capture of Algiers by the French in 1830 meant the end of pirate strongholds on the northern coasts of Africa.

## Pirates of the Spanish Main

It must be kept in mind that piracy on any large scale depended for its existence on ports of refuge and the resultant markets for disposing of the plunder. Although the Mediterranean refuges had been destroyed, the extended use of the oceans had in the meantime developed other resorts for pirates, of which the most notorious were the West Indies, the islands of the Pacific and of the Indian Ocean, and the east coast of Africa. The term " Spanish Main," of our romantic reading, did not mean the high seas, but the American mainland coasts ruled by Spain. These resorts of pirates increased the dangers of the seas, and arms remained a necessity for the protection of merchantmen.

It was in this period that the infant merchant marine of the American Colonies received its hard education in armed resistance against plunder on the seas. Not only did our early mariners have to arm against pirates, but they were also compelled to defend themselves against another enemy. Privateers had come into use by the warring powers, especially England and France, in the wars that preceded the American Revolution.

The privateer, as its name implies, was

A PRIVATEER OF THE WAR OF 1812: THE LETTER OF MARQUE GRAND
TURK, OF SALEM, 14 GUNS, AT MARSEILLES, 1815

a privately owned ship to which its Government had given letters of marque, empowering it to wage war against an enemy's shipping. Such ships were allowed to receive the profits from their prizes; and in the various wars between England and France the merchants of the two countries equipped many such ships as a matter of private venture for profit. Many of these merchants were undoubtedly successful in making money, but the tactical results of privateering were merely matters of give and take, and it is doubtful if either power gained any real advantage from the use of privateers.

### Era of American Privateers

It remained for the American merchant marine first to make privateering a real factor in warfare on the sea. Our sailors, in their struggle to maintain their commerce against pirates and privateers, had become notably skillful in their dangerous profession. American seamen, on their armed merchantmen, had fought their predatory enemies in all parts of the world. Their ships were of the best design and noted for their speed. This constant life of adventure had developed a resourcefulness in all circumstances of danger which had equipped them for offense as well as defense.

Consequently, in the War of the Revolution and in the War of 1812, when American merchants equipped their armed merchantmen as privateers and manned them with seamen taught in this school of raiding warfare, the American privateers were more efficient than any that had been used in warfare. In both wars these privateers inflicted such unprecedented damage that their ravages accomplished more than anything else to make Great rBitain give an advantageous peace after each of these wars.

Authorities unite in describing the influence on the British public mind of the losses inflicted by these American raiders of commerce. This public sentiment was not to be wondered at, when one realizes that, in the War of 1812, the Americans captured 1,300 prizes of the value of $39,000,000—enormous figures for those days.

We should also remember that, in spite of their great successes, after peace had been made, the American ships returned to peaceful trade and did not yield to the

A TYPICAL AMERICAN ARMED MERCHANTMAN: THE BRIG TENEDOS, OF
BOSTON, LYING AT SMYRNA, JULY 4, 1834

tendency of armed merchantmen to become privateers—and then to become pirates! There were notable outbreaks of this kind of piracy after many of the old treaties of peace. The last instance of this was after the peace of 1815. In fact, Nelson always maintained that privateers were no better than pirates.

### Steady Decrease of Piracy

With accessions from the privateers to swell the numbers of the pirates on the seas, merchantmen were still forced to carry arms after the treaties of 1815. But in the long years of peace that followed, with the extension of commerce and the growth of trading colonies in all parts of the world, the refuges for pirates decreased rapidly.

An interesting account of the extirpation of pirates in the West Indies, by Rear Admiral Caspar Gooodrich, U. S. N., has been appearing in the recent Proceedings of the United States Naval Institute. The islands of the Pacific also became peaceful settlements, and by degrees the former haunts of piracy became safe for peaceful commerce.

The destruction of pirates in Borneo by the British Navy, aided by Rajah Brooke, made an end of the last communities which may be said to have systematically engaged in piracy. After this the pirate became a furtive wanderer upon the seas, with no refuge except by concealment. There were a few ports where the pirate might trade and refit, by connivance with corrupt officials or smugglers, but this was a heavy drain on the booty, and the Jolly Roger became an unprofitable flag to sail under. Even such unreliable havens grew more and more dangerous, with no wars to divert the attention of the navies and coast guards, and the avowed pirate, the rakish craft of story, disappeared from the seas.

### Armed Ships of Later Days

Yet, far along through the nineteenth century it was necessary for merchantmen to be armed on certain voyages. The Red Rover was no longer to be dreaded, but in the Eastern seas, and even in the Mediterranean, a ship becalmed was in great danger. The peaceful small craft of the native coasts frequently became pirates at such opportunities, and there were many desperate fights and many tragedies long after the actual pirates had disappeared from the seas.

The writer well remembers the time when a couple of serviceable guns amidships were considered necessary for such voyages, and these guns were not for appearances, but the crews were trained to handle them to prevent native craft from using sweeps to close in on a becalmed ship and overpower her.

AMERICAN ARMED MERCHANTMAN, WITH SIDES PAINTED IN IMITATION OF A
MAN-OF-WAR: BARQUE STAMBOUL, OF BOSTON, AT MARSEILLES, 1844

These latest of the old armed merchantmen were often also painted with the white streak and many dummy ports to imitate men-of-war, as shown in the picture of the Stamboul. This camouflage, in addition to the actual guns, was a great protection, as can be imagined. The man-of-war also used to imitate the merchantmen by painting out its ports, giving a slovenly guise to its rigging, and thus inducing this kind of gentry to attack the man-of-war—of course with disastrous results to the pirates! The U. S. S. St. Lawrence made use of this last ruse to lure to destruction one of the few privateers sent out by the South in the civil war.

With the advent of steam, the increased use and policing of the sea and the civilization of the coasts from commercial settlements, these last remnants of piracy disappeared. Privateering had been abolished by the Declaration of Paris, (April, 1856.) " Privateering is and remains abolished." In our civil war the Confederates attempted to revive this practice; but they had no ships of any ability to keep the seas, and this attempt was short lived. Consequently, at the dawn of the twentieth century it is fair to say that an armed merchantman was as much an anachronism as a galleon.

The idea of converting the great liners into auxiliary warships in times of war had been adopted, especially by the British and German Navies, but these were to be essentially warships. Their status is sharply defined by The Hague Convention, (1907,) and it will be evident from the following extracts that these ships are not to be considered armed merchantmen, but improvised warships pure and simple.

" A merchant ship converted into a warship " must be " under immediate control and responsibility of the power of the flag which it flies." It must " bear the external marks which distinguish the warships of their nationality." Its " commander must be duly commissioned " and its " crew subject to military discipline." It must " observe the laws and customs of war," and the belligerent must as soon as possible announce conversion " in the list of warships." It will be seen at once that all this is outside of the definition of an armed merchantman.

In international law the status of a ship is determined by its employment, and it has been established that merchantmen are allowed to arm for defense only. Such an armament does not abate their rights as traders engaged in lawful commerce. It is also established that, although an armed merchantman may resist an attack by an enemy ship, only a man-of-war can attack a man-of-war. It must also be noted that any act of resistance against a man-of-war forfeits all the rights of the merchantman to immunity from sinking as a peaceful trader. Keeping these principles in mind will help the reader to understand the real status of an armed merchantman.

## Fear of Auxiliary Cruisers

From these definitions it can be seen that in the twentieth century, following established usages on the seas, there was no use for arms on a merchantman. Pirates and privateers had disappeared, and there was no object in arming against a man-of-war. Yet Great Britain had announced an intention of arming merchantmen. This was not a defense against U-boats, whose ravages had not been foreseen, but it was to protect merchantmen against the class of converted warships which has been described.

In 1913 Winston Churchill, then First Lord of the Admiralty, had stated that there was " good reason to believe that " a considerable number of foreign mer- " chant steamers may be rapidly con- " verted into armed ships by the mount- " ing of guns." The statement plainly shows that Great Britain had feared Germany would improvise a fleet of commerce destroyers by arming merchantmen in foreign ports, or on the high seas. This is confirmed by the First Lord's statement: " It would be obviously ab- " surd to meet the contingency of con- " siderable numbers of foreign armed " merchantmen by building an equal " number of cruisers."

As a matter of fact, nothing of the kind happened in the present war. The German commerce destroyers which did so much damage were, for the most part, regular cruisers of which the location should have been known and against which it was folly to arm merchantmen. But, expecting raids from these extemporized cruisers, Great Britain early in the war armed many of her merchant steamers and notified the Secretary of State of the United States that these armed merchantmen would use our harbors.

## Status Carefully Defined

The British Government carefully defined the status of these ships in notes culminating in the following, which may be said fairly to describe the essentials of an armed merchantman before the complications brought about by the submarine. The note is from the British Ambassador to the Secretary of State:

BRITISH EMBASSY,
Washington, Aug. 25, 1914.

Sir: With reference to Mr. Barclay's notes Nos. 252 and 259 of the 4th and 9th of August, respectively, fully explaining the position taken up by his Majesty's Government in regard to the question of armed merchantmen, I have the honor, in view of the fact that a number of British armed mechantmen will now be visiting United States ports, to reiterate that the arming of British merchantmen is solely a precautionary measure adopted for the purpose of defense against attack from hostile craft.

I have at the same time been instructed by his Majesty's Principal Secretary of State for Foreign Affairs to give the United States Government the fullest assurances that British merchant vessels will never be used for purposes of attack, that they are merely peaceful traders armed only for defense, that they will never fire unless fired upon, and that they will never, under any circumstances, attack any vessel. I have, &c.,

CECIL SPRING-RICE.

The German Government promptly assumed the position that the purpose of such armament was " armed resistance " against German cruisers. Such a re- " sistance is contrary to international " law, because a merchantman is not per- " mitted military defense against a man- " of-war: such action would entitle a " man-of-war to sink the merchantman " with her crew and passengers."*

This contention was half true and half false. It was true that the act of resistance against a man-of-war forfeited the immunities of a merchantman, but this act of resistance did not in any way make an outlaw of the resisting ship. The tendency to apply the law of " franctireur " is evident here. This inexorable ruling that a civilian who offers armed resistance to military forces forfeits his

---

*Promemoria of the German Government, Oct. 13, 1914.

life cannot be stretched to apply to the merchantman as the civilian of the sea.

The extreme application of this would be that a duly commissioned motor boat might hold up a huge armed steamer, and any act of resistance would make that ship an outlaw liable to destruction by any other warship. One of our Judges in an important case declared that the law was founded on common sense.

International law on the sea, especially, may be so described as the product of generations of the common sense of the world in questions of right and wrong on the seas.

The American Secretary of State at this time (1914) very properly decided that such ships were to be treated as regular merchantmen, in so far as their armament was to serve exclusively for purposes of defense. As the submarine had not then been developed as a commerce destroyer, there was not much made of the matter, and thus the position of the armed merchantman remained unchanged.

## Complications Due to U-Boats

But with the astonishing leap of the submarine into the rôle of the most efficient commerce destroyer that has ever been seen, all this was ended. At once, from the very nature of the U-boat, there arose a mass of complications such as never before had been known in international law on the seas.

The following change in directions to British armed merchantmen, early in 1915, shows vividly the immediate effect of the use of the U-boats against commerce on the seas: " If a submarine is " obviously pursuing a ship by day, and " it is evident to the master that she has " hostile intentions, the ship pursued " should open fire in self-defense, not- " withstanding the submarine may not " have committed a definite hostile act, " such as firing a gun or torpedo."*

The Germans maintained that such orders were equivalent to arming merchantmen for attacks on submarines, and then followed the involved controversies over the use of the U-boat. A great deal of this is outside the province of this article, but one way of keeping the mind

*Feb. 25, 1915.

clear in this matter is to remember the established standing of the armed merchantman as described.

The armed merchantman, in the common sense of the applied law, was armed for defense against pirates, privateers, and small fry among the men-of-war. Pirates and privateers had disappeared, and cutters and such small deer were also extinct. Consequently, for practical purposes, as the first months of the war proved, the armed merchantman was useless. Resisting the ordinary man-of-war was out of the question—and there was nothing else in sight.

## Submarine Outlawry

Suddenly there appeared the U-boat, the most extraordinary combination of weakness and strength ever devised. Obviously here was a warship that might be resisted, and its double life above and below the water made it something to which all existing laws could not be applied. It was plain at once, from the makeup of the U-boat and the limitations of its crew, that the submarine could not carry out the prescribed program of visit, search, taking off the crew, putting on board a prize crew—or else destroying the prize. This, with the added element of its great vulnerability, made it evident that there must be some modifications of the existing rules.

If the Germans had attempted to reach a solution of this problem in accordance with the common sense of sea usage, and with due regard for ordinary humanity, Germany might have retained some of the respect of the world. It is idle to consider in what manner these rules might have been drawn, because the German Government has deliberately chosen to throw aside all dictates of humanity in the use of the submarine. It has made no attempt to deserve the good opinion of the world. The chosen policy of the German Government is ruthless destruction of ships, enemy and neutral alike, without any decent regard for the lives of the passengers and crews.

When the official representative of Germany cold-bloodedly advised sinking without trace the Argentine ships, it was evident that there was no limit to the cynical cruelty of the present German Government. Argentina had been specially friendly to Germany, yet this Government of Germany treated the friendly nation as few of the most hardened of the old pirates would have treated their friends. In fact, the merchantman is now armed against tactics that would have disgraced the worst of the pirates in their own eyes.

# The Romance of the UC-12
## Revelations of a Submarine's Log

*Dr. Walter W. Seton, an English writer familiar with Italian affairs, is responsible for the following dramatic bit of history:*

THE Italian naval authorities have recently lifted the veil of mystery which shrouded the story of submarine UC-12. The story begins in May, 1915, a very short while after the declaration of war by Italy upon Austria. It will be remembered that, in spite of the alliance in arms between Austria and Germany, Germany was not included in the declaration of war, and remained outwardly, at all events, on friendly terms with Italy until August, 1916.

There was, however, plenty of ground for supposing that the friendliness of Germany was outward only, and that she was in reality secretly aiding Austria in every possible way. Toward the end of June, 1915, the Italian mine-sweepers, while performing their daily task near one of the Italian naval bases in the Adriatic, suddenly came upon a new form of secret destruction, consisting of a barrier of twelve mines in the water.

They were carefully cleared away and the mine-sweepers continued day after day their accustomed work, when suddenly another barrier of mines was found in very much the same position. It was not difficult to guess how the mines got there; they could only have been placed there by a submarine, which was able to cruise below the water and in secret to lay her deadly eggs. The Italians determined that the next attempt on the part of the submarine should be less successful, and should, on the other hand, result in her own destruction.

They had to wait for some time and possess their souls in patience until March 16, 1916, when the enemy submarine ventured once again into the waters of the naval base to lay another batch of eggs. She ventured in, but this time she did not make her escape silently and unobserved, for she fell a victim to the Italian mines which were lying in readiness for her. A loud explosion made it known to the Italian watchers that their plan had succeeded. That might have been the end of the story of the UC-12, an end which has doubtless come to many another U-boat during the present war.

But the enterprise of the Italian commander of the naval base gave a fresh turn to the story and brought to light facts which proved the duplicity of Germany once again. The water in which the submarine met her fate was not particularly deep, and a brilliant idea occurred to the commander of attempting to salve the vessel and to send her out repaired, refitted, and re-equipped as a unit in the Italian Submarine Service.

It was not an easy task to undertake, for the commander knew well that the sunken submarine almost certainly carried her usual cargo of mines. After divers had first been sent down to ascertain where the submarine lay and the condition in which she was, she was cautiously fished up to the surface a broken, tangled mass, apparently quite useless. It was not, however, until she reached the surface that her previous history began to be understood. She then stood revealed as the UC-12, built in Germany at the Weser Dockyard by the firm Ditta Siemens Schuckert.

It was now clear that while Germany

remained nominally on terms of friendship with her former ally, Italy, she had lent one of her submarines to operate in the service of Austria in the Adriatic and to lay mines in Italian waters. But how did the submarine make her way from the harbor of her birth to the Adriatic? That is a question which may well be asked, and it would not be an easy one to answer were it not for the fact that on board the UC-12 was found her log from birth to death. She had made her trial trip on the Weser, after which she was towed through the Kiel Canal in May, 1915; at Kiel she took on board the mines which she was to be sent to sow in Italian waters.

After having made her trials she was sent in three pieces by rail from Kiel to Pola, where she arrived on June 24, 1915. She left her German flag at Pola and adopted instead an Austrian flag, but, being ready for all emergencies, she was provided also with the British flag and a French flag, so as to be able to pose as an ally, and also with a Greek flag, in case it became necessary for her to become a neutral. These flags were found on board the submarine when she was raised to the surface.

The log contained records of her cruises on July 25, 1915, and Aug. 15, 1915, the two dates upon which she had been engaged in laying down mines in the Italian waters. It must not be supposed, however, that UC-12 was unoccupied between her second mine-laying exploit in August, 1915, and her third attempt in March, 1916. In December, 1915, she had been carrying a cargo of rifles from the Austrian base of Cattaro to Port Bardia in Cyrenaica, for the benefit of the rebels against the Italian Government.

In February, 1916, also UC-12 had been active in the Adriatic. She was round about Durazzo while the Italians were engaged in transporting the remains of the Serbian Army from the eastern to the western side of the Adriatic. Such was the revelation of the log of UC-12. But an investigation of the mangled remains of the ship and her crew proved even more completely the perfidy of Germany and the connivance of Austria. Her crew was German, too. There was absolutely nothing Austrian on board the submarine except the Austrian flag.

For many months Italian naval engineers were busy on the remains of UC-12. It was an ambitious task to salve her, but it has been accomplished, and not long ago UC-12 was once again placed in commission, and took to the water, flying the Tricolore, emblem of the position claimed by Italy as Queen of the Adriatic.

## British Navy Has Transported 13,000,000 Men

Premier Lloyd George in an address to Parliament on Oct. 29, 1917, summarized the war activities of the British Navy and gave some illuminating figures. He said:

But for the navy, disaster would have fallen upon the allied cause. Prussia would be mistress of Europe and, through Europe, of the world. Despite hidden foes, despite illegitimate naval warfare, despite black piracy, the navy has preserved the highways of the seas for Britain and her allies. Since the beginning of the war the navy has insured the safe transportation to the British and allied armies of 13,000,000 men, 2,000,000 horses, 25,000,000 tons of explosives and supplies, and 51,000,000 tons of coal and oil.

The losses of men out of the whole 13,000,000 were only 3,500, of which only 2,700 were lost through the action of the enemy. Altogether, 130,000,000 tons have been transported by British ships.

# Military Operations of the War

### By Major Edwin W. Dayton,

*Major Third Battalion, Fifteenth New York Infantry*

## X.—The Spring and Summer of 1916 on the Russian Front

THE Hindenburg axiom that the war was to be won on the eastern front appeared to suffer some loss of prestige as 1915 ended. In that fatal year the Germans had conquered all Western Russia, from Courland to Bukowina, and, in addition to the loss of cities, fortresses, and provisions, the Russians had lost men to an unparalleled number. The killed, wounded, and prisoners totaled over 2,000,000 men, and the territory lost amounted to 65,000 square miles.

Such a defeat would have seemed sufficient to eliminate any nation, and yet so vast was the reserve power of Russia that the German hope was doomed to bitter disappointment in the following year, when great Russian armies resumed the offensive in Volhynia, Galicia, and Bukowina. In the pursuit of the retreating Russian armies in the Summer of 1915 great numbers of prisoners had been taken in rearguard battles and in beleagured fortresses, but nowhere along that long front did the Germans succeed in cutting off any army. In each sector the Russians fought their way clear of the flanking forces with which von Hindenburg sought to envelop them, and although defeated and depleted, all the Russian armies succeeded in preserving an efficient nucleus upon which, in the Winter, new levies could be grafted.

The most tangible fruit of victory for the Germans seemed to be the winning to the Teuton side of Bulgaria, which in October, 1915, decided to join the ranks of the Central Powers, and thereby insured an open road through middle Europe from the Baltic to the Mediterranean. The more immediate result which had been hoped for failed, for the Russian fighting spirit was still too strong to be quenched, and the armies which, according to von Hindenburg's theory, ought to

have been freed for use on the western front had still to face eastward. Russia had suffered an overwhelming defeat, but still remained a dangerous factor in the war.

The German campaign in the north had

GENERAL A. A. BRUSILOFF

been halted before Riga and Dvinsk, and all through the frozen Winter months it was supposed that plans were maturing for the capture of both cities when Spring arrived. In the south at Christmas time General Ivanoff attempted to take Czernowitz, but failed, and in the next few months there was little more than local trench fighting to record, although a number of desperate battles were fought around the bridgehead of Uscieszko in January and February. About the middle of March the Austrians were driven out of this strong position, and the Russians effected the crossing of the Dniester.

## Battles at Lake Narotch

About the middle of March, 1916, an important offensive was developed against von Hindenburg's lines seventy miles south of Dvinsk, where, between Lakes Narotch and Vishnevsky, four Russian corps belonging to General Ewart's right centre and under the immediate command of General Baluyeff began an attack which lasted for a month.

A victory here would have reopened a road to Vilna and Kovno, two of the most important places captured by the Germans in 1915, and so the Germans resisted desperately the Russian effort to break their lines in this sector. Eight battles were fought among the marshes and sand hills between the lakes, and at the cost of some 12,000 casualties, the Russians won part of the German first line positions. All the ground won was lost in one day, (April 28,) when an overwhelming bombardment with high explosive shells paved the route for a powerful infantry attack, which smashed a way through Russian regiments, whose losses were as high as 75 per cent. Ewart's effort was a costly failure so far as the intention to break through the German lines below Lake Narotch was concerned, but it is generally believed to have spoiled von Hindenburg's plan to assail Riga early in April, when the waters of the gulf would have been open to the German fleet while the Russian naval forces were still bottled up by the ice further north.

## Brusiloff's Great Attack

In May, 1916, the Austrian armies of the Archduke Karl smashed the Italian defenses and seemed destined to overrun the Venetian Plains. In France the Germans, after months of furious battling, were close to Verdun. The British and French had not yet opened their campaign north of the Somme. A diversion especially for the sake of Italy was greatly needed, and Brusiloff, the brilliant cavalryman, hero of the Russian campaign in the Carpathians in 1914-15, replaced Ivanoff in command of the southern army group along the battle front from the Pripet marshes southward to the Rumanian frontier, a distance of nearly 300 miles.

On June 3, after a twelve-hour bombardment, the Russian infantry attacked at many places on that long line. In the region of the famous Volhynian triangle, between Lutsk and Rovno, the armies of Kaledin and Sakharoff stormed and broke the Austrian front under the Archduke Joseph Ferdinand. Achieving an overwhelming success, the Russians drove forward, and on June 6 took Lutsk with enormous booty of heavy guns, shells, and prisoners. Two days later Rojetche and Dubno fell, and the Russians held again all the Volhynian fortresses. On June 13 Kolki was captured, and after a severe battle Svidniki on the Stokhod was taken. In less than a fortnight the armies of Kaledin and Sakharoff had advanced fifty miles to the Galician border and captured over 70,000 Austrian prisoners and fifty-three guns.

The seriousness of the situation was apparent, and von Hindenburg began to send reinforcements into the threatened sectors under von Ludendorff. In Volhynia von Linsingen resumed the command and conducted a series of counterattacks during the latter weeks of June.

Further toward the north, where the Germans defended stubbornly their important centre of railway communications at Baranovitchi, General Rogoza's Fourth Russian Army fought hard against the forces of General von Woyrsch, but after promising early successes the Russians were halted by Prussian and Silesian troops. In the middle of July von Woyrsch tried to recover some of the ground lost in the first days of the month, but both sides appeared to have reached the limit of their power for offense, and the fighting in this sector gradually died down.

## Checked by Linsingen

In June the Russian line under the impetus of Kaledin's successes had bulged ominously on a wide curve from Czartorysk to Radziviloff. The salient of this advance west of Lutsk was along the route toward Vladimir-Volynsk, while an equal advance northwest of Lutsk was

AMERICA'S NEW ARMIES IN TRAINING

Members of the Hospital Corps at Camp Wadsworth, Spartanburg, S. C., Learning How to Remove Wounded Men from the Trenches.

(Photo © International Film Service.)

A TYPICAL SCENE AT A NEW ARMY CAMP

Recruits Going Through Different Stages of Training. Those in the Foreground Are Ready with Pick and Shovel to Start Trench Digging.

(Photo © International Film Service.)

getting dangerously close to Kovel. at Svidniki. The task of arresting this Russian success was assigned to von Linsingen, who directed a series of heavy counterattacks in the latter half of June. The Russians were driven back from Svidniki, and Kovel was saved.

Had Kaledin succeeded in taking this

GENERAL LECHITSKY

city, with its radiating railways, it is probable that the whole German line in the south would have been compelled to fall back to the line of the Bug, a strong, natural line of defense, where it had been thought in the previous year the Germans might be content finally to establish their new military frontier.

Below Czartorysk, along the River Styr, furious battles were fought, and the town of Gadomitchi was won and lost several times. Along the road Lutsk-Vladimir-Volynsk the Austrians attacked in great force and drove Kaledin's men back fully five miles to a position running through Zaturtsy and Bludov.

While Kaledin had been threatening Kovel further to the south, Sakharoff's army crossed the Sereth and advanced toward Brody. Still further down on that long line the army of Scherbacheff made a number of thrusts against the enemy.

Along the line of the Tarnopol-Lemberg railway von Bothmer's Austro-German forces gave the Russians a severe check. Below this sector, however, the Russians defeated the enemy along the Stripa River and captured Buczacz. This part of the line might apparently have been pushed much further toward the west had it not been for the check on the north.

### Lechitsky's Successes in Bukowina

While these great battles were being fought in Volhynia and Galicia, Lechitsky carried Brusiloff's left flank forward in great successes through Bukowina. On June 4 the attacks began, and after many desperate hand-to-hand battles with the bayonet the picked troops of Hungary, under Pflanzer-Baltin, were compelled to yield ground. Within a week the Russians advanced to Dabronovtse and captured nearly 20,000 Austrians. The enemy retreated all through the region between the River Dniester and Czernowitz, with the Russian infantry close on their heels. On June 12 Horodenka, twenty miles north of Czernowitz, was captured, and the Russians gained control of the roads above the city. In great confusion the badly demoralized Austrian forces continued to retreat along the line of the Pruth. Sadagora was evacuated and thousands of prisoners were picked up daily as the Russians advanced. About June 16 the Pruth was crossed, and on the 17th Czernowitz was captured.

Lechitsky pursued tirelessly, crossed the Sereth, and took Kuty, Pistyn, and Radantz. In the last week of June he was in Kimpolung, the most southerly town of Bukowina. Here the Russian left flank, in a wonderful victory, was far down against the Rumanian frontier and close to the Carpathian passes at Kirlibaba and Dorna Watra.

The great Russian advance through Volhynia, Galicia, and Bukowina had in three weeks of victorious battles along a front of several hundred miles gained the one really great success of the war for the Allies. In addition to notable advances in the two northerly provinces, Bukowina had been entirely recovered. Nearly 200,000 prisoners were captured, with over 200 cannon and about 650 machine guns.

The Russian victories, particularly in Bukowina, were so threatening to Austria as to compel the immediate withdrawal of every man who could be spared from the forces which had been on the verge of a successful invasion of Northern Italy. This campaign of Brusiloff was one of the very few instances in the whole war where the Allies succeeded in rescuing a small adherent to their cause from impending disaster. The credit belongs entirely to Russia, and ought not to be forgotten in later days of evil fortune, when internal dissensions robbed the great eastern nation of the power to continue the splendid successes won by the skill of her Generals and the courage of her soldiers in the Summer of 1916. Russia had Austria in full retreat and apparently on the verge of a catastrophe, which was only averted by the most vigorous measures of Germany's ablest Generals, with heavy reinforcements so distributed as to restore the shattered morale of the Austrian armies.

### Brusiloff's Further Victories

When June ended with Bukowina securely held by the Russian right, Brusiloff found his next great task along the middle Dniester, where Bothmer's army covered Halicz. Kovel, Brody, and ultimately Lemberg, remained, too, as chief objectives still to be won.

As July began General Ewart renewed the Russian effort against Baranovitchi, and although powerful infantry and artillery attacks won initial successes, the Russian effort in this sector was ultimately defeated with very heavy losses.

At the same time, south of the Pripet marshes, General Lesch delivered a great attack on a front of more than twenty-five miles east of the Styr River, in the region of Kolki. Here the Czartorysk salient had been a bloody battleground for long months. On the night of July 4 Lesch's men crossed the Styr above Rafalovka and were soon a dozen miles to the west of the river. A heavily fortified position at Vulka-Galuziskaya was stormed in heavy fighting, and several towns in the direction of Kolki fell. The

Czartorysk salient collapsed, and the Russian cavalry rode into Manievitche station, midway between the Styr and the Stokhod, on the line of the Kovel-Sarny railroad. Above this Lesch's right flank reached the Stokhod just south of the Pripet marshes. By the end of the first week in July the Russians were across the Stokhod, having driven the Austro-Germans back fully twenty-five miles and captured more than 12,000 prisoners. They were within twenty miles of Kovel, a main objective.

The Austrians had concentrated heavy reinforcements below the Lutsk salient for a great counterstroke, but Brusiloff, aware of their intention, struck hard before the Austrian concentration was completed. In quick, hard attacks on July 16 Sakharoff's men smashed several Austrian and one German division, and captured at Mikhailovka, on the Lipa, great stores of munitions. The Austrians retreated west on the Lipa to Gorochoff, losing en route about 13,000 men taken prisoners, with thirty cannon. Within the next week the Russians, pressing on, took Berestechko, southwest of the junction of the Lipa and the Styr, with still another 12,000 prisoners. After several days of hard fighting in forests and marshes, Brody was stormed on July 28, and 14,000 prisoners, with forty-nine guns, captured. Driving on tirelessly, the Russians advanced southward, and early in August won a number of villages about the upper Sereth, and by the 10th of the month were within a few miles of the Tarnopol line.

On the northern sector, meanwhile, the Russian armies made further progress along the Stokhod and captured several thousand Germans, with a number of guns. On Aug. 3 a hard battle occurred at Rudka Marynska, a strongly fortified village, which the Germans lost and later recaptured. About this time the Russian line had advanced to within some twenty-five miles of Kovel, and seemed well nigh irresistible, although facing an army composed principally of Germans.

### Austrian Debacle in Galicia

About the time when Lechitsky was winning Bukowina the Austrians in Galicia were retreating rapidly, and by

MAP OF THE REGION OF RUSSIA'S GREAT ADVANCE IN THE CAMPAIGNS OF 1916

the end of June were behind the Dniester River and holding the bridgeheads from Halicz to Nishnioff. Proceeding against the Austrian right rear, the Russian commander on June 28 started an attack northwest of Czernowitz in the direction of Kolomea, and on the first day captured over 10,000 officers and men.

GENERAL VON LINSINGEN

The next day Kolomea fell, and the panic-stricken Austrians were in headlong flight. On June 30 a brigade of Circassian cavalry captured Tlumatch, south of the Dniester, but with the arrival of German reinforcements the Austrian resistance stiffened, and on July 2 the Russians were driven out of Tlumatch.

Further to the south the Russian successes were uninterrupted, and town after town was captured, until, on July 8, Delatyn, twenty miles west of Kolomea, on the Pruth, was taken. Between June 22 and July 8 in this region more than 31,000 Austrian officers and men were captured.

In July heavy rains raised raging floods in the two great rivers, Pruth and Dniester, and the attacks were arrested, but on Aug. 7 Lechitsky recaptured Tlumatch and fought his way to

the banks of the Dniester. On Aug. 10 he was in Stanislau and Scherbacheff's men crossed the Zlota Lipa River, one of the numerous tributaries flowing into the Dniester from the north. The Austrians under General Bothmer were threatened on both flanks and once more were compelled to yield ground by retreating to a new position, whose centre was at Brzezany with the left back of Zboroff, along the Tarnopol-Lemberg railway.

The net results of Brusiloff's great offensive were enormous. Besides vast quantities of supplies of every description, fully 400,000 prisoners were taken and 7,000 square miles of territory recaptured of the 65,000 square miles lost in the previous year.

### Rumania in the War

As Summer ended, Russian efforts were diverted to helping Rumania, whose declaration of war against the Teutons was the signal for an attack upon Southern Austria. For a few weeks this gave promise of great things. Very shortly, however, the tide there turned, and von Falkenhayn and von Mackensen swept over Rumania almost as completely as the Teuton military machine had crushed Serbia in the previous year.

Having declared war on Aug. 27, 1916, Rumania rushed troops into Transylvania, a much-coveted Austrian province, which lay just north of the frontier. Defeats soon sobered Rumanian enthusiasm, and the German campaign under the two great Teuton tacticians worked out with a cruel precision that never seemed to suffer much more than temporary inconveniences from the opposition of the combined Rumanian and Russian Armies. Bucharest fell on Dec. 6, 1916, and the survivors of the defending armies were huddled away across country into Eastern Moldavia. The Teutons closed up to the Danube at Braila and held the country, except the valley of the Sereth, from the Danube up to the mountains in the northeast corner of the country. What was left of the Rumanian Government settled in Jassy, close to the Pruth, which forms the border between Rumania and Russia.

In a few months von Mackensen captured 10,000 square miles of territory rich in wheat fields and oil lands. The Rumanian-Russian losses were fully 400,-000 men. The losses here much more than offset the gains of Brusiloff in the north. The crushing of Rumania was a fresh evidence of the inability of the Allies to give efficient help to small nations drawn into the vortex of the war on their side. The Teutons were content to leave them unmolested in Moldavia, while the invaders have remained undisturbed masters of all the rest of the country since the end of 1916.

## Teutons Regain Initiative

An astonishing feature of the war in 1916 was the ability of the Germans to produce great mobile reserves whenever and wherever needed. A number of divisions were hurried over from the western front, and with large reserve bodies from Germany united to stop the dangerous Russian offensive in Volhynia, Galicia, and the Balkans. Austria brought troops back from the Italian campaign, and at least two divisions of Turks were brought up to the threatened area.

By the middle of October the Germans were attacking on a front of 300 miles from the Pinsk marshes to the Rumanian frontier, and in November, in a battle on the Stokhod, 4,000 Russian prisoners were taken with the front-line positions. The initiative had once more passed into the hands of the Germans, and by early December the Russian-Rumanian defenses in the south were being smashed to pieces, while further north, where Brusiloff had been winning great victories in the Summer, the Russians were again reduced to the defensive, and at places it was a precarious defense.

Early in December, in the high tide of German successes, the German Chancellor announced the willingness of Germany and her allies to discuss peace. At the end of the month the Allies published their refusal to listen to any proposals until Germany should have first been punished.

In March, 1917, the whole war situation was seriously affected by the Russian revolution, which banished the Czar and all royalty and created a republic. The Russian Army was seriously crippled by the spirit of independence which followed the passage of laws relieving soldiers from the duty of saluting their own officers. In many places whole regiments refused to fight at all, and with very little effort the Germans recovered all the ground which the Russians had so valiantly captured during the previous Summer. Kerensky, the popular idol of the nation, although not a soldier, went to the south, and by his personal influence induced the Russian soldiers to remember their duty to their country. For a while in the Spring a part of the forces seemed like the splendid fighting organization of 1916, but a sip from the cup of liberty had intoxicated the army as well as the civil population, and no great concerted aggressive effort could be induced. In places all along the line from north to south Russian and German troops fraternized in No Man's Land. At the same time in other sectors other regiments preserved their morale and still fought for the honor and integrity of Russia.

In midsummer of 1917 absolute chaos reigned in Russia. Kronstadt, the fortification defending Petrograd, was for a time in the hands of a commune, and while the authority of the Central Government was finally acknowledged, it is still matter of grave doubt whether a German fleet would meet much resistance if it should pass through the Gulf of Finland into the Neva en route toward Petrograd.

Riga, the important northern naval base, which had valiantly held out against every German attack for a year, has passed into German hands, as well as all the waters of the great Gulf of Riga and the islands along the coast at Moon Sound. When Riga fell the defenses along the Dvina River, which had been impregnable for a year, crumbled, and the Teutons, crossing easily, marched some distance toward Petrograd. The folly of becoming involved in a Winter campaign among the frozen lakes and marshes of that northern interior soon became apparent to the Germans, and their troops were drawn back to the line of the Dvina, where they are likely for the present at least to maintain that military frontier, established at the end of von Hindenburg's great campaign of 1915.

### Effects of Russia's Collapse

Germany's military interests will be best served by the creation of several independent small States, such as Finland promises to be. Buffer States of that type on the east would reduce to an absolute minimum the need for German troops on that side. That it has already been possible to withdraw great numbers of troops has been indicated by the appearance in the Alps of great German armies, which in a few weeks in this Autumn of 1917 have undone all that had been accomplished by Italian valor along the Isonzo in a year and a half of bloody warfare. If it should prove to be possible for von Hindenburg to take the bulk of his forces from the east and use them successfully to crush separate elements of the Allies, such as Italy, while holding the western line fairly steady, then the soundness of his proposition that Germany must win the war in the east would be well accredited. The year 1915 proved that driving Russian armies back in successive defeats meant little toward ultimate victory if the necessity remained to keep great armies out there ready to repel counter-attacks. If the loss of all internal cohesion in Russia changes that condition, then von Hindenburg will become a very successful prophet so far as theory goes.

Practically, however, it will not bring victory to Germany now, for the great resources of the United States will soon begin to tip the scale heavily against all that the Teuton can do. The same situation two years ago, after the end of von Hindenburg's great drive in the Summer of 1915, would have been serious if not disastrous for the Allies. In 1917 it is serious, but can no longer be disastrous for the Allies as a whole, although it may prove to be so for Italy.

[The author of this valuable series has been called to service in France, where he will take an active part in the great drama whose chief military events he has narrated in these pages. The series will be concluded next month with an article bringing the other phases of the war down to the present year.—Editor.]

# 38,000,000 Men Bearing Arms

The United States War Department, on Oct. 22, 1917, issued estimates based on published reports from various countries, showing that at least 38,000,000 men are bearing arms in the war—27,500,000 on the side of the allies and 10,-600,000 on the side of the Central Powers. These figures do not include naval personnel strength, which would raise the total several millions. Against Germany's 7,000,000, Austria's 3,000,000, Turkey's 300,000, and Bulgaria's 300,000 are arrayed the following armed forces: Russia, 9,000,000; France, 6,000,000; Great Britain, 5,000,000; Italy, 3,000,000; Japan, 1,400,000; United States, more than 1,000,000; China, 541,000; Rumania, 320,000; Serbia, 300,000; Belgium, 300,000; Greece, 300,000; Portugal, 200,000; Montenegro, 40,000; Siam, 36,000; Cuba, 11,000, and Liberia, 400.

Military experts do not regard these figures as entirely accurate, but believe they represent in round numbers the comparative strength of the contending armies.

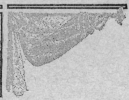

# The Beginnings of the War

## A Review of the Antecedent Causes and the Thirteen Critical Days

### By M. Louise McLaughlin

THE Balkan States, where occurred the inception of the great war, had long been a menace to the peace of Europe, more through the fault of their more powerful neighbors than through any sins of their own. Some of these States had occupied the position of distinct nationalities for more than a thousand years. Indeed, Serbia appears in a map of Europe of the time of Charlemagne, not quite in its present position nor including within its limits its present capital, the ancient town of Nissa. The Rumini are also in evidence in several places. In a map of the latter half of the tenth century, Serbia still occupies its position, then including within its borders both Belgrade and Nissa, while the great kingdom of the Bulgarians occupies nearly all the remainder of the Balkan Peninsula. Bosnia is represented apparently under the title of Bosona, while Prussia is a little country scarcely the size of Serbia, on the shore of the Baltic, separated from Serbia and Bulgaria by Polonia and the Kingdom of Hungary. As subsequent changes brought into dominance the great powers, France, Germany, Russia, and Austria, the natural riches of the Balkan States, as well as the possession of ports on southern seas, aroused covetous plans and gave rise to various intrigues for the attainment of influence over them or actual ownership by their powerful neighbors.

Bosnia, at whose capital of Serajevo the murder of the Archduke Ferdinand occurred, is, with the adjoining province of Herzegovina, under the control of Austria. The original kingdom, founded in 1378, was conquered by the Turks in 1463.

In 1877, when Russia made war against Turkey in defense of Bulgaria and especially because of the atrocities committed by the Turks against the Christian inhab-

itants, she apparently desired to placate Austria and to prevent that power from interfering with her plans; to this end she entered into a secret agreement to recognize the claim of Austria to an interest in the administration of the provinces of Bosnia and Herzegovina. On this occasion it was necessary for Russia to go through Rumania, just as in 1914 it seemed necessary for Germany to go through Belgium in her advance upon France, but, as Rumania did not resist, that country was merely occupied.

Later, when Russia had suffered defeat at Plevna, Rumania was called upon to assist, and through her aid Russia was finally victorious, and almost under the walls of Constantinople forced the Turks to sign the Treaty of San Stefano. Rumania in return for the aid given was made an independent State. Bulgaria also became an independent kingdom, and the interest gained by Russia through these circumstances was important on account of the possession by Bulgaria of seaports on the Aegean Sea.

### The Congress of Berlin

Aware of this, the other European powers saw a menace to the balance of power and insisted on bringing the matter before an international conference. Accordingly, the Congress of Berlin was called in 1878. Bismarck presided. England was represented by Lords Beaconsfield and Salisbury, Russia by Prince Gortchakoff.

The great Chancellor had two objects in view—he desired an alliance with Austria and he also wished to retain friendly relations with Russia. The decisions of the Congress of Berlin were satisfactory to neither of the parties directly concerned. Russia was not permitted to place the boundary line between her dominions and those of Turkey where she desired, as England, through an unfortunate blunder of the Russian representative, had become aware of the extreme concession that Russia was prepared to make and insisted on that. The Turkish delegates were themselves surprised when it developed during the proceedings that a secret agreement had been made between their Sultan and England that the Island of Cyprus was to be ceded to her as the price of her intervention.

The provisions of the Treaty of San Stefano with regard to Rumania and Bulgaria were allowed to stand, the occupation of Bosnia and Herzegovina by Austria was permitted, and Serbia, having aided Russia in the war, was granted independence. The province of Tunisia, which Italy had expected to obtain, was given to France. Russia took from Rumania the province of Bessarabia and gave in return that of Dobrudja. The arbitrary provisions of the Congress of Berlin did not satisfy all the participants, but the peace of Europe had been retained for the time being. The next year Bismarck attained his desire of an alliance with Austria, thus preventing what he had feared—an alliance between that country and France.

## Friction in Colonial Matters

It was about this time that, contrary to his previous policy, Bismarck began to take an interest in colonial expansion for Germany. France became involved in colonial friction with England, and, having taken possession of Tunisia in 1881, thereby incurred the anger of Italy. In 1889 an important treaty was arranged between England and Germany by which Germany came into possession of Samoa. Referring to this in a speech in Parliament, Lord Salisbury said:

This morning you have learned of an arrangement concluded between us and one of the Continental States with whom, more than with others, we have for years maintained sympathetic relations. The arrangement, above all, is interesting as an indication that our relations with the German Nation are all that we could desire.

In February, 1900, Lord Rosebery said: " The Government made pressing " overtures to Germany and to the United " States for an alliance last December." But the influence which finally culminated in the Triple Entente of England, France,

and Russia had now begun to be effective in the policy of M. Delcassé, the French Minister.

The Fashoda incident had brought M. Delcassé into office through the resignation of his predecessor, M. Hanotaux. The difficulty caused by this affair almost led to war between England and France. In 1882 the British had undertaken to crush a native rebellion in Egypt and had bombarded the City of Alexandria, afterward landing troops, which were still in occupation. The other powers had protested in vain.

There had been some trouble as to the failure of Great Britain to carry out certain treaty rights of France in regard to fisheries on the coast of Newfoundland, and now a more serious difficulty arose as to the Sudan. A French expeditionary force was in that country when a rumor arose as to a possible intention of diverting the waters of the Nile. Great Britain promptly annexed the Sudan, and when Colonel Marchand, the leader of the French expedition, finally made his way to Fashoda, a village on the Nile, he found Kitchener in possession, and after a conference was obliged to withdraw. France was not in a position to defend her claim against England by force of arms, although feeling in regard to the incident ran high in France. Her Minister, M. Hanotaux, was obliged to resign.

M. Delcassé, succeeding to the office, endeavored to maintain peaceful relations, although the task was not an easy one, with Italy also assuming a hostile attitude with regard to Tunisia. In 1902 an agreement was made with Italy which contained a proviso that she would not join in an aggressive war against France. This probably influenced Italy's action in 1914. Italy was also induced to accept a revision of the Tunisian treaty, thus recognizing the claims of France to that province.

## Rise of the Triple Entente

The idea of war with Germany was never very far from the thought of French politicians after 1870, and, indeed, war was barely averted in 1875. M. Delcassé did not like Germany, but in his policy of conciliation he even drew upon himself the charge of having " sold out to the Germans " because he went to Russia to intercede with the Government of that country to withhold opposition to the German project of a railway to the East. In his quest of a defensive alliance, however, he turned to Great Britain. The new order of things, which changed the ancient enemies into allies and resulted in the formation of the Triple Entente, had given signs of its approach, from the time, indeed, when it might have been expected—the retirement of Bismarck. From this time the change in the relations of Germany and Russia may be dated. Bismarck's intention was always to retain the friendship of Russia, and a disagreement on this subject between the young Kaiser and the aged Chancellor is supposed to have led to the latter's retirement in 1890. The following year the alliance between France and Russia was consummated, although the full text of this alliance was not made public until 1897 upon the occasion of the visit of the Czar Nicholas to Paris. Great resentment was felt in Germany when the terms of this alliance were known, and the war party did not conceal its dissatisfaction with the Kaiser for his policy of maintaining peace.

It was three years before this that the photograph of the Kaiser, with his arm encircling the shoulder of the Czar, was taken, upon the occasion of the latter's bethrothal to the cousin of the Kaiser. When this picture was exhibited in a shop window of Paris, at the time of the Czar's visit in 1897, the Parisians objected so strongly that it had to be removed.

But the dominating force of Bismarck no longer controlled the politics of Europe, and it became more and more evident that the other countries resented the exercise of German influence and entertained a growing fear of German military power. It was after the Boer war that the enmity developing in England became apparent. Great Britain, humiliated by the mismanagement of that war and the criticisms her conduct toward the Boers had called forth, was inclined to meet the overtures of France. The Associated Chambers of Commerce of London passed a resolution in favor of an arbitration treaty with France in the interests of trade. King Edward visited Paris, and President Loubet and M. Delcassé returned the visit. It is understood that King Edward was largely instrumental in establishing friendly relations with France, and it is also believed that his personal association with the Kaiser, his nephew, had not been agreeable.

## Entente Cordiale Signed

The " Entente Cordiale " between England and France was signed in 1904. By the entente the two Governments pledged themselves not to interfere with each other, or, rather, " to afford to one " another their diplomatic support in " order to obtain the execution of the " clauses of the present declaration re- " garding Egypt and Morocco." The secret portions of the treaty were not made public until seven years afterward.

When, the following year after the entente was signed, the Kaiser arrived at Tangier in his yacht and, in a speech to the Sultan, offered his services if needed, and also expressed his intention of safeguarding the interests of Germans in Morocco, the French people, who were not aware of the underlying causes, were extremely indignant. The secret portion of the entente, which related to a possible partition of Morocco, would appear to have come to the knowledge of the Kaiser. Great Britain had desired to protect her interests in Gibraltar, and in the event of a partition of Morocco, while not demanding a share, asked that the portion lying opposite her possessions should belong to Spain, and that that country should give a pledge that no fortification would be erected thereon which could menace the British occupation of Gibraltar. As this portion of the treaty was not made public until 1911, the action of the Kaiser indicated that he had learned of its provisions. His visit to Tangier was also timed after the defeat of the Russians by the Japanese at Liao-Yang. France, not being prepared to fight, was obliged to consent to the demand of public opinion in Germany, which insisted that a conference of the powers should be held and that M. Delcassé should be asked to resign.

A conference of the powers was held at Algeciras in Spain in 1906. At this conference it appeared that Germany did not have the support of the other nations, as all those taking part voted against her except Austria and Morocco. Among those who thus voted were Belgium and the United States, although the fact of the presence of our representative was withheld from the Senate. Again the war party of Germany regretted the settlement of this matter by diplomacy, in which they did not excel, instead of the sword, which at this time they could have drawn with every prospect of success. The maintenance of peace, however, seemed to be most desired, and efforts at conciliation continued to be made.

### Austria's Annexation of Bosnia

But again the Eastern question arose. A revolution in Turkey overthrew the Government of Abdul Hamid. In power, the party of the Young Turks undertook to assert their sovereignty over Bosnia and Herzegovina. Austria, ignoring the fact that the Congress of Berlin had merely given her a protectorate over those provinces, annexed them. In this act she was upheld by Germany, and the protests of the other powers were overruled. On account of interest in Slav nationalities, the Czar especially was insistent, but, as the Kaiser threatened war rather than abandon the support of his ally, Russia was forced to withdraw opposition, which she was the more willing to do, as she was then in no condition to undertake a war against Germany and Austria.

The affair of Agadir was the next menace to the peace of Europe, the scene being again laid in Morocco. There were German interests in that country, and there had been complaints of unequal treatment in commercial matters. It had been rumored that France was preparing to assume a protectorate over the territory. A military expedition had been sent to Fez, ostensibly to protect the interests of the French residents. Germany protested by sending a warship to Agadir. The crisis produced threatened to be serious, but at last the Kaiser recognized the French protectorate of Morocco and as a compensation received a rather useless bit of territory in the Congo.

### The Treaty of Bucharest

Italy now proceeded to take from Turkey her last remaining colonies in Africa, engaging in a war with the Turks without either the consent or participation of her allies. This war was followed by the war of the Balkan Alliance against Turkey in 1912. Earlier in this year a treaty had been made between Bulgaria and Serbia, from which it appeared that Serbia desired access to the Adriatic, while Bulgaria's object was the independence of Macedonia. The Serbians, cherishing a national spirit that had been aroused through the efforts of Austria to keep them in subjection, aspired to a union of those nationalities of the Balkan Peninsula which had a common origin or spoke similar languages. Austria opposed this aspiration and undertook to protect Albania from Serbia. The result of the war of the Balkan Alliance was in favor of Serbia, and Bulgaria was forced to accept a solution which she had gone to war to prevent.

The Treaty of Bucharest, which ended the war, has been pronounced one of the most iniquitous ever perpetrated. The demand to have it laid before the powers for revision was refused. Germany and Austria resented the advantages gained by Serbia and considered the result a victory for Russia. Serbia, on account of their common Slav origin, was the protégé of Russia, and on her own part recognized the advantage of the friendship of her northern neighbor, while that power realized that through Serbia lay the route to southern seas. Austria's policy was to subject Serbia to her domination and to frustrate any ambitions as to Pan-Slavonic development. Under these conditions, and with the Balkan question still unsettled, the peace of Europe was unstable.

In 1913 Germany passed a law giving a great increase to her army; Russia also voted enormous military credits, and France lengthened the enforced term of service in her army from two to three years. The stage was set for the great war, and on June 28, 1914, the incentive to trouble was given in the assassination of the heir to the Austrian throne, the Archduke Franz Ferdinand, and his wife at Serajevo.

## The Fatal Thirteen Days

With the constantly increasing preparations for war, the endless speculations as to when it would begin, with everybody on the qui vive and the young German officers drinking to " The Day," it was evident that the provocation that would set a match to the tinder would not be far to seek. The increase in the German Navy and the extension of German competition in the commerce of all the marts of the world had also been a source of concern to England, while the German project of a railway from Hamburg to Bagdad was regarded by that country as inimical to her interests in the East. The crime of Serajevo precipitated the crisis.

The history of the great war begins with the first of the " Fatal Thirteen Days," July 23, 1914. On that day Austria sent an ultimatum to Serbia containing ten demands, with the request that an answer be returned within forty-eight hours. The important demand included in the ultimatum was that in which Serbia was asked to permit the collaboration of Austria " for the suppression of the subversive movement directed against the territorial integrity of the monarchy." It would seem that Austria had chosen the time as an opportune occasion to humiliate and browbeat Serbia.

At the moment Great Britain was occupied with the home-rule conference, and the ultimatum was sent on the very day that the conference failed and civil war in Ulster seemed inevitable. The President of France and his Prime Minister were in Russia, the French Ambassador to Serbia had gone away from the capital, the Russian Ambassador was about to leave for a fortnight's vacation, and left after receiving the assurance that the situation was not critical. It was evident that Germany knew of the action of her ally and was prepared to give her support. The demand of Austria, however, to be permitted to take part in the investigation of the crime which had been committed was felt to be an infringe-

ment upon the sovereign rights of Serbia which that country could not permit.

On July 24 the British Ambassador at Vienna reported to his Government that the Russian Chargé d'Affaires, having been received by the Austrian Minister of Foreign Affairs, had given as his own personal opinion that the Austrian note had been so drawn as to render its acceptance as it stood impossible, and that it was both unusual and peremptory in its terms. The Austrian Minister replied that unless the demands were accepted by 4 P. M. the following day the Austrian Minister at Belgrade had instructions to leave. On the same day the German Ambassador at Paris made known the hope of his Government that the conflict might be confined to Austria and Serbia.

On Saturday, July 25, Austria refused to extend the time limit imposed on Serbia. The British Chargé d'Affaires at Berlin reported a conversation had that day with the Secretary of State in which the latter said he " did not know what " Austria-Hungary had ready on the " spot, but he admitted quite freely that " the Austro - Hungarian Government " wished to give Serbia a lesson, and they " meant to take military action." This seemed to be the general opinion among the Ambassadors.

## Serbia's Answer to Austria

Serbia's answer, in which she accepted eight out of the ten demands of Austria, was dated upon this day. As to the remaining two demands, she declined to permit Austrian officials to conduct the investigation of her citizens, as such action would be a reflection on her sovereignty; but she offered to place the matter before The Hague Tribunal or the great powers. The Austrian Minister at Belgrade spent forty minutes in considering the answer and left for Vienna.

Sunday, July 26. The British Ambassador at St. Petersburg reported a conversation with the German Ambassador in which, in reply to his question if the Russian Government might not be induced to intervene on account of kindred nationality, the German Ambassador said that everything would depend on the personality of the Russian Minister for Foreign Affairs—but he did not think that official would take a step which would open up so many frontier questions; besides, France was not at all in a condition to make war.

On this day Sir Edward Grey proposed that the four powers most directly interested should authorize their Ambassadors to meet and seek some formula of agreement, while in the meantime neither Serbia, Austria, nor Russia should enter into military preparations. France and Italy agreed to this, and the proposition was also favored by Russia, who had already made overtures to Austria for the purpose of entering into direct conversations. Germany, while appearing to approve of this suggestion on principle, objected that it would be tantamount to calling Austria and Russia before an international court, which was out of the question. M. Cambon, the French Ambassador at Berlin, pointed out that in such a crisis the matter of form might be disregarded, and if a peaceful solution could not be found, the responsibility would rest with Germany. The German diplomat still refused.

Monday, July 27. Sir Edward Grey informed his Ambassador at St. Petersburg that he had learned from German and Austrian sources that they believed that Russia would not take action as long as Austria agreed not to take Serbian territory.

### Austria Refuses a Parley

Tuesday, July 28. The Austrian Ambassador at Berlin assured the British Ambassador that a general war was most unlikely, that Russia neither wanted nor was in a condition to make war. This seemed to be the opinion in the German capital. On this day, however, the offer of Russia to discuss the matter with Austria was refused, and the Austrian Premier withheld from his Ambassador at St. Petersburg the authority to hold conversations with the Russian authorities in regard to the terms of the note to Serbia.

Austria declared war upon Serbia.

Wednesday, July 29. The Italian Minister made a suggestion to the British Ambassador at Rome to the effect that, as it appeared Germany was desirous of

maintaining friendly relations with England, it would be well if she were given to understand that the latter country would act with France and Russia. To the entreaty of the French Ambassador, however, Sir Edward Grey replied: " In " the present case the dispute between " Austria and Serbia is not one in which " we feel called upon to take a hand. " Even if the question were one between " Austria and Russia we should not feel " called upon to take a hand in it. It " would then be a question of the su- " premacy of Teuton or Slav—a struggle " for supremacy in the Balkans—and our " idea has always been to avoid being " drawn into a war over the Balkan " question."

It was on this day that the Kaiser, according to his letter, given to our Ambassador, Mr. Gerard, on Aug. 10, for transmission to President Wilson, received the verbal message from his brother, Prince Henry, which had previously been transmitted by telegraph. This message, he asserts, was to the effect that King George, in a conversation with Prince Henry, had assured him that England would remain neutral " if war broke out on the Continent involving Germany, France, Austria, and Russia "; but King George flatly denies ever having sent such a message.

The German Chancellor promised that if England would stand aside, Germany would seek no territorial aggrandizement from France, although he would make no promises as to French colonies. Also he would guarantee to respect the neutrality of Belgium if she did not side with France.

### Britain's Attitude Made Clear

Thursday, July 30. Sir Edward Grey refused the German offer of the previous day. What Germany asked, he said, was in effect

to stand by while French colonies were taken and France is beaten, so long as Germany does not take French territory as distinct from her colonies. From the material point of view such a prospect is unacceptable, for France, without further territory being taken from her, could be so crushed as to lose her position as a great power and become subordinate to German policy. Altogether apart from that, it would be a disgrace for us to make this bargain at the expense of France, a disgrace from which the good name of this country would never recover. The Chancellor also asks us to bargain away whatever obligation or interest we have as regards the neutrality of Belgium; we could not entertain this bargain, either.

At 2 o'clock on this morning the German Ambassador at St. Petersburg had a second interview with the Russian Minister of Foreign Affairs, and asked M. Sazonoff to offer some suggestion that could be telegraphed to his Government as a last hope. M. Sazonoff then drew up and handed to the Ambassador the following formula:

If Austria, recognizing that her conflict with Serbia has assumed character of question of European interest, declares herself ready to eliminate from her ultimatum points which violate sovereignty of Serbia, Russia engages to stop all military preparations.

### Austria Recedes a Step

Learning of the military preparations of Russia, Count von Berchtold, the Austrian Premier, agreed to permit the resumption of diplomatic conversations, saying that his former refusal to permit this interchange with the Russian officials had been based on a misunderstanding, and begging the Russian Ambassador to do all in his power to remove the false impression that "Austria had brutally banged the door on negotiations." He also informed Paris and London that Austria had no intention of impugning the sovereign rights of Serbia. The Russian Ambassador at Vienna in his turn gave assurance that his Government would take into consideration the demands of Austria in "a far more generous spirit than was expected." At St. Petersburg the Austrian Ambassador accepted the discussion proposed, and agreed to accept the mediation of the powers suggested by Sir Edward Grey and drafted by the Russian Minister.

Jules Cambon, the French Ambassador at Berlin, informed his Government of an extraordinary council which he believed had been held at Potsdam the previous evening, consisting of the military authorities under the Presidency of the Emperor, and which "had decided upon mobilization, a fact which explains the Lokal-Anzeiger's special edition, [con-taining the order for mobilization,] but that various influences [England's statement that she reserves full liberty of action, exchange of telegrams between the Czar and Wilhelm II.] have caused the serious measures which have been determined upon to be suspended."

### Kaiser to President Wilson

Referring to the situation at this point, the Kaiser, in his letter to President Wilson, says that his Ambassador at London communicated to him the position of England as given by Sir Edward Grey in a private conversation—that England would not move even if Russia was involved with Austria—but if Germany entered the conflict "she would take quick de-"cisions and grave measures; i. e., if I "left my ally Austria in the lurch to "fight alone, England would not touch "me." Continuing (Part 4):

"This communication being directly "counter to the King's message to me, I "telegraphed to H. M., on the 29th or 30th, "thanking him for kind messages through "my brother and begging him to use all "his power to keep France and Russia— "his allies—from making any warlike "preparations calculated to disturb my "work of mediation, stating that I was in "constant communication with H. M. the "Czar.

"In the evening the King kindly an-"swered that he had ordered his Govern-"ment to use every possible influence with "his allies to refrain from taking any "provocative military measures. At the "same time H. M. asked me if I would "transmit to Vienna the British proposal "that Austria was to take Belgrade and a "few Serbian towns and a strip of coun-"try as a 'main-mise' to make sure that "the Serbian promises on paper should "be fulfilled in reality. This proposal "was in the same moment telegraphed to "me from Vienna for London, quite in "conjunction with the British proposal; "besides, I had telegraphed to H. M. the "Czar the same as an idea of mine, be-"fore I received the two communications "from Vienna and London, as both were "of the same opinion.

"I immediately transmitted the tele-"grams vice versa to Vienna and Lon-"don. I felt that I was able to tide the "question over and was happy at the "peaceful outlook."

The telegrams here referred to have not appeared in the German official reports of the diplomatic proceedings. Mr. Gerard, to whom the Kaiser's cablegram was given for transmission, relates that directly after receiving it he was questioned in regard to its contents by a certain person in high authority whose identity he did not wish to disclose. Requesting that the cablegram be shown to him, this personage suggested that it would be best in the interest of good feeling between Germany and America that it should not be published. This precaution evidently applied to the closing paragraph, (Part 7,) in which the Kaiser said that the neutrality of Belgium " had to be violated on strategical grounds." Why that admission should have been considered imprudent then, or why the publication three years afterward when we were at war with Germany was considered as an important confession, it is difficult to understand, when Chancellor von Bethmann Hollweg, on the very day that the act was committed, announced the fact that they " found it necessary to enter Belgian territory."

## The Kaiser to the Czar

But we have left the Kaiser at the close of the day when he was " happy at the peaceful outlook." That night a telegram was sent to the Czar and received by the latter at 1 o'clock A. M., which was worded by the Kaiser as follows:

My Ambassador has been instructed to call the attention of your Government to the dangers and serious consequences of mobilization. This is what I told you in my last telegram. Austria-Hungary has mobilized only against Serbia, and no more than part of her army. If it is the case, as your telegram and the communication of your Government indicate, that Russia is mobilizing against Austria-Hungary, the success of the mission of mediation with which you amicably intrusted me, and which I accepted at your request, will be endangered or perhaps made impossible. The whole burden of the decision to be arrived at now rests on your shoulders, which will have to bear the responsibility of war or peace.

The reply to this telegram was received in Berlin at 1:20 P. M. and was as follows:

The military measures which have now been taken were decided upon five days ago as a precaution against the preparations of Austria. I hope most sincerely that these measures will not in any way hinder your mediation, which I value very greatly.

Meanwhile the Kaiser, as he states in his letter to President Wilson, was in the act of preparing a letter to the Czar " to inform him that Vienna, London, and Berlin were agreed about the treatment of affairs " when he received a telephone message from his Chancellor that " the " night before the Czar had given the " order to mobilize the whole of the Rus- " sian Army, which was, of course, also " meant against Germany; whereas up " till then the southern armies had been " mobilized against Austria."

From this time the Kaiser openly manifested his resentment at the action of the Czar and adopted the aggressive attitude that within forty-eight hours precipitated the war. He stated that he considered the Czar's reply to his telegram evasive, and was evidently angered at what he construed as a defiance from Russia.

## Czar's Efforts for Peace

A light has been thrown upon the conduct of the Czar recently, which absolves him from deliberate intention to produce the result which followed. It has been pointed out that demobilization at the demand of the Kaiser would have been the deepest possible humiliation for Russia, yet in the trial of the Russian General Soukhomlinoff on the charge of treason by the revolutionary authorities it was brought out that the Czar actually did give an order for arrest of mobilization, which upon the night in question was changed by General Januschkevitch because of news which he said had been received of mobilization by Germany. On being informed of this in the morning, the Czar was said to have thanked the General for his action.

The efforts of the Czar to preserve peace are made plain, but also the fact that he was manipulated by one of his officers, or that they were both the victims of false information.

Mr. Gerard says that in Berlin peace talk continued, but that on the afternoon of this day he had a conversation with Baron Beyens, the Minister from Belgium, and Jules Cambon, the French Ambassador, who were very much depressed, and who told him that nothing could now prevent war but the intervention of the United States.

Acting on his own responsibility, Mr. Gerard sent this letter to the Chancellor:

Your Excellency: Is there nothing that my country can do? Nothing that I can do toward stopping this dreadful war? I am sure the President would approve any act of mine looking toward peace. Yours ever, (Signed) JAMES W. GERARD.

To this no reply was sent.

Friday, July 31. Mr. Gerard cabled the State Department that a general European war was inevitable.

At 2 P. M. the Kaiser telegraphed to the Czar:

I undertook to mediate between your Government and the Austro-Hungarian Government. While this negotiation was still proceeding your troops were mobilized against Austria-Hungary, my ally, and, in consequence of this, as I have already informed you, my intervention has become almost illusory. In spite of this, I continued.

I have just received reliable information of serious warlike preparations on my eastern frontier, and, as I am responsible for the security of my empire, I am obliged to adopt similar measures of defense.

I have done everything possible in my efforts to keep the peace, and it is not I who will bear the responsibility of the frightful disaster which at present menaces the whole civilized world.

Even now it depends only upon you to prevent it. No one threatens the honor and authority of Russia, and she might very well have awaited the result of my intervention.

No reply was given to this telegram, and the same day an official summons was sent to Russia to demobilize within twelve hours. It is definitely asserted that a telegram from the Czar offering to place the matters at issue before The Hague Tribunal, which received no reply, was deliberately omitted from the German diplomatic record. Indeed, all the events which led to the crisis have been the subject of bitter controversy. For, although there are those who, like stormy petrels, ride this whirlwind with evident delight, no one wants to assume the responsibility of having started it, and it has been the peculiarity of this war that every nation that has entered it, those of the Central Powers as well as those of the Allies, has proclaimed that it did so in self-defense.

At 7 P. M., the same hour at which the demand upon Russia to demobilize was made, the Kreigsgefahrzustand, or "condition of danger of war," was proclaimed in Berlin.

## German and Russian Mobilization

Aug. 1. At 5 P. M. the order for mobilization of the German Army was given, and at 7:10 P. M., the twelve hours of the ultimatum to Russia having expired, war was declared against that country.

Perhaps the most important of the controversies that have been waged as to the responsibility for the breaking out of the war has been that in regard to the dates of mobilization in Germany and Russia. We have, as given above, the official time of Germany's order for mobilization as reported by our Ambassador, Mr. Gerard—5 P. M. on Aug. 1. The Czar, in his telegram to the Kaiser on the 30th, admitted that the military preparations of Russia had been decided upon five days before, thus apparently giving the Russian mobilization a precedence of about six days before that of Germany. Christopher Schnurrer, a graduate of the University of Leipsic, has recently been arrested in this country, and among his effects was found a card issued by the Imperial Government of Germany directing him to report for military duty on July 17, 1914. This agrees with the stories that were current about the time of the breaking out of the war, going to show that Germany had anticipated the event by summoning officers of her army on leave at distant points to return; and that some of them had been making their way from Canada and remote parts of the United States ten days or two weeks before war was declared.

That, on account of the trouble between Austria and Serbia, Germany had considered the possibility of being drawn into a war with Russia, was admitted in the diplomatic correspondence published in THE NEW YORK TIMES of Aug. 24, 1914, known as the German White Paper. In this document the following statement was made: "We are fully aware in this "connection that warlike moves on the "part of Austria-Hungary against Serbia "would bring Russia into the question "and might draw us into a war in ac- "cordance with our duties as an ally."

This accounted for preparations made by Germany for mobilization. The increase in the German Army the previous year, the military preparations of Russia, and the lengthened term of service in the French Army; in fact, all the efforts of the great powers to be prepared for the emergency had previously indicated the state of apprehension that existed.

It was expected that France would enter into the war. Her Premier had said that she would act as her interests demanded, but to insure the neutrality of Italy it was felt that France should abstain from aggressive movements, and her troops were ordered to retire ten kilometers from the border of Germany.

## German Invasion of Belgium

Aug. 2. At 7 P. M. the German Government announced to Belgium its purpose to violate the neutrality of that country, either with or without her consent. Accompanying the note was the assurance that "the German troops with "their iron discipline will respect per-"sonal liberty and personal property of "the individual in Belgium, just as they "did in France in 1870." Article 4 of this communication also contained the warning: "Should Belgium oppose the "German troops, and in particular should "she throw difficulties in the way of "their march by resistance of the fort-"resses on the Meuse, or by destroying "railroads, tunnels, or other similar "works, Germany will to her regret be "compelled to consider Belgium an ene-"my."

In the Reichstag that day, Chancellor von Bethmann Hollweg said:

"We are now in a state of necessity, "and necessity knows no law—anybody "who is threatened as we are threat-"ened and is fighting for his highest "possessions can have only one thought "—how he is to hack his way through."

Monday, Aug. 3. At 7 o'clock in the morning Belgium delivered her reply, that she was resolved to repulse by every means in her power any attack upon her rights.

Later in the day, the Germans, having crossed the frontier, the King of the Belgians appealed to England for diplomatic intervention.

## Great Britain and Belgium

Tuesday, Aug. 4. On this day the climax arrived which threw the great powers of Europe into the war, and which has now drawn into its toils nearly the whole world. The German Chancellor stated to the Reichstag the events which had led to the declaration of war against Russia. With regard to France, while he admitted that the French had agreed to respect a zone of ten kilometers from the border, he asserted that in reality aggressions had been made on German territory (in Alsace-Lorraine) by "bomb-throwing fliers, cavalry patrols, invading companies." Proof of this has not been given, and the Kaiser does not refer to it definitely in his letter to President Wilson, stating the case in relation to France as follows:

In a telegram from London my Ambassador informed me he understood the British Government would guarantee neutrality of France and wished to know whether Germany would refrain from attack. I telegraphed to H. M. personally that mobilization being carried out could not be stopped, but if H. M. could guarantee with his armed forces the neutrality of France I would *refrain from attacking her, leave her alone*, and employ my troops elsewhere. H. M. answered that he thought my offer was based on a misunderstanding; and, as far as I can make out, Sir E. Grey never took my offer into serious consideration. He never answered it. Instead, he declared England had to defend Belgian neutrality, which had to be violated by Germany on strategical grounds, news having been received that France was already preparing to enter Belgium, and the King of the Belgians having refused my petition for a free passage under guarantees of his country's freedom.

Proof of a possible French invasion of Belgian territory has not been furnished; on the contrary, it is said that the French troops near the border were opposite the German frontier, not the Belgian.

As to possible occupation of Belgium by England in the event of a war with Germany, even without the request or consent of that country, proof that this had been discussed was alleged to have been found by the Germans in the archives of Antwerp, although the documents, which they have since published, indicate that the matter never went any further than certain conversations between the Military Attachés of England and Belgium in 1906, and again in 1912, over hypothetical situations. The King of the Belgians has published a statement in which, referring to the conversation reported by General Ducarme to the Minister of War in 1906, he says that so fearful was he of any act that could be construed as unneutral that he caused these matters to be communicated to the German Military Attaché at Berlin, and therefore, when the Germans went through the archives at Antwerp they knew exactly what they would find. When it became known that the Dutch contemplated fortifying the mouth of the Scheldt, both Great Britain and France protested. It was there that the possible landing of troops had been contemplated.

## Early Diplomatic Conversations

In 1911 the Belgian representative at Berlin objected that the plans should also take into account an arrangement with Germany in the event of an invasion of Belgium by France and England. In the conversation between the Military Attachés Lieutenant Bridges and General Jungbluth in 1912, the former said that England could send an army of 160,000 men even if Belgium did not demand aid. To this the Belgian General objected that Belgium's consent would be necessary. Colonel Bridges answered that he was aware of that, but as the Belgians would not be able to prevent the passage of the Germans through their country, England would send troops into Belgium in any case. General Jungbluth contended that the Belgians would be perfectly able to prevent the passage of the Germans.

Details were discussed even in the earlier conversations as to the amount of time which would be required for the arrival of the British troops and if the Belgian preparations were sufficient for defense during the time, perhaps ten days, which must elapse before the landing was accomplished.

On the other hand, it is said that there were evidences of preparation on the part of Germany for the invasion of Belgium in the numerous railways leading in the direction of the frontier, ten of which had been constructed, while eight more were under construction when most of them were unnecessary for the traffic of the region. In fact, the strategic importance of this region was recognized by both sides, and Flanders was again to be made the battlefield of the nations. To the fact that it had suffered so much through wars, Fergusson attributed the circumstance that it was so rich in architectural monuments, because the country had been so impoverished that it was unable to follow the custom of more prosperous places and destroy the fine mediaeval structures to give way to more modern but less beautiful productions.

## Belgium's Neutrality Guaranteed

In 1830, when the independence of Belgium was demanded and obtained from Holland, its permanent neutrality as a State not strong enough to defend itself was guaranteed by the powers. In 1839 the Quintuple Treaty, made when Lemberg and Luxemburg had been divided between Belgium and the Netherlands, again guaranteed this neutrality. Although the German Empire as it is constituted today was not in existence at that time, the neutrality of Belgium had been understood as amply guaranteed by Bismarck, and Herr von Jagow had remarked in the Reichstag in 1913 that Germany was resolved to respect those conventions.

Mr. Gerard characterized the Kaiser's excuse for the violation of Belgian neutrality on the score of " strategical reasons," and because the King of the Belgians had refused free passage to his troops under a guarantee of his country's freedom, as weak; remarking that " it would, indeed, inaugurate a new era in the intercourse of nations if a small nation could only preserve its freedom by at all times, on request, granting free passage to the troops of a powerful neighbor on the march to attack an adjoining country." In fact it would be a new order of things if this were not done, but it is to be hoped that after this the custom will be discontinued. The Kaiser's method, although a custom more honored in the breach than the observance, is one that has been practiced many times without even the promise of freedom to the country whose rights are thus violated.

## England's Safety Involved

The fact that this was Belgium and that the neutrality of that country was essential as a defensive measure for England changed the situation. The possibility of making the coast of Flanders and that of Northwestern France a base for hostile demonstrations against England would, of course, be of vital importance to that country. It was probably in anticipation of such a contingency that a secret clause had been incorporated into the entente between England and France providing that in case of war with Germany the French coast would be protected by England. This was the reason why England could not proceed as in 1870 to arrange that Belgian neutrality should be respected by France and Germany.

In 1870 France had proposed to take possession of Belgium, and England had demanded that both France and Germany should sign treaties guaranteeing Belgian neutrality for the duration of the war. These treaties were signed by France and the North German Federation on Aug. 9 and 26, respectively, in 1870, to be observed during the war and one year thereafter, when matters were to continue as before. Now the secret agreement of the entente bound England to aid France as an ally, but the fact was unknown even to the members of the British Cabinet until it was revealed in the speech of Sir Edward Grey before Parliament on Aug. 2, 1914. This revelation led to the resignation of John Burns, Minister of Commerce, and that of two other members of the Cabinet, Lord Trevelyan and Mr. Morley, who thus renounced their political careers as a protest against the situation into which Sir Edward Grey had led the country. The leader of the Labor Party also resigned, and Arthur Ponsonby publicly denounced the practices of the Minister for Foreign Affairs in a letter in which he said that they had been assured again and again that Great Britain was under no obligation to go to the assistance of France, while now they found themselves so hopelessly involved that there was no retreat. Through the provisions of the entente and the agreement for the defense of the coasts of France, England was now definitely aligned with the enemies of Germany.

On Aug. 4 Great Britain protested against the violation of Belgian neutrality and delivered to the German Government what was practically an ultimatum to the effect that if the neutrality of that country was not respected and a favorable reply received by midnight, the British Ambassador would demand his passports.

## Bethmann's Reichstag Speech

In his speech before the Reichstag on this day the Chancellor said:

Concerning the French complaints in regard to violations of the border, I have received from the Chief of the General Staff the following report: Only one offense has been committed. Contrary to an emphatic order, a patrol of the Fourteenth Army Corps, led by an officer, crossed the border on Aug. 2. They apparently were killed. Only one man returned. However, long before the crossing of the border French fliers were dropping bombs in Southern Germany, and at Schluchtpass the French troops had attacked our border troops. [These assertions were never substantiated by Germany, and are denounced by France as falsehoods.]

Until the present our troops have confined their activity to the protection of our borders. They are now on the defense, and necessity knows no law.

Our troops have occupied Luxemburg, and perhaps have also found it necessary to enter Belgian territory. This is contrary to international law. The French Government has declared in Brussels that it will respect the neutrality of Belgium as long as the enemy respects it. We know, however, that France was ready to attack us. France could wait, but we could not, because a French attack on our lower Rhine flank would have proved fatal.

So we were forced to disregard the justified protests of the Luxemburg and Belgian Governments. We shall try to make good the injustice we have committed as soon as our military goal has been reached. When one is threatened as we are, and when one is fighting for a supreme good, one must consider only how victory can be gained.

That evening, in discussing Great Britain's decision with the British Ambassador, the Chancellor said:

Just for a word—neutrality, a word

which in time of war is so often disregarded—just for a scrap of paper, Great Britain was going to make war on a kindred nation who desired nothing better than to be friends with her. * * * What Great Britain had done was unthinkable, it was like striking a man from behind while he was fighting for his life against two assailants.

England entered the war at midnight. Germany on this day declared war against France, Belgium, and England.

In the outlining of the historical facts cited above no account has been taken of the emotional phase of the situation, out of which has grown a mass of evidence from which it will be extremely difficult to separate the true from the false. We are dealing now with history. What has been cited above indicates the questions at issue. They are still unsettled, insoluble in the heat of conflict.

A recent report seems to strengthen the general belief that the war was the result of a deep-laid plan of the Central Powers, which are represented as having held a conference some weeks before the ultimatum of Austria to Serbia, in which all the possibilities were discussed. It is said that when a few days after this meeting Chancellor von Bethmann Hollweg became convinced that England would enter the war, he wished to withdraw, but it was too late. Among the Allies a settled belief has grown that the German plan involved nothing less than world conquest; that the invasion of Belgium included the plan of obtaining possession of Dunkirk and Calais, whence as a base, and by the aid of submarines, the commerce of the world could be controlled, and whence an expedition could separate the armies of Belgium and France and obtain possession of Paris. Whether this ambitious scheme had a place in the minds of the German military party or not, we can, with the evidence at hand, but leave in the realm of conjecture.

# Legend of the Belgian Francs-Tireurs

## Investigations of the Belgian Documentary Bureau

*Germany has from the beginning based its defense of the atrocities in Belgium upon the assertion that the German soldiers were fired upon by armed Belgian civilians, usually called " francs-tireurs" or " free-shooters." Michel Annebault, a French writer, has dealt with this charge in the appended article, based on the investigations of the Belgian Documentary Bureau:*

THANKS to the notes of the Belgian Documentary Bureau, drawn from the best and surest sources, the German campaign intended to accredit the legend of an organization of Belgian francs-tireurs may be seen in its true light as a villainous fabrication. That campaign was begun with a pamphlet entitled " Confessions of the Belgian Press," (" Der Franktireurkrieg in Belgien: Geständnis der Belgischen Presse.") The Belgian Documentary Records contain this comment: " The publication in question contains no word or mark to indicate who is responsible for it or whence it emanates; yet the leading newspapers of Germany and Austria, including the official organs, have published long analyses of it and given it the benefit of wide publicity."

The German pamphlet accuses the Belgian Government of having instituted, on Aug. 8, 1914, a commission of inquiry " with the object of throwing light upon the violations of international law in Belgium." It pretends that there could not then be any question of violation, as Germany had only just crossed the frontier. [The frontier was crossed on the 3d.] The Belgian Government, it adds, had therefore gone faster than the events. But, either through negligence or through disdain for the truth, a few pages further along the pamphlet cites extracts from the Belgian press reporting the burning and pillaging of the first Belgian towns by the imperial troops.

The German pamphlet then accuses the Belgian Government of having organized that famous war of francs-tireurs, exciting the civil population to rebel against the conquering soldiers. It pretends to find proof of this in the royal decree of Aug. 5, which, according to the Belgian Documentary Bureau, " called into action the reserve regiments of the Civil Guard, and which corresponded with the general call of a nation to arms, issued through one or two Belgian newspapers of the same date." The argumentation of the pamphlet, fantastic in its smallest details, confuses the calling of the Civil Guard reserves with the organization of a war of francs-tireurs.

The Belgian Documentary Bureau goes on to give the antecedents of the Civil Guard, its rules and objects since its creation. It verifies the date and the calling of its inactive members to arms by the decree of the King on Aug. 5. It is shown that there was here no measure of illegal revolt, but a call foreseen in the laws of the guard. But Germany scorns these distinctions.

The German pamphlet continues to accuse the Belgian Government of inciting the civil population to take part in the hostilities. Now, that accusation falls of its own weight when one examines the State telegrams addressed on Aug. 4 to the administrative authorities of the 2,600 communes of the country, reminding them of the duties of the civil population in time of war. Besides, the official advice was reproduced daily by the press. Upon what documents, then, is the accusation based? Upon certain wild stories in the allied press, which gave way, in the first hours of the war, to partisanship, to the demand for legends, to the popular thirst for heroism and exaltation. With a view, evidently very human, to singing the praises of our soldiers and the courage of communities basely attacked, we at that time created the Romanesque and the fantastic. Witness the episode of the " Battle of the Francs-Tireurs of Herstal ":

Two thousand German soldiers, arriving before the arms factory at Herstal, were greeted by a hail of bullets. All the houses, even the smallest, had been transformed into veritable fortresses. Barricades had been thrown up in the streets. The women and children supplied the fighters with ammunition. Repulsed at first, the Germans returned to the charge; then the women poured boiling oil and water on the soldiers, who rolled on the ground, howling with pain. * * *

The Belgian Documentary Bureau adds with reason: " This story is really too sensational to be true." Nevertheless, Germany took note of these newspaper tales, and a part of its accusation is based on them. Since then we have reached a stage of greater modesty and more exactness. The accounts of pillage, thefts, and combats in the cities and the open country are written with names, dates, and details, after the manner of official statements. We have learned that phraseology is a dangerous thing in the hands of those who mutilate even a language.

If one follows the series of studies devoted to the legend of the Belgian francs-tireurs, one finds that the Belgian Documentary Bureau has devoted itself, throughout its notes, to refuting the German accusations, sometimes so inconsistent, with dates and precise facts of undeniable validity. Furthermore, on the subject of combats in which Belgian civilians are represented as taking part, the bureau denounces the sensational unreliability of certain Belgian journals, as exemplified in passages taken from their columns; it shows how they " illustrated with false photographs " the accusations in the German pamphlet.

Finally, it cites before the allied and neutral public the German White Book of May 10, 1915, on the warfare of Belgian civilians, contrary to the law of nations. What bearing has this new White Book on the subject? Does it furnish serious and unpublished documents on the pretended culpability of the Belgian civil population? No; it is nothing but a piece of propaganda, a " copious repetition of grievances long since known and refuted."

The Documentary Records then take up the study of the facts themselves— the fight of the people of Dinant, the case of the curate of Battice, the official protest of Bishop Heylem of Namur, the Austrian ecclesiastical inquiry into the Belgian clergy's participation in the alleged war of armed civilians, the German legends and neutral comments; the bureau gives not only the dates and names, but also the depositions of witnesses. It is piling proofs upon proofs, thus creating one of the strongest indictments of German duplicity and falsehood. * * * The time will come, indeed, when the last of the neutrals will cease to be tempted to search for truth in German documents, knowing them in advance to be mutilated, distorted, and falsified. At the same time they will find that the Belgian Documentary Bureau has done a valuable service in bringing together the simple facts, dates, and names, and in formulating unanswerable official statements, both individual and collective, of all kinds of German barbarity in Belgium.

## La France Vous Salue, Étoiles!

Par EUGENE HOLLANDE
[Le Revue Bleue, Paris]

La France vous salue, étoiles!
Blanches étoiles dans l'azur du fier drapeau
Qui sur Paris flotta si beau
Qu'un frisson fraternel en courut dans nos moëlles,
Voici l'ovation des vivats et des fleurs!
Etoiles du drapeau dont chantent les couleurs,
Etoiles! entendez la France qui salue
Votre triomphante venue!
Nos façades avaient dès longtemps marié
La soie
De nos drapeaux amis qu'un même souffle éploie.
Mais voici que Paris au grand coeur a crié
Sa généreuse joie,
Quand sur les étendards de ce peuple géant
De l'Amérique si lointaine,
Il a vu pour sa cause et pour la cause humaine
Entrer dans le combat le ciel d'outre-Océan,
Témoin auguste
Des champions du Juste
Accourus s'immoler sans regret et sans peur.
Etoiles! dites-leur,
Dites à ces vaillants de la mort volontaire
Que l'honneur de leur race et de leur libre terre
A jamais est en eux!

# THE KAISER'S RESPONSIBILITY

## A Former Ambassador's Analysis of Official Documents Convicts the German Emperor of Forcing the War

### By David Jayne Hill

David Jayne Hill, United States Ambassador to Germany from 1908 to 1911, in the subjoined article—prepared for THE NEW YORK TIMES—has made a new and close analysis of the official reports bearing on the commencement of the war, with the result that he definitely convicts the German Emperor of having caused the great conflict. The Kaiser's acts in the initial crisis, especially as seen now in the light of his recently published telegram to President Wilson, show that Wilhelm's later professions of sympathy with the idea that "in the future the material power of arms must be superseded by the moral power of right" are insincere.

## I.—Germany's Plan to Localize the Conflict

LET us address ourselves to the standard of conduct by which the German Government wishes to be judged, namely, by the nature of the Kaiser's efforts to preserve peace. First of all, allow him to speak for himself. This he has done in his personal telegram to the President of the United States, written on Aug. 10, 1914, first published in August, 1917. It is in substance a detailed statement of the Kaiser's reasons for not desiring the mediation of the President with a view to ending the war and a justification of his desire to continue it.

In this telegram the Kaiser's first point is a complaint against England, which had entered the war on Aug. 4, after the invasion of Belgium. The charge is made that Prince Henry had informed the Kaiser that King George V. had empowered him to give verbal assurance "that England would remain neutral if war broke out on the Continent involving Germany and France, Austria and Russia."

The belief that England would take no part in a Continental war had other grounds than the alleged assurance of the King, for as is well known the German Embassy at London had assured the Kaiser that the internal condition of British affairs absolutely precluded such participation. Although it is officially denied in England that the assurance given by Prince Henry was ever authorized by the King, it is certain that Prince

Henry was in London and that he conversed with George V. The most charitable interpretation of the conversation is that one or the other did not understand the scope of the inquiry made or the implications of the answer, for the journey of Prince Henry was undertaken before there was any actual casus belli and when it was apparently possible that the Austro-Serbian controversy, in which England had no direct interest, might be settled in a judicial manner.

### The Kaiser's Early Intentions

The Austrian ultimatum to Serbia was presented on July 23, and the reply of Serbia was not received at Vienna until the evening of July 25. It was on Sunday, July 26, that Prince Henry, as he informs us in the telegram he sent to King George on July 30, after his return to Berlin, was received by the King at Buckingham Palace. For the message the King had sent to the Kaiser, whatever it was, Prince Henry says in his telegram, "William was very thankful." So far as the Prince's language is concerned, we might suppose the message was that in case any danger of war should arise the King would use all possible means to help in preserving peace. But the Kaiser assures us in his telegram to the President that this was not the message he had sought and which Prince Henry had said he was "thankful for." The grateful communication, according to the Kaiser, was that

France and Germany, Russia and Austria, might fight it out without any interference on the part of England.

Before the Serbian answer was known, therefore, Kaiser William was not only expecting a general Continental war, but he was arranging to confine it to these four powers, a situation which would give to the Central Powers every advantage and the prospect of speedy triumph.

Until July 30, then, the Kaiser, as he himself informs us, was looking for a conflict of arms in which England would take no part. What he was "thankful for," according to his own version of the King's message, which may have been a mistaken one, was not that England would assist in preventing war, but that he could have it on his own terms. This was all he had sought. For peace he had spoken no favorable word.

## Giving Austria a Free Hand

Did he know of the contents of the Austrian ultimatum before July 26, when Prince Henry had his conversation with King George? He may not have dictated the note, but he already knew its contents and had approved them.

> From the beginning of the conflict [reports the German White Book] we assumed the position that there were here concerned the affairs of Austria alone. * * * We therefore directed our efforts toward the localizing of the war and toward convincing the other powers that Austria-Hungary had to appeal to arms in justifiable self-defense, forced upon her by the conditions.

It was also known that Serbia, otherwise helpless, would ask for a hearing by the other powers, particularly Russia, which was to be denied her. On the 26th Russia was warned by the Kaiser that any military measures to defend Serbia from an armed attack by Austria would be followed by German mobilization, and that German mobilization "means war." It was distinctly declared that an attempt on the part of Russia to secure the independence of Serbia as a sovereign State " would unchain a European war." The alternative presented to war was abject submission to the subjugation of Serbia, as the annexa-

tion of Bosnia and Herzegovina had been reluctantly submitted to in 1909 under a similar threat.

On that same day, July 26, Sir Edward Grey made a proposal to submit the differences between Austria-Hungary and Serbia to a conference of the Ambassa-

DAVID JAYNE HILL

dors of Germany, France, and Italy under his Chairmanship. But, the Kaiser then believing that England's intervention was not to be seriously considered, the German White Book asserts:

> We declared in regard to this proposal that we could not, however much we approved the idea, participate in such a conference, as we could not call Austria in her dispute with Serbia before a European tribunal. Faithful to our principle that mediation should not extend to the Austro-Serbian conflict, which is to be considered as a purely Austro-Hungarian affair, but merely to the relations of Austria-Hungary and Russia, we continued our endeavors to bring about an understanding between these two powers.

That is, the "understanding" impressed upon Russia was that any intervention to prevent the attack of Austria upon Serbia would be answered by war, while that impressed upon Austria-

Hungary was that no interference with her humiliation of Serbia would be permitted.

Then, on July 30, came the great disappointment, which Kaiser William frankly sets forth as a personal grievance, and even as a breach of faith on the part of England. " On the 30th," states the next point in his telegram to the President, " my Ambassador in Lon-
" don reported that Sir Edward Grey, in
" course of a ' private ' conversation, told
" him that if the conflict remained local-
" ized between Russia—not Serbia—and
" Austria, England would not move, but
" if we ' mixed ' in the fray she would
" take quick decisions and grave
" measures, i. e., if I left my ally, Austria,
" in the lurch to fight alone, England
" would not touch me."

Here was a turning point. The war between Germany and France, Austria and Russia was then to be blocked. Kaiser William was no longer " thankful." Matters were taking a serious turn. There might be no war at all under these new conditions. Germany's bluff of Russia on the 26th was called by England on the 30th.

To comprehend what this meant to the Kaiser's plans it is important to note what had been occurring in this interval.

## Germany Against Peace

On July 27 the Russian Chargé d'Affaires at Berlin wrote to the Minister for Foreign Affairs at St. Petersburg:

> Before my visit to the Minister for Foreign Affairs today his Excellency had received the French Ambassador, who endeavored to induce him to accept the Britis\ proposal for action in favor of peace, such action to be taken simultaneously at St. Petersburg and at Vienna by Great Britain, Germany, Italy, and France. Cambon suggested that these powers should give their advice to Vienna in the following terms: " To abstain from all action which might aggravate the situation. * * * *Jagow refused point blank to accept this suggestion* in spite of the entreaties of the Ambassador.
>
> *Russian Orange Book, No.* 39.

On July 29 the British Ambassador at Berlin telegraphed Sir Edward Grey:

> I was sent for again today by the Imperial Chancellor, who told me that he regretted to state that the Austro-Hungarian Government, to whom he had at once communicated your opinion, had answered that events had marched too rapidly and that *it was therefore too late* to act upon your suggestion that the Serbian reply might form a basis of discussion.
>
> *British Diplomatic Correspondence, No.* 75.

On the same day, July 29, Czar Nicholas telegraphed to Kaiser William:

> I am glad you are back in Germany. In this serious moment I ask you earnestly to help me. An ignominious war has been declared against a weak country, and in Russia the indignation, which I fully share, is tremendous. I fear that very soon I shall be unable to resist the pressure exercised upon me and that I shall be forced to take measures which will lead to war. To prevent a calamity, as a European war would be, I urge you in the name of our old friendship to do all in your power to restrain your ally from going too far.
>
> *German White Book, No.* 21.

Now follows the telegraphic correspondence of the two Emperors, very actively prosecuted during July 29-31, consisting on the side of the Czar in urgent appeals to the Kaiser to moderate the military procedure of his ally, Austria-Hungary, and on the part of the Kaiser in emphatic demands upon the Czar that he take no military action to stay the attack of Austria upon Serbia, but to remain passive.

The one important observation to be made with regard to the " mediation " which the Kaiser undertook between Austria and Russia is that in the German White Book, published in August, 1914, to show Germany's attitude before the declaration of war by Kaiser William, although the correspondence between the Kaiser and the Czar is published in full, *there is not one word of any attempt on the part of the Kaiser to influence the action of Austria-Hungary against provoking a conflict with Russia!* The part Austria was to play had been already arranged, and the support Germany was to give was fully understood. There is no documentary evidence that the mediation Kaiser William had professed to be engaged in ever actually occurred. The Kaiser's rôle consisted solely until July 30 in flashing his sword in the face of the Czar, with the determination that Europe should have nothing to say about it.

## II.—The Kaiser and King George

With July 30, for the reason already stated, a new chapter opened in the Kaiser's negotiations. He has himself written the introduction to it, and here it is:

This communication (the German Ambassador's telegram of July 30, above referred to) being directly counter to the King's message to me, I telegraphed to H. M. on the 29th and 30th thanking him for his kind messages through my brother, and begging him to use all his power to keep France and Russia, his allies, from making any warlike preparations calculated to disturb my work of mediation, stating that I was in constant communication with H. M. the Czar. In the evening the King kindly answered that he had ordered his Government to use every possible influence with his allies to refrain from taking any provocative military measures. At the same time H. M. asked me if I would transmit to Vienna the British proposal that Austria was to take Belgrade and a few other Serbian towns, and a strip of country, as a " main mise " to make sure that the other Serbian promises on paper should be fulfilled in reality. This proposal was in the same moment telegraphed to me from Vienna for London, quite in conjunction with the British proposal. Besides, I had telegraphed to H. M. the Czar, the same as an idea of mine, before I received the two communications from Vienna and London, as both were of the same opinion.

I immediately transmitted the telegrams vice versa, Vienna and London. I felt that I was able to tide the question over and was happy at the peaceful outlook.

The lack of precision in the Kaiser's statements requires a comment upon his general accuracy as a historian. So far as the records show, it was not by direct communication with King George, but through Prince Henry, that the King was asked to use all his power to keep France and Russia from making any warlike preparations, and it was through the Prince also that he received the reply. (See Nos. 1 and 2 of telegrams exchanged between London and Berlin.) In his telegram of July 30 to King George, Prince Henry expresses the opinion that the neutrality of Russia and France is, perhaps, " the only possible means of preserving the peace of Europe "—which is equivalent to saying that Germany would not tolerate any interference with regard to the rights of Serbia, and rather than do so would unchain a general European war.

### King George's Peace Plea

In his reply to Prince Henry, King George does not say, as the Kaiser reports, that he " had ordered his Government to use every possible influence with his allies to refrain from taking any provocative military measures." What he says is:

I earnestly desire that such a misfortune as a European war—the evil of which could not be remedied—may be prevented. My Government is doing the utmost possible in order to induce Russia and France to postpone further military operations, provided that Austria declares herself satisfied with the occupation of Belgrade and the neighboring Serbian territory as a pledge of a satisfactory settlement of her demands, while at the same time the other countries suspend their preparations for war. I rely on William applying his great influence in order to induce Austria to accept this proposal. In this way he will prove that Germany and England are working together to prevent what would be an international catastrophe. Please assure William that I am doing all I can, and will continue to do all in my power, to maintain the peace of Europe.

The Kaiser informs us that he received the same proposal " from Vienna for London," that he had telegraphed this as his own idea to the Czar, and that he immediately transmitted the telegrams, vice versa, to Vienna and London. The way of peace was thus apparently clearly opened.

### Was This Message Suppressed?

Did the Kaiser in reality act in the sense he has here indicated, or is his statement merely an expression of what as a faithful mediator he ought to have done? The question is of crucial importance.

It is a singular fact that the German White Book in explaining the origin of the war makes no mention of any such message to the Czar. The whole incident is passed over without a reference; and is thus treated, like the Russian proposal that the Austro-Serbian question be referred to The Hague Tribunal, as a matter of no importance. The German White Book purports to give the entire telegraphic correspondence between the Kaiser and the Czar, but there is in it no allusion to a suggestion by the Kaiser similar to the British proposal or of that proposal itself in any form. No proposal was made by the Kaiser to the Czar except unconditional abstention from any intervention on behalf of Serbia under penalty of a European war. The British proposal referred to by the Kaiser as opening the door for peace *was never at any time or in any form communicated by the German Government to the Czar or the Russian Government!*

The Kaiser himself, as we shall soon see, expressly states that he was about to send the British proposal to the Czar, but did not send it. He left the Czar in ignorance of the open door of peace and closed it by a declaration of war.

### Sir Edward Grey's Proposal

The British proposal was never publicly referred to in Germany until Nov. 9, 1916, when Chancellor Bethmann Hollweg justified his Government against the charge by Sir Edward Grey by informing the Reichstag that on July 30, 1914, he had sent the following instruction to the German Ambassador at Vienna:

> Should the Austro-Hungarian Government refuse all mediation, we are confronted with a conflagration in which England would go against us, and Italy and Rumania, according to all indications, would not be with us; so that with Austria-Hungary we should confront three great powers. Germany, as the result of England's hostility, would have to bear the chief brunt of the fight. The political prestige of Austria-Hungary, the honor of her arms, and her justified claims against Serbia can be sufficiently safeguarded by the occupation of Belgrade or other places. We therefore urgently and emphatically ask the Vienna Cabinet to consider the acceptance of mediation on the proposed conditions. Responsibility for the consequences which may otherwise arise must be extraordinarily severe for Austria-Hungary and ourselves.

" The Austro-Hungarian Government," he continues, " acceded to our urgent representations " by giving its Ambassador in Berlin the following instructions:

> I ask your Excellency most sincerely

to thank Herr von Jagow, the Secretary of State for Foreign Affairs, for the information given through Herr von Tschirschki, and to declare to him that, *despite the change in the situation which has since arisen trrowgh the Russian mobilization,* we are quite ready to consider the proposals of Sir Edward Grey for a settlement between us and Serbia. *A condition of our acceptance is, of course, that our military action against Serbia should meanwhile proceed,* and that the English Cabinet should induce the Russian Government *to bring to a standstill the Russian mobilization directed against us,* in which case also we, as a matter of course, will at once cancel our defensive countermeasures forced upon us in Galicia.

The Chancellor does not, however, profess that this answer was sent to Russia.

### Talk of Mediation

Confessedly, it was fear of England that on July 30 changed the attitude of the German Government. " Should the " Austro-Hungarian Government refuse " all mediation we are confronted with a " conflagration in which England would " go against us." The mediation which had up to this point been refused was now advised by the German Government. " Responsibility for the circumstances " that may otherwise arise must be ex- " traordinarily severe for Austria-Hun- " gary and ourselves," concludes the note.

Let us see, then, how Germany acquitted herself of this responsibility:

> While I was preparing a note to H. M. the Czar the next morning [that is, the 31st of July] to inform him that Vienna, London, and Berlin were agreed about the treatment of affairs, I received the telephones from H. E. the Chancellor that on the night before the Czar had given the order to mobilize the whole of the Russian Army, which was, of course, also meant against Germany; whereas up till then the southern armies had been mobilized against Austria.

That report, without waiting for confirmation, although it was known that weeks would be required for an effective Russian mobilization against Germany, put an end to all Germany's efforts for peace.

Regarding the time of receiving this report the Kaiser's mind was evidently in some confusion. In his telegram to the President he says " in the morning," but in his telegram to King George of July 31 he says: " Your proposals coincide with my ideas and with the communication which I have *this evening* received from Vienna, and which I have passed on to London. I have just heard from the Chancellor that intelligence has just reached him that Nicholas this evening has ordered the mobilization of his entire fleet and army." (*Telegram No. 3.*)

### Czar Kept in the Dark

An entire day thus passed and Nicholas had not been informed by the Kaiser of the British proposal. But he had received from the Czar the following telegram, dated at 2 o'clock that day:

I thank you cordially for your mediation, which permits the hope that everything may yet end peaceably. It is *technically impossible* to discontinue our military preparations, which have been made necessary by the Austrian mobilization. *It is far from us to want war. As long as the negotiations between Austria and Serbia continue my troops will undertake no provocative action. I give you my solemn word thereon.* I confide with all my faith in the grace of God, and I hope for success of your mediation in Vienna, for the welfare of our countries, and the peace of Europe.

On that same day the Russian Minister for Foreign Affairs had sent to all Russian Embassies and Legations the following message to be delivered to all Governments:

If Austria consents to stay the march of her troops on Serbian territory, and if, recognizing that the Austro-Serbian conflict has assumed the character of a question of European interest, she admits that the great powers may examine the satisfaction which Serbia can accord to the Austro-Hungarian Government without injury to her rights as a sovereign State or her independence, Russia undertakes to maintain her waiting attitude.

### All for Peace But Germany

Austria also, at the same time the reply was made to the British proposals, sent this to all embassies and legations:

Negotiations dealing with the situation are proceeding between the Cabinets at Vienna and St. Petersburg, and we hope that they may lead to a general understanding.

At the same time Sir Edward Grey, in a telegram, declared:

If Germany could get any reasonable proposal put forward which made it clear that Germany and Austria were striving to preserve European peace and that Russia and France would be unreasonable if they rejected it, I would support it at St. Petersburg and Paris, and go to the length of saying that if Russia and France would not accept it his Majesty's Government would have nothing more to do with the consequences.

On that very day, apparently before the Austrian reply had been received, the German Government sent an ultimatum to Russia which it was known it was technically impossible to accept, and the next day, the twelve-hour limit of time not having been observed, on Aug. 1, war on Russia was formally declared.

## III.—What Rendered War Inevitable

What rendered war inevitable, according to the Kaiser's statement, was that on July 31 a general order of mobilization was issued by the Czar. It mattered nothing that it would require weeks to render the order really effective as against Germany, and that the Czar had assured him, in a telegram dated 2 P. M. of the day war was declared:

I comprehend that you are forced to mobilize, but I should like to have from you, viz., *that these measures do not mean war, and that we shall continue to negotiate for the welfare of our two countries and the universal peace which is so dear to our hearts.* With the aid of God it must be possible to our long-tried friendship to prevent the shedding of blood. I expect with full confidence your urgent reply.

*German White Book. No number.*

Not content to meet Russian mobilization with German mobilization, which the Russian Minister of Foreign Affairs was assured by the German Ambassador even on Aug. 1 " did not mean war," (*Russian Orange Book, No. 70,*) and wholly ignoring the Czar's expressed belief that " these measure do not mean war " and his disposition " to negotiate for the welfare of our two countries and the universal peace," the declaration of war was without delay presented at St. Petersburg.

And what was going on in Germany in these last days of July? On July 30 the Russian Ambassador at Berlin had telegraphed his Foreign Office, " I learn that the order for the mobilization of the German Army and Navy has just been issued." A few hours later this was contradicted and explained by the statement that " the news sheets had been printed in advance so as to be ready for all eventualities, and they were put on sale this afternoon, but that they have now been confiscated."

This step has been considered by Sir Edward Grey as a provocative measure, intended to incite Russia and technically to put her in the wrong. Chancellor von Bethmann Hollweg indignantly denies this, and it is not necessary to insist upon it. It is a fact, however, that " the threatening state of war " (Kriegsgefahrzustand) was announced on July 31.

### French Ambassador's Telegram

An interesting light is thrown upon the subject by the telegram of the French Ambassador, Jules Cambon, sent to the French Minister of Foreign Affairs on July 30, which reads as follows:

Herr von Jagow telephoned to me at 2 o'clock that the news of the German mobilization which had spread an hour before was false, and asked me to inform you of this urgently; the Imperial Government is confiscating the extra editions of the papers which announced it. But neither this communication nor these steps diminish my apprehension with regard to the plans of Germany.

It seems certain that the Extraordinary Council held yesterday evening at Potsdam with the military authorities under the Presidency of the Emperor decided on mobilization, and this explains the preparation of the special edition of the Lokal-Anzeiger, but that from various causes (the declaration of Great Britain that she reserved her entire liberty of action, the exchange of telegrams between the Czar and William II.) the serious measures which had been decided upon were suspended.

One of the Ambassadors with whom I have very close relations saw Herr Zimmermann at 2 o'clock. According to the Under Secretary of State the military authorities are very anxious that mobilization should be ordered, because every delay makes Germany lose some of her advantages. Nevertheless, up to the present the haste of the General Staff, which sees war in mobilization, had been successfully prevented. In any case, mobilization may be decided upon at any moment. I do not know who had issued in the Lokal-Anzeiger, a paper which is usually semi-official, premature news calculated to cause excitement in France.

Further, I have the strongest reasons to believe *that all the measures for mobilization* which can be taken before the publication of the general order of mobilization *have already been taken here,* and that *they are anxious here to make us publish our mobilization first,* in order to attribute the responsibility to us.

*French Yellow Book, No.* 105.

It was after all this, and while the Czar was not informed by the Kaiser of his latest stroke of " mediation " with Austria, that the Russian general order had been issued. Does it appear that the Kaiser was looking for peace or for war? Was there not still, on Aug. 1, 1914, a chance for averting the European catastrophe?

## IV.—The Fateful Responsibility

There is, however, a fourth development, from some points of view the most interesting of all, in Kaiser William's explanation of the origin of the war. Here is his final statement:

In a telegram from London my Ambassador informed me he understood the British Government would guarantee the neutrality of France and wished to know whether Germany would refrain from attack. I telegraphed to his Majesty the King personally that mobilization being already carried out could not be stopped,

but if H. M. could guarantee with his armed forces the neutrality of France I would refrain from attacking her, leave her alone, and employ my troops elsewhere. H. M. answered that he thought my offer was based on a misunderstanding, and as far as I can make out, Sir E. Grey never took my offer into serious consideration. He never answered it. Instead he declared that England had to defend Belgian neutrality, which had to be violated by Germany on strategical grounds, news having been received that France was already preparing to enter

Belgium and the King of the Belgians having refused my petition for a passage under guarantee of his country's freedom. I am most grateful for the President's message.

The general mobilization of the German Army is officially reported to have been ordered at 5 o'clock in the afternoon of Aug. 1. The telegram referred to by the Kaiser from the German Ambassador at London had also been sent on that day. In his reply to King George regarding its suggestion, sent in the evening of that day, Kaiser William said: "For technical reasons the mobilization which I have already ordered this afternoon on two fronts—east and west—must proceed according to arrangements made. A counterorder cannot now be given" Was it really a military impossibility to arrest this mobilization which, according to Berlin, had only just been set in motion? Why, then, was not the Czar's plea of "technical reasons" equally good, if not better? But Kaiser William had refused to listen to this, even when accompanied with the most solemn pacific assurances.

## Gave No Pacific Assurances

But the Kaiser did not give any pacific assurances. He would "refrain from attacking France, leave her alone, and employ his troops elsewhere" on condition that H. M. "would guarantee with his armed forces" the neutrality of France! The telegram to arrest mobilization, the Kaiser said, had come "too late." His troops were on the track of a victim. They insisted on being used somewhere.

Had this condition on the French frontier been created since 5 o'clock of that same afternoon, when, as the Kaiser said in his telegram to the King, (No. 6,) his troops were "being kept back by telegraph and telephone from crossing the French frontier"?

Here is what President Poincaré telegraphed to King George on July 31:

The military preparations which are being undertaken by the Imperial Government, especially *in the immediate neighborhood of the French frontier, are being pushed forward every day with fresh vigor and speed.* France, resolved to continue to the very end to do all that lies within

her power to maintain peace, has, up to the present confined herself solely to the most indispensable precautionary measures. But it does not appear that her prudence and moderation serve to check Germany's action; indeed, quite the reverse.
—*Collected Diplomatic Documents, p. 542.*

## Germany the Sole Aggressor

We have now reached the fateful day, Aug. 1, 1914. What was the international situation on that day? Was it, as the German peace proposals profess, "a fatal enchainment of events" that caused the war? There was no war with Russia and France until the Kaiser declared it. There was no desire for war on the part of Russia, France, and England, which were doing all in their power to avert it. There was mobilization in Russia, but it was incomplete, and the honor of the Czar was pledged to the fact that it did not mean war.

In his explanation of his conduct to the President the Kaiser does not claim that Germany was attacked, or that there was any invasion of German soil. He even recited his telegram to the effect that unless the neutrality of France was guaranteed by England's armed forces, he intended to attack her, and only on that condition would he "leave her alone." Nothing that France herself could say or do would save her. In order to attack her successfully, he informs us, "Belgian neutrality had to be violated by Germany on strategical grounds." The reason for this he first wrote was, "*Knowledge* having been received that France was already preparing to enter Belgium"; but knowing this to be demonstrably false and that it was idle to maintain it, he struck out "knowledge," and substituted "*news*," as the photograph of his telegram discloses.

## War Willed by the Kaiser

The Kaiser knew on Aug. 1 that Great Britain had previously asked France and Germany separately if the neutrality of Belgium would be respected, that France had promptly replied in the affirmative, and that by his own orders an answer had been withheld by the Imperial Foreign Office. He knew that the decision to strike France through Belgium had been made before there was any "news" on the subject. In spite of the solemn assurance given by the Government in the Reichstag on May 2, 1913, that "the neutrality of Belgium is guaranteed by international treaty," the passage through Belgium was a part of the Kaiser's military plans.

In view of what we know of German military movements, the Kaiser's reply that the telegram regarding the possible neutrality of France had come "too late" to arrest mobilization was undoubtedly the truth, but it was not too late to prevent the war. Even after the declaration had been formally delivered at 5 P. M. of Aug. 1 at St. Petersburg, its operation could have been suspended by a telegram, the Czar's word of honor that his mobilization did not mean war could have been made the reason for a suspension, and the British proposal, which Austria had accepted the day before, but which the Kaiser had never communicated to the Czar, might have been sent to him with the statement that all the others had agreed to it. In that case there would be no need of a European war, and the Austro-Serbian question, after the occupation of Belgrade as a hostage, could have been pacifically and amicably settled.

### The Czar's Illuminating Telegram

That this interpretation of the situation is correct is proved by the telegram of the Czar to King George, sent on Aug. 1, immediately after the Kaiser's declaration of war. Referring to the British proposals, to which Austria had agreed, but of which the Kaiser, the trusted mediator, had given him no information, he says:

I would gladly have accepted your proposals had not German Ambassador this afternoon presented a note to my Government declaring war. Ever since presentation of the ultimatum at Belgrade, Russia has devoted all her efforts to finding some pacific solution of the question raised by Austria's action. Object of that action was to crush Serbia and make her a vassal of Austria. Effect of this would have been to upset balance of power in Balkans, which is of such vital interest to my empire. Every proposal, including that of your Government, was rejected by Germany and Austria, and it was only when favorable moment for bringing

pressure to bear on Austria had passed that Germany showed any disposition to mediate. Even then she did not put forward any precise proposal. Austria's declaration of war on Serbia forced me to order a partial mobilization, though, in view of threatening situation, my military advisers strongly advised a general mobilization owing to quickness with which Germany can mobilize in comparison with Russia. I was eventually compelled to take this course in consequence of complete Austrian mobilization, of the bombardment of Belgrade, of concentration of Austrian troops in Galicia, and of secret military preparations being made in Germany. That I was justified in doing so is proved by Germany's sudden declaration of war, which was quite unexpected by me, as I have given most categorical assurances to the Emperor William that my troops would not move so long as mediation negotiations continued.

In this solemn hour I wish to assure you once more that I have done all in my power to avert war. Now that it has been forced on me, I trust your country will not fail to support France and Russia. God bless and protect you.—*Collected Diplomatic Documents, p. 537.*

It was only England's insistence on an effort for peace that caused the German Government to put the British proposal before Austria, and only the fear of England's action—as the note of instruction of July 31 to the German Ambassador at Vienna plainly says—that induced the Kaiser to urge Austria's acceptance.

### Placing the Responsibility

On Aug. 1, when the fatal plunge was finally made at 5 P. M., the situation was again altered. By emphasizing Russia's war preparations, which in extent bore no comparison with those of Germany, and by failing to inform Russia of Austria's real attitude regarding the British proposal, the Kaiser believed he had successfully played England and loaded upon Russia the whole responsibility for the war. With Lichnowsky's telegram suggesting the neutrality of France through England's influence in his hands, he now had even more than what Prince Henry had said he was "thankful for"—the evident indisposition of England to engage in the war and even the possible neutrality of France. Prevent the war under these conditions? By no means.

France might be spared if England would guarantee with her armed forces, military and naval, that France would not regard her treaty obligations with Russia and would offer no resistance. Very eager was he, who spoke with such resentment of leaving his " Austrian ally in the lurch," either to force France to violate her treaty obligations to Russia or, in order to crush her, himself to violate the most sacred of pledges by extorting from Belgium the privilege of attacking France by the possession of her forts and the use of her territory as the price of Belgium's " freedom "!

### The Kaiser's Guilt

If one wishes to know the state of the Kaiser's mind on the day he declared war and lighted the conflagration which has set the whole world ablaze, let him read and reread that telegram of Aug. 1 to King George when the Kaiser believed for a short time that all which his embassy at London had told him was true; that England was weak, divided, preoccupied, and would be in a short, swift war after all a negligible quantity. Let the reader grasp the lofty arrogance of it. The Kaiser hopes " France will not be nervous! " He is holding back his troops by telegraph and telephone from crossing the frontier. The Chancellor telegraphs to London that Germany will give England until 7 P. M. on Monday, Aug. 3, to furnish it armed guarantee that France will remain neutral. If not, then— And England is now accused of having caused the war!

And today, with this record behind her, balked and hemmed in on sea and land by walls of steel that are closing in upon her like the shears of fate, Germany professes to accept all that she has for years strenuously opposed—the idea of obligatory arbitration, disarmament, respect for law; but without confession, without contrition, without a surrender of property to which she has no right except that of the housebreaker, and without formally abandoning her lust for gain through annexations and indemnities. This to a conscientious mind would seem monstrous; but to say that the Kaiser has kept the pledge for peace he is said to have made twenty-six years ago and " to the last moment has directed his efforts toward settling the conflict by peaceful means," is to reveal an absence of a sense of responsibility so complete as to justify a suspicion of untrustworthiness regarding every profession which such a Government may make.

# Russia's Mobilization as a Cause of War

## Testimony of General Yanushkevitch

THE fateful call to arms in Russia has been charged from the beginning with being responsible for precipitating the war. The German Kaiser and Chancellor have repeatedly asserted that Germany's course was due to Russian mobilization. As late as Sept. 5, 1917, Chancellor Michaelis, referring to the testimony given at the Soukhomlinoff trial by the Russian Chief of Staff, General Yanushkevitch, stated that " it was calculated to destroy the legend of Germany's guilt of starting the war." He further said: " It is now irrefutably established that it was not Germany who chose the time for the war, but a military party surrounding the Czar, which was under the influence of France and England."

The testimony of General Yanushkevitch on this point was reported in the Novoe Vremya of Petrograd as follows:

At first it was decided to declare only a partial mobilization of four districts, in order to frighten Austria-Hungary, but afterward this question was reconsidered, and on July 30, after my report to the ex-Czar, the order of the Senate for the general mobilization was signed by him. In my insistence on the general mobilization I said then that it was necessary definitely to manifest our relationships not only to Austria, but also to Germany, who was backing her up. Coming from Peterhof, I appeared at a sitting of the Council of Ministers, and brought the order as to the mobilization signed the sovereign.

But the same day, about 11 o'clock in the evening, I was called up on the telephone by the sovereign. The question was put to me in what stage was the mobilization. I answered that the matter was already in motion. The further question was put to me, was it not possible not to declare a general mobilization; was it not possible to substitute for it a partial mobilization with reference merely to Austria-Hungary. I replied that that would be exceedingly difficult, that it would threaten catastrophic consequences, that 400,000 reserves had already been called up. Then it was definitely stated to me by the ex-Czar that he had received a telegram from Wilhelm, in which the latter guaranteed on his word of honor that if the general mobilization was not declared the relationships between Russia and Germany would remain friendly as in the past.

After this conversation with the ex-Czar I drove to the Minister for Foreign Affairs, Sazonoff, and convinced him that it was then impossible to alter the general mobilization. It was decided that in the morning he should make a fresh report to the sovereign. He did make that report, and at half-past 4 on the following day a Court Council was held, in which the Minister for Foreign Affairs, Sazonoff, the War Minister, Soukhomlinoff, and I took part. In some ten minutes we decided that there was no possibility of revoking the general mobilization, and that a revocation would be fatal for Russia.

General Yanushkevitch remarked that the contents of all his telephonic conversations, including those with the Czar, were well known to the German General Staff. Every time he got into telephonic connection with any one he heard the sound of the joining up of a third wire.

When General Yanushkevitch had finished, the accused General Soukhomlinoff rose and asked that he might be allowed to supplement the former's deposition. He said:

### Soukhomlinoff's Testimony

On the night of July 30 the ex-Emperor rang me up and ordered me to revoke the mobilization. I received a direct order, a definite order, which did not admit of argument. I went cold all over. The mobilization had already been declared, and the revocation of it threatened a catastrophe. What was I to do? I knew that it was impossible to annul the mobilization, that to do so was technically impractica-

ble, that we should have God knows what confusion in Russia. I felt that I was lost. The Chief of the General Staff has just spoken of this; ask him if you do not believe me. Half an hour after the conversation with the sovereign, General Yanushkevitch rang me up. He told me that the sovereign had informed him of the stoppage of the mobilization. " And what answer did you give him? " I asked Yanushkevitch. " I replied that for technical reasons that was impossible, but, nevertheless, the Czar ordered that the mobilization should be stopped." General Yanushkevitch asked me what was to be done. I answered him: " Do nothing." I heard through the telephone how a sigh of relief burst from him. On the following morning, I lied to the sovereign, telling him that the mobilization was taking place only in the southwestern districts. That day I was beside myself. I knew that full mobilization was being carried out, and that there was no possibility of stopping it. Happily that same day the monarch was talked over, and I received thanks for the excellent carrying out of the mobilization. In the other event I should long ago have been in penal servitude.

Passages from General Soukhomlinoff's diary were then put in, which confirmed this statement in every particular.

## Decision for Mobilization

General Yanushkevitch was again called to settle the point whether the Czar had desired a complete revocation of the mobilization, or merely its restriction to the four southwestern military districts. The ex-Chief of Staff said that he could not recall the details of his conversation with General Soukhomlinoff, but he distinctly remembered that with the ex-Emperor he discussed only the question of substituting a partial for a general mobilization. General Yanushkevitch made the following further interesting statement:

On July 29, when the decision as to mobilization existed but had not yet been declared, the ex-Emperor charged me to tell the German Ambassador, Pourtales, the declaration of mobilization by Russia was not an act of hostility to Germany, and to assure him that Russia intended to maintain friendly relations to Germany. I told S. D. Sazonoff of this commission. The Minister had a very poor opinion of the ex-German Ambassador. He said that Count Pourtales would put his own interpretation on it, and advised me rather to

# THE FRENCH DRIVE IN FLANDERS

Some of the Ground Gained by the French. The Officer Is Examining the New German Defensive Positions.
*(Photo Pays de France.)*

LE MORT HOMME AS IT IS TODAY

The Famous Hill After It Had Been Swept by French Artillery Fire and Captured by French Infantry.
(Photo Pictorial Press.)

discuss the matter with the German military agent, who understood these questions better.

The military agent came on my invitation to the General Staff. Previously he had always appeared in military uniform, arrived punctually at the appointed hour, and spoke only Russian. That day he kept me waiting for him a whole hour, appeared in civilian clothes, and spoke only French. I pointed out that Russia cherished no aggressive aims against Germany. The Major replied that, unfortunately, mobilization had begun in Russia. I assured him that it had not yet begun. Then the military agent, with excessive confidence, declared that he had more precise information on that point. I gave him the word of honor of the Chief of the General Staff that at that moment, exactly 3 o'clock on July 29, mobilization had not yet been declared. I fixed that important point in my memory in all its details. The Major did not believe me. I offered to put it into writing. He politely declined. I considered it right to give him such a note, because, as a matter of fact, at that moment there was no mobilization. The order with regard to it was still in my pocket.

In the report printed in the Retch, the opening of General Yanushkevitch's statement reads as follows:

When the inevitability of war became clear I insisted to the Emperor on the necessity of declaring a general mobilization, and not a partial one, because it was obvious that Germany was backing up Austria and that war with Germany was inevitable. The monarch replied that a general mobilization threatened war not only with Austria but also with Germany. However, regarding this war as inevitable, I insisted on the declaration of general mobilization, and on July 29 went to the Council of Ministers, where I secured the signatures of the three Ministers necessary under our law for the declaration of mobilization.

## French Historian's Comment

*Joseph Reinach, the French historian, commenting on the foregoing testimony, summed up the case as follows:*

Germany believed the other day that it had found some sort of argument on its side in the testimony of General Yanushkevitch at the Soukhomlinoff trial. It seems that the Russian Emperor, on July 29, about 5 or 6 o'clock in the evening, on the advice of his Ministers of War and of Foreign Affairs, ordered a general mobilization; and that he tried to suspend the order later in the evening upon receipt of a telegram from the German Emperor. We have reason to believe the facts are accurately stated.

Leaving out of account the Czar's attempt to revoke his order in the evening, the decree for the general mobilization of the Russian Army on the 29th was simply a reply to the official order mobilizing the whole Austrian Army, which had been signed on the 28th. (Dispatch of Schebeko to Sazonoff, Orange Book, No. 47.) The order for the general mobilization of the German Army was signed on the 29th. The signature of an order is one thing, the promulgation of it is another thing. The promulgation of all three decrees for general mobilization took place on the same day—the 31st—Austria's at 1 o'clock in the morning, Russia's in the forenoon, Germany's at noon.

The German Emperor has never yet tried to explain why he did not accept the proposition of the Czar Nicholas " to submit the Austro-Serbian problem to The Hague Conference," (July 29;) nor why, on the same date, having refused the first British proposal of a conference, he repulsed the new British proposition that he himself should decide upon the method of mediation to be undertaken by the four powers—Germany, Great Britain, France, and Italy—between Austria and Russia; nor why, on Aug. 1, he declared war on Russia, when on the same day Austria had accepted mediation upon " the litigious points of her ultimatum to Serbia," and even upon the main issue, as shown on Aug. 1 by the declarations of the Austrian Ambassador at St. Petersburg and of the Austrian Ambassador at London.

The Kaiser is so well aware that he prepared, willed, and let loose this war at his own hour that no proposition will ever come from him offering to submit the question of the responsibility for the war to a neutral commission whose competence and impartiality shall be above suspicion.

# The Kaiser and King George

## Documents That Refute the German Emperor's Statement About British Neutrality

CURRENT HISTORY MAGAZINE for September printed a hitherto unpublished telegram sent by the German Emperor to President Wilson on Aug. 10, 1914, and made public by former Ambassador Gerard, in which the Kaiser stated that King George had sent him a verbal assurance that " England would remain neutral if war broke out on the Continent involving Germany and France, Austria and Russia." The official documents of the correspondence between King George and the Kaiser were printed in the North German Gazette in the third week of the war, and it will be observed that the statement he ascribed to King George in his cablegram to President Wilson was not justified by the actual context of the telegrams as they appear in the German official documents.

The documents on the exchange of views between Germany and France as officially promulgated by Germany in the North German Gazette Aug. 21, 1914, were as follows:

*Official documents relating to the political exchange of views between Germany and England immediately before the outbreak of the war are published below. These communications elucidate the fact that Germany was prepared to spare France provided England remained neutral and guaranteed the neutrality of France.*

Telegrams exchanged between London and Berlin, July 30-Aug. 2, 1914:

### No. 1.

His Royal Highness Prince Henry of Prussia to his Majesty King George, dated July 30, 1914.

I arrived here yesterday, and have communicated what you were so good as to say to me at Buckingham Palace last Sunday to William, who was very thankful to receive your message.

William, who is very anxious, is doing his utmost to comply with the request of Nicholas to work for the maintenance of peace. He is in continued telegraphic communication with Nicholas, who has today confirmed the news that he has ordered military measures which amount to mobilization, and that these measures were taken five days ago.

We have also received information that France is making military preparations, while we have not taken measures of any kind, but may be obliged to do so at any moment if our neighbors continue their preparations. This would then mean a European war.

If you seriously and earnestly desire to prevent this terrible misfortune, may I propose to you to use your influence on France, and also on Russia, that they should remain neutral? In my view this would be of the greatest use. I consider that this is a certain, and perhaps the only possible, way of maintaining the peace of Europe. I might add that Germany and England should now, more than ever, give each other mutual support in order to prevent a terrible disaster, which otherwise appears inevitable.

Believe me that William is inspired by the greatest sincerity in his efforts for the maintenance of peace. But the military preparations of his two neighbors may end in compelling him to follow their example for the safety of his own country, which otherwise would remain defenseless. I have informed William of my telegram to you, and I hope that you will receive my communication in the same friendly spirit which has inspired it.

(Signed) HENRY.

### No. 2.

His Majesty King George to his Royal Highness Prince Henry of Prussia, dated July 30, 1914.

Thanks for your telegram. I am very glad to hear of William's efforts to act with Nicholas for the maintenance of peace. I earnestly desire that such a misfortune as a European war—the evil of which could not be remedied—may be prevented. My Government is doing the utmost possible in order to induce Russia and France to postpone further military preparations, provided that Austria declares herself satisfied with the occupation of Belgrade and the neighboring Serbian territory as a pledge for a satisfactory settlement of her demands, while at the same time the other countries suspend their preparations for war. I rely on William applying his great influence in order to induce Austria to accept this proposal. In this way he will prove that Germany and England are working together to prevent what would be an international catastrophe. Please assure William that I am doing all I can, and will continue to do all that lies in my power, to maintain the peace of Europe.

(Signed) GEORGE.

### No. 3.

His Majesty the Emperor William to his Majesty King George, dated July 30, 1914.

Many thanks for your friendly communication. Your proposals coincide with my ideas, and with the communication which I have this evening received from Vienna, and which I have passed on to London. I have just heard from the Chancellor that intelligence has just reached him that Nicholas this evening has ordered the mobilization of his entire army and fleet. He has not even awaited the result of the mediation in which I am engaged, and he has left me completely without information. I am traveling to Berlin to assure the safety of my eastern frontier, where strong Russian forces have already taken up their position.     (Signed) WILLIAM.

### No. 4.

His Majesty King George to his Majesty the Emperor William, dated Aug. 1, 1914.

Many thanks for your telegram of last night. I have sent an urgent telegram to Nicholas, in which I have assured him of my readiness to do everything in my power to further the resumption of the negotiations between the powers concerned.     (Signed) GEORGE.

### No. 5.

German Ambassador at London to the German Imperial Chancellor, dated Aug. 1, 1914.

Sir Edward Grey has just called me to the telephone and has asked me whether I thought I could declare that in the event of France remaining neutral in a German-Russian war we would not attack the French. I told him that I believed that I could assume responsibility for this.     (Signed) LICHNOWSKY.

### No. 6.

His Majesty the Emperor William to his Majesty King George, dated Aug. 1, 1914.

I have just received the communication of your Government offering French neutrality under the guarantee of Great Britain. To this offer there was added the question whether, under these conditions, Germany would refrain from attacking France. For technical reasons the mobilization which I have already ordered this afternoon on two fronts—east and west—must proceed according to the arrangements made. A counterorder cannot now be given, as your telegram unfortunately came too late; but if France offers me her neutrality, which must be guaranteed by the English Army and Navy, I will naturally give up the idea of an attack on France and employ my troops elsewhere. I hope that France will not be nervous. The troops on my frontier are at this moment being kept back by telegraph and by telephone from crossing the French frontier.

(Signed) WILLIAM.

### No. 7.

German Imperial Chancellor to the German Ambassador at London, dated Aug 1, 1914.

Germany is ready to agree to the English proposal in the event of England guaranteeing, with all her forces, the unconditional neutrality of France in the conflict between Germany and Russia. Owing to the Russian challenge, German mobilization occurred today, before the English proposals were received. In consequence our advance to the French frontier cannot now be altered. We guarantee, however, that the French frontier will not be crossed by our troops until Monday, Aug. 3, at 7 P. M., in case England's assent is received by that time.

(Signed) BETHMANN HOLLWEG.

### No. 8.

His Majesty King George to his Majesty the Emperor William, dated Aug. 1, 1914.

In answer to your telegram, which has just been received, I believe that there must be a misunderstanding with regard to a suggestion which was made in a friendly conversation between Prince Lichnowsky and Sir Edward Grey, when they were discussing how an actual conflict between the German and the French Army might be avoided, so long as there is still a possibility of an agreement being arrived at between Austria and Russia. Sir Edward Grey will see Prince Lichnowsky early tomorrow morning, in order to ascertain whether there is any misunderstanding on his side.

(Signed) GEORGE.

### No. 9.

German Ambassador at London to the German Imperial Chancellor, dated Aug. 2, 1914.

The suggestions of Sir Edward Grey, based on the desire of creating the possibility of lasting neutrality on the part of England, were made without any previous inquiry of France, and without knowledge of the mobilization, and have since been given up as quite impracticable.

(Signed) LICHNOWSKY.

# The Systematic Exploitation of Belgium

*Germany is draining every department of Belgium's economic life, its commerce, agriculture, and industry, as well as the public and private savings of the nation. A careful estimate of the extent of these depredations, up to the Autumn of 1917, by the Nouvelles de France is here translated for CURRENT HISTORY MAGAZINE.*

IT was by means of requisitions that the Germans first sapped the commerce and industry of Belgium. From the first days of the invasion the military authorities have levied innumerable requisitions, the greater part of which have had nothing to do with the support of the troops of occupation, and these requisitions have been multiplied incessantly, both by the local authorities and by the Berlin Government. In general, no trace of these military exactions is to be found in the regularly published official documents, except when they are made under official orders from the central military authorities, and such documents are seldom accessible outside of Belgium.

On the other hand, the requisitions ordered by the civil Government of the occupied territory are made by virtue of orders published in the Official Bulletin of Laws and Decrees for the Occupied Territory, (*Gesetz und Verordnungsblatt für die okkupierten Gebiete Belgiens.*) Up to Sept. 12, 1916, there appeared in this bulletin eighty-nine orders dealing with 400 different kinds of raw materials and manufactured products. (See pictures and text in " Les Déportations Belges à la Lumière des Documents Allemands," by Fernand Passelecq: Paris, Berger-Levrault, 1917, pp. 133-157.) From September, 1916, to July 6, 1917, fifty-one new orders were published in the Official Bulletin, most of them striking at products not yet seized by preceding orders. True, some decrees merely order the declaration of certain products, without calling for their seizure, but the seizure usually follows closely upon the declaration.

To the requisitions of products and raw materials must be added the carrying away of tools. A great number of factories have been systematically robbed of their machinery, which has been transported to Germany.

These diverse requisitions, prescribed by the civil authorities, have been executed ever since August, 1914, in accordance with a preconceived and carefully studied plan worked out by Walter Rathenau for the German War Ministry.

## Belgium in Fetters

These civil requisitions, in conjunction with those of the military authorities, have ruined Belgian commerce and industry, attacking, as they do, every branch of activity, some striking the factories, farms, and domestic trade, others placing fetters upon exports and imports, as well as upon the transport of merchandise. They have been completed by interdicting certain public works in Belgium, and by forbidding the continuance of certain manufactures and the employment of men upon them, with a view to keeping the raw materials for German industries.

Finally, the working population itself has been struck directly. It was, indeed, by a Machiavellian calculation that the Germans caused an enforced state of unemployment in Belgium, in order that this might be used as a pretext for deporting Belgian workingmen to Germany to serve in the war industries of the empire. (See " Les Déportations Belges," pp. 3, 107, 180, 225.)

The deportations for forced service took away from Belgium, in the period from October, 1916, to the end of January, 1917, at least 120,000 men. Since then, under pressure of the universal public conscience and the official protests of neutrals, the Germans have had to promise to renounce the violent removal of workers for compulsory labor in Germany; but *they continue to practice such deportations for forced service on the German front in France*, as well as recruiting for Germany by means of false promises and moral constraint.

## " German Industrial Bureau "

This latter manoeuvre has been revealed unintentionally by the German press itself. Two circular letters appeared in the newspapers in June, 1917, inviting German manufacturers who are in need of men to get them from the German Industrial Bureau, (Deutsches Industrie Büro,) that is to say, from the same organization which at the time of the violent deportations in the Winter of 1916-17 was already doing business in Belgium, trying to force the designated victims to sign at the moment of departure a contract making them appear to be voluntary workers in Germany.

The two circulars, proving that this German Industrial Bureau is still active in Belgium, appeared in the Hamburger Nachrichten, (Morgen Ausgabe, June 19, 1917;) the Münchener Zeitung, and the Münchener Neueste Nachrichten, No. 302—both of June 18, 1917.

Nor are these circulars the only German documents in which can be found an official confession that the pillage of Belgium is still going on for the benefit of German industry and German warfare. A new proof of it may be found in a circular by Mr. Schröder, Director of the Federation of German Metallurgists, dated Jan. 2, 1917, stating that by order of the Bureau of Munitions and Arms (Department of Manufactures) he is commissioned to serve as intermediary to procure for German factories the mechanical equipments obtained in the occupied countries.

The Germans have pushed their monopoly of Belgian industries to such lengths that they have not hesitated to commit infractions of the common law, such as the violation of trade secrets. A typical case is that of Dr. Emile Bronnert, who, armed with a permit from the War Ministry at Berlin, gained control of the industrial secrets of the artificial silk factory of Obourg, in the Province of Hainaut, at the end of 1916.

## Exactions of Money

Not content with exhausting Belgium's commercial and industrial vitality, the Germans have drained its financial resources with equal tyranny, as follows:

1. After establishing the compulsory circulation of the mark at the rate of 1.25 francs, they applied—for purposes both of terrorization and of lucre—the iniquitous principle of *collective responsibility* for individual infractions of their complex regulations. Under this principle the German authorities have made a practice of inflicting large fines upon communities and heads of families. Besides these there were the special war contributions levied in 1914 at the time of the invasion. The war contributions and fines known with certainty through official documents already exceed 200,000,000 francs, or $40,000,000. (See " Les Déportations des Belges," p. 158, note, and p. 176, Section B.) Many of them date from the period before December, 1914.

2. By an order issued Dec. 10, 1914, Belgium was struck with a war levy out of all proportion with the needs of the occupying army. First fixed at 40,000,-000 francs a month, it was increased successively to 50,000,000, then to 60,000,-000 francs ($12,000,000) a month, under the orders of Nov. 20, 1916, and May 21, 1917. The total paid up to Aug. 10, 1917, was 1,440,000,000 francs, or $288,000,000.

3. The Germans inflicted upon Belgium a whole series of taxes, either by creating new ones or by modifying the existing scale of imposts, all in violation of The Hague Convention.

4. On Sept. 12, 1916, the Germans seized 430,000,000 marks, constituting the cash balances—in German bank notes—of the Banque Nationale and the Société Générale de Belgique, which are not Government banks, but private corporations enjoying rights of issue under State regulation. The Germans compelled the deposit of these funds in the Reichsbank upon conditions wholly to their advantage and very burdensome for the Belgian banks. (See " Les Déportations Belges," pp. 158-159.)

## Germany's Total Plunder

Though it is impossible at present to establish the full total of Belgium's losses, some outstanding facts and figures—necessarily incomplete — can be cited:

A war levy of $288,000,000 up to Aug. 10, 1917.

Individual war contributions and fines of about $40,000,000 up to the end of the year 1914.

The carrying away of tools and machinery and the requisitions of raw materials, $400,000,000 up to the end of January, 1915, according to the estimate of a German, Dr. Ludwig Ganghofer, a special correspondent of the Münchener Neueste Nachrichten. (See that journal, issue of Feb. 26, 1916.)

Losses due to forced idleness of workmen and the cessation of industry: These are enormous, but the data are still insufficient to furnish even an estimate.

General destruction of resources and economic wealth—not counting the destruction of property, which is going on continually: The official Norddeutsche Allgemeine Zeitung, in a dispatch from Brussels dated Dec. 29, 1914, and reproduced by the whole German press, estimated the total up to the end of 1914 at "five billions" (marks or francs?).

Thus, if we estimate the total only of the definite items above mentioned at 8,000,000,000 francs, ($1,600,000,000,) we shall have a moderate valuation of the loss, and one certainly far below the reality. To figure out the total damage to be repaired in Belgium it would be necessary to add several more billions of francs. As for the advantages gained by Germany from the occupation and exploitation of Belgium, it will suffice to recall the testimony of General von Bissing, former Military Governor, who wrote in his "Political Testament," (edition annotated by F. Passelecq, Paris, Van Oest, 1917, p. 9):

"Before quitting the military and "strategic viewpoint I must call atten- "tion to the fact that the industrial "territory of Belgium is of great value, "not only in time of peace, but also in "case of war. The supplementary ad- "vantages which we have derived in the "present war from Belgian industries, "by the carrying away of machines, &c., "must be accounted fully as great as the "injury caused to the enemy by the dep- "rivation of these resources. The im- "mediate importance of the industrial "region of Belgium does not exhaust the "interest of the subject for us. *With- "out Belgian coal, what would have be- "come of our policy of exchange with "Holland and the northern countries? "The 23,000,000 tons taken annually "from the Belgian coal mines have given "us a monopoly on the Continent which "has contributed to assure our exist- "ence.*"

# A Protest From the Mayor of Lille

The following poignant letter of protest from the Mayor of Lille, in Northern France, is dated July 17, 1917, and offers fresh proof of the continuous nature of the extortions practiced by the German invaders upon the unfortunate inhabitants of the occupied regions. The original text appeared in the Paris Figaro of Oct. 13, and is here translated for CURRENT HISTORY MAGAZINE:

*The Mayor of Lille to His Excellency General von Gravenitz:*

EXCELLENCY:

I have received your letter of July 4, No. 13917, and its contents have caused me profound stupefaction.

Scarcely have we paid over the money for a forced levy of 24,000,000 francs, when you demand the payment of a new sum of 33,000,000.

During the first year of the occupation, when the City of Lille still possessed a large proportion of its resources, you demanded from it, in various forms, the sum of 28,000,000 francs. During the second year, a total of 30,000,000. And during the third year, when the city is in the deepest distress, when its trade is annihilated, its stores closed, its industries destroyed, you double the tribute and raise it to the sum of 60,000,000 francs.

Such exactions, *ceaselessly increasing,* are as exorbitant as they are unjustifiable. They are contrary to the spirit and the letter of The Hague Convention. They are in absolute contradiction to the comment made upon that convention by the German General Staff itself, as I clearly showed in my correspondence of last year. These fixed contributions, devoid of all justification, rest upon the most arbitrary basis. In place of diminishing, they increase in proportion as the requisitions, ruins, and devastations accumulate upon the unhappy city.

In closing you threaten us with the most rigorous punishments in case of resistance to your will, notably with a fine of more than 1,000,000 francs for every day in arrears.

In these circumstances, if nothing were involved except my personal security and that of a few notables, I would not hesitate to reply with a formal refusal to ex-

actions which seem to me to be an abuse of power and a violation of right. But the destiny of a whole population, weakened by three years of sufferings, is at stake, and I do not feel that I have the courage to expose the people to new rigors.

Consequently I come to declare to you, in the name of the City Council, whose spokesman I am, that the City of Lille, bowed under oppression, isolated from the outer world, powerless to appeal to any tribunal from the arbitrary tyranny to which it is subjected, will pay the new tribute on the dates indicated, but that it will pay with the knife at its throat.

The Mayor of Lille,
CHARLES DELESALLE.

# A Chapter of German Atrocities
## Inhumanity on Land and Sea

CURRENT HISTORY MAGAZINE *in previous issues has printed various official and well-authenticated stories of atrocities, and it will present further details from time to time, as they are revealed, so that this lamentable phase of the world war may be definitely recorded.*

H. PERRY ROBINSON, a correspondent in France for The Associated Press, on Oct. 15, 1917, sent the following account of the act of Germans in firing on the Red Cross:

" In the mud wilderness where the armies now confront each other there are many German dead and wounded out in front of our lines. German stretcher parties are continually at work retrieving the latter. In this service they come close up to our posts and are never by any chance molested. When they have come close to our line our men have more than once seen them hit by German shells.

" Our stretcher parties are also moving about, and so far from their being respected it is a fact that in some units the proportion of casualties among the stretcher bearers has been higher than among the infantry in the fighting line. Some of these casualties, of course, are caused accidentally by shellfire, but a much greater number are the result of deliberate sniping by the Germans, who know quite well whom they are shooting.

" Two days ago a stretcher party was at work when German snipers deliberate-

ly shot three out of four members, killing each one, for the range was short. A British officer in a shell hole close by saw what was happening. He jumped from the hole, seized a Red Cross flag, and, waving it conspicuously before him, marched straight toward the place where the snipers were hiding. He floundered through the mud till he was close by the German position, and the Germans, presumably out of curiosity, held their fire.

" Our officer spoke German well, and when he came within earshot his tongue lashed those Germans as they had rarely been talked to before, pointing to German stretcher parties moving about unmolested, and pouring out his soul in the strongest language he could command.

" The Germans listened in silence. When the officer finished he turned and floundered back again, tossed away the flag, and resumed his place in the shell hole. There's no doubt whatever of the substantial exactness of this incident.

" The German theory of the Red Cross differs entirely from that of all civilized nations. All international Red Cross workers in neutral countries are perfectly aware of the fact that the German

Red Cross is not an organization of mercy, but is as much part of the German military machine as the German artillery, or anything else.

"The Germans have been purposefully bombing hospitals, just as they have torpedoed hospital ships. In conjunction with other things such as stated above it unquestionably shows a deliberate policy which is quite intelligible, the fact being that the Germans know what the Red Cross means to them, and argue that in attacking our Red Cross they are striking at a legitimate military object. In the early days of the war I myself heard German prisoners captured in Belgium declare in all sincerity their belief that Belgian and British nurses and doctors went out on the battlefield for the purpose of murdering German wounded. It was useless to argue with them."

## Firing on Lifeboats

Bryan Wood, an American, whose ship was torpedoed off the Irish coast on Oct. 12, 1917, made the following statement of deliberate firing on lifeboats by the submarine:

"We were attacked early this morning off the Irish coast by two German submarines, which shelled us unmercifully, the shells piercing our steamer fast and furious. One of our party of horsemen named James Fringer, an American, of Roanoke, Va., was killed outright in one of the lifeboats after he had left the ship. Forty-seven of us had got into two lifeboats in order to escape the shells, when the Germans fired on us in the open boats. This was deliberately done to murder us, as we were quite defenseless. A fireman was struck by a shell in the boat, where he lay wounded and unable to rise, in dreadful agony, until rescued by a trawler, when everything possible was done to alleviate his suffering; but the poor fellow died on the rescuing steamer after lingering twenty minutes.

"There were two submarines firing shells and shrapnel at the steamer, when we succeeded in launching only two lifeboats from the starboard side, the lifeboats on the port side being shot away. We managed to get clear of our ship, when the nearest submarine, which was

within measurable distance of us, directed its guns on us. Both the open boats were badly damaged by the shells, which pierced their sides and injured several of their inmates in a fearful manner. One poor fellow lost his eye, the shot carrying away his nose. Another lost his leg, which was shot away. Several of us were wounded dreadfully."

## Deportation of Young Girls

The following letter was recently published in the French newspapers. It was written by a young girl, who relates her experiences when she was forcibly deported from her home and held at hard labor for months without being permitted to communicate with her parents:

BRETEUIL, Aug. 24, 1917.

Sir: I send the following letter so that you may know the truth of what happened in the occupied districts of France, where I have just returned after five months' detention in Belgium.

I lived with my mother and two sisters at —— (Aisne.) On Oct. 11, 1916, the German authorities announced that all the young girls and women without children must appear for roll call the next morning at 5 o'clock at the City Hall. I went. The German policemen classified us and divided us into batches. They chose haphazard twenty young girls and women without telling us for what purpose.

When, despite tears and weeping, the final selection was made they told the people that were chosen to come to the station next morning with their luggage, without permitting their parents to object or even know where they were going. Three young girls from ——, who had been selected, refused; they were forced to obey the policemen, who went to their homes and took them away by force. They were sent off next morning and were treated, during the entire period of their exile, as recalcitrant prisoners.

The mother of one of them, when she found that her nineteen-year-old daughter was being taken from her, resisted the policeman; after having been ill-treated she was put in jail for fifteen days and her daughter was taken just the same. From the 15th of October the parents of the deported girls ceaselessly demanded their return. Dec. 6 the German headquarters, then under the command of X., decided that they might return if others would take their places. Fresh anxiety, fresh anguish.

On Dec. 7 orders were given to the different Mayors that they must furnish complete lists of girls and women without children, without any regard to class, honorability, or conduct.

I and one of my sisters were chosen. My mother, who was very ill, begged permission to keep one of us. I remained on the list and was ordered to the station to leave that same night. More than 150 of us assembled at headquarters. The roll was called in the courtyard of a hotel, and the next day at noon we were put on the train without our parents knowing why or where we were being taken. We traveled as far as X., where we arrived at 7 o'clock on a bitter cold evening. Here soldiers were awaiting us. We were divided according to our districts and sent to the small neighboring villages. In the middle of the night and without knowing where we were going, I was hoisted into a cattle car with my luggage, with four young girls from M. and three from A. At 1 o'clock in the morning we arrived at S., a village of eighty-five inhabitants.

There we were conducted to a deserted house where soldiers had been quartered—it was nothing but a ruin—without being given food or fire. We passed a horrible night, and the next morning the nine of us tried to settle down in this wretched shelter. Two days later we were ordered to report for work, and from the 8th of December until March we were compelled to work under German authority, commanded by soldiers to do the hardest kind of man's work; hauling manure, sorting potatoes. We had to gather up all the mattresses belonging to civilians and empty and refill the straw beds of the German soldiers.

We suffered from cold, and especially from hunger. We were forbidden to touch the piles of potatoes. Sometimes a soldier, more humane than his fellows, let us take a few potatoes.

The greatest cruelty was the strict refusal to let us write to our parents. My mother, like the others, begged the German headquarters for news of us; petitions were signed. Never, from December, 1916, to March, 1917, did she have one word of news. Neither did I. The grief of all our parents was increased by the knowledge that we were mixed in with women of ill repute. I assure you this was the most criminal thing the Germans did—to force us to live in this vile promiscuousness.

In the beginning of March we heard rumors that our native regions had been evacuated. We thought we should never be able to find our families again. We were evacuated March 15 to Belgium; I, without knowing where my mother was.

At the end of much searching I finally found my family. My mother had nearly died of grief, and my own health was so shattered that I have not yet recovered. At Evian, on Aug. 15, I met a young girl who had been deported like me and who had only succeeded in finding her family

a few weeks before. Ten other girls, who were sent to work in the Ardennes, have had no direct news from their families, who are now in Belgium.

## Much Cannot Be Told

Dr. Leon Dabo, an artist and a member of the commission that went from the United States to investigate alleged atrocities in France, made the following statement on Nov. 1, 1917, at a dinner of the Merchants' Association of New York City in the Hotel Astor:

" All that the correspondents send over about the atrocities that have been committed, all the inhumanities, all the bestialities, that no paper can possibly publish—they are not only true, but the worst of them cannot be told. To return from France and to come in contact with America's men and women, to see the civilians on the streets with clean linen on, to see women fashionably dressed, to see the shops wide open, selling the gewgaws of other days; coming from France, coming from the land of the widow, of the orphan, of the maimed, then only did I realize that we as Americans know nothing, nothing, of the slime of the beast.

" One of my distinguished predecessors has just told you that our women and our girls have been protected from the fate that befell the women of France and of Belgium by the British Navy. Men, believe it, it is absolutely true. It is more than true. I have been in a hospital in the Department of Meuse of France where there are nearly a thousand girls; not one is 18 years of age, and all will be mothers. Eleven per cent., in addition, are stark mad."

## The Horrors of War

Harry Lauder, the Scotch comedian, made the following statement from a rostrum in New York City on Oct. 22:

" Read all you can find and look at all the pictures obtainable of the havoc that has been done by earthquake, cyclone, and volcanic eruption in the past and you will not find anything that can compare with the destruction wrought by the Hun. It is so hellish that it outdoes the elements of God in the might of their wrath.

" In one of our hospitals I saw a poor fellow who had one eye and half of his face blown away, and he talked with his mouth twisted up toward his ear. I asked how he received his frightful injuries, and he replied that it was through picking up a fountain pen in a German dugout just after it was captured. 'I was one of the first over the top,' said this remnant of a human, 'and as I fell forward in the dugout from which the Germans had just fled rather hurriedly, I noticed a fountain pen on the floor and put it into my pocket. Two days later I wanted to write a letter home to my wife and children and took the pen out to use it instead of a pencil. As I unscrewed the cap there was a violent explosion, and half of my face was blown clean off, as you see now.'

"I will try to give you a faint idea of what the destruction in France means. You are riding in a military automobile along a road made all but impassable by deep shell holes, pieces of charred wood, and loose stones. The officer who is escorting you explains that you are passing over the site on which three months ago there was a thriving village of 3,000 inhabitants. All that remains are a few curbstones that mark the former location of sidewalks. The town with its people have been wiped out by the Hun as if they had never been.

"I have here a piece of barbed wire which I obtained from a trench before Arras. It is six inches long and has twenty-four barbs, which hold a piece of tartan so firmly that it cannot be torn away except in threads. That little shred of cloth is all that remains of a Highland soldier who was hit by a shell as he struck the entanglements.

"I could tell you of deeds that I have seen and heard of committed by the Hun that would haunt your sleep, and not one word of exaggeration. By the memory of my boy who laid down his life for the cause, you may rely upon it that I would not tell a lie."

## A Message of Thanks From the Queen of Rumania

*Queen Marie of Rumania said to an Associated Press correspondent at Jassy on Oct. 23, 1917:*

The mothers, children, and soldiers of Rumania bless America's great name. Each sufferer well knows that Rumania's ally overseas has come to the rescue in the time of trouble, and as their Queen I voice their gratitude to America, which is the whole-hearted expression of the eight millions of my people. The noble ideals of President Wilson, with which I am in sympathy, touch closely our country, for Rumania entered the struggle in the hope of realizing national unity with the other four million Rumanians beyond the Carpathians. King Ferdinand himself has been the exponent of the principles of democracy. In a message to Parliament before the war he proposed, on his own initiative, that there be a fairer division of lands among the people, and he intended to set the first example by surrendering large estates to be divided among the peasants. In the same message he asked the widest political rights for all his subjects, who previously had voted according to the amount of taxes paid. Later, in answering a petition from the Jews, the King pledged the same rights to them, also.

# Atrocities in Serbia

## Report of Neutral Investigators Regarding Barbarities Committed by Austrians, Hungarians, and Bulgars

*The Holland section of the League of Neutral Countries, in the Autumn of 1917, published the subjoined report, signed by the three officers constituting the permanent committee of the league. After stating that they are in possession of numerous documents, Serbian Government reports, and individual depositions, and that these have been subjected to careful sifting for historical facts, they declare that they have no hesitation in formulating the grave accusations here set forth:*

DEPORTATIONS from Serbia began with the driving forth of 5,000 men, women, and children by the Austrians at the time of the occupation of Belgrade. Because of bad housing and insufficient food one-half of these unfortunates succumbed to typhoid fever in less than a year.

The Bulgarians made their first use of deportations in the countries that had been given to Serbia by the peace of Bucharest in 1913, notably in Southern Serbia and a part of Macedonia. Thus they deported into Bulgaria almost all the Serbian families of Prizren and Prishtina; from Prilep, 170; from Krushevo, 70. At the end of 1915 an order was given to assemble and conduct away all the male population between the ages of 15 and 70 years from the districts of Veles, Poretch, and Prilep, where already torrents of blood had been shed.

The Bulgarian Bishop of Kitchevo, who had just been appointed, protested. He wrote to King Ferdinand that such a measure would demonstrate to the whole world that Macedonia sympathized with Serbia and not with the Bulgarians. This argument may have had some effect; at any rate, the King ordered that the deportations should cease, although the men might already be on the road. However, 500 notables and their families were selected and interned in the environs of Sofia. Their property was immediately confiscated by the Bulgarian Government and most of their houses were rented to Mohammedans.

### Austro-Hungarian Methods

When the Rumanians declared war the deportations were continued in still greater numbers, both by the Austrians and by the Bulgars, reaching their maximum after the capture of Monastir. The victims always included men, women, and children, but especially men of 17 to 70 years. A special method was applied to boys. In May, 1916, the reopening of the schools was announced, and the enrollment lists were accessible. The Austro-Hungarian authorities had the lists copied, and the deportations were based on these.

### Many Thousands Deported

Not less than nine internment camps for Serbs were established in Austria-Hungary, three of the principal ones being situated in the Danube marshes, where the health conditions are extremely bad; the most distant are the camps of Heinrichsgrüs in Bohemia and Braunau in Upper Austria, near the German frontier. In that at Braunau there are not less than 35,000 Serbians; it is quite correct, therefore, to speak of deportations en masse. Among these interned prisoners one finds high officials of the Serbian Government, members of the Council of State, Deputies, besides physicians, lawyers, merchants, &c. The sanitary conditions are very bad in these places, where the Serbs are obliged to live in great wooden barracks that are penetrated by wind and rain; they are ill-fed, and are compelled to sleep upon straw on the ground, where the children, especially, are dying in great numbers. At Braunau there was an epidemic of typhus.

Like the Austrians and Hungarians, the Bulgars have been making deportations since July, 1916, from all the Serbian territory they occupy. The northern part of the country is subject to Bulgarian rule. The families deported by the Bulgarians alone in the last six months of 1916 are estimated at 10,000.

The Bulgarians are inhumane in their treatment of prisoners. They do not permit these unfortunates to prepare themselves, or to take away from their homes even the most indispensable articles, as the Germans do in Belgium. At Nish prominent persons were made prisoner in the streets without permitting them to say good-bye to their families.

The largest Serbian internment camp in Bulgaria is situated in a swampy plain near Sofia, where the families are housed in miserable sheds, and where they are dying of cold, hunger, and wretched sanitary conditions. Thus without any military necessity a part of the Serbian population has been systematically killed. What is the object of such actions? The answer will be found in what follows.

The Austrians, like the Bulgars, began these persecutions at the time of the invasion. They professed a desire to respect the Greek Catholic religion, but they have deported a large number of priests, and have taken possession of churches, seeking to introduce into them the Roman Catholic faith. The Julian calendar, which is intimately connected with the Greek faith, is forbidden, though it is permitted in Bosnia.

## Stamping Out the Language

The attempts against the language of the nation are these:

1. The interdiction of the Cyrilian script, which is also in use among the Russians. In all the names of the streets the Russian characters are replaced by Latin letters; the books and newspapers printed in those characters are forbidden to circulate, though permitted in Bosnia, where even the official journal is printed in both kinds of characters.

2. The confiscation of collections of national poems, though these patriotic songs tell of battles against the Turks and contain absolutely nothing against Austria.

3. The seizure of certain books, among others the poems of Raditchevitch and Zinaï, both Hungarian subjects, whose poems for fifty years have been popular among the Serbs in Hungary; also a book by Dr. Bakitch, former rector of the University of Belgrade, on national education.

4. The closing of the Serbian primary schools, whose teachers have all been dismissed; the opening of a certain number of primary schools organized like those of Hungary, where instruction in German and Hungarian is compulsory, though in Bosnia these languages are not taught. The pupils wear the Austrian uniform and are told that the Emperor of Austria is their sovereign. The placing of hundreds of boys between the ages of 9 and 19 years, (the Austrian Reichspost of Dec. 6, 1916, speaks of more than 800, but according to Serbian advices they number nearly 2,000,) especially collegians, in the camp at Braunau, where they work on the land of the celebrated abbey, and where the monks are trying to make them instruments of Austrian propaganda.

## Destroying the Serbian Church

It has long been known that the Museum of Belgrade was pillaged immediately after the Austrian occupation. The same thing has happened to the Ethnographical Museum, which contained objects of high value. Not a single souvenir of the history or the life of the nation has been left there. The Bulgars have gone still further; they have deported into Bulgaria all the priests of the Serbian Church. The Bulgarian Synod has sent priests from Bulgaria and subjected all the occupied country to the Bulgarian Exarchate, which was obtained by force from the Sultan in 1871, but which the other Orthodox Greek Churches regard as schismatic. All the Serbian churches and convents have been pillaged. All the inscriptions recording the foundation of these institutions by Serbian Princes have been broken with axes. The famous convents of Ravanitza and Manassia have suffered most, though they date from the thirteenth century and had been respected even by the Turks.

Furthermore, whatever the Bulgars have found written in the Serbian language they have destroyed absolutely.

With this object they have made house-to-house search, and have confiscated all the books and manuscripts, even those of the churches, courts, and archives. All these were burned — until the Minister of Commerce at Sofia ordered all papers to be sent to the national printing office, stating that they would make good material for manufacturing paper.

Immediately after occupation the Bulgarian authorities compelled the Serbs, whose family names usually end in "itch," to change that termination to "off," like those of Bulgarian families.

Naturally, it was also at Belgrade that the Serbian teachers were interned; they were replaced by Bulgarians and the Bulgarian language was made compulsory. The children were compelled to learn the popular Bulgarian songs and heard the war explained from the Bulgar viewpoint; they were given to understand that henceforth they were Bulgarians. A great number of reading rooms were opened, whose names recall Bulgarian patriots, and through these centres the authorities are spreading every sort of writing in favor of Bulgarian chauvinism. Thus they are trying to kill the spirit of the Serbian people.

## Recruiting for the Army

As long ago as October, 1916, Prime Minister Pashitch formulated a protest in the name of the Serbian Government against the recruiting of Serbs by the Bulgars. Since then the Serbian Government has received many Bulgarian newspapers that speak openly of such recruiting. These publications refer to Macedonia, but from other sources it is learned that compulsory recruiting has also been introduced into Old Serbia, so that thousands of Serbs are said to have been forced to fight in the Bulgarian army against their own country. We do not know whether Bulgaria has denied this accusation, which is extremely grave.

## Atrocities in Serbia

In Macedonia the Bulgars began immediately after their arrival to put to death the authorities of cities and towns. These murders reached extreme propor-

tions in the three districts of Macedonia which we have mentioned in connection with deportations. The deported victims were generally the objects of the greatest cruelty. Some were obliged to make the journey on foot, poorly clad, without shoes, in the terrible cold; they were given only half a loaf of bread a week. The Bulgarian soldiers drove them onward with blows from rifle stocks, like cattle; many died on the way.

The Austrian soldiers acted with the same brutality, driving children with the bayonet, so that many had to be taken to the hospital at Szegedin; women about to become mothers were forced to march with the rest. Many priests were killed by the Bulgarian troops. By a refinement of cruelty the Serbs who fled are prevented from corresponding with their families who remained behind.

We have believed in these circumstances that it was our duty to cite the facts more in detail than ordinarily. Before the Austro-Hungarian and Bulgarian Governments can clear themselves of the odium imposed by this simple enumeration of facts, they will have to try to draw up a denial of its truth. We believe that such a denial will be very difficult to formulate.

## Trying to Destroy a Nation

The mass of documents placed at our disposal has left a profound impression of an attempt to achieve the complete ruin of a free nation by means the most brutal and cruel. Among all the horrors of war practiced en masse against an entire nation, the worst certainly is the wholesale murder of the Armenians by the Turks under the indifferent or approving eye of the Germans. The systematic destruction of the Serbian Nation is a pendant to the enslavement of Belgium. The latter, perhaps, has suffered more in certain regards, because it is nearer to one of the fronts, but in other respects there is something still more grave in the treatment inflicted upon the Serbians; and the civilized world has known less about it.

Le Temps of Paris has expressed a desire to see the neutral Governments realize that they also have signed the international conventions which have been violated, adding that now is the moment to protest, since they have neglected thus far to do so. We also have formerly expressed the same hope, but our disillusionment has been too great; we will not return to that prayer again. Happily the neutrals that have the power to do so are going to oppose themselves to these crimes, abandoning their neutrality. The only thing we can do is to take care that, later, no one can say that from Holland no voice was raised against such barbarities.

*Permanent Committee of the League of Neutral Countries:*

> NIERMEIJER, President.
> DE LA FAILLE, Home Secretary.
> DIEPENBROCK, Foreign Secretary.

# Austria Favors a Croatian State

EMPEROR CHARLES of Austria-Hungary received a deputation on Oct. 3, 1917, from the Croatian Diet. The President, Dr. Medakovitch, in an address of homage, expressed the wish of the Croat nation for unity. He emphasized its agreement with the kingdom of Hungary quite in the sense of the Hungarian public law, which the Austrian Premier accepted when he declared that the Hungarian Government wished to demand the reincorporation of Dalmatia with Croatia and thus also with the Hungarian State. This was a unionist declaration by the Croatian Diet and implied the alienation of the Serbs in that body, which till the outbreak of the war constituted the sharpest opposition to Serbo-Croatian policy in the interests of Croatism. The Croats now desire the union of Dalmatia, also Bosnia and Herzegovina, as well as the conquered territories, (Montenegro and part of Serbia,) with Croatia. A great Croatia —under Hungary—is their object.

The Emperor Charles replied to the address of homage by praising the Croats' heroism during the war, and declaring that it filled him with joy. They described as the basis of their political activity the bonds established by centuries of history and by laws which comprehend one and the same State community of the Crown of St. Stephen. By defending this State community they could count, within the limits legally settled for their activity—having as its aim the consolidation as well as the intellectual and economic development of the Croat Nation—on the same benevolent feelings on his side as his predecessors on the throne always cherished for the Croat Nation.

The comment by a leading Vienna statesman on the declaration of the Emperor is:

First, this Imperial manifesto will be valued as a success of the new Hungarian Government, which will be able to appeal to it as proof that it can reckon in its efforts for the reincorporation of Dalmatia on the Emperor's demand. The Emperor's declaration should also press into the background the Serbian tendency in Croatia and strengthen the unionist policy of which the representatives adopt the standpoint of the compromise concluded with Hungary in 1863. The Emperor's statement should not be without far-reaching effect in Austria also. While he referred to legally fixed limits for the efforts of a union of the Croats, he indirectly adopted a position against the Slovene plans for the foundation of a South Slav State which should embrace also South Styria, Trieste, Carinthia, and Carniola. For there are no legal limits for this plan of a union of Southern Slavs in a State independent of Hungary. The Slovenes in the Reichsrath must, therefore, be strengthened in their attitude of opposition by the Emperor's utterances and hold fast to a tactical community with Czech union. Against this, the breaking loose of the Croat Deputies from this community is not impossible. If Dalmatia were united with Hungary-Croatia, the Slavs would be weakened in the Reichsrath by the votes of the Croatian Deputies. This possibility will lend a new impulse to the Czechs' opposition. They will, however, undoubtedly utilize the Emperor's statement as an occasion for stronger representation of their demand for a Czech-Slovene State, to the creation of which the new Hungarian Government is strongly opposed. From the circumstance that the Hungarian Government has succeeded in obtaining the Emperor's assent for a solution of the South Slav question corresponding to Hungarian influence it may be deduced that the creation of a Czech-Slovene State cannot count on support in authoritative circles in Vienna at the present time.

# The Reorganization of Rumania

## Story of a Year's Progress Toward Recovery
## From the Disastrous Reverses of 1916

*The French authorities, who were largely instrumental in rehabilitating the shattered military and economic forces of Rumania, have furnished many important facts to the writer of the subjoined article, which is translated for* CURRENT HISTORY MAGAZINE *from Nouvelles de France.*

SINCE December, 1916, when the Rumanian Army fell back behind the Sereth River, Rumania has found two-thirds of its territory invaded by the enemy and its remaining area reduced to the one province of Moldavia. Here the Government, after a hasty exodus from Bucharest, established itself at Jassy with all the institutions of the country, and with the greater part of the population of the capital and the larger cities—Braila, Buzen, Craiova—and even a fairly large contingent of the rural population from Muntenia, Bukowina, and Transylvania. It is Moldavian Rumania, cut off from all communications with Europe, save through Russia, that has had to furnish a refuge for the exiles, hastily improvise hospitals, barracks, offices for the various Government departments from Bucharest, lodge and feed the refugees, care for the wounded and dying soldiers, and provide, besides, for the needs of the Russians co-operating with the Rumanian Army.

Moldavian Rumania found itself denuded of almost everything; even the yield of cereals, important in ordinary times, was scarcely sufficient, because the country's chief agricultural production comes from the plains of the Danube. Even with its cereals, the cattle that have disappeared, and the oil wells that have been destroyed, Rumania had to import some of these commodities before the war. Also meat, butter, milk, vegetables, oil, fats, firewood, had reached very high prices by the beginning of 1917. Colonial commodities and coal were almost totally lacking, clothes and shoes very scarce.

Finally the scarcity of food created a terrible epidemic of spotted typhus, to which were added epidemics of intermittent fever, cholera, and dysentery. Many physicians and nurses of both sexes succumbed to the scourge in tending the patients. It was while struggling against all these difficulties that Rumania, with the help of her allies, achieved her military and economic reorganization and prepared her social transformation. She has done more; she is even giving thought to the period after the war.

### Reorganizing the Army

So far as Rumania's military reorganization is concerned, it has been largely the work of the French mission commanded by General Berthelot and seconded by the devotion of all the Rumanians, from the King to the most humble soldier.

The army had undergone very heavy losses during the retreat, but it had not been reduced to the point of not being able to reorganize. The men from 16 to 50 years had been called to the colors, and in the course of the Winter the army was re-established. About 50,000 wounded were restored to health, and the effectives were increased: (1) by the new recruits of 17 to 18 years, (60,000 in a separate contingent;) (2) by the men of 42 to 50 years; (3) a very large contingent of recuperated men—exempted, excused, invalided men of the period before the war; (4) by a great number of men from the rear who were poured into the fighting regiments.

The officers had suffered less heavy losses, proportionally, and in the course of reorganization the staffs were entirely reconstructed. Schools for officers were established in several centres of Moldavia. Many superior officers were removed and replaced by younger men whose ability had been demonstrated in the course of the campaign. General

Averscu, who had shown his courage, energy, and military capacity, was named for the commanding position to which his conduct had entitled him. The long delay of the Winter was utilized by all the officers in becoming familiar with French methods; these have now replaced the old methods, which were rather German than Rumanian.

The morale of the men has completely changed in this new atmosphere. The warlike qualities of the Rumanian soldier, which are of the first order, have been perfectly understood and brought out by the officers of the French mission.

## Military Equipment

All the efforts made by Rumania before the war to furnish a suitable equipment for its army had been insufficient, as Rumania has no large manufacturing industries. At the beginning of the campaign whole divisions could be seen with nothing but the old equipment, and many of the men were without shoes. During the four months of fighting the stocks could not be replenished, and if the Germans found nothing of this sort in the territory which they occupied, it was because the nation's military supplies had long been exhausted.

At the present moment, (October, 1917,) the improvement is noteworthy. The men are wearing the French helmet. The boot has disappeared and is replaced by the legging. In general the men now look like French troopers.

The German guns and other war material predominant at the moment of Rumania's entry into the conflict have been replaced largely by French arms—field artillery, machine guns, repeating rifles—which the Rumanian soldier handles skillfully. France has provided most of these arms. The artillery is well mounted, the accessories for the heavy guns are ample, the anti-aircraft guns are very good. The knife bayonet has been replaced by the French bayonet.

The army also has an abundance of telephones, of wire, and of trench tools, which were lacking in the Autumn of 1916. The equipment, besides, continues to be increased and completed by constant arrivals, which come by way of Russia.

## New Sanitary Measures

The engineering service has developed in a way unknown before the war, and the system back of the lines has been completely recast; the food supply methods are modeled on those of the French Quartermaster's Department, and are working admirably. Aviation, too, is developing.

The epidemics have been checked by sanitary measures, in which Dr. J. Cantacuzene has especially distinguished himself, and by the creation of numerous hospitals, isolation camps, hygienic precautions, police surveillance; everything has been foreseen and realized, thanks to the activity and courage of Rumanian, French, and English physicians, such as Dr. Clunet, Dr. Bottesco, and many other victims of duty and of science, who have not hesitated to sacrifice their lives. The nurses, with the Queen at their head, have given them devoted aid.

The chief cause of the spread of epidemics was scarcity of food, and this has been effectively combated, first by measures of restriction and the prevention of monopoly, then by stimulating farm labor in Moldavia, and, finally, by improving transportation. The Autumn sowing was done in time, and the harvest promises to be abundant. It includes all the Rumanian cereals, which are of excellent quality. As for petroleum, a few wells are still running very near the front, in the district of Bacau, and are sufficient to provide for the needs of the railways.

Transport facilities, unfortunately, are very meagre in Moldavia, and the food supplies had to be brought in all last Winter over the single railway that connects Rumania and Russia by way of Ungheni. The famine was due primarily to lack of transport. The chaos of the Russian railways during the last months of the old régime was accountable for the fact that Russia could then send only four carloads of food a day for the Russian Army, the Rumanian Army, and the civil population of the country, which exceeds three millions. The new Russian régime immediately improved this situation by sending twenty-five carloads a

# THE BATTLE IN THE MUD IN FLANDERS

An Example of the Difficulties with Which the British Had to Contend During the Fighting in Flanders.
(British Official Photograph.)

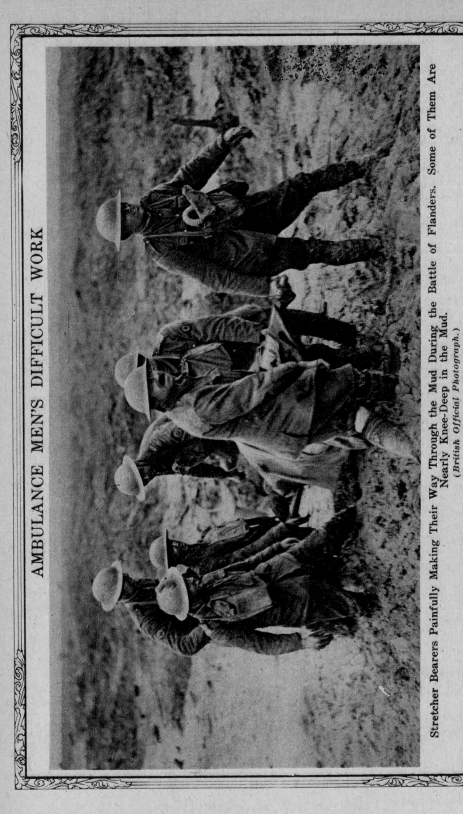

AMBULANCE MEN'S DIFFICULT WORK

Stretcher Bearers Painfully Making Their Way Through the Mud During the Battle of Flanders. Some of Them Are Nearly Knee-Deep in the Mud.
(British Official Photograph.)

day. It is thus doing all it can to supply Rumania with wheat, oil, coal, farm products, fish, clothes, and shoes.

The gold reserves of the Rumanian National Bank, which amounted to $120,-000,000 at the time of the declaration of war, were put in a safe place when the Government was removed to Jassy. Contributions have been paid in Moldavia under fairly good conditions. Important loans have been made to Rumania by her allies—notably by England, which has lent her $200,000,000—and the Rumanian Government is using these funds entirely for armament.

## Social Reform Measures

While fighting famine and fever, and while toiling to restore her army, Rumania has at the same time been busy transforming her social organism in behalf of fuller democracy. For some years before the war the Rumanian Parliament had been at work on an important project of agrarian reform, which was to lead to the partition of private domains and the distribution of State lands among the peasants.

A large number of Rumanian peasants were formerly land owners, for an old national tradition held that the defender of the soil should possess a share of it, and that after a war the soldier, whatever his rank, should be rewarded with a fair allotment of land. But many events during the Turco-Phanariot period helped to dispossess the Rumanian soldier-laborer of his property. After 1848 the peasants again became proprietors to some degree, but in the subsequent years the rapid increase of population, which, by inheritance, involved the dividing of small farms into still smaller parcels, had reduced the peasant class to a rural proletariat. The people lived by work in the fields, but not their fields.

This abnormal situation has long been a matter of concern to political thinkers in Rumania, without distinction of party. For fifteen years they had been preparing the way for agrarian reform, first by isolated attempts, then notably by the creation of farmers' unions and rural banks, which produced excellent results. The Government, which was already studying the question when the war came, and which had put it into the legislative program, could not leave it in suspense, and, after providing for the most urgent needs of the moment, hastened to take it up again.

## Germany Takes a Hand

Aside from these general reasons, a new danger threatened to plunge the country into an era of internal troubles. The Germans, through their agents and spies, who had been swarming for forty years in Rumania, knew the social situation there to its minutest detail; they were not slow in using the agrarian troubles as a weapon.

In order to attract the sympathies of the rural population in the invaded regions, and to procure supplies without expense, they gave private estates unconditionally to the peasants. This manoeuvre, which obliged the peasant to work without wages for Germany—under the fallacious pretext that he was being taught agriculture and was enriching himself—did not prevent the Germans from driving this same peasant, with cudgel blows, to dig trenches under the bullets of the Rumanian soldiers. At the same time that Germany was assuring herself provisions during the war she was preparing a bloody revolution in Rumania after the coming of peace.

The Rumanians had to parry this scheme. King Ferdinand was the first to offer his domains, and in several proclamations to the soldiers he solemnly promised them agrarian reform and universal suffrage. The Government of Mr. Bratiano, which Take Jonescu and three Conservative Ministers have joined, thus making the "Cabinet of Sacred Unity," has just caused Parliament to pass these two reform measures, which are so fully in harmony with the democratic principles of the Entente Allies.

# Rumania's Efforts and Aspirations

*Dr. Constantine Angelscu, the new Rumanian Minister to the United States, issued a statement late in October, the essential parts of which are given herewith:*

THE first phase of our entry into the great struggle was fraught with immense sacrifices and sufferings. Our front, more than 1,200 kilometers (750 miles) in extent, had to be defended by us single-handed, for the help we had been led to expect did not arrive. But the courage of our soldiers did not fail.

Unhappily, we sustained losses amounting to over 50,000 killed and 150,000 wounded. And that was not the full extent of our calamities. There was our retreat in Moldavia, the heartrending exodus of the inhabitants of the occupied territories, rich and poor, old men, women, and children, abandoning their homes before the advance of the hated enemy; and our enforced destruction of the oil wells in Rumania, representing hundreds and hundreds of millions of francs in value, as well as of our stores of cereals and our factories, to prevent their falling into the hands of the invaders. To these indescribable misfortunes were added other sufferings which culminated in an epidemic of exanthematic typhus, which claimed an immense number of victims. In spite of all this, however, my country did not lose faith, but remained profoundly attached to the common cause. Our sorely tried army awaited with passionate ardor the moment when it could turn the tables on the enemy, and when that moment came it did so in most magnificent fashion. In the battles of Marashesti men were seen to throw away their steel helmets and their coats, and, thus freed, fall on the enemy with tremendous fury. Many are the heroic deeds that have been related of them.

When, in consequence of the condition of internal affairs in Russia, the order came from Petrograd to stop the Rumanian offensive, our officers and men wept from disappointment. Later Mackensen assumed the offensive. His object was to conquer Moldavia also on the occasion of the first anniversary of the entry of Rumania into the war, and, once in the possession of the whole of Rumanian territory, the Germans had the intention of proclaiming a new régime. They reckoned without the valor of the Rumanian soldier. As a matter of fact, Rumania saved the eastern front. The offensive of Mackensen was definitely broken, and the Rumanian Army, with our chivalrous King at its head, is absolutely confident that it is no longer possible to break through the Rumanian front.

Forty years ago Rumania began her career as a political State, allying herself with Russia, and was true to her principle of being in the Near East a loyal and firm co-operator in the work of civilization and stability. In following her destiny she never was a source of embarrassment to Europe. Among the Near Eastern States, Hungary included, Rumania alone has been able to preserve her national individuality throughout the centuries. While Bulgaria became a Turkish province, while Hungary was under the dominion for a space of two centuries of Ottoman Pashas, while Russia herself had not yet succeeded in breaking through the iron ring of the Mongols, Rumania preserved her national existence, and, moreover, was a tower of strength to the Christian peoples of the Balkans. It was on Rumanian territory that the renascence of Bulgaria was engineered and that as a rule all the patriots of Christian countries on the right bank of the Danube found a safe asylum.

What we ask for is the amalgamation of our race in the region of the Carpathians and safe frontiers in the Balkans. Our historic and political right to the territories of Hungary inhabited by the people of Rumanian race is established beyond question. More than 4,000,000 Rumanians who have determined to be and have remained Rumanians for something like 2,000 years, in spite of all the persecutions of the Magyars, reside there in compact masses. These populations have consistently maintained throughout the centuries spiritual relations with their brethren beyond the mountains. The Rumanian peasant of Hungary calls Rumania " the country," meaning his country. And the union is not only spiritual but territorial, for the chain of the Rumanian Carpathians is, as it were, the backbone of Rumania. Our Hungarian congeners have never ceased to claim to belong to us. In 1867, when the Austro-Hungarian compromise was effected and Transylvania, Rumanian at heart, was sacrificed on the altar of dualism, the duped Rumanians were consoled with the law of nationalities. Under that law our brethren have been subjected to the most cruel persecutions. Even women and children have been made to expiate their fidelity to their race.

Dominated by the obsession of endeavoring to establish an exclusively Magyar State in a polyglot country, wherein the Hungarians are in a minority in the territories inhabited by Rumanians, all Hungarian Governments without exception have endeavored to denationalize the Rumanian population by violence, but have made no impression on the dogged determination of that population to remain Rumanian. That is why we Rumanians of Rumania have always had our eyes turned toward the Carpathians, and have never in our history renounced our aspirations after national reunion in spite of diplomatic arrangements imposed on us by hard necessity.

## The Jews in Rumania

*M. Take Jonescu, in an address to the Rumanian Chamber on Oct. 21, 1917, referred to the Jewish question in these words:*

From the standpoint of every reasonable man it was impossible that we should attach to our country provinces in which there were Jews whom we should have had to make into Rumanian citizens, Jews who would have fought under the enemy's flag, and at the same time that we should allow our own Jews, some of whom have fought under our flag, to remain strangers to us. No one can admit such an idea. It is for this reason that the fourth point that we should consider closely is the Jewish question, and that we should deal with it by a broad-minded, comprehensive resolution, which should have no reserves, and that we should deal with it honestly, as a country ought to do that has pledged its word and keeps its promises.

I have brought this question before the House because I wish the Jews throughout the country to know that if it was natural and legitimate that this question should be fought when we were still undecided, to fight it from now onward is both useless and unjust. Unjust, because the mere granting of rights cannot solve a question of this sort. When the Jews are fellow-citizens like ourselves, we are determined that they should not be foreigners to us, and that we should not appear to be their brothers while being really their enemies. We shall have to undertake a second task, a social task, a task of brotherhood, and this will be carried out all the better if foreigners refrain from interfering in a question as to which we have said our last word.

As for myself, I shall not lay down my arms until the Jewish question has been solved as I have stated that it should be solved.

# Australasia's Record in the War

## By Robert Sumner Winn

### An Australian Journalist

AUSTRALASIA is geographically further away from the main theatre of the greatest of wars than any other part of the world. Yet it has played a notable part in this war. The Commonwealth of Australia and the Dominion of New Zealand—democratic, advanced, and essentially British—have freely given men, money, ships, munitions, and other supplies; fought valiantly on land and sea, legislated radically, and worked zealously for the allied cause and the overthrow of present-day Germany. Various South Sea islands—British and French colonies or dependencies—have made proportionate efforts and sacrifices.

Australia alone of the continents has never had a hostile shot fired at it or upon it; and until August, 1914, it was a country almost without military traditions. True, Australians in numbers had fought in the South African war, but the Australian people had never been menaced by invasion; much less have they experienced a battle upon their soil. A comprehensive system of military training, based upon the recommendations of Lord Kitchener and in some respects characteristically progressive, had been put into operation, but too soon before the war broke out to make it of value. A federal military academy (Duntroon) and a federal naval academy (Jervis Bay) had been established, but only the former long enough to help meet the crisis. Because of connection with Great Britain, and because of Britain's sea power, because of fear of Asia, and because of the visit of the American battleship fleet in 1908, there was an Australian Navy in the fateful Summer of 1914. But this navy was young, somewhat incomplete, and untried—a quasi-experiment in British imperial relations.

Neighboring New Zealand had likewise never been threatened by an enemy. But there had at least been a war there, that of the sixties, between the white settlers and the Maoris, the martial aborigines whom it required trained British troops to master. New Zealanders, too, had engaged in the South African war. New Zealand had a competent system of military training in 1914; but owing to a policy which had centred upon representation in the British Navy rather than upon a semi-independent navy, like that of Australia, the dominion in the naval sense was only nominally defended.

Of the South Sea islands participating in the war not one save perhaps French New Caledonia knew anything military except from tribal feuds or European punitive expeditions in an era ending upward of half a century before. But British Australasia dealt Germany and German prestige several severe and totally unexpected blows at the very outset of the war. While Belgium and Northern France were being overrun by the Kaiser's armies most of Germany's empire in the Pacific was easily falling captive to the arms of Australia and New Zealand. Administrative Germany had greatly misconceived or underrated Australasian loyalty; Australasia had greatly overrated Germany's strength in the Pacific.

## Taking Samoa and New Guinea

A New Zealand military force under Colonel Robert Logan, an Otago farmer-militia man, convoyed by the battle cruiser Australia, flagship of the fledgling Australian Navy; the cruiser Melbourne, also of that navy, and other warships descended upon German Samoa at the end of August, 1914, took it without resistance, and hoisted the Union Jack over Apia.

An Australian naval and military force, under Colonel William Holmes, a Sydney city official, but a military enthusiast and a veteran of the South African war, obliged Dr. Haber, the Acting Governor of German New Guinea, to surrender that extensive territory at Herbertshohe in New Britain (Neu Pommern) the latter part of September. Colonel Holmes's expedition was convoyed and materially assisted by virtually the entire Australian Navy, under command of its then active head, the British Admiral Sir George Patey—the Australia, the cruiser Sydney, the destroyers Parramatta, Warrego, and Yarra; the submarines AE-1 and AE-2, and other units. In the sole engagement of this campaign —a series of sharp skirmishes in the jungle for the possession of the German wireless station some miles from Herbertshohe—the attacking Australian naval reservists were successful. Their losses were small. Those of the Germans were somewhat heavier, and they had to blow up the plant. Never before had Australians been on the offensive or Australian blood been shed in action so near Australia.

Within two months from the beginning of the war, Australia, with her navy acting under the British Admiralty, and New Zealand had contributed largely to the destruction of the German Pacific wireless chain and the seizure and occupation of Germany's Pacific colonies. What the two Governments did not do Japan did. The operations against German New Guinea, a big and scattered colony, and German Samoa had been suggested by the British Government; the work was expeditiously carried out by Australasia. Germany, aside from other deprivations, was cut off from sources of tropical products invaluable for her conduct of the war, copra and, to a less degree, rubber and cacao.

## Work of Australian Navy

Admiral Count von Spee's squadron, including the more or less formidable Scharnhorst and Gneisenau, was at this stage an important factor in the war, particularly as it affected the Pacific. The Australia, a battle cruiser of 19,000 tons, patrolled an extensive sector of that ocean northeast of the Fiji group in order, if possible, to prevent German concentration; and subsequently by virtue of her superior speed and armament she was instrumental in driving the German warships into South Ameri-

can waters and to their annihilation off the Falkland Islands by Admiral Sturdee.

Since then the Pacific has been considered safe for the Allies; German Samoa and German New Guinea have been successfully administered respectively by the New Zealand and Australian Governments pending the terms of peace; and the Australian Navy has entered more closely into Great Britain's scheme of naval defense. During the war the Commonwealth has augmented its navy by a cruiser and three destroyers. Australasia was fired at once by the war, but for a short time it did not altogether realize the Central Powers' onset or Germany's organization and might. Men flocked to the colors, and mobilization, equipment, and training were begun upon lines believed to have the most method and merit. By the last of October, 1914, after offers of military units to the British Government for use in any quarter, Australia had ready an expeditionary force of about 20,000 men and New Zealand one of about 8,000.

The dispatch of these two forces, which were combined in one, to Egypt, the destination which had been fixed upon, was a military feat which has yet to be equaled. Approximately 30,000 men—infantry, artillery, and cavalry— went from the antipodes to the Suez Canal without hitch, accident, or loss. It is 6,750 sea miles from Albany, Western Australia, where the transports mobilized, to Suez; and when the New Zealanders reached Egypt they had traversed more than 9,500 sea miles. In point of distance and relative number this carriage of troops constitutes a record.

## Destroying the Crusier Emden

The Australian cruiser Sydney encountered and defeated the famous German raiding cruiser Emden during this historic voyage. The time was early November. The Emden, under command of Captain Müller, had accounted for twenty-one British merchantmen, a Russian transport, and a French destroyer; raided Penang and bombarded Madras, and caused the Allies loss amounting to $12,500,000. The Sydney, commanded by the British Captain Glossop, but manned largely by Australians, was one of the warships convoying the troopships. The Emden swooped down upon the Eastern Extension Cable Company's station at Cocos Island in the Indian Ocean, intending to destroy it and cut the cable. The island's distress signals, which the Emden's wireless could not drown, were heard by the escorting warships, and the Sydney was detached to save the station. She came upon the Emden the next day. After a short but hot fight, in which her heavier and better served guns wrought havoc, she put the Emden to flight. The sinking raider was run ashore on North Keeling Island and her surviving officers and crew surrendered. The Sydney's casualties were less than twenty; those of the Emden were much greater, the killed alone numbering more than a hundred. This was the four-year-old Australian Navy's victorious "baptism of fire."

## The "Anzacs" at Gallipoli

The word "Anzac" was coined and immortalized by Australasian troops in the Levant. Initially their presence in Egypt, their first training ground, late in 1914 and early in 1915 was timely, because of the recently proclaimed British protectorate of Egypt and the necessity of defending the Suez Canal. Virtually only the high command of these troops included any but professional soldiers, and only a sprinkling of the rank and file had ever before been on active service. The great majority of them were men suddenly transplanted from prosaic pursuits to modern warfare. Although raw and rather undisciplined soldiers, they represented the best blood in the two dominions—the flower of their manhood.

It was in the allied attempts to take the Dardanelles during the Spring and Summer of 1915 that Australasians revealed to the world their prowess and morale. The last of April the Australian and New Zealand Army Corps—whence "Anzac" is derived—landed upon the Gallipoli Peninsula. The corps was part of the army under General Sir Ian Hamilton, before which had been set the task of forcing a way to Constantinople.

It gained a foothold at "Anzac" cove near Gaba Tepeh in the early hours of a day which Australasia will always hold was a heroic one. The fortified steeps commanding the beach were stormed and taken with the bayonet by scrambling, shouting, impetuous Queenslanders, South Australians, and West Australians— bushmen and miners—in defiance of all the accepted rules of war. Theoretically, the heights were impregnable, and actually the Turkish fire was deadly to a degree, but the defenders were driven back. Moreover, the positions taken were not relinquished until the end of the campaign.

So far as the Australasians were involved, the remaining seven months of the ill-starred Gallipoli campaign were characterized by like courage and dash in action, and by a mixture of resourcefulness, tenacity, and sang froid in trenches, practically under constant fire, which challenged the admiration of their friends and the respect of their enemies. Throughout the vicissitudes of the campaign the "Anzacs" were under an officer singularly adapted to their temperament and spirit, General Sir William Birdwood of the British Army. In the bloody engagements hinging upon Suvla Bay New Zealanders penetrated the Turkish lines deeper than any other of the allied forces at any stage of the campaign. They are said to have glimpsed the Dardanelles.

## Work of Premier Hughes

Meanwhile, William M. Hughes, Australia's Labor Attorney General, had focused worldwide attention upon the German "metal ring." A trust of giant proportions and ramifications, he averred, with headquarters at Frankfort-on-the-Main, was dominating and manipulating for German ends the Australian output of zinc, lead, and copper ores essential for British munitions; and among the disguised instruments of the trust were the German Metallgesellschaft and the British firm known as Mertons. He followed up his attacks by compelling Australian mining companies to sever their German connections and to become all-British; establishing a Governmental metal exchange for Britain's benefit, and bringing about an investigation in England of the nation's metal business. Eventually drastic action such as his in Australia was taken there.

Early in 1916 Mr. Hughes, who had become the Prime Minister of the Commonwealth, landed in England. After becoming head of the Australian Government he had organized a Governmental pool for supplying Great Britain and her confederates with Australian wheat on a large scale. This scheme was one of the first foodstuff conservation measures born of the war, and it was unique of its kind. Later, while in England, he bought the Strath Line of cargo steamers for the Commonwealth for the transportation of its wheat. This, too, was a novel stroke.

By reason of his picturesque story, pronounced anti-German sentiments, fiery "win-the-war" speeches, and decided leanings toward British tariff reform, the Australian Prime Minister stirred not only Great Britain but the other world powers as well. In some quarters he was —and is—hailed as one of the outstanding figures of the war. His British visit culminated in his attending in an advisory capacity the Entente conference in Paris in the middle of 1916, which formulated an allied economic union and German trade penalization after the war.

## Conscription in New Zealand

New Zealand was not only the first British oversea dominion to meet the overwhelming fact of the war by the formation of a Coalition Government, but next after Great Britain it was the first British community to adopt the conscription principle. [See CURRENT HISTORY MAGAZINE, November, 1916, Pages 318-320.] The Coalition Government, headed by William F. Massey as Prime Minister and Sir Joseph Ward as Finance Minister, came into being in 1915. These two Ministers took part in the British Imperial War Conference in London in 1917. Compulsory military service in order to keep the dominion's oversea forces at full strength came into effect the latter part of 1916. The Coalition Government's rule of action was not to displace the voluntary system but to sup-

plement it by the conscriptive system. New Zealand lays claim to having furnished more troops for the war in proportion to her population than any other British State save Britain herself. From among about 1,000,000 persons the dominion has raised an army of some 80,000 men.

Mr. Hughes's proposal that Australia adopt conscription having been defeated in a referendum upon that issue in October, 1916, [see CURRENT HISTORY MAGAZINE, December, 1916, Pages 446-449,] the Commnowealth's forces, totaling about 362,000 men since the beginning of the war, are volunteers. New Zealand's 80,000 men are divided between volunteers and conscripts. The Commonwealth and the Dominion, in the former of which the Defense Minister is Senator George F. Pearce and in the latter Colonel Sir James Allen, equip and maintain their warrior sons throughout—from training camp to firing line. The enormous expense entailed has been met by taxation and by successful internal loans aggregating many millions of pounds sterling.

## On European Battlefields

Since the Spring of 1916 the bulk of Australasia's fighting men has been merged with the allied armies on the western front; and they have taken part in the successive "pushes" on that front, as attested by their deeds at Pozières, Mouquet Farm, Bullecourt, Messines, and other places. Australasian cavalry and camelry have been conspicuous in the British operations on the Sinai Peninsula and in Southern Palestine, and there are Australasian units in Mesopotamia. General Birdwood—"the soul of Anzac"—has been the Australians' commander in France.

Contributions to war funds, Red Cross, Australasian, Belgian, French, and others, for relief purposes or for the prosecution of the war, have probably been greater per head in the South Pacific than in any other quarter of the globe. They mount up into the millions. What Australasian women have done toward raising these funds is incalculable.

Maoris are in the New Zealand ranks and their war cry, "We will fight on forever and ever," has been heard on European battlefields. The Cook Islands and Niue Island—a speck in the vast Pacific —have also furnished New Zealand with native recruits. Fijians are among the polyglot war workers in France. The Fiji, Gilbert, and Ellice groups; the little Kingdom of Tonga; Ocean and Niue Islands have aided Britain with gifts of money. Norfolk Island, peopled by de-

scendants of the mutineers of the Bounty, Lord Howe Island and the Chatham Islands have given men from their slender numbers. The French possessions in the Pacific, New Caledonia, the Loyalty Islands, and the Society Islands have provided the republic with devoted conscripts, whites and kanakas, some of whom were in the hell of Verdun.

# The English in India

## A Summary of What They Have Done

ON Oct. 15, 1917, Edwin S. Montague, M. P., Secretary of State for India, announced that he was proceeding to India, his journey being "the direct outcome of the British "Government's declaration in Parliament "that its policy in India is to develop self- "governing institutions with a view to the "progressive realization of representative "government. Electoral bodies have "sprung up," added Mr. Montague, "and there are in most provinces today "councils which have power to pass "resolutions and to act in an advisory "capacity, although they have little re- "sponsibility or real power. The mem- "bers of these legislative units have be- "gun to tire of a situation in which they "are little more than debaters, and we "shall be glad to provide food for this "developing civic appetite. Today the "British people have begun to realize "that India has proved herself worthy "of a larger part in the imperial plan. "India is now assured of a place in all "future imperial war conferences."

A further step is thus taken in the long task of giving India peace, security, law, and liberty.

On the last day of the year 1600 Queen Elizabeth granted a charter to a group of English merchants to trade in the Orient, with the title the East India Company. Seven years later, in 1607, another group of Englishmen formed a trading post at Jamestown in Virginia, a region named for the same Queen Elizabeth. From these two beginnings

grew, on the one hand, the British Indian Empire, with an area of 1,800,000 square miles and a population of over 300,000,- 000; and, on the other, the United States of America, with an area of 3,600,000 square miles and a population of 100,- 000,000. Needless to say that neither group of English traders had the remotest idea or wish that any such result should follow.

For nearly 150 years no very large results did follow. Then, in 1740, Frederick the Great turned the Pragmatic Sanction into a scrap of paper, and seized territories belonging to the Austrian Princess Maria Theresa. This act enkindled a war in Europe, in which England and France took opposite sides. As a result, England and France were presently at war, not only in Europe, but also in America, Africa, and Asia; and George Washington in Pennsylvania and Clive in India were colleagues and fellow-officers fighting together in the British armies. This war made England pre-eminent over France in North America and India; there are still remnants of French territory in both: the little Islands of St. Pierre and Miquelon in the Gulf of St. Lawrence, with West Indian islands; and, in India, French settlements like Pondicherry in Madras and Chandranagore in Bengal.

The English traders in India, after the 150 years, had still no territory. In 1756 the youthful Mohammedan Viceroy of Bengal, Siraj-ud-Daula, in a quarrel with some of his relations, captured Calcutta, and shut 146 English men and women in a dungeon sixteen feet square, the Black Hole of Calcutta. Only 23 came out alive. To punish this atrocity Clive, with a small force of 1,000 English troops, defeated the Viceroy at Plassey on June 25, 1757, drove him from his capital, Murshidabad, and put a new Viceroy, Mir Jafar, in his place. This was the beginning of territorial power in India, after a century and a half of trading in silk and indigo.

When Plassey was fought and won on the bank of an arm of the Ganges, there were three classes of political powers in India. To the first class belonged the Mogul (or Mongol) Empire, built up by military adventurers descended from Genghis Khan; of these, the greatest were Baber, who invaded India, and Akbar, the gifted and enlightened contemporary of Queen Elizabeth. But by 1757 the Mogul despotism had fallen into the last stages of decay; it was divided into provinces, under Nawabs (Nabobs) or Viceroys, who were as bad administrators as the Mohammedans in Turkey or in Egypt. Their single idea was to farm the taxes for as much as possible, the tax-farmers then extracting the last possible penny from the downtrodden cultivators. This fiscal system has been a fertile source of evil and oppression in Mohammedan rule wherever it has been established.

Beginning with the regions about Calcutta, the English merchants at first undertook to gather the revenues, (while not owning the territories,) and began by making a valuation of the land, on which a fixed rate of taxation was then levied. Fixity of taxation, as against the rapacious exactions of greedy tax-farmers, was the first boon conferred by England on India; and it should be added that perhaps no country in the world which possesses a strong and stable Government is so lightly taxed, the total of revenue from all sources amounting to a charge of less than $1.50 per head each year. As, therefore, the decaying Mogul Empire (which we have called the first class of political powers in India at the time of Clive's victory) fell to pieces, the Eng-

lish merchants gathered up the pieces and gave them a sound administration at an extremely low cost. There is one exception: the Viceroyalty of Hyderabad, in area equal to Great Britain, is still governed by a Mohammedan Viceroy, or Nizam, though under British supervision. In this whole region taken over from the Mogul invaders, the English on no occasion fought against any really indigenous native power, but only against foreign conquerors of alien religion who had carried the sword of Mohammed into India. They were exactly in the position of the Turks in Greece, Serbia, Bulgaria, and Rumania, and governed about as badly.

The second class of political powers in India were the old Hindu States, which, though badly shaken by the Moslem raids, invasions, and conquests, had managed to survive, with a remnant of their former glory. Wherever it has been possible, the English have conserved these ancient States under their hereditary Princes, and have, in every possible way, secured their development along indigenous lines, carefully guarding native customs, religions, and languages. Most notable of these ancient Hindu States are the princedoms of Rajputana, in Western India, whose princely houses trace their ancestry back for hundreds, even for thousands of years; and the large Hindu State of Mysore, in Southern India, which has several very ancient seats of Sanskrit learning. The total area of these native States, both Hindu and Mohammedan, (the latter representing foreign conquest and invasion,) is over 700,000 square miles, or over one-third of the whole area of India.

While these States are under native rule, they in no sense represent popular or democratic government; they are, on the contrary, Oriental despotisms, tempered by English political control.

In the third class of political powers in India at the time of Plassey were two new States: the Mahratta States, based on recent raids and conquests by predatory hill tribes, and the Sikh Confederacy, an aggressive military theocracy;

both bent on subjugating the rest of India. It was against these two new powers that most of the English wars in India were waged. The Mahratta wars were fought by the Marquis of Wellesley, whose younger brother, as Duke of Wellington, was making history in Europe. In both Sikh wars the Sikhs, not the English, were the aggressors; they were closed by the battles of Sobraon and Gujarat, which brought the Punjab under English rule, shortly before the Mutiny of 1857. In this Mutiny the Sikhs fought enthusiastically on the side of the English, as the Boers have fought on the English side in the world war.

Since 1857, save for a few frontier wars provoked by raids from beyond the border, all India has enjoyed unbroken peace for the first time in many centuries. This Pax Britannica has now lasted for sixty years. India has, further, enjoyed a system of just and impartial laws, administered everywhere in the local languages and dialects. These laws fall into two groups. In the first are criminal laws, like the Indian Penal Code, which apply to all persons in India, native and European alike, with modern commercial laws, like the Contract act. In the second class are the laws regulating family affairs, including the devolution of property. The British principle is in all cases to conserve the existing family laws; thus Hindu inheritance cases are decided under the laws of Manu; Mohammedan cases under the Koran and the law books that have grown out of it. The same principle holds good for less-developed communities.

England has thus given India (1) unbroken peace; (2) one of the most efficient and least costly administrations in the world; (3) the development of all indigenous religions, institutions, languages, along indigenous lines; (4) Western inventions, like railroads, telegraph, Post Offices, sanitation.

## "Soldiers Back of the Lines"

The bravest battle that ever was fought!
        Shall I tell you where and when?
On the maps of the world you will find it not—
        'Tis fought by the mothers of men.
Nay, not with cannon or battle shot,
        With sword or nobler pen!
Nay, not with eloquent words of thought
        From mouths of wonderful men;
But deep in the walled-up woman's heart—
        Of woman that would not yield,
But bravely, silently, bore her part—
        Lo, there is that battlefield!
No marshaling troop, no bivouac song,
        No banner to gleam and wave;
But, oh! their battles, they last, they last,
        From babyhood to the grave.
Yet faithful still, as a bridge of stars,
        She fights in her walled-up town—
Fights on and on in endless wars,
        Then silent, unseen, goes down.
Oh, ye with banners and battle shot,
        And soldiers to shout and praise,
I tell you the kingliest victories fought
        Were fought in those silent ways.
Oh, spotless woman in a world of shame,
        With splendid and silent scorn,
Go back to God as white as you came—
        This kingliest warrior born.

AUSTRIAN OFFICERS AS WAR PRISONERS IN A RUSTIC SUMMERHOUSE IN SIBERIA

# In the War Prisons of Eastern Siberia

## By George P. Conger

The author of this article has recently returned to the United States after a year and a half as Y. M. C. A. Secretary in Siberian prison camps.

SIBERIA may be seen as it really is by going to the region which extends 500 miles north of Vladivostok. There the world contacts by way of the Pacific have given a new impetus to the civilization which, mainly in the last fifty years, has made its way from European Russia to the Far East. Compared with many other parts of Russia, this region is highly developed. Of its principal cities, Vladivostok, the terminus of the Trans-Siberian Railroad, has 75,000 inhabitants, and is one of the most important ports in the world.

From Vladivostok the Chinese Eastern Railroad runs 450 miles northward to Habarovsk, a city of 45,000 inhabitants, commandingly situated on a bluff facing the great sweep of waters which mark the confluence of the Ussuri and Amur rivers. From Habarovsk the newly opened Amur Railroad, crossing the river by one of the longest bridges in the world, leads westward through a rich mining and timber district to Blagoviestchensk, a curious provincial capital with 50,000 people, across the Amur from Manchuria.

Just over the Manchurian frontier,

which is not far from any of the prosperous towns along the rivers and railroads, there is a wild region, inhabited chiefly by robber bands, who sometimes have whole villages to themselves, where they live subject to no law save their own primitive codes. Their presence just over the borders has made it necessary for Russia to keep large garrisons in some of the Siberian towns and villages.

The modern trend of things in these towns was reflected before the war in the barracks provided for the garrisons. Some of the buildings were of the old pioneer type—one-story houses built of squared logs. A Siberian loghouse is by no means to be despised; some of the fine residences in every city are built in this way. The houses are heated by immense sheet-iron stoves, which are built with them.

### Brick Barracks for Prisoners

In the garrison towns of Eastern Siberia this older type of barracks had, however, been largely replaced by modern brick buildings—usually of two stories, with concrete floors and whitewashed walls. Within the barracks the long rooms were equipped with double-decked wooden platforms, which served the soldiers as a combination of bedstead, wardrobe, dining table, and writing desk. The soldiers, recruited largely from the peasantry, had practically the same food in the barracks as at home; it consisted principally of soup, "kasha," black bread, and tea.

The Russian soup resembles a stew; it usually contains meat and vegetables, especially cabbage. "Kasha" is a cereal food, which is like boiled buckwheat; the Russian way is to put it into one's soup as we might croutons. Russian black bread is more nearly brown—heavy and coarse, but very nutritious.

When the war broke out, some of these regiments were sent to the front, leaving their barracks empty; and as soon as Russia began taking prisoners, thousands of Germans, Austrians, and Turks were sent out to Serbia to fill up the empty buildings. There have been as many as 50,000 prisoners in the district, but constant transfers have now considerably affected the numbers. The proportion of Austrians to Germans is roughly four to one; there are fewer Turks than Germans.

## Misguided Attempts to Escape

At first these prisoners, more than six thousand miles from the front, were allowed some liberty. At one camp, charmingly located on an arm of the Pacific, the prisoner officers had the privilege of sea-bathing; at other places they were allowed to come quite freely into the towns to make purchases. But the neighboring Chinese frontier was too alluring, and some of the men, who knew how easy it is to walk in a day or two from one European country to another, decided to try walking from one Asiatic country to another; so several parties attempted to escape. They reckoned without the vast distances and the cold, and some starved or froze to death out in the wilderness. They reckoned also without the Russian Cossacks, who knew every foot of the country except the international boundry line; many of the escaping prisoners were recaptured. Some who escaped these things were captured by robbers. I have heard that some escaping prisoners were even eaten by the huge Amur tigers, which are larger, and, if anything, fiercer, than those of Bengal. Altogether only a small proportion of prisoners ever reached China and the shelter of those German oganizations which have since figured among the causes of China's entry into the war.

The effect of the attempts to escape was what might have been expected. The Russians built huge wooden stockades around the barracks and confined the remaining prisoners inside. These stockades are of thick boards, twelve or fifteen feet high, topped with three rows of barbed wire and guarded night and day by sentries. The stockades are in most cases of generous size. In Eastern Siberia there are between twenty and thirty such inclosures, varying in size from those accommodating twenty-five men to one immense affair large enough to hold 10,000; they are located at Habarovsk, Blagoviestchensk, Nikolsk-Ussurisk, and other smaller towns.

### Prisoners Well Treated

The private soldiers among the prisoners were placed on practically the same food and given the same accommodations as the Russian soldiers had before they went to the front. Several times, where there was a possible choice of barracks, the prisoners were placed in new brick buildings, while the regiments guarding them occupied the older log structures.

Prisoner officers were separated from soldiers, kept in stockades by themselves, and usually treated much better. It strikes many persons as curious that each group of nations engaged in the war should be paying a monthly salary to the enemy prisoner officers whom it has captured. Germany pays her Russian prisoner officers about 100 marks a month, and Russia pays her captive Germans about the same sum, or 50 rubles. Out of this latter sum the prisoner officers in Siberia pay for their food and side purchases; their lodging is gladly furnished them without charge.

The officers were not obliged to sleep on the wooden platforms, but, like the Russian officers in neighboring barracks, were provided with iron cots. In some camps the feeding of the officers was let out to private contractors; in others, the officers managed their own kitchens. One officers' camp in Eastern Siberia has a cook who was formerly chef of one of the large hotels of Budapest. As a general thing, the problem of foodstuffs has not been acute in this region, because the railroad service was so nearly paralyzed that little could be shipped away, and the large quantities produced had to be locally consumed.

### American Shoes in Favor

As the clothing of officers and men has worn out, new supplies have been secured through various relief agencies. No articles of clothing are in greater favor among the prisoners than American shoes. Europe and Asia, as represented there, unite in admitting their superiority. It is worth noting that last Winter, at a time when private shippers were vainly offering fortunes to secure freight cars leaving Vladivostok, trainloads of supplies for the prison camps were being shipped out.

Apparently Russia did not at first plan to have prisoners of war work; but, especially after the reports showing that Germany was employing her Russian prisoners to good advantage, the Russians began to follow suit. Large numbers of men were retransferred from Eastern Siberia to European Russia; and of all the hundreds of thousands of Austrians captured during General Brusiloff's great drive in 1916, only a few were sent out to Eastern Siberia. These few were mainly officers, and for the most part very young officers. One day one of them asked me to telegraph to Austria that he had received no news from his grandmother.

Three classes of prisoners are exempt from work, and even if they wish to work are, in the vast majority of cases, not allowed to do so. These are officers, invalids, and " intelligentsia." The latter comprise the one-year volunteers of the German Army and the better-educated or professionally trained men; they are usually confined in the private soldiers' camps, but in barracks or rooms by themselves.

In every camp the musicians are organized into orchestras, which play almost every night in many tea rooms and restaurants in the towns. Siberia has never heard such music as since the war began. These orchestras are capable of everything from ragtime to symphony concerts.

A well-known sculptor from Central Europe has since his imprisonment executed some remarkably lifelike heads of the now gradually disappearing Siberian aborigines; these will in future years form some of the treasures of one of the local museums. Some of the prison camps have studios for the painters who have been taken in the war; one camp had in its studio eleven Academicians from Vienna and Budapest.

The private soldiers who have remained in the East work on the roads, farms, parks, or in private establishments in the cities. They are often obliged to work long hours, but at a leisurely pace. All the carpenters, cobblers, and tailors are kept busy, and are on the whole the most contented of the prisoners. Interior decorators have been in great demand; if the war lasts much longer they will have left their memorials in every church and theatre in the region.

The tradition of the old convict camps leads many persons to ask particularly about prisoners working in Siberia. The general answer is that the prisoners who have been obliged to work in Siberia are for the most part those who would naturally expect to be working if they were at home or in their own armies. I have heard tales of hardship and cruelty, coming from remote and inaccessible workcamps; but there are two sides to all those stories, and from what I know of the Russians I am just as ready to believe that in the small, scattered camps there is even more kindliness and freedom than is afforded the prisoners in the larger centres. I remember particularly the case of a young lawyer from Berlin who the last time I saw him, in one of the larger camps, told me he hoped that the Russians would allow him to be transferred to one of the work-camps somewhere out on the big farms; he was looking forward to relief from the endless monotony of life inside the stockade.

Take it altogether, it is not the prisoners who work who are to be pitied —it is those who are not allowed to work. One day in an officers' camp I met a prisoner who had recently been transferred from another inclosure. He pointed to a fringe of scrub timber on a hill in the distance and said: "That looks good, over there—I have looked at a board fence for a year and a half." My work was to help relieve the monotony of the board fence and all that it stood for—and wherever possible to turn it to positive account by enabling the men to utilize the time on their hands. The whole thing was undertaken on a reciprocal basis; work like mine for the Germans and Austrians in Siberia made it possible for other men to work in Central Europe for the allied prisoners there.

## Studious Germans and Austrians

The Germans and Austrians occupied much of their time in study. At first it was impossible to secure books in any language but Russian; the prisoner schools were equipped for awhile with these textbooks, which the prisoner who had a general knowledge of Russian translated for the men who served as teachers of the various subjects treated. Many of the prisoners spoke English or French, the more proficient among them organized study groups, and all the camps soon came to contain good sized language schools. Some of the prisoners have learned four or five languages during their imprisonment; it is noticeable that some of the Germans devote considerable attention to commercial Spanish. The prisoner schools taught everything from the alphabet up to literary and scientific subjects of university grade. Some boys have been able to learn trades in the camps, and even to secure three years' apprenticeship there. In the course of time thousands of German books arrived for the prisoners, and many advanced students in particular received material enabling them to continue studies interrupted by the war.

The prisoners were all greatly interested in the belated foreign newspapers which reached them. For a long time only two were allowed in the camps—

The London Times and the Paris Temps. The restriction was made in order to save the time of the Russian censors rather than because of any distrust of other English or French papers. Not only all German and American but all neutral newspapers were banned; it was only after America entered the war that I was able to secure permission for the prisoners to receive THE NEW YORK TIMES. I had accumulated a file of THE TIMES, and accordingly turned it over to the prisoners. One of the officers told me that, whenever such papers were brought into the camps, some one who knew English well was selected to translate them aloud, while a group around him listened for hours together.

Religious services for the prisoners were conducted by their own priests, pastors, rabbis, and mullahs. Services in progress in more than one camp were upset by reprisals enforced because of reports concerning the treatment of some Russian priests who were prisoners in Austria.

In general, the camps were well equipped with facilities for recreation. Most of the officers' camps were provided with theatres, tennis courts, football grounds, promenades, and rustic gardens. One camp where common soldiers were confined included a veritable park of thickly planted trees. Some camps had bowling alleys; in one or two there was room enough for a Hungarian game which bears some resemblance to baseball.

Since the Russian revolution the Russian Soldiers' Committees, in exercise of their new powers, have modified these arrangements somewhat by concentrating the prisoners in certain camps, in order to lessen the work of guarding so many points. But these changes have not been such as to impose upon the prisoners either cold, or desolation, or cruelty.

## Mental Attitude of Prisoners

What do the prisoners think about the war? It was not my work to discuss it with them, but of course I heard a good deal of it here and there. My impression is that in their attitudes they fall into groups which are pretty clearly marked along national lines.

The Germans—upstanding, neat, polite, precise—outwardly, at least, maintain their hostilities and their pride more rigidly than the other prisoners. At the time of General Brusiloff's greatest success they said merely that it would prolong the war; asked if they still thought Germany would win, they answered, wonderingly, "How can it be otherwise?" When the telegram came saying that Rumania had entered the war against them, one officer, whom I happened to overhear when the Russian commandant asked him what he thought of it, said, "The more enemies the more glory." I visited some of the highest German officers in Siberia after America had entered the war; they were personally as friendly as ever, and they said nothing to me about the international situation; but I think if a neutral had been there he would have said that they looked grave.

The Austrians are quite different. The Russian commandant of one of the most important camps in the country told me that as between Germans and Austrians the problem of maintaining camp discipline admitted of no comparison. When this commandant finishes his book dealing with his experiences there he will have some curious tales to tell of messages which, as camp censor, he has intercepted in the camp mail, and which reveal bitterness between the Austrians and Germans.

## All Longing for Peace

The Austrians are much more ready to talk about war and about peace than are the Germans. An officer in one Austrian camp told me that from morning to night they discussed among themselves the question when peace would come. Another went so far as to say, "If I could get the two Emperors at a table together, I'd soon end the war." Still another, after assuring me that the French and the Italians were not civilized, ("keine Kulturvöker,") said, dramatically, pointing to a map of Central Europe on the wall: "That is a heap of ruins! That is a sea of blood! The future lies with America, and if I were young I would go there." This does not mean that they are all ready to give up; a representative Hungarian officer in one camp during a period of Russian success at the front, solemnly said: "If one considers it logically, (Wenn man ganz logisch denkt,) there is no other possibility than victory for us." One or two indications which I observed lead me to think that the prisoners rather expect to lose this war, but count on another one which is to follow this. One day in an officers' camp I caught just a glimpse of a notebook kept by a prisoner; unless I am mistaken it was inscribed "Taktik," and contained notes of secret conferences on military science. One Hungarian prisoner even said that in twenty years there would be another war.

The Czechs in one camp agreed to enlist in the Russian Army if the Russians would set them free; but before the arrangement was completed the Austrians in the camp heard of it and attacked the Czechs, who had to be rescued and removed by the Russian garrison.

The Turks were a puzzle to every one. In one camp the Russian commandant spoke Armenian; in another one Turk spoke French; in a third one man spoke English with a true New York flavor. For the rest, communication with the Turks was difficult. One evening at sunset I saw a group of Turks out in the prison yard, kneeling on their prayer rugs and praying toward Mecca. I asked one of the Russians if any one had told the Turks that Arabia was in revolt and Mecca on the brink of being captured by the rebels. "No," said he; "they would not believe it if one told them; they believe that there isn't even any war—that the whole thing is illusion."

I think all the prisoners have expected peace long before this. In one camp there is a door on which the camp prophets and soothsayers have recorded their predictions and dreams and hopes concerning the date of peace. As one date after another has been passed by both the European and the lagging Russian calendar, fresh dates have been added, so that there are always some just ahead. But some of the dates once predicted are now almost three years old!

# A Historic Peace Conference

## The Congress of Vienna and Its Workings
## Viewed as a Precedent of Timely Interest

### By Allan Westcott

THE congress which assembled at Vienna in September, 1814, after the Napoleonic wars, was the most important since that which had negotiated the Peace of Westphalia in 1648. The diplomats gathered at the Austrian capital held in their hands the fate of some 32,000,000 " souls," to adopt the word then current—the population of States and provinces cast adrift at Napoleon's fall. It was their formidable task, assigned to them by the Peace of Paris, (May 30, 1814,) to establish " a real and durable equilibrium " after a quarter of a century of war. The importance of the congress may be measured also by its results, the undoing of which, it has been said, constitutes a major part of nineteenth century history.

Among royalty in attendance were two Emperors, Alexander I. of Russia and Francis of Austria, and the Kings of Prussia, Bavaria, Denmark, and Württemberg; while the vast halls of the Hofburg were thronged with sovereigns or some-time sovereigns of petty States, and with half the nobility of Europe. The rulers and Princes met each day before dinner to discuss the disposition of their property, and engaged in lively disputes, bargains, and exchanges, much like some immense family assembled to settle an estate. Their views, however, were not always consulted or regarded by the diplomats in actual control.

Each of the great powers was represented by four or more plenipotentiaries. Talleyrand, who had broken with Napoleon in time to gain favor with his Bourbon successor, headed the delegation of France. Castlereagh represented England until February, 1815, when he was succeeded by Wellington. Prussia's chief delegate, Prince von Hardenburg, was, by reason of his deafness, always accompanied by the gifted von Humboldt, brother of the scientist. For Russia, the Czar was often his own spokesman, with the Polish Prince Czartoryski, Prince Nesselrode, and the Corsican Pozzo di Borgo as his chief advisers. Metternich, Austrian Minister of State and Foreign Affairs, was President of the Congress and its most conspicuous figure. Each of these leaders was supported by a corps of political and military experts. In addition there were representatives of nearly every minor European State, of the Pope, the Jews, the Free Cities, the German Catholics, the banking and other business interests.

While the chief diplomats dealt with the more important problems, their subordinate colleagues took up the yeoman labor of the Congress, attending committees, drawing up agreements, and carrying out details. According to the " Memoirs " of Gagern, much of the work was accomplished by a small group of men, including Gentz, who was Secretary of the congress; Wessenberg of Austria, Dalberg and La Besnardière of France, Clancarty of England, and von Humboldt.

### Methods of Metternich

To amuse and also to distract the assemblage, Metternich provided a continual round of military spectacles, hunts, theatricals, concerts, fêtes, and balls. Conspicuous among the celebrations was a gorgeous ceremony commemorating the martyrdom of Louis XVI. The Czar in particular took keen delight in these festivities. They cost the bankrupt treasury of Austria over 30,000,000 florins, but they gave the Austrian minister free play for his favorite policy of diplomacy by intrigue.

" Le Congrès danse," remarked Prince de Ligne, " mais il ne marche pas." But the diplomats of the Four Allies—Austria, Great Britain, Prussia, and Russia —were not idle; they were empowered, and they fully intended, to take matters into their own hands. The congress had assembled in accordance with the Thirty-second Article of the Peace of Paris, consisting of four identic treaties between Louis XVIII. and the Four Allies, to which Spain, Portugal, and Sweden were accessories, and which restored to France her boundaries virtually as they were in 1792. This agreement not only outlined the main tasks of the congress, but in secret articles provided that all general European questions should be settled " on a basis agreed upon by the allied powers." In other words, the Allies were to decide all important matters; the function of the congress was to give its passive sanction to their decrees. On this principle—if on nothing else—the four powers were a unit.

## Talleyrand's Diplomacy

It was the main object of Talleyrand to break up this combination and secure for France her former influence in European affairs. In this he was assisted by the fact, already mentioned, that the coalition—less through generosity than through their unwillingness to see any other power strengthened by the crippling of France—had restored to that nation her old frontiers. Expecting little or no material gain from the congress, Talleyrand could afford to assume a lofty attitude and pose as the champion of high principles and the friend of small States.

When, on September 30, the French and the Spanish Plenipotentiaries were kindly invited to attend a conference of the Four Powers, Talleyrand at once launched his attack. Throwing aside a protocol, each clause of which began with the phrase, " The Allies agree," he professed his complete mystification as to the meaning of the term allies. The war was over, Napoleon at Elba—against whom, then, were they allied? He pointed to the public clause of the Paris Treaties which gave a voice in the congress to " all powers on either side engaged in the war." He pressed for an immediate opening of the general congress as the only authority from which

a special " steering " committee could derive its powers; and he threatened to leave the congress should his request be denied. After prolonged and stormy sittings of this inner circle, on Oct. 5 and 8, his policy gained at least a partial triumph by the concession that the Preliminary Committee should be composed of all the eight signatories of the Peace of Paris—France, Spain, Portugal, and Sweden, in addition to the Four Allies. Having thus demonstrated that France was not a negligible factor, and having secured a voice and vote in the main council, Talleyrand no longer concerned himself about a convocation of all delegates. The formal opening, put off till Nov. 1, was again postponed, and, in fact, never occurred; so that, in the paradoxical language of Secretary Gentz, the congress came into existence only by the signing of its final act.

The control thus exercised by the Committee of Eight, in which Spain, Portugal, and Sweden played but slight part, was a definite recognition of the principle which has since prevailed, that affairs of Europe should be under supervision of the major powers.

In the congress, however, the minor States were not without a voice. The work, so far as it was not accomplished by informal conferences and discussion, was divided among committees. The main committee itself met but seldom, and then usually to pass upon the conclusions of subordinate bodies. Of these there were many, notably the Committee for a German Federal Constitution, Committees for the Italian States, the Swiss Confederation, the Netherlands, the Navigation of Rivers, the Prohibition of the Slave Trade. The membership of these committees consisted of representatives of both major and minor States whose interests were particularly concerned.

## The Allies Divided

To complete the recovery of France and give her a virtual ascendency in the congress it was essential that the Allies should be divided among themselves and forced to seek her support. This came about less through the machinations of Talleyrand than through the inherent

THE CONGRESS OF VIENNA

Metternich is the prominent standing figure to the left of the centre. Lord Castlereagh is seated
in the centre. Talleyrand is the second seated delegate from the extreme right.

weakness of a coalition held together, like the Allies in the present war, chiefly by a sense of common danger. In this case the rock upon which the coalition split was the fate of Saxony and Poland. In 1813, independently from the other allies, Russia and Prussia had entered into a compact by which Prussia agreed to turn over her share of Poland to Russia, in return for compensations elsewhere. In accordance with this bargain, Prussia now asserted her claim to Saxony, which was already occupied by her forces. Both these transactions Talleyrand saw fit resolutely to oppose, utilizing Austria's fear of a greater Prussia planted on her immediate frontiers, and the objections of both Austria and England to immense Russian acquisitions toward the west. Briefly, the diplomatic tangle resulted in a secret offensive and defensive alliance, Jan. 3, 1815, of France, Austria, and Great Britain against the northern powers.

Russia and Prussia receded, and in the end got less than they bargained for. But it was only upon Napoleon's return from Elba that the powers were able to patch up their differences, hasten negotiations, and reach the terms set down in the final act. This was signed June 9, a week before Waterloo.

### The Balance of Power

The principles applied in the territorial and other adjustments then agreed upon are more significant than the changes themselves. The chief aim throughout was to establish a safe equilibrium or balance which should protect Europe against the ascendency of any one power or even any probable combination of powers. The means employed to this end was a system of buffer States, especially on the French frontier—Belgium and Luxemburg joined to Holland as a protection for England and the German States, the Kingdom of Sardinia re-established in Western Italy with the addition of Genoa, the Swiss Confederation again set up as a neutralized State, the German Confederation created as an element of safety in Central Europe.

So far as compatible with this policy, the principle of legitimacy, or hereditary right, was respected, though there were inevitable violations and sacrifices. Regard for this principle was in a sense respect for the spirit of nationality, which at that time manifested itself chiefly in the form of loyalty to a ruling house. But the national principle was violated in the short-lived union of Catholic Belgium and Protestant Holland, in the complete failure to redress the wrongs of Poland, in the turning over of the Genoese Republic to the House of Savoy, in the acquisitions of Austria in Italy and of Prussia in Saxony, and in a general tendency to shift populations, like cattle, from one ruler to another, without regard for popular consent.

In certain other respects the congress was more progressive. It guaranteed the Germanic Constitution, which in turn provided that Constitutions should be granted to the States in the Confederation. In response to the insistent demands of British sentiment, it took a definite stand for the prohibition of the slave trade. As an important step toward freer commercial intercourse among nations, the Committee on the Navigation of Rivers set up the principle of free peace-time navigation on streams forming boundaries or flowing through more than one State, and established codes for the navigation of the Rhine, the Scheldt, and the Meuse. This precedent was followed later in the system of international control for the lower Danube, and is applicable to present-day problems of water routes and trade channels.

### " World Safe for Kings "

The predominant spirit of the diplomats at the congress, however, was reactionary, and out of sympathy with the more liberal thought of the age. Their desire for a permanent peace was no less genuine than that of statesmen today, but it was a peace the watchword of which might have been, " a world made safe for Kings."

Hence, in spite of the Czar's liberal enthusiasms and England's admiration of her own form of government, the tendency of this congress—a tendency even more strongly manifested in the congresses of the next decade—was opposition to popular government as the chief danger which threatened the status quo. In the words of the Hungarian historian Reich, " The congress introduced that system of reaction, of obscurantism, of police persecution, that made the period from 1815 to 1848 one filled with the most shameful outrages against the liberty of the people." The Five Powers— which Metternich euphemistically called the " moral pentarchy "—attempted, under Austrian leadership, to stifle liberalism wherever it appeared and in whatever form. Their task, foredoomed to failure, was to pour living national organisms into a rigid unchangeable mold.

### Aims of Entente Allies

The aims and ideals of the Allies today are in this respect fundamentally different from those of the victors in the Napoleonic conflict. Whereas Napoleon, at least in his earlier campaigns, had behind him the forces of democracy, these forces are now combined against the last exponents of autocratic rule. Even if the diplomacy of the coming peace settlement should lag behind the spirit of the times, its every act will be subject to the pressure of public opinion to an extent undreamed of a century ago. The press at the time of the Vienna Congress was merely an instrument which statesmen could employ to play upon public opinion, if the effort were thought worth while. At the Algeciras Conference of 1906, on the other hand, it is said that there were more newspaper men present than there were diplomats. The next peace congress will presumably be thrown open to the scrutiny of the world.

It is safe to assume, therefore, that a world " made safe for democracy " will be something very different from the political system devised at the Congress of Vienna. There is reason to suppose that the next peace conference will exercise as much restraint toward the defeated powers as was shown toward France after the elimination of Napoleon; that, while adopting the principle of nationality, it will make an effort to break down commercial and other barriers between nations; that it will seek to establish, not a fixed order, which is impossible, but machinery that will reduce international friction in the accomplishment of those changes inevitable in national growth and decay. In the attainment of these ends the Congress of Vienna offers abundant counsels in avoidance and has put the sign " No thoroughfare " over some old and wornout roads.

# Armed and Armored Automobiles in the War

[By Arrangement with the Revue Scientifique, Paris]

*A French officer, who signs himself " Captain A. M.," has contributed to the Revue Scientifique this illuminating historical study of " Les Auto-Mitrailleuses," as the French call the whole class of armed automobiles to which the " tanks " belong.*

**M**ODERN scientific skill in the present war has made realities of many romancers' dreams. Jules Verne is surpassed, Wells is almost equaled, by the industries of war. Apropos of this English novelist's book, "The Land Dreadnought," did there not appear in the gigantic battle of the Somme—to the astonishment of the troopers and the astounding of the journalists—strange engines, armored and armed, that laughed at trenches and shell holes, walking over them with ease? In the French offensive on the Aisne, in the Spring of 1917, the "artillery of assault" also had its share of glory. These heavy English and French war chariots were not the only fighting vehicles that appeared during the campaign: fast auto machine guns also played their part.

But all these engines have not been created wholly since August, 1914. A good many years before the war the Governments were busy trying to utilize the progress of automobiles to create some kind of mobile fort; and during preceding wars certain of these vehicles, armored or not, appeared on the battle-fields. Their achievements were not equal to those of their decendants today, but it is none the less interesting to follow the history of these applications of mechanical invention to the science of war.

In 1861 a Frenchman named Balbi presented to Napoleon III. a tower protected with armor and moved by steam. It carried two guns, and its armor was pierced with loopholes for rifles. A system of scythes revolving around a vertical axis and operated by steam prevented approach to the vehicle. Experiments produced good results, but the idea was not followed up.

In 1873 a man named Bouyn invented a car whose propulsion was based on a principle analogous to that of the caterpillar "tank," which will be discussed later; strongly armored, this vehicle was intended to be powerfully armed. But only about 1900 [after the gasoline engine had solved the motor problem] was the idea really put into practice; the automobile was applied to the art of war, not only as a vehicle of transport but as an instrument of combat, armed and protected with armor.

The inventors who undertook to apply modern technics to war quickly realized the important rôle which explosion-motor vehicles could play if they were armed with that effective weapon, the machine gun. But two theories divided them: some sought after an armored car that should furnish the greatest amount of protection for the men on it and for the vital machinery; others, condemning the weight and slowness of the armored car, contended for the unprotected auto machine gun, light and swift, capable of accompanying the cavalry and taking the enemy by surprise.

[Here the author gives a brief history of the unprotected "auto-mitrailleuse," which was used to some extent by the French in the early battles of this war, but which was soon abandoned as impractical, except for use against aircraft; in that rôle, armed with " 75s," it is still employed successfully. After stating that the first armored car was the work of an English engineer, Simms, he continues:]

In 1902 there appeared at the automobile show in Paris an armored auto machine gun constructed by Charron, Girardot & Voigt. In that same year experiments were made in the United States with automobiles carrying Colt machine guns and bearing shields to protect the gunners. In 1903 Captain Edwin Dayton of New York built "Dayton's automobile fort," an armored vehicle that could be transformed into a little fort. A test was made, in the course of which this engine was run upon a bridge of boats; in nine minutes it was transformed into a metal trench with battlements, the whole having thirty feet front, prolonged with sacks of earth brought by the automobile itself.*

## Progress in European Countries

In France General Metzinger, member of the Superior War Council, declared that in tests made at the manoeuvres of the Ninth and Eighteenth Corps near Montélimar the auto cannon, especially the auto machine gun, showed considerable progress.

England, where the automobile industry took on a great development, though less quickly than in France, was busy applying this new mode of locomotion to the army. Even before France she used motor cycles on a large scale for military purposes. Her attention was also attracted to the question of the armored automobile. Tests were made in 1901 with protected motor cars bearing machine guns or rapid-fire cannon. Armored autos were even used in London to carry policemen during strikes. In 1904 a test was made of an automobile farm wagon with two cylinders of eighteen horse power, transformable into an armored tractor, bullet proof, serving for the transport of the wounded on the firing line.

The question particularly interested Austria, whose Technical Military Committee ordered of the firm of Daimler at Wiener Neustadt an armored automobile which made very satisfactory trials before the Austrian Minister of War, leaving the solid roads, traversing meadows and plowed fields, crossing ditches, and climbing slopes of 35 degrees. This machine, with the same framework as the

others of that firm, had both axles turned by motors, which enabled it to move over any kind of ground, thanks to the total traction. The rear of the body consisted of a steel tower provided with bearings upon which a cupola could turn. By this means the machine gun could aim in all directions through an embrasure in the wall of the cupola. Two gunners operated the weapon, which was provided with 14,000 cartridges. The armor was of nickel-steel plates about one-sixth of an inch thick covering the whole vehicle down to one-half of the wheels. The machine without the guns weighed about two tons. A motor of forty horse power gave it a speed of about thirty miles an hour.

## Germany Slow to Accept It

A car of the same sort was presented to the German War Minister in 1905. After trial it was rejected on the ground that it could not carry sufficiently heavy armor. Besides, unlike Austria, Germany showed little interest in armored automobiles. * * * She was still far away, in 1905, from the hundreds of such machines that were sent through Belgium to the north of France in August, 1914. The value of this modern fighting machine came to light very slowly in Germany. * * *

In 1906 the house of Charron, Girardot & Voigt built for Russia an armored automobile that was tested in the manoeuvres at Mans and at those of Krasnoe Selo in the presence of the Czar. This was a 25-30 horse power machine, completely protected by plates that were proof against rifle bullets at fifty yards. The driver could see his way through loopholes at the height of his eyes. In the rear an eclipse turret served for the firing of a Hotchkiss gun that could be pointed in all directions; it was provided with 5,000 cartridges. It carried 120 litres of gasoline and 60 of oil, sufficient to go 400 miles. The speed was about 25 miles, and the weight, with five men, about three tons. These machines cost $16,000 each.

Germany and Great Britain both ordered machines of this model from the house of Charron, but that firm refused to deliver them to any other power than

Russia, the ally of France. It offered one to the French Government for use in Morocco, but the authorities preferred the unprotected Genty auto machine gun. * * *

When war broke out in 1914, and the formidable masses of the German Army began marching through Belgium toward France, a myriad of armored enemy automobiles appeared, often far in advance of the vanguard, or far outside the zone of march, and began requisitioning supplies and terrorizing the population. Our [French] cavalry had to bear their swift and unexpected raids. Like the cruiser that awaits with anguish the instant of the submarine's attack, the regiment that knows a swift armored auto machine gun is prowling in the neighborhood must necessarily suffer from depressing anxiety.

Germany, wonderfully prepared, found us in this regard, as in others, a little lacking. But we and our allies went to work. On Sept. 10, 1914, a Belgian auto machine gun achieved a magnificent raid through the German lines at Antwerp, where it surprised a squadron of Uhlans, threw it into confusion, shot it to pieces, and disappeared.

## French Armored Cars

It was also in September, 1914, that auto machine guns first appeared in the French Army in considerable numbers. But these were still mostly imperfect attempts, machines hard to operate and poorly protected with wood or thin sheet iron. Two ingenious examples were built in the Normand works at Havre, each armed with a Hotchkiss gun mounted on a bulwark base with a ratchet arrangement that enabled it to be raised and lowered. This machine could be installed behind a hillock, shooting over it; a large shield was attached to the gun support; two gunners were thus easily protected from direct or even from slanting fire. A low circular armor protected the space back of the gun, and the motor was likewise protected. Two machines of the same type were armed with 37-millimeter guns.

During the war of movement—before the trench warfare began—we unfor-tunately had very few machines; and soon the trenches came to immobilize the lines and bar the roads to automobiles. Armored cars found only few and fugitive opportunities to get into action at the front; one could no longer count upon swift raids and overwhelming surprises. There were only actions of limited scope, in which, however, these war machines could play a useful part.

For example, on Oct. 11, 1914, in the north of France, an auto mitrailleuse found itself on watch among the outposts of a village that was attacked by the Germans in the morning mists; its presence was certainly unknown to the enemy, upon whom it opened through the fog a surprise fire at close range, barring the entrance to the principal street, where the assaulting columns were assembling. Then, when the enemy finally entered the village, forcing our troops, inferior in numbers, to retire, the auto machine gun was able to follow without ceasing to shoot, a thing that infantry gunners could not do.

But soon the armored automobiles were kept in the cantonments at the rear unloading light artillery and carrying it to the trenches. Where were the fine dreams of epic raids?

## Exploits in Galicia

On other fronts, however, where the fighting was not held in forced immobility, raids with these machines continued to be possible. The Russian official reports of the campaign in Galicia in 1916 particularly mention the services rendered by the Belgian armored automobiles, whose ardent and audacious crews were able to accomplish wonders. In October, 1916, such an auto remained for two weeks within the enemy's lines, penetrating to a depth of ninety miles and returning unscathed. One can imagine what a bold crew in such a machine could accomplish so far from the firing line by surprising troops who supposed themselves to be entirely safe. The Belgian auto machine gun corps in Russia was several times cited for bravery in the commander's orders, and received the congratulations of the Czar. The Caucasus witnessed similar exploits by British automobiles.

The French armored automobiles, which were very imperfect at first, were gradually perfected; their armor was strengthened both by extending and by thickening it; besides, the machines became more manageable; the earlier ones were too long and difficult to turn, even on an ordinary road; at the end of 1914 I saw an auto mitrailleuse which, in making a half turn, went off into a field, stuck in the mud, and, caught there by the enemy's artillery fire, had to be abandoned for a time by the crew, who took refuge in a neighboring cellar while waiting for the bombardment to cease. Auto machine guns were afterward built with two steering wheels, one in front and one behind, with several speeds for each.

## Coming of the Tank

As the French front was fortified more and more, with defenses accumulating—wire entanglements, concrete trenches, shelters for armored machine guns—to such a point that the German press grew lyric over the inexpugnable strength of its war front; and as the armored and armed automobile stood chilled by inaction, there appeared upon the British front, to the amazement of the combatants, a war monster that seemed to have emerged from the dreams of some scientific romancer. The effect was startling, so much so that something like a legend sprang up around these land battleships, and the press printed descriptions that were as fantastic as imaginative. Their exploits were spread abroad, veiled in a mystery that heightened their strangeness, and the taking of the sugar mill at Courcelette, where the animal overturned a solid wall upon the backs of the German defenders, popularized the glory of "Crème de Menthe."

Where the light armored automobile was powerless, there was need of a machine heavily armored and heavily armed, which could move along—slowly, indeed, but heedless of obstacles—over any terrain, even that which was honeycombed with shell holes and cut up with trenches.

These new English movable forts, officially designated by the initials H. M. L. S., (His Majesty's Land Ships,) and familiarly known as "tanks," (because the workmen who had built them pretended, in order to guard the secret, that they were making oil tanks,) were constructed in the greatest secrecy, and appeared for the first time in the battle of the Somme, in September, 1916. The Germans, in their passion for monopoly, pretended that the invention was purely German, the work of a Königsberg engineer, who created it in 1913, as the Lokal-Anzeiger stated " in the interests of historical truth."

[The machine is an adaptation of the American caterpillar tractor, manufactured at Peoria, Ill. Hundreds of these unarmored tractors were sold to the British Government, which added the armor and armament.—Translator.]

## Mechanism of the Monster

The veil covering the tanks has been lifted somewhat, and even the moving-picture camera has shown them in action. If the details of their machinery are still secret, the principle is now known. The mode of locomotion is the old system of caterpillar wheels already in use for some years in farm machinery and heavy artillery tractors. The sustaining base is formed of two rolling tracks placed on the sides under the vehicle, and formed of a great number of wooden plates united by joints in an endless chain, so that the lower portions constantly rest on the ground in a long flat surface. The plates are sufficiently large to hinder the sinking of the heavy vehicle in soft soil. They are ribbed so as to grip the ground. These chains pass over sprocket wheels, with which they articulate; the turning of a pair of the wheels communicates the power from the motor to the endless chains, which thus move along the ground. The body of the vehicle rests on simple carrying wheels, which travel on the carpet constantly displaced beneath them. The direction is altered by varying the speed of one of the chains, which is done by means of differentials; the driver can even stop one of the chains, or make the two run in opposite directions, so as to turn the machine around.

The tanks also have two guide wheels at the rear. Besides, the caterpillar chains slope upward in front at an angle

BRITISH "TANK" AND AMERICAN ARMORED CAR IN A LIBERTY LOAN PARADE

of thirty or forty degrees, enabling the machine to lift itself up steep grades while the rear continues to push. These land battleships are armed with machine guns at front and rear; a turret resting on corbels at each side contains two cannon. France, too, has her " tanks," which made their appearance in the battle of April 16, 1917. They are officially designated under the general name of " artillery of assault." Already they have had the honor to be cited in army orders, and the cinematograph is popularizing their strange aspect, which is different from that of their English brethren.

The United States, which is never behind hand with scientific appliances, also possesses gigantic forts on wheels.

## " Spurlos Versenkt "

### By GEORGE W. GALE

Steal out, sea wolves, from your lair,
　Out to the slaughter you seek;
Wage not the fight that is fair;
　War on the helpless, the weak.
Grant them no moment of grace,
　Heed not their pleadings and wails,
" *Sink without leaving a trace,*"
　DEAD MEN TELL NO TALES.

A stab in the dark, then—away!
　A sneer at the fear-stricken crew,
At the women and children—your prey;
　'Tis victory, glory, for you.
Prowl on, sea wolves, to the chase,
　Moloch, your god, never fails;
" *Sink without leaving a trace,*"
　DEAD MEN TELL NO TALES.

Cincinnati, Ohio.

# Japanese-American Agreement

## Reciprocal Notes Recognize Japan's Interests in China and Pledge Japan's Active Aid in the War

THE far-reaching agreement of Nov. 2, 1917, between Japan and the United States regarding China was first announced in a cable dispatch from Peking on Nov. 5, and the news was confirmed with full details and text by Secretary Lansing on Nov. 6. The arrangement was the culmination of the work of the special Japanese mission headed by Viscount Ishii, and was the result of extended conversations between him and Secretary Lansing regarding Japan's part in the war and her relations with China.

The primary point settled was the recognition by the United States of Japan's special interests in China, but no less important was the collateral pledge given by Japan that she would immediately begin taking a more active part in the European war. It was announced unofficially at Washington that Japan had consented to furnish a great amount of tonnage for transport purposes and to risk her warships in European waters, these being her immediate contribution to the allied and American cause. It was also said that she had expressed a willingness to send troops. The promise of American steel and iron adequate to Japan's needs was an item on the other side of the agreement.

A score of torpedo-boat destroyers and other Japanese warships have long been aiding the Allies in the Mediterranean; but at the time of the Washington negotiations Japan's fleet was concluding extensive naval manoeuvres on the Korean coast and in neighboring Japanese waters. Nearly 100 warships, aggregating more than 500,000 tons, participated. It was understood that this fleet was preparing to take an active part in the war.

### The Lansing-Ishii Agreement

The Lansing-Ishii agreement of Nov. 2, 1917, is an extension of the Root-Takahira "gentlemen's agreement" of Nov. 30, 1908, which engages the United States and Japan mutually to respect the possessions of the other in the region of the Pacific Ocean and to support the prin-

VISCOUNT ISHII,
*Head of Japanese Mission*

ciple of equal opportunity for the commerce and industry of all nations in China. The new pact commits the United States Government to a recognition of Japan's special interests in China —similar to ours in Mexico—growing out of the close proximity of the two countries. Great Britain and Russia had already recognized the special interests in question. The agreement also reaffirms the principle of the "open door."

No alliance has been entered into between the Governments at Tokio and Washington, and there is no understanding concerning any resort to force to prevent China from falling a prey to the cupidity of other nations. At the same time the agreement is believed to insure China against aggression. It marks the fruition of the efforts of John Hay, begun at the outbreak of the Boxer uprising seventeen years ago, and makes known to all the world that China must stand as a political and territorial entity.

The arrangement between Japan and the United States took the form of an exchange of identical notes dated Nov. 2 between Mr. Lansing, as Secretary of State of the United States, and Viscount Ishii, the Special Japanese Ambassador, who came to this country at the head of a mission of distinguished Japanese military and naval officers and civilian officials for the ostensible purpose of making known to this Government the satisfaction of the Japanese Government over the entrance of the United States into the war against Germany. But the notes exchanged in regard to China show that the purpose of the Japanese Government in sending a special mission here had a wider significance.

## Text of the Agreement

Following is the State Department's announcement:

On Friday, Nov. 2, 1917, the Secretary of State and Viscount Ishii, the special Japanese Ambassador, exchanged at the Department of State the following notes dealing with the policy of the United States and Japan in regard to China:

DEPARTMENT OF STATE,
WASHINGTON, NOV. 2, 1917.

Excellency: I have the honor to communicate herein my understanding of the agreement reached by us in our recent conversations touching the questions of mutual interest to our Governments relating to the Republic of China.

In order to silence mischievous reports that have from time to time been circulated, it is believed by us that a public announcement once more of the desires and intentions shared by our two Governments with regard to China is advisable.

The Governments of the United States and Japan recognize that territorial propinquity creates special relations between countries, and, consequently, the Government of the United States recognizes that Japan has special interests in China, particularly in the part to which her possessions are contiguous.

The territorial sovereignty of China, nevertheless, remains unimpaired, and the Government of the United States has every confidence in the repeated assurances of the Imperial Japanese Government that, while geographical position gives Japan such special interests, they

have no desire to discriminate against the trade of other nations or to disregard the commercial rights heretofore granted by China in treaties with other powers.

The Governments of the United States and Japan deny that they have any purpose to infringe in any way the independence or territorial integrity of China, and they declare, furthermore, that they always adhere to the principle of the so-called " open door," or equal opportunity for commerce and industry in China.

Moreover, they mutually declare that they are opposed to the acquisition by any Government of any special rights or privileges that would affect the independence or territorial integrity of China, or that would deny to the subjects or citizens of any country the full enjoyment of equal opportunity in the commerce and industry of China.

I shall be glad to have your Excellency confirm this understanding of the agreement reached by us.

Accept, Excellency, the renewed assurance of my highest consideration.

(Signed) ROBERT LANSING.

His Excellency, Viscount Kikujiro Ishii, Ambassador Extraordinary and Plenipotentiary of Japan, on special mission.

---

THE SPECIAL MISSION OF JAPAN.
WASHINGTON, NOV. 2, 1917.

Sir: I have the honor to acknowledge the receipt of your note of today, communicating to me your understanding of the agreement reached by us in our recent conversations touching the questions of mutual interest to our Governments relating to the Republic of China.

I am happy to be able to confirm to you, under authorization of my Government, the understanding in question set forth in the following terms:

[Here the Special Ambassador repeats the language of the agreement as given in Secretary Lansing's note.]

(Signed) K. ISHII.

Ambassador Extraordinary and Plenipotentiary of Japan, on special mission.

Honorable Robert Lansing, Secretary of State.

## Secretary Lansing's Statement

In his statement accompanying the announcement Secretary Lansing said:

Viscount Ishii and the other Japanese Commissioners who are now on their way back to their country have performed a service to the United States as well as to Japan which is of the highest value.

There had unquestionably been growing up between the peoples of the two countries a feeling of suspicion as to the motives inducing the activities of the other in the Far East, a feeling which, if unchecked, promised to develop a serious situation. Rumors and reports of improper intentions were increasing and were more and more believed. Legitimate commercial and industrial enterprises without ulterior motive were presumed to have political significance, with the result that opposition to those enterprises was aroused in the other country.

The attitude of constraint and doubt thus created was fostered and encouraged by the campaign of falsehood which for a long time had been adroitly and secretly carried on by Germans, whose Government as a part of its foreign policy desired especially to so alienate this country and Japan that it would be at the chosen time no difficult task to cause a rupture of their good relations. Unfortunately there were people in both countries, many of whom were entirely honest in their beliefs, who accepted every false rumor as true, and aided the German propaganda by declaring that their own Government should prepare for the conflict which they asserted was inevitable, that the interests of the two nations in the Far East were hostile, and that every activity of the other country in the Pacific had a sinister purpose.

### German Machinations Frustrated

Fortunately this distrust was not so general in either the United States or Japan as to affect the friendly relations of the two Governments, but there is no doubt that the feeling of suspicion was increasing and the untrue reports were receiving more and more credence in spite of the earnest efforts which were made on both sides of the Pacific to counteract a movement which would jeopardize the ancient friendship of the two nations.

The visit of Viscount Ishii and his colleagues has accomplished a great change of opinion in this country. By frankly denouncing the evil influences which have been at work, by openly proclaiming that the policy of Japan is not one of aggression, and by declaring that there is no intention to take advantage commercially or industrially of the special relations to China created by geographical position, the representatives of Japan have cleared the diplomatic atmosphere of the suspicions which had been so carefully spread by our enemies and by misguided or overzealous people in both countries. In a few days the propaganda of years has been undone, and both nations are now able to see how near they came to being led into the trap which had been skillfully set for them.

Throughout the conferences which have taken place Viscount Ishii has shown a sincerity and candor which dispelled every doubt as to his purpose and brought the two Governments into an attitude of confidence toward each other which made it possible to discuss every question with frankness and cordiality. Approaching the subjects in such a spirit and with the mutual desire to remove every possible cause of controversy, the negotiations were marked by a sincerity and goodwill which from the first insured their success.

### Principle of Non-Interference

The principal result of the negotiations was the mutual understanding which was reached as to the principles governing the policies of the two Governments in relation to China. This understanding is formally set forth in the notes exchanged and now made public. The statements in the notes require no explanation. They not only contain a reaffirmation of the " open door " policy, but introduce a principle of non-interference with the sovereignty and territorial integrity of China, which, generally applied, is essential to perpetual international peace, as clearly declared by President Wilson, and which is the very foundation also of Pan Americanism, as interpreted by this Government.

The removal of doubts and suspicions and the mutual declaration of the new doctrine as to the Far East would be enough to make the visit of the Japanese Commission to the United States historic and memorable, but it accomplished a further purpose, which is of special interest to the world at this time, in expressing Japan's earnest desire to co-operate with this country in waging war against the German Government. The discussions, which covered the military, naval, and economic activities to be employed, with due regard to relative resources and ability, showed the same spirit of sincerity and candor which characterized the negotiations resulting in the exchange of notes.

### Japan Pledges Help in War

At the present time it is inexpedient to make public the details of these conversations, but it may be said that this Government has been gratified by the assertions of Viscount Ishii and his colleagues that their Government desired to do its part in the suppression of Prussian militarism and was eager to co-operate in every practical way to that end. It might be added, however, that complete and satisfactory understandings upon the matter of the naval co-operation in the Pacific for the purpose of attaining the common object against Germany and her allies have been reached between the representative of the Imperial Japanese Navy, who is attached to the special mission of Japan, and the representative of the United States Navy.

It is only just to say that the success which has attended the intercourse of the

Japanese Commission with American officials and with private persons as well is due in large measure to the personality of Viscount Ishii, the head of the mission. The natural reserve and hesitation which are not unusual in negotiations of a delicate nature disappeared under the influence of his open friendliness, while his frankness won the confidence and good-will of all. It is doubtful if a representative of a different temper could in so short a time have done as much as Viscount Ishii to place on a better and firmer basis the relations between the United States and Japan. Through him the American people have gained a new and higher conception of the reality of Japan's friendship for the United States, which will be mutually beneficial in the future.

Viscount Ishii will be remembered in this country as a statesman of high attainments, as a diplomat with a true vision of international affairs, and as a genuine and outspoken friend of America.

## Statement by Viscount Ishii

The following statement by Viscount Ishii was given out by the Japanese Embassy:

My final departure from Washington affords a fit occasion for me to express once more to the American people my deep sense of gratitude for the cordial reception and hospitality accorded to the special mission of Japan. The spontaneous and enthusiastic manifestations of friendship and good-will toward us on all hands have profoundly impressed not only the members of the mission, but the whole Japanese people. The kindly feeling and fraternal spirit always existing between the two nations have never been more emphatically testified to.

Believing as I do in frank talking, I have tried as best I could in my public utterances in this country to tell the truth and the facts about my country, the aspirations and motives which spur my nation. For, to my mind, it is misrepresentation and the lack of information that allow discordance and distrust to creep in in the relationship between nations. I am happy to think that at a time when the true unity and co-operation between the allied nations are dire necessities, it has been given me to contribute in my small way to a better understanding and appreciation among the Americans with regard to Japan.

The new understanding in regard to the line of policy to be followed by Japan and America respecting the Republic of China augurs well for the undisturbed maintenance of the harmonious accord and good neighborhood between our two countries. It certainly will do away with all doubts that have now and then shadowed the Japanese-American relationship. It cannot fail to defeat for all time the pernicious efforts of German agents, to whom every new situation developing in China always furnished so fruitful a field for black machinations. For the rest, this new understanding of ours substantiates the solidity of comradeship which is daily gaining strength among the honorable and worthy nations of the civilized world.

It is a great pleasure for me to add that this declaration has been reached as an outcome of free exchange of frank views between the two Governments. I cannot pay too high a tribute to the sincerity and farsightedness of Secretary Lansing, with whom it was my privilege to associate in so pleasurable a way. It is my firm belief that so long as the two Governments maintain a perfectly appreciative attitude toward each other, so long as there is no lack of statesmanship to guide public opinion, the reign of peace and tranquillity in our part of the world will remain unchallenged.

Government officials at Washington objected to the tendency to refer to the new agreement as a recognition of a Japanese Monroe Doctrine. It would be more accurate, they said, to regard it as applying the principle which in this hemisphere is known as Pan-Americanism. The Monroe Doctrine, it was contended, was based on the principle of national safety—the national safety of the United States—while Pan Americanism was altruistic in that it was based on preserving the integrity of all the nations involved, and was therefore international. The Lansing-Ishii agreement contained a recognition of the principle that all the nations concerned were to see that the territorial integrity of China was respected.

Comment of the British press, irrespective of party, was commendatory of the Japanese-American pact. The Japanese press, with minor exceptions, also accepted the arrangement with highly favorable comments. Chinese sentiment was divided on the subject, and on Nov. 9 the Chinese Ambassador at Tokio presented a formal protest to the Japanese Government against its course in acting on a Chinese problem without consulting the Government of China.

# THE EUROPEAN WAR AS SEEN BY CARTOONISTS

[French Cartoon]

## Von Tirpitz, the U-Boat Shepherd

—*By a French Artist*

Little von Tips has lost her ewe ships,
And cannot tell where to find 'em;
Let them alone, they won't come home—
They're leaving no tales behind 'em.

# The Entente and China

—From the Lustige Blaetter, Berlin.

The Entente have been watching China so long that they have themselves acquired Oriental eyes.

# Samson and Delilah

—From The Passing Show, London

Russian anarchy has shorn the giant of his strength.

# Perverted Offspring

*—From Novi Satirikon, Petrograd.*

KROPOTKIN (Grandfather of the Russian Revolution): "Do you know, that grandson of ours is quite the wrong style?"

BRESHKO-BRESHKOVSKAYA (Grandmother of the Revolution): "Yes, he is too German in his ways."

# Columbia's Greater Task

—*Charles Dana Gibson in the Red Cross Magazine*

# The Height of Culture

—*From The Chicago Herald.*

# The Crown Prince's Load

—*From a Drawing by G. Bonfitz.*

It is growing heavier every day, and he must carry it all his life.

[English Cartoon]

# The Witches' Sabbath

—From The Passing Show, London.

The three German Queens (of Russia, Sweden, and Greece) singing:

> "Round about the cauldron go;
> In the poisoned entrails throw. * * *
> Double, double toil and trouble;
> Fire burn and cauldron bubble."

["Macbeth," Act IV., Scene 1.]

# The German Eagle Defeated

*—From a drawing by E. O. Hempel.*

With little to wear and nothing to eat but rations of shame and infamy.

[American Cartoon]
## Camouflage

—*Brooklyn Eagle.*

[English Cartoon]
## The Three Musketeers

—*The Bystander, London.*

" Tommy," " Poilu," and " Sammy "
marching together to victory.

[American Cartoon]
## German Plotting

—*Philadelphia Evening Ledger.*

" Better stick to murder, Willie;
you're too blamed clumsy to cheat! "

[French Cartoon]
## American Troops in Battle

—*La Baionnette, Paris.*

THE KAISER'S COMMENT: " Dirty
business! "

# Before the Examining Board

—From *Thé Sketch, London.*

The conscript's own view of how he looks while the doctors are examining him.

# Italy's Peril

—*From The New York Herald*

"Lo!  The fell monster with the deadly sting,
  Who passes mountains, breaks through fenced walls
  And firm embattled spears, and with his filth
  Taints all the world."—Dante's Inferno.

# How Peace May Come

The Kaiser's Farewell:

*—From De Amsterdammer, Amsterdam.*

Mine is the duty, mine the choice,
    To stem or swell the flood,
And I have but to raise my voice
    To stop this tide of blood.

The whole earth rocks, the towers shake,
    I will the victim be!
Farewell, my friends, one last handshake,
    Farewell, remember me!

[Free translation from Tollens's "Jan van Schaffelaar."]

[Swiss Cartoon]

# First Fruits of the Papal Peace Note

—*From Nebelspalter, Zurich.*

"What have we for dinner today?"
"Roast peace dove, Father, in three styles—Flanders, Verdun, and Isonzo."

# Germany Demands a Million Loan in Return for Coal

—From De Amsterdammer, Amsterdam.

TREUB (Dutch Statesman): "Don't let her catch you! Look at the other one she has in her prison!" [Switzerland.]

# The Songbirds of the Battle Front

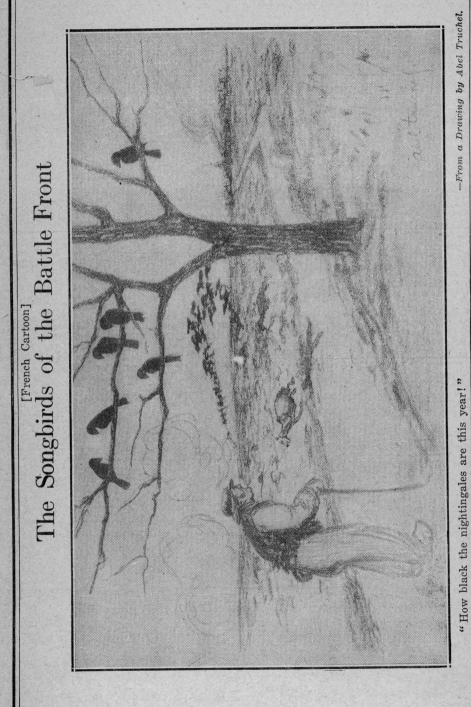

"How black the nightingales are this year!"

—From a Drawing by Abel Truchet.

# The Man Who Slew His God

—*Norman Lindsay in Sydney Bulletin.*

The war, started by the German war lord, is destroying autocracy.

# The Useless Scarecrow

—*From The New York Times.*

UNCLE SAM: "I reckon it's time to begin shooting."

## A Real Halloween Scare

—*Duluth Herald.*

## The Same Could Happen to Bread and Meat

—*Dallas News.*

## Hold Fast, Italy!

## At His Throat

## Knitting to Beat the Dutch

## The Lion and the Mouse

*—All from The Baltimore American.*

## It's Thoroughly Aroused Now

—*Portland Oregonian.*

## The Beast of All the Ages

—*Charleston News.*

## Two Birds With One Stone

—*New York Tribune.*

## Sinking Without Leaving a Trace

—*Brooklyn Eagle.*